CurrentLaw

STATUTES

1994

VOLUME THREE

AUSTRALIA
The Law Book Company
Brisbane : Sydney : Melbourne : Perth

CANADA
Carswell
Ottawa : Toronto : Calgary : Montreal : Vancouver

Agents:
Steimatzky's Agency Ltd., Tel Aviv;
N. M. Tripathi (Private) Ltd., Bombay;
Eastern Law House (Private) Ltd., Calcutta;
M.P.P. House, Bangalore;
Universal Book Traders, Delhi;
Aditya Books, Delhi;
MacMillan Shuppan KK, Tokyo;
Pakistan Law House, Karachi

Current Law

STATUTES

1994

VOLUME THREE

SWEET & MAXWELL EDITORIAL TEAM
SARAH ANDREWS
MELANIE BHAGAT
CAROLINE EADIE
ALICE EMMOTT
PHILIPPA JOHNSON
ALA KUZMICKI
SOPHIE LOWE
JON PEAKE
CERI PICKERING

W. GREEN EDITORIAL TEAM
ELANOR BOWER
CHARLOTTE HALL
PETER NICHOLSON

LONDON

SWEET & MAXWELL

EDINBURGH

W. GREEN

1995

Published by
SWEET & MAXWELL LIMITED
of South Quay Plaza, 183 Marsh Wall, London,
and W. GREEN LIMITED
of Alva Street, Edinburgh,
Typeset by MFK Typesetting Ltd., Hitchin, Herts.
and printed in Great Britain
by The Bath Press,
Bath, Avon.

ISBN This Volume only : 0 421 51930 4
As a set : 0 421 51900 2

All rights reserved.
U.K. statutory material in this publication is acknowledged as Crown copyright.
No part of this publication may be reproduced or transmitted in any form or by any means, or
stored in any retrieval system of any nature, without prior written permission, except for permitted
fair dealing under the Copyright, Designs and Patents Act 1988, or in accordance with the terms of
a licence issued by the Copyright Licensing Agency in respect of photocopying and/or repro-
graphic reproduction. Application for permission for other use of copyright material including
permission to reproduce extracts in other published works shall be made to the publishers. Full
acknowledgment of author, publisher and source must be given.

©
Sweet & Maxwell Ltd.
1995

CONTENTS

Chronological Table . . . . *page* v
Index of Short Titles vii

CHRONOLOGICAL TABLE

VOLUME THREE

Annotators' names are in italic

VOLUME THREE

*c.*29. Police and Magistrates' Courts Act 1994
   Rudi F. Fortson, LL.B., Barrister at Law of the Middle Temple and Neil Walker, LL.B., PhD., Department of Law, University of Edinburgh
30. Education Act 1994
   William Hinds, Lecturer in Law, University of Leeds
31. Firearms (Amendment) Act 1994
32. Sale of Goods (Amendment) Act 1994
   W.H. Thomas, Solicitor, Editor of the Encyclopedia of Consumer Law
33. Criminal Justice and Public Order Act 1994
   H.H.J. Richard May, Circuit Judge on the Midland and Oxford Circuit and Mr J.J. McManus LL.B., PhD., Senior Lecturer in Law, University of Dundee
34. Marriage Act 1994
35. Sale and Supply of Goods Act 1994
   W.H. Thomas, Solicitor, Editor of the Encyclopedia of Consumer Law
36. Law of Property (Miscellaneous Provisions) Act 1994
   Sidney Ross, Barrister, Middle Temple and Lincoln's Inn
37. Drug Trafficking Act 1994
   Rudi F. Fortson, LL.B., Barrister at Law of the Middle Temple
38. European Union (Accessions) Act 1994
39. Local Government *etc.* (Scotland) Act 1994
   C.M.G. Himsworth, Faculty of Law, University of Edinburgh
40. Deregulation and Contracting Out Act 1994
   Professor Alan Page, Professor of Public Law, University of Dundee
41. Consolidated Fund (No. 2) Act 1994

INDEX OF SHORT TITLES

STATUTES 1994

(References are to chapter numbers of 1994)

Consolidated Fund (No. 2) Act 1994 41
Criminal Justice and Public Order Act 1994 33
Deregulation and Contracting Out Act 1994 40
Drug Trafficking Act 1994 37
Education Act 1994 30
European Union (Accessions) Act 1994 38
Firearms (Amendment) Act 1994 31
Law of Property (Miscellaneous Provisions) Act 1994 36
Local Government *etc.* (Scotland) Act 1994 39
Marriage Act 1994 34
Police and Magistrates' Courts Act 1994 29
Sale and Supply of Goods Act 1994 35
Sale of Goods (Amendment) Act 1994 32

POLICE AND MAGISTRATES' COURTS ACT 1994*

(1994 c. 29)

ARRANGEMENT OF SECTIONS

PART I

POLICE

CHAPTER I

PRINCIPAL AMENDMENTS OF POLICE ACT 1964

Police areas

SECT.
1. Police areas.

Forces outside London

2. Police forces and police authorities.
3. Membership of police authorities etc.
4. Functions of police authorities.
5. Chief constables.
6. Deputy and assistant chief constables.
7. Other members of police forces.
8. Police fund.
9. Supply of goods and services.
10. Civilian employees.
11. Appointment of officers.
12. Questions by local councillors.

General

13. Provision of advice and assistance to international organisations etc.
14. Alteration of police areas.
15. Functions of Secretary of State.
16. Reports from police authorities.
17. Police grant and other grants.
18. Regulations for police forces.
19. Appeals against dismissal etc.
20. Inspectors of constabulary.
21. Reports from inspectors of constabulary.
22. Assistant inspectors and staff officers.
23. Common services.
24. Grants by local authorities.
25. Acceptance of gifts and loans.
26. Police officers engaged on service outside their force.

CHAPTER II

OTHER PROVISIONS ABOUT THE POLICE

Financial provisions

27. Precepts.
28. Approval of decisions about precepts.
29. Directions as to minimum budget.
30. Revenue accounts and capital finance.
31. Financial administration.
32. Initial financing of new police authorities.
33. Validation of past grants.

Complaints against and conduct of police officers

34. Reference of matters other than complaints to Complaints Authority.
35. Steps to be taken after investigation of complaint.
36. Powers of Complaints Authority as to disciplinary proceedings.
37. Repeal of certain provisions about discipline.
38. Saving for certain complaints procedures.

---

* Annotations by Rudi F. Fortson, LL.B., Barrister at Law, of the Middle Temple and Neil Walker, LL.B., PhD., Department of Law, University of Edinburgh.

Reorganisation of local government

39. Police areas in England: alterations under Local Government Act 1992.
40. Police areas in Wales: alterations under Local Government Act 1972.

Miscellaneous

41. Metropolitan police: assistant commissioners.
42. Application of Firearms Act 1968 to civilian staff.
43. Application to police authorities of enactments relating to local authorities etc.
44. Minor and consequential amendments.
45. Application of certain provisions to new police authorities.
46. Interpretation of Part I.

PART II

POLICE (SCOTLAND)

47. Constitution of police force.
48. Deputy and assistant chief constables.
49. Civilian employees.
50. Provision of advice and assistance to international organisations etc.
51. Chief constables' annual reports.
52. Regulations for police forces.
53. Fixed term appointments etc.
54. Power of Secretary of State to give directions to police authorities.
55. Appeals against dismissal etc.
56. Expenditure in safeguarding national security.
57. Duty of inspectors of constabulary.
58. Assistant inspectors of constabulary and staff officers to inspectors of constabulary.
59. Common services.
60. Constables engaged on service outside their force.
61. Examination of handling of complaints against constables.
62. Transmission of criminal statistics.
63. Other amendments of 1967 Act.
64. Delegation of functions of Scottish police authority.
65. Interpretation of Part II.

PART III

POLICE (NORTHERN IRELAND)

66. Regulations for administration, etc. of Royal Ulster Constabulary.
67. Regulations for administration, etc. of reserve constables.
68. Minor and consequential amendments.

PART IV

MAGISTRATES' COURTS

Magistrates' courts committees

69. Alteration of magistrates' courts committee areas.
70. Constitution of magistrates' courts committees.
71. Regulations as to constitution etc. of magistrates' courts committees.
72. Supplementary provisions as to magistrates' courts committees.
73. General powers and duties of magistrates' courts committees.
74. Reports and plans.

Justices' chief executives, justices' clerks and staff

75. Appointment and functions of justices' chief executive.
76. Appointment and removal of justices' clerks.
77. Justices' chief executives and justices' clerks to be employed under contracts of service.
78. Independence of justices' clerk and staff in relation to legal functions.

Inner London area

79. Magistrates' courts committee for inner London area.
80. Organisation of justices' clerks in inner London area.
81. Division of work in inner London area.
82. Pensions etc. of justices' chief executives, justices' clerks and staff in inner London area.

Administrative and financial arrangements

83. Administrative and financial arrangements for magistrates' courts.
84. Local authority land appropriated to magistrates' courts purposes.
85. Regulations as to accounts and audit.

Inspectors of the magistrates' courts service

86. Inspectors of the magistrates' courts service.
87. Powers of inspectors.

Default powers

88. Default powers.

Studies by Audit Commission

89. Studies by Audit Commission.

General

90. Regulations under Justices of the Peace Act 1979.
91. Minor and consequential amendments.
92. Interpretation of Part IV.

PART V

SUPPLEMENTARY

93. Repeals.
94. Commencement and transitional provisions.
95. Police: co-operation on implementation.
96. Extent.
97. Short title.

SCHEDULES:
   Schedule 1—Schedule to be inserted in Police Act 1964: police areas.
   Schedule 2—Schedules to be inserted in Police Act 1964: police authorities.
   Schedule 3—Schedule to be inserted in Police Act 1964: appeals tribunals.
   Schedule 4—Application to police authorities of enactments relating to local authorities.
     Part I—Amendments of local government enactments.
     Part II—Amendments of other enactments.
   Schedule 5—Police: minor and consequential amendments.
     Part I—Amendments of Police Act 1964.
     Part II—Amendments of other enactments.
   Schedule 6—Schedule to be inserted in Police (Scotland) Act 1967: appeals tribunals.
   Schedule 7—Continuing functions of Receiver for the Metropolitan Police District in relation to pensions etc. of court staff.
   Schedule 8—Magistrates' courts: minor and consequential amendments.
     Part I—Amendments of Justices of the Peace Act 1979.
     Part II—Amendments of other enactments.
   Schedule 9—Repeals.
     Part I—Police.
     Part II—Magistrates' courts.

An Act to make provision about police areas, police forces and police authorities; to make provision for England and Wales about magistrates' courts committees, justices' clerks and administrative and financial arrangements for magistrates' courts; and for connected purposes.

[21st July 1994]

PARLIAMENTARY DEBATES
   Hansard, H.L. Vol. 551, cols. 457, 1269; Vol. 552, cols. 101, 181, 292, 353, 423, 517, 591, 633, 940; Vol. 553, cols. 104, 188, 390, 747; Vol. 557, col. 11; H.C. Vol. 242, col. 110; Vol. 246, col. 156.
   The Bill was discussed in Standing Committee between May 10–June 26, 1994.

GENERAL NOTE

Following the publication of two White Papers: *Police Reform: the Government's proposals for the police service in England and Wales* (Cm. 2281 1993) and *A New Framework for Local Justice* (Cm. 1829 1993), the Police and Magistrates' Courts Bill was introduced in the Lords towards the end of 1993. Some members of the legislature questioned whether or not the better course would have been to split the Bill in two in order to give separate consideration to the reform of the police, and the administration of magistrates' courts, respectively. This did not find favour with the legislature, presumably on the basis that the measures introduced in Pt. IV, albeit important, are administrative in nature and thus it was prudent to accommodate them in this Act, but *cf.* the speech of Baroness Miller (*Hansard*, H.L. Vol. 551, col. 539). One reason for separating the reforms into two Acts would have been to dispel the notion that there remains an affinity between the police and magistrates' courts which previously earned the latter the name "Police Courts".

It is not the purpose of the Act to alter the jurisdiction of magistrates' courts or to give statutory effect to recommendations made by the Royal Commission on Criminal Justice (1993) (see recommendations 114 to 120; Chap. 6). It might be said that the Act missed a valuable opportunity to take on board the recommendations of the Royal Commission but the short answer appears to be that the Government considered that the Criminal Justice and Public Order Act 1994 (c. 33) was the more appropriate vehicle for introducing reforms of that sort because they could readily be accommodated under the umbrella of Pt. III of that Act ("Course of Justice; Evidence, Procedure, Etc.").

As was pointed out during the parliamentary debates (*Hansard*, H.C. Vol. 142, col. 147), the efficiency of the magistrates' courts is vital to the adm᙮ istration of justice in England and Wales. According to the Government's own figures (*Criminal Statistics, England and Wales*, HMSO, 1993) 1.96 million defendants appeared before a magistrates' court in 1991 of which 894,000 cases related to summary motoring offences; 75 per cent of the cases were not remanded but the average number of adjournments per case had increased by 25 per cent since 1986. An average of 18 weeks elapsed between the date proceedings were initiated, and concluded, before the magistrates' court for offences that could or must be tried on indictment. In all of this the role of the Crown Prosecution Service must be taken into account. The CPS discontinued approximately 11 per cent of cases in the magistrates' court during 1991. Formal cautioning by police appears to range between 20 per cent of "known offenders in South Wales to 45 per cent in Humberside" but it seems clear that any change of police practice as to the number of persons cautioned could have a significant impact on the courts' business and, indeed, on the amount of work undertaken by the police in dealing with each case.

The Government statistics also shed considerable light on the performance and structure of the police. Of the staff employed by the 43 police forces in England and Wales some 127,100 members were police officers and almost 47,000 were civilian staff. Whereas the number of police officers has risen by 6.3 per cent since 1981, the number of civilian staff grew by 24 per cent. A ratio of almost one civilian to every three police officers may be viewed as being indicative of wasted resources but the Government claims that the rise in strength of civilian employees has made possible the deployment of operational duties of approximately 4,000 uniform officers between 1982 and 1988 "at less than half the cost of the same number of police officers" (see *Information on the Criminal Justice System in England and Wales*, HMSO, 1993 at p. 69). Some 63 per cent of government expenditure on the criminal justice system is on the police.

It has to be recognised that putting more officers on operational duties will result in an increase in the need for administrative support and it would be idle to pretend that the valuable safeguards introduced under the Police and Criminal Evidence Act 1984 (c. 60) (and the related Codes of Practice) have not contributed to a marked increase over recent years in the volume of paperwork handled by the police, *e.g.* custody records which are now becoming highly detailed documents in many cases. In one or two well publicised instances, the police have complained that their officers have to perform a disproportionate amount of paperwork to "process" every arrest made. Much of the relevant (and necessary) paperwork involved in the investigation of a case could not easily be removed from the responsibility of the arresting officer, *e.g.* the making of a statement or the recording of exhibits but the case for using civilian staff to release officers to perform as many hours as are reasonably practicable, on operational duties is obvious. This is arguably all the more important when one bears in mind various observations of the Royal Commission on Criminal Justice (1993) to the effect that police performance should be measured on the basis of the quality of work performed and that officers should be assessed on the basis of their "skills, abilities and attitudes rather than chiefly on number of arrests, searching and stops in the street" (see para. 62).

Significantly, the Royal Commission attached importance to the need for clear lines of supervision and accountability of the police and individual officers (para. 63). The Royal Commission recommended that, "as a first step", job descriptions should be drawn up for "supervising ranks" including sergeants "who should work as supervisors as well as having their own case-loads" (para. 59). It is easy to understand why the Royal Commission included sergeants as being part of the line of supervision and accountability but their inclusion also demonstrates the difficulties involved in maximising the amount of time officers can spend on pure "policing" without unduly compromising their administrative obligations which form part of the machinery for an effective system of supervision and accountability of the police.

The sentiments of the Royal Commission do not appear to have gone unheeded in the Police and Magistrates' Courts Act 1994 because s.15 introduces four new provisions (ss.28A, 28B, 28C and 28D) into the Police Act 1964 (c. 48) to empower the Secretary of State to set "performance targets" for meeting objectives for the policing of the areas of all police authorities. Further power is vested in the Secretary of State to require the inspectors of the constabulary to carry out an inspection under s.38 of the Police Act 1964 (see s.20 of the 1994 Act) and thereafter directions may be given to the Police Authority to "take such measures as may be specified in the direction" (s.28D as introduced by s.15 of the 1994 Act).

The Government's White Paper *Police Reform* criticised the present system insofar as it results in "overlapping responsibilities, unnecessary controls, and confused lines of accountability" (para. 2.22). The Government argued that there should be "unitary management structure within the police force" (para. 3.8) and that the chief constable should have responsibilities for personnel management decisions (para. 3.6). However, under the 1994 Act, Parliament now holds the reins somewhat more tightly than the White Paper indicated would be the case because the ranks within a police force must include an assistant chief constable but not that of deputy chief constable (s.6 which amends s.6 of the Police Act 1964). The latter rank is abolished. In any event, appointments and promotions to the rank of assistant chief constable shall be subject to the approval of the Secretary of State (see s.6) and the 1994 Act strengthens the supervisory role of the Home Secretary considerably.

One of the themes of the 1994 Act is to instill a sense of "business management" into the running of the police service. This theme manifested itself, in the history of the Act, in ways which may be surprising if not controversial. Thus, commercial sponsorship of an activity undertaken by the Police Authority, is now given statutory footing (see s.25). This may (constructively) allow companies to sponsor (for example) information packs on the dangers of drug or alcohol abuse which would then be distributed to schools and colleges. By contrast, provisions made for the introduction of fixed-term contracts for the ranks of superintendent and above, are less likely to be welcomed: see s.18(3) which amends s.33 of the Police Act 1964 and s.53 of the 1994 Act.

On a more subtle level, ss.34–38 (complaints against the police) and s.55 (appeals against dismissal) reflect the changes in parliamentary thinking towards control over the police. Thus, s.37 removes a failure to comply with a code of practice (made under the Police and Criminal Evidence Act 1984) as a disciplinary offence, yet an officer acquitted of a criminal offence may still face an equivalent disciplinary charge. Both of these controversial provisions – quite contrary to what the Police and Criminal Evidence Act 1984 expressly provided – are, apparently, part of the Government's strategy to ensure that "police managers" have greater flexibility in the "management of police staff" than was previously the case (see para. 3.29 of the White Paper, *Police Reform*) and gives police managers freedom to regulate their own affairs at an internal managerial level. Note the emphasis being placed by the Government on the importance of applying managerial skills and ethics.

Just as the magistrates' court system has a very high proportion of lay justices within the system (at an obvious cost benefit) so the Government seems to be looking to increase police personnel by expanding the current number of special constables (19,000) to a target number of 30,000 (see para. 6.4 of the White Paper). Although concern might be expressed that this target figure (if achieved) will create problems of supervision and control, this expansion is designed to meet concerns that the present assignment of officers to policing the streets does not discourage the creation of so-called vigilante groups. There is enough flexibility, under the combined effect of both the 1994 Act and the Police Act 1964, to deal with these issues.

An object lesson in democracy

The history of this Act is not straightforward. The Bill was introduced into the Lords in December 1993 where it received an almost instantly hostile reception. High quality debates in that House soon followed, resulting in a large number of amendments being considered by the Lords in Committee, and in the Committee On Re-commitment (March 1, 1994) and again on Report (March 17, 1994). The Bill was brought from the Lords on March 25, 1994 and read for a second time in the House of Commons on April 26, 1994. A substantial number of further amendments were considered by the House of Commons Standing Committee D between May 10 and June 28, 1994 with a third reading of the Bill in the House of Commons on July 5, 1994. The Bill was again considered by the Lords on July 18, 1994 and received Royal Assent on July 21, 1994.

Rarely has there been a Bill which has received such critical scrutiny in a non-partisan way and it is not without good reason that Lord Simon of Glaisdale was moved to say:

"I cannot remember a measure that has been debated and discussed with equal ability. That applies not only to the Front Bench spokesman, to whom we are irredeemably in debt, but also to those on the Back Benches who brought so much experience and expertise to the measure". (*Hansard*, H.L. Vol. 553, col. 806).

Earl Ferrers made the same point but summarised the mood of the Chamber during debates when he said:

"Your Lordships' House has carried out its function of putting the Government's proposals to the test, in a manner which, I may respectfully hope, will not necessarily be repeated with quite the same vigour on any other Bills with which I may in future have the privilege of being involved. I should like to thank the noble Lords from all parts of the House for the contributions which they have made, some of which, I might say, have been more helpful than others, but all of which have contributed to the rich tapestry of debate which this Bill has experienced". (*Hansard*, H.L. Vol. 553, col. 797).

Some attempt was made to stem the flood of criticism by, among others, Lord Finsberg and Baroness Miller. The latter remarked that "it was inevitable that there should be an instant outcry from some quarters – some of them not previously noted for their support for the police – against the Bill, even before its terms were published" (*Hansard*, H.L. Vol. 551, col. 540). In fact, many of the criticisms were non-partisan and came from sources that could scarcely be marginalised (still less dismissed) as being anti-establishment or anti-police. Certainly, from an early stage, it was apparent that the Police and Magistrates' Courts Bill was not one which was going to receive an easy passage through Parliament so that by the middle of January 1994, three former Home Secretaries, the Lord Chief Justice, a bishop, a former chief constable, and an array of senior and distinguished members of the House of Lords joined forces in attacking various aspects of it. It is important to put this attack into context. Few commentators challenged the proposition that the administration of the police and the magistrates' courts required reform in the interests of efficiency and effectiveness. Thus, notwithstanding his reservations, Viscount Whitelaw regarded the Bill as an important measure which "carefully considered and modified ... can be of great value to the British police service in the future" (*Hansard*, H.L. Vol. 551, col. 481). The Lord Chief Justice did not seek to attack Pts. I, II or III of the Bill.

There was, without question, much genuine concern about specific provisions and details of the Bill which called for thorough scrutiny but, for many participants in the debates in both Houses of Parliament, the Bill was also an opportune moment to make a "stand" against what was perceived to be the growing power of the Executive and the weakening of local government in favour of central government, and to question the merits in regulating the public sector in ways familiar to the private commercial sector. Whatever might be said about the merits of the arguments advanced, the points made brought very clearly into focus the interaction between the various organs of the legislative process – and represent a significant lesson in the history of Parliament. At a time when a highly critical public are questioning the justification for retaining the House of Lords as a political institution (or at all) – and questioning the need for a second Chamber – no one but the least charitable, could doubt that the quality of the debates were generally of the highest, and the speeches well researched, well prepared and fearlessly presented. This is not to belittle in any way the contribution made by the House of Commons. All of this is more than just part of the legislative process; it exemplifies "an important lesson" for the reasons given by Lord Simon of Glaisdale:

"Your Lordships' House is much freer and more enabled to act as a forum of state for the discussion of these grave constitutional measures than, it must be said, the House of Commons. I was always proud to be a Member of the other place. Why is that so? One has only to think in the context of this Bill that your Lordships have among you five former Secretaries of State at the Home Office. At one point, three of them intervened significantly and decisively. Another also contributed to our deliberations. We have among our Members a former Permanent Secretary and three Ministers of State in that department, in addition to the noble Earl. No other legislative assembly in the world can show such a galaxy of relevant talent. Lord Lieutenants of counties, the Governor of the Isle of Wight and a number of justices of the peace supplemented the knowledge and brought their influence to bear. It would be quite inappropriate to try to list them all.

That means that your Lordships' House as at present constituted is in a wonderful constitutional position to review a constitutional measure such as this. It can be done in the way that it has been done; that is, by negotiations between Front Benchers who trust each other. It can be done by influence brought to bear by former Ministers of the department and by all the Back Benchers with the knowledge to which I have referred.

Perhaps I may add that among noble Lords who intervened in that way, some were hereditary Peers and some were Life Peers by appointment. *Therefore, when, as at the moment, the future of a Second Chamber is being canvassed, your Lordships and the general public will, I think, wish to look at what has happened and why and how it has happened with regard to this Bill. Your Lordships need feel no modesty in view of the fact that you have improved the Bill out of all recognition*" [emphasis added] (*Hansard*, H.L. Vol. 553, col. 805).

This is an important statement which should not be lightly overlooked in future debates on the merits or need for a second chamber. The Bill (particularly as originally drafted) threw up constitutional issues of considerable importance – some of which have yet to be fully addressed. The main thrust of the criticisms were aimed at provisions which struck at the so-called doctrine of the "separation of powers". Thus, Lord Ackner complained:

"We have been moving backwards … with ever-increasing centralisation, the process is advanced by which the Executive creeps nearer and nearer to running the administration of justice. The pursuit of power and the Executive's concept of what constitutes value for money are the motive forces" (*Hansard*, H.L. Vol. 553, col. 803).

The Lord Chief Justice scrutinised the impact that the Bill would have on the independence of the magistracy, while Viscount Whitelaw, Lord Callaghan and Lord Carr questioned whether the Government's original proposals would result in a truly non-political police force (see *Hansard*, H.L. Vol. 551, col. 457 *et seq.*). Lord Ackner summarised the position of the opponents in these terms:

"the provisions in the Bill … propose a substantial move towards centralisation of policing and away from the tripartite relationship of police, Home Office and local police authorities. This tripartite relationship is clearly a constitutional safeguard of enormous importance which prevents policing falling under national political control. Central appointments, combined with the placing of the chief constable on short-term contracts and performance-related pay, clearly carry a danger of replacing the operational independence of the chief constable with effective control of policing by the Home Secretary. Its provisions, super-added to those in the magistrates' courts section of the Bill, emphasise the Government's obsession with central control" (*Hansard*, H.L. Vol. 551, col. 510).

It is perhaps surprising that this particular Bill should have attracted so much biting criticism from so many eminent individuals as if this Bill, alone, was capable of undermining the constitutional framework of the U.K. However, there are signs that the intensity of the attack was symptomatic of the existence of deep-rooted grievances over the reorganisation of government and a warning that the tide, in the growth of Executive power, needed to be stemmed. If this analysis is valid then it may explain the impatience shown by Lord Ackner who took a much broader look at events leading up to the introduction of this Bill:

"My Lords, it is a very remarkable, deeply depressing and much to be regretted fact that since 1989 the Government have managed to antagonise virtually every component part of the administration of justice. Through my noble and learned friend the Lord Chancellor and his department, they have alienated the Bar, the solicitors and the professional judges. They are now bent on alienating the lay judges – the magistrates – who, without fees or other remuneration, deal efficiently, as we have been told, with 97 per cent of our criminal cases. In addition they are intent on affronting their legal advisers, the justices clerks, by destroying their time honoured autonomy.

Not to be outdone by this sorry achievement, the Government, through the Home Secretary and his department, have alienated the police, the probation officers and some, if not a majority of, prison governors and officers; and most recently, as a specious Christmas present, the victims of violent crime, the White Paper published last month savagely reducing the compensation to which in future they will be entitled". (*Hansard*, H.L. Vol. 551, col. 506).

Lord Ackner suggested that these results were the product of "twin driving forces", being first, the pursuit of power and, secondly, the use as a yardstick for decision-making of financial value for money rather than the interests of justice. Financial value being determined by the Executive and not by judicial decision.

In 1989 a previous Lord Chief Justice, Lord Lane, remarked:

"The signs are that it will extend still further, and one asks whether we are now seeing tools being fashioned which by some future, perhaps less scrupulous, government may be used to weaken the independent administration of justice" (*Official Report*, April 7, 1989, col. 1331).

Lord Ackner described that passage as "a highly prophetic observation" and continued:

"The matters to which I have referred I hope demonstrate to your Lordships how strongly the tide towards Executive domination is flowing – a tide which is eroding judicial independence, so fundamental to the protection of democracy".

Lord Williams of Mostyn reinforced the attack when he remarked that:

"The Chief Secretary [to the Treasury] spoke of two great institutions. One has always been, and presently remains, a locally accountable police force; and the second has been an impartial magistracy trusted by the people and wholly contemptuous of any attempt to direct it by central authority. With one Bill this present Administration are doing their best to subvert both of these great institutions. We owe the public servants in the police service and the magistracy our duty. I believe our duty is that in these two central respects this Bill must be amended so that these vices are withdrawn from it" (*Hansard*, H.L. Vol. 551, col. 506).

The employment of words such as "contemptuous", "subvert" and "vices" are rarely heard in speeches emanating from the House of Lords against an "Administration". Lord Archer suggested that the White Paper *A Framework for Local Justice* was not an offer for consultation on whether the proposals should be implemented but on how they should be implemented and added:

"It was not a Member of the opposition parties who first used the expression 'an elective dictatorship' ... if a government hope for co-operation from those for whom they are providing legislative instructions there are wiser ways of proceeding" (*ibid.*, col. 519).

In reading the relevant parliamentary material, it is therefore advisable to keep one eye on the wider issue which both Houses of Parliament sought to examine, namely the structure of our democratic system of government and the need to ensure that a constitution has in place an effective system of safeguards to maintain an appropriate balance of freedoms, rights and restrictions on liberty in the regulation of human affairs within that system.

The House of Lords were particularly successful in bringing about major changes to the nature and structure of the Bill. These changes were matched by speeches – most notably in the Lords – reflecting on the successes which had been achieved and commending the legislative process which allowed for free and effective debate. As will be seen, the Government clearly heeded the wealth of protest and the Bill has been substantially amended to reflect much of the opposition expressed.

The original structure of the Bill

What was the stated intention of Government when the Bill was introduced into the House of Lords and, notwithstanding the criticism, how much of the original Bill has survived? The first question is in part answered by the speech of the Lord Chancellor when he moved that the Bill be read for a second time. In dealing with the reforms of the police the Lord Chancellor said:

"The most substantial provisions in this Bill are in Parts I and IV. Part I will reform the structure of the police service in England and Wales. Its purpose is to improve the management and organisation of the police service, so that it is better able to combat crime. The reforms in this Part were foreshadowed in the White Paper on *Police Reform* which was published in June last year. Part IV will strengthen and modernise the administration of magistrates' courts. Parts II and III make changes affecting the police in Scotland and Northern Ireland respectively.

The organisation of police forces in England and Wales is based on the tripartite structure of chief constables, police authorities and the Home Secretary. The Bill will strengthen that structure by making the changes necessary to provide effective policing into the 21st Century. Our objective is to establish a framework for the management and structure of the service which will allow policemen and women to tackle crime and to protect local communities in the most effective way" (*Hansard*, H.L. Vol. 551, col. 457).

There was agreement in both Houses that the principal objective of the Bill should be to tackle crime not just efficiently but effectively and that therefore the police needed to be restructured. The Lord Chief Justice expressly avoided commenting on those parts of the Bill which dealt with reform of the police and indeed, the Lord Chief Justice supported the Lord Chancellor in his desire to secure greater efficiency in the magistrates' courts by amalgamating some committee areas and establishing an inspectorate to report to him on the organisation and management of those courts. There also seems to have been general agreement with the Lord Chancellor that:

"The present arrangements involve too many controls by the Home Secretary and central government over the details of local expenditure. They prevent the best use being made of the available resources" (*ibid.*, col. 457).

However, the Lord Chancellor continued:

"We propose to abolish those controls and to give more power to local police authorities and to chief constables, whose business it is to provide a service to their local communities.

Each police force will be maintained, as now, by a police authority. We intend to strengthen local police authorities so that they are better equipped to carry out their responsibilities" (*Hansard*, H.L. Vol. 551, col. 457).

So far as magistrates' courts were concerned, the Lord Chancellor suggested that the Bill would bring the administrative structure of the magistrates' courts service, which has remained essentially unaltered for the past 50 years, up-to-date. The reforms proposals were designed to enable the magistrates' courts to deal better with the challenges that the service now faces without undermining its local nature, and without interfering with the independence of the magistracy. It was intended that the reforms should have a threefold objective, namely:

"First, magistrates' courts committees, who are responsible for running the service locally, should be better able to fulfil their responsibilities.

Secondly, there should be a clear line of management accountability from the courts to the magistrates' courts committees at local level. I am in turn accountable, as the responsible Minister, to your Lordships and the other place, for the administration of the magistrates' courts service. I therefore need some means, consistent with the local nature of the service, of discharging that accountability. This is not the type of direct line management accountability exercised by the magistrates' courts committees. It is of a more general nature. Nevertheless, it needs to be clear if I am to undertake my responsibilities. Thirdly, we want to ensure, in case there is any doubt that the proposals might do otherwise, that the independence of judicial decisions made by magistrates in individual cases remains secure" (*Hansard*, H.L. Vol. 553, col. 797).

Reforming the structure and management of the Police

Police authorities play a major part in the administration of the police. They were, therefore, a major focus of attention by the Government. The Government originally proposed that police authorities should be smaller, with their own budget and be able to take decisions without being overruled by the local authority. Accordingly, it was suggested that every authority should be of the same size (16 members) irrespective of the size of the area over which the authority would have jurisdiction, and irrespective of the particular problems associated with that area. Of the 16 members, eight were to be members of relevant councils (thus preserving some democratic control), three were to be magistrates, and the five other members were to be drawn from the locality but appointed by the Home Secretary. The Chairman was to be appointed by the Home Secretary.

There was very little about these proposals which did not come under scrutiny and attack. Why, for example, did the government propose an even number of members? Was it an attempt to prevent decisions by way of a simple majority? Why should it be left to the Home Secretary to appoint the Chairman and not the membership of the authority? Most controversially of all, why should the local authority lose its controlling influence over decisions taken by the authority in favour of central government? Ironically the Government, in the White Paper *Police Reform* (Cm. 2281), believed that their proposals would lead to wider local representation not least because the previous system put a limit on persons who could be members so that only magistrates or local councillors could be appointed and therefore persons from different walks of life, who could make a valuable contribution, would be excluded (see para. 2.19 of the White Paper). This is a valid criticism but there are, of course, other ways of drawing members from the local community than having them be appointed by the Home Secretary.

The Government also made the valid point that the structure of police authorities, under the original system, meant that their ability to reflect the views of local people about policing, in the strategic direction of the force, was limited because the different types of police authority (single county forces, forces covering two or more forces, and metropolitan forces) had different levels of powers and different degrees of autonomy. It was therefore appropriate to introduce consistency into the structure of police authorities and in the organisation of police forces. However, the argument focused on the balance of power between the relevant local councils and central government for the management of the police, and the proportions in which that power should be divided. The Lord Chancellor sought to demonstrate that the original proposals did not amount to centralised policing ("it is precisely the reverse", see *Hansard*, H.L. Vol. 551, col. 458) by pointing out that powers would be taken away from the Home Secretary and given to police authorities and chief constables.

In this debate, the role of the Home Secretary was of crucial importance. According to the White Paper *Police Reform* (see Chap. 5), he was no longer to be concerned with such things as the number of police officers but he would be expected to give a "clear steer" on priorities and to call upon the chief constable to account to him for the performance of the force, to call for a report from the chief constable, to promote "consistency of approach between forces through national guide-lines", to provide some equipment and training and to control expenditure given that some 51 per cent of police funding comes from central government. In turn, the Home Secretary would be accountable to Parliament and thus, so it was argued, the proposed reforms would put right that which was lacking, namely, they would ensure that the Home Secretary could answer to Parliament "for a service for which he has no direct responsibility" (para. 2.14). However, why does the Home Secretary need to be directly responsible for the service? Why is it not enough for him simply to report to Parliament on the performance of various forces and to encourage pressure to be applied to those local forces which are falling short of what is required or is acceptable? Part of the Government's answer is to be found in what the White Paper describes as a "new partnership between the public and the police" (chap. 6). Realistically, the Government admitted (in para. 6.3) that this partnership is "not new" and that what it really seeks to do is to "revitalise community support for the police". Such an objective received – as it should – cross-party support but many of the opponents to the original draft of the Bill asked how centralisation would engender that support.

Recent publicity over the role of special constables, private security firms, and "neighbourhood watches", or the extension of duties of the "Parks Police" to "neighbourhood patrols", has highlighted many of the issues which are relevant to an inquiry as to what is expected both of the public, and the Government, in pursuance of this new and revitalised partnership for policing. Some of these issues become confused when they are discussed in the context of cost and efficiency. There are presently 19,000 special constables but the Government would like to increase this figure to 30,000 (para. 6.5). The Government believes that there is scope for much greater use of such constables in support of regular officers but some of the debates questioned how much of their use is influenced by economics rather than by desirability and efficiency.

The Government acknowledges that "value for money and efficiency are fundamental to the Government's proposals for the police service" (para. 10.5). Few denied in Parliament that efficiency is an important objective but there was much greater debate as to whether the "value for money" concept is entirely appropriate in the context of policing. In any event, what does "value for money" mean beyond ensuring that the police operate "effectively and efficiently"? The Government drew attention to the fact that there are presently 43 police forces in England and Wales (27 county forces, 8 combined police areas, 6 metropolitan forces plus the Metropolitan Police and City of London Police; see para. 10.2). It asked whether so many forces makes the most use of the resources available for policing (see para. 10.5). This gave rise to extensive debates as to whether some or all of the forces should be amalgamated. The Government was not slow to face this issue head-on in the White Paper (para. 10.11) by indicating that it intends to ensure "that it will be possible to implement a programme of police force amalgamations in the future when the time is right". It added that the "boundaries of police force areas will be determined by Orders made by the Secretary of State" (para. 10.12).

Special consideration was given to policing London. Not surprisingly, concern was expressed in Parliament that the Bill would open the way to amalgamation of the police – a claim which was refuted by the Lord Chancellor (see *Hansard*, H.L. Vol. 551, col. 458), who explained that the Government had no "predetermined view that a particular size of police force is better than any other". What, then, is intended by the Government in amending s.21 of the Police Act 1964 (see s.14 of the 1994 Act)? The Government's response is that changes to the shape of the force would only be made if it would lead to more effective policing but it was seen as "sensible to allow for the possibility of change in the number or shape of forces, should any alterations become necessary . . . ." (*Hansard*, H.L. Vol. 551, cols. 458, 459). This proposition was not fundamentally challenged, but there was objection to a provision which was perceived as giving the Secretary of State "absolute power to carry through amalgamations without any need for a local inquiry" (*Hansard*, H.L. Vol. 551, col. 471). Amendments were considered in terms of introducing a requirement that a public inquiry should be held whenever an amalgamation was considered but the Act (s.14) largely reflects the original terms of the Bill.

Applying business ethics/standards to the Police Force

An attempt to draw a parallel between the management of the police and the management of a business has raised familiar arguments as to the function of the State in the development of law and order. Lord Lester adopted the criticism of an experienced chairperson of an inner London family proceeding court (Paula Davies; see *Hansard*, H.L. Vol. 551, col. 489) that justice is not just another product and that a legal service cannot be measured like a manufactured product, and he complained that Pt. IV of the Bill introduced what he called "a major erosion in response to Treasury demands to show value for money". In a similar context the Lord Chief Justice remarked:

"A cult seems to have developed and to be invading the whole of the public sector whereby fixed-term contracts and performance pay are seen as the panaceas which will give us managerial efficiency. They may indeed be useful tools in a purely managerial context, but in a judicial context, or where there exists a judicial element, they can have no place" (*Hansard*, H.L. Vol. 551, col. 476).

Police funding

At this stage of the commentary it is as well not to lose sight of s.8 (police fund), s.17 (central funding), s.24 (grants by local authorities), s.25 (acceptance of gifts and loans) and s.23 (provision of common services). It is well understood that the Government provides the bulk of the funds which finance the police but local authorities also provide a substantial amount of finance. Section 25 now empowers the police to provide for the commercial sponsorship of any activity undertaken by the police authority and the hope is that the Treasury will not see this provision as a substitute for the provision of grant funding. Indeed the Government believes that sponsorship is unlikely to produce more than 1 per cent of police funds and they recognise that police authorities will not be able to predict the flow of funds from sponsorship (Standing Committee D, June 14, 1994, col. 348).

Concern has already been expressed that police efficiency and effectiveness is being hampered by a lack of resources. The Government's White Paper *Police Reform* (Cm. 2281) revealed that overall expenditure on the police service for 1993/1994 was estimated at £6.2 billion amounting to an increase of some 88 per cent over a period of 10 years (para. 2.9). Just in excess of 50 per cent of funding is provided by the Home Secretary. He has the responsibility of approving expenditure on capital items and equipment, and for any increase in the establishment of the police force. He also approves the appointment by police authorities of senior officers – which, of course, has resource implications. The White Paper, *Police Reform*, said very little about the balance of funding (as between central and local government) or as to how the funds were to be raised and distributed. Paragraph 9.13 of the White Paper suggested that the costs incurred in providing "essential central services" to the police service might be recovered by a variety of mechanisms. The White Paper did not elaborate on that suggestion in any detail but gave, as an example, "charging for the use of services by allowing police authorities to contract to purchase the services they need".

Putting police forces on a quasi-commercial footing has certain dangers to the efficient running of the police force which may not be immediately apparent. This is more fully dealt with below (see ss.24 and 25 of the 1994 Act). The problem is new, at least in terms of its scale. The police have long received donations from grateful members of the public but the police have facilities which could, in theory, be made commercially available to others and, conversely, the police also have to pay for certain services which they use. The use of experts (forensic services) is a good example. Placing budgetary constraints upon the police leads to the risk that the police will not seek to use the services that they should, on the grounds of cost. The police may hope that they have gathered enough evidence to mount a successful prosecution but to put a law enforcement agency in a position whereby it has to decide, for example, whether an admission of guilt is an adequate reason for not seeking supporting scientific evidence, is of questionable merit.

It will be seen that s.20 of the 1994 Act amends s.38 of the Police Act 1964 to ensure that the reports of inspectors examine the efficiency and *effectiveness* of the police. Clearly, effectiveness cannot be divorced from resources, and yet s.23 amends s.41 of the Police Act 1964 in a way which might cause concern, or at least should require a high degree of scrutiny. The new s.41 empowers the Home Secretary to provide and maintain or contribute to the provision of organisations, facilities and services as he considers necessary or expedient for "prompting the efficiency or effectiveness of the police": see s.41(1), as amended. This provision includes forensic science services but it equally applies to police training centres and other services ripe for privatisation.

By virtue of the new s.41(2) of the Police Act 1964 changes may be made for the use of facilities and services provided by the Home Secretary. The police already pay for certain services (*e.g.* forensic science) on an item-for-item basis. But s.41 goes further and although the 1994 Act is claimed to give police authorities and chief constables the freedom to make day-to-day managerial decisions, s.41(3) empowers the Home Secretary to direct (by regulation) that police forces should use particular facilities or services whether or not they are provided or maintained by the Home Secretary. Whether the police wish to use some, all, or none of the available services or facilities will be a matter for the police – subject to their obligation to be "efficient and effective". This topic is further considered below in relation to ss.8 and 23, but the twin concepts of efficiency and effectiveness must involve a realistic assessment by the government of the day as to what is attainable within the limits of funding. These issues may also call for an examination of quality control of the services or facilities provided and that, in turn, may involve the introduction of schemes of accreditation. In practice, the police will have to make a judgment as to whether a particular service should be employed within the financial constraints of their budget. The concern is that this judgement may be over-influenced by considerations of cost rather than of need.

Changes made by the Government to the Bill

The Government reflected on many of the criticisms made of the original provisions of the Bill and, on March 1, 1994, Earl Ferrers indicated that the Government would amend the Bill so that the standard size of the police authority would increase from 16 to 17 members with a power given to the Home Secretary to increase the size of the authority to reflect the local circumstances and need of the relevant authority, the number of councillors was increased to nine, the police authority could select a shortlist of suitable candidates to be appointed to the authority by the Home Secretary, the selection panels would be drawn up at local level and the chairman would be appointed by the members of the police authority (*Hansard*, H.L. Vol. 552, col. 943).

When those proposals were announced there was relief that the Government had taken on board the main thrust of the complaints levelled against Pts. I, II and III of the Bill. Earl Ferrers remarked that "this is not a question of humiliation; it is a matter of Parliament saying what it thinks about the Bill and the Government saying that they will try to take note of it" (*Hansard*,

H.L. Vol. 552, col. 961). However, anxieties remained and thus s.3 as it now appears embodies further refinements made in respect of this difficult topic.

Along with the reforms of the police authority there exist measures designed to streamline the structure of the police force itself. Section 6 of the Act will have the effect of abolishing the rank of deputy chief constable but it is apparent that other ranks may disappear by regulations made by the Secretary of State (see *Hansard*, H.L. Vol. 551, cols. 459, 460). This position has been justified on the grounds that many forces have already gone a long way towards restructuring the line of management and reducing the number of middle management posts. Some questioned whether the reduction in the number of ranks would not result in a reduction of morale (see *Hansard*, H.L. Vol. 552, col. 154).

Commencement
By s.94(3) of the Act, s.3 and Sched. 2 (in the terms prescribed by s.94(3)) and ss.13, 26, 50, 60, 63(4), 63(7)(a), paras. 17 to 20 of Sched. 5 and s.44 in so far as it relates to paras. 17–20 of Sched. 5, came into force on July 21, 1994.

Part IV, Sched. 8, Pt. II, Sched. 9 and part of s.93 shall come into force on such day as the Lord Chancellor may appoint.

The remaining provisions of the Act shall come into force on such days as the Secretary of State shall appoint, and see now five commencement orders made under the Act; S.I. 1994 Nos. 2025 (C. 38), 2151 (C. 44), 2594 (C. 55), 3075 (C. 72) (S. 163) and 3262 (C. 83).

ABBREVIATIONS
The 1967 Act: Police (Scotland) Act 1967 (c. 77).
The 1984 Act: Police and Criminal Evidence Act 1984 (c. 60).
The 1994 Act: Police and Magistrates' Courts Act 1994 (c. 29).
Police Reform: Police Reform: the Government's proposals for the police service in England and Wales (cm. 2281).

PART I

POLICE

CHAPTER I

PRINCIPAL AMENDMENTS OF POLICE ACT 1964

GENERAL NOTE
The Lord Chancellor explained the Government's original intentions as follows:
"Clause 2 provides for the establishment of the new police authorities outside London. They will, in future, be smaller bodies. They will be free-standing with their own money and their own standard spending assessments. Decisions about policing will be taken by the police authority. They will not be taken by a committee of a local authority which can be overruled by the local authority. It will be possible for local people from any background who have relevant skills or expertise to be members of the authority. Each will have a total of 16 members. Of those, eight are to be members of relevant councils, three are to be magistrates and five will be independent members, appointed by the Home Secretary. The Home Secretary made an announcement in another place yesterday about how those members will be appointed. My noble friend Lord Ferrers also set out the details of this announcement for your Lordships. I hope that the detailed arrangements involving a published job description and personal profile, and short-listing by regional panels, will help to allay concerns about the independence of those members. Rules governing the appointment of members, including eligibility for appointment, tenure of office and allowances, are set out in Schedule 2 to the Bill. This also provides for the appointment of the chairman to the authority, who will be chosen by the Home Secretary from the overall membership" (*Hansard*, H.L. Vol. 551, col. 457).

Considerable objection was taken to the Government's initial proposals. On the one hand it could be said that the object was merely to ensure that the police were accountable to Parliament by streamlining the system for controlling and managing the police by way of a system of "tiers", built within a pyramid, so that each "tier" would operate according to a defined set of rules yet be accountable to the Home Secretary – who is himself accountable to Parliament. Accountability was very much a theme of the *Police Reform* White Paper (Cm. 2281). In para. 2.14 of that paper, the Government complained that:
"the Home Secretary is expected to answer to Parliament for a service for which he has no direct responsibility. The Government provides the majority of funding, but the size of the contribution which the Home Secretary is required to make is not within his control".

The Government also made the point that if the Home Secretary considered that a police authority is not maintaining an adequate and efficient force then he could only (and as a last resort) withhold payment of grant monies or require a Chief Constable to retire "in the interests of efficiency" (para. 2.17). The Government believed that the ability of police authorities to discharge their responsibilities efficiently and effectively was "undermined by their status as subordinate parts of local government" (para. 2.18). Central to this analysis was the constitution of police authorities. It was pointed out that only local councillors or magistrates could be appointed members of these authorities and thus excluded "people in many walks of life who would be able to make a valuable contribution ..." (para. 2.19). The Government proposed that there should be broader local representation in the membership (para. 4.21) and the White Paper *Police Reform* also proposed that each police authority would have 16 members in order to do away with large, unwieldy (and less efficient) authorities.

It is, perhaps, worth emphasising that the Government was anxious to ensure that representation was "local". The White Paper made it clear that the Government sought to permit the Home Secretary to use his power of appointment to bring in five people with relevant knowledge and experience but it added "that might include people with management or financial experience ..." but "the appointees will not necessarily be people from business backgrounds" (paras. 4.21 and 4.22). The Government made no secret of its desire to see the police authorities run in a business-like fashion and, indeed, drew a parallel between the problems faced by the police and other large organisations. The model for reform was that the police service should "use the best techniques of modern management commonplace in the private sector and increasingly in other parts of the public sector ..." (para. 3.1).

Lord Carr (former Home Secretary) remarked that good policing needs efficiency but it also needs more: "to be truly effective, good policing must carry a natural authority with the people whom it is serving" (*Hansard*, H.L. Vol. 551, col. 490). He made the point that to many people the police must represent the "people's police" and not the "Government's police" and that a truly non-political police force is an essential pillar of democracy. This theme represented the backdrop against which many of the speeches in both Houses of Parliament were made. It was the basis upon which considerable argument was mounted that control of the police must be local. Lord Knights, in supporting the criticism that the original draft of the Bill was in danger of infringing long-standing constitutional principles, relied on the Desborough Committee's description of the police as acting:

"not as agents of Government, exercising powers derived from that fact, but as citizens representing the rest of the community, their powers resting on the support, both moral and physical, of their fellow citizen": see *Hansard*, H.L. Vol. 551, cols. 492, 493.

Police areas

Police areas

1.—(1) For section 1 of the 1964 Act there shall be substituted—

"Police areas

Police areas

1.—(1) England and Wales shall be divided into police areas.

(2) The police areas referred to in subsection (1) of this section shall be—

    (a) those listed in Schedule 1A to this Act (subject to any amendment made to that Schedule by an order under section 21 or 21A of this Act, section 58 of the Local Government Act 1972, or section 17 of the Local Government Act 1992), together with

    (b) the City of London police area and the metropolitan police district.

(3) References in Schedule 1A to any local government area are to that area as it is for the time being, but excluding any part of it within the metropolitan police district."

(2) For Schedule 1 to the 1964 Act there shall be substituted (as Schedule 1A) the Schedule set out in Schedule 1 to this Act.

DEFINITIONS

"city of London police area": s.62 of the Police Act 1964.

"metropolitan police district": s.62 of the Police Act 1964; s.44 of the 1994 Act.

Forces outside London

Police forces and police authorities

2. For sections 2, 2A and 3 of the 1964 Act there shall be substituted—

"Forces outside London

Maintenance of police forces
2. A police force shall be maintained for every police area for the time being listed in Schedule 1A to this Act.

Establishment of police authorities
3.—(1) There shall be a police authority for every police area for the time being listed in Schedule 1A to this Act.

(2) A police authority established under this section for any area shall be a body corporate to be known by the name of the area with the addition of the words "Police Authority"."

DEFINITIONS
"police area": s.1 of the Police Act 1964.
"police authority": s.62 of the Police Act 1964; s.44 of the 1994 Act.

Membership of police authorities etc.

3.—(1) After section 3 of the 1964 Act there shall be inserted—

"Membership of police authorities etc.
3A.—(1) Subject to subsection (2) of this section, each police authority established under section 3 of this Act shall consist of seventeen members.

(2) The Secretary of State may by order provide in relation to a police authority specified in the order that the number of its members shall be a specified odd number greater than seventeen.

(3) A statutory instrument containing an order made under subsection (2) of this section shall be laid before Parliament after being made.

(4) Schedules 1B and 1C to this Act shall have effect in relation to police authorities established under section 3 and the appointment of their members.

Reductions in size of police authorities
3B.—(1) This section applies to any order under subsection (2) of section 3A of this Act which varies or revokes an earlier order so as to reduce the number of a police authority's members.

(2) Before making an order to which this section applies, the Secretary of State shall consult—
(a) the authority,
(b) the councils which are relevant councils in relation to the authority for the purposes of Schedule 1B to this Act, and
(c) any panel (or magistrates' courts committee which is responsible, or is represented on a joint committee which is responsible, for the appointment of members of the authority.

(3) An order to which this section applies may include provision as to the termination of the appointment of the existing members of the authority and the making of new appointments or re-appointments."

(2) After Schedule 1A to the 1964 Act there shall be inserted (as Schedules 1B and 1C) the Schedules set out in Schedule 2 to this Act.

DEFINITIONS
  "police authority": s.62 of the Police Act 1964; s.44 of the 1994 Act.

GENERAL NOTE
  This provision should be read in conjunction with ss.4, 14, 16 of and Sched. 2 to the 1994 Act and ss.3, 4 and 28 of the Police Act 1964.
  Although it was always proposed that the Police Authority would be retained as the vehicle for securing the maintenance of the police force, in reality, it would have become a very different body (under the Government's original scheme) because it would have put the Home Secretary in charge of it. He would have been able to appoint his own nominees to the police authority with the further power to appoint his own chairman so that the majority of members of the authority would no longer be members of the local authority. This provoked criticism that "members of a police authority would be expected to act on behalf of local people as the customers of the service which the police force provides" (*per* Lord McIntosh, *Hansard*, H.L. Vol. 551, col. 467) and that the tripartite system (chief officer, local police authorities and the Home Secretary) would be replaced by the Home Secretary commanding both the police authorities and the chief constables (*ibid.*, col. 465). Other critics suggested that the Government was endeavouring to "centralise" the management of the police by devolving local democratic control. Some suggested that the Bill would open the way to the amalgamation of various police forces. The Lord Chancellor was at pains to make it clear that this was not the intention of the Government:
  "The Government believe that these changes in the Bill will help the police to deal with those things which are of greatest concern to local people. This is not centralisation of policing, as is often suggested. It is precisely the reverse. It is giving away to police authorities and to chief constables various powers which the Home Secretary presently has. It is making those local police authorities stronger, more independent and more influential. It is enabling policing to be done locally, to be the responsibility of local people, and for policing to be accountable to local people.
  The Bill makes no changes to the existing pattern of police forces, nor to the areas which they cover. I can make it absolutely clear that the Government have no plans for police force amalgamation" (*Hansard*, H.L. Vol. 551, col. 458).
  This did not entirely allay the fears of a number of members of the House of Lords who pointed to the provision of cl. 10 (now s.14), which amends s.21 of the Police Act 1964 so as to give the Secretary of State power to alter police areas, and boundaries, by Order. There is nothing in this provision which would require the Secretary of State to hold, say, a public inquiry before he reached a decision (a point canvassed during debate; see *Hansard*, H.L. Vol. 553, col. 190) and thus, it was said, this provision might yet be used to amalgamate forces (see the speech of Lord McIntosh, *Hansard*, H.L. Vol. 551, col. 465). The new s.21B of the Police Act 1964 is intended to go some way to allaying those fears. Thus, the Lord Chancellor said:
  "Under Clause 10 [now s.14] the Secretary of State may make changes to police force boundaries by order. This includes changes to the Metropolitan Police district. But the clause places a requirement on the Secretary of State, if he decides that a change is desirable in the interests of efficiency or effectiveness, to consult interested parties, to give his reasons for any proposed change, and to consider objections to the plan. A change proposed by the Secretary of State can only be made if it is approved by both Houses of Parliament" (*Hansard*, H.L. Vol. 551, cols. 458, 459).
  As to the size that a particular police force should be in a particular area (bearing in mind that the police would be required to be accountable to the public for their performance) the Lord Chancellor said:
  "We have no predetermined view that a particular size of police force is better than any other. We would only wish to make changes if there were good arguments that it would lead to more effective policing. However, we intend that the legislation should lay the basis of policing for many years to come. It is, therefore, sensible to allow for the possibility of change in the number or shape of forces, should any alterations become necessary in future" (*Hansard*, H.L. Vol. 551, col. 458).
  However, the main area of dispute concerned the size of the police authorities and their constitution. This is covered by ss.3 and 4 and should be read in conjunction with Scheds. 2, 3 and 4 of the 1994 Act. When the Bill was introduced into the Lords, the Lord Chancellor described the proposals as follows:
  "Clause 3 [now s.3] sets out the general functions and duties of the new police authorities. The primary duty of each police authority will be to secure the maintenance of an efficient and effective police force for the area. This duty is slightly different from the duty under the 1964

Act as it stands, which is to maintain an adequate and efficient force. This small but important change will ensure that police authorities give priority not only to achieving value for money with the resources available, but also to ensure that the results are consistent with the objectives that have been set. Similar changes are made by the Bill to other references in the 1964 Act to efficiency. In the l990s, and beyond, we should equally be concerned with effectiveness.

For the first time, there will be a duty on each local police authority to produce a costed local policing plan, setting out its priorities for the forthcoming year. They will do this together with the chief constable, and in so doing, they must take account of the views of local people. The Bill requires this plan to be published. Each police authority will also be required to publish an annual report, assessing how far the plans for the previous year have been achieved. Local people will be able to see clearly what their local police are doing with their money and how well they are doing it" (*Hansard*, H.L. Vol. 551, col. 458).

These proposals were attacked on a number of grounds. To make sense of the complaints it is important to have regard to the original wording of the Bill (then cl. 2 and its Schedules). Under that proposal, each police authority was to have consisted of 16 members, of whom eight were to be members of a "relevant council" appointed in accordance with the original schedule; three were to be magistrates and five to be appointed by the Secretary of State. The chairman was to be appointed – not by the authority – but by the Secretary of State. This was attacked on the grounds that only half of the members would be members of the local authority and thus the Secretary of State would command the police authorities. This, it was said, struck at the heart of the tripartite system of policing between chief officers, local police authorities and the Home Secretary – a system which had been in force since the Municipal Corporations Act 1835 (repealed by Municipal Corporations Act 1882 (c. 50)), the Local Government Act 1888 (c. 41) and the Police Act 1964 (c. 48). These initial proposals did not enhance local democratic power but, on the contrary, moved power towards central government. The wisdom of so acting was questioned by Viscount Whitelaw who said:

"Is it wise particularly at a time when community policing is being rightly stressed? Is there not a danger that local councils would tend to lose interest in their police forces? That would certainly be a loss. I know from experience that many of those councils are proud of their police and are closely interested in their local force" (*Hansard*, H.L. Vol. 551, col. 481).

The proposals also meant that every police authority – no matter how small or large the force – was of exactly the same size; 16 members. Furthermore, the figure itself must have been arbitrarily determined and did not take into account local needs. These measures were therefore seen as being designed to put power into the hands of the Home Secretary and not merely as a way of providing a fountain of accountability. Thus, Lord Harris of Greenwich said:

"These provisions have nothing whatever to do with the efficiency of the British Police service; they have to do with the power of a Home Secretary in future ... The risk to the independence of chief officers, which is the bulwark of our present system, is obvious ... The measure before us today raises issues of the utmost constitutional gravity ... This country does not have a written constitution or a constitutional court. This House is the final guardian of the liberties of the British people" (*Hansard*, H.L. Vol. 551, col. 474).

With these objections in mind, the Government reflected on their position and on March 1, 1994, Earl Ferrers on behalf of the Government restated the Government's intention in respect of the proposed reforms:

"One of the great virtues of this Bill, I thought, was its overriding objective to move power or responsibility – call it what you will – away from Whitehall and down to the locality, to police authorities and to chief constables ... The operational independence of chief officers of police is paramount. That was an anxiety which was expressed by your Lordships and I want to make it quite clear that that is a cardinal principle which underlies all the Government's proposals.

It was in relation to that operational independence of chief officers that questions about the composition of the police authority became linked with other features of the Bill, such as the setting of objectives, the monitoring of performance, the terms of appointment of chief officers, and so on. I do not complain that the House felt strongly about these matters. They are vitally important, and it is right that any changes which may have an impact on these matters should be scrutinised through and through.

I must confess, however, that I had mixed feelings about the task which we faced. It seemed that there was no doubt about the strength of feeling of some of your Lordships. There was rather more doubt, however, about the solutions" (*Hansard*, H.L. Vol. 552, col. 941).

The Government then indicated the amendments which it sought to introduce on Report:

"However, the amendments which we propose to table for the Report stage, and which will relate to the composition of the police authority, would have the following effects:

The standard size of a police authority would increase from 16 to 17. The Home Secretary would have the power, as proposed earlier, to increase its size where local circumstances made the Home Secretary consider that it was desirable to do so. There would be no upper limit on the size of the police authority, although the aim would be to keep authorities as small as possible.

The 17 members of a police authority would consist of nine councillors, three magistrates, and five independent members. That would always leave local councillors in a majority over everyone else.

Where the Secretary of State increased the size of the authority, the local authority members would always be in a majority of one, and the numbers of magistrates and independent members would be increased in proportion to the overall size of the authority.

It would greatly simplify my explanation of the other features of the arrangements, and it might conceivably also ease your Lordships' comprehension of them, if I were to explain the arrangements entirely in terms of the standard sized police authority of 17 members.

The five independent members would be co-opted by the other members of the police authority; that is, by the nine councillors and the three magistrates. It would be they, and only they, who would choose the five independent members. They would do that from a list of 10 names, which would be forwarded to them by the Home Secretary. The Home Secretary would choose the 10 names, which he will forward to the police authority, from a shortlist of 20 which would be provided to him by a local selection panel. In considering which 10 names to forward to the police authority the Home Secretary would have an opportunity to identify those candidates who seemed to him to be the strongest. I should emphasise one point. The Home Secretary would have no power to forward to the police authority any name which had not been on the short list which he had received from the selection panel.

The selection panels would be drawn up at local level. There would not be, as we had proposed previously, six regional panels. We now propose that there should be one selection panel for each police area.

A selection panel would consist of three people. One panel member would be chosen by the councillors and magistrates on the police authority. They could choose someone from among themselves, or they could choose some other local person of independent judgment from outside the police authority. The second panel member would be appointed by the Home Secretary. He would also be a local person of independent judgment, almost certainly from outside the police authority. The third panel member, who would also be required to be a local person, would be appointed by the other two panel members. In other words, the third panel member would be chosen by the police authority's choice and the Home Secretary's choice" (*Hansard*, H.L. Vol. 552, col. 943).

By the combination of s.3 and Sched. 2, a police authority will consist of 17 (or in some cases, more) members, of which nine are to be members of a "relevant council" and the election of the chairperson is now a matter for the authority.

Functions of police authorities

4. For section 4 of the 1964 Act there shall be substituted—

"General functions of police authorities

4.—(1) It shall be the duty of every police authority established under section 3 of this Act to secure the maintenance of an efficient and effective police force for its area.

(2) In discharging its functions, every police authority established under section 3 of this Act shall have regard to—

    (a) any objectives determined by the Secretary of State under section 28A of this Act,

    (b) any objectives determined by the authority under section 4A,

    (c) any performance targets established by the authority, whether in compliance with a direction under section 28B or otherwise, and

    (d) any local policing plan issued by the authority under section 4B.

(3) In discharging any function to which a code of practice issued under section 28C of this Act relates, a police authority established under section 3 of this Act shall have regard to the code.

(4) A police authority shall comply with any direction given to it by the Secretary of State under section 28B or 28D of this Act.

Local policing objectives

4A.—(1) Every police authority established under section 3 of this Act shall, before the beginning of each financial year, determine objectives for the policing of the authority's area during that year.

(2) Objectives determined under this section may relate to matters to which objectives determined under section 28A of this Act also relate, or to other matters, but in any event shall be so framed as to be consistent with the objectives determined under that section.

(3) Before determining objectives under this section a police authority shall—

(a) consult the chief constable for the area, and

(b) consider any views obtained by it in accordance with arrangements made under section 106 of the Police and Criminal Evidence Act 1984 (arrangements for obtaining the views of the community on policing).

Local policing plans

4B.—(1) Every police authority established under section 3 of this Act shall, before the beginning of each financial year, issue a plan setting out the proposed arrangements for the policing of the authority's area during the year ("the local policing plan").

(2) The local policing plan shall include a statement of the authority's priorities for the year, of the financial resources expected to be available and of the proposed allocation of those resources, and shall give particulars of—

(a) any objectives determined by the Secretary of State under section 28A of this Act,

(b) any objectives determined by the authority under section 4A, and

(c) any performance targets established by the authority, whether in compliance with a direction under section 28B or otherwise.

(3) A draft of the local policing plan shall be prepared by the chief constable for the area and submitted by him to the authority for it to consider.

(4) Before issuing a local policing plan which differs from the draft submitted by the chief constable under subsection (3) of this section, a police authority shall consult the chief constable.

(5) A police authority shall arrange for the local policing plan to be published in such manner as appears to it to be appropriate, and shall send a copy of the plan to the Secretary of State.

Annual reports by police authorities

4C.—(1) As soon as possible after the end of each financial year every police authority established under section 3 shall issue a report relating to the policing of the authority's area for the year.

(2) A report issued under this section for any year by a police authority shall include an assessment of the extent to which the local policing plan for that year has been carried out.

(3) A police authority shall arrange for every report issued by it under this section to be published in such manner as appears to it to be appropriate, and shall send a copy of the report to the Secretary of State."

DEFINITIONS
"police authority": s.62(b) of the Police Act 1964; s.44 of the 1994 Act.
"police force": s.62(c) of the Police Act 1964; s.44 of the 1994 Act.

GENERAL NOTE

Functions of police authorities and the role of chief constables
Described by the Government as "probably the single most important [section]" in the Act (Standing Committee D, May 17, 1994, col. 130, *per* Mr MacLennan), this provision forms part

of the Government's aim to provide the Home Secretary with the powers he needs to give a "clear steer" (or indication) to the police authority and the chief constable in respect of the required objectives and performance targets expected of the police. However, this section must also be read in conjunction with s.15 which amends s.28 of the Police Act 1964 by the addition of s.28A (setting objectives for police authorities); s.28B (setting of performance targets); s.28C (codes of practice for police authorities) and s.28D (power vested in the Secretary of State to give directions to police authorities after receipt of an adverse report made to the Home Secretary); and see s.16 of the 1994 Act. The stated aim of this provision is to set out a "clear chain of accountability" (Standing Committee D, May 19, 1994, col. 162, Mr Wardle).

It is intended that the police authorities should have the protection of the public and the detection of crime at the top of the agenda, but crime prevention and the involvement of the community in policing are also regarded as being important objectives. The general duty is thus set out in subs. (1) but it will be noted that the police authority need do no more than "have regard to" any objectives, performance targets and local policing plans referred to in subs. (2). Of course, the reality is that any significant failure to comply with these statutory functions may result in both adverse publicity and the imposition of financial sanctions against the offending police authorities. Critics of s.4 expressed concern at the amount of bureaucracy and correspondence that might unnecessarily result between civil servants in order to comply with these measures (Standing Committee D, May 19, 1994, col. 144). However, the Government believes that the relevant parties should be able to work together without incurring unnecessary paperwork. This view is founded, in part, on the belief that chief officers and police authorities "usually get on with each other" because they have "common goals, ideals and common values" and thus it is hoped that the parties will "on almost all occasions ... agree objectives and the policing plan" (*per* Mr Wardle, Parliamentary Under-Secretary of State for the Home Department, Standing Committee D, May 19, 1994, col. 163).

The Government has pointed out that the statutory measures, set out in this section, do not mean that police authorities have no influence over the operational policies adopted by the force. In discharging their responsibilities, the police authority will be expected to determine local objectives after consulting the local community and the chief constable. The police authority will then set performance targets and policing priorities. Any local policing plan should be prepared by the chief constable and submitted to the police authority for its consideration. The Government recognise that the policing plan will grow out of the police budget – for which the police authority will be held responsible – and it will thus be accountable to the Home Secretary. Making sure that the police carry out these various targets and objectives, is the responsibility of the chief constable whose authority, in that regard, is enshrined by s.5 of the 1994 Act.

The Lord Chancellor introduced the Government's original set of proposals as follows: "Clauses 2 to 8 [now ss.2 to 10] are crucial in giving local police authorities and chief constables defined responsibilities and in enabling them to get on with the job without unnecessary interference. The Bill also ensures that there will be a clear framework for setting police priorities and measuring performance. Clause 11 [s.15] enables the Home Secretary to set key objectives for policing and to require police authorities to set performance targets for measuring the achievement of these objectives. The clause also enables him to issue codes of practice relating to the exercise of police authority functions.

The Government are confident that all police authorities will be well equipped to ensure that the force provides a high quality service. Some provision needs to be made, however, for the eventuality of a police authority which fails to meet its obligations. Clause 11 also enables the Secretary of State to direct a police authority to take remedial measures, where a special inspection report indicates that a police force is not efficient or not effective. The power will only be available as a last resort, where there is independent evidence from an inspector of constabulary that a police authority is failing in its duties" (*Hansard*, H.L. Vol. 551, col. 459). Much of these provisions has remained intact.

Chief constables

5. For section 5 of the 1964 Act there shall be substituted—

"General functions of chief constables

5.—(1) A police force maintained under section 2 of this Act shall be under the direction and control of the chief constable appointed under section 5A.

(2) In discharging his functions, every chief constable shall have regard to the local policing plan issued by the police authority for his area under section 4B of this Act.

Appointment and removal of chief constables
5A.—(1) The chief constable of a police force maintained under section 2 of this Act shall be appointed by the police authority responsible for maintaining the force, but subject to the approval of the Secretary of State and to regulations under Part II of this Act.

(2) Without prejudice to any regulations under Part II of this Act or under the Police Pensions Act 1976, the police authority, acting with the approval of the Secretary of State, may call upon the chief constable to retire in the interests of efficiency or effectiveness.

(3) Before seeking the approval of the Secretary of State under subsection (2) of this section, the police authority shall give the chief constable an opportunity to make representations and shall consider any representations that he makes.

(4) A chief constable who is called upon to retire under subsection (2) of this section shall retire on such date as the police authority may specify or on such earlier date as may be agreed upon between him and the authority."

Deputy and assistant chief constables

6. For section 6 of the 1964 Act there shall be substituted—

"Assistant chief constables
6.—(1) The ranks that may be held in a police force maintained under section 2 of this Act shall include that of assistant chief constable (but not that of deputy chief constable); and in every such police force there shall be at least one person holding that rank.

(2) Appointments and promotions to the rank of assistant chief constable shall be made, in accordance with regulations under Part II of this Act, by the police authority after consultation with the chief constable and subject to the approval of the Secretary of State.

(3) Subsections (2), (3) and (4) of section 5A of this Act shall apply to an assistant chief constable as they apply to a chief constable.

(4) A chief constable shall after consulting his police authority designate a person holding the rank of assistant chief constable to exercise all the powers and duties of the chief constable—

(a) during any absence, incapacity or suspension from duty of the chief constable, or

(b) during any vacancy in the office of chief constable.

(5) No more than one person shall be authorised to act by virtue of a designation under subsection (4) of this section at any one time; and a person so authorised shall not have power to act by virtue of that subsection for a continuous period exceeding three months except with the consent of the Secretary of State.

(6) The provisions of subsection (4) of this section shall be in addition to, and not in substitution for, any other enactment which makes provision for the exercise by any other person of powers conferred on a chief constable."

DEFINITIONS
"police authority": ss.3, 62 of the Police Act 1964; s.44 of the 1994 Act.

GENERAL NOTE
This section (formerly cl. 5) will have the effect of abolishing the rank of deputy chief constable and it is apparent that other ranks may be removed by Regulation.

The abolition of the deputy chief constable follows in the wake of the Sheehy Inquiry, into *Police Responsibilities and Rewards* (Cm. 2280), which examined the need for a variety of ranks within the police as well as pay and conditions of service. It was s.6 of the Police Act 1964 which required a force to appoint a deputy chief constable and to perform all the powers and duties of the chief constable for a period of up to three months (except with the consent of the Secretary of

State) during the absence, incapacity, suspension of duty, or vacancy in the post of the chief constable. The abolition of the rank of deputy chief constable does not mean that a vacuum is created by the temporary absence of a chief constable. This is because s.6 permits the chief constable to designate an assistant chief constable to perform his duties during his absence. To what extent these reforms achieve any real saving or benefit remains to be seen.

Not surprisingly, this proposal was originally met with some concern but the purpose of abolishing the rank of deputy chief constable is said to be to "streamline the top management ranks of the service" (*per* Earl Ferrers, *Hansard*, H.L. Vol. 552, col. 154). Earl Ferrers went on to explain the reason for the reduction of ranks:

"We felt that the ranks of chief superintendent and chief inspector should be abolished. The purpose of removing those is to enable further streamlining of the management hierarchy by simplifying the structure. That will provide clearer and more direct communications. It will enable those police officers with the greatest ability – which is important – to move more quickly through the ranks. It will also provide chief constables with the opportunity to exchange middle management posts for more police officers on the beat.

The need for streamlining the forces' management structures has been accepted for a long time. Indeed, many forces have gone a long way towards reducing the number of middle management posts. But the existing rank structure, which has six separate ranks, from sergeant to assistant chief constable, hinders forces achieving the optimum management restructuring. … Traditionally, although I accept that it is not so in every case, a person may be a sergeant and become an inspector, then a chief inspector and move up to superintendent. Then he becomes a chief superintendent and moves up through that grade. Under the new proposal there will be only two hurdles to overcome. Once a person has finished being a sergeant he becomes an inspector. Thereafter he will be able to move right up the chain. The most able people will move up to the top the most quickly. There will then be a hurdle to jump to reach the office of superintendent. The most efficient will be able to move quickly up the structure until they come to the position of assistant chief constable.

There have been occasions when forces have identified a chief superintendent's post, a superintendent's post or a chief inspector's post. We feel that if the two middle-ranking structures are done away with, it will enable the movement of people through those ranks to be quicker and that the best people will get to the top earlier than they would otherwise have done.

The noble Lord, Lord Knights, referred to public order situations. The police have a separate mechanism for designating authority to people in those circumstances. They have gold, silver and bronze insignia. As the noble Lord will know only too well, those are imposed on the rank structure specifically for the purpose of providing for clarity of command in public order situations. Changing the rank structure does not affect that.

I accept that it is difficult for people who are in those posts. When one has risen in a disciplined service to the rank of, say, chief superintendent, one feels an understandable pride at having done so. If that rank does not exist in the future, that person will inevitably feel a degree of regret. However, if one is trying to look at the structure for the future, it is better to have the command simpler and quicker so that there will be a more streamlined structure in the future than there has been in the past. For those reasons we consider the change important".

These views have prevailed despite some reservation: see the speech of Baroness Hilton, *Hansard*, H.L. Vol. 552, col. 159.

Other members of police forces

7. In section 7 of the 1964 Act (other members of police forces) in subsection (1)—

(a) for the words "section 1" there shall be substituted the words "section 2",

(b) the words ", deputy chief constable" shall be omitted, and

(c) after the word "superintendent" there shall be inserted the words ", chief inspector".

DEFINITIONS
"deputy chief constable": s.6 of the Police Act 1964.
"police forces": s.62(c) of the Police Act 1964.

GENERAL NOTE
This provision brings the Police Act 1964 into line with the reforms introduced by the 1994 Act in respect of the ranks which may exist within a police force; see s.7 of the Police Act 1964.

Because the rank of deputy chief constable is abolished under the 1994 Act it follows that amendments were required in respect of both ss.6 and 7 of the Police Act 1964.

Police fund

8. For section 8 of the 1964 Act (financial provisions) there shall be substituted—

> **"Police fund**
> 8.—(1) Each police authority established under section 3 of this Act shall keep a fund to be known as the police fund.
> (2) Subject to any regulations under the Police Pensions Act 1976, all receipts of the police authority shall be paid into the police fund and all expenditure of the authority shall be paid out of that fund.
> (3) Accounts shall be kept by each police authority of payments made into or out of the police fund."

DEFINITIONS
"police authority": ss.3, 62 of the Police Act 1964; s.44 of the 1994 Act.

GENERAL NOTE
Police funding is derived from central and local government sources. The implications of para. 9.13 of the White Paper (suggesting that the costs incurred in providing "essential central services", to the police service, might be recovered by a variety of mechanisms) may not be immediately apparent, but it is a topic which requires detailed and critical examination. Under this heading, it is appropriate to have in mind the provisions of s.25 of the 1994 Act, which adds s.53B to the Police Act 1964 so as to permit the police authority to accept gifts and loans in connection with the discharge of any of its functions. This controversial provision means that the police authority may now raise money through sponsorship but an amendment (to prohibit the Secretary of State from taking into account the amount of any gift or loan accepted by the authority in determining the amount of grant to be made to the authority under the 1994 Act) was narrowly defeated (see Standing Committee D, June 14, 1994, col. 334). The Government indicated that a police authority is not expected to be able to rely on and to take into account income from the acceptance of gifts or loans as it cannot be predicted how long it would continue to be a source of income and it is unlikely to prove to be a regular source of income. Of course, much may depend on the results of this provision. Successful schemes which are forecasted as being likely to attract an amount falling within a sufficiently high range of figures may, ultimately, tempt the Treasury to reduce the amount of the grant if only to encourage police authorities to improve, or to persist in, their entrepreneurial skills.

As said above, putting police forces on a quasi-commercial footing poses certain dangers to the efficient running of the police force which may not be immediately apparent. For example, forensic evidence is a powerful tool in the detection and apprehension of criminals. The fact that incriminating (or damning) evidence may be obtained in a variety of ways may in itself serve as a deterrent to further offending – but this fact loses some of its impact if would-be offenders (contemplating the commission of so-called "minor" offences) believe that the use of forensic science services are unlikely to be deployed against them, on the grounds of cost, thus reducing the magnitude of risk of being apprehended – at least in the mind of the offender. Concern has already been expressed that the budgetary constraints placed upon the police now mean that they are not making full or appropriate use of forensic services. Thus, Dr Angela Gallop (of Forensic Access) wrote in the *Journal of the Forensic Science Service* (1994, p. 126):

> "We must set to, again and again, at meetings such as this one, to hammer home the principles on which the future of our profession needs to be established. Important among these are that the police must have unconstrained access to the best forensic science available. There should be no question of their having to impose restrictions on the scope of scientific examinations on cost grounds, or having to use substandard facilities because they are cheaper. By the same token, in every case where scientific evidence is going to be presented by the prosecution, the defence should as of right be free to instruct whomsoever it pleases, but again in the sure knowledge that the expert it chooses is properly and demonstrably qualified and in the particular fields at issue.

All this will require two things: a new approach to funding for scientific services both for the prosecution and the defence and not necessarily involving the complete abandonment of direct charging, and a new robust system of accreditation and regulation. This must be transparently dependent on knowledge, training and expertise, and genuine ability, and policed by a properly constituted body with an appropriate number of sharp teeth and the power to use them effectively.

All of this has been said before, and will need saying again until sufficient people realize that Rome is burning, and that playing the fiddle is no way to respond".

The significance of this statement merits further explanation because on one hand it provides a warning, if only by example, of the problems that can arise if the administration of justice and law enforcement were to be run on purely commercial principles. The Forensic Science Service (FSS) provides independent scientific support to the investigation of crime, and similar support is provided to the police serving London by the Metropolitan Police Forensic Science Laboratory. However, as para. 9.5 of the White Paper *Police Reform* makes plain, the FSS is also a "Next Steps Agency" and it has been so since April 1991. The FSS now aims to recover its full costs through direct charges to its customers. According to the White Paper (para. 9.5):

"... the changes have created a more customer-orientated business and are prompting a new approach to the way in which police decisions are being made about the use of forensic science in criminal cases".

The question is whether this "new approach" is producing desirable results. At a lecture sponsored by the Criminal Bar Association on June 18, 1994, Dr Gallop clearly did not think so and had this to say on the question of resources (and other matters):

"There is currently no system of regulation or accreditation of forensic scientists which means that any Tom, Dick or Harriet with the most minimal of scientific qualifications and not necessarily any forensic science experience, can set themselves up as forensic scientists. ... Some experts who came to check the work I'd done for the police didn't know how to use a microscope properly or have the faintest idea how to read a blood grouping plate.

In 1991 the Forensic Science Service became a Government agency and the police were free to go where they liked for scientific help and advice. Obviously, with tight budgets very much in mind, they are attracted by cheaper alternatives to the traditional laboratories and they have started to use other outfits who are jumping on the bandwagon but who have little idea about the particular requirements of forensic science work and no real experience of the necessary background against which to set their findings.

Over and above all of this, the police are becoming increasingly reluctant to ask scientists to visit scenes of crime, and ever more selective in the items they send to the laboratory for examination. This means that there is an increasing danger of the evidence the scientist produces, and particularly his interpretation of it, being unbalanced in the context of the case at issue. There has always been a general paucity of information available to scientists working for the police, and this seems set to exacerbate the problem.

All this means that it is more than ever important for defence lawyers to make sure that they have proper scientific help and advice, not just to check what has been found and the interpretation placed on it by police scientists, but also whether and to what extent the findings might be explained as the result of some sort of unwitting contamination, as well as the consequences on the defence case of the selection of items that were examined.

But budgetary problems don't affect just the prosecution. Most criminal defence work seems to be funded by Legal Aid and it can be very difficult to persuade Legal Aid Boards as to the extent and depth of scientific investigations required by the defence if the prosecution's scientific evidence is to be properly bottomed. Solicitors are increasingly required to obtain estimates from different scientists and then exhorted to go for the cheapest. In an entirely unregulated field, this is a recipe for disaster because obviously someone who has no real idea of what needs to be done, or how to go about it, will provide a much lower estimate than someone who does".

Russell Stockdale BSc., C.Biol., Fl.Biol., expressed similar concerns when he said:

"The police now have to pay for the work which is done in the laboratories on an item-by-item basis. A seriously concerning, insidious effect of these changes is relevant to my talk today for it has emerged that, in some areas, police have apparently taken to opening sealed exhibit bags in order to have a quick look to see whether they think they can see potential trace evidence on the items and that it is worth the cost of sending them to be examined. Of course, none of this is ever recorded. The consequences of this sort of behaviour, induced by the need to save money, are incalculable when it comes to the safety of evidence derived from fibre and other microscopic traces. Any system which encourages it, however indirectly, is fatally flawed and needs to be thrown out.

Another unacceptable consequence of direct charging this time the fault of forensic scientists themselves is the unrecorded examination of items in order to avoid running up what might be seen to be an over large bill to the police. ... I have to say that I have been appalled at the damage done to the [Forensic Science] Service in the name of efficiency, effectiveness and economy, and even more appalled that the Metropolitan Police Laboratory here in London, is contemplating going down the same road.

Forensic science is losing its way and this is something which should be of great concern to all of you here today. Financial pressures of one sort or another are making the work of many of the police scientists increasingly vulnerable and, at the same time, constraints on Legal Aid are making it less likely that it will be investigated properly on behalf of the defence. To this extent, I echo Dr Gallop's warning that forensic science will continue to feature in miscarriages of justice unless and until the profession is properly regulated, realistically funded and appropriately managed".

The Government's view was explained by the Lord Chancellor as follows:
"Part I also puts into place a new system of police funding. Clause 13 [section 17] replaces the current provisions on police grant, under which the Home Secretary refunds 51 per cent of police expenditure. In future, each police authority will receive a cash limited amount of police grant. The Secretary of State is required to report in another place on how he proposes to allocate police grant and he must secure the approval of that House to his proposals.

The new police authorities will also receive funding through revenue support grant, non-domestic rates and the council tax. Clause 22 [section 22] establishes the new police authorities as major precepting bodies for local government finance purposes.

The Bill will also reinforce the independent scrutiny of police performance. It makes important changes to the role of Her Majesty's inspectors of constabulary. Clause 16 [section 20] extends their statutory responsibilities to the inspection of the Metropolitan Police. Clause 17 [section 21] requires that all inspection reports are published and that every police authority publishes a response. This will help to provide much greater openness about what the police are doing and how well they are doing it" (*Hansard*, H.L. Vol. 551, col. 459).

Except by way of two small (but not unimportant) amendments, the original wording of cl. 13 (now s.17) has remained intact. The effect of the section is to substitute a new s.31 of the Police Act 1964. Earl Ferrers described the new s.31 as having been carefully drafted to permit its application to all police authorities without exception. It has been designed to require the Secretary of State to determine the amount of grant to be made to each authority and it allows him to use rules or a formula to allocate part of the total amount available. It also requires him to state the considerations he took into account in deciding how much to give and to whom; see *Hansard*, H.L. Vol. 552, col. 362. In other words, the Secretary of State would be accountable to the House of Commons for his determinations in respect of the allocation of funding to various police authorities but he is allowed a degree of latitude in deciding how much grant should be received by different police authorities.

Not surprisingly, concern was expressed as to what machinery would be put in place for consultation between the Home Office and the police in order to determine how funds should be distributed. During 1994, discussions took place among the Home Office, the local authority associations and the Association of Chief Police Officers about grant distribution formulae for 1995/1996. These discussions seem to have proceeded on the basis that the grant should be divided roughly 51 per cent (central funds) and 49 per cent (local finance) and this approach received the support of the legislature. However, because local authorities will continue to play a major part in the management of police services, concern was expressed that the Bill merely provided that the Secretary of State should determine the basis of his grant only with the "approval" of the Treasury rather than in consultation with the local authority associations or associations' representatives of chief police officers. For this reason, an amendment (no. 99) was moved in the Lords to make such consultation mandatory. However, upon the Minister of State for the Home Office (Earl Ferrers) undertaking to give further consideration to that aspect of the legislation, amendment 99 was withdrawn; *Hansard*, H.L. Vol. 552, col. 363.

The Minister did not think it necessary to impose upon the Home Secretary a statutory obligation to consult either with the local authorities or chief constables. The reason given for this approach was twofold. First, the Home Secretary will, in any event, consult widely with the chief constables and the local authorities on the distribution of police funding (*supra*, col. 363). Without further explanation, it could be argued that if this is truly the intention of the Home Office, then why not put that process on an open statutory footing? However, the answer seems to be that the Department of the Environment will be expected to use the same formula as the Home Office in distributing its share of the funding to the police authorities but the Department of the Environment is already "bound to a process of consultation" with the local authority associations. "Therefore, to bind the Home Secretary as well in a similar way would appear to duplicate the process", *per* Earl Ferrers (*ibid.*, col. 364). The Minister recognised that this process did not, as yet, include chief constables, but the Home Secretary "wants to be able to discuss his proposed distribution formula simultaneously with the local authorities representatives and chief constables" (col. 364). This explanation was accepted by the Legislature (the new s.31(2) of the Police Act 1964 having been enacted in the form originally proposed by the Government) even though it was not explained on what basis the Department of the Environment is "bound to a process of consultation". Nevertheless, there is no good reason for thinking that intentions declared by the Government will not be put into practice. In any event, the necessary safeguard may be said to be found in the new subss. (3) and (6) of s.31 of the 1964 Act which provide that a report shall be prepared by the Secretary of State (and laid before Parliament) stating the considerations which he took into account in making the determination.

The initial drafts of the new subss. 31(4) and (5) of the Police Act 1964 – which appeared in cl. 13 of the Bill – were amended (in part on the initiative of the Government). It had been proposed that in determining the allocation among police authorities of the whole or any part of the aggregate amount of grants, the Secretary of State could exercise his discretion by applying a set of rules "decided upon by him and then applied without modification by reference to the particular circumstances of each authority" and that the rules may be different for different authorities or different classes of authority.

Those words in quotes were removed by amendment 100 (moved in the Lords *Hansard*, H.L. Vol. 553, col. 206) and in their place were substituted the words "such formulae or other rules as he considers appropriate"; see now s.17 of the 1994 Act.

The original draft for revising s.31 of the Police Act 1964 (as it appeared in cl. 13 of the Bill) was capable of a number of interpretations and criticisms (politely described by Lord McIntosh as an "opaque subsection": *Hansard*, H.L. Vol. 553, col. 205). Earl Ferrers explained that the new s.31(4) of the 1964 Act was not intended to allow the Secretary of State to do what he likes (see *Hansard*, H.L. Vol. 552, col. 368) but to allow him to allocate all or part of a police specific grant by adopting rules which depend upon the individual circumstances of each police authority. The phrase "applied without modification" was to embrace formulae such as fixing a grant by determining that it shall be payable "for every 1,000 residents or every 100 road miles".

The amended wording to the new s.31(4) (see amendments Nos. 100 and 101 to the Bill, moved on March 15, 1994) were thus intended to clarify the Government's intentions – not to change its effect. Earl Ferrers suggested that a formula "is more rigid than a rule" – presumably on the basis that to every rule there are, or will be, exceptions – and thus the words "without modification" became redundant. However, it is submitted that there is force in the view put forward by Lord McIntosh (*Hansard*, H.L. Vol. 553, col. 206) that the expression "formulae" is a "safer term" but it is doubtful that the words "other rules" are any less discretionary than the original wording of cl. 13 of the Bill. This is because the very expression "*other* rules" must suggest that the "formulae" envisaged will not always be rigid in application – particularly in cases where the formulae consist of rules to which there will probably be exceptions.

A local authority may make grants to any police authority established under s.3 of the 1994 Act whose police area falls wholly or partly within the county, district, county borough or borough; see s.24 of the 1994 Act which adds a new s.53A to the Police Act 1964.

Supply of goods and services

9. After section 8 of the 1964 Act there shall be inserted—

> **"Supply of goods and services**
>   8A. Subsections (1) to (3) of section 1 of the Local Authorities (Goods and Services) Act 1970 (supply of goods and services by local authorities) shall apply to a police authority established under section 3 of this Act as they apply to a local authority, except that in their application to a police authority the references in those subsections to a public body shall be read as references to any person."

DEFINITIONS
    "police authority": ss.3, 62(b) of the Police Act 1964; s.44 of the 1994 Act.

GENERAL NOTE
    This technical, and seemingly bland provision, is not without importance to the extent that it demonstrates the Government's commitment to ensure that the police authority have much greater control over their own affairs and those of the police than was previously the case. Critics of that development might point to this measure as indicating the extent to which local government is losing influence in the political arena.

Civilian employees

10. For section 10 of the 1964 Act there shall be substituted—

> **"Civilian employees**
>   10.—(1) A police authority established under section 3 of this Act

may employ persons to assist the police force maintained by it or otherwise to enable the authority to discharge its functions.

(2) A police authority shall exercise its powers under section 101 (and section 107) of the Local Government Act 1972 so as to secure that, subject to subsection (3) of this section, any person employed by the authority under this section is under the direction and control of the chief constable of the police force maintained by the authority.

(3) Subsection (2) of this section shall not apply to such of the persons employed by the authority as may be agreed between the chief constable and the authority or, in the absence of agreement, as may be determined by the Secretary of State.

(4) The powers of direction and control referred to in subsection (2) of this section include the powers of engagement and dismissal."

DEFINITIONS
    "police authority": ss.3, 62(b) of the Police Act 1964; s.44 of the 1994 Act.

GENERAL NOTE
    Section 107 of the Local Government Act 1972 (c. 70) empowers the police authority to discharge some of its functions by the use of civilians employed by the police authority. This may be true in the case of chief officers, treasurers, or advisers. Scene of Crime Officers may in fact be civilians. Section 10 of the 1994 Act amends s.10 of the Police Act 1964 so that the chief constable has the statutory power to be responsible for managing the force and all those who work for him.

Appointment of officers

11. After section 10 of the 1964 Act there shall be inserted—

"Appointment of clerk
    10A. A police authority established under section 3 of this Act shall appoint a person to be the clerk to the authority.

Appointment of persons not employed by police authorities
    10B. Where a police authority established under section 3 of this Act is required or authorised by any Act—
    (a) to appoint a person to a specified office under the authority, or
    (b) to designate a person as having specified duties or responsibilities,
then, notwithstanding any provision of that Act to the contrary, the authority may appoint or designate either a person employed by the authority under section 10 of this Act, or a person not holding any office or employment under the authority."

DEFINITIONS
    "police authority": ss.3, 62(b) of the Police Act 1964; s.44 of the 1994 Act.

GENERAL NOTE
    This was added without objection when the Bill was being examined by Standing Committee D, June 23, 1994, col. 514.

Questions by local councillors

12. For section 11 of the 1964 Act (questions on police matters by members of constituent councils) there shall be substituted—

"Questions on police matters at council meetings
    11.—(1) Every relevant council shall make arrangements (whether by

standing orders or otherwise) for enabling questions on the discharge of the functions of a police authority to be put by members of the council at a meeting of the council for answer by a person nominated by the authority for that purpose.

(2) On being given reasonable notice by a relevant council of a meeting of that council at which questions on the discharge of the police authority's functions are to be put, the police authority shall nominate one or more of its members to attend the meeting to answer those questions.

(3) In this section "relevant council" has the same meaning as in Schedule 1 B to this Act."

DEFINITIONS
  "police authority": ss.3, 62(b) of the Police Act 1964; s.44 of the 1994 Act.
  "relevant council": s.3(1) of the 1994 Act inserting s.3B into the Police Act 1964.

General

Provision of advice and assistance to international organisations etc.

13. After section 15 of the 1964 Act there shall be inserted—

"Provision of advice and assistance to international organisations etc.
  15A.—(1) Subject to the provisions of this section, a police authority may provide advice and assistance—
   (a) to an international organisation or institution, or
   (b) to any other person or body which is engaged outside the United Kingdom in the carrying on of activities similar to any carried on by the authority or the chief officer of police for its area.

(2) The power conferred on a police authority by subsection (1) of this section includes a power to make arrangements under which a member of the police force maintained by the authority is engaged for a period of temporary service with a person or body within paragraph (a) or (b) of that subsection.

(3) The power conferred by subsection (1) of this section shall not be exercised except with the consent of the Secretary of State or in accordance with a general authorisation given by him.

(4) A consent or authorisation under subsection (3) of this section may be given subject to such conditions as the Secretary of State thinks fit.

(5) Nothing in this section authorises a police authority to provide any financial assistance by—
   (a) making a grant or loan,
   (b) giving a guarantee or indemnity, or
   (c) investing by acquiring share or loan capital.

(6) A police authority may make charges for advice or assistance provided by it under this section.

(7) In its application in relation to the metropolitan police this section shall apply—
   (a) as if the power conferred by subsection (1) were conferred on the Commissioner of Police of the Metropolis (and accordingly as if the references in subsections (1)(b) and (2) to a police authority were omitted), and
   (b) as if in subsection (6) the reference to a police authority were a reference to the Receiver for the Metropolitan Police District.

(8) The provisions of this section are without prejudice to the Police (Overseas Service) Act 1945 and section 10 of the Overseas Development and Co-operation Act 1980."

DEFINITIONS
"police authority": ss.3, 62(b) of the Police Act 1964; s.44 of the 1994 Act.

GENERAL NOTE
This was inserted by the House of Commons on July 5, 1994 (*Hansard*, H.L. Vol. 246, col. 156). The provision deals with the service overseas of British police officers so as to permit them to serve abroad not only with foreign governments but also with international organisations such as the United Nations.

Alteration of police areas

14. For section 21 of the 1964 Act there shall be substituted—

"Power to alter police areas by order

21.—(1) The Secretary of State may by order make alterations in police areas in England and Wales other than the City of London police area.

(2) The alterations that may be made by an order under subsection (1) of this section include alterations that result in a reduction or an increase in the number of police areas, but not alterations that result in the abolition of the metropolitan police district.

(3) The Secretary of State shall not exercise his power under subsection (1) of this section to make alterations unless either—

   (a) he has received a request to make the alterations from the police authority for each of the areas (other than the metropolitan police district) affected by them, or

   (b) it appears to him to be expedient to make the alterations in the interests of efficiency or effectiveness.

(4) The Secretary of State shall exercise his power to make orders under this section in such a way as to ensure that none of the following areas—

   (a) a county in which there are no district councils,

   (b) a district in any other county,

   (c) a county borough in Wales, and

   (d) a London borough,

is divided between two or more police areas.

(5) Subsection (4) shall not have effect so as to prevent the maintenance of any part of the boundary of the metropolitan police district as it exists at the commencement of section 1 of the Police and Magistrates' Courts Act 1994.

Alteration of Welsh police areas on local government reorganisation

21A.—(1) The Secretary of State shall by order made before 1st April 1996 make such alterations to police areas in Wales as he considers necessary or expedient in connection with the reorganisation of local government in Wales taking place on that date.

(2) The alterations that may be made by an order under subsection (1) of this section include alterations that result in a reduction or an increase in the number of police areas, but not alterations that result in the division of any county or county borough between two or more police areas.

(3) The Secretary of State shall make an order under subsection (1) of this section only after he has consulted every body within the following paragraphs which is in existence when the order is made—

   (a) the police authorities established under section 3 of this Act for the police areas altered by the order;

(b) the police authorities which are to be superseded by the police authorities mentioned in paragraph (a) of this subsection;

(c) the county councils which—
    (i) are the councils of counties wholly or partly within the police areas altered by the order, and
    (ii) are to cease to exist on 1st April 1996 by virtue of the Local Government (Wales) Act 1994;

(d) the councils of the counties and county boroughs established by virtue of that Act which are wholly or partly within the police areas altered by the order;

and such other persons as he considers appropriate.

Objections to alterations proposed by Secretary of State

21B.—(1) Before making an order under section 21 of this Act by virtue of paragraph (b) of subsection (3) of that section, the Secretary of State shall give notice of his proposal to—

(a) the police authority for every area (other than the metropolitan police district) that he proposes to alter,

(b) the council of every county, district, county borough or London borough wholly or partly within any area (other than the metropolitan police district) that he proposes to alter,

(c) the council of every London borough, county or district all or part of which would under the proposal be brought into or left out of the metropolitan police district, and

(d) such other persons as he considers appropriate.

(2) A notice under subsection (1) of this section shall—

(a) specify the proposed alterations and describe the general nature of any related provisions proposed to be included in the order,

(b) set out the Secretary of State's reasons for proposing the alterations, and

(c) specify a date before which any objections to the proposals are to be delivered to the Secretary of State.

(3) The date specified under subsection (2)(c) of this section shall fall after the end of the period of four months beginning with the date of the notice.

(4) Where objections have been duly delivered to the Secretary of State by a person notified under subsection (1) of this section, the Secretary of State shall before making the order under section 21 of this Act—

(a) consider the objections, and

(b) give to that person a further notice stating whether he accepts the objections and, if he does not, giving his reasons.

(5) Where the Secretary of State has given a notice under subsection (1) of this section specifying proposed alterations, the provisions of an order making the alterations may be inconsistent with the notice so far as it describes the general nature of the provisions, and may contain provisions not referred to in the notice.

Orders altering police areas supplementary provisions

21C.—(1) The power to make orders under section 21 or 21A of this Act includes power to make such supplementary and transitional provision as the Secretary of State thinks necessary or expedient, including—

(a) provision as to the membership of a police authority;

(b) provision for the transfer of property, rights and liabilities;

(c) provision for the transfer of members of police forces and other persons;

(d) provision as to pending legal proceedings.

(2) Without prejudice to subsection (1) of this section, the power to make orders under section 21 or 21A of this Act includes power—

    (a) to amend Schedule 1A to this Act and section 76 of the London Government Act 1963 (extent of metropolitan police district), and

    (b) to amend any other enactment, and any instrument made under any enactment, where the amendment is consequential on any provision of the order.

(3) No order shall be made under section 21 of this Act by virtue of paragraph (b) of subsection (3) of that section unless a draft of the order has been laid before and approved by resolution of each House of Parliament.

(4) An order to which subsection (3) of this section applies, and which would apart from this subsection be treated for the purposes of the standing orders of either House of Parliament as a hybrid instrument, shall proceed in that House as if it were not such an instrument.

(5) A statutory instrument containing an order under section 21 or 21A of this Act, other than an order to which subsection (3) of this section applies, shall be subject to annulment in pursuance of a resolution of either House of Parliament."

DEFINITIONS

    "any enactment": s.64 of the Police Act 1964.
    "police area": s.62 of the Police Act 1964.
    "police authority": ss.3, 62(b) of the Police Act 1964; s.44 of the 1994 Act.

GENERAL NOTE

    See the General Note to s.3 above. The chief constable has the responsibility for carrying out operational decisions and he alone is intended to exercise direction and control over his force. However, the Government recognises that the police authority is bound to have a voice about matters connected with the policing of its area. Just as the Home Secretary has been empowered to ask the chief constable to provide a report, so it is provided by s.14 that the Home Secretary may require a report from the police authority. To make provision for one but not for the other was thought to be incongruous; see Standing Committee D, May 24, 1994, col. 281.

Functions of Secretary of State

15. After section 28 of the 1964 Act there shall be inserted—

"Setting of objectives for police authorities

28A.—(1) The Secretary of State may by order determine objectives for the policing of the areas of all police authorities established under section 3 of this Act.

(2) Before making an order under this section the Secretary of State shall consult—

    (a) persons whom he considers to represent the interests of police authorities established under section 3 of this Act, and

    (b) persons whom he considers to represent the interests of chief constables of forces maintained by those authorities.

(3) A statutory instrument containing an order under this section shall be laid before Parliament after being made.

Setting of performance targets

28B.—(1) Where an objective has been determined under section 28A of this Act, the Secretary of State may direct police authorities to establish levels of performance ("performance targets") to be aimed at in seeking to achieve the objective.

(2) A direction under this section may be given to all police authorities established under section 3 of this Act or to one or more particular authorities.

(3) A direction given under this section may impose conditions with which the performance targets must conform, and different conditions may be imposed for different authorities.

(4) The Secretary of State shall arrange for any direction given under this section to be published in such manner as he thinks fit.

Codes of practice

28C.—(1) The Secretary of State may issue codes of practice relating to the discharge by police authorities established under section 3 of this Act of any of their functions.

(2) The Secretary of State may from time to time revise the whole or part of any code of practice issued under this section.

(3) The Secretary of State shall lay before Parliament a copy of any code of practice, and of any revision of a code of Practice, issued by him under this section.

Power to give directions to police authorities after adverse reports

28D.—(1) The Secretary of State may at any time require the inspectors of constabulary to carry out, for the purposes of this section, an inspection under section 38 of this Act of any police force maintained under section 2 of this Act.

(2) Where a report made to the Secretary of State under section 38 of this Act on an inspection carried out for the purposes of this section states—

(a) that, in the opinion of the person making the report, the force inspected is not efficient or not effective, or

(b) that in his opinion, unless remedial measures are taken, the force will cease to be efficient or will cease to be effective,

the Secretary of State may direct the police authority responsible for maintaining the force to take such measures as be specified in the direction."

DEFINITIONS
  "police authority": ss.3, 62(b) of the Police Act 1964; s.44 of the 1994 Act.

Reports from police authorities

16. After section 29 of the 1964 Act there shall be inserted—

"Reports from police authorities

29A.—(1) A police authority shall, whenever so required by the Secretary of State, submit to the Secretary of State a report on such matters connected with the discharge of the authority's functions, or otherwise with the policing of its area, as may be specified in the requirement.

(2) A requirement under subsection (1) of this section may specify the form in which a report is to be given.

(3) The Secretary of State may arrange, or require the police authority to arrange, for a report under this section to be published in such manner as he thinks fit."

DEFINITIONS
  "police authority": ss.3, 62(b) of the Police Act 1964; s.44 of the 1994 Act.

GENERAL NOTE
  See the General Note to ss.4 and 5 above.

Police grant and other grants

17. For section 31 of the 1964 Act there shall be substituted—

"**Police grant**
31.—(1) Subject to the following provisions of this section, the Secretary of State shall for each financial year make grants for police purposes to—
(a) police authorities for areas other than the metropolitan police district, and
(b) the Receiver for the Metropolitan Police District;
and in those provisions references to police authorities shall be taken as including references to the Receiver.
(2) For each financial year the Secretary of State shall with the approval of the Treasury determine—
(a) the aggregate amount of grants to be made under this section, and
(b) the amount of the grant to be made to each authority;
and any determination may be varied by further determinations under this subsection.
(3) The Secretary of State shall prepare a report setting out any determination under subsection (2) of this section, and stating the considerations which he took into account in making the determination.
(4) In determining the allocation among police authorities of the whole or any part of the aggregate amount of grants, the Secretary of State may exercise his discretion by applying such formulae or other rules as he considers appropriate.
(5) The considerations which the Secretary of State takes into account in making a determination under subsection (2) of this section, and the formulae and other rules referred to in subsection (4), may be different for different authorities or different classes of authority.
(6) A copy of every report prepared under subsection (3) of this section shall be laid before the House of Commons, and no payment of grant shall be made unless the report setting out the determination of its amount has been approved by resolution of that House.
(7) A grant to a police authority under this section shall be paid at such time, or in instalments of such amounts and at such times, as the Secretary of State may with the approval of the Treasury determine; and any such time may fall within or after the financial year concerned.
(8) Where in consequence of a further determination under subsection (2) of this section the amount of an authority's grant is less than the amount already paid to it for the year concerned, a sum equal to the difference shall be paid by the authority to the Secretary of State on such day as he may specify; but no sum shall be payable by an authority under this subsection unless the report setting out the further determination has been approved by resolution of the House of Commons.

Grants for capital expenditure
31A.—(1) The Secretary of State may make grants in respect of capital expenditure incurred (or to be incurred) for police purposes by—
(a) police authorities for areas other than the metropolitan police district, and
(b) the Receiver for the Metropolitan Police District.
(2) Grants under this section may be made either unconditionally or subject to conditions.
(3) The Secretary of State shall exercise his powers under this section only with the approval of the Treasury.

Grants for expenditure on safeguarding national security
31B.—(1) The Secretary of State may make grants in respect of expenditure incurred (or to be incurred) for police purposes by—
(a) police authorities for areas other than the metropolitan police district, and
(b) the Receiver for the Metropolitan Police District,
in connection with safeguarding national security.
(2) Grants under this section may be made either unconditionally or subject to conditions.
(3) The Secretary of State shall exercise his powers under this section only with the approval of the Treasury."

GENERAL NOTE
See the General Note to ss.8 and 9 above.

Regulations for police forces

18.—(1) Section 33 of the 1964 Act (regulations for the administration etc. of police forces) shall be amended as follows.
(2) In subsection (2) (which lists certain matters with respect to which regulations may be made) for paragraph (e) (discipline) there shall be substituted—
"(e) the conduct, efficiency and effectiveness of members of police forces and the maintenance of discipline;".
(3) After that subsection there shall be inserted—
"(3) Without prejudice to the powers conferred by this section, regulations under this section shall—
(a) establish, or make provision for the establishment of, procedures for cases in which a member of a police force may be dealt with by dismissal, requirement to resign, reduction in rank, reduction in rate of pay, fine, reprimand or caution, and
(b) make provision for securing that any case in which a senior officer may be dismissed or dealt with in any of the other ways mentioned in paragraph (a) of this subsection is decided—
(i) where he is an officer of the metropolitan police force, by the Commissioner of Police of the Metropolis, and
(ii) where he is an officer of any other force, by the police authority which maintains the force or by a committee of that authority.
For the purposes of this subsection "senior officer" means a member of a police force holding a rank above that of superintendent.
(3A) In relation to any matter as to which provision may be made by regulations under this section, the regulations may, subject to subsection (3)(b) of this section,—
(a) authorise or require provision to be made by, or confer discretionary powers on, the Secretary of State, police authorities, chief officers or other persons, or
(b) authorise or require the delegation by any person of functions conferred on him by or under the regulations."
(4) After subsection (4) there shall be inserted—
"(4A) Regulations under this section as to conditions of service shall secure that appointments for fixed terms are not made except where the person appointed holds the rank of superintendent or a higher rank."
(5) In subsection (5) the words "and may" onwards shall be omitted.

DEFINITIONS
"chief officer of police": s.62(b) of the Police Act 1964.
"police authority": ss.3, 62(b) of the Police Act 1964; s.44 of the 1994 Act.
"police force": s.62(c) of the Police Act 1964.

GENERAL NOTE
This provision (which should be read in conjunction with ss.17 and 19, and ss.34 to 38) was dealt with by the Lord Chancellor as follows:

"Clause 14 [section 18] allows for greater flexibility in regulations relating to conditions of service. It also ensures that regulations concerning fixed term appointments may not be made for officers below superintendent rank".

In the Government's White Paper *Police Reform* (Cm. 2281) it is said that, in the light of the Sheehy Inquiry Report, "there are likely to be changes to police rank structure, pay and conditions of service" (para. 1.8). The recommendations made in the Report were met with strong opposition both from the police and from some members of an anxious public who sought reassurance that changes in the structure of the police would lead to a more efficient and productive force to fight crime. Relevant to that issue is the morale of the police, and many of the speeches in both Houses of Parliament were directed to that aspect.

There is much in the recommendations and proposals of the Sheehy Inquiry which did not find its way into the Bill but cl.14 (now section 18) is primarily an enabling provision that will permit the Secretary of State to provide for procedures for cases in which a police officer may be dismissed, or otherwise subject to management action, and to make provision for fixed-term appointments other than for officers of the rank of superintendent or above. The Government had argued in their White Paper *Police Reform* that the changes in police organisation, and the emphasis on increased accountability, involve very different roles and responsibilities for officers in all ranks compared with those that applied when the Edmund-Davies Committee reported in 1979 (see para. 3.24). This is not a topic which can be examined without a consideration of the measures for dealing with misconduct. So far as that aspect is concerned, perhaps the most telling passage in the White Paper is to be found at para. 3.29 which (by implication) suggests that the rationale for changing existing procedures on discipline is:

"to bring them more in line with wider management practice while recognising the particular vulnerability of police officers to false complaints" (See also para. 7.20).

The prospect of fixed-term contracts caused concern but the Government regard them as being consistent with increased emphasis on performance and accountability in the police and reflect established arrangements in other employment sectors (*Hansard*, H.L. Vol. 552, col. 383). The Government conceded that the idea of such contracts is that a chief constable can take the job and if he is very successful the contract can be renewed. Alternatively, at the end of his contract, he can move on to somewhere else. "It introduces an area of flexibility", *per* Earl Ferrers (*Hansard*, H.L. Vol. 552, col. 388). As if to pre-empt the suggestion that this would be unfair, Earl Ferrers pointed to a recommendation made in 1992 by the Police Negotiating Board, for a pay settlement which included acceptance of the principle of fixed-term appointments for chief constables. Earl Ferrers recognised that what may be right for chief constables may not be right for superintendents even though the Government clearly categorise such posts as senior management. Accordingly, the Government does not rule out fixed-term contracts for them either (*Hansard*, H.L. Vol. 552, col. 383).

The Government proposed that fixed-term contracts should be capable of extension but not an unlimited extension and it cannot be ruled out that there may be different contracts applicable to different parts of the country (*Hansard*, H.L. Vol. 552, col. 387).

Discipline in the Police Service
The Lord Chancellor described the main provisions of this Part of the Act as having the following objectives, namely, that:

"Part I of the Bill paves the way for procedures to deal with police officers whose performance is unsatisfactory and for simplified procedures for dealing with misconduct by police officers. These provisions give effect to the results of the consultation process which followed the publication of the Government's proposals on police discipline last year. The Bill does not itself establish new procedures for police discipline. But the provisions of Clause 14 [*section 18*] and Clauses 29 to 33 [*sections 34 to 37*] enable revised procedures to be introduced, and Clause 15 [*section 19*] and Schedule 3 make provision for new appeals tribunals to be established".

The provisions in ss.14 to 17 inclusive should be read in conjunction with ss.34 to 38 inclusive. The Government was anxious to establish procedures so that the police force can deal with one of its members by dismissal, the requirement to resign, reduction in rank, reduction in rate of pay and reprimand or caution; see, for example, the wording of s.18 of the 1994 Act. Regulations may be made for the administration of police forces to ensure the conduct and efficiency of police officers under s.33 of the Police Act 1964. By virtue of s.46 of the 1964 Act, the Police Advisory Board must be consulted before regulations are made and staff associations are represented on the Board but the *consent* of that Board will not be required. The Government hope that by simplifying the disciplinary system the process of dealing with complaints can be made more efficient and productive both to the service and to the public but it would also seem that the Government are trying to make various disciplinary matters more a question of managerial decision and thus if a person is thought to have done something criminally wrong, he will be taken before a court and subjected to the criminal standard of proof but (whether convicted or not) the police may have to consider whether they wish the person concerned to remain in the police force. That would be a disciplinary matter which, according to the Government, should not be subject to the criminal burden of proof but which should be subject to some lesser standard, such as that applied in civil cases; see *Hansard*, H.L. Vol. 552, cols. 379, 380.

This is clearly a matter of considerable importance and was addressed to some extent by Earl Ferrers (*Hansard*, H.L. Vol. 552, col. 444). It seems that the thinking is that proof, according to the criminal standard, would constrain the way in which the hearing would work and would require it to concentrate on particular issues and to admit only evidence of a type that would be acceptable in a criminal court. The purpose of such disciplinary determinations is not to ascertain: "... whether it is proved that he or she has committed a criminal offence but whether, in the light of his or her action, any corrective action needs to be taken".

As part of the package (to streamline disciplinary proceedings) the Government has also enacted s.37 which, it will be noted, has the effect of preventing the operation of various provisions of the Police and Criminal Evidence Act 1984 (c. 60) including the application of s.67(8) of the 1984 Act which makes it a disciplinary offence to fail to comply with a Code of Practice. On one view, it is arguable that not all breaches of the Codes of Practice should amount to a disciplinary offence. However, it is not clear whether a flagrant breach of the Codes would be enough to bring the offending member of the police within the terms of s.34 of the 1994 Act. The scope of s.34(a) caught the attention of House of Commons, Standing Committee D, June 14, 1994, col. 349. At least one member of that committee (Alun Michael) saw no reason for the repeal but the explanation given (by Charles Wardle) on that occasion was as follows:

"Section 67 of the Police and Criminal Evidence Act 1984 ... includes the subsection, currently under discussion, which provides that failure to comply with any provision of the code shall make the officer concerned liable to disciplinary proceedings. The subsection is not without difficulty even at present, because many provisions of the code are discretionary rather than mandatory. We have, therefore, thought it advisable to repeal it and to make a provision of similar effect in the police disciplinary regulations to be introduced under the Bill. This way of proceeding will permit greater flexibility in the event of revision of the codes of practice.

There is no intention to cease to make breaches of the codes of practice the subject of police discipline. The provision will be replaced by one of similar effect in the regulations to be issued once the Bill has become law. I hope that with that assurance the Hon. Gentleman will feel able to withdraw this amendment.

Mr Michael: What will happen in the period between Royal Assent and the new disciplinary codes being published?

Mr Wardle: The law as it now is will apply. The existing law stands".

Revising the Codes of Practice is actively under review and was indeed a topic raised by the Royal Commission on Criminal Justice (1992).

Against that provision may be contrasted s.37(f) of the 1994 Act which, at one stage during the Bill's history, had been removed from the Bill only to be restored by the House of Commons. Section 104 of the Police and Criminal Evidence Act 1984 prevents a police officer convicted or acquitted of a criminal offence being charged with an equivalent disciplinary offence. The effect of s.37(f) is to remove that protection. Not surprisingly s.37(f) is open to the criticism that it exposes an accused officer to "double jeopardy". This was a matter fully canvassed before both Houses of Parliament. Indeed, what is now s.37(f) of the 1994 Act was originally part of cl. 32 of the Bill, but it was heavily attacked in the House of Lords and an amendment (no. 128) was successfully moved deleting this provision from the Bill on the third day in Committee (*Hansard*, H.L. Vol. 552, col. 456). The argument against what is now s.37(f) was distilled by Lord Renton. It should be noted that his arguments addressed another provision (cl. 32(e)) which would have withdrawn the legal representation of officers at disciplinary proceedings pursuant to s.102 of the Police and Criminal Evidence Act 1984. Lord Renton said:

"Perhaps I can remind the Committee of the provisions of the Police and Criminal Evidence Act as they stand. Section 102 allows the legal representation of officers on disciplinary hearings in cases where the officer is at risk of demotion, requirement to resign or dismissal. In view of the tradition of justice in this country, it is unthinkable that a police officer – perhaps quite a junior officer without even an O-level or two – should not have legal representation at a hearing at which he may be dismissed and thereby could be ruined for life. I regard this as a very serious matter indeed. Section 104(1) and (2) of the Police and Criminal Evidence Act 1984 prevents an officer acquitted of a criminal offence from being disciplined by his force in respect of the same actions. It has for hundreds of years been part of our legal system that no one shall be tried twice for the same offence. But by repealing that section of the Act that is just what we should be imposing upon the police. I do not think that it is right to do so" (*Hansard*, H.L. Vol. 552, col. 448).

Baroness Hilton put the issue somewhat differently when she said:

"The Government persist in drawing a false analogy with the world of business. They appear to think that the police service have some difficulty in dismissing officers. The Metropolitan Police dismisses around 60 officers a year as a result of disciplinary proceedings. That does not suggest, if one extrapolates it to the rest of the country, that there is any particular difficulty in getting rid of the small minority of officers who should no longer be serving, and that is with the current system of the right to legal representation. There seems to be a curious obsession with wanting to remove the barriers to being able to dismiss officers who should not be in the police service. I do not understand that obsession. It suggests a negative view of the police service. It ignores the fact that more than 99 per cent of police officers are carrying out their duties in a dedicated and enthusiastic fashion. Inevitably, in any profession, there are some who do not behave as they should. The present situation does not inhibit the police service from dismissing those who should be dismissed" (*Hansard*, H.L. Vol. 552, col. 447).

However, when the matter came to be considered by the House of Commons in Standing Committee D, an amendment was successfully moved (no. 177) to restore s.104(1) and (2) of the Police and Criminal Evidence Act 1984 into the framework of s.37 of the 1994 Act. The Government's position was expressed by Mr Charles Wardle when he said:

"The amendment will restore to the Bill the proposed repeal of section 104(1) and (2) of the Police and Criminal Evidence Act 1984 that was removed in another place at an earlier stage. Those parts of section 104 prevent police disciplinary action being taken in any case where an officer has been acquitted by a criminal court of an offence that is, in substance, the same as the disciplinary offence. The argument has been offered in the past that to deal with an officer for breaches of police discipline once he has been acquitted for the actions in question was to try him twice for the same offence. I do not accept that argument. A police disciplinary hearing is not and never has been a court of law.

The issues are entirely different. Whatever an officer did or did not do may have been entirely uncriminal as the court may have decided – but that does not necessarily mean that he or she behaved in a fitting way for a police officer. Acquittals may be made on technical grounds at the same time as an officer's actions may have been shown in court to have been utterly unfitting for a police officer.

This part of section 104 has never been an easy provision to administer. It is often difficult to determine whether the substance of a disciplinary offence is the same as the equivalent crime and certainly the two issues are likely to involve different requirements for the mental element.

These problems will be greatly magnified in future when the matters to be decided by senior police officers will be very different. In future police managers will no longer be seeking to consider a series of particular charges, which could be regarded as equivalent to particular criminal charges, but will be looking at the whole pattern of events and whether an officer lived up to police standards throughout.

It would make a nonsense of such an approach if police managers had to exclude from their consideration that group of an officer's actions which had come under the scrutiny of the court when acquitting him. As I have said, acquittal of a particular criminal accusation cannot be held to carry the inevitable implication that an officer behaved in all respects as befits a police officer" (Standing Committee D, June 14, 1994, col. 350).

This did not satisfy all members of the committee and the contrary argument was taken up by Michael O'Brien who developed some of the arguments raised in the Lords:

"The Government amendment would ... deny to police officers the same rights that effectively exist for ordinary members of the public. It is a contradiction of the evidence submitted in 1981 by the Home Office to the Royal Commission on criminal procedure which refers to section 104 of the Police and Criminal Evidence Act 1984, which was a repetition of section 11 of the Police Act 1976, and to the concept of double jeopardy. The Home Office said:

'it becomes important therefore in the interests of natural justice to ensure that police officers enjoy the protection of the same rights as those enjoyed by other members of the public. To this end, it is a cardinal principle that a police officer should not, as a consequence of a complaint against him, be exposed to the risk of double jeopardy.'

That means that a police officer should not be placed in jeopardy for exactly the same charge on two separate occasions. That principle is outlined in the landmark case of *Connelly v. Director of Public Prosecutions* in 1964. If a police officer is acquitted in a court and then tried for exactly the same charge in proceedings, he could be placed in jeopardy twice. If he were in breach of a different disciplinary rule, current rules with section 104 in place allow him to be dealt with because he would have breached a different sort of disciplinary rule.

The Government ... will say that police disciplinary proceedings are not the same as a court. I should like to hear the Minister try to convince a police officer who has faced a fine or a trial of that. Several times I have represented police officers who have been charged. Such officers are often under considerable pressure. In one case an officer was under threat of proceedings for two years, during which he was suspended. It seems that such officers are to be placed under pressure again in disciplinary proceedings. That is unacceptable.

Although the current applicability of section 104 is limited, it serves, within its limited context, a fundamental principle that is important to ordinary police officers – that when they are acquitted in court they cannot be subject to disciplinary procedures alleging substantially the same offence.

The Minister's proposal is unacceptable to police officers. Perhaps senior police officers are in favour of it but junior officers, who will bear most of the brunt of it, find it unacceptable. They would be placed in jeopardy twice and the principles of natural justice, which have existed in this country since the 13th Century, would be contradicted. The Minister should withdraw the proposal" (Standing Committee D, June 14, 1994, col. 351).

The matter was ventilated again in the Lords on July 18, 1994 (*Hansard*, H.L. Vol. 557, col. 28) and although the Lords agreed with the Commons in their amendment it can hardly be said to have been universally approved by them.

By s.34 (formerly cl. 29), s.88 of the Police and Criminal Evidence Act 1984 (c. 60) is amended by substituting the words "behaving in a manner which would justify disciplinary proceedings" in place of the existing words of s.88, namely, "an offence against discipline". Originally, cl. 29 was drafted very differently by removing the words "an offence against discipline". This would have meant that offences against discipline, which were not criminal offences, would not have been capable of being referred to the Police Complaints Authority. Not surprisingly, this caused some anxiety. The wording of s.34 was said "substantially [to] restore the position to what it was" (*Hansard*, H.L. Vol. 552, col. 440) but on one view the terms of s.34 must now be wider in scope than hitherto and thus extend the scope of references to the Police Complaints Authority.

Appeals against dismissal etc.

19.—(1) For section 37 of the 1964 Act (disciplinary appeals to Secretary of State) there shall be substituted—

> **"Appeals against dismissal etc.**
> 37.—(1) A member of a police force who is dismissed, required to resign or reduced in rank by a decision taken in proceedings under regulations made in accordance with subsection (3) of section 33 of this Act may appeal to a police appeals tribunal against the decision except where he has a right of appeal to some other person; and in that case he may appeal to a police appeals tribunal from any decision of that other person as a result of which he is dismissed, required to resign or reduced in rank.
>
> (2) Where a police appeals tribunal allows an appeal it may, if it considers that it is appropriate to do so, make an order dealing with the appellant in a way—
> (a) which appears to the tribunal to be less severe than the way in which he was dealt with by the decision appealed against, and
> (b) in which he could have been dealt with by the person who made that decision.
>
> (3) The Secretary of State may make rules as to the procedure on appeals to police appeals tribunals under this section.
>
> (4) Rules made under this section may make provision for enabling a police appeals tribunal to require any person to attend a hearing to give evidence or to produce documents, and may, in particular, apply subsections (2) and (3) of section 250 of the Local Government Act 1972 with such modifications as may be set out in the rules.

(5) A statutory instrument containing rules made under this section shall be laid before Parliament after being made.

(6) Schedule 5 to this Act shall have effect in relation to appeals under this section."

(2) For Schedule 5 to the 1964 Act there shall be substituted the Schedule set out in Schedule 3 to this Act.

DEFINITIONS
"police force": s.62 of the Police Act 1964.

GENERAL NOTE

Appeals against dismissal or resignation

Section 19 of the 1994 Act is the product of some amendment to what was originally cl. 15 of the Bill. The section substitutes s.37 in the Police Act 1964 (and note Sched. 3 to the 1994 Act which inserts the structure of an Appeals Tribunal into the Police Act 1964). It will be seen from the wording of the new s.37(1) of the 1964 Act that an appeal may be made depending on three results: (i) dismissal, (ii) requirement to resign and (iii) a reduction in rank. By s.37(2) of the 1964 Act, the Police Appeals Tribunal may make any order dealing with the appellant in a way which is "less severe" than the course originally ordered.

This represents a significant shift away from the position initially taken when the Bill was introduced in the Lords. Clause 15 did not then embrace the case of a person reduced in rank and where an appeal was successful the tribunal was empowered only to substitute a reduction of rank, reduction in pay, a fine, or to reprimand or caution the appellant. Furthermore, the Bill also included a controversial provision to remove the right to be legally represented at the hearing of the tribunal. This has also been reversed. As Lord Harris graphically demonstrated (*Hansard*, H.L. Vol. 552, col. 391), an inspector who with 15 years' service, and a reduction in rank to constable, stood to lose a considerable sum of money (for example some £140,000) and under the Government's original proposal, there would have been no right of appeal and no legal representation. Viscount Mountgarret suggested that such a state of affairs threatened to undermine the right of police officers to the natural justice to which they are entitled and that the analogy between a police tribunal and an industrial tribunal was invalid. However, the Government's proposals were based on the notion that disciplinary procedures needed to be streamlined and simplified in order to expedite proceedings and, furthermore, such an approach was consistent with the Government's overall strategy for enabling the police force in question to manage their internal affairs in a business-like manner. Thus, Earl Ferrers said that he did not believe a tribunal should be granted the power to "interfere in the internal management of the police force" on the grounds that a tribunal could not as readily form a judgement as to whether the person concerned was capable of performing the duties of the higher rank; this was a managerial question (see *Hansard*, H.L. Vol. 552, col. 395). In any event, the Government believed that it would be rare for a police force to take action as severe as that described by Lord Harris unless the officer's offence was very great (*Hansard*, H.L. Vol. 553, col. 210). However, even if that proposition is valid, then that might have been a further reason why such offenders should have a right of appeal and be legally represented on the hearing of that appeal.

Notwithstanding the above, the Government agreed to reconsider its position on this issue and, after an indication given by the Government on March 1, 1994, that police officers who had been reduced in rank would be given an avenue of appeal to the Police Appeal Tribunal, the House of Lords moved amendments nos. 105, 107, 112 to 114, and amendments nos. 137 to 142, which affect Scotland, on March 15, 1994.

The Government was not prepared to go further and to extend a right of appeal to the tribunal in cases where a lesser penalty (such as a fine, or a reprimand) was imposed on an officer. It had been argued that a constable and a sergeant who jointly committed a disciplinary offence might find that the sergeant was entitled to appeal to a tribunal (if he was reduced in rank to constable) but the constable who was merely fined wasn't, and that this was an unfair approach. The Government resisted that criticism on the grounds that the obvious distinction was that the sergeant's penalty was much more severe and that the attempts being made to simplify the disciplinary procedures would be frustrated if the complaints of the critics were met.

Inspectors of constabulary

20.—(1) Section 38 of the 1964 Act (appointment and functions of inspectors of constabulary) shall be amended as follows.

(2) In subsection (2) for the word "efficiency" onwards there shall be sub-

stituted the words "efficiency and effectiveness of, every police force maintained for a police area".

(3) In subsection (3) after the word "efficiency" there shall be inserted the words "and effectiveness".

DEFINITIONS
"police area": s.62 of the Police Act 1964.
"police force": s.62 of the Police Act 1964.

GENERAL NOTE
Whereas s.38 of the Police Act 1964 speaks of "efficiency", the 1994 Act adds the word "effectiveness" to s.38. Some might argue – with some justification – that Parliament is indulging in cosmetic niceties. Clearly, there is a technical difference between efficiency and effectiveness. However, it is difficult to believe that Parliament, in 1964, overlooked effectiveness as part of the remit of the inspectors. Nevertheless, the Government have at least put the matter beyond doubt (if there was doubt) and it serves to emphasise the Government's desire to see that performance targets are both set and achieved.

Reports from inspectors of constabulary

21. After section 38 of the 1964 Act there shall be inserted—

"Publication of reports

38A.—(1) Subject to subsection (2) of this section, the Secretary of State shall arrange for any report received by him under section 38(2) of this Act to be published in such manner as he thinks fit.

(2) The Secretary of State may exclude from publication under subsection (1) of this section any part of a report if, in his opinion, the publication of that part—
   (a) would be against the interests of national security, or
   (b) might jeopardise the safety of any person.

(3) The Secretary of State shall send a copy of the published report—
   (a) (except where he is himself the police authority) to the police authority maintaining the police force to which the report relates, and
   (b) to the chief officer of police of that police force.

(4) The police authority shall invite the chief officer of police to submit comments on the published report to the authority before such date as it may specify.

(5) The police authority shall prepare comments on the published report and shall arrange for—
   (a) its comments,
   (b) any comments submitted by the chief officer of police in accordance with subsection (4) of this section, and
   (c) any response which the authority has to the comments submitted by the chief officer,
to be published in such manner as the authority thinks fit.

(6) The police authority (except where it is the Secretary of State) shall send a copy of any document published under subsection (5) of this section to the Secretary of State."

DEFINITIONS
"chief police officer": s.62(b) of the Police Act 1964.
"police authority": s.62(b) of the Police Act 1964.
"police force": s.62(c) of the Police Act 1964.

GENERAL NOTE
While s.38 of the Police Act 1964 expressly provided that the inspectors shall inspect and report to the Secretary of State on the "efficiency" (and now the "effectiveness") of the police

forces (see s.20 above), s.38 did not expressly permit the publication of the report. This has been put right by the insertion of a new s.38A into the Police Act 1964 but the Home Secretary retains a discretion to prohibit publication of any part of a report if it would be against the interests of national security, or where disclosure might jeopardise the safety of any person. It could be argued that the existence of this discretion is all the more needed where inspectors are now clearly under a duty to examine the *effectiveness* of a force, *e.g.* in relation to surveillance techniques employed by a particular force to tackle certain types of crime, such as terrorism, and where disclosure would reveal not only the methods employed but also their effectiveness. On the other hand, s.38A(2)(a) is expressly directed to matters of national security – not national interest – so it is to be hoped that this distinction does not become fudged in practice. Challenging the correctness of the Home Secretary's decision to exclude information under s.38A(2) is likely to prove difficult and it is not clear to what extent the Home Secretary would be under an obligation to make known the content of the excluded material in the event that his decision was challenged.

Assistant inspectors and staff officers

22. In section 39 of the 1964 Act for subsection (1) (appointment of assistant inspectors of constabulary and staff officers) there shall be substituted—
    "(1) The Secretary of State may appoint assistant inspectors of constabulary.
    (1A) Members of a police force may be appointed by the Secretary of State to be assistant inspectors of constabulary or to be staff officers to the inspectors of constabulary."

DEFINITIONS
"police force": s.62 of the Police Act 1964.

GENERAL NOTE
    The significant difference between the old and new s.39(1) of the 1964 Act is that the Home Secretary may now appoint members of a police force to act as "assistant inspectors" who presumably carry a greater degree of responsibility than "staff officers" to the inspector.

Common services

23. For section 41 of the 1964 Act there shall be substituted—

"Common services
    41.—(1) The Secretary of State may provide and maintain, or may contribute to the provision or maintenance of, such organisations, facilities and services as he considers necessary or expedient for promoting the efficiency or effectiveness of the police.
    (2) Charges may be made for the use of facilities and services provided by the Secretary of State (or by organisations provided or maintained by him) under subsection (1) of this section.
    (3) The Secretary of State may by regulations make provision for requiring all police forces in England and Wales to use specified facilities or services, or facilities or services of a specified description, (whether or not provided under subsection (1) of this section) if he considers that it would be in the interests of the efficiency or effectiveness of the police for them to do so.
    (4) Before making regulations under this section, the Secretary of State shall consult—
        (a) persons whom he considers to represent the interests of police authorities, and
        (b) persons whom he considers to represent the interests of chief officers of police."

Definitions
"chief officer of police": s.62(b) of the Police Act 1964.
"police authority": s.62(b) of the Police Act 1964.
"police force": s.62(c) of the Police Act 1964.

General Note
See the General Note to Pt. I of the Act, and to s.8 of the Act. It will be seen that s.23 amends s.41 of the Police Act 1964 so that s.41(1) is now phrased in very broad terms. Unlike the old s.41(1) which refers to particular types of establishments, *e.g.* police colleges, the new s.41 does not but it seems clear that the new s.41(1) is intended to widen the range of services which could be made available to the police. On the other hand, s.41 now has two new subsections so that, by s.41(2), a change may be made in respect of services provided by the Secretary of State and, by s.41(3), the police may be required by the Secretary of State to use specified facilities or services if the Home Secretary (after consultation) considers that it would be in the interests of the efficiency or effectiveness of the police for them to do so.

Grants by local authorities

24. Before section 54 of the 1964 Act there shall be inserted—

"Grants by local authorities
53A.—(1) The council of a county, district, county borough or London borough may make grants to any police authority established under section 3 of this Act whose police area falls wholly or partly within the county, district, county borough or borough.

(2) The council of a London borough, county, or district which falls wholly or partly within the metropolitan police district may make grants for police purposes to the Receiver for the Metropolitan Police District.

(3) Grants under this section may be made unconditionally or, with the agreement of the chief officer of police for the police area concerned, subject to conditions.

(4) This section applies to the Council of the Isles of Scilly as it applies to a county council."

Definitions
"chief officer of police": s.62(b) of the Police Act 1964.
"police area": s.62(a) of the Police Act 1964.
"police purposes": s.64(1) of the Police Act 1964.

General Note
See the General Note to ss.8, 23 and 25.

Acceptance of gifts and loans

25. After section 53A of the 1964 Act there shall be inserted—

Acceptance of gifts and loans
53B.—(1) A police authority may, in connection with the discharge of any of its functions, accept gifts of money, and gifts or loans of other property, on such terms as the authority thinks fit.

(2) The terms on which gifts or loans are accepted under subsection (1) of this section may include terms providing for the commercial sponsorship of any activity of the police authority or of the police force maintained by it.

(3) In the application of this section to the metropolitan police, for the references to the police authority there shall be substituted references to the Receiver for the Metropolitan Police District."

DEFINITIONS
"police authority": s.62(b) of the Police Act 1964.

GENERAL NOTE

Section 25 (originally cl. 21) amends s.53 of the Police Act 1964 by inserting s.53B into the latter Act. At first sight it is perhaps surprising to find a provision which is so widely drawn. On one construction it seems to meet the case of the police authority which wishes to ensure that donations from members of the public, or gifts amounting to an expression of thanks, are properly received by the police authority but this is not what the legislature had in mind. Unfortunately, the 1994 Act does not seek to offer any definitions relevant to the new section. It must, presumably, now be left to the courts to determine what is meant by "gifts", "loans", "gifts . . . of other property" and "loans of other property". Is a reward a "gift" for the purposes of the section? If the answer were to be given in the affirmative then this is exactly the opposite of what Parliament actually intended. Because this issue may become a matter of some importance the following extracts from the debates in the House of Lords may be of assistance:

Lord Knights: "The question of rewards is rather different, I believe, from the question of gifts or money. In my experience, the word 'rewards' has been held to cover money or gifts which are given, usually by a victim, to reward or to say 'thank you' to people who have helped to recover his property or who have given help that has led to the conviction of a criminal, rather than rewards to the police authority or rewards or gifts to the police themselves. Rewards have a special connotation in police circles. They are not gifts to the police or to the police authority. As I have said, they are gifts from a victim or a company, offered in order to gain information that may lead to the solution of a particular crime. They have to be handled very carefully. I do not believe that they fall within the responsibility of the police authority; they are much more matters to be handled by the police themselves in their dealings with victims, complainants and people who have offended against them.

I do not believe that police authorities should become involved in what can often be a difficult and complicated matter when it comes to prosecuting someone. Allegations can quickly be made that prosecutions have been brought about or affected by way of gifts or inducements of one kind or another. This matter is better left to be handled by the police or the Crown Prosecution Service' rather than involving the police authorities. I do not believe that it would be appropriate for rewards to be handled by members of a police authority" (*Hansard*, H.L. Vol. 552, col. 424).

Earl Ferrers: "Gifts are different from rewards. I agree with the noble Lord when he said that all these matters have to be dealt with very carefully indeed for fear that one might induce some notion of bribery or return for services rendered. That would be wholly undesirable.

Clause 21(1) enables the police service to accept gifts of money 'on such terms as the authority thinks fit' – for example, for sponsoring work in relation to crime prevention or community relations. We do not believe that the terms should be further extended to cover the acceptance of financial rewards. Those rewards would probably be offered in return for specific achievements, such as solving certain crimes. They would almost certainly give rise to anxieties about police impartiality and the operational independence of the police as well as the impression that those companies or organisations with wealth might have an undue influence over policing matters.

Rewards would be most likely to be offered in return for police activities which are, and must continue to be, funded through government expenditure. It would be wrong for a company to be able to offer to reward the police for their success in a particular operation. It can offer rewards to the public to encourage them to co-operate with the police but not to the police 'for services rendered'.

The Bill allows individuals or organisations wishing to make a general contribution to the police to do so in the form of a gift. We believe that that is the right way to treat gifts to the police service" (*Hansard*, H.L. Vol. 552, col. 424).

This response did not entirely satisfy the members of the House of Lords and accordingly, Earl Ferrers explained the Government's position and intentions in greater detail (*Hansard*, H.L. Vol. 552, col. 429):

"... all possible steps must be taken to ensure that there is no corruption or thought of corruption.

The purpose of Clause 21 [now section 25 of the 1994 Act] is to formalise the existing position as regards gifts and sponsorship and to allow those forces which are active in that area to continue with their programmes. There are all sorts of examples of ventures which involved gifts, loans and sponsorships. They include, for example, support for regional neighbourhood watch conferences which I understand General Accident has sponsored. There have also been loans of cars fitted with crime prevention devices which Vauxhall have provided and there are publicity booklets and schools liaison information packs which could also be funded in that way. Clause 21 will give forces a clear legal basis on which to operate".

Commercial sponsorship

The new s.53B of the Police Act 1964, introduced by s.25 of the 1994 Act, also enables the police authority to receive monies or property by engaging in "commercial sponsorship" activities. The Government acknowledged that this represents a fairly recent development in the history of policing but explained its significance as follows:

"... we are now encouraging the police, the communities and organisations to work together to co-operate against crime. If it is possible for some of those institutions to fund something, then that should be encouraged. ..." (*Hansard*, H.L. Vol. 552, col. 429).

However, having regard to the wording of the new s.53B(1) of the Police Act 1964 confusion arose as to when it would not be proper under this provision for the police authority to accept gifts and what could be done if complaint was made that the authority should have declined to have accepted the gift or the loan. This aspect was explained by Earl Ferrers as follows:

"... it is our intention to make use of Clause 11 of the Bill, which enables the Secretary of State to issue codes of practice to provide the means to control the use of gifts, loans and sponsorship ... the codes of practice will come into operation as soon as possible after Royal Assent. ... The clause is a method of trying to clarify the law ... if a crime prevention conference was sponsored by an organisation I do not think it would be wrong to state that fact on the leaflet.

Such points are precisely those which will have to be covered by the codes of practice. Nevertheless, it will be for the police authorities to determine the terms upon which gifts, loans and sponsorship might be accepted. ... It is the police authority, not the chief constable, which will have the responsibility for saying whether such sponsorship should be offered and for determining the terms that would apply. Those concerned would need to have regard to any relevant code of practice issued by the Secretary of State. The latter would set out what should and should not be permitted. Police authorities would also be expected to have due regard for the issues of probity and propriety, which would also be set out in the codes of practice.

It is not, and it has never been, our intention that gifts, loans or sponsorship should be used by forces to replace planned activity. They represent a way in which the police service and the community as a whole can work together in partnership to deliver an improved level of service. They would bring the police service more into line with other public services and offer the police further flexible opportunities" (*Hansard*, H.L. Vol. 552, col. 424).

The Government explained that it would be open to the police authority to accept, reject, or attach suitable conditions to the acceptance of any gift or loan:

"Police authorities would not be under any obligation to accept offers. We would expect police authorities to think very carefully about any conditions that they might want to make before accepting gifts, loans or sponsorship ... if the police had to investigate an organisation which was sponsoring an activity [that] may be inconvenient and uncomfortable, but it would not be the first time that the police have had to investigate people of great probity. It does happen. I do not see that there would be any difficulty in such a case" (*Hansard*, H.L. Vol. 552, col. 430).

This vexed topic received very close scrutiny in the House of Commons, Standing Committee D, June 14, 1994, col. 322. The opponents to this provision argued that it could, "at one extreme", lead to sponsorship of core police functions so that a local constable could be sponsored by companies unless it was regarded as competition. The Government's Draft Code of Practice stated that:

"... The terms on which gifts or loans are accepted may allow commercial sponsorship of certain police force activities" (Standing Committee D, June 14, 1994, col. 322).

Alun Michael M.P. said that sentence was in contrast to another passage which read:

"... Gifts, loans and sponsorship are particularly suitable for multi-agency work such as crime prevention, community relations work and victim support schemes. ... It is not, however, intended that forces should actively solicit gifts, loans or sponsors" (Standing Committee D, June 14, 1994, col. 332).

However, that draft of the Code did not prohibit the soliciting of gifts and loans and it therefore remains to be seen how the codes will be developed to permit (or restrict) the police authorities to act in a commercial way. The Government believes that through sponsorship, many forces are able to fund additional activities that benefit the community and give the example of the service provided by "Yellow Pages" to the Metropolitan Police in promoting "Operation Bumblebee".

Amendments designed to preclude the acceptance of gifts or loans which may interfere with the operational independence of the chief constable, and to require the police authority to publish in its annual report the identity of those making gifts or loans (and the amounts involved) were narrowly defeated during the examination by Standing Committee D, June 14, 1994, col. 334.

Police officers engaged on service outside their force

26. After section 53B of the 1964 Act there shall be inserted—

"Police officers engaged on service outside their force
53C.—(1) For the purposes of this section "relevant service" means—
(a) temporary service on which a person is engaged in accordance with arrangements made under section 15A(2) of this Act,
(b) central service (as defined in section 43(5) of this Act) on which a person is engaged with the consent of the appropriate authority,
(c) service the expenses of which are payable under section 1 (1) of the Police (Overseas Service) Act 1945, on which a person is engaged with the consent of the appropriate authority,
(d) service in the Royal Ulster Constabulary, on which a person is engaged with the consent of the Secretary of State and the appropriate authority, or
(e) service pursuant to an appointment under section 10 of the Overseas Development and Co-operation Act 1980, on which a person is engaged with the consent of the appropriate authority.

(2) In subsection (1) of this section "appropriate authority" has the same meaning as in section 43 of this Act.

(3) Subject to subsections (4) to (7) of this section, a member of a police force engaged on relevant service shall be treated as if he were not a member of that force during that service; but, except where a pension, allowance or gratuity becomes payable to him out of money provided by Parliament by virtue of regulations made under the Police Pensions Act 1976—
(a) he shall be entitled at the end of the period of relevant service to revert to his police force in the rank in which he was serving immediately before the period began, and
(b) he shall be treated as if he had been serving in that force during the period of relevant service for the purposes of any scale prescribed by or under regulations made under section 33 of this Act fixing his rate of pay by reference to his length of service.

(4) In the case of relevant service to which subsection (1)(c) of this section refers, the reference in subsection (3) to regulations made under the Police Pensions Act 1976 shall be read as including a reference to regulations made under section 1 of the Police (Overseas Service) Act 1945.

(5) A person may, when engaged on relevant service, be promoted in his police force as if he were serving in that force; and in any such case—
(a) the reference in paragraph (a) of subsection (3) of this section to the rank in which he was serving immediately before the period of relevant service began shall be construed as a reference to the rank to which he is promoted, and
(b) for the purposes mentioned in paragraph (b) of that subsection he shall be treated as having served in that rank from the time of his promotion.

(6) A member of a police force who—
(a) has completed a period of relevant service within paragraph (a), (b) or (e) of subsection (1) of this section, or
(b) while engaged on relevant service within paragraph (c) of that subsection, is dismissed from that service by the disciplinary authority established by regulations made under section 1 of the Police (Overseas Service) Act 1945 or is required to resign as an alternative to dismissal, or

    (c) while engaged on relevant service within paragraph (d) of that subsection, is dismissed from that service or is required to resign as an alternative to dismissal,

may be dealt with under regulations made in accordance with subsection (3) of section 33 of this Act for anything done or omitted while he was engaged on that service as if that service had been service in his police force; and section 37 of this Act shall apply accordingly.

    (7) For the purposes of subsection (6) of this section a certificate certifying that a person has been dismissed, or required to resign as an alternative to dismissal, shall be evidence of the fact so certified, if—

    (a) in a case within paragraph (b) of that subsection, it is given by the disciplinary authority referred to in that paragraph, or

    (b) in a case within paragraph (c) of that subsection, it is given by or on behalf of the Chief Constable of the Royal Ulster Constabulary, or such other person or authority as may be designated for the purposes of this subsection by order of the Secretary of State."

DEFINITIONS
  "police force": s.62(c) of the Police Act 1964.
  "relevant service": s.53C(1) of the Police Act 1964.

GENERAL NOTE
  This provision was added to the Bill in the House of Commons on July 5, 1994 (*Hansard*, H.C. Vol. 246, col. 158) and agreed by the House of Lords on July 18 (*Hansard*, H.L. Vol. 557, col. 26). The purpose of this provision is to provide continuity of service and entitlements for officers who are engaged on service outside their force.
  The scope of these provisions is largely self-explanatory.

CHAPTER II

OTHER PROVISIONS ABOUT THE POLICE

Financial provisions

Precepts

    27.—(1) In section 39 of the Local Government Finance Act 1992, in subsection (1) (list of major precepting authorities) for paragraphs (b) and (c) there shall be substituted—

    "(b) a police authority established under section 3 of the Police Act 1964;".

    (2) In section 54 of that Act (designation of authorities whose budget requirements are to be limited), in subsection (3) (classes of authorities to be treated on same principles) for paragraph (f) there shall be substituted—

    "(f) police authorities established under section 3 of the Police Act 1964;".

DEFINITIONS
  "police authority": s.62(b) of the Police Act 1964.

GENERAL NOTE
  The Local Government Act 1992 (c. 19) designates those authorities whose budget requirements are to be limited. Obviously, this is a matter of considerable importance in the context of the wider discussion as to the funding of the police; see the commentary to ss.8 and 25 and see the General Note to Pt. I of the Act. The question here is who should be responsible for determining the level at which the precept should be set. As the Government has pointed out, if the police authority fails to fulfil any of its statutory obligations (including the setting of the budget) then all the members of the police authority will be liable to surcharge – a heavy responsibility. Given

the limited proposition of local authority representations who will be entitled to have a place on the police authority, it is perhaps not surprising to find that s.27 seeks to strike a balance between the rights of non-council members to decide on the level at which the precept should be set. The effect of the Act is that at least half of all police authority members should be in favour of the level of the precept (see Standing Committee D, June 14, 1994, col. 348).

Approval of decisions about precepts

28.—(1) A police authority established under section 3 of the 1964 Act shall not—
  (a) issue a precept under section 40 of the Local Government Finance Act 1992, or
  (b) make the calculations required by section 43 of that Act,
except by a decision of the authority which complies with subsection (2) below.
  (2) A decision complies with this subsection only if the members approving it—
  (a) constitute at least half of the total membership at the time of the decision, and
  (b) include more than half of the members (at that time) appointed under paragraph 2 of Schedule 1B to the 1964 Act (local authority appointees).

Directions as to minimum budget

29.—(1) The power of the Secretary of State to give directions under section 28D of the 1964 Act to a police authority established under section 3 of that Act shall include power to direct the authority that the amount of its budget requirement for any financial year (under section 43 of the Local Government Finance Act 1992) shall not be less than an amount specified in the direction.
  (2) The power exercisable by virtue of subsection (1) above, and any direction given under that power, are subject to any limitation imposed under Chapter V of Part I of the Local Government Finance Act 1992.
  (3) A direction shall not be given by virtue of subsection (1) above in relation to a financial year at any time after the end of the preceding December.
  (4) Where the Secretary of State gives a direction to a police authority under subsection (1) above any precept issued or calculation made by the authority under Part I of the Local Government Finance Act 1992 which is inconsistent with the direction shall be void.

DEFINITIONS
  "police authority": s.62(b) of the Police Act 1964.

GENERAL NOTE
  Where an inspector of constabulary provides an adverse report to the Home Secretary then s.29 permits him to give the police authority directions which may impinge on the level of the budget of that authority. Minimum levels of expenditure may also be determined by the Home Secretary.

Revenue accounts and capital finance

30. In section 39 of the Local Government and Housing Act 1989, in subsection (1) (authorities to which provisions about revenue accounts and capital finance apply) for paragraph (j) there shall be substituted—
  "(j) a police authority established under section 3 of the Police Act 1964;".

DEFINITIONS
    "police authority": ss.3, 62(b) of the Police Act 1964.

Financial administration

31. In section 111 of the Local Government Finance Act 1988, in subsection (2) (definition of "relevant authority" for the purposes of provisions regulating financial administration) for paragraph (e) there shall be substituted—
    "(e) a police authority established under section 3 of the Police Act 1964,".

DEFINITIONS
    "police authority": ss.3, 62(b) of the Police Act 1964.

Initial financing of new police authorities

32.—(1) The Secretary of State may make grants to any police authority established under section 3 of the 1964 Act in respect of expenditure incurred (or to be incurred) by it at any time before the beginning of its first precepting year.

(2) Without prejudice to any other powers to borrow, a police authority established under section 3 of the 1964 Act may borrow by way of temporary loan or overdraft from a bank or otherwise any sums which it may require for the purpose of meeting its expenditure before the beginning of its first precepting year.

(3) The sums borrowed by an authority under this section shall not exceed such amount as the Secretary of State may determine, and shall be repaid before the end of its first precepting year.

(4) In this section the "first precepting year" of a police authority is the financial year in which revenue is first received by it as a result of a precept issued by it under Part I of the Local Government Finance Act 1992.

DEFINITIONS
    "police authority": ss.3, 62(b) of the Police Act 1964.

Validation of past grants

33.—(1) Any deductions made from grants under section 31 of the 1964 Act for any period ended after 31st March 1980 and before the passing of this Act on account of common services expenditure shall be deemed to have been made in accordance with that section and any order made under it.

(2) In subsection (1) above "common services expenditure" means expenditure incurred by the Secretary of State under—
    (a) section 41 (common services) of the 1964 Act, or
    (b) section 44 (Police Federations) of that Act, or
    (c) section 4 of the Police Act 1969 (Police Council for the United Kingdom) or section 1 of the Police Negotiating Board Act 1980.

Complaints against and conduct of police officers

Reference of matters other than complaints to Complaints Authority

34. In section 88 of the Police and Criminal Evidence Act 1984 (references of matters other than complaints to the Complaints Authority), in paragraph (a) for the words "an offence against discipline" there shall be substituted the words "behaved in a manner which would justify disciplinary proceedings".

GENERAL NOTE
    The purpose of this provision was broadly explained by Earl Ferrers (*Hansard*, H.L. Vol. 552, col. 441). The Police Complaints Authority can accept a reference on any matter which may justify disciplinary proceedings. Previously, an officer could be disciplined for misconduct under the discipline regulations which covered a wide range of matters that could give rise to

complaint. However, the Government believes that: "the cumbersome, legalistic, and lengthy nature of these procedures has meant that little could be done formally to encourage police officers to improve their performance". This is a reference to conduct which extends beyond the conduct specified in the discipline regulations and includes acts which could cause harm to members of the public. The Government also believes that there is "public interest in ensuring that its police service acts properly". The new procedure is intended to remove the process for dealing with complaints from the strictures of court-like proceedings and to deal with matters as if the question is: "[was] the officer doing what he is paid to do in the way required or not?" (*per* Earl Ferrers, *Hansard*, H.L. Vol. 552, col. 442).

By rejecting the formal approach adopted by our courts and tribunals, the Government believes that it is no longer necessary to adhere to a rule which requires every allegation to be proved to the criminal standard of proof because the relevant issue to be determined is whether "in the light of his or her actions, any corrective action needs to be taken by police managers": see *Hansard*, H.L. Vol. 552, cols. 442 and 444. This formula is, of course, not free of difficulty. For example, there are likely to be issues which directly involve an allegation that a criminal offence has been committed and which may involve an allegation of dishonest conduct. The 1994 Act does not seem to address that problem or to distinguish between issues (or cases) where proof of an allegation to the criminal standard is desirable, and issues (or cases) which can satisfactorily be proved to a lower standard of proof. The short answer may be that this distinction was regarded by the Government as being inappropriate if the complaints procedure was intended to form part of the on-going managerial process of staff appraisal. This is because public confidence in the police is presently a fragile element in the balance of law and order. There have been numerous and well-publicised cases where the public complain that officers who have fallen short of what is expected of them, appear to carry on serving in the force regardless of their conduct so that public confidence is damaged (rightly or wrongly).

Some complaints obviously involve allegations that the officer or officers concerned have committed one or more criminal offences and yet, if the officers concerned were to be judged in accordance with the rules of the appropriate court of law, the decision would work in their favour even if, prima facie, there was substance in the complaint. The dilemma is whether the police service – having regard to its unique position and role in society – should be able to take preventative (albeit harsh) action to avoid the risk of misconduct occurring or whether the course of public justice must be allowed to take its course. There is a strong argument for saying that any decision which is liable to affect an officer's reputation, standing or earning potential, cannot be allowed to run in a way which is incapable of scrutiny in appropriate cases. It is perhaps with these considerations in mind that Earl Ferrers has said that an application of the criminal standard of proof could cause problems and require evidence of a type that would be acceptable in a criminal court. Strictly speaking, this proposition confuses the standard by which evidence should be judged, with wholly separate rules relating to the evidence which may be admitted to meet that standard, but the important point is that the Government does not want to see disciplinary proceedings becoming so formal in nature that they impede good management. The dilemma, which this issue throws up, is perhaps illustrated by what seems to be an inconsistent view on the part of the Government expressed by Earl Ferrers, when he said:

"I expect chief officers to require in the future, just as much as they did in the past, to be *convinced of the truth of an allegation* that a police officer had performed an offending action ..." [emphasis added] (*Hansard*, H.L. Vol. 552, col. 442).

Can one be "convinced" if the evidence falls short of the criminal standard of proof? The reality is that the Government are looking for a speedy resolution of complaints in the context of the provision of a service by the police, to the public, which should be managed and executed in a business-like fashion. The danger is that serious allegations against officers will not be judged in a satisfactorily disciplined manner to avoid a miscarriage of justice.

Steps to be taken after investigation of complaint

35.—(1) Section 90 of the Police and Criminal Evidence Act 1984 (steps to be taken after investigation: general) shall be amended as follows.

(2) In subsection (3), paragraph (ii) and the word "and" immediately preceding it shall be omitted.

(3) In subsection (4), paragraph (b) and the word "and" immediately preceding it shall be omitted.

(4) In subsection (5)—

(a) for the words "Subject to section 91(1) below" there shall be substituted the words "In such cases as may be prescribed by regulations made by the Secretary of State", and

(b) for the words "preferred disciplinary charges" onwards there shall be substituted the words "brought (or proposes to bring) disciplinary proceedings in respect of the conduct which was the subject of the investigation and, if not, giving his reasons".

(5) Subsection (6) shall be omitted.

(6) In subsection (7)—

(a) for the words "Subject to section 91(1) below" there shall be substituted the words "In such cases as may be prescribed by regulations made by the Secretary of State", and

(b) for the words "preferred disciplinary charges" onwards there shall be substituted the words "brought (or proposes to bring) disciplinary proceedings in respect of the conduct which was the subject of the investigation and, if not, giving his reasons".

(7) Subsection (8) shall be omitted.

(8) In subsection (9) for the words "the chief officer" onwards there shall be substituted the words "then, if the chief officer is required by virtue of regulations under subsection (5) or (7) above to send the Authority a memorandum, he shall at the same time send them a copy of the complaint, or of the record of the complaint, and a copy of the report of the investigation".

(9) In subsection (10)—

(a) in paragraph (a) for the words "prefer disciplinary charges" onwards there shall be substituted the words "bring disciplinary proceedings, it shall be his duty to bring and proceed with them; and", and

(b) in paragraph (b) for the words "preferred such charges" there shall be substituted the words "brought such proceedings".

DEFINITIONS
"authority": s.83(1) of the Police and Criminal Evidence Act 1984.
"chief officer": s.62(b) of the Police Act 1964.
"complaint": s.84(4) of the Police and Criminal Evidence Act 1984.
"disciplinary proceedings": s.84(4) of the Police and Criminal Evidence Act 1984.

GENERAL NOTE
See the General Note to s.34 above. The provisions in s.35 are largely self-explanatory but the obligations placed on investigators to pursue complaints should be noted. Thus, where proceedings are not brought against officers, reasons should be given (see s.35(4)(b), and note the terms of s.35(9)(a)).

Powers of Complaints Authority as to disciplinary proceedings

36.—(1) Section 93 of the Police and Criminal Evidence Act 1984 (powers of Complaints Authority as to disciplinary charges) shall be amended as follows.

(2) In subsection (1) for the words "preferred disciplinary charges" onwards there shall be substituted the words "brought disciplinary proceedings or does not propose to do so, the Authority may recommend him to bring such proceedings".

(3) In subsection (2) for the words "withdraw charges which he has preferred" there shall be substituted the words "discontinue disciplinary proceedings that he has brought".

(4) In subsection (3) for the words "prefer such charges" onwards there shall be substituted the words "bring disciplinary proceedings, they may direct him to do so".

(5) In subsection (5) for the words "prefer and proceed with charges specified in" there shall be substituted the words "comply with".

(6) For subsection (6) there shall be substituted—

"(6) The Authority may withdraw a direction given under this section."

(7) For subsections (7) and (8) there shall be substituted—
"(7) A chief officer shall—
(a) advise the Authority of what action he has taken in response to a recommendation or direction under this section, and
(b) furnish the Authority with such other information as they may reasonably require for the purpose of discharging their functions under this section."

DEFINITIONS
"authority": s.83(1) of the Police and Criminal Evidence Act 1984.

Repeal of certain provisions about discipline

37. The following provisions of the Police and Criminal Evidence Act 1984 shall cease to have effect—
(a) section 67(8) (failure to comply with a code of practice is a disciplinary offence);
(b) section 92 (powers of Complaints Authority to direct reference of reports etc. to Director of Public Prosecutions);
(c) section 94 (disciplinary tribunals);
(d) section 97(4) (review of complaints procedure and reports by Complaints Authority);
(e) section 101 (discipline regulations);
(f) in section 104, subsections (1) and (2) (which prevent a police officer convicted or acquitted of a criminal offence being charged with an equivalent disciplinary offence).

DEFINITIONS
"authority": s.84(4) of the Police and Criminal Evidence Act 1984.

GENERAL NOTE
See the General Notes to ss.18, 34 and 35 above.

Saving for certain complaints procedures

38. The amendment, by any provision of this Act, of Part IX of the Police and Criminal Evidence Act 1984 shall not affect any procedures established by virtue of section 96 of that Act (constabularies maintained by authorities other than police authorities) before the amendment comes into force.

Reorganisation of local government

Police areas in England: alterations under Local Government Act 1992

39.—(1) The Local Government Act 1992 shall be amended as follows.
(2) In section 14(5) (matters on which Local Government Commission to make recommendations) after paragraph (d) there shall be added—
"(e) whether, in connection with any recommended structural or boundary change, there should be any change in police areas (including any change resulting in a reduction or increase in the number of police areas)".
(3) In section 15 (procedure on a review) in subsections (3)(c) and (4)(c) (duty to deposit draft and final recommendations with affected councils) after the word "council" there shall be inserted the words "or police authority".
(4) In section 17 (implementation of recommendations), in subsection (3)(g) for the words "and election" there shall be substituted the words ", election and membership".
(5) After subsection (5) of section 17 there shall be added—

"(6) The Secretary of State shall exercise his power to make orders under this section in relation to police areas in such a way as to ensure that none of the following areas—

(a) a county in which there are no district councils,

(b) a district in any other county, and

(c) a London borough,

is divided between two or more police areas; but this subsection shall not have effect so as to prevent the maintenance of any part of the boundary of the metropolitan police district as it exists at the commencement of section 1 of the Police and Magistrates' Courts Act 1994."

(6) In section 18, subsection (2) and paragraph (a) of subsection (4) shall cease to have effect.

(7) In section 19(2) (provision that may be made by regulations), in paragraph (a) after the words "local authority" in each place where they occur there shall be inserted the words "or police authority".

DEFINITIONS

"police area": s.62(a) of the Police Act 1964.
"police authority": s.62(b) of the Police Act 1964.

GENERAL NOTE

Under s.14 of the Local Government Act 1992 (c. 19), the Local Government Commission is required to make recommendations about structural or boundary changes in local government. The powers of the Commission might not have extended to police authorities without the introduction of s.39. The purpose of s.39(5) is to ensure that certain areas of England and Wales are not divided between two or more police authorities.

Police areas in Wales: alterations under Local Government Act

40.—(1) The Local Government Act 1972 shall be amended as follows.

(2) In section 54(1) (changes that may be proposed by Welsh Local Government Boundary Commission) after paragraph (e) there shall be added—

"(f) a change in police areas (including a change resulting in a reduction or increase in the number of police areas) in connection with a change in local government areas".

(3) In section 58 (implementation of Commission's reports) after subsection (3) there shall be inserted—

"(3A) The Secretary of State shall exercise his power to make orders under this section in relation to police areas in such a way as to ensure that no county or county borough is divided between two or more police areas."

(4) In section 60 (procedure for reviews)—

(a) in subsection (2)(a)(i) (duty to consult local authorities etc.) after the word "area" there shall be inserted the words "and the police authority for any police area";

(b) in subsection (2)(c) (duty to deposit documents with councils, etc.) after the words "principal council" there shall be inserted the words "or police authority", and after the word "such" there shall be inserted the word "principal";

(c) in subsection (5)(b) (further duty to deposit documents with councils, etc.) after the words "principal council" there shall be inserted the words "or police authority", and after the word "such" there shall be inserted the word "principal".

(5) In section 67 (provision that may be made by orders), in subsection (5)(b) for the words "and election" there shall be substituted the words ", election and membership".

DEFINITIONS
   "principal council": s.270(1) of the Local Government Act 1992.

GENERAL NOTE
   See the General Note to s.39, above.

Miscellaneous

Metropolitan police: assistant commissioners

41. In section 2 of the Metropolitan Police Act 1856 (power to appoint six assistant commissioners of police—
   (a) the word "six", and
   (b) the words "and upon every vacancy" onwards,
shall be omitted.

Application of Firearms Act 1968 to civilian staff

42. In section 54 of the Firearms Act 1968 (application of Act to Crown Servants) for subsection (3) (which provides that members of police forces are deemed to be in the service of Her Majesty) there shall be substituted—
   "(3) For the purposes of this section and of any rule of law whereby any provision of this Act does not bind the Crown, a person shall be deemed to be in the service of Her Majesty if he is—
      (a) a member of a police force, or
      (b) a person employed by a police authority who is under the direction and control of a chief officer of police."

DEFINITIONS
   "chief officer of police": s.62(b) of the Police Act 1964.
   "police authority": s.62(b) of the Police Act 1964.
   "police force": s.62(c) of the Police Act 1964.

Application to police authorities of enactments relating to local authorities etc.

43. Schedule 4 to this Act (which makes amendments relating to the application of enactments to police authorities, including amendments providing for them to be treated as local authorities for certain purposes) shall have effect.

Minor and consequential amendments

44. Schedule 5 to this Act (which makes minor and consequential amendments relating to the police) shall have effect.

Application of certain provisions to new police authorities

45.—(1) Any relevant legislative provision which, immediately before the passing of this Act, applied to police authorities constituted in accordance with section 2 of the 1964 Act shall, except where the context otherwise requires, apply in the same way to police authorities established under section 3 of the 1964 Act (as substituted by section 2 of this Act).
   (2) Subsection (1) above is subject to any provision to the contrary made by or under this Act.

(3) For the purposes of subsection (1) above, a provision is a "relevant legislative provision" if it is a provision (other than a provision which applies only to specified police authorities) of an instrument which—
(a) was made before the passing of this Act under a public general Act, and
(b) is of a legislative character.

Interpretation of Part I

46. In this Part of this Act "the 1964 Act" means the Police Act 1964.

PART II

POLICE (SCOTLAND)

GENERAL NOTE

Creeping centralisation: a variation on a theme
The Scottish provisions in Pt. II of the PCMA 1994 are in many respects similar to the provisions for England and Wales in Pt. I. There is significant common ground in the measures expanding the authority of central government and of their appointees, the Inspectorate of Constabulary, over local police forces and police authorities. These include new powers on the part of the Secretary of State to impose a cash limit on the general police grant payable to police authorities (see *Hansard*, H.C. Vol. 228, cols. 306–307, *per* Mr Ian Lang), to make special provision for expenditure safeguarding national security (s.56), and to give directions to police authorities to remedy inefficient or ineffective policing where this is certified by the Inspectorate (s.54). Additionally, there is a general widening of the powers of the Inspectorate to inquire, on behalf of the Secretary of State, into the workings of police forces (s.57). Another echo from Pt. I is sounded in the provisions securing the managerial autonomy of Chief Constables to decide upon the size and rank profile of their force (s.47) and to direct and control civilian employees (s.49), and in the power of police authorities to delegate their remaining functions to the Chief Constable (s.64). Also common to both jurisdictions are the Sheehy-inspired reforms which introduce fixed-term appointments for very senior ranks (s.53), providing additional leverage for the exercise of central influence, and which reduce the rank structure (ss.47 and 48). Other common provisions, included as part of a more general overhaul of personnel policy concerned with narrowing the gap between the conditions of employment of police officers and those of other public and private sector employees, involve a departure from a restrictive reliance on a quasi-military discipline code and the establishment of a more extensive framework for investigating the conduct and efficiency of police officers (s.54), together with a new police appeals tribunal (Sched. 6).
In other important respects, however, the Scottish provisions are different from those south of the border. Most notably, the composition of police authorities, substantially changed in England and Wales to diminish the influence of local government and to enhance the authority of the centre, remains unaltered. Neither is there a Scottish equivalent to the powers of the Secretary of State to establish national policing objectives and related performance targets for England and Wales, or to the duties of the police authority to have regard to these national standards in developing its own objectives and local policing plan. On the other hand, some measures enhancing the influence of the centre are peculiar to Scotland in their substance or effect. The Secretary of State may now prescribe matters to be included in the annual reports of chief constables (s.51). His power to facilitate and direct the provision of central services is increased to a level similar to that of England and Wales, but from a significantly lower baseline than in England and Wales (s.59). Finally, at the request of a complainer, the Scottish Inspectorate may require a chief constable to re-investigate certain types of complaint (s.61).
Despite the absence of two of the major centralising planks of the new regime for England and Wales, the Scottish provisions arguably represent just as radical a shift towards the centre and away from the local government element. As regards the concentration of power at the national level, while there may be no specific legislative provision for objectives and performance targets, the measures allowing central direction of police authorities on grounds of efficiency and effectiveness and imposing new reporting obligations on chief constables presuppose the development and application of a similar steering mechanism at the centre (see *Hansard*, H.C. Vol. 228, cols. 306–307, *per* Mr Ian Lang). Indeed, over the past few years, the Scottish Inspectorate,

mandated by the 1991 Justice Charter for Scotland and complemented in their efforts by the Scottish Accounts Commission, which has a similar statutory responsibility to audit efficiency by reference to performance standards (see the Local Government Act 1992 (c. 19), ss.1–3), has been just as active as its sister body in England and Wales in developing a set of embryonic national policy guidelines to inform the use of these new statutory powers, in particular, the Inspectorate has pursued this end through the elaboration of a matrix of performance indicators and associated monitoring devices. Against this background, the fact that the legislative framework is less explicit and less comprehensive in Scotland may count for little. In fact, by rendering the new central powers less detailed and less transparent, the Scottish legislation may even permit these powers to be utilised in a more flexible and less accountable manner.

Although Scottish police authorities remain comprised solely of local authority members, a number of factors have combined to erode their standing within the traditional tripartite relationship with national government and local constabularies to an extent comparable with England and Wales. Indeed, it may be partly *because* no attempt was made to reconstitute Scottish police authorities in the image of central government that their powers have been settled at such a modest level. Under the new system for developing objectives, plans and performance indicators, police authorities in England and Wales are given an explicit policy-making role alongside central government. The Government's willingness to allow police authorities this strategic brief may not have been unrelated to their confident anticipation that other key aspects of their Bill would prevail and the membership of these authorities would duly become subject to close influence from the centre. In the event, with the decision of the Government, under intense political pressure, to drop its plans to end the local government majority on police authorities, and to abandon its proposals for the Secretary of State to appoint the chair of the police authority and to nominate his own members, the restructuring of police authorities in England and Wales has proved to be rather less radical than envisaged. Arguably, the police authorities have been allocated a role which might have been denied them if the fate of attempts to restrict their independent power-base had been foreseen, and which was denied in advance to their counterparts in Scotland where no similar restriction was ever contemplated.

The absence of an explicit policy-making role for Scottish police authorities is compounded by two other developments. First, the delegation to the chief constable of the police authority's functions in respect of the supply and deployment of personnel (ss.47 and 49), and potentially in respect of the supply of other resources also (s.64), threatens its traditional role in providing and maintaining the infrastructure of the force. There may well be strong arguments in favour of the devolution to the operational level of decisions about resource management and deployment. However, if police authorities are not allocated a more strategic role in lieu of this traditional remit, then the danger arises that they become deprived of any effective function, trapped between the pincers of a Government strategy which concentrates policy making at the centre and leaves resource and personnel management to the professionals.

Secondly, the capacity of police authorities to retain their position within the tripartite structure against these legislative inroads is likely to be hindered by wider local government reorganisation. Under the existing two-tier local government system in Scotland, the boundaries of Scottish police forces, with only two exceptions (the Lothian and Borders Constabulary and the Northern Constabulary), have been coterminous with those of the upper-tier authorities, the regional councils. In the majority of cases, therefore, it has been possible to supply the membership of police authorities from a single local authority and so avoid resort to joint committees. The extensive restructuring of the Scottish local authority system envisaged under the Local Government etc. (Scotland) Act 1994 (c. 39) means that this will no longer be possible. While it is not proposed, under this scheme for reorganisation, to alter the boundaries of police forces (although this will be made easier in future, as s.35 of the Local Government etc. (Scotland) Act 1994 has a similar effect to s.14 of the present Act in respect of England and Wales in removing the requirement on the Secretary of State to hold a public local inquiry prior to any alteration of police areas), the present two-tier system of regional and local authorities is to be replaced by a single-tier system organised on a new territorial basis. As a consequence, four of the existing six single authority police areas will be reconstituted as joint police areas requiring joint police committees (see s.34 of the Local Government etc. (Scotland) Act 1994). For example, Strathclyde police area, the largest in Scotland, will cover 12 local authority areas and be serviced by a joint police authority comprising representatives of all constituent authorities.

In England and Wales, successive local government reorganisations have meant that joint police committees, or boards, have been much more prevalent than in Scotland. The evidence of the workings of such joint boards, particularly in the metropolitan areas after the abolition by the Local Government Act 1985 (c. 51) of the metropolitan county councils with their powerful unitary police authorities, is that they are significantly more fragmented and much less influential than unitary bodies (see, *e.g.* "The New Police Authorities", B. Loveday, *Policing and*

Society, (1991) Vol. 1, no. 3). If a similar fate awaits Scottish joint committees, it may be that at the very point when the legal foundations of police authorities have been weakened in Scotland, they may also become less well-equipped organisationally to rise to the defence of their position as major political players within the tripartite system.

The legislative process in Scotland

The reform of the constitutional arrangements for policing in Scotland, therefore, is arguably just as profound as that achieved in England and Wales. Compared to the scenario for England and Wales, however, the Scottish position appears to be less the result of the application of an explicit policy blueprint, than the cumulative effect of various loosely assembled statutory bits and pieces. This impression is borne out when the history of Pt. II of the PMCA 1994 is considered. Part I of the PMCA 1994 emerged from two key policy documents published in June 1993, namely the *Sheehy Inquiry into Police Responsibilities and Rewards* (cm. 2280) and the White Paper on *Police Reform* (cm. 2281). Although only a limited investigation of the Scottish police was undertaken, Sheehy's remit did include Scotland, and when the Government signalled its selective acceptance of the inquiry's recommendations (see *Hansard*, H.C. Vol. 233, cols. 975–989, *per* Mr Michael Howard), legislative proposals were duly drafted for both jurisdictions. The White Paper, however, did not refer to Scotland. The first sign that some of its constitutional proposals were, nevertheless, intended to be applied to Scotland, emerged in a statement to the House of Commons by the Secretary of State for Scotland, Ian Lang, in the month following the publication of the White Paper (see *Hansard*, H.C. Vol. 228, cols. 306–307).

In a short speech, the Secretary of State largely confined himself to a description of the proposals earmarked for Scotland. By comparison to the White Paper, there was no detailed attempt to justify particular proposals or to articulate a general philosophy underpinning the overall package. The Government's economy of output also meant that there was little scope for public discussion of the proposals in the period leading up to the publication of the Bill in December 1993.

The Government's abbreviated approach to policy formation on a matter which was both of considerable constitutional importance and of direct concern to two powerful Scottish interest groups, namely the police and the local authorities, helps to explain the vehemence of the opposition expressed when the Bill finally emerged. It was immediately attacked by Dr Ian Oliver, president of the Association of Chief Police Officers (Scotland), as "centralising and politicising the police in a way which . . . is unhealthy" and "as a radical constitutional move the Government may come to regret" (*The Scotsman*, December 18, 1993). This theme was expanded upon in an open letter to the Scottish newspapers by Dr Oliver and representatives of the other two Scottish police staff associations published on January 14, 1994, the week before the Bill was introduced into the Lords. In turn, this provoked an angry reaction from the Scottish home affairs minister, Lord Fraser of Carmyllie, who accused the police staff associations of confusing the issue by muddling up discussion of proposals exclusive to England and Wales with discussion of the Scottish provisions; he also claimed that their analysis lacked objectivity, in that they failed to acknowledge the benefits to be derived from the proposals augmenting the managerial autonomy of forces alongside their criticism of the Bill's centralising thrust (*The Scotsman*, January 15, 1994).

This unusual rift between Government and police leaders in Scotland was reflected in the refusal of Lord Fraser to accede to a request from four chief constables for a special meeting of the Police Advisory Board for Scotland to consider the Bill (*Scotland on Sunday*, January 16, 1994). It was also evident in the perseverance of the Scottish police staff associations with their campaign of opposition to the Bill even after it had embarked on its passage through the two Houses. The police proved to be effective lobbyists, both in the Lords, where their main channel was the Scottish Peers Association, and later in the Commons, where all the Opposition parties were well briefed as to the nature and extent of professional concern. As a result of their efforts, the police achieved a number of minor amendments, and one major concession. The original cl. 45, which would have empowered the Secretary of State to require police forces, on the grounds of efficiency, to participate in campaigns or operations which others had already adopted, was singled out by the staff associations as a particularly intrusive and insensitive measure of centralisation, in that it appeared to sanction direct operational control by central government. It was eventually withdrawn at Committee stage in the Lords, Lord Fraser intimating that compulsory measures had been rendered unnecessary by receipt of a memorandum of co-operation from the Scottish Chief Constables committing their forces to voluntary participation in joint activities where appropriate (see *Hansard*, H.L. Vol. 552, cols. 477–478).

If this signalled the re-emergence of a more pragmatic tone in discussions between police and the Government, no such thawing was evident in relations between the Government and the major Opposition parties. Their differences remained more fundamental; this was partly because the Opposition were just as concerned with the erosion of the position of police authorities, as regards which no concessions were granted during the progress of the Bill, as they were with the reduction in the autonomy of the Chief Constable; it was also partly because disagreement over the adequacy of the political process struck a more general chord. After the introduction of the Bill, the Labour Party, through their Home Affairs Minister, John McFall, contended that the Government's refusal to contemplate separate Scottish legislation on such an important matter, belied their commitment, made after their taking-stock exercise undertaken in the wake of the 1992 election (see *Scotland in the Union: a Partnership for Good*, 1993, cm. 2225), to make Scottish Government more responsive to Scottish needs. Menzies Campbell, the Liberal Democrat home affairs spokesman, argued that the Scottish policing measures in the Police and Magistrates' Courts Bill, together with provisions relating to the privatisation of Scottish prisons contained in the Criminal Justice and Public Order Bill (which received Royal Assent on November 3, 1994) published the previous month, clearly demonstrated how important Scottish criminal justice measures were "being dragged in on the coat-tails of English measures" (*The Scotsman*, December 18, 1993). The Scottish National Party home affairs spokesman, Fergus Ewing, claimed that the Scottish Office attitude was "a symptom of Scotland's democratic deficit" (*Scotland on Sunday*, January 16, 1994).

At every stage of the parliamentary proceedings, and with increasing intensity as the Bill passed from the Lords to the Commons, the Opposition parties developed the twin arguments that the Bill lacked detailed justification of its Scottish provisions, and a distinctively Scottish procedure through which these provisions could be discussed. The major debates on the floor of each House were only marginally concerned with the Scottish dimension. Further, the Standing Committee in the House of Commons, the forum best equipped to engage in detailed debate, numbered only four Scottish M.P.s amongst its 29 members and devoted only two of its 17 sittings to the Scottish provisions. Accordingly, at its third and final reading in the House of Commons, Tony Worthington, for Labour, could still claim with some justification that "Pt. II of the Bill applies to Scotland, yet it has not been discussed and no policy documents have been issued. The Minister with responsibility for policing in Scotland has not made a public statement on why the changes are necessary. That is contemptuous ..." (*Hansard*, H.C. Vol. 246, cols. 284–285).

Constitution of police force

47.—(1) For section 3 of the 1967 Act there shall be substituted—

     "Establishments of police forces
     3.—(1) A police force shall consist of a chief constable, regular constables and special constables.
     (2) In subsection (1) above—
          'regular constables' means constables (including probationary constables) to whom both pay and allowances are, by virtue of section 26 of this Act, payable; and
          'special constables' means constables to whom allowances only are so payable.".
     (2) In section 7 of that Act (assignment of ranks)—
     (a) in subsection (1)—
          (i) the words ", deputy chief constable" and ", chief superintendent and" shall be omitted; and
          (ii) after the word "superintendent" there shall be inserted the words ", chief inspector, inspector, sergeant and constable."; and
     (b) subsection (2) shall be omitted.
     (3) In section 8(1) (appointment of police cadets), the words "and subject to the approval of the police authority and the Secretary of State as to numbers" shall be omitted.
     (4) In section 14(1) (extra policing of locality where works are being constructed), the words "(whether by the appointment of temporary constables or otherwise)" shall be omitted.
     (5) In section 26(2)(d) (regulations as to retirement of certain constables), the words "or temporary" shall be omitted.

DEFINITIONS
   "constable": s.51(1) of the 1967 Act, as amended by s.63(9)(a).
   "rank": s.51(1) of the 1967 Act.
   "the 1967 Act": s.65.

GENERAL NOTE
   This section has three main purposes, each broadly concerned with the constitution of Scottish police forces. First, it removes the controls exercised by police authorities and the Secretary of State over the number of police officers and cadets in Scottish police forces, and also over the number of officers in each rank. Secondly, by removing the requirement that "regular constables" be "whole-time constables", it allows part-time working to be introduced for regular constables in Scotland. Thirdly, effectively it abolishes the ranks of chief superintendent and deputy chief constable.

Subs. (1)
   This subsection substitutes a new s.3 of the 1967 Act. Under the previous s.3, special constables provided the only recognised category of part-time constables, with regular constables defined as whole-time constables. Under the new subsection, special constables are treated as a separate category, and the definition of regular constables is no longer restricted to whole-time constables. This aspect of the substituted s.3 was the subject of debate and revision prior to and during the Lords stages of the Bill. In the original cl. 42, the Secretary of State was empowered to define and modify the status of constable by regulation. In a letter to the Scottish newspapers (see *The Scotsman*, January 14, 1994), and in their concerted lobby of the Lords, the three Scottish police staff associations (the Association of Chief Police Officers (Scotland), the Association of Scottish Police Superintendents and the Scottish Police Federation), expressed concern at the leeway this allowed the Government to depart from the existing model of police organisation. These concerns were articulated by Opposition peers in Committee, where it was claimed that the delegation of powers to the Secretary of State was "another manifestation of the spread of the virus of centralisation" (*Hansard*, H.L. Vol. 552, col. 467, *per* Lord Campbell of Alloway). In particular, it was feared that the new powers might be used to support a policy of deregulation or privatisation of policing services, or to reinforce the existing functional division of labour within police organisations. Lord Fraser of Carmyllie, the Minister of State at the Scottish Office with responsibility for home affairs, sought to reassure the Lords that the purpose of the more flexible definition of constable was the more limited one of encouraging part-time working and job sharing, as an incentive to recruit and retain female constables who are significantly underrepresented in the Scottish forces (cols. 468–470). This specific objective met with the general approval of the Lords, although they remained of the view that the method chosen to achieve it was unduly open-ended. The present formula, which removes the broad discretion of the Secretary of State but which still allows the detailed arrangements for part-time working to be set out in regulations under s.26 of the 1967 Act, was eventually agreed at Report stage in the Lords (*Hansard*, H.L. Vol. 553, cols. 401–402).
   The new s.3 achieves two other substantive changes. It removes the reference to the obsolete category of temporary constables. More significantly, it removes the control previously exercised by the police authority, acting with the consent of the Secretary of State, over the number of police officers in each force. This increase in the managerial autonomy of the chief constable is identical to that achieved for England and Wales under s.4 of the present Act, which in turn gives effect to one of the recommendations in the White Paper on *Police Reform* (cm. 2281, 1993, para. 3.6).

Subs. (2)
   This subsection amends s.7(1) of the 1967 Act such that the list of ranks which the Secretary of State is required to prescribe may be held in Scottish forces includes all nine existing ranks except those of chief superintendent and deputy chief constable. The flattening of the rank structure achieved by this provision in conjunction with s.48(1), is based upon the recommendations of the Sheehy Report *Police Responsibilities and Rewards* (1993 cm. 2280.I, paras. 3.51 and 3.53). Sheehy, however, had also sought to abolish a third rank, namely chief inspector. The Government initially adhered to this position but relented when the Bill reached the Commons. Nevertheless, the reduction in the Scottish rank structure settled upon by the Government drew criticism in both Houses over and above that directed towards the application of the same policy to England and Wales in Pt. I of the 1994 Act (ss.6 and 7 above).
   The Government's case was based upon considerations of managerial efficiency and the desirability of retaining within the Scottish police a rank structure identical to that in England and Wales (see Standing Committee D, June 14, 1994, cols. 369–370, 377–379, *per* Lord James Douglas Hamilton). Furthermore, assurances were given that despite the down-grading of many

officers at chief superintendent and deputy chief constable rank, an inevitable consequence of restructuring, no officers would have their pay reduced (*Hansard*, H.L. Vol. 553, col. 179, *per* Earl Ferrers).

In terms of managerial efficiency, it was claimed that a less top heavy management structure would facilitate clearer and more direct lines of communication and would allow the best officers to progress more swiftly through the ranks. Against this, it was argued from the Opposition benches, again with the backing of the three Scottish police staff associations, that the abolition of two ranks might weaken the chain of command without yielding any clear benefit (see Standing Committee D, June 14, 1994, cols. 369–373, 380–381, *per* Mr John McFall, and cols. 373–377, 382–383, *per* Mr Tony Worthington). In particular, while there might be scope for some streamlining of the higher managerial ranks beyond what had already taken place in recent years, this could be achieved by pruning within the existing rank structure rather than by the wholesale removal of ranks. An inflexible approach would deprive chief constables of the capacity to adjust their command arrangements to local needs, and might interfere with the clear chain of command required for the policing of major incidents and occasions. Government suggestions that a satisfactory demarcation of responsibilities could be retained by differentiating roles within ranks, it was claimed, amounted to an admission of the inevitability of an extensive division of labour within the modern police, so reinforcing, rather than negating, the argument for the retention of the more elaborate rank structure. As to the enhancement of promotion opportunities, it was pointed out by the Opposition that it was unclear whether there existed a problem which required addressing. Currently operating fast-track schemes together with early compulsory retirement ages already ensured a steady turnover of senior management.

The Government's secondary argument, that it was important to retain an identical rank structure north and south of the border, rests on the benefits of a co-ordinated approach for joint operations and for training and the advantages of a common career structure. While the relevance of these considerations was conceded by the police staff associations, this line of argument fails to acknowledge that the merits of administrative uniformity might be outweighed by the need to respond to local conditions. In any event, if, as the Opposition argued, the case for retaining the existing rank structure in Scotland is also persuasive in England and Wales, uniformity could be equally well safeguarded by maintaining the status quo *ante*.

Subsection (2) also repeals s.7(2) of the 1967 Act which requires authorisation by the police authority and the Secretary of State of the number of officers in each rank. This increase in the managerial autonomy of the chief constable complements the new power under subs. (1) to decide the overall establishment of the force.

Subs. (3)

This subsection removes the requirement in s.8(1) of the 1967 Act for approval by the police authority and Secretary of State of the number of cadets in a police force. It thus reinforces the policy of greater control by the chief constable over manpower.

Subss. (4) and (5)

These subsections make amendments to the 1967 Act consequential upon the removal of the category of "temporary constables" under subs. (1) above.

Deputy and assistant chief constables

48. For sections 5 and 5A of the 1967 Act there shall be substituted—

"Assistant chief constables

5.—(1) The ranks that may be held in a police force maintained under section 1 of this Act shall include that of assistant chief constable (but not that of deputy chief constable); and in every such police force there shall be at least one person holding that rank.

(2) Appointments and promotions to the rank of assistant chief constable shall be made, in accordance with regulations under Part II of this Act, by the police authority after consultation with the chief constable and subject to the approval of the Secretary of State.

(3) Subsections (4) to (7) of section 4 of this Act shall apply to an assistant chief constable as they apply to a chief constable.

(4) A chief constable shall, after consulting the police authority for the area for which his force is maintained, designate a person holding the rank of assistant chief constable to exercise all the powers and duties of the chief constable—

(a) during any absence, incapacity or suspension from duty of the chief constable, or

(b) during any vacancy in the office of chief constable.

(5) No more than one person shall be authorised to act by virtue of a designation under subsection (4) of this section at any one time; and a person so authorised shall not have power to act by virtue of that subsection for a continuous period exceeding three months except with the consent of the Secretary of State.

(6) The provisions of subsection (4) of this section shall be in addition to, and not in substitution for, any other enactment which makes provision for the exercise by any other person of powers conferred on a chief constable.".

DEFINITIONS

"enactment": s.51(1) of the 1967 Act.

"rank": s.51(1) of the 1967 Act.

"the 1967 Act": s.65.

GENERAL NOTE

This section makes provision for Scotland similar to the provisions made for England and Wales by s.6. It substitutes a new s.5 in the 1967 Act in place of the existing ss.5 and 5A. The effect of the new section is to reinforce s.47 by formally abolishing the rank of deputy chief constable, and to provide for the appointment and dismissal of assistant chief constables. It also provides for an assistant chief constable to act in place of the chief constable during the latter's absence or incapacity.

New subs. 5(1) of the 1967 Act

This provides that the ranks in police forces in Scotland are to include the rank of assistant chief constable, that there is to be at least one officer of that rank in each force, but that there is to be no rank of deputy chief constable.

The abolition of the deputy rank, in accordance with the Government's qualified acceptance of the streamlining philosophy of the Sheehy Report (cm. 2280I, para. 3.53), was challenged by the Opposition on two counts (Standing Committee D, June 14, 1994, cols. 384–385, *per* Mr Tony Worthington). First, it could leave a force without effective leadership in the absence of the Chief Constable. This concern is answered, at least in part, by the inclusion of subs. (4), considered below. Secondly, as the deputy chief constable, apart from his deputising function, performs a number of specific tasks, most significantly that of administering force discipline, who is to assume future responsibility for these tasks? The Government answered that such tasks could be performed by one or more assistant chief constables, as they have sufficient authority to act as adequate replacements (Standing Committee D, June 14, 1994, cols. 385–386, *per* Lord James Douglas-Hamilton). In the case of the disciplinary function, this would require a change in the Police Discipline (Scotland) Regulations 1967 (SI 1967 No. 1021) made under s.26(2)(e) of the 1967 Act (as amended by s.52 of the present Act), which establishes the deputy chief constable as the responsible rank. In any case, however, the changes anticipated under s.52 below will require more radical reform of the present discipline regulations. The Government also argued that, since the designated assistant chief constable in respect of any particular function need not be the acting deputy under subs. (4), managerial flexibility would be enhanced. Finally, the Government also promised in Committee that they would retain the same number of senior officer posts in each force – the deputy post being replaced by an additional assistant chief constable, thereby reinforcing their claim that police forces will not be deprived of necessary senior management resources.

New subs. 5(2) of the 1967 Act

This subsection substantially re-enacts s.5(5) of the 1967 Act insofar as it relates to the rank of assistant chief constable. It provides for appointments and promotions to the rank of assistant chief constable to continue to be made by the police authority after consultation with the chief constable and subject to the approval of the Secretary of State.

New subs. 5(3) of the 1967 Act

This subsection re-enacts s.5(6) of the 1967 Act insofar as it relates to the rank of assistant chief constable. It applies, to assistant chief constables, parts of s.4 of the 1967 Act which govern the resignation, dismissal and retirement in the interests of efficiency of chief constables.

New subs. 5(4) of the 1967 Act
This subsection provides that the chief constable of each force must, after consulting his police authority, designate one of the assistant chief constables in his force to act in his place during his own absence, incapacity or suspension, or while there is a vacancy in the office of chief constable. While this ensures that the abolition of the deputy rank does not create an authority vacuum in the absence of the Chief Constable, the conditions attached to the new power entail that the deputy function will be performed on a temporary basis only.

New subs. 5(5) of the 1967 Act
This subsection provides that there can only be one acting chief constable at any time, and reinforces the temporary nature of the role by stipulating that a designation cannot last for longer than three months except with the consent of the chief constable.

New subs. 5(6) of the 1967 Act
This subsection ensures against conflict with other provisions relating to the exercise by any other person of powers conferred on a chief constable, by providing that the provisions of the new subs. 5(4) shall be additional to, and not in substitution for, any other such provisions. In including this subsection, the Government may have had particularly in mind the new subs. (2B) of s.63 of the Local Government (Scotland) Act 1973 (c. 63) inserted by s.64 of the present Act. By virtue of this provision the chief constable is permitted to sub-delegate to a subordinate officer, or to a civilian, such functions of the police authority as have been delegated to him under the new subs. (2A) of s.63 of the 1973 Act, also inserted by s.64 of the present Act.

Civilian employees

49. For section 9 of the 1967 Act there shall be substituted—

"Civilian employees
9.—(1) A police authority may employ for the assistance of the con-stables of a police force maintained for their area, or otherwise to enable the authority to discharge their functions, officers who are not constables.
(2) The police authority shall exercise their powers under section 56 (and section 63) of the Local Government (Scotland) Act 1973 so as to secure that, subject to subsection (3) below, any person employed by the authority under subsection (1) above is under the direction and control of the chief constable of the police force.
(3) Subsection (2) above shall not apply to such of the persons employed by the authority as may be agreed between the chief constable and the authority or, in the absence of agreement, as may be determined by the Secretary of State.
(4) The powers of direction and control referred to in subsection (2) above include the powers of engagement and dismissal.".

DEFINITIONS
"constable": s.51(1) of the 1967 Act, as amended by s.63(9)(a).
"functions": s.51(1) of the 1967 Act.
"officer": s.51(1) of the 1967 Act.
"the 1967 Act": s.65.

GENERAL NOTE
This section makes provision for Scotland similar to that made by s.10 for England and Wales. It replaces s.9 of the 1967 Act which provides for police authorities to employ civilians for the assistance of constables. The effect of the new section is to place civilians under the direction and control of the Chief Constable, and also to remove controls by the police authority and the Secretary of State over the number of such civilians. Like s.10, s.49 is influenced by the rec-ommendations of the White Paper on *Police Reform*, although it stops short of implementing

the White Paper's proposal that "civilian staff employed for police purposes should be employed by the chief constable, not the police authority" (cm. 2281, 1993, para. 3.8). The new section, together with s.47, represents a policy initiative which significantly increases the managerial autonomy of chief constables in respect of personnel matters.

New subs. 9(1) of the 1967 Act
This subsection provides for a police authority to employ civilians both to assist the police force maintained by the authority and to allow the authority to carry out its own administrative functions in respect of policing.

New subs. 9(2) of the 1967 Act
This subsection requires a police authority to exercise its powers under ss.56 and 63 of the Local Government (Scotland) Act 1973 to secure that, subject to subs. (3) below, any civilians employed by the authority are to come under the direction and control of the chief constable (see also s.64, discussed below). This will allow chief constables to assume control over the whole range of civilian staff currently assisting police forces, whether working in an operational or in an administrative capacity. The significance of this is underlined if the growing importance of civilian staff in recent years is appreciated. For example, between 1990 and 1993, the civilian establishment rose from 3,521 to 4,045.5, an increase of 15 per cent, while the regular force establishment rose from 14,045 to 14,205, an increase of only 1 per cent. This reflects the pursuit over the last decade of a concerted Government policy of civilianisation of tasks which are deemed not to require police powers or experience (see *H.M. Chief Inspector of Constabulary for Scotland: Report for the Year ended 31 December 1993*, 1994, cm. 2587, paras. 47–51, 67–68).

New subs. 9(3) of the 1967 Act
This subsection creates an exception to the rule in subs. (2) above that civilian staff be under the control of the chief constable. It allows the police authority to retain control of such civilian staff as are necessary to provide it with independent advice and administrative support. The staff to come under the control of the police authority for these purposes are to be agreed between the chief constable and the police authority, or, if such agreement is not possible, are to be determined by the Secretary of State. The Opposition objected to this as allowing insufficient flexibility to police authorities. It was argued that, given the considerable additional leeway allowed to chief constables in this and other provisions, it was anomalous that the police authority was not entitled to appoint its own advisers without reference to and the agreement of either the chief constable or the Secretary of State (Standing Committee D, June 14, 1994, col. 387, *per* Mr John McFall).

New subs. 9(4) of the 1967 Act
This subsection gives chief constables the powers of engagement and dismissal of civilians under their control. It was argued by the Opposition that as the police authority remains the legal employer of the civilian staff and would be responsible for any action taken by a civilian employee at an industrial tribunal, it should retain ultimate power, after consulting with the chief constable, to approve the civilian establishment and conditions of service. Removal of the powers of the police authority and Secretary of State in this regard would also mean that there was no means of controlling a possible abuse of discretion by the chief constable, such as a policy of mass redundancies (Standing Committee D, June 14, 1994, cols. 387–389, *per* Mr John McFall and Mr Tony Worthington). In refusing to reconsider the provision, the Government argued that its policy of decentralisation required control to be devolved to the chief constable, and that the police authority could continue to exert a significant indirect influence over civilian numbers through its control of the overall budget. Further, any general abuse of power could be guarded against by the Secretary of State by resort to his general powers to make directions as regards the general efficiency of the force under s.26A of the 1967 Act, as inserted by s.54 of the present Act, and his powers to make regulations in respect of the conduct of individual officers under s.26 of the 1967 Act, as amended by s.52 of the present Act (Standing Committee D, June 14, 1994, cols. 389–390, *per* Lord James Douglas-Hamilton).

Provision of advice and assistance to international organisations etc.

50. After section 12 of the 1967 Act there shall be inserted—

"Provision of advice and assistance to international organisations etc.
    12A.—(1) Subject to the provisions of this section, a police authority may provide advice and assistance—

    (a) to an international organisation or institution, or
    (b) to any other person or body which is engaged outside the United
        Kingdom in the carrying on of activities similar to any carried on
        by the authority or the chief constable of a force maintained by it.

    (2) The power conferred on a police authority by subsection (1) of this section includes a power to make arrangements under which a constable of the force maintained for the area of the authority is engaged for a period of temporary service with a person or body within paragraph (a) or (b) of that subsection.

    (3) The power conferred by subsection (1) of this section shall not be exercised except with the consent of the Secretary of State or in accordance with a general authorisation given by him.

    (4) A consent or authorisation under subsection (3) above may be given subject to such conditions as the Secretary of State thinks fit.

    (5) Nothing in this section authorises a police authority to provide any financial assistance by—
    (a) making a grant or loan,
    (b) giving a guarantee or indemnity, or
    (c) investing by acquiring share or loan capital.

    (6) A police authority may make charges for advice and assistance provided by it under this section.

    (7) The provisions of this section are without prejudice to the Police (Overseas Service) Act 1945 and section 10 of the Overseas Development and Co-operation Act 1980.".

DEFINITIONS

"the 1967 Act": s.65.

GENERAL NOTE

    This section, which was introduced after minimal debate at Report stage in the Commons, adds a new s.12A to the 1967 Act dealing with service overseas by Scottish officers. The same substantive provision is applied to England and Wales by s.13. Read together with s.60, the new section has the principal effect of permitting police officers from Scottish forces to serve abroad not only with foreign governments, which is already possible by virtue of the Police (Overseas Service) Act 1945 (c. 17) and the Overseas Development and Co-operation Act 1980 (c. 63), but also with international organisations and other agencies engaged in policing activities outwith the U.K.

Subs. (1) of s.12A of the 1967 Act

    This subsection permits a police authority to provide advice and assistance both to international organisations or institutions and to other persons or bodies engaged in policing activities outside the U.K. International organisations and institutions include the United Nations and the Council of Europe. This would, for example, allow British police officers to serve with the International Criminal Tribunal for the former Yugoslavia recently established by the United Nations Security Council (*Hansard*, H.L. Vol. 557, col. 21, *per* Earl Ferrers). Within the category of other bodies the institutions of the European Union are presumably included. The significance of this lies in the fact that under the terms of Title VI of the Treaty on European Union, introduced into U.K. law by the European Communities (Amendment) Act 1993, provision is made for the establishment of a new European Police Office to be known as Europol (Art. K.1.(9)), to which officers from domestic forces may be seconded.

Subs. (2) of s.12A of the 1967 Act

    This subsection makes it clear that the power of a police authority to provide advice and assistance includes a power to arrange for a constable of the force maintained for the area to be engaged in temporary service.

Subss. (3) and (4) of s.12A of the 1967 Act

    These subsections provide that the power conferred by subs. (1) shall only be exercised with the consent of the Secretary of State and subject to such conditions as he thinks fit.

Subss. (5) and (6) of s.12A of the 1967 Act
These subsections prevent a police authority from providing assistance of a financial nature to an international organisation or other relevant overseas body or person and permit an authority to charge for any services provided under this section.

Chief constables' annual reports

51. In section 15(1) of the 1967 Act (submission of general report by chief constable on policing—
(a) for the word "May" there shall be substituted the word "July";
(b) for the words "general report in writing on" there shall be substituted the words "report in writing on such matters as the Secretary of State may prescribe as respects, and generally as respects,"; and
(c) for the words "year ended on 31st December last preceding" there shall be substituted the words "twelve months ending on 31st March in that year".

DEFINITIONS
"prescribe": s.51(1) of the 1967 Act.
"the 1967 Act": s.65.

GENERAL NOTE
This section amends s.15 of the 1967 Act, which refers to the annual reports of chief constables. First, it provides that annual reports to police authorities should be for the financial year rather than the calendar year, and that, consequently, they should be submitted by the end of July rather than the end of May. The same change is made for England and Wales by virtue of para. 2(2)(a) of Sched. 5 to the present Act. Secondly, it enables the Secretary of State to prescribe matters to be covered in the chief constable's report in addition to the general policing of the force area.

Para. (a)
This paragraph provides that annual reports should be submitted by the end of May rather than the end of July, in consequence of the change brought about by para. (c) of the present section (discussed below).

Para. (b)
This specifies that the annual report shall include matters to be prescribed by the Secretary of State. According to the Government, the purpose of this provision is to allow: "the Secretary of State ... to ask all chief constables to say in their report what they are doing in relation to issues of current importance that are of substantial concern to the public", and thereby "to underpin the accountability of the police" (Standing Committee D, June 16, 1994, col. 399, *per* Lord James Douglas-Hamilton). Consistent reporting by forces on matters of major interest would render the actions of the police more transparent and would build upon the recommendations in the *Justice Charter for Scotland*, published by the Scottish Office in November 1991, which urged greater public consultation by the police and the dissemination of accessible information on police performance.
In the debate at Committee stage in the Commons, the Opposition challenged this new provision as unnecessary and as potentially oppressive and misleading (Standing Committee D, June 16, 1994, cols. 394–407). Under s.15(2) of the 1967 Act the Secretary of State already has a power to request reports on specific policing matters from the chief constable. Detailed reports on police forces may also be sought through the Inspectorate of Constabulary under s.33 of the 1967 Act, and remedial action taken under ss.26A–C of the 1967 Act (inserted by s.54 of the present Act). Arguably, these are the appropriate avenues to pursue if the Government seeks information on policing either for public consumption or for its own purposes in developing and monitoring policy. By contrast, the annual report has traditionally provided an opportunity for public reflection on the performance of his force by the chief constable. If he were required to abide by terms of reference set by the Secretary of State, his independent view might be compromised. Further, if the type of information requested was quantifiable data organised by refer-

ence to performance indicators, as has been the case with the publication of information in other public services such as education, and as is already the case with requests of information made by the inspectors of constabulary (see *H.M. Chief Inspector of Constabulary for Scotland: Report for the Year ended 31 December 1993*, 1994, cm. 2587, paras. 52–53), then the prospect of the production of unduly crude and selective "league tables" of police performance would be raised, so distorting rather than augmenting public understanding.

There is some merit in both sides of the argument. By bringing more information into the public domain, the new measure does have the potential to enhance public accountability. Against that, perhaps the wrong instrument has been chosen to achieve this, and it will succeed only in blurring the constitutionally important distinction between chief constable and Secretary of State. This could be avoided by the publication of separate information under the Government's own authority, although the publication of too many reports might itself lead to public confusion and apathy.

Para. (c)
This paragraph provides that the annual report should cover the financial year rather than the calendar year. According to the Notes on Clauses produced to assist the Government in steering the Bill through the Commons, this alteration is justified by the fact that police forces are funded by financial year and chief constables can best account for their use of funds over that same period.

Regulations for police forces

52.—(1) Section 26 of the 1967 Act (regulations as to government and administration of police forces) shall be amended as follows.

(2) In subsection (2) (which lists certain matters with respect to which regulations may be made), for paragraph (e) there shall be substituted—
"(e) the conduct and efficiency of constables;".

(3) After that subsection there shall be inserted—
"(2A) Without prejudice to the powers conferred by this section, regulations under this section shall—
(a) establish, or make provision for the establishment of, procedures for cases in which a constable may be dealt with by dismissal, requirement to resign, reduction in rank, reduction in rate of pay, fine, reprimand or caution; and
(b) make provision for securing that any case in which a constable who holds a rank above that of superintendent may be dismissed, or dealt with in any of the other ways mentioned in paragraph (a) above, is decided by the police authority of the area for which the force is maintained.

(2B) In relation to any matter as to which provision may be made by regulations under this section, the regulations may, subject to subsection (2A)(b) above—
(a) authorise or require provision to be made by, or confer discretionary powers on, the Secretary of State, police authorities, chief constables or other persons; or
(b) authorise or require the delegation by any person of functions conferred on him by or under the regulations.

(2C) Without prejudice to the generality of subsection (2A)(a) above, regulations under this section shall specify the circumstances in which, for the purposes of section 40A(2) of this Act, proceedings by virtue of that subsection are to be taken to have commenced.".

(4) Subsection (7) shall be omitted.

DEFINITIONS
"constable": s.51(1) of the 1967 Act, as amended by s.63(9)(a).
"efficiency": s.51(3A) of the 1967 Act, as inserted by s.63(9)(b).
"functions": s.51(1) of the 1967 Act.
"rank": s.51(1) of the 1967 Act.
"the 1967 Act": s.65.

GENERAL NOTE

This section amends s.26 of the 1967 Act, which requires the Secretary of State to make regulations as to the government and administration of police forces. The general purpose of the section, which is similar to that of s.14 in respect of England and Wales, is to provide, in combination with s.55 below, a broader and more graduated system for dealing with misconduct and inefficiency on the part of individual constables than was available under the 1967 Act. Under the previous system, no sanctions were available to deal with an inefficient officer. Only the misbehaving officer who was held to be in breach of the discipline code could be the subject of sanctions. If the discipline code was invoked, only limited options were available to avoid the full panoply of a disciplinary hearing (see the Police Discipline (Scotland) Regulations 1967 (SI 1967 No. 1021) as amended). Regulations to be made under the amended framework of s.26 will focus specifically upon inefficiency as well as misconduct, and will provide a range of investigatory and adjudicatory procedures appropriate to the seriousness of the offence.

Subs. (1)

This subsection introduces the amendments to s.26 of the 1967 Act.

Subs. (2)

This subsection substitutes a new s.26(2)(e) of the 1967 Act. In place of the previous reference to "the maintenance of discipline in police forces", it refers to "the conduct and efficiency of constables". This enables the Secretary of State to make regulations for dealing with unsatisfactory performance by police officers as well as misconduct. The new provision was amended at Report stage in the Lords to omit all reference to discipline, thus reinforcing the new focus upon a wider range of conduct. In this respect, the Scottish amendment represents a more radical break than the equivalent English provisions in s.14, which retains a reference to discipline in order to remain coherent with the provisions of the Police and Criminal Evidence Act 1984 (c. 60) relating to the Police Complaints Authority, which has no jurisdiction in Scotland (see *Hansard*, H.L. Vol. 553, col. 404, *per* Lord Fraser of Carmyllie). Echoing the misgivings of the police staff associations, the Opposition expressed some concern in debate that the increased scope of the amended provision might allow relatively minor forms of misconduct to be the subject of relatively severe sanctions, with only limited rights of appeal; the fact that the substance of the new system would be contained in regulations rather than in the primary legislation reinforced this concern (Standing Committee D, June 16, 1994, col. 407, *per* Mr Tony Worthington).

New subs. (2A) of s.26 of the 1967 Act

This subsection requires that, without prejudice to the powers conferred by s.26 generally, regulations shall be made to provide a formal procedure which is required to be followed for cases in which officers may be dealt with by dismissal, requirement to resign, reduction in rank or rate of pay, fine, reprimand or caution. The "without prejudice" clause was inserted at Report stage in the Lords and makes clear that formal proceedings under s.26 may, if regulations so provide, be disposed of by means other than those here specified, such as a warning. It also ensures that regulations may provide, as the existing discipline code does, that warnings may be used to dispose of a case at an earlier stage, before the matter of conduct or efficiency is deemed to be sufficiently serious to bring the officer before a formal hearing. The Government made it clear, moreover, that the new regulations under s.26 would not prescribe a detailed procedure to be followed prior to the issue of a warning at the earlier stage, so emphasising the relative informality of this type of disposal (*Hansard*, H.L. Vol. 553, cols. 206–207, *per* Lord Fraser of Carmyllie). This answers a concern expressed by the Opposition on behalf of the Scottish police staff associations at the earlier Committee stage that the fullest range of disciplinary options should be included within the regulations (*Hansard*, H.L. Vol. 552, col. 480, *per* Lord Carmichael of Kelvingrove).

Regulations under s.26 are also required to provide that where the officer holds a rank above superintendent, the case will be decided by the police authority of the area for which the force is maintained. This retains the distinction between ACPO-rank officers and other officers in respect of the investigation and sanctioning of their conduct which was previously provided for in s.26(7) of the 1967 Act, now repealed by subs. (4) of this section.

New subs. (2B) of s.26 of the 1967 Act

This subsection provides that regulations under s.26 may authorise or require the exercise of discretionary powers by certain persons, and may authorise or require the delegation by any person of the powers conferred by the regulations on that person. Such authorisation or delegation, however, may not override the stipulation in subs. (2A)(b) above as to the authority required to deal with an officer above the rank of superintendent.

New subs. (2C) of s.26 of the 1967 Act
Inserted at Report stage in the Lords, this provides that without prejudice to the generality of subs. (2A)(a) above, regulations under s.26 shall specify for the purposes of s.40A(2) of the 1967 Act, as inserted by s.61 of the present Act, when proceedings taken under regulations under subs. (2A)(a) can be taken to have commenced. New s.40A empowers inspectors of constabulary to direct a chief constable to reconsider the handling of a complaint, but, to ensure against double jeopardy, s.40A(2) stipulates that no such direction shall be given as regards so much of a complaint as has been, or is, the subject of proceedings against the constable by virtue of subs. (2A)(a) above. In order to clarify the circumstances in which the new s.40A applies, a precise definition is required of when proceedings can be taken to have commenced, and that is the purpose of the present subsection.

Fixed term appointments etc.

53.—(1) Section 26 of the 1967 Act shall be further amended—
(a) by inserting, after the words "administration of" in subsection (1), the words ", and the conditions of service in,"; and
(b) by inserting after subsection (5)—
"(5A) Regulations under this section as to conditions of service shall secure that appointments for fixed terms are not made except where the person appointed holds the rank of superintendent or a higher rank.".
(2) Section 23 of the 1967 Act (chief constables affected by amalgamations or local government reorganisation) shall be amended as follows—
(a) in subsection (2), for the word "deputy" there shall be substituted "assistant";
(b) in subsection (3), after the word "Act" there shall be inserted "and to subsection (3A) below"; and
(c) after subsection (3) there shall be inserted—
"(3A) If a chief constable was appointed for a term which expires within three months of his becoming a constable of a police force by virtue of this section, subsection (3) above shall have effect as if the reference in it to three months were a reference to that term.".

DEFINITIONS
"constable": s.51(1) of the 1967 Act, as amended by s.63(9)(a).
"rank": s.51(1) of the 1967 Act.
"the 1967 Act": s.65.

GENERAL NOTE
The main purpose of this section is to introduce fixed-term appointments for senior police officers. The principle of fixed-term appointments, which are provided for in substantially similar terms for England and Wales under s.18(4), was proposed for all ranks in the Sheehy Report (*Inquiry into Police Responsibilities and Rewards*: cm. 2280-I, 1993, chap. 12), but was only adopted by the Government in respect of ranks of superintendent and above.

Subs. (1)(a)
This subsection extends s.26 of the 1967 Act to empower the Secretary of State to make regulations as to the conditions of service in police forces as well as to the government and administration of forces. This ties in with the reference to regulations as to conditions of service in the new s.26(5A) of the 1967 Act, inserted by subs. (1)(b) below.

Subs. (1)(b)
This is the key provision of the section, inserting a new s.26(5) into the 1967 Act to specify that, under his general power to make regulations as to conditions of service, the Secretary of State may make regulations as to fixed-term appointments at superintendent level and above. Ironically, given the controversy surrounding this provision, the text is actually couched in negative terms, as a limitation on the Secretary of State's powers excluding reference to junior ranks. Strictly speaking, under the broad terms of s.26, he had previously possessed the power to introduce fixed-term contracts more generally, although no regulations were ever made to that effect.
Despite the reference to the superintendent rank, the Government has repeatedly emphasised that its plans to introduce fixed-term contracts apply only to chief constables and assistant

chief constables in the first instance, and that a decision whether to extend the principle to superintendents will only be made in the light of experience of the more limited scheme. The Government has also developed its thinking on other matters associated with fixed-term appointments. It was suggested to the Association of Chief Police Officers and the Association of Chief Police Officers (Scotland) (which, by virtue of s.26(9) of the 1967 Act, may be consulted before any regulations are made under subs. (5A)), that the minimum period of appointment should be for four years, and that it may be extended on a rolling basis to a maximum of seven years in the case of chief constable and 10 years in the case of assistant chief constable. The Government is also considering what arrangements should be made to compensate people for the risk inherent in a fixed-term appointment that it may not be renewed or a new appointment secured before the person has qualified to receive a pension (*Hansard*, H.L. Vol. 553, cols. 164–165, *per* Earl Ferrers).

The Government defends the principle of fixed-term appointments by reference to the importance of the individual accountability of senior officers for their professional performance. Despite this, and despite the various qualifications and modifications introduced by the Government, the provision was subject to intense critical scrutiny in both Houses. Fixed-term contracts, it was argued, might undermine the vocational nature of policing and the associated high and constant level of professional commitment expected of officers, in that a lengthy career could no longer be guaranteed beyond a certain rank. Uncertainty could also affect recruitment and retention levels, and could act as a brake on the aspirations of highly promising officers who gained rank early in their careers. Perhaps most significantly, fixed-term contracts might compromise the independence of chief officers from political interference by police authorities and the Secretary of State, each of whom has a role in the appointment of senior officers under ss.4 and 5 of the 1967 Act. Given the general centralising drift of the Act, most apparent in Pt. I but also evident in the Scottish provisions (see particularly s.51 above, and ss.54–57 below), this fear has been expressed most strongly with regard to the influence exerted by the Secretary of State. If, for example, a force was involved in the policing of a high-profile industrial dispute, in whose outcome the Government had a particular interest, the temporary appointee at chief officer level might be unusually vulnerable to political influence (see, *e.g.* Standing Committee D, June 16, 1994, cols. 408–410, *per* Mr John McFall).

Subs. (2)

This subsection amends s.23 of the 1967 Act which makes special provision for chief constables whose forces cease to exist because of amalgamations and who are not appointed as chief constable of the new force and do not accept office at any other rank in that force. Previously, such a person, by virtue of s.23(2), would have been appointed to the rank of deputy chief constable in the new force for a period of three months. Under the amended provision, given the abolition of the rank of deputy under ss.48 and 63 of the present Act, an officer in such a position will instead be appointed to the rank of assistant chief constable on a temporary basis. Further, by virtue of the new subs. (3A) of s.23, if such a chief officer was on a fixed-term appointment which expired prior to the end of the three-month period, his substitutional appointment to the rank of assistant chief constable would also terminate at that earlier date.

Power of Secretary of State to give directions to police authorities

54. After section 26 of the 1967 Act there shall be inserted—

"Power to give directions to police authority after adverse report

26A.—(1) The Secretary of State may at any time require the inspectors of constabulary to carry out, for the purposes of this section, an inspection under section 33(3) of this Act of any police force maintained under section 1 of this Act.

(2) Where a report made to the Secretary of State on an inspection carried out for the purposes of this section states—

(a) that, in the opinion of the person making the report, the force inspected is not efficient; or

(b) that in his opinion, unless remedial measures are taken, the force will cease to be efficient,

the Secretary of State may direct the police authority or joint police committee for the area for which the force is maintained to take such measures as may be specified in the direction.

Police efficiency: allocation of funds

26B. Without prejudice to the generality of subsection (2) of section 26A of this Act, the Secretary of State may under that subsection direct a police authority or joint police committee to allocate from their income, to the purpose of ensuring that a police force is efficient, such amounts as he shall specify.

Duty of compliance

26C. It shall be the duty of a police authority or joint police committee to comply with any direction given to them under section 26A or 26B of this Act.".

DEFINITIONS
"efficient": s.51(3A) of the 1967 Act, as inserted by s.63(9)(b).
"the 1967 Act": s.65.

GENERAL NOTE
This section inserts three new sections into the 1967 Act. They provide for sanctions to be used by the Secretary of State where a police authority, in the opinion of the inspectors of constabulary, fails to maintain an efficient police force. As with the original cl. 45 empowering the Secretary of State to direct police forces to participate in joint activities, which was eventually dropped by the Government at Report stage in the House of Lords, this provision attracted criticism from both the police staff associations and the Opposition as vesting unnecessarily broad powers in the Secretary of State. Compared to cl. 45, however, criticism was selective and relatively muted, and, unlike the earlier clause, the Government was not prepared to sacrifice either the principle underlying their provision or any of its detailed mechanisms.

According to the Government, the main purpose of the new section is to provide the Secretary of State with the means to remedy an inefficiency caused by a police authority, whether on account of failure to provide sufficient funding or otherwise, without resort to the drastic step of withdrawing the central police grant altogether under s.32 of the 1967 Act. It is conceived of as a reserve power, to be used only *in extremis*, and particularly useful as a deterrent. The arguments against various aspects of the new provision are considered below.

New s.26A of the 1967 Act
This new section is equivalent to the new s.28D of the Police Act 1964, inserted by s.15 of the present Act. It empowers the Secretary of State to give directions to a police authority which, in the opinion of an inspector of constabulary, has failed, or may be about to fail, to secure the maintenance of an efficient police force.

Subs. (1) of s.26A of the 1967 Act
This subsection provides the Secretary of State with the power to carry out, for the purposes of this section, an inspection under s.33(3) of the 1967 Act (as substituted by s.57 of the present Act) of any police force. Such inspections would be additional to the normal inspections which inspectors carry out in accordance with their existing statutory duty under s.33(3) of the 1967 Act to visit and inquire into any matter concerning or relating to the operation of a police force or of police forces generally. Arguably, this new power is unnecessary, as s.33(3), particularly with the substitution of a wider formula for the original under s.57 below, is already sufficiently broad to cover the situation in question. This is rather underlined by the terms of the new provision, which is *ex facie* otiose, amounting to a permission to use an *existing* power rather than the creation of a new power. Alternatively, s.33(3) may be understood as being limited to general inquiries, with the present provision designed for a more specific type of inquiry, *i.e.* one which is undertaken in anticipation of the possibility of the Secretary of State requiring to use his remedial powers under subs. 26A(2) and new s.26B below.

Subs. (2) of s.26A of the 1967 Act
This subsection provides that where the Secretary of State has required an inspection under subs. (1), and the report made by the inspector states that, in his opinion, the force in question is not efficient or will cease to be efficient unless remedial measures are taken, the Secretary of State may direct the police authority responsible for maintaining the force to take such measure as he specifies in the direction.

This somewhat circular formulation attracted criticism as being unduly permissive. Read literally, it requires "no necessary relationship between the nature of the report of the inspector of constabulary and the remedies to be found in that respect" (*Hansard*, H.L. Vol. 552, col. 491, *per* Lord McIntosh of Haringey). Arguably, such a connection is implicit, and any attempt to direct remedial measures unrelated to the discovered inefficiency would be *ultra vires.* Perhaps a more serious concern relates to the general scope of permissible remedial measures. Seeking to draw upon the same example used to illustrate the centralising dangers of the abortive original cl. 45, the Opposition raised the prospect at Committee stage in the House of Commons of a direction being made to secure a vigorous campaign against possession of offensive weapons in force areas where this was not presently considered a priority (Standing Committee D, June 16, 1994, col. 415, *per* Mr John McFall). For the Government, Lord James Douglas-Hamilton reassured the Committee that such a matter would come under the operational independence of the Chief Constable, and so would be outwith the competence of the police authority, which is concerned only with efficiency, and is immune from remedial treatment under the present provision (col. 416). However, the boundary between considerations of overall efficiency, on the one hand, which, in Lord James Douglas-Hamilton's own phrase, concerns the "provision of an adequate and competent service" (col. 419), and operational considerations, on the other hand, is a notoriously blurred one. This blurring may be all the more pronounced, given that, by virtue of s.63(9)(b) of the present Act, any reference to efficiency shall be construed to refer to the wider concept of effectiveness also. As is clearly demonstrated under the new s.26B below, considerations of efficiency and effectiveness often impinge upon operational issues.

New s.26B of the 1967 Act
This new section, which has broadly equivalent effect to s.29(1) of the Act, for England and Wales, gives the Secretary of State the more specific power to direct the police authority to allocate additional funding from its income to its police force where there has been an adverse report by an inspector of constabulary under s.26A(1) above. Unlike s.26A(2), there is a clear requirement on the part of the Secretary of State to relate the remedy to the inefficiency. Arguably, this may still allow the Secretary of State to encroach upon the operational independence of the chief constable. In the Lords, in order to illustrate the constraints upon the discretion of the Secretary of State secured by the requirement of a causal link between inefficiency and remedy, the Government minister suggested that if the inefficiency was located in the conduct of a criminal investigation, then any additional funding would have to be directed specifically to that investigation rather than, say, to the purchase of new motorvehicles for the traffic department (*Hansard,* H.L. Vol. 552, col. 490, *per* Lord Fraser of Carmyllie). However, the conduct of a criminal investigation provides a prime example of a matter which falls within the operational competence of the Chief Constable, albeit related to questions of overall efficiency and effectiveness inasmuch as an insufficient level of general resources might compromise investigative capacity in particular cases. By directing the deployment of resources to a specific operation in the name of efficiency, therefore, the Secretary of State might, in effect, be usurping the traditional role of the chief constable to decide upon the operational priorities of the force.

New s.26C of the 1967 Act
This new section places a duty on a police authority to comply with any direction given to it under ss.26A or 26B.

Appeals against dismissal etc.

55.—(1) For section 30 of the 1967 Act there shall be substituted—

"Appeals against dismissal etc.
30.—(1) A constable who is dismissed, required to resign or reduced in rank by a decision taken in proceedings under regulations made in accordance with subsection (2A) of section 26 of this Act may appeal to a police appeals tribunal against the decision except where he has a right of appeal to some other person; and in that case he may appeal to such a tribunal from any decision of that other person as a result of which he is dismissed, required to resign or reduced in rank.
(2) Where a police appeals tribunal allows an appeal it may, if it considers that it is appropriate to do so, make an order dealing with the appellant in a way—
(a) which appears to the tribunal to be less severe than the way in which he was dealt with by the decision appealed against; and
(b) in which he could have been dealt with by the person who made that decision.
(3) The Secretary of State may make rules as to the procedure on appeals under this section to a police appeals tribunal.

(4) Rules made under this section may make provision for enabling a police appeals tribunal to require any person to attend a hearing to give evidence or to produce documents and may, in particular, apply subsections (4) and (5) of section 210 of the Local Government (Scotland) Act 1973 with such modifications as may be set out in the rules.

(5) Schedule 3 to this Act shall have effect in relation to appeals under this section.

(6) Rules made under this section may make such supplementary and transitional provision as the Secretary of State thinks necessary or expedient in consequence of the coming into operation of an amalgamation scheme, amending scheme or revoking scheme while an appeal under this section is pending; and without prejudice to the generality of this subsection, such provision may in particular include modifications to Schedule 3 to this Act in that Schedule's application to any case affected by the making of such a scheme.".

(2) For Schedule 3 to the 1967 Act there shall be substituted the Schedule set out in Schedule 6 to this Act.

DEFINITIONS
"amalgamation scheme": s.51(1) of the 1967 Act.
"amending scheme": s.51(1) of the 1967 Act.
"constable": s.51(1) of the 1967 Act, as amended by s.63(9)(a).
"rank": s.51(1) of the 1967 Act.
"revoking scheme": s.51(1) of the 1967 Act.
"the 1967 Act": s.65.

GENERAL NOTE
This section replaces s.30 of the 1967 Act, thereby providing arrangements for appeals to a new appeals tribunal for officers dismissed, required to resign or reduced in rank. Under the original s.30, an officer dealt with for an offence against discipline had a right of appeal to the Secretary of State.

New subs. 30(1) of the 1967 Act
This subsection provides that a police officer who is dismissed, required to resign or reduced in rank may appeal directly to a new appeals tribunal (established by subs. (2) and Sched. 6 below), except where he has a right of appeal to some other person; and in the latter case he may appeal to a police appeals tribunal against any decision of that other person as a result of which he was dismissed, required to resign or reduced in rank. By contrast, disposals which involve less severe sanctions will be dealt with internally, but there may be an appeal from the initial decision to the chief constable.

In the original Bill, rights of appeal to an external tribunal were only available where the officer was dismissed or required to resign. An amendment was proposed at Committee stage in the Lords which would have extended rights of appeal to officers who had been penalised in any of the ways set out in the new s.26(2A)(a) of the 1967 Act, as inserted by s.52(3) of the present Act. At Report stage in the Lords, the final enacted version was proposed as a compromise solution by the Government, which was concerned to retain the approach developed in s.52 of a graduated treatment of individual misconduct and inefficiency within police forces.

New subs. 30(2) of the 1967 Act
This subsection provides that, when it allows an appeal, an appeals tribunal may deal with the applicant in a manner less severe than he was dealt with by the decision appealed against, but in which he could have been dealt with by the person who made that decision.

New subss. 30(3) and (4) of the 1967 Act
These subsections deal with the power of the Secretary of State to make rules of procedure for the conduct of appeals before a police appeals tribunal. These may include powers for the tribunal to require any person to attend to give evidence or to produce documents, and would make it an offence for any person to refuse to meet such a requirement.

New subs. 30(6) of the 1967 Act
Inserted at Report stage in the Lords, this subsection provides that the rules of procedure under subs. (3) above may make provision for the proper completion of appeals pending the

time when an amalgamation, or an amending or revoking scheme comes into operation, and may include modifications to Sched. 3 (disciplinary appeals procedure) to the 1967 Act insofar as it applies to any case affected by the making of such a scheme.

Subsection (2) of the present Act substitutes a new Sched. 3 to the 1967 Act, applied in relation to appeals under this section by subs. (4) above. The new Schedule is set out in Sched. 6 to the present Act.

Expenditure in safeguarding national security

56. After section 32 of the 1967 Act there shall be inserted—

"Grants for expenditure on safeguarding national security

32A.—(1) The Secretary of State may make grants in respect of expenditure incurred (or to be incurred) by a police authority or joint police committee in connection with safeguarding national security.

(2) Grants under this section may be made either unconditionally or subject to conditions.

(3) The Secretary of State shall exercise his powers under this section only with the approval of the Treasury.".

DEFINITIONS
"the 1967 Act": s.65.

GENERAL NOTE
This section inserts a new s.32A into the 1967 Act empowering the Secretary of State to make grants in respect of expenditure incurred, or to be incurred, by police authorities or joint police committees in connection with safeguarding national security. An equivalent provision for England and Wales is provided for under s.17 of the present Act which inserts a new s.31B into the Police Act 1964.

New s.32A(1) of the 1967 Act
This subsection contains the basic power to make grants in respect of national security. Some concern was expressed in the Lords by members of the Scottish Peers Association, who had consulted with the police staff associations, that the provision was insufficiently wide-ranging to cover the types of unexpected and exceptional expenditure not easily catered for within normal budgeting arrangements under s.32 of the 1967 Act, which authorises the payment of a general police grant by the Secretary of State to police authorities (*Hansard*, H.L. Vol. 552, cols. 499–500, *per* Lady Saltoun of Abernethy). For the most part, special expenditure by way of royal protection or diplomatic protection—for example, with regard to the Edinburgh European Council summit of December 1992—could be taken into account in the normal budget-setting process, and special provision duly made. However, if a major security operation was required for an event which cropped up at short notice, or there was a major public incident requiring an extensive police response, would these eventualities be covered by the new provision? The meaning of "national security" is notoriously vague, its scope not being clearly delimited. Also, "safeguarding" suggests a preventive role, rather than a response after a breach of national security has already taken place (*Hansard*, H.L. Vol. 552, col. 500, *per* Lord Renton).

For the Government, it was argued that the new provision was intended to be narrowly drawn, as it was felt that exceptions to the normal dual system of local-central police funding should be kept to a minimum (*Hansard*, H.L. Vol. 552, col. 501, *per* Lord Fraser of Carmyllie). It was meant to cover operations, "often ... co-ordinated", dealing with "threats from terrorists" (Standing Committee D, June 16, 1994, col. 421, *per* Lord James Douglas-Hamilton), although it was unclear whether this was deemed to be its sole purpose. Neither was it clear whether, to take Lord Renton's point, it would also cover police responses to terrorist incidents, as with the Lockerbie incident, or, whether, as in that case, additional central funding would continue to be made available under the general authority of s.32.

New s.32A(2) of the 1967 Act
This subsection allows grants under subs. (1) to be made either unconditionally or subject to conditions.

New s.32A(3) of the 1967 Act
This subsection requires the Secretary of State to have the approval of the Treasury before exercising his powers under this section, as is also the case with general police grant under s.32(1) of the 1967 Act.

Duty of inspectors of constabulary

57. For subsection (3) of section 33 of the 1967 Act (inspectors of constabulary), there shall be substituted—

"(3) It shall be the duty of the inspectors of constabulary, on being directed to do so by the Secretary of State, to visit and inquire into any matter concerning or relating to the operation of a police force or of police forces generally; and, without prejudice to the generality of this subsection, such matters may include the state and efficiency of, and of the buildings and equipment used by, the force or forces.".

DEFINITIONS
"efficiency": s.51(3A) of the 1967 Act, as inserted by s.63(9)(b).
"the 1967 Act": s.65.

GENERAL NOTE
This section substitutes a new s.33(3) in the 1967 Act. Whereas previously it was the duty of inspectors of constabulary under the direction of the Secretary of State to visit and inquire into the state and efficiency of police force and of the buildings used by such forces, this duty has now been expanded in two respects. First, while inspections may still cover the specific matters mentioned, they can now also cover any other matter concerning or relating to the operation of a police force. Secondly, inspections may now cover matters relating to police forces generally, and need not be restricted to particular forces.

These two changes reflect developments in the role and functions of the Inspectorate in recent years, and establish a firmer statutory foundation with regard to these developments. The first reflects a general broadening and deepening of the annual inspection of and report upon each force carried out by the Inspectorate. In particular, since 1991 the Inspectorate has established a new system whereby each force is subject to a primary inspection every second year, with an intermediate inspection in alternate years. The scope of the primary inspection, which involves a thorough performance review of all the functions of the force under scrutiny, is more adequately covered by the new statutory formulation. Secondly, since 1991 the Inspectorate has also established a series of thematic inspections into particular aspects of policing in all Scottish forces. In 1993, for example, thematic inspections were completed in relation to the issues of misuse of drugs and equal opportunities (*H.M. Chief Inspector of Constabulary for Scotland: Report for the year ended 31 December 1993*, cm. 2587, para. 4).

Assistant inspectors of constabulary and staff officers to inspectors of constabulary

58. In section 34 of the 1967 Act, for subsection (1) (appointment of assistant inspectors of constabulary and their staff officers) there shall be substituted—

"(1) The Secretary of State may appoint assistant inspectors of constabulary.

(1A) Constables may be appointed under subsection (1) above or to be staff officers to inspectors of constabulary.".

DEFINITIONS
"constable": s.51(1) of the 1967 Act, as amended by s.63(9)(a).
"the 1967 Act": s.65.

GENERAL NOTE
This section, which replaces subs. (1) of s.34 of the 1967 Act with new subss. (1) and (1A), makes provision for Scotland similar to s.22 for England and Wales concerning the appointment of assistant inspectors of constabulary and of staff officers to the inspectors of constabulary. It permits serving police officers to be appointed as staff officers and also as assistant inspectors. As it stood, s.34(1) had provided, by implication, that serving police officers could only be appointed as staff officers to the Inspectorate.

Common services

59. For section 36 of the 1967 Act there shall be substituted—

"Common services

36.—(1) After consulting the Joint Central Committee and such bodies or associations as appear to the Secretary of State to be representative of police authorities or of chief constables or superintendents (such consultation being in the following provisions of this section referred to as "relevant consultation"), he may, either directly or indirectly, provide and maintain such facilities and services, or establish and maintain such institutions and organisations, as he considers necessary or expedient for promoting the efficiency of the police.

(2) The Secretary of State may, after relevant consultation, by regulations make provision for requiring all police forces in Scotland to use specified facilities or services, or facilities or services of a specified description, (whether or not provided under subsection (1) above) if he considers that it would be in the interests of the efficiency of the police for them to do so.

(3) The Secretary of State may, after relevant consultation, by order determine the charges to be payable for facilities and services provided under or by virtue of subsection (1) above, make provision as regards their payment and make provision for the recovery, other than by such charges, of expenses incurred by him in providing the facilities and services.

(4) A statutory instrument containing an order under subsection (3) above shall be subject to annulment in pursuance of a resolution of either House of Parliament.

(5) Any expenses falling on a police authority or joint police committee by virtue of subsection (3) above shall be defrayed in like manner as other expenses incurred for the purposes of this Act by the authority or committee.

(6) The Secretary of State may, after relevant consultation, in any order under subsection (3) above apply that order, or any provision of that order, to other expenses specified in the order, being expenses incurred by him for the purposes of police forces generally.".

DEFINITIONS
    "efficiency": s.51(3A) of the 1967 Act, as inserted by s.63(9)(b).
    "Joint Central Committee": s.51(1) of the 1967 Act.
    "the 1967 Act": s.65.

GENERAL NOTE
    This section substitutes a new s.36 of the 1967 Act making wider provision for the maintenance by the Secretary of State of common services for the benefit of the Scottish police service generally. The section makes provision similar to s.23 for England and Wales, which substitutes a new s.41 of the Police Act 1964. The new Scottish provision, however, represents a more radical departure than the new provision for England and Wales. While the original s.41 of the 1964 Act already made wide-ranging and relatively detailed provision for common services, the original s.36 of the 1967 Act was limited to the provision of central training (original subs. (1)) and a vague power to make regulations in respect of "expenses ... incurred by [the Secretary of State] for the purposes of police forces generally" (original subs. (5)).

New subs. 36(1) of the 1967 Act
    This subsection empowers the Secretary of State, after consulting the Joint Central Committee of the Police Federation and such bodies or association as appear to him to be representative of police authorities or chief constables or superintendents, to make direct or indirect provision for and maintain such facilities and services, and to establish and maintain such institutions and organisations as he considers necessary or expedient for promoting the efficiency of the police. The consultation requirement, which also applies to subss. (2), (3) and (6) below, did not originally include the Joint Central Committee, but this unintentional omission was corrected by the Government at Report stage in the Lords.

The new powers conferred are very broadly conceived. Not only do they cover all common services currently provided under s.36 of the 1967 Act, including training, recruitment publicity, forensic facilities and the Scottish Criminal Records Office, but, arguably, they also include certain services which overlap the remit of police authorities under s.2 of the 1967 Act, and which could bring the Secretary of State into conflict with police authorities. In *R. v. Secretary of State for the Home Department, ex p. Northumbria Police Authority* [1989] Q.B. 26, a case under the 1964 Act in England, it was decided that "organisations and services ... [the Home Secretary] considers necessary and expedient for promoting the efficiency of the police" under s.41 include the supply of plastic baton rounds and CS gas from a central store, even if this is disapproved of by the local police authority which has the general duty under s.4(4) of the 1964 Act (equivalent to s.2(3) of the 1967 Act), to provide "equipment" required for policing purposes. As the new s.36(1) of the 1967 Act is similar to, but broader than the original s.41 of the 1964 Act, a Scottish court faced with a similar case of conflict between the Secretary of State and the police authority over facilities appropriate to local policing, may well come to the same conclusion and allow the will of central Government to prevail.

New subs. 36(2) of the 1967 Act
Whereas subs. (1) is concerned with the Secretary of State's power to facilitate policing through the provision of common services, this subsection concerns his power, by means of regulation, to require police forces to use specified facilities and services, or facilities or services of a specified description, where he considers it to be in the interests of the efficiency of the police service as a whole for them to do so. As indicated by the Notes on Clauses, such common facilities might include a common radio system to improve communications, or a common database to widen access to information, where the usefulness of such a service might be reduced if one or two forces failed to participate. It was anticipated by the Government that the circumstances in which this type of issue might arise would be rare.

New subss. 36(3) and (4) of the 1967 Act
This subsection empowers the Secretary of State, by order, to make arrangements for payment for facilities and services provided under subs. (1). Under the original s.36(4) of the 1967 Act provision was made for the Secretary of State to recover 49 per cent of the expenses incurred by him in establishing and maintaining services. The Secretary of State may still use the method of cost recovery, but may now, in the alternative, fund the service by requiring individual police forces to pay charges according to the level of demand which they make on a service. It will also be possible for payment for services provided on behalf of the Secretary of State to be made to some other party, such as a private contractor. An order made under subs. (3) must be the subject of the negative resolution procedure in both Houses of Parliament.

New subs. 36(5) of the 1967 Act
This subsection provides for police authorities or joint committees to meet any expenses falling on the Scottish police force under subs. (3) in the same way as other expenses incurred by them under the 1967 Act.

New subs. 36(6) of the 1967 Act
This subsection substantially re-enacts the original subs. (5) of the 1967 Act. It permits the Secretary of State to apply any order under subs. (3) to any other expenses specified in the order, being expenses incurred by him for the purposes of police forces generally. It thus effectively allows him to extend the remit of subs. (3) beyond the matters covered in subs. (1), provided they are for general policing purposes. While the attractiveness to Government of such an open-ended extension of their powers in respect of common service was undeniable in the context of the original s.36, which was otherwise narrowly restricted to training matters, its value under the new, more comprehensive framework is more questionable.

Constables engaged on service outside their force

60. After section 38 of the 1967 Act there shall be inserted—

"Constables engaged on service outside their force
     38A.—(1) For the purposes of this section "relevant service" means—
       (a) temporary service on which a person is engaged in accordance with arrangements made under section 12A(2) of this Act,
       (b) central service (as defined by section 38(5) of this Act) on which a person is engaged with the consent of the appropriate authority,

(c) service the expenses of which are payable under section 1(1) of the Police (Overseas Service) Act 1945, on which a person is engaged with the consent of the appropriate authority,

(d) service in the Royal Ulster Constabulary, on which a person is engaged with the consent of the Secretary of State and the appropriate authority, or

(e) service pursuant to an appointment under section 10 of the Overseas Development and Co-operation Act 1980, on which a person is engaged with the consent of the appropriate authority.

(2) In subsection (1) of this section "appropriate authority" has the same meaning as in section 38 of this Act.

(3) Subject to subsections (4) to (7) of this section, a constable of a police force engaged on relevant service shall be treated as if he were not a constable of that force during that service; but except where a pension, allowance or gratuity becomes payable to him out of money provided by Parliament by virtue of regulations made under the Police Pensions Act 1976—

(a) he shall be entitled at the end of the period of relevant service to revert to his police force in the rank in which he was serving immediately before the period began, and

(b) he shall be treated as if he had been serving in that force during the period of relevant service for the purposes of any scale prescribed by or under regulations made under section 26 of this Act fixing his rate of pay by reference to his length of service.

(4) In the case of relevant service to which subsection (1)(c) of this section refers, the reference in subsection (3) of this section to regulations made under the Police Pensions Act 1976 shall be read as including a reference to regulations made under section 1 of the Police (Overseas Service) Act 1945.

(5) A person may, when engaged on relevant service, be promoted in his police force as if he were serving in that force; and in any such case—

(a) the reference in paragraph (a) of subsection (3) of this section to the rank in which he was serving immediately before the period of relevant service began shall be construed as a reference to the rank to which he is promoted, and

(b) for the purposes mentioned in paragraph (b) of that subsection he shall be treated as having served in that rank from the time of his promotion.

(6) A constable who—

(a) has completed a period of relevant service within paragraph (a), (b) or (e) of subsection (1) of this section,

(b) while engaged on relevant service within paragraph (c) of that subsection, is dismissed from that service by the disciplinary authority established by regulations under section 1 of the Police (Overseas Service) Act 1945 or is required to resign as an alternative to dismissal, or

(c) while engaged on relevant service within paragraph (d) of that subsection, is dismissed from that service or required to resign as an alternative to dismissal,

may be dealt with under regulations made in accordance with subsection (2A) of section 26 of this Act for anything done or omitted while he was engaged on that service as if that service had been service in his police force; and section 30 of this Act shall apply accordingly.

(7) For the purposes of subsection (6) of this section a certificate certifying that a person has been dismissed, or required to resign as an alternative to dismissal, shall be evidence of the fact so certified, if—

(a) in a case within paragraph (b) of that subsection, it is given by the disciplinary authority referred to in that paragraph, or

(b) in a case within paragraph (c) of that subsection it is given by or on behalf of the Chief Constable of the Royal Ulster Constabulary, or such person or authority as may be designated for the purposes of this subsection by order of the Secretary of State.".

DEFINITIONS
"constable": s.51(1) of the 1967 Act, as amended by s.63(9)(a).
"rank": s.51(1) of the 1967 Act.
"the 1967 Act": s.65.

GENERAL NOTE
This section, which was introduced after minimal debate at Report stage in the Commons, adds a new s.38A to the 1967 Act dealing with service overseas by Scottish officers. The same substantive provision is applied to England and Wales by s.26. Read together with s.50, the new section has the principal effect of permitting police officers from Scottish forces to serve abroad not only with foreign Governments, which is already possible by virtue of the Police (Overseas Service) Act 1945 (c. 17) and the Overseas Development and Co-operation Act 1980 (c. 63), but also with international organisations and other agencies engaged in policing activities outwith the U.K. Whereas s.50 deals with the general powers of police authorities to permit service overseas, the present section deals with the conditions of service of seconded officers.

Subs. 38A(1) of the 1967 Act
This subsection applies the substantive terms of the section to police officers seconded to service abroad, and also to officers engaged in temporary service with the Royal Ulster Constabulary, and to persons temporarily employed on central service under s.38(5) of the 1967 Act, or employed under the terms of a collaboration agreement between two or more forces under s.12 of the 1967 Act.

Subs. 38A(2) of the 1967 Act
This subsection provides that a constable engaged in service outside his force in any of the capacities specified in subs. (1) shall be treated as if he were not a constable of that force during his outside service, subject to certain qualifications and exceptions. One such set of qualifications and exceptions concerns a constable's pension rights under the Police Pensions Act 1976 (c. 35). On account of these rights, he shall be entitled to revert to his original rank at the end of his period of outside service, and he shall be deemed to have served continuously in his own force throughout the period of outside service. Other qualifications and exceptions are contained in subss. (4)–(7) below.

Subss. 38A(4)–(7) of the 1967 Act
These subsections provide for the possibility of a constable being promoted in his own force or being dismissed or required to resign from the police service during his period of outside service.

Examination of handling of complaints against constables

61. After section 40 of the 1967 Act there shall be inserted—

"Examination of handling of complaints against constables
40A.—(1) Where a member of the public has made a complaint to the chief constable of a police force against a constable of that force the inspectors of constabulary may, at the request of the member of the public, examine the manner in which the chief constable has dealt with the complaint.

(2) Where the inspectors of constabulary have carried out an examination under subsection (1) above, they shall report their findings to the person who made the complaint and send a copy of that report to the chief constable and to the constable against whom the complaint was made; and they may direct the chief constable to reconsider the complaint and may instruct him to have regard, in doing so, to such further information as may have become available (whether or not as a result of the examination) after he dealt with the complaint; but no such direction shall be given as respects so much of the complaint as has been, or is, the subject of proceedings against the constable by virtue of section 26(2A)(a) of this Act.

(3) On making a direction under subsection (2) above, the inspectors of constabulary shall notify the constable against whom the complaint was made and the person who made it that they have done so; and the outcome of any reconsideration carried out by virtue of that subsection shall be communicated forthwith to the inspectors of constabulary, who shall—

    (a) report the outcome, and their own findings as regards the outcome, to that constable and to that person; and

    (b) communicate those findings to the chief constable.

(4) Where an examination has been carried out under subsection (1) above—

    (a) the Secretary of State may require the inspectors of constabulary to submit to him, and

    (b) the police authority for the area for which the police force in question is maintained may require the inspectors of constabulary to submit to them,

a written report concerning that examination and a copy of any report under subsection (3)(a) above consequent on that examination.".

DEFINITIONS

"constable": s.51(1) of the 1967 Act, as amended by s.63(9)(a).
"the 1967 Act": s.65.

GENERAL NOTE

This section inserts s.40A into the 1967 Act, providing inspectors of constabulary with the power to consider representations from complainers dissatisfied with the way the police have handled their complaints, and, where appropriate, to direct the chief constable to re-examine the case. In Scotland, there is no independent body with overall responsibility for the investigation of complaints against the police equivalent to the Police Complaints Authority for England and Wales established under s.83 and Sched. 4 to the Police and Criminal Evidence Act 1984 (c. 60). The Government is of the view that this absence can be justified by reference to the general distinctiveness of the Scottish police and criminal justice systems, particularly as there is a long tradition of investigation of complaints of a criminal character by the Procurator Fiscal. However, insofar as the Scottish position makes it all the more important that the general public be assured that their complaints are being examined thoroughly and objectively, the new power conferred by this section may be beneficial (*Hansard*, H.L. Vol. 552, col. 504, *per* Lord Fraser of Carmyllie).

Some concern was expressed at Committee stage in the House of Lords as to whether the Inspectorate was an appropriate body to exercise this type of power. As its traditional role has been to advise the Secretary of State, the conferral of a power to give directions to chief constables could be viewed as a considerable constitutional innovation (*Hansard*, H.L. Vol. 552, cols. 503–504, *per* Lords Renton and Harris of Greenwich). For the Government, it was pointed out that since, by virtue of s.40 of the 1967 Act, a duty is already imposed upon inspectors of constabulary to keep themselves informed as to the manner in which complaints made by members of the public against the police are dealt with by the police, the new power may be seen as a development of the existing position rather than a radically new departure (*Hansard*, H.L. Vol. 552, col. 505, *per* Lord Fraser of Carmyllie). It is undeniable, however, that, if s.61 is considered together with ss.54 and 57, there is a significant trend within Pt. II of the Act towards increasing the authority of the Inspectorate within the overall arrangements for the control and direction of the Scottish police.

Subs. 40A(1) of the 1967 Act

This subsection enables inspectors of constabulary, when requested to do so by a member of the public, to examine the way in which that individual's initial complaint was dealt with by the chief constable of the force concerned. Concern was expressed by Opposition members at Committee stage in the Lords, echoing the views of the police staff associations, that the new provision would give *carte blanche* to frivolous or malicious complainers, and would waste police time and cause unnecessary worry to the subjects of complaints. It was suggested that a "good cause" proviso be introduced to avoid that danger (*Hansard*, H.L. Vol. 552, col. 502, *per* Earl of Winchelsea and Nottingham). In rejecting this suggestion, the Government argued that the effectiveness of independent scrutiny as a means of bolstering public confidence in the integrity of the complaints system would be undermined if access was not unconditional. Moreover, unless there was some form of further investigation, it would be difficult to determine in advance whether any particular claim was, in fact, frivolous or mischievous. In any event, the use of the permissive "may" in the present subsection would allow the Inspectorate discretion to take no further action where an approach from a member of the public was manifestly unfounded (*Hansard*, H.L. Vol. 552, cols. 502–503, *per* Lord Fraser of Carmyllie). When the issue was returned to at Committee stage in the Commons (Standing Committee D, June 16, 1994, cols. 423–424, *per* Mr Robert MacLennan), the Government agreed to consider whether it was necessary to issue guidelines to inspectors informing the exercise of their discretion in such cases (Standing Committee D, June 16, 1994, col. 424, *per* Lord James Douglas-Hamilton).

Subs. 40A(2) of the 1967 Act
This subsection provides that on completion of their examination under subs. (1), inspectors of constabulary will report their findings to the complainer, the constable(s) complained against, and the relevant chief constable.

The subsection also empowers inspectors of constabulary to direct the chief constable to reconsider a complaint. In so doing, inspectors of constabulary can instruct the chief constable to take account of any further information which may have come to light since the complaint was first investigated, whether or not this information was revealed by the inspector's examination of the case. However, any direction to reconsider a complaint will not extend to any part of the case which has already been, or is, the subject of proceedings against a constable by virtue of the new s.26(2A) of the 1967 Act, as inserted by s.52(3) of the present Act.

The purpose of this exception is to guard against the dangers of double jeopardy, raised on behalf of the police staff associations in both the Lords (*Hansard*, H.L. Vol. 552, cols. 503–506, *per* Lord Harris of Greenwich) and the Commons (Standing Committee D, June 16, 1994, cols. 422–423, *per* Mr John McFall). Although the Government conceded the importance of avoiding double jeopardy, it was of the view that this could not be treated as a categorical principle, but would have to be balanced against the wider object of the section to ensure public confidence in the efficacy of the system for investigating complaints against the police (*Hansard*, H.L. Vol. 552, cols. 504–507, *per* Lord Fraser of Carmyllie). Subsection (2) prevents re-investigation by the chief constable provided any prior investigation had reached the stage where proceedings had formally commenced under the new arrangements in s.26(2A). Reinvestigation would not, therefore, be prevented where a previous investigation was discontinued at an earlier, informal stage, after initial inquiry failed to reveal any basis for further inquiry. Further, as an amendment introduced by the Government at Report stage in the Lords ensured (*Hansard*, H.L. Vol. 553, col. 409, *per* Lord Fraser of Carmyllie), neither would reinvestigation be prevented just because the complaint had been the subject of criminal charges against the constable. While the actions of the Procurator Fiscal in investigating criminal charges cannot be the subject of later scrutiny by the Inspectorate, if the conduct to which these charges refer raises separate questions of police misconduct, then there is no bar to further investigation on the latter count merely because the Procurator Fiscal decides not to proceed to a criminal trial. Finally, it should also be noted that initial reinvestigation by the Inspectorate under subs. (1) is competent irrespective of whether the matter has already been the subject of proceedings which have reached the stage of formal commencement under s.26(2A). The protection against double jeopardy only applies at and beyond the point at which the chief constable is formally directed to reconsider a case.

Subs. 40A(3) of the 1967 Act
This subsection obliges inspectors of constabulary, when they have directed a chief constable to reconsider a case, to notify this to the constable(s) complained against and the complainer. It also requires that the outcome be communicated to the inspectors of constabulary who will report the outcome, and their own comments on the outcome, to the constable(s) complained against and the complainer, and also report these further comments to the chief constable. The duty on the Inspectorate to make and report further comments was introduced at Report stage in the Lords for the sake of "completeness" of the reinvestigation process (*Hansard*, H.L. Vol. 553, col. 410, *per* Lord Fraser of Carmyllie).

Subs. 40A(4) of the 1967 Act
This subsection provides that where inspectors of constabulary have examined a complaint at the request of a member of the public, both the Secretary of State and the local police authority may require inspectors of constabulary to submit a written report of their examination of any complaint under this section together with a copy of any report under subs. (3) detailing their own findings on the outcome of their examination.

Transmission of criminal statistics

62. In section 47 of the 1967 Act (criminal statistics)—
  (a) in subsection (1), for the words "the year to 31st December last pre-ceding" there shall be substituted the words "such period as the Secretary of State may specify in the direction"; and
  (b) for subsection (2) there shall be substituted—
  "(2) The Secretary of State shall prepare such reports as he considers appropriate from such statements as he receives by virtue of subsection (1) above; and he shall lay any such report before Parliament and send a copy of it to each police authority.".

DEFINITIONS
  "the 1967 Act": s.65.

GENERAL NOTE
  This section amends s.47(1) of the 1967 Act and substitutes a new s.47(2) of the 1967 Act. The effect of these changes is to introduce a more flexible system for the reporting and dissemination of criminal statistics.

Amended subs. 47(1) of the 1967 Act
  This provides that statements on criminal statistics from the chief constable to the Secretary of State shall not be restricted to the calendar year, but shall instead relate to any period specified by the Secretary of State.

New subs. 47(2) of the 1967 Act
  This dispenses with the set criteria (number of reported offences, number of persons taken into custody by the police, etc.), in accordance with which the Secretary of State, under the original subs. (2), was obliged to prepare reports for submission to Parliament and to police authorities. The Secretary of State may now prepare such reports as he considers appropriate from statements received by virtue of s.47(1) of the 1967 Act. This will permit the Secretary of State to prepare statistical bulletins as and when such information becomes available. Depending upon the spirit in which it is interpreted by the Secretary of State, the new provision could lead to a more or less detailed and frequent dissemination of statistical information.

Other amendments of 1967 Act

63.—(1) The 1967 Act shall be amended in accordance with this section.
  (2) In section 6(2) (application of certain provisions of 1967 Act to con-stables below rank of assistant chief constable) the words "a deputy chief constable" shall be omitted.
  (3) In section 7(3) (assignment of lower rank), for the words from "as to" to the end there shall be substituted the words "made in accordance with section 26(2A) of this Act".
  (4) In section 24 (effect of amalgamation scheme on constables engaged in service other than with their own force)—
  (a) in subsection (1) for the words from "either" to "transferred force" there shall be substituted the words "a person is engaged in relevant service within the meaning of section 38A of this Act";
  (b) in subsection (2) for the word "overseas" in each of the three places where it occurs there shall be substituted the word "relevant"; and
  (c) in subsection (3), the words from "and the expression" onwards shall be omitted.
  (5) In section 31 (requirement for chief constable to retire in interests of efficiency)—
  (a) in subsection (2)—
      (i) for the words "a deputy or" there shall be substituted the word "an"; and
      (ii) the words "or deputy" shall be omitted; and
  (b) in subsection (4), the words "or deputy" shall be omitted.

(6) In section 32(1) (payment towards expenses of police authorities and joint police committees) after the words "19(6)" there shall be inserted the words ", section 32A".

(7) In section 38—

(a) in subsection (3A), for the words "subsection (1) above" there shall be substituted the words "section 38A(3) of this Act"; and

(b) in subsection (5) (interpretation), in the definition of "central service" for the words "service as a staff officer to the inspectors of constabulary" there shall be substituted the words "temporary service under section 34 of this Act".

(8) In section 42(1) (offence of causing disaffection amongst constables), the words "or to commit breaches of discipline" shall be omitted.

(9) In section 51 (interpretation)—

(a) in subsection (1), the definitions of "regular constable", "special constable" and "temporary constable" shall be omitted; and

(b) after subsection (3) there shall be inserted—

"(3A) Any reference in this Act to efficiency or to being efficient shall be construed, except where the context otherwise requires, as including, respectively, a reference to effectiveness or to being effective.".

(10) In Schedule 2 (transitory provisions for purposes of amalgamation schemes), paragraph 2 shall be omitted.

DEFINITIONS
"amalgamation schemes": s.51(1) of the 1967 Act.
"constable": s.51(1) of the 1967 Act, as amended by s.63(9)(a).
"efficiency": s.51(3A) of the 1967 Act, as inserted by s.63(9)(b).
"rank": s.51(1) of the 1967 Act.
"the 1967 Act": s.65.

GENERAL NOTE
This section makes minor and consequential amendments to various provisions in the 1967 Act. Subsections (2), (3) and (5) remove various references to the ranks of deputy chief constable and chief superintendent, abolished by ss.47 and 48 above. Subsections (3), (8) and (10) make amendments consequential upon the replacement of the existing internal discipline system by new procedures for investigating the conduct and efficiency of officers under ss.52 and 55 above. Subsection (9) amends the interpretation section in the 1967 Act; of particular importance, especially in respect of s.54 above, is the redefinition of "efficient" to include "effective". Subsections (4), (6) and (7) make other minor and consequential amendments to the 1967 Act.

Delegation of functions of Scottish police authority

64. In section 63 of the Local Government (Scotland) Act 1973 (arrangements as to police authority functions etc.), after subsection (2) there shall be inserted—

"(2A) The officers who may discharge functions of a police authority in pursuance of arrangements under section 56(1) or (2) of this Act shall include the chief constable of the police force.

(2B) Where, pursuant to arrangements made by virtue of subsection (2A) above, a chief constable may discharge functions of a police authority, he may himself arrange for the discharge of any of the functions in question by a constable of the police force or by a person who is employed by the authority but is not under their direction and control.".

DEFINITIONS
"constable": s.51(1) of the 1967 Act, as amended by s.63(9)(a).
"functions": s.51(1) of the 1967 Act.
"officer": s.51(1) of the 1967 Act.

GENERAL NOTE
The purpose of this section, which was introduced at Report stage in the Commons, is to allow devolution of managerial responsibility from the police authority to the chief constable, and

from the chief constable to subordinate officers within his force or to civilian staff. This is achieved by inserting new subss. (2A) and (2B) in s.63 of the Local Government (Scotland) Act 1973 (c. 63). On behalf of the Government it was emphasised that the new powers, which were presented as an important part of their overall package of police reform, were permissive not mandatory; it is for police authorities and chief constables to decide on matters of delegation, although the Secretary of State intends to issue guidelines on delegation of financial management after appropriate consultation (*Hansard*, H.C. Vol. 246, col. 161, *per* Lord James Douglas-Hamilton).

New subs. (2A) of s.63 of the 1973 Act
   This subsection clarifies the capacity of the police authority to delegate powers to the chief constable. For instance, it reinforces the capacity of the police authority under s.49(2) above to ensure that civilians employed by itself are under the effective direction and control of the chief constable. It may also be used in due course to delegate a broader range of functions presently carried out by the police authority under s.2 of the 1967 Act relating to the provision and maintenance of vehicles, equipment, land, buildings, etc.

New subs. (2B) of s.63 of the 1973 Act
   This subsection provides that a chief constable to whom powers are delegated by virtue of subs. (2A) can arrange for the further delegation of these responsibilities to less senior members of his force, or to civilians under his direction and control by virtue of s.49(2) of the present Act.

Interpretation of Part II

   65. In this Part of this Act "the 1967 Act" means the Police (Scotland) Act 1967.

GENERAL NOTE
   This section defines references in Pt. II of the present Act to "the 1967 Act" as references to the Police (Scotland) Act 1967.

PART III

POLICE (NORTHERN IRELAND)

Regulations for administration, etc. of Royal Ulster Constabulary

   66.—(1) Section 25 of the Police Act (Northern Ireland) 1970 (regulations for administration, etc. of Royal Ulster Constabulary) shall be amended as follows.
   (2) Subsection (5) (Treasury concurrence required for certain regulations) shall be omitted.
   (3) For subsections (6) and (7) there shall be substituted—
      "(5A) In relation to any matter as to which provision may be made by regulations under this section (other than the matters mentioned in subsection (2)(e) and (f)), the regulations may—
         (a) authorise or require provision to be made by, or confer discretionary powers on, the Secretary of State, the Police Authority, the Chief Constable or other persons; or
         (b) authorise or require the delegation by any person of functions conferred on him by or under the regulations.
      (5B) Regulations under this section as to conditions of service shall secure that appointments for fixed terms are not made except where the person appointed holds the rank of superintendent or a higher rank.
      (6) Where regulations under subsection (2)(a) vary the ranks held by members of the Royal Ulster Constabulary, the regulations may make consequential amendments to any statutory provision (including this Act) containing a reference to any rank held by a member of that Constabulary."

Regulations for administration etc. of reserve constables

67.—(1) Section 26 of the Police Act (Northern Ireland) 1970 (regulations for administration, etc. of reserve constables) shall be amended as follows.

(2) Subsection (3) (Treasury concurrence required for certain regulations) shall be omitted.

(3) At the end there shall be added—

"(4) In relation to any matter as to which provision may be made by regulations under this section (other than the matters mentioned in subsection (2)(cc) and (d)), the regulations may—

    (a) authorise or require provision to be made by, or confer discretionary powers on, the Secretary of State, the Police Authority, the Chief Constable or other persons; or

    (b) authorise or require the delegation by any person of functions conferred on him by or under the regulations."

Minor and consequential amendments

68.—(1) The Police Act (Northern Ireland) 1970 shall have effect subject to the following minor and consequential amendments.

(2) Section 10(5) (Treasury concurrence required for certain regulations relating to police cadets) shall be omitted.

(3) In section 34 (orders and regulations)—

    (a) for subsection (1) there shall be substituted—

"(1) Regulations and orders under this Act (other than orders under section 4(3)) shall be subject to annulment in pursuance of a resolution of either House of Parliament and section 5 of the Statutory Instruments Act 1946 shall apply accordingly.";

    (b) after subsection (1) there shall be inserted—

"(1A) The following regulations shall not be made without the concurrence of the Treasury, namely—

    (a) regulations under section 10 for regulating pensions;

    (b) regulations under section 25 providing for any of the matters specified in subsection (2)(k) of that section;

    (c) regulations under section 26 providing for the matter specified in subsection (2)(f) of that section.";

    (c) in subsection (3) for the words from "sections" to "reserve constables and" there shall be substituted the words "section 10(4) (making provision with respect to allowances of".

(4) In section 35 (interpretation) in the definition of "senior officer" for the words from "means" onwards there shall be substituted the words "means an officer above the rank of superintendent".

Part IV

Magistrates' courts

GENERAL NOTE

Magistrates' Court reforms

The initial response to the Government's original proposals regarding reform of the Magistrates' Courts was one of strong opposition. The main complaint was the suggestion that, as originally drafted, the proposals would challenge the independence of the magistracy and of the justices' clerks in their performance of various judicial functions. The Lord Chancellor described the initial proposals in Pt. IV of the Bill as follows:

"Part IV of the Bill deals with the Government's proposals for the reform of the magistrates' courts service in England and Wales. These reforms relate to the management of the service. They will not affect the judicial decision taken in individual cases.

The 1989 scrutiny on the administration of the magistrates' courts found some serious and fundamental flaws in the management and organisational structure of the service. It concluded:

'There is no coherent management structure for the service. At the national level, the role of the Home Office is so uncertain, and its powers so limited, that it might be truer to say that there are 105 local services, each run by a committee of magistrates. But the local structure is just as confused, with 285 justices' clerks enjoying a semi-autonomous status, under committees which are fundamentally ill-suited to the task of management. It is impossible to locate clear management responsibility or accountability anywhere in the structure'.

The scrutiny proposed a radical solution, that the magistrates' courts service should be restructured as a single national service, operated as an executive agency. We rejected this option. It had little support in the service, which broadly opposed the ending of local management of the service. However, the weaknesses identified by the scrutiny still needed to be addressed. We published our proposals for this in a White Paper in February 1992".

The parliamentary debates suggest that the response from interested parties to the White Paper *Police Reform* were largely negative (see *Hansard*, H.L. Vol. 553, col. 797) but the Lord Chancellor described the main objectives of the intended legislation as being threefold:

"First, magistrates' courts committees, who are responsible for running the service locally, should be better able to fulfil their responsibilities. Secondly, there should be a clear line of management accountability from the courts to the magistrates' courts committees at local level. I am in turn accountable, as the responsible Minister, to your Lordships and the other place, for the administration of the magistrates' courts service. I therefore need some means, consistent with the local nature of the service, of discharging that accountability. This is not the type of direct line management accountability exercised by the magistrates' courts committees. It is of a more general nature. Nevertheless, it needs to be clear if I am to undertake my responsibilities. Thirdly, we want to ensure, in case there is any doubt that the proposals might do otherwise, that the independence of judicial decisions made by magistrates in individual cases remains secure.

Although it is evident from what I have already said, it is worth my emphasising that it is no part of my intention to seek direct managerial control. Had the proposals in the original scrutiny been implemented, I have no doubt that a wide range of detailed controls would have been necessary. As it is, the proposals in this Bill will do no more than provide me with the minimum level of control consistent with my accountability to Parliament".

The use of the phrase "managerial control" may have proved to be something of a catalyst for the speeches which were to follow. A number of contributors to the debates focused their attention on measures introduced by the Government (not just in respect of this particular piece of legislation) in an attempt to analyse the extent to which those measures were balanced between managerial efficiency on the one hand, and ensuring that justice is not only done but also seen to be done, on the other. Thus, the Lord Chief Justice said:

"It is a truism that justice should be seen to be done as well as be done. It follows from this that the arrangements we make for justice to be administered must serve not only the requirements of justice itself but also the way the public perceive its institutions and those who work in them. We shall fail in our duty if we allow this Bill to pass in a way which allows the impression to be given that the advice magistrates receive or the judicial decisions taken by their clerks are no longer a matter of their own discretion, but are instead liable to influence by the executive, either through the terms under which they are employed or because they may feel under pressure from a superior officer as to the way in which they exercise them" (*Hansard*, H.L. Vol. 551, col. 478).

Despite the force of this speech (and others) it is, of course, important to keep the attack in context. There is much in the original Bill which has remained unscathed and there was a consensus that reform of the police and the administration of the magistrates' court was overdue. By the time the House of Lords considered the Bill on its Third reading there was also a consensus that the Bill was one which was by then significantly improved.

The original proposals for Magistrates' Court reform

These were described by the Lord Chancellor as follows:

"There are a number of provisions in Part IV of the Bill to which I should like to draw your Lordships' attention. Clause 62 [now section 69] will enable me to amalgamate magistrates' courts committees. There are at present 105 magistrates' courts committee areas. Some are very small, covering for example, the smallest counties and metropolitan districts. Many are much larger. The largest area has over 400 times more work than the smallest. I have published to the service my preliminary conclusions as to the geographical areas of the new committees. I do not propose that all magistrates' courts committee areas should be of the same size. But many of the smallest committees cannot use their resources as flexibly as the larger ones, and this results in a loss of potential for improved value for money, and lower levels of service to the public than would otherwise be possible. I propose that there should be local consultation before making particular orders. The object of such a course is that full account can be taken of local circumstances" (*Hansard*, H.L. Vol. 551, col. 461).

As to the constitution of the magistrates' committees, the Lord Chancellor said:

"The constitution of magistrates' courts committees needs to be better structured to fulfil the task of providing strategic direction for their local service. Committees will be smaller than at present. They will no longer be primarily representational bodies, but their members will be appointed by a selection panel made up of representatives of local benches, to ensure that the choice of committee members will continue to rest firmly with the local magistracy. They will be able to co-opt up to two members who may be, but need not be, magistrates. If there is a clear weakness in a committee's membership which they decline to rectify by co-option, I envisage that I could do so by making up to two appointments myself.

Magistrates' courts committees comprise volunteers giving their services in their own time. It is not easy for them directly to manage the staff of the courts. Therefore I propose that they should have the assistance of a single head of service, to whom they can delegate much of the day-to-day administration of the service. The head of service will be the line manager of all the committee's staff. Without this managerial control, there will continue to be no proper accountability to the magistrates' courts committee from the staff delivering the service, which was one of the important weaknesses identified by the 1989 scrutiny. I can think of no other public service which does not have a single head who is accountable to those responsible for delivering the service" (*Hansard*, H.L. Vol. 551, cols. 461, 462).

There had been some criticism that the Government's proposals were made without taking sufficient or appropriate soundings, but (for reasons explained in greater detail elsewhere) this was a superficial complaint and, indeed, there is evidence that the Government felt fortified in the correctness of their approach in the light of the responses received. Thus, the Lord Chancellor said:

"This principle is already recognised in some parts of the service and those magistrates' courts committees who have already appointed a head of service in advance of this legislation have, I believe, secured benefits" (*Hansard*, H.L. Vol. 551, col. 462).

Originally, the Government sought radically to alter the terms and conditions of employment for justices' clerks.

"All chief justices' clerks and justices' clerks should have a contract of employment with their committee. This is clearly much more satisfactory than the present arrangements under which justices' clerks hold office (and can be dismissed) at the pleasure of the committee. I also want to be sure that magistrates' courts committees have in place a proper framework for managing their staff.

I accordingly propose that contracts between magistrates' courts committees and senior staff should contain certain broad provisions. I envisage that these provisions will include the fixing of a term to the contract – although this may be rolling – and provide for an element of remuneration to be linked to performance. None of these provisions will affect existing office holders, and I do not seek any powers to vary contracts of service between magistrates' courts committees and their staff once they are in force". (*per* the Lord Chancellor, *Hansard*, H.L. Vol. 551, col. 462).

On the issue of the independence and accountability of the justices' clerks (and the proposed chief justices' clerks), the Lord Chancellor said:

"I know that in clarifying the accountability of justices' clerks to their magistrates' courts committees in administrative matters, some people fear that the independent advice given to magistrates in court will be undermined. Having given this matter considerable thought, I am satisfied that those fears are groundless. For example, where the justices' clerk is also the head of service, there is no evidence or suggestion that there has been any interference with judicial independence. As confirmation of this and to put the matter beyond doubt, I propose that it be declared, as appears on the face of the Bill, that in giving advice to magistrates in court, or in exercising the delegated functions of a single justice, justices' clerks may not be subject to management direction, neither local nor national. That provision is incorporated on the face of the Bill and would govern any exercise of delegated powers under it" (*Hansard*, H.L. Vol. 551, col. 462).

The debate on the independence of the justices' clerks became tied in with other aspects of the Government's proposals, not least conditions and terms of employment, and performance targets:

"The Magistrates' Courts Service Inspectorate has, following the White Paper, already been set up and I propose in this Bill to place it on a statutory footing. The Inspectorate's remit will extend only to the administration of the magistrates' courts service, not the judicial work of the courts.

I also propose to issue in directions the standards of performance that I expect the magistrates' courts service to achieve. The Inspectorate will examine the performance of the service against these standards. If the required standards are not achieved, or the service is unsatisfactory in other ways, the Inspectorate will provide guidance on how improvements can be made. I expect that the vast majority of problems will be resolved in this way. As is normal for any organisation, there needs to be some reserve powers for use on those very rare occasions when a committee, without reasonable excuse, continues to fail in its duties. This Bill therefore proposes a number of incremental steps that I can take in these unusual circumstances. Clearly, the circumstances would be exceptional and all other remedies would have been tried". (*per* the Lord Chancellor, *Hansard*, H.L. Vol. 551, col. 463).

Some justification for pursuing these proposals was founded on the fact that many of the reforms proposed in this part of the Bill are already in place in one area of the country or another. Thus:

"Various committees have appointed either a single justices' clerk to be the head of the staff, or have appointed an equivalent of the chief justices' clerk. The benefits of flexible organisation within larger magistrates' courts committee areas have been exploited by many committees, who have, for example, concentrated their administrative support in a few locations. A number of employees of the magistrates' courts service have fixed-term contracts. Where the reforms I propose have been brought into effect locally, they have been shown to bring benefits to the management of the service. ... The Bill also brings the administrative structure of the magistrates' courts service, which has remained essentially unaltered for the past 50 years, up-to-date. The reforms will better enable it to deal with the challenges that the service now faces without undermining its local nature, and they will not interfere with the independence of the magistracy" (*Hansard*, H.L. Vol. 551, col. 463).

The Government's proposals were attacked on a variety of grounds but perhaps none more fiercely than cl. 70 (significantly remodelled in s.78) which is now limited to making specific provision for the independence of justices' clerks and staff in relation to legal functions, but which previously embraced the post of "chief justices' clerk" and which gave rise to the allegation that the chief justices' clerk was not merely concerned with administration but was also part of the judicial decision-making process.

However, considerable changes were made to the Bill and these may be summarised as follows. It is no longer part of the scheme of the legislation that justices' clerks should be appointed on fixed-term contracts or on performance-related pay. The chairman of the magistrates' court committee is no longer intended to be a post occupied by a person whose election is approved by the Lord Chancellor and some steps have been taken to try and clarify the position of the justices' clerk (as well as that of the Justices' Chief Executive – formerly described as the "chief justices' clerk") in so far as their duties, powers and responsibilities are concerned. One would not normally expect a change in title to be much more than nomenclature but there was considerable anxiety that the executive role, of the "justices' chief executive" might merge with any judicial role performed either by himself or by the clerks to the justices. This is not a straightforward issue and is examined in greater detail below.

Magistrates' courts committees

Alteration of magistrates' courts committee areas

69.—(1) A magistrates' courts committee may at any time submit to the Lord Chancellor written proposals—

(a) for the replacement of two or more magistrates' courts committees (including the committee submitting the proposals) with a single magistrates' courts committee or with two or more magistrates' courts committees in relation to areas different from the existing magistrates' courts committee areas, or

(b) for the replacement of the committee submitting the proposals with two or more magistrates' courts committees.

(2) Before submitting such proposals, the magistrates' courts committee shall consult—

(a) the magistrates for their area or any other existing magistrates' courts committee area to which the proposal relates,

(b) any other magistrates' courts committee to which the proposal relates, and

(c) every interested authority.

(3) Whether or not proposals have been submitted to him under subsection (1) above, the Lord Chancellor may by order made by statutory instrument provide—

(a) for the replacement of two or more magistrates' courts committees with a single magistrates' courts committee or with two or more magistrates' courts committees relating to areas which are different from the existing magistrates' courts committee areas, or

(b) for the replacement of a magistrates' courts committee with two or more magistrates' courts committees.

(4) The Lord Chancellor shall not make an order under subsection (3) above unless he is satisfied that the making of the order is likely to contribute to an overall increase in the efficiency of the administration of the magistrates' courts for the magistrates' courts committee area or areas to which the order relates.

(5) Before making an order under subsection (3) above, other than an order which implements proposals submitted to him under subsection (1) above, the Lord Chancellor shall consult—

(a) the magistrates for each of the existing magistrates' courts committee areas to which the order relates,

(b) the magistrates' courts committees to which the proposal relates, and

(c) every interested authority.

(6) For the purposes of subsection (5) above, an order shall be taken to implement proposals if it implements them without alteration or the departures from the proposals do not, in the opinion of the Lord Chancellor, effect important alterations in the proposals.

(7) Where proposals under subsection (1) above or an order under subsection (3) above would (apart from this subsection) divide a petty sessions area between the areas of two or more magistrates' courts committees, the proposals or order shall provide for a consequential alteration of petty sessions areas.

(8) An order under subsection (3) above may contain such consequential and transitional provisions as appear to the Lord Chancellor to be necessary or expedient, including—

(a) provision for the transfer of property, rights and liabilities,

(b) provision for the management or custody of transferred property (whether real or personal), and

(c) provision for any magistrates' courts committee coming into existence by virtue of the order to be constituted under section 22 of the 1979 Act as a body corporate, and to incur liabilities, before the date on which the functions of any existing magistrates' courts committee are transferred to it.

(9) A statutory instrument containing an order under subsection (3) above shall be subject to annulment in pursuance of a resolution of either House of Parliament.

(10) In this section—

"existing magistrates' courts committee area" means a magistrates' courts committee area existing by virtue of—

(a) section 19(2) of the 1979 Act (as amended by section 79(4) of this Act),

(b) an order made under section 19(3) of that Act before the commencement of this section, or

(c) a previous order under subsection (3) above;

"interested authority", in relation to any proposal or order, means the council of every local authority whose area includes any of the existing magistrates' courts committee areas to which the proposal or order relates, or part of any such area;

"local authority" means any unitary authority or any county council so far as they are not a unitary authority; and

"unitary authority" means—

    (a) the council of any county so far as they are the council for an area for which there are no district councils,

    (b) the council of any district comprised in an area for which there is no county council,

    (c) a county borough council,

    (d) a London borough council, or

    (e) the Common Council of the City of London.

(11) Any order made under subsection (3) of section 19 of the 1979 Act (power to establish a single magistrates' courts committee for a joint committee area) before the commencement of this section shall continue to have effect notwithstanding the repeal of that subsection by this Act, but subject to any subsequent order under subsection (3) above.

(12) Until 1st April 1996, the definition of "unitary authority" in subsection (10) above shall have effect with the omission of paragraph (c).

DEFINITIONS

"magistrate": s.70 of the Justices of the Peace Act 1979.

"petty sessions area": s.92(2) of the Justices of the Peace Act 1979.

GENERAL NOTE

The main statutory provisions that regulate the administration of the magistrates' courts are to be found in the Justices of the Peace Act 1979 (c. 55). The primary purpose of the 1994 Act is to amend the 1979 Act. There had been some concern that the original proposals set out in the Bill were with a view to abolishing the lay magistracy but these views seem to have been unfounded (*Hansard*, H.L. Vol. 552, col. 525). Such an objective seems unlikely to be attainable – at least over a short period of time – given that the total number of magistrates is now in the region of 30,000. The cost of putting into place an alternative structure would be considerable.

The responsibility of accounting to Parliament for the administration of magistrates' courts fell upon the Home Secretary, but more recently, the Lord Chancellor and the Lord Chancellor's Department now shoulder much of this responsibility. The Lord Chancellor also carries the responsibility for the supply of magistrates' courts and this means that the Lord Chancellor must also distribute monies from central funds between the various magistrates' courts committees. As the Lord Chancellor pointed out (*Hansard*, H.L. Vol. 552, col. 527) the magistrates' courts committees have the power to amalgamate on their own initiative and this means that they may amalgamate local benches without the approval of the local benches concerned. Although the amalgamation of local benches has occurred, it seems that there has not been an instance where two or more magistrates' courts committees have done so. This Act seeks to give the Lord Chancellor power to take that step either upon his own initiative or upon the written proposals of a magistrates' courts committee. Clearly, an amalgamation will only be truly effective if it has the goodwill of the parties affected.

The Lord Chancellor's intentions in putting forward the measures in s.69 of the 1994 Act is "to bring decision-making to a reasonably local level" and not to centralise the process of important decision-making (*Hansard*, H.L. Vol. 552, col. 529). With that in mind, it is not the intention of the Lord Chancellor to amalgamate without full consultation with the relevant parties including the paying authorities. On the other hand, Lord McIntosh made the point that although the Bill and the debates proceed on the basis that the provisions are about amalgamations, that need not necessarily be the case, and the provisions are equally relevant if one is talking about an alteration in the structure of the committees. If that were to occur then regional committees might be created which would have jurisdiction over local committees and this, it was argued, would be a move towards centralisation which means that despite the provisions in relation to consultation, the Lord Chancellor's Department would be able to "enforce alteration, amalgamation or division against the advice of those who are consulted" (*Hansard*, H.L. Vol. 552, col. 531).

There is much force, in theory, in those views and indeed the Lord Chancellor agreed that if one pursued the logic advanced by Lord McIntosh then one could end up with a single authority. However, the Lord Chancellor contends that the allocation of money is within local units and accordingly, unless the decision-making on the allocation of money is at the centre, the provisions in the Act will decentralise.

Subsection (4) was added by the House of Lords (by way of amendment no. 7 moved by the Lord Chancellor on March 24, 1994) in order to take account of the views expressed by various members of the House of Lords during earlier debates. It was intended further to endorse the principle that an amalgamation should only take place after careful consideration of local circumstances and with "a good deal of encouragement to local initiative" (*Hansard*, H.L. Vol. 553, col. 760).

Constitution of magistrates' courts committees

70. For section 20 of the 1979 Act there shall be substituted—

"Constitution of magistrates' courts committees

20.—(1) A magistrates' courts committee shall, subject to subsections (2) to (4) below, be composed of magistrates for the area to which the committee relates, chosen in accordance with regulations under section 21 of this Act.

(2) Not more than two other members, who need not be justices of the peace, may be either—

(a) co-opted by a magistrates' courts committee to the committee with the approval of the Lord Chancellor, or

(b) appointed by the Lord Chancellor to the committee.

(3) The chief metropolitan stipendiary magistrate shall by virtue of his office be a member of the inner London magistrates' courts committee.

(4) Until such day as the Lord Chancellor may by order made by statutory instrument appoint, two members of the inner London magistrates' courts committee shall be other metropolitan stipendiary magistrates appointed by the chief metropolitan stipendiary magistrate.

(5) In subsections (3) and (4) above "the inner London magistrates' courts committee" means the magistrates' courts committee for an area consisting of or including the whole of the inner London area or, if there is no such committee, every magistrates' courts committee for any area which consists of or includes any part of the inner London area."

DEFINITIONS
"inner London area": s.2(1)(a) of the Justices of the Peace Act 1979.

GENERAL NOTE
There was general agreement that it is important that magistrates' courts committees should manage their own affairs and that co-opted members should only be proposed locally. Put shortly, the objection which has been levelled against what is now s.70(2)(b) is that the Lord Chancellor cannot be the best person to know who best to appoint under that section. The Lord Chancellor did not disagree with that proposition but asked for this provision as a fallback provision if he needed to use it in the interests of justice as a whole (*Hansard*, H.L. Vol. 552, col. 538). The extent to which this provision is invoked must, in theory, depend on the attitude of the Lord Chancellor (who then holds office), given that finding a suitable formula for restricting the exercise of that provision proved elusive by the time the Bill received Royal Assent. The intention of the Bill in respect of the size of magistrates' courts committees is to make them responsible for the management of the local magistrates' courts service. That would enable them to be the responsible authority for that service within the locality. The Lord Chancellor was concerned to ensure that the responsible authority should not be too large and that 12 members "would be about right". Many will welcome the Lord Chancellor's approach that membership on a committee for a Lord Lieutenant should not be automatic but that co-opting members should be left as a "local arrangement". If a Lord Lieutenant was interested in a position on the committee he could then be appointed either as a co-opted member or by the election procedure. If he was not interested then he would not be taking a place which could be occupied by someone else who was interested. However, some questioned whether this was a sufficient reason for giving power to the Lord Chancellor to appoint members (see *Hansard*, H.L. Vol. 552,

col. 543) and there were calls for the power to be restricted and safeguards added to the legislation for the removal of those who are either unsuitable or unfit (*ibid.*, col. 541).

A magistrates' courts committee shall be composed of magistrates in accordance with regulations made under s.21 of the Justices of the Peace Act 1979 as amended by s.71 of the 1994 Act. By virtue of those amendments, regulations shall provide for the members of the committee to be chosen by a selection panel in accordance with the terms of the regulations. Regulations may lay down an upper limit for the number of members of a magistrates' courts committee (see s.71). The initial version of the Bill (cl. 64) permitted the Lord Chancellor to regulate both the upper and lower limits for the number of committee members, but it was not the intention of the Lord Chancellor to set a lower limit (*ibid.*, col. 545). The upper limit was 35 and had been reduced to 20. The Act further reduces the number to 12.

Regulations as to constitution etc. of magistrates' courts committees

71.—(1) Section 21 of the 1979 Act (powers of Lord Chancellor in relation to magistrates' courts committees) shall be amended as follows.

(2) After subsection (1) there shall be inserted—

"(1A) Any such regulations shall provide for the members referred to in section 20(1) of this Act to be chosen by a selection panel constituted in accordance with the regulations."

(3) For subsection (2) there shall be substituted—

"(2) Any such regulations may—

(a) lay down an upper limit for the number of members of a magistrates' courts committee (inclusive of the members referred to in subsections (2), (3) and (4) of section 20 of this Act), and

(b) enable the Lord Chancellor to direct that, in relation to any magistrates' courts committee to which the direction is given, any members co-opted or appointed under subsection (2) of that section are to be left out of account in applying the upper limit.

(2A) Any such regulations may also make different provision in relation to the magistrates' courts committees for areas which consist of or include the whole or any part of the inner London area from that made in relation to other committees."

DEFINITIONS
"Inner London area": s.2(1)(a) of the Justices of the Peace Act 1979.

GENERAL NOTE
See the General Note to s.70 above.

Supplementary provisions as to magistrates' courts committees

72.—(1) Section 22 of the 1979 Act (supplementary provisions as to magistrates' courts committees) shall be amended in accordance with this section.

(2) For subsection (1) there shall be substituted—

"(1) Subject to subsection (1A) below, a magistrates' courts committee shall appoint one of their members to be chairman of the committee.

(1A) Until such day as the Lord Chancellor may by order made by statutory instrument appoint, the chief metropolitan stipendiary magistrate shall by virtue of his office be the chairman of any magistrates' courts committee for an area which consists of or includes the whole of the inner London area."

(3) Subsection (2) shall be omitted.

(4) At the end of subsection (4) there shall be added the words "which may, if they include at least one member of the committee, also include persons who are not members".

(5) After subsection (4) there shall be inserted—

"(4A) A magistrates' courts committee may also arrange for the discharge of any of their functions—

(a) by the chairman of the committee, or
(b) by the justices' chief executive."
(6) At the end there shall be added—

"(8) A magistrates' courts committee shall, on at least one occasion in every calendar year, admit members of the public to a meeting of the committee.

(9) The minutes of proceedings of every meeting of a magistrates' courts committee shall be open to inspection by members of the public at the offices of the committee, except to the extent that the committee determine that the minutes disclose information of a confidential nature.

(10) Copies of any minutes which are open to inspection under subsection (9) above shall be made available to the public on payment of such reasonable fee as the magistrates' courts committee may in any case determine.

(11) A magistrates' courts committee making a determination under subsection (9) above shall state their reasons for regarding the information in question as being of a confidential nature."

DEFINITIONS
"inner London area": s.2(1)(a) of the Justices of the Peace Act 1979.

GENERAL NOTE
By s.72 of the 1994 Act (which amends s.22 of the Justices of the Peace Act 1979) a magistrates' courts committee shall appoint one of their members to be its chairman. Clause 65 of the original version of the Bill also contained a provision which stipulated that the appointment would cease at the end of a "prescribed period" unless the continuation of the appointment was approved by the Lord Chancellor before the end of that period. This provision was deleted from the Bill with the agreement of the Lord Chancellor (*Hansard*, H.L. Vol. 552, col. 548) who discussed the matter with delegates of the national organisations representing those who work and serve in the magistrates' courts service. The provision was described, by the Lord Chancellor, as designed to make the Lord Chancellor accountable in Parliament for the magistrates' courts service but: "... the important thing is that the justice system in the magistrates' courts should be locally managed" (*ibid.*, col. 548).

General powers and duties of magistrates' courts committees

73. After section 22 of the 1979 Act there shall be inserted—

"General powers and duties of magistrates' courts committees
22A.—(1) A magistrates' courts committee shall be responsible for the efficient and effective administration of the magistrates' courts for their area.
(2) A magistrates' courts committee may, in particular—
(a) allocate administrative responsibilities among the justices' chief executive, the justices' clerks and the staff of the committee, and
(b) determine the administrative procedures to be followed by any of the persons mentioned in paragraph (a) above.
(3) It shall be the duty of every magistrates' courts committee to provide courses of instruction for justices' clerks and for staff of the committee.
(4) The Lord Chancellor may give directions to magistrates' courts committees requiring each of them, in discharging their responsibilities under subsection (1) above, to meet specified standards of performance.
(5) The Lord Chancellor may also give directions to magistrates' courts committees requiring each of them to take specified steps, at such intervals as may be specified—
(a) for the purpose of keeping the magistrates for their area informed as to the activities of the committee, or

(b) for the purpose of ascertaining the views of those magistrates on particular matters related to the functions of the committee.

(6) In discharging their responsibilities under subsection (1) above, a magistrates' courts committee shall have regard to the needs of court users who are disabled; and so long as any direction under subsection (4) above is in force the standards of performance required under that subsection must include standards relating to the provision made for such court users.

(7) A direction under this section may be given to all magistrates' courts committees or to one or more particular committees.

(8) The Lord Chancellor shall arrange for any direction given under this section to be published in such manner as he thinks fit."

DEFINITIONS
"justices' clerk": s.70 of the Justice of the Peace Act 1979.
"magistrates' courts committee area": s.70 of the Justices of the Peace Act 1979.

GENERAL NOTE
Section 73 of the 1994 Act inserts s.22A into the Justices of the Peace Act 1979. By s.22A(1) a magistrates' courts committee shall be responsible for the efficient and effective administration of the magistrates' courts for its area. An amendment was moved in the Lords to extend this provision to have regard to the needs of disabled people (*Hansard*, H.L. Vol. 552, col. 551). Apart from the fact that it is highly unlikely that this provision could be construed as embracing the quality of the environment in which court administration is carried out, the amendment was withdrawn after the Lord Chancellor gave a detailed account of the steps being taken by the Government to give effect to the amendment in other ways:
   "It is highly important that the public service, and the magistrates' courts service in particular, should be accessible to all members of society". (*per* the Lord Chancellor, *Hansard*, H.L. Vol. 552, col. 551).
The guidance in respect of new buildings is contained in the Magistrates' Courts Design Guide (1991), which covers the provision of facilities for disabled persons.

Section 22A(2)(a) of the Justices of the Peace Act 1979
This provision and the need for it were explained by the Lord Chancellor (*Hansard*, H.L. Vol. 552, cols. 554, 555) as follows:

"This is simply an administrative power given to the magistrates' courts committees. It is not a power to the Lord Chancellor. The provision gives the magistrates' courts committees power to allocate administrative responsibilities among the various persons who are there specified. I believe that it is a proper capacity and freedom to manage for the committees and that in order that they should manage effectively ... they should have this power. It is not a direction; it is simply a power to make the allocation. They may not need to exercise the power in great detail. On the other hand, the committees may in some circumstances consider that they should exercise it. That is a matter entirely for them. No power of the Lord Chancellor is involved ... the power is a power; it is by no means exclusive. It is intended as a specific power allowing the allocation of administrative responsibilities. I am not clear that without the subsection it would be proper for the magistrates' courts committee necessarily to allocate the administrative responsibilities in that way. It is important that the committees should have that power. I believe that it is desirable that the provision should be spelt out to that level of detail. The level is not great, but it gives the committees the overall responsibility for allocation. ... I do not believe that at present it would improve the Bill to take that specific power away from the magistrates' courts committees. The assumption appears to be that, if the provision is taken away, nothing is removed, but I am not certain that that is so".

Section 22A(4) of the Justices of the Peace Act 1979
The need for this power and the extent to which it is likely to be used in practice was described by the Lord Chancellor as follows:

"I am not particularly keen to be impaled upon a fork. I say that it may be necessary to use these powers. If in some situations they may require to be used, once is required to have them in the Bill. I hope and pray that I shall never have to find any magistrates' court committee in default. I strongly believe that it is highly unlikely that that will ever happen. Nevertheless, it is a wise proposal.... The question is: is it absolutely beyond the bounds of possibility that some of these standards may be required? ... there is also the question of helping people by using the experience of others to show what standards are appropriate to deal with these matters. To circulate best practice is a useful thing to do. Even if my view on the numbers ultimately proves to be correct, we will still have a large number of magistrates' courts committees. It is important that standards of performance should be available ... it may be that examples of standards set and attained by others will help us to improve our own. ... I would feel very unhappy if I had to exercise any default power at all in respect of a magistrates' court committee. But I would feel it much safer to exercise default powers against a proved failure to meet a statutory standard than to proceed on any other basis. It is true that I would wish to do everything that I possibly could by informal means to avoid such a default. But if it comes to exercising a statutory default power, the Lord Chancellor would need to have very secure grounds on which to stand. A necessary part of that is specifying what is required before a default is found. I hope and believe that in most cases if that happened the default would be rectified without any further procedure.... I do not accept that the fact that the Lord Chancellor is given powers to do certain things necessarily means that he will require to exercise those powers. That depends on events that unfold in the future" (*Hansard*, H.L. Vol. 552, cols. 559, 560).

Reports and plans

74. After section 24B of the 1979 Act there shall be inserted—

"Reports and plans
24C.—(1) The Lord Chancellor may by regulations made by statutory instrument require magistrates' courts committees to submit to him such reports and plans, in relation to matters for which they are responsible, as may be prescribed.
(2) Any report or plan required by regulations under this section—
(a) shall be prepared in the prescribed manner, after such consultation as may be prescribed, and within such time as may be prescribed,
(b) shall be in the prescribed form,
(c) shall be sent to such persons as may be prescribed, and
(d) shall be made available to the public on payment of such reasonable fee as the magistrates' courts committee may in any case determine.
(3) The Lord Chancellor may direct any one or more magistrates' courts committees to produce such additional reports or plans in relation to matters for which they are responsible as may be specified in the direction."

DEFINITIONS
"magistrates' courts committee": s.19(1) of the Justices of the Peace Act 1979.
"prescribed": s.70 of the Justices of the Peace Act 1979.

Justices' chief executives, justices' clerks and staff

Appointment and functions of justices' chief executive

75. After section 24C of the 1979 Act there shall be inserted—

"Justices' chief executives, justices' clerks and staff

Appointment of justices' chief executive
24D.—(1) Every magistrates' courts committee shall appoint a justices' chief executive.
(2) A person may not be appointed as justices' chief executive unless—
(a) the magistrates' courts committee have submitted to the Lord Chancellor, in accordance with regulations, an application for approval of one or more persons offering themselves for the appointment,

(b) the Lord Chancellor has approved one or more of those persons, and

(c) the person appointed is a person so approved.

(3) For the purposes of subsection (2) above, appointment as justices' chief executive does not include, in relation to a person employed as such under a contract for a fixed term, re-appointment on the expiry of that term.

(4) Where the Lord Chancellor declines to approve any person who is named in an application under subsection (2)(a) above, he shall inform the magistrates' courts committee of the reasons for his decision.

(5) A person may not be appointed as justices' chief executive unless he is eligible under section 26 of this Act for appointment as justices' clerk.

(6) A person may not be appointed both as justices' chief executive and as justices' clerk for a petty sessions area unless the Lord Chancellor has agreed that he may hold both appointments.

(7) Where, in accordance with subsection (6) above, a person holds an appointment as justices' chief executive with an appointment as justices' clerk for a petty sessions area, he shall not exercise any functions as justices' clerk for the petty sessions area unless authorised to do so (either generally or in any particular case) by the magistrates' courts committee for the area which includes that petty sessions area.

(8) In this section "regulations" means regulations made by the Lord Chancellor by statutory instrument.

Functions of justices' chief executive

24E.—(1) The justices' chief executive in relation to any magistrates' courts committee shall—

(a) act as clerk to the committee, and

(b) subject to and in accordance with any directions given by the committee, carry on the day to day administration of the magistrates' courts for the area to which the committee relates.

(2) A justices' chief executive may arrange for his functions under subsection (1)(a) above to be exercised by any member of the staff of the magistrates' courts committee.

(3) It shall be the duty of the justices' chief executive to make arrangements for discussions relating to law, practice and procedure among the justices' clerks for petty sessions areas within the area of the committee."

DEFINITIONS

"justices' clerk": s.70 of the Justices of the Peace Act 1979.

"magistrates' courts committee": s.19(1) of the Justices of the Peace Act 1979.

GENERAL NOTE

When the Bill was introduced into the House of Lords, the Government's intention was to create a post (originally with the title "Chief Justices' Clerk") whose functions and responsibilities would require the appointee to act as a head of service and yet to perform judicial or quasi-judicial functions. The name was changed by an amendment moved by the Lord Chancellor on March 24, 1994 (*Hansard*, H.L. Vol. 553, col. 767).

It follows from the above that it was envisaged that his tasks might be both of an executive and judicial nature but this was criticised as threatening the independence of the judiciary or at least was liable to infringe the so-called doctrine of the separation of powers. It was therefore vital to clarify the duties and powers that would attach to the creation of this post. Thus, Lord Peyton suggested that:

"... it is important that there should be a very clear dividing line about the duties and powers. I believe that there are people now in post who are carrying out the kind of administrative duties which could easily be done by someone called a chief justices' clerk but which could, in my view, be done better – because there would be less misunderstanding – if he were called a chief executive ..." (*Hansard*, H.L. Vol. 552, col. 561).

The Lord Chief Justice again focused on the challenge to the independence of the judiciary if the proposed post had been enacted in its original form. Thus, he said:

"I see no prospect that the essential distinction between administrative functions on the one hand, and judicial and legal functions on the other, can possibly be maintained if the new office-holder is both qualified and denominated as a justices' clerk. On the contrary, the proposal is bound to lead to the distinction becoming blurred, and to serving justices' clerks being made (whatever assurances my noble and learned friend gives now) to feel accountable to their "chief" for both sets of functions.

Moreover, there is no reason that I can see why the new head of service should be required to be legally qualified (though of course if a local committee wants him to be then that should be a matter for them). In my noble and learned friend's own department I know from personal experience that lawyers work for or under administrators without any difficulty and, in particular, without any impairment of "clear lines of accountability". The circuit administrator who heads the court service in the Crown Court on each circuit does not have to be legally qualified. Some are, some are not. But the important point is that a circuit administrator does not, and cannot, come into court and exercise judicial or advisory functions in the legal process. Nor does he train judicial officers" (*Hansard*, H.L. Vol. 552, col. 564).

In response to these criticisms, the Lord Chancellor made the point that the original proposals were not made without consultation or, indeed, without the approval of some of the interested parties.

"The various organisations in the magistrates' courts service responded in November 1993 to the Government's White Paper of February 1992. That response was agreed by the Central Council of the Magistrates' Courts Committees, the Magistrates' Association, the Justices' Clerks' Society, the Association of Magisterial Officers and the Standing Conference of Clerks to Magistrates' Courts Committees" (*Hansard*, H.L. Vol. 552, col. 572).

After the responses were received by the Government, it seems that various parties changed their views. By that time, the Government felt fortified in pursing their original proposals on the basis of the information gleaned during the consultation process. Thus, the honorary secretary of the Justices' Clerks' Society had said by way of a letter that:

'... We question whether someone without experience as a justices' clerk would have an in-depth feel for the workings of the system. The unique and sometimes apparently paradoxical role of a justices' clerk needs a degree of insight and sensitivity not always obvious to the outsider, even if a lawyer.

In addition to being legally qualified as a barrister or solicitor (assuming also that the postholder would be required to have demonstrated management competencies) we suggest that for a person to become a chief justices' clerk he must be eligible for appointment as a justices' clerk under the Justices of the Peace Act 1979, section 26 and be the current holder of such a post ... The Society is of the view that the head of service should be qualified under section 26 of the Justices of the Peace Act 1979 and also hold or have formerly held the office of justices' clerk".

The letter then moved on to deal with the administrative and judicial functions which the new post was likely to have:

"Whilst the job description of the chief justices' clerk requires the execution of mainly administrative functions, it is in our view imperative that the chief justices' clerk possesses a thorough understanding of the role and duties of justices' clerks and relationships between justices' clerks and magistrates.

Inter-agency relations locally and regionally would be strengthened if the head of service is perceived by those within and outside the service to possess the qualities, qualifications, experience and competencies as those sought and demanded of justices' clerks. The Society is of the opinion therefore that the title to be given to the head of service should be 'Chief Justices' Clerk' " (*Hansard*, H.L. Vol. 552, col. 571).

By February 22, 1994, the views of the Justices' Chief Clerks Society had changed due, it was suggested, to an increasing awareness of the dangers of what the Government had proposed: see *Hansard*, H.L. Vol. 552, cols. 578 and 579. The Lord Chief Justice expressed concern that the new s.24E of the Justices of the Peace Act 1979 (see s.75 of the 1994 Act) imposed a duty on the head of service to: "make arrangements for discussions relating to law, practice and procedure ...", and there was thus a danger that he would use these powers to influence the way justices' clerks advise the Bench and indeed the way they exercise their own judicial functions. (*Hansard*, H.L. Vol. 552, col. 565). This topic has also been addressed by the Justices' Clerks' Society in the following terms:

"Justices' clerks and court clerks must be free when sitting in court to give such legal advice as they believe appropriate to assist the magistrates in carrying out their judicial functions. However, the desirability of achieving consistency of advice on a particular point throughout a magistrates' courts committee area is also a relevant consideration ... it has to be recognised that many points will continue to arise in court which will require an immediate decision. It would be most unfortunate if there was an unnecessary over-use of the legal forum resulting in delays in court following adjournments of hearings pending discussions at the next meeting of the group.

The legal forum, we have no doubt, provides the best way forward in this difficult area and, in doing so, uses the knowledge and experience of all justices' clerks within the committee's area as a way of improving the legal support given to benches ... it is important to stress that if a justices' clerk has a firm view on any point which arises, even if he is completely at variance with his colleagues, then he should be free to give that advice to his magistrates. Justices' clerks are independent practitioners and the legal forum would give an opportunity to discuss and persuade, allowing those present to reflect on the views of colleagues and change their minds, if necessary. Alternatively, they might be able, with better arguments and research to persuade their colleagues to change their minds subsequently. *Whatever the outcome, justices' clerks must feel free to give the advice which they believe to be correct.* Until a categorical answer is given in the High Court to issues where there is more than one interpretation, then each such interpretation, assuming it to be one of merit, will remain valid. This in our view, is a fundamental constitutional point which needs to be emphasised". [emphasis added] (*Hansard*, H.L. Vol. 552, col. 571).

The passage highlighted in that extract, explains (in part) the purpose behind s.78 of the 1994 Act (formerly cl. 71). It is designed to re-emphasise the need for justices' clerks to retain their independence to advise freely in relation to the exercise of their legal functions. In an earlier speech, Lord Chief Justice regarded it as "absolutely fundamental" that:

"... nobody providing legal directions or advice to a tribunal of fact, or who is taking decisions which affect the rights or liabilities of parties to proceedings, should be or appear to be susceptible to outside influences of any kind. ... We shall fail in our duty if we allow this Bill to pass in a way which allows the impression to be given that the advice magistrates receive or the judicial decisions taken by their clerks are no longer a matter of their discretion but are instead liable to influence by the executive, either through the terms under which they are employed or because they may feel under pressure from a superior officer as to the way in which they exercise them" (*Hansard*, H.L. Vol. 552, col. 561).

The Lord Chief Justice gave the example of the executive who complained that the throughput of cases in their courts was "too thin, that they have been granting too much legal aid and that they ought to be granting adjournments less frequently" and that the justices' clerks might respond accordingly so as to "achieve favour with the chief"(*Hansard*, H.L. Vol. 552, col. 578). In a later debate (*Hansard*, H.L. Vol. 553, col. 768), Lord Ackner sought to move an amendment which was designed to extend the scope of s.78 or, at least, to make it clear that justices' clerks should be free to give advice either in respect of a particular case or in relation to cases generally, whether such advice is given in the course of training, or in discussions relating to law, practice or procedure, or otherwise; see *Hansard*, H.L. Vol. 553, col. 768). The Lord Chancellor successfully argued against that amendment on the grounds that it would be a recipe for confusion if different justices' clerks were advising different benches to apply different sets of propositions.

The Lord Chancellor agreed to change the title of the head of service but he did not want to remove the word "Justice" from it because to do so would be a "retrograde step" (*Hansard*, H.L. Vol. 552, col. 573). However, the mere fact that there was support for the Government's initial proposals could not, by itself, answer the question whether it was good constitutional law to have a post that blurred administrative and judicial functions. It will be appreciated from the above that there was much discussion on this vexed topic. However, when considering the criticisms levelled against the original proposals, it should be borne in mind that many of the complaints have not gone unheeded and therefore the 1994 Act no longer contains provisions which formed part of the original draft for ss.75–78. Thus, fixed-term contracts are no longer required, no longer is a chief justices' executive automatically to be treated as a justices' clerk (the Lord Chancellor must now agree that he may hold both appointments), and the chief justices' clerk is incapable of exercising the functions of a justices' clerk unless the Lord Chancellor agrees that he may hold both appointments and is authorised to exercise the functions of a justices' clerk by the magistrates' courts committee for the relevant area: see s.75. It therefore became unnecessary for s.78 to contain the provision (as the original clause did) that the chief justices' clerk would not be subject to the direction of the magistrates' courts committee "or any other person". In other words, the separation of powers between the executive and the judiciary has been upheld to that extent.

Section 75 (formerly cl. 68 of the Bill) which adds a new s.24D to the Justices of the Peace Act 1979, requires the Lord Chancellor to approve the appointment of the justices' chief executive from a shortlist of candidates put before him. The Lord Chancellor's intention was to allow the magistrates' courts committee to choose whether they want to put up a list or whether they want to put up the one person they selected. The Lord Chancellor expressed no view as to which course he preferred. There were objections to this procedure based primarily on the argument that the Lord Chancellor should have no part in the appointment of justices' chief executives at all.

Inspectors of the magistrates' courts service
There is a team of 17 inspectors of which one is the chief inspector, four are senior inspectors and 12 are ordinary inspectors. Of the four senior inspectors, one is a former deputy clerk to the magistrates and another is a magistrate. The intention of the Lord Chancellor is that all reports of the chief inspector will be published along with an annual report (*Hansard*, H.L. Vol. 552, cols. 606, 607).

Appointment and removal of justices' clerks

76. For section 25 of the 1979 Act (and the heading "Justices' clerks and their staffs" immediately preceding it) there shall be substituted—

> **"Appointment and removal of justices' clerks**
> 25.—(1) Justices' clerks shall be appointed by the magistrates' courts committee; and a magistrates' courts committee may appoint more than one justices' clerk for any petty sessions area.
> (2) A person may not be appointed as justices' clerk unless—
> (a) the magistrates' courts committee have submitted to the Lord Chancellor, in accordance with regulations, an application for approval of one or more persons offering themselves for the appointment,
> (b) the Lord Chancellor has approved one or more of those persons, and
> (c) the person appointed is a person so approved.
> (3) For the purposes of subsection (2) above, appointment as justices' clerk does not include, in relation to a person employed as such under a contract for a fixed term, re-appointment on the expiry of that term.
> (4) Where the Lord Chancellor declines to approve any person who is named in an application under subsection (2)(a) above, he shall inform the magistrates' courts committee of the reasons for his decision.
> (5) The approval of the Lord Chancellor shall be required—
> (a) for any decision to increase the number of justices' clerks in a petty sessions area or to have more than one justices' clerk in a new petty sessions area, or
> (b) for the removal of the justices' clerk for a petty sessions area where the magistrates for the area do not consent to the removal.
> (6) A magistrates' courts committee shall consult the magistrates for any petty sessions area—
> (a) on the appointment of a justices' clerk for the area, except in the case of a re-appointment on the expiry of a fixed term, or
> (b) on the removal of a justices' clerk for the area.
> (7) Before—
> (a) approving any persons under subsection (2) above, or
> (b) approving the removal of a justices' clerk,
> the Lord Chancellor shall consider any representations made to him by the magistrates for the petty sessions area concerned; and before approving the removal of a justices' clerk the Lord Chancellor shall also consider any representations made to him by the clerk.
> (8) For the purposes of subsections (5) to (7) above, removal as justices' clerk shall be taken to include, in relation to a person employed as

such under a contract for a fixed term, the expiry of that term without renewal in any case where the clerk has not consented to the failure to renew.

(9) In this section "regulations" means regulations made by the Lord Chancellor by statutory instrument."

DEFINITIONS

"magistrates' courts committees": s.19(1) of the Justices of the Peace Act 1979.
"petty sessions area": s.4 of the Justices of the Peace Act 1979.

GENERAL NOTE

Historically, the magistrates' courts committee exercised considerable latitude in the selection or removal of justices' clerks but for many years this has been subject to two broad controls. First, the committee is required to consult magistrates of the relevant petty sessional division. This obligation remains unchanged. Secondly, the committee was obliged to seek the approval of the Home Secretary of the proposed appointment or removal after considering any representations of the Magistrates (or the justices' clerk in the case of his proposed removal). This task now falls to the Lord Chancellor but the 1994 Act gives the Lord Chancellor greater powers of supervision and control by requiring that the committee submits one or more candidates for his approval *in accordance with regulations* made by him (see s.25(2) and (9)).

It is important to keep these revised selection and removal procedures in proportion. Under the old procedure the committee could submit just one name for approval. Under the new model the committee is required to submit a list of "one or more persons offering themselves" for appointment. By definition that does not mean that the committee is obliged to submit more than one candidate for approval. Where the Lord Chancellor approves, say, four candidates out of five, it remains for the committee to select the suitable candidate.

There is nothing on the face of the new s.25 of the Justices of the Peace Act 1979, which entitles the Lord Chancellor to indicate his preferred order of suitable candidates. His power, in theory, seems to be confined either to approving or to declining to approve a particular candidate for appointment. Where the Lord Chancellor declines to approve any person then, by s.25(4), he is obliged to inform the magistrates' court committee of the reasons for his decision. The provision was inserted into the Bill by amendment (no. 22) moved by the Lord Chancellor on March 24, 1994 (*Hansard*, H.L. Vol. 553, col. 767) and puts into statutory form assurances which the Lord Chancellor gave to the House of Lords in Committee on February 22, 1994 (*Hansard*, H.L. Vol. 552, cols. 595, 598) namely that he would give reasons for not approving a particular candidate. The Lord Chancellor pointed out that "within living memory" there has never been a refusal to approve – a point which the Lord Chancellor reinforced when he said:

"I believe that it would be extremely unlikely that the Lord Chancellor would require to disapprove anyone whom a Magistrates' Courts Committee has in mind to approve and who is appropriately qualified" (*Hansard*, H.L. Vol. 553, col. 767).

The Lord Chancellor was not persuaded that it would be appropriate to publish criteria for the approval of any justices' clerk or to furnish reasons to the committee for approving a particular candidate; an amendment to that effect, moved by Lord Peyton, was withdrawn: see *Hansard*, H.L. Vol. 552, col. 595.

The reasoning behind that particular amendment is, at first sight, attractive but it would be difficult to articulate criteria which would be apt to cover every candidate. In fact, to invite the Lord Chancellor to give reasons to the Committee for approval might (unwittingly or otherwise) cause a Lord Chancellor to express an order of preference between candidates which would be a result inconsistent with s.25 of the Justices of the Peace Act 1979. In any event, it has to be remembered that s.26 of the Justices of the Peace Act 1979 (as amended by ss.91 and 93 and Sched. 8, para. 10, and Sched. 9) already specifies the statutory qualifications required for appointment as a justices' clerk and it could be said that if it is appropriate to publish criteria for approval, then the proper place for that to be done is in s.26.

Justices' chief executives and justices' clerks to be employed under contracts of service

77. After section 26 of the 1979 Act there shall be inserted—

"Justices' chief executives and justices' clerks to be employed under contracts of service

    26A.—(1) Except as provided by this Act, a justices' chief executive or justices' clerk—

(a) shall be employed by the magistrates' courts committee, on such terms as they may determine, and

(b) shall hold and vacate office in accordance with the terms of his contract of service.

(2) Subsection (1) above shall not have effect in relation to any person appointed by a magistrates' courts committee before the commencement of this section as justices' clerk for a petty sessions area so long as he—

(a) continues to hold office as a justices' clerk for that area or for any one or more petty sessions areas including any part of that area, and

(b) has not entered into a contract of service after the commencement of this section.

(3) Any justices' clerk in relation to whom, by virtue of subsection (2) above, subsection (1) above does not have effect shall hold office during the pleasure of the magistrates' courts committee concerned."

DEFINITIONS
"justices chief executive": s.75 of the 1994 Act.
"justices clerk": s.70 of the Justices of the Peace Act 1979.
"Magistrates' Courts Committee": s.19(1) of the Justices of the Peace Act 1979.

GENERAL NOTE
During the course of the debates, in the House of Lords, the Lord Chief Justice remarked:

"A cult seems to have developed and to be invading the whole of the public sector whereby fixed-term contracts and performance pay are seen as the panaceas which will give us managerial efficiency. They may indeed be useful tools in a purely managerial context, but in a judicial context, or where there exists a judicial element, they can have no place.
    I suspect that the noble Earl, Lord Ferrers, will, in replying to this debate, say that those elements of the contract are intended merely to affect the way in which justices' clerks discharge their administrative responsibilities, and that their independence in respect of their judicial functions is safeguarded by Clause 71. I can only say that I would regard such an answer as a pious hope, but unrealistic. A clerk is a single officer with a single contract of employment. The terms should be a matter between him or her and the employing committee. It should not be required to contain terms inimical to the proper exercise of judicial functions by virtue of ministerial direction" (*Hansard*, H.L. Vol. 551, col. 476).
    The protest of the Lord Chief Justice (and others) did not go unheeded because it will be seen that, although s.76 speaks of "fixed-term contracts", the 1994 Act now makes it clear that the terms of a contract of service are a matter between the justices' clerk and the Magistrates' Courts Committee: see s.77, inserting s.26A into the Justices of the Peace Act 1979. Clerks, who held office prior to the commencement of s.77, will continue to serve during the pleasure of the committee. Some clerks may prefer a greater degree of certainty of tenure and thus s.26A(2)(b) permit existing office holders to opt for a contract of service. Once that step is taken, there is no turning back.

Independence of justices' clerk and staff in relation to legal functions

78. After section 30 of the 1979 Act there shall be inserted—

"Independence of justices' clerk and staff in relation to legal functions

30A.—(1) When exercising the functions specified in subsection (2) below or giving advice to justices of the peace in an individual case—

(a) a justices' clerk shall not be subject to the direction of the magistrates' courts committee, the justices' chief executive or any other person, and

(b) any member of the staff of a magistrates' courts committee shall not be subject to the direction of that committee or of the justices' chief executive (when acting as such).

(2) The functions referred to in subsection (1) above are functions conferred by rules made in accordance with section 144 of the Magistrates' Courts Act 1980 by virtue of section 28(1) or (1A) of this Act."

DEFINITIONS
"justices clerk": s.70 of the Justices of the Peace Act 1979.
"Magistrates' Courts Committee": s.19(1) of the Justices of the Peace Act 1979.

GENERAL NOTE
There was considerable discussion, in both Houses of Parliament, about the need or the wisdom to insert s.30A into the Justices of the Peace Act 1979. The Lord Chief Justice said:

"There are very real dangers here. I cannot overstress that to insert a clause proclaiming judicial independence, even if it were written in capital letters or red ink, will be no guarantee of such independence if specific provisions elsewhere in the Act, or in the Lord Chancellor's blueprint for clerks' contracts, in fact operate against judicial independence or appear to do so. What is sought to be done is this. One puts in place provisions which would obviously create a grave danger to independence, so obviously that one recognises that one has to do something about it. What does one do? One does not change the provisions so as to prevent that danger arising but waves a wand and puts in a clause which simply says that that danger shall not arise". (*Hansard*, H.L. Vol. 551, col. 477).
Lord Ackner observed:

"The Government have taken the concern which has been expressed sufficiently seriously to seek to make special provision in Clause 71. According to the side note, it preserves the "Independence of chief justices' clerk, justices' clerk ... in relation to legal functions". That provision, which wrongly presupposes that a firm line can be drawn between legal and administrative matters, is particularly noteworthy for two quite separate reasons. First, that it should ever have become necessary in an Act of Parliament to provide a specific assurance that what the Act provides is to have no impact on the independence of the judiciary underlines the very danger of the provisions which have necessitated that assurance. Secondly, the magistrates and their clerks are totally unmoved by the Government's assurance to be found encapsulated in this clause. They remain convinced that the Executive will use its control of their clerks to manipulate the judicial decision-making process. Speaking entirely for myself, I have every sympathy for the magistrates and their clerks taking such a view". (*Hansard*, H.L. Vol. 551, col. 509).
Much later in the history of the Bill, Mr Paul Boateng returned to the issue as follows:

"... there must be a guarantee of independence in relation to the three separate and important functions that a justices' clerk is called on to perform – the discharge of statutory duties, the giving of advice to the magistracy and the handling of individual cases. Those three essential elements must be protected. They were identified by the Lord Chief Justice and by a former Lord of Appeal in Ordinary, Lord Ackner, in the other place.
    Those elements are threatened by a Government who, while introducing legislation that superimposes the powers of the Treasury on those of justices and their clerks, subordinate the interests of justice to those of the market and a Treasury determined to claw back the deficit created by the Government. As it stands, the legislation fails to preserve the necessary independence. There is nothing more important than that, and we shall return to the matter on Third Reading. There is nothing more important than the independence of the judiciary, and the independence of the justices' clerks in the context of the administration of justice.
    We are not satisfied with the clause as it stands, we seek to strengthen it, and we shall divide the House in order to do so" (*Hansard*, H.C. Vol. 246, col. 261).
It is not surprising that Mr Boateng referred to the speeches of the Lord Chief Justice and Lord Ackner (above) but they must be studied very carefully in the context of the Bill as originally drafted and not as the Act now appears. Both of their Lordships saw s.30A (then cl. 71) as suggesting the existence of a hidden agenda when that provision was contrasted with other provisions which were then part of the Bill but which have since been removed – notably the proposal that the Lord Chancellor should be empowered to direct the inclusion of terms within a contract of employment, *e.g.* performance targets. Accordingly, there remains limited mileage in boarding a bandwagon which is now unlikely to reach any useful destination.

Inner London area

Magistrates' courts committee for inner London area

79.—(1) Section 35 of the 1979 Act (under which the committee of magistrates for the inner London area is constituted) shall cease to have effect.

(2) The body corporate constituted under that section shall remain in existence, but as a magistrates' courts committee for the inner London area constituted in accordance with Part II of the 1979 Act.

(3) Any reference in any document to the committee of magistrates shall have effect, in relation to any time after the commencement of subsection (2) above, as a reference to the magistrates' courts committee for the inner London area.

(4) In section 19(2) of the 1979 Act (areas to which magistrates' courts committees relate) for the word "and" at the end of paragraph (c) there shall be substituted the words—

"(cc) the inner London area; and".

(5) Section 38(2) of the 1979 Act (which confers administrative functions on the chief metropolitan stipendiary magistrate) shall cease to have effect.

(6) Subsections (2) and (3) above have effect subject to any order made under section 69 of this Act after the commencement of subsection (2) above.

DEFINITIONS

"inner London area": s.2(1)(a) of the Justices of the Peace Act 1979.
"Magistrates' Courts Committee": s.19(1) of the Justices of the Peace Act 1979.
"stipendiary magistrate": s.70 of the Justices of the Peace Act 1979; s.31(3).

GENERAL NOTE

Section 79 must be read in conjunction with ss.80, 81, 82, 91 and Sched. 8, para. 16.

The Justices of the Peace Act 1979, s.35, made provision for the committee of magistrates for the inner London area who were empowered (by s.36) to organise the inner London area into petty sessional divisions. The appointment of justices' clerks and other officers, to service the inner London area and the City of London, was governed by s.37. The chief metropolitan stipendiary magistrate shouldered the responsibility of carrying on the day-to-day administration of the magistrates' courts in London; see s.38 of the Justices of the Peace Act 1979.

Sections 35, 36, and 37 are now wholly repealed by the 1994 Act (see ss.79, 80, 91 and Sched. 8, para. 16). Instead, the division of work in the inner London area is now governed by the insertion of s.34A into the Justices of the Peace Act 1979 by s.81 of the 1994 Act. The purpose of the revised structure is to bring magistrates' courts in London closer into line with other such courts in England and Wales.

Organisation of justices' clerks in inner London area

80.—(1) Section 37 of the 1979 Act (which obliges the committee of magistrates for the inner London area to appoint a principal chief clerk and chief clerks, together with such senior deputy chief clerks, deputy chief clerks and other officers as may be necessary) shall cease to have effect.

(2) Any person who, immediately before the commencement of subsection (1) above, holds office as principal chief clerk for the inner London area shall be taken to have been appointed by the magistrates' courts committee for the inner London area as justices' chief executive in accordance with section 24D of the 1979 Act.

(3) Any person who, immediately before the commencement of subsection (1) above, holds office as chief clerk for any petty sessional division of the inner London area or for the youth courts or family proceedings courts for that area and the City of London shall be taken to have been appointed by the magistrates' courts committee for the inner London area in accordance with section 25 of the 1979 Act as a justices' clerk for that petty sessional division or, as the case requires, in accordance with section 34B of that Act as a justices' clerk for those courts.

(4) Except as provided by subsections (5) to (7) of section 25 of the 1979 Act, any person to whom subsection (2) or (3) above applies shall hold and vacate office in accordance with the terms of his appointment or, if he has

entered into a contract of service (whether before or after the commencement of subsection (1) above), in accordance with the terms of his contract of
service.

(5) The abolition by virtue of subsection (1) above of the statutory offices
of senior deputy chief clerk and deputy chief clerk shall not affect the continuation of the contract of service of any person who holds either of those
offices immediately before the commencement of that subsection.

(6) A person who is employed under a contract of service to which subsection (5) above applies shall not be dismissed from his employment without
the approval of the Lord Chancellor; and before approving the dismissal of
any such person the Lord Chancellor shall consider any representations
made by him.

(7) Any reference in any instrument or document to the chief clerk for any
petty sessional division of the Inner London area or for the youth courts or
family proceedings courts for that area and the City of London shall have
effect, in relation to any time after the commencement of subsection (1)
above, as a reference to the justices' clerk for that petty sessional division or,
as the case may be, for those courts.

Division of work in inner London area

81. After section 34 of the 1979 Act there shall be inserted—

"Division of work in inner London area
    34A.—(1) There shall be established for the purposes of this section a
committee consisting of the following members—
    (a) the chief metropolitan stipendiary magistrate,
    (b) six lay justices appointed by the chairmen of the petty sessional
         divisions of the inner London area, and
    (c) six metropolitan stipendiary magistrates appointed by the chief
         metropolitan stipendiary magistrate.
    (2) The lay justices eligible for appointment under paragraph (b) of
subsection (1) above include any of the chairmen referred to in that
paragraph.
    (3) The members of the committee shall hold office for a period of
twelve months, but shall be eligible for re-appointment.
    (4) The chief metropolitan stipendiary magistrate shall be the chair-
man of the committee.
    (5) It shall be the duty of the committee—
    (a) to keep under consideration the division of work in the inner
         London area between the metropolitan stipendiary magistrates
         and the lay justices, and
    (b) to give general directions to any magistrates' courts committee
         for any area which consists of or includes the whole or any part of
         the inner London area as to the division of the work."

Pensions etc. of justices' chief executive, justices' clerks and staff in inner London area

82.—(1) Schedule 7 (which re-enacts certain provisions relating to the
functions of the Receiver for the Metropolitan Police District with respect to
pensions etc. of court staff) shall have effect.

(2) The Lord Chancellor may by order make provision with respect to
pensions, allowances or gratuities payable to or in respect of inner London
court staff, or any class of inner London court staff.

(3) An order under subsection (2) above may—
    (a) itself make provision with respect to the pensions, allowances or
         gratuities which, subject to the fulfilment of such requirements and

conditions as may be prescribed by the order, are to be or may be paid to or in respect of inner London court staff, or any class of inner London court staff, or

(b) provide that the civil service provisions are to have effect, with such modifications as may be prescribed by the order, in relation to the payment by such persons as may be so prescribed, out of such funds as may be so prescribed, of pensions, allowances and gratuities to or in respect of inner London court staff, or any class of inner London court staff.

(4) Without prejudice to the generality of subsections (2) and (3) above, an order under subsection (2)—

(a) may include all or any of the provisions referred to in paragraphs 1 to 11 of Schedule 3 to the Superannuation Act 1972, and

(b) may make different provision as respects different classes of persons and different circumstances.

(5) Paragraphs 1 to 11 of Schedule 3 to the Superannuation Act 1972 shall have effect, in their application for the purposes of this section, as if references to regulations were references to an order under this section and references to the Secretary of State were references to the Lord Chancellor.

(6) Subsections (3) and (4) of section 7 of the Superannuation Act 1972 (which relate to increases under the Pensions (Increase) Act 1971) shall have effect in relation to an order under subsection (2) above as they have effect in relation to regulations under that section.

(7) The Lord Chancellor may by order repeal or amend any of the relevant enactments, whether or not he makes provision under subsection (2) above.

(8) An order under subsection (2) or (7) above may make such consequential, transitional, incidental or supplemental provision (including provision amending or repealing any provision of this Act, the 1979 Act or any other enactment) as the Lord Chancellor thinks necessary or expedient.

(9) Before making an order under subsection (2) or (7) above the Lord Chancellor shall consult—

(a) the inner London magistrates' courts committee,

(b) such local authorities as appear to him to be concerned,

(c) the Receiver for the Metropolitan Police District, and

(d) such representatives of other persons likely to be affected by the proposed order as appear to him to be appropriate.

(10) An order under subsection (2) or (7) above shall be made by statutory instrument which shall be subject to annulment in pursuance of a resolution of either House of Parliament.

(11) In this section—

"the civil service provisions" has the meaning given by section 15(1) of the Superannuation (Miscellaneous Provisions) Act 1967,

"inner London court staff" means the justices' chief executive employed by the inner London magistrates' courts committee, any justices' clerk for the inner London area and staff of the inner London magistrates' courts committee,

"the inner London magistrates' courts committee" means the magistrates' courts committee for an area consisting of or including the inner London area or, if there is no such committee, every magistrates' courts committee for any area which consists of or includes any part of the inner London area, and

"the relevant enactments" means—

(a) Schedule 7 to this Act, and

(b) section 15 of the Superannuation (Miscellaneous Provisions) Act 1967 (superannuation of metropolitan civil staffs) so far as it relates to the persons mentioned in subsection (1)(a)(ii) of that section.

DEFINITIONS
"inner London area": s.2(1)(a) of the Justices of the Peace Act 1979.
"justices' clerk": s.70 of the Justices of the Peace Act 1979.
"Magistrates' courts committee": s.19(1) of the Justices of the Peace Act 1979.

GENERAL NOTE
As the Lord Chancellor has pointed out (*Hansard*, H.L. Vol. 557, col. 37) the 1994 Act is designed to bring the funding of the inner London magistrates' courts into line with such courts elsewhere in England and Wales by "severing its links with the Receiver of the Metropolitan Police". Section 82, and amendments to the Superannuation (Miscellaneous Provisions) Act 1967 (c. 28) (see Sched. 8) and s.46 of the Local Government Act 1992 (c. 70) (see Sched. 8) are intended to allow the existing arrangements to continue:

"until such time as the best pension arrangements can be made. This includes ensuring that the pension expectations of staff will be fulfilled" (*per* Lord Chancellor, *Hansard*, H.L. Vol. 557, col. 37).

Administrative and financial arrangements

Administrative and financial arrangements for magistrates' courts

83.—(1) For sections 55 and 56 of the 1979 Act there shall be substituted—

"Duties of local authorities
    55.—(1) Subject to the provisions of this Act, the paying authority or authorities in relation to any magistrates' courts committee shall provide the petty sessional court-houses and other accommodation, and the goods and services, proper for the performance of the functions of—
        (a) the magistrates for the magistrates' courts committee area,
        (b) the magistrates' courts committee,
        (c) any other committee of the magistrates for that area, or
        (d) the justices' clerks for any part of the magistrates' courts committee area.
    (2) Subsection (1) above shall not require the paying authority or authorities to provide any current item or class of current items if the magistrates' courts committee have notified the authority or authorities that they intend to obtain that item or class of items otherwise than from that authority or any of those authorities.
    (3) For the purposes of subsection (2) above "current item" means any goods or services which are of such a kind that expenditure incurred by a paying authority on providing them would not be capital expenditure.
    (4) Where there is one paying authority in relation to a magistrates' courts committee, that authority shall pay the expenses of the committee.
    (5) Where there are two or more paying authorities in relation to a magistrates' courts committee, each of those authorities shall pay a proper proportion of those expenses.
    (6) For the purposes of subsections (4) and (5) above the expenses of a magistrates' courts committee shall be taken to include—
        (a) expenses incurred by them in obtaining goods and services which are proper for the purposes mentioned in subsection (1) above but which by virtue of subsection (2) above the paying authority or authorities are not required to provide;
        (b) the sums payable under Part II of this Act on account of a person's salary or expenses as justices' chief executive or as justices' clerk for any part of the magistrates' courts committee area, the remuneration of any staff employed by the committee and the remuneration of any court security officers employed (whether by the committee or a paying authority) under section 76(2)(a) of

the Criminal Justice Act 1991 in relation to petty sessions areas within the magistrates' courts committee area together with—

    (i) secondary Class I contributions payable in respect of any such person, staff or officers under Part I of the Social Security Contributions and Benefits Act 1992, and

    (ii) state scheme premiums so payable under Chapter III of Part III of the Pension Schemes Act 1993;

  (c) the sums payable under any contract entered into (whether by any such magistrates' courts committee or a paying authority) under section 76(2)(b) of the Criminal Justice Act 1991; and

  (d) so far as they are not otherwise provided for, all other costs incurred, with the general or special authority of the magistrates' courts committee, by the justices for the magistrates' courts committee area.

(7) Nothing in subsection (1), (4) or (5) above shall require any paying authority to incur any expenditure or make any payment which would—

  (a) cause the net cost to it in any year of the matters mentioned in subsection (1) of section 59 of this Act to exceed the amount which, in relation to that authority and that year, is for the time being determined by the Lord Chancellor under subsection (3)(b) of that section, or

  (b) cause its capital expenditure in any year in pursuance of functions under this Part of this Act to exceed the amount which, in relation to that authority and that year, is for the time being determined by the Lord Chancellor under subsection (4)(b) of that section;

and in determining any such net cost as is mentioned in paragraph (a) above there shall be disregarded any such capital expenditure as is mentioned in paragraph (b) above.

(8) Subject to section 16(2) of this Act, any accommodation provided under this section for any justice, justices' clerk or justices' chief executive may be outside the area for which the justices act and, in the case of a petty sessional court-house, shall be deemed to be in that area for the purposes of the jurisdiction of the justices when acting in the court-house.

(9) Two or more paying authorities may arrange for accommodation, goods or services provided for the purposes of this section by one of them to be used also as if provided for those purposes by the other or each of the others.

(10) In this section—

    "paying authority" in relation to a magistrates' courts committee, means any responsible authority whose area comprises all or part of the area to which the committee relates;

    "responsible authority" means any unitary authority or any county council so far as they are not a unitary authority; and

    "unitary authority" means—

      (a) the council of any county so far as they are the council for an area for which there are no district councils,

      (b) the council of any district comprised in an area for which there is no county council,

      (c) a county borough council,

      (d) a London borough council, or

      (e) the Common Council of the City of London.

(11) Until 1st April 1996, the definition of "unitary authority" in subsection (10) above shall have effect with the omission of paragraph (c).

Provisions supplementary to s.55

56.—(1) Subject to the provisions of this section—

(a) the petty sessional court-houses and other accommodation, goods and services to be provided by the paying authority, or each of the paying authorities, under section 55 of this Act,

(b) the salary to be paid to a justices' clerk or justices' chief executive and to staff of a magistrates' courts committee, and

(c) the nature and amount of the expenses which a magistrates' courts committee may incur in the discharge of any functions or may authorise to be incurred,

shall be such as may from time to time be determined by the magistrates' courts committee after consultation with the paying authority or authorities.

(2) Where the expenses of a magistrates' courts committee (including any sums which are taken by section 55(6) of this Act to be such expenses) fall to be borne by more than one paying authority, any question as to the manner in which they are to be borne by the authorities concerned shall be determined by agreement between those authorities and the magistrates' courts committee concerned or, in default of such agreement, shall be determined by the Lord Chancellor.

(3) Any paying authority which is aggrieved by a determination of a magistrates' courts committee under subsection (1) above may, within one month from the receipt by the authority of written notice of the determination, appeal to the Lord Chancellor, whose decision shall be binding upon the magistrates' courts committee and any authority concerned.

(4) The approval of the Lord Chancellor shall be required for any determination under subsection (1) above reducing the salary of a justices' clerk or justices' chief executive, unless the justices' clerk or justices' chief executive concerned consents to the reduction.

(5) In this section "paying authority" has the same meaning as in section 55 of this Act."

(2) Section 57 of the 1979 Act (application of sections 55 and 56 to outer London areas and City of London) and section 58 of that Act (arrangements for inner London area corresponding to those under section 55 of that Act) shall cease to have effect.

DEFINITIONS
    "capital expenditure": s.70 of the Justices of the Peace Act 1979.
    "justices' clerk": s.70 of the Justices of the Peace Act 1979.
    "magistrate": s.70 of the Justices of the Peace Act 1979.
    "Magistrates' Courts Committee area": s.70 of the Justices of the Peace Act 1979.

GENERAL NOTE
    See the General Note to s.82 above. This provision ensures that magistrates' courts funding is provided by the local authorities and puts the funding for the inner London magistrates' courts on the same basis as magistrates' courts in the rest of England and Wales and thus removes that responsibility from the Receiver of the Metropolitan Police. One consequence of breaking an association with the Receiver of the Metropolitan Police is to weaken the criticism that magistrates' courts are "police courts".

Local authority land appropriated to magistrates' courts purposes

84. After section 59 of the 1979 Act there shall be inserted—

"Local authority land appropriated to magistrates' courts purposes
    59A.—(1) Where after the commencement of this section a responsible authority appropriate any land owned by them to magistrates' courts purposes, the authority shall be taken for the purposes of section

59(2) of this Act to incur, in the year in which the appropriation is made, capital expenditure in pursuance of their functions under this Part of this Act of an amount equal to the open market value of the land at the time of the appropriation.

(2) In subsection (1) above—

"land" includes any interest in land,

"magistrates' courts purposes" means the purposes of being provided under section 55(1) of this Act as a petty sessional courthouse or other accommodation, and

"responsible authority" has the same meaning as in section 55 of this Act."

DEFINITIONS
"capital expenditure": s.70 of the Justices of the Peace Act 1979.

GENERAL NOTE
Section 84 inserts s.59A into the Justices of the Peace Act 1979 so as to provide land for use by the Magistrates' Courts Committees – *e.g.* for court room accommodation and which entitles the committee to seek capital funding for the purpose.

Regulations as to accounts and audit

85. After section 62 of the 1979 Act there shall be inserted—

"Regulations as to accounts and audit
62A.—(1) The Lord Chancellor may by regulations made by statutory instrument require magistrates' courts committees—

(a) to keep prescribed accounts and prescribed records in relation to those accounts, and

(b) to cause any such accounts to be audited in accordance with the regulations.

(2) In subsection (1) above "prescribed" means prescribed by the regulations."

DEFINITIONS
"Magistrates' Courts Committees": s.19(1) of the Justices of the Peace Act 1979.

Inspectors of the magistrates' courts service

Inspectors of the magistrates' courts service

86.—(1) The Lord Chancellor may appoint such number of inspectors of the magistrates' courts service (to be known collectively as "Her Majesty's Magistrates' Courts Service Inspectorate') as he may consider appropriate.

(2) The Lord Chancellor shall appoint one of the persons so appointed to be Her Majesty's Chief Inspector of the Magistrates' Courts Service.

(3) It shall be the duty of inspectors of the magistrates' courts service—

(a) to inspect and report to the Lord Chancellor on the organisation and administration of magistrates' courts for each magistrates' courts committee area, and

(b) to discharge such other functions in connection with the organisation and administration of magistrates' courts as the Lord Chancellor may from time to time direct.

(4) Her Majesty's Chief Inspector of the Magistrates' Courts Service shall make an annual report to the Lord Chancellor as to the discharge of the

functions of the Inspectorate and the Lord Chancellor shall, within one month of receiving the report, lay a copy of it before each House of Parliament.

(5) The Lord Chancellor shall make to or in respect of inspectors of the magistrates' courts service such payments by way of remuneration, allowances or otherwise as he may with the approval of the Treasury determine.

(6) Any person appointed by the Lord Chancellor before the commencement of this section as an inspector of the magistrates' courts service, or as Her Majesty's Chief Inspector of the Magistrates' Courts Service, shall be taken to have been appointed under this section.

DEFINITIONS
"Magistrates' Courts Committees": s.19(1) of the Justices of the Peace Act 1979.

GENERAL NOTE
By virtue of this provision the Inspectorate will be required to examine the efficiency and effectiveness of the structure and administration of the magistrates' courts in each committee area. Section 86 should therefore be read in conjunction with s.87.

Powers of inspectors

87.—(1) Subject to subsection (2) below, an inspector of the magistrates' courts service exercising his functions under section 86 above shall have at all reasonable times—
   (a) a right of entry to any court-house or other premises occupied by a magistrates' courts committee, and
   (b) a right to inspect, and take copies of, any records kept by a magistrates' courts committee, and any other documents containing information relating to the administration of the magistrates' courts for their area, which he considers relevant to the discharge of his functions.
(2) Subsection (1) above does not entitle an inspector—
   (a) to be present when a magistrates' court is hearing proceedings in private, or
   (b) to attend any private deliberations of the justices of the peace.
(3) The records referred to in paragraph (b) of subsection (1) above include records kept by means of a computer; and an inspector exercising the power to inspect records conferred by that subsection—
   (a) shall be entitled at any reasonable time to have access to, and inspect and check the operation of, any computer and associated apparatus or material which is or has been in use in connection with the records in question, and
   (b) may require—
      (i) the person by whom or on whose behalf the computer is or has been so used, or
      (ii) any person having charge of, or otherwise concerned with the operation of, the computer, apparatus or material,
to afford him such reasonable assistance as he may require.

DEFINITIONS
"Magistrates' Courts Committees": s.19(1) of the Justices of the Peace Act 1979.

GENERAL NOTE
This provision should read in conjunction with s.86 above.
Although s.87(1) gives inspectors a right of entry to any courthouse, that right is limited to entry at a reasonable time and does not permit inspectors to be present when the court is having proceedings in private or when the justices are deliberating in private. It would seem that no notice need be given by the inspectors to the Magistrates' Court Committee of their intention to exercise any of their powers under s.87. It is inconceivable that any court would refuse entry to

any inspector but it is not inconceivable that difficulties may arise as to whether particular documents (or class of documents) can properly be said to relate to the administration of the court and not to some other purposes.

Default powers

Default powers

88.—(1) The Lord Chancellor may make an order under subsection (3) below if he is of the opinion that, without reasonable excuse, a magistrates' courts committee—

(a) are failing properly to discharge any duty imposed on them by or under any enactment, or

(b) have so failed and are likely to do so again.

(2) Before making an order under subsection (3) below, the Lord Chancellor shall give a written warning to the magistrates' courts committee specifying the default or defaults to which the order relates.

(3) An order under this subsection shall—

(a) state that the Lord Chancellor is of the opinion mentioned in subsection (1) above, and

(b) provide either or both of the following—

(i) that, on the making of the order, the chairman of the committee is to vacate his office as chairman, or

(ii) that, on the making of the order, one or more specified members of the committee (who may include the chairman but may not consist of all the members of the committee) are to vacate their office.

(4) If, after making an order under subsection (3) above, the Lord Chancellor remains of the opinion mentioned in subsection (1) above, he may make an order—

(a) stating that he remains of that opinion, and

(b) providing—

(i) that all the members of the committee are to vacate their office on the making of the order, and

(ii) that for a specified period, not exceeding three months, beginning with the making of the order the committee is to consist of persons nominated by the Lord Chancellor (who need not be justices of the peace).

(5) An order under subsection (4) above shall provide for new members of the committee to be chosen, in accordance with regulations under section 21 of the 1979 Act, to take office at the end of the specified period.

(6) In relation to the magistrates' courts committee for an area which consists of or includes the whole or any part of the inner London area, the reference in subsection (3)(b)(ii) above to members of the committee does not include the chief metropolitan stipendiary magistrate; and where an order under subsection (4) above is made in relation to any such committee, subsections (3) and (4) of section 20 of the 1979 Act (under which the chief metropolitan stipendiary magistrate and other stipendiary magistrates are members of the committee) shall not have effect in relation to the committee during the period specified in the order.

DEFINITIONS
    "inner London area": s.2(1)(a) of the Justices of the Peace Act 1979.
    "magistrates' courts committee": s.19(1) of the Justices of the Peace Act 1979.
    "stipendiary magistrate": s.70 of the Justices of the Peace Act 1979.

GENERAL NOTE
    The powers conferred on the Lord Chancellor under this provision go very much further than just exercising a supervisory role over the organisation and administration of magistrates' courts within a Magistrates' Courts Committee area.

It entitles the Lord Chancellor to determine (if necessary to adjudicate) whether a Magistrates' Courts Committee without reasonable excuse, either is failing to discharge any statutory duty or (where it has so failed) is likely to fail again. Nevertheless it must be emphasised that the powers conferred under s.88 are clearly intended to be measures of last resort and they are likely to be applied only in cases where there has been an obvious and serious dereliction of duty on the part of all or some members of the committee.

By subs. (1) it is for the Lord Chancellor to decide whether he can properly be of the opinion mentioned in that subsection. The inclusion of the words "without reasonable excuse" suggests that before the Lord Chancellor can give a written warning under subs. (2), he should first give the committee the opportunity to make representations to him. It is apparent from the wording of subs. (1)(a) that the Lord Chancellor need not wait for the default to occur before exercising his powers under this section but, if that is the position, then it is not entirely easy to understand why the draftsman thought it necessary to add the restrictive condition in subs. (1)(b) that, in circumstances where the committee have actually failed, they "are likely to do so again". One answer may be that the Lord Chancellor is entitled to assume (under subs. (1)(a)) that the failure is likely to continue but he cannot make a similar assumption that any default is likely to be repeated for the purpose of subs. (1)(b). It therefore seems that the Lord Chancellor will be in a stronger position if he strikes "while the iron is hot" rather than waiting until after a default has manifested itself before taking action under the section.

A written warning given by the Lord Chancellor under subs. (2) will inevitably be followed by a reasonable period for consultation and rectification before the Lord Chancellor would take the drastic step of issuing an order under subs. (3).

Once an order is made then, subject to subs. (4), the decision of the Lord Chancellor is final without any statutory right of appeal under the 1994 Act. However, subs. (4) envisages that the committee (or any member of the committee) may request the Lord Chancellor to reconsider his decision but, if his reply remains the same then the options open to the Lord Chancellor seem to be more limited (yet more drastic) than his powers under subs. (3). This is because subs. (3) enables the Lord Chancellor to order that all or some members of the committee should vacate their office whereas subs. (4) requires the Lord Chancellor to order that *every* member of the committee should vacate their office and to nominate replacements for a term not exceeding three months, after which period new members will be chosen under s.21 of the Justices of the Peace Act 1979. This may prove to be something of a disincentive in cases where only some members of the committee are subject to an order under subs. (3) and the remainder are not. The defaulters may not wish to invite the Lord Chancellor to reconsider his decision, to do so might jeopardise the position of the non-offending remainder.

Studies by Audit Commission

Studies by Audit Commission

89.—(1) The Audit Commission may, at the request of a magistrates' courts committee, undertake or promote comparative and other studies—

    (a) designed to enable the Commission to make recommendations for improving economy, efficiency and effectiveness in the performance of the committee's functions, and

    (b) for improving the financial or other management of the committee.

(2) Any magistrates' courts committee which has requested a study in accordance with subsection (1) above, and any officer or member of such a committee, shall provide the Audit Commission, or any person authorised by it, with such information as it or he may reasonably require for the carrying out of the study.

(3) The Audit Commission shall charge the magistrates' courts committee concerned such fees for any study carried out under subsection (1) above as will cover the full cost of carrying it out.

(4) In this section "the Audit Commission" means the Audit Commission for Local Authorities and the National Health Service in England and Wales.

General

Regulations under Justices of the Peace Act 1979

90. After section 69 of the 1979 Act there shall be inserted—

    "Regulations
        69A. A statutory instrument containing (whether alone or with other

provisions) regulations made by virtue of section 12, 21, 24C, 24D(2), 25(2) or 62A of this Act shall be subject to annulment in pursuance of a resolution of either House of Parliament."

Minor and consequential amendments

91.—(1) Schedule 8 to this Act (which makes minor and consequential amendments relating to magistrates' courts) shall have effect.

(2) The repeal of subsections (1), (2) and (4) of section 27 of the 1979 Act does not affect any justices' clerks in relation to whom section 26A(1) of the 1979 Act does not have effect.

(3) The repeal of sections 36 and 36A of the 1979 Act does not affect the division of the inner London area into petty sessional divisions as existing immediately before the commencement of the repeal or the names of those petty sessional divisions.

Interpretation of Part IV

92.—(1) In this Part of this Act "the 1979 Act" means the Justices of the Peace Act 1979.

(2) Expressions used in this Part of this Act and in the 1979 Act have the same meaning in this Part as in that Act.

PART V

SUPPLEMENTARY

Repeals

93. The enactments mentioned in Schedule 9 to this Act (which include spent enactments) are hereby repealed to the extent specified in the third column of that Schedule.

Commencement and transitional provisions

94.—(1) Except as provided by subsections (2) and (3) below, the preceding sections of, and the Schedules to, this Act shall come into force on such day as the Secretary of State may by order appoint.

(2) The following provisions of this Act—

Part IV and Schedule 8, and

Part II of Schedule 9 and section 93 so far as it relates to that Part of that Schedule,

shall come into force on such day as the Lord Chancellor may by order appoint.

(3) The following provisions of this Act—

(a) section 3 and Schedule 2, so far as they relate to—

(i) the power to make orders under the section inserted by section 3, or

(ii) the power to make regulations under paragraph 11 of the Schedule entitled Schedule 1C set out in Schedule 2,

(b) sections 13 and 50,

(c) sections 26 and 60, subsections (4) and (7)(a) of section 63, and paragraphs 17 to 20 of Schedule 5, so far as they relate to service in accordance with arrangements made under section 15A(2) of the Police Act 1964 or section 12A(2) of the Police (Scotland) Act 1967, and

(d) section 44, so far as it relates to paragraphs 17 to 20 of Schedule 5,

shall come into force on the passing of this Act.

(4) An order under subsection (1) or (2) above may appoint different days for different purposes or different areas.

(5) The power to make orders under subsection (1) or (2) above includes power to make such transitional provisions and savings as appear to the Secretary of State or, as the case may be, the Lord Chancellor to be necessary or expedient.

(6) Without prejudice to the generality of subsection (5) above, an order under subsection (1) above may make provision—

(a) for the co-existence, for such period as may be prescribed by the order, of the police authorities to be established under section 3 of the Police Act 1964 ("the new police authorities") and the police authorities which they are to supersede ("the old police authorities"); for the division of functions between them; for the performance by the old police authorities, before the new police authorities come into existence, of functions prescribed by the order and for consequential and supplementary matters (including the modification of the application in relation to them of provisions of this or any other Act or of any instrument);

(b) for the transfer and apportionment of property, and for the transfer, apportionment and creation of rights and liabilities;

(c) for the transfer of members of police forces and other persons;

(d) as to pending legal proceedings;

(e) for the Secretary of State, or any other person nominated by or in accordance with the order, to determine any matter requiring determination under or in consequence of the order;

(f) as to the payment of fees charged, or expenses incurred, by any person nominated to determine any matter by virtue of paragraph (e) above.

(7) Without prejudice to the generality of subsection (5) above, an order under subsection (2) above may make provision—

(a) for the transfer and apportionment of property, and for the transfer, apportionment and creation of rights and liabilities;

(b) for the Lord Chancellor, or any other person nominated by or in accordance with the order, to determine any matter requiring determination under or in consequence of the order;

(c) as to the payment of fees charged, or expenses incurred, by any person nominated to determine any matter by virtue of paragraph (b) above.

(8) An order under this section shall be made by statutory instrument which, if the order contains provisions made by virtue of subsections (5) to (7) above, shall be subject to annulment in pursuance of a resolution of either House of Parliament.

Police: co-operation on implementation

95.—(1) It shall be the duty of the relevant authorities and their staff to co-operate with each other, and generally to exercise their functions, so as to facilitate the implementation of this Act and any transfer of functions, property or staff made under it.

(2) In subsection (1) above "relevant authorities" means the police authorities to be established under section 3 of the Police Act 1964 and the police authorities which they are to supersede, and

(a) where the police authority to be superseded is a committee of a council constituted in accordance with section 2 of that Act, that council, and

(b) where the police authority to be superseded is a combined police authority constituted in accordance with section 3(4) of that Act, the constituent councils.

Extent

96.—(1) The following provisions of this Act extend to England and Wales only—

sections 1 to 41 together with Schedules 1 to 3;

Part IV together with Schedule 8;
Schedules 4 and 5 so far as they relate to enactments which extend to
    England and Wales only.
(2) Part II of, together with Schedule 6 to, this Act extends to Scotland
only.
(3) The following provisions of this Act extend to Northern Ireland (and in
the case of Part III to Northern Ireland only)—
sections 43 and 44 together with Schedules 4 and 5 so far as they relate to
    enactments which extend there;
Part III;
Part V.
(4) The provisions of Schedule 9 to this Act have the same extent as the
enactments repealed.
(5) Except as provided by subsections (3) and (4) above, this Act does not
extend to Northern Ireland.

Short title

97. This Act may be cited as the Police and Magistrates' Courts Act 1994.

SCHEDULES

Section 1   SCHEDULE I

SCHEDULE TO BE INSERTED IN POLICE ACT 1964: POLICE AREAS

"SCHEDULE 1A

POLICE AREAS

England (except London)

Name of police area	Extent
Avon and Somerset	The counties of Avon and Somerset
Bedfordshire	The county of Bedfordshire
Cambridgeshire	The county of Cambridgeshire
Cheshire	The county of Cheshire
Cleveland	The county of Cleveland
Cumbria	The county of Cumbria
Derbyshire	The county of Derbyshire
Devon and Cornwall	The counties of Devon and Cornwall and the Isles of Scilly
Dorset	The county of Dorset
Durham	The county of Durham
Essex	The county of Essex
Gloucestershire	The county of Gloucestershire
Greater Manchester	The metropolitan districts of Bolton, Bury, Manchester, Oldham, Rochdale, Salford, Stockport, Tameside, Trafford and Wigan
Hampshire	The counties of Hampshire and Isle of Wight
Hertfordshire	The county of Hertfordshire
Humberside	The county of Humberside
Kent	The county of Kent
Lancashire	The county of Lancashire
Leicestershire	The county of Leicestershire
Lincolnshire	The county of Lincolnshire
Merseyside	The metropolitan districts of Knowsley, Liverpool, St. Helens, Sefton and Wirral
Norfolk	The county of Norfolk
Northamptonshire	The county of Northamptonshire

Northumbria	The county of Northumberland and the metropolitan districts of Gateshead, Newcastle upon Tyne, North Tyneside, South Tyneside and Sunderland
North Yorkshire	The county of North Yorkshire
Nottinghamshire	The county of Nottinghamshire
South Yorkshire	The metropolitan districts of Barnsley, Doncaster, Rotherham and Sheffield
Staffordshire	The county of Staffordshire
Suffolk	The county of Suffolk
Surrey	The county of Surrey
Sussex	The counties of East Sussex and West Sussex
Thames Valley	The counties of Berkshire, Buckinghamshire and Oxfordshire
Warwickshire	The county of Warwickshire
West Mercia	The counties of Hereford and Worcester and Shropshire
West Midlands	The metropolitan districts of Birmingham, Coventry, Dudley, Sandwell, Solihull, Walsall and Wolverhampton
West Yorkshire	The metropolitan districts of Bradford, Calderdale, Kirklees, Leeds and Wakefield
Wiltshire	The county of Wiltshire

Wales

Name of police area	Extent
Dyfed Powys	The counties of Dyfed and Powys
Gwent	The county of Gwent
North Wales	The counties of Clwyd and Gwynedd
South Wales	The counties of Mid Glamorgan, South Glamorgan and West Glamorgan"

Section 3   SCHEDULE 2

SCHEDULES TO BE INSERTED IN POLICE ACT 1964: POLICE AUTHORITIES

"SCHEDULE IB

POLICE AUTHORITIES ESTABLISHED UNDER SECTION 3

Membership of police authorities

1.—(1) Where, by virtue of section 3A of this Act, a police authority is to consist of seventeen members—
   (a) nine of those members shall be members of a relevant council appointed under paragraph 2 of this Schedule,
   (b) five shall be persons appointed under paragraph 5, and
   (c) three shall be magistrates appointed under paragraph 8.

(2) Where, by virtue of an order under subsection (2) of that section, a police authority is to consist of more than seventeen members—
   (a) a number which is greater by one than the number of members provided for in paragraphs (b) and (c) of this sub-paragraph shall be members of a relevant council appointed under paragraph 2 of this Schedule,
   (b) such number as may be prescribed by the order, not exceeding one third of the total membership, shall be persons appointed under paragraph 5, and
   (c) the remainder shall be magistrates appointed under paragraph 8.

Appointment of members by relevant councils

2.—(1) In the case of a police authority in relation to which there is only one relevant council, the members of the police authority referred to in paragraph 1(1)(a) or (2)(a) of this Schedule shall be appointed by that council.

(2) In any other case, those members shall be appointed by a joint committee consisting of persons appointed by the relevant councils from among their own members.

3. The number of members of the joint committee, and the number of those members to be appointed by each relevant council, shall be such as the councils may agree or, in the absence of agreement, as may be determined by the Secretary of State.

4.—(1) A council or joint committee shall exercise its power to appoint members of a police authority under paragraph 2 of this Schedule so as to ensure that, so far as practicable, the members for whose appointment it is responsible reflect—

    (a) in the case of appointments by a council, the balance of parties for the time being prevailing among the members of the council, and

    (b) in the case of appointments by a joint committee, the balance of parties for the time being prevailing among the members of the relevant councils taken as a whole.

(2) The members referred to in sub-paragraph (1)(a) and (b) of this paragraph do not include any member of a relevant council who is disqualified for being appointed as or being a member of the police authority under paragraph 13 of this Schedule.

Appointment of independent members

5. The members of a police authority referred to in paragraph 1(1)(b) or (2)(b) of this Schedule shall be appointed—

    (a) by the members of the police authority appointed under paragraph 2 or 8,

    (b) from among persons on a short-list prepared by the Secretary of State in accordance with Schedule 1C to this Act.

6.—(1) Every police authority shall arrange for a notice stating—

    (a) the name of each of its members appointed under paragraph 5 of this Schedule, and

    (b) such other information relating to him as the authority considers appropriate,

to be published in such manner as it thinks fit.

(2) A police authority shall send to the Secretary of State a copy of any notice which it has arranged to be published under sub-paragraph (1) of this paragraph.

Appointment of magistrates

7. The members of a police authority referred to in paragraph 1(1)(c) or (2)(c) of this Schedule—

    (a) must be magistrates for an area all or part of which constitutes or forms part of the authority's area, and

    (b) shall be appointed in accordance with paragraph 8 of this Schedule;

and in that paragraph and paragraph 9 references to a panel are references to a selection panel established under regulations made in accordance with section 21(1A) of the Justices of the Peace Act 1979.

8.—(1) Where there is a panel for an area which constitutes or includes the police authority's area, that panel shall make the appointment.

(2) Where the area of more than one panel falls wholly or partly within the police authority's area, the appointment shall be made by a joint committee consisting of representatives from the panels concerned.

(3) The number of members of a joint committee, and the number of those members to be appointed by each panel, shall be such as the panels may agree or, in the absence of agreement, as may be determined by the Lord Chancellor.

9. In relation to any appointment made at a time when no panels have been established, paragraph 8 of this Schedule shall have effect as if for any reference to a panel there were substituted a reference to a magistrates' courts committee.

Chairman

10.—(1) A police authority shall at each annual meeting appoint a chairman from among its members.

(2) The appointment under sub-paragraph (1) of this paragraph shall be the first business transacted at the meeting.

(3) On a casual vacancy occurring in the office of chairman, an appointment to fill the vacancy shall be made—

    (a) at the next meeting of the authority (other than an extraordinary meeting), or

    (b) if that meeting is held within fourteen days after the date on which the vacancy occurs and is not an annual meeting, not later than the next following meeting.

Disqualification

11. A person shall be disqualified for being appointed as a member of a police authority if he has attained the age of seventy years.

12.—(1) Subject to sub-paragraphs (3) and (4) of this paragraph, a person shall be disqualified for being appointed as or being a member of a police authority if—

(a) he holds any paid office or employment appointments to which are or may be made or confirmed by the police authority or any committee or sub-committee of the authority, or by a joint committee on which the authority are represented, or by any person holding any such office or employment;

(b) a bankruptcy order has been made against him or his estate has been sequestrated or he has made a composition or arrangement with, or granted a trust deed for, his creditors;

(c) he is subject to a disqualification order under the Company Directors Disqualification Act 1986, or to an order made under section 429(2)(b) of the Insolvency Act 1986 (failure to pay under county court administration order); or

(d) he has within five years before the date of his appointment or since his appointment been convicted in the United Kingdom, the Channel Islands or the Isle of Man of an offence, and has had passed on him a sentence of imprisonment (whether suspended or not) for a period of not less than three months.

(2) A paid employee of a police authority who is employed under the direction of a joint board, joint authority or joint committee on which the authority is represented and any member of which is appointed on the nomination of some other police authority shall be disqualified for being appointed as or being a member of that other police authority.

(3) Where a person is disqualified under sub-paragraph (1)(b) of this paragraph by reason that a bankruptcy order has been made against him or his estate has been sequestrated, the disqualification shall cease—

(a) unless the bankruptcy order is previously annulled or the sequestration of his estate is recalled or reduced, on his obtaining a discharge; and

(b) if the bankruptcy order is annulled or the sequestration of his estate is recalled or reduced, on the date of that event.

(4) Where a person is disqualified under sub-paragraph (1)(b) of this paragraph by reason of his having made a composition or arrangement with, or granted a trust deed for, his creditors and he pays his debts in full, the disqualification shall cease on the date on which the payment is completed, and in any other case it shall cease at the end of the period of five years beginning with the date on which the terms of the deed of composition or arrangement or trust deed are fulfilled.

(5) For the purposes of sub-paragraph (1)(d) of this paragraph, the date of a conviction shall be taken to be the ordinary date on which the period allowed for making an appeal or application expires or, if an appeal or application is made, the date on which the appeal or application is finally disposed of or abandoned or fails by reason of its non-prosecution.

13. Without prejudice to paragraphs 11 and 12 of this Schedule, a member of a relevant council shall be disqualified for being appointed as or being a member of a police authority under paragraph 2 of this Schedule if he was elected for an electoral division or ward wholly within the metropolitan police district.

14.—(1) Without prejudice to paragraphs 11 and 12 of this Schedule, a person shall be disqualified for being appointed as a member of a police authority under paragraph 5 of this Schedule if—

(a) he has not yet attained the age of twenty-one years, or

(b) neither his principal or only place of work, nor his principal or only place of residence, has been in the area of the authority during the whole of the period of twelve months ending with the day of appointment.

(2) Without prejudice to paragraphs 11 and 12 of this Schedule, a person shall be disqualified for being a member so appointed if, at any time, neither his principal or only place of work, nor his principal or only place of residence, is within that area.

15.—(1) Without prejudice to paragraphs 11 and 12 of this Schedule, a person shall be disqualified for being appointed as a member of a police authority under paragraph 5 of this Schedule, and for being a member so appointed, if he is—

(a) a member of the council for a county, district, county borough or London borough which is wholly or partly within the area of the police authority;

(b) a magistrate eligible for appointment to the police authority under paragraph 8 of this Schedule;

(c) a member of the selection panel for the police authority's area established under Schedule 1C to this Act;

(d) a member of a police force;

(e) an officer or employee of a police authority; or

(f) an officer or employee of a relevant council.

(2) A person shall not be regarded for the purposes of sub-paragraph (1)(f) of this paragraph as an employee of a relevant council by reason of his holding—

(a) the post of head teacher or principal of a school, college or other educational institution or establishment which is maintained or assisted by a local education authority; or

(b) any other post as a teacher or lecturer in any such school, college, institution or establishment.

Tenure of office

16. Subject to the following paragraphs (and to the provisions of any order under section 3A(2) of this Act), a person shall hold and vacate office as a member of a police authority in accordance with the terms of his appointment.

17.—(1) A person shall be appointed to hold office as a member for—

(a) a term of four years or a term expiring on his attaining the age of seventy years, whichever is the shorter, or

(b) such shorter term as the body appointing him may determine in any particular case.

(2) A person shall not, by virtue of sub-paragraph (1)(b) of this paragraph, be appointed under paragraph 5 of this Schedule for a term shorter than four years without the approval of the Secretary of State.

18.—(1) A person may at any time resign his office as a member, or as chairman, by notice in writing to the police authority.

(2) Where a member appointed under paragraph 5 of this Schedule resigns his office as a member under sub-paragraph (1) of this paragraph, he shall send a copy of the notice to the Secretary of State.

19.—(1) A member of a relevant council appointed to be a member of a police authority under paragraph 2 of this Schedule shall cease to be a member of the authority if he ceases to be a member of the council (and does not on the same day again become a member of the council).

(2) A magistrate appointed to be a member of a police authority under paragraph 8 of this Schedule shall cease to be a member of the authority if he ceases to be a magistrate for an area all or part of which constitutes or forms part of the authority's area.

20.—(1) A police authority may remove a member from office by notice in writing if—

(a) he has been absent from meetings of the police authority for a period longer than three consecutive months without the consent of the authority,

(b) he has been convicted of a criminal offence (but is not disqualified for being a member under paragraph 12 of this Schedule),

(c) the police authority is satisfied that the member is incapacitated by physical or mental illness, or

(d) the police authority is satisfied that the member is otherwise unable or unfit to discharge his functions as a member.

(2) Where a police authority removes a member under sub-paragraph (1) of this paragraph, it shall give notice of that fact—

(a) in the case of a member appointed under paragraph 2 or 8 of this Schedule, to the body which appointed him, and

(b) in the case of a member appointed under paragraph 5, to the Secretary of State.

21. A council or joint committee may remove from office a member of a police authority appointed by it under paragraph 2 of this Schedule with a view to appointing another in his place if it considers that to do so would further the object provided for by paragraph 4.

22. If a chairman of a police authority ceases to be a member, he shall also cease to be chairman.

Eligibility for re-appointment

23. A person who ceases to be a member, otherwise than by virtue of paragraph 20 of this Schedule, or ceases to be chairman, may (if otherwise eligible) be re-appointed.

Validity of acts

24. The acts and proceedings of any person appointed to be a member or chairman of a police authority and acting in that office shall, notwithstanding his disqualification or want of qualification, be as valid and effectual as if he had been qualified.

25. The proceedings of a police authority shall not be invalidated by a vacancy in the membership of the authority or in the office of chairman or by any defect in the appointment of a person as a member or as chairman.

Allowances

26.—(1) A police authority may make to its chairman and other members such payments by way of reimbursement of expenses and allowances as the Secretary of State may, with the approval of the Treasury, determine.

(2) Payments made under sub-paragraph (1) of this paragraph may differ according to whether the recipient is a chairman or other member or was appointed under paragraphs 2, 5 or 8 of this Schedule.

Interpretation

27.—(1) For the purposes of this Schedule, a council is a "relevant council" in relation to a police authority if—
  (a) it is the council for a county, district, county borough or London borough which constitutes, or is wholly within, the authority's police area, and
  (b) in the case of a district council, the district is not in a county having a county council within paragraph (a).

(2) In determining for the purposes of sub-paragraph (1) of this paragraph whether a county or district is wholly within a police area, any part of the county or district which is within the metropolitan police district shall be disregarded.

SCHEDULE 1C

POLICE AUTHORITIES: SELECTION OF INDEPENDENT MEMBERS

Selection panels

1.—(1) There shall be a selection panel for each police area for the time being listed in Schedule 1A to this Act.

(2) Each selection panel shall consist of three members, one of whom shall be appointed by each of the following—
  (a) the designated members of the police authority for the area;
  (b) the Secretary of State;
  (c) the two members of the panel appointed by virtue of paragraphs (a) and (b) of this sub-paragraph.

(3) A designated member may be appointed as a member of a selection panel by virtue of paragraph (a) (but not paragraph (b) or (c)) of sub-paragraph (2) of this paragraph.

(4) In this Schedule "designated member" means a member appointed under paragraph 2 or 8 of Schedule 1B to this Act.

2. A person shall be disqualified for being appointed as or being a member of a selection panel if, by virtue of paragraph 11, 12, 14 or 15(1)(d) to (f) of Schedule 1B to this Act, he is disqualified—
  (a) for being appointed under paragraph 5 of that Schedule as a member of the police authority for the panel's area, or
  (b) for being a member so appointed.

3.—(1) A person shall be appointed to hold office as a member of a selection panel for a term of two years, or for a term expiring on his attaining seventy years of age, whichever is the shorter.

(2) A person may at any time resign his office as a member by notice in writing to the persons who under paragraph 1 of this Schedule would be required to appoint his successor.

(3) A person shall not cease to be a member by reason only that any of the persons appointing him cease to hold the positions by virtue of which they appointed him.

4. A member of a selection panel may be removed from office by notice in writing by the persons who, under paragraph 1 of this Schedule, would be required to appoint his successor ("the appointer") if—
  (a) the member has been absent from two consecutive meetings of the selection panel without the consent of the panel,
  (b) the member has been convicted of a criminal offence (but is not disqualified for being a member under paragraph 2 of this Schedule),
  (c) the appointer is satisfied that the member is incapacitated by physical or mental illness, or
  (d) the appointer is satisfied that the member is otherwise unable or unfit to discharge his functions as a member.

5. A person who ceases to be a member of a selection panel, otherwise than by virtue of paragraph 4 of this Schedule may (if otherwise eligible) be re-appointed.

6.—(1) The acts and proceedings of any person appointed to be a member of a selection panel and acting in that office shall, notwithstanding his disqualification or want of qualification, be as valid and effectual as if he had been qualified.

(2) Subject to the provisions of any regulations made under paragraph 11 of this Schedule, the proceedings of a selection panel shall not be invalidated by—

(a) a vacancy in the membership of the panel, or

(b) a defect in the appointment of a person as a member.

7.—(1) A police authority shall make to members of the selection panel for the authority's area such payments by way of reimbursement of expenses and allowances as it may determine.

(2) A police authority shall—

(a) provide the selection panel for the authority's area with such accommodation, and such secretarial and other assistance, as they may reasonably require, and

(b) meet any expenses incurred by the panel in the exercise of their functions.

Functions of selection panel

8.—(1) Where appointments to a police authority are to be made under paragraph 5 of Schedule 1B to this Act, the selection panel for the authority's area shall nominate persons willing to be candidates for appointment.

(2) Unless the selection panel are able to identify only a smaller number, the number of persons to be nominated by a selection panel under this paragraph on any occasion shall be a number four times greater than the number of appointments to be made under paragraph 5 of Schedule 1B to this Act.

(3) A selection panel shall notify the Secretary of State of—

(a) the name of each person nominated by it under this paragraph, and

(b) such other information regarding those persons as it considers appropriate.

9. A person shall not be nominated under paragraph 8 of this Schedule in relation to an authority if, by virtue of paragraph 11, 12, 14 or 15 of Schedule 1B to this Act, he is disqualified for being appointed as a member of the authority under paragraph 5 of that Schedule.

10. In exercising their functions a selection panel shall have regard to the desirability of ensuring that, so far as reasonably practicable, the persons nominated by them under paragraph 8 of this Schedule—

(a) represent the interests of a wide range of people within the community in the police area, and

(b) include persons with skills, knowledge or experience in such fields as may be specified for the purposes of this paragraph in regulations made under paragraph 11 of this Schedule.

11.—(1) The Secretary of State may make regulations as to—

(a) the procedures to be followed in relation to the selection of persons for nomination under paragraph 8 of this Schedule, and

(b) the conduct of the proceedings of selection panels.

(2) Without prejudice to the generality of sub-paragraph (1) of this paragraph, regulations under this paragraph may—

(a) make provision (including provision imposing time limits) as to the procedures to be adopted when inviting applications or suggestions for nomination under paragraph 8 of this Schedule, and for dealing with applications and suggestions received;

(b) make provision specifying the fields referred to in paragraph 10 of this Schedule;

(c) prescribe matters, in addition to those mentioned in paragraph 10 of this Schedule, to which a selection panel is to have regard in carrying out any of its functions;

(d) provide for decisions of a selection panel to be taken by a majority of the members.

(3) Regulations under this paragraph may make different provision for different cases and circumstances.

(4) A statutory instrument containing regulations under this paragraph shall be subject to annulment in pursuance of a resolution of either House of Parliament.

Secretary of State's short-list

12.—(1) Where the Secretary of State receives a notice under paragraph 8(3) of this Schedule, he shall as soon as practicable prepare a short-list of candidates and send it to the police authority concerned.

(2) Subject to paragraph 13 of this Schedule, the candidates on the short-list prepared by the Secretary of State shall be persons nominated by the selection panel, and their number shall be one half of the number of those persons.

(3) Where the number of persons nominated by the panel is an odd number, the number to be short-listed by the Secretary of State shall be one half of the number nominated reduced by one.

13.—(1) This paragraph has effect where the number of persons nominated by the selection panel is less than twice the number of vacancies to be filled by appointments under paragraph 5 of Schedule 1B.

(2) The Secretary of State may himself nominate such number of candidates as, when added to the number nominated by the selection panel, equals twice the number of vacancies; and if he does so, paragraph 12 of this Schedule shall have effect as if the selection panel had nominated the Secretary of State's nominees as well as their own.

14. The Secretary of State shall give to the designated members any information regarding the persons on his short-list which they request and which he has received under paragraph 8 of this Schedule."

Section 19 SCHEDULE 3

SCHEDULE TO BE INSERTED IN POLICE ACT 1964: APPEALS TRIBUNALS

"SCHEDULE 5

APPEALS

Police appeals tribunals

1.—(1) In the case of an appeal by a senior officer, the police appeals tribunal shall consist of three members appointed by the Secretary of State, of whom—

(a) one shall be a person chosen from a list of persons who have a seven year general qualification within the meaning of section 71 of the Courts and Legal Services Act 1990 and have been nominated by the Lord Chancellor for the purposes of this Schedule,

(b) one shall be a member of a police authority, other than the relevant police authority, and

(c) one shall be a person who—

(i) is (or has within the previous five years been) an Inspector of Constabulary, or

(ii) has within the previous five years been (and is no longer) the Commissioner of Police of the Metropolis.

(2) The member of the police appeals tribunal to whom sub-paragraph (1)(a) of this paragraph applies shall be the chairman.

2.—(1) In the case of an appeal by a member of a police force who is not a senior officer, the police appeals tribunal shall consist of four members appointed by the relevant police authority, of whom—

(a) one shall be a person chosen from the list referred to in paragraph 1(1)(a) of this Schedule,

(b) one shall be a member of the authority or, where the authority is the Secretary of State, a person nominated by him,

(c) one shall be a person chosen from a list maintained by the Secretary of State of persons who are (or have within the last five years been) chief officers of police, other than a person who is (or has at any time been) the chief officer of police of the force maintained by the relevant authority, and

(d) one shall be a retired officer of appropriate rank.

(2) The member of the police appeals tribunal to whom sub-paragraph (1)(a) of this paragraph applies shall be the chairman.

Notice of appeal

3. An appeal shall be instituted by giving notice of appeal within the time prescribed by rules made under section 37 of this Act.

Respondent

4. On any appeal the respondent shall be such person as may be prescribed by rules made under section 37 of this Act.

Casting vote

5. Where there is an equality of voting among the members of a police appeals tribunal, the chairman shall have a second or casting vote.

Hearing

6.—(1) A police appeals tribunal may determine a case without a hearing but shall not decide to do so unless both the appellant and the respondent have been afforded an opportunity to make written or, if either so requests, oral representations and any such representations have been considered.

(2) Where a hearing is held, the appellant shall have the right to appear by a serving member of a police force or by counsel or a solicitor; and the respondent shall have the right to appear by an officer of the police force or by the clerk or other officer of the police authority or by counsel or a solicitor.

Effect of orders

7.—(1) Where an appeal is allowed, the order shall take effect by way of substitution for the decision appealed against, and as from the date of that decision or, where that decision was itself a decision on appeal, the date of the original decision appealed against.

(2) Where the effect of the order made by the police appeals tribunal is to reinstate the appellant in the force or in his rank, he shall, for the purpose of reckoning service for pension and, to such extent (if any) as may be determined by the order, for the purpose of pay, be deemed to have served in the force or in his rank continuously from the date of the original decision to the date of his reinstatement.

(3) Where the effect of the order made by the police appeals tribunal is to reinstate the appellant in the force and he was suspended for a period immediately preceding the date of the original decision or any subsequent decision, the order shall deal with the suspension.

Remuneration and expenses

8. Members of a police appeals tribunal shall be—
(a) paid such remuneration, and
(b) reimbursed for such expenses,
as the Secretary of State may determine.

Costs

9.—(1) An appellant shall pay the whole of his own costs unless the police appeals tribunal directs that the whole or any part of his costs are to be defrayed out of the police fund of the relevant police authority.

(2) Subject to sub-paragraph (1) of this paragraph, all the costs and expenses of an appeal under section 37 of this Act, including the costs of the respondent and any remuneration or expenses paid by virtue of paragraph 8 of this Schedule, shall be defrayed out of the police fund of the relevant police authority.

Interpretation

10. In this Schedule—
(a) "senior officer" means a member of a police force holding a rank above that of superintendent,
(b) "relevant police authority" means the police authority which maintains the police force of which the appellant is a member, and
(c) "retired officer of appropriate rank" means—
    (i) where the appellant was, immediately before the proceedings, of the rank of superintendent, a retired member of a police force who at the time of his retirement was of that rank, and
    (ii) in any other case a retired member of a police force who at the time of his retirement was of the rank of chief inspector or below."

SCHEDULE 4

APPLICATION TO POLICE AUTHORITIES OF ENACTMENTS RELATING TO LOCAL AUTHORITIES

PART I

AMENDMENTS OF LOCAL GOVERNMENT ENACTMENTS

Local Government (Records) Act 1962

1. In section 2 of the Local Government (Records) Act 1962 (acquisition and deposit of records), in subsection (6) after the words "City of London," there shall be inserted the words "to a police authority established under section 3 of the Police Act 1964,".
2. In section 8 of that Act (interpretation), in subsection (1), in the definition of "local authority" after the words "City of London" there shall be inserted the words ", a police authority established under section 3 of the Police Act 1964,".

Local Government Act 1966

3. In section 11 of the Local Government Act 1966 (grants for expenditure due to ethnic minority population), in subsection (2) after the words "apply to" there shall be inserted the words "a police authority established under section 3 of the Police Act 1964 and".

Local Government Grants (Social Need) Act 1969

4. In section 1 of the Local Government Grants (Social Need) Act 1969 (provision for grants), in subsection (3) after the word "include" there shall be inserted the words "a police authority established under section 3 of the Police Act 1964 and".

Local Authorities (Goods and Services) Act 1970

5. In section 1 of the Local Authorities (Goods and Services) Act 1970 (supply of goods and services by local authorities), in subsection (4), in the definition of "public body" after the words "local authority" there shall be inserted the words ", any police authority established under section 3 of the Police Act 1964, any".

Local Government Act 1972

6. In section 94 of the Local Government Act 1972 (disability of members of authorities for voting on account of interest in contracts, etc.), in subsection (5)(b) (receipt of certain allowances not to be treated as a pecuniary interest) after the words "176 below" there shall be inserted the words "or paragraph 26 of Schedule 1B to the Police Act 1964".
7. In section 98 of that Act, in subsection (1A) (application to joint authorities of provisions about members' interests) after the words "joint authority" there shall be inserted the words "and a police authority established under section 3 of the Police Act 1964".
8. In section 99 of that Act (meetings and proceedings of local authorities) after the words "joint authorities," there shall be inserted the words "police authorities established under section 3 of the Police Act 1964".
9.—(1) Section 100J of that Act (application to joint authorities etc. of provisions relating to access to meetings and documents) shall be amended as follows.
(2) For subsection (1)(e) there shall be substituted—
"(e) a police authority established under section 3 of the Police Act 1964;".
(3) In subsection (4), in paragraph (a)—
(a) for the words "combined police authority" there shall be substituted the words "police authority established under section 3 of the Police Act 1964", and
(b) for the word "which" there shall be substituted the words "or other person that".
10.—(1) Section 107 of that Act (application to police authorities of provisions relating to the discharge of functions by local authorities) shall be amended as follows.
(2) In subsection (1)—
(a) the words "104 and" shall be omitted, and
(b) after the words "those sections" there shall be inserted the words "and section 104".
(3) In subsection (3) for the words "for the purposes of" there shall be substituted the word "by".

(4) After subsection (3) there shall be inserted—

"(3A) Where pursuant to arrangements made by virtue of subsection (3) above—

(a) a chief officer of police, or

(b) the deputy of a chief officer of police,

may discharge functions of a police authority, he may himself arrange for the discharge of any of those functions by a member of the police force or by a person who is employed by the authority but is not under the authority's direction and control."

(5) In subsection (8) for the words "for the purposes of" there shall be substituted the word "by".

(6) Subsections (9) and (10) shall be omitted.

11.—(1) Section 146A of that Act (application to police authorities of miscellaneous powers of local authorities) shall be amended as follows.

(2) In subsection (1)—

(a) at the beginning there shall be inserted the words "Subject to subsection (1A) below,", and

(b) after the words "joint authority" there shall be inserted the words "and a police authority established under section 3 of the Police Act 1964".

(3) After subsection (1) there shall be inserted—

"(1A) A police authority established under section 3 of the Police Act 1964 shall not be treated—

(a) as a local authority for the purposes of section 112, 139, 140A or 140C above, or

(b) as a principal council for the purposes of section 122 above."

12. In section 223 of that Act (appearance of local authorities in legal proceedings), in subsection (2) after the words "joint authority" there shall be inserted the words ", a police authority established under section 3 of the Police Act 1964".

13. In section 228 of that Act (inspection of documents), in subsection (7A) after the words "joint authority" there shall be inserted the words "or a police authority established under section 3 of the Police Act 1964".

14. The words "and a police authority established under section 3 of the Police Act 1964" shall be inserted after the words "joint authority"—

(a) in section 229 of that Act (photographic copies of documents), in subsection (8);

(b) in section 231 of that Act (service of notices on local authorities, etc.), in subsection (4);

(c) in section 232 of that Act (public notices), in subsection (1A);

(d) in section 233 of that Act (service of notices by local authorities), in subsection (11); and

(e) in section 234 of that Act (authentication of documents), in subsection (4).

15.—(1) Schedule 12 to that Act (meetings and proceedings of local authorities) shall be amended as follows.

(2) In sub-paragraph (1) of paragraph 6A after the words "joint authority", there shall be inserted the words "or a police authority established under section 3 of the Police Act 1964".

(3) In paragraph 6B—

(a) after the word "that" there shall be inserted "(a)", and

(b) for the words "members in the case of a joint authority", there shall be substituted the words ", and

(b) in the case of a police authority established under section 3 of the Police Act 1964, sub-paragraphs (2) and (3) of paragraph 5 shall not apply and if the chairman is absent from a meeting of such an authority another member chosen by the members of the authority present shall preside."

(4) In paragraph 46, after the words "joint authority" there shall be inserted the words "and a police authority established under section 3 of the Police Act 1964".

Local Government Act 1974

16. In section 25 of the Local Government Act 1974 (authorities subject to investigation by Commission for Local Administration), in subsection (1) for paragraph (ca) there shall be substituted—

"(ca) any police authority established under section 3 of the Police Act 1964;".

Local Government (Miscellaneous Provisions) Act 1976

17. In section 30 of the Local Government (Miscellaneous Provisions) Act 1976 (power to forgo repayment of remuneration paid to deceased employees), for subsection (3) (police authorities to be treated as local authorities and police officers to be treated as their employees) there shall be substituted—

"(3) For the purposes of this section a member of a police force which is maintained by a police authority (other than the Secretary of State) shall be treated as employed by the authority and references to employment shall be construed accordingly."

18. In section 44 of that Act (interpretation), in subsection (1), in paragraph (a) of the definition of "local authority" after the words "of this Act," there shall be inserted the words "a police authority established under section 3 of the Police Act 1964 and".

Local Government, Planning and Land Act 1980

19. In section 2 of the Local Government, Planning and Land Act 1980 (duty of authorities to publish information), in subsection (1)—
   (a) in paragraph (j) the words from "a police committee" to "in Scotland", and
   (b) in paragraph (k) the words from "a combined" to "in Scotland",
shall be omitted.

20. In section 20 of that Act (interpretation of provisions relating to direct labour organisations), in subsection (1), in paragraph (a)(i) of the definition of "local authority" after the words "borough council," there shall be inserted the words "a police authority established under section 3 of the Police Act 1964".

21. In section 99 of that Act (directions to dispose of land), in subsection (4) after paragraph (db) there shall be inserted—
   "(dc) a police authority established under section 3 of the Police Act 1964;".

22. In Schedule 16 to that Act (bodies to whom provisions of Part X relating to registration of land apply) after paragraph 5B there shall be inserted—
   "5C. A police authority established under section 3 of the Police Act 1964."

Local Government (Miscellaneous Provisions) Act 1982

23. In section 33 of the Local Government (Miscellaneous Provisions) Act 1982 (enforceability by local authorities of certain covenants relating to land), in subsection (9)(a) after the words "Residuary Body" there shall be inserted the words ", a police authority established under section 3 of the Police Act 1964".

24. In section 41 of that Act (lost and uncollected property), in subsection (13), in the definition of "local authority" after paragraph (c) there shall be inserted—
   "(ca) a police authority established under section 3 of the Police Act 1964; and".

Local Government Finance Act 1982

25. In section 12 of the Local Government Finance Act 1982 (accounts subject to audit), in subsection (2) for paragraph (g) there shall be substituted—
   "(g) a police authority established under section 3 of the Police Act 1964;".

26. In section 19 of that Act (declaration that item of account is unlawful), in subsection (7) at the end there shall be added the words "and a police authority established under section 3 of the Police Act 1964".

27. In section 20 of that Act (recovery of amount not accounted for etc.), in subsection (10) at the end there shall be added the words "and a police authority established under section 3 of the Police Act 1964".

28. After section 28A of that Act there shall be inserted—

"Delivery of documents relating to police authorities to Secretary of State

28B.—(1) The Commission shall send to the Secretary of State a copy of any report of which a copy is sent to the Commission under section 18(4) above and which relates to a police authority established under section 3 of the Police Act 1964.

(2) If it appears to the Commission appropriate to do so, it may send to the Secretary of State a copy of any document—
   (a) which relates to one or more police authorities established under section 3 of the Police Act 1964, and
   (b) which has been sent (or a copy of which has been sent) by the Commission to a police authority established under that section."

Local Government Act 1986

29. In section 6 of the Local Government Act 1986 (interpretation of provisions relating to publicity and promotion of homosexuality), in subsection (2)(a) after the entry relating to the Broads Authority there shall be inserted—
   "a police authority established under section 3 of the Police Act 1964,".

30. In section 9 of that Act (interpretation of provisions relating to the transfer of mortgages), in subsection (1)(a) after the entry relating to the Common Council there shall be inserted—
   "a police authority established under section 3 of the Police Act 1964,".

Local Government Act 1988

31. In section 1 of the Local Government Act 1988 (defined authorities for provisions on competition), in subsection (1) for paragraph (e) there shall be substituted—
"(e) a police authority established under section 3 of the Police Act 1964,".
32. In Schedule 2 to that Act, in the list of public authorities to which provisions on public supply or works contracts apply, for the entry relating to police authorities there shall be substituted—
"A police authority established under section 3 of the Police Act 1964."

Local Government Finance Act 1988

33. In section 112 of the Local Government Finance Act 1988 (financial administration as to combined police and fire authorities), in subsection (2) for paragraph (a) there shall be substituted—
"(a) any police authority established under section 3 of the Police Act 1964, and".
34. In section 114 of that Act (functions of the chief finance officer as regards reports), in subsection (2), for the words "or officer of the authority" there shall be inserted the words "of the authority, a person holding any office or employment under the authority, a member of a police force maintained by the authority,".

Local Government and Housing Act 1989

35. In section 5 of the Local Government and Housing Act 1989 (designation and reports of monitoring officer)—
   (a) in subsection (1), after the words "paid service" there shall be inserted the words "(or, in the case of a police authority established under section 3 of the Police Act 1964, the clerk to the authority)";
   (b) in subsection (2), for the words "sub-committee or officer of the authority", in both places where they occur, there shall be substituted the words "or sub-committee of the authority, by any person holding any office or employment under the authority"; and
   (c) in subsection (3), for the words "head of the authority's paid service" there shall be substituted the words "person who is for the time being designated as the head of the authority's paid service under section 4 above".
36. In section 13 of that Act (voting rights of members of certain committees who are not members of the relevant local authority)—
   (a) in subsection (4)(h) for the words "paragraphs (a) to (g)" there shall be substituted the words "paragraphs (b) to (g)", and
   (b) in subsection (9) for the words "paragraphs (a) to (j)" there shall be substituted the words "paragraphs (a) to (f) or (h) to (j)".
37. In section 18 of that Act (allowances for local authority members), in subsection (5)(a) for the words "paragraphs (d) and (j)" there shall be substituted the words "paragraphs (d), (g) and (j)".
38. In section 21 of that Act, in subsection (1) (definition of local authority for purposes of various provisions relating to their members, officers, staff and committees etc.) for paragraph (g) there shall be substituted—
"(g) a police authority established under section 3 of the Police Act 1964;".
39. In section 67 of that Act (application of provisions relating to companies in which local authorities have interests), in subsection (3) (definition of local authority) for paragraph (i) there shall be substituted—
"(i) a police authority established under section 3 of the Police Act 1964;".
40. In section 101 of that Act (housing grants for improvements and repairs), in subsection (3) (bodies ineligible to apply for grants) after paragraph (e) there shall be inserted—
"(ea) a police authority established under section 3 of the Police Act 1964;".
41. In section 152 of that Act (interpretation etc. of provision relating to power of local authorities to impose charges) subsections (1)(f) and (2)(g) shall be omitted.
42. In section 155 of that Act (emergency assistance to local authorities), after subsection (4)(e) there shall be inserted—
"(ea) a police authority established under section 3 of the Police Act 1964;".
43. In section 157 of that Act (commutation of, and interest on, periodic payments of grants etc.), in subsection (6) for paragraph (g) there shall be substituted—
"(g) a police authority established under section 3 of the Police Act 1964;".
44. In Schedule 1 to that Act (political balance on local authority committees etc.—

(a) in paragraph 2(1)(a) for the words "paragraphs (f) to (j)" there shall be substituted the words "paragraphs (f) or (h) to (j)", and
(b) in paragraph 4(1), in paragraph (a) of the definition of "relevant authority" for the words "paragraphs (a) to (c) or (f) to (j)" there shall be substituted the words "paragraphs (a) to (c), (f) or (h) to (j)".

Local Government Finance Act 1992

45. In section 19 of the Local Government Finance Act 1992 (exclusion of Crown exemption in certain cases), in subsection (3) for paragraph (c) there shall be substituted—
"(c) a police authority established under section 3 of the Police Act 1964; and".

PART II

AMENDMENTS OF OTHER ENACTMENTS

Trustee Investments Act 1961

46. In section 11 of the Trustee Investments Act 1961 (local authority investment schemes), in subsection (4)(a) after the words "the Broads Authority" there shall be inserted the words ", a police authority established under section 3 of the Police Act 1964".
47. In Part II of Schedule 1 to that Act (list of narrower-range investments requiring advice), in paragraph 9, in sub-paragraph (d) for the words "a combined police authority" onwards there shall be substituted the words "a police authority established under section 3 of the Police Act 1964;".

Leasehold Reform Act 1967

48. In section 28 of the Leasehold Reform Act 1967 (retention or resumption of land required for public purposes), in subsection (5), in paragraph (a) for the words "any combined police authority" onwards there shall be substituted the words "any police authority established under section 3 of the Police Act 1964; and".

Post Office Act 1969

49. In section 7 of the Post Office Act 1969 (powers of the Post Office) after subsection (1) there shall be inserted—
"(1AA) In subsection (1)(e) above, "local authority" includes a police authority established under section 3 of the Police Act 1964."

Employment Agencies Act 1973

50. In section 13 of the Employment Agencies Act 1973, in subsection (7) (cases in which Act is not to apply), in paragraph (f) after the words "local authority" there shall be inserted the words ", a police authority established under section 3 of the Police Act 1964".

Race Relations Act 1976

51. In section 71 of the Race Relations Act 1976 (local authorities: general statutory duty) after the word "includes" there shall be inserted the words "a police authority established under section 3 of the Police Act 1964 and".

Rent (Agriculture) Act 1976

52. In section 5 of the Rent (Agriculture) Act 1976 (no statutory tenancy where landlord's interest belongs to Crown or to local authority, etc.), in subsection (3) after paragraph (b) there shall be inserted—
"(baa) a police authority established under section 3 of the Police Act 1964;".

Rent Act 1977

53. In section 14 of the Rent Act 1977 (landlord's interest belonging to local authority, etc.) after paragraph (c) there shall be inserted—
"(caa) a police authority established under section 3 of the Police Act 1964;".

Justices of the Peace Act 1979

54. In section 64 of the Justices of the Peace Act 1979 (disqualification in certain cases of justices who are members of local authorities), in subsection (6) (definition of local authority) for the word "and" (in the first place where it occurs) there shall be substituted the words "a police authority established under section 3 of the Police Act 1964,".

Acquisition of Land Act 1981

55. In section 17 of the Acquisition of Land Act 1981 (compulsory purchase of local authority and statutory undertakers' land), in subsection (4), in the definition (for the purposes of subsection (3)) of "local authority"—
   (a) in paragraph (a) after the words "City of London" there shall be inserted the words ", a police authority established under section 3 of the Police Act 1964"; and
   (b) in paragraph (b) at the end there shall be added the words "or a police authority established under section 3 of the Police Act 1964."

Stock Transfer Act 1982

56. In Schedule 1 to the Stock Transfer Act 1982 (securities that can be transferred through a computerised system), in paragraph 7(1) for the word "or" at the end of paragraph (b) there shall be substituted—
   "(ba) any police authority established under section 3 of the Police Act 1964; or".

County Courts Act 1984

57. In section 60 of the County Courts Act 1984 (right of audience for officer of local authority in proceedings brought by authority), in subsection (3), in the definition of "local authority" after the words "borough council" there shall be inserted the words ", a police authority established under section 3 of the Police Act 1964".

Housing Act 1985

58. In section 4 of the Housing Act 1985 (interpretation), in paragraph (e) (definition of "local authority")—
   (a) after the words "Broads Authority" (in the first place where they occur) there shall be inserted the words ", in sections 438, 441, 442, 443 and 458 includes the Broads Authority and a joint authority established by Part IV of the Local Government Act 1985",
   (b) the words "sections 438, 441, 442, 443, 458, 460(3)" shall be omitted, and
   (c) after the words "Broads Authority" (in the second place where they occur) there shall be inserted the words ", a police authority established under section 3 of the Police Act 1964 and".

Housing Associations Act 1985

59. In section 106 of the Housing Associations Act 1985 (minor definitions), in subsection (1), in the definition of "local authority"—
   (a) for the words "sections 84(5) and 85(4)" there shall be substituted the words "section 84(5)", and
   (b) at the end there shall be added the words "and in section 85(4) includes such a joint authority and a police authority established under section 3 of the Police Act 1964".

Landlord and Tenant Act 1985

60. In section 38 of the Landlord and Tenant Act 1985 (minor definitions), in the definition of "local authority" after the words "Broads Authority" there shall be inserted the words ", a police authority established under section 3 of the Police Act 1964 and".

Landlord And Tenant Act 1987

61. In section 58 of the Landlord and Tenant Act 1987, in subsection (1) (definition of "exempt landlord"), in paragraph (a) after the word "Scilly," there shall be inserted the words "a police authority established under section 3 of the Police Act 1964".

Housing Act 1988

62. In Schedule 1 to the Housing Act 1988 (tenancies which cannot be assured tenancies), in paragraph 12 (local authority tenancies, etc.) after sub-paragraph (2)(f) there shall be added the words "and
   (g) a police authority established under section 3 of the Police Act 1964."

Town and Country Planning Act 1990

63. In section 252 of the Town and Country Planning Act 1990 (procedure for making of orders relating to highways), in subsection (12), in the definition of "local authority" after the words "London borough," there shall be inserted the words "a police authority established under section 3 of the Police Act 1964,".

Section 44   SCHEDULE 5

POLICE: MINOR AND CONSEQUENTIAL AMENDMENTS

PART I

AMENDMENTS OF POLICE ACT 1964

1.—(1) Section 12 of the Police Act 1964 (reports by chief constables to police authorities) shall be amended as follows.

(2) In subsection (1)—

(a) for the words "calendar year" there shall be substituted the words "financial year", and

(b) the words "in writing" shall be omitted.

(3) After subsection (1) there shall be inserted—

   "(1A) A chief constable shall arrange for a report submitted by him under subsection (1) of this section to be published in such manner as he thinks fit."

(4) In subsection (2) the words "in writing" shall be omitted.

(5) After subsection (2) there shall be inserted—

   "(2A) A report submitted under subsection (2) of this section shall be in such form as the police authority may specify."

(6) After subsection (3) there shall be inserted—

   "(3A) The police authority may arrange, or require the chief constable to arrange, for a report under subsection (2) of this section to be published in such manner as the authority thinks fit."

2.—(1) Section 13 (collaboration agreements) shall be amended as follows.

(2) In subsection (1) after the word "efficiently" there shall be inserted the words "or effectively".

(3) After subsection (6) there shall be added—

   "(7) The provisions of this section shall not prejudice the power of a police authority to act jointly, or co-operate in any other way, with any person where to do so is calculated to facilitate, or is conducive or incidental to, the discharge of any of the authority's functions."

3. In section 17(1) (appointment of police cadets) the words "and subject to the approval of the police authority as to numbers" shall be omitted.

4. In section 19(3) (jurisdiction of special constables) after the words "City of London', in each place where they occur, there shall be added the words "police area".

5. In section 25, subsection (5) (five representatives of Cambridge University to be members of police authority for area including Cambridge) shall be omitted.

6. In section 28 (general duty of Secretary of State) after the word "efficiency" there shall be inserted the words "and effectiveness".

7.—(1) Section 29 (removal of chief constables etc.) shall be amended as follows.

(2) At the end of subsection (1) there shall be added the words "or effectiveness".

(3) In subsection (2) for the words "a deputy or assistant chief constable" there shall be substituted the words "an assistant chief constable".

8.—(1) Section 30 (reports by chief constables to the Secretary of State) shall be amended as follows.

(2) After subsection (1) there shall be inserted—

   "(1 A) A requirement under subsection (1) of this section may specify the form in which a report is to be given.

   (1 B) The Secretary of State may arrange, or require the chief constable to arrange, for a report under this section to be published in such manner as the Secretary of State thinks fit."

(3) In subsection (2) for the words "calendar year" there shall be substituted the words "financial year".

9. In section 42 (research) after the word "efficiency" there shall be inserted the words "or effectiveness".

10.–(1) Section 43 (central service on police duties) shall be amended as follows.

(2) In subsection (3A), for the words "subsection (1) above" there shall be substituted the words "section 53C(3) of this Act".

(3) In subsection (5) for the words "service as a staff officer to the inspectors of constabulary" there shall be substituted the words "temporary service under section 39 of this Act".

11.—(1) Section 44 (Police Federations) shall be amended as follows.

(2) In subsection (1A) for the words "disciplinary proceedings" there shall be substituted the words "proceedings brought under regulations made in accordance with subsection (3) of section 33 of this Act or with subsection (2A) of section 26 of the Police (Scotland) Act 1967".

(3) In subsection (1B) for the words "the Secretary of State" there shall be substituted the words "a police appeals tribunal".

12. In section 53 (causing disaffection) in subsection (1) the words "or to commit breaches of discipline" shall be omitted.

13. In section 56 (metropolitan and City of London police funds) in paragraph (a) after the words "City of London" there shall be added the words "police area".

14.—(1) Section 58 (chief officers affected by amalgamations or local government reorganisations) shall be amended as follows.

(2) In subsection (1), for the words "or Part II of the Local Government Act 1958" there shall be substituted the words ", section 58 of the Local Government Act 1972 or section 17 of the Local Government Act 1992".

(3) In subsection (2) for the word "deputy" there shall be substituted the word "assistant".

(4) After subsection (3) there shall be inserted—

"(3A) If a chief constable was appointed for a term which expires within three months of his becoming a member of a police force by virtue of this section, subsection (3) shall have effect as if the reference to three months were a reference to that term."

15. For section 62 (meaning of "police area" etc.) there shall be substituted—

"Meaning of "chief officer of police" etc.

62. Except where the context otherwise requires, in this Act—
"chief officer of police" means—

(a) in relation to a police force maintained under section 2 of this Act, the chief constable,

(b) in relation to the metropolitan police force, the Commissioner of Police of the Metropolis, and

(c) in relation to the City of London police, the Commissioner of the City of London Police;

"City of London police area" means the City of London as defined for the purposes of the Acts relating to the City of London police;

"metropolitan police district" means that district as defined in section 76 of the London Government Act 1963;

"police area" (or "police district') means a police area provided for by section 1 of this Act;
"police authority" means—

(a) in relation to a police area listed in Schedule 1A to this Act, the authority established under section 3 of this Act,

(b) in relation to the metropolitan police district, the Secretary of State, and

(c) in relation to the City of London police area, the Common Council;

"police force" means a force maintained by a police authority;
"police fund" means—

(a) in relation to a force maintained under section 2, the fund kept by that force's police authority under section 8 of this Act,

(b) in relation to the metropolitan police, the metropolitan police fund, and

(c) in relation to the City of London Police, the fund out of which the expenses of the City police are paid."

PART II

AMENDMENTS OF OTHER ENACTMENTS

Offices, Shops and Railway Premises Act 1963

16. In section 90 of the Offices, Shops and Railway Premises Act 1963 (interpretation), in subsection (1), in the definition of "police authority" for the words "the Police Pensions Act 1921" there shall be substituted the words "the Police Pensions Act 1976".

Pensions (Increase) Act 1971

17. In Schedule 2 to the Pensions (Increase) Act 1971 (list of official pensions for the purposes of that Act), in paragraph 15, for sub-paragraph (b) there shall be substituted—

"(b) was engaged on service pursuant to an appointment under section 10 of the Overseas Development and Co-operation Act 1980, being service in respect of which section 53C of the Police Act 1964 or, as the case may be, section 38A of the Police (Scotland) Act 1967 had effect; or

(ba) was engaged on temporary service in accordance with section 15A(2) of the Police Act 1964 or section 12A(2) of the Police (Scotland) Act 1967; or".

Overseas Pensions Act 1973

18. In section 2 of the Overseas Pensions Act 1973 (which makes provisions for superannuation schemes as respects certain overseas service), in subsection (2), for paragraph (d) there shall be substituted—

"(d) a person who is—
(i) a member of a police force engaged on relevant service within the meaning of section 53C(1)(a), (c) or (e) of the Police Act 1964 (service under section 15A of the Police Act 1964, under section 1(1) of the Police (Overseas Service) Act 1945 or pursuant to an appointment under section 10 of the Overseas Development and Co-operation Act 1980), or
(ii) a constable of a police force engaged on relevant service within the meaning of section 38A(1)(a), (c) or (e) of the Police (Scotland) Act 1967 (service under section 12A of that Act, section 1(1) of the Police (Overseas Service) Act 1945 or pursuant to an appointment under section 10 of the Overseas Development and Co-operation Act 1980),
and who is incapacitated or dies as a result of an injury sustained or disease contracted during that service;".

Police Pensions Act 1976

19. In section 7 of the Police Pensions Act 1976 (payment of pensions and contributions), in subsection (2), for paragraph (b) there shall be substituted—

"(b) an officer engaged on service pursuant to an appointment under section 10 of the Overseas Development and Co-operation Act 1980;

(ba) a person engaged on temporary service in accordance with arrangements made under section 15A(2) of the Police Act 1964 or section 12A(2) of the Police (Scotland) Act 1967;

(bb) a person engaged on service in the Royal Ulster Constabulary, whose service is or was for the time being service in respect of which the provisions of section 53C of the Police Act 1964 or, as the case may be, section 38A of the Police (Scotland) Act 1967 have or had effect;".

20.—(1) Section 11 of that Act (interpretation) shall be amended as follows.

(2) In subsection (1), for paragraph (a) there shall be substituted—

"(a) service as an officer pursuant to an appointment under section 10 of the Overseas Development and Co-operation Act 1980;

(aa) temporary service in accordance with arrangements made under section 15A(2) of the Police Act 1964 or section 12A(2) of the Police (Scotland) Act 1967;

(ab) service in the Royal Ulster Constabulary in respect of which the provisions of section 53C of the Police Act 1964 or, as the case may be, section 38A of the Police (Scotland) Act 1967 have effect;".

(3) In subsection (2)(b) after the words "subsection (1)" there shall be inserted "(aa), (ab),"

(4) In subsection (3—

(a) in paragraph (b) after the words "subsection (1)(a)," there shall be inserted "(aa), (ab),", and

(b) after the words "body in" there shall be inserted the words "or with".

Police Negotiating Board Act 1980

21.—(1) Section 1 of the Police Negotiating Board Act 1980 shall be amended as follows.

(2) In subsection (1) (which provides for a Board of persons representing the interests of authorities maintaining police forces and of members of police forces) at the end of paragraph (b) there shall be inserted—

"(c) the Commissioner of Police of the Metropolis, and
(d) the Secretary of State,".

(3) In subsection (3) (consultation) for the words "referred to in" there shall be substituted the words "of the persons referred to in paragraphs (a), (b) and (c) of".

Finance Act 1981

22. In section 107 of the Finance Act 1981 (sale of houses at discount by local authorities etc.), in subsection (3)(k) for the words "section 62(b)" there shall be substituted the words "section 62".

Aviation Security Act 1982

23. In section 31 of the Aviation Security Act 1982 (application to Scotland,etc.), in subsection (2)(b) for the words from "from" to "paragraph" there shall be substituted the words "following 'area or,' ".

Police and Criminal Evidence Act 1984

24. In section 84 of the Police and Criminal Evidence Act 1984 (general provision relating to police complaints and discipline), in subsection (4)—
(a) in the definition of "senior officer" for the words "chief superintendent" there shall be substituted the word "superintendent", and
(b) at the end there shall be added—
" 'disciplinary proceedings' means proceedings identified as such by regulations under section 33 of the Police Act 1964."

25. In section 85 of that Act (investigation of complaints: standard procedure)—
(a) subsection (8) shall be omitted, and
(b) in subsection (10) for the words "a criminal or disciplinary charge" there shall be substituted the words "criminal or disciplinary proceedings".

26. In section 86 of that Act (investigation of complaints against senior officers), in subsection (2) for the words "a criminal or disciplinary charge" there shall be substituted the words "criminal or disciplinary proceedings".

27. In section 89 of that Act (supervision of investigations by Complaints Authority), in subsection (12) for the word "charge" there shall be substituted the word "proceedings".

28. Section 91 of that Act (steps to be taken where accused has admitted charges) shall cease to have effect.

29. In section 95 of that Act (manner of dealing with complaints etc.—
(a) for the words "adequate and efficient" there shall be substituted the words "efficient and effective", and
(b) after the word "efficiency" there shall be inserted the words "and effectiveness".

30. In section 96 of that Act (constabularies maintained by authorities other than police authorities), in subsection (1) after the word "corresponding" there shall be inserted the words "or similar".

31. In section 99 of that Act (regulations), in subsection (2) after paragraph (e) there shall be inserted—
"(ea) for enabling the Authority to relinquish the supervision of the investigation of any complaint or other matter;".

32. In section 100 of that Act, in subsection (6) (regulations to which affirmative parliamentary procedure applies)—
(a) after paragraph (a) there shall be inserted—
"(aa) of section 90(5) or (7) above;", and
(b) in paragraph (b) for the words "section 99(2)(b) or (e)" there shall be substituted the words "section 99(2)(b), (e) or (ea)".

33. For section 102 of that Act (representation at disciplinary proceedings) there shall be substituted—

"Representation at disciplinary and other proceedings
102.—(1) A police officer of the rank of superintendent or below may not be dismissed, required to resign or reduced in rank by a decision taken in proceedings under regulations made in accordance with section 33(3)(a) of the Police Act 1964 unless he has been given an opportunity to elect to be legally represented at any hearing held in the course of those proceedings.

(2) Where an officer makes an election to which subsection (1) above refers, he may be represented at the hearing, at his option, either by counsel or by a solicitor.

(3) Except in a case where an officer of the rank of superintendent or below has been given an opportunity to elect to be legally represented and has so elected, he may be represented at the hearing only by another member of a police force.

(4) Regulations under section 33 of the Police Act 1964 shall specify—
(a) a procedure for notifying an officer of the effect of subsections (1) to (3) above,
(b) when he is to be notified of the effect of those subsections,and
(c) when he is to give notice whether he wishes to be legally represented at the hearing.

(5) If an officer—

(a) fails without reasonable cause to give notice in accordance with the regulations that he wishes to be legally represented; or

(b) gives notice in accordance with the regulations that he does not wish to be legally represented,

he may be dismissed, required to resign or reduced in rank without his being legally represented.

(6) If an officer has given notice in accordance with the regulations that he wishes to be legally represented, the case against him may be presented by counsel or a solicitor whether or not he is actually so represented."

34.—(1) Section 105 of that Act (guidelines) shall be amended as follows.

(2) In subsection (1)—

(a) after the words "issue guidance" there shall be inserted the words "to police authorities,"

(b) for paragraph (b) there shall be substituted—

"(b) under regulations made under section 33 of the Police Act 1964 in relation to the matters mentioned in subsection (2)(e) of that section;", and

(c) after the word "and", in the third place where it occurs, there shall be inserted the words "police authorities and".

(3) For subsection (3) there shall be substituted—

"(3) A failure on the part of a police authority or a police officer to have regard to any guidance issued under subsection (1) above shall be admissible in evidence on any appeal from a decision taken in proceedings under regulations made in accordance with subsection (3) of section 33 of the Police Act 1964."

(4) In subsection (4)—

(a) the words from "affecting" to "charges", and

(b) the words "and are not governed by section 104 above",

shall be omitted.

35.—(1) Section 107 of that Act (police officers performing duties of higher rank) shall be amended as follows.

(2) In subsection (1) for the words "he has been" onwards there shall be substituted—

"(a) he has been authorised by an officer holding a rank above the rank of superintendent to exercise the power or, as the case may be, to give his authority for its exercise, or

(b) he is acting during the absence of an officer holding the rank of superintendent who has authorised him, for the duration of that absence, to exercise the power or, as the case may be, to give his authority for its exercise."

(3) In subsection (2) for the words "chief superintendent" there shall be substituted the word "superintendent".

36.—(1) Schedule 4 to that Act (Police Complaints Authority) shall be amended as follows.

(2) For paragraph 1(6) (appointment of two deputy chairmen) there shall be substituted—

"(6) The Secretary of State may appoint not more than two of the members of the Authority to be deputy chairmen."

(3) In paragraph 3(4) (grounds on which members can be removed) after paragraph (d) there shall be inserted—

"(da) he has acted improperly in relation to his duties, or".

Public Order Act 1986

37. In section 15 of the Public Order Act 1986 (delegation of functions of chief officer of police), for the words "a deputy or", in both places where they occur, there shall be substituted the word "an".

Channel Tunnel Act 1987

38.—(1) Section 14 of the Channel Tunnel Act 1987 (arrangements for the policing of the tunnel system) shall be amended as follows.

(2) In subsections (1), (2) and (3) for the words "of the county of Kent" there shall be substituted the words "maintained for the Kent police area".

(3) In subsections (4) and (5—

(a) for the words "police committee for the county of Kent" there shall be substituted the words "Kent Police Authority", and

(b) for the word "committee", in the second place where it occurs, there shall be substituted the word "Authority".

Tribunals and Inquiries Act 1992

39. In section 7 of the Tribunals and Inquiries Act 1992 (which restricts Ministers' powers to remove members of tribunals listed in Schedule 1 to that Act), in subsection (2) (tribunals to which that section does not apply)—

(a) after "36(a)," there shall be inserted "36A,", and

(b) for the words "or 56(a)" there shall be substituted the words ", 56(a) or 57a".

40.—(1) Schedule 1 to that Act (tribunals under general supervision of Council on Tribunals) shall be amended as follows.

(2) In Part I (tribunals under the direct supervision of the Council), after paragraph 36 there shall be inserted—

"Police	36A. An appeals tribunal constituted in accordance with Schedule 5 to the Police Act 1964 (c. 48)."

(3) In Part II (tribunals under the supervision of the Scottish Committee of the Council), after paragraph 57 there shall be inserted—

"Police	57A. An appeals tribunal constituted in accordance with Schedule 3 to the Police (Scotland) Act 1967 (c. 77)."

Section 55   SCHEDULE 6

SCHEDULE TO BE INSERTED IN POLICE (SCOTLAND) ACT 1967: APPEALS TRIBUNALS

"SCHEDULE 3

APPEALS

Police Appeals Tribunals

1.—(1) In the case of an appeal by a senior officer, the police appeals tribunal shall consist of three members appointed by the Secretary of State, of whom—

(a) one shall be a person chosen from a list of persons who have been nominated by the Lord President of the Court of Session for the purposes of this Schedule;

(b) one shall be a member of a police authority, other than the relevant police authority; and

(c) one shall be a person who is (or has within the previous five years been) an inspector of constabulary.

(2) The member of the police appeals tribunal to whom sub-paragraph (1)(a) of this paragraph applies shall be the chairman.

2.—(1) In the case of an appeal by a constable who is not a senior officer, the police appeals tribunal shall consist of four members appointed by the relevant police authority, of whom—

(a) one shall be a person chosen from the list referred to in paragraph 1(1)(a) of this Schedule;

(b) one shall be a member of the authority;

(c) one shall be a person chosen from a list maintained by the Secretary of State of persons who are (or have within the last five years been) chief constables, other than a person who is (or has at any time been) chief constable of the police force; and

(d) one shall be a retired constable of appropriate rank.

(2) The member of the police appeals tribunal to whom sub-paragraph (1)(a) of this paragraph applies shall be the chairman.

Notice of appeal

3. An appeal shall be instituted by giving notice of appeal within the time prescribed by rules under section 30 of this Act.

Respondent

4. On any appeal the respondent shall be the person prescribed by rules under section 30 of this Act.

Casting vote

5. Where there is an equality of voting among the members of a police appeals tribunal, the chairman shall have a second or casting vote.

Hearing

6.—(1) A police appeals tribunal may determine a case without a hearing but shall not decide to do so unless both the appellant and the respondent have been afforded an oppor- tunity to make written or, if either so requests, oral representations and any such represen- tations have been considered.

(2) Where a hearing is held, the appellant shall have the right to be represented by a serving constable or by an advocate or a solicitor; and the respondent to be represented by a constable of the force maintained by, or an officer of, the relevant police authority or by an advocate or a solicitor.

Effect

7.—(1) Where an appeal is allowed, the order shall take effect by way of substitution for the decision appealed against, and as from the date of that decision or, where that decision was itself a decision on appeal, the date of the original decision appealed against.

(2) Where the effect of the order made by the police appeals tribunal is to reinstate the appellant in the force, or in his rank he shall, for the purposes of reckoning service for pension and to such extent (if any) as may be determined by the order for the purposes of pay, be deemed to have served in the force or in that rank continuously from the date of the original decision to the date of his reinstatement.

(3) Where the effect of the order made by the police appeals tribunal is to reinstate the appellant in the force and he was suspended for a period immediately preceding the date of the original decision or any subsequent decision, the order shall deal with the suspension.

Tribunal remuneration and expenses

8. Members of a police appeals tribunal shall be—
(a) paid such remuneration; and
(b) reimbursed for such expenses,
as the Secretary of State may determine.

Expenses of proceedings

9.—(1) An appellant shall pay the whole of his own expenses unless the police appeals tribunal directs that the whole or any part of those expenses are to be paid by the relevant police authority.

(2) Subject to sub-paragraph (1) of this paragraph, all the expenses of an appeal under section 30 of this Act, including the expenses of the respondent and any remuneration or expenses paid by virtue of paragraph 8 of this Schedule, shall be paid by the relevant police authority.

Interpretation

10. In this Schedule—
(a) "senior officer" means a constable holding a rank above that of superintendent;
(b) "relevant police authority" means the police authority for the area for which the police force of which the appellant is a constable is maintained; and
(c) "retired constable of appropriate rank" means—
      (i) where the appellant was, immediately before the proceedings, of the rank of superintendent, a retired constable who at the time of his retirement was of that rank, and
      (ii) in any other case a retired constable who at the time of his retirement was of the rank of chief inspector or below.".

DEFINITIONS
"constable": s.51(1) of the 1967 Act, as amended by s.63(9)(a).
"prescribe": s.51(1) of the 1967 Act.
"rank": s.51(1) of the 1967 Act.

GENERAL NOTE
Section 55(2) above substitutes a new Sched. 3 to the 1967 Act. The present Schedule sets out the new Sched. 3, detailing the rule governing the conduct of the appeals process provided for under s.55(1). The original Sched. 3, read in conjunction with the original s.30 of the 1967 Act, provided a procedure whereby an officer dealt with for an offence against discipline could appeal to the Secretary of State. The new Sched. 3 establishes a new police appeals tribunal as a

final appeal body for the more serious types of disposals under the new framework for treating cases of individual misconduct and inefficiency, introduced by ss.52 and 55 above. The new appeals tribunal is, in effect, two different bodies with different memberships. One deals with appeals by senior officers above the rank of superintendent (para. 1) from the decision of the police authority (s.26(2A)(a) of the 1967 Act, as inserted by s.52(3) above), while the other deals with appeals by officers of more junior rank (para. 2) from an original or appellate decision in proceedings internal to a police force (s.30(1) of the 1967 Act, as substituted by s.55 above).

Section 82   SCHEDULE 7

CONTINUING FUNCTIONS OF RECEIVER FOR THE METROPOLITAN POLICE DISTRICT IN RELATION TO
PENSIONS ETC. OF COURT STAFF

1. In this Schedule—
  "court staff" has the same meaning as in section 59 of the 1979 Act,
  "the inner London magistrates' courts committee" has the same meaning as in section 82 of this Act,
  "the Receiver" means the Receiver for the Metropolitan Police District, and
  "responsible authority" has the same meaning as in section 55 of the 1979 Act.
2. The Receiver shall pay out of the metropolitan police fund any superannuation benefits payable in respect of justices' clerks and other officers employed by the committee of magistrates or the inner London magistrates' courts committee under any enactment or instrument applied to those clerks or other officers by regulations having effect in accordance with section 15(9) of the Superannuation (Miscellaneous Provisions) Act 1967, other than benefits payable by the London Residuary Body, and any superannuation contributions and other payments for which the inner London magistrates' courts committee may be liable as their employer under any such enactment or instrument.
3. Nothing in paragraph 2 above shall require the Receiver to incur any expenditure or make any payment which would cause the net cost to him in any year of the matters mentioned in paragraph 4 below to exceed the amount which in relation to that year, is for the time being determined by the Lord Chancellor under paragraph 5(b) below.
4. The Lord Chancellor may out of money provided by Parliament pay to the Receiver grants towards the net cost to the Receiver in any year—
  (a) of the Receiver's functions under paragraph 2 above, and
  (b) of the Receiver's functions corresponding to those of responsible authorities under regulations made, or having effect as if made, under section 7 of the Superannuation Act 1972 with respect to court staff.
5. The amount of any grant under paragraph 4 above towards the net cost to the Receiver in any year of the matters mentioned in that paragraph shall not exceed 80 per cent of whichever of the following is the less, namely—
  (a) that net cost, and
  (b) the amount which, in relation to that year, is for the time being determined for the purposes of this paragraph by the Lord Chancellor.
6. In subsections (5), (6) and (7) of section 59 of the 1979 Act (grants by Lord Chancellor to responsible authorities)—
  (a) references to that section include references to this Schedule, and
  (b) references to the matters mentioned in subsection (1) of that section include references to the matters mentioned in paragraph 4 above.

Section 91   SCHEDULE 8

MAGISTRATES' COURTS: MINOR AND CONSEQUENTIAL AMENDMENTS

PART I

AMENDMENTS OF JUSTICES OF THE PEACE ACT 1979

1.—(1) Section 12 of the 1979 Act (travelling, subsistence and financial loss allowances) shall be amended as follows.
(2) In subsection (5) for paragraph (b) there shall be substituted—
  "(b) in relation to the inner London area—
        (i) the council of the inner London borough which is or includes the petty sessions area for which the justice acts, or
        (ii) where the justice acts for a petty sessions area which is partly included in two or more inner London boroughs, the councils of those boroughs;".

(3) After that subsection there shall be inserted—

"(5A) Where by virtue of subsection (5)(b)(ii) above an allowance under this section is payable jointly by two or more inner London boroughs, the manner in which it is to be borne by each of them shall be determined by agreement between them or, in default of agreement, by the Lord Chancellor."

2.—(1) Section 17 (chairman and deputy chairmen of justices) shall be amended as follows.

(2) In subsection (1), after the words "for the area" there shall be inserted the words "; and any contested election for the purposes of this section shall be held".

(3) In subsection (2), for the words "subsection (3)" there shall be substituted the words "subsections (2A) and (3)".

(4) After subsection (2) there shall be inserted—

"(2A) Subsection (2) above shall not confer on any chairman or deputy chairman of the justices the right to preside in court if, under rules made under the next following section, he is ineligible to preside in court."

3. In section 18 (rules as to chairmanship and size of bench) in subsection (2)—

(a) in paragraph (b), after the words "petty sessions area" there shall be inserted the words "(including any procedure for nominating candidates at any such election)", and

(b) for paragraph (c) there shall be substituted—

"(c) as to courses of instruction to be completed by justices before they may preside in court;

(d) as to the approval of justices, by committees of justices constituted in accordance with the rules, before they may preside in court, as to the justices who may be so approved and as to the courts to which the approval relates; and

(e) as to circumstances in which a justice may preside in court even though requirements imposed by virtue of paragraph (c) or (d) above are not satisfied in relation to him."

4.—(1) Section 19 (general provisions as to magistrates' courts committees) shall be amended as follows.

(2) In subsection (1), for the words from "in relation to" to "this Act or" there shall be substituted the words "as are or may be conferred on them by or under this or any other Act and such other functions relating to matters of an administrative character".

(3) In subsection (2), for the words "subsection (3) below" there shall be substituted the words "section 69 of the Police and Magistrates' Courts Act 1994 and to any order made under subsection (3) of this section before the commencement of that section".

(4) Subsections (3) and (4) shall be omitted.

5. In section 22 (supplementary provisions as to magistrates' courts committees), in subsection (3) for the words "section 20" there shall be substituted the words "section 21".

6.—(1) Section 23 (powers and duties of committee as to petty sessional divisions) shall be amended as follows.

(2) In subsection (1)—

(a) the words from "acting" to "boroughs" shall cease to have effect, and

(b) for the words "the county, district or borough" there shall be substituted the words "their area".

(3) In subsection (2) for the words "the county, district or borough, as the case may be" there shall be substituted the words "their area".

(4) In subsection (4) for the words "a non-metropolitan county or metropolitan district or any of the outer London boroughs", in both places where they occur, there shall be substituted the words "an area".

7.—(1) Section 24 (procedure relating to section 23) shall be amended as follows).

(2) In subsection (1)(a)—

(a) for the words "council of the" there shall be substituted the words "council of every",

(b) the word "outer" shall be omitted, and

(c) for the word "concerned" there shall be substituted the words "which includes all or part of the area".

(3) In subsection (2)—

(a) for the words "council of the" there shall be substituted the words "council of every",

(b) the word "outer" shall be omitted, and

(c) for the word "concerned" there shall be substituted the words "which includes all or part of the area".

(4) In subsection (5)—

(a) the words "in a non-metropolitan county, metropolitan district or outer London borough" shall be omitted, and

(b) at the end there shall be inserted the words "or by section 69 of the Police and Magistrates' Courts Act 1994".

8.—(1) Section 24A (alteration of names of petty sessions areas outside inner London area) shall be amended as follows.

(2) In subsection (1) the words "for an area mentioned in section 19(2) above other than the City of London" shall be omitted.

(3) After subsection (2) there shall be inserted—

"(2A) Nothing in this section shall enable the name of the petty sessions area consisting of the City of London to be changed."

9. In section 24B (procedure relating to section 24A), for the words "outer London borough" in subsections (1)(a) and (2) there shall be substituted the words "London borough".

10.—(1) Section 26 (qualifications for appointment as justices' clerk) shall be amended as follows.

(2) In subsection (1) the words "of any class or description" and, in paragraph (a), the words from "and is within" to "that class or description" shall be omitted.

(3) For subsection (3) there shall be substituted—

"(3) A person not having the qualification which is required by subsection (1)(a) above may be appointed as justices' clerk if at the time of the appointment he is a barrister or solicitor and has served for not less than five years as assistant to a justices' clerk."

(4) Subsections (2), (4) and (5) shall be omitted.

11.—(1) Section 27 (conditions of service and staff of justices' clerks) shall be amended as follows.

(2) Subsections (1) to (5) and (7) and (9) shall be omitted.

(3) For subsection (6) there shall be substituted—

"(6) A magistrates' courts committee may employ staff on such terms as they think fit."

(4) At the end of subsection (8) there shall be added the words "or approved by the Lord Chancellor in accordance with the rules".

12. In section 28 (general powers and duties of justices' clerks), in subsection (1A), paragraphs (b) and (c) shall be omitted.

13. In section 30 (person acting as substitute clerk to justices), in subsection (1) the words "outside the inner London area" shall be omitted.

14. In section 32 (allocation and sittings of metropolitan stipendiary magistrates), in subsection (1), for the words "constituted under section 36 of this Act" there shall be substituted the words "of the inner London area".

15. After section 34A of the 1979 Act there shall be inserted—

"Justices' clerks for youth courts and family proceedings courts

Appointment of justices' clerks for youth courts and family proceedings courts

34B.—(1) The inner London magistrates' courts committee shall appoint one or more justices' clerks for the youth courts and family proceedings courts for the metropolitan area.

(2) Subsections (2) to (4), (5)(b), (6) and (7) of section 25 of this Act have effect in relation to any justices' clerk appointed under subsection (1) above as they have effect in relation to a justices' clerk for a petty sessions area, but with the substitution for any reference to the magistrates for a petty sessions area of a reference to the justices of the peace who are members of the youth court panel for the metropolitan area or (as the case may be) of a family panel for that area, other than any such justice whose name is for the time being entered on the supplemental list.

(3) In this section—

"the inner London magistrates' courts committee" means the magistrates' courts committee for an area consisting of or including the whole of the inner London area or, if there is no such committee, all the magistrates courts' committees for areas which consist of or include any part of the inner London area acting jointly; and

"the metropolitan area" means the inner London area and the City of London."

16. Section 36 (petty sessional divisions in inner London area) and section 36A (alteration of names of petty sessions area in inner London area) shall be omitted.

17. In section 42 (no petty sessional divisions in the City) for the words "section 41 above" there shall be substituted the words "this Act".

18.—(1) Section 53 (indemnification of justices and justices' clerks) shall be amended as follows.

(2) In subsection (3), in paragraph (b), for the words "the local authority" there shall be substituted the words "any paying authority".

(3) After subsection (3) there shall be inserted—

"(3A) Where there are two or more paying authorities in relation to any justice or justices' clerk, any question as to the extent to which the funds required to indemnify him are to be provided by each authority shall be determined by agreement between those authorities and the magistrates' courts committee concerned or, in default of such agreement, shall be determined by the Lord Chancellor."

(4) In subsection (4) for the words "this section" there shall be substituted the words "subsection (3) above".

(5) For subsection (5) there shall be substituted—

"(5) In this section—

"justices' clerk" includes any person appointed by a magistrates' courts committee to assist a justices' clerk,

"local funds", in relation to a justice or justices' clerk, means funds out of which the expenses of the magistrates' courts committee for the area for which he acted at the material time are payable, and

"paying authority", in relation to a justice or justices' clerk, means any authority which is a paying authority for the purposes of section 55 of this Act in relation to the magistrates' courts committee for the area for which he acted at the material time."

19.—(1) Section 59 (grants by Lord Chancellor to responsible authorities) shall be amended as follows.

(2) In subsection (1)—

(a) in paragraph (b) after the word "7" there shall be inserted the words "or 24", and

(b) for the word "and" immediately following that paragraph there shall be substituted—

"(bb) of their functions under any regulations having effect by virtue of paragraph 13(1) of Schedule 1 to this Act; and".

(3) For subsection (8) there shall be substituted—

"(8) In this section—

"court staff" means justices' chief executives, justices' clerks and staff of magistrates' courts committees, and

"responsible authority" has the same meaning as in section 55 of this Act."

20. In section 62 (defaults of justices' clerks and their staffs), in subsection (1), for the words "a person employed to assist a justices' clerk" there shall be substituted the words "any staff of a magistrates' courts committee".

21. In section 63 (courses of instruction), in subsection (5), for the words "and their staffs" there shall be substituted the words "and for staff of magistrates' courts committees".

22. In section 70 (interpretation), for the definition of "magistrate" there shall be substituted—

" 'magistrate'—

(a) in relation to a commission area, means a justice of the peace for the commission area, other than a justice whose name is for the time being entered in the supplemental list,

(b) in relation to a part of a commission area, means a person who (in accordance with paragraph (a) of this definition) is a magistrate for that area and ordinarily acts in and for that part of it, and

(c) in relation to a magistrates' courts committee area, means a person who (in accordance with paragraphs (a) and (b) of this definition) is a magistrate for that area or any part of that area;

'magistrates' courts committee area' means the area to which a magistrates' courts committee relates;".

23. In Schedule 1, in paragraph 17 (saving for superannuation provisions), for the words "55 to 58" there shall be substituted the words "55 and 56".

PART II

AMENDMENTS OF OTHER ENACTMENTS

London Building Acts (Amendment) Act 1939

24. In section 151 of the London Building Acts (Amendment) Act 1939 (Crown exemptions), in subsection (1)(bb) the words from "the magistrates' courts" to "City of London)" shall be omitted and for the words "that area" in the second place where they occur there shall be substituted the words "the inner London area within the meaning of the Justices of the Peace Act 1979".

Superannuation (Miscellaneous Provisions) Act 1967

25. In section 15 of the Superannuation (Miscellaneous Provisions) Act 1967 (superannuation of metropolitan civil staffs), in subsection (1)(a)(ii), for the words from "or other officer" to "that area" there shall be substituted the words ", as a justices' chief executive for that area or as staff of the magistrates' courts committee for that area".

Pensions (Increase) Act 1971

26. In Schedule 2 to the Pensions (Increase) Act 1971 (list of official pensions for the purposes of that Act), in paragraph 47, at the end of paragraph (b) there shall be added the words—
"or as staff of such a committee; or
(c) service as a justices' chief executive."

27. In Schedule 6 to that Act (employments relevant to section 13(2) of that Act), in paragraph (d) after the words "for that area" there shall be inserted the words "or by any magistrates' courts committee whose area includes all or part of that area".

Juries Act 1974

28. In Schedule 1 to the Juries Act 1974, in Group B of Part I (persons ineligible) for the entry beginning "Justices' clerks" there shall be substituted—
"Justices' chief executives, justices' clerks and justices' clerks' assistants."

Domestic Proceedings and Magistrates' Courts Act 1978

29. In section 30 of the Domestic Proceedings and Magistrates' Courts Act 1978 (provisions as to jurisdiction and procedure), in subsection (1) for the words "the committee of magistrates' " there shall be substituted the words "a magistrates' courts committee".

Magistrates' Courts Act 1980

30. In section 70 of the Magistrates' Courts Act 1980 (jurisdiction of magistrates' courts in inner London for domestic proceedings), for the words "committee of magistrates" in subsections (1) and (2) there shall be substituted the words "magistrates' courts committee whose area consists of or includes that petty sessions area".

31. In section 145 of that Act, subsection (1)(d) (by virtue of which rules may make provision as to the extent to which a justices' clerk may engage in practice as a legal representative) shall be omitted.

Road Traffic Offenders Act 1988

32. In section 82 of the Road Traffic Offenders Act 1988 (accounting for fixed penalties in England and Wales), for subsection (2) there shall be substituted—
"(2) Where, in England and Wales, a justices' clerk for a petty sessions area comprised in the area of one magistrates' courts committee ("the first committee") discharges functions in connection with a fixed penalty for an offence alleged to have been committed in a petty sessions area comprised in the area of another magistrates' courts committee ("the second committee")—
(a) the paying authority or authorities in relation to the second committee must make to the paying authority or authorities in relation to the first committee such payment in connection with the discharge of those functions as may be agreed between all the paying authorities concerned or, in default of such agreement, as may be determined by the Lord Chancellor, and
(b) any such payment between paying authorities shall be taken into account in determining for the purposes of section 59 of the Justices of the Peace Act 1979 the net cost to the responsible authorities of the functions referred to in subsection (1) of that section.
(2A) In subsection (2) above "paying authority" and "responsible authority" have the same meaning as in section 55 of the Justices of the Peace Act 1979."

Criminal Justice Act 1991

33.—(1) Section 76 of the Criminal Justice Act 1991 (provision of courts security officers) shall be amended as follows.

(2) In subsections (1)(b) and (2), for the words "responsible authority" there shall be substituted the words "paying authority or authorities".

(3) In subsection (3)—
(a) the words from "in relation to" to "inner London area" shall be omitted, and
(b) for the words "responsible authority" there shall be substituted the words "paying authority or authorities".

(4) In subsection (4), for the words from "in relation to" to "responsible authority" there shall be substituted the words "any paying authority".

(5) Subsection (5) shall be omitted.

(6) For subsection (6) there shall be substituted—

"(6) In this section—

'the committee', in relation to a petty sessions area, means the magistrates' courts committee whose area consists of or includes that petty sessions area, and

'paying authority', in relation to a committee, has the same meaning as in section 55 of the 1979 Act."

34. In section 77 of that Act (powers and duties of court security officers), in subsection (5)—

(a) in paragraph (a), for the words "chief clerk" there shall be substituted the words "justices' chief executive", and

(b) in paragraph (b), for the words from "employed to" to "by him" there shall be substituted the words "of the magistrates' courts committee authorised by such a justices' chief executive or clerk".

Local Government Finance Act 1992

35. In section 46 of the Local Government Finance Act 1992 (special items for purposes of section 45), in subsection (2)(d) for the words from "the magistrates' courts" to "that area" there shall be substituted the words "the probation service in the inner London area or the functions referred to in paragraph 4 of Schedule 7 to the Police and Magistrates' Courts Act 1994".

Section 93   SCHEDULE 9

REPEALS

PART I

POLICE

Chapter	Short Title	Extent of repeal
19 & 20 Vict. c. 2.	The Metropolitan Police Act 1856.	In section 2 the word "six" and the words "and upon every vacancy" onwards.
49 & 50 Vict. c. 38.	The Riot (Damages) Act 1886.	In section 9, paragraph (a) of the definition of "compensation authority".
54 & 55 Vict. c. 43.	The Forged Transfers Act 1891.	In section 2, in paragraph (ab) of the definition of "local authority" the words "a combined police authority or".
2 Edw. 7 c. 28.	The Licensing Act 1902.	In section 6(1) the words "(within the meaning of the Police Act 1890)".
9 & 10 Geo. 6 c. 17.	The Police (Overseas Service) Act 1945.	Section 2(1), (1A) and (2). Section 3(1) and (2).
9 & 10 Geo. 6. c. 18.	The Statutory Orders (Special Procedure) Act 1945.	In section 11(1), in paragraph (aa) of the definition of "local authority" the words "a combined police authority or".
12, 13 & 14 Geo. 6 c. 5.	The Civil Defence Act 1948.	In section 9(1), in paragraph (aa) of the definition of "local authority" the words "a combined police authority or".
1963 c. 18.	The Stock Transfer Act 1963.	In section 4(1), in paragraph (aa) of the definition of "local authority" the words "a combined police authority or".
1964 c. 48.	The Police Act 1964.	Section 6A. In section 7(1) the words ", deputy chief constable". Section 9. In section 12, in subsections (1) and (2) the words "in writing". In section 17(1) the words "and subject to the approval of the police authority as to numbers". Sections 22, 23, and 24. Section 25(5). In section 26(1) the words "and to the county fund" and the words "and to the general fund" onwards. In section 27, the definition of "amalgamation scheme", "constituent area", "constituent authority", "local fund" and "officer".

Chapter	Short Title	Extent of repeal
		In section 29(2) the words "or deputy".
		In section 29(4) the words "or deputy".
		In section 33(5) the words "and may" onwards.
		Section 43(1) to (3).
		In section 43(5) the words "and "police regulations" " onwards.
		In section 53(1) the words "or to commit breaches of discipline".
		Section 58(6).
		In section 60(1) the words "(other than orders on appeals under section 37)".
		In section 60(2) the words "(other than such orders as aforesaid)".
		Schedules 3, 4 and 8.
		In Schedule 9, the entry relating to the Police (Overseas Service) Act 1945.
1965 c. 12.	The Industrial and Provident Societies Act 1965.	In section 31(a)(ia) the words "a combined police authority or".
1965 c. 63.	The Public Works Loans Act 1965.	In section 2(1)(a)(ia) the words "a combined police authority or".
1967 c. 77.	The Police (Scotland) Act 1967.	In section 6(2), the words "a deputy chief constable".
		In section 7(1), the words "deputy chief constable", and ", chief superintendent and".
		Section 7(2).
		In section 8(1), the words "and subject to the approval of the police authority and the Secretary of State as to numbers".
		In section 14(1), the words "(whether by the appointment of temporary constables or otherwise)".
		In section 24(3) the words from "and the expression" onwards.
		In section 26, in subsection (2)(d), the words "or temporary"; and subsection (7).
		In section 31, in each of subsections (2) and (4), the words "or deputy".
		Section 38(1) to (3).
		In section 38(5), the words from ""police regulations"" onwards.
		In section 42(1), the words "or to commit breaches of discipline".
		In section 51(1), the definitions of "regular constable", "special constable" and "temporary constable".
		In Schedule 2, paragraph 2.
		In Schedule 4, the entry relating to the Police (Overseas Service) Act 1945.
1968 c.13.	The National Loans Act 1968.	In Schedule 4, in paragraph 1(a)(ia) the words "a combined police authority or".
1969 c. 51.	The Development of Tourism Act 1969.	In section 14(2)(a)(ia) the words "a combined police authority or".
1969 c. 63.	The Police Act 1969.	Section 2.
1971 c. 23.	The Courts Act 1971.	Section 53(5).
		In section 53(6) the words "or subsection (5)".
		In section 53(7) the words "and (b) any amalgamation" onwards.

Chapter	Short Title	Extent of repeal
1971 c. 56.	The Pensions (Increase) Act 1971.	In Schedule 3, in paragraph 6(1)(a)(ia) the words "a combined police authority or".
1972 c. 70.	The Local Government Act 1972.	Section 101(9)(c). In section 107(1)(b) the words "104 and". Section 107(9) and (10). In section 168(5)(aa) the words "a combined police authority or". In section 196, subsections (2) to (4), (6) and (9).
1976 c. 35.	The Police Pensions Act 1976.	In Schedule 2, paragraph 1, in paragraph 5 the words "43(1) and" and in paragraph 6 the words from "1948" to "in both".
1980 c. 10.	The Police Negotiating Board Act 1980.	In section 1(1) the word "and" at the end of paragraph (a).
1980 c. 63.	The Overseas Development and Co-operation Act 1980.	Section 11.
1980 c. 65.	The Local Government, Planning and Land Act 1980.	In section 2(1), in paragraph (j) the words from "a police committee" to "in Scotland", and in paragraph (k) the words from "a combined" to "in Scotland".
1980 c. 66.	The Highways Act 1980.	In Schedule 6, in paragraph 3(3)(a)(ia) the words "a combined police authority or".
1981 c. 64.	The New Towns Act 1981.	In section 80(1), in paragraph (aa) of the definition of "local authority" the words "a combined police authority or".
1981 c. 67.	The Acquisition of Land Act 1981.	In section 7(l), in paragraph (aa) of the definition of "local authority" the words "a combined police authority or". In Schedule 4, paragraph 13.
1982 c. 32.	The Local Government Finance Act 1982.	In Schedule 5, paragraph 2.
1982 c. 36.	The Aviation Security Act 1982.	In section 30(3)(c) the words "or, if that area is a county, to employment by the police authority or the county council".
1984 c. 27.	The Road Traffic Regulation Act 1984.	Section 97(2).
1984 c. 60.	The Police and Criminal Evidence Act 1984.	Section 67(8). Section 85(8). In section 90(3), paragraph (ii) and the word "and" immediately preceding it. In section 90(4), paragraph (b) and the word "and" immediately preceding it. Section 90(6) and (8). Sections 91 and 92. Section 94. Section 97(4). In section 99(2), in paragraph (k) the words "other than" onwards. Sections 101 and 103. Section 104(l) and (2). In section 105, in subsection (4) the words from "affecting" to "charges" and the words "and are not governed by section 104 above". Section 108(2) and (3). In section 108(6) the words "section 58(2) of the Police Act 1964 and" and the words "both of".

Chapter	Short Title	Extent of repeal
		In Schedule 4, in paragraph 11, sub-paragraph (a)(ii) and sub-paragraph (b)(iii) and the word "or" immediately preceding it.
		In Schedule 6, paragraphs 14 and 15.
1985 c. 43.	The Local Government (Access to Information) Act 1985.	In Schedule 2, paragraph 5.
1985 c. 51.	The Local Government Act 1985.	Sections 24 and 25.
		In section 29(1) the words ", joint magistrates' committee or magistrates' courts committee" and the words "or committee".
		In section 29(3) the words "and any alteration" onwards.
		In section 30(1) the words ", joint magistrates' committee and magistrates' courts committee".
		In section 30(2), paragraph (c) and the word "and" immediately preceding it.
		Section 32(8).
		In section 36 the words ", joint magistrates' committee or magistrates' courts committee", and the words "from a constituent council" in the second place where they occur.
		In section 37 the word "police,".
		In section 42, subsections (1)(a) and (2)(a), and in subsection (3) the word "police,".
		In the tables in Parts II to IV of Schedule 10, in column 1 the words "Joint magistrates' committee" and column 2.
		In the table in Part V of Schedule 10, in column 1 the words "Magistrates:" onwards and column 2.
		In the tables in Parts VI and VII of Schedule 10, in column 1 the words "Joint magistrates' committee" and column 2.
		In Schedule 11, paragraph 1.
1985 c. 68.	The Housing Act 1985.	In section 4(e) the words "sections 438, 441, 442, 443, 458, 460(3)".
1986 c. 32.	The Drug Trafficking Offences Act 1986.	Section 35.
1986 c. 63.	The Housing and Planning Act 1986.	In Schedule 5, paragraph 20.
1988 c. 1.	The Income and Corporation Taxes Act 1988.	In section 842A(2)(e).
1988 c. 41.	The Local Government Finance Act 1988.	In section 111(2), paragraphs (f) and (1).
1989 c. 42.	The Local Government and Housing Act 1989.	Section 5(4)(a).
		Section 13(4)(a).
		In section 21(1)(i) the word "police,".
		In section 39(1)(g) the word "police,".
		In section 67(3)(k) the word "police,".
		Section 152(1)(f).
		In section 152(2), paragraph (g) and the word "police," in paragraph (i).
		In Schedule 1, paragraph 2(1)(c).
1990 c. 8.	The Town and Country Planning Act 1990.	In section 336(1), in paragraph (aa) of the definition of "local authority" the words "a combined police authority or".
1990 c. 41.	The Courts and Legal Services Act 1990.	In Schedule 10, paragraph 22.

Chapter	Short Title	Extent of repeal
1992 c. 14.	The Local Government Finance Act 1992.	In section 19(3), paragraph (d), the word "and" at the end of paragraph (e), and paragraph (f). In section 46, subsections (2)(a) and (3)(a).
1992 c. 19.	The Local Government Act 1992.	In section 14(5), the word "and" at the end of paragraph (c). In section 18, subsections (2) and (4)(a). In Schedule 3, paragraphs 3, 4 and 5.
1993 c. 25.	The Local Government (Overseas Assistance) Act 1993.	In section 1(10), paragraph (b) and in paragraph (d) the word "police".
1994 c. 19.	The Local Government (Wales) Act 1994.	Section 24.

Act of the Parliament of Northern Ireland

Chapter	Short Title	Extent of repeal
1970 c. 9 (N.I.).	The Police Act (Northern Ireland) 1970.	Section 10(5). Section 25(5). Section 26(3).

PART II

MAGISTRATES' COURTS

Chapter	Short Title	Extent of repeal
60 & 61 Vict. c. 26.	The Metropolitan Police Courts Act 1897.	Sections 3, 4, 7 and 11.
2 & 3 Geo. 6 c. xcvii.	The London Building Acts (Amendment) Act 1939.	In section 151(1)(bb) the words from "the magistrates' courts" to "City of London)".
14 & 15 Geo. 6 c. 65.	The Reserve and Auxiliary Forces (Protection of Civil Interests) Act 1951.	In section 48 the words "or justices' clerk".
7 & 8 Eliz. 2 c. 45.	The Metropolitan Magistrates' Court Act 1959.	In section 3(1) the words "and the metropolitan magistrates' courts". In section 4(2) the words "of the metropolitan magistrates' courts".
1964 c. 42.	The Administration of Justice Act 1964.	In Schedule 3, in part II, paragraph 29.
1968 c. 65.	The Gaming Act 1968.	In Schedule 2, in paragraph 2(2), in the definition of "the clerk to the licensing authority", the words from "(or, in the case" to "committee of magistrates)".
1974 c. 23.	The Juries Act 1974.	In Schedule 1, in Group B of Part I, the words from "Clerks and other officers" to magistrates courts administration)".
1979 c. 55.	The Justices of the Peace Act 1979.	In section 12(7), the words from "which" onwards. In section 18(2), the word "and" at the end of paragraph (b). Section 19(3) and (4). In section 21(1), the words "(except as provided by subsection (2) below)".

Chapter	Short Title	Extent of repeal
		Section 22(2).
		In section 23, in subsection (1) the words from "acting" to "boroughs".
		In section 24, in subsections (1)(a) and (2), the word "outer" and in subsection (5) the words "in a non-metropolitan county, metropolitan district or outer London borough".
		In section 24A(1), the words from "for an area" to "City of London".
		In section 26, in subsection (1) the words "of any class or description" and, in paragraph (a), the words from "and is within" to "that class or description" and subsections (2), (4) and (5).
		In section 27, subsections (1) to (5) and (7) and (9).
		Section 28(1A)(b) and (c).
		In section 30(1), the words "outside the inner London area".
		Sections 35 to 38.
		Sections 53(6).
		Sections 57 and 58.
		In section 59(1)(b), the words "or, in the case of the Receiver, his corresponding functions".
		In section 63, subsection (2) and, in subsection (4), the words "or subsection (2)" and "or committee of magistrates".
		In section 70, the definitions of "joint committee area" and "the Receiver".
1980 c. 43.	The Magistrates' Courts Act 1980.	Section 68(7).
		Section 141(3).
		Section 145(1)(d).
1985 c. 51.	The Local Government Act 1985.	Section 12(4)(a), (5), (6), (8)(c) and (9).
1988 c. 33.	The Criminal Justice Act 1988.	Sections 164(3) and 165.
1990 c. 41.	The Courts and Legal Services Act 1990.	Section 10(3) to (5).
		In Schedule 18, paragraph 25(4)(c).
1991 c. 53.	The Criminal Justice Act 1991.	In section 76, in subsection (3), the words from "in relation to" to "inner London area" and subsection (5).
		Section 79.
		Section 93(1) and (2).
		In Schedule 11, in paragraph 40(2)(k), the words "35(3), 37(1)" and paragraph 41(2)(c).
1992 c. 6.	The Social Security (Consequential Provisions) Act 1992.	In Schedule 2, paragraph 58.
1993 c. 48.	The Pension Schemes Act 1993.	In Schedule 8, paragraph 12.

INDEX

References are to sections and Schedules

COMMENCEMENT, 94

COMPLAINTS AGAINST POLICE OFFICER,
Complaints Authority,
    powers of, 36
    reference to, 34
disciplinary provisions repealed, 37
steps to be taken after investigation of complaint, 35

DISCIPLINARY APPEALS, 19, SCHED. 3

EXTENT, 96

INSPECTORS OF CONSTABULARY,
appointment and functions, 20
assistant inspectors, 22
reports from, 21
staff officers, 22

MAGISTRATES' COURTS,
administrative and financial arrangements,
    accounts and audit, 85
    local authorities,
        duties of, 83
        land of, appropriated to courts purposes, 84
Audit Commission, studies by, 89
committees,
    areas, alteration of, 69
    constitution of, 70
        regulations as to, 71
    powers and duties, 73
        failure to discharge duties: Lord Chancellor's default powers, 88
    reports and plans, 74
    supplementary provisions, 72
inner London area,
    committees, 79
    division of work, 81
    justices' clerks, organisation of, 80
inspectors of magistrates' courts service,
    appointment of, 86
    powers of, 87
interpretation, 92
justices' chief executive,
    appointment of, 75
    contract of service, 77
    functions of, 75
    pensions, 82
justices' clerks,
    appointment and removal of, 76
    contracts of service, 77

MAGISTRATES' COURTS—*cont.*
justices' clerks—*cont.*
    independence of, 78
    pension, 82
minor and consequential amendments, 91,
    Sched. 8
regulations under Justices of the Peace Act
    1979, 90

METROPOLITAN POLICE,
assistant commissioners, 41

POLICE AREAS,
names of, 1, Sched. 1
objection to alterations, 14
power to alter by order, 14
Welsh, on local government reorganisation,
    14, 40

POLICE AUTHORITIES,
advice and assistance to international
    organisations, 13
appointment of officers, 11
civilian employees, 10
co-operation in implementing this Act, 95
codes of practice, 15
directions to, following adverse reports, 15
financial provisions,
    administration, 31
    minimum budget, directions as to, 29
    new authorities: initial financing, 32
    precepts, 27
        approval of decisions about, 28
    revenue accounts and capital finance, 30
functions of, 4
    annual reports, 4
    general functions, 4
    local policing objectives, 4
    local policing plans, 4
gifts and loans to, 25
grants to,
    capital expenditure, for, 15
    financial provisions,
        valuation of past, 33
    generally, 17
    local authorities, by, 24
    national security, for safeguarding, 17
interpretation, 47
legislative provisions, applicability of, 45
local authorities, treated as, 43, Sched. 4
maintenance of, 2
membership of, 3, Sched. 2
minor and consequential amendments, 44,
    Sched. 5
police fund, 8
questions by local councillors, 12
reduction in size of, 3, Sched. 2

POLICE AUTHORITIES—*cont.*
  reports from, 16
  setting objectives for, 15
    performance targets, 15
  supply of goods and services, 9
POLICE FORCES,
  appeals against dismissal, 19, Sched. 3
  chief constables,
    appointment and removal, 5
    deputy and assistant chief constables, 6
  general functions, 5
  co-operation in implementing this Act, 95
  common services, 23
  Firearms Act 1968: application to civilian
    staff, 42
  maintenance of, 2
  officers engaged on service outside their
    force, 26
  officers other than chief, deputy and assist-
    ant chief constables, 7
  regulations for, 18
POLICE (NORTHERN IRELAND),
  minor and consequential amendments, 68
  regulations for administration of reserve
    constables, 67
  of RUC, 66
POLICE (SCOTLAND)
  advice and assistance to international
    organisations, 50
  appeals against dismissal etc., 55, Sched. 6
  chief consables, annual reports, 51

POLICE (SCOTLAND)—*cont.*
  civilian employees, 49
  common services, 59
  complaints against constables, 61
  constables engaged on service outside their
    force, 60
  criminal statistics, transmission of, 62
  delegation of functions of police authority,
    64
  deputy and assistant chief constables, 48
  directions to police authorities, 54
  establishment of police forces, 47
  fixed term appointments, 53
  inspectors of constabulary,
    assistant inspectors and staff officers to,
      58
    duty of, 57
  interpretation, 65
  minor amendments, 63
  national security, expenditure on safe-
    guarding, 56
  regulation of police forces, 52

REPEALS, 93, Sched. 9

SHORT TITLE, 97

TRANSITIONAL PROVISIONS, 94

EDUCATION ACT 1994*

(1994 c.30)

ARRANGEMENT OF SECTIONS

PART I

TEACHER TRAINING

The Teacher Training Agency

SECT.
1. The Teacher Training Agency.
2. Membership, &c. of the agency.

Funding

3. The funding agencies.
4. Qualifying activities and eligible institutions.
5. Grants, loans and other payments.
6. Provisions supplementary to s.5.
7. Grants to the funding agencies.
8. Directions by the Secretary of State.
9. Joint exercise of functions.
10. Efficiency studies.
11. Research.

Supplementary provisions

12. Power of schools to provide courses of initial teacher training.
13. Grants for teacher training.
14. Qualification of teachers, &c.
15. Duty to provide information, &c.
16. Additional, supplementary and ancillary functions.
17. The Teaching as a Career Unit: transfer of property and staff.
18. Power to reimburse certain payments to persons formerly employed in teacher training.
19. Interpretation.

PART II

STUDENTS' UNIONS

20. Meaning of "students' union".
21. Establishments to which Part II applies.
22. Requirements to be observed in relation to students' unions.

PART III

GENERAL PROVISIONS

23. Orders and directions.
24. Consequential amendments.
25. Extent.
26. Commencement.
27. Short title and citation.

SCHEDULES:
Schedule 1—The Teacher Training Agency.
Schedule 2—Consequential amendments.

An Act to make provision about teacher training and related matters; to make provision with respect to the conduct of students' unions; and for connected purposes. [21st July 1994]

---

* Annotations by William Hinds, Lecturer in Law, University of Leeds.

PARLIAMENTARY DEBATES
Hansard, H.L. Vol. 550, col. 819; Vol. 552, cols. 1540, 1601; Vol. 553, cols. 11, 589, 746, 836, 855, 917, 1388; Vol. 557, col. 55; H.C. Vol. 242, col. 597; Vol. 246, col. 334.
The Bill was discussed in Standing Committee E between May 10, 1994 and June 21, 1994.

INTRODUCTION AND GENERAL NOTE
The Education Act 1994 is significantly shorter than its immediate predecessor, the Education Act 1993 and the other major measures of recent years, the Further and Higher Education Act 1992 and the Education Reform Act 1988. It was described by the Secretary of State as: "the last pieces of the jigsaw" based on "the principles driving our reform—choice, democracy and accountability" (Mr J. Patten, *Hansard*, H.C. Vol. 242, col. 609). The Act deals with two areas only, teacher training and student unions. Prior to the presentation of the Bill to Parliament, two separate consultation papers dealing with these topics had been issued and the Bill was substantially based on the proposals in those papers. The paper dealing with teacher training, issued in September 1993, proposed institutional changes for funding teacher training and the process of accreditation of courses. A Teacher Training Agency would be established to administer funding in place of the Higher Education Funding Council for England and (to a limited extent) the Secretary of State himself. Two options were proposed in relation to accreditation, one involving the new agency but neither was, in the event, adopted. It was also proposed that the new agency would have a promotional and advisory role, replacing the existing Teaching as a Career Unit.

The Bill which was presented to Parliament following the consultation process provided for the creation of the new Teacher Training Agency as a funding agency for teacher training. It was also given responsibility for funding educational studies generally, including research into educational issues, a proposal which was subsequently abandoned. In addition the agency would accredit institutions which provided courses, successful completion of which would lead to qualified teacher status. One aspect of the Bill which proved politically most controversial was that schools, or consortia of schools, could be accredited institutions for this purpose even though they were not involved with any higher education institution. An amendment compelling such involvement was passed, against the Government's wishes, by the House of Lords but was then removed by the House of Commons. The Bill also proposed, as envisaged by the consultation paper, that the Teacher Training Agency would have a promotional and information distributing role.

Although the Bill was substantially amended during its parliamentary passage, the Act provides for the Teacher Training Agency to be established with three functions: funding teacher training; accrediting institutions providing teacher training; and promoting teaching as a career. The Agency has only a limited role in relation to research; it has a power to commission or carry out research but the main channel for funding educational research will continue to be the higher education funding councils. The Act gives effect to the central policy aim of allowing schools to undertake programmes of teacher training and the Teacher Training Agency is directed to have regard to the desirability of establishing and maintaining an appropriate balance between such courses and others.

Different arrangements are established for Wales. Here, for reasons of size, no new body is established and the Higher Education Funding Council for Wales will act as the funding body for teacher training and accredit institutions providing teacher training. In exercising its funding and accreditation functions the Council will operate in parallel to the Teacher Training Agency.

Part II of the original Bill was also based on proposals in a consultation paper, issued in July 1993, following a statement by the Secretary of State to the House of Commons on the reform of student unions. The proposals would have placed considerable limitations on the lawful activities of student unions employing public funds, which would be confined to a core area, anything beyond which would need to be financed from other sources. In addition a series of requirements for the general conduct of students' unions would be imposed. The Bill was very heavily criticised at the Second Reading in the House of Lords and the Government subsequently came forward with substantial amendments at Committee stage, with further amendments at later stages of the passage of the Bill through the House of Lords and the House of Commons.

The Act does not seek to regulate the activities which students' unions may undertake but imposes upon higher and further education institutions a duty to ensure that students' unions operate in a fair and democratic manner and are accountable for their finances. It requires institutions to take such steps as are reasonably practicable to secure that students' unions comply with a number of specific requirements. These relate, *inter alia*, to the constitution of unions, requiring them to be written, subject to regular review, to provide for election to major offices by secret ballot of members and to limit the tenure of sabbatical offices. Elections and the financial affairs of unions must be supervised by the institution in question. The financial reports and procedures for allocation of resources to groups or clubs must be fair and made available to students. Procedures relating to affiliation to external organisations are regulated. Complaints procedures must be established for students in relation to dealings with unions. The Act requires that union membership should be voluntary. This was a major policy aim of the Act, which, as well as giving students a right to opt out of union membership, provides that they should not be unfairly disadvantaged as a result of having done so and should have access to a complaints procedure if they claim that they have been. The right to opt out and any arrangements made for such students must be brought to the attention of students and potential students. Institutions are also required to issue a code of practice regarding compliance with the requirements of the Act. The provisions relating to students' unions apply to Scotland as well as to England and Wales.

The scheme of the Act

The Act is divided into three parts: Pt. I concerns teacher training; Pt. II concerns students' unions and lays down requirements to be observed in relation to them; Pt. III contains general provisions.

Part I: Teacher Training

Sections 1 and 2 and Sched. 1 provide for the establishment, functions, objectives, proceedings and membership of the Teacher Training Agency.

Sections 3 and 4 define the funding agencies for teacher training in England and Wales and the activities and institutions qualifying for funding.

Sections 5 and 6 confer power on the funding agencies to provide funding, deal with the conditions on which it may be provided and factors which the funding agencies should take into account.

Sections 7 and 8 confer power on the Secretary of State to make grants to the funding agencies, the conditions which may be imposed and empower the Secretary of State to give directions to the funding agencies.

Sections 9, 10 and 11 provide for the joint exercise of functions with other funding bodies, the carrying out of efficiency studies and the conduct or commissioning of research.

Section 12 empowers schools or consortia of schools to provide teacher training.

Sections 13 and 14 deal with grants for teacher training, accreditation of institutions and qualification to teach.

Section 15 deals with the provision of information or advice by the Teacher Training Agency, the exchange of information with the other funding agencies and the provision of information to the funding agencies.

Sections 16 and 17 empower the Secretary of State to confer additional, supplementary or ancillary functions upon the funding agencies and to transfer to the Teacher Training Agency the property, rights and liabilities of the Teaching as a Career Unit.

Section 18 confers power upon Higher Education Funding Councils to reimburse payments to certain persons formerly employed in teacher training.

Section 19 is an interpretation section.

Part II: Students' Unions

Sections 20 and 21 define students' unions and the establishments to which the Act applies.

Section 22 lays down requirements to be observed in relation to students' unions.

Part III: General Provisions

Sections 23–27 provide for the making of orders and directions, consequential amendments and the extent, commencement and citation of the Act.

ABBREVIATIONS

The 1944 Act	: The Education Act 1944.
The 1988 Act	: The Education Reform Act 1988.
The 1992 Act	: The Further and Higher Education Act 1992.
The 1993 Act	: The Education Act 1993.
HEFCW	: Higher Education Funding Council for Wales.
OFSTED	: Office for Standards in Education.
The Agency	: Teacher Training Agency.

PART I

TEACHER TRAINING

The Teacher Training Agency

The Teacher Training Agency

1.—(1) There shall be established a body corporate to be known as the Teacher Training Agency to exercise—
  (a) their functions as a funding agency under this Part,
  (b) the function of providing information and advice on teaching as a career, and
  (c) such other functions as may be conferred on them by or under this Part.

(2) The objectives of the agency in exercising their functions shall be—
  (a) to contribute to raising the standards of teaching;
  (b) to promote teaching as a career;
  (c) to improve the quality and efficiency of all routes into the teaching profession;
  (d) to secure the involvement of schools in all courses and programmes for the initial training of school teachers;
and generally to secure that teachers are well fitted and trained to promote the spiritual, moral, social, cultural, mental and physical development of pupils and to prepare pupils for the opportunities, responsibilities and experiences of adult life.

(3) Except where corresponding functions in relation to Wales are conferred on another person or body, the functions of the agency are exercisable in relation to England and Wales generally; but the agency shall not do anything in relation to Wales, or institutions or students in Wales, except at the request of the Secretary of State.

DEFINITIONS
  "funding agency": s.3(1).
  "pupils": s.114(1) of the Education Act 1944; s.14(6) of the Further and Higher Education Act 1992.
  "schools": s.14(5) of the Further and Higher Education Act 1992; s.304(1) of the Education Act 1993.
  "training": s.19(4).

GENERAL NOTE
  The Teacher Training Agency has been created to confer upon a single body functions previously exercised by a number of other bodies. It will have responsibility for funding institutions providing teacher training, previously provided primarily by the Higher Education Funding Council for England. Some funding was being provided, for experimental school-based training, directly by the Secretary of State for Education under his general grant-making powers. It will also have responsibility for accreditation of institutions providing courses of teacher training. Courses were previously accredited by the Secretary of State following recommendations by the Council on the Accreditation of Teacher Education, which is to be wound up. It will also take over the promotional work of the Teaching as a Career Unit, which will also be wound up.

Subs. (1)
  This establishes the Teacher Training Agency as a body corporate to exercise the specific functions conferred upon it by subs. (1)(a) and (b) and other functions conferred upon it by or under Pt. I of the Act. The Agency will be a non-departmental public body responsible to the Secretary of State. Its accounts will be examined by the Comptroller and Auditor General (Sched. 1, para. 16) but it is not proposed to bring it within the jurisdiction of the Parliamentary Commissioner for Administration (Mr T. Boswell, Parliamentary Under-Secretary of State, Standing Committee E, May 24, 1994, col. 218).
  Functions as a funding agency. The Agency will provide funding to institutions providing "qualifying activities"; primarily, but not exclusively, the provision of teacher training. The functions of the Agency in this respect are set out in ss.3–6.

Information and advice on teaching as a career. The Agency will take over the remit in this respect of the Teaching as a Career Unit, which is being wound up. Provision is made in s.16 for the Secretary of State to transfer by order to the Agency the property, rights and liabilities of the unit.

Such other functions. In addition to its functions in relation to funding, the Agency will, when the necessary regulations have been made, have responsibility for the accreditation of institutions providing courses of initial teacher training, successful completion of which will lead to qualified teacher status: this is achieved by s.14(1) and (2). The Agency will also have power to confer licensed teacher status under s.14(3). In addition, the Agency has powers under s.10 to arrange for studies designed to improve economy, efficiency and effectiveness in the management and operations of an institution to which it is giving financial support and, under s.11, the power to carry out or commission research with a view to improving the training of teachers or the standards of teaching. It also has a duty to provide information or advice relating to matters for which they are responsible to the Secretary of State at his request and may do so on their own initiative (see s.15). Power is conferred by s.13 to make grants in relation to teacher training. Section 2(5) and Sched. 1, para. 1 confer a general power to do anything that appears to the Agency to be necessary or expedient for the purpose of, or in connection with, the discharge of their functions and specifically confers powers in relation to the acquisition and disposition of property, the entering into of contracts and also regulates other financial transactions. In addition s.16(1) empowers the Secretary of State to confer or impose additional functions related to their general objectives as defined in subs. (2).

Subs. (2)

This sets out the general objectives that the Agency should pursue in exercising the functions conferred upon it by subs. (1). The general objectives of the Agency are designed as a framework and are deliberately phrased in broad and general terms. It was not thought appropriate to incorporate more specific requirements, for example, in relation to special educational needs. Desirable criteria for courses of initial teacher training were a matter for the Secretary of State to determine and for the Agency to take into account in exercising its functions in relation to accreditation and funding of institutions (Mr T. Boswell, Parliamentary Under-Secretary of State, Standing Committee E, May 19, 1994, col. 131).

Contribute to raising of standards of teaching. It was an assumption in the consultation paper upon which the Act was based that action was necessary to achieve this objective and that the new Agency was an appropriate mechanism to this end.

Promote teaching as a career. Subsection (2)(b) reflects the function imposed on the Agency by subs. (1)(b).

All routes into the teaching profession. One argument for the creation of the Agency was that the existing system was unnecessarily fragmented. The objective in para. (c) is also interrelated with the objective in para. (d).

Securing the involvement of schools. A major policy objective of the Act was the creation of systems for teacher training that were school-based to a greater extent than previously. In particular, schools or groups of schools were to be able to undertake the organisation of their own programmes of teacher training. Power to do so is conferred upon the governing bodies of schools by s.12(1). Provision of such courses by schools is voluntary. The Agency has no power to compel their provision. The objective imposed upon the Agency by subs. (2)(d) is to ensure that all courses of teacher training, by whomsoever provided, involve schools in training programmes and courses.

Generally to secure etc. This was an amendment to the Bill in its original form. Section 1 of the 1988 Act and the Education (Schools) Act 1992 (c. 38), s.2 have broadly comparable provisions and the amendment was designed to ensure that the Agency's approach to its work took account of these factors. The requirement is intended to be both a separate objective and a qualification of the objectives set out in subs. (2)(a) to (d). "The amendment will require the Agency to take account of spiritual, moral and other imperatives in pursuing all of its objectives" (Baroness Blatch, Minister of State, *Hansard*, H.L. Vol. 553, col. 837).

Subs. (3)

The Act establishes separate systems in relation to teacher training for England and Wales. The Agency is to be the funding agency for teacher training courses and programmes in England and will accredit institutions providing teacher training. In Wales the funding and accreditation agency will be the Higher Education Funding Council for Wales. The explanation for this different approach is the smaller number of schools and teacher training institutions in Wales, which would make the creation of a parallel Teacher Training Agency for Wales inappropriate (see Baroness Blatch, Minister of State, *Hansard*, H.L. Vol. 550, col. 820). Subsection (3) makes clear that where functions in relation to Wales are conferred upon another person or body the functions of the Agency are not exercisable in relation to Wales. As well as the principal functions relating to funding and accreditation conferred upon HEFCW, s.10 provides for the commissioning of efficiency studies; s.11 the carrying out of or commissioning of research; and s.16(2) empowers the Secretary of State to confer supplementary functions upon HEFCW. As subs. (3) provides, other functions of the Agency are exercisable in relation to Wales but only at the request of the Secretary of State. There is provision in s.9 for the joint exercise of their functions by the two funding agencies and in s.15(2) for the interchange of information.

Secretary of State. See the note to s.2(1).

Membership, &c. of the agency

2.—(1) The Teacher Training Agency shall consist of between eight and twelve members appointed by the Secretary of State, of whom one shall be so appointed as chairman.

(2) In appointing the members of the agency the Secretary of State shall have regard to the desirability of including persons who appear to him—
  (a) to have experience of, and to have shown capacity in—
      (i) teaching in schools,
      (ii) teaching in higher education (other than training teachers), or
      (iii) training teachers, or
  (b) to have held, and to have shown capacity in, any position carrying responsibility for—
      (i) the provision of education in schools,
      (ii) the provision of higher education (other than the training of teachers), or
      (iii) the training of teachers;
and in appointing such persons he shall have regard to the desirability of their being currently engaged in the provision of, or in carrying responsibility for, such matters.

(3) In considering the appointment of members in accordance with subsection (2) the Secretary of State shall have regard to the desirability of including persons whose relevant experience or responsibility is, or was, in or in relation to—
  (a) institutions of a denominational character, or
  (b) teaching persons with special educational needs.

(4) In appointing the members of the agency the Secretary of State shall also have regard to the desirability of including persons who appear to him to have experience of, and to have shown capacity in, industrial, commercial or financial matters or the practice of any profession.

(5) Schedule 1 has effect with respect to the agency.

DEFINITIONS
"denominational character": s.19(2).
"higher education": s.120(1) of and Sched. 6 to the Education Reform Act 1988; s.90(1) of the Further and Higher Education Act 1992.
"schools": s.14(5) of the Further and Higher Education Act 1992; s.304(1) of the Education Act 1993.
"special educational needs": s.19(3).
"training": s.19(4).

GENERAL NOTE
The size and composition of the Funding Agency is broadly similar to that of the other educational funding agencies, the Further and Higher Education Funding Councils and the Funding Agency for Schools. Members are to be appointed by the Secretary of State with reference, *mutatis mutandis*, to broadly similar criteria, although these are slightly more detailed than in relation to the other agencies. In addition to persons with experience of teaching in schools or higher education, training teachers or responsibility for the provision of these, experience of and capacity in industrial, commercial or financial matters or the practice of a profession is a qualifi-

cation. Specific provision is made for experience in relation to denominational education and special educational needs.

Subs. (1)
The Agency is to be slightly smaller in membership than the Higher Education Funding Council for England, reflecting its more limited functions (see Baroness Blatch, Minister of State, *Hansard*, H.L. Vol. 552, col. 1621). As with those bodies the members will be appointed by the Secretary of State. The appointment of the first Chairman was announced while the Bill was proceeding through Parliament (Standing Committee E, June 14, 1994, col. 225).

Secretary of State. The general rule of interpretation is that Secretary of State means one of Her Majesty's principal Secretaries of State (see the Interpretation Act 1978, Sched. 1). Section 17(4) provides, however, that, unless otherwise defined, expressions in the Act have the same meaning as in the 1944 Act. References to the Secretary of State in the 1994 Act will therefore be to the Secretary of State for Education or the Secretary of State for Wales. See Secretary of State for Education and Science Order 1964 (S.I. 1964 No. 490); Transfer of Functions (Science) Order 1992 (S.I. 1992 No. 1296); Transfer of Functions (Wales) Order 1970 (S.I. 1970 No. 1536); Transfer of Functions (Wales) Order 1978 (S.I. 1978 No. 274).

Subs. (2)
The criteria for appointment are listed in subs. (2). The Secretary of State is to "have regard to the desirability" of appointing persons with the appropriate qualifications so the subsection does not impose an obligation to appoint members who qualify under the listed criteria. It was stressed that members should not be regarded as representing particular interest groups, so that a more prescriptive categorisation of qualifications for membership would not be appropriate.

"[M]embers should be chosen for the personal contribution which they can make and not in any representative capacity. But ... there is a range of areas of experience and expertise to which it would be right to require the Secretary of State to have regard in considering possible members" (Baroness Blatch, Minister of State, *Hansard*, H.L. Vol. 553, col. 871). The subsection contains a rather more detailed list of criteria than the Bill in its original form. Subsection (2)(a) makes clear that experience and capacity in actual teaching in schools or higher education or actual training of teachers is a qualification rather than merely responsibility for the provision of education in schools or higher education. It is clear from *R.* v. *Croydon London Borough Council*, ex p. *Leney* [1987] 85 L.G.R. 466 that "provision of education" is not confined to experience as a teacher but could include experience of educational administration as a school governor. Subsection (2)(b) will allow for educational administration as a separate qualification. Subsection (2)(a)(ii) was an amendment inserted to separate, as qualifications, teaching in higher education generally from training teachers in higher education.

Currently engaged in. This would not exclude persons who have relevant experience but have now retired.

Subs. (3)
Denominational character. This is an amendment to the original Bill which was included to make clear that the interest of denominational institutions would be given due consideration. Concern had been expressed by the Bishop of Guildford that, as a substantial amount of teacher training was provided in such institutions, their interests should be specifically recognised. It should be noted that there is no specific requirement to consult with representatives of denominations prior to appointments as there is in s.3(4) of the 1993 Act.

Special educational needs. This was again an amendment to the Bill as originally drafted intended to give particular emphasis to this area of education.

Subs. (5)
Schedule 1 provides for the appointment of a Chief Officer, tenure of members of the agency, salaries, allowances and pensions. It confers a power to appoint staff, to establish committees and to delegate functions. It provides for the procedure of the Agency, its accounts and imposes a duty to make an annual report. It provides that the Agency shall not be a servant or agent of the Crown and confers certain supplementary powers upon it.

Funding

The funding agencies

3.—(1) Any reference in this Part to a funding agency is—
  (a) in relation to institutions in England, to the Teacher Training Agency, and

(b) in relation to institutions in Wales, to the Higher Education Funding Council for Wales.

(2) The references above to institutions in England and in Wales are to institutions whose activities are carried on, or principally carried on, in England or, as the case may be, in Wales; but both references include the Open University.

Any dispute as to which funding agency any functions are exercisable by shall be determined by the Secretary of State.

(3) The funding agencies shall be responsible for administering funds made available to them by the Secretary of State and others for the purpose of providing financial support for the carrying on by eligible institutions of qualifying activities.

DEFINITIONS
"eligible institutions": s.4(2).
"funding agency": subs. (1).
"Higher Education Funding Council for Wales": s.62(1)(a) of the Further and Higher Education Act 1992.
"qualifying activities": s.4(1).
"Teacher Training Agency": s.1(1).

GENERAL NOTE
This section defines funding agencies as being the Teacher Training Agency and the Higher Education Funding Council for Wales. As noted in relation to s.1(3), different institutions are to be employed for the purpose of funding teacher training in England and Wales. Institutions within the jurisdiction of the respective funding agencies are defined in subs. (2). Any disputes as to which funding agency should exercise particular functions are to be determined by the Secretary of State. The principal function of the funding agencies is defined in subs. (3) which confers upon them responsibility for administering funds made available to them, whether from the Secretary of State or elsewhere, for the purpose of providing financial support for qualifying activities in eligible institutions.

Qualifying activities and eligible institutions

4.—(1) The activities qualifying for funding under this Part ("qualifying activities") are—

(a) the provision of teacher training;

(b) the provision of facilities, and the carrying on of other activities, by eligible institutions which the governing bodies of the institutions consider it necessary or desirable to provide or carry on for the purpose of or in connection with activities within paragraph (a);

(c) the provision by any person of services for the purposes of, or in connection with, such activities.

(2) The institutions eligible for funding under this Part ("eligible institutions") are—

(a) any institution within the higher or further education sector,

(b) any school, and

(c) any other institution or body designated by order of the Secretary of State,

and any partnership or association of eligible institutions, or body established by one or more such institutions, for the purpose of carrying on qualifying activities.

(3) The Secretary of State may by order provide for references in this Part to the governing body of an institution, in relation to an institution which is conducted by a company, to be read as references to the governing body provided for in the instrument of government, or to the company or to both.

(4) In relation to a nursery school which is maintained by a local education authority references in this Part to the governing body shall be construed as references to the authority.

DEFINITIONS
"further education": s.14(1)–(4) of the Further and Higher Education Act 1992.
"higher education": s.90(1) of the Further and Higher Education Act 1992; s.120(1) of and
Sched. 6 to the Education Reform Act 1988.
"institution within the higher or further education sector": s.91(3), (5) of the Further and
Higher Education Act 1992.
"nursery school": s.9(4) of the Education Act 1944.
"school": s.14(5) of the Further and Higher Education Act 1992; s.304(1) of the Education
Act 1993.
"training": s.19(4).

GENERAL NOTE
    This section provides for the activities qualifying for funding under s.5 and defines the insti-
tutions which are entitled to receive funding. Qualifying activities are the provision of teacher
training and ancillary activities and the provision of facilities for the same (subs. (1)). Eligible
institutions are higher and further education institutions, schools and other institutions or
bodies designated by the Secretary of State (subs. (2)). The provision of teacher training by
schools alone was a central policy aim of the Act. Eligibility for funding by the funding agencies
of such courses is provided for in subs. (2) and s.12(1) empowers schools to provide the courses.
Subsection (2)(b) allows other institutions or bodies to be designated as eligible by the Secretary
of State. No criteria are provided for such designation. A Diocesan Board was instanced by the
Government as a body that might be appropriate for designation (Mr R. Squire, Parliamentary
Under-Secretary of State, Standing Committee E, May 24, 1994, col. 187). Any such designation
must be by order which must be made by way of statutory instrument, subject to the negative
resolution procedure (s.23(1)). Subsections (3) and (4) provide for the interpretation of references to "governing body" in the Act in relation to institutions conducted by companies and
nursery schools.

Grants, loans and other payments

5.—(1) A funding agency may—
  (a) make grants, loans or other payments in respect of expenditure
      incurred or to be incurred by the governing body of an eligible insti-
      tution for the purposes of activities qualifying for funding under this
      Part by virtue of section 4(1)(a) or (b), and
  (b) make grants, loans or other payments in respect of expenditure
      incurred or to be incurred for the purposes of the provision of services
      as mentioned in section 4(1)(c),
subject in each case to such terms and conditions as the funding agency think
fit.
    (2) The terms and conditions on which a funding agency may make any
grants, loans or other payments under this section may in particular—
  (a) enable the funding agency to require the repayment, in whole or in
      part, of sums paid by the agency if any of the terms and conditions
      subject to which the sums were paid is not complied with, and
  (b) require the payment of interest in respect of any period during which a
      sum due to the funding agency in accordance with any of the terms and
      conditions remains unpaid.
    (3) The terms and conditions shall not relate to the application of any sums
derived otherwise than from a funding agency.
    (4) In exercising their functions under this section a funding agency shall
have regard—
  (a) generally, to any forecasts of demand for newly-qualified teachers
      notified to them by the Secretary of State; and
  (b) in relation to any particular institution, to any assessment of the qual-
      ity of education provided by the institution—
            (i) made by either of Her Majesty's Chief Inspectors of Schools,
      or
            (ii) to which the agency think it appropriate to have regard or to
      which the Secretary of State directs them to have regard.

DEFINITIONS
"activities qualifying for funding": s.4(1).
"eligible institutions": s.4(2).
"funding agency": s.3(1).
"Her Majesty's Chief Inspectors of Schools": s.18(1) of the Education (Schools) Act 1992.

GENERAL NOTE
This section sets out the central power of the funding agencies in their capacity as such. It is responsible for the distribution of funds made available to it by the Secretary of State under s.7(1). The funds are for the qualifying activities defined in s.4(1) and may be made available to eligible institutions as defined in s.4(2). The funding agencies provide funds by way of grant, loan or other payment which may be subject to such terms or conditions as the agency thinks fit (subs. (1)). Such conditions may provide for repayment (with interest) if any of the terms or conditions are not met. Such conditions may not relate to sums received from other sources than the funding agency. In making funding decisions the funding agencies are required to have regard to forecasts of demand for newly-qualified teachers notified to them by the Secretary of State and assessments of the quality of the education provided by institutions in receipt of funds (subs. (4)). The provisions relating to the making of payments, terms and conditions and repayment are broadly similar to those regarding grants by the higher and further education funding Councils; see ss.5 and 65 of the 1992 Act. The duty to have regard to the quality of education imposed by subs. (4)(b) is more specific than that imposed on the further and higher education funding councils, although the latter are required to make provision for the assessment of the quality of education in institutions receiving financial support: ss.9 and 70 of the 1992 Act.

Subs. (1)
Governing body. As under ss.5 and 65 of the 1992 Act, payments are made to the governing body, not to the institution as such. The intention is to preserve individual accountability for monies received. Section 4(3) confers power, in relation to an institution which is a company, for the Secretary of State to provide by order for the reference to "governing body" to be read as a reference to the company, so that responsibility would rest upon the company rather than the governing body.
Think fit. The terms and conditions which may be imposed are limited by s.5(3), which prevents the funding agency imposing conditions in relation to funds not received from the agency and by s.6(3), requiring consultation with interested bodies before exercising a discretion to impose terms or conditions. In addition the Secretary of State may, under s.7, impose terms or conditions when making grants to the funding agencies which, in turn, must be imposed upon institutions to which payments are made. The width of the funding agencies' discretion would also be limited by general principles of judicial review.

Subs. (3)
This subsection would prevent an institution from being required to repay sums paid by a funding agency from money obtained from other sources or the imposition of other restrictions on the use of such money. The funding agencies are under a duty, under s.6(1)(b), to have regard to the desirability of not discouraging institutions from developing alternative sources of finance. It was said by the Government in relation to that provision that there was no intention to reduce public funding if institutions succeeded in obtaining finance from elsewhere (see Baroness Blatch, Minister of State, *Hansard*, H.L. Vol. 552, col. 1656).

Subs. (4)
Forecasts of demand. It is made clear here that forecasting demand for teachers in the future is to remain a responsibility of the Secretary of State and that the funding agencies must take account of these in making its funding decisions. Suggestions in Parliament that the funding agencies should themselves undertake a forecasting role were not accepted by the Government.
Assessment of the quality of education. Subsection (4)(b)(i) was introduced as an amendment at a very late stage in the Bill's parliamentary passage to make explicit the role of OFSTED in assessing courses and advising the funding agencies on the accreditation of institutions. A duty is imposed on the funding agencies to have regard to assessments by the Chief Inspectors of Schools but the Act does not, as such, confer any new power to conduct inspections. Power already exists in relation to schools but in relation to higher education institutions the Secretary of State announced that he would make it a condition of his grant to the Agency under s.7(1) that the Agency should make it a condition of grants to individual institutions under s.5(1) that they must allow an unrestricted right to inspect activities on which the Agency's funds are spent (see Mr J. Patten, *Hansard*, H.C. Vol. 246, col. 357).

Provisions supplementary to s.5

6.—(1) In exercising their functions in relation to the provision of financial support for qualifying activities the funding agencies shall have regard to the desirability of—

(a) establishing and maintaining in relation to courses for initial training of school teachers an appropriate balance between school-centred courses and other courses; and

(b) not discouraging any institution for whose activities financial support is provided under this Part from maintaining or developing its funding from other sources.

(2) For the purposes of subsection (1)(a) a "school-centred course" means a course provided by a school or schools, or by a partnership or association consisting wholly or mainly of schools or by a body established by a school or institutions consisting wholly or mainly of schools.

(3) Before exercising their discretion under section 5(1)(a) or (b) with respect to the terms and conditions to be imposed in relation to any grants, loans or other payments, a funding agency shall consult such of the following bodies as appear to them to be appropriate to consult in the circumstances—

(a) such bodies representing the interests of eligible institutions as appear to the funding agency to be concerned, and

(b) the governing body of any particular eligible institution which appears to the funding agency to be concerned.

(4) In exercising their functions in relation to the provision of financial support for qualifying activities a funding agency shall have regard (so far as they think it appropriate to do so in the light of any other relevant considerations) to the desirability of maintaining—

(a) what appears to them to be an appropriate balance in the support given by them as between institutions which are of a denominational character and other institutions, and

(b) any distinctive characteristics of any eligible institution for whose activities financial support is provided under this Part.

(5) In exercising their functions a funding agency shall take such steps as appear to them appropriate to secure that the governing body of any institution which provides a course of initial teacher training funded by the agency makes available such information relating to the course, in such manner and to such persons, as the agency may require.

DEFINITIONS

"eligible institutions": s.4(2).

"funding agencies": s.3(1).

"governing body": s.4(3) and (4).

"institutions which are of a denominational character": s.19(2).

"school": s.14(5) of the Further and Higher Education Act 1992; s.304(1) of the Education Act 1993.

"school-centred course": subs. (2).

GENERAL NOTE

This section contains limits on the powers of the funding agencies under s.5(1) to make payments to qualifying institutions, by specifying other matters than those in s.5(4) to which the funding agencies must have regard. They must have regard to the desirability of establishing and maintaining an appropriate balance between school-centred courses and others (see subs. (1)(a)) and an appropriate balance between support given to institutions of a denominational character and others (see subs. (4)(a)). They must have regard to any distinctive characteristics of an institution receiving support (see subs. (4)(b)) and to the desirability of not discouraging institutions receiving support from obtaining funding from other sources. In addition the funding agencies must consult the governing bodies of, and other bodies representing the interests of, eligible institutions before imposing terms and conditions in relation to payments under s.5(1)(a) and (b) (see subs. (3)). The funding agencies must take steps to ensure that institutions receiving support make available such information about courses of teacher training as the agency may require (see subs. (5)).

Subs. (1)

Establishing and maintaining. This requires the funding agencies to take into account, when making funding decisions, the desirability of first establishing and then maintaining a balance between school-centred courses and other courses. School-centred courses are defined in subs. (2). This requirement gives expression to a major policy objective of the Act which allows schools or consortia of schools to organise their own courses of teacher training (see s.12(1)). This policy objective was identified in the consultation paper: "schools should not only act as full partners with higher education institutions but should also be able, if they wish, to play the leading role in planning and providing courses" (see The Government's Proposals for the Reform of Initial Teacher Training, para. 1.6).

The policy objective was stressed during the passage of the Bill through Parliament: "schools should have the freedom to choose whether they work with higher education partners as long as they meet the necessary standards as judged by the Teacher Training Agency ..." (*per* Mr J. Patten, Secretary of State, *Hansard*, H.C. Vol. 242, col. 606). This objective was also politically the most contentious and resulted in amendments to the Bill in the House of Lords, against the wishes of the Government, requiring schools organising courses of teacher training to do so only in partnership with, and accredited by, institutions of higher education. The revised Bill was amended again by the House of Commons to confer freedom on schools to organise courses without higher education involvement.

Not discouraging. The intention is that institutions should have the incentive to develop additional sources of funding and should not receive reduced funding from the funding agencies if they do so.

See also Baroness Blatch, Minister of State: "The purpose of this subsection is not to pressurise institutions into maximising their non-teacher training funding. On the contrary, it is to afford institutions a protection, so that funding is not automatically reduced pound for pound every time they identify a charitable or other private source of funding" (*Hansard*, H.L. Vol. 552, col. 1656). There are similar provisions in ss.6(2) and 66(2) of the 1992 Act.

Subs. (2)

School-centred course. This is here defined to include courses provided by an association or partnership or a body established by institutions consisting mainly of schools, as well as wholly of schools.

Subs. (3)

The same duty to consult before imposing terms or conditions on payments is imposed upon the funding agencies as upon the higher and further education funding councils under ss.6(1) and 66(1) of the 1992 Act. On requirements for consultation, see *R.* v. *Brent London Borough Council*, ex p. *Gunning* (1985) 84 L.G.R. 168; *R.* v. *Secretary of State for Social Services*, ex p. *Association of Metropolitan Authorities* [1986] 1 W.L.R. 1.

Subs. (4)

The contribution of denominational institutions to teacher training was stressed in the debates in Parliament. This subsection requires the funding agencies to take account of the desirability of maintaining a balance between these and other institutions and of the distinctive characteristics of eligible institutions. There is a comparable provision in s.66(3) of the 1992 Act.

Subs. (5)

This subsection requires funding agencies to ensure that information about courses provided by funded institutions is made available. This subsection was a government amendment to the Bill in the House of Lords. The principle that information should be made available was accepted; however, it was not thought appropriate to list matters about which information should be made available in detail considering this unduly prescriptive and rigid. The funding agencies are given a discretion as to what information should be provided to which recipients. It was stated by the Government that the Secretary of State would draw the attention of the funding agencies in his initial remit letter to the importance of full information being provided (Baroness Blatch, Minister of State, *Hansard*, H.L. Vol. 553, col. 1442).

Grants to the funding agencies

7.—(1)The Secretary of State may make grants to the funding agencies of such amounts and subject to such terms and conditions as he may determine.

(2) The terms and conditions subject to which grants are made by the Secretary of State to a funding agency—

(a) may in particular impose requirements to be complied with in respect of every institution, or every institution falling within a class or description specified in the terms and conditions, being requirements to be complied with in the case of any institution to which the requirements apply before financial support of any amount or description so specified is provided by the agency in respect of activities carried on by the institution, but

(b) shall not otherwise relate to the provision of financial support by the agency in respect of activities carried on by any particular institution or institutions.

(3) Such terms and conditions may not be framed by reference—

(a) to particular courses of study or programmes of research (including the contents of such courses or programmes and the manner in which they are taught, supervised or assessed), or

(b) to criteria for the selection and appointment of academic staff and for the admission of students.

(4) Such terms and conditions may in particular—

(a) enable the Secretary of State to require the repayment, in whole or in part, of sums paid by him if any of the terms and conditions subject to which the sums were paid is not complied with, and

(b) require the payment of interest in respect of any period during which a sum due to the Secretary of State in accordance with any of the terms and conditions remains unpaid.

DEFINITIONS

"funding agencies": s.3(1).

GENERAL NOTE

This section empowers the Secretary of State to make grants to the funding agencies subject to terms and conditions (subs. (1)). The power is in similar terms to that conferred upon the Secretary of State in relation to grants to higher education funding councils under s.68 of the 1992 Act and contains, in subs. (3), the same prohibition on the imposition of terms and conditions relating to particular courses of study or research programmes or the criteria for selecting staff or students. Subsection (4) provides that the Secretary of State may require the repayment by an eligible institution of all or part of the grant if they are not fulfilled and that interest may be payable.

Subs. (1)

Terms and conditions. There is no duty to consult before imposing terms or conditions parallel to those imposed by s.6(3) in relation to terms and conditions imposed by funding agencies on payments to eligible institutions under s.5(1). The power to impose terms and conditions is supplemented by the power given to the Secretary of State by s.8 to give directions to the funding agencies. As noted in relation to s.5(4)(b), the Secretary of State stated his intention to impose a condition requiring access by inspectors to higher education institutions providing courses of teacher training (*Hansard*, H.C. Vol. 246, col. 357).

Subs. (2)

This subsection enables the Secretary of State to impose conditions in relation to all institutions or classes of institution which must be met before they are eligible for funding but may not otherwise relate to particular institutions. The power is identical to that in relation to grants by the Secretary of State to the higher education funding councils under s.68 of the 1992 Act.

Subs. (3)

Terms and conditions may not relate to particular courses of study or programmes of research or criteria for selection of staff or admission of students. This subsection "precisely replicates certain safeguards for academic freedom in the Further and Higher Education Act 1992, relating to the Secretary of State's grants to the Higher Education Funding Councils. We have provided exactly the same restrictions on the terms and conditions that the Secretary of State may apply to his grants to the [Agency]" (*per* Baroness Blatch, Minister of State, *Hansard*, H.L. Vol. 552, col. 1669).

Subs. (4)

This subsection confers a specific power to recover grants in whole or in part and to require payments of interest if terms and conditions are not complied with. Again the power is identical to that conferred upon the Secretary of State in relation to grants to higher education funding councils under s.68 of the 1992 Act. A similar power is conferred upon the teacher training funding agencies in relation to individual institutions under s.5(2).

Directions by the Secretary of State

8.—(1) In exercising their functions under this Part a funding agency shall comply with any directions under this section.

(2) The Secretary of State may give general directions to a funding agency about the exercise of their functions.

(3) If it appears to the Secretary of State that the financial affairs of an eligible institution have been or are being mismanaged he may, after consulting the agency and the institution, give such directions to the funding agency about the provision of financial support in respect of the activities carried on by the institution as he considers are necessary or expedient by reason of the mismanagement.

(4) Directions under this section shall be contained in an order made by the Secretary of State.

DEFINITIONS

"eligible institutions": s.4(2).

"funding agency": s.3(1).

GENERAL NOTE

This section empowers the Secretary of State to give directions to the Agency and HEFCW, with which those bodies are obliged to comply. The Secretary of State already possessed such powers in relation to HEFCW under s.81 of the 1992 Act, upon which this section is modelled. Some concern was expressed in Parliament at the width of the powers granted to the Secretary of State by this section.

Subs. (1)

This subsection imposes a duty on the Agency and HEFCW to comply with directions from the Secretary of State.

Subs. (2)

This confers a power on the Secretary of State to give general directions to the funding agencies. This was described as a fall-back power which would allow urgent action to be taken in an unexpected situation.

"It is unlikely that we should ever need to use this in practice ... But since the Secretary of State is ultimately accountable to Parliament for the use of the agencies' funds, it would be improper for him to have no such power when in practice he could one day face a real need for action" (*per* Baroness Blatch, Minister of State, *Hansard*, H.L. Vol. 552, col. 1670). The power to make general directions under this subsection is in relation to any of the functions of the funding agencies, primarily but not exclusively, administration of funds and is not explicitly confined to a situation of emergency (see the General Notes to s.1(1) and s.8(1)). It was stated in relation to the joint exercise of functions permitted by s.9 that it would be open to the Secretary of State to issue a direction requiring co-operation between funding agencies (Mr T. Boswell, Parliamentary Under-Secretary of State, Standing Committee E, June 14, 1994, col. 236). Unlike the position in relation to directions under subs. (3) there is no requirement for consultation before action is taken, on the ground that if it was necessary to invoke the power, speed would be essential (see Baroness Blatch, Minister of State, *Hansard*, H.L. Vol. 553, col. 621). Contrast the requirement in s.9(3) of the 1993 Act requiring consultation before directions are issued to a funding authority for schools, unless, in the opinion of the Secretary of State, it is not reasonably practicable to do so for reasons of urgency.

Subs. (3)

Power to give directions in relation to individual institutions is confined to cases of financial mismanagement. This subsection replicates s.81(3) of the 1992 Act. Financial mismanagement is not defined but would seem to extend to incompetence as well as wilful default or fraud.

Subs. (4)

Directions must be by way of order made by statutory instrument subject to the negative resolution procedure: see s.23(1). There is a power to revoke or vary such directions: see s.23(3).

Joint exercise of functions

9.—(1) A funding agency and any other relevant funding body may exercise any of their functions jointly where it appears to them that to do so—

(a) will be more efficient, or

(b) will enable them more effectively to discharge any of their functions.

(2) In subsection (1) "other relevant funding body" means the other funding agency, the Higher Education Funding Council for England, a further education funding council or a funding authority for schools.

DEFINITIONS

"funding agency": s.3(1).

"funding authority for schools": s.5(1) of the Education Act 1993.

"further education council": s.1(1) and (6) of the Further and Higher Education Act 1992.

"Higher Education Funding Council for England": s.62(1)(a) of the Further and Higher Education Act 1992.

"other relevant funding body": subs. (2).

GENERAL NOTE

This section provides for the joint exercise of functions by the funding agencies and between either or both of them and other relevant funding bodies (see subs. (1)). The latter are the Higher Education Funding Council for England, further education funding councils and funding authorities for schools (see subs. (2)). Joint exercise of functions must be in the interests of efficiency or more effective discharge of their functions (see subs. (1)). No specific matters on which joint exercise of functions is required are laid down. It would be open to the Secretary of State under s.8 to issue a direction requiring co-operation between funding agencies and powers exist to give directions to the other relevant funding agencies under ss.56 and 81 of the 1992 Act and s.9 of the 1993 Act. The section would not permit delegation of functions as opposed to their joint exercise.

Efficiency studies

10.—(1) A funding agency may arrange for the promotion or carrying out by any person of studies designed to improve economy, efficiency and effectiveness in the management or operations of an institution which is receiving financial support under this Part.

(2) A person promoting or carrying out such studies at the request of a funding agency may require the governing body of the institution concerned—

(a) to furnish him, or a person authorised by him, with such information, and

(b) to make available to him, or a person authorised by him, for inspection their accounts and such other documents,

as he may reasonably require for that purpose.

DEFINITIONS

"funding agency": s.3(1).

GENERAL NOTE

This section enables the funding agencies to arrange for the conduct of efficiency studies into the management or operations of institutions receiving financial support from them. A similar power is enjoyed by further and higher education funding councils under s.83 of the 1992 Act and a duty is imposed upon funding authorities for schools to arrange value for money studies of grant maintained schools by s.8(1) of the 1993 Act. Value for money studies are defined, in part, by s.8(3)(b) of the 1993 Act in similar terms to the efficiency studies referred to in subs. (1). The agencies are thus able to perform a function similar to that of the Audit Commission which can conduct such studies in relation to various public bodies. The Audit Commission may, indeed, conduct such studies in relation to the funding agencies themselves or the governing bodies receiving financial support from them. This power is conferred by Sched. 2, para. 8(5), amending s.220 of the Education Reform Act 1988. In relation to such studies concerning the funding agencies, they can only be conducted at the request of the agency. With respect to studies relating to the governing body of an institution receiving financial support from a funding agency, they may be requested either by the governing body concerned or a funding agency. The present section empowers a funding agency to require such a study in relation to an institution to be conducted by any person chosen by the agency in question. Proposals that such a person should be one approved by the Audit Commission were not accepted.

"The Government believe strongly that value for money is best secured by open competition ... The Agency should be free to choose between competitive tenders" (*per* Mr R. Squire, Parliamentary Under-Secretary of State, Standing Committee E, June 14, 1994, col. 241).

Subs. (1)

Studies are those designed to improve economy, efficiency and effectiveness in the management or operation of the agencies, or institutions receiving financial support from the agencies. These terms are not defined but it was made clear that they were concerned with value for money studies and not direct financial supervision. The section: "empowers the agency to commission value for money studies across all or some of its funded institutions to improve economy, efficiency and effectiveness. It is not concerned with the auditing arrangements of all the individual institutions that it funds" (*per* Baroness Blatch, Minister of State, *Hansard*, H.L. Vol. 553, col. 1446). Nor was it concerned with the normal financial accountability of the agencies for the use of their funds (*per* Baroness Blatch, *ibid.*).

Subs. (2)

This subsection empowers the person conducting such a study to require the governing body of the institution concerned to provide information or documents reasonably required for the purpose.

Research

11. A funding agency may carry out or commission such research as they consider appropriate with a view to improving—
   (a) the training of teachers, or
   (b) the standards of teaching.

DEFINITIONS
   "funding agency": s.3(1).

GENERAL NOTE

The Bill as originally drafted included, as one of the activities qualifying under, what is now s.4 of the Act, "the provision of higher education in, or the undertaking of research into, the theory, practice and management of education". Considerable disquiet was expressed in the House of Lords about the effect of the transfer of funding in this area from the Higher Education Funding Council for England to the Agency, particularly in relation to research. A government amendment removed this category as one qualifying for funding by the Agency. At the same time, what is now s.11 of the Act was introduced as an amendment to the Bill. Its purpose is to make it clear that the Agency and HEFCW can commission research directed towards improvement in teacher training or teaching standards. While such research would not be an activity qualifying for funding under s.4, the Agency has authority to finance such research by virtue of its supplementary powers under Sched. 1, para. 1 to do anything which appears to them to be necessary or expedient for the purpose of, or in connection with, the discharge of their functions, including entering into contracts. HEFCW already has such powers under Sched. 1, para. 1 to the 1992

Act. While this section confers discretion upon the agencies as to the nature and extent of the research carried out or commissioned, it was indicated that the agencies would have a research budget and would be expected to be concerned with matters like "improving courses and teaching methods in a fairly direct way" (*per* Mr T. Boswell, Parliamentary Under-Secretary of State, Standing Committee E, June 14, 1994, cols. 246 and 247).

Supplementary provisions

Power of schools to provide courses of initial teacher training

12.—(1) The governing body of any county, voluntary or maintained special school, or of any grant-maintained school, may—

(a) provide courses of initial training for school teachers, or

(b) join in a partnership or association with other eligible institutions, or (alone or jointly with other eligible institutions) establish a body, for the purpose of providing such courses.

(2) Courses of initial teacher training so provided shall be open only to persons holding a degree or equivalent qualification granted by a United Kingdom institution or an equivalent degree or other qualification granted by a foreign institution.

For this purpose—

(a) a "United Kingdom institution" means an institution established in the United Kingdom, other than one which is, or is affiliated to or forms part of, an institution whose principal establishment is outside the United Kingdom; and

(b) a "foreign institution" means any institution other than a United Kingdom institution.

(3) In relation to an exercise of the powers conferred by subsection (1), the governing body shall have all the same supplementary and incidental powers as it has in relation to the conduct of the school.

(4) The above provisions have effect notwithstanding any provisions of the instrument of government or articles of government for the school.

(5) For the purposes of section 12 or 13 of the Education Act 1980 or section 96 of the Education Act 1993 (procedure in case of certain proposals for alteration of school) an exercise of the powers conferred by this section, or ceasing to exercise them, shall not be treated as involving a significant change in the character of the school.

(6) Any exercise by the governing body of a school of the powers conferred by this section shall not be treated, for the purposes of—

(a) sections 33 to 43 of the Education Reform Act 1988 (financing of schools maintained by local education authorities), or

(b) Chapter VI of Part II of the Education Act 1993 (funding of grant-maintained schools),

as being undertaken for the purposes of the school.

(7) Nothing in this section shall be construed as affecting the power of the governing body of a school, as an ordinary incident of the conduct of the school—

(a) to provide training for persons employed as teachers at the school, or

(b) to participate in the provision of teacher training as part of a course provided by another institution.

DEFINITIONS
  "county school": s.91(2) of the Education Act 1944.
  "foreign institution": subs. (2)(b).
  "governing body": s.4(3) and (4).
  "grant-maintained school": s.22(1) of the Education Act 1993.
  "institution of higher education": s.91(5) of the Further and Higher Education Act 1992.
  "maintained special school": s.182(2) of the Education Act 1993.
  "United Kingdom institution": subs. (2)(a).
  "voluntary school": s.15 of the Education Act 1944.

GENERAL NOTE

This section gives effect to a key element of the policy regarding teacher training upon which the Act is based. It allows for the provision of courses of initial teacher training by schools or associations of schools, without any involvement by higher education institutions (see subs. (1)). Power to decide on the provision of such courses is conferred upon the governing body of schools (see subs. (1)) and is not to be treated as involving a significant change in the character of the school so as to bring into play the procedural provisions of the Education Act 1980, ss.12 and 13 and s.96 of the 1993 Act (subs. (5)). The power conferred will be available notwithstanding any provisions in the instrument or articles of government of the school (subs. (4)). Any such courses are to be open only to graduates (subs. (2)).

Subs. (1)

This subsection confers upon the governing body of any county, voluntary or maintained special school or grant-maintained school the power to provide courses of initial teacher training. Such courses may be provided by one school or in an association or partnership with other schools or by a body established for the purpose by a school or schools. It is also open to a school or schools to enter into an association or partnership with, or establish a body in association with, other institutions eligible for funding by the Agency, which, by virtue of s.4(2), is any institution within the higher or further education sector and any institution or body designated by the Secretary of State. It is thus open to a school or schools to provide courses in conjunction with a higher education institution but they are not compelled to do so. The possibility of a school or schools alone, without any involvement by a higher education institution, providing teacher training courses was politically one of the most controversial elements of the Act and was one of the major policies it sought to implement. An amendment to the Bill in the House of Lords would have required that courses could only be provided in conjunction with higher education institutions; this was rejected by the House of Commons.

A single school may provide teacher training courses but it is envisaged that, in practice, consortia of schools will do so. The pilot schemes already undertaken took this form. Accreditation of the institution by the funding agencies and consequent funding would be based on advice from OFSTED that course provision satisfied criteria specified by the Secretary of State. It was stated for the Government that the criteria would include experience of teaching in more than one school and that one school alone would be unable to provide that (Mr R. Squire, Parliamentary Under-Secretary of State, Standing Committee E, May 24, 1994, col. 186).

Subs. (2)

This was an amendment to the Bill as originally drafted. Concern was expressed that students taking teacher training courses organised by schools might not be graduates and would have had no higher education at all. This subsection was introduced as a government amendment in the House of Lords to make it clear that such courses would be open only to students holding a degree or equivalent qualification.

Subs. (5)

This subsection states that a decision to provide teacher training courses is not to be treated as involving a significant change in the character of the school. If it was so treated, by virtue of the Education Act 1980, ss.12 and 13 and s.96 of the 1993 Act, consultation, publication of proposals, opportunity for objection and, in most cases, the approval of the Secretary of State would be required. It was said for the Government that the change of character provisions would be too cumbersome and in the case of county and controlled schools could only be initiated by a local education authority and not the governing body (Baroness Blatch, Minister of State, *Hansard*, H.L. Vol. 553, col. 36).

Subs. (6)

The purpose of this subsection is to ring-fence school budgets to prevent cross-subsidy to finance initial teacher training courses. Such courses must cover their costs. It is envisaged that the costs will be met partly by grants from the funding agencies and partly by charging fees to students. Schedule 2, para. 8(3) amends s.106 of the 1988 Act to permit fees to be charged for teacher training. The fees would be met by awards to students. The mandatory awards and student loan provisions are to be extended to such courses to harmonise student support arrangements. Schedule 2, paras. 2 and 9 have this effect. There is nothing to prohibit schools from charging fees which are higher than those which would be reimbursed under the mandatory grant. Such additional income could be spent for the general purposes of the school (Baroness Blatch, Minister of State, *Hansard*, H.L. Vol. 553, cols. 33 to 34).

Subs. (7)

This subsection ensures that some forms of teacher training are not affected by the provisions of s.12. Subsection (7)(a) is intended to apply to teacher training under the licensed or overseas trained teachers schemes. The financial limitations in subs. (6) and the restriction of training to graduates in subs. (2) would not therefore apply to such training. The intention of subs. (7)(b) is that schools co-operating with other institutions, particularly those in higher education, where the latter are the funded course providers, should not be caught by s.12.

Grants for teacher training

13.—(1) Section 50 of the Education (No. 2) Act 1986 (grants for teacher training, &c.) is amended as follows.

(2) In subsection (1) (power of Secretary of State to make provision for payment of grants), omit "by him".

(3) In subsection (3)(b)—

(a) omit "by the Secretary of State" in the first place where it occurs; and

(b) for "by the Secretary of State" in the second place where it occurs substitute "in accordance with the regulations".

(4) After subsection (3) insert—

"(3A) Grants shall be payable in accordance with the regulations by the Secretary of State or, in the case of grants to facilitate and encourage the training of teachers, by the Teacher Training Agency or the Secretary of State according as the regulations may provide.".

(5) Until the coming into force of the first regulations made under section 50 as amended by this section, the Education (Bursaries for Teacher Training) Regulations 1988 shall have effect as if so made and as if references therein to the Secretary of State included the Teacher Training Agency.

DEFINITIONS

"Teacher Training Agency": s.1(1).

GENERAL NOTE

This section amends existing legislation to take account of the assumption by the Agency of functions previously exercised by the Secretary of State. The Education (No. 2) Act 1986, s.50 conferred power on the Secretary of State to make regulations providing for the payment of grants by him to facilitate and encourage the training of teachers. The effect of s.13 is that the power will now extend to making regulations providing for payments by the Agency and the imposition of conditions on such payments by the Agency. Until the coming into force of such regulations, the Education (Bursaries for Teachers) Regulations 1988 (S.I. 1988 No. 1397) are, by virtue of subs. (5), to have effect as if made under s.50 of the Education (No. 2) Act 1986 in its amended form and as if references therein to the Secretary of State included the Agency.

Qualification of teachers, &c.

14.—(1) In section 218 of the Education Reform Act 1988 (regulations as to qualification of teachers, &c.), after subsection (2) (meaning of "qualified teacher") insert—

"(2A) Regulations under subsection (2)(a) above may make provision—

(a) by reference to the successful completion of a course of initial training for teachers in schools at an accredited institution; and

(b) conferring on the Teacher Training Agency or the Higher Education Funding Council for Wales such functions in relation to accreditation or otherwise as may be prescribed.".

(2) In paragraph 2 of Schedule 3 to the Education (Teachers) Regulations 1993 (persons who are qualified teachers), after sub-paragraph (1) insert—

"(1A) The person—

(a) holds a degree or equivalent qualification granted by a United Kingdom institution or an equivalent degree or other qualification granted by a foreign institution, and

(b) has successfully completed a course of initial training for teachers in schools at an accredited institution in England or Wales.

For the purposes of this sub-paragraph—

(a) a "United Kingdom institution" means an institution established in the United Kingdom, other than one which is, or is affiliated to or forms part of, an institution whose principal establishment is outside the United Kingdom;

(b) a "foreign institution" means any institution other than a United Kingdom institution; and

(c) an "accredited institution" means an institution accredited by the Teacher Training Agency or, in Wales, by the Higher Education Funding Council for Wales as a provider of courses satisfying such criteria as may from time to time be specified by the Secretary of State.".

The above amendment shall not be taken as prejudicing the power to make further regulations revoking or amending the provision inserted.

(3) In section 218(3) of the Education Reform Act 1988 (power to provide for exceptions to requirement that only qualified teachers be employed), for "persons licensed to teach by the Secretary of State" substitute "persons licensed or otherwise authorised to teach by the Secretary of State or the Teacher Training Agency".

(4) In section 232(6) of that Act (power to make different provision for Wales), in the list of provisions to which the power does not apply, omit the reference to section 218(1)(a) (requirement that only qualified teachers be employed).

DEFINITIONS

"accredited institution": subs. (2).

"foreign institution": subs. (2).

"Higher Education Funding Council for Wales": s.62(1)(a) of the Further and Higher Education Act 1992.

"qualified teacher": subs. (1); s.218(2) of the Education Reform Act 1988.

"Teacher Training Agency": s.1(1).

"United Kingdom institution": subs. (2).

GENERAL NOTE

This section provides for the accreditation powers of the Agency and HEFCW. Power is conferred to make regulations conferring functions upon these bodies in relation to accreditation. This was defined as: "the official approval of a qualification as an acceptable preparation for entering a profession" (*per* Baroness Blatch, Minister of State, *Hansard*, H.L. Vol. 553, col. 1399). Prior to the Act qualified teacher status was obtained by successful completion of a course of teacher training accredited by the Secretary of State. This section allows for accreditation powers to be conferred upon the funding agencies. The intention is that the funding agencies will accredit institutions and successful completion of a course of teacher training at an accredited institution will lead to qualified teacher status. In making decisions on accreditation the funding agencies will act on the advice of OFSTED and the Secretary of State will continue to set criteria which courses must satisfy (Baroness Blatch, Minister of State, *Hansard*, H.L. Vol. 550, cols. 820 to 821).

Subs. (1)

This subsection amends the definition of qualified teacher in s.218(2) of the 1988 Act to include, on the making of regulations to that effect, a person who has successfully completed a course of teacher training at an accredited institution. It also confers the power to make regulations conferring functions in relation to accreditation on the funding agencies. It is envisaged that when the necessary regulations have been made and all institutions accredited, the power of the Secretary of State to accredit courses will be repealed (Baroness Blatch, Minister of State, *Hansard*, H.L. Vol. 553, col. 1397).

Subs. (2)

This subsection amends the Education (Teachers) Regulations 1993 (S.I. 1993 No. 543) defining qualified teacher status to include a person who has completed a course of teacher training at an accredited institution and has a degree or equivalent qualification from a U.K. or foreign institution. The definition of "accredited institution" makes clear that satisfaction of course criteria specified by the Secretary of State is a prerequisite for accreditation by the funding agencies. Subsection (2) expressly preserves the power to amend or revoke the regulations, as amended by the subsection. Amendment of the regulations could not remove the requirement that students taking school-centred courses of initial teacher training must be graduates, as this is also required by s.12(2) of the present Act.

Subs. (3)

This subsection amends s.218(3) of the 1988 Act to allow the Agency as well as the Secretary of State to confer licensed teacher status or to otherwise confer authority to teach. It is envisaged that the Agency will take over the general administration of the licensed teacher scheme.

Subs. (4)

The effect of this subsection is that different provision may be made in Wales in relation to the qualification of teachers.

Duty to provide information, &c.

15.—(1) The Teacher Training Agency—

(a) shall provide the Secretary of State (in such manner as he may from time to time determine) with such information or advice relating to matters for which they are responsible as he may from time to time require, and

(b) may provide the Secretary of State with such information or advice relating to such matters as they think fit.

(2) The Teacher Training Agency and the Higher Education Funding Council for Wales shall give each other such information as they may require for the purposes of the exercise of their functions under this Part.

(3) The following shall give the Teacher Training Agency or the Higher Education Funding Council for Wales such information as they may require for the purpose of the exercise of their functions under this Part—

(a) the governing body of any institution receiving, or which has received or applied for, any grant, loan or other payment under this Part;

(b) any local education authority.

DEFINITIONS

"Higher Education Funding Council for Wales": s.62(1)(a) of the Further and Higher Education Act 1992 (c. 13).

"Teacher Training Agency": s.1(1).

GENERAL NOTE

This section imposes a duty on the Agency to provide the Secretary of State with information or advice when requested and confers a power to do so when the Agency thinks fit (see subs. (1)). The Agency and HEFCW are under a duty to provide each other with information on request (see subs. (2)). Governing bodies of institutions applying for, receiving, or having received, funding and local education authorities are under a duty to provide information to the funding agencies on request (see subs. (3)).

Subs. (1)

The subsection distinguishes between information and advice provided at the request of the Secretary of State, where the Secretary of State may determine the form in which it is given, and information and advice provided of the Agency's own volition. A power to impose requirements as to form was seen by the Government as essential to allow, for example, the Secretary of State to require confidentiality in relation to an individual institution's finances (Baroness Blatch, Minister of State, *Hansard*, H.L. Vol. 553, col. 946). The wording here differs from s.69(1) of the 1992 Act, which applies in relation to HEFCW. Under that section the Secretary of State may determine the form in which all information or advice is provided. In addition to the power granted to require information here, Sched. 1, para. 10 provides for attendance at meetings of the Agency or its committees by a representative of the Secretary of State, who may also require copies of documents issued to agency or committee members. A representative of the Chief Inspector of Schools in England has the same rights under Sched. 1, para. 11. The Secretary of State already has these rights in relation to HEFCW under Sched. 1, para. 11 to the 1992 Act. More general information about the Agency's performance of its functions is required by

Sched. 1, para. 17, which imposes a duty to make an annual report to the Secretary of State which must be laid before Parliament and which the Agency may publish. The Agency will be expected to produce other documentation, including a corporate plan, and to comply with the Government's open government initiatives (Mr R. Squire, Parliamentary Under-Secretary of State, Standing Committee E, May 24, 1994, cols. 211, 213).

Additional, supplementary and ancillary functions

16.—(1) The Secretary of State may by order confer or impose on the Teacher Training Agency such additional functions as he considers they may appropriately discharge having regard to their general objectives.

(2) The Secretary of State may by order confer or impose on the Higher Education Funding Council for Wales such functions supplementary to their functions as a funding agency as he thinks fit.

For the purposes of this subsection a function is a supplementary function in relation to the Council if it is exercisable for the purposes of—

(a) the exercise by the Secretary of State of functions of his under any enactment, or

(b) the doing by the Secretary of State of anything he has power to do apart from any enactment,

and it relates to, or to the activities of, an eligible institution.

(3) Before making an order under subsection (1) or (2) the Secretary of State shall carry out such consultation as appears to him to be appropriate.

(4) The Teacher Training Agency and the Higher Education Funding Council for Wales shall carry out such activities ancillary to their functions under this Part as the Secretary of State may direct.

DEFINITIONS

"eligible institution": s.4(2).

"Higher Education Funding Council for Wales": s.62(1)(a) of the Further and Higher Education Act 1992.

"Teacher Training Agency": s.1(1).

GENERAL NOTE

This section empowers the Secretary of State to confer additional functions upon the Agency (see subs. (1)), supplementary functions upon the Higher Education Funding Council for Wales (see subs. (2)) and ancillary functions upon both (see subs. (4)). Limits are placed upon the Secretary of State's powers by the requirement that additional functions must be related to the general objectives of the Agency and supplementary functions must be functions that are already within the powers (statutory or otherwise) of the Secretary of State. In addition, the Secretary of State is under a duty to consult before exercising his powers to confer or impose additional or supplementary functions (see subs. (3)).

Subs. (1)

The Secretary of State may confer or impose additional functions on the Agency. In committee in the House of Lords, Viscount St. Davids gave the example of the Agency helping to arrange admissions (*Hansard*, H.L. Vol. 553, col. 66). This power extends to new functions; it is not intended to be confined, as is subs. (2), to existing powers of the Secretary of State (Viscount St. Davids, *ibid.*). The only constraint is the requirement that the Secretary of State must have regard to the general objectives of the Agency. The power is exercisable only in relation to the Agency, not HEFCW and any order made under this subsection must be made by statutory instrument subject to the negative resolution procedure (s.22(1)).

Subs. (2)

In relation to HEFCW there is a power to confer or impose supplementary functions. This is subject to the qualification that the function is already within the powers (statutory or otherwise) of the Secretary of State and it must relate to the activities of an eligible institution. As with subs. (1), the power granted must be exercised by statutory instrument subject to the negative resolution procedure (see s.23(1)).

Subs. (3)

The Secretary of State is required to consult before exercising his powers under subss. (1) and (2). Consultation is such as appears to him to be appropriate. There is no specification of who must be consulted, although the Secretary of State's exercise of his discretion would be subject to the test of *Wednesbury* reasonableness (*Associated Provincial Picture Houses* v. *Wednesbury Corporation* [1948] 1 K.B. 223).

Subs. (4)

This confers a power on the Secretary of State to require both the Agency and HEFCW to carry out ancillary activities. This power is exercisable by direction not order and is not therefore required to be exercised by statutory instrument. It is also not subject to the consultation requirement imposed in relation to the powers contained in subss. (1) and (2). Ancillary functions were described by Baroness Blatch in the House of Lords as by definition matters of a technical matter which did not require Parliamentary scrutiny and that a requirement to consult would be heavy-handed (*Hansard*, H.L. Vol. 553, col. 68).

The Teaching as a Career Unit: transfer of property and staff

17. The Secretary of State may by order provide for the transfer to the Teacher Training Agency of the property, rights and liabilities (including rights and liabilities arising under contracts of employment) of the Teaching as a Career Unit.

DEFINITIONS

"Teacher Training Agency": s.1(1).

GENERAL NOTE

This section provides for the transfer to the Agency of the property, rights and liabilities (including those arising under contracts of employment) of the Teaching as a Career Unit. This was a non-Departmental public body established as a limited company which had the function of promoting teaching and advising those considering it as a career, including former teachers planning to return. These functions will now be performed by the Agency in accordance with s.1(1)(b). The Act makes no provision for Wales on this point.

Power to reimburse certain payments to persons formerly employed in teacher training

18.—(1) A higher education funding council may make payments, subject to such terms and conditions as they think fit, to—
  (a) the governing body of a grant-maintained school or grant-maintained special school, or
  (b) a further education corporation or the governing body of any institution designated under section 28 of the Further and Higher Education Act 1992,
in respect of expenditure incurred or to be incurred by that body in making safeguarded salary payments to which this section applies.

(2) This section applies to payments made to a person who in consequence of a direction given by the Secretary of State under—
  (a) regulation 3(2) of the Further Education Regulations 1975,
  (b) regulation 15 of the Education (Schools and Further Education) Regulations 1981, being a direction relating to a course for the training of teachers, or
  (c) regulation 16 of those Regulations,
ceased before April 1, 1989 to be employed in a college for the training of teachers, or in a department for the training of teachers in any other establishment of further education.

(3) The amount of the safeguarded salary payment is the amount by which, in consequence of the matters mentioned in subsection (2), a person's salary exceeds that which would normally be appropriate to the post held by him.

(4) A body to which subsection (1)(a) or (b) applies shall give to a higher education funding council such information as the council may require for the purposes of the exercise of their power under that subsection.

DEFINITIONS

"further education funding council": s.1(1) and (6) of the Further and Higher Education Act 1992.

"grant-maintained school": s.22(1) of the Education Act 1993.
"grant-maintained special school": ss.182(3) and 187(3)(b) of the Education Act 1993.
"higher education funding council": s.62(1) of the Further and Higher Education Act 1992.

GENERAL NOTE

This section empowers higher education funding councils to make payments to the governing bodies of the institutions listed in respect of certain salary payments. Following the reorganisation of teacher training in the 1970s and early 1980s a number of people employed in teacher training establishments were redeployed in jobs in schools and further education colleges at lower salaries. A scheme was established to provide salary enhancements. The necessary funds have been paid by successive funding bodies to local education authorities. Subsection (1) provides for the payment, in respect of safeguarded salary payments, to be made directly by the funding councils to the institutions concerned. Safeguarded salary payments are defined in subs. (3) as the amount by which, in virtue of the payments made under the scheme, a person's salary exceeds that which would normally be appropriate for the post held by him. Persons in receipt of such payments are defined in subs. (2).

Interpretation

19.—(1) In this Part—
"denominational character", in relation to an institution, shall be construed in accordance with subsection (2) below;
"eligible institution" has the meaning given by section 4(2);
"funding agency" has the meaning given by section 3(1);
"governing body"—
(a) in relation to an institution conducted by a company, shall be construed in accordance with any order under section 4(3), and
(b) in relation to a nursery school maintained by a local education authority, shall be construed in accordance with section 4(4);
"qualifying activities" has the meaning given by section 4(1);
"special educational needs" shall be construed in accordance with subsection (3) below; and
"training", in relation to teachers, shall be construed in accordance with subsection (4) below.
(2) For the purposes of this Part an institution is of a denominational character if—
(a) at least one-quarter of the members of the governing body of the institution, or in the case of a school at least one-fifth, are persons appointed to represent the interests of a religion or religious denomination, or
(b) any of the property held for the purposes of the institution is held upon trusts which provide that, in the event of the discontinuance of the institution, the property concerned shall be held for, or sold and the proceeds of sale applied for, the benefit of a religion or religious denomination, or
(c) any of the property held for the purposes of the institution is held on trust for or in connection with—
(i) the provision of education, or
(ii) the conduct of an educational institution,
in accordance with the tenets of a religion or religious denomination.
(3) For the purposes of this Part persons with special educational needs are—
(a) children with special educational needs as defined in section 156 of the Education Act 1993, or
(b) persons (other than children within the meaning of that section) who—

(i) have a significantly greater difficulty in learning than the majority of persons of their age, or

(ii) have a disability which either prevents or hinders them from making use of educational facilities of a kind generally provided for persons of their age.

(4) It is hereby declared that references in this Part (and elsewhere in the Education Acts) to training, in relation to teachers, include any training or education with the object of fitting persons to be teachers, or better teachers.

(5) Other expressions, if used in this Part and in the Education Act 1944, have the same meaning in this Part as in that Act.

GENERAL NOTE

This section is an interpretation section which applies to Pt. I of the Act.

Subs. (2)

Like the virtually identical definitions in ss.6(4) and 66(4) of the 1992 Act this does not confine "denominational character" to the Christian religion.

Subs. (3)

This extends the definition of special educational needs contained in s.156 of the 1993 Act, which applies only to persons under the age of 19 who are registered pupils at a school (s.156(5)). The definition adopted in the present Act includes these but also applies to persons of any age. In respect of such persons it is otherwise modelled on the definition in s.156(2)(a) and (b) of the 1993 Act.

Subs. (4)

This provides that teacher training is to be interpreted in the Education Acts 1944 to 1994 as including education and training with the object of fitting persons to be teachers or better teachers. This subsection and the consequential amendment to subs. (1) were inserted as government amendments in the House of Lords to meet the objection that education was a more appropriate term to employ than training to describe the process of qualification for the teaching profession. The initial government response had been that "training" was a term of art and that introduction of the term "education" into the present Act could cause confusion with regard to earlier legislation.

"We have never had any problem with the principle that the education element is every bit as important a part of a teacher's preparation as the element of training in, for example, classroom skills ... These amendments put beyond doubt that the term 'teacher training' includes teacher education" (*per* Baroness Blatch, Minister of State, *Hansard*, H.L. Vol. 553, col. 1454).

PART II

STUDENTS' UNIONS

Meaning of "students' union"

20.—(1) In this Part a "students' union" means—

(a) an association of the generality of students at an establishment to which this Part applies whose principal purposes include promoting the general interests of its members as students; or

(b) a representative body (whether an association or not) whose principal purposes include representing the generality of students at an establishment to which this Part applies in academic, disciplinary or other matters relating to the government of the establishment.

(2) References in this Part to a students' union include an association or body which would fall within subsection (1) if for the references to the generality of students at the establishment there were substituted a reference to—

(a) the generality of undergraduate students, or graduate students, at the establishment; or

(b) the generality of students at a particular hall of residence of the establishment.

(3) References in this Part to a students' union include an association or body which consists wholly or mainly of—

(a) constituent or affiliated associations or bodies which are themselves students' unions within subsection (1) or (2), or

(b) representatives of such constituent or affiliated associations,

and which fulfils the functions of a students' union within subsection (1) or (2) in relation to students at an establishment to which this Part applies.

(4) An association or body may be a students' union within the meaning of this Part in relation to more than one establishment but not in relation to establishments generally in the United Kingdom or a part of the United Kingdom.

(5) References in this section to an association of the generality of students, or of any description of students, include—

(a) any association which the generality of students, or of students of that description, may join, whether or not it has in membership a majority of them, and

(b) any association which would fall within paragraph (a) if the references there to students were confined to full-time students;

and references to a representative body whose principal purposes include representing the generality of students, or of any description of students, shall be similarly construed.

DEFINITIONS
"establishment": s.21(1) and (2).

GENERAL NOTE
This section defines the meaning of "students' union" for the purposes of the Act.

"It is intended to cover all students' unions in publicly-funded further or higher education in the two sectors. It is based on ... the widest possible set of definitions based on the actual position ..." (*per* Mr T. Boswell, Parliamentary Under-Secretary of State, Standing Committee E, col. 338, June 16, 1994). Student organisations take a variety of forms: at one extreme there are representative bodies covering the whole institution; at the other there are small, specific clubs, bringing together like-minded individuals. In between there are a range of organisations. The Act intends to cover any body which provides services to, or for, the generality of students, rather than specific groups. However, organisations representing some particular categories of students within an institution are included, *e.g.* undergraduates at an Oxford or Cambridge college or residents in a particular hall of residence. The general definition in s.20(1) defines two main types of student unions. These are either an association of students at an establishment whose principal purposes include promoting the general interests of its members as students, or a representative body representing students in relation to academic, disciplinary or other matters relating to the government of the establishment (see s.20(1)). Such an association or representative body must be concerned with the generality of students at an establishment (see s.20(1)) but s.20(2) includes within the definition the generality of undergraduate or graduate students only at an establishment or the generality of students at a particular hall of residence. It is not however necessary that a majority of the eligible students are actually members (see s.20(5)). Associations of bodies which are themselves students' unions are included (see s.20(3) and (4)).

Subs. (1)
The general definition here includes two types of students' unions which are concerned with the generality of students at an establishment. The first is an association of students whose principal purpose is to promote the interests of its student members. The second is a representative body whose chief purpose is to represent students in relation to the government of the institution they attend and, in particular, academic and disciplinary matters. The subsection requires that students' unions should be associations of, or represent, the generality of students at an establishment. This would exclude associations of, or bodies representing, particular categories of students at an establishment (subject to subss. (2) and (5)). The effect of subs. (5) is that it is not necessary for the generality of students actually to be members, provided they are eligible for membership and that only full-time students need be eligible.

Subs. (2)
This subsection brings within the definition bodies not concerned with the generality of students at an establishment. Subsection (2)(a) provides that unions of graduate or postgraduate students alone will constitute students' unions. Thus where there are separate unions for gradu-

ate and undergraduate students at an establishment, both will constitute students' unions. The effect of subs. (2)(b) is that associations of, or bodies representing, students at halls of residence will also constitute students' unions. Associations of particular categories of students, *e.g.* law students, would not be covered.

Subs. (3)

This subsection: "deals with unions that are associations of lower tier unions, such as the university-wide unions at Oxford and Cambridge universities" (*per* Mr T. Boswell, Parliamentary Under-Secretary of State, Standing Committee E, June 16, 1994, col. 338). If these fulfil the functions of a students' union under subss. (1) or (2), they will themselves constitute students' unions. By virtue of s.21(1)(g) colleges forming constituent parts of a university will be establishments to which the Act applies and associations of, or bodies representing, the generality of students at such colleges will constitute students' unions within subs. (1). Where such unions affiliate to a university-wide union, the effect of subs. (3) is that the latter will also constitute a students' union.

Subs. (4)

This subsection deals with the situation where a single union covers a number of separate establishments rather than the constituent parts of an establishment, for example, the students' union of a town which has several higher education establishments. It does however exclude unions which relate to establishments generally in the U.K. or part of it. So, for example, the National Union of Students will not be caught by the Act.

Subs. (5)

This subsection achieves two results. It firstly provides that a union may be an association or body representing the generality of students even though the majority of students may not be members. One of the principal objectives of this Part of the Act was to make provision for students to opt out of union membership (achieved by s.22(2)(c)). The subsection ensures that a union would not cease to be such if a majority of students at an establishment chose to do so. It would also cover the situation where parallel unions existed at an establishment. The second effect of subs. (5) is that if an establishment has a large number of part-time students, and those students are not eligible for union membership, the generality requirement will still be satisfied in relation to a union for full-time students. It was made clear in the House of Lords, where this subsection was introduced as an amendment, that eligibility for membership was a matter for each establishment to determine. Concern had been expressed that considerable problems would be caused for institutions with large numbers of part-time students, particularly in relation to the requirements for secret ballots in s.22(2).

"The extent of union membership is of course determined by each institution in its union constitution. The Government have no plan to change or reduce institutions' discretion in this area" (*per* Baroness Blatch, Minister of State, *Hansard*, H.L. Vol. 553, col. 598). The reference to the generality of any description of students will cover the case of organisations which are students' unions by virtue of subs. (2).

Establishments to which Part II applies

21.—(1) The establishments in England and Wales to which this Part applies are—

    (a) any university receiving financial support under section 65 of the Further and Higher Education Act 1992;

    (b) any institution conducted by a higher education corporation or further education corporation within the meaning of that Act;

    (c) any institution designated under section 129 of the Education Reform Act 1988 as eligible to receive support from funds administered by a higher education funding council;

    (d) any institution designated under section 28 of the Further and Higher Education Act 1992 as eligible to receive support from funds administered by a further education funding council;

    (e) any institution substantially dependent on financial support under section 6(5) of that Act (certain institutions providing facilities for part-time, or adult, further education);

(f) any institution designated, or of a description designated, by order of the Secretary of State;

(g) any college, school or hall in an establishment within any of the above paragraphs.

(2) The establishments in Scotland to which this Part applies are—

(a) any institution within the higher education sector for the purposes of section 56(2) of the Further and Higher Education (Scotland) Act 1992;

(b) any college of further education (within the meaning of section 36(1) of that Act), the board of management of which, or in respect of which an appropriate person, is in receipt of a grant, loan or other payment as mentioned in section 4(1) of that Act;

(c) any central institution within the meaning of section 135(1) of the Education (Scotland) Act 1980;

(d) any institution designated, or of a description designated, by order of the Secretary of State.

(3) For the purposes of subsection (1)(e) an institution is substantially dependent on financial support under section 6(5) of the Further and Higher Education Act 1992 in any year in which such support amounts to 25 per cent. or more of its income.

For this purpose "year" means an accounting year of the institution, and "income" means receipts of any description, including capital receipts.

(4) In subsection (1)(g) "college" includes any institution in the nature of a college.

(5) References in this Part to the governing body of an establishment are to the executive governing body which has responsibility for the conduct of affairs of the establishment and the management and administration of its revenue and property.

Definitions

"further education corporation": s.17(1) of the Further and Higher Education Act 1992.

"further education funding council": ss.91(2) and 1(1) of the Further and Higher Education Act 1992.

"higher education corporation": s.90(1) of the Further and Higher Education Act 1992.

"higher education funding council": ss.91(4), 61(1) and (6) of the Further and Higher Education Act 1992.

General Note

This section defines the establishments in England, Wales and Scotland to which this Part of the Act applies. The provisions dealing with students' unions, unlike the rest of the Act, apply in Scotland as well as England and Wales. The intention was to define the establishments "in an inclusive and general way to cover all those in the public sector in further and higher education" (*per* Mr T. Boswell, Parliamentary Under-Secretary of State, Standing Committee E, col. 338, June 16, 1994).

Subs. (1)

(a) University here will include institutions with the power to award degrees under royal charter (see *St. David's College, Lampeter* v. *Minister of Education* [1951] 1 All E.R. 559). Such charters are granted by the Privy Council under the College Charters Act 1871. Additionally, s.77(1) of the 1992 Act confers power on the Privy Council to authorise the use of the title "university" by any institution within the higher education sector and, by s.77(4), such an institution is to be treated as a university for all purposes. Subsection (1)(a) is, however, confined to universities in receipt of public funds under s.65 of the 1992 Act and would not apply to a privately funded institution.

(b) This includes, among establishments to which the Act applies, those providing further as well as higher education. "The reforms will apply in further education just as much as in higher education" (*per* Baroness Blatch, Minister of State, *Hansard*, H.L. Vol. 553, col. 1459).

(c) Section 129 of the 1988 Act empowered the Secretary of State to designate certain categories of institution as eligible to receive public funding through the then Polytechnics and Colleges Funding Council. These included colleges grant-aided by the Secretary of State and some institutions assisted by local education authorities. Such designated institutions are brought within the present Act. The power of designation was continued in amended form by s.72 of the 1992 Act, which omits reference to the current funding of the institution and allows designation if its full-time equivalent enrolment number for courses of higher education exceeds 55 per cent. of its total full-time equivalent enrolment number.

(d) This supplements the provision in subs. (1)(a) relating to further education. As an alternative to incorporation as a further education corporation, an institution may be designated under s.28 of the 1992 Act as eligible to receive funding from the further education funding councils. Such institutions must be principally concerned with the provision either of education for 16 to 18 year olds or courses of higher or further education. They must in addition be either voluntary-aided schools or institutions assisted by local education authorities or grant-aided institutions. Such designated institutions will be establishments to which this Act applies.

(e) This includes within the Act institutions, such as adult education and community colleges, which do not receive funding directly from the further education funding councils but through their local further education funding corporation. Section 6(5) of the 1992 Act provides for appropriate requests for funding by such institutions to be forwarded to the further education funding councils.

(f) Power is here conferred on the Secretary of State to designate further institutions, or categories of institutions, as establishments to which the Act applies. The Act contains no criteria for such designation. Such designation must be contained in an order made by statutory instrument subject to the negative resolution procedure: s.23.

(g) This makes it clear that constituent parts of establishments within the preceding definitions will themselves constitute establishments to which the Act applies. Organisations which fall within the definition in s.19 of "students' union" at colleges, schools or halls of residence will thus be included. So, for example Junior Common Rooms at Oxford and Cambridge colleges will constitute students' unions. Subsection (4) defines college as including any institution in the nature of a college but the term is not otherwise defined. As subs. (1)(g) refers to colleges within one of the institutions referred to in subs. (1)(a) to (f), the intention must be to refer to constituent parts of institutions like Oxford and Cambridge universities which have a collegiate structure. School is not defined; the expression is sometimes used to refer to a department or faculty within an institution, *e.g.* School of Law. It does not seem to have been the intention, however, that organisations of particular categories of students within an institution, *e.g.* law students (other than the specific cases referred to in s.20(2)) should constitute students' unions. "Hall" in this subsection is not defined. Halls of residence are specifically covered by s.20(2)(b) though hall may be intended here in a wider sense, *e.g.* St. Edmund Hall, Oxford (which would also, by virtue of subs. (4), constitute a college for this purpose).

Subs. (2)

This contains the parallel provisions in relation to Scotland. As in the case of England and Wales, the Act applies to both higher and further education. The establishments to which the Act applies are universities and other institutions designated by the Secretary of State as eligible to receive funding under the Further and Higher Education (Scotland) Act 1992; colleges of further education in receipt of payments under that Act; educational establishments for the provision of further education recognised as central establishments in accordance with regulations made by the Secretary of State and other institutions or classes of institution designated by the Secretary of State. No criteria are given for such designation which must be by order made by statutory instrument subject to the negative resolution procedure (s.23).

Subs. (3)

This defines substantial dependence on financial support under s.6(5) of the 1992 Act for the purposes of subs. (1)(e) as 25 per cent. or more of income (which includes capital receipts) received during an accounting year of the institution. The accounting year in further and higher education usually runs from August 1 to July 31.

Subs. (5)

The Act imposes, in s.21, a series of duties on governing bodies of establishments to which it applies in relation to the conduct of students' unions. This subsection defines "governing body" in functional terms as the executive body responsible for the conduct of the affairs of the establishment and the management and administration of its revenue and property. The definition differs from that adopted in s.90(1) of the 1992 Act, although it is modelled on that adopted there for "governing body" in relation to a university that did not constitute a higher education corporation. This will apply here to all establishments subject to the Act, which includes, *inter alia*, higher and further education corporations.

Requirements to be observed in relation to students' unions

22.—(1) The governing body of every establishment to which this Part applies shall take such steps as are reasonably practicable to secure that any students' union for students at the establishment operates in a fair and democratic manner and is accountable for its finances.

(2) The governing body shall in particular take such steps as are reasonably practicable to secure that the following requirements are observed by or in relation to any students' union for students at the establishment—
  (a) the union should have a written constitution;
  (b) the provisions of the constitution should be subject to the approval of the governing body and to review by that body at intervals of not more than five years;
  (c) a student should have the right—
       (i) not to be a member of the union, or
       (ii) in the case of a representative body which is not an association, to signify that he does not wish to be represented by it,
    and students who exercise that right should not be unfairly disadvantaged, with regard to the provision of services or otherwise, by reason of their having done so;
  (d) appointment to major union offices should be by election in a secret ballot in which all members are entitled to vote;
  (e) the governing body should satisfy themselves that the elections are fairly and properly conducted;
  (f) a person should not hold sabbatical union office, or paid elected union office, for more than two years in total at the establishment;
  (g) the financial affairs of the union should be properly conducted and appropriate arrangements should exist for the approval of the union's budget, and the monitoring of its expenditure, by the governing body;
  (h) financial reports of the union should be published annually or more frequently, and should be made available to the governing body and to all students, and each such report should contain, in particular—
       (i) a list of the external organisations to which the union has made donations in the period to which the report relates, and
       (ii) details of those donations;
  (i) the procedure for allocating resources to groups or clubs should be fair and should be set down in writing and freely accessible to all students;
  (j) if the union decides to affiliate to an external organisation, it should publish notice of its decision stating—
       (i) the name of the organisation, and
       (ii) details of any subscription or similar fee paid or proposed to be paid, and of any donation made or proposed to be made, to the organisation,
    and any such notice should be made available to the governing body and to all students;
  (k) where the union is affiliated to any external organisations, a report should be published annually or more frequently containing—
       (i) a list of the external organisations to which the union is currently affiliated, and
       (ii) details of subscriptions or similar fees paid, or donations made, to such organisations in the past year (or since the last report),

and such reports should be made available to the governing body and to all students;

(l) there should be procedures for the review of affiliations to external organisations under which—

(i) the current list of affiliations is submitted for approval by members annually or more frequently, and

(ii) at such intervals of not more than a year as the governing body may determine, a requisition may be made by such proportion of members (not exceeding 5 per cent.) as the governing body may determine, that the question of continued affiliation to any particular organisation be decided upon by a secret ballot in which all members are entitled to vote;

(m) there should be a complaints procedure available to all students or groups of students who—

(i) are dissatisfied in their dealings with the union, or

(ii) claim to be unfairly disadvantaged by reason of their having exercised the right referred to in paragraph (c)(i) or (ii) above,

which should include provision for an independent person appointed by the governing body to investigate and report on complaints;

(n) complaints should be dealt with promptly and fairly and where a complaint is upheld there should be an effective remedy.

(3) The governing body of every establishment to which this Part applies shall for the purposes of this section prepare and issue, and when necessary revise, a code of practice as to the manner in which the requirements set out above are to be carried into effect in relation to any students' union for students at the establishment, setting out in relation to each of the requirements details of the arrangements made to secure its observance.

(4) The governing body of every establishment to which this Part applies shall as regards any students' union for students at the establishment bring to the attention of all students, at least once a year—

(a) the code of practice currently in force under subsection (3),

(b) any restrictions imposed on the activities of the union by the law relating to charities, and

(c) where the establishment is one to which section 43 of the Education (No.2) Act 1986 applies (freedom of speech in universities and colleges), the provisions of that section, and of any code of practice issued under it, relevant to the activities or conduct of the union.

(5) The governing body of every establishment to which this Part applies shall bring to the attention of all students, at least once a year, and shall include in any information which is generally made available to persons considering whether to become students at the establishment—

(a) information as to the right referred to in subsection (2)(c)(i) and (ii), and

(b) details of any arrangements it has made for services of a kind which a students' union at the establishment provides for its members to be provided for students who are not members of the union.

(6) In subsections (2), (4) and (5) the expression "all students" shall be construed as follows—

(a) in relation to an association or body which is a students' union by virtue of section 20(1), the reference is to all students at the establishment;

(b) in relation to an association or body which is a students' union by virtue of section 20(2), the reference is to all undergraduate, or all graduate, students at the establishment or to all students at the hall of residence in question, as the case may be;

(c) in relation to an association or body which is a students' union by virtue of section 20(3), the reference is to all the students who by virtue section 20(1) or (2) are comprehended by that expression in relation to its constituent or affiliated associations or bodies.

(7) In this section the expression "members", in relation to a representative body which is not an association, means those whom it is the purpose of the union to represent, excluding any student who has exercised the right referred to in subsection (2)(c)(ii).

(8) In subsection (2)(j) to (1) the references to affiliation to an external organisation, in relation to a students' union for students at an establishment, include any form of membership of, or formal association with, an organisation whose purposes are not confined to purposes connected with that establishment.

(9) Subsection (2)(d) and (1)(ii) (elections and affiliations: requirements to hold secret ballot of all members) do not apply in the case of an open or distance learning establishment, that is, an establishment where the students, or the great majority of them, are provided with materials for private study and are not required to attend the establishment to any significant extent or at all.

DEFINITIONS
"affiliation to an external organisation": subs. (8).
"all students": subs. (6).
"establishment": s.21(1) and (2).
"governing body": s.21(5).
"members": subs. (7).
"students' union": s.20.

GENERAL NOTE
This section is the key section of this part of the Act, laying down requirements for the conduct of students' unions and the implementation of those requirements by institutions. Duties are imposed on governing bodies, generally, to take steps to ensure the fair, democratic and financially accountable conduct of students' unions (see s.22(1)) and specifically to ensure that a series of requirements are complied with (see s.22(2)). These relate to the constitution of students' unions, requiring them to be written and subject to approval and review by the establishment concerned (see subs. (2)(a) and (b)). Holding of sabbatical office is regulated, major offices must be filled by election by secret ballot of all members and the establishment must oversee the proper conduct of elections (see subs. (2)(d)–(f)). The principle of voluntary membership is provided for and safeguards to prevent discrimination against non-members are laid down (see subs. (2)(c) and (m)(ii)). There must be supervision of the financial affairs of students' unions and publication of financial information (see subs. (2)(g) and (h)). Allocation of resources to groups or clubs is regulated, as is affiliation to, or donations to, external organisations (see subs. (2)(i)–(m)). A complaints procedure is required and the governing body of each establishment must issue a code of practice relating to the observance of the requirements of the section (see subs. (2)(m) and (n) and subs. (3)). The governing body must bring the code of practice and other information to the attention of students, in particular their right to opt out and alternative provision of facilities for students who have done so (see subss. (4) and (5)).

Subs. (1)
This subsection imposes a general duty of supervision on governing bodies of the conduct of the affairs of students' unions at their establishments.

Reasonably practicable. The duties imposed upon governing bodies by this and the following subsection are not absolute. Discretion is granted as to how the requirements are to be satisfied and it was recognised by the Government that local circumstances would allow for varying solutions.

"The responsibility for putting the requirements into action will lie with the particular institution concerned. It will be for the institution to introduce those requirements in its own way. The provisions offer flexibility to operate and address specific points of principle in a way that makes sense. That is where the words, 'take such steps as are reasonably practicable' come into play, as they relate to each institution" (*per* Baroness Blatch, Minister of State, *Hansard*, H.L. Vol. 553, col. 615).

Subs. (2)
This subsection contains the detailed requirements which governing bodies must take reasonably practicable steps to ensure are satisfied.

Reasonably practicable. See the note to subs. (1).

Student should have the right. This gives effect to the principle that membership of students' unions should be voluntary. The proposal in the original version of the Bill, foreshadowed by the consultation paper, was that beyond a core area of activity, available to all students, students' union activities should be "on an opt in, voluntary subscription basis" (see The Government's Proposals for Student Union Reform, para. 2). The substantial government amendments to this Part of the Bill in the House of Lords replaced this with the present provision, and the freedom of choice which this creates was stressed as a major underlying policy objective (Baroness Blatch, Minister of State, *Hansard*, H.L. Vol. 553, cols. 594, 597). The right conferred by subs. (2)(c) is reinforced by the duty imposed on governing bodies by subs. (5)(a) to inform students and potential students of their right to opt out, the provisions regarding alternative arrangements for students who have done so (subss. (2)(c) and (5)(b)) and the complaints procedure to be provided for students who claim to have been disadvantaged as a result of doing so (subs. (2)(m)(ii)).

Students ... should not be unfairly disadvantaged. The provision of alternative services for students who decide to opt out of union membership was the subject of considerable debate in Parliament. The duty placed upon establishments is to take steps to ensure that such students are not unfairly disadvantaged in respect of access to facilities and subs. (5)(b) imposes a duty to provide information about arrangements that have been made to provide services, while subs. (2)(m)(ii) provides for a complaints procedure in such cases. How such services are to be provided is a matter for establishments themselves to determine.

"It is important to note that it will be for institutions to decide how to provide for opted-out students either directly or through the student union" (*per* Baroness Blatch, Minister of State, *Hansard*, H.L. Vol. 553, col. 618). As originally drafted, the Bill imposed no direct obligation on institutions to provide services and the Minister of State spoke several times of a moral obligation on institutions to do so (*Hansard*, H.L. Vol. 553, col. 618; *Hansard*, H.L. Vol. 553, col. 969). The proviso in subs. (2)(c) that opted-out students should not be unfairly disadvantaged was introduced as an amendment in Committee in the House of Commons to impose a duty to ensure the provision of at least some services. It was envisaged that one form of provision would be for the institution to arrange with the students' union for the latter to provide, by agreement, access to some facilities by non-members. An alternative way institutions could fulfil their obligations would be by the provision of separate parallel facilities. The Government stressed that there was no intention of alteration of the existing funding arrangements allowing the provision of facilities (see Mr T. Boswell, Parliamentary Under-Secretary of State, Standing Committee E, cols. 344, 345, June 21, 1994). The Act does not specify what services should be provided. That again was regarded as a matter for local determination by institutions.

"It is not for the Government to say what services should be available: that is quite properly a matter for the institution to decide. I emphasise that in initiating the measures, we are leaving matters to local decision wherever possible and not seeking to prescribe in concrete the exact procedures to be followed" (*per* Mr T. Boswell, Parliamentary Under-Secretary of State, Standing Committee E, col. 344, June 21, 1994). Welfare services, catering and sport were suggested as possible examples of services that might be made available, while voting rights in union affairs were seen as something that clearly would not be open to non-members. The duty to provide services is intended to apply only to students who have opted out of union membership; no duty is cast upon institutions to provide services for students who are ineligible for union membership.

"Let me make it quite clear for the record that the Bill does nothing to adjust the membership arrangements set up at local level. If an institution's part-time students were not union members under the constitution of that union, the Bill would require no change and there would be no obligation to provide services to those who were constitutionally excluded from the union, as well as those who might seek to opt out" (*per* Mr T. Boswell, Parliamentary Under-Secretary of State, Standing Committee E, June 21, 1994, col. 386).

Major union offices. A secret ballot of all members is required for election to these. The Act again does not specify what constitutes major union offices. Again a degree of individual discretion is permitted here.

"I would expect the requirement to apply to the union president and others with a significant role in running the union" (*per* Baroness Blatch, Minister of State, *Hansard*, H.L. Vol. 553, col. 617). The Minister of State also said: "We have left it to the institutions themselves to determine which shall be the main offices subject to secret ballot" and referred to a women's officer as one that could be regarded as major or not at the discretion of the governing body (*Hansard*, H.L. Vol. 553, col. 953). This discretion will be constrained by the principle of *Wednesbury* unreasonableness (*Associated Provincial Picture Houses Ltd.* v. *Wednesbury Corporation* [1948] 1 KB 223).

All members. The Bill as originally drafted would have entitled all students to vote in elections. The Bill was amended in Committee in the House of Lords to provide that students who had opted out of union membership could not vote and further amended on Report to exclude from voting students who were not eligible for union membership under the terms of its constitution. It was accepted that eligibility for membership was a matter for each institution to determine.

"The effect will be to enable each institution and union, as now, to determine which categories of student are eligible for membership of the student union, and which in consequence are able to vote" (*per* Baroness Blatch, Minister of State, *Hansard*, H.L. Vol. 553, col. 955).

Fairly and properly conducted. The precise form of supervision is left to each institution but it is envisaged that scrutiny should not be left to the union itself.

"It will be for the governing bodies to decide how to satisfy themselves that union elections are properly and fairly conducted either directly or through delegation to an appropriate official, such as the returning officer. It is important to ensure that it is not delegated to the union itself" (*per* Baroness Blatch, Minister of State, *Hansard*, H.L. Vol. 553, col. 617).

Sabbatical union office. The purpose of this was stated to be: "to provide no platform for the career student politician" (*per* Baroness Blatch, Minister of State, *Hansard*, H.L. Vol. 553, col. 597).

Paid elected union office. This is intended to ensure that a student who having graduated continued to hold or took up union office would be caught by the rule limiting tenure of office to two years.

A list of the external organisations ... donations. Subsection (2)(k) requires the publication of a list of external organisations to which the union is affiliated and payments made to such organisations. Subsection (2)(h) provides that the financial report which the subsection requires to be published should contain similar details of donations to organisations to which the union is not affiliated. There is, however, no duty to give prior notice of such donations as there is in relation to decisions to affiliate to external organisations under subs. (2)(j). This is on the ground that donations could not then be made at short notice and that, unlike affiliation, did not involve a commitment of the union to the organisation in question. Any improper donations would be a matter for the regular financial supervision which governing bodies are required to undertake under subs. (2)(g) and the general requirements of charity law. Those students' unions which are charities will have power to make donations only provided they are in conformity with their educational purposes.

Procedure for allocating resources. The requirement that procedures for allocating resources to groups and clubs should be fair as well as written and available to students was an amendment inserted at Committee in the House of Commons. The governing body will be under a duty to take steps to ensure that procedures are fair and aggrieved group or club members would have a right to invoke the complaints procedure provided for in subs. (2)(m). It appears that fair here is intended to include substantive as well as procedural fairness. When this point was raised in the House of Lords the Minister of State said: "there is a procedural element involved: namely, that the procedures should be fair and democratic; that the procedures should be set out; and that the issue of membership and non-membership should be properly addressed. However, in the case of allocating resources to clubs and societies, it was felt important ... to address the issue of fairness" (*per* Baroness Blatch, *Hansard*, H.L. Vol. 557, col. 91).

Affiliate to an external organisation. Affiliation to external organisations is dealt with in some detail in subs. (2)(j)–(l). It is defined in subs. (8) as any form of membership of, or formal association with, an organisation whose purposes are not confined to purposes connected with the establishment in question. Any such affiliation must be in pursuit of the objects for which the union is established and within the limits of the powers allowed by their constitutions. Such affiliations, however, are intended to be: "those which are made by the students' union in the name of the generality of students" (*per* Baroness Blatch, Minister of State, *Hansard*, H.L. Vol. 553, col. 619). The Minister stated that clubs and societies, such as sports clubs, affiliating to a national association would not be affected. Affiliation by the union itself to such an association would, however, be covered (Baroness Blatch, Minister of State, *Hansard*, H.L. Vol. 553, col. 959). Notice of a decision to affiliate must be given (see subs. (2)(j)), a list of affiliations and payments made to affiliated organisations must be published at least annually (see subs. (2)(k)), the current list of affiliations must be approved by members at least annually and the question of continued affiliation may be put to a secret ballot of members at least annually on the request of a specified proportion of members not exceeding 5 per cent. Subject to the limits imposed, governing bodies are at liberty to specify the relevant periods and the proportion of students who may request a ballot on affiliation. The form in which information about affiliation is issued is also left to the discretion of governing bodies; it must be made available to all students but there is no requirement that it should be published to each individual student. The manner in which annual approval of affiliations is obtained is also not specified, provided that it is given by the membership. Approval by a meeting would be sufficient; there is no requirement for a ballot under subs. (2)(l)(i). The Bill as originally drafted would have required annual ballots on all affiliations; the present proposals were introduced as a Government amendment in the House of Lords.

Complaints procedure. The duty to establish a complaints procedure is in respect of two matters. Firstly, dissatisfaction on the part of a student or group of students in dealings with the union. This does not permit complaints that the governing body is not properly complying with its duties under this section. An amendment to allow general complaints that the requirements for the conduct of students' unions contained in this section were not being observed was not acceptable to the Government on the grounds that governing bodies could be expected to comply with statutory requirements and that a further layer of supervision was unnecessary. Complaints must be by a student or group of students directly affected.

"If nobody is directly affected by a perceived grievance, a person may complain to the governing body of the institution that it is in breach of its obligations under [s.22(2)]. The person could ultimately complain to a court" (*per* Mr T. Boswell, Parliamentary Under-Secretary of State, Standing Committee E, col. 384, June 21, 1994). Secondly, specific complaints may be made that a student has been unfairly disadvantaged by exercising the right to opt-out conferred by subs. (2)(c). A similar *locus standi* requirement would apply in this case. The complaints procedure must provide for an independent person to investigate and report on complaints. While "independent person" is not defined it was envisaged that such a person would not be connected with the institution. It was stated by the Parliamentary Under-Secretary of State that the complaints procedure was designed: "to provide for an impartial element outside the institution where necessary" (Standing Committee E, col. 360, June 21, 1994). The selection of the person concerned and their qualifications is left to the institution concerned. The power of the independent person investigating the complaint is to report only, but subs. (2)(n) imposes a duty on the governing body to provide an effective remedy when a complaint is upheld.

Subs. (3)

The governing body is under a duty to prepare and issue a code of practice regarding compliance with the requirements imposed by subs. (2). The code is expected to give details of the substantive arrangements which institutions have made to ensure compliance, including details of the complaints procedure.

"We are seeking to ensure that the substance of the machinery for meeting requirements is dealt with, and not just the procedures" (*per* Mr T. Boswell, Parliamentary Under-Secretary of State, Standing Committee E, col. 392, June 21, 1994). The Bill in its original form provided for the Secretary of State to issue a code of guidance to which governing bodies would have been expected to have regard but in relation to the present provision in the Act it was stressed that it was for individual institutions to determine what provision should be made, particularly given the range of institutions covered by the Act (see Standing Committee E, col. 388, June 21, 1994).

Subs. (4)

Code of practice. The requirement in subs. (4)(a) was inserted by an amendment introduced in the House of Commons to ensure that establishments not merely drew up a code of practice but also took steps to draw it to the attention of students.

Restrictions imposed. The duty imposed here is a separate requirement to give students information on restrictions imposed by the law relating to charities. It was not envisaged by the Government that this would form part of the code of practice issued by institutions. Considerable stress was, however, laid on the impact of charity law on the activities of students' unions, given that most would enjoy charitable status. For judicial consideration of the charitable status of students' unions in higher education institutions, see *Att.-Gen.* v. *Ross* [1985] 3 All E.R. 334. It was announced that the Attorney-General proposed to issue revised guidance on the impact of the law relating to charities on students' unions (Mr T. Boswell, Parliamentary Under-Secretary of State, Standing Committee E, col. 358, June 21, 1994).

Freedom of speech in universities and colleges. The Education (No. 2) Act 1986, s.43 imposes duties on those concerned in the government of certain establishments to take steps to ensure freedom of speech for members, students, employees and visiting speakers. This includes a duty to issue a code of conduct and to take steps to ensure that it is complied with. Subsection (4)(c) now imposes a duty to bring to the attention of all students the provisions of the legislation and the code of conduct issued by the institution, insofar as it affects the activities of the union. For judicial consideration of s.43, see *R.* v. *University of Liverpool*, ex p. *Caesar-Gordon* [1991] 1

Q.B. 124. The Act applies to all establishments within the further and higher education sectors. Establishments for the purposes of the present Act which do not fall within those categories will not therefore be affected by subs. (4)(c).

Subs. (5)

Information must be given at least annually to students of their right to opt out of union membership and of any alternative facilities made available to them if they do. The facilities must be of a kind which a students' union at that establishment provides for its members. The same information must be included in information provided generally to potential students. Again it is not specified how this information should be provided.

Subs. (9)

The requirement to hold secret ballots for elections to all major union offices and, when required by the appropriate number of students, continued affiliation to organisations, does not apply to the Open University or any other distance-learning establishment. Concern had been expressed at the difficulty and cost of balloting large numbers of students scattered all over the country and the Government introduced an amendment in the House of Lords to exclude such institutions. The other provisions of the Act will apply.

PART III

GENERAL PROVISIONS

Orders and directions

23.—(1) Any power of the Secretary of State to make orders under Part I or II shall be exercised by statutory instrument which shall be subject to annulment in pursuance of a resolution of either House of Parliament.

(2) Orders under Part I or II may make different provision for different cases, circumstances or areas and may contain such incidental, supplementary or transitional provisions as the Secretary of State thinks fit.

(3) Any power conferred by Part I to give directions includes power, exercisable in the same manner and subject to the same conditions or limitations, to revoke or vary directions previously given.

DEFINITIONS

"statutory instrument": s.1 of the Statutory Instruments Act 1946.

GENERAL NOTE

This section provides for powers to make orders which are conferred upon the Secretary of State by Pts. I and II of the Act to be exercised by statutory instrument subject to the negative resolution procedure and confers a power to revoke or vary directions when a power to give directions is conferred.

Subs. (1)

Secretary of State. See the note to s.2(1).

To make orders. Power to make orders is conferred by ss.4(3), 8, 16(1) and (2), 17 and 26.

Subs. (3)

Directions. The power to give directions conferred by s.8 must be exercised by order (s.8(4)). Power to give directions is also conferred by s.16(4) and Sched. 1, para. 5(2).

Consequential amendments

24. The enactments specified in Schedule 2 are amended in accordance with that Schedule, the amendments being consequential on the provisions of this Act.

Extent

25.—(1) The following provisions of this Act extend to England and Wales—

Part I (teacher training),
Part II (students' unions),
the provisions of Schedule 2 (consequential amendments) so far as relating to enactments which extend to England and Wales,
the other provisions of this Part so far as relating to the above provisions.
(2) The following provisions of this Act extend to Scotland—
Part II (students' unions),
the provisions of Schedule 2 (consequential amendments) so far as relating to enactments which extend to Scotland,
the other provisions of this Part so far as relating to the above provisions.
(3) The following provisions of this Act extend to Northern Ireland—
the provisions of Schedule 2 (consequential amendments) so far as relating to enactments which extend to Northern Ireland,
the other provisions of this Part so far as relating to the above provisions.

Commencement

26. The provisions of this Act come into force on such day as the Secretary of State may appoint by order made by statutory instrument; and different days may be appointed for different provisions and for different purposes.

Short title and citation

27.—(1) This Act may be cited as the Education Act 1994.
(2) The Education Acts 1944 to 1993 and this Act may be cited together as the Education Acts 1944 to 1994.

SCHEDULES

Section 2(5)   SCHEDULE 1

THE TEACHER TRAINING AGENCY

Supplementary powers

1.—(1) The agency may, subject to sub-paragraph (2), do anything which appears to them to be necessary or expedient for the purpose of or in connection with the discharge of their functions, including in particular—
(a) acquiring and disposing of land and other property,
(b) entering into contracts,
(c) investing sums not immediately required for the purpose of the discharge of their functions, and
(d) accepting gifts of money, land or other property.
(2) The agency shall not borrow money.

Chief officer

2.—(1) One of the members of the agency shall be the chief officer.
(2) The first chief officer shall be appointed as such by the Secretary of State and shall hold and vacate office in accordance with the terms of his appointment.
(3) Each subsequent chief officer shall be appointed by the agency with the approval of the Secretary of State on such terms and conditions (including terms with respect to tenure and vacation of office) as the agency may with the approval of the Secretary of State determine.
(4) On approval by the Secretary of State of the person to be appointed on any occasion as chief officer of the agency and the terms and conditions of his appointment, the Secretary of State shall—
(a) if that person is not already a member of the agency, appoint him as a member for the same term as the term of his appointment as chief officer, or
(b) if he is already such a member but his term of appointment as such ends before the term of his appointment as chief officer ends, extend his term of appointment as a member so that it ends at the same time as the term of his appointment as chief officer.

Tenure of members of the agency

3.—(1) A person shall hold and vacate office as a member or as chairman or chief officer of the agency in accordance with the terms of his appointment and shall, on ceasing to be a member, be eligible for re-appointment.

(2) A person may at any time by notice in writing to the Secretary of State resign his office as a member or as chairman of the agency.

4. If the Secretary of State is satisfied that a member of the agency—

(a) has been absent from meetings of the agency for a period longer than six consecutive months without the permission of the agency, or

(b) is unable or unfit to discharge the functions of a member,

the Secretary of State may by notice in writing to that member remove him from office and thereupon the office shall become vacant.

Salaries, allowances and pensions

5.—(1) The agency—

(a) shall pay to their members such salaries or fees, and such travelling, subsistence or other allowances, as the Secretary of State may determine, and

(b) shall, as regards any member in whose case the Secretary of State may so determine, pay or make provision for the payment of such sums by way of pension, allowances and gratuities to or in respect of him as the Secretary of State may determine.

(2) If a person ceases to be a member of the agency and it appears to the Secretary of State that there are special circumstances which make it right that he should receive compensation, the Secretary of State may direct the agency to make to that person a payment of such amount as the Secretary of State may determine.

(3) The agency shall pay to the members of any of their committees who are not members of the agency such travelling, subsistence and other allowances as the Secretary of State may determine.

(4) A determination or direction of the Secretary of State under this paragraph requires the approval of the Treasury.

Staff

6.—(1) The agency may appoint such employees as they think fit.

(2) The agency shall pay to their employees such remuneration and allowances as the agency may determine.

(3) The employees shall be appointed on such other terms and conditions as the agency may determine.

(4) A determination under sub-paragraph (2) or (3) requires the approval of the Secretary of State given with the consent of the Treasury.

7.—(1) Employment with the agency shall be included among the kinds of employment to which a scheme under section 1 of the Superannuation Act 1972 can apply.

(2) The agency shall pay to the Treasury, at such times as the Treasury may direct, such sums as the Treasury may determine in respect of the increase attributable to sub-paragraph (1) in the sums payable out of money provided by Parliament under that Act.

(3) Where an employee of the agency is, by reference to that employment, a participant in a scheme under section 1 of that Act and is also a member of the agency, the Treasury may determine that his service as such a member shall be treated for the purposes of the scheme as service as an employee of the agency (whether or not any benefits are payable to or in respect of him by virtue of paragraph 5).

Committees

8.—(1) The agency may establish a committee for any purpose.

(2) The number of the members of a committee established under this paragraph, and the terms on which they are to hold and vacate office, shall be fixed by the agency.

(3) Such a committee may include persons who are not members of the agency.

(4) The agency shall keep under review the structure of committees established under this paragraph and the scope of each committee's activities.

Delegation of functions

9. The agency may authorise the chairman, the chief officer or any committee established under paragraph 8 to exercise such of their functions as they may determine.

Proceedings

10. Without prejudice to any other rights the Secretary of State may require to be accorded to him as a condition of any grants made to the agency under this Act—

(a) a representative of the Secretary of State shall be entitled to attend and take part in any deliberations (but not in decisions) at meetings of the agency or of any committee of the agency, and

(b) the agency shall provide the Secretary of State with such copies of any documents distributed to members of the agency or of any such committee as he may require.

11.—(1) Her Majesty's Chief Inspector of Schools in England, or a representative of his, shall be entitled to attend and take part in any deliberations (but not in decisions) at meetings of the agency or of any committee of the agency.

(2) The agency shall provide Her Majesty's Chief Inspector of Schools in England with such copies of any documents distributed to members of the agency or of any such committee as he may require.

12. The validity of any proceedings of the agency or of any committee of the agency shall not be affected by a vacancy among the members or by any defect in the appointment of a member.

13. Subject to the preceding provisions of this Schedule, the agency may regulate their own procedure and that of any of their committees.

Application of seal and proof of instruments

14. The application of the seal of the agency shall be authenticated by the signature—
(a) of the chairman or of some other person authorised either generally or specially by the agency to act for that purpose, and
(b) of one other member.

15. Every document purporting to be an instrument made or issued by or on behalf of the agency and to be duly executed under the seal of the agency, or to be signed or executed by a person authorised by the agency to act in that behalf, shall be received in evidence and be treated, without further proof, as being so made or issued unless the contrary is shown.

Accounts

16.—(1) It shall be the duty of the agency—
(a) to keep proper accounts and proper records in relation to the accounts,
(b) to prepare in respect of each financial year of the agency a statement of accounts, and
(c) to send copies of the statement to the Secretary of State and to the Comptroller and Auditor General before the end of the month of August next following the financial year to which the statement relates.

(2) The statement of accounts shall comply with any directions given by the Secretary of State with the approval of the Treasury as to—
(a) the information to be contained in it,
(b) the manner in which the information contained in it is to be presented, or
(c) the methods and principles according to which the statement is to be prepared,
and shall contain such additional information as the Secretary of State may with the approval of the Treasury require to be provided for the information of Parliament.

(3) The Comptroller and Auditor General shall examine, certify and report on each statement received by him in pursuance of this paragraph and shall lay copies of each statement and of his report before each House of Parliament.

(4) In this paragraph "financial year" means the period beginning with the date on which the agency is established and ending with the 31st March following that date, and each successive period of twelve months.

Annual reports

17. The agency—
(a) shall make an annual report to the Secretary of State, who shall lay a copy of it before each house of Parliament; and
(b) may arrange for any such report to be published in such manner as the agency consider appropriate.

Status of agency

18. The agency shall not be regarded as the servant or agent of the Crown or as enjoying any status, immunity or privilege of the Crown; and the property of the agency shall not be regarded as property of, or property held on behalf of, the Crown.

DEFINITIONS
"financial year": para. 16(4).

GENERAL NOTE
This Schedule contains more detailed provisions for the organisation and procedure of the Agency provided for in s.2(5). Its provisions follow closely those for the further and higher

education funding councils (ss.1, 62 of and Sched. 1 to the 1992 Act). Like those bodies, the Agency is a non-departmental public body responsible to the Secretary of State who appoints the members (s.2(1), subject to the considerations to which s.2(2)–(4) directs him to have regard) and may remove them for absence or incapacity (para. 4). The Secretary of State appoints the first Chief Officer and subsequent appointments require his approval (para. 2). The terms of appointment of members and the Chief Officer are determined by the Secretary of State (paras. 2 and 3) as are salaries and other payments to members (para. 5). The Secretary of State may require that his representative be permitted to attend meetings of the Agency and its committees, and he may require that he be provided with papers distributed to members (para. 10).

Para. 1

This confers ancillary powers of owning property, making contracts, investing money and receiving gifts, although the Agency is prohibited by subpara. (2) from borrowing money.

Para. 2

The period of office and other terms of appointment of members are to be determined by the Secretary of State. If not already a member of the Agency, or if his or her term of appointment as a member is due to expire before the period of appointment as Chief Officer, the Secretary of State must appoint the Chief Officer as a member or extend the term of membership as the case may be (subpara. 4). The qualifications for membership to which the Secretary of State is directed to have regard by s.2(2)–(4) will therefore apply to the Chief Officer.

Para. 3

The Secretary of State will make provision for tenure and other terms of office. Specific provision is made for the reappointment of retiring members and for resignation by members.

Para. 4

The Secretary of State may remove members for absence, unfitness or inability to discharge office.

Para. 5

Payments to members (including committee members who may not necessarily be members of the Agency) may only be made following a determination by the Secretary of State, subject to the approval of the Treasury. There is a power to direct the payment of compensation, in special circumstances, to a member on leaving office (subpara. (2)). No particular form is provided for determinations, directions under this paragraph or Treasury approval. Provision is made by s.22(3) for the revocation or variation of directions.

Para. 6

Determinations by the Agency as to the payment and other terms of employment of staff require the approval of the Secretary of State and the Treasury. The decision to appoint staff will be taken by the Agency.

Para. 7

This provision enables staff to be admitted to the Principal Civil Service Pension Scheme in accordance with the Superannuation Act 1972, s.1.

Para. 8

The Agency may establish committees for any purpose, but is not required to do so. Contrast the requirement for the appointment of regional committees imposed on the Further Education Funding Council for England by Sched. 1, para. 9 to the 1992 Act. Committee members need not be members of the Agency (subpara. (3)).

Para. 10

The involvement of the Secretary of State in the working of the Agency is provided for by conferring upon him a right that his representative should attend meetings of the Agency and its committees and to require the provision of copies of documents distributed to members and committee members. Schedule 1, para. 11 to the 1992 Act, and Sched. 1, para. 10 to the 1993 Act conferred the same power in respect of the Further and Higher Education Funding Councils and the Funding Agency for Schools.

Para. 11

Section 5(2) requires the Agency to have regard to assessments of the quality of education provided by institutions made by H.M. Chief Inspector of Schools. This paragraph grants the same rights to him as are conferred upon the Secretary of State under para. 10.

Para. 16
This provides for financial accountability to Parliament through the supervision of the Comptroller and Auditor General. Statements of accounts must be provided to the latter and to the Secretary of State, who is empowered to give directions, with the approval of the Treasury, as to the information to be contained, its presentation, and methods and principles of presentation. Power is also given (see subs. (3)) to require additional information for Parliament.

Para. 17
This imposes a duty on the Agency to prepare an annual report for the Secretary of State, which must be laid before Parliament. The Agency may publish the report.

Para. 18
The Agency does not enjoy Crown immunity or benefit from any privilege of the Crown. As a public body it will be subject to judicial review; *cf. R.* v. *Higher Education Funding Council,* ex p. *Institute of Dental Surgery* [1994] 1 All E.R. 651.

Section 24   SCHEDULE 2

CONSEQUENTIAL AMENDMENTS

Public Records Act 1958 (c.51)

1. In Schedule 1 to the Public Records Act 1958 (definition of public records), in Part II of the Table at the end of paragraph 3 (organisations whose records are public records) insert at the appropriate place—
  "Teacher Training Agency".

Education Act 1962 (c. 12)

2. In section 4 of the Education Act 1962 (awards &c. by local education authorities and Secretary of State: supplementary provisions), after subsection (1) insert—
  "(1A) In those sections any reference to an institution other than a university or college includes a reference to an institution providing a course which qualifies for funding under Part I of the Education Act 1994.".

Superannuation Act 1972 (c.11)

3. In Schedule 1 to the Superannuation Act 1972 (employments to which a scheme under section 1 of that Act can apply), at the end of the list of "Other Bodies" insert—
  "Teacher Training Agency.".

House of Commons Disqualification Act 1975 (c.24)

4. In Part III of Schedule 1 to the House of Commons Disqualification Act 1975 (disqualifying offices), at the appropriate place insert—
  "Any member of the Teacher Training Agency in receipt of remuneration.".

Sex Discrimination Act 1975 (c.65)

5.—(1) The Sex Discrimination Act 1975 is amended as follows.
  (2) In section 23A (discrimination by further education and higher education funding councils), for "1992" substitute "1994".
  (3) After section 23C (discrimination by Funding Agency for Schools or Schools Funding Council for Wales) insert—

"Discrimination by Teacher Training Agency
  23D. It is unlawful for the Teacher Training Agency in carrying out their functions under Part I of the Education Act 1994 to do any act which constitutes sex discrimination.".
  (4) In section 25 (general duty in public sector of education)—
  (a) in subsections (2) and (4) for "and 23C" substitute ", 23C and 23D"; and
  (b) after subsection (6)(e) insert—
  "(f) the Teacher Training Agency.".

Race Relations Act 1976 (c.74)

6.—(1) The Race Relations Act 1976 is amended as follows.
  (2) In section 18A (discrimination by further education and higher education funding councils), for "1992" substitute "1994".
  (3) After section 18C (discrimination by Funding Agency for Schools or Schools Funding Council for Wales) insert—

"Discrimination by Teacher Training Agency

18D. It is unlawful for the Teacher Training Agency in carrying out their functions under Part I of the Education Act 1994 to do any act which constitutes racial discrimination.".

(4) In section 19 (general duty in public sector of education)—

(a) in subsections (2) and (4) for "and 18C" substitute ", 18C and 18D"; and

(b) after subsection (6)(e) insert—

"(f) the Teacher Training Agency.".

Education (Fees and Awards) Act 1983 (c.40)

7. In section 1 of the Education (Fees and Awards) Act 1983 (regulations as to fees payable by foreign students), in subsection (3) (institutions to which the section applies) after paragraph (d) insert—

"(e) any institution eligible for funding under Part I of the Education Act 1994 (teacher training).".

Education Reform Act 1988 (c.40)

8.—(1) The Education Reform Act 1988 is amended as follows.

(2) In section 9(1A) (prohibition of conditions as to religious worship, &c.), after "further education" insert "or teacher training".

(3) In section 106 (prohibition of charges, &c. in maintained schools), in subsection (1A) (exceptions from prohibition) after paragraph (b) insert—

"; or

(c) teacher training.".

(4) In section 218 (school and further and higher education regulations)—

(a) the subsection (2A) inserted by section 291 of the Education Act 1993 is renumbered (2B), and

(b) at the beginning of that subsection for "The regulations" substitute "Regulations under subsection (2) above".

(5) In section 220 (extension of functions of Audit Commission)—

(a) in subsection (1), after paragraph (a) insert—

"(aa) a funding agency under Part I of the Education Act 1994 or the governing body of an institution receiving financial support under that Part, or"; and

(b) in subsection (2), omit the word "and" following paragraph (bd) and after paragraph (c) insert—

"(d) with respect to studies relating to a funding agency under Part I of the Education Act 1994, the agency; and

(e) with respect to studies relating to the governing body of an institution receiving financial support under that Part, the appropriate funding agency or the governing body.".

Education (Student Loans) Act 1990 (c.6)

9. In section 1 of the Education (Student Loans) Act 1990 (loans for students of certain institutions), in subsection (3)(a) (meaning of "institutions receiving support from public funds"), after "institutions receiving grants under section 65 of the Further and Higher Education Act 1992" insert "or under section 5 of the Education Act 1994".

Further and Higher Education Act 1992 (c.13)

10.—(1) The Further and Higher Education Act 1992 is amended as follows.

(2) In section 70(1)(a) (assessment by higher education funding councils of quality of education provided by institutions), omit "under this Part of this Act".

(3) In section 90(1) (interpretation), in the definition of "the Education Acts", for "1993" substitute "1994".

GENERAL NOTE

This schedule makes consequential changes to existing Acts of Parliament.

INDEX

References are to sections and Schedules

ACCREDITED INSTITUTIONS, 14
AMENDMENTS, 24, Sched. 2

COMMENCEMENT, 26

EFFICIENCY STUDIES, 10
EXTENT, 25

FUNDING,
  Funding Agencies,
    defined, 3
    directions from Secretary of State, 8
    efficiency studies, 10
    grants to,
      power to make, 7(1)
      terms and conditions of, 7(2)–(3)
    joint exercise of functions, 9
    research by, 11
  grants, loans and other payments,
    consultations as to, 6(3)
    information from governing bodies, 6(5)
    matters to be taken into account, 5(4),
      6(4)
    power to make, 5(1)
    school-centred and non-school-centred
      courses, 6(1)–(2)
    terms and conditions, 5(2)–(3)
  institutions eligible, 4(2)–(4)
  qualifying activities, 4(1)

HIGHER EDUCATION FUNDING COUNCIL FOR
  WALES, 3(2), 14(2)(c), 16(4)

INTERPRETATION, 19

ORDERS AND DIRECTIONS, 23

RESEARCH, 11

SAFEGUARD SALARY PAYMENTS, 18
SHORT TITLE, 27
STUDENTS' UNIONS,
  meaning of, 20
  qualifying establishments, 21
  requirements to be observed, 22

TEACHER TRAINING,
  grants for, 13
  initial,
    availability of, 12(2)
    power of schools to provide, 12
  qualified teachers, 14
TEACHER TRAINING AGENCY,
  constitution, 2(5), Sched. 1
  establishment, 1(1)
  functions, 1(1)
    supplementary, 16
  information for Secretary of State,
    duty to provide, 15
  membership,
    appointment, 2(2)
    number of members, 2(1)
    qualifications, 2(2)–(4)
  objectives, (1)(2)
  Teaching as a Career Unit, transfer of, 17
TEACHING AS A CAREER UNIT, 17

FIREARMS (AMENDMENT) ACT 1994

(1994 c. 31)

An Act to create a new offence of possessing a firearm or imitation firearm with intent to cause fear of violence; to apply certain provisions of the Firearms Act 1968 to imitation firearms; and for connected purposes.

[21st July 1994]

PARLIAMENTARY DEBATES
Hansard, H.C. Vol. 243, col. 1102; H.L. Vol. 556; cols. 843; 1846; Vol. 557, col. 252.

INTRODUCTION
This Act provides for the amendment of the Firearms Act 1968 (c. 27) to include an offence of possession of a firearm with intent to cause fear of violence (new s.16A). Sched. 6, Pt. I of the 1968 Act is amended accordingly to include reference to the appropriate punishment on indictment for the offence.

Possession of firearm or imitation firearm with intent to cause fear of violence

1.—(1) After section 16 of the Firearms Act 1968 ("the 1968 Act") there shall be inserted the following section—

"**Possession of firearm with intent to cause fear of violence**
16A. It is an offence for a person to have in his possession any firearm or imitation firearm with intent—
(a) by means thereof to cause, or
(b) to enable another person by means thereof to cause,
any person to believe that unlawful violence will be used against him or another person."

(2) In Part I of Schedule 6 to that Act (prosecution and punishment of offences), after the entry relating to section 16 there shall be inserted the following entry—

"Section 16A	Possession of firearm with intent to cause fear of violence.	On indictment	10 years or a fine; or both.	—"

Application of sections 20 and 46 of 1968 Act to imitation firearms

2.—(1) In section 20 of the 1968 Act (trespassing with firearms), after the word "firearm", in both places where it occurs, there shall be inserted the words "or imitation firearm".

(2) In subsection (1)(b) of section 46 of that Act (power of search with warrant), after the word "firearm" there shall be inserted the words ", imitation firearm".

(3) In Part I of Schedule 6 to that Act—
(a) in the entry relating to section 20(1), in the second column, after the word "firearm" there shall be inserted the words "or imitation firearm" and, in the third column, after the words "but not" there shall be inserted the words "in the case of an imitation firearm or"; and
(b) in the entry relating to section 20(2), in the second column, after the word "firearm" there shall be inserted the words "or imitation firearm".

Northern Ireland

3.—(1) Sections 1 and 2 above do not extend to Northern Ireland.

(2) An Order in Council under paragraph 1(1)(b) of Schedule 1 to the Northern Ireland Act 1974 (legislation for Northern Ireland in the interim period) which contains a statement that it is made only for purposes corresponding to those of sections 1 and 2 above—

(a) shall not be subject to paragraph 1(4) and (5) of that Schedule (affirmative resolution of both Houses of Parliament); but

(b) shall be subject to annulment in pursuance of a resolution of either House of Parliament.

Short title and commencement

4.—(1) This Act may be cited as the Firearms (Amendment) Act 1994.

(2) This Act shall come into force at the end of the period of two months beginning with the day on which it is passed.

(3) This Act shall not have effect in relation to anything done before it comes into force.

INDEX

References are to sections

COMMENCEMENT, 4

IMITATION FIREARMS, 2

NORTHERN IRELAND PROVISIONS, 3

POSSESSION OF FIREARM WITH INTENT TO CAUSE FEAR OF VIOLENCE, 1

SHORT TITLE, 4

TRESPASSING WITH FIREARMS, 2

SALE OF GOODS (AMENDMENT) ACT 1994*

(1994 c. 32)

An Act to abolish the rule of law relating to the sale of goods in market overt. [3rd November 1994]

PARLIAMENTARY DEBATES

Hansard, H.L. Vol. 550, col. 950; Vol. 551, cols. 209, 1038, 1352; Vol. 557, col. 967; H.C. Vol. 242, col. 564; Vol. 243, col. 1076; Vol. 246, col. 1341.

The Bill was discussed in Standing Committee C on May 10, 1994.

INTRODUCTION

The purpose of this Act is to abolish the rule of law relating to the sale of goods in market overt. It is an English rule of law that the buyer of goods acquires no better title to them than the seller had; *nemo dat quod non habet*. This ancient principle is put into statutory form by s.21 of the Sale of Goods Act 1979 (c. 54). A thief has no title to what he steals and therefore no one who buys them from him or a purchaser from him can obtain any title. There is one exception to this rule, not to be found in Wales, Scotland or Northern Ireland (nor in the Irish Republic), which permits title to be acquired by a buyer of goods to which the seller had no title, *i.e.* a sale in market overt.

The market overt rule has existed since before 1189 or was created by statute or charter. Where goods are sold in market overt according to the usage of the market, good title passes to an innocent purchaser, buying in good faith and without notice of the lack of, or taint to, the seller's title. There is some protection in the case of stolen goods (see below) and, should a sale be rescinded or the goods in some way come back into the possession of the seller, the true owner's title is reconstituted.

In order to come within the rule of market overt, the sale must take place within the boundaries of the market place on the usual market day and between sunrise and sunset. The goods must be on open display and of a kind normally bought and sold in the market, although the seller does not have to be a trader at the market. Any market tolls must be paid, otherwise the sale is voidable. The rule is contained in s.22(3) of the Sale of Goods Act 1979.

Nowadays the rule applies mostly to the ancient street markets, the best known of which is probably Bermondsey market, although the principle is as valid in any open, public and legally constituted market or fair (see *Lee* v. *Bayes* (1856) 18 C.B. 599). A sale by private treaty at a market where auctions are usual is still within the rule (see *Bishopsgate Motor Finance Corporation* v. *Transport Brakes (Winsor Garage, Third Party)* [1949] 1 K.B. 322).

An exception to the rule of sales in open market was made in the Middle Ages for the City of London. Every part of a shop to which the public have access without permission is market overt every day of the week except Sundays and holidays for the sale of the type of goods normally handled by the trader. During the debate of the Bill it was said that there had been no claims of market overt in the City of London for 80 years.

When someone is convicted of any offence connected to the theft of any goods, the court may order anyone having possession of the goods to restore them to the true owner, or may order the defendant to pay compensation equal to the value of the goods to the true owner. This remedy is almost unheard of where there has been a sale in market overt, and there has been a belief that the remedy was not available in such cases.

The Bill, which was introduced by Lord Renton, was supported by the police, antiques dealers and auction houses (whose irritation was justifiably directed at what Lord Oliver called "a senseless and antisocial medieval survival") as well as The Law Society and organisations representing consumers.

During its Second Reading, the Minister of State, Lord Strathclyde, indicated some reservation on the part of the Government. The Department of Trade and Industry published a consultation document *Transfer of Title: Sections 21 to 26 of the Sale of Goods Act 1979* which invited views on the whole issue of the protection of innocent purchasers. One of the propositions in that document was the abolition of market overt. Despite the Government's caution, and desire to await the outcome of the consultation process, the Bill was taken through all stages in the House of Lords and the Commons.

COMMENCEMENT

The Act will come into force on January 3, 1995 and will apply to any contract made after that date.

---

*Annotations by W. H. Thomas, Solicitor, Editor of The Encyclopedia of Consumer Law.

Repeal of s.22(1) of the Sale of Goods Act 1979

1. Section 22(1) (relating to the sale of goods in market overt) of the Sale of Goods Act 1979 is hereby repealed.

GENERAL NOTE

This section repeals s.22(1) of the Sale of Goods Act 1979 thus ensuring that the historic rule of *nemo dat quod non habet* is restored for sales of stolen goods in street markets and other open, legally constituted markets and fairs. The rule of market overt has never applied to car-boot sales and any sales taking place outside the formal boundaries of the market or fair.

Consequential repeals

2.—(1) Section 47 of the Laws in Wales Act 1542 (sale of stolen goods in a fair or market in Wales) is hereby repealed.

(2) In section 7(3) of the Sea Fisheries (Shellfish) Act 1967 (protection of fisheries for shellfish), the words "sold in market overt or" shall be omitted.

GENERAL NOTE

The purpose of this section is to repeal two existing statutory references to market overt.

Section 7 of the Sea Fisheries (Shellfish) Act 1967 (c. 83) provides that shellfish removed from a bed remain the absolute property of the owner or grantees unless disposed of under their authority. It provides one exception in the case of market overt. The repeal is necessary to prevent an accidental retention of the rule in connection with shellfish.

The Laws in Wales Act 1542 (34 & 35 Hen. 8, c. 39) laid down that title could not pass in the case of stolen goods sold at a market in Wales. The 1994 Act makes that the case throughout the U.K. The rest of the 1542 Act was repealed by the Welsh Language Act 1993 (c. 38); the present repeal removes the 1542 Act from the Statute Book.

Short title, commencement and extent

3.—(1) This Act may be cited as the Sale of Goods (Amendment) Act 1994.

(2) This Act shall apply to any contract for sale of goods which is made after this Act comes into force.

(3) This Act shall come into force at the end of the period of two months beginning with the day on which it is passed.

(4) Section 1 and this section extend to Northern Ireland.

GENERAL NOTE

This section makes it clear that the Act is not retrospective and that it comes into effect on January 3, 1995.

It also ensures that the new law is applied in Northern Ireland. Formerly, although there was no market overt in Ireland, title acquired in market overt in England was recognised.

INDEX

References are to sections

COMMENCEMENT, 3(2)–(3)

EXTENT, 3(4)

MARKET OVERT,
  fisheries, 2(2)
  repeal of 1979 Act as to, 1

SHELLFISH, 2(2)
SHORT TITLE, 3(1)

WALES,
  sale of stolen goods, 2(1)

CRIMINAL JUSTICE AND PUBLIC ORDER ACT 1994*

(1994 c. 33)

ARRANGEMENT OF SECTIONS

PART I

YOUNG OFFENDERS

Secure training orders

SECT.
1. Secure training orders.
2. Secure training orders: supplementary provisions as to detention.
3. Supervision under secure training order.
4. Breaches of requirements of supervision of persons subject to secure training orders.
5. Provision etc. of secure training centres.
6. Management of secure training centres.
7. Contracting out of secure training centres.
8. Officers of contracted out secure training centres.
9. Powers and duties of custody officers employed at contracted out secure training centres.
10. Intervention by Secretary of State in management of contracted out secure training centres.
11. Contracted out functions at directly managed secure training centres.
12. Escort arrangements and officers.
13. Protection of custody officers at secure training centres.
14. Wrongful disclosure of information relating to offenders detained at secure training centres.
15. Interpretation of sections 7 to 14.

Custodial sentences for young offenders

16. Long term detention of young offenders.
17. Maximum length of detention for young offenders.
18. Accommodation of young offenders sentenced to custody for life.

Secure accommodation for certain young persons

19. Extension of kinds of secure accommodation.
20. Secure remands for young offenders.
21. Cost of secure accommodation.
22. Management of secure accommodation.

Arrest of young persons in breach of conditions of remand

23. Liability of young persons to arrest for breaking conditions of remand.

Police detention of young persons

24. Detention of arrested juveniles after charge.

PART II

BAIL

25. No bail for defendants charged with or convicted of homicide or rape after previous conviction of such offences.

---

*Annotations by H.H.J. Richard May, a Circuit Judge on the Midland and Oxford Circuit and Mr J.J. McManus LL.B., Ph.D., Senior Lecturer in Law, University of Dundee.

26. No right to bail for persons accused or convicted of committing offence while on bail.
27. Power for police to grant conditional bail to persons charged.
28. Police detention after charge.
29. Power for police to arrest for failure to answer to police bail.
30. Reconsideration of decisions granting bail.

PART III

COURSE OF JUSTICE: EVIDENCE, PROCEDURE, ETC.

Imputations on character

31. Imputations on character.

Corroboration

32. Abolition of corroboration rules.
33. Abolition of corroboration requirements under Sexual Offences Act 1956.

Inferences from accused's silence

34. Effect of accused's failure to mention facts when questioned or charged.
35. Effect of accused's silence at trial.
36. Effect of accused's failure or refusal to account for objects, substances or marks.
37. Effect of accused's failure or refusal to account for presence at a particular place.
38. Interpretation and savings for sections 34, 35, 36 and 37.
39. Power to apply sections 34 to 38 to armed forces.

Juries

40. Disqualification for jury service of persons on bail in criminal proceedings.
41. Jury service: disabled persons.
42. Jury service: excusal on religious grounds.
43. Separation of jury during consideration of verdict.

Procedure, jurisdiction and powers of magistrates' courts

44. Transfer for trial instead of committal proceedings.
45. Extension of procedures enabling magistrates' courts to deal with cases in which accused pleads guilty.
46. Criminal damage, etc. as summary offence: relevant sum.
47. Recovery of fines, etc. by deduction from income support.

Sentencing: guilty pleas

48. Reduction in sentences for guilty pleas.

Publication of reports in young offender cases

49. Restrictions on reports of proceedings in which children or young persons are concerned.

Child testimony

50. Video recordings of testimony from child witnesses.

Intimidation, etc., of witnesses, jurors and others

51. Intimidation, etc., of witnesses, jurors and others.

Criminal appeals

52. Circuit judges to act as judges of criminal division of Court of Appeal.
53. Expenses in criminal appeals in Northern Ireland Court of Appeal.

PART IV

POLICE POWERS

Powers of police to take body samples

54. Powers of police to take intimate body samples.
55. Powers of police to take non-intimate body samples.

56. Fingerprints and samples: supplementary provisions.
57. Retention of samples in certain cases.
58. Samples: intimate and non-intimate etc.
59. Extension of powers to search persons' mouths.

Powers of police to stop and search

60. Powers to stop and search in anticipation of violence.

PART V

PUBLIC ORDER: COLLECTIVE TRESPASS OR NUISANCE ON LAND

Powers to remove trespassers on land

61. Power to remove trespassers on land.
62. Supplementary powers of seizure.

Powers in relation to raves

63. Powers to remove persons attending or preparing for a rave.
64. Supplementary powers of entry and seizure.
65. Raves: power to stop persons from proceeding.
66. Power of court to forfeit sound equipment.

Retention and charges for seized property

67. Retention and charges for seized property.

Disruptive trespassers

68. Offence of aggravated trespass.
69. Powers to remove persons committing or participating in aggravated trespass.

Trespassory assemblies

70. Trespassory assemblies.
71. Trespassory assemblies: power to stop persons from proceeding.

Squatters

72. Violent entry to premises: special position of displaced residential occupiers and intending occupiers.
73. Adverse occupation of residential premises.
74. Protected intending occupiers: supplementary provisions.
75. Interim possession orders: false or misleading statements.
76. Interim possession orders: trespassing during currency of order.

Powers to remove unauthorised campers

77. Power of local authority to direct unauthorised campers to leave land.
78. Orders for removal of persons and their vehicles unlawfully on land.
79. Provisions as to directions under s.77 and orders under s.78.
80. Repeal of certain provisions relating to gipsy sites.

PART VI

PREVENTION OF TERRORISM

81. Powers to stop and search vehicles, etc. and persons.
82. Offences relating to terrorism.
83. Investigations into activities and financial resources of terrorist organisations.

PART VII

OBSCENITY AND PORNOGRAPHY AND VIDEOS

Obscene publications and indecent photographs of children

84. Indecent pseudo-photographs of children.
85. Arrestable offences to include certain offences relating to obscenity or indecency.

86. Indecent photographs of children: sentence of imprisonment.
87. Publishing, displaying, selling or distributing etc. obscene material in Scotland: sentence of imprisonment.

Video recordings

88. Video recordings: increase in penalties.
89. Video recordings: restriction of exemptions.
90. Video recordings: suitability.
91. Enforcement by enforcing authorities outside their areas.

Obscene, offensive or annoying telephone calls

92. Obscene, offensive or annoying telephone calls: increase in penalty.

PART VIII

PRISON SERVICES AND THE PRISON SERVICE

CHAPTER I

ENGLAND AND WALES

Prisoner escorts

93. Arrangements for the provision of prisoner escorts.
94. Powers and duties of prisoner custody officers acting in pursuance of such arrangements.
95. Breaches of discipline by prisoners under escort.

Contracted out prisons etc.

96. Contracted out parts of prisons, etc.
97. Temporary attachment of prison officers.
98. Prisoners temporarily out of prison.

Miscellaneous

99. Contracted out functions at directly managed prisons.
100. Provision of prisons by contractors.

Supplemental

101. Minor and consequential amendments.

CHAPTER II

SCOTLAND

Prisoner escorts

102. Arrangements for the provision of prisoner escorts.
103. Monitoring of prisoner escort arrangements.
104. Powers and duties of prisoner custody officers performing escort functions.
105. Breaches of discipline by prisoners under escort.

Contracted out prisons

106. Contracting out of prisons.
107. Officers of contracted out prisons.
108. Powers and duties of prisoner custody officers employed at contracted out prisons.
109. Breaches of discipline by prisoners temporarily out of contracted out prison.
110. Consequential modifications of 1989 Act, prison rules and directions.
111. Intervention by the Secretary of State.

Contracted out functions

112. Contracted out functions at directly managed prisons.

Provision of new prisons

113. Provision of new prisons.

Supplemental

114. Prisoner custody officers: general provisions.
115. Wrongful disclosure of information.
116. Minor and consequential amendments.
117. Interpretation of Chapter II.

CHAPTER III

NORTHERN IRELAND

Prisoner escorts

118. Arrangements for the provision of prisoner escorts.
119. Monitoring etc. of prisoner escort arrangements.
120. Powers and duties of prisoner custody officers acting in pursuance of such arrangements.
121. Breaches of discipline by prisoners under escort.

Supplemental

122. Certification of custody officers.
123. Protection of prisoner custody officers.
124. Wrongful disclosure of information.
125. Interpretation of Chapter III.

CHAPTER IV

THE PRISON SERVICE

126. Service in England and Wales and Northern Ireland.
127. Inducements to withhold services or to indiscipline.
128. Pay and related conditions.

PART IX

MISCELLANEOUS AMENDMENTS: SCOTLAND

129. Transfer of persons detained by police and customs officers.
130. Detention and release of children: Scotland.
131. Conditions in licence of released prisoner: requirement for Parole Board recommendations.
132. Provision for standard requirements in supervised release orders in Scotland.
133. Extension of categories of prisoner to whom Part I of Prisoners and Criminal Proceedings (Scotland) Act 1993 applies.
134. Amendment of provisions continued in effect for certain prisoners by Prisoners and Criminal Proceedings (Scotland) Act 1993.
135. Further amendment of Schedule 6 to the Prisoners and Criminal Proceedings (Scotland) Act 1993: application of "new provisions".

PART X

CROSS-BORDER ENFORCEMENT

136. Execution of warrants.
137. Cross-border powers of arrest etc.
138. Powers of arrest etc.: supplementary provisions.
139. Search powers available on arrests under sections 136 and 137.
140. Reciprocal powers of arrest.
141. Aid of one police force by another.

PART XI

SEXUAL OFFENCES

Rape

142. Rape of women and men.

Male rape and buggery

143. Male rape and buggery.

Revised penalties for certain sexual offences

144. Revised penalties for buggery and indecency between men.

Homosexuality

145. Age at which homosexual acts are lawful.
146. Extension of Sexual Offences Act 1967 to the armed forces and merchant navy.
147. Homosexuality on merchant ships and in the armed forces: Northern Ireland.
148. Amendment of law relating to homosexual acts in Scotland.

PART XII

MISCELLANEOUS AND GENERAL

The Parole Board

149. Incorporation of the Parole Board.
150. Powers to recall prisoners released on licence.

Prisons: powers in relation to prisoners, visitors and others

151. Powers to test prisoners for drugs.
152. Powers of search by authorised employees in prisons.
153. Prohibited articles in Scottish prisons.

Harassment, alarm or distress

154. Offence of causing intentional harassment, alarm or distress.

Offence of racially inflammatory publication etc. to be arrestable

155. Offence of racially inflammatory publication etc. to be arrestable.

Prohibition on use of cells from embryos or foetuses

156. Prohibition on use of cells from embryos or foetuses.

Increase in certain penalties

157. Increase in penalties for certain offences.

Extradition procedures

158. Extradition procedures.
159. Backing of warrants: Republic of Ireland.

Constabulary powers in United Kingdom waters

160. Extension of powers, etc., of constables to United Kingdom waters.

Obtaining computer-held information

161. Procuring disclosure of, and selling, computer-held personal information.
162. Access to computer material by constables and other enforcement officers.

Closed-circuit television by local authorities

163. Local authority powers to provide closed-circuit television.

Serious fraud

164. Extension of powers of Serious Fraud Office and of powers to investigate serious fraud in Scotland.

Copyright and illicit recordings: enforcement of offences

165. Enforcement of certain offences relating to copyright and illicit recordings.

Ticket touts

166. Sale of tickets by unauthorised persons.

Taxi touts

167. Touting for hire car services.

General

168. Minor and consequential amendments and repeals.
169. Power of Secretary of State to make payments or grants in relation to crime prevention, etc.
170. Security costs at party conferences.
171. Expenses etc. under Act.
172. Short title, commencement and extent.

SCHEDULES:

Schedule 1—Escort Arrangements: England and Wales.
Schedule 2—Certification of Custody Officers: England and Wales.
Schedule 3—Bail: Supplementary Provisions.
Schedule 4— Transfer for Trial.
Schedule 5—Magistrates' Courts: Dealing with cases where accused pleads guilty.
Schedule 6—Certification of Prisoner Custody Officers: Scotland.
Schedule 7—Certification of Prisoner Custody Officers: Northern Ireland.
Schedule 8—Increase in Penalties.
Schedule 9—Minor Amendments.
Schedule 10—Consequential Amendments.
Schedule 11—Repeals.

An Act to make further provision in relation to criminal justice (including employment in the prison service); to amend or extend the criminal law and powers for preventing crime and enforcing that law; to amend the Video Recordings Act 1984; and for purposes connected with those purposes.   [3rd November 1994]

PARLIAMENTARY DEBATES
Hansard, H.C. Vol. 235, cols. 20, 123; Vol. 238, col. 23; Vol. 240, cols. 648, 649; Vol. 241, cols. 35, 169, 214, 361; Vol. 248, cols. 282, 445; H.L. Vol. 554, cols. 380, 413, 926; Vol. 555, cols. 10, 78, 134, 482, 541, 609, 697, 1084, 1085, 1166, 1589, 1665, 1818, 1889; Vol. 556, cols. 10, 74, 131, 179, 530, 1141, 1222, 1386, 1454, 1516, 1580, 1643, 1714, 1761; Vol. 557, col. 141; Vol. 558, cols. 445, 476.
The Bill was discussed in Standing Committee B between January 18 and March 15, 1994.

INTRODUCTION AND GENERAL NOTE
In July 1993 the Royal Commission on Criminal Justice produced its Report (Cm. 2263). In October 1993 at a political party conference the Home Secretary announced 27 measures to deal with crime. It is against the background of these two events that this Act must be seen. Some of the recommendations of the Royal Commission feature in the Act. On the other hand, in some cases (notably on the right to silence) its recommendations were ignored. Likewise, many of the measures announced by the Home Secretary feature in the Act.
The purpose of introducing this Act appears to have been to produce a comprehensive piece of legislation, covering a wide range of issues. That purpose may well have been achieved. However, substantial amendments were made to the Bill during its passage through Parliament and much was added to it (often due to the efforts of backbench Members of Parliament and Peers). The result is an Act the focus of which is difficult to discern.

Arrangement of the Act

Part I—Young Offenders
This Part of the Act is designed to increase the power of the courts to deal with persistent young offenders and young offenders who commit serious crime. It is particularly aimed at the younger age group. Thus it provides for a new custodial sentence in the form of a secure training order. The order will be available to punish persistent young offenders (of either sex) aged between 12 and 14 who have committed three or more imprisonable offences and who have failed to respond to community sentences. The order will be served in two parts: the first in custody; and the second, an equal term, under supervision in the community. The maximum sentence will be two years, served in equal parts in and out of custody. According to the Home Secretary, this provision is aimed at a small hard core of persistent young offenders of this age

(*Hansard*, H.C., Vol. 235, col. 23). 200 places are to be created in five regional centres (not in Scotland). Formerly, offenders of this age could not be sentenced to custody except for grave crimes under s.53 of the Children and Young Persons Act 1933.

In a further increase of the courts' powers, s.53 of the 1933 Act is amended in order to reduce the age at which a sentence of long-term detention may be passed; the age is reduced from 14 to 10. Similarly, the maximum length of detention in a young offender institution for offenders aged 15 to 17 is increased from 12 to 24 months.

Part II—Bail

The Home Secretary told the House of Commons that it was estimated that 50,000 offences were committed every year by people on bail and the aim of Pt. II is to restrict the grant of bail and thus help to ensure that it is only given when the public will not be put at risk (*ibid.*, col. 25). Accordingly, this Part provides that (a) bail may not be granted to a person charged with murder, manslaughter or rape who has a previous conviction for such an offence; (b) an exception to the right to bail will now apply when a person is charged with an indictable offence, alleged to have been committed while he was on bail; (c) the police are now given new powers to release a person on bail subject to conditions and to arrest without warrant a person who is in breach of police bail; and (d) magistrates may now re-consider a grant of bail if new information comes to light.

Part III—Course of Justice: Evidence, Procedure, etc.

This Part makes important changes to the law of criminal evidence. First, following an amendment moved by Lord Ackner, a defendant who makes imputations on the character of a deceased victim of a crime will now be liable to have his own convictions revealed to the jury. Secondly, the corroboration rules are abolished. This follows the recommendation of the Law Commission in its Report on Corroboration (Cm. 1620). This means that judges will no longer be required to warn juries against the dangers of convicting on the uncorroborated evidence of accomplices and complainants in sexual cases. Thirdly, the law is amended to allow inferences to be drawn against defendants who, when questioned, fail to mention facts relied on in their defence at trial or fail to account for their presence at a particular place or for marks or substances found upon them. Inferences may similarly be drawn against a defendant who fails to give evidence. (The law had previously forbidden the drawing of inferences in these circumstances and required judges to warn juries accordingly). These changes are based on experience in Northern Ireland where similar laws are enacted. They were originally recommended by the Criminal Law Revision Committee as long ago as 1972 in its Eleventh Report (Cmnd. 4991), but no steps were taken at the time to put them into legislation. It appears that their hour has now come. These changes were described by the Home Secretary as steps to redress the balance of justice which had tilted too far in favour of the guilty and against protecting society (*ibid.*, col. 25).

There are also important procedural changes in this Part, the most important of which is the abolition of committal proceedings and their replacement by a transfer for trial procedure based on that used in serious fraud cases. Provision is also made, following a recommendation by the Royal Commission, for circuit judges to sit in the Court of Appeal (Criminal Division). Changes are made in sentencing practice: for instance, the existing practice of allowing a discount in sentence for a plea of guilty is now put into statutory form. The Criminal Justice Act 1991 is amended to allow the court a discretion whether in most cases to obtain a pre-sentence report before passing sentence (Sched. 9): the position thus in general reverts to what it was before the passing of the Criminal Justice Act 1991.

Part IV—Police Powers

Following a recommendation of the Royal Commission, police powers to take body samples for the purpose of DNA testing are enlarged and brought into line with powers to take fingerprints. Previously such samples could only be taken for the investigation of serious arrestable offences. The Royal Commission recommended that the power to take non-intimate samples without consent should be extended to include assault and burglary. However, this Part goes further and permits the police to take samples from any person charged with a recordable offence *i.e.* generally, an offence punishable by imprisonment. Samples may now be retained and used for the purposes of comparison. The objective is to build a national data base.

This Part also gives the police extended powers to stop and search people and vehicles in anticipation of violence. The power is to search for offensive weapons or dangerous instruments. This power may only be exercised in a particular area for a limited time when a senior police officer reasonably believes that serious violence may break out.

Part V—Public Order: Collective Trespass or Nuisance on Land

This Part of the Act gives the police wide powers to deal with trespassers who create problems of public order in the countryside. The powers are mainly concerned with large-scale trespass by squatters, participants in raves and hunt saboteurs. The new powers under this Part may be summarised as follows.

(a) Powers are given to remove trespassers with six or more vehicles on land: failure to comply with a police direction to leave will amount to an offence. The purpose of this measure is to provide a remedy against trespassers which is speedier than that available under the civil law.

(b) The police are given wide powers to deal with raves both by stopping people going to them and directing people present at such gatherings to disperse; failure to leave after such a direction will amount to an offence and the police are then empowered to seize vehicles and sound equipment.

(c) An offence of aggravated trespass is introduced by the Act. The offence is committed when a person trespasses on land in the open air and seeks to obstruct or disrupt those engaged in a lawful activity. This provision is aimed at restricting the activities of hunt saboteurs and other demonstrators. If the police reasonably believe that trespassers will seek to disrupt a lawful activity they will have powers to direct such trespassers to leave the land: if a trespasser fails to comply with the direction, he commits an offence.

(d) In addition, the police will have powers to prevent a "trespassory assembly", *i.e.* an assembly of 20 or more people held on land to which the public has limited or no right of access.

(e) Remedies against squatting are provided under this Part of the Act. An amendment to the Rules of the Supreme Court will allow an owner or occupier to apply to a county court for an interim possession order which will require the squatter to leave within 24 hours. Failure to comply with the order is an offence under this Act and the police may arrest without warrant a person committing such an offence and may enter property in order to do so.

(f) Local authorities are given a power to direct unauthorised campers to leave land: failure to comply with the order is an offence and the local authority may apply to magistrates for an order authorising it to enter land and take such steps as are reasonably necessary to enforce the order including entering the land and removing any vehicles. A person wilfully obstructing such enforcement commits an offence.

Part VI—Prevention of terrorism

The police are given new powers under this Part, based on powers already in existence in Northern Ireland, and aimed at combating terrorism. The powers are to stop and search both pedestrians and vehicles and their occupants. The purpose is to safeguard the public against the dual threat of vehicle bombs and small devices carried by individual terrorists (Home Secretary, *ibid.*, col. 30). This Part also creates two offences connected with the possession of articles or information for terrorist purposes.

Part VII—Obscenity and Pornography and Videos

The purpose of this Part of the Act is to strengthen the law against pornography. This is necessary partly because of the advances in modern technology. Thus it is made an offence to deal in child pornography simulated by computer graphics. The police are given an immediate power of arrest of those trading in obscene material and child pornography. On a separate but related topic, the offence of making obscene or offensive telephone calls is now made imprisonable for the first time.

Part VIII—Prison Services and the Prison Service

This Part deals in particular with two aspects of the prison service. First, it increases the powers of the Home Secretary to contract-out prisons and prison services in England and Wales. Secondly it clarifies the employment position of prison officers. Thus, provision is made for prison officers to benefit from employment protection rights on the same basis as other Crown employees, although retaining their status as constables. However, it is unlawful to induce a prison officer to take industrial action.

Part IX—Miscellaneous Amendments: Scotland

Part X—Cross-Border Enforcement

The police had concerns about the difficulties of cross-border enforcement of warrants and a consultation paper was produced. This Part introduces powers allowing police forces to execute warrants and arrest suspects across borders in the U.K.

Part XI—Sexual Offences

As originally drafted, the Bill did not contain references to sexual offences. However, as a result of substantial amendment in both Houses of Parliament (moved by backbenchers) this Part was added during the passage of the Bill. The main effects of this Part on the law relating to sexual offences are as follows:

(a) The offence of rape is redefined to include male rape and rape within marriage.

(b) The age at which two men may engage in consensual homosexual acts in private is reduced to 18.

(c) The buggery of one person by another is not now unlawful provided it takes place in private and both parties are at least 18.

Part XII—Miscellaneous and General

This Part contains a hotch-potch of measures, mostly added by way of amendment during the passage of the Bill through Parliament. The measures include the incorporation of the Parole Board, the provision of new powers of search to prison officers, the creation of a new offence of causing intentional harassment, alarm or distress, the prohibition on the use of human embryos and foetuses for fertility services and the creation of offences in relation to touting tickets and taxis.

Scottish Perspective

It is perhaps in the areas of criminal law and criminal procedure that Scots Law has best managed to preserve a different character from the other legal systems within the U.K. Given this, there must accordingly be problems when Parliament attempts to cover all U.K. jurisdictions in one criminal law statute. Such problems are manifest in this Act. It requires 10 subsections to the short title, commencement and extent section (s.172) to detail which sections, parts and chapters of the Act apply to which parts of the U.K. And it requires the mind of a crossword champion to distil from these subsections which are the relevant ones for Scotland. A list in simple numerical order is appended hereto.

As it applies to Scotland, this Act is, in effect, a miscellaneous provisions measure. Several of the changes introduced were required by omissions in recent purely Scottish legislation (*e.g.* the Prisoners and Criminal Proceedings (Scotland) Act 1993 (c.9)). It might seem appropriate that Scotland should piggy-back on an English measure to have mistakes remedied as quickly as possible. But bringing Scotland into the frame may have done Scotland no favours. Scotland is also to have applied to it measures which are a response to problems experienced in England and Wales about which little concern had been expressed north of the border. In view of the fact that it is now known that session 1994–95 is to see a Scottish Criminal Justice Bill, patience may have been better counsel. These matters are, however, only clear with hindsight. Rather than bemoan the new provisions which perhaps Scotland did not need, it should be acknowledged that an early opportunity has been taken to remedy some deficiencies and that not all of the provisions of the Act are to be applied to Scotland. Indeed, in addition to offering general comments on the provisions applying to Scotland, it is worth a little space here to outline the parts which apply only south of the border, and to speculate on the reasons, not least to stress how differently Scotland tackles some of the issues.

Parts I–IV—sections 1–60

With the exception of s.47(3)(4), which authorises the Secretary of State to permit deductions from benefit for payment of fines transferred to Scotland from English and Welsh courts and s.49, which extends restrictions on reporting of proceedings involving children or young persons in English and Welsh cases to Scotland (and will require Scottish editors to be fully familiar with English legal terminology; s.49(11)), none of these parts of the Act apply to Scotland. Part I introduces secure training orders for 12–15-year-olds, extends the maximum period of detention for those aged 10–17 and extends the range of secure accommodation for young persons convicted of, or charged with, serious offences. Scotland is not covered, presumably because the present legal structure, which permits the Lord Advocate to proceed in the ordinary courts against anyone over the age of eight and allows local authorities to provide secure accommodation as required by individual cases (Social Work (Scotland) Act 1968 (c. 49)), covers this need. The Scottish system may not be perfect, but it certainly has legal provisions enabling appropriate responses to be made to the small number of youngsters who might pose a serious threat to society.

Part II changes the English the Welsh law relating to bail. Both north and south of the border, there have been considerable public concerns about "abuse of bail". In societies which hold to the presumption of innocence, this always seems a bit of a paradox. Indeed many of the problems flow directly from the time taken to bring people to trial, and the cause of this lies at the door of the criminal justice system rather than the offender. It is understood that the Scottish Bill for session 1994–95 will contain amendments to the present bail provision in Scotland, which is governed by the Bail (Scotland) Act 1980 and the *Wheatly* guidelines and which has never in practice allowed bail on murder charges.

Part III

Few of these attempts to make convictions more easily obtained would find ready acceptance in Scotland. Sections 32 and 33 confirm a marked difference between the jurisdiction on the matter of corroboration. While Scottish common law still generally requires evidence from two separate sources to obtain a conviction, the requirement south of the border is further reduced from an already low base. Sections 34 to 39 implement the contentious policy on inferences from an accused's silence and do not apply in Scotland. It is understood that the new Scottish Bill is to extend at least a similar provision to Scotland. Section 48 introduces a discretion to reduce sentences because of early guilty pleas, an idea which was discussed by the Thomson Committee in Scotland but not accepted. Section 50 allows video recordings of testimony from child witnesses, a practice permitted in Scotland under the Prisoners and Criminal Proceedings (Scotland) Act 1993 (c. 9).

Part IV

With the exception of s.60, the Act brings English law into line with Scots law in relation to police powers to take non-intimate bodily samples (s.28 of the Prisoners and Criminal Proceedings (Scotland) Act 1993 (c. 9)). Section 60 applies only in England and Wales and allows police stop and search powers on the authority of only a senior police officer when it is believed that incidents involving serious violence may take place anywhere in that senior police officer's area.

Part V

With the exception of the provisions relating to squatters and the power to remove unauthorised campers, the public order provisions of the Act apply to Scotland, and detailed comments are offered under the individual sections (ss.61 to 71). While the provisions applying to Scotland only aroused any opposition in Scotland very late in the Bill's progress through Parliament, there was little demand, or indeed need, for the new power north of the border. The common law offences of breach of the peace, conduct likely to cause a breach of the peace and conspiracy to breach the peace provided adequate cover against the behaviour targeted in these actions. Squatting has not been a problem in Scotland on the same scale as, for example, in London. Unauthorised campers, in the persons of "new age travellers" and other "travelling people", do, however, exist, but Scottish practice has been to use the civil law as a mechanism for dealing with the issue. There are criminal law powers contained in the Trespass (Scotland) Act 1865 governing both squatting and illegal camping. Clearly, therefore, the problem is not a new one, and Scotland tackled it a long time ago.

Part VI

This amends the Prevention of Terrorism (Temporary Provisions) Act 1989 which is a U.K. statute.

Part VII

Section 84 updates the law relating to indecent images of children and increases the penalties for possession of such images. Sections 86 and 87 increase the penalties for publishing, displaying, selling or distributing indecent photographs or other obscene material. It is not thought that the existing maxima have been much used in Scotland. Sections 88 to 92 amend U.K. statutes regulating video recordings and obscene telephone calls.

Part VIII

Chapters I, II and III apply respectively to England and Wales, Scotland and Northern Ireland and effectively introduce the same provisions to each jurisdiction but against very different backgrounds. Chapter II (ss.102–117) creates powers for the Secretary of State for Scotland to arrange for the appointment of prisoner escorts, to contract-out whole prisons, parts of prisons or functions within prisons, to recognise any building or floating structure as a prison and to recognise and regulate prison custody officers. Under the Prisons (Scotland) Act 1989, only the Secretary of State could appoint prison officers (s.3(1)), make contracts and do other acts necessary for the maintenance of prisons and prisoners and have the legal estate of a prison vested in him (s.36). These restrictions prohibited the development of alternative mechanisms for providing prison places and staffing and are now withdrawn.

Escorting prisoners outwith prisons has traditionally been organised differently north and south of the border. The main responsibility for bringing prisoners to and from criminal courts in Scotland has lain with the police, with prison officer escorts being used for production of prisoners in civil cases, in inter-prison transfers and for other out-of-prison reasons. In England and

Wales almost all escorts were provided by the prison service. In either situation, escorts are expensive, especially given the unpredictable duration of court proceedings, and the need to have staff available for the longest possible time they may be required. Where those staff may have other duties, in the prison or as police officers, the unpredictability of escort commitments makes organising staffing very difficult. Accordingly, a specialist escort service makes logistical and financial sense, presuming that it can also meet the security requirements of the task.

While there have been privatised prisons south of the border for several years, Scotland has not been able to develop this idea until now. The Scottish Prison Service (SPS) became an agency in 1993 and, like most other public bodies, has been subject to market-testing procedures. As part of an industrial relations settlement on the implementation of a staffing structure review in 1994, it has been agreed that market testing will be suspended for four years and that no existing prison will be privatised. However, the Chief Executive of SPS announced at the same time that negotiations are underway for the provision of a new prison using the powers obtained in Pt. VIII of the Act. The most likely area for this experiment is in the provision of accommodation for remand prisoners.

The Act (s.107(1)) makes clear that private contractors will be responsible for appointing their own staff, but that these staff must be approved under a certification scheme which is to be established by the Secretary of State. The private contractor's director is to have the same powers as a prison governor, except in relation to reporting to the Secretary of State on the running of the prison, investigating allegations against members of staff at the prison, dealing with disciplinary charges against prisoners and, except in an emergency, removing prisoners from association or authorising the application to a prisoner of any control or restraint (s.107(2)(3)(4)). In addition to the director, the Secretary of State must appoint a controller to any contracted-out prison and this controller is to carry out the functions not required of the director. In addition, the Secretary of State retains the power to appoint a Crown servant to take over control of any contracted-out prison when it appears to the Secretary of State that the director has lost, or is likely to lose, effective control within it or that this step is necessary to preserve the safety of any person or prevent serious damage to any property (s.111). Accordingly, ultimate responsibility for the contracted-out prison still lies with the Secretary of State.

Chapter IV (s.126–128) of Pt. VIII applies to the whole of the U.K. Section 126 has no relevance to Scotland since the Scottish prison officer has not had the powers or privileges of a constable and has not, therefore, been subject to restrictions of the normal rights of an employee. It may also be though that s.127 is irrelevant to Scotland, where the trade unions involved in prisons have generally acted very responsibly in relation to industrial action. However, ss.127 and 128 apply fully to Scotland. Section 127 renders any person who induces a prison officer to withhold his services or commit a breach of discipline liable in damages to the Secretary of State. It thus effectively rules out organised strike action. Section 128 provides for the Secretary of State to make regulations for the establishment of a mechanism for the determination of rates of pay and allowances and other related terms and conditions of employment of prison officers.

Part IX

This Part introduces minor amendments into the Scottish legislation. Thus s.129 permits persons detained under s.2(1) of the Criminal Justice (Scotland) Act 1980 or s.48(1) of the Criminal Justice (Scotland) Act 1987 to be moved to another place during the period of detention and for intimation of any such move to be given to any person to whom such intimation of the detention has been given.

Sections 130–135 correct errors and omissions in the Prisoners and Criminal Proceedings (Scotland) Act 1993. Section 130 brings the release arrangements for child detainees more closely into line with the arrangements for adults and young offenders. Section 131 allows for the variation of license terms for released prisoners. Section 132 enables standard requirements to be included in supervised release orders by Act of Adjournal. Section 133 brings prisoners sentenced to discretionary life sentences by courts martial under the same provisions as those sentenced by civilian courts. Section 134 makes further provision for prisoners sentenced before the coming into operation of the 1993 Act to assimilate their treatment with that of those sentenced after that date, but without withdrawing any better entitlement they may have had. Section 135 extends the new provisions in relation to released discretionary life prisoners to all such prisoners and makes provision for those prisoners who are serving sentences passed before and after the coming into force of the 1993 Act.

Part X

This provides for greater co-operation between or among the police forces in the different parts of the U.K., validates warrants issued in one part for execution in another part and permits reciprocal powers of arrest.

Part XI

This changes the law in relation to certain sexual offences, but only the section relating to the age of consent for homosexual acts (s.145) and that relating to homosexuality in the armed forces and merchant navy (s.146) apply to Scotland. Scots common law knows rape only as an offence by a male against a female and involving vaginal penetration. Thus ss.142–144 have no relevance to Scotland.

Part XII

This Part is properly described as "Miscellaneous and General". The sections which *do not* apply to Scotland involve changes in the English parole system (ss.149 and 150), provisions relating to harassment, alarm or distress (s.154), an amendment to the Police and Criminal Evidence Act 1984 (s.155) and the provisions relating to ticket touting (s.166) and taxi touting (s.167). The sections which do apply to Scotland amend the Prisons (Scotland) Act 1989 (ss.151 and 153), amend the Human Fertilisation and Embryology Act 1990 (s.156), increase penalties for certain offences (s.157 and Sched. 8, Pt. I), amend extradition procedures (s.158) and the Backing of Warrants (Republic of Ireland) Act 1965, extend police powers to sea and other waters within the seaward limits of the territorial sea (s.160(2)), amend the Data Protection Act 1984 and the Computer Misuse Act 1990 (ss.161 and 162), empower local authorities to provide closed-circuit television for crime prevention purposes, extend the powers and duties of the Lord Advocate in relation to serious and complex frauds (s.164(3)(4)) and amend the Copyright, Designs and Patents Act 1988.

Commencement

Sections 61, 63, 65, 68–71, 81, 83, 90, 127, 128, 142–148, 158 and 171 came into force on the passing of the Act. It is understood that the intention of the Scottish Office is to seek to implement the remaining parts of the Act which apply to Scotland in early 1995.

Sections applicable to Scotland

Sections 47(3)(4); 49; 61–71; 81; 82; 83(2)(3)(4)(5); 84(5)(6)(7); 87–93; 95; 101(8); 102–117; 126–128; 129–135; 136–141; 145(2); 146(2)(4); 148; 151(2); 152(2); 153; 156; 157(1)(2)(3)(5)(7)(9); 158; 159; 160(2); 161–165; 168–171.

Commencement

The Act received Royal Assent on November 3, 1994. Sections 5–15, 61, 63, 65, 68–71, 77–81, 83, 93–101, 126–128, 142–147, 150, 158(1), (3) and (4), 166–167 and Sched. 9, para. 45 came into force on Royal Assent. Sections 159(1), (2) and (4) and s.82 came into force on December 19, 1994 and January 3, 1995, respectively. The following provisions were brought into force on January 9, 1995: ss.16, 151, and 168 (to the extent necessary to bring into force Sched. 9, paras. 34 and 41, Sched. 10, paras. 40 and 69 and Sched. 11, the entries relating to s.24 of the Magistrates' Courts Act 1980 (c. 43), s.126 of the Criminal Justice Act 1988 (c. 33), s.64 of the Criminal Justice Act 1991 (c. 53) and s.67(2) of the Criminal Justice Act 1933 (c. 36).

Section 52 came into force on January 11, 1995. The following provisions were brought into force on February 3, 1995: ss. 17, 18, 23, 24, 31–33, 40–43, 46–51, 64(1) to (3), 66(6) and (10) to (13), 67(3) to (5), (8) and (9), 72–74, 84–88, 91, 92, 136–141, 152–155, 157 (and Sched. 8), 160–164, 169, 170 and 168 (to the extent necessary to bring into force Sched. 9, paras. 1–33, 35–36, 37(1) and (2), 39–40, 42–45, 47–53 and Sched. 10, paras. 7, 8, 11, 13, 14, 17, 18, 25, 27–29, 31, 37–38, 45, 47, 52, 63(2) and 68. Section 53 came into force on February 2, 1995. The remainder will come into force on dates set by Order, likely to be later in 1995.

Abbreviations

The 1952 Act: The Prison Act 1952.
The 1982 Act: The Criminal Justice Act 1982.
The 1991 Act: The Criminal Justice Act 1991.
The 1992 Act: The Criminal Justice Act 1992.

Part I

Young Offenders

Secure training orders

Secure training orders

1.—(1) Subject to section 8(1) of the Criminal Justice Act 1982 and section 53(1) of the Children and Young Persons Act 1933 (sentences of custody for life and long term detention), where—

(a) a person of not less than 12 but under 15 years of age is convicted of an imprisonable offence; and

(b) the court is satisfied of the matters specified in subsection (5) below, the court may make a secure training order.

(2) A secure training order is an order that the offender in respect of whom it is made shall be subject to a period of detention in a secure training centre followed by a period of supervision.

(3) The period of detention and supervision shall be such as the court determines and specifies in the order, being not less than six months nor more than two years.

(4) The period of detention which the offender is liable to serve under a secure training order shall be one half of the total period specified by the court in making the order.

(5) The court shall not make a secure training order unless it is satisfied—

(a) that the offender was not less than 12 years of age when the offence for which he is to be dealt with by the court was committed;

(b) that the offender has been convicted of three or more imprisonable offences; and

(c) that the offender, either on this or a previous occasion—

  (i) has been found by a court to be in breach of a supervision order under the Children and Young Persons Act 1969, or

  (ii) has been convicted of an imprisonable offence committed whilst he was subject to such a supervision order.

(6) A secure training order is a custodial sentence for the purposes of sections 1 to 4 of the Criminal Justice Act 1991 (restrictions etc. as to custodial sentences).

(7) Where a court makes a secure training order, it shall be its duty to state in open court that it is of the opinion that the conditions specified in subsection (5) above are satisfied.

(8) In this section "imprisonable offence" means an offence (not being one for which the sentence is fixed by law) which is punishable with imprisonment in the case of a person aged 21 or over.

(9) For the purposes of this section, the age of a person shall be deemed to be that which it appears to the court to be after considering any available evidence.

(10) This section shall have effect, as from the day appointed for each of the following paragraphs, with the substitution in subsections (1) and (5)—

(a) of "14" for "12";

(b) of "13" for "14";

(c) of "12" for "13";

but no substitution may be brought into force on more than one occasion.

DEFINITIONS

"custodial sentence": s.3(1) of the Criminal Justice Act 1991 (c. 53).

"imprisonable offence": subs. (8).

"secure training centre": s.5(2).

"secure training order": subss. (2)(6).

"supervision order": s.11 of the Children and Young Persons Act 1969 (c. 54).

GENERAL NOTE

This section provides the courts with new powers to pass custodial sentences. It extends the existing powers to pass custodial sentences on those aged 15 and 16 to a younger age group. The section introduces a new sentence in the form of the "secure training order," aimed at persistent juvenile offenders. (For a recent report on research conducted on behalf of the Home Office into such offenders see Hagell and Newburn: "Persistent Young Offenders" (1994) Policy Study Institute, London). The court may now make such an order upon a young person of either sex aged 12 to 14 years: the order will entail a maximum period of 12 months' detention in a secure training centre, followed by supervision for a similar period. The section does not apply to cases of murder or any other case where the sentence is fixed by law as imprisonment for life: see note on subs. (1) below.

Various conditions must be met before a secure training order is made. The first conditions relate to the offence. An order may not be made unless the "seriousness" or other criteria in ss.1–4 of the 1991 Act are met: subs. (6). Thus, the court may not make an order in circumstances where a person over the age of 14 may not be sent into custody. The other conditions are set out in subs. (5) and relate to the offender. He must (a) have been aged not less than 12 at the time of the offence; (b) have been convicted of at least three imprisonable offences; (c) have failed to respond to community supervision either by re-offending while subject to such an order or failing to comply with its requirements. It may be thought that three imprisonable offences is setting the threshold of persistence rather low. However, this will allow the court the opportunity to consider the nature of the offences which are bound to vary widely in gravity. There is no indication in the section as to whether the three imprisonable offences relate to previous convictions on separate occasions or to convictions on the same occasion (including those for which the offender appears before the court). It is submitted that in the absence of an indication in the section the latter meaning must prevail. However, other criteria will prevent an order being made under this section on a first offender *e.g.* the requirement that the offender must have failed to respond to a community sentence in the past.

Providing the above conditions are met the court has a complete discretion in making an order under this section. It must be doubted whether many such orders will be passed on children as young as this. (The Government has said that it will create 200 places in five regional secure training centres to cover England and Wales: the scheme does not extend to Scotland). On the other hand, the courts will be provided with a weapon (where none existed before) with which to deal with the truly persistent offender of this age.

Subs. (1)

By s.8(1) of the 1982 Act, a person between the ages of 18 and 21 convicted of an offence, the fixed penalty for which is imprisonment for life, shall be sentenced to custody for life. Section 53(1) of the Children and Young Persons Act 1933 as amended by this Act is the subject of the Note to s.16, *post.*

Subs. (5)

A *supervision order* (under s.11 of the Children and Young Persons Act 1969) is an order by a court placing a child or young person under the supervision of a local authority designated by the order or of a probation officer. By the 1991 Act, s.6(4)(a), a supervision order is a community order. As to supervision orders under this Act, see further s.3.

Subs. (6)

A *custodial sentence* (s.31(1)(b) of the 1991 Act) includes "… a sentence of detention in a young offender institution".

Secure training orders: supplementary provisions as to detention

2.—(1) The following provisions apply in relation to a person ("the offender") in respect of whom a secure training order ("the order") has been made under section 1.

(2) Where accommodation for the offender at a secure training centre is not immediately available—

    (a) the court may commit the offender to such place and on such conditions—

        (i) as the Secretary of State may direct, or

        (ii) as the Secretary of State may arrange with a person to whom this sub-paragraph applies,

    and for such period (not exceeding 28 days) as the court may specify or until his transfer to a secure training centre, if earlier;

    (b) if no such accommodation becomes or will become available before the expiry of the period of the committal the court may, on application, extend the period of committal (subject to the restriction referred to in paragraph (a) above); and

    (c) the period of detention in the secure training centre under the order shall be reduced by the period spent by the offender in such a place.

(3) The power conferred by subsection (2)(b) above may, subject to section 1(4), be exercised from time to time and the reference in subsection (2)(b) to the expiry of the period of the committal is, in the case of the initial extension, a reference to the expiry of the period of the committal under subsection (2)(a) above and, in the case of a further extension, a reference to

the expiry of the period of the previous committal by virtue of this subsection.

(4) Where the circumstances of the case require, the Secretary of State may transfer the offender from a secure training centre to such other place and on such conditions—

(a) as the Secretary of State may direct, or

(b) as the Secretary of State may arrange with a person to whom this paragraph applies;

and the period of detention in the secure training centre under the order shall be reduced by the period spent by the offender in such a place.

(5) The persons to whom subsections (2)(a)(ii) and (4)(b) apply are local authorities, voluntary organisations and persons carrying on a registered childrens' home.

(6) Where the Secretary of State is satisfied that exceptional circumstances exist which justify the offender's release on compassionate grounds he may release the offender from the secure training centre; and the offender shall, on his release, be subject to supervision for the remainder of the term of the order.

(7) A person detained in pursuance of directions or arrangements made for his detention shall be deemed to be in legal custody.

(8) In this section "local authority", "voluntary organisation" and "registered children's home" have the same meaning as in the Children Act 1989.

DEFINITIONS
"local authority": subs. (8).
"offender": subs. (1).
"order": subs. (1).
"registered children's home": subs. (8).
"secure training centre": s.5(2).
"secure training order": s.1(2)(6).
"voluntary organisation": subs. (8).

GENERAL NOTE
This section makes provision for cases when a secure training order is made but no place in a secure training centre is immediately available. It gives the court power to commit an offender to alternative accommodation specified by the Home Secretary. The period of committal is limited to 28 days, but the court may then extend the period. The court thus retains control of the case. The section puts no limit on the number of extensions. However, it must be anticipated that in practice the court will not be prepared to give indefinite extensions if accommodation in a training centre is not available within a reasonable time. The Home Secretary may determine where the accommodation shall be or may contract with other bodies (set out in subs. (5)) to provide it. The section does not prohibit the use of police cells or prison for this purpose. During the passage of the Act through Parliament the Government was pressed to rule this possibility out, but declined to do so. Thus, such accommodation would be available for use in exceptional circumstances. The section also permits the Home Secretary (a) to transfer an offender from a secure training centre to alternative accommodation (subs. (4)): examples might include a transfer for hospital treatment or psychiatric care; and (b) to release the offender on compassionate grounds.

Subs. (8)
The Children Act 1989, s.105(1), defines (i) *local authority* as "... in relation to England and Wales, the council of a county, a metropolitan district, a London Borough, or the Common Council of the City of London" (ii) *registered children's home* "as in s.63" [*i.e.* a children's home registered under Pt. VIII of the Children Act 1989]; *voluntary organisation* as "a body (other than a public or local authority) whose activities are not carried on for profit".

Supervision under secure training order

3.—(1) The following provisions apply as respects the period of supervision of a person ("the offender") subject to a secure training order.

(2) The offender shall be under the supervision of a probation officer, a social worker of a local authority social services department or such other person as the Secretary of State may designate.

(3) The category of person to supervise the offender shall be determined from time to time by the Secretary of State.

(4) Where the supervision is to be provided by a social worker of a local authority social services department, the social worker shall be a social worker of the local authority within whose area the offender resides for the time being.

(5) Where the supervision is to be provided by a probation officer, the probation officer shall be an officer appointed for or assigned to the petty sessions area within which the offender resides for the time being.

(6) The probation committee or local authority shall be entitled to recover from the Secretary of State the expenses reasonably incurred by them in discharging their duty under this section.

(7) The offender shall be given a notice from the Secretary of State specifying—
    (a) the category of person for the time being responsible for his supervision; and
    (b) any requirements with which he must for the time being comply.

(8) A notice under subsection (7) above shall be given to the offender—
    (a) before the commencement of the period of supervision; and
    (b) before any alteration in the matters specified in subsection (7)(a) or (b) comes into effect.

(9) The Secretary of State may by statutory instrument make rules for regulating the supervision of the offender.

(10) The power to make rules under subsection (9) above includes power to make provision in the rules by the incorporation by reference of provisions contained in other documents.

(11) A statutory instrument made under subsection (9) above shall be subject to annulment in pursuance of a resolution of either House of Parliament.

(12) The sums required by the Secretary of State for making payments under subsection (6) shall be defrayed out of money provided by Parliament.

DEFINITIONS
    "offender": subs. (1).
    "secure training order": s.1(2)(6).

GENERAL NOTE
    This section makes provision for the supervision period of an offender subject to a secure training order. Supervision will normally be provided by a probation officer or social worker from the petty session area or local authority where the offender resides. However, subs. (2) gives the Home Secretary a wider power to designate other persons to supervise: the purpose of which is to provide flexibility. Thus an employee of a registered charity with which a local authority has entered into a contract for the supervision of young offenders could be designated; as could anyone with the necessary qualifications *e.g.* a retired social worker or one who has left to bring up a family. Supervision will be subject to inspection under rules formulated under subs. (9) (discussed below). It will also be subject to requirements specified by the Home Secretary (subs. 9). It is not known what the requirements may be: the section is silent upon the point. The legislation must have been framed in this way in order to allow flexibility in relation to individual orders. Section 65(5) of the 1991 Act gives the Home Secretary similar powers in relation to persons released from young offender institutions.
    Subsection (9) allows the Home Secretary to make rules by statutory instrument to regulate supervision. This rule-making power is subject only to negative resolution of either House of Parliament: subs. (11). Subsection (10) gives the Home Secretary an apparently wide power to incorporate in the rules the provisions of any other document. However, it would appear that the purpose of subss. (9) and (10) is to allow the Home Secretary to make rules by means of statutory instrument to apply national standards to supervision orders. National standards were issued in 1992 for probation and other community disposals. These standards are to be revised and will then presumably cover supervision orders. A similar power exists in s.37(7) of the 1991 Act in relation to the supervision of offenders released on licence. For breaches of the requirements of supervision, see s.4, below. It should be noted that a supervision order under this section is not to be confused with a supervision order under the Children and Young Persons Act 1969 (c. 54), s.11.

Breaches of requirements of supervision of persons subject to secure training orders

4.—(1) Where a secure training order has been made as respects an offender and it appears on information to a justice of the peace acting for a relevant petty sessions area that the offender has failed to comply with requirements under section 3(7)(b) the justice may issue a summons requiring the offender to appear at the place and time specified in the summons before a youth court acting for the area or, if the information is in writing and on oath, may issue a warrant for the offender's arrest requiring him to be brought before such a court.

(2) For the purposes of this section a petty sessions area is a relevant petty sessions area in relation to a secure training order—

(a) if the secure training centre is situated in it;

(b) if the order was made by a youth court acting for it; or

(c) if the offender resides in it for the time being.

(3) If it is proved to the satisfaction of the youth court before which an offender appears or is brought under this section that he has failed to comply with requirements under section 3(7)(b) that court may—

(a) order the offender to be detained in a secure training centre for such period, not exceeding the shorter of three months or the remainder of the period of the secure training order, as the court may specify, or

(b) impose on the offender a fine not exceeding level 3 on the standard scale.

(4) Where accommodation for an offender in relation to whom the court decides to exercise their powers under subsection (3)(a) above is not immediately available, paragraphs (a), (b) and (c) of subsection (2) and subsections (5), (7) and (8) of section 2 shall apply in relation to him as they apply in relation to an offender in respect of whom a secure training order is made.

(5) For the purposes of this section references to a failure to comply include references to a contravention.

DEFINITIONS
"relevant petty sessions area": subs. (2).
"secure training order": s.1(2)(6).
"secure training centre": s.5(2).

GENERAL NOTE
This section deals with breaches of the requirements of a supervision order. It provides that a person subject to a secure training order who has failed to comply with the requirements of his supervision (which includes contravening them: subs. (5)) may on summons be brought before a youth court. If it appears on information to a justice of the peace that there may have been non-compliance he may issue a summons or a warrant for the offender's arrest (subs. (1)). In the latter case the information must be in writing and on oath. Presumably, it will usually be for the person charged with supervising the offender to supply the information (as happens for instance in the case of a breach of probation) although the section does not restrict the category of person who may do so. It must then be proved under subs. (3) to the satisfaction of the court that the offender has failed to comply with the requirements of the order under s.3(7)(b). Proof to this standard is not uncommon. It will be a matter for the court to decide what information will satisfy it. These matters are not normally disputed and a report from the relevant probation officer or social worker will suffice. However, a court must ensure that it is satisfied of the breach because of the consequences of such a finding. Accordingly, there may be occasions when it is necessary to hear evidence on the point. If the court is so satisfied it may order that the offender be detained for a further period in a secure training centre or fined. The period of detention may not exceed three months or the remainder of the period of the secure training order (whichever is the shorter): subs. (3)(*a*). The offender's parent or guardian will be liable to pay any fine imposed under this section: Children and Young Persons Act 1933 (c. 12), s.55.

Youth Court: s.70(1) of the 1991 Act: "Juvenile courts shall be renamed youth courts ..."

Provision etc. of secure training centres

5.—(1) Section 43 of the Prison Act 1952 (which enables certain institutions for young offenders to be provided and applies provisions of the Act to them) shall be amended as follows.

(2) In subsection (1), after paragraph (c), there shall be inserted the following paragraph, preceded by the word "and"—

"(d) secure training centres, that is to say places in which offenders not less than 12 but under 17 years of age in respect of whom secure training orders have been made under section 1 of the Criminal Justice and Public Order Act 1994 may be detained and given training and education and prepared for their release".

(3) After subsection (4), there shall be inserted the following subsection—

"(4A) Sections 16, 22 and 36 of this Act shall apply to secure training centres and to persons detained in them as they apply to prisons and prisoners.".

(4) In subsection (5), for the words "such centres" there shall be substituted the words "centres of the descriptions specified in subsection (4) above".

(5) After subsection (5), there shall be inserted the following subsection—

"(5A) The other provisions of this Act preceding this section, except sections 5, 5A, 6(2) and (3), 12, 14, 19, 25, 28 and 37(2) and (3) above, shall apply to secure training centres and to persons detained in them as they apply to prisons and prisoners, but subject to such adaptations and modifications as may be specified in rules made by the Secretary of State.".

DEFINITIONS

"secure training centre": subs. (2).

GENERAL NOTE

This section enables the Home Secretary to provide secure training centres and applies provisions of the 1952 Act to them, subject to modifications which may be contained in rules. Section 43 of the 1952 Act was re-enacted by s.11 of the 1982 Act.

Subs. (2)

By s.43 of the 1952 Act (as substituted, see above), the Secretary of State may provide remand centre and young offender institutions. The new para. (d) added to s.43(1) allows the provision of secure training centres for offenders in respect of whom *secure training orders* have been made. For the meaning of secure training order, see s.1, *ante*. The reference to "offenders not less than 12 but under 17" may be explained by the fact that a two-year order under s.1 may be made on a 14-year-old which will still be in force on his 16th birthday; hence the reference to "under 17". Emphasis will be placed on training and education in the centres. For the rules governing the provision of training and education see s.6 below and the notes thereto.

Subs. (3)

The sections of 1952 Act referred to in the new s.43(4A) thereto relate to the photographing and measuring of prisoners (s.16), the removal of prisoners for judicial and other purposes (s.22), and the acquisition of land for prisons (s.36).

Subs. (5)

The new s.43(5A) of the 1952 Act applies that Act to secure training centres except as regards the Annual Report of the Prison Commissioners (s.5), the appointment and functions of H.M. Chief Inspector of Prisons (*ibid.* s.5A), the appointment and functions of Boards of Visitors, (*ibid.* s.6(2)(3)), the place of confinement of prisoners (*ibid.* s.12), cells (*ibid.*), the right of a justice to visit a prison (*ibid.* s.19), remission for good conduct and release on licence (*ibid.* s.25), temporary discharge of prisoners on account of ill-health (*ibid.* s.28) and certain provisions relating to the closing of prisons (*ibid.* s.37(2)(3)). Rules made under s.47 of the 1952 Act (as amended by s.6 of this Act, *q.v. post*) will provide for the inspection of secure training centres and the appointment of independent persons to visit such centres, and for the temporary release of persons detained in them.

Management of secure training centres

6.—(1) Section 47 of the Prison Act 1952 (rules for the regulation and management of prisons and certain institutions for young offenders) shall be amended as follows.

(2) In subsection (1), for the words between "remand centres" and "respectively", there shall be substituted the words ", young offender institutions or secure training centres".

(3) After subsection (4), there shall be inserted the following subsection—

"(4A) Rules made under this section shall provide for the inspection of secure training centres and the appointment of independent persons to visit secure training centres and to whom representations may be made by offenders detained in secure training centres.".

(4) In subsection (5), for the words between "remand centre" and "not" there shall be substituted the words ", young offender institution or secure training centre".

DEFINITIONS
"secure training centre": s.5(2).

GENERAL NOTE
This section enables rules to be made under the 1952 Act for the regulation and management of secure training centres. These statutory rules will set the standards which contractors must meet. (The contractors will provide and run the centres: see s.8, below). Subsection (3) requires rules to be made for inspection and visiting by independent persons. The rules will be introduced to set minimum standards and requirements and include rules concerning the functions of a director and a monitor, the induction and assessment of trainees and the development and review of a personalised training plan for each trainee. There will be rules about food, clothing, education, training, health care, visits, inspection arrangements, independent visitors, representations in grievance procedure, privileges, control, discipline and religious observance: Minister of State, Home Office, H.C. Official Report, Standing Committee B, col. 218. No rules had been drafted before the Act received the Royal Assent.

Section 5 of this Act (*q.v. ante*) excludes certain provisions of the 1952 Act from applying to secure training centres. This section enables alternative provision to be made by means of Rules.

Contracting out of secure training centres

7.—(1) The Secretary of State may enter into a contract with another person for the provision or running (or the provision and running) by him, or (if the contract so provides) for the running by sub-contractors of his, of any secure training centre or part of a secure training centre.

(2) While a contract for the running of a secure training centre or part of a secure training centre is in force the centre or part shall be run subject to and in accordance with the Prison Act 1952 and in accordance with secure training centre rules subject to such adaptations and modifications as the Secretary of State may specify in relation to contracted out secure training centres.

(3) Where the Secretary of State grants a lease or tenancy of land for the purposes of any contract under this section, none of the following enactments shall apply to it, namely—

(a) Part II of the Landlord and Tenant Act 1954 (security of tenure);

(b) section 146 of the Law of Property Act 1925 (restrictions on and relief against forfeiture); and

(c) section 19 of the Landlord and Tenant Act 1927 and the Landlord and Tenant Act 1988 (covenants not to assign etc.).

In this subsection "lease or tenancy" includes an underlease or sub-tenancy.

(4) In this section—

(a) the reference to the Prison Act 1952 is a reference to that Act as it applies to secure training centres by virtue of section 43 of that Act; and

(b) the reference to secure training centre rules is a reference to rules made under section 47 of that Act for the regulation and management of secure training centres.

Definitions
     "secure training centre": s.5(2).
     "secure training centre rules": s.15.
     "sub-contractor": s.15.

General Note
     This section enables the Home Secretary to contract-out the provision and running of secure
training centres (or parts of a secure training centre). These centres may be contrasted with
directly-managed secure training centres (i.e. directly managed by the Home Secretary) which
are the subject of s.11, below.
     Secure training centre rules: s.15 refers to the meaning given by subs. (4)(b) of this section
which in turn refers to s.47 of the 1952 Act but *note* that that section, in relation to secure training
centres, is amended by s.6 of this Act, *ante.*

Officers of contracted out secure training

8.—(1) Instead of a governor, every contracted out secure training centre
shall have—
     (a) a director, who shall be a custody officer appointed by the contractor
          and specially approved for the purposes of this section by the Sec-
          retary of State; and
     (b) a monitor, who shall be a Crown servant appointed by the Secretary of
          State;
and every officer of such a secure training centre who performs custodial
duties shall be a custody officer who is authorised to perform such duties or
an officer of a directly managed secure training centre who is temporarily
attached to the secure training centre.
     (2) The director shall have such functions as are conferred on him by the
Prison Act 1952 as it applies to secure training centres and as may be conferred on him by secure training centre rules.
     (3) The monitor shall have such functions as may be conferred on him by
secure training centre rules and shall be under a duty—
     (a) to keep under review, and report to the Secretary of State on, the run-
          ning of the secure training centre by or on behalf of the director; and
     (b) to investigate, and report to the Secretary of State on, any allegations
          made against custody officers performing custodial duties at the
          secure training centre or officers of directly managed secure training
          centres who are temporarily attached to the secure training centre.
     (4) The contractor and any sub-contractor of his shall each be under a duty
to do all that he reasonably can (whether by giving directions to the officers of
the secure training centre or otherwise) to facilitate the exercise by the monitor of all such functions as are mentioned in or imposed by subsection (3)
above.

Definitions
     "contracted out secure training centre": s.15.
     "contractor": s.15.
     "custodial duties": s.15.
     "custody officer": s.12(3).
     "director": subs. (1)(a).
     "monitor": subs. (1)(b).
     "secure training centre": s.5(2).
     "secure training centre rules": s.15.
     "subcontractor": s.15.

General Note
     This section provides for the officers of a contracted-out secure training centre and specifies
the duties and functions of the director and monitor of the centre. It will be the responsibility of
the director to run the centre; whereas the monitor will be responsible to the Home Secretary for
seeing that the contract is correctly carried out. This is not the first time that the idea of a monitor

has appeared in current legislation. Section 81 of the 1991 Act provides for the appointment of monitors in relation to prison escorts.

Secure training centre rules: see Note to s.7, *ante*.

Powers and duties of custody officers employed at contracted out secure training centres

9.—(1) A custody officer performing custodial duties at a contracted out secure training centre shall have the following powers, namely—

(a) to search in accordance with secure training centre rules any offender who is detained in the secure training centre; and

(b) to search any other person who is in or who is seeking to enter the secure training centre, and any article in the possession of such a person.

(2) The powers conferred by subsection (1)(b) above to search a person shall not be construed as authorising a custody officer to require a person to remove any of his clothing other than an outer coat, headgear, jacket or gloves.

(3) A custody officer performing custodial duties at a contracted out secure training centre shall have the following duties as respects offenders detained in the secure training centre, namely—

(a) to prevent their escape from lawful custody;

(b) to prevent, or detect and report on, the commission or attempted commission by them of other unlawful acts;

(c) to ensure good order and discipline on their part; and

(d) to attend to their wellbeing.

(4) The powers conferred by subsection (1) above, and the powers arising by virtue of subsection (3) above, shall include power to use reasonable force where necessary.

DEFINITIONS

"contracted out secure training centre": s.15.
"custodial duties": s.15.
"custody officer": s.12(3).
"secure training centre": s.5(2).
"secure training centre rules": s.15.

GENERAL NOTE

This section defines the powers and duties of custody officers performing custodial duties in the contracted-out secure training centres. Subsection 1(b) permits a custody officer to search any person who is in or who is seeking to enter a centre. Subsection (2) restricts the power of such an officer to "require" a person to remove his clothing. Thus an officer cannot require someone to submit to a "strip" search. These restrictions are based on similar restrictions applied to the powers of the police to search arrested persons by s.32(4) of the Police and Criminal Evidence Act 1984. However, subs. (2) goes further than s.32(4) because it allows headgear to be removed. This power was added by way of amendment during the passage of the Bill through the House of Commons. The change was made because something, such as soft drug, could be hidden in a hat. The word "headgear" was subsequently substituted for the word "hat". Presumably, this change was made for greater clarification and to avoid disputes as to whether some forms of headgear were hats or not. It is anticipated that Home Office guidance will be issued to the effect that religious headgear, such as turbans, will not normally be required to be removed. However, there is nothing in the section to prevent it. Subsection (3) does not appear to set out the duties of the custody officer with any great degree of precision. Subsection (4) permits an officer to use "reasonable force" when carrying out his duties under subss. (1) and (3). The concept of reasonable force is a familiar one; it plays an important part in the law of self-defence. By analogy with that law, it will presumably be a matter of question and degree in each case under subs. (3) whether the use of force was reasonable. What was reasonable in a particular case will depend on the circumstances. However, it will not be sufficient for the officer merely to assert that the force was reasonable. On the other hand, his state of mind would be taken into account in assessing what was reasonable.

Secure training centre rules: see General Note to s.7, *ante*.

Intervention by Secretary of State in management of contracted out secure training centres

10.—(1) This section applies where, in the case of a contracted out secure training centre, it appears to the Secretary of State—

(a) that the director has lost, or is likely to lose, effective control of the secure training centre or any part of it; and

(b) that the making of an appointment under subsection (2) below is necessary in the interests of preserving the safety of any person, or of preventing serious damage to any property.

(2) The Secretary of State may appoint a Crown servant to act as governor of the secure training centre for the period—

(a) beginning with the time specified in the appointment; and

(b) ending with the time specified in the notice of termination under subsection (4) below.

(3) During that period—

(a) all the functions which would otherwise be exercisable by the director or monitor shall be exercisable by the governor;

(b) the contractor and any sub-contractor of his shall each do all that he reasonably can to facilitate the exercise by the governor of those functions; and

(c) the officers of the secure training centre shall comply with any directions given by the governor in the exercise of those functions.

(4) Where the Secretary of State is satisfied—

(a) that the governor has secured effective control of the secure training centre or, as the case may be, the relevant part of it; and

(b) that the governor's appointment is no longer necessary for the purpose mentioned in subsection (1)(b) above,

he shall, by a notice to the governor, terminate the appointment at a time specified in the notice.

(5) As soon as practicable after making or terminating an appointment under this section, the Secretary of State shall give a notice of the appointment, or a copy of the notice of termination, to the contractor, any sub-contractor of his, the director and the monitor.

DEFINITIONS

"contracted out secure training centre": s.15.

"contractor": s.15.

"custody officer": s.12(3).

"director": subs. 8(1)(a).

"monitor": subs. 8(1)(b).

"secure training centre": s.5(2).

"subcontractor": s.15.

GENERAL NOTE

This section provides for the intervention of the Home Secretary at a contracted-out secure training centre in the event of a loss of control or in the interests of safety. It follows the wording of s.88 of 1991 Act (which makes similar provision in the case of contracted-out prisons) except that the latter section refers to a "controller" instead of a "monitor". *N.B.* that s.88 is amended by s.101 of this Act, q.v. *post*, in respect of sub-contractors.

Contracted out functions at directly managed secure training centres

11.—(1) The Secretary of State may enter into a contract with another person for any functions at a directly managed secure training centre to be performed by custody officers who are provided by that person and are authorised to perform custodial duties.

(2) Section 9 shall apply in relation to a custody officer performing contracted out functions at a directly managed secure training centre as it applies in relation to such an officer performing custodial duties at a contracted out secure training centre.

(3) In relation to a directly managed secure training centre, the reference in section 13(2) of the Prison Act 1952 (legal custody of prisoners) as it applies to secure training centres to an officer of the prison shall be construed as including a reference to a custody officer performing custodial duties at the secure training centre in pursuance of a contract under this section.

(4) Any reference in subsections (1), (2) and (3) above to the performance of functions or custodial duties at a directly managed secure training centre includes a reference to the performance of functions or such duties for the purposes of, or for purposes connected with, such a secure training centre.

DEFINITIONS
"contracted out functions": s.15.
"custodial duties": s.15.
"directly managed secure training centre": s.15.

GENERAL NOTE
This section allows for staff from contracted-out secure training centres to give support to directly-managed establishments and facilitates contracting-out of functions within directly-managed secure training centres. Unlike the previous section there is no parallel for this section in the 1991 Act relating to prisons, but a new section (s.88A) has been added by s.99 of this Act, *post*, to provide similar powers in relation to prisons.

Escort arrangements and officers

12.—(1) The provisions of Schedule 1 to this Act (which make provision for escort arrangements for offenders detained at a secure training centre) shall have effect.

(2) The provisions of Schedule 2 to this Act shall have effect with respect to the certification of custody officers.

(3) In this Part, "custody officer" means a person in respect of whom a certificate is for the time being in force certifying—
  (a) that he has been approved by the Secretary of State for the purpose of performing escort functions or custodial duties or both in relation to offenders in respect of whom secure training orders have been made; and
  (b) that he is accordingly authorised to perform them.

DEFINITIONS
"custodial duties": s.15.
"custody officer": subs. (3).
"escort arrangements": s.15.
"escort functions": s.15.
"secure training centre": s.5(2).
"secure training order": s.1(2)(6).

GENERAL NOTE
This section gives effect to Sched. 1 (which makes provision for escort arrangements for offenders detained in a secure training centre) and Sched. 2 (which makes provision for the certification of custody officers of a secure training centre to carry out escort functions and custodial duties). The Schedule creates an offence of making a false statement to obtain certification. *Note* that s.80 of the 1991 Act is amended by s.93, *post*, to make the prisoner escort legislation compatible with that provided by this section and Sched. 1.

Escort arrangements and escort functions are defined by s.15 as those specified by Sched. 1, *post*.

Protection of custody officers at secure training centres

13.—(1) Any person who assaults a custody officer—
  (a) acting in pursuance of escort arrangements;
  (b) performing custodial duties at a contracted out secure training centre; or
  (c) performing contracted out functions at a directly managed secure training centre,

shall be liable on summary conviction to a fine not exceeding level 5 on the standard scale or to imprisonment for a term not exceeding six months or to both.

(2) Any person who resists or wilfully obstructs a custody officer—

(a) acting in pursuance of escort arrangements;

(b) performing custodial duties at a contracted out secure training centre; or

(c) performing contracted out functions at a directly managed secure training centre,

shall be liable on summary conviction to a fine not exceeding level 3 on the standard scale.

(3) For the purposes of this section, a custody officer shall not be regarded as acting in pursuance of escort arrangements at any time when he is not readily identifiable as such an officer (whether by means of a uniform or badge which he is wearing or otherwise).

DEFINITIONS

"contracted out functions": s.15.
"contracted out secure training centre": s.15.
"custodial duties": s.15.
"custody officer": s.12(3).
"directly managed secure training centre": s.15.
"escort arrangements": s.15.

GENERAL NOTE

The object of this section is to provide for the protection of custody officers in the performance of their duties at secure training centres. To this end, two offences are created: assault on such an officer (subs. (1)); and resisting or wilfully obstructing him (subs. (2)). The offence of assault carries the same penalty as assault on a police officer in the execution of his duties. The section is based on s.90 of the 1991 Act which creates similar offences in relation to prisoner custody officers. In subs. (1) *assault* must be given its ordinary common law meaning. Thus it may be defined as an act by which a person intentionally or recklessly applies unlawful force to another or causes another to apprehend immediate personal violence. The offence of assault carries the same penalty as assault on a police officer in the execution of his duties set out in s.51 of the Police Act 1964 (as amended). It has been held under s.51, above, that a person wilfully obstructs a police officer if he deliberately does an act which in fact prevents a constable from carrying out his duties or makes it more difficult for him to do so and if he knows or intends that it will have that effect: *Lewis v. Cox* [1984] C.L.Y. 676. The effect of subs. (3) is that an officer will not be treated as acting in pursuance of escort arrangements unless he is "readily identifiable" as such. Whereas this may be thought to provide a not very meritorious defence in some cases, it should ensure that officers in these circumstances wear their badges or other identification in order to retain the protection of the section.

Wrongful disclosure of information relating to offenders detained at secure training centres

14.—(1) A person who—

(a) is or has been employed (whether as a custody officer or otherwise) in pursuance of escort arrangements or at a contracted out secure training centre; or

(b) is or has been employed to perform contracted out functions at a directly managed secure training centre,

commits an offence if he discloses, otherwise than in the course of his duty or as authorised by the Secretary of State, any information which he acquired in the course of his employment and which relates to a particular offender detained at a secure training centre.

(2) A person guilty of an offence under subsection (1) above shall be liable—

(a) on conviction on indictment, to imprisonment for a term not exceeding two years or a fine or both;

(b) on summary conviction, to imprisonment for a term not exceeding six
months or a fine not exceeding the statutory maximum or both.

DEFINITIONS
"contracted out functions": s.15.
"contracted out secure training centre": s.15.
"custody officer": s.12(3).
"directly managed secure training centre": s.15.
"escort arrangements": s.15.

GENERAL NOTE
This section makes it an offence for a person employed in pursuance of escort, custodial or
other duties at a secure training centre to disclose any information which he may have acquired
in the course of his employment and which relates to a particular offender detained at a secure
training centre. The purpose is to prevent unauthorised disclosures which may harm young
offenders. Such an offence would involve a serious breach of trust: hence, the provision of a
severe penalty.

Interpretation of sections 7 to 14

15. In sections 7 to 14—
"contracted out functions" means any functions which, by virtue of a
contract under section 11, fall to be performed by custody officers;
"contracted out secure training centre" means a secure training centre
or part of a secure training centre in respect of which a contract
under section 7(1) is for the time being in force;
"the contractor", in relation to a contracted out secure training centre,
means the person who has contracted with the Secretary of State
for the provision or running (or the provision and running) of it;
"custodial duties" means custodial duties at a secure training centre;
"directly managed secure training centre" means a secure training centre which is not a contracted out secure training centre;
"escort arrangements" means the arrangements specified in paragraph
1 of Schedule 1 to this Act;
"escort functions" means the functions specified in paragraph 1 of
Schedule 1 to this Act;
"escort monitor" means a person appointed under paragraph 2(1)(a) of
Schedule 1 to this Act;
"secure training centre rules" has the meaning given by section 7(4)(b);
and
"sub-contractor", in relation to a contracted out secure training centre,
means a person who has contracted with the contractor for the running of it or any part of it.

DEFINITIONS
"custody officer": s.12(3).
"secure training centre": s.5(2).

GENERAL NOTE
This section defines the terms used in ss.7 to 14.
Escort monitor (not referred to in this Act otherwise than in Sched. 1) is under Sched. 1, para.
2(1)(a): "a Crown servant whose duty it shall be to keep the arrangements under review and to
report on them to the Secretary of State". Paragraph 2(1)(b) provides for a panel of lay
observers. Paragraph 2(2) provides that it is "the duty of an escort monitor to investigate and to
report to the Secretary of State on any allegations made against custody officers acting in pursuance of escort arrangements." For *escort arrangement* and *escort functions* see the General Note
to s.12.

Custodial sentences for young offenders

Long term detention of young offenders

16.—(1) Section 53 of the Children and Young Persons Act 1933 (which provides for the long term detention of children and young persons for certain grave crimes) shall be amended as follows.

(2) In subsection (1), for the words after "conditions" there shall be substituted—
"—
    (a) as the Secretary of State may direct, or
    (b) as the Secretary of State may arrange with any person.".

(3) In subsection (2), for the words from the beginning to the words "and the court" there shall be substituted the following—
"(2) Subsection (3) below applies—
    (a) where a person of at least 10 but not more than 17 years is convicted on indictment of—
        (i) any offence punishable in the case of an adult with imprisonment for fourteen years or more, not being an offence the sentence for which is fixed by law, or
        (ii) an offence under section 14 of the Sexual Offences Act 1956 (indecent assault on a woman);
    (b) where a young person is convicted of—
        (i) an offence under section 1 of the Road Traffic Act 1988 (causing death by dangerous driving), or
        (ii) an offence under section 3A of the Road Traffic Act 1988 (causing death by careless driving while under influence of drink or drugs).
(3) Where this subsection applies, then, if the court".

(4) For the words from "as the" in subsection (3) to the end of the section there shall be substituted—
"—
    (a) as the Secretary of State may direct, or
    (b) as the Secretary of State may arrange with any person.
(4) A person detained pursuant to the directions or arrangements made by the Secretary of State under this section shall, while so detained, be deemed to be in legal custody.".

GENERAL NOTE
This section amends s.53(2) of the Children and Young Persons Act 1933 by reducing the age at which a young person may receive a Crown Court sentence of long-term detention. The age is reduced from 14 to 10. The maximum age remains the same at 17. Subsection (3) replaces s.64 of the 1991 Act in extending the category of offence to which s.53 applies to include indecent assault on a woman. The section also enables the Home Secretary to contract with independent providers of secure accommodation for the placement of children and young persons so detained. Such a sentence may be passed where "the court is of the opinion that none of the other methods in which the case may legally be dealt with is suitable": s.53(2). A sentence of this kind may only be passed for the most serious offences; and the younger the age of the child, the more serious the crime will have to be before a sentence under this section will be appropriate.

Child means a person under the age of 14 years (Children and Young Persons Act 1933 (c. 12), s.107(1)).

Young person means a person between the ages of 14 and 18 (*ibid.* as amended by the 1991 Act, s.68, Sched. 8).

Maximum length of detention for young offenders

17.—(1) Section 1B of the Criminal Justice Act 1982 (maximum length of detention in young offender institution for offenders aged 15, 16 or 17 years) shall be amended as follows.

(2) In subsection (2)(b), for the words "12 months" there shall be substituted the words "24 months".

(3) In subsection (4), for the words "12 months" there shall be substituted the words "24 months".

(4) In subsection (5), for the words "12 months" in both places where they occur there shall be substituted the words "24 months".

GENERAL NOTE

This section increases the maximum length of detention in a young offender institution for 15, 16, and 17-year-olds. The effect of this section which amends s.1B of the 1982 Act (as amended by the 1992 Act, s.63(2)) is to increase the maximum length of detention in a young offender institution for offenders aged between 15 and 17. The maximum length of detention is increased from 12 months to 24 months. But by subs. (5) of s.1(B) (as amended by this section) where the *total term* exceeds 24 months so much of the term as exceeds 24 months shall be treated as remitted. Subsection (6) defines *total term* as "(a) in the case of an offender sentenced (whether or not on the same occasion) to two or more terms of detention in a young offender institution which are consecutive or wholly or partly concurrent, the aggregate of those terms; (b) in the case of any other offender, the term of the sentence in a young offender institution in question".

This section will bring sentences available for 15 to 17-year-olds into line with those for younger persons under secure training orders: s.1, *ante.* Until the enactment of the 1991 Act 17-year-olds were liable to the same penalties as adults. The changes embodied in this section reflect the views of the Council of H.M. Circuit Judges in its evidence to the Home Affairs Select Committee. The purpose is to give the Crown Court greater flexibility in dealing with young offenders who have committed offences which are serious, but not so grave as to merit long term detention under s.53 of the Children and Young Persons Act 1933. An example might be a case of unlawful wounding, *e.g.* a stabbing. In such a case the maximum sentence for an adult is five years imprisonment, but under the previous legislation, a 17-year-old was liable only to a maximum of 12 months' detention. This section corrects that disparity. The sentencing powers of magistrates are unaffected.

Accommodation of young offenders sentenced to custody for life

18.—(1) In section 1C of the Criminal Justice Act 1982 (young offenders sentenced to detention in a young offender institution to be detained in such an institution unless the Secretary of State otherwise directs)—
  (a) in subsection (1), after the words "young offender institution" there shall be inserted the words "or to custody for life" and for the words "such an institution" there shall be substituted the words "a young offender institution"; and
  (b) in subsection (2), after the words "in a young offender institution" there shall be inserted the words "or to custody for life".

(2) Subsections (6) and (7) of section 12 of the Criminal Justice Act 1982 (which provide for the detention of young offenders sentenced to custody for life in a prison unless the Secretary of State otherwise directs) are hereby repealed.

(3) In section 43(1) of the Prison Act 1952 (which relates to the institutions for the detention of young offenders which may be provided by the Secretary of State), in paragraph (aa), at the end, there shall be inserted the words "or to custody for life".

GENERAL NOTE

This section (by amending s.1C of the 1982 Act and repealing subss. (6) and (7) of s.12 of the 1982 Act) provides that a young person sentenced to custody for life shall be detained in a young offender institution unless the Home Secretary directs otherwise.

Secure accommodation for certain young persons

Extension of kinds of secure accommodation

19.—(1) Section 23 of the Children and Young Persons Act 1969 (remands and committals to local authority accommodation) shall be amended by the insertion, in subsection (12), in the definition of "secure accommodation", after the words "community home", of the words ", a voluntary home or a registered children's home", and, at the end of that subsection, of the words "but, for the purposes of the definition of "secure accommodation", "local authority accommodation" includes any accommodation falling within section 61(2) of the Criminal Justice Act 1991.".

(2) In the Children Act 1989, Schedules 5 and 6 (which provide for the regulation of voluntary homes and registered childrens' homes respectively) shall be amended as follows, that is to say—

(a) in Schedule 5, in paragraph 7(2) (regulations as to conduct of voluntary homes)—

(i) head (f) (power to prohibit provision of secure accommodation) shall be omitted; and

(ii) after that head, there shall be inserted the following—

"(ff) require the approval of the Secretary of State for the provision and use of accommodation for the purpose of restricting the liberty of children in such homes and impose other requirements (in addition to those imposed by section 25) as to the placing of a child in accommodation provided for that purpose, including a requirement to obtain the permission of any local authority who are looking after the child;"; and

(b) in Schedule 6, in paragraph 10(2) (regulations as to conduct, etc. of registered childrens' homes)—

(i) head (j) (power to prohibit use of accommodation as secure accommodation) shall be omitted; and

(ii) after that head, there shall be inserted the following—

"(jj) require the approval of the Secretary of State for the provision and use of accommodation for the purpose of restricting the liberty of children in such homes and impose other requirements (in addition to those imposed by section 25) as to the placing of a child in accommodation provided for that purpose, including a requirement to obtain the permission of any local authority who are looking after the child.".

(3) In section 61 of the Criminal Justice Act 1991 (provision by local authorities of secure accommodation)—

(a) in subsection (2), at the end, there shall be inserted the words "or by making arrangements with voluntary organisations or persons carrying on a registered childrens' home for the provision or use by them of such accommodation or by making arrangements with the Secretary of State for the use by them of a home provided by him under section 82(5) of the Children Act 1989"; and

(b) in subsection (5), at the end, there shall be inserted the words "and expressions, other than "local authority", used in the Children Act 1989 have the same meanings as in that Act.".

GENERAL NOTE

This section amends provisions in the Children Act 1989 which prevent the use of private or voluntary children's homes for secure accommodation. It also amends provisions in the Children and Young Persons Act 1969 and the 1991 Act which govern remands to secure accommodation. The section enables local authorities to make arrangements with voluntary organisations or persons carrying on registered children's homes for the provision by them of approved secure accommodation. Local authorities will thus be able to make placements (under the Children Act 1989) in approved secure accommodation provided by the voluntary and private sector. Such accommodation will be subject to the same criteria as apply to the public sector. No child can be placed in such accommodation unless the criteria in s.25 of the Children Act 1989 are met.

Subs. (1)

Secure accommodation is defined by s.23 of the Children and Young Persons Act 1969 (as substituted by s.60(1) of the 1991 Act and amended by this subsection) as follows: "… accommodation which is provided in a community home, a voluntary home or a registered children's home, for the purpose of restricting liberty, and is approved for that purpose by the Secretary of State; …" but for the purposes of secure accommodation: "local authority accommodation" includes any accommodation falling within s.61(2) of the 1991 Act. For s.61(2) see the note to subs. (3) below.

Subs. (2)
This subsection allows the use of voluntary homes and registered children's homes, but only with the approval of the Secretary of State.

Subs. (3)
The effect of the amendment is that certain words used in s.61 now have the meanings given to them by the Children Act 1989, s.105(1): local authority, voluntary organisation, registered children's home. See General Note to s.2, *ante*.

Secure remands for young offenders

20. In section 23(5) of the Children and Young Persons Act 1969 (as substituted by section 60 of the Criminal Justice Act 1991) (conditions for imposing a security requirement in case of young persons remanded to local authority accommodation), for the words "young person who has attained the age of fifteen" there shall be substituted the words—
  (a) "person who has attained the age of fourteen";
  (b) "person who has attained the age of thirteen"; or
  (c) "person who has attained the age of twelve";
but no substitution may be brought into force on more than one occasion.

GENERAL NOTE
This section extends the court's powers to remand young persons to local authority accommodation with a security requirement to those aged 12 to 14. This provision may be brought into force initially for 14-year-olds and subsequently for 13 and then 12-year-olds.
Security requirement, by the Children and Young Persons Act 1969, as substituted by the 1991 Act, s.60(1), is "a requirement that the person in question be placed in secure accommodation". For the definition of *secure accommodation* see the General Note to s.19(1), *ante*; and for the definition of *local authority accommodation*, see *ibid*.

Cost of secure accommodation

21. After section 61 of the Criminal Justice Act 1991 there shall be inserted the following section—

"Cost of secure accommodation
61A.—(1) The Secretary of State may, in relation to any costs incurred by a local authority in discharging their duty under section 61(1) above—
  (a) defray such costs to such extent as he considers appropriate in any particular case;
  (b) defray a proportion to be determined by him from time to time of such costs; and
  (c) defray or contribute to such costs in accordance with a tariff to be determined by him from time to time.
(2) The Secretary of State may require any person providing secure accommodation to transmit to him, at such times and in such form as he may direct, such particulars as he may require with respect to any costs to which this section applies.
(3) Payments under this section shall be made out of money provided by Parliament.".

GENERAL NOTE
This section provides for the costs incurred by local authorities in complying with court-ordered remands to local authority accommodation with a security requirement to be defrayed by the Secretary of State either on a case by case basis or according to a proportion of such costs or a tariff structure determined by the Secretary of State.

Management of secure accommodation

22.—(1) The Children Act 1989 shall be amended as follows.

(2) In section 53 (provision and management of community homes)—

(a) in subsection (3) (homes which may be community homes)—

(i) in paragraph (a), for the words "managed, equipped and maintained" there shall be substituted the words "equipped, maintained and (subject to subsection (3A)) managed"; and

(ii) in paragraph (b)(i), for the words "management, equipment and maintenance" there shall be substituted the words "equipment, maintenance and (subject to subsection (3B)) management"; and

(b) after subsection (3) there shall be inserted the following subsections—

"(3A) A local authority may make arrangements for the management by another person of accommodation provided by the local authority for the purpose of restricting the liberty of children.

(3B) Where a local authority are to be responsible for the management of a community home provided by a voluntary organisation, the local authority may, with the consent of the body of managers constituted by the instrument of management for the home, make arrangements for the management by another person of accommodation provided for the purpose of restricting the liberty of children.".

(3) In Part II of Schedule 4 (management of controlled and assisted community homes)—

(a) in paragraph 3(4), after the word "managers" there shall be inserted the words ", except in so far as, under section 53(3B), any of the accommodation is to be managed by another person."; and

(b) in paragraph 3(5), after the word "body" there shall be inserted the words "; and similarly, to the extent that a contract so provides, as respects anything done, liability incurred or property acquired by a person by whom, under section 53(3B), any of the accommodation is to be managed".

DEFINITIONS
"child": s.105(1) of the Children Act 1958 (c. 65).
"community homes": s.53(1).
"managers": Sched. 4, Pt. II, para. 3(3) of the Children Act 1989 (c. 41).

GENERAL NOTE
This section enables local authorities to contract-out the management of secure accommodation in community homes and, with the consent of the managers (constituted by an Instrument of Management and comprising usually two-thirds local authority and one-third voluntary organisation managers), to contract out secure accommodation in controlled community homes.

Section 53(1) of the Children Act 1989 enacts that "every local authority shall make such arrangements as they consider appropriate for securing that homes ("community homes") are available (a) for the care and accommodation of children looked after by them; and (b) for purposes connected with the welfare of children (whether or not looked after by them), and may do so jointly with one or more other local authorities."

Arrest of young persons in breach of conditions of remand

Liability of young persons to arrest for breaking conditions of remand

23. After section 23 of the Children and Young Persons Act 1969 there shall be inserted the following section—

"Liability to arrest for breaking conditions of remand

23A.—(1) A person who has been remanded or committed to local authority accommodation and in respect of whom conditions under subsection (7) or (10) of section 23 of this Act have been imposed may be arrested without warrant by a constable if the constable has reasonable grounds for suspecting that that person has broken any of those conditions.

(2) A person arrested under subsection (1) above—

(a) shall, except where he was arrested within 24 hours of the time appointed for him to appear before the court in pursuance of the remand or committal, be brought as soon as practicable and in any event within 24 hours after his arrest before a justice of the peace for the petty sessions area in which he was arrested; and

(b) in the said excepted case shall be brought before the court before which he was to have appeared.

In reckoning for the purposes of this subsection any period of 24 hours, no account shall be taken of Christmas Day, Good Friday or any Sunday.

(3) A justice of the peace before whom a person is brought under subsection (2) above—

(a) if of the opinion that that person has broken any condition imposed on him under subsection (7) or (10) of section 23 of this Act shall remand him; and that section shall apply as if he was then charged with or convicted of the offence for which he had been remanded or committed;

(b) if not of that opinion shall remand him to the place to which he had been remanded or committed at the time of his arrest subject to the same conditions as those which had been imposed on him at that time.".

GENERAL NOTE

This section amends s.38(6) of Police and Criminal Evidence Act 1984 in order to reduce the age at which the police may detain young persons in police cells after arrest but prior to their appearance in court. The section applies when no local authority secure accommodation is available and there is a risk to the public of serious harm from the youngsters. The minimum age was 15: it is now reduced to 12. This provision is in line with the other sections of the Act which make provision for the secure confinement of 12 to 14-year-olds.

In this section "arrested juvenile" is defined by the Police and Criminal Evidence Act 1984 (c. 60), s.37(15). For "custody officer", see *ibid.*, s.36, and "police detention", *ibid.*, s.118(2).

Police detention of young persons

Detention of arrested juveniles after charge

24. In section 38(6) of the Police and Criminal Evidence Act 1984 (detention of arrested juveniles after charge), in paragraph (b), for the words "age of 15 years" there shall be substituted the words "age of 12 years".

GENERAL NOTE

Section 38(6) (as amended by this and previous legislation) of the Police and Criminal Evidence Act 1984 now reads "the custody officer shall, unless he certifies (a) that by reason of such circumstances as are specified in the certificate, it is impracticable for him to do so; or (b) in the case of an arrested juvenile who has attained the *age of 12 years*, that no secure accommodation is available and that keeping him in other local authority accommodation would not be adequate to protect the public from serious harm from him, secure that the arrested juvenile is moved to local authority accommodation." The words in italics are those substituted by this section.

PART II

BAIL

No bail for defendants charged with or convicted of homicide or rape after previous conviction of such offences

25.—(1) A person who in any proceedings has been charged with or convicted of an offence to which this section applies in circumstances to which it applies shall not be granted bail in those proceedings.

(2) This section applies, subject to subsection (3) below, to the following offences, that is to say—
(a) murder;
(b) attempted murder;
(c) manslaughter;
(d) rape; or
(e) attempted rape.

(3) This section applies to a person charged with or convicted of any such offence only if he has been previously convicted by or before a court in any part of the United Kingdom of any such offence or of culpable homicide and, in the case of a previous conviction of manslaughter or of culpable homicide, if he was then sentenced to imprisonment or, if he was then a child or young person, to long-term detention under any of the relevant enactments.

(4) This section applies whether or not an appeal is pending against conviction or sentence.

(5) In this section—
  "conviction" includes—
    (a) a finding that a person is not guilty by reason of insanity;
    (b) a finding under section 4A(3) of the Criminal Procedure (Insanity) Act 1964 (cases of unfitness to plead) that a person did the act or made the omission charged against him; and
    (c) a conviction of an offence for which an order is made placing the offender on probation or discharging him absolutely or conditionally;
  and "convicted" shall be construed accordingly; and
  "the relevant enactments" means—
    (a) as respects England and Wales, section 53(2) of the Children and Young Persons Act 1933;
    (b) as respects Scotland, sections 205 and 206 of the Criminal Procedure (Scotland) Act 1975;
    (c) as respects Northern Ireland, section 73(2) of the Children and Young Persons Act (Northern Ireland) 1968.

(6) This section does not apply in relation to proceedings instituted before its commencement.

DEFINITIONS
"conviction": subs. (5).
"relevant enactments": subs. (5).

GENERAL NOTE
This section provides that bail shall not be granted to a person charged with or convicted of murder, attempted murder, rape, attempted rape or manslaughter, where that person has a previous conviction for any of those offences and, in the case of a previous conviction for manslaughter, was sentenced to imprisonment or long-term detention. This section can only apply in a very limited number of cases indeed. Under the pre-existing law bail would not normally have been granted in cases of this sort. However, this section removes the court's discretion and bail must be withheld. The apparent purpose is to protect the public and to increase public confidence in the courts' ability to afford protection.
Bail in criminal proceedings is defined in the Bail Act 1976, s.1(1) and *bail, ibid.* s.1(2): see General Note to s.26, *post.*

No right to bail for persons accused or convicted of committing offence while on bail

26. In Part I of Schedule 1 to the Bail Act 1976 (exceptions to right to bail for imprisonable offences)—
  (a) after paragraph 2, there shall be inserted the following paragraph—
    "2A. The defendant need not be granted bail if—
      (a) the offence is an indictable offence or an offence triable either way; and

(b) it appears to the court that he was on bail in criminal proceedings on the date of the offence."; and

(b) in paragraph 9, after the words "paragraph 2" there shall be inserted
the words "or 2A".

GENERAL NOTE

This section creates an addition to the exceptions to the right to bail which are set out in Sched.
1 to the Bail Act 1976. It applies where a defendant is accused or convicted of an indictable
offence, or one triable either way, which appears to have been committed while he or she was on
bail. A court will now be able to remand a defendant in custody in these circumstances without
any other exception applying *i.e.* a substantial likelihood that the defendant would abscond,
re-offend or interfere with witnesses. The court will still be required to have regard to the nature
and seriousness of the offence and to the circumstances of the defendant as set out in para. 9 of
the Schedule. The section was introduced because of the high incidence of crimes committed by
persons on bail: 50,000 a year, according to the Home Office. However, the fact that a defendant
had committed an alleged offence while on bail was always a matter for the court to consider
when deciding whether to withhold bail on the ground that he was likely to commit further
offences. Accordingly, it must be seen whether this provision makes a great deal of practical
difference to decisions as to granting or withholding bail.

By the Bail Act 1976, s.1(2) *bail* means "bail grantable under the law (including the common
law) for the time being in force" and *bail in criminal proceedings*, by *ibid*. s.1(1), means "(a) bail
grantable or in connection with proceedings for an offence to a person who is accused or convicted of the offence, or (b) bail grantable in connection with an offence to a person who is under
arrest for the offence or for whose arrest for the offence a warrant (endorsed for bail) is being
issued."

Indictable offence: an offence which, if committed by an adult, is triable on indictment,
whether it is exclusively so triable or triable either way: Sched. 1 of the Interpretation Act 1978.

Offence triable either way: an offence, other than an offence triable on indictment only by
virtue of Pt. V of the Criminal Justice Act 1988 which, if committed by an adult, is triable either
on indictment or summarily, *ibid*.

Bail: bail in criminal proceedings.

Power for police to grant conditional bail to persons charged

27.—(1) Part IV of the Police and Criminal Evidence Act 1984 (detention
of persons, including powers of police to grant bail) shall have effect with the
following amendments, that is to say, in section 47 (bail after arrest)—

(a) in subsection (1), for the words after "in accordance with" there shall
be substituted the words "sections 3, 3A, 5 and 5A of the Bail Act 1976
as they apply to bail granted by a constable"; and

(b) after subsection (1) there shall be inserted the following subsection—

"(1A) The normal powers to impose conditions of bail shall be
available to him where a custody officer releases a person on bail under section 38(1) above (including that subsection as applied by section 40(10) above) but not in any other cases.

In this subsection, "the normal powers to impose conditions of
bail" has the meaning given in section 3(6) of the Bail Act 1976.".

(2) Section 3 of the Bail Act 1976 (incidents including conditions of bail in
criminal proceedings) shall be amended as follows—

(a) in subsection (6), the words "(but only by a court)" shall be omitted;

(b) at the end of subsection (6) there shall be inserted—

"and, in any Act, "the normal powers to impose conditions of bail"
means the powers to impose conditions under paragraph (a), (b) or
(c) above";

(c) after subsection (9), there shall be inserted the following subsection—

"(10) This section is subject, in its application to bail granted by a
constable, to section 3A of this Act.".

(3) After section 3 of the Bail Act 1976 there shall be inserted the following
section—

"Conditions of bail in case of police bail

3A.—(1) Section 3 of this Act applies, in relation to bail granted by a custody officer under Part IV of the Police and Criminal Evidence Act 1984 in cases where the normal powers to impose conditions of bail are available to him, subject to the following modifications.

(2) Subsection (6) does not authorise the imposition of a requirement to reside in a bail hostel or any requirement under paragraph (d).

(3) Subsections (6ZA), (6A) and (6B) shall be omitted.

(4) For subsection (8), substitute the following—

"(8) Where a custody officer has granted bail in criminal proceedings he or another custody officer serving at the same police station may, at the request of the person to whom it was granted, vary the conditions of bail; and in doing so he may impose conditions or more onerous conditions.".

(5) Where a constable grants bail to a person no conditions shall be imposed under subsections (4), (5), (6) or (7) of section 3 of this Act unless it appears to the constable that it is necessary to do so for the purpose of preventing that person from—

    (a) failing to surrender to custody, or

    (b) committing an offence while on bail, or

    (c) interfering with witnesses or otherwise obstructing the course of justice, whether in relation to himself or any other person.

(6) Subsection (5) above also applies on any request to a custody officer under subsection (8) of section 3 of this Act to vary the conditions of bail.".

(4) The further amendments contained in Schedule 3 to this Act shall have effect.

DEFINITIONS

"bail hostel": s.2(2) of the Bail Act 1976 (c. 63), as inserted by the Magistrates' Courts Act 1980 (c. 43).

"custody officer": s.36 of the Police and Criminal Evidence Act 1984 (c. 60).

"vary": s.2(2) of the Bail Act 1976 (c. 63).

GENERAL NOTE

Under s.38 of the Police and Criminal Evidence Act 1984 the police (in the person of the custody officer) have power to admit a defendant to bail pending his appearance in court. However, there is no power under that section to attach conditions to bail. The police wished to have that power in order that more defendants could be admitted to bail. It was felt that in some cases a person could be safely admitted to bail provided that a condition applied; but that, if there were no condition, it would not be safe to bail him. An example might be a case arising from a domestic dispute where a necessary condition of bail would be a requirement that the defendant did not visit his former wife's home.

The Royal Commission on Criminal Justice (1986, Cmnd. 2263) recommended that the police should have the additional power of releasing on bail subject to conditions (para. 5.22). The Commission pointed out that in many cases suspects are brought before the courts to make applications for bail even though the police might be willing to grant bail themselves; and if there were a power to release on condition, it would reduce the suspect's liability to attend court. It would also enable the police to release more suspects on bail while enquiries continued.

Section 26 follows the Commission's recommendation. This section, along with Sched. 3, provides a police power to attach conditions to bail after the defendant has been charged (and to vary those conditions). It is thus hoped to achieve a reduction in those held overnight in police cells. Section 43B of the Magistrates' Court Act 1980, as inserted by Sched. 3, will give a magistrates' court (on an application by a defendant) power to vary the conditions imposed by a custody officer or grant unconditional bail. However, the court also has power under the section either to impose more onerous conditions or to withhold bail. Accordingly, a defendant should be aware of these powers before making an application.

Subs. (1)

This subsection relates to police bail. By s.47 of the Police and Criminal Evidence Act 1984 the police powers under that Act to release persons on bail is a release on bail granted in accordance with the Bail Act 1976 (subs. (1)). By subs. (3) "references to bail are references to bail subject to a duty (a) to appear before a magistrates' court at such time and such place; or (b) to attend the police station at such time, as the custody officer may appoint."

As to the *normal powers to impose conditions of bail* see note to subs. (2) below.

Subs. (2)

Section 3(6) of the Bail Act 1976, as amended by this subsection enacts that a person granted bail in criminal proceedings "... may be required ... to comply, either before release on bail or later, with such requirements as appear to be necessary to secure that (a) he surrenders to custody, (b) he does not commit an offence while on bail, (c) he does not interfere with witnesses or otherwise obstruct the course of justice whether in relation to himself or any other person, (d) he makes himself available for the purpose of enabling inquiries or a report to be made to assist in dealing with him for the offence, and, in any Act, 'the normal powers to impose conditions of bail' means the powers to impose conditions under paragraphs (a)(b) or (c) above".

Subs. (3)

Bail hostel has the same meaning as in the Powers of Criminal Courts Act 1973: Bail Act 1976 (c. 63), s.2(2).

Vary: "in relation to bail, means imposing further conditions after bail is granted, or varying or rescinding conditions": *ibid.*

Police detention after charge

28.—(1) Section 38 of the Police and Criminal Evidence Act 1984 (which requires an arrested person charged with an offence to be released except in specified circumstances) shall be amended as follows.

(2) In subsection (1)(a), for sub-paragraphs (ii) and (iii) there shall be substituted the following sub-paragraphs—

"(ii) the custody officer has reasonable grounds for believing that the person arrested will fail to appear in court to answer to bail;

(iii) in the case of a person arrested for an imprisonable offence, the custody officer has reasonable grounds for believing that the detention of the person arrested is necessary to prevent him from committing an offence;

(iv) in the case of a person arrested for an offence which is not an imprisonable offence, the custody officer has reasonable grounds for believing that the detention of the person arrested is necessary to prevent him from causing physical injury to any other person or from causing loss of or damage to property;

(v) the custody officer has reasonable grounds for believing that the detention of the person arrested is necessary to prevent him from interfering with the administration of justice or with the investigation of offences or of a particular offence; or

(vi) the custody officer has reasonable grounds for believing that the detention of the person arrested is necessary for his own protection;".

(3) After subsection (2), there shall be inserted the following subsection—

"(2A) The custody officer, in taking the decisions required by subsection (1)(a) and (b) above (except (a)(i) and (vi) and (b)(ii)), shall have regard to the same considerations as those which a court is required to have regard to in taking the corresponding decisions under paragraph 2 of Part I of Schedule 1 to the Bail Act 1976.".

(4) After subsection (7), there shall be inserted the following subsection—

"(7A) In this section "imprisonable offence" has the same meaning as in Schedule 1 to the Bail Act 1976.".

GENERAL NOTE

This section amends s.38 of the Police and Criminal Evidence Act 1984, to add a new power for a custody officer to detain a person charged with an imprisonable offence if the officer has reasonable grounds for believing that the person would commit an offence if released. The section, as now amended, requires that the custody officer in exercising his powers under the section should have regard to the same considerations as a court when deciding whether to withhold bail under the Bail Act 1976.

The detention referred to in the new subparagraphs to s.38 of the Police and Criminal Evidence Act 1984 is, by subs. (1) of that section, *police detention*, which is defined by the Police and Criminal Evidence Act 1984, s.118(2) in the following terms.

A person is in police detention for the purposes of that Act "if (a) he has been taken to a police station after being arrested for an offence; or (b) he is arrested at a police station after attending voluntarily at the station or accompanying a constable to it, and is detained there, or is detained elsewhere, in the charge of a constable, except that a person who is at a court after being charged is not in police detention for those purposes."

Power for police to arrest for failure to answer to police bail

29.—(1) Part IV of the Police and Criminal Evidence Act 1984 (detention of persons, including powers of police to grant bail) shall be amended as follows.

(2) After section 46 there shall be inserted the following section—

"Power of arrest for failure to answer to police bail

46A.—(1) A constable may arrest without a warrant any person who, having been released on bail under this Part of this Act subject to a duty to attend at a police station, fails to attend at that police station at the time appointed for him to do so.

(2) A person who is arrested under this section shall be taken to the police station appointed as the place at which he is to surrender to custody as soon as practicable after the arrest.

(3) For the purposes of—

(a) section 30 above (subject to the obligation in subsection (2) above), and

(b) section 31 above,

an arrest under this section shall be treated as an arrest for an offence.".

(3) In section 34 after subsection (6), there shall be inserted the following subsection—

"(7) For the purposes of this Part of this Act a person who returns to a police station to answer to bail or is arrested under section 46A below shall be treated as arrested for an offence and the offence in connection with which he was granted bail shall be deemed to be that offence.".

(4) In consequence of the foregoing amendments—

(a) in section 37(1), paragraph (b) shall be omitted;

(b) in sections 41(9), 42(11) and 43(19), at the end, there shall be inserted the words "; but this subsection does not prevent an arrest under section 46A below.";

(c) in section 47, subsection (5) shall be omitted;

(d) in section 47(6), for the words "is detained under subsection (5) above" there shall be substituted the words "who has been granted bail and either has attended at the police station in accordance with the grant of bail or has been arrested under section 46A above is detained at a police station"; and

(e) in section 47(7), at the end, there shall be inserted the words "; but this subsection does not apply to a person who is arrested under section 46A above or has attended a police station in accordance with the grant of bail (and who accordingly is deemed by section 34(7) above to have been arrested for an offence).".

(5) This section applies whether the person released on bail was granted bail before or after the commencement of this section.

GENERAL NOTE

This section (by adding a new section, s.46(A), to the Police and Criminal Evidence Act 1984) provides the police with a new power, namely, to arrest a person who has failed to answer to police bail. It obviates the need for an application to a magistrate when a person, bailed on condition that he attend at the police station, fails to do so. The police may now arrest the person without a warrant. A person arrested under this power must be taken as soon as practicable to the police station where he was granted bail. If it is not practicable to take him to that police station the provisions of s.30 of the Police and Criminal Evidence Act 1984 (which deals with arrests elsewhere than at a police station) will apply. A person arrested under this power may also be arrested for a further offence under s.31 of the Police and Criminal Evidence Act 1984.

Reconsideration of decisions granting bail

30. After the section 5A of the Bail Act 1976 inserted by Schedule 3 to this Act there shall be inserted the following section—

> **"Reconsideration of decisions granting bail**
> 5B.—(1) Where a magistrates' court has granted bail in criminal pro-ceedings in connection with an offence, or proceedings for an offence, to which this section applies or a constable has granted bail in criminal proceedings in connection with proceedings for such an offence, that court or the appropriate court in relation to the constable may, on appli-cation by the prosecutor for the decision to be reconsidered,—
>> (a) vary the conditions of bail,
>> (b) impose conditions in respect of bail which has been granted unconditionally, or
>> (c) withhold bail.
>
> (2) The offences to which this section applies are offences triable on indictment and offences triable either way.
>
> (3) No application for the reconsideration of a decision under this section shall be made unless it is based on information which was not available to the court or constable when the decision was taken.
>
> (4) Whether or not the person to whom the application relates appears before it, the magistrates' court shall take the decision in accordance with section 4(1) (and Schedule 1) of this Act.
>
> (5) Where the decision of the court on a reconsideration under this section is to withhold bail from the person to whom it was originally granted the court shall—
>> (a) if that person is before the court, remand him in custody, and
>> (b) if that person is not before the court, order him to surrender him-self forthwith into the custody of the court.
>
> (6) Where a person surrenders himself into the custody of the court in compliance with an order under subsection (5) above, the court shall remand him in custody.
>
> (7) A person who has been ordered to surrender to custody under subsection (5) above may be arrested without warrant by a constable if he fails without reasonable cause to surrender to custody in accordance with the order.
>
> (8) A person arrested in pursuance of subsection (7) above shall be brought as soon as practicable, and in any event within 24 hours after his arrest, before a justice of the peace for the petty sessions area in which he was arrested and the justice shall remand him in custody.
>
> In reckoning for the purposes of this subsection any period of 24 hours, no account shall be taken of Christmas Day, Good Friday or any Sunday.
>
> (9) Magistrates' court rules shall include provision—
>> (a) requiring notice of an application under this section and of the grounds for it to be given to the person affected, including notice of the powers available to the court under it;
>> (b) for securing that any representations made by the person affected (whether in writing or orally) are considered by the court before making its decision; and

(c) designating the court which is the appropriate court in relation to the decision of any constable to grant bail.".

GENERAL NOTE

This section (by inserting s.5B into the Bail Act 1976) enables a magistrates' court (on application by the prosecutor) to reconsider a decision to grant bail either by the court or the police. Such an application may only be made where a person is charged with a serious offence: it may not be made in relation to a person charged with a summary offence only (subs. (2)). Subsection (1) allows a court to re-consider decisions by the police to grant bail (a power not previously available to justices) but no application may be made in relation to police bail granted before charge (subs. (1)). No application may be made under this section unless it is on new information which was not available to the court or the police when the original decision was taken (subs. (3)).

The purpose of the section is to allow the prosecution to make an application only in two situations: (a) if information comes to light which might have been relevant to the original bail decision and of which the court was unaware; or (b) there has been a change of circumstances. While s.4(1) of the Bail Act 1976 requires the court to re-consider bail on each occasion a defendant appears before it, the Divisional Court in *R. v. Nottingham Justices, ex p. Davies* [1980] C.L.Y. 433 held that justices could only hear an application where there was a change of circumstances since the original application. Furthermore, Sched. 1, Pt. IIA of the Act provides that after the first hearing at which the court refused bail the court need not hear arguments as to fact and law which it has heard previously. However, under the present section magistrates are not bound by a previous decision and may re-consider it. Similarly, the court may re-consider a bail decision if new information comes to light before a defendant's next scheduled appearance (without having to wait for that appearance).

The effect of subs. (4) is to retain the defendant's right to bail on an application under this section: bail may only be withheld in accordance with s.4(1) and Sched. 1 to the Bail Act 1976. Since the court is not bound by any previous decision, subs. (1) empowers it to vary any conditions, to impose conditions where none existed or to withhold bail.

Under subs. (9) rules must be made requiring notice to be given to the defendant of an application under this section and ensuring that his representations are considered by the court. However, if a defendant does not appear and the court decides to withhold bail, he must be remanded in custody on his next appearance in court, whether as a result either of his surrender to custody or as a result of his arrest: subss. (5)–(8).

Magistrates' courts rules means "rules made under s.15 of the Justices of the Peace Act 1949" (Bail Act 1976 (c. 63), s.2(2)).

Offence "includes an alleged offence" (*ibid.*).

Surrender to custody means "in relation to a person released on bail, surrender himself into the custody of the court or of the constable (according to the requirements of the grant of bail) at the time and place for the time being appointed for him to so do" (*ibid.*).

Conditions of bail: see note to s.27(2), *ante.*

PART III

COURSE OF JUSTICE: EVIDENCE, PROCEDURE, ETC.

Imputations on character

Imputations on character

31. In section 1 of the Criminal Evidence Act 1898 there shall be inserted at the end of sub-paragraph (ii) of paragraph (f) the words "the deceased victim of the alleged crime; or".

GENERAL NOTE

This section amends s.1(f)(ii) of the Criminal Evidence Act 1898 in order to render the accused liable to cross-examination as to his bad character if he makes imputations about the deceased victim. The Court of Criminal Appeal in *R. v. Biggin* [1920] K.B. 213 held that an attack on the victim of murder did not entitle the prosecution to cross-examine the defendant as to character since the dead man was not the prosecutor. This section overrules that decision which had been accepted as the law since 1920. The section is not limited in its scope to cases of murder; and it would appear to apply to any case in which the victim has died. Thus, if a defendant puts in the driving convictions of the deceased in a case of causing death by dangerous driving, he will be at risk of having his own convictions put before the court. The reason for introducing this amendment was because it was felt right that the jury should know the character of the person making an attack on the character of the deceased. An example given during debate involved a defendant charged with murder who alleges that he was defending himself against a homosexual attack by the victim (the "Portsmouth defence"): *Hansard*, H.L. Vol. 556, col. 1246, July 5, 1994. (The section was inserted during the passage of the Bill through the House of Lords as a result of an amendment by Lord Ackner).

Corroboration

Abolition of corroboration rules

32.—(1) Any requirement whereby at a trial on indictment it is obligatory for the court to give the jury a warning about convicting the accused on the uncorroborated evidence of a person merely because that person is—
  (a) an alleged accomplice of the accused, or
  (b) where the offence charged is a sexual offence, the person in respect of whom it is alleged to have been committed,
is hereby abrogated.

(2) In section 34(2) of the Criminal Justice Act 1988 (abolition of requirement of corroboration warning in respect of evidence of a child) the words from "in relation to" to the end shall be omitted.

(3) Any requirement that—
  (a) is applicable at the summary trial of a person for an offence, and
  (b) corresponds to the requirement mentioned in subsection (1) above or that mentioned in section 34(2) of the Criminal Justice Act 1988,
is hereby abrogated.

(4) Nothing in this section applies in relation to—
  (a) any trial, or
  (b) any proceedings before a magistrates' court as examining justices,
which began before the commencement of this section.

GENERAL NOTE

This section abolishes the "corroboration rules" *i.e.* the common law requirement that judges warn juries of the danger of convicting on the uncorroborated evidence of a complainant in a sexual offence or of an accomplice (and the similar rule applying to magistrates). Until recently, it was considered that the evidence of accomplices and complainants in sexual cases was inherently unreliable: in the case of an accomplice because he may give false evidence in order to obtain a lighter sentence; in the case of complainants in sexual cases because they may give false evidence due to a motive such as shame, neurosis, or spite. Ideas about these matters have now changed. The corroboration rules were criticised for their complexity and for the problems in directing juries upon them. For instance, Lord Taylor C.J. said that this area of the law had become "arcane, technical and difficult to convey": *R.* v. *Cheema* [1994] 1 W.L.R. 147. In 1991 the Law Commission in its Report: "Corroboration of Evidence in Criminal Trials" (Cmnd. 1620) recommended that these rules should be abolished. These views were accepted by the Royal Commission on Criminal Justice which endorsed the recommendation (Cmnd. 2263, para. 8.35). This section is based upon the Law Commission's recommendation. The effect of the section is that judges are no longer required to warn juries that it is dangerous to convict in reliance on the evidence of the witnesses in the above categories and magistrates are no longer required so to direct themselves.

The Law Commission recommended that the corroboration rules should be abolished without replacement. The Commission concluded that no new rules should be introduced because defendants receive adequate protection from the general law and practice of criminal trials; and the creation of new rules could lead to unnecessary formality and the unjustified categorisation of witnesses. (*op. cit.*, para. 2.23). The Commission said that the effect of their recommendation would be that (a) witnesses now within the corroboration rules would be treated, as other witnesses already are, on their merits; and (b) the courts would not be prevented from developing new principles for the general guidance of trial judges in relation to particular kinds of witness (*ibid.*, paras. 3.12–3.15). Accordingly, the Commission took the view that judges should be left free to comment on the evidence in the way that their experience and judgment suggests will most fairly and effectively assist the jury. These views were accepted by the Royal Commission on Criminal Justice which recommended that where a warning from the judge is required it should be tailored to the particular circumstances of the case (*ibid.*).

Thus, an accomplice may have no motive for lying, in which case there is no need for a warning of any sort. On the other hand, there may be a danger in some cases that he is lying to save his own skin. If the judge thinks that there is such a danger, which may be unperceived by the jury in a particular case, no doubt he will point it out to them. In any case, the judge is already under an obligation to warn the jury to proceed with caution if there is material to suggest that a witness's evidence may be tainted by an improper motive: *R. v. Beck* [1982] C.L.Y. 563. The Law Commission anticipated that trial judges would adopt the direction in *Beck* to cases where an accomplice may have an interest to serve in giving evidence; and if the judges did not adopt it, the Court of Appeal would require them to do so (*op.cit.*, para. 3.19).

There is no longer an obligation on the judge to warn the jury in a sexual case that it is dangerous to convict in reliance on the evidence of the complainant alone. Indeed, in many cases it is submitted that it would be wrong to give such a warning. For instance, to suggest that a woman may be motivated by neurosis, jealousy or spite (when there is no ground for doing so) may be to make an irrelevant comment and one which may sound gratuitously offensive. If such a danger does exist in a particular case the judge should warn the jury of it; but it is not necessary in every case, regardless of the issues. The Law Commission said that the judge may wish to speak about the way in which evidence fits together rather than the "corroboration" of one piece of evidence by another because it would be a misdirection to give the impression that evidence which was "corroborative" in the former strict sense continued to have some special legal effect, or should be treated by the jury in some special way (*op. cit.*, para. 4.13.). It has been suggested that a Practice Direction should be issued to cover the appropriate directions in these circumstances. However, the Minister of State, Home Office, reported to the House of Lords that the Lord Chief Justice had concluded that a Practice Direction was not necessary and that if further guidance proves to be needed, then it will fall to the Court of Appeal to provide it: *Hansard*, H.L. Vol. 556, col. 1263, July 5, 1994.

It seems to follow that the complicated rules as to what evidence is capable of amounting to corroboration have also ceased to have effect. The Law Commission thought so. They said that with the abolition of the requirement to give a corroboration warning these rules would cease to have any standing or purpose (*op. cit.*, para. 4.12). The Commission drew attention to the South Australian case of *Pahuja* [1987] 30 A.Crim.R. 118 where the Court of Criminal Appeal held that the abolition of the requirement to give the corroboration warning in sexual cases had resulted in the falling of the associated rules.

The effect of subs. (2) is to ensure that the abolition of the corroboration rules (as enacted in this section) should apply to the evidence of children as it does to that of adults.

Abolition of corroboration requirements under Sexual Offences Act 1956

33.—(1) The following provisions of the Sexual Offences Act 1956 (which provide that a person shall not be convicted of the offence concerned on the evidence of one witness only unless the witness is corroborated) are hereby repealed—

    (a) section 2(2) (procurement of woman by threats),
    (b) section 3(2) (procurement of woman by false pretences),
    (c) section 4(2) (administering drugs to obtain or facilitate intercourse),
    (d) section 22(2) (causing prostitution of women), and
    (e) section 23(2) (procuration of girl under twenty-one).
    (2) Nothing in this section applies in relation to—
    (a) any trial, or
    (b) any proceedings before a magistrates' court as examining justices,
which began before the commencement of this section.

GENERAL NOTE

This section abolishes the corroboration requirements in relation to procuration and other offences under the Sexual Offences Act 1956. These repeals follow logically the abolition of the common law rules relating to corroboration in s.32, *ante*. They are based on the recommendation of the Law Commission in its Report: "Corroboration of Evidence in Criminal Trials"

(1991, Cmnd. 1620, para. 4.37). For a general discussion on the abolition of the corroboration rules, see the General Note to s.32, *ante.*

Inferences from accused's silence

Effect of accused's failure to mention facts when questioned or charged

34.—(1) Where, in any proceedings against a person for an offence, evidence is given that the accused—

(a) at any time before he was charged with the offence, on being questioned under caution by a constable trying to discover whether or by whom the offence had been committed, failed to mention any fact relied on in his defence in those proceedings; or

(b) on being charged with the offence or officially informed that he might be prosecuted for it, failed to mention any such fact,

being a fact which in the circumstances existing at the time the accused could reasonably have been expected to mention when so questioned, charged or informed, as the case may be, subsection (2) below applies.

(2) Where this subsection applies—

(a) a magistrates' court, in deciding whether to grant an application for dismissal made by the accused under section 6 of the Magistrates' Courts Act 1980 (application for dismissal of charge in course of proceedings with a view to transfer for trial);

(b) a judge, in deciding whether to grant an application made by the accused under—

(i) section 6 of the Criminal Justice Act 1987 (application for dismissal of charge of serious fraud in respect of which notice of transfer has been given under section 4 of that Act); or

(ii) paragraph 5 of Schedule 6 to the Criminal Justice Act 1991 (application for dismissal of charge of violent or sexual offence involving child in respect of which notice of transfer has been given under section 53 of that Act);

(c) the court, in determining whether there is a case to answer; and

(d) the court or jury, in determining whether the accused is guilty of the offence charged,

may draw such inferences from the failure as appear proper.

(3) Subject to any directions by the court, evidence tending to establish the failure may be given before or after evidence tending to establish the fact which the accused is alleged to have failed to mention.

(4) This section applies in relation to questioning by persons (other than constables) charged with the duty of investigating offences or charging offenders as it applies in relation to questioning by constables; and in subsection (1) above "officially informed" means informed by a constable or any such person.

(5) This section does not—

(a) prejudice the admissibility in evidence of the silence or other reaction of the accused in the face of anything said in his presence relating to the conduct in respect of which he is charged, in so far as evidence thereof would be admissible apart from this section; or

(b) preclude the drawing of any inference from any such silence or other reaction of the accused which could properly be drawn apart from this section.

(6) This section does not apply in relation to a failure to mention a fact if the failure occurred before the commencement of this section.

(7) In relation to any time before the commencement of section 44 of this Act, this section shall have effect as if the reference in subsection (2)(a) to the grant of an application for dismissal was a reference to the committal of the accused for trial.

DEFINITIONS
"officially informed": subs. (4).

GENERAL NOTE
This section provides that the court or jury, in determining whether the defendant is guilty of the offence charged (or a court in determining whether there is a case to answer), may draw such inferences as appear proper from evidence that, on being questioned under caution by the police about the offence before being charged (or on being charged), the defendant failed to mention any fact relied on in his defence which in the circumstances existing at the time he could reasonably have been expected to mention. Subsection (4) applies the section to questioning by others charged with investigating offences or charging offenders: an example might be customs officers. The requirement that the questioning should be under caution was added by amendment in the House of Lords after the original clause ran into opposition because of the lack of safeguards for the suspect.

The Royal Commission on Criminal Justice recommended against any interference with the right to silence on the ground that it would work adversely against the most vulnerable suspects ((1993) HMSO, Cmnd. 2263, paras. 4.20–4.24.). However, it has been pointed that there is now greater protection for suspects than formerly existed: *i.e.* greater access to legal advice and the introduction of tape recording of interviews ((1989) Report of the Working Group on the Right of Silence, Home Office, para. 39). In fact, s.34 is based on the recommendations of the Criminal Law Revision Committee's Eleventh Report of 1972; and the wording of the section is based on that in the Draft Bill attached to the Report (Cmnd. 4991, para. 28). The Committee said that a suspect would not lose the "right of silence" in the sense that it is no offence to refuse to answer questions, but if he chooses to exercise the right he will risk having an adverse inference drawn against him at trial. The Committee thought that to forbid the jury or magistrates from drawing whatever inferences are reasonable from the failure of the accused, when interrogated, to mention a defence put forward at trial was contrary to common sense; and, without helping the innocent, gave an unnecessary advantage to the guilty.

Before an adverse inference can be drawn under the section the jury must be satisfied that: (a) on being questioned the defendant failed to mention the fact; (b) the fact is relied on in his defence; and (c) in the circumstances existing at the time, he could reasonably have been expected to mention the fact. The Criminal Law Revision Committee said that the words "any fact relied on in his defence" are intended to apply to any definite statement made by a witness at the hearing and supporting the case for the defence *e.g.* an alibi, consent in a case of rape, innocent association in an indecency case or, in a handling case, a belief that the goods were not stolen (*op. cit.*, para. 33). It is submitted that the jury must be directed that before drawing any inference they must be satisfied that: (a) at the time the defendant was questioned he knew the fact; (b) there is no innocent explanation for his failure to mention it; and (c) in the circumstances existing at the time (including his knowledge of the case against him) he could reasonably have been expected to mention it (Report of the Home Office Working Group, *ante*, Appendix D).

The effect of the section is to bring to an end the need for the mandatory direction to the jury that no inference is to be drawn against the accused because of his failure to answer questions. Instead, if satisfied on the above matters, the jury must determine what inference it will be proper to draw from the defendant's failure to mention a fact. It is submitted that the inference to be drawn must be limited to a conclusion that the defendant's evidence in relation to the fact is untrue; and the jury must be so directed. Thus, the Home Office Working Group on the Right of Silence considered that the inference to be drawn from a defendant's failure to answer questions should not be one of guilt (for that would be to change the burden of proof) but only an inference that the particular defence is untrue. Magistrates must direct themselves in the same way as a jury is directed. It will be a matter for them in a summary trial to decide what inference may properly be drawn from the defendant's failure to mention a fact.

Section 38 of the present Act provides a measure of protection to the accused. That section provides that an accused may not have a case transferred for trial, have a case to answer or be convicted solely on an inference drawn under s.34 (s.38(3)) and the court must not refuse an application for dismissal of a charge of serious fraud or of a violent or sexual offence involving a child on such a ground (s.38(4)). Similarly, the court's powers to exclude evidence as a matter of law or discretion are not affected by s.34 (s.38(6)). Section 38(5) provides that nothing in s.34 prejudices the operation of any statutory provision which renders any answer or evidence inadmissible.

This section will be brought into effect when a revised Code of Practice (issued by the Home Secretary under s.66 of Police and Criminal Evidence Act 1984) has been laid before Parliament. A revised Code is necessary in order to accommodate a new form of caution, required as a result of the changes made by this section. At the time of writing no new caution has been issued.

According to the Minister of State, Home Office (*Hansard*, H.L. Vol. 556, col. 1393, July 17, 1994) the proposed caution will follow the caution in use in Northern Ireland. First, it will remind the suspect that he is not obliged to answer questions and that any answers may be given in evidence. Secondly, it will warn him of the potential dangers of remaining silent.

This section is modelled on Art. 3 of the Criminal Evidence (Northern Ireland) Order 1988 (S.I. 1987/1988 N.I. 20) which already provides for the circumstances in which inferences may be drawn from the accused's failure to mention particular facts when questioned. Paragraph 61 of Sched. 10, *post*, amends Art. 3 in order to being it into line with the requirement in this section that the questioning must be under caution before any inference may be drawn.

Effect of accused's silence at trial

35.—(1) At the trial of any person who has attained the age of fourteen years for an offence, subsections (2) and (3) below apply unless—

(a) the accused's guilt is not in issue; or

(b) it appears to the court that the physical or mental condition of the accused makes it undesirable for him to give evidence;

but subsection (2) below does not apply if, at the conclusion of the evidence for the prosecution, his legal representative informs the court that the accused will give evidence or, where he is unrepresented, the court ascertains from him that he will give evidence.

(2) Where this subsection applies, the court shall, at the conclusion of the evidence for the prosecution, satisfy itself (in the case of proceedings on indictment, in the presence of the jury) that the accused is aware that the stage has been reached at which evidence can be given for the defence and that he can, if he wishes, give evidence and that, if he chooses not to give evidence, or having been sworn, without good cause refuses to answer any question, it will be permissible for the court or jury to draw such inferences as appear proper from his failure to give evidence or his refusal, without good cause, to answer any question.

(3) Where this subsection applies, the court or jury, in determining whether the accused is guilty of the offence charged, may draw such inferences as appear proper from the failure of the accused to give evidence or his refusal, without good cause, to answer any question.

(4) This section does not render the accused compellable to give evidence on his own behalf, and he shall accordingly not be guilty of contempt of court by reason of a failure to do so.

(5) For the purposes of this section a person who, having been sworn, refuses to answer any question shall be taken to do so without good cause unless—

(a) he is entitled to refuse to answer the question by virtue of any enactment, whenever passed or made, or on the ground of privilege; or

(b) the court in the exercise of its general discretion excuses him from answering it.

(6) Where the age of any person is material for the purposes of subsection (1) above, his age shall for those purposes be taken to be that which appears to the court to be his age.

(7) This section applies—

(a) in relation to proceedings on indictment for an offence, only if the person charged with the offence is arraigned on or after the commencement of this section;

(b) in relation to proceedings in a magistrates' court, only if the time when the court begins to receive evidence in the proceedings falls after the commencement of this section.

DEFINITIONS
"legal representative": s.38(1).

GENERAL NOTE

This section permits the court or jury, in determining whether the accused is guilty of the offence charged, to draw such inferences as appear proper from the failure of the defendant to give evidence at his trial or his refusal (without good cause) to answer questions: subs. (3). However, unless informed that he intends to give evidence, the court must satisfy itself that the accused is aware that he can give evidence and that if he does not do so (or refuses to answer questions) inferences may be drawn: subs. (2). If the accused is unrepresented it will be necessary for the court to bring this provision to his attention. If he is represented and the court is informed that he will not be giving evidence, presumably the court is entitled to infer that he has been informed of the consequences by those representing him. The section applies both to proceedings on indictment and in the magistrates' court. However, the section does not render the accused compellable to give evidence on his own behalf and it provides that the accused shall not be guilty of contempt by reason of his refusal to be sworn: subs. (4). To that extent the rules under s.1 of the Criminal Evidence Act 1898 are preserved.

The section does not apply if the accused is a child, *i.e.* under the age of 14 (subs. (1)) or if it appears to the court that his mental or physical condition makes it undesirable for him to be called (subs. (1)(b)). Presumably, it will be for the court to determine whether this latter consideration applies. However, it is submitted that it will be unusual for it to apply since, if it did, the accused should not normally be on trial at all. On the other hand, the section may apply if an accused, having been sworn, refuses to answer any question without good cause; but the section provides that a person shall not be taken to have refused to answer a question without good cause if he is entitled to refuse to answer on the ground of privilege or the court, in the exercise of its general discretion, excuses him from doing so: subs. (5). Thus, the judge's powers to restrain unfair, oppressive or inadmissible questioning remains intact, but if the accused refuses to answer a question for some other alleged reason (*e.g.* fear of reprisal or unwillingness to incriminate another) it will be open to the jury to draw an inference from the refusal. (See also s.38(5) and (6) for the retention of the judge's powers).

This section closely follows the recommendation of the Criminal Law Revision Committee in its Eleventh Report (1972) Cmnd. 4991, para. 110. (The Bill as originally drafted contained the Committee's recommendation that the court should call on the accused to give evidence. This provision met strong opposition and was abandoned during the passage of the Bill through the House of Commons). The Criminal Law Revision Committee considered that the same kinds of adverse inference, such as common sense dictates, should be drawn from the accused's failure to give evidence as those drawn from his failure to mention a fact on which he intends to rely at trial. (See General Note to s.34, *ante* for a discussion of such inferences). In the same vein, Lord Diplock said in *Haw Tua Tan v. Public Prosecutor; Tan Ah Tee v. Public Prosecutor; Low Hong Eng v. Public Prosecutor* [1981] C.L.Y. 401 (a Privy Council case involving a provision, similar to s.35, under the law of Singapore) that such inferences will depend on the circumstances of the particular case and is a question to be decided by applying ordinary common sense.

The Criminal Law Revision Committee stressed that their proposal depended on there being a prima facie case against the accused: "failure to give evidence may be of little or no significance if there is no case against him, or a weak one. But the stronger the case is, the more significant will be his failure to give evidence" (*op. cit.*, para. 110). It is submitted that normally the proper inference would not be that the defendant is guilty, but to conclude that a line of defence or a suggestion by counsel on his behalf (*e.g.* that he was acting in self-defence) was not true because it was unsupported by evidence from the defendant himself. Indeed, s.36(3) provides that a defendant shall not be convicted solely on an inference drawn under s.30. However, in *Murray v. D.P.P.* [1993] C.L.Y. 3941 the House of Lords held that the inferences which may be drawn under Art. 4 of the Criminal Evidence (Northern Ireland) Order 1988 (S.I. 1987/1988 N.I. 20) (a provision in similar terms to s.35) are not limited to specific inferences from specific facts but include an inference that the accused is guilty of the offence charged. In that case Lord Slynn said that this did not mean that the court can conclude that simply because the accused does not give evidence that he is guilty. "There must be some basis derived from the circumstances which justify the inference ... [If] parts of the prosecution case had so little evidential value that they called for no answer, a failure to deal with specific matters cannot justify an inference of guilt. On the other hand, if aspects of the evidence taken alone or in combination ... clearly call for an explanation which the accused ought to be in a position to give, if an explanation exists, then a failure to give any explanation may as a matter of common sense allow the drawing of an inference that there is no explanation and that the accused is guilty" (pp. 160–161).

The prohibition under s.1 of the Criminal Evidence Act 1898 against comment by the prosecution on the defendant's failure to give evidence has been abolished by s.148 and Sched. 11, post. As a result, comment by the prosecution is now permissible. The common law permitted the judge to comment on the defendant's failure to give evidence. However, that right was latterly much circumscribed and the conventional direction required the judge to stress that the jury must not assume that the jury was guilty because he had not given evidence (*R. v. Bathurst* [1968] C.L.Y. 909; *Martinez-Tobin* [1994] 1 W.L.R. 388). The judge is now free to comment as he thinks fit.

Article 4 of the Criminal Evidence (Northern Ireland) Order 1988 permitted the court to draw inferences if the accused, having been called on to do so, refused to give evidence. Article 4 is amended by Sched. 10, para. 61, *post*. The effect of the amendment is to delete the reference to the court's calling on the accused and to replace it with a procedure which follows the procedure in this section; the amendment also provides that Art. 4 applies to officers of customs and excise as it applies to constables. For a discussion of *Murray v. D.P.P.* [1993] C.L.Y. 3941, criticism of drawing inferences from common sense and argument for statutory guidance, see Jackson J.; *Inferences from Silence—From Common Law to Common Sense* (1993) 44 N.I.L.Q. 103.

Effect of accused's failure or refusal to account for objects, substances or marks

36.—(1) Where—
(a) a person is arrested by a constable, and there is—
    (i) on his person; or
    (ii) in or on his clothing or footwear; or
    (iii) otherwise in his possession; or
    (iv) in any place in which he is at the time of his arrest,
any object, substance or mark, or there is any mark on any such object; and
(b) that or another constable investigating the case reasonably believes that the presence of the object, substance or mark may be attributable to the participation of the person arrested in the commission of an offence specified by the constable; and
(c) the constable informs the person arrested that he so believes, and requests him to account for the presence of the object, substance or mark; and
(d) the person fails or refuses to do so,
then if, in any proceedings against the person for the offence so specified, evidence of those matters is given, subsection (2) below applies.
(2) Where this subsection applies—
(a) a magistrates' court, in deciding whether to grant an application for dismissal made by the accused under section 6 of the Magistrates' Courts Act 1980 (application for dismissal of charge in course of proceedings with a view to transfer for trial);
(b) a judge, in deciding whether to grant an application made by the accused under—
    (i) section 6 of the Criminal Justice Act 1987 (application for dismissal of charge of serious fraud in respect of which notice of transfer has been given under section 4 of that Act); or
    (ii) paragraph 5 of Schedule 6 to the Criminal Justice Act 1991 (application for dismissal of charge of violent or sexual offence involving child in respect of which notice of transfer has been given under section 53 of that Act);
(c) the court, in determining whether there is a case to answer; and
(d) the court or jury, in determining whether the accused is guilty of the offence charged,
may draw such inferences from the failure or refusal as appear proper.
(3) Subsections (1) and (2) above apply to the condition of clothing or footwear as they apply to a substance or mark thereon.
(4) Subsections (1) and (2) above do not apply unless the accused was told in ordinary language by the constable when making the request mentioned in subsection (1)(c) above what the effect of this section would be if he failed or refused to comply with the request.
(5) This section applies in relation to officers of customs and excise as it applies in relation to constables.

(6) This section does not preclude the drawing of any inference from a failure or refusal of the accused to account for the presence of an object, substance or mark or from the condition of clothing or footwear which could properly be drawn apart from this section.

(7) This section does not apply in relation to a failure or refusal which occurred before the commencement of this section.

(8) In relation to any time before the commencement of section 44 of this Act, this section shall have effect as if the reference in subsection (2)(a) to the grant of an application for dismissal was a reference to the committal of the accused for trial.

GENERAL NOTE

Since this section and s.37 are so similar in concept, it will be convenient to discuss them together. Section 36 provides that where the accused fails or refuses to account for objects, substances or marks on him at the time of his arrest, the court or jury may draw such inferences from that failure or refusal as appear proper. Section 37 provides that if the accused fails or refuses to account for his presence at a particular place, at or about the time the offence for which he was arrested was committed, the court or jury may draw such inferences from the failure or refusal as appear proper. The sections apply both to summary trials and trials on indictment. They are aimed at situations such as those where an accused is found at the time of a burglary at a warehouse with an incriminating article (*e.g.* a crowbar) or in incriminating circumstances (*e.g.* on the roof) and fails to offer an explanation, but produces one for the first time at trial. In these circumstances no inference could previously be drawn from the failure of the accused to give an explanation at the time; and juries had to be so directed. A court or jury may now draw an inference in these circumstances.

Before these provisions may be brought into effect it must be shown that: (a) the police reasonably believed that the presence of the object, etc. , or the presence of the accused at the particular place may be attributable to the participation of the accused in an offence; (b) the accused was informed of this belief and requested to account for the object, etc. , or to account for his presence; and (c) the accused was told in ordinary language the effect if he failed or refused to comply with the request. Thus the accused should be left in no doubt as to the consequences of failing to provide an explanation. However, it will be for the court or jury to determine what inference to draw from the failure: no doubt the most obvious being that the explanation advanced at trial is not true. These provisions are modelled on those in the Criminal Evidence (Northern Ireland) Order 1988. They contain (as does the 1988 Order) protection for the suspect in that the accused may not have a case transferred for trial, have a case to answer or be convicted solely on an inference drawn under these sections (s.38(3)) and the rules as to the inadmissibility of evidence (and exclusion under the court's discretion) are not affected by the provisions of these sections: (s.38(5)(6)).

Effect of accused's failure or refusal to account for presence at a particular place

37.—(1) Where—
(a) a person arrested by a constable was found by him at a place at or about the time the offence for which he was arrested is alleged to have been committed; and
(b) that or another constable investigating the offence reasonably believes that the presence of the person at that place and at that time may be attributable to his participation in the commission of the offence; and
(c) the constable informs the person that he so believes, and requests him to account for that presence; and
(d) the person fails or refuses to do so,
then if, in any proceedings against the person for the offence, evidence of those matters is given, subsection (2) below applies.

(2) Where this subsection applies—
(a) a magistrates' court, in deciding whether to grant an application for dismissal made by the accused under section 6 of the Magistrates'

Courts Act 1980 (application for dismissal of charge in course of proceedings with a view to transfer for trial);

(b) a judge, in deciding whether to grant an application made by the accused under—

(i) section 6 of the Criminal Justice Act 1987 (application for dismissal of charge of serious fraud in respect of which notice of transfer has been given under section 4 of that Act); or

(ii) paragraph 5 of Schedule 6 to the Criminal Justice Act 1991 (application for dismissal of charge of violent or sexual offence involving child in respect of which notice of transfer has been given under section 53 of that Act);

(c) the court, in determining whether there is a case to answer; and

(d) the court or jury, in determining whether the accused is guilty of the offence charged,

may draw such inferences from the failure or refusal as appear proper.

(3) Subsections (1) and (2) do not apply unless the accused was told in ordinary language by the constable when making the request mentioned in subsection (1)(c) above what the effect of this section would be if he failed or refused to comply with the request.

(4) This section applies in relation to officers of customs and excise as it applies in relation to constables.

(5) This section does not preclude the drawing of any inference from a failure or refusal of the accused to account for his presence at a place which could properly be drawn apart from this section.

(6) This section does not apply in relation to a failure or refusal which occurred before the commencement of this section.

(7) In relation to any time before the commencement of section 44 of this Act, this section shall have effect as if the reference in subsection (2)(a) to the grant of an application for dismissal was a reference to the committal of the accused for trial.

DEFINITIONS
"place": s.38(1).

GENERAL NOTE
This section provides that where the accused fails or refuses to account for his presence at a particular place at the time of his arrest, the court or jury may draw such inferences from that failure or refusal as appear proper. For discussion, see General Note to s.36, *ante*.

Interpretation and savings for sections 34, 35, 36 and 37

38.—(1) In sections 34, 35, 36 and 37 of this Act—

"legal representative" means an authorised advocate or authorised litigator, as defined by section 119(1) of the Courts and Legal Services Act 1990; and

"place" includes any building or part of a building, any vehicle, vessel, aircraft or hovercraft and any other place whatsoever.

(2) In sections 34(2), 35(3), 36(2) and 37(2), references to an offence charged include references to any other offence of which the accused could lawfully be convicted on that charge.

(3) A person shall not have the proceedings against him transferred to the Crown Court for trial, have a case to answer or be convicted of an offence solely on an inference drawn from such a failure or refusal as is mentioned in section 34(2), 35(3), 36(2) or 37(2).

(4) A judge shall not refuse to grant such an application as is mentioned in section 34(2)(b), 36(2)(b) and 37(2)(b) solely on an inference drawn from such a failure as is mentioned in section 34(2), 36(2) or 37(2).

(5) Nothing in sections 34, 35, 36 or 37 prejudices the operation of a provision of any enactment which provides (in whatever words) that any answer or evidence given by a person in specified circumstances shall not be admissible in evidence against him or some other person in any proceedings or class of proceedings (however described, and whether civil or criminal).

In this subsection, the reference to giving evidence is a reference to giving evidence in any manner, whether by furnishing information, making discovery, producing documents or otherwise.

(6) Nothing in sections 34, 35, 36 or 37 prejudices any power of a court, in any proceedings, to exclude evidence (whether by preventing questions being put or otherwise) at its discretion.

DEFINITIONS
"giving evidence": subs. (5).

GENERAL NOTE
   This section provides for interpretation and savings for ss.34–37. Subsection (3) provides that a person shall not have a case transferred for trial, have a case to answer or be convicted solely on the grounds of refusal or failure to answer questions. Subsections (5) and (6) ensure that the sections do not prejudice the statutory rules relating to the admissibility of evidence or the court's discretion to exclude evidence.

Power to apply sections 34 to 38 to armed forces

39.—(1) The Secretary of State may by order direct that any provision of sections 34 to 38 of this Act shall apply, subject to such modifications as he may specify, to any proceedings to which this section applies.
   (2) This section applies—
   (a) to proceedings whereby a charge is dealt with summarily under Part II of the Army Act 1955;
   (b) to proceedings whereby a charge is dealt with summarily under Part II of the Air Force Act 1955;
   (c) to proceedings whereby a charge is summarily tried under Part II of the Naval Discipline Act 1957;
   (d) to proceedings before a court martial constituted under the Army Act 1955;
   (e) to proceedings before a court martial constituted under the Air Force Act 1955;
   (f) to proceedings before a court martial constituted under the Naval Discipline Act 1957;
   (g) to proceedings before a disciplinary court constituted under section 50 of the Naval Discipline Act 1957;
   (h) to proceedings before the Courts-Martial Appeal Court;
   (i) to proceedings before a Standing Civilian Court; and it applies wherever the proceedings take place.
   (3) An order under this section shall be made by statutory instrument and shall be subject to annulment in pursuance of a resolution of either House of Parliament.

GENERAL NOTE
   This section enables the sections concerning the inferences from silence to be applied to disciplinary proceedings in the armed forces, with any modifications necessary because of the differences between such proceedings and their civilian counterparts.

Juries

Disqualification for jury service of persons on bail in criminal proceedings

40.—(1) A person who is on bail in criminal proceedings shall not be qualified to serve as a juror in the Crown Court.

(2) In this section "bail in criminal proceedings" has the same meaning as in the Bail Act 1976.

DEFINITIONS
"bail in criminal proceedings": s.1(1) of the Bail Act 1976.

GENERAL NOTE
This section provides that a person who is on bail in criminal proceedings shall not be qualified to serve on a jury. The list of persons disqualified from jury service set out in the Juries Act 1974 (c. 23), Sched. 1, Pt. II does not contain people in this category. The Royal Commission on Criminal Justice pointed out that it was thus possible for a person to sit on a jury while on bail for an offence that is similar to the one for which the defendant is to be tried. As a result, the Commission recommended that persons on bail be disqualified (Cmnd. 2263, para. 8.59). This section gives effect to that recommendation.

Subs. (2)
"Bail in criminal proceedings"—see General Note to s.26.

Jury service: disabled persons

41. After section 9A of the Juries Act 1974 there shall be inserted the following section—

> "**Discharge of summonses to disabled persons only if incapable of acting effectively as a juror**
> 9B.—(1) Where it appears to the appropriate officer, in the case of a person attending in pursuance of a summons under this Act, that on account of physical disability there is doubt as to his capacity to act effectively as a juror, the person may be brought before the judge.
> (2) The judge shall determine whether or not the person should act as a juror; but he shall affirm the summons unless he is of the opinion that the person will not, on account of his disability, be capable of acting effectively as a juror, in which case he shall discharge the summons.
> (3) In this section "the judge" means any judge of the High Court or any Circuit judge or Recorder.".

DEFINITIONS
"judge": subs. (3).

GENERAL NOTE
The purpose of this amendment to the Juries Act 1974 is to provide a procedure for discharging from jury service a person with a physical disability. As the section shows, there is a presumption in favour of a such a person serving on a jury. As a result, the judge must affirm the jury summons unless he is of the opinion that the person could not act effectively as a juror on account of his or her disability. This section was added to the Act after an amendment was moved by Lord Ashley of Stoke.

Jury service: excusal on religious grounds

42. In Schedule 1 to the Juries Act 1974, in Part III (Persons excusable as of right), after the entry entitled *Medical and other similar professions*, there shall be inserted the following—

> *"Members of certain religious bodies*
>
> A practising member of a religious society or order the tenets or beliefs of which are incompatible with jury service.".

GENERAL NOTE
This section (resulting from an amendment proposed by Lord Archer of Sandwell) clarifies the reasons for which a person may be excused from jury service on religious grounds.

Separation of jury during consideration of verdict

43.—(1) For section 13 of the Juries Act 1974 (under which a jury may be allowed to separate at any time before they consider their verdict) there shall be substituted—

"Separation

13. If, on the trial of any person for an offence on indictment, the court thinks fit, it may at any time (whether before or after the jury have been directed to consider their verdict) permit the jury to separate.".

(2) The amendment made by subsection (1) above shall not have effect in relation to a trial where a direction to the jury to consider their verdict has been given before the commencement of this section.

GENERAL NOTE

This section (by substituting a new s.13 into the Juries Act 1974) will allow a court to permit a jury to separate at any time, whether before or after it has retired to consider its verdict. Section 13 (as originally drafted) only enabled a court to permit a jury to separate at any time before their retirement. Once the jury had retired to consider their verdict no separation was permissible. The section reflected the practice as it had long been recognised. Any failure to follow this practice was capable of amounting to a material irregularity: *R. v. Goodson* [1975] C.L.Y. 1816. As a result, in longer cases (where a jury has found it impossible to reach verdicts during a day's sitting) the practice has been for arrangements to be made for the jury to spend the night in a hotel. This practice was criticised as too rigid. This new section will give the court a discretion whether to permit a jury to separate after its retirement or whether to go to a hotel. The exercise will no doubt depend on the circumstances of the particular case and any dangers of interference with or influence upon that jury. Whereas it might be permissible for a jury to separate in a fraud trial the same might not be so in a terrorist trial.

Procedure, jurisdiction and powers of magistrates' courts

Transfer for trial instead of committal proceedings

44.—(1) The functions of a magistrates' court as examining justices are hereby abolished.

(2) The provisions set out in Part I of Schedule 4 to this Act as sections 4 to 8C of the Magistrates' Courts Act 1980 shall be substituted for sections 4 to 8 of that Act (which provide for the functions of magistrates' courts as examining justices).

(3) The amendments specified in Part II of that Schedule shall also have effect.

(4) Subsections (1) and (2) above do not apply in relation to proceedings in which a magistrates' court has begun to inquire into a case as examining justices before the commencement of this section.

DEFINITIONS

"co-accused": s.5(6) of the Magistrates' Courts Act 1980 (as amended by Sched. 4, Pt. I to the present Act).

"magistrates' court": s.148(1) of the Magistrates' Courts Act 1980.

"publish": s.8A(13) of the Magistrates' Courts Act 1980 (as enacted by Sched. 4, Pt. I to the present Act).

"relevant programme": s.8A(13) of the Magistrates' Courts Act 1980 (as enacted by Sched. 4, Pt. I to the present Act).

"relevant time": s.8A(13) of the Magistrates' Courts Act 1980 (as enacted by Sched. 4, Pt. I to the present Act).

"transfer for trial": s.4 of the Magistrates' Courts Act 1980 (as substituted by Sched. 4, Pt. I to the present Act).

GENERAL NOTE

This section abolishes committal proceedings, formerly held under s.6 of the Magistrates' Courts Act 1980. These proceedings derived from the ancient function of magistrates as examining justices with a duty to examine witnesses in order to take statements. The function then evolved into an examination of the prosecution case to be held before a person could be put on trial (which function is abolished by sub. (1)). The purpose of this examination was to ensure that there was a case against the accused and to protect him from oppressive or unfounded charges. After such examination the justices could either commit the accused for trial or discharge him. Under s.6 of the Magistrates' Courts Act 1980, committal proceedings could either be by way of a full hearing under s.6(1), known as an "old style" committal, or under s.6(2) of the Act, without consideration of the evidence by the magistrates, a proceeding known as a "paper committal".

Over the years there have been numerous calls for reform of committal proceedings. Thus, in 1981, the Royal Commission on Criminal Procedure recommended that they should be replaced because they were ineffective as a screening procedure (Cmnd. 8092, para. 8.30): the Commission recommended instead a procedure to allow applications for discharge to be made. In 1986 the Fraud Trials Committee described committal proceedings as containing serious deficiencies in allowing abuse by defendants and leading to unnecessary delays and duplication of effort. The Committee recommended that they should be abolished in fraud cases and should be replaced by a procedure for transfer (Report, para. 4.31). This recommendation was brought into effect in cases of serious and complex fraud by the 1987 Act. Finally, in 1993 the Royal Commission on Criminal Justice pointed out that the great majority of committals were a formality and that "old style" committals only represented 7 per cent of all committal proceedings. The Commission thought that there were better ways of enabling magistrates' courts to weed out the weak cases which should not proceed to trial. They recommended that committal proceedings should be abolished and replaced by a procedure to permit submissions of no case to be made on paper before trial (Cmnd. 2263, para. 6.26). As will be seen, this recommendation forms the basis for the procedure set out in Sched. 4. (The Commission also recommended that these applications should only be heard by a legally qualified tribunal *i.e.* by the Crown Court in the case of an indictable only offence and by a stipendiary magistrate in the case of an either way offence. This recommendation was not followed in Sched. 4.)

This section and Sched. 4 substitute new sections, namely, ss.4–8C in the Magistrates' Courts Act 1980. These sections provide for transfer of trial proceedings in the place of committal proceedings. The result is to replace the committal hearing by a procedure which retains the justices' power to dismiss a case, but which provides for automatic transfer to the Crown Court without a hearing in all other cases. The effect of the new provisions may be summarised as follows. In the case of an indictable only offence, or an either way offence which the court decides is more suitable for trial on indictment or if the defendant elects such a trial, the prosecutor must serve on the court and the defendant a notice of the prosecution case, including the evidence. The defendant may then make an application in writing for dismissal of the charge, which the prosecutor will have the opportunity to oppose, also in writing. Oral representations may not be made except, with leave, in cases of complexity or difficulty or if the defendant is unrepresented. The parties are not entitled to be present when the court hears an application for dismissal unless they have been allowed to make oral representations. Reporting restrictions apply to such applications. The court must dismiss a case if there is insufficient evidence against a defendant to put him on trial by jury. On the other hand, if the application is dismissed, or no application for dismissal is made, the court must transfer the case to the Crown Court for trial. On transfer the court may bail the defendant or remand him in custody to appear at the Crown Court.

Subs. (3)

Schedule 4, Pt. II, contains consequential amendments to other legislation resulting from the abolition of committal proceedings.

Extension of procedures enabling magistrates' courts to deal with cases in which accused pleads guilty

45. The amendments to the Magistrates' Courts Act 1980 specified in Schedule 5 (being amendments designed principally to extend the procedures applicable in magistrates' courts when the accused pleads guilty) shall have effect.

DEFINITIONS

"magistrates' court": s.148(1) of the Magistrates' Courts Act 1980.

GENERAL NOTE

This section, together with Sched. 5, extends the procedures enabling magistrates' courts to deal with cases in which the accused pleads guilty and does not wish to appear before the court.

Criminal damage, etc. as summary offence: relevant sum

46.—(1) In subsection (1) of section 22 of the Magistrates' Courts Act 1980 (under which, where an offence of or related to criminal damage or, in certain circumstances, an offence of aggravated vehicle-taking, is charged and it appears clear to the magistrates' court that the value involved does not exceed the relevant sum, the court is to proceed as if the offence were triable only summarily) in the second paragraph (which states the relevant sum), for "£2,000" there shall be substituted "£5,000".

(2) Subsection (1) above does not apply to an offence charged in respect of an act done before this section comes into force.

DEFINITIONS
"aggravated vehicle taking": s.12A of the Theft Act 1968.
"criminal damage": s.1 of the Criminal Damage Act 1971.
"magistrates' court": s.148(1) of the Magistrates' Courts Act 1980.
"value involved": s.22(10) of the Magistrates' Courts Act 1980.

GENERAL NOTE
This section amends Sched. 2 to the Magistrates' Courts Act 1980 so that offences of criminal damage must be tried summarily if the value of the property damaged or destroyed is £5,000 or less. Two reasons were given by the Government for this change. First, the Lord Chief Justice's mode of trial guidelines advise that summary trial is appropriate in cases where the value is less than £10,000 and, secondly, that when thresholds were raised by a factor of two-and-a-half in the 1991 Act criminal damage was inadvertently omitted: Minister of State, Home Office, Parl. Debs, Standing Committee B, cols. 497–498.

Recovery of fines, etc. by deduction from income support

47.—(1) In section 89 of the Magistrates' Courts Act 1980 (which gives a magistrates' court power to make a transfer of fine order), after subsection (2) there shall be inserted the following subsection—

"(2A) The functions of the court to which subsection (2) above relates shall be deemed to include the court's power to apply to the Secretary of State under any regulations made by him under section 24(1)(a) of the Criminal Justice Act 1991 (power to deduct fines etc. from income support).".

(2) In section 90 of the Magistrates' Courts Act 1980 (which gives a magistrates' court power to transfer a fine to Scotland), after subsection (3) there shall be inserted the following subsection—

"(3A) The functions of the court which shall cease to be exercisable by virtue of subsection (3) above shall be deemed to include the court's power to apply to the Secretary of State under regulations made by him under section 24(1)(a) of the Criminal Justice Act 1991 (power to deduct fines from income support).".

(3) In section 24(3) of the Criminal Justice Act 1991 (which relates to the Secretary of State's power to authorise deduction of fines etc. from income support), after paragraph (b) there shall be inserted the following paragraph—

"(c) the reference in paragraph (a) to "the court" includes a reference to a court to which the function in that paragraph has been transferred by virtue of a transfer of fine order under section 89(1) or (3) or 90(1)(a) of the 1980 Act (power of magistrates' court to make transfer of fine order) or under section 403(1)(a) or (b) of the Criminal Procedure (Scotland) Act 1975 (analogous provision as respects Scotland) and a reference to a court to which that function has been remitted by virtue of section 196(2) of the said Act of 1975 (enforcement of fine imposed by High Court of Justiciary).".

(4) In section 403 of the Criminal Procedure (Scotland) Act 1975 (which gives a court of summary jurisdiction in Scotland power to make a transfer of fine order), after subsection (4) there shall be inserted the following subsection—

"(4A) The functions of the court to which subsection (4) above relates shall be deemed to include the court's power to apply to the Secretary of

State under any regulations made by him under section 24(1)(a) of the Criminal Justice Act 1991 (power to deduct fines etc. from income support).".

DEFINITIONS
"fine": s.24(4) of the 1991 Act.
"income support": s.24(4).

GENERAL NOTE
This section provides for a court to apply to deduct fines, etc., from income support in respect of fines transferred from another court.

Sentencing: guilty pleas

Reduction in sentences for guilty pleas

48.—(1) In determining what sentence to pass on an offender who has pleaded guilty to an offence in proceedings before that or another court a court shall take into account—
   (a) the stage in the proceedings for the offence at which the offender indicated his intention to plead guilty, and
   (b) the circumstances in which this indication was given.
   (2) If, as a result of taking into account any matter referred to in subsection (1) above, the court imposes a punishment on the offender which is less severe than the punishment it would otherwise have imposed, it shall state in open court that it has done so.

GENERAL NOTE
It has long been a cardinal principle of sentencing practice that a plea of guilty is a mitigating factor which entitles the defendant to a discount in sentence (varying according to the circumstances of the case, but usually of between one quarter and one third). This is because a plea of guilty amounts to an indication of remorse on the part of the defendant and also because such a plea leads to a saving of public time and money. The earlier in the proceedings that the plea is entered, the greater the discount: a very late plea may involve a minimal discount. "It should be appreciated by those advising defendants in criminal cases that if their clients put up tactical pleas and then change them to pleas of guilty when they are finally arraigned, they cannot expect to get the same discount for a plea of guilty as they would have done if they had pleaded guilty from the beginning": *R. v. Hollington and Emmens* [1986] C.L.Y. 815 *per* Lawton L.J. It is usual for the sentencer in any sentencing remarks to mention a plea of guilty as a factor in mitigation (although not the extent of the discount).
   This section requires the court, when passing sentence, to take account of the timing and other circumstances of a plea of guilty and, where a discount is given, to indicate the fact. These requirements reflect the present practice (as outlined above) and put it into statutory form. The Royal Commission on Criminal Justice called for "greater articulation" of these principles (Cmnd. 2263, para. 7.46); and this section represents Parliament's response. The purpose must be to put the practice on a mandatory, as opposed to a discretionary, footing. The effect of the section will be to oblige the court to take into account the "stage in the proceedings" at which the defendant "indicated his intention" to plead guilty. It is to be noted that the section does not say "entered" his plea. Presumably, an indication by his legal representative would be sufficient. However experience shows that such an indication is not the same as the plea in fact being entered. An indication may be reversed and there cannot be certainty about it. On the other hand, the court will be able to take these matters into account when considering all the "circumstances". The obligation placed on the court in subs. (2) to state the fact that the sentence has been discounted adds another item to the lengthening list of matters which now have to be mentioned.

Publication of reports in young offender cases

Restrictions on reports of proceedings in which children or young persons are concerned

49. For section 49 of the Children and Young Persons Act 1933 (restrictions on reports of proceedings in which children or young persons are concerned) there shall be substituted—

"Restrictions on reports of proceedings in which children or young persons are concerned

49.—(1) The following prohibitions apply (subject to subsection (5) below) in relation to any proceedings to which this section applies, that is to say—

(a) no report shall be published which reveals the name, address or school of any child or young person concerned in the proceedings or includes any particulars likely to lead to the identification of any child or young person concerned in the proceedings; and

(b) no picture shall be published or included in a programme service as being or including a picture of any child or young person concerned in the proceedings.

(2) The proceedings to which this section applies are—

(a) proceedings in a youth court;

(b) proceedings on appeal from a youth court (including proceedings by way of case stated);

(c) proceedings under section 15 or 16 of the Children and Young Persons Act 1969 (proceedings for varying or revoking supervision orders); and

(d) proceedings on appeal from a magistrates' court arising out of proceedings under section 15 or 16 of that Act (including proceedings by way of case stated).

(3) The reports to which this section applies are reports in a newspaper and reports included in a programme service; and similarly as respects pictures.

(4) For the purposes of this section a child or young person is "concerned" in any proceedings whether as being the person against or in respect of whom the proceedings are taken or as being a witness in the proceedings.

(5) Subject to subsection (7) below, a court may, in relation to proceedings before it to which this section applies, by order dispense to any specified extent with the requirements of this section in relation to a child or young person who is concerned in the proceedings if it is satisfied—

(a) that it is appropriate to do so for the purpose of avoiding injustice to the child or young person; or

(b) that, as respects a child or young person to whom this paragraph applies who is unlawfully at large, it is necessary to dispense with those requirements for the purpose of apprehending him and bringing him before a court or returning him to the place in which he was in custody.

(6) Paragraph (b) of subsection (5) above applies to any child or young person who is charged with or has been convicted of—

(a) a violent offence,

(b) a sexual offence, or

(c) an offence punishable in the case of a person aged 21 or over with imprisonment for fourteen years or more.

(7) The court shall not exercise its power under subsection (5)(b) above—

(a) except in pursuance of an application by or on behalf of the Director of Public Prosecutions; and

(b) unless notice of the application has been given by the Director of Public Prosecutions to any legal representative of the child or young person.

(8) The court's power under subsection (5) above may be exercised by a single justice.

(9) If a report or picture is published or included in a programme service in contravention of subsection (1) above, the following persons, that is to say—

   (a) in the case of publication of a written report or a picture as part of a newspaper, any proprietor, editor or publisher of the newspaper;
   (b) in the case of the inclusion of a report or picture in a programme service, any body corporate which provides the service and any person having functions in relation to the programme corresponding to those of an editor of a newspaper,

shall be liable on summary conviction to a fine not exceeding level 5 on the standard scale.

(10) In any proceedings under section 15 or 16 of the Children and Young Persons Act 1969 (proceedings for varying or revoking supervision orders) before a magistrates' court other than a youth court or on appeal from such a court it shall be the duty of the magistrates' court or the appellate court to announce in the course of the proceedings that this section applies to the proceedings; and if the court fails to do so this section shall not apply to the proceedings.

(11) In this section—

"legal representative" means an authorised advocate or authorised litigator, as defined by section 119(1) of the Courts and Legal Services Act 1990;

"programme" and "programme service" have the same meaning as in the Broadcasting Act 1990;

"sexual offence" has the same meaning as in section 31(1) of the Criminal Justice Act 1991;

"specified" means specified in an order under this section;

"violent offence" has the same meaning as in section 31(1) of the Criminal Justice Act 1991;

and a person who, having been granted bail, is liable to arrest (whether with or without a warrant) shall be treated as unlawfully at large.".

DEFINITIONS

"child": s.107(1) of the Children and Young Persons Act 1933.

"concerned": s.49(4) of the Children and Young Persons Act 1933 as substituted by this section.

"legal representative": s.49(11) of the Children and Young Persons Act 1933 as substituted by this section.

"proceedings": s.49(2) of the Children and Young Persons Act 1933 as substituted by this section.

"programme/programme service": s.49(11) of the Children and Young Persons Act 1933 as substituted by this section.

"sexual offence": s.49(11) of the Children and Young Persons Act 1933 as substituted by this section.

"specified": s.49(11) of the Children and Young Persons Act 1933 as substituted by this section.

"violent offence": s.49(11) of the Children and Young Persons Act 1933 as substituted by this section.

GENERAL NOTE

This section re-states the existing prohibition in s.49 of the Children and Young Persons Act 1933 (as amended) on identifying juveniles who are concerned in proceedings in youth courts and appeals from those courts. The section previously permitted the court (and the Secretary of State) to dispense with the prohibition where to do so is necessary to avoid injustice to a child. This power is retained for the court and a new power is added. This power enables the court to dispense with the prohibition in circumstances where a child or young person has been charged with or convicted of a violent, sexual or serious offence and is unlawfully at large. This provision is aimed at juveniles who may represent a danger to the public and where, for instance, the publication of a photograph may assist the police in identifying and catching them. The section removes the power of the Secretary of State to dispense with the prohibition. However, since the Secretary of State never used the power, its loss will make little difference.

Subs. (11)
    Authorised advocate: "means any person (including a barrister or solicitor) who has a right of audience granted by an authorised body in accordance with the provisions of this Act": Courts and Legal Services Act 1990 (c. 41), s.119(1).
    Authorised litigator: "means any person (including a solicitor) who has a right to conduct litigation granted by an authorised body in accordance with the provisions of this Act": *ibid.*

Scottish perspective
    The restrictions imposed by this section are also to apply to publication in Scotland of the specified proceedings in England and Wales. Difficulties have arisen previously when publication has been prohibited by legislation or by court order in only one of the jurisdictions and the media in the other jurisdiction has exercised its freedom effectively to undermine the restrictions. Given the seemingly insatiable appetite of sections of the media for any salacious news, and the inability of geographical boundaries to restrict cross border publication, this provision is very necessary. Scottish editors will, however, need to acquaint themselves with the foreign concepts contained in this section.

Child testimony

Video recordings of testimony from child witnesses

50. In section 32A of the Criminal Justice Act 1988, in subsection (5)(b), the word "adequately" shall be inserted after the words "dealt with".

GENERAL NOTE
    Section 32A of the 1988 Act, which was added by s.54 of the 1991 Act, deals with video recordings of testimony of child witnesses. This section amends subs. (5) of that section so that the subsection now reads: "Where a video recording is admitted under this section (a) the child witness shall be called by the party who tendered it in evidence; (b) that witness shall not be examined in chief on any matter which, in the opinion of the court, has been dealt with *adequately* in his recorded testimony." The purpose of the amendment (printed in italics) is presumably to clarify the circumstances in which any form of examination in chief is permissible. The policy of the Act is that the recording should stand in the place of examination in chief. Accordingly, any further examination of the child by the party calling him or her is not to be encouraged.

Intimidation, etc., of witnesses, jurors and others

Intimidation, etc., of witnesses, jurors and others

51.—(1) A person who does to another person—
  (a) an act which intimidates, and is intended to intimidate, that other person;
  (b) knowing or believing that the other person is assisting in the investigation of an offence or is a witness or potential witness or a juror or potential juror in proceedings for an offence; and
  (c) intending thereby to cause the investigation or the course of justice to be obstructed, perverted or interfered with,
commits an offence.
  (2) A person who does or threatens to do to another person—
  (a) an act which harms or would harm, and is intended to harm, that other person;
  (b) knowing or believing that the other person, or some other person, has assisted in an investigation into an offence or has given evidence or particular evidence in proceedings for an offence, or has acted as a juror or concurred in a particular verdict in proceedings for an offence; and
  (c) does or threatens to do the act because of what (within paragraph (b)) he knows or believes,

commits an offence.

(3) A person does an act "to" another person with the intention of intimi-dating, or (as the case may be) harming, that other person not only where the act is done in the presence of that other and directed at him directly but also where the act is done to a third person and is intended, in the circumstances, to intimidate or (as the case may be) harm the person at whom the act is directed.

(4) The harm that may be done or threatened may be financial as well as physical (whether to the person or a person's property) and similarly as respects an intimidatory act which consists of threats.

(5) The intention required by subsection (1)(c) and the motive required by subsection (2)(c) above need not be the only or the predominating intention or motive with which the act is done or, in the case of subsection (2), threatened.

(6) A person guilty of an offence under this section shall be liable—

  (a) on conviction on indictment, to imprisonment for a term not exceed-ing five years or a fine or both;

  (b) on summary conviction, to imprisonment for a term not exceeding six months or a fine not exceeding the statutory maximum or both.

(7) If, in proceedings against a person for an offence under subsection (1) above, it is proved that he did an act falling within paragraph (a) with the knowledge or belief required by paragraph (b), he shall be presumed, unless the contrary is proved, to have done the act with the intention required by paragraph (c) of that subsection.

(8) If, in proceedings against a person for an offence under subsection (2) above, it is proved that he did or threatened to do an act falling within para-graph (a) within the relevant period with the knowledge or belief required by paragraph (b), he shall be presumed, unless the contrary is proved, to have done the act with the motive required by paragraph (c) of that subsection.

(9) In this section—

    "investigation into an offence" means such an investigation by the po-lice or other person charged with the duty of investigating offences or charging offenders;

    "offence" includes an alleged or suspected offence;

    "potential", in relation to a juror, means a person who has been sum-moned for jury service at the court at which proceedings for the offence are pending; and

    "the relevant period"—

        (a) in relation to a witness or juror in any proceedings for an offence, means the period beginning with the institution of the proceedings and ending with the first anniversary of the con-clusion of the trial or, if there is an appeal or reference under section 17 of the Criminal Appeal Act 1968, of the conclusion of the appeal;

        (b) in relation to a person who has, or is believed by the accused to have, assisted in an investigation into an offence, but was not also a witness in proceedings for an offence, means the period of one year beginning with any act of his, or any act believed by the accused to be an act of his, assisting in the investi-gation; and

        (c) in relation to a person who both has, or is believed by the accused to have, assisted in the investigation into an offence and was a witness in proceedings for the offence, means the period beginning with any act of his, or any act believed by the accused to be an act of his, assisting in the investigation and ending with the anniversary mentioned in paragraph (a) above.

(10) For the purposes of the definition of the relevant period in subsection (9) above

(a) proceedings for an offence are instituted at the earliest of the following times—

    (i) when a justice of the peace issues a summons or warrant under section 1 of the Magistrates' Courts Act 1980 in respect of the offence;

    (ii) when a person is charged with the offence after being taken into custody without a warrant;

    (iii) when a bill of indictment is preferred by virtue of section 2(2)(b) of the Administration of Justice (Miscellaneous Provisions) Act 1933;

(b) proceedings at a trial of an offence are concluded with the occurrence of any of the following, the discontinuance of the prosecution, the discharge of the jury without a finding, the acquittal of the accused or the sentencing of or other dealing with the accused for the offence of which he was convicted; and

(c) proceedings on an appeal are concluded on the determination of the appeal or the abandonment of the appeal.

(11) This section is in addition to, and not in derogation of, any offence subsisting at common law.

DEFINITIONS

"does an act 'to' ": subs. (3).
"harm": subs. (4).
"intending/intention": subs. (5)
"investigation into an offence": subs. (9)
"motive": subs. (5).
"offence": subs. (9).
"potential": subs. (9).
"relevant period": subss. (9) and (10).

GENERAL NOTE

This section provides for a new offence of intimidating or harming a juror or witness (or a person assisting in the investigation of an offence). The purpose is to provide greater protection than the common law can give to witnesses and jurors. It is aimed at protecting them before, during and after a trial or investigation. Thus, the offence may be committed in one of two ways, set out in subss. (1) and (2). Under subs. (1) it must be proved that the defendant, knowing or believing that the victim was a juror or witness (or was assisting in the investigation of an offence) did an act which intimidated (and was intended to intimidate) the alleged victim. Under subs. (2) it must be proved that the defendant, knowing or believing that the victim (or some other person) had assisted in an investigation or had been a witness or juror, did or threatened to do an act which harmed or would have harmed the victim (and was intended to do so). When these matters have been proved the section provides that a statutory presumption should apply. Thus, once it is proved under subs. (1) that the defendant did the intimidatory act with the necessary intent, knowledge or belief, subs. (7) provides that (unless the contrary is proved) he shall be presumed to have intended to obstruct, pervert or interfere with the investigation or the course of justice. The effect is that once the intention to intimidate is proved the burden of proving the defendant's intention to obstruct or interfere is removed from the prosecution. The burden shifts to the defence to prove that the defendant did not have the intent. The standard of proof when the burden is on the defence in circumstances such as these is not as high as that on the prosecution. The standard is the civil standard *i.e.* on the balance of probability. Subsection (8) makes similar provision in relation to the offence under subs. (2). Provided that the prosecution prove that the defendant harmed or threatened to harm the victim, knowing or believing that the victim had assisted the investigation or had been a witness or juror, the burden of proving that he did not do so because of that knowledge or belief shifts to the defence. However, in this case, the presumption against the defendant only comes into play provided that he did the act complained of within a period of a year of the end of the trial (or appeal) or the victim's beginning to assist in the investigation: subs. (2), as defined in subs. (9). The reason for this restriction is that it was felt that the presumption that the defendant was acting from motives of revenge should not operate after one year. After this period has elapsed the prosecution may still bring a charge under subs. (2), but the presumption will not operate and all the elements of the offence must be proved. From an abundance of caution it is provided that the intention or

33–59

motive in the respective sections need not be the only or predominating intention or motive: subs. (5). As a result of subs. (11) the common law offence of perverting the course of justice is not affected by this section. However, that offence may only be committed before or during the subsistence of the proceedings: it cannot apply after the proceedings are over; and the statutory presumptions will not apply.

Criminal appeals

Circuit judges to act as judges of criminal division of Court of Appeal

52.—(1) Section 9 of the Supreme Court Act 1981 (which provides for certain judges to act on request in courts rather than that to which they were appointed) shall have effect with the amendments specified in subsections (2) to (5) below.

(2) In subsection (1)—

(a) after the words "Table may", there shall be inserted the words ", subject to the proviso at the end of that Table,";

(b) in the Table, in column 2, in the entry specifying the court relating to entry 5 in column 1 (Circuit judges), after the words "High Court" there shall be inserted the words "and the Court of Appeal"; and

(c) at the end of the Table there shall be inserted the following—
"The entry in column 2 specifying the Court of Appeal in relation to a Circuit judge only authorises such a judge to act as a judge of a court in the criminal division of the Court of Appeal.".

(3) In subsection (2)—

(a) in the definition of "the appropriate authority" after the words "High Court" there shall be inserted the words "or a Circuit judge"; and

(b) at the end, there shall be inserted the following—
"but no request shall be made to a Circuit judge to act as a judge of a court in the criminal division of the Court of Appeal unless he is approved for the time being by the Lord Chancellor for the purpose of acting as a judge of that division.".

(4) In subsection (5), for the words "subsection (6)" there shall be substituted the words "subsections (6) and (6A)".

(5) After subsection (6) there shall be inserted the following subsection—
"(6A) A Circuit judge or Recorder shall not by virtue of subsection (5) exercise any of the powers conferred on a single judge by sections 31 and 44 of the Criminal Appeal Act 1968 (powers of single judge in connection with appeals to the Court of Appeal and appeals from the Court of Appeal to the House of Lords).".

(6) The further amendments specified in subsections (7) to (9) below (which supplement the foregoing amendments) shall have effect.

(7) In section 55 of the Supreme Court Act 1981 (composition of criminal division of Court of Appeal)—

(a) in subsections (2) and (4), at the beginning, there shall be inserted the words "Subject to subsection (6),"; and

(b) after subsection (5), there shall be inserted the following subsection—
"(6) A court shall not be duly constituted if it includes more than one Circuit judge acting as a judge of the court under section 9.".

(8) After section 56 of the Supreme Court Act 1981 there shall be inserted the following section—

"Circuit judges not to sit on certain appeals

56A. No Circuit judge shall act in the criminal division of the Court of Appeal as a judge of that court under section 9 on the hearing of, or shall determine any application in proceedings incidental or preliminary to, an appeal against—

(a) a conviction before a judge of the High Court; or

(b) a sentence passed by a judge of the High Court.".

(9) After the section 56A of the Supreme Court Act 1981 inserted by subsection (8) above there shall be inserted the following section—

"Allocation of cases in criminal division

56B.—(1) The appeals or classes of appeals suitable for allocation to a court of the criminal division of the Court of Appeal in which a Circuit judge is acting under section 9 shall be determined in accordance with directions given by or on behalf of the Lord Chief Justice with the concurrence of the Lord Chancellor.

(2) In subsection (1) "appeal" includes the hearing of, or any application in proceedings incidental or preliminary to, an appeal.".

DEFINITIONS

"appeal": s.56B of the Supreme Court Act 1981 as inserted by subs. (9).
"appropriate authority": s.9(2) of the Supreme Court Act 1981 as amended by subs. (3).

GENERAL NOTE

This section, by amending s.9 of the Supreme Court Act 1981, enables circuit judges (approved by the Lord Chancellor) to sit in the Court of Appeal (Criminal Division) at the request of the Lord Chief Justice. The section implements a recommendation of the Royal Commission on Criminal Justice (1993) H.M.S.O., Cmnd. 2263, para. 10.82. The Commission, observing that the Court of Appeal should include more judges with current experience of trying criminal cases, said that this need would be best met by appointing suitably qualified circuit judges to sit as members of the Court. Judicial statistics show that in 1991 five per cent of the work of the Crown Court was done by High Court judges while 67 per cent was done by circuit judges. The Commission recommended that senior circuit judges nominated by the Lord Chief Justice should be able to sit as members of the full court. However the Commission said that they should not be members in the full sense. To that end the Commission recommended that no more than one circuit judge should sit as part of any full court; that circuit judges should not act as single judges and should not sit on a court reviewing a case tried by a High Court judge. These recommendations have been followed in the section.

Expenses in criminal appeals in Northern Ireland Court of Appeal

53.—(1) After section 28(2) of the Criminal Appeal (Northern Ireland) Act 1980 (certain expenses to be defrayed up to amount allowed by the Master (Taxing Office)) there shall be inserted the following subsections—

"(2A) Where a solicitor or counsel is dissatisfied with the amount of any expenses allowed by the Master (Taxing Office) under subsection (2)(a) above, he may apply to that Master to review his decision.

(2B) On a review under subsection (2A) the Master (Taxing Office) may confirm or vary the amount of expenses allowed by him.

(2C) An application under subsection (2A) shall be made, and a review under that subsection shall be conducted, in accordance with rules of court.

(2D) Where a solicitor or counsel is dissatisfied with the decision of the Master (Taxing Office) on a review under subsection (2A) above, he may appeal against that decision to the High Court and the Lord Chancellor may appear and be represented on any such appeal.

(2E) Where the Lord Chancellor is dissatisfied with the decision of the Master (Taxing Office) on a review under subsection (2A) above in relation to the expenses of a solicitor or counsel, he may appeal against that decision to the High Court and the solicitor or barrister may appear or be represented on any such appeal.

(2F) On any appeal under subsection (2D) or (2E) above the High Court may confirm or vary the amount of expenses allowed by the Master (Taxing Office) and the decision of the High Court shall be final.

(2G) The power of the Master (Taxing Office) or the High Court to vary the amount of expenses allowed under subsection (2)(a) above includes power to increase or reduce that amount to such extent as the

Master or (as the case may be) the High Court thinks fit; and the reference in subsection (2) above to the amount allowed by the Master (Taxing Office) shall, in a case where that amount has been so varied, be construed as a reference to that amount as so varied.".

(2) Subsection (1) above does not have effect in relation to expenses allowed by the Master (Taxing Office) under section 28(2)(a) of the Criminal Appeal (Northern Ireland) Act 1980 before the date on which that subsection comes into force.

GENERAL NOTE
This section, by amending s.28 of the Criminal Appeal (Northern Ireland Act) 1980, provides new rights of appeal against determinations of criminal legal aid expenses incurred in connection with proceedings in the Northern Ireland Court of Appeal. Until now there has been no appeal from the decision of the Master. Under this section there will first be a right to apply to the Master for a review of his decision; and then a right of appeal to the High Court against the decision. The Lord Chancellor will also have a right of appeal to the High Court.

PART IV

POLICE POWERS

Powers of police to take body samples

Powers of police to take intimate body samples

54.—(1) Section 62 of the Police and Criminal Evidence Act 1984 (regulation of taking of intimate samples) shall be amended as follows.

(2) After subsection (1) there shall be inserted the following subsection—
"(1A) An intimate sample may be taken from a person who is not in police detention but from whom, in the course of the investigation of an offence, two or more non-intimate samples suitable for the same means of analysis have been taken which have proved insufficient—
  (a) if a police officer of at least the rank of superintendent authorises it to be taken; and
  (b) if the appropriate consent is given.".

(3) In subsection (2)—
(a) after the word "authorisation" there shall be inserted the words "under subsection (1) or (1A) above"; and
(b) in paragraph (a), for the words "serious arrestable offence" there shall be substituted the words "recordable offence".

(4) In subsection (3), after the words "subsection (1)" there shall be inserted the words "or (1A)".

(5) In subsection (9)—
(a) for the words "or saliva" there shall be substituted the words "or a dental impression"; and
(b) at the end there shall be inserted the words "and a dental impression may only be taken by a registered dentist".

DEFINITIONS
"appropriate consent": s.65 of the Police and Criminal Evidence Act 1984.
"intimate sample": s.65 of the Police and Criminal Evidence Act 1984 as substituted by s.58(2) of the present Act.
"non-intimate sample": s.65 of the Police and Criminal Evidence Act 1984 as substituted by s.58(3) of this Act.
"recordable offence": s.118 of the Police and Criminal Evidence Act 1984.
"registered dentist": s.58(4).
"serious arrestable offence": s.116 of the Police and Criminal Evidence Act 1984.
"sufficient/insufficient": s.58(4).

GENERAL NOTE
This section (by amending s.62 of the Police and Criminal Evidence Act 1984) provides the police with a power to take intimate samples from persons not in police detention. The power

may be exercised in circumstances where two earlier non-intimate samples have proved insufficient. It only applies in relation to an investigation of a "recordable" offence. Recordable offences are listed in The National Police Records (Recordable Offences) Regulations 1985 and are generally those punishable by imprisonment. By amending s.62 to provide that an intimate sample may now be taken in connection with the investigation of "recordable" offences (and not, as previously, only in connection with "serious arrestable" offences) Parliament in subs. (3) has enlarged police powers, but has brought the power to take samples into line with that to take fingerprints. (The Royal Commission on Criminal Justice had merely recommended that the power to take non-intimate samples without consent should be extended by a re-classification of serious arrestable offences to include assault and burglary). Section 58, *post*, now classifies a dental impression as an intimate sample. Subsection (5) provides that a dental impression may only be taken by a registered dentist. As a result, a court or jury may draw an adverse inference under s.62(10) from a defendant's failure to provide a dental impression. (This follows a recommendation of the Royal Commission at para. 2.31 of its Report, Cmnd. 2263).

Powers of police to take non-intimate body samples

55.—(1) Section 63 of the Police and Criminal Evidence Act 1984 (regulation of taking of non-intimate samples) shall be amended as follows.

(2) After subsection (3), there shall be inserted the following subsections—

"(3A) A non-intimate sample may be taken from a person (whether or not he falls within subsection (3)(a) above) without the appropriate consent if—

    (a) he has been charged with a recordable offence or informed that he will be reported for such an offence; and

    (b) either he has not had a non-intimate sample taken from him in the course of the investigation of the offence by the police or he has had a non-intimate sample taken from him but either it was not suitable for the same means of analysis or, though so suitable, the sample proved insufficient.

(3B) A non-intimate sample may be taken from a person without the appropriate consent if he has been convicted of a recordable offence.".

(3) In subsection (4), in paragraph (a), for the words "serious arrestable offence" there shall be substituted the words "recordable offence".

(4) After subsection (8), there shall be inserted the following subsection—

"(8A) In a case where by virtue of subsection (3A) or (3B) a sample is taken from a person without the appropriate consent—

    (a) he shall be told the reason before the sample is taken; and

    (b) the reason shall be recorded as soon as practicable after the sample is taken.".

(5) In subsection (9), after the words "subsection (8)" there shall be inserted the words "or (8A)".

(6) After subsection (9) there shall be inserted the following subsection—

"(10) Subsection (3B) above shall not apply to persons convicted before the date on which that subsection comes into force.".

DEFINITIONS

"appropriate consent": s.65 of the Police and Criminal Evidence Act 1984.

"non-intimate sample": s.65 of the Police and Criminal Evidence Act 1984 as amended by s.58(3) of this Act.

"recordable offence": s.118 of the Police and Criminal Evidence Act 1984.

"serious arrestable offence": s.116 of the Police and Criminal Evidence Act 1984.

"sufficient/insufficient": s.58(4).

GENERAL NOTE

This section (by amending s.63 of the Police and Criminal Evidence Act 1984) provides the police with a power to take non-intimate samples without consent from persons whether in detention or not. This power may only be exercised in connection with the investigation of recordable offences (from persons charged with or convicted of a recordable offence) and in circumstances where a previous sample has proved insufficient or no sample has been taken. Subsection (4) requires that reasons must be given to a suspect before samples are taken. The section in this and other respects is similar in its terms to s.61 of the Police and Criminal Evidence Act 1984. The amendment in subs. (3) substituting "recordable" for "serious arrestable" offences should be noted: for comment, see General Note to s.54, *ante*. Following a recommendation of the Royal Commission on Criminal Justice (Report, Cmnd. 2263, para. 2.29), s.58 *post* re-classifies saliva as a non-intimate sample. As a result, mouth swabs may now be taken under this section without consent. Experience in Northern Ireland (where the police already have power to take mouth swabs without consent) has given impetus to the introduction of this section. It has been pointed out that the taking of non-intimate samples does not require specialist or invasive procedures and can be carried out by trained police officers: Minister of State, Home Office (*Hansard*, H.L. Vol. 555, col. 599). However, the legislation does not go as far as the Royal Commission on Criminal Justice recommended. The Commission said that because DNA profiling is now so powerful a diagnostic technique and so helpful in establishing guilt or innocence, the police should have powers to take non-intimate samples without consent whether or not DNA profiling is relevant to the particular offence: Report, Cmnd. 2263, para. 2.35).

Appropriate consent, recordable offence, serious arrestable offence, see General Note to s.54, *ante*.

Fingerprints and samples: supplementary provisions

56. The following section shall be inserted after section 63 of the Police and Criminal Evidence Act 1984—

"Fingerprints and samples: supplementary provisions

63A.—(1) Fingerprints or samples or the information derived from samples taken under any power conferred by this Part of this Act from a person who has been arrested on suspicion of being involved in a recordable offence may be checked against other fingerprints or samples or the information derived from other samples contained in records held by or on behalf of the police or held in connection with or as a result of an investigation of an offence.

(2) Where a sample of hair other than pubic hair is to be taken the sample may be taken either by cutting hairs or by plucking hairs with their roots so long as no more are plucked than the person taking the sample reasonably considers to be necessary for a sufficient sample.

(3) Where any power to take a sample is exercisable in relation to a person the sample may be taken in a prison or other institution to which the Prison Act 1952 applies.

(4) Any constable may, within the allowed period, require a person who is neither in police detention nor held in custody by the police on the authority of a court to attend a police station in order to have a sample taken where—

(a) the person has been charged with a recordable offence or informed that he will be reported for such an offence and either he has not had a sample taken from him in the course of the investigation of the offence by the police or he has had a sample so taken from him but either it was not suitable for the same means of analysis or, though so suitable, the sample proved insufficient; or

(b) the person has been convicted of a recordable offence and either he has not had a sample taken from him since the conviction or he has had a sample taken from him (before or after his conviction) but either it was not suitable for the same means of analysis or, though so suitable, the sample proved insufficient.

(5) The period allowed for requiring a person to attend a police station for the purpose specified in subsection (4) above is—

(a) in the case of a person falling within paragraph (a), one month beginning with the date of the charge or one month beginning with the date on which the appropriate officer is informed of the fact that the sample is not suitable for the same means of analysis or has proved insufficient, as the case may be;

(b) in the case of a person falling within paragraph (b), one month beginning with the date of the conviction or one month beginning with the date on which the appropriate officer is informed of the fact that the sample is not suitable for the same means of analysis or has proved insufficient, as the case may be.

(6) A requirement under subsection (4) above—

(a) shall give the person at least 7 days within which he must so attend; and

(b) may direct him to attend at a specified time of day or between specified times of day.

(7) Any constable may arrest without a warrant a person who has failed to comply with a requirement under subsection (4) above.

(8) In this section "the appropriate officer" is—

(a) in the case of a person falling within subsection (4)(a), the officer investigating the offence with which that person has been charged or as to which he was informed that he would be reported;

(b) in the case of a person falling within subsection (4)(b), the officer in charge of the police station from which the investigation of the offence of which he was convicted was conducted.".

DEFINITIONS

"appropriate officer": subs. (8).

"fingerprint": s.65 of the Police and Criminal Evidence Act 1984.

"samples [intimate/non-intimate]": s.65 of the Police and Criminal Evidence Act 1984 as amended by s.58(2)(3) of the present Act.

"recordable offence": s.118(1) of the Police and Criminal Evidence Act 1984.

"sufficient, insufficient": s.58(4).

GENERAL NOTE

This section inserts a new s.63A into the Police and Criminal Evidence Act 1984. The purpose is to clarify the power to compare fingerprints or samples (taken from a person arrested on suspicion of being involved in a recordable offence) against existing records: subs. (1). This power is, of course, of great importance in relation to DNA samples. Schedule 10, paras. 56–58 insert into ss.61–63 of the Police and Criminal Evidence Act 1984, a requirement that suspects be warned of this possibility. Subsection (2) permits hair (other than pubic hair) to be plucked as well as cut (for Northern Ireland, see Sched. 9, para. 39, below). This provision is based on the recommendation of the Royal Commission on Criminal Justice (Cmnd. 2263, para. 2.28). The distinction is that plucked hair contains part of the root and thus may be capable of producing DNA evidence. Subsection (3) permits samples to be taken in prisons and similar institutions. Subsection (4) enables the police to require a person to attend a police station for the purpose of providing a sample. This power may only be exercised in the case of a person who has been charged or convicted of a recordable offence and in circumstances where no sample has been taken or the sample has proved insufficient.

Recordable offence: see General Note to s.54, *ante*.

Retention of samples in certain cases

57.—(1) Section 64 of the Police and Criminal Evidence Act 1984 (which prescribes the situations in which fingerprints and samples must be destroyed) shall be amended as follows.

(2) In subsections (1), (2) and (3), after the words "they must" there shall be inserted the words ", except as provided in subsection (3A) below,".

(3) After subsection (3), there shall be inserted the following subsections—

"(3A) Samples which are required to be destroyed under subsection (1), (2) or (3) above need not be destroyed if they were taken for the purpose of the same investigation of an offence of which a person from whom one was taken has been convicted, but the information derived from the sample of any person entitled (apart from this subsection) to its destruction under subsection (1), (2) or (3) above shall not be used—

(a) in evidence against the person so entitled; or

(b) for the purposes of any investigation of an offence.

(3B) Where samples are required to be destroyed under subsections (1), (2) or (3) above, and subsection (3A) above does not apply, information derived from the sample of any person entitled to its destruction under subsection (1), (2) or (3) above shall not be used—

(a) in evidence against the person so entitled; or

(b) for the purposes of any investigation of an offence.".

DEFINITIONS

"fingerprints": s.65 of the Police and Criminal Evidence Act 1984.
"samples [intimate/non-intimate]": *ibid.*, as amended by s.58, *post.*

GENERAL NOTE

This section amends s.64 of the Police and Criminal Evidence Act 1984. That section provided for the destruction of fingerprints or samples of people who were cautioned, cleared of the offence, or not suspects in the first place. The amendment in this section permits the retention of samples if taken for the purpose of an investigation of an offence, as a result of which, a person from whom a sample was taken was convicted (subs. (3)). This provision is due to the advance of modern technology *i.e.* the use of mass spectrometers to process a number of samples together and the practice of putting a number of samples into machines together to secure the same level of distortion. The result is that all the samples then have to be retained in order to retain one sample. A safeguard against misuse of retained samples is provided by subs. (3) which renders such samples inadmissible in evidence against the supplier and provides that they may not be used for the purpose of any investigation of an offence. The Royal Commission on Criminal Justice had commented that in these circumstances it should be possible only to keep a DNA sample on a data base for statistical purposes. That objective has been achieved by the section. The same problem does not arise in relation to fingerprints which are unique to the individual who has provided them.

Fingerprints: see General Note to s.56, *ante.*

Samples: intimate and non-intimate etc.

58.—(1) Section 65 of the Police and Criminal Evidence Act 1984 (which contains definitions of intimate and non-intimate samples and other relevant definitions) shall be amended as follows.

(2) For the definition of "intimate sample" there shall be substituted—

" "intimate sample" means—

(a) a sample of blood, semen or any other tissue fluid, urine or pubic hair;

(b) a dental impression;

(c) a swab taken from a person's body orifice other than the mouth;".

(3) For the definition of "non-intimate sample" there shall be substituted—

" "non-intimate sample" means—

(a) a sample of hair other than pubic hair;

(b) a sample taken from a nail or from under a nail;

(c) a swab taken from any part of a person's body including the mouth but not any other body orifice;

(d) saliva;

(e) a footprint or a similar impression of any part of a person's body other than a part of his hand;".

(4) After the definition of "non-intimate sample" there shall be inserted the following definitions—

" "registered dentist" has the same meaning as in the Dentists Act 1984;

"speculative search", in relation to a person's fingerprints or samples, means such a check against other fingerprints or samples or against information derived from other samples as is referred to in section 63A(1) above;

"sufficient" and "insufficient", in relation to a sample, means sufficient or insufficient (in point of quantity or quality) for the purpose of enabling information to be produced by the means of analysis used or to be used in relation to the sample.".

GENERAL NOTE
Subsection (1) amends the definition of "intimate samples" in s.65 of the Police and Criminal Evidence Act 1984. The definition now includes a dental impression and excludes a mouth swab: for a comment on these amendments see General Note to s.54, *ante*. Subsection (2) amends the definition of "non-intimate" samples in s.65 to include saliva and a mouth swab: see General Note to s.55, *ante*, for a comment.

Registered dentist, by the Dentists Act 1984 (c. 24), s.14, means a person registered in the dentists' register but note that s.14 allows for temporary registration.

Extension of powers to search persons' mouths

59.—(1) In section 65 of the Police and Criminal Evidence Act 1984 (definitions for purposes of Part V: treatment of persons by police), after the definition of "intimate sample" there shall be inserted the following definition—
   " "intimate search" means a search which consists of the physical examination of a person's body orifices other than the mouth;".
   (2) In section 32 of that Act (powers of search upon arrest), in subsection (4), at the end, there shall be inserted "but they do authorise a search of a person's mouth".

DEFINITIONS
"intimate search": subs. (1).

GENERAL NOTE
This section amends s.65 of the Police and Criminal Evidence Act 1984 to extend the powers of search upon arrest in order to permit the searching of a person's mouth. The effect of this change is to allow the removal of substances such as drugs from a suspect's mouth.

Powers of police to stop and search

Powers to stop and search in anticipation of violence

60.—(1) Where a police officer of or above the rank of superintendent reasonably believes that—
   (a) incidents involving serious violence may take place in any locality in his area, and
   (b) it is expedient to do so to prevent their occurrence,
he may give an authorisation that the powers to stop and search persons and vehicles conferred by this section shall be exercisable at any place within that locality for a period not exceeding twenty four hours.
   (2) The power conferred by subsection (1) above may be exercised by a chief inspector or an inspector if he reasonably believes that incidents involving serious violence are imminent and no superintendent is available.
   (3) If it appears to the officer who gave the authorisation or to a superintendent that it is expedient to do so, having regard to offences which have, or are reasonably suspected to have, been committed in connection with any incident falling within the authorisation, he may direct that the authorisation shall continue in being for a further six hours.
   (4) This section confers on any constable in uniform power—
   (a) to stop any pedestrian and search him or anything carried by him for offensive weapons or dangerous instruments;
   (b) to stop any vehicle and search the vehicle, its driver and any passenger for offensive weapons or dangerous instruments.
   (5) A constable may, in the exercise of those powers, stop any person or vehicle and make any search he thinks fit whether or not he has any grounds for suspecting that the person or vehicle is carrying weapons or articles of that kind.

(6) If in the course of a search under this section a constable discovers a dangerous instrument or an article which he has reasonable grounds for suspecting to be an offensive weapon, he may seize it.

(7) This section applies (with the necessary modifications) to ships, aircraft and hovercraft as it applies to vehicles.

(8) A person who fails to stop or (as the case may be) to stop the vehicle when required to do so by a constable in the exercise of his powers under this section shall be liable on summary conviction to imprisonment for a term not exceeding one month or to a fine not exceeding level 3 on the standard scale or both.

(9) Any authorisation under this section shall be in writing signed by the officer giving it and shall specify the locality in which and the period during which the powers conferred by this section are exercisable and a direction under subsection (3) above shall also be given in writing or, where that is not practicable, recorded in writing as soon as it is practicable to do so.

(10) Where a vehicle is stopped by a constable under this section, the driver shall be entitled to obtain a written statement that the vehicle was stopped under the powers conferred by this section if he applies for such a statement not later than the end of the period of twelve months from the day on which the vehicle was stopped and similarly as respects a pedestrian who is stopped and searched under this section.

(11) In this section—
     "dangerous instruments" means instruments which have a blade or are sharply pointed;
     "offensive weapon" has the meaning given by section 1(9) of the Police and Criminal Evidence Act 1984; and
     "vehicle" includes a caravan as defined in section 29(1) of the Caravan Sites and Control of Development Act 1960.

(12) The powers conferred by this section are in addition to and not in derogation of, any power otherwise conferred.

DEFINITIONS
     "dangerous instruments": subs. (10).
     "offensive weapon": subs. (10).
     "vehicle": subs. (10).

GENERAL NOTE
     Police powers to stop and search people and vehicles are governed by Pt. I of the Police and Criminal Evidence Act 1984 and the Code of Practice issued under s.66 of that Act. This power may only be exercised if a police officer has reasonable grounds for suspecting that he will find stolen or prohibited articles: s.1(3) of the 1984 Act. Thus a police officer is only permitted under this legislation to search a person for weapons if he reasonably suspects that the person has a weapon in his possession. There is no general power under the 1984 Act to search individuals or a group of people in anticipation that violence is likely to occur or because a violent incident has taken place. Such violent incidents have grown in number since the enactment of the 1984 Act. For instance, the carrying of knives and other weapons has led to the deaths of 16 police officers in that time.

     Accordingly, after representations from police organisations, this section was introduced during the Report stage of the Bill in the House of Commons. The Government said that it had been persuaded that the need to meet the test of reasonable suspicion inhibits effective preventive action by the police when they believe that violence is likely to break out (Minister of State, Home Office, H.C., Official Report, Parl. Debs, Vol. 241, No. 81, col. 69). The purpose of the section is to enable the police to search for weapons in a particular locality and for a limited period of time in anticipation of serious violence. The object is to enable them to prevent violent disorder involving the use of offensive weapons. To this end, the section empowers a superintendent (or officer of higher rank) to authorise, within a specified area, uniformed officers to stop and search pedestrians, vehicles and their occupants for offensive weapons or dangerous instruments (*i.e.* having a blade or sharp point). Subsection (2) allows these powers to be carried out by an inspector. The purpose of this provision is to cater for an emergency when trouble occurs suddenly and a superintendent is not available.

The power in this section may only be exercised where the authorising officer reasonably believes that serious incidents of violence may take place in any locality in his area and it is expedient to authorise the exercise of the powers in order to prevent such acts occurring: subs. (1). What is reasonable is not defined. Whether the officer reasonably believes that incidents of violence will take place is a question of fact which will depend on the circumstances of the particular case. However, a reasonable belief pre-supposes reasonable grounds for the belief. The Minister of State said that the belief should be based on sound professional judgment and that if it is shown to be arbitrary or irrational there would be grounds for considering it to be unlawful (*ibid.*, col. 71). The reference in the subsection to "his area" seems to suggest the geographical area of responsibility of the authorising officer. "Locality" is not defined in the section (or elsewhere in the Act). Presumably, it simply means "place".

The power to stop and search under the section is exercisable for a period not exceeding 24 hours: subs. (1). However, the power may be extended for six hours if it appears "expedient" to the authorising officer to extend it: subs. (3). In deciding whether to do so, the officer must have regard to offences committed or "reasonably suspected" to have been committed: subs. (3). These provisions are aimed at circumstances such as those which might arise if violence has already broken out and a further six hours is necessary to deal with it.

Subsection (4) sets out the powers of police officers to stop and search which the section confers. It is to be noted that there is no requirement for the exercise of those powers that the officer should have grounds for suspecting that the person or vehicle is carrying weapons: subs. (5). Failure to stop when required to do so by a constable in the exercise of his powers under the section is a summary offence punishable by one month's imprisonment or a fine or both: subs. (8). It would appear that it will not be a defence to a charge under subs. (8) for the defendant to say that he was unaware of the authorisation. On the other hand, it would be grounds for mitigation. Accordingly, it will be necessary for news that an order has been made to be widely disseminated. The authorisation must be in writing and must give details of the locality and period to which it applies: subs. (8). Consideration should be given in each case as to how this may most effectively be made known in the relevant locality.

Subs. (10)

Offensive weapon under s.1(9) of the Police and Criminal Evidence Act 1984 is "any article (a) made or adapted for use for causing injury to persons; or (b) intended by the person having it with him for such use by him or by some other person".

Caravan under s.29(1) of the Caravan Sites and Control of Development Act 1960 "means any structure designed or adapted for human habitation which is capable of being moved from one place to another (whether by being towed, or by being transported on a motor vehicle or trailer), and any motor vehicle so designed or adapted, but does not include any railway rolling stock which is for the time being on rails forming part of a railway system, or (b) any tent". The Caravan Sites Act 1968 (c. 52), ss.13 and 16, extends the definition to include twin-unit caravans but excludes certain caravan-like structures over a certain length, width or internal height.

PART V

PUBLIC ORDER: COLLECTIVE TRESPASS OR NUISANCE ON LAND

Powers to remove trespassers on land

Scottish perspective

Trespass in Scotland has generally been a civil law subject. Under common law, persons have, in the main, been entitled to pass over private land provided (a) the occupier has not forbidden them to do so, (b) there is no court order prohibiting them from doing so *and* (c) they do not cause any damage to heritable or moveable property legitimately on the land. Failure to comply with any court order may lead to the imposition of a penalty, including imprisonment, but remedies all lay in the civil courts. There are some statutory exceptions to this general rule (for example under the Game Acts, the Firearms Act, the Railway Acts and Merchant Shipping Acts). Section 3 of the Trespass (Scotland) Act 1865 prohibits only lodging, occupying or encamping on any land without the consent of the owner or legal occupier. Perhaps this explains why sections 72–80 do not apply to Scotland.

Power to remove trespassers on land

61.—(1) If the senior police officer present at the scene reasonably believes that two or more persons are trespassing on land and are present there with the common purpose of residing there for any period, that reasonable steps have been taken by or on behalf of the occupier to ask them to leave and—

(a) that any of those persons has caused damage to the land or to property on the land or used threatening, abusive or insulting words or behaviour towards the occupier, a member of his family or an employee or agent of his, or

(b) that those persons have between them six or more vehicles on the land,

he may direct those persons, or any of them, to leave the land and to remove any vehicles or other property they have with them on the land.

(2) Where the persons in question are reasonably believed by the senior police officer to be persons who were not originally trespassers but have become trespassers on the land, the officer must reasonably believe that the other conditions specified in subsection (1) are satisfied after those persons became trespassers before he can exercise the power conferred by that subsection.

(3) A direction under subsection (1) above, if not communicated to the persons referred to in subsection (1) by the police officer giving the direction, may be communicated to them by any constable at the scene.

(4) If a person knowing that a direction under subsection (1) above has been given which applies to him—

(a) fails to leave the land as soon as reasonably practicable, or

(b) having left again enters the land as a trespasser within the period of three months beginning with the day on which the direction was given,

he commits an offence and is liable on summary conviction to imprisonment for a term not exceeding three months or a fine not exceeding level 4 on the standard scale, or both.

(5) A constable in uniform who reasonably suspects that a person is committing an offence under this section may arrest him without a warrant.

(6) In proceedings for an offence under this section it is a defence for the accused to show—

(a) that he was not trespassing on the land, or

(b) that he had a reasonable excuse for failing to leave the land as soon as reasonably practicable or, as the case may be, for again entering the land as a trespasser.

(7) In its application in England and Wales to common land this section has effect as if in the preceding subsections of it—

(a) references to trespassing or trespassers were references to acts and persons doing acts which constitute either a trespass as against the occupier or an infringement of the commoners' rights; and

(b) references to "the occupier" included the commoners or any of them or, in the case of common land to which the public has access, the local authority as well as any commoner.

(8) Subsection (7) above does not—

(a) require action by more than one occupier; or

(b) constitute persons trespassers as against any commoner or the local authority if they are permitted to be there by the other occupier.

(9) In this section—

"common land" means common land as defined in section 22 of the Commons Registration Act 1965;

"commoner" means a person with rights of common as defined in section 22 of the Commons Registration Act 1965;

"land" does not include—

(a) buildings other than—

(i) agricultural buildings within the meaning of, in England and Wales, paragraphs 3 to 8 of Schedule 5 to the

Local Government Finance Act 1988 or, in Scotland, section 7(2) of the Valuation and Rating (Scotland) Act 1956, or

(ii) scheduled monuments within the meaning of the Ancient Monuments and Archaeological Areas Act 1979;

(b) land forming part of—

(i) a highway unless it falls within the classifications in section 54 of the Wildlife and Countryside Act 1981 (footpath, bridleway or byway open to all traffic or road used as a public path) or is a cycle track under the Highways Act 1980 or the Cycle Tracks Act 1984; or

(ii) a road within the meaning of the Roads (Scotland) Act 1984 unless it falls within the definitions in section 151 (2)(a) (ii) or (b) (footpaths and cycle tracks) of that Act or is a bridleway within the meaning of section 47 of the Countryside (Scotland) Act 1967;

"the local authority", in relation to common land, means any local authority which has powers in relation to the land under section 9 of the Commons Registration Act 1965;

"occupier" (and in subsection (8) "the other occupier") means—

(a) in England and Wales, the person entitled to possession of the land by virtue of an estate or interest held by him; and

(b) in Scotland, the person lawfully entitled to natural possession of the land;

"property", in relation to damage to property on land, means—

(a) in England and Wales, property within the meaning of section 10(1) of the Criminal Damage Act 1971; and

(b) in Scotland, either—

(i) heritable property other than land; or

(ii) corporeal moveable property,

and "damage" includes the deposit of any substance capable of polluting the land;

"trespass" means, in the application of this section—

(a) in England and Wales, subject to the extensions effected by subsection (7) above, trespass as against the occupier of the land;

(b) in Scotland, entering, or as the case may be remaining on, land without lawful authority and without the occupier's consent; and

"trespassing" and "trespasser" shall be construed accordingly;

"vehicle" includes—

(a) any vehicle, whether or not it is in a fit state for use on roads, and includes any chassis or body, with or without wheels, appearing to have formed part of such a vehicle, and any load carried by, and anything attached to, such a vehicle; and

(b) a caravan as defined in section 29(1) of the Caravan Sites and Control of Development Act 1960;

and a person may be regarded for the purposes of this section as having a purpose of residing in a place notwithstanding that he has a home elsewhere.

DEFINITIONS

"common land": subs. (9) and s.22 of the Commons Registration Act 1965.

"commoner": *ibid.*

"damage": subs. (9).

"land": subs. (9).

"local authority": subs. (9).

"occupier": subss. (7) and (9).

"property": subs. (9).

"trespass": subss. (7) and (9).

"vehicle": subs. (9) and s.29(1) of the Caravan Sites and Control of Development Act 1960.

GENERAL NOTE

This section replaces s.39 of the Public Order Act 1986, which is repealed (s.148, Sched. 11). It enables a police officer to direct trespassers on land to leave the land where the occupier has taken steps to ask them to do so, *either* if any of the trespassers has caused damage or if they have been threatening, abusive or insulting, *or* if they have between them six or more vehicles on the land. Failure to obey such a direction, or return to the land as a trespasser within three months of the direction, is an offence. The intention of the legislation, by criminalising trespass in these circumstances, is to provide a remedy against trespassers which is speedier than the new accelerated process under the civil law (see General Notes to ss.75–76, *post*) and will not involve the occupier in the expense of litigation. But the circumstances in which the criminal law may be invoked are somewhat narrower than under the civil law: not every act of trespass will have criminal implications.

Subs. (1)

The *conditions* in which a direction may be given are set out in this subsection. There must be a *trespass to land* (an "unjustifiable intrusion by one person upon land in the possession of another": *Clerk and Lindsell*, 16th ed. 23–01) by two or more persons. The following should be noted:—

(1) The restriction in subs. (9) to trespass as against the occupier of the land except in the case of common land (see note to subs. (7), below). Knowledge by the trespassers of the trespass is not necessary: *Clerk and Lindsell*, above, 23–05. Section 39 required that there be an *entry by trespass*: note that this section refers to *presence on land* and that, by subs. (2) (which is new) persons not originally on land as trespassers may become so (see below).

(2) There must be a *common purpose to reside.* These words are not defined but must be taken to have their everyday meaning: *reside*: dwell permanently or for a considerable amount of time, have one's settled or usual abode, live in or at a particular place: Shorter Oxford English Dictionary.

(3) The trespassers may have caused *damage to the land or property on the land*: s.39 referred only to property on the land. *Land* includes crops growing on the land. It also includes *common land* (which is defined in the note to subs. (9), below, and the *damage* done to them will, presumably, include writing graffiti, urinating on the land and leaving litter about: see Standing Committee B, col. 533. In *Roe v. Kingerlee* [1986] C.L.Y. 533 the Divisional Court held that what constitutes "damage" within the Criminal Damage Act 1971 is a matter of fact and degree: it is a matter for the justices, applying common sense, to decide. For the definition of *property* see note to subs. (9) below. The definition includes fences, stiles and animals: see Standing Committee B, col. 537; but hedges presumably count as land.

(4) Alternatively the trespassers may have *used threatening, abusive or insulting behaviour towards the occupier of the land, a member of his family or an employee or agent of his. Threatening* carries its ordinary meaning and will be a question of fact according to the circumstances (*Brutus v. Cozens* [1972] C.L.Y. 706) as will *insulting* and *abusive* (*D.P.P. v. Clarke; Lewis, O'Connel and O'Keefe* [1992] C.L.Y. 1129 (a decision under s.5 of the Public Order Act 1986); but rude and offensive words are not necessarily insulting (*R. v. Ambrose (Peter Thomas)* [1973] C.L.Y. 602). *Occupier* is defined by subs. (9). In *Atkin v. D.P.P.* [1990] C.L.Y. 1156 (a decision under s.4 of the Public Order Act 1986) the Divisional Court held that the words "uses towards another person" in s.4 meant "uses in the presence of and in the direction of another person directly". So it would seem that threats against a farmer made to *e.g.* his wife would not come within the section unless the farmer was actually present.

(5) The third alternative is that the trespassers may have caused no damage and used no threatening words etc. but may have brought *six or more vehicles* on to the land. *Vehicles* includes caravans: see further the General Note to s.60, *ante*. Section 39 referred to 12 or more vehicles: the reduction in number no doubt reflects the tendency of New Age travellers (at whom the legislation is chiefly directed) to travel in groups of one less than 12. It is not clear what the application of the section would be to two or more apparently separate groups of trespassers who have set up on different parts of the same piece of land but who have altogether six or more vehicles: presumably it would be necessary to establish the common purpose of residence (see above).

If these conditions are fulfilled the senior police officer *present at the scene* may direct any or all of the trespassers to leave the land and *to remove any vehicles or other property they have with them on the land.* The words in italics were not in s.39 of the Public Order Act 1986: (i) *note* that the senior police officer present need not be high-ranking (and see further the note to subs. (3) below); (ii) *remove any vehicles etc.* : *Krumpa v. D.P.P.* [1989] C.L.Y. 870 (see note to subs. (4) below) highlighted the omission in s.39 of any explicit reference to the removal of vehicles. The direction need not be given to each individual trespasser; it may be given generally, *e.g.* by loudhailer.

For police power to remove vehicles, see s.62, *post*.

Subs. (2)

This provision empowers the senior police officer, in a situation where persons did not originally enter the land as trespassers but have become so, that is, where the owner gave them
permission to enter the land but has since withdrawn his permission, to direct the trespassers to
leave the land. This will include land in respect of which an access agreement applies under the
National Parks and Access to the Countryside Act 1949; and land where the occupier, while not
having given specific permission to individuals, has tolerated the trespass *e.g.* hikers and ram-
blers. But they must have, or the police officer must reasonably believe that they have, fulfilled
the conditions set out in subs. (1), above.

Subs. (3)

This subsection, which was also not in s.39 of the Public Order Act 1986, enables the direction
under subs. (1) actually to be communicated to the trespassers by a police constable who is not
necessarily the senior police officer at the scene.

Subs. (4)

This subsection creates the offence of failing to obey the direction given under subs. (1). The
wording is the same as that in s.39(2) of the Public Order Act 1986. See subs. (6) as to defences. A
trespasser to whom the direction has been given must leave the land as soon as is reasonably
practicable. In *Krumpa v. D.P.P.* it was held that the test is as soon as *objectively* reasonably
practicable, not when a reasonable police officer believed was practicable, and must depend on
the circumstances. This would cover the situation where vehicles were in too great a state of
disrepair to be moved as in *Krumpa*; on the other hand, trespassers who then failed to repair
their vehicle would not be being reasonable. *Knowledge* that the direction has been given is an
essential ingredient of the offence and must be proved by the prosecution: *Gaumont British
Distributors Ltd v. Henry* [1939] 2 K.B. 711.

Subs. (6)

This subsection sets out the defences to a charge under subs. (4). It is similar to the defences in
the Public Order Act 1986 except that the former requirement to show that the accused had not
entered the land as a trespasser is replaced by a requirement to show that he was not *on* the land
as a trespasser. As for reasonable excuse for failing to leave the land, see *Krumpa*, above. It is to
be noted that the subsection places the burden of proof of these defences upon the defendant.
The standard of proof (as is normal when a burden is on the defence in a criminal case) is the civil
standard, *i.e.* on the balance of probability: *R. v. Carr-Briant* [1943] K.B. 607.

Subss. (7) and (8)

There was no provision in s.39 of the Public Order Act 1986 for dealing with mass incursions
by persons (such as those at whom the section is directed) on to common land. These subsections
deal with such situations. For a definition of *common land*, see below. All or any of the commoners, or the local authority if there is a public right of access to the common land, may ask the
police for a direction under subs. (1). *Note* that, by subs. (8), if one commoner permits persons on
to the land they will not become trespassers as against the other commoners or the local
authority.

Subs. (9)

Common land under the Commons Registration Act 1965 (c. 64), s.22(1) "means (a) land
subject to rights of common (as defined by this Act) whether these rights are exercisable at all
times or only during limited periods; waste land of a manor not subject to rights of common, but
does not include a town or village green or any land which forms part of a highway". *Land*
"includes land covered with water". *Rights of common* "includes cattlegates or beastgates (by
whatever name known) and rights of sole or several vesture of herbage or of sole or several
pasture but does not include rights held for a term of years or from year to year". *Town or village
green* means land which has been allotted by or under any Act for the exercise or recreation of
the inhabitants of any locality or on which the inhabitants of any locality have a customary right
to indulge in lawful sports or pastimes or on which the inhabitants of any locality have indulged
in such sports and pastimes as of right for not less than 20 years": Commons Registration Act
1965 (c. 64), s.22(1).

Local Authority. Section 9 of the Commons Registration Act 1965 gave powers to local
authorities to protect common land against unlawful interference. For the purposes of the 1965
Act a local authority is "... the council of a county, London borough or county district, the
council of a parish ...": s.22 of the Commons Registration Act 1965, as amended.

Property is defined by Criminal Damage Act 1971 (c. 48), s.10, as "property of a tangible nature, whether real or personal, including money and (a) including wild creatures which have been tamed or are ordinarily kept in captivity...; but (b) not including mushrooms growing wild on any land, or any flowers, fruit or foliage or a plant growing wild on any land".

Vehicle includes *caravan*: for the definition of which see General Note to s.60, *ante*.

Scottish perspective

Subs. (1)
This requires three elements to be present before the section can be operated: (a) there is more than one trespasser; (b) there is a common purpose to reside on the land; and either (c) that the persons have caused damage to the land or used threatening, abusive or insulting words or behaviour, or (d) have possession of six or more vehicles on the land.

This section is thus fairly restricted and, if the interpretation given to "resides" is at all similar to that given to "lodges" in s.3 of the Trespass (Scotland) Act 1865, may be more difficult to enforce than the earlier Act.

Subs. (9)
The definition of "trespass" for Scottish purposes is the first statutory definition ever given. It should be noted that the definition is purely for the application of this section and it thus does not restrict the common law right to pass over private land.

Supplementary powers of seizure

62.—(1) If a direction has been given under section 61 and a constable reasonably suspects that any person to whom the direction applies has, without reasonable excuse—

(a) failed to remove any vehicle on the land which appears to the constable to belong to him or to be in his possession or under his control; or

(b) entered the land as a trespasser with a vehicle within the period of three months beginning with the day on which the direction was given,

the constable may seize and remove that vehicle.

(2) In this section, "trespasser" and "vehicle" have the same meaning as in section 61.

Definitions
"trespasser": subs. (2), s.61(9).
"vehicle": subs. (2), s.61(9).

General Note
This section provides a power for the police to seize the vehicles of persons who have failed to comply with a direction under s.56 or who have re-entered the land as trespassers within three months.

The power is new and arises from the power under s.61(1), *ante*, which the police have to direct persons who are trespassers within paras. (a) and (b) of that subsection also to remove their vehicles and other property which they have with them on the land. *Note* that the section applies only to vehicles and not to other property about which a direction under s.61(1) may be made. It will not only cover situations where the trespassers have departed leaving their vehicles behind them but also situations where the trespassers delay departure, unreasonably claiming, for instance, that their vehicles are too dilapidated to be moved. *Note* that where trespassers have left the land and then return their re-entry, for the section to be effective, must be as a trespasser.

In his possession or under his control. Presumably, the trespasser who claims that a vehicle (which appears to be his) is not, in fact, in his possession or under his control must prove that this is not so. The phrase is similar to that in the Powers of Criminal Courts Act, 1971 (c. 62), s.43(1), which deals with forfeiture of property used or intended to be used for committing an offence.

Powers in relation to raves

Powers to remove persons attending or preparing for a rave

63.—(1) This section applies to a gathering on land in the open air of 100 or more persons (whether or not trespassers) at which amplified music is played during the night (with or without intermissions) and is such as, by reason of its loudness and duration and the time at which it is played, is likely to cause serious distress to the inhabitants of the locality; and for this purpose—

(a) such a gathering continues during intermissions in the music and, where the gathering extends over several days, throughout the period during which amplified music is played at night (with or without intermissions); and

(b) "music" includes sounds wholly or predominantly characterised by the emission of a succession of repetitive beats.

(2) If, as respects any land in the open air, a police officer of at least the rank of superintendent reasonably believes that—

(a) two or more persons are making preparations for the holding there of a gathering to which this section applies,

(b) ten or more persons are waiting for such a gathering to begin there, or

(c) ten or more persons are attending such a gathering which is in progress,

he may give a direction that those persons and any other persons who come to prepare or wait for or to attend the gathering are to leave the land and remove any vehicles or other property which they have with them on the land.

(3) A direction under subsection (2) above, if not communicated to the persons referred to in subsection (2) by the police officer giving the direction, may be communicated to them by any constable at the scene.

(4) Persons shall be treated as having had a direction under subsection (2) above communicated to them if reasonable steps have been taken to bring it to their attention.

(5) A direction under subsection (2) above does not apply to an exempt person.

(6) If a person knowing that a direction has been given which applies to him—

(a) fails to leave the land as soon as reasonably practicable, or

(b) having left again enters the land within the period of 7 days beginning with the day on which the direction was given,

he commits an offence and is liable on summary conviction to imprisonment for a term not exceeding three months or a fine not exceeding level 4 on the standard scale, or both.

(7) In proceedings for an offence under this section it is a defence for the accused to show that he had a reasonable excuse for failing to leave the land as soon as reasonably practicable or, as the case may be, for again entering the land.

(8) A constable in uniform who reasonably suspects that a person is committing an offence under this section may arrest him without a warrant.

(9) This section does not apply—

(a) in England and Wales, to a gathering licensed by an entertainment licence; or

(b) in Scotland, to a gathering in premises which, by virtue of section 41 of the Civic Government (Scotland) Act 1982, are licensed to be used as a place of public entertainment.

(10) In this section—

"entertainment licence" means a licence granted by a local authority under—

(a) Schedule 12 to the London Government Act 1963;

(b) section 3 of the Private Places of Entertainment (Licensing) Act 1967; or

(c) Schedule 1 to the Local Government (Miscellaneous Provisions) Act 1982;

"exempt person", in relation to land (or any gathering on land), means the occupier, any member of his family and any employee or agent of his and any person whose home is situated on the land;

"land in the open air" includes a place partly open to the air;

"local authority" means—

    (a) in Greater London, a London borough council or the Common Council of the City of London;

    (b) in England outside Greater London, a district council or the council of the Isles of Scilly;

    (c) in Wales, a county council or county borough council; and

"occupier", "trespasser" and "vehicle" have the same meaning as in section 61.

(11) Until 1st April 1996, in this section "local authority" means, in Wales, a district council.

DEFINITIONS

"entertainment licence": subs. (10).
"exempt persons": subs. (10).
"land in the open air": subs. (10).
"local authority": subs. (10).
"music": subs. (1)(b).
"occupier": subs. (10), s.61(9).
"trespasser": subs. (10), s.61(9).
"vehicle": subs. (10), s.61(9).

GENERAL NOTE

This section, together with ss.64–67, deals with *raves*, which, like the New Age travellers at whom ss.61 and 62 are directed, are a phenomenon of the 1990s. The word "rave", which appears only in the headnote and is not specifically defined by the statute, is a term derived from pop music culture; it is perhaps the first occasion in which such a term has appeared in an Act of Parliament. It must now be taken to mean an event of the kind described in subs. (1), see below.

The facts in *R. v. Shorrock (Peter)* [1993] C.L.Y. 3014 provide a good example of a rave, although the event concerned was actually described as an "acid house party". A weekend event was held on a field in Lancashire. The defendant gave permission for the event to be held, but absented himself for its duration. The event was publicised by posters which did not give the actual venue but gave telephone numbers from which information could be obtained—a common device at such events and designed to circumvent attempts to stop them. It was attended by between three and five thousand people. Loud music was played during the night (as well as the day) which caused noise and disturbance to local residents. An injunction, restraining the holding of the event, had been obtained by the police but, although it was read aloud at the site of the party, it had no effect. *Shorrock* was prosecuted successfully for committing a public nuisance. This new legislation is designed to prevent such events from being held at all.

It should be noted that the holding of a "rave" is not in itself an offence; the offence is that of failing to obey a police direction to leave the land on which the rave is being held. And *note also* that (unlike s.61, *ante* and ss.68, 70 and 73, *post*) trespass is not an element.

Subs. (1)

A *rave* is a gathering on land in the open air of 100 or more persons at which amplified music is played so loudly and so long at night that it is likely to cause serious distress to the inhabitants of the locality. (As to events where an entertainment licence has been issued, see note to subs. (9), below.) The persons at the gathering may be present either with the permission of the occupier or as trespassers.

The *music* concerned is defined by subs. (1)(b) as sounds wholly or predominantly characterised by the emission of a series of repetitive beats, and is clearly aimed at certain types of rock music. In practice, whether a particular type of rock music is within or without the definition will be a matter of fact. The same test will apply to music which is not rock music at all, but is music which has a predominant beat. The music must be *amplified*: this is not defined but must mean amplified by means of sound equipment as defined in s.64(6). The gathering should be continuous but the music need not be played throughout.

Land in the open air includes land partly in the open air (subs. (10)), for instance, a barn or an aircraft hangar with the doors open; but not such buildings with the doors shut: Standing Committee B, col. 582. Whatever the level of noise in the latter case, the section will not apply.

As to police powers to enter the land to ascertain if a rave is taking or is going to take place and powers of seizure, see s.64, *post*.

Subss. (2) and (5)

This subsection gives the police power to deal with such gatherings by making directions for persons to leave the land and to take with them their vehicles and other property. The direction must be given by an officer of the rank of superintendent or above. The officer must reasonably believe that a gathering within subs. (1) is to be held and that either two or more persons are making preparations for it, or 10 or more persons are waiting for it to begin, or 10 or more persons are attending it. The direction to leave is to be given to those persons. The subsection does not apply to *exempt persons* (subs. (5)) who are, by subs. (10), the occupier of the land, his family, his employees and anyone whose home is on the land. The officer may be required to justify his belief that the section applied although only between two and 10 persons were present at the material time. This he will only be able to do by reference to the circumstances as they existed at the time.

Subss. (3) and (4)

There is no requirement for the superintendent to actually be present at the gathering; the direction may be communicated to the persons concerned by any constable at the scene (subs. (3)) who should take reasonable steps to bring it to their attention (subs. (4)).

Subss. (6) (7) and (8)

Failure to leave the land as soon as reasonably practicable or re-entry within seven days is a summary offence (subs. (6)). Defences are available (subs. (7)): see the General Note to s.61(6), *ante*, for comment on the similar defences available under that section. There is a power to arrest without warrant (subs. (8)).

Subs. (9)

Outside Greater London, entertainment licences are granted by the district council. In Greater London, they are granted by a London borough council (in the City of London, by the Common Council). These bodies also grant licences in respect of which a licence is required under the Private Places of Entertainment (Licensing) Act 1967.

Scottish perspective

It is thought that most "raves" in Scotland take place in buildings and will not, therefore, be covered by this section. Scotland was originally excluded from all the sections relating to raves. Fear that this might result in rave organisers moving north ensured the extension of the provisions to Scotland.

Supplementary powers of entry and seizure

64.—(1) If a police officer of at least the rank of superintendent reasonably believes that circumstances exist in relation to any land which would justify the giving of a direction under section 63 in relation to a gathering to which that section applies he may authorise any constable to enter the land for any of the purposes specified in subsection (2) below.

(2) Those purposes are—

(a) to ascertain whether such circumstances exist; and

(b) to exercise any power conferred on a constable by section 63 or subsection (4) below.

(3) A constable who is so authorised to enter land for any purpose may enter the land without a warrant.

(4) If a direction has been given under section 63 and a constable reasonably suspects that any person to whom the direction applies has, without reasonable excuse—

(a) failed to remove any vehicle or sound equipment on the land which appears to the constable to belong to him or to be in his possession or under his control; or

(b) entered the land as a trespasser with a vehicle or sound equipment within the period of 7 days beginning with the day on which the direction was given,

the constable may seize and remove that vehicle or sound equipment.

(5) Subsection (4) above does not authorise the seizure of any vehicle or sound equipment of an exempt person.

(6) In this section—

"exempt person" has the same meaning as in section 63;
"sound equipment" means equipment designed or adapted for amplifying music and any equipment suitable for use in connection with such equipment, and "music" has the same meaning as in section 63; and
"vehicle" has the same meaning as in section 61.

DEFINITIONS
"exempt person": s.63(10).
"music": s.63(1)(b).
"sound equipment": subs. (6).
"vehicle": ss.61(9) and 63(10).

GENERAL NOTE
This section provides that a police officer of the rank of superintendent or above may authorise any constable to enter land to ascertain whether a rave is being or is likely to be held (subss. (1) and (2)). No warrant is required (subs. (3)). It also, by subs. (4), provides a power for the police to seize vehicles or sound equipment of persons failing to comply with a direction under s.63 or arrested for an offence.

Note that the section applies only to vehicles and sound equipment and not to "other property" which the persons concerned may have been directed to move under s.63, *ante, e.g.* stages, lighting equipment and tents. For the power to retain and dispose of or destroy vehicles and sound equipment, see s.67, *post*. As in the case of s.62, *ante*, this section covers not only situations where those concerned depart leaving vehicles and sound equipment behind them but also situations where they re-enter the land as trespassers.

As to the meaning of *vehicle* see the General Note to s.61; and for comments on *in his possession or control* see the General Note to s.62. The occupier of the land, his family and employees, and anyone else living on the land are *exempt* from the powers of seizure under subs. (4): subs. (5).

Raves: power to stop persons from proceeding

65.—(1) If a constable in uniform reasonably believes that a person is on his way to a gathering to which section 63 applies in relation to which a direction under section 63(2) is in force, he may, subject to subsections (2) and (3) below—

(a) stop that person, and
(b) direct him not to proceed in the direction of the gathering.

(2) The power conferred by subsection (1) above may only be exercised at a place within 5 miles of the boundary of the site of the gathering.

(3) No direction may be given under subsection (1) above to an exempt person.

(4) If a person knowing that a direction under subsection (1) above has been given to him fails to comply with that direction, he commits an offence and is liable on summary conviction to a fine not exceeding level 3 on the standard scale.

(5) A constable in uniform who reasonably suspects that a person is committing an offence under this section may arrest him without a warrant.

(6) In this section, "exempt person" has the same meaning as in section 63.

DEFINITIONS
"exempt person": s.63(10).

GENERAL NOTE
This section provides the police (constables and above) with the power to stop a person from proceeding to a rave (as per s.63, *ante*). A police officer can only do so within a five-mile radius of the boundary of the site of the rave. The power does not apply to *exempt persons* (as to whom, see s.63, *ante*). However, the application of the section is not confined to those proceeding to a

rave by road: it would cover situations where the people concerned have left their cars more than five miles away and are making their way to the rave by bicycle or across the fields on foot. A person who fails to comply with a police direction under this section commits an offence: subs. (4). There is a power of arrest under the section: subs. (5).

Power of court to forfeit sound equipment

66.—(1) Where a person is convicted of an offence under section 63 in relation to a gathering to which that section applies and the court is satisfied that any sound equipment which has been seized from him under section 64(4), or which was in his possession or under his control at the relevant time, has been used at the gathering the court may make an order for forfeiture under this subsection in respect of that property.

(2) The court may make an order under subsection (1) above whether or not it also deals with the offender in respect of the offence in any other way and without regard to any restrictions on forfeiture in any enactment.

(3) In considering whether to make an order under subsection (1) above in respect of any property a court shall have regard—

(a) to the value of the property; and

(b) to the likely financial and other effects on the offender of the making of the order (taken together with any other order that the court contemplates making).

(4) An order under subsection (1) above shall operate to deprive the offender of his rights, if any, in the property to which it relates, and the property shall (if not already in their possession) be taken into the possession of the police.

(5) Except in a case to which subsection (6) below applies, where any property has been forfeited under subsection (1) above, a magistrates' court may, on application by a claimant of the property, other than the offender from whom it was forfeited under subsection (1) above, make an order for delivery of the property to the applicant if it appears to the court that he is the owner of the property.

(6) In a case where forfeiture under subsection (1) above has been by order of a Scottish court, a claimant such as is mentioned in subsection (5) above may, in such manner as may be prescribed by act of adjournal, apply to that court for an order for the return of the property in question.

(7) No application shall be made under subsection (5), or by virtue of subsection (6), above by any claimant of the property after the expiration of 6 months from the date on which an order under subsection (1) above was made in respect of the property.

(8) No such application shall succeed unless the claimant satisfies the court either that he had not consented to the offender having possession of the property or that he did not know, and had no reason to suspect, that the property was likely to be used at a gathering to which section 63 applies.

(9) An order under subsection (5), or by virtue of subsection (6), above shall not affect the right of any person to take, within the period of 6 months from the date of an order under subsection (5), or as the case may be by virtue of subsection (6), above, proceedings for the recovery of the property from the person in possession of it in pursuance of the order, but on the expiration of that period the right shall cease.

(10) The Secretary of State may make regulations for the disposal of property, and for the application of the proceeds of sale of property, forfeited under subsection (1) above where no application by a claimant of the property under subsection (5), or by virtue of subsection (6), above has been made within the period specified in subsection (7) above or no such application has succeeded.

(11) The regulations may also provide for the investment of money and for the audit of accounts.

(12) The power to make regulations under subsection (10) above shall be exercisable by statutory instrument which shall be subject to annulment in pursuance of a resolution of either House of Parliament.

(13) In this section—

"relevant time", in relation to a person—

(a) convicted in England and Wales of an offence under section 63, means the time of his arrest for the offence or of the issue of a summons in respect of it;

(b) so convicted in Scotland, means the time of his arrest for, or of his being cited as an accused in respect of, the offence;

"sound equipment" has the same meaning as in section 64.

DEFINITIONS

"relevant time": subs. (13).

"sound equipment": subs. (13), s.64(6).

GENERAL NOTE

This section relates to the forfeiture of sound equipment (as defined by s.64(6), *ante*) used at raves. It applies only to sound equipment and not to vehicles or other property. It adds to the number of specific statutes authorising forfeiture (such as the Misuse of Drugs Act 1971, Firearms Act 1968, Obscene Publications Act 1959) as well as the general power under the Powers of Criminal Courts Act 1971. Like other powers of forfeiture, the order will deprive the owner of any rights he may have in the forfeited property.

The effect of the section is that where a person is convicted by a magistrates' court of an offence under s.63(6) relating to raves, the court may also order the forfeiture of sound equipment seized from him or which was under his possession or control (as to which see General Note to s.62, *ante*) (subs. (1)): this is irrespective of any other punishment (subs. (2)).

Subsection (3), which repeats the wording of s.43(1A) of the Powers of Criminal Courts Act 1971 requires the court to have regard to the value of the property and the likely financial and other effects on the offender when considering whether to make an order under this section. In *R. v. Highbury Corner Stipendiary Magistrates' Court ex p. Di Matteo* [1991] C.L.Y. 1125 the divisional court held that (a) both these matters *must* be considered when a court is considering an order under s.43, and (b) if the defendant is being sentenced for more than one offence, the court must consider the total effect of the sentence. Thus, in *R. v. Buddo* [1983] C.L.Y. 809 it was held that, in that case, a forfeiture order plus a prison sentence was "overdoing the punishment": the subsection requires that the forfeiture order be part of the totality of the punishment. Where several persons are convicted and it is held that the responsibility of each person for the offence is the same (and they are sentenced accordingly) it is wrong to make an order of forfeiture against one only: *R. v. Ottey* [1985] C.L.Y. 787.

The magistrates' court making the order may order the delivery of the sound equipment to a claimant (other than the offender against whom the order has been made) provided it appears to the court that he is the owner of the equipment (subs. (5)). This would appear to require the claimant to provide some evidence of ownership. Such a claim must be made within six months of the forfeiture order being made (subs. (7)) and the claimant must satisfy the court that he had either not consented to the equipment being in the possession of the offender or that he had not known (and had no reason to suspect) that it was to be used in a rave (subs. (8)). The making of an order for delivery of the property does not affect the right of anyone to commence proceedings for the recovery of the sound equipment but *note* that such a right ceases at the end of six months from making the order for delivery (subs. (9)).

Retention and charges for seized property

Retention and charges for seized property

67.—(1) Any vehicles which have been seized and removed by a constable under section 62(1) or 64(4) may be retained in accordance with regulations made by the Secretary of State under subsection (3) below.

(2) Any sound equipment which has been seized and removed by a constable under section 64(4) may be retained until the conclusion of proceedings against the person from whom it was seized for an offence under section 63.

(3) The Secretary of State may make regulations—
(a) regulating the retention and safe keeping and the disposal and the destruction in prescribed circumstances of vehicles; and
(b) prescribing charges in respect of the removal, retention, disposal and destruction of vehicles.

(4) Any authority shall be entitled to recover from a person from whom a vehicle has been seized such charges as may be prescribed in respect of the removal, retention, disposal and destruction of the vehicle by the authority.

(5) Regulations under subsection (3) above may make different provisions for different classes of vehicles or for different circumstances.

(6) Any charges under subsection (4) above shall be recoverable as a simple contract debt.

(7) Any authority having custody of vehicles under regulations under subsection (3) above shall be entitled to retain custody until any charges under subsection (4) are paid.

(8) The power to make regulations under subsection (3) above shall be exercisable by statutory instrument which shall be subject to annulment in pursuance of a resolution of either House of Parliament.

(9) In this section—
"conclusion of proceedings" against a person means—
(a) his being sentenced or otherwise dealt with for the offence or his acquittal;
(b) the discontinuance of the proceedings; or
(c) the decision not to prosecute him,
whichever is the earlier;
"sound equipment" has the same meaning as in section 64; and
"vehicle" has the same meaning as in section 61.

DEFINITIONS
"conclusion of proceedings": subs. (9).
"sound equipment": subs. (9), s.64(6).
"vehicle": subs. (9), s.61(9).

GENERAL NOTE
This section provides for the retention of property seized and the imposition of charges under regulations (which have not yet been made). Such property may be held until the conclusion of proceedings against the persons from whom it was seized, that is, his conviction and sentence or acquittal or the discontinuance of those proceedings or the decision not to prosecute. It applies to vehicles seized under ss.62(1) and 64(4) and to sound equipment seized under s.64(4). It does not apply to "other property" which the police may have directed be moved from the land but which, if it is not moved, they have no power to seize themselves. The Minister envisaged (Standing Committee B, col. 605) that the regulations would allow for fair warning to be given so that the owners of vehicles could remove them themselves.

The power under this section is *not* a power of forfeiture. As a result, the rights, if any, of the person from whom the property was seized will not be affected. However, it should be noted that there will be a power under regulations to dispose of or destroy the items concerned.

Disruptive trespassers

Offence of aggravated trespass

68.—(1) A person commits the offence of aggravated trespass if he trespasses on land in the open air and, in relation to any lawful activity which persons are engaging in or are about to engage in on that or adjoining land in the open air, does there anything which is intended by him to have the effect—
(a) of intimidating those persons or any of them so as to deter them or any of them from engaging in that activity,

  (b) of obstructing that activity, or

  (c) of disrupting that activity.

  (2) Activity on any occasion on the part of a person or persons on land is "lawful" for the purposes of this section if he or they may engage in the activity on the land on that occasion without committing an offence or trespassing on the land.

  (3) A person guilty of an offence under this section is liable on summary conviction to imprisonment for a term not exceeding three months or a fine not exceeding level 4 on the standard scale, or both.

  (4) A constable in uniform who reasonably suspects that a person is committing an offence under this section may arrest him without a warrant.

  (5) In this section "land" does not include—

  (a) the highways and roads excluded from the application of section 61 by paragraph (b) of the definition of "land" in subsection (9) of that section; or

  (b) a road within the meaning of the Roads (Northern Ireland) Order 1993.

DEFINITIONS

  "land": subs. (5).

  "lawful activity": subs. (2).

GENERAL NOTE

This section provides that people who trespass on land and seek to deter by intimidation, obstruct or disrupt other people engaged in a lawful activity commit a summary offence of aggravated trespass. (*Note* that the offence is committed when the act of aggravated trespass occurs. Thus, the requirement in other sections of this Act that the offence is not committed unless there is a failure to obey a direction to leave the land is not found in this section).

The section is aimed at all forms of violent mass protest. Thus, much of the discussion in Parliament concentrated on the activities of "hunt saboteurs" (*i.e.*, groups of protesters whose aim is to disrupt and prevent hunting). Other forms of mass protest (such as demonstrations intended to halt the construction of roads) also come within the ambit of the section. But, as worded, its effect is much wider. Debates in Parliament referred to the fact that the section would apply to any demonstration, however minor, on private land where the demonstrators were trespassers and not just to "hunt saboteurs." The Government confirmed that this was its intention.

For the section to apply there must be *a trespass on land in the open air*. The offence can be committed by *one person*: the section does not require him to be with others. *Trespass* is not defined: see the General Note to s.61, *ante*, for comment, but *note* that the restriction in s.61(9) whereby trespass is confined to trespass as against the occupier is not extended to this section. The distinction in the earlier sections between entry on the land as a trespasser and becoming a trespasser when already on the land is not drawn. The trespass must be committed *in the open air*: the inclusion of "partly in the open air" in the definition of "open air" in s.63 has not been extended to this section; presumably this means that a demonstration in e.g. a covered stand at a racecourse or football stadium will not be covered.

The person trespassing must do some act which is *intended* to intimidate other persons lawfully on the land from carrying on a lawful activity, or to obstruct or disrupt that activity. (It need not have that effect). A mere intent is not sufficient: the intention must be evinced by the person doing something. Such an action with such an intention will constitute the offence of *aggravated trespass* (subs. (1)). There is a power of arrest without warrant for the offence (subs. (4)). (There is an additional offence of failing to obey a direction to leave the land, see s.69(3), *post*).

Intimidate, obstruct, and *disrupt* are not defined and may be taken to have their common meanings: respectively, "to force to or to deter from some action by threats or violence", "to interrupt, to render difficult, impede, hinder or retard", "to break or burst asunder": Shorter Oxford English Dictionary. *Note* that the Public Order Act 1986 (c. 64), ss.12, 14, refers to "serious disruption": presumably the disruption envisaged by this section is of a lesser degree. Many otherwise lawful actions will thus be rendered unlawful if committed with an intent to intimidate etc, *e.g.* blowing a hunting horn so as to distract hounds.

A *lawful activity* is one which is not either an offence or a trespass (subs. (2)). It would therefore appear that where a hunt trespasses it will not be a lawful activity and that, as a result, an anti-hunt protest which takes place on land where the hunt is trespassing will not come within the section.

Scottish perspective

The Scottish common law offences of breach of the peace and conduct liable to cause a breach of the peace were perfectly adequate to deal with hunt saboteurs and others covered by this section. Both are arrestable offences and carry maximum penalties considerably higher than that specified in subs. (3). A difficulty may arise for the Scottish courts in giving meaning to the term "trespass" in subs. (1). It will be recalled that the definition of that term for Scotland in s.61(9) was limited to that section.

Powers to remove persons committing or participating in aggravated trespass

69.—(1) If the senior police officer present at the scene reasonably believes—

(a) that a person is committing, has committed or intends to commit the offence of aggravated trespass on land in the open air; or

(b) that two or more persons are trespassing on land in the open air and are present there with the common purpose of intimidating persons so as to deter them from engaging in a lawful activity or of obstructing or disrupting a lawful activity,

he may direct that person or (as the case may be) those persons (or any of them) to leave the land.

(2) A direction under subsection (1) above, if not communicated to the persons referred to in subsection (1) by the police officer giving the direction, may be communicated to them by any constable at the scene.

(3) If a person knowing that a direction under subsection (1) above has been given which applies to him—

(a) fails to leave the land as soon as practicable, or

(b) having left again enters the land as a trespasser within the period of three months beginning with the day on which the direction was given,

he commits an offence and is liable on summary conviction to imprisonment for a term not exceeding three months or a fine not exceeding level 4 on the standard scale, or both.

(4) In proceedings for an offence under subsection (3) it is a defence for the accused to show—

(a) that he was not trespassing on the land, or

(b) that he had a reasonable excuse for failing to leave the land as soon as practicable or, as the case may be, for again entering the land as a trespasser.

(5) A constable in uniform who reasonably suspects that a person is committing an offence under this section may arrest him without a warrant.

(6) In this section "lawful activity" and "land" have the same meaning as in section 68.

DEFINITIONS

"land": subs. (6), s.68.

"lawful activity": subs. (6), s.68.

GENERAL NOTE

This section enables the senior police officer present on land to order persons whom he reasonably believes are committing, have committed or intend to commit the offence of aggravated trespass to leave the land. *Note* that the offence need not actually have been or be committed. There is no requirement that the police officer be high-ranking. There is a power of arrest without warrant. A person disobeying such a direction or returning to the land as a trespasser within three months is guilty of a summary offence. *Note* that this offence is separate to that of aggravated trespass. The three-month period is intended to extend the protection of the Bill to *e.g.* sporting activities which take place over several weeks or longer: see Standing Committee B, col. 638.

Trespassory assemblies

Trespassory assemblies

70. In Part II of the Public Order Act 1986 (processions and assemblies), after section 14, there shall be inserted the following sections—

"Prohibiting trespassory assemblies

14A.—(1) If at any time the chief officer of police reasonably believes that an assembly is intended to be held in any district at a place on land to which the public has no right of access or only a limited right of access and that the assembly—
(a) is likely to be held without the permission of the occupier of the land or to conduct itself in such a way as to exceed the limits of any permission of his or the limits of the public's right of access, and
(b) may result—
(i) in serious disruption to the life of the community, or
(ii) where the land, or a building or monument on it, is of historical, architectural, archaeological or scientific import-ance, in significant damage to the land, building or monument,
he may apply to the council of the district for an order prohibiting for a specified period the holding of all trespassory assemblies in the district or a part of it, as specified.
(2) On receiving such an application, a council may—
(a) in England and Wales, with the consent of the Secretary of State make an order either in the terms of the application or with such modifications as may be approved by the Secretary of State; or
(b) in Scotland, make an order in the terms of the application.
(3) Subsection (1) does not apply in the City of London or the metro-politan police district.
(4) If at any time the Commissioner of Police for the City of London or the Commissioner of Police of the Metropolis reasonably believes that an assembly is intended to be held at a place on land to which the public has no right of access or only a limited right of access in his police area and that the assembly—
(a) is likely to be held without the permission of the occupier of the land or to conduct itself in such a way as to exceed the limits of any permission of his or the limits of the public's right of access, and
(b) may result—
(i) in serious disruption to the life of the community, or
(ii) where the land, or a building or monument on it, is of historical, architectural, archaeological or scientific import-ance, in significant damage to the land, building or monument,
he may with the consent of the Secretary of State make an order pro-hibiting for a specified period the holding of all trespassory assemblies in the area or a part of it, as specified.
(5) An order prohibiting the holding of trespassory assemblies oper-ates to prohibit any assembly which—
(a) is held on land to which the public has no right of access or only a limited right of access, and
(b) takes place in the prohibited circumstances, that is to say, without the permission of the occupier of the land or so as to exceed the limits of any permission of his or the limits of the public's right of access.

(6) No order under this section shall prohibit the holding of assemblies for a period exceeding 4 days or in an area exceeding an area represented by a circle with a radius of 5 miles from a specified centre.

(7) An order made under this section may be revoked or varied by a subsequent order made in the same way, that is, in accordance with subsection (1) and (2) or subsection (4), as the case may be.

(8) Any order under this section shall, if not made in writing, be recorded in writing as soon as practicable after being made.

(9) In this section and sections 14B and 14C—

"assembly" means an assembly of 20 or more persons;

"land", means land in the open air;

"limited", in relation to a right of access by the public to land, means that their use of it is restricted to use for a particular purpose (as in the case of a highway or road) or is subject to other restrictions;

"occupier" means—

(a) in England and Wales, the person entitled to possession of the land by virtue of an estate or interest held by him; or

(b) in Scotland, the person lawfully entitled to natural possession of the land,

and in subsections (1) and (4) includes the person reasonably believed by the authority applying for or making the order to be the occupier;

"public" includes a section of the public; and

"specified" means specified in an order under this section.

(10) In relation to Scotland, the references in subsection (1) above to a district and to the council of the district shall be construed—

(a) as respects applications before 1st April 1996, as references to the area of a regional or islands authority and to the authority in question; and

(b) as respects applications on and after that date, as references to a local government area and to the council for that area.

(11) In relation to Wales, the references in subsection (1) above to a district and to the council of the district shall be construed, as respects applications on and after 1st April 1996, as references to a county or county borough and to the council for that county or county borough.

Offences in connection with trespassory assemblies and arrest therefor

14B.—(1) A person who organises an assembly the holding of which he knows is prohibited by an order under section 14A is guilty of an offence.

(2) A person who takes part in an assembly which he knows is prohibited by an order under section 14A is guilty of an offence.

(3) In England and Wales, a person who incites another to commit an offence under subsection (2) is guilty of an offence.

(4) A constable in uniform may arrest without a warrant anyone he reasonably suspects to be committing an offence under this section.

(5) A person guilty of an offence under subsection (1) is liable on summary conviction to imprisonment for a term not exceeding 3 months or a fine not exceeding level 4 on the standard scale or both.

(6) A person guilty of an offence under subsection (2) is liable on summary conviction to a fine not exceeding level 3 on the standard scale.

(7) A person guilty of an offence under subsection (3) is liable on summary conviction to imprisonment for a term not exceeding 3 months or a fine not exceeding level 4 on the standard scale or both, notwithstanding section 45(3) of the Magistrates' Courts Act 1980.

(8) Subsection (3) above is without prejudice to the application of any principle of Scots Law as respects art and part guilt to such incitement as is mentioned in that subsection.".

DEFINITIONS

"assembly": subs. (9).
"City of London": Public Order Act 1986, s.16.
"land": subs. (9).
"limited": subs. (9).
"occupier": subs. (9).
"public": subs. (9).
"specified": subs. (9).

GENERAL NOTE

This section amends the Public Order Act 1986 by adding to it two new sections, ss.14A and 14B, which include new provisions in respect of *trespassory assemblies*. The section is similar to s.13 of the Public Order Act 1986 which empowers the prohibiting of public processions and created offences connected therewith (see Standing Committee B, col. 647). This section is designed to prevent such activities as mass gatherings at Stonehenge to observe the midsummer solstice.

Note that the offences created by the sections are not the holding of a trespassory assembly as such, but offences relating to trespassory assemblies which have been prohibited by order of the relevant local authority. See new s.14B, below.

New s.14A of the Public Order Act 1986

This section provides for the prohibition of *trespassory assemblies*. The concept of a trespassory assembly is new. The phrase is not specifically defined by this or any other section but, its meaning is clear from subss. (1)(a) and (5). It is an *assembly* ("of 20 or more persons": subs. (9)) held on land to which the public has no or only limited right of access. For the section to apply, the assembly must be:

(1) held on *land in the open air* (subs. (9)); not partly in the open air, see General Note to s.68, *ante*; and

(2) *trespassory*, that is, it must take place without the consent of the occupier of the land (*i.e.*, the person who is entitled to possession of the land by virtue of an estate or interest held by him); or, it must conduct itself in such a way that it exceeds any permission that the occupier may have given. If there is a limited right of public access to such land the assembly must conduct itself in a way beyond those limits.

If a trespassory assembly is likely to take place which may result in either a serious disruption to the life of the community or the likelihood of damage to the land on which the assembly is to be held (*note*: the land on which the assembly is to be held, not *e.g.* the field next to it), or a building or monument on that land, any of which is of significant historical, archaeological, architectural or scientific interest, then the chief officer of police may apply to the council of the district for an order prohibiting the holding of the assembly. The chief officer may delegate his power to apply for such an order to an assistant or a deputy chief constable (Public Order Act 1986 (c. 64), s.15, as amended by Sched. 10, *post*).

If the order is granted (subs. (2)) there will be limits as to time and geographical area (subs. (6)). For London, see subss. (3) and (4).

New s.14B of the Public Order Act 1986

This section creates summary offences, arrestable without warrant, for breaches of an order under s.14A: organising a prohibited assembly (subs. (1)); taking part in such an assembly (subs. (2)); inciting another to organise or take part in such an assembly (subs. (3)).

These sections, while comparable with s.13 of the Public Order Act 1986, may be contrasted with s.14 which deals with *public assemblies* "an assembly of 20 or more persons in a public place which is wholly or partly open to the air": s.16 of the Public Order Act 1986. The essential difference between the two is that a public assembly is lawful although failure to observe conditions imposed under the section may be a criminal offence, whereas a trespassory assembly is unlawful although it will not become criminal until there is an order prohibiting it.

Scottish perspective

The definition of "limited right of access" given in the new s.14A(9) is probably wide enough to encompass the traditional Scottish common law provision regulating access to private land.

The saving provision in the new s.14B(8) of the Scots common law of art and part guilt is probably superfluous.

Trespassory assemblies: power to stop persons from proceeding

71. After the section 14B inserted by section 70 in the Public Order Act 1986 there shall be inserted the following section—

"Stopping persons from proceeding to trespassory assemblies

14C.—(1) If a constable in uniform reasonably believes that a person is on his way to an assembly within the area to which an order under section 14A applies which the constable reasonably believes is likely to be an assembly which is prohibited by that order, he may, subject to subsection (2) below—

(a) stop that person, and

(b) direct him not to proceed in the direction of the assembly.

(2) The power conferred by subsection (1) may only be exercised within the area to which the order applies.

(3) A person who fails to comply with a direction under subsection (1) which he knows has been given to him is guilty of an offence.

(4) A constable in uniform may arrest without a warrant anyone he reasonably suspects to be committing an offence under this section.

(5) A person guilty of an offence under subsection (3) is liable on summary conviction to a fine not exceeding level 3 on the standard scale.".

DEFINITIONS
   "assembly": s.14A of the Public Order Act 1986 (inserted by s.70 of this Act, see *ante.*)

GENERAL NOTE
   This section inserts a new section, s.14C, into the Public Order Act 1986 and provides a police power to direct persons reasonably believed to be going to a trespassory assembly not to proceed. It is similar to s.65, *ante*, which confers a similar power in respect of persons going to "raves". See the General Note to s.65 for further comment.

Squatters

Violent entry to premises: special position of displaced residential occupiers and intending occupiers

72.—(1) Section 6 of the Criminal Law Act 1977 (which penalises violence by a person for securing entry into premises where a person on the premises is opposed and is known to be opposed to entry) shall be amended as follows.

(2) After subsection (1), there shall be inserted the following subsection—

"(1A) Subsection (1) above does not apply to a person who is a displaced residential occupier or a protected intending occupier of the premises in question or who is acting on behalf of such an occupier; and if the accused adduces sufficient evidence that he was, or was acting on behalf of, such an occupier he shall be presumed to be, or to be acting on behalf of, such an occupier unless the contrary is proved by the prosecution.".

(3) In subsection (2), at the beginning, there shall be inserted the words "Subject to subsection (1A) above,".

(4) Subsection (3) (which is superseded by the provision made by subsection (2) above) shall be omitted.

(5) In subsection (7), at the end, there shall be inserted the words "and section 12A below contains provisions which apply for determining when any person is to be regarded for the purposes of this Part of this Act as a protected intending occupier of any premises or of any access to any premises.".

DEFINITIONS
    "displaced residential occupier": ss.12(3)–(5) of the Criminal Law Act 1977.
    "protected intending occupier": s.12A of the Criminal Law Act 1977, as inserted by s.74 of this Act.

GENERAL NOTE
    This section amends s.6 of the Criminal Law Act 1977 by extending the "self-help" defences provided by that section to "protected intending occupiers".
    Section 6(1) of the Criminal Law Act 1977 made it a summary offence for a person without lawful authority to use or threaten violence for the purpose of securing entry to premises on which, to his knowledge, there was someone present. By s.6(2) the section applied to persons with any interest in or right to possession or occupation of the premises. Section 6(3), however, provided a defence for a *displaced residential occupier* (as defined by s.12 of the Criminal Law Act 1977 see below) or person acting on his behalf, the effect of which was that such persons were entitled to use or threaten to use violence to gain entry to such premises.
    The effect of the amendments made by this section is that the "self-help defence" is now extended to *protected intending occupiers*, as defined by a new s.12A (for which see *post*). It may be *noted* that the definition refers to *individuals* not persons (in contrast to the definition of displaced residential occupiers): for comment, see note to s.74, *post*. Persons acting *on behalf of* such occupiers, if they have evidence to show that that is what they are, will be presumed to be such unless the contrary is proved.
    However, such occupiers, whether existing or intending, are not given *carte blanche* to use unlimited force. The force used must be "reasonable". The use of excessive force will amount to the commission of a criminal offence.
    For a remedy under the criminal law alternative to the use of force (except by the police), see the new s.7 of the Criminal Law Act 1977, as substituted by s.73, *post*.
    For a detailed commentary on s.6, of the Criminal Law Act 1977, apart from the amendments made by this section, see the Note by Prof. Edward Griew in *The Criminal Law Act 1977* (1978), Sweet & Maxwell.
    Displaced residential occupier: s.12(3)–(5) of the Criminal Law Act 1977 provides:
    "(3) Subject to subsection (4) below, any person who was occupying any premises as a residence immediately before being excluded from occupation by anyone who entered those premises, or any access to those premises, as a trespasser is a displaced residential occupier of the premises for the purposes of this Part of this Act so long as he continues to be excluded from occupation of the premises by the original trespasser or by any subsequent trespasser.
    (4) A person who was himself occupying the premises in question as a trespasser immediately before being excluded from occupation shall not by virtue of subsection (3) above be a displaced residential occupier of the premises for the purposes of this Part of this Act.
    (5) A person who by virtue of subsection (3) above is a displaced residential occupier of any premises shall be regarded for the purposes of this Part of this Act as a displaced residential occupier also of any access of those premises."

Adverse occupation of residential premises

73. For section 7 of the Criminal Law Act 1977 (trespassers failing to leave premises after being requested to do so by specified persons to be guilty of an offence) there shall be substituted the following section—

"Adverse occupation of residential premises
    7.—(1) Subject to the following provisions of this section and to section 12A(9) below, any person who is on any premises as a trespasser after having entered as such is guilty of an offence if he fails to leave those premises on being required to do so by or on behalf of—
    (a) a displaced residential occupier of the premises; or
    (b) an individual who is a protected intending occupier of the premises.
    (2) In any proceedings for an offence under this section it shall be a defence for the accused to prove that he believed that the person requiring him to leave the premises was not a displaced residential occupier or protected intending occupier of the premises or a person acting on behalf of a displaced residential occupier or protected intending occupier.

(3) In any proceedings for an offence under this section it shall be a defence for the accused to prove—
  (a) that the premises in question are or form part of premises used mainly for non-residential purposes; and
  (b) that he was not on any part of the premises used wholly or mainly for residential purposes.

(4) Any reference in the preceding provisions of this section to any premises includes a reference to any access to them, whether or not any such access itself constitutes premises, within the meaning of this Part of this Act.

(5) A person guilty of an offence under this section shall be liable on summary conviction to imprisonment for a term not exceeding six months or to a fine not exceeding level 5 on the standard scale or to both.

(6) A constable in uniform may arrest without warrant anyone who is, or whom he, with reasonable cause, suspects to be, guilty of an offence under this section.

(7) Section 12 below contains provisions which apply for determining when any person is to be regarded for the purposes of this Part of this Act as a displaced residential occupier of any premises or of any access to any premises and section 12A below contains provisions which apply for determining when any person is to be regarded for the purposes of this Part of this Act as a protected intending occupier of any premises or of any access to any premises.".

DEFINITIONS
  "protected intending occupier": s.12A of the Criminal Law Act 1977, as inserted by s.74 of this Act.

GENERAL NOTE
  This section, which, like s.72, was introduced at Commons Committee stage, replaces s.7 of the Criminal Law Act 1977 with a new s.7. The major difference between the old and new sections is that the definition of *protected intending occupier* is expanded and shifted to a new s.12A of the 1977 Act, see s.74, *post.*
  Subsection (1) of new s.7 follows (in the main) the wording of old s.7 and makes it a summary offence for a trespasser to fail to leave premises, having been required to do so by a displaced residential occupier or a protected intending occupier. The premises in question must be wholly or partly residential (subs. (3) re-enacting old subs. (7)). *Premises* includes *access* to them (subs. (4) replacing old subs. (9)). For the definition of both words, see below.
  The section applies to trespassers who have entered the premises unlawfully (not *e.g.* to tenants who have outstayed their tenancy). There is no requirement that the trespasser be given a reasonable time within which to leave. Where a person is charged with an offence under subs. (1) there is a defence that the individual requiring him to leave was not in fact a protected intending occupier, see s.12A(9) (s.74), *post*). (There is no similar defence under s.12 where the individual concerned is a displaced residential occupier). Where the section provides the accused with a defence if some matter is proved (subss. (2) and (3)) the burden of proof is on the defence and the standard of proof is on the balance of probabilities: see the General Note to s.61, *ante.*
  The power of arrest without warrant given by subs. (6) (originally subs. (10)) is supplemented by powers of arrest and search under s.11 of the Criminal Law Act 1977.
  False in a material particular: a statement may be false by omission, even if literally true (*R. v. Lord Kylsant* [1932] 1 K.B. 442). As to *material particular* in the Theft Act 1968 (c. 60), s.17(1) (a), see *R. v. Mallett* [1978] C.L.Y. 507.
  For a fuller consideration of the original s.7, which should be read in the light of the changes made by this section, see Prof. Edw. Griew's commentary in *The Criminal Law Act 1977* (1978), Sweet & Maxwell. There has been very little authority on s.7 since it was enacted. However, see *R. v. Forest Justices, ex p. Hartman* [1992] C.L.Y. 1130 (cited in the General Note to the next section).
  As to the phrase, *on behalf of,* see the General Note to the previous section.
  Access, Premises: s.12(1) of the Criminal Law Act 1977 provides:
  "**12.**—(1) In this Part of this Act—
    (*a*) "premises" means any building, any part of a building under separate occupation, any land ancillary to a building, the site comprising any building or buildings together with

any land ancillary thereto, and (for the purposes only of sections 10 and 11 above) any other place; and

(b) "access" means, in relation to any premises, any part of any site or building within which those premises are situated which constitutes an ordinary means of access to those premises (whether or not that is its sole or primary use)."

Protected intending occupiers: supplementary provisions

74. After section 12 of the Criminal Law Act 1977 there shall be inserted the following section—

"Protected intending occupiers: supplementary provisions

"**12A.**—(1) For the purposes of this Part of this Act an individual is a protected intending occupier of any premises at any time if at that time he falls within subsection (2), (4) or (6) below.

(2) An individual is a protected intending occupier of any premises if—

(a) he has in those premises a freehold interest or a leasehold interest with not less than two years still to run;

(b) he requires the premises for his own occupation as a residence;

(c) he is excluded from occupation of the premises by a person who entered them, or any access to them, as a trespasser; and

(d) he or a person acting on his behalf holds a written statement—

(i) which specifies his interest in the premises;

(ii) which states that he requires the premises for occupation as a residence for himself; and

(iii) with respect to which the requirements in subsection (3) below are fulfilled.

(3) The requirements referred to in subsection (2)(d)(iii) above are—

(a) that the statement is signed by the person whose interest is specified in it in the presence of a justice of the peace or commissioner for oaths; and

(b) that the justice of the peace or commissioner for oaths has subscribed his name as a witness to the signature.

(4) An individual is also a protected intending occupier of any premises if—

(a) he has a tenancy of those premises (other than a tenancy falling within subsection (2)(a) above or (6)(a) below) or a licence to occupy those premises granted by a person with a freehold interest or a leasehold interest with not less than two years still to run in the premises;

(b) he requires the premises for his own occupation as a residence;

(c) he is excluded from occupation of the premises by a person who entered them, or any access to them, as a trespasser; and

(d) he or a person acting on his behalf holds a written statement—

(i) which states that he has been granted a tenancy of those premises or a licence to occupy those premises;

(ii) which specifies the interest in the premises of the person who granted that tenancy or licence to occupy ("the landlord");

(iii) which states that he requires the premises for occupation as a residence for himself; and

(iv) with respect to which the requirements in subsection (5) below are fulfilled.

(5) The requirements referred to in subsection (4)(d)(iv) above are—

(a) that the statement is signed by the landlord and by the tenant or licensee in the presence of a justice of the peace or commissioner for oaths;

(b) that the justice of the peace or commissioner for oaths has sub-scribed his name as a witness to the signatures.

(6) An individual is also a protected intending occupier of any premises if—

(a) he has a tenancy of those premises (other than a tenancy falling within subsection (2)(a) or (4)(a) above) or a licence to occupy those premises granted by an authority to which this subsection applies;

(b) he requires the premises for his own occupation as a residence;

(c) he is excluded from occupation of the premises by a person who entered the premises, or any access to them, as a trespasser; and

(d) there has been issued to him by or on behalf of the authority referred to in paragraph (a) above a certificate stating that—

(i) he has been granted a tenancy of those premises or a licence to occupy those premises as a residence by the authority; and

(ii) the authority which granted that tenancy or licence to occupy is one to which this subsection applies, being of a description specified in the certificate.

(7) Subsection (6) above applies to the following authorities—

(a) any body mentioned in section 14 of the Rent Act 1977 (land-lord's interest belonging to local authority etc.);

(b) the Housing Corporation;

(c) Housing for Wales; and

(d) a registered housing association within the meaning of the Housing Associations Act 1985.

(8) A person is guilty of an offence if he makes a statement for the purposes of subsection (2)(d) or (4)(d) above which he knows to be false in a material particular or if he recklessly makes such a statement which is false in a material particular.

(9) In any proceedings for an offence under section 7 of this Act where the accused was requested to leave the premises by a person claiming to be or to act on behalf of a protected intending occupier of the premises—

(a) it shall be a defence for the accused to prove that, although asked to do so by the accused at the time the accused was requested to leave, that person failed at that time to produce to the accused such a statement as is referred to in subsection (2)(d) or (4)(d) above or such a certificate as is referred to in subsection (6)(d) above; and

(b) any document purporting to be a certificate under subsection (6)(d) above shall be received in evidence and, unless the contrary is proved, shall be deemed to have been issued by or on behalf of the authority stated in the certificate.

(10) A person guilty of an offence under subsection (8) above shall be liable on summary conviction to imprisonment for a term not exceeding six months or to a fine not exceeding level 5 on the standard scale or to both.

(11) A person who is a protected intending occupier of any premises shall be regarded for the purposes of this Part of this Act as a protected intending occupier also of any access to those premises.".

DEFINITIONS

"protected intending occupier": s.12A(2)–(7) of the Criminal Law Act 1977, as inserted by this section.

GENERAL NOTE

This section inserts a new s.12A into the Criminal Law Act 1977 and defines who is a protected intending occupier of premises for the purposes of that Act.

The definition is wider than that contained in the old s.7(2)–(5) of the Criminal Law Act 1977. It now applies to an individual who requires the premises concerned as a residence and who is excluded from those premises (or from access thereto (subs. (11)) by a person who has entered the premises (or any access thereto) as a trespasser. *N.B.* that this definition refers to an individual as opposed to a person: *Halsbury's Statutes*, 4th edition in the Note to the original s.7 suggests that "the word [individual] is used instead of the word "person" in order, presumably, to exclude bodies of persons corporate or incorporate": p. 706). The definition applies if the individual falls into any of the three following categories.

(1) The individual may have a freehold interest or a leasehold interest with not less than two years still to run. The original legislation required that the leasehold interest should have at least 21 years still to run. It also required that the interest, whether freehold or leasehold, should have been acquired for money or moneys' worth. So the protection of the Act now extends to individuals who have acquired their interest by *e.g.* will or gift. The individual (or someone acting on his behalf: see General Note to s.73, *ante*) must hold a written statement to that effect which he has signed in the presence of, and which has been witnessed by, a justice of the peace or a commissioner for oaths (subss. (2) and (3)).

(2) Or the individual may be a private tenant (with a tenancy which may be less than two years) or a licensee with a licence granted by a freeholder or leaseholder (whose lease has more than two years to run). He must have a statement to that effect signed by himself and his landlord, signed and witnesses as in (1) above (subss. (4) and (5)). This provision is new and did not appear in s.7 of the Criminal Law Act 1977.

It is a summary offence knowingly or recklessly to make a statement which is false in a material particular (subs. (8)).

(3) Or the individual may be a tenant or licensee of a local authority, the Housing Corporation, Housing for Wales, or a registered housing association. He must have a certificate granted to him by the authority etc. concerned (subss. (6) and (7)).

The statement or certificate concerned must be produced on request by the intending protected occupier (or person acting on his behalf) and failure to do so is a defence for a person charged under s.7(1) with failing to leave the premises (subs. (9)(a)). In *R. v. Forest Justices, ex p. Hartman* [1992] C.L.Y. 1130 it was held that the whole of a certificate need not be shown to the person requesting it so long as that person was able to read those matters required to be certified in it. A document containing such a statement or certificate is admissible as evidence (subs. (9)(b)).

In each of the above cases it is necessary that the intended occupier requires the premises for his own occupation as a residence. This requirement applied under s.7(2), but not s.7(4) of the Criminal Law Act 1977, see *R. v. Forest Justices, ex p. Hartman, ante*.

Interim possession orders: false or misleading statements

75.—(1) A person commits an offence if, for the purpose of obtaining an interim possession order, he—

(a) makes a statement which he knows to be false or misleading in a material particular; or

(b) recklessly makes a statement which is false or misleading in a material particular.

(2) A person commits an offence if, for the purpose of resisting the making of an interim possession order, he—

(a) makes a statement which he knows to be false or misleading in a material particular; or

(b) recklessly makes a statement which is false or misleading in a material particular.

(3) A person guilty of an offence under this section shall be liable—

(a) on conviction on indictment, to imprisonment for a term not exceeding two years or a fine or both;

(b) on summary conviction, to imprisonment for a term not exceeding six months or a fine not exceeding the statutory maximum or both.

(4) In this section—

"interim possession order" means an interim possession order (so entitled) made under rules of court for the bringing of summary proceedings for possession of premises which are occupied by trespassers;

"premises" has the same meaning as in Part II of the Criminal Law Act
1977 (offences relating to entering and remaining on property); and
"statement", in relation to an interim possession order, means any statement, in writing or oral and whether as to fact or belief, made in or
for the purposes of the proceedings.

DEFINITIONS
"interim possession order": subs. (4).
"premises": subs. (4).
"statement": subs. (4).

GENERAL NOTE
A new procedure for evicting unauthorised occupants of premises (squatters) will be introduced by an amendment to the Rules of the Supreme Court. The new procedure will provide
that a person entitled to immediate possession of a building or part of a building may apply to a
county court for an interim possession order provided notice of an intention to commence proceedings has been given to the alleged squatter. The applicant will be required to attend before
the judge (a circuit judge) who will decide whether to make an order. The occupier will not be
given notice of the hearing and will have no opportunity to set out a defence at this stage. Before
the judge can make an interim possession order, he must be satisfied that the applicant has
complied with the requirements of the procedure and has a strong case for possession based on
the civil standard of proof. The judge may require undertakings to be given to protect the occupier in the event that the interim order is set aside. If the judge is not satisfied, the application will
be adjourned to a date when both parties can be present. Where this happens, the existing summary procedure will apply. If an interim possession order is made, the order will require the
alleged squatter to leave the premises within 24 hours of service of the order. At the same time
the judge will fix a return day for confirmation of the order in open court. For the effect of failure
to obey an order for interim possession order, see s.76, *post.* This summary of the procedure has
been taken from the Lord Chancellor's Consultation Paper, published March 1994.
   This section creates offences of knowingly or recklessly making a statement false or misleading in a material particular so as to obtain or resist the making of an interim possession order
(subss. (1) and (2)). The offence is triable summarily or on indictment (subss. (2) and (3)).

Subs. (1)
   False or misleading in a material particular: see the General Note to s.73, *ante.*

Subs. (3)
   Premises is defined by the Criminal Law Act 1977 Pt. II. See the General Note to s.73, *ante.*

Interim possession orders: trespassing during currency of order

76.—(1) This section applies where an interim possession order has been
made in respect of any premises and served in accordance with rules of court;
and references to "the order" and "the premises" shall be construed
accordingly.
   (2) Subject to subsection (3), a person who is present on the premises as a
trespasser at any time during the currency of the order commits an offence.
   (3) No offence under subsection (2) is committed by a person if—
   (a) he leaves the premises within 24 hours of the time of service of the
       order and does not return; or
   (b) a copy of the order was not fixed to the premises in accordance with
       rules of court.
   (4) A person who was in occupation of the premises at the time of service
of the order but leaves them commits an offence if he re-enters the premises
as a trespasser or attempts to do so after the expiry of the order but within the
period of one year beginning with the day on which it was served.
   (5) A person guilty of an offence under this section shall be liable on summary conviction to imprisonment for a term not exceeding six months or a
fine not exceeding level 5 on the standard scale or both.
   (6) A person who is in occupation of the premises at the time of service of
the order shall be treated for the purposes of this section as being present as a
trespasser.

(7) A constable in uniform may arrest without a warrant anyone who is, or whom he reasonably suspects to be, guilty of an offence under this section.

(8) In this section—

"interim possession order" has the same meaning as in section 75 above and "rules of court" is to be construed accordingly; and

"premises" has the same meaning as in that section, that is to say, the same meaning as in Part II of the Criminal Law Act 1977 (offences relating to entering and remaining on property).

DEFINITIONS

"interim possession order": subs. (8), s.75(4).
"order": subs. (1).
"premises": subs. (8).
"rules of court": subs. (8).

GENERAL NOTE

This section provides that where an interim possession order has been made in respect of any premises and served in accordance with rules of court (subs. (1)) any person who is present on the premises as a trespasser at any time during the currency of the order commits an offence (subs. (2)). But where the person leaves the premises within 24 hours of the time of service of the order (and does not return) or a copy of the order is not fixed to the premises in accordance with rules of the court no offence is committed (subs. (3)). It is also an offence if a person who was on the premises when the order was served and who has left then re-enters or attempts to do so as a trespasser after the expiry of the order but within one year of the date of service of the order (subs. (4)). Both offences are triable summarily and punishable by imprisonment or fine (subs. (5)). *Note* that a person who is in occupation of the premises at the time of service of the order shall be treated for the purposes of the section as a trespasser (subs. (6)): such a person may not be the person who was on the premises at the time when the interim possession order was applied for. It gives a constable in uniform the power to arrest without warrant a person whom he reasonably suspects to have committed this offence (subs. (7)). In order to effect an arrest under this section the police power to enter premises has been extended: Sched. 10, para. 53 *post*, amending s.17 of the Police and Criminal Evidence Act 1984.

As to interim possession orders, see the General Note to s.75, *ante*.

Powers to remove unauthorised campers

Power of local authority to direct unauthorised campers to leave land

77.—(1) If it appears to a local authority that persons are for the time being residing in a vehicle or vehicles within that authority's area—

(a) on any land forming part of a highway;

(b) on any other unoccupied land; or

(c) on any occupied land without the consent of the occupier,

the authority may give a direction that those persons and any others with them are to leave the land and remove the vehicle or vehicles and any other property they have with them on the land.

(2) Notice of a direction under subsection (1) must be served on the persons to whom the direction applies, but it shall be sufficient for this purpose for the direction to specify the land and (except where the direction applies to only one person) to be addressed to all occupants of the vehicles on the land, without naming them.

(3) If a person knowing that a direction under subsection (1) above has been given which applies to him—

(a) fails, as soon as practicable, to leave the land or remove from the land any vehicle or other property which is the subject of the direction, or

(b) having removed any such vehicle or property again enters the land with a vehicle within the period of three months beginning with the day on which the direction was given,

he commits an offence and is liable on summary conviction to a fine not exceeding level 3 on the standard scale.

(4) A direction under subsection (1) operates to require persons who re-enter the land within the said period with vehicles or other property to leave and remove the vehicles or other property as it operates in relation to the persons and vehicles or other property on the land when the direction was given.

(5) In proceedings for an offence under this section it is a defence for the accused to show that his failure to leave or to remove the vehicle or other property as soon as practicable or his re-entry with a vehicle was due to illness, mechanical breakdown or other immediate emergency.

(6) In this section—

"land" means land in the open air;

"local authority" means—

(a) in Greater London, a London borough or the Common Council of the City of London;

(b) in England outside Greater London, a county council, a district council or the Council of the Isles of Scilly;

(c) in Wales, a county council or a county borough council;

"occupier" means the person entitled to possession of the land by virtue of an estate or interest held by him;

"vehicle" includes—

(a) any vehicle, whether or not it is in a fit state for use on roads, and includes any body, with or without wheels, appearing to have formed part of such a vehicle, and any load carried by, and anything attached to, such a vehicle; and

(b) a caravan as defined in section 29(1) of the Caravan Sites and Control of Development Act 1960;

and a person may be regarded for the purposes of this section as residing on any land notwithstanding that he has a home elsewhere.

(7) Until 1st April 1996, in this section "local authority" means, in Wales, a county council or a district council.

DEFINITIONS

"land": subs. (6).

"local authority": subss. (6) and (7).

"occupier": subs. (6).

"vehicle": subs. (6).

GENERAL NOTE

This section replaces s.10 of the Caravan Sites Act 1968 which, with the rest of Pt. II of that Act, is repealed by s.80, *post*. Section 10 applied only to unauthorised camping by gypsies in caravans in designated areas (as to which see the General Note to s.80, *post*). It made such camping a summary offence.

This section, unlike s.10 of the Caravan Sites Act 1968, provides a remedy under the criminal law against unauthorised camping by any person (not just gypsies) in any vehicle (not just caravans) in any place (not just designated areas). But *note* that it is not the unauthorised camping which is an offence (as it was under s.10) but the failure to obey a direction given under subs. (1), below.

Subsection (1) gives local authorities the power to direct that persons residing on land in a vehicle or vehicles remove themselves, their vehicles(s) and their other property from the land. The land may be occupied, unoccupied, or part of a highway.

The references in subs. (1)(b) and (c) to land which is "unoccupied/occupied" is repeated from s.10(1)(b) and (c) of the Caravan Sites Act 1968. In that Act it caused problems: "The meaning of 'occupied' land and the references to 'consent of the occupier' do create difficulties of interpretation": *per* Woolf J. in *Stubbings v. Beaconsfield Justices and Others* (1987) 54 P. & C.R. 327. It was held in that case that the definition of "occupier" in the Caravan Sites and Control of Development Act 1960 could not be imported into the Caravan Sites Act 1968 which did not define the word. In this Act "occupier" is defined; but when it comes to deciding what is "unoccupied" land the definition may not be of much help. In *Stebbings v. Beaconsfield JJ.*, above, the court referred with approval to what Lord Denning had said in *Newcastle City Council v. Royal Newcastle Hospital* [1959] C.L.Y. 2760: "Legal possession is not the same as occupation. Occupation is a matter of fact and only exists where there is sufficient measure of control; see *Pollock and Wright on Possession in the Common Law*, at pp. 12, 13. There must be something actually done on the land, not necessarily on the whole, but on part in respect of the whole. No-one would describe a bombed site or an empty unlocked house as "occupied" by anyone; but everyone would say that a farmer "occupies" the whole of his farm even though he does not set foot on the woodlands within it from one year's end to another" It would appear that common land etc. will be, for these purposes, unoccupied.

N.B. that the person must be *residing in* the vehicle: the section seems not to apply to persons who put up tents or "benders" (huts made of branches etc.) and reside in those. But such persons, by causing *damage* to the land, however slight, may come within s.61, *ante*. *Note also* that the land must be *in the open air*: the extension of this phrase to land "partly in the open air" in s.63 does not occur in this section. So it would seem that where the vehicle is driven into a barn or other building the section will not apply. But other legislation might apply, *e.g.* six or more vehicles, or violent, etc. behaviour towards the occupier (s.61, *ante*), entry secured by violence (Criminal Law Act 1977, s.6, as amended) refusing to leave the premises if residential (*ibid.*, s.7, as substituted by s.73, *ante*) failure to leave a building contrary to an interim possession order (s.76, *ante*).

As to powers to remove vehicles and persons unlawfully on land, see s.78, *post*.

By subs. (4), where a direction has been given, it applies to persons who re-enter the land within three months of the direction being given. The direction must specify the land concerned and be served on the persons concerned but need not name them unless there is only one person (subs. (2)). As to provisions for service, see s.79, *post*.

Subsection (3) makes failure to obey such a direction a summary offence, as is re-entry on the land within three months of the giving of a direction.

Subsection (5) (replacing s.10(2) of the Caravan Sites Act 1968) provides defences, namely that failure to obey the direction was as a result of illness, mechanical breakdown or other immediate emergency. (The burden of establishing these defences is on the defendant; the civil standard of proof will apply: see the General Note to s.61, *ante*). *Note* that *vehicle* includes vehicles not "in a fit state for use on roads" (subs. (6), not in the Caravan Sites Act 1968): there must be occasions when it is difficult to establish whether a vehicle which is not in a fit state has actually broken down mechanically (and an unfit vehicle which is not broken down mechanically may expose the driver to penalties for road traffic offences if it is taken off the land and on to the road).

Subsection (6). Vehicle includes *caravan*: see the General Note to s.61, *ante*.

Orders for removal of persons and their vehicles unlawfully on land

78.—(1) A magistrates' court may, on a complaint made by a local authority, if satisfied that persons and vehicles in which they are residing are present on land within that authority's area in contravention of a direction given under section 77, make an order requiring the removal of any vehicle or other property which is so present on the land and any person residing in it.

(2) An order under this section may authorise the local authority to take such steps as are reasonably necessary to ensure that the order is complied with and, in particular, may authorise the authority, by its officers and servants—

    (a) to enter upon the land specified in the order; and

    (b) to take, in relation to any vehicle or property to be removed in pursuance of the order, such steps for securing entry and rendering it suitable for removal as may be so specified.

(3) The local authority shall not enter upon any occupied land unless they have given to the owner and occupier at least 24 hours notice of their intention to do so, or unless after reasonable inquiries they are unable to ascertain their names and addresses.

(4) A person who wilfully obstructs any person in the exercise of any power conferred on him by an order under this section commits an offence and is liable on summary conviction to a fine not exceeding level 3 on the standard scale.

(5) Where a complaint is made under this section, a summons issued by the court requiring the person or persons to whom it is directed to appear before the court to answer to the complaint may be directed—

    (a) to the occupant of a particular vehicle on the land in question; or

(b) to all occupants of vehicles on the land in question, without naming him or them.

(6) Section 55(2) of the Magistrates' Courts Act 1980 (warrant for arrest of defendant failing to appear) does not apply to proceedings on a complaint made under this section.

(7) Section 77(6) of this Act applies also for the interpretation of this section.

DEFINITIONS

"land": subs. (7), s.77(6).
"local authority": subs. (7), s.77(6).
"occupier": subs. (7), s.77(6).
"vehicle": subs. (7), s.77(6).

GENERAL NOTE

This section provides for the enforcement of directions made under s.77, *ante*. It, together with s.79, *post*, replaces s.11 of the Caravan Sites Act 1960 (as substituted by the Local Government, Planning and Land Act 1980 (c. 65), s.174), which, with the rest of Pt. II of the Caravan Sites Act 1968, is repealed by s.80, *post*. Section 11 applied only to gypsies and their caravans and was only effective within designated areas (as to which, see the General Note to s.80, *post*).

Subsection (1) (replacing s.11(1) of the Caravan Sites Act 1968, which referred only to caravans) enacts that a local authority may *complain* to a magistrates' court that a direction made under s.77(1) has not been complied with. Where such a complaint is made, a *summons* issued by a magistrates' court may be directed to the occupant or occupants of the vehicles concerned without naming them. As to service of the order, see s.79, *post*. By subs. (1) the magistrates' court may then make an *order* that the direction be complied with. The order will authorise the local authority, *i.e.* its officers and servants, to take such steps as are reasonably necessary to enter the land and to remove vehicle(s) and other property. The order may specify what needs to be done to the vehicles etc. in order to make them suitable for removal (subs. (2): s.10(2) of the Caravan Sites Act 1968). Twenty four hours' notice should be given to the owner or occupier unless it is not practicable to ascertain their names and addresses (subs. (3): s.10(3) of the Caravan Sites Act 1968).

Wilful obstruction of such an order is a summary offence (*note* that this is in addition to the offence of failing to obey a direction under s.77) (subs. (4)). The parallel subsection (s.10(4) of the Caravan Sites Act 1968) referred to "international obstruction". "Wilful obstruction" is a return to the phraseology of the Police Act 1964 (c. 48), s.51(3) (wilful obstruction of a police officer in the execution of his duty). This phraseology must be deliberate; presumably, it signifies that the numerous cases on wilful obstruction of the police may apply to obstruction under this section (in so far as they can be applied to the officers or servants of a local authority). There must be an *obstruction i.e.* "the doing of any act which makes it more difficult for the police to carry out their duty": *Rice v. Connolly* [1966] C.L.Y. 9240 *per* Lord Parker C.J. This will include not only such acts of physical obstruction as forcible resistance or putting up a barrier or digging a trench but also acts designed to make it difficult or impossible for the person exercising the power to do so. Thus the main offenders in the "Peace Convoy" cases, below, refused to stop their vehicles when ordered by the police to do so. The obstruction must be *wilful*, and the intention to obstruct must be proved. Simply to intervene to assist the person obstructed is not an offence: *Willmott v. Atack* [1976] C.L.Y. 527. Refusing to help the person obstructed is not wilful obstruction, but in *Ricketts v. Cox* [1982] C.L.Y. 2359 abusive and obscene language and trying to walk away from the scene was held to be an "obstruction". In *R. v. Forde (James)* [1985] C.L.Y. 634, a case which concerned s.23(4) of the Misuse of Drugs Act 1971 ("internationally obstructs a person in the exercise of his powers...") in a definition which is clear and concise and so may be of assistance (although the word concerned is "intentional" not "wilful") the Court of Appeal held that the act of obstruction must have been intended to obstruct the exercise of powers and must actually have done so.

N.B. that passengers in the vehicle may be guilty of aiding and abetting the driver: *Smith v. Reynolds* [1986] C.L.Y. 659 (the "Peace Convoy" cases). But it must be proved that they must have encouraged, and have intended to do so, the main offender by remaining present.

Vehicle: see the General Note to s.61, *ante*.

Provisions as to directions under s.77 and orders under s.78

79.—(1) The following provisions apply in relation to the service of notice of a direction under section 77 and of a summons under section 78, referred to in those provisions as a "relevant document".

(2) Where it is impracticable to serve a relevant document on a person named in it, the document shall be treated as duly served on him if a copy of it is fixed in a prominent place to the vehicle concerned; and where a relevant document is directed to the unnamed occupants of vehicles, it shall be treated as duly served on those occupants if a copy of it is fixed in a prominent place to every vehicle on the land in question at the time when service is thus effected.

(3) A local authority shall take such steps as may be reasonably practicable to secure that a copy of any relevant document is displayed on the land in question (otherwise than by being fixed to a vehicle) in a manner designed to ensure that it is likely to be seen by any person camping on the land.

(4) Notice of any relevant document shall be given by the local authority to the owner of the land in question and to any occupier of that land unless, after reasonable inquiries, the authority is unable to ascertain the name and address of the owner or occupier; and the owner of any such land and any occupier of such land shall be entitled to appear and to be heard in the proceedings.

(5) Section 77(6) applies also for the interpretation of this section.

DEFINITIONS
 "land": subs. (5), s.77(6).
 "local authority": subs. (5) s.77(6).
 "occupier": subs. (5), s.77(6).
 "relevant document": subs. (1).
 "vehicle": subs. (5), s.77(6).

GENERAL NOTE
 This section provides for the service of documents under ss.77 and 78. It replaces s.10(7)–(9) of the Caravan Sites Act 1968 which referred only to summonses and caravans, reflecting the narrower application of that Act.
 Vehicle: see the General Note to s.61.

Repeal of certain provisions relating to gipsy sites

80.—(1) Part II of the Caravan Sites Act 1968 (duty of local authorities to provide sites for gipsies and control of unauthorised encampments) together with the definition in section 16 of that Act of "gipsies" is hereby repealed.

(2) In section 24 of the Caravan Sites and Control of Development Act 1960 (power to provide sites for caravans—
 (a) in subsection (2), after paragraph (b) there shall be inserted the following—
 ", or
  (c) to provide, in or in connection with sites for the accommodation of gipsies, working space and facilities for the carrying on of such activities as are normally carried on by them,"; and
 (b) in subsection (8), at the end, there shall be inserted the words "and "gipsies" means persons of nomadic habit of life, whatever their race or origin, but does not include members of an organised group of travelling showmen, or persons engaged in travelling circuses, travelling together as such.".

(3) The repeal by subsection (1) above of section 8 of the said Act of 1968 shall not affect the validity of directions given under subsection (3)(a) of that section; and in the case of directions under subsection (3)(c), the council may elect either to withdraw the application or request the Secretary of State to determine the application and if they so request the application shall be treated as referred to him under section 77 of the Town and Country Planning Act 1990.

(4) The repeal by subsection (1) above of the definition of "gipsies" in section 16 of the said Act of 1968 shall not affect the interpretation of that word in the definition of "protected site" in section 5(1) of the Mobile Homes Act 1983 or in any document embodying the terms of any planning permission granted under the Town and Country Planning Act 1990 before the commencement of this section.

(5) Section 70 of the Local Government, Planning and Land Act 1980 (power to pay grant to local authorities in respect of capital expenditure in providing gipsy caravan sites) is hereby repealed so far as it extends to England and Wales except for the purposes of applications for grant received by the Secretary of State before the commencement of this section.

DEFINITIONS

"gypsy": s.24(8) of the Caravan Sites Act 1968, as substituted by this section.

GENERAL NOTE

Subs. (1)

This subsection repeals Pt. II of the Caravan Sites Act 1968. Part II made it mandatory for local authorities to provide sites for gypsies (s.6), allocated the duty of providing sites to the county council and the duty of running them to district councils (s.7), made provision for the acquisition of land for such sites (s.8), empowered the Secretary of State to direct local authorities to provide sites (s.9), enacted that it was an offence for a gypsy to camp on an unauthorised site in a designated area (s.10, see further s.77, *ante*), enabled the local authority to make an order requiring the removal of any caravan stationed on that site and any person residing in it (s.11, see further s.78, *ante*), and empowered the Minister to make a certain area a designated area if it appeared to him that adequate provision had been made in that area for the accommodation of gypsies residing in or resorting to that area (s.12). For new provisions as to unauthorised camping and removal of vehicles unlawfully on land, see ss.72 and 78, *ante*. The remainder of Pt. II is not replaced.

Subs. (2)

By s.1(3) of the Caravan Sites and Control of Development Act 1960 "the expression 'caravan site' means land on which a caravan is stationed for the purposes of human habitation and land which is used in conjunction with land on which a caravan is so situated." Section 24(2) provides for local authorities to do anything which appears to them desirable in connection with such sites, and in particular (a) to acquire land which is in use as a caravan site, or (b) to provide for the use of those occupying caravan sites any services or facilities for their health or convenience. The effect of this subsection is to allow local authorities to provide working space and facilities for normal gypsy activities. The definition of *gypsy* in s.16 of the Caravan Sites Act 1968, repealed by subs. (1) of this section, is repeated in this subsection adding the definition to s.24(8) of the Caravan Sites and Control of Development Act 1960. The definition is "not confined to members of the Romany race" (*Halsbury's Statutes* 4th ed. p. 512), but the Court of Appeal has made it clear that the persons concerned must follow a nomadic way of life, but moving with a purpose in mind as necessary and characteristic of their lives: persons who moved from place to place as the fancy might take them and without any connection between the movement and their means of livelihood fell outside the statutory definition (*R. v. South Hams D.C. ex p. Gibb, The Times,* June 8, 1994).

Subs. (4)

Protected site: by the Mobile Homes Act 1983 (c. 34), s.5(10): " 'protected site' does not include any land occupied by a local authority as a caravan site providing accommodation for gypsies ... but, subject to that, has the same meaning as in Part I of the Caravan Sites Act 1968 (c. 52), s.1(1)". By the 1968 Act "... a protected site is any land in respect of which a site licence is required under Part I of the Caravan Sites and Control of Development Act 1960 or would be so required if para. 11 of Sched. 1 to that Act (exemption of land occupied by local authorities) were omitted, not being land in respect of which the relevant planning permission or site licence (a) is expressed to be granted for holiday use only; or (b) is otherwise so expressed or subject to such conditions that there are times of the year when no caravan may be situated on the land for human habitation."

PART VI

PREVENTION OF TERRORISM

Powers to stop and search vehicles, etc. and persons

81.—(1) In Part IV of the Prevention of Terrorism (Temporary Provisions) Act 1989 (powers of arrest, detention and control of entry) there shall be inserted, before section 14, the following section—

> **"Powers to stop and search vehicles etc. and persons**
>
> 13A.—(1) Where it appears to—
>
> (a) any officer of police of or above the rank of commander of the metropolitan police, as respects the metropolitan police area;
>
> (b) any officer of police of or above the rank of commander of the City of London police, as respects the City of London; or
>
> (c) any officer of police of or above the rank of assistant chief constable for any other police area,
>
> that it is expedient to do so in order to prevent acts of terrorism to which this section applies he may give an authorisation that the powers to stop and search vehicles and persons conferred by this section shall be exercisable at any place within his area or a specified locality in his area for a specified period not exceeding twenty eight days.
>
> (2) The acts of terrorism to which this section applies are—
>
> (a) acts of terrorism connected with the affairs of Northern Ireland; and
>
> (b) acts of terrorism of any other description except acts connected solely with the affairs of the United Kingdom or any part of the United Kingdom other than Northern Ireland.
>
> (3) This section confers on any constable in uniform power—
>
> (a) to stop any vehicle;
>
> (b) to search any vehicle, its driver or any passenger for articles of a kind which could be used for a purpose connected with the commission, preparation or instigation of acts of terrorism to which this section applies;
>
> (c) to stop any pedestrian and search any thing carried by him for articles of a kind which could be used for a purpose connected with the commission, preparation or instigation of acts of terrorism to which this section applies.
>
> (4) A constable may, in the exercise of those powers, stop any vehicle or person and make any search he thinks fit whether or not he has any grounds for suspecting that the vehicle or person is carrying articles of that kind.
>
> (5) This section applies (with the necessary modifications) to ships and aircraft as it applies to vehicles.
>
> (6) A person is guilty of an offence if he—
>
> (a) fails to stop or (as the case may be) to stop the vehicle when required to do so by a constable in the exercise of his powers under this section; or
>
> (b) wilfully obstructs a constable in the exercise of those powers.
>
> (7) A person guilty of an offence under subsection (6) above shall be liable on summary conviction to imprisonment for a term not exceeding six months or a fine not exceeding level 5 on the standard scale or both.
>
> (8) If it appears to a police officer of the rank specified in subsection (1)(a), (b) or (c) (as the case may be) that the exercise of the powers conferred by this section ought to continue beyond the period for which their exercise has been authorised under this section he may, from time to time, authorise the exercise of those powers for a further period, not exceeding twenty eight days.

(9) Where a vehicle is stopped by a constable under this section, the driver shall be entitled to obtain a written statement that the vehicle was stopped under the powers conferred by this section if he applies for such a statement not later than the end of the period of twelve months from the day on which the vehicle was stopped; and similarly as respects a pedestrian who is stopped under this section for a search of anything carried by him.

(10) In this section—

"authorise" and "authorisation" mean authorise or an authorisation in writing signed by the officer giving it; and

"specified" means specified in an authorisation under this section.

(11) Nothing in this section affects the exercise by constables of any power to stop vehicles for purposes other than those specified in subsection (1) above.".

(2) In consequence of the insertion in Part IV of the Prevention of Terrorism (Temporary Provisions) Act 1989 of section 13A, for the title to that Part, there shall be substituted the following title—

"POWERS OF ARREST, STOP AND SEARCH, DETENTION AND CONTROL
OF ENTRY".

(3) For the purposes of section 27 of the Prevention of Terrorism (Temporary Provisions) Act 1989 (temporary provisions), the provisions inserted in that Act by this section shall be treated, as from the time when this section comes into force, as having been continued in force by the order under subsection (6) of that section which has effect at that time.

DEFINITIONS

"acts of terrorism": s.13A of the Prevention of Terrorism (Temporary Provisions) Act 1989, as inserted by this section.

"authorise/authorisation": s.13A of the Prevention of Terrorism (Temporary Provisions) Act 1989, as inserted by this section.

"specified": s.13A of the Prevention of Terrorism (Temporary Provisions) Act 1989, as inserted by this section.

GENERAL NOTE

This section amends Pt. IV of the Prevention of Terrorism (Temporary Provisions) Act 1989, by inserting a new s.13A, to empower a police officer of at least the rank of Assistant Chief Constable (or equivalent) to authorise uniformed officers in his force to stop and search pedestrians and vehicles and their occupants for articles which could be used in connection with terrorism. This power may be exercised where it appears to the officer "expedient to do so in order to prevent acts of terrorism": subs. (1). The expression "acts of terrorism" is defined in subs. (2) as referring both to terrorism connected with Northern Ireland (which contains the real thrust of the section) and to international terrorism unconnected with any part of the U.K. except Northern Ireland. The reason for this definition is to limit the scope of the section to terrorism, experience of which leads to the conclusion that the powers are or might be needed (*Hansard*, H.L. Vol. 555, col. 1205). The authorisation must be for a specified period not exceeding 28 days: subs. (1). The power conferred by the section includes a power to stop pedestrians and search anything which they are carrying: subs. (3). The section also creates associated summary offences of failure to stop and wilful obstruction punishable by imprisonment of up to six months a fine or both: subss. (6) and (7).

These powers are aimed at detecting vehicle bombs and small devices carried by individual terrorists. They are based on powers already in existence in the Northern Ireland (Emergency Provisions) Act 1991. "Expedient" is not defined in the section. It may be contrasted with the concept of "reasonableness" in s.60, *ante*, which governs the authorisation of stop and search powers in anticipation of violence. Presumably the intention is to give the police a wider discretion in relation to terrorist offences. ("Expedient" appears earlier in s.4 of the Prevention of Terrorism (Temporary Provisions) Act 1989 which deals with the powers of the Home Secretary to make exclusion orders). The Shorter Oxford English Dictionary defines "expedient" as "advantageous; fit, proper or suitable to the circumstances of the case". This definition seems to fit what would appear to be the intention of the section *i.e.* that the police should use the powers when suitable in the circumstances in order to prevent terrorism. In England and Wales no prosecution for offences under s.13A may be brought without the consent of the D.P.P.: Sched. 10, para. 63, *post.* See Sched. 10, para 62, *post.*, as to the powers to take intimate and non-intimate samples.

By s.20(1) of the Prevention of Terrorism (Temporary Provisions) Act 1989, *aircraft* "includes hovercraft"; *ship* "includes every description of vehicle used in navigation"; *terrorism* "means the use of violence for political ends, and includes any use of violence for the purpose of putting the public or any section of the public in fear" (but see the definition of *acts of terrorism* in s.13A(2), above), and *vehicle* "includes a train and parts of a train".

Offences relating to terrorism

82.—(1) The Prevention of Terrorism (Temporary Provisions) Act 1989 shall be amended by the insertion, as Part IVA of that Act, of the following provisions—

"PART IVA

OFFENCES AGAINST PUBLIC SECURITY

Possession of articles for suspected terrorist purposes

16A.—(1) A person is guilty of an offence if he has any article in his possession in circumstances giving rise to a reasonable suspicion that the article is in his possession for a purpose connected with the commission, preparation or instigation of acts of terrorism to which this section applies.

(2) The acts of terrorism to which this section applies are—

(a) acts of terrorism connected with the affairs of Northern Ireland; and

(b) acts of terrorism of any other description except acts connected solely with the affairs of the United Kingdom or any part of the United Kingdom other than Northern Ireland.

(3) It is a defence for a person charged with an offence under this section to prove that at the time of the alleged offence the article in question was not in his possession for such a purpose as is mentioned in subsection (1) above.

(4) Where a person is charged with an offence under this section and it is proved that at the time of the alleged offence—

(a) he and that article were both present in any premises; or

(b) the article was in premises of which he was the occupier or which he habitually used otherwise than as a member of the public,

the court may accept the fact proved as sufficient evidence of his possessing that article at that time unless it is further proved that he did not at that time know of its presence in the premises in question, or, if he did know, that he had no control over it.

(5) A person guilty of an offence under this section is liable—

(a) on conviction on indictment, to imprisonment for a term not exceeding ten years or a fine or both;

(b) on summary conviction, to imprisonment for a term not exceeding six months or a fine not exceeding the statutory maximum or both.

(6) This section applies to vessels, aircraft and vehicles as it applies to premises.

Unlawful collection, etc. of information

16B.—(1) No person shall, without lawful authority or reasonable excuse (the proof of which lies on him)—

(a) collect or record any information which is of such a nature as is likely to be useful to terrorists in planning or carrying out any act of terrorism to which this section applies; or

(b) have in his possession any record or document containing any such information as is mentioned in paragraph (a) above.

(2) The acts of terrorism to which this section applies are—

(a) acts of terrorism connected with the affairs of Northern Ireland; and

(b) acts of terrorism of any other description except acts connected solely with the affairs of the United Kingdom or any part of the United Kingdom other than Northern Ireland.

(3) In subsection (1) above the reference to recording information includes a reference to recording it by means of photography or by any other means.

(4) Any person who contravenes this section is guilty of an offence and liable—

(a) on conviction on indictment, to imprisonment for a term not exceeding ten years or a fine or both;

(b) on summary conviction, to imprisonment for a term not exceeding six months or a fine not exceeding the statutory maximum or both.

(5) The court by or before which a person is convicted of an offence under this section may order the forfeiture of any record or document mentioned in subsection (1) above which is found in his possession.".

(2) For the purposes of section 27 of the Prevention of Terrorism (Temporary Provisions) Act 1989 (temporary provisions), the provisions constituting Part IVA of that Act inserted by this section shall be treated, as from the time when those provisions come into force, as having been continued in force by the order under subsection (6) of that section which has effect at that time.

(3) This section shall come into force at the end of the period of two months beginning with the date on which this Act is passed.

GENERAL NOTE

This section, by adding two new sections to the Act, ss.16A and 16B, creates two new offences under the Prevention of Terrorism (Temporary Provisions) Act 1989. The offence under s.16A involves possession of an article in circumstances giving rise to a reasonable suspicion that the possession is for a purpose connected with acts of terrorism. The offence under s.16B involves the collection, recording or possession of any information which is likely to be useful to terrorists in planning or carrying out any act of terrorism. (The expression "acts of terrorism" is defined in subs. (2) of each section: for a comment on the phraseology, see the General Note to s.81, *ante*). The sections are based on ss.30 and 31 of the Northern Ireland (Emergency Provisions) Act 1991. In England and Wales no prosecution for offences under ss.16A and 16B may be brought without the consent of the D.P.P.: Sched. 10, para. 63, post. Both offences are serious: if tried on indictment, they carry a maximum sentence of 10 years' imprisonment.

Section 16A is unusual in creating an offence based on "reasonable suspicion"; and then casting a burden on the defence of disproving that the defendant had the article for the purpose alleged. Thus, the prosecution have merely to prove that the defendant was in possession of the article in circumstances giving rise to a reasonable suspicion. If this is proved, the burden of proving that the article was not in his possession for a terrorist purpose switches to the defendant: subs. (3). Furthermore, evidence that the defendant and the article were both in premises of which he was the occupier or habitual user may be accepted by the court as sufficient evidence of his possession of the article, unless he proves that he did not know of its presence in the premises: subs. (4). The result is that the section (a) contains an offence provable by reasonable suspicion and (b) makes provision for the burden of proof to change on two occasions. Such a provision has been characterised as draconian. However, the explanation for this unusual offence is to be found in the unusual circumstances which have led to its enactment.

The offence under s.16(B) is committed by a person either collecting or recording information of such a nature as is likely to be useful to terrorists in planning or carrying out any act of terrorism or having in his possession any record or document containing any such information. This would include collecting such information as names, addresses and telephone numbers. However, the section does not limit the scope of the information. Any information useful to terrorists or of a nature likely to be of use to them comes within the section. It is a defence for the defendant to show that he has lawful authority or a reasonable excuse to collect or record the information or possess it. The burden of proving this defence is placed specifically on him. According to the usual principles he must establish the defence on the balance of probabilities. The reason for placing the burden on the defendant is that he is in the best position to provide an explanation. (The same justification is used in cases where a statute impliedly casts a burden on an accused: *R. v. Hunt (Richard)* [1987] C.L.Y. 796). Thus, if the defence is that the defendant is an investigative journalist, the defendant should without difficulty be able to show that he or she had the information for the purposes of journalism.

Premises by the Prevention of Terrorism (Temporary Provisions) Act 1989, "includes any place and in particular includes (a) any vehicle, vessel or aircraft; (b) any offshore installation as defined in s.1 of the Mineral Working (Offshore Installations) Act 1971 (as substituted by s.24 of the Oil and Gas Enterprise Act 1982); and (c) any tent or movable structure".

Vehicle is not defined in the main Act but is included within the definition of "ship" in s.20(1), see note to s.81, *ante*.

Investigations into activities and financial resources of terrorist organisations

83.—(1) In Schedule 7 to the Prevention of Terrorism (Temporary Provisions) Act 1989, in Part I (England, Wales and Northern Ireland)—
- (a) in paragraph 3 (orders for production of excluded or special procedure material)—
    - (i) in sub-paragraph (2) for the words from "he may make" to "shall" there shall be substituted the words "he may order a person who appears to him to have in his possession, custody or power any of the material to which the application relates, to—" and after the word "possession" where it subsequently appears in that sub-paragraph there shall be inserted in both places the words ", custody or power"; and
    - (ii) in sub-paragraph (5)(b)(ii), for the words from "in possession" to the end there shall be substituted the words "has the material in his possession, custody or power";
- (b) in paragraph 4(6) (order for production made to government department)—
    - (i) after the word "possession" where it first appears there shall be inserted the words ", custody or power"; and
    - (ii) for the words "be in possession of" there shall be substituted the words "have in his possession, custody or power"; and
- (c) in paragraph 8(1) (orders of Secretary of State authorising searches for certain investigations), at the end, there shall be inserted the words "or an offence under section 27 of the Northern Ireland (Emergency Provisions) Act 1991".

(2) In Schedule 7 to the Prevention of Terrorism (Temporary Provisions) Act 1989, in Part II (Scotland)—
- (a) in paragraph 12 (order for production of material—
    - (i) in sub-paragraph (2) for the words from "he may make" to "shall" there shall be substituted the words "he may order a person who appears to him to have in his possession, custody or power any of the material to which the application relates, to—" and after the word "possession" where it subsequently appears in that sub-paragraph there shall be inserted in both places the words ", custody or power";
    - (ii) in sub-paragraph (5)(b)(ii), for the words from "in possession" to the end there shall be substituted the words "has the material in his possession, custody or power"; and
- (b) in paragraph 13(5) (order for production made to government department)—

(i) after the word "possession" where it first appears there shall be inserted the words ", custody or power"; and

(ii) for the words "be in possession of" there shall be substituted the words "have in his possession, custody or power".

(3) In Schedule 5 to the Northern Ireland (Emergency Provisions) Act 1991, in paragraph 2 (investigative powers of authorised investigators), after sub-paragraph (1), there shall be inserted the following sub-paragraph—

"(1A) An authorised investigator may by notice in writing require any such person to furnish specified information relevant to the investigation within a specified time or such further time as the investigator may allow and in a specified manner or in such other manner as the investigator may allow.".

(4) For the purposes of section 27 of the Prevention of Terrorism (Temporary Provisions) Act 1989 (temporary provisions) the amendments made in that Act by subsections (1) and (2) above shall be treated, as from the time when those subsections come into force, as having been continued in force by the order under subsection (6) of that section which has effect at that time.

(5) For the purposes of section 69 of the Northern Ireland (Emergency Provisions) Act 1991 (temporary provisions) the amendments made in that Act by subsection (3) above shall be treated, as from the time when that subsection comes into force, as having been continued in force by the order under subsection (3) of that section which has effect at that time.

GENERAL NOTE

This section makes three amendments to legislation connected with the investigation of terrorism.

Subsections (1) and (2) amend Sched. 7 to the Prevention of Terrorism (Temporary Provisions) Act 1989 to enable the police to apply for a production order to require an individual to produce material which is in his possession, custody or power. As originally drafted the Schedule only permitted an order to relate to material in the possession of the person subject of the order. The effect of the amendment is to allow an order to be made where material is held on behalf of one person by another. Thus, a person will not be able to evade an order by moving material from his physical possession.

Subsection (1)(c) amends para. 8 of Sched. 7 to empower the Secretary of State to authorise search warrants and production orders in connection with the offence of directing a terrorist organisation under s.27 of the Northern Ireland (Emergency Provisions) Act 1991. The purpose of this amendment is to protect material from disclosure while investigations are still continuing.

Subsection (3) amends Sched. 5 to the 1991 Act to enable investigators appointed under s.57 of that Act to require answers in writing to questionnaires. Previously, the investigators, appointed to help investigate terrorist finances, could only require people to attend for interview. The amendment is intended to allow the investigators to operate more flexibly. Thus an interview may be quite unnecessary in the case of a person willing to give information or a person willing to do so if required.

Subs. (1)

Schedule 7, paras. 3 and 4, to the Prevention of Terrorism (Temporary Provisions) Act 1989, relate to orders by a judge for the production of excluded or special procedure material, including items subject to legal privilege, for the purposes of a terrorist investigation. Schedule 7 defines a *terrorist investigation* as "any investigation to which s.17(1) of this Act applies", and items subject to legal privilege, excluded material and special procedure material as having "the meanings given by ss.10 to 14 of the Police and Criminal Evidence Act 1984". Schedule 7 originally applied only to material as defined by the Schedule in the possession of a person. The changes made by the subsection extend this to possession, custody or control, none of which are defined. It is not immediately obvious what these words add, since a person is usually held to be in possession of an article if he is knowingly in control of it. Presumably, the object of the change is to put the matter beyond doubt.

Subs. (3)

Schedule 5 to the Northern Ireland (Temporary Provisions) Act 1991 defines authorised investigator as "a person authorised under s.57 of this Act to exercise the powers conferred by Sched. 5"; and the investigation (in relation to an authorised investigator) as "the investigation for the purpose of which those powers are exercisable by him".

Scottish perspective

Sections 81–83
These amendments to the Prevention of Terrorism (Temporary Provisions) Act 1989 are effective U.K.-wide. The new ss.13A(2), 16A(2) and 16B(2) make clear that the provision does not apply to acts of terrorism connected solely with Scotland, England and Wales. The new s.16A(2) places the burden of proving innocence on the person reasonably believed to be in possession of any article in circumstances giving rise to reasonable suspicion that the article could be used for terrorist purposes. Equally, s.16A(3) creates a rebuttable presumption that a person is in possession of an article if he is the occupier, habitual user of, or simply present in premises on which the article is found. Section 83(2) amends Pt. II of Sched. 7 to the 1989 Act to add "custody or power" to "possession", to enable orders for the production of materials to be made against anyone associated with potentially terrorist related material. These further extensions of police powers in relation to essentially Northern Ireland related terrorism may seem strangely timed.

PART VII

OBSCENITY AND PORNOGRAPHY AND VIDEOS

Obscene publications and indecent photographs of children

Indecent pseudo-photographs of children

84.—(1) The Protection of Children Act 1978 shall be amended as provided in subsections (2) and (3) below.

(2) In section 1 (which penalises the taking and distribution of indecent photographs of children and related acts)—

  (a) in paragraph (a) of subsection (1)—

      (i) after the word "taken" there shall be inserted the words "or to make", and the words following "child" shall be omitted;

      (ii) after the word "photograph" there shall be inserted the words "or pseudo-photograph";

  (b) in paragraphs (b), (c) and (d) of subsection (1), after the word "photographs" there shall be inserted the words "or pseudo-photographs";

  (c) in subsection (2), after the word "photograph" there shall be inserted the words "or pseudo-photograph"; and

  (d) in paragraphs (a) and (b) of subsection (4), after the word "photographs" there shall be inserted the words "or pseudo-photographs".

(3) In section 7 (interpretation)—

  (a) in subsection (3), at the end, there shall be inserted the words "and so as respects pseudo-photographs"; and

  (b) for subsection (4) there shall be substituted the following subsection—

    "(4) References to a photograph include—

      (a) the negative as well as the positive version; and

      (b) data stored on a computer disc or by other electronic means which is capable of conversion into a photograph.".

  (c) after subsection (5) there shall be inserted the following subsections—

    "(6) 'Child', subject to subsection (8), means a person under the age of 16.

    (7) 'Pseudo-photograph' means an image, whether made by computer-graphics or otherwise howsoever, which appears to be a photograph.

    (8) If the impression conveyed by a pseudo-photograph is that the person shown is a child, the pseudo-photograph shall be treated for all purposes of this Act as showing a child and so shall a pseudo-photograph where the predominant impression conveyed is that the person shown is a child notwithstanding that some of the physical characteristics shown are those of an adult.

(9) References to an indecent pseudo-photograph include—
(a) a copy of an indecent pseudo–photograph; and
(b) data stored on a computer disc or by other electronic means which is capable of conversion into a pseudo-photograph.".

(4) Section 160 of the Criminal Justice Act 1988 (which penalises the possession of indecent photographs of children) shall be amended as follows—
(a) in subsection (1), after the word "photograph" there shall be inserted the words "or pseudo-photograph" and the words from "(meaning" to "16)" shall be omitted; and
(b) in paragraphs (a), (b) and (c) of subsection (2), after the word "photograph" there shall be inserted the words "or pseudo-photograph"; and
(c) in subsection (5), the reference to the coming into force of that section shall be construed, for the purposes of the amendments made by this subsection, as a reference to the coming into force of this subsection.

(5) The Civic Government (Scotland) Act 1982 shall be amended as provided in subsections (6) and (7) below.

(6) In section 52 (which, for Scotland, penalises the taking and distribution of indecent photographs of children and related acts)—
(a) in paragraph (a) of subsection (1)—
(i) after the word "taken" there shall be inserted the words "or makes"; and
(ii) for the words from "of a" to the end there shall be substituted the words "or pseudo-photograph of a child";
(b) in paragraphs (b), (c) and (d) of subsection (1), after the word "photograph" there shall be inserted the words "or pseudo-photograph"; and
(c) in subsection (2), at the beginning there shall be inserted "In subsection (1) above "child" means, subject to subsection (2B) below, a person under the age of 16; and";
(d) after subsection (2), there shall be added—
"(2A) In this section, "pseudo-photograph" means an image, whether produced by computer-graphics or otherwise howsoever, which appears to be a photograph.
(2B) If the impression conveyed by a pseudo-photograph is that the person shown is a child, the pseudo-photograph shall be treated for all purposes of this Act as showing a child and so shall a pseudo-photograph where the predominant impression conveyed is that the person shown is a child notwithstanding that some of the physical characteristics shown are those of an adult.
(2C) In this section, references to an indecent pseudo-photograph include—
(a) a copy of an indecent pseudo-photograph;
(b) data stored on a computer disc or by other electronic means which is capable of conversion into a pseudo-photograph.".
(e) in subsection (3)—
(i) in paragraph (a), for the words "3 months" there shall be substituted the words "6 months"; and
(ii) in paragraph (b), for the words "two years" there shall be substituted the words "3 years";
(f) in subsection (4), and in paragraphs (a) and (b) of subsection (5), after the word "photograph" there shall be inserted the words "or pseudo-photograph"; and
(g) for subsection (8)(c) there shall be substituted—
"(c) references to a photograph include—
(i) the negative as well as the positive version; and
(ii) data stored on a computer disc or by other electronic means which is capable of conversion into a photograph.".

(7) In section 52A (which, for Scotland, penalises the possession of indecent photographs of children)—

(a) in subsection (1), for the words from "of a" to "16)" there shall be substituted the words "or pseudo-photograph of a child";
(b) in subsection (2), in each of paragraphs (a) to (c), after the word "photograph" there shall be inserted the words "or pseudo-photograph";
(c) in subsection (3)—
    (i) after the word "to" there shall be inserted the words "imprisonment for a period not exceeding 6 months or to"; and
    (ii) at the end there shall be added the words "or to both.";
(d) in subsection (4), after the word "(2)" there shall be inserted the words "to (2C)".

(8) The Protection of Children (Northern Ireland) Order 1978 shall be amended as provided in subsections (9) and (10) below.

(9) In Article 2 (interpretation)—
(a) in paragraph (2)—
    (i) in the definition of "child", after "child" there shall be inserted the words "subject to paragraph (3)(c)";
    (ii) for the definition of "photograph" there shall be substituted the following definitions—
    " "indecent pseudo-photograph" includes—
        (a) a copy of an indecent pseudo-photograph; and
        (b) data stored on a computer disc or by other electronic means which is capable of conversion into a pseudo-photograph;
    "photograph" includes—
        (a) the negative as well as the positive version; and
        (b) data stored on a computer disc or by other electronic means which is capable of conversion into a photograph;
    "pseudo-photograph" means an image, whether made by computer-graphics or otherwise howsoever, which appears to be a photograph;";
(b) in paragraph (3)—
    (i) in sub-paragraph (a), after the word "photograph" there shall be inserted the words "or pseudo-photograph";
    (ii) in sub-paragraph (b), at the end, there shall be inserted the words "and so as respects pseudo-photographs; and";
    (iii) after sub-paragraph (b) there shall be inserted the following sub-paragraph—
    "(c) if the impression conveyed by a pseudo-photograph is that the person shown is a child, the pseudo-photograph shall be treated as showing a child and so shall a pseudo-photograph where the predominant impression conveyed is that the person shown is a child notwithstanding that some of the physical characteristics shown are those of an adult.".

(10) In Article 3 (which, for Northern Ireland, penalises the taking and distribution of indecent photographs of children and related acts)—
(a) in sub-paragraph (a) of paragraph (1)—
    (i) after the word "taken" there shall be inserted the words "or to make";
    (ii) after the word "photograph" there shall be inserted the words "or pseudo-photograph";
(b) in sub-paragraphs (b), (c) and (d) of paragraph (1), after the word "photographs" there shall be inserted the words "or pseudo-photographs";
(c) in sub-paragraphs (a) and (b) of paragraph (3), after the word "photographs" there shall be inserted the words "or pseudo-photographs".

(11) Article 15 of the Criminal Justice (Evidence, etc.) (Northern Ireland) Order 1988 (which, for Northern Ireland, penalises the possession of indecent photographs of children) shall be amended as follows—

  (a) in paragraph (1), after the word "photograph" there shall be inserted the words "or pseudo-photograph" and the words from "(meaning" to "16)" shall be omitted;

  (b) in sub-paragraphs (a), (b) and (c) of paragraph (2), after the word "photograph" there shall be inserted the words "or pseudo-photograph"; and

  (c) in paragraph (6), the reference to the coming into operation of that Article shall be construed, for the purposes of the amendments made by this subsection, as a reference to the coming into force of this subsection.

DEFINITIONS

"child": s.7(6)(8) of the Protection of Children Act 1978 as inserted by this section.
"photograph": s.7(3) of the Protection of Children Act 1978 as amended by this section.
"pseudo-photograph": s.7(7)–(9) of the Protection of Children Act 1978 as inserted by this section.

GENERAL NOTE

The purpose of this section is to strike at computer pornography. This is a comparatively new phenomenon. For instance, of 976 prosecutions concerning pornography in 1991 only seven concerned computer pornography. This section, together with Sched. 10 paras. 37 and 38, amend the Protection of Children Act 1978 and s.160 of the Criminal Justice Act 1988. The effect is to make it an offence to make, distribute, advertise or possess pornography, simulated by computer graphics or other means, which appears to be an indecent photograph of a child ("a pseudo-photograph"). The definition of "pseudo-photograph" is wide enough to cover an image (which appears to be a photograph) made by any form of technology. This would include images received via telephone transmission or bulletin boards. The purpose of the section is to preclude a defence that a "pseudo photograph" is not a photograph.

Subss. (8) to (11)

These subsections make corresponding provision for Northern Ireland by amending Arts. 2 and 3 of the Protection of Children (Northern Ireland) Order 1978 and Art. 15 of the Criminal Justice (Evidence, etc.) (Northern Ireland) Order 1988.

Indecent photograph, as defined by the Protection of Children Act 1978 (c. 37) s.7(2) "includes an indecent film, a copy of an indecent photograph or film, and an indecent photograph comprised in a film."

Photographs, as defined by s.7(3) of the Protection of Children Act 1978 as amended by this Act, "(including those comprised in a film) shall, if they show children and are indecent, be treated for all purpose of this Act as indecent photographs of children, and so as respects pseudo-photographs".

Scottish perspective

There is little evidence that the taking or distribution of indecent photographs of children is a particular problem in Scotland, or that there was any need for an increase in the maximum penalty for these offences. However, developments in technology have necessitated the broadening of the definition of photograph to include pseudo-photographs and the consequent broadening of the definition of child to include any representation appearing to depict a person under the age of 16.

Arrestable offences to include certain offences relating to obscenity or indecency

85.—(1) The Police and Criminal Evidence Act 1984 shall be amended as follows.

  (2) In section 24(2) (arrestable offences), after paragraph (e), there shall be inserted the following paragraphs—

  "(f) an offence under section 2 of the Obscene Publications Act 1959 (publication of obscene matter);

(g) an offence under section 1 of the Protection of Children Act 1978 (indecent photographs and pseudo-photographs of children);".

(3) At the end of Part II of Schedule 5 (serious arrestable offences mentioned in section 116(2)(b)) there shall be inserted the following paragraphs—

"Protection of Children Act 1978 (c. 37)

14. Section 1 (indecent photographs and pseudo-photographs of children).

Obscene Publications Act 1959 (c. 66)

15. Section 2 (publication of obscene matter).".

(4) The Police and Criminal Evidence (Northern Ireland) Order 1989 shall be amended as provided in subsections (5) and (6) below.

(5) In Article 26(2) (arrestable offences), after sub-paragraph (e), there shall be inserted the following sub-paragraph—

"(f) an offence under Article 3 of the Protection of Children (Northern Ireland) Order 1978 (indecent photographs and pseudo-photographs of children).".

(6) At the end of Part II of Schedule 5 (serious arrestable offences mentioned in Article 87(2)(b)) there shall be inserted the following paragraph—

"Protection of Children (Northern Ireland) Order 1978
(1978 N.I. 17)

13. Article 3 (indecent photographs and pseudo-photographs of children).".

DEFINITIONS
"arrestable offence": s.24(1) of the Police and Criminal Evidence Act 1984.
"pseudo-photograph": s.7(7)–(9) of the Protection of Children Act 1978 as inserted by s.79 of this Act, *ante.*
"serious arrestable offence": s.116 of the Police and Criminal Evidence Act 1984.

GENERAL NOTE
The purpose of this section is to provide for an immediate power of arrest of those trading in obscene material and child pornography. Thus the section provides that offences under s.2 of the Obscene Publications Act 1959 (publishing an obscene article, or possessing an obscene article for publication for gain) and under s.1 of the Protection of Children Act 1978 (taking, showing, advertising, distributing or possessing with a view to distributing indecent photographs or pseudo-photographs of a child under the age of 16) shall be arrestable offences; and serious arrestable offences under the Police and Criminal Evidence Act 1984. It also provides that offences under Art. 3 of the Protection of Children (Northern Ireland) Order 1978 shall be arrestable offences and serious arrestable offences for the purposes of the Police and Criminal Evidence (Northern Ireland) Order 1989. Amendments to the 1978 Act and to 1978 Northern Ireland Order are made by Sched. 10, paras. 37, 38, *post.*

Obscene, as defined by s.1(1) of the Obscene Publications Act 1959, means that "an article shall be deemed to be obscene if its effect or (where the article comprises two or more distinct items) the effect of any one of its items is, if taken as a whole, such as to tend to deprave and corrupt persons who are likely, having regard to all relevant circumstances, to read, see or hear all the matter contained or embodied in it."

Publication: note that this now includes the transmission of electronic data: Sched 9, para. 3, *post.*

Indecent photographs of children: sentence of imprisonment

86.—(1) In section 160(3) of the Criminal Justice Act 1988 (which makes a person convicted of certain offences relating to indecent photographs of children liable to a fine not exceeding level 5 on the standard scale) there shall be inserted after the word "to" the words "imprisonment for a term not exceeding six months or" and at the end the words ", or both".

(2) In Article 15(3) of the Criminal Justice (Evidence, etc.) (Northern Ireland) Order 1988 (which makes a person convicted in Northern Ireland of certain offences relating to indecent photographs of children liable to a fine not exceeding level 5 on the standard scale) there shall be inserted after the word "to" the words "imprisonment for a term not exceeding 6 months or" and at the end the words ", or both".

GENERAL NOTE
    This section increases the maximum penalty for the offence under s.160 of the Criminal Justice Act 1988 and under Art. 15(3) of the Criminal Justice (Evidence) (Northern Ireland) Order 1988 (possessing an indecent photograph of a child under the age of 16) to include imprisonment for a term not exceeding six months.

Publishing, displaying, selling or distributing etc. obscene material in Scotland: sentence of imprisonment

87. In section 51(3) of the Civic Government (Scotland) Act 1982 (which makes persons convicted in summary proceedings in Scotland of certain offences relating to obscene material liable, among other penalties, to imprisonment for a period not exceeding 3 months and persons convicted there on indictment of such offences liable, among other penalties, to imprisonment for a period not exceeding two years), for the words "3 months" there shall be substituted the words "6 months" and for the words "two years" there shall be substituted the words "3 years".

GENERAL NOTE
    Again, there is little evidence that previous maximum penalties for these offences were felt to be insufficient in Scotland.

Video recordings

Video recordings: increase in penalties

88.—(1) The following provisions of the Video Recordings Act 1984 (which create offences for which section 15(1) and (3) prescribe maximum fines of, in the case of sections 9 and 10, £20,000 and, in the case of other offences, level 5) shall be amended as follows.

(2) In section 9 (supplying videos of unclassified work), after subsection (2), there shall be inserted the following subsection—
    "(3) A person guilty of an offence under this section shall be liable—
    (a) on conviction on indictment, to imprisonment for a term not exceeding two years or a fine or both,
    (b) on summary conviction, to imprisonment for a term not exceeding six months or a fine not exceeding £20,000 or both.".

(3) In section 10 (possessing videos of unclassified work for supply), after subsection (2), there shall be inserted the following subsection—
    "(3) A person guilty of an offence under this section shall be liable—
    (a) on conviction on indictment, to imprisonment for a term not exceeding two years or a fine or both,
    (b) on summary conviction, to imprisonment for a term not exceeding six months or a fine not exceeding £20,000 or both.".

(4) In section 11 (supplying videos in breach of classification), after subsection (2), there shall be inserted the following subsection—
    "(3) A person guilty of an offence under this section shall be liable, on summary conviction, to imprisonment for a term not exceeding six months or a fine not exceeding level 5 on the standard scale or both.".

(5) In section 12 (supplying videos in places other than licensed sex shops), after subsection (4), there shall be inserted the following subsection—
    "(4A) A person guilty of an offence under subsection (1) or (3) above shall be liable, on summary conviction, to imprisonment for a term not

exceeding six months or a fine not exceeding level 5 on the standard scale or both.".

(6) In section 14 (supplying videos with false indication as to classification), after subsection (4), there shall be inserted the following subsection—

"(5) A person guilty of an offence under subsection (1) or (3) above shall be liable, on summary conviction, to imprisonment for a term not exceeding six months or a fine not exceeding level 5 on the standard scale or both.".

(7) The amendments made by this section shall not apply to offences committed before this section comes into force.

DEFINITIONS
"sex shop": s.12(5) of the Video Recordings Act 1984.
"supply": s.1(4) of the Video Recordings Act 1984.
"video": See General Note to s.91, *post*.

GENERAL NOTE
This section increases the penalties for offences under the Video Recordings Act 1984. Previously the most serious offences (*i.e.* supplying unclassified videos and possessing the same for supply under ss. 9 and 10 of the Act) were only triable summarily and the maximum penalty was a fine of £20,000. This section makes these offences imprisonable for the first time. Under it they are triable either way: the maximum punishment for those tried on indictment is two years' imprisonment and an unlimited fine; and for those tried summarily six months' imprisonment (the maximum fine remains the same). The other offences under the Act may only be tried summarily. However, the section provides that the maximum penalty for offences under ss. 11, 12 and 14 shall be six months' imprisonment or a fine of £5,000.

Sched. 10, para. 52, *post*, amends section 13 and substitutes a new section 15 (time-limit for prosecutions).

Video recordings: restriction of exemptions

89.—(1) Section 2 of the Video Recordings Act 1984 (exempted works) shall be amended as follows.

(2) In subsection (1), after the words "subsection (2)" there shall be inserted the words "or (3)".

(3) In subsection (2)—
  (a) after paragraph (c), there shall be inserted the following paragraph—
      "(d) techniques likely to be useful in the commission of offences;"; and
  (b) for the word "designed" (in both places) there shall be substituted the word "likely".

(4) After subsection (2), there shall be inserted the following subsection—

"(3) A video work is not an exempted work for those purposes if, to any significant extent, it depicts criminal activity which is likely to any significant extent to stimulate or encourage the commission of offences.".

DEFINITIONS
"exempted work": s.2(1) and (2) of the Video Recordings Act 1984.
"video recording work": see General Note to s.91, *post*.

GENERAL NOTE
This section amends s.2 of the Video Recordings Act 1984 in order to restrict the number of video works which are exempt from classification by the British Board of Film Classification. Such works will not be exempt either if they depict criminal activity to any significant extent or if they stimulate or encourage the commission of offences.

Video recordings: suitability

90.—(1) After section 4 of the Video Recordings Act 1984 there shall be inserted the following sections—

"Criteria for suitability to which special regard to be had

4A.—(1) The designated authority shall, in making any determination as to the suitability of a video work, have special regard (among the other relevant factors) to any harm that may be caused to potential viewers or, through their behaviour, to society by the manner in which the work deals with—

  (a) criminal behaviour;

  (b) illegal drugs;

  (c) violent behaviour or incidents;

  (d) horrific behaviour or incidents; or

  (e) human sexual activity.

(2) For the purposes of this section—

  "potential viewer" means any person (including a child or young person) who is likely to view the video work in question if a classification certificate or a classification certificate of a particular description were issued;

  "suitability" means suitability for the issue of a classification certificate or suitability for the issue of a certificate of a particular description;

  "violent behaviour" includes any act inflicting or likely to result in the infliction of injury;

and any behaviour or activity referred to in subsection (1)(a) to (e) above shall be taken to include behaviour or activity likely to stimulate or encourage it.

Review of determinations as to suitability

4B.—(1) The Secretary of State may by order make provision enabling the designated authority to review any determination made by them, before the coming into force of section 4A of this Act, as to the suitability of a video work.

(2) The order may in particular provide—

  (a) for the authority's power of review to be exercisable in relation to such determinations as the authority think fit;

  (b) for the authority to determine, on any review, whether, if they were then determining the suitability of the video work to which the determination under review relates, they—

    (i) would issue a classification certificate, or

    (ii) would issue a different classification certificate;

  (c) for the cancellation of a classification certificate, where they determine that they would not issue a classification certificate;

  (d) for the cancellation of a classification certificate and issue of a new classification certificate, where they determine that they would issue a different classification certificate;

  (e) for any such cancellation or issue not to take effect until the end of such period as may be determined in accordance with the order;

  (f) for such persons as may appear to the authority to fall within a specified category of person to be notified of any such cancellation or issue in such manner as may be specified;

  (g) for treating a classification certificate, in relation to any act or omission occurring after its cancellation, as if it had not been issued;

  (h) for specified provisions of this Act to apply to determinations made on a review subject to such modifications (if any) as may be specified;

  (i) for specified regulations made under section 8 of this Act to apply to a video work in respect of which a new classification certificate has been issued subject to such modifications (if any) as may be specified.

(3) In subsection (2) above "specified" means specified by an order made under this section.

(4) The Secretary of State shall not make any order under this section unless he is satisfied that adequate arrangements will be made for an appeal against determinations made by the designated authority on a review.

(5) The power to make an order under this section shall be exercisable by statutory instrument which shall be subject to annulment in pursuance of a resolution of either House of Parliament.

(6) In this section "suitability" has the same meaning as in section 4A of this Act.".

(2) In section 7(2) of the Video Recordings Act 1984 (contents of classification certificates), in paragraph (a), after the words "viewing by children", there shall be inserted the words "or young children".

DEFINITIONS
"potential viewer": s.4A(2) of the Video Recordings Act 1984, as inserted by this section.
"specified": subs. (3).
"suitability": s.4A(2) of the Video Recordings Act 1984, as inserted by this section.
"video work": see General Note to s.91, *post.*
"violent behaviour": s.4A(2) of the Video Recordings Act 1984, as inserted by this section.

GENERAL NOTE
This section, by inserting a new section into the Video Recordings Act 1984, establishes statutory criteria for the classification of videos by the designated authority, the British Board of Film Classification. The authority must have special regard to any harm which may be caused to potential viewers (or, indirectly, to society) by the portrayal of the activities set out in the section. These criteria are not exhaustive. This section was added to the Bill in response to an amendment introduced by David Alton M.P.

Enforcement by enforcing authorities outside their areas

91.—(1) The Video Recordings Act 1984 shall have effect with the following amendments.

(2) In section 16A (enforcement)—
(a) after subsection (1) there shall be inserted the following subsections—
    "(1A) Subject to subsection (1B) below, the functions of a local weights and measures authority shall also include the investigation and prosecution outside their area of offences under this Act suspected to be linked to their area as well as the investigation outside their area of offences suspected to have been committed within it.
    (1B) The functions available to an authority under subsection (1A) above shall not be exercisable in relation to any circumstances suspected to have arisen within the area of another local weights and measures authority without the consent of that authority.";
(b) in subsection (4), for the words "Subsection (1)" there shall be substituted the words "Subsections (1) and (1A)";
(c) after subsection (4), there shall be inserted the following subsection—
    "(4A) For the purposes of subsections (1A), (1B) and (2) above—
    (a) offences in another area are "linked" to the area of a local weights and measures authority if—
        (i) the supply or possession of video recordings in contravention of this Act within their area is likely to be or to have been the result of the supply or possession of those recordings in the other area; or
        (ii) the supply or possession of video recordings in contravention of this Act in the other area is likely to be or to have been the result of the supply or possession of those recordings in their area; and

(b) "investigation" includes the exercise of the powers conferred by sections 27 and 28 of the Trade Descriptions Act 1968 as applied by subsection (2) above;

and sections 29 and 33 of that Act shall apply accordingly.".

(3) After section 16A there shall be inserted the following sections—

"Extension of jurisdiction of magistrates' courts in linked cases

16B.—(1) A justice of the peace for an area to which section 1 of the Magistrates' Courts Act 1980 applies may issue a summons or warrant under and in accordance with that section as respects an offence under this Act committed or suspected of having been committed outside the area for which he acts if it appears to the justice that the offence is linked to the supply or possession of video recordings within the area for which he acts.

(2) Where a person charged with an offence under this Act appears or is brought before a magistrates' court in answer to a summons issued by virtue of subsection (1) above, or under a warrant issued under subsection (1) above, the court shall have jurisdiction to try the offence.

(3) For the purposes of this section an offence is "linked" to the supply or possession of video recordings within the area for which a justice acts if—

(a) the supply or possession of video recordings within his area is likely to be or to have been the result of the offence; or

(b) the offence is likely to be or to have been the result of the supply or possession of video recordings in his area.

Extension of jurisdiction of sheriff in linked cases

16C.—(1) Subsection (4) of section 287 of the Criminal Procedure (Scotland) Act 1975 (jurisdiction of sheriff as respects offences committed in more than one district) shall apply in respect of linked offences, whether or not alleged to have been committed by one and the same person, as that subsection applies in respect of offences alleged to have been committed by one person in more than one sheriff court district which, if committed in one of those districts, could be tried under one complaint.

(2) For the purposes of subsection (1) above, offences are linked if, being offences under this Act, they comprise the supply or possession of video recordings each within a different sheriff court district but such supply or possession within the one district is likely to be, or to have been, the result of such supply or possession within the other.

Extension of jurisdiction of magistrates' courts in Northern Ireland in linked cases

16D.—(1) Paragraph (2) of Article 16 of the Magistrates' Courts (Northern Ireland) Order 1981 (jurisdiction of magistrates' court as respects offences committed in another division) shall apply in respect of linked offences as that paragraph applies in respect of summary offences committed in other county court divisions.

(2) For the purposes of subsection (1) above, an offence is a linked offence if the supply or possession of video recordings within one county court division is likely to be or to have been the result of the supply or possession of those recordings in another such division.".

DEFINITIONS
"investigation": s.16A(4A(b)) of the Video Recordings Act 1984 as inserted by this section.
"linked": ss.16A(4A(a)) and 16B(3) of the Video Recordings Act 1984 as inserted by this section.

GENERAL NOTE

This section amends the Video Recordings Act 1984 (by inserting a new s.16A) in order to permit a local weights and measures authority to investigate and prosecute offences (under the Act) outside its area if linked to that area. In addition, by inserting new ss.16B–D, the section makes a corresponding extension in the jurisdiction of the relevant courts in order to deal with linked offences. Those courts are as follows: magistrates' courts in England and Wales and in Northern Ireland, and sheriff courts in Scotland.

By the Video Recordings Act 1984 (c. 39), s.1(3) as amended by Sched. 9, para. 22, *post.*, video recording "means any disc or any other device capable of storing electronically magnetic tape containing information by the use of which the whole or part of a video work may be produced" and video work "means any series of visual images (with or without sound) (a) produced electronically by the use of information contained on any disc or any other device capable of storing data electronically on magnetic tape, and (b) shown as a moving picture": (*ibid.*, s.1(2)).

Supply "means supply in any manner, whether or not for reward, and therefore includes supply by way of sale, letting on hire, exchange or loan: and references to 'a supply' are to be interpreted accordingly": *ibid.*, s.1(4).

Scottish perspective

Sections 88–91

These sections are a response to an apparent public concern about the potential adverse effects of video recordings on the behaviour especially of young people. Section 88 increases penalties for offences relating to the classification of videos. Section 89 restricts the categories of videos exempted from control by the Video Recordings Act 1984 and effectively removes the *mens rea* requirement by substituting "likely to be useful in the commission of offences ..." for "designed to be useful ...". Section 90 tightens the procedures for determining the suitability of video recordings and s.91 extends the jurisdiction of trading standards officers to operate outwith their area in relation to video recording offences committed within it, and the jurisdiction of Sheriffs to deal with such offences when committed outwith their geographical area but linked to similar offences within that area.

Obscene, offensive or annoying telephone calls

Obscene, offensive or annoying telephone calls: increase in penalty

92.—(1) In section 43(1) of the Telecommunications Act 1984 (which makes a person convicted of certain offences relating to improper use of public telecommunication systems liable to a fine not exceeding level 5 on the standard scale), for the words "a fine not exceeding level 3 on the standard scale" there shall be substituted the words "imprisonment for a term not exceeding six months or a fine not exceeding level 5 on the standard scale or both".

(2) Subsection (1) above does not apply to an offence committed before this section comes into force.

GENERAL NOTE

This section increases the maximum penalty for the offence under s.43(1) of the Telecommunications Act 1984 (making improper use of a public telecommunication system) to imprisonment for a term not exceeding six months or a fine not exceeding level 5 on the standard scale, or both. The purpose is to increase the penalty available to the courts for making obscene, offensive or annoying phone calls. (Surveys suggest that about 10 million such calls are made every year). The offence becomes imprisonable for the first time. However, it remains a summary offence. As originally drafted, the section provided for imprisonment of three months and a fine not exceeding level 4. These penalties were increased after debate in the Committee of the House of Commons.

By the Telecommunications Act 1984 (c. 12), s.4(1): " 'telecommunications system' means a system for the conveyance through the agency of electric, magnetic, electro-magnetic, electro-chemical or electro-mechanical energy, of (a) speech, music and other sounds; (b) visual images; (c) signals serving for the impartation (whether as between persons and persons, things and things or persons and things) of any matter otherwise than in the form of sounds or visual images; or (d) signals serving for the actuation or control of machinery or apparatus". By s.9 of the Act a public telecommunications system is a telephone system under Pt. II of the Act.

PART VIII

PRISON SERVICES AND THE PRISON SERVICE

CHAPTER I

ENGLAND AND WALES

Prisoner escorts

Arrangements for the provision of prisoner escorts

93.—(1) In subsection (1) of section 80 (arrangements for the provision of prisoner escorts) of the Criminal Justice Act 1991 ("the 1991 Act")—
  (a) for paragraph (a) there shall be substituted the following paragraph—
    "(a) the delivery of prisoners from one set of relevant premises to another;";
  (b) in paragraph (b), for the words "such premises" there shall be substituted the words "the premises of any court"; and
  (c) for paragraphs (c) and (d) there shall be substituted the following paragraph—
    "(c) the custody of prisoners temporarily held in a prison in the course of delivery from one prison to another; and".
  (2) After that subsection there shall be inserted the following subsection—
    "(1A) In paragraph (a) of subsection (1) above 'relevant premises' means a court, prison, police station or hospital; and either (but not both) of the sets of premises mentioned in that paragraph may be situated in a part of the British Islands outside England and Wales.".
  (3) In subsection (3) of that section, for the words "a warrant of commitment" there shall be substituted the words "a warrant or a hospital order or remand" and for the words "that warrant" there shall be substituted the words "the warrant, order or remand".
  (4) After that subsection there shall be inserted the following subsection—
    "(4) In this section—
      'hospital' has the same meaning as in the Mental Health Act 1983;
      'hospital order' means an order for a person's admission to hospital made under section 37, 38 or 44 of that Act, section 5 of the Criminal Procedure (Insanity) Act 1964 or section 6, 14 or 14A of the Criminal Appeal Act 1968;
      'hospital remand' means a remand of a person to hospital under section 35 or 36 of the Mental Health Act 1983;
      'warrant' means a warrant of commitment, a warrant of arrest or a warrant under section 46, 47, 48, 50 or 74 of that Act.".
  (5) In subsection (1) of section 92 of that Act (interpretation of Part IV), for the definition of "prisoner" there shall be substituted the following definition—
      " 'prisoner' means any person for the time being detained in legal custody as a result of a requirement imposed by a court or otherwise that he be so detained;".
  (6) In subsection (3) of that section—
  (a) for the words from "kept" to "accommodation)" there shall be substituted the words "remanded or committed to local authority accommodation under section 23 of the 1969 Act"; and
  (b) for the words "section 80(1)(c) to (e)" there shall be substituted the words "section 80(1)(c) or (e) or (1A)".
  (7) After that subsection there shall be inserted the following subsection—
    "(4) In sections 80, 82 and 83 above, 'prison'—
      (a) so far as relating to the delivery of prisoners to or from a prison situated in Scotland, includes a remand centre or young offenders

institution within the meaning of section 19 of the Prisons (Scotland) Act 1989; and
  (b) so far as relating to the delivery of prisoners to or from a prison situated in Northern Ireland, includes a remand centre or young offenders centre.".

DEFINITIONS
  "hospital": s.80(4) of the Criminal Justice Act 1991, as inserted by this section.
  "hospital order": s.80(4) of the Criminal Justice Act 1991, as inserted by this section.
  "hospital remand": s.80(4) of the Criminal Justice Act 1991, as inserted by this section.
  "prisoner": s.92(1) of the Criminal Justice Act 1991, as substituted by this section.
  "relevant premises": s.80(1A) of the Criminal Justice Act 1991, as inserted by this section.
  "warrant": s.80(4) of the Criminal Justice Act 1991, as inserted by this section.

GENERAL NOTE
  This section extends the power of the Home Secretary to make prisoner escort arrangements under s.80 of the 1991 Act to include delivery of prisoners to a hospital. The section also enables the delivery of prisoners by prisoner custody officers between England and Wales and Scotland, Northern Ireland, the Channel Islands and the Isle of Man.
  Hospital under the Mental Health Act 1983 (c. 20), "means (a) any health service hospital within the meaning of the National Health Service Act 1977; and (b) any accommodation provided by a local authority and used as a hospital by or on behalf of the Secretary of State under that Act".
  Prison under the Criminal Justice Act 1991 (c. 53), s.92(1), "includes a young offender institution or remand centre".

Powers and duties of prisoner custody officers acting in pursuance of such arrangements

94.—(1) For subsection (4) of section 82 of the 1991 Act (powers and duties of prisoner custody officers acting in pursuance of such arrangements) there shall be substituted the following subsection—
  "(4) Where a prisoner custody officer acting in pursuance of prisoner escort arrangements is on any premises in which the Crown Court or a magistrates' court is sitting, it shall be his duty to give effect to any order of that court made—
    (a) in the case of the Crown Court, under section 34A of the 1973 Act (power of Court to order search of persons before it); or
    (b) in the case of a magistrates' court, under section 80 of the 1980 Act (application of money found on defaulter).".
  (2) After subsection (2) of section 6 of the Imprisonment (Temporary Provisions) Act 1980 (detention in the custody of a police constable) there shall be inserted the following subsection—
  "(3) Any reference in this section to a constable includes a reference to a prisoner custody officer (within the meaning of Part IV of the Criminal Justice Act 1991) acting in pursuance of prisoner escort arrangements (within the meaning of that Part).".

DEFINITIONS
  "constable": s.6 of the Imprisonment (Temporary Provisions) Act 1980, as amended by this section.
  "prisoner": s.93, *ante.*

GENERAL NOTE
  Subsection (1) (by substituting a new subs. (4) in s.82 of the 1991 Act) imposes a duty on prisoner custody officers to search prisoners at magistrates' courts on the order of the court. The duty already exists in relation to prisoners at a Crown Court. However, the section re-states this duty.
  Subsection (2) extends to a contractor the power to hold in custody prisoners sentenced by the courts in respect of whom it is not practicable to secure admission to the place where they are to be detained. Thus, prisoner custody officers may hold prisoners in police cells if they cannot be conveyed to prison. The purpose is to remove from the police the obligation of caring for con-

victed prisoners after sentence when no prison is available to them. Typically, this power may be used when a prisoner is sentenced by a court at a time which makes it too late to deliver him to prison. The question whether the Police and Criminal Evidence Act 1994 applied in these circumstances was raised in Committee in the House of Commons. Some doubts were raised; however, the Government view was that it did not, since s.118(2) of the 1984 Act applies that Act only to a person detained in the charge of a constable (Standing Committee B, col. 7876, February 15, 1994).

Prisoner custody officer under the Criminal Justice Act 1991, ss.89(1) and 92(1), "means a person in respect of whom a certificate is for the time being in force certifying (a) that he has been approved by the Secretary of State for the purpose of performing escort functions or custodial duties or both; and (b) he is accordingly authorised to perform them." *Custodial duties*, by the Criminal Justice Act 1991, s.89(3), means "custodial duties at a contracted out prison." By a new subs. (1A) to s.92 of the 1991 Act, such duties "include a reference to custodial duties in relation to a prisoner who is outside such a prison for temporary purposes": s.98, *post.* For the certification of prisoner custody officers see Sched. 10 to the 1991 Act, as amended by later legislation including s.101(9) of this Act, *post.*

Prisoner escort arrangements: s.80(1) and (2) of the 1991 Act, as amended by s.94, *ante.*

Breaches of discipline by prisoners under escort

95. For section 83 of the 1991 Act there shall be substituted the following section—

"Breaches of discipline by prisoners under escort

83.—(1) This section applies where a prisoner for whose delivery or custody a prisoner custody officer has been responsible in pursuance of prisoner escort arrangements is delivered to a prison.

(2) For the purposes of such prison rules as relate to disciplinary offences, the prisoner shall be deemed to have been—

(a) in the custody of the governor of the prison; or

(b) in the case of a contracted out prison, in the custody of its director,

at all times during the period for which the prisoner custody officer was so responsible.

(3) In the case of any breach by the prisoner at any time during that period of such prison rules as so relate, a disciplinary charge may be laid against him by the prisoner custody officer.

(4) Nothing in this section shall enable a prisoner to be punished under prison rules for any act or omission of his for which he has already been punished by a court.

(5) In this section 'prison rules', in relation to a prison situated in a part of the British Islands outside England and Wales, means rules made under any provision of the law of that part which corresponds to section 47 of the 1952 Act.".

DEFINITIONS

"prison rules": s.83(5) of the Criminal Justice Act 1991, as substituted by this section.
"prisoner": s.93, *ante.*

GENERAL NOTE

This section, by inserting a new s.83 into the 1991 Act, clarifies the power of a prison custody officer to lay disciplinary charges against a prisoner for breaches of discipline when under escort. The charges will be heard in the prison to which the prisoner is delivered.

Contracted out prisons etc.

Contracted out parts of prisons, etc.

96. For section 84 of the 1991 Act there shall be substituted the following section—

"Contracting out prisons etc.

84.—(1) The Secretary of State may enter into a contract with another person for the provision or running (or the provision and running) by him, or (if the contract so provides) for the running by sub-contractors of his, of any prison or part of a prison.

(2) While a contract under this section for the running of a prison or part of a prison is in force—

   (a) the prison or part shall be run subject to and in accordance with sections 85 and 86 below, the 1952 Act (as modified by section 87 below) and prison rules; and

   (b) in the case of a part, that part and the remaining part shall each be treated for the purposes of sections 85 to 88A below as if they were separate persons.

(3) Where the Secretary of State grants a lease or tenancy of land for the purposes of any contract under this section, none of the following enactments shall apply to it, namely—

   (a) Part II of the Landlord and Tenant Act 1954 (security of tenure);

   (b) section 146 of the Law of Property Act 1925 (restrictions on and relief against forfeiture);

   (c) section 19(1), (2) and (3) of the Landlord and Tenant Act 1927 and the Landlord and Tenant Act 1988 (covenants not to assign etc.); and

   (d) the Agricultural Holdings Act 1986.

In this subsection 'lease or tenancy' includes an underlease or sub-tenancy.

(4) In this Part—

   'contracted out prison' means a prison or part of a prison for the running of which a contract under this section is for the time being in force;

   'the contractor', in relation to a contracted out prison, means the person who has contracted with the Secretary of State for the running of it; and

   'sub-contractor', in relation to a contracted out prison, means a person who has contracted with the contractor for the running of it or any part of it.".

DEFINITIONS
   "contracted out prisons": s.84(4) of the Criminal Justice Act 1991, as substituted by this section.
   "contractor": s.84(4) Criminal Justice Act 1991, as substituted by this section.
   "sub-contractor": s.84(4) of the Criminal Justice Act 1991, as substituted by this section.

GENERAL NOTE
   This section provides for the contracting-out of the running of part of a prison. It also provides that a contractor may (with the Home Secretary's consent) sub-contract the running of a prison or part of a prison.

Temporary attachment of prison officers

97.—(1) At the end of subsection (1) of section 85 of the 1991 Act (officers of contracted out prisons) there shall be inserted the words "or a prison officer who is temporarily attached to the prison".

(2) At the end of paragraph (b) of subsection (4) of that section there shall be inserted the words "or prison officers who are temporarily attached to the prison".

(3) For subsection (3) of section 87 of that Act (consequential modifications of 1952 Act) there shall be substituted the following subsection—

   "(3) Section 8 (powers of prison officers) shall not apply in relation to a prisoner custody officer performing custodial duties at the prison.".

(4) After subsection (4) of that section there shall be inserted the following subsection—

   "(4A) Section 11 (ejectment of prison officers and their families refusing to quit) shall not apply.".

(5) At the end of subsections (6) and (7) of that section there shall be inserted the words "or a prison officer who is temporarily attached to the prison".

DEFINITIONS
    "contracted out prisons": s.84(4) of the Criminal Justice Act 1991, as amended by s.96, *ante.*

GENERAL NOTE
    This section amends provisions in Pt. IV of the 1991 Act to permit prison officers from directly-managed prisons to give aid and support to contracted out prisons. (Such support would most likely be necessary in the case of a loss or potential loss of control of the prison). The section ensures that in these circumstances prison officers have the necessary legal powers to carry out their duties. (Section 99, *post,* contains similar provisions for aid from contracted out prisons to directly managed prisons). *Custodial duties; prisoner custody officer:* see General Note to s.94, *ante.*

Prisoners temporarily out of prison

98. After subsection (1) of section 92 of the 1991 Act (interpretation of Part IV) there shall be inserted the following subsection—
    "(1A) Any reference in this Part to custodial duties at a contracted out prison includes a reference to custodial duties in relation to a prisoner who is outside such a prison for temporary purposes.".

DEFINITIONS
    "contracted out prisons": s.84(2) of the Criminal Justice Act 1991, as amended by s.94, *ante.*
    "prisoner": s.93, *ante.*

GENERAL NOTE
    This section provides that prisoner custody officers may exercise custodial duties when a prisoner is temporarily outside a contracted out prison (*e.g.* in hospital or on a prison farm). *Custodial duties:* see General Note to s.94, *ante.*

Miscellaneous

Contracted out functions at directly managed prisons

99. After section 88 of the 1991 Act there shall be inserted the following section—

"Contracted out functions

Contracted out functions at directly managed prisons
    88A.—(1) The Secretary of State may enter into a contract with another person for any functions at a directly managed prison to be performed by prisoner custody officers who are provided by that person and are authorised to perform custodial duties.
    (2) Section 86 above shall apply in relation to a prisoner custody officer performing contracted out functions at a directly managed prison as it applies in relation to such an officer performing custodial duties at a contracted out prison.
    (3) In relation to a directly managed prison—
       (a) the reference in section 13(2) of the 1952 Act (legal custody of prisoners) to an officer of the prison; and
       (b) the reference in section 14(2) of that Act (cells) to a prison officer, shall each be construed as including a reference to a prisoner custody officer performing custodial duties at the prison in pursuance of a contract under this section.
    (4) Any reference in subsections (1) to (3) above to the performance of functions or custodial duties at a directly managed prison includes a

reference to the performance of functions or such duties for the purposes of, or for purposes connected with, such a prison.

(5) In this Part—

'contracted out functions' means any functions which, by virtue of a contract under this section, fall to be performed by prisoner custody officers;

'directly managed prison' means a prison which is not a contracted out prison.".

DEFINITIONS

"contracted out functions": s.88A(5) of the Criminal Justice Act 1991, as inserted by this section.

"directly managed prison": s.88A(5) of the Criminal Justice Act 1991, as inserted by this section.

GENERAL NOTE

This section, by inserting a new s.88A in the Criminal Justice Act 1988, enables the Home Secretary to contract out functions at directly managed prisons: subs. (1). The section also enables prisoner custody officers from a contracted out prison to assist in a directly managed prison: subs. (2). It thus complements the provisions of s.97, *ante. Custodial duties; prisoner custody officer*: see General Note to s.94, *ante.*

Provision of prisons by contractors

100.—(1) For subsection (2) of section 33 of the Prison Act 1952 (power to declare buildings etc. to be prisons) there shall be substituted the following subsection—

"(2) The Secretary of State may provide new prisons by declaring to be a prison—

(a) any building or part of a building built for the purpose or vested in him or under his control; or

(b) any floating structure or part of such a structure constructed for the purpose or vested in him or under his control.".

(2) Subsections (3) and (4) below apply where the Secretary of State enters into a contract with another person ("the contractor") for the provision by him of a prison.

(3) Section 33(2) of the Prison Act 1952 shall have effect as if it also included references to—

(a) any building or part of a building built by the contractor for the purpose or vested in him or under his control; and

(b) any floating structure or part of such a structure constructed by the contractor for the purpose or vested in him or under his control.

(4) Nothing in section 35(1) of that Act (prison property to be vested in the Secretary of State) shall require the prison or any real or personal property belonging to the prison to be vested in the Secretary of State.

DEFINITIONS

"contractor": s.84(2) of the Criminal Justice Act 1991, as substituted by s.96 of this Act.

GENERAL NOTE

By amending s.33 of the Prison Act 1952, this section enables the Home Secretary to provide that a prison ship or a "maritime detention facility" is a new prison. It thus clarifies the question whether such facilities may be used as a prison or not. The section also enables any building or floating structure provided by a contractor to be a prison. It is apparently intended that these facilities should only be used as a contingency measure to relieve overcrowding: (Standing Committee B, col. 826, February 17, 1994).

Prison (s.92(1) of the 1991 Act) includes a young offender institution or remand centre but not a naval, military or airforce prison (s.53(1) of the Prison Act 1952).

Subs. (4)

The Prison Act 1952 (c. 52), s.35(1) provides as follows:

"Every prison and all real and personal property belonging to a prison shall be vested in the Secretary of State and may be disposed of in such manner as the Secretary of State, with the consent of the Treasury, may determine."

Supplemental

Minor and consequential amendments

101.—(1) In subsection (5) of section 85 of the 1991 Act (officers of contracted out prisons), for the words "The contractor shall" there shall be substituted the words "The contractor and any sub-contractor of his shall each".

(2) In subsection (3)(b) of section 88 of that Act (intervention by the Secretary of State), for the words "the contractor shall" there shall be substituted the words "the contractor and any sub-contractor of his shall each".

(3) In subsection (5) of that section, after the words "the contractor," there shall be inserted the words "any sub-contractor of his,".

(4) In subsection (3) of section 89 of that Act (certification of prisoner custody officers), for the words "contracted out prison" there shall be substituted the words "contracted out or directly managed prison".

(5) In subsections (1) and (3) of section 90 of that Act (protection of prisoner custody officers), for the words from "acting" to "prison" there shall be substituted the words—

> "(a) acting in pursuance of prisoner escort arrangements;
> (b) performing custodial duties at a contracted out prison; or
> (c) performing contracted out functions at a directly managed prison,".

(6) In subsection (1) of section 91 of that Act (wrongful disclosure of information), for the words from "is or has been" to "prison" there shall be substituted the words—

> "(a) is or has been employed (whether as a prisoner custody officer or otherwise) in pursuance of prisoner escort arrangements, or at a contracted out prison; or
> (b) is or has been employed to perform contracted out functions at a directly managed prison,".

(7) In subsection (1) of section 92 of that Act (interpretation of Part IV)—
(a) after the words "In this Part" there shall be inserted the words "unless the context otherwise requires";
(b) in the definitions of "contracted out prison" and "contractor", for the words "section 84(2)" there shall be substituted the words "section 84(4)";
(c) after those definitions there shall be inserted the following definitions—

> " 'contracted out functions' and 'directly managed prison' have the meanings given by section 88A(5) above;";

(d) after the definition of "prison" there shall be inserted the following definitions—

> " 'prison officer' means an officer of a directly managed prison;
> 'prison rules' means rules made under section 47 of the 1952 Act;"; and

(e) after the definition of "prisoner escort arrangements" there shall be inserted the following definition—

> " 'sub-contractor' has the meaning given by section 84(4) above.".

(8) After subsection (7) of section 102 of the 1991 Act (short title, commencement and extent) there shall be inserted the following subsection—

> "(7A) Sections 80, 82 and 83 above, so far as relating to the delivery of prisoners to or from premises situated in a part of the British Islands outside England and Wales, extend to that part of those Islands.".

(9) For sub-paragraph (1) of paragraph 3 of Schedule 10 to that Act (certification of prisoner custody officers) there shall be substituted the following sub-paragraph—

"(1) This paragraph applies where at any time—

(a) in the case of a prisoner custody officer acting in pursuance of prisoner escort arrangements, it appears to the prisoner escort monitor for the area concerned that the officer is not a fit and proper person to perform escort functions;

(b) in the case of a prisoner custody officer performing custodial duties at a contracted out prison, it appears to the controller of that prison that the officer is not a fit and proper person to perform custodial duties; or

(c) in the case of a prisoner custody officer performing contracted out functions at a directly managed prison, it appears to the governor of that prison that the officer is not a fit and proper person to perform custodial duties.".

(10) In sub-paragraph (2) of that paragraph, for the words "or controller" there shall be substituted the words "controller or governor".

DEFINITIONS
"contracted out functions": s.88A(5) of the Criminal Justice Act 1991, as substituted by s.99 of this Act.
"contractor": s.84(2) of the Criminal Justice Act 1991, as substituted by s.96 of this Act, *ante*.
"directly managed prison": s.88A(5) of the Criminal Justice Act 1991, as substituted by s.99 of this Act, *ante*.
"prisoner escort arrangements": s.94, *ante*.
"sub-contractor": s.84(2) of the Criminal Justice Act 1991, as substituted by s.96 of this Act, *ante*.

GENERAL NOTE
This section provides for minor amendments made necessary by other sections in this Chapter. *Custodial duties*; *prisoner custody officer*: see General Note to s.94, *ante*.

CHAPTER II

SCOTLAND

Prisoner escorts

Arrangements for the provision of prisoner escorts

102.—(1) The Secretary of State may make arrangements for any of the functions specified in subsection (2) below ("escort functions") to be performed in such cases as may be determined by or under the arrangements by prisoner custody officers who are authorised to perform such functions.

(2) Those functions are—

(a) the transfer of prisoners from one set of relevant premises to another;

(b) the custody of prisoners held on court premises (whether or not they would otherwise be in the custody of the court) and their production before the court;

(c) the custody of prisoners temporarily held in a prison in the course of transfer from one prison to another; and

(d) the custody of prisoners while they are outside a prison for temporary purposes.

(3) In paragraph (a) of subsection (2) above, "relevant premises" means—

(a) the premises of any court, prison, police station or hospital; or

(b) the premises of any other place from or to which a prisoner may be required to be taken under the Criminal Procedure (Scotland) Act 1975 or the Mental Health (Scotland) Act 1984;

and either (but not both) of the sets of premises mentioned in that paragraph may be situated in a part of the British Islands outside Scotland.

(4) Arrangements made by the Secretary of State under this section ("prisoner escort arrangements") may include entering into contracts with other persons for the provision by them of prisoner custody officers.

(5) Any person who, under a warrant or hospital order, is responsible for the performance of any such function as is mentioned in subsection (2) above shall be deemed to have complied with that warrant or order if he does all that he reasonably can to secure that the function is performed by a prisoner custody officer acting in pursuance of prisoner escort arrangements.

(6) In this section—

"hospital" has the same meaning as in the Mental Health (Scotland) Act 1984;

"hospital order" means an order for a person's detention in, or admission to and detention in, a hospital under section 174, 174A, 175, 375A or 376 of the Act of 1975 or section 70 of the Act of 1984; and

"warrant" means a warrant for committal, a warrant for arrest, a warrant under section 69, 73, 74 or 75 of the Act of 1984, a transfer direction under section 71 of that Act or any other warrant, order or direction under the Act of 1975 or the Act of 1984 requiring a person to be taken to a particular place.

GENERAL NOTE

Prisoner escorts in Scotland have generally been carried out (a) by the police, when prisoners are being taken to or from prisons and courts in relation to criminal proceedings against them, and (b) by prison officers in all other circumstances. There is considerable, but variable, daily movement to and from prisons, to courts, for both civil and criminal purposes, to children's hearings, to hospitals and for compassionate visits to families or funerals. Providing staff on the regular complement for these purposes is difficult and costly. These new provisions will enable the establishment of a specialised escort service.

Provision is made for the members of the escort service to be certificated by the Secretary of State (s.114 and Sched. 6). This should ensure that recruitment and training procedures are appropriate. The officers are empowered to act in relation to transfers of prisoners, custody within courts, within or between prisons and in any other place outside a prison where a prisoner may temporarily be (subss. (2)(3)). At least one of the transmit points must be within Scotland (*ibid.*). (The service may be a public one or provided under contract with an outside body (subs. (4)).

Monitoring of prisoner escort arrangements

103.—(1) Prisoner escort arrangements shall include the appointment of a prisoner escort monitor, that is to say, a Crown servant whose duty it shall be—

(a) to keep the arrangements under review and to report on them to the Secretary of State;

(b) to investigate and report to the Secretary of State on any allegations made against prisoner custody officers acting in pursuance of the arrangements; and

(c) to report to the Secretary of State on any alleged breaches of discipline on the part of prisoners for whose transfer or custody such officers so acting are responsible.

(2) In section 7(2) (functions of Her Majesty's Chief Inspector of Prisons for Scotland) of the 1989 Act—

(a) after "Inspector" there shall be inserted "—(a)"; and

(b) at the end there shall be inserted—

"; and

(b) to inspect the conditions in which prisoners are transported or held in pursuance of prisoner escort arrangements (within the meaning of section 102 of the Criminal Justice and Public Order Act 1994) and to report to the Secretary of State on them.".

GENERAL NOTE

Perhaps to allay public fears about the operation of the new provision, but also to ensure that allegations against prison custody officers and breaches of discipline by those under their custody can be dealt with, the Act requires the appointment of a crown servant to monitor the new arrangements. The jurisdiction of this post extends to all escort services whether provided by the private sector or not. The remit of H.M. Chief Inspector of Prisons is also extended to cover such services, though it should be borne in mind that the Inspectorate has no role in relation to investigations of individual complaints or grievances.

Powers and duties of prisoner custody officers performing escort functions

104.—(1) A prisoner custody officer acting in pursuance of prisoner escort arrangements shall have power to search—
   (a) any prisoner for whose transfer or custody he is responsible in accordance with the arrangements; and
   (b) any other person who is in or is seeking to enter any place where any such prisoner is or is to be held and any article in the possession of such a person.

(2) The power conferred by subsection (1)(b) above to search a person shall not be construed as authorising a prisoner custody officer to require a person to remove any of his clothing other than an outer coat, jacket, headgear and gloves.

(3) A prisoner custody officer shall, as respects prisoners for whose transfer or custody he is responsible in pursuance of prisoner escort arrangements, have the duty—
   (a) to prevent their escape from legal custody;
   (b) to prevent, or detect and report on, the commission or attempted commission by them of other unlawful acts;
   (c) to ensure good order and discipline on their part;
   (d) to attend to their wellbeing; and
   (e) to give effect to any directions as to their treatment which are given by a court.

(4) Where a prisoner custody officer acting in pursuance of prisoner escort arrangements is on any premises in which a court of summary jurisdiction is sitting he shall have the duty to give effect to any order of the court under section 395(2) of the Criminal Procedure (Scotland) Act 1975 requiring an offender to be searched.

(5) The powers conferred by subsection (1) above and the powers arising by virtue of subsections (3) and (4) above shall include power to use reasonable force where necessary.

(6) Prison rules may make provision in relation to—
   (a) the power conferred by subsection (1) above; and
   (b) the duty imposed by subsection (3)(d) above.

GENERAL NOTE

The powers of search, of both prisoners and visitors, accorded to prison custody officers are the same as those available to prison officers (see further ss.152 and 153 *infra.*). The power granted by subs. (4) relates to the ability of a summary court on imposing a fine to order that the person be searched and any money on his person taken in payment of that fine.

Breaches of discipline by prisoners under escort

105.—(1) Where a prisoner for whose transfer or custody a prisoner custody officer has been responsible in pursuance of prisoner escort arrangements is delivered to a prison, he shall be deemed, for the purposes of such prison rules as relate to breaches of discipline, to have been—
   (a) in the custody of the governor of the prison; or
   (b) in the case of a contracted out prison, in the custody of its director,

at all times during the period for which that officer was so responsible, and that officer may bring a charge of breach of such rules as so relate against the prisoner in respect of any such time.

(2) Nothing in subsection (1) above shall render a prisoner liable to be punished under prison rules for any act or omission of his for which he has already been punished by a court.

(3) In this section "prison rules", in relation to a prison situated in a part of the British Islands outside Scotland, means rules made under any provision of the law of that part which corresponds to section 39 of the 1989 Act.

GENERAL NOTE

Breaches of discipline and the procedures for dealing therewith are detailed in rr. 99–101 of the Prisons and Young Offenders Institutions (Scotland) Rules 1994 (S.I. 1994 No. 1931 (S.85)). Subsection (2) prohibits double jeopardy.

Contracted out prisons

Contracting out of prisons

106.—(1) The Secretary of State may enter into a contract with another person for the provision or running (or the provision and running) by him, or (if the contract so provides) for the running by sub-contractors of his, of any prison or part of a prison in Scotland.

(2) While a contract under this section for the running of a prison or part of a prison is in force—

(a) the prison or part shall be run subject to and in accordance with—
   (i) sections 107 and 108 below; and
   (ii) the 1989 Act and prison rules and directions made under or by virtue of that Act (all as modified by section 110 below); and
(b) in the case of a part, that part and the remaining part shall each be treated for the purposes of sections 107 to 112 below as if they were separate prisons.

(3) Where the Secretary of State grants a lease for the purpose of any contract under this section, none of the following enactments shall apply to it—

(a) sections 4 to 7 of the Law Reform (Miscellaneous Provisions) (Scotland) Act 1985 (irritancy clauses); and
(b) the Agricultural Holdings (Scotland) Act 1991.

In this subsection "lease" includes a sub-lease.

(4) In this Chapter—

"contracted out prison" means a prison or part of a prison for the running of which a contract under this section is for the time being in force;

"the contractor", in relation to a contracted out prison, means the person who has contracted with the Secretary of State for the running of it; and

"sub-contractor", in relation to a contracted out prison, means a person who has contracted with the contractor for the running of it or any part of it.

GENERAL NOTE

The Prisons (Scotland) Act 1989 empowered only the Secretary of State to run prisons, appoint staff and carry full responsibility for what happened in prisons. Accordingly, private prisons, or parts of prisons, were not possible without this change in the law. Subsection (2) ensures that essentially the same legal régime will apply to private prisons as applies to the public sector. Subsection (3) ensures that the Secretary of State does not have to wait for the statutory five years before terminating a lease if a contractor contravenes an intrancy clause in any lease (a power which could, under both Acts, have been achieved in contract).

It is understood that negotiations are shortly to start with a view to the commissioning of a contracted-out prison, probably for remand prisoners, in the near future.

Officers of contracted out prisons

107.—(1) Instead of a governor, every contracted out prison shall have—
(a) a director, who shall be a prisoner custody officer appointed by the contractor and specially approved for the purposes of this section by the Secretary of State; and
(b) a controller, who shall be a Crown servant appointed by the Secretary of State,
and every officer of such a prison who performs custodial duties shall be a prisoner custody officer who is authorised to perform such duties or a prison officer who is temporarily attached to the prison.

(2) Subject to subsection (3) below, the director shall have the same functions as are conferred on a governor by the 1989 Act and by prison rules.

(3) The director shall not—
(a) have any function which is conferred on a controller by virtue of subsection (4) below;
(b) inquire into a disciplinary charge brought against a prisoner, conduct ... hearing of such a charge or make, remit or mitigate an award in respect of such a charge; or
(c) except in cases of urgency, order the removal of a prisoner from association with other prisoners, the temporary confinement of a prisoner in a special cell or the application to a prisoner of any other special control or restraint.

(4) The controller shall have such functions as may be conferred on him by prison rules and shall be under a duty—
(a) to keep under review, and report to the Secretary of State on, the running of the prison by or on behalf of the director; and
(b) to investigate, and report to the Secretary of State on, any allegations made against prisoner custody officers performing custodial duties at the prison or prison officers who are temporarily attached to the prison.

(5) The contractor and any sub-contractor of his shall each be under a duty to do all that he reasonably can (whether by giving directions to the officers of the prison or otherwise) to facilitate the exercise by the controller of all such functions as are mentioned in or conferred by subsection (4) above.

(6) Every contracted out prison shall have a medical officer, who shall be a registered medical practitioner appointed by the contractor or, if the contract provides for the running of the prison by a sub-contractor, by the sub-contractor.

GENERAL NOTE
Directors or private prisons are to have the same powers and duties as governors of ordinary prisons, save for those relating to disciplinary infractions and segregation and restraint of prisoners. These powers, and the power to investigate allegations against prison custody officers, are vested in the controller, an official to be appointed by the Secretary of State. The controller is also to have the duties of keeping the running of the whole prison under review and reporting to the Secretary of State. The Secretary of State thus retains a general duty of superintendence of prisoners. Subsection (6) repeats the provision in s.3(1) of the Prisons (Scotland) Act 1989 in relation to the appointment of a medical officer; it may be thought strange that there is no equivalent of s.3(2) of the 1989 Act, which requires the appointment of a chaplain to each prison.

Powers and duties of prisoner custody officers employed at contracted out prisons

108.—(1) A prisoner custody officer performing custodial duties at a contracted out prison shall have power to search—
(a) any prisoner who is confined in the prison or for whose custody he is responsible; and

(b) any other person who is in or is seeking to enter the prison and any article in the possession of such a person.

(2) The power conferred by subsection (1)(b) above to search a person shall not be construed as authorising a prisoner custody officer to require a person to remove any of his clothing other than an outer coat, jacket, headgear and gloves.

(3) A prisoner custody officer performing custodial duties at a contracted out prison shall, as respects the prisoners for whose custody he is responsible, have the duty—

(a) to prevent their escape from legal custody;
(b) to prevent, or detect and report on, the commission or attempted commission by them of other unlawful acts;
(c) to ensure good order and discipline on their part; and
(d) to attend to their wellbeing.

(4) The powers conferred by subsection (1) above and the powers arising by virtue of subsection (3) above shall include power to use reasonable force where necessary.

GENERAL NOTE
This section gives prison custody officers the same powers of search of prisoners and visitors as are accorded to prison officers (see also ss.152, 153 *infra.*).

Breaches of discipline by prisoners temporarily out of contracted out prison

109.—(1) This section applies where a prisoner custody officer who performs custodial duties at a contracted out prison is responsible for the custody of a prisoner who is outside the prison for temporary purposes.

(2) For the purposes of such prison rules as relate to breaches of discipline the prisoner shall be deemed to have been in the custody of the director of the prison at all times during the period for which the prisoner custody officer was so responsible, and that officer may bring a charge of breach of such rules as so relate against the prisoner in respect of any such time.

(3) Nothing in subsection (1) above shall render a prisoner liable to be punished under prison rules for any act or omission of his for which he has already been punished by a court.

GENERAL NOTE
This section extends the operation of the disciplinary provisions of the Prisoners and Young Offenders Institutions (Scotland) Rules 1994 (S.I. 1994 No. 1931 (S.85)) (rr. 99–101) to cover periods when prisoners outside prison are in the custody of prison custody officers.

Consequential modifications of 1989 Act, prison rules and directions

110.—(1) In relation to a contracted out prison, the provisions specified in subsections (2) to (7) below shall have effect subject to the modifications so specified.

(2) In section 3 of the 1989 Act (general superintendence of prisons)—
(a) in subsection (1), the words from "who shall appoint" to the end shall be omitted; and
(b) subsection (3) shall not apply.

(3) In sections 9(5), 11(4), 15(1) and (3) (various functions of the governor of a prison), 33A (power of governor to delegate functions), 34 (duty of governor where prisoner dies), 39(8) and (12) (prison rules), 41(4) (detention of person suspected of bringing prohibited article into prison) and 41B(3) (testing prisoners for drugs) of that Act, in prison rules and in directions made by virtue of section 39(8) of that Act the reference to the governor shall be construed as a reference to the director.

(4) In sections 11(4) (execution of certain warrants by prison officers etc.), 13(b) (legal custody of prisoners), 33A (power of governor to delegate functions), 40(1) (persons unlawfully at large), 41(3), (4), (6) and (8) (detention

of person suspected of bringing prohibited article into prison) and 41B(1) (testing prisoners for drugs) of that Act, the reference to an officer of a prison (or, as the case may be, a prison officer) shall be construed as a reference to a prisoner custody officer performing custodial duties at the prison or a prison officer temporarily attached to the prison.

(5) Section 36 of that Act (vesting of prison property in Secretary of State) shall have effect subject to the provisions of the contract entered into under section 106 above.

(6) Sections 37 (discontinuance of prison), 41(2A) and (2B) (power to search for prohibited articles) and 41A (powers of search by authorised employees) of that Act shall not apply.

(7) In prison rules, in subsection (8) of section 39 of that Act (directions supplementing prison rules) and in any direction made by virtue of that subsection, the reference to an officer of a prison (or, as the case may be, a prison officer) shall be construed as including a reference to a prisoner custody officer performing custodial duties at the prison.

GENERAL NOTE

This section makes the necessary amendments to the Prisons (Scotland) Act 1989 to account for the creation of prison custody officers and the new power of the Secretary of State to contract out prisons or parts of prisons.

Intervention by the Secretary of State

111.—(1) This section applies where, in the case of a contracted out prison, it appears to the Secretary of State—
  (a) that the director has lost or is likely to lose effective control of the prison or any part of it; and
  (b) that the making of an appointment under subsection (2) below is necessary in the interests of preserving the safety of any person or preventing serious damage to any property.

(2) The Secretary of State may appoint a Crown servant to act as governor of the prison for the period—
  (a) beginning with the time specified in the appointment; and
  (b) ending with the time specified in the notice of termination under subsection (4) below.

(3) During that period—
  (a) all the functions which would otherwise be exercisable by the director or the controller shall be exercisable by the governor;
  (b) the contractor and any sub-contractor of his shall each do all that he reasonably can to facilitate the exercise by the governor of those functions; and
  (c) the officers of the prison shall comply with any directions given by the governor in the exercise of those functions.

(4) Where the Secretary of State is satisfied—
  (a) that the governor has secured effective control of the prison or, as the case may be, the relevant part of it; and
  (b) that the governor's appointment is no longer necessary as mentioned in subsection (1)(b) above,
he shall, by a notice to the governor, terminate the appointment at a time specified in the notice.

(5) As soon as practicable after making or terminating an appointment under this section, the Secretary of State shall give a notice of the appointment, or a copy of the notice of termination, to the contractor, any sub-contractor of his, the director and the controller.

GENERAL NOTE

The provisions of this section stress that the Secretary of State retains an ultimate responsibility for the custody of prisoners and allows him, when he is of the opinion that the director has lost or is likely to lose effective control of the prison or parts of it, in the interests of preserving the safety of any prisoner or preventing serious damage to any property, to appoint a Crown servant to run the prison. It is to be presumed that any contract with the provider of a private prison or service will provide for reimbursement of expenses incurred by the Secretary of State in such circumstances.

Contracted out functions

Contracted out functions at directly managed prisons

112.—(1) The Secretary of State may enter into a contract with another person for any functions at a directly managed prison to be performed by prisoner custody officers who are provided by that person and are authorised to perform custodial duties.

(2) Sections 108 and 109 above shall apply in relation to a prisoner custody officer performing contracted out functions at a directly managed prison as they apply in relation to such an officer performing custodial duties at a contracted out prison, but as if the reference in section 109(2) to the director of the contracted out prison were a reference to the governor of the directly managed prison.

(3) In relation to a directly managed prison, the references to an officer of a prison (or, as the case may be, a prison officer) in the provisions specified in subsection (4) below shall each be construed as including a reference to a prisoner custody officer performing custodial duties at the prison in pursuance of a contract under this section.

(4) Those provisions are—

(a) section 11(4) of the 1989 Act (execution of certain warrants by prison officers etc.);

(b) section 13(b) of that Act (legal custody of prisoners);

(c) section 33A of that Act (power of governor to delegate functions);

(d) subsection (8) of section 39 of that Act (directions supplementing prison rules) and directions made by virtue of that subsection;

(e) section 40(1) of that Act (persons unlawfully at large);

(f) section 41(3), (4), (6) and (8) of that Act (prohibited articles); and

(g) prison rules.

(5) Section 41(2A) and (2B) of the 1989 Act (search of person suspected of bringing prohibited article into prison) shall not apply in relation to a prisoner custody officer performing contracted out functions at a directly managed prison.

(6) Any reference in the foregoing provisions of this section to the performance of functions or custodial duties at a directly managed prison includes a reference to the performance of functions or such duties for the purposes of, or for purposes connected with, such a prison.

(7) In this Chapter—

"contracted out functions" means any functions which, by virtue of a contract under this section, fall to be performed by prisoner custody officers; and

"directly managed prison" means a prison which is not a contracted out prison.

GENERAL NOTE

While the provision of a wholly contracted-out prison is likely in the near future, an agreement reached in October 1994, on the introduction of a new staffing system, included an undertaking that the powers contained in this section will not be used until 1998 at the earliest. If these powers are used, the section requires that staff performing any contracted-out function must be authorised prison custody officers (subs. (1)) and will have the same powers as a prison officer, except for the power to search visitors (subs. (4)(5)).

Provision of new prisons

Provision of new prisons

113.—(1) The Secretary of State may declare to be a prison—
(a) any building or part of a building built or adapted for the purpose; and
(b) any floating structure or part of such a structure constructed or adapted for the purpose,
whether vested in, or under the control of, the Secretary of State or any other person.

(2) Section 106(1) and subsection (1) above are without prejudice to the Secretary of State's powers under the 1989 Act with respect to the provision of prisons.

(3) A declaration under subsection (1) above—
(a) shall have effect for the purposes of the 1989 Act and any other enactment (including an enactment contained in subordinate legislation);
(b) shall not be sufficient to vest the legal estate in any building or structure in the Secretary of State; and
(c) may be revoked by the Secretary of State at any time other than a time when the prison to which it relates is a contracted out prison.

(4) Nothing in section 36 of the 1989 Act (prison property to be vested in the Secretary of State) shall require the legal estate in—
(a) any prison provided under a contract entered into under section 106(1) above;
(b) any prison declared to be such under subsection (1) above and not vested in the Secretary of State; or
(c) any heritable or moveable property belonging to any prison mentioned in paragraph (a) or (b) above,
to be vested in the Secretary of State.

GENERAL NOTE

Subsection (1) enables the Secretary of State to declare any building or floating structure to be a prison, provided it has been built or adapted for this purpose. Accordingly, there is some restriction on what might otherwise be too wide a power, but it is now possible for Scotland to revert to 19th century practices (and follow contemporary New York State ones) of having "prison hulks". Subsections (3) and (4) alter the requirements in s.36 of the Prisons (Scotland) Act 1989 that legal estate in every prison and in all heritable and moveable property belonging to a prison must be vested in the Secretary of State.

Supplemental

Prisoner custody officers: general provisions

114.—(1) In this Chapter "prisoner custody officer" means a person in respect of whom a certificate is for the time being in force certifying—
(a) that he has been approved by the Secretary of State for the purpose of performing escort functions or custodial duties or both; and
(b) that he is accordingly authorised to perform them.

(2) Schedule 6 to this Act shall have effect with respect to the certification of prisoner custody officers.

(3) Prison rules may make provision regarding the powers and duties of prisoner custody officers performing custodial duties.

GENERAL NOTE

Taken with Sched. 6 to the Act, this section requires that any person to be appointed as a prison custody officer must obtain a certificate from the Secretary of State authorising the person so to act. The schedule provides for appropriate character checks and training before the grant of any certificate and for the suspension or revocation of certificates where an escort monitor, controller or governor considers, in circumstances to be prescribed by prison rules, or the Secretary of State, on receipt of a report from an escort monitor, controller or governor or in any other circumstances, decides this is appropriate (paras. 3 and 4). It shall be an offence for anyone knowingly or recklessly to make false statement for the purposes of obtaining a certificate (para. 5).

Wrongful disclosure of information

115.—(1) A person who—

(a) is or has been employed (whether as a prisoner custody officer or otherwise) in pursuance of prisoner escort arrangements, or at a contracted out prison; or

(b) is or has been employed to perform contracted out functions at a directly managed prison,

shall be guilty of an offence if he discloses, otherwise than in the course of his duty or as authorised by the Secretary of State, any information which he acquired in the course of his employment and which relates to a particular prisoner.

(2) A person guilty of an offence under subsection (1) above shall be liable—

(a) on conviction on indictment, to imprisonment for a term not exceeding two years or a fine or both;

(b) on summary conviction, to imprisonment for a term not exceeding six months or a fine not exceeding the statutory maximum or both.

GENERAL NOTE

A similar restriction is placed on prison custody officers under r. 131 of the Prisons and Young Offenders Institutions (Scotland) Rules 1994, with sanctions available under the Code of Discipline made by authority of r. 132. The independence of the prison custody officers brings with it the possibility of punishments in the form of fines and/or imprisonment. Prison custody officers are not covered by the Code of Discipline.

Minor and consequential amendments

116.—(1) In section 19(4)(b) of the 1989 Act (remand centres and young offenders institutions), for "33" there shall be substituted "33A".

(2) Section 33 of that Act (miscellaneous duties of prison governor) shall cease to have effect.

(3) After section 33 of that Act there shall be inserted the following section—

"Power of governor to delegate functions

33A. Rules made under section 39 of this Act may permit the governor of a prison to authorise an officer of the prison, or a class of such officers, to exercise on his behalf such of the governor's functions as the rules may specify.".

(4) In section 39 of that Act (prison rules)—

(a) in subsection (1), after "Act" there shall be inserted "or any other enactment";

(b) in subsection (8), for "the purpose so specified" there shall be substituted "any purpose specified in the rules"; and

(c) after subsection (11), there shall be inserted the following subsection—

"(12) Rules made under this section may (without prejudice to the generality of subsection (1) above) confer functions on a governor.".

GENERAL NOTE

Section 33(2) of the Prisons (Scotland) Act 1989 imposed an obligation on the governor of each prison to perform certain tasks (*e.g.* the visiting of the whole of the prison and seeing each prisoner every day) which it is neither practicable nor sensible for a senior manager to perform. The new s.33A, as inserted by subs. (3), creates a power to enable delegation of such of these functions as may be prescribed by rules. Section 39 of the Prisons (Scotland) Act 1989 has already been amended by Sched. 9 of the Prisoners and Criminal Proceedings (Scotland) Act 1993.

Interpretation of Chapter II

117.—(1) In this Chapter, except where otherwise expressly provided—
"the 1989 Act" means the Prisons (Scotland) Act 1989;
"contracted out prison" and "the contractor" have the meanings given
    by section 106(4) above;
"contracted out functions" and "directly managed prison" have the
    meanings given by section 112(7) above;
"custodial duties" means custodial duties at a contracted out or a
    directly managed prison;
"escort functions" has the meaning given by section 102(1) above;
"prison" includes—
        (a) any prison other than a naval, military or air force prison; and
        (b) a remand centre or young offenders institution within the
    meaning of section 19 of the 1989 Act;
"prison officer" means an officer of a directly managed prison;
"prison rules" means rules made under section 39 of the 1989 Act;
"prisoner" means any person who is in legal custody or is deemed to be
    in legal custody under section 215 or 426 of the Criminal Procedure
    (Scotland) Act 1975;
"prisoner custody officer" has the meaning given by section 114(1)
    above;
"prisoner escort arrangements" has the meaning given by section 102(4)
    above; and
"sub-contractor" has the meaning given by section 106(4) above.
(2) Any reference in this Chapter to custodial duties at a contracted out or
directly managed prison includes a reference to custodial duties in relation to
a prisoner who is outside such a prison for temporary purposes.
(3) In sections 102(1) to (3), 104 and 105 above, "prison"—
(a) so far as relating to the transfer of prisoners to or from a prison situ-
    ated in England and Wales, includes a young offender institution and a
    remand centre; and
(b) so far as relating to the transfer of prisoners to or from a prison situ-
    ated in Northern Ireland, includes a young offenders centre and a
    remand centre.

CHAPTER III

NORTHERN IRELAND

Prisoner escorts

Arrangements for the provision of prisoner escorts

118.—(1) The Secretary of State may make arrangements for any of the
following functions, namely—
(a) the delivery of prisoners from one set of relevant premises to another;
(b) the custody of prisoners held on the premises of any court (whether or
    not they would otherwise be in the custody of the court) and their
    production before the court;
(c) the custody of prisoners temporarily held in a prison in the course of
    delivery from one prison to another; and
(d) the custody of prisoners while they are outside a prison for temporary
    purposes;
to be performed in such cases as may be determined by or under the arrangements by prisoner custody officers who are authorised to perform such
functions.
(2) In paragraph (a) of subsection (1) above, "relevant premises" means a
court, prison, police station or hospital; and either (but not both) of the sets

of premises mentioned in that paragraph may be situated in a part of the British Islands outside Northern Ireland.

(3) Arrangements made by the Secretary of State under this section ("prisoner escort arrangements") may include entering into contracts with other persons for the provision by them of prisoner custody officers.

(4) Any person who, under a warrant or a hospital order or remand, is responsible for the performance of any such function as is mentioned in subsection (1) above shall be deemed to have complied with that warrant, order or remand if he does all that he reasonably can to secure that the function is performed by a prisoner custody officer acting in pursuance of prisoner escort arrangements.

(5) In this section—
> "hospital" has the same meaning as in the Mental Health (Northern Ireland) Order 1986;
> "hospital order" means an order for a person's admission to hospital under Article 44, 45, 49 or 50 of that Order, or section 11 or 13 of the Criminal Appeal (Northern Ireland) Act 1980;
> "hospital remand" means a remand of a person to hospital under Article 42 or 43 of the Mental Health (Northern Ireland) Order 1986;
> "warrant" means a warrant of commitment, a warrant of arrest or a warrant under Article 52, 53, 54, 56 or 79 of that Order.

DEFINITIONS
> "hospital": subs. (5).
> "hospital order": subs. (5).
> "hospital remand": subs. (5).
> "prison": s.125(1)(3).
> "prisoner": s.125(1).
> "prisoner custody officer": ss.122(1), 125(1).
> "prisoner escort arrangements": subs. (3), s.125(1).
> "relevant premises": subs. (2).
> "warrant": subs. (5).

GENERAL NOTE
> This section makes similar arrangements for prisoner escorts in Northern Ireland to those which exist in England and Wales (Criminal Justices Act 1991, s.80, as amended by s.93, *ante*), and Scotland, (s.102, *ante*) so that prisoners in custody can be moved from one set of "relevant premises" to another. *Note* that, by subs. (2), such premises may be outside Northern Ireland. Legal "custody" refers both to sentenced prisoners and to those held in police cells: Minister of State, Home Office, Standing Committee B, col. 869, Feb. 17, 1994 (see the definition of "prisoner" in s.125(1)), *post.* The section is similar to the arrangements for the escort of offenders detained at secure training centres: Sched. 1, *post.* The section allows for the "contracting-out" of prisoner escort functions. The Minister announced (Standing Committee B, col. 868) that there were no plans for the private sector to escort high-risk terrorist prisoners.

Monitoring etc. of prisoner escort arrangements

119.—(1) Prisoner escort arrangements shall include the appointment of a prisoner escort monitor, that is to say, a Crown servant whose duty it shall be to keep the arrangements under review and to report on them to the Secretary of State.

(2) It shall also be the duty of a prisoner escort monitor to investigate and report to the Secretary of State on—
> (a) any allegations made against prisoner custody officers acting in pursuance of the arrangements; and
> (b) any alleged breaches of discipline on the part of prisoners for whose delivery or custody such officers so acting are responsible.

DEFINITIONS
> "prisoner": s.125(1).
> "prisoner custody officer": ss.122(1), 125(1).
> "prisoner escort monitor": subs. (1).

GENERAL NOTE

This section provides for the appointment of a Crown Servant to act as a prisoner escort monitor with responsibility to the Secretary of State for Northern Ireland for keeping prisoner escort arrangements under review, investigating and reporting on any allegations made against prisoner custody officers and reporting on any alleged breach of discipline by prisoners. It is similar to the provisions of the 1991 Act, s.81, which apply to England and Wales and the provisions in Sched. 1, *post*, relating to offenders detained at secure training centres (except that there is no provision for a panel of lay observers).

Powers and duties of prisoner custody officers acting in pursuance of such arrangements

120.—(1) A prisoner custody officer acting in pursuance of prisoner escort arrangements shall have the following powers, namely—

(a) to search in accordance with rules made by the Secretary of State any prisoner for whose delivery or custody he is responsible in accordance with the arrangements; and

(b) to search any other person who is in or is seeking to enter any place where any such prisoner is or is to be held and any article in the possession of such a person.

(2) The powers conferred by subsection (1)(b) above to search a person shall not be construed as authorising a prisoner custody officer to require a person to remove any of his clothing other than an outer coat, hat, jacket or gloves.

(3) A prisoner custody officer shall have the following duties as respects prisoners for whose delivery or custody he is responsible in pursuance of prisoner escort arrangements, namely—

(a) to prevent their escape from lawful custody;

(b) to prevent, or detect and report on, the commission or attempted commission by them of other unlawful acts;

(c) to ensure good order and discipline on their part;

(d) to attend to their wellbeing; and

(e) to give effect to any directions as to their treatment which are given by a court,

and the Secretary of State may make rules with respect to the performance by prisoner custody officers of their duty under paragraph (d) above.

(4) Where a prisoner custody officer acting in pursuance of prisoner escort arrangements is on any premises in which a magistrates' court is sitting, it shall be his duty to give effect to any order of that court made under Article 110 of the Magistrates' Courts (Northern Ireland) Order 1981 (application of funds found upon defaulter).

(5) The powers conferred by subsection (1) above and the powers arising by virtue of subsections (3) and (4) above shall include power to use reasonable force where necessary.

(6) The power to make rules under this section shall be exercisable by statutory instrument which shall be subject to annulment in pursuance of a resolution of either House of Parliament.

DEFINITIONS

"prisoner": s.125(1).
"prisoner custody officer": ss.122(1), 125(1).
"prisoner escort arrangements": ss.118(3), 125(1).
"rules": s.125(1).

GENERAL NOTE

This section sets out the powers and duties of prisoner custody officers performing escort functions under this Chapter of Pt. VIII. It gives a power to prisoner custody officers to search both prisoners and any person in or seeking to enter a place where the prisoner is held and any article on such person. The power to oblige a prisoner to remove his outer coat, jacket, hat or gloves (subs. (2)) is wider than the equivalent in s.82(2) of the 1991 Act, which refers only to outer coat, jacket and gloves. In s.104, *ante*, which relates to Scotland, and Sched. 1, *post*, which relates to secure training centres, the equivalent word is "headgear". The duties laid down by subs. (3) are similar to those laid on prisoner custody officers in England and Wales by s.82(3) of the 1991 Act.

Subs. (4)
Article 110, Magistrates' Courts (Northern Ireland) Order 1981 (S.I. 1981 No. 1675 (N.I. 26)), empowers a magistrates' court, where a person has been adjudged to pay a sum by a court, to order that person to be searched. The English equivalent is the Magistrates' Courts Act 1980 (c. 43), s.80.

Subs. (5)
Reasonable force: see the General Note to s.136, *post.*

Breaches of discipline by prisoners under escort

121.—(1) This section applies where a prisoner for whose delivery or custody a prisoner custody officer has been responsible in pursuance of prisoner escort arrangements is delivered to a prison.

(2) For the purpose of such prison rules as relate to disciplinary offences, the prisoner shall be deemed to have been in the custody of the governor of the prison at all times during the period for which the prisoner custody officer was so responsible.

(3) In the case of any breach by the prisoner at any time during the period of such prison rules as so relate, a disciplinary charge may be laid against him by the prisoner custody officer.

(4) Nothing in this section shall enable a prisoner to be punished under prison rules for any act or omission of his for which he has already been punished by a court.

(5) In this section "prison rules", in relation to a prison situated in a part of the British Islands outside Northern Ireland, means rules made under any provision of the law of that part which corresponds to section 13 of the Prison Act (Northern Ireland) 1953.

DEFINITIONS
    "prison": s.125(1)(3).
    "prisoner": s.125(1).
    "prisoner custody officer": ss.122(1), 125(1).
    "rules": subs. (5), s.125(1).

GENERAL NOTE
    This section provides that where a prisoner has been delivered to a prison by a prisoner custody officer he shall be deemed for the purposes of disciplinary proceedings to have been in the custody of the governor of a prison. The equivalent legislation for England and Wales is s.95 of this Act, *ante*, and for Scotland, s.105, *ante*. But this section, unlike the other two, refers only to "prisons" and not to "contracted-out prisons". At the time the Bill was debated in the House of Commons there were no plans to privatise prisons in Northern Ireland (Standing Committee B, col. 872).

Subss. (2) and (5)
    Prison rules: the relevant rules for Northern Ireland are the Prison Rules 1982 No. 170 as amended by the Prison Rules 1982 No. 248.

Supplemental

Certification of custody officers

122.—(1) In this Chapter "prisoner custody officer" means a person in respect of whom a certificate is for the time being in force certifying—
    (a) that he has been approved by the Secretary of State for the purpose of performing escort functions; and
    (b) that he is accordingly authorised to perform them.

(2) Schedule 7 to this Act shall have effect with respect to the certification of prisoner custody officers.

(3) In this section and Schedule 7 to this Act "escort functions" means the functions specified in section 118(1) above.

DEFINITIONS
"escort functions": subs. (3).
"prisoner custody officer": ss.122(1), 125(1).

GENERAL NOTE
This section, with Sched. 7 which it introduces, provides for the Secretary of State for Northern Ireland to issue certificates approving prisoner custody officers for the purposes of performing prisoner escort duties. The equivalent legislation in England and Wales is s.89 (as amended by s.101(4), *ante*) and Sched. 10 to the 1991 Act, and in Scotland, s.114, *ante*, and Sched. 6, *post*. Sched. 7, *post*, provides for the issue, suspension and revocation of certificates. A false statement made for the purpose of obtaining a certificate is an offence: Sched. 7, para. 5. Provision with regard to persons detained in secure training centres is made by s.12(2), *ante*, and Sched. 2, *post*.

Protection of prisoner custody officers

123.—(1) Any person who assaults a prisoner custody officer acting in pursuance of prisoner escort arrangements shall be liable on summary conviction to a fine not exceeding level 5 on the standard scale or to imprisonment for a term not exceeding six months or to both.

(2) Article 18(2) of the Firearms (Northern Ireland) Order 1981 (additional penalty for possession of firearms when committing certain offences) shall apply to offences under subsection (1) above.

(3) Any person who resists or wilfully obstructs a prisoner custody officer acting in pursuance of prisoner escort arrangements shall be liable on summary conviction to a fine not exceeding level 3 on the standard scale.

(4) For the purposes of this section, a prisoner custody officer shall not be regarded as acting in pursuance of prisoner escort arrangements at any time when he is not readily identifiable as such an officer (whether by means of a uniform or badge which he is wearing or otherwise).

DEFINITIONS
"prisoner custody officer": ss.122(1), 125(1).
"prisoner escort arrangements": ss.118(3), 125(1).

GENERAL NOTE
This section provides that it will be an offence to assault, resist or wilfully obstruct a prisoner custody officer acting in pursuance of his duties. He will only be regarded as acting in pursuance of his duties if at the time, he is readily identifiable as a prisoner custody officer either by badge, uniform or otherwise. These offences will be included in the list of offences for which there will be an additional penalty if when committing them a person has in his possession a firearm or imitation firearm. The equivalent legislation in England and Wales is s.90 of the 1991 Act (as amended by s.101(5), *ante*). There is a similar provision with regard to persons detained in secure training centres: s.13, *ante*. For further comment, see Note to s.13.

Subs. (3)
"*Wilfully obstructs*": see the General Note to s.13, *ante*.

Wrongful disclosure of information

124.—(1) A person who is or has been employed (whether as a prisoner custody officer or otherwise) in pursuance of prisoner escort arrangements shall be guilty of an offence if he discloses, otherwise than in the course of his duty or as authorised by the Secretary of State, any information which he acquired in the course of his employment and which relates to a particular prisoner.

(2) A person guilty of an offence under subsection (1) above shall be liable—

(a) on conviction on indictment, to imprisonment for a term not exceeding two years or a fine or both;

(b) on summary conviction, to imprisonment for a term not exceeding six months or a fine not exceeding the statutory maximum or both.

DEFINITIONS
"prisoner custody officer": ss.122(1), 125(1).
"prisoner escort arrangements": ss.118(3), 125(1).

GENERAL NOTE
This section provides that a person who has been employed in pursuance of prisoner escorting arrangements shall be guilty of an offence if he discloses without authority any information which he acquired in the course of his employment and which relates to a particular prisoner. The equivalent legislation in England and Wales is s.91 (as amended by s.101(6), *ante*) of the 1991 Act and in Scotland s.115, *ante*. For further comment see Note to s.14, *ante*, relating to disclosure of information connected with persons detained in secure training centres.

Interpretation of Chapter III

125.—(1) In this Chapter—
"prison" includes a young offenders centre or remand centre;
"prisoner custody officer" has the meaning given by section 122(1) above;
"prison rules" means rules made under section 13 of the Prison Act (Northern Ireland) 1953;
"prisoner" means any person for the time being detained in lawful custody as the result of a requirement imposed by a court or otherwise that he be so detained;
"prisoner escort arrangements" has the meaning given by section 118(3) above.
(2) Sections 118, 119(1) and (2)(a), 120 and 122 to 124 above, subsection (1) above and Schedule 7 to this Act shall have effect as if—
(a) any reference in section 118(1), 119(1), 120 or 124 above to prisoners included a reference to persons remanded or committed to custody in certain premises under section 51, 74 or 75 of the Children and Young Persons Act (Northern Ireland) 1968 or ordered to be sent to a training school under section 74 or 78 of that Act; and
(b) any reference in section 118(1)(c) or (d) or (2) above to a prison included a reference to such premises or training school.
(3) In sections 118, 120 and 121 above, "prison"—
(a) so far as relating to the delivery of prisoners to or from a prison situated in England and Wales, includes a remand centre or young offender institution; and
(b) so far as relating to the delivery of prisoners to or from a prison situated in Scotland, includes a remand centre or young offenders institution within the meaning of section 19 of the Prisons (Scotland) Act 1989.

GENERAL NOTE
This section is the interpretation section for ss.110 to 116.

CHAPTER IV

THE PRISON SERVICE

Service in England and Wales and Northern Ireland

126.—(1) The relevant employment legislation shall have effect as if an individual who as a member of the prison service acts in a capacity in which he has the powers or privileges of a constable were not, by virtue of his so having those powers or privileges, to be regarded as in police service for the purposes of any provision of that legislation.
(2) In this section "the relevant employment legislation" means—

(a) the Employment Protection (Consolidation) Act 1978 and the Trade Union and Labour Relations (Consolidation) Act 1992; and

(b) the Industrial Relations (Northern Ireland) Order 1976, the Industrial Relations (No. 2) (Northern Ireland) Order 1976 and the Industrial Relations (Northern Ireland) Order 1992.

(3) For the purposes of this section a person is a member of the prison service if he is an individual holding a post to which he has been appointed for the purposes of section 7 of the Prison Act 1952 or under section 2(2) of the Prison Act (Northern Ireland) 1953 (appointment of prison staff).

(4) Except for the purpose of validating anything that would have been a contravention of section 127(1) below if it had been in force, subsection (1) above, so far as it relates to the question whether an organisation consisting wholly or mainly of members of the prison service is a trade union, shall be deemed always to have had effect and to have applied, in relation to times when provisions of the relevant employment legislation were not in force, to the corresponding legislation then in force.

(5) Subsection (6) below shall apply where—

(a) the certificate of independence of any organisation has been cancelled, at any time before the passing of this Act, in consequence of the removal of the name of that organisation from a list of trade unions kept under provisions of the relevant employment legislation; but

(b) it appears to the Certification Officer that the organisation would have remained on the list, and that the certificate would have remained in force, had that legislation had effect at and after that time in accordance with subsection (1) above.

(6) Where this subsection applies—

(a) the Certification Officer shall restore the name to the list and delete from his records any entry relating to the cancellation of the certificate;

(b) the removal of the name from the list, the making of the deleted entry and the cancellation of the certificate shall be deemed never to have occurred; and

(c) the organisation shall accordingly be deemed, for the purposes for which it is treated by virtue of subsection (4) above as having been a trade union, to have been independent throughout the period between the cancellation of the certificate and the deletion of the entry relating to that cancellation.

DEFINITIONS
"relevant employment legislation": subs. (2).
"member of the prison service": subs. (3).

GENERAL NOTE
The purpose of this section (together with s.127 and 128, *post*) has been said to be "to put industrial relations in the prison service on a proper footing": Standing Committee B, col. 881, February 22, 1994. The background is to be found in s.8 of the Prison Act 1952 which provides that: "Every prison officer while acting as such shall have all the powers, authority, protection and privileges of a constable". From time to time the courts have drawn attention to this section. Thus, in *Home Office v. Robinson and The Prison Officers' Association* [1982] C.L.Y. 1117 the Employment Appeal Tribunal held that, since s.8 of the 1952 Act gave a prison officer the powers etc. of a constable, he did not have the right to bring a claim for unfair dismissal to an industrial tribunal. Similarly, in *McLaren v. The Home Office* [1991] C.L.Y. 2994, Woolf L.J. referred to the fact that a prison officer had, by reason of s.8, while acting as such, the powers etc. of a police officer. In November 1993 the Prison Officers' Association threatened industrial action. The Home Secretary obtained an injunction forbidding the action on the ground that it was unlawful. The effect of this decision was that prison officers did not have, and never had had, the right to belong to a trade union or to take industrial action. (Constables do not have the right to belong to a trade union the police representative institutions are specifically recognised by the Police Act 1964, Pt. III).

Accordingly, this section provides for prison officers to benefit from employment protection rights on the same basis as other Crown employees and for them to be represented by trade unions, although their status as constables continues.

Subs. (3)

Section 7 of the Prison Act 1952 provides that every prison shall have a governor, a Church of England chaplain and a medical officer (registered under the Medical Acts) and such other officers as may be necessary; every prison in which women are received shall have a sufficient number of women officers; a prison which is in the opinion of the Secretary of State large enough, may have a deputy governor or deputy chaplain or both. (Note that by s.101(7), *ante,* amending Criminal Justice Act 1991, s.92(1) *prison officer* "means an officer of a directly managed prison". For the definition of *directly managed prison* see s.99, *ante.*)

The Prison Act (Northern Ireland) 1953 No. 18, s.2(2), provides: "The Ministry shall appoint the governors, medical officers, and such other officers as appear to it to be necessary."

Subs. (4)

The purpose of this subsection is to protect third parties who had in good faith entered into legal and contractual relationships with the Prison Officers' Association (POA) on the assumption that it was a properly constituted trade union, including the POA's own employees. Such employees now have the "full range of employment protection rights that other Crown employees have, notably access to industrial tribunals": Standing Committee B, col. 883, February 22, 1994. But there is one important limitation: an action which would contravene s.127, *post* (inducements to withhold services or to indiscipline). As a consequence not only will the POA in future be unable to call for industrial action but calls made previous to this Act, which had been thought to be lawful, will remain unlawful. The Government refused to allow an amendment to make such previous calls to action lawful: "one cannot go back and wipe the slate clean": Minister of State, Home Office, H.C. Comm. Deb. 883.

Scottish perspective

It should be noted that Scottish prison officers were not accorded the powers and privileges of a constable in the exercise of their duties and thus did not suffer any legal limitations on their industrial activities.

Inducements to withhold services or to indiscipline

127.—(1) A person contravenes this subsection if he induces a prison officer—

(a) to withhold his services as such an officer; or

(b) to commit a breach of discipline.

(2) The obligation not to contravene subsection (1) above shall be a duty owed to the Secretary of State.

(3) Without prejudice to the right of the Secretary of State, by virtue of the preceding provisions of this section, to bring civil proceedings in respect of any apprehended contravention of subsection (1) above, any breach of the duty mentioned in subsection (2) above which causes the Secretary of State to sustain loss or damage shall be actionable, at his suit or instance, against the person in breach.

(4) In this section "prison officer" means any individual who—

(a) holds any post, otherwise than as a chaplain or assistant chaplain or as a medical officer, to which he has been appointed for the purposes of section 7 of the Prison Act 1952 or under section 2(2) of the Prison Act (Northern Ireland) 1953 (appointment of prison staff),

(b) holds any post, otherwise than as a medical officer, to which he has been appointed under section 3(1) of the Prisons (Scotland) Act 1989, or

(c) is a custody officer within the meaning of Part I of this Act or a prisoner custody officer, within the meaning of Part IV of the Criminal Justice Act 1991 or Chapter II or III of this Part.

(5) The reference in subsection (1) above to a breach of discipline by a prison officer is a reference to a failure by a prison officer to perform any duty

imposed on him by the prison rules or any code of discipline having effect under those rules or any other contravention by a prison officer of those rules or any such code.

(6) In subsection (5) above "the prison rules" means any rules for the time being in force under section 47 of the Prison Act 1952, section 39 of the Prisons (Scotland) Act 1989 or section 13 of the Prison Act (Northern Ireland) 1953 (prison rules).

(7) This section shall be disregarded in determining for the purposes of any of the relevant employment legislation whether any trade union is an independent trade union.

(8) Nothing in the relevant employment legislation shall affect the rights of the Secretary of State by virtue of this section.

(9) In this section "the relevant employment legislation" has the same meaning as in section 126 above.

DEFINITIONS
"breach of discipline": subs. (5).
"custody officer": s.12(3).
"prison officer": subs. (4).
"relevant employment legislation": subs. (9), s.126(2).

GENERAL NOTE
This section limits the employment rights conferred on prison officers by s.126, *ante*, in one important respect: it is unlawful, and therefore a tort, to induce a prison officer to withhold his services or to commit a breach of discipline, *i.e.* to take industrial action: subs. (1). As in other similar torts in trade union law, it is the inducement that is unlawful: actually withholding services or committing breaches of discipline will not be within the section. The tort created by this section is actionable only by the Home Secretary (subs. (2)). He is entitled to apply for an injunction to prevent an apprehended breach of the duty (under this section) without the need to show that he would suffer any actual loss or damage (subs. (3) introduced in the House of Lords). If a third party wishes to bring an action against the trade union it must do so under s.235A of the Trade Union and Labour Relations (Consolidation) Act 1992 which was inserted by the Trade Union Reform and Employment Rights Act 1992, which extended to third parties rights of redress for losses incurred as a result of industrial disputes in contravention of the procedures laid down in the main Act.

Prisoner custody officers and custody officers of secure training centres, who are not members of the prison service within the meaning of s.126(3), *ante* (see the General Note to the section), are *prison officers* for the purposes of this section (subs. (4)(c)). Thus, where prisoner custody officers or custody officers are induced to take industrial action against their employer, the Secretary of State may seek the appropriate legal remedy. But chaplains, assistant chaplains and medical officers, who are part of the prison service (see s.126, *ante*) do not come within this section: the Government felt that the ethical and professional codes which regulate the conduct of chaplains and doctors were sufficient: Standing Committee B, col. 888, February 22, 1994. Subsection (7), however, provides that a trade union representing prison officers is still, for all the limitations on its powers enacted by this section, a trade union.

Scottish perspective
Scotland has never witnessed the kind of industrial action by prison officers which was seen in England in the early summer of 1986. Nevertheless, this provision applies throughout the U.K. and renders organised strike action illegal. The provision applies equally to prison officers and prison custody officers. The present Code of Discipline governing Scottish prison officers is dated July 1993.

Pay and related conditions

128.—(1) The Secretary of State may by regulations provide for the establishment, maintenance and operation of procedures for the determination from time to time of—

(a) the rates of pay and allowances to be applied to the prison service; and
(b) such other terms and conditions of employment in that service as may appear to him to fall to be determined in association with the determination of rates of pay and allowances.

(2) Before making any regulations under this section the Secretary of State shall consult with such organisations appearing to him to be representative of persons working in the prison service and with such other persons as he thinks fit.

(3) The power to make regulations under this section shall be exercisable by statutory instrument subject to annulment in pursuance of a resolution of either House of Parliament.

(4) Regulations under this section may—

(a) provide for determinations with respect to matters to which the regulations relate to be made wholly or partly by reference to such factors, and the opinion or recommendations of such persons, as may be specified or described in the regulations;

(b) authorise the matters considered and determined in pursuance of the regulations to include matters applicable to times and periods before they are considered or determined;

(c) make such incidental, supplemental, consequential and transitional provision as the Secretary of State thinks fit; and

(d) make different provision for different cases.

(5) For the purposes of this section the prison service comprises all the individuals who are prison officers within the meaning of section 127 above, apart from those who are custody officers within the meaning of Part I of this Act or prisoner custody officers within the meaning of Part IV of the Criminal Justice Act 1991 or Chapter II or III of this Part.

DEFINITIONS
"prison service": subs. (5).

GENERAL NOTE
This section gives the Secretary of State power to make regulations concerning procedures for determining pay and related terms of employment of officers of prisons (subs. (1)). The Secretary of State must consult with such organisations as appear to him to be representative of persons working in the prison service (this could include organisations other than trade unions) and other persons as he thinks fit (subs. (2)). Subsection (4) provides for the content of the regulations and is unspecific about what that content will actually be.

Prison officers in this section do not include chaplains, assistant chaplains or medical officers, nor custody officers of contracted-out secure training centres, nor prisoner custody officers at contracted-out prisons: in the debate on s.126, *ante*, the Minister said: "It would be entirely for the private sector to ... determine pay and conditions": Standing Committee B, col. 906.

Scottish perspective
It is not known whether there is to be a separate body to determine pay and conditions of prison employees in Scotland. This provision does not apply to prison custody officers in contracted out prisons or escort services.

PART IX

MISCELLANEOUS AMENDMENTS: SCOTLAND

Transfer of persons detained by police and customs officers

129.—(1) In subsection (1) of section 2 of the Criminal Justice (Scotland) Act 1980 (detention of suspect at police station or other premises)—

(a) after the word "premises" there shall be inserted the words "and may thereafter for that purpose take him to any other place"; and

(b) for the word "there" there shall be substituted the words "at the police station, or as the case may be the other premises or place".

(2) In subsection (4) of that section—

(a) after paragraph (a) there shall be inserted the following paragraph—

"(aa) any other place to which the person is, during the detention, thereafter taken;"; and

(b) in paragraph (f), for the words "departure from the police station or other premises" there shall be substituted the words "release from detention".

(3) In section 3(1)(b) of that Act (intimation to solicitor and other person of detention under section 2)—

(a) for the words "in a police station or other premises" there shall be substituted the words "and has been taken to a police station or other premises or place"; and

(b) for the words "place where he is being detained" there shall be substituted the words "police station or other premises or place".

(4) In subsection (1) of section 48 of the Criminal Justice (Scotland) Act 1987 (detention of suspect by customs officer)—

(a) after the word "premises" there shall be inserted the words "and may thereafter for that purpose take him to any other place"; and

(b) for the word "there" there shall be substituted the words "at the customs office, or as the case may be the other premises or place.".

(5) In subsection (5) of that section—

(a) after paragraph (a) there shall be inserted the following paragraph—

"(aa) any other place to which the person is, during the detention, thereafter taken;"; and

(b) in paragraph (f), for the words "departure from the customs office or other premises" there shall be substituted the words "release from detention".

(6) In section 49(1) of that Act (intimation to solicitor and other person of detention under section 48)—

(a) for the words "at a customs office or other premises" there shall be substituted the words "and has been taken to a customs office or other premises or place"; and

(b) for the words "place where he is being detained" there shall be substituted the words "customs office or other premises or place".

GENERAL NOTE

Neither the Criminal Justice (Scotland) Act 1980 nor the Criminal Justice (Scotland) Act 1987 allowed a person detained under the six-hour power to be moved from the police or customs premises where first detained or taken to on detention to any other premises. This provision alters the situation, subject to the protection that any solicitor or any other person notified of the detention must also be notified of the change in location.

Detention and release of children: Scotland

130.—(1) In section 7 of the Prisoners and Criminal Proceedings (Scotland) Act 1993 (children detained in solemn proceedings), after subsection (1) there shall be inserted—

"(1A) The Secretary of State may by order provide—

(a) that the reference to—

(i) four years, in paragraph (a) of subsection (1) above; or

(ii) four or more years, in paragraph (b) of that subsection,

shall be construed as a reference to such other period as may be specified in the order;

(b) that the reference to—

(i) half, in the said paragraph (a); or

(ii) two thirds, in the said paragraph (b),

shall be construed as a reference to such other proportion of the period specified in the sentence as may be specified in the order.

(1B) An order under subsection (1A) above may make such transitional provision as appears to the Secretary of State necessary or expedient in connection with any provision made by the order.".

(2) In section 45(3) of that Act (procedure in respect of certain orders), for the words "7(6)" there shall be substituted "7(1A) or (6)".

(3) In Schedule 6 to that Act (transitional provisions and savings)—

(a) in paragraph 8, after the word "revoked" there shall be inserted "by virtue of paragraph 10 of this Schedule"; and

(b) after paragraph 9 there shall be added—

"10. Section 17 of this Act shall apply in respect of a release on licence under paragraph 4 of this Schedule as that section applies in respect of the release on licence, under Part I of this Act, of a long-term prisoner.".

(4) In section 39(7) of the Prisons (Scotland) Act 1989 (award of additional days), at the end there shall be added—

"; and the foregoing provisions of this subsection (except paragraph (b)) shall apply in respect of a person sentenced to be detained under section 206 of the 1975 Act, the detention not being without limit of time, as those provisions apply in respect of any such short-term or long-term prisoner.".

GENERAL NOTE

This provision further assimilates the treatment of child detainees with that accorded to adults in relation to release arrangements under the Prisoners and Criminal Proceedings (Scotland) Act 1993 and disciplinary procedures under the Prisons (Scotland) Act 1989.

Conditions in licence of released prisoner: requirement for Parole Board recommendations

131. In section 12(3)(a) of the Prisoners and Criminal Proceedings (Scotland) Act 1993 (requirement of Parole Board recommendations for inclusion of conditions in licences of certain released prisoners), after the word "inclusion" there shall be inserted the words "or subsequent insertion, variation or cancellation".

GENERAL NOTE

The Prisons and Criminal Proceedings (Scotland) Act 1993 had only allowed the Parole Board to direct the inclusion of conditions in the release licence of a discretionary life prisoner at the time of release.

Provision for standard requirements in supervised release orders in Scotland

132. In section 212A of the Criminal Procedure (Scotland) Act 1975 (which makes provision for the supervised release of short-term prisoners)—

(a) in subsection (2)—

(i) for the words from "and", where it occurs immediately after paragraph (a), to the end of sub-paragraph (i) of paragraph (b), there shall be substituted—

"(b) comply with—

(i) such requirements as may be imposed by the court in the order;"; and

(ii) at the end there shall be added—

"; and

(c) comply with the standard requirements imposed by virtue of subsection (3)(a)(i) below"; and

(b) in subsection (3), for paragraph (a) there shall be substituted—

"(a) shall—

(i) without prejudice to subsection (2)(b) above, contain such requirements (in this section referred to as the "standard requirements"); and

(ii) be as nearly as possible in such form,

as may be prescribed by Act of Adjournal;".

GENERAL NOTE

The Prisons and Criminal Proceedings (Scotland) Act 1993 created for the first time a "supervised release order" under which a court, when sentencing someone to between one and four years' imprisonment, can order that the person be subject to compulsory supervision on release for up to 12 months. This amendment allows standard conditions for such licences to be set by means of Act of Adjournal.

Extension of categories of prisoner to whom Part I of Prisoners and Criminal Proceedings (Scotland) Act 1993 applies

133. In section 10(4) of the Prisoners and Criminal Proceedings (Scotland) Act 1993 (interpretation of expression "transferred life prisoner")—
  (a) in paragraph (a), after the word "Scotland" there shall be inserted the words "or a court-martial"; and
  (b) in paragraph (b)—
      (i) for the word "(whether" there shall be substituted—
      ", or in the case of a sentence imposed by a court martial in Scotland to a prison in Scotland (in either case whether";
      (ii) after sub-paragraph (ii) there shall be inserted—
      "; or
          (iii) rules made under section 122(1)(a) of the Army Act 1955 (imprisonment and detention rules); or
          (iv) rules made under section 122(1)(a) of the Air Force Act 1955 (imprisonment and detention rules); or
          (v) a determination made under section 81(3) of the Naval Discipline Act 1957 (place of imprisonment or detention),"; and
      (iii) at the end there shall be added—
      "; and in this subsection "prison" has the same meaning as in the 1989 Act.".

<small>GENERAL NOTE</small>
In its definition of "discretionary life prisoners", the Prisoners and Criminal Proceedings (Scotland) Act 1993 omitted to include those sentenced to life imprisonment by courts martial for offences other than murder and transferred to serve their sentence in Scotland.

Amendment of provisions continued in effect for certain prisoners by Prisoners and Criminal Proceedings (Scotland) Act 1993

134.—(1) In Schedule 6 to the Prisoners and Criminal Proceedings (Scotland) Act 1993 (transitional provisions and savings)—
  (a) in paragraph 1—
      (i) in the definition of "existing provisions", at the end there shall be added "except that an amendment or repeal effected by any enactment shall apply for the purposes of the existing provisions if expressly stated to do so"; and
      (ii) in the definition of "new provisions", after the word "amended" there shall be added "by this Act"; and
  (b) in paragraph 2(1), for the words from "and to" to "Schedule" there shall be substituted—
      ", to the following provisions of this Schedule and to the exception in the definition of "existing provisions" in paragraph 1 above,".
(2) Sections 18 (constitution and functions of Parole Board etc.), 22 (release on licence of persons serving determinate sentences), 28 (revocation of licences and conviction of prisoners on licence) and 42(3) (exercise of power to make rules etc.) of the Prisons (Scotland) Act 1989, being provisions which, notwithstanding their repeal by the Prisoners and Criminal Proceedings (Scotland) Act 1993, are "existing provisions" for the purposes of that Act of 1993, shall for those purposes be amended in accordance with the following subsections.
(3) In the said section 18, for subsections (3) and (4) there shall be substituted—
      "(3A) The Secretary of State may by rules make provision with respect to the proceedings of the Board, including provision—

(a) authorising cases to be dealt with in whole or in part by a pre-scribed number of members of the Board in accordance with such procedure as may be prescribed;

(b) requiring cases to be dealt with at prescribed times; and

(c) as to what matters may be taken into account by the Board (or by such number) in dealing with a case.

(3B) The Secretary of State may give the Board directions as to the matters to be taken into account by it in discharging its functions under this Part of this Act; and in giving any such directions the Secretary of State shall in particular have regard to—

(a) the need to protect the public from serious harm from offenders; and

(b) the desirability of preventing the commission by offenders of fur-ther offences and of securing their rehabilitation.".

(4) In each of the said sections 22 and 28, after subsection (1) there shall be inserted—

"(1A) The Secretary of State may by order provide that, in relation to such class of case as may be specified in the order, subsection (1) above shall have effect subject to the modification that for the word "may" there shall be substituted the word "shall".".

(5) In the said section 22, at the beginning of subsection (7) there shall be inserted the words "In a case where the Parole Board has recommended that a person be released on licence, and by virtue of subsection (1A) above such release is then mandatory, no licence conditions shall be included in the licence, or subsequently inserted, varied or cancelled in it, except in accord-ance with recommendations of the Board; and in any other case".

(6) In the said section 42—

(a) in each of subsections (1) and (4), for the words "22(2)" there shall be substituted "22(1A) or (2), 28(1A),"; and

(b) in subsection (3), for the word "(3)" there shall be substituted "(3A)".

GENERAL NOTE

The drafters of the Prisoners and Criminal Proceedings (Scotland) Act 1993 were concerned to ensure that persons sentenced before the implementation of the Act did not lose any entitle-ment to earlier consideration for release than that provided in the Act. As a result of this con-cern, the Act did not alter existing arrangements for parole consideration for such prisoners and decreed that changes in the function of the Parole Board should not affect them. It is now con-sidered that, while the principle was correct, the procedural restrictions were unnecessary. Accordingly, this section now empowers the Secretary of State to use the same procedures for reviewing all prisoners, although those sentenced before October 1, 1993 retain the qualifying dates specified by the old law.

Further amendment of Schedule 6 to the Prisoners and Criminal Proceed-ings (Scotland) Act 1993: application of "new provisions"

135. In Schedule 6 to the Prisoners and Criminal Proceedings (Scotland) Act 1993 (transitional provisions and savings), after paragraph 6 there shall be inserted the following paragraphs—

"6A.—(1) This paragraph applies where a prisoner sentenced before the relevant date to a sentence of imprisonment for life for an offence the sentence for which is not fixed by law has been (whether before, on or after that date) released on licence under the 1989 Act.

(2) Without prejudice to section 22(6) of the 1989 Act, in a case to which this paragraph applies, the new provisions shall apply as if the prisoner were a discretionary life prisoner, within the meaning of sec-tion 2 of this Act, whose licence has been granted under subsection (4) of that section of this Act on his having served the relevant part of his sentence.

6B.—(1) This paragraph applies where—

(a) a prisoner was, at the relevant date, serving a sentence or sentences of imprisonment, on conviction of an offence, passed before that date and that sentence was for a term of, or as the case may be those sentences fall to be treated as for a single term of, two or more years; and

(b) on or after that date he is, or has been, sentenced to a further term or terms of imprisonment, on conviction of an offence, to be served consecutively to, or concurrently with, the sentence or sentences mentioned in head (a) above.

(2) In a case to which this paragraph applies—

(a) the sentence or sentences mentioned in head (b) of sub-paragraph (1) above shall be treated as a single term with the sentences mentioned in head (a) of that sub-paragraph and that single term as imposed on or after the relevant date (so however that nothing in the foregoing provisions of this head shall affect the application of sections 39(7) (which makes provision as respects the award of additional days for breaches of discipline) and 24 (which makes provision as respects remission for good conduct) of the 1989 Act); and

(b) the new provisions shall apply accordingly, except that—

(i) where the prisoner is a long-term prisoner by virtue only of the aggregation provided for in head (a) of this sub-paragraph, he shall be released unconditionally on the same day as he would have been but for that aggregation;

(ii) where, notwithstanding the aggregation so provided for, the prisoner remains a short-term prisoner, subsection (1) of section 1 of this Act shall in its application be construed as subject to the qualification that the prisoner shall be released no earlier than he would have been but for that aggregation;

(iii) that section shall in its application be construed as if for subsection (3) there were substituted—

"(3) Without prejudice to subsection (1) above and to sub-paragraph (2)(b)(i) of paragraph 6B of Schedule 6 to this Act, after a prisoner to whom that paragraph applies has either served one-third of the sentence, or as the case may be sentences, mentioned in sub-paragraph (1)(a) of that paragraph, or (if it results in a later date of release) has served twelve months of that sentence or those sentences, the Secretary of State may, if recommended to do so by the Parole Board under this section, release him on licence; and where such a prisoner has been released on licence under section 22 of the 1989 Act, that licence shall be deemed to have been granted by virtue of this subsection.";

(iv) section 11(1) shall in its application be construed as if the sentence referred to were the further term or terms mentioned in head (b) of sub-paragraph (1) above; and

(v) section 16 shall in its application be construed as if the original sentence (within the meaning of that section) were the further term or terms so mentioned.".

<small>GENERAL NOTE</small>

The new para. 6A to Sched. 6 to the Prisoners and Criminal Proceedings (Scotland) Act 1993 ensures that discretionary life sentence prisoners released before that Act came into force will have the same (greatly improved) rights as those governed by the Act if they are recalled to custody.

The new para. 6B corrects an omission in the Prisoners and Criminal Proceedings (Scotland) Act 1993, which did not specifically address the position where a prisoner serving a parole eligible sentence imposed before implementation of that Act received a subsequent custodial sentence, whether concurrent with or consecutive to the existing sentence, after the implementation date. The situation could thus have arisen where parole was granted on the earlier sentence but the person would be required to return to prison at the end of the parole period to serve the new sentence. Paragraph 6B eliminates that potential nonsense by allowing the release under the old system, and thus not denying the prisoner his right to be considered for parole, but providing that, instead of returning to custody for the second sentence, the parole licence will continue until the date on which the person would have been due to be released unconditionally from the second sentence. Accordingly, the new sentence is given real meaning, but not at the cost of interrupting successful reintegration into the community.

PART X

CROSS-BORDER ENFORCEMENT

Execution of warrants

136.—(1) A warrant issued in England, Wales or Northern Ireland for the arrest of a person charged with an offence may (without any endorsement) be executed in Scotland by any constable of any police force of the country of issue or of the country of execution as well as by any other persons within the directions in the warrant.

(2) A warrant issued in—

(a) Scotland; or

(b) Northern Ireland,

for the arrest of a person charged with an offence may (without any endorsement) be executed in England or Wales by any constable of any police force of the country of issue or of the country of execution as well as by any other persons within the directions in the warrant.

(3) A warrant issued in—

(a) England or Wales; or

(b) Scotland,

for the arrest of a person charged with an offence may (without any endorsement) be executed in Northern Ireland by any constable of any police force of the country of issue or of the country of execution as well as by any other persons within the directions in the warrant.

(4) A person arrested in pursuance of a warrant shall be taken, as soon as reasonably practicable, to any place to which he is committed by, or may be conveyed under, the warrant.

(5) A constable executing a warrant—

(a) under subsection (1), (2)(b) or (3)(a) of this section may use reasonable force and shall have the powers of search conferred by section 139;

(b) under subsection (2)(a) or (3)(b) of this section shall have the same powers and duties, and the person arrested the same rights, as they would have had if execution had been in Scotland by a constable of a police force in Scotland.

(6) Any other person within the directions in a warrant executing that warrant under this section shall have the same powers and duties, and the person arrested the same rights, as they would have had if execution had been in the country of issue by the person within those directions.

(7) This section applies as respects—

(a) a warrant of commitment and a warrant to arrest a witness issued by a judicial authority in England, Wales or Northern Ireland as it applies to a warrant for arrest; and

(b) a warrant for committal, a warrant to imprison (or to apprehend and imprison) and a warrant to arrest a witness issued by a judicial authority in Scotland as it applies to a warrant for arrest.

(8) In this section "judicial authority" means any justice of the peace or the judge of any court exercising jurisdiction in criminal proceedings; and any reference to a part of the United Kingdom in which a warrant may be executed includes a reference to the adjacent sea and other waters within the seaward limits of the territorial sea.

DEFINITIONS
"judicial authority": subs. (8).

GENERAL NOTE
This and the following sections in this Part arose from a joint Home Office/Scottish Office Consultation Paper and responses thereto. The Paper had addressed the problems raised in a report produced by the police forces of Cumbria, Northumbria, Dumfries and Galloway and Lothian and Borders which discussed the difficulties of police officers wishing to act across the Border. The sections were introduced by the Minister of State, Home Office in Committee in the House of Commons: Standing Committee B, cols. 1101 *et seq.*

Previous to the sections coming into force the relevant legislation provided that: (1) warrants of arrest issued in Scotland could be executed in England and Wales by any constable acting within his area; (2) warrants of arrest issued in England and Wales or Northern Ireland could be executed in Scotland by any constable appointed for a police area in like manner as any such warrant issued in Scotland; (3) warrants of arrest issued in England and Wales or Scotland could be executed in Northern Ireland by any member of the Royal Ulster Constabulary or the Royal Ulster Constabulary Reserve: Criminal Law Act 1977 (c. 45), s.38(1)–(3) as amended by the Magistrates' Courts Act 1980 (c. 43) and the Magistrates' Courts (Northern Ireland) Order 1981 (S.I. 1981 No. 1675 (N.I. 26)).

This section enables a warrant of arrest issued in any of the three U.K. jurisdictions (England and Wales; Scotland; Northern Ireland) to be executed in any other of those jurisdictions either by a constable of a police force of the country in which the warrant was issued, or by a constable of a police force of the country in which the warrant is to be executed (subss. (1)(2)(3)); or by a person authorised in the warrant to do so (subs. (6)). Thus a Scottish or RUC officer may arrest a person in Scotland on a warrant issued in Northern Ireland, but a constable of a police force in which the warrant of arrest has neither been issued nor is to be executed, has no such power unless he is named in the warrant: thus a constable of an English police force cannot arrest in Scotland a person in respect of whom a warrant of arrest has been issued in Northern Ireland.

Subs. (5)(a)
A constable executing a warrant issued in England and Wales or Northern Ireland for the arrest of a person in another jurisdiction of the U.K. may use reasonable force and has the powers of search under s.139, *post. Reasonable force*: such force as is reasonable in the circumstances. All the circumstances, including the nature and degree of the force used, the gravity of the offence, the harm that the use of force might occasion, and the possibility of effecting the arrest by other means, must be taken into account. As to arrest without warrant, see s.137, *post.* And as to powers of search see s.139, *post.*

Subs. (5)(b)
A constable who executes a warrant of arrest in England and Wales or Northern Ireland which has been issued in Scotland has the powers in respect of that warrant which he would have under Scottish law. This applies whether the constable is of a Scottish police force or an English or Welsh force or the RUC.

Scottish perspective
Some may see in this, and subsequent sections, a move towards the creation of a national police force. However, the main impact should be to eliminate a purely formal process of endorsing warrants from other parts of the U.K. and subs. (6) ensures that the same protections are available to the arrested person as would have been available in the jurisdiction where the warrant is issued.

Cross-border powers of arrest etc.

137.—(1) If the conditions applicable to this subsection are satisfied, any constable of a police force in England and Wales who has reasonable grounds for suspecting that an offence has been committed or attempted in England or Wales and that the suspected person is in Scotland or in Northern Ireland may arrest without a warrant the suspected person wherever he is in Scotland or in Northern Ireland.

(2) If the condition applicable to this subsection is satisfied, any constable of a police force in Scotland who has reasonable grounds for suspecting that an offence has been committed or attempted in Scotland and that the suspected person is in England or Wales or in Northern Ireland may, as respects the suspected person, wherever he is in England or Wales or in Northern Ireland, exercise the same powers of arrest or detention as it would be competent for him to exercise were the person in Scotland.

(3) If the conditions applicable to this subsection are satisfied, any constable of a police force in Northern Ireland who has reasonable grounds for suspecting that an offence has been committed or attempted in Northern Ireland and that the suspected person is in England or Wales or in Scotland may arrest without a warrant the suspected person wherever he is in England or Wales or in Scotland.

(4) The conditions applicable to subsection (1) above are—
(a) that the suspected offence is an arrestable offence; or
(b) that, in the case of any other offence, it appears to the constable that service of a summons is impracticable or inappropriate for any of the reasons specified in subsection (3) of section 138.

(5) The condition applicable to subsection (2) above is that it appears to the constable that it would have been lawful for him to have exercised the powers had the suspected person been in Scotland.

(6) The conditions applicable to subsection (3) above are—
(a) that the suspected offence is an arrestable offence; or
(b) that, in the case of any other offence, it appears to the constable that service of a summons is impracticable or inappropriate for any of the reasons specified in subsection (3) of section 138.

(7) It shall be the duty of a constable who has arrested or, as the case may be detained, a person under this section—
(a) if he arrested him in Scotland, to take the person arrested either to the nearest convenient designated police station in England or in Northern Ireland or to a designated police station in a police area in England and Wales or in Northern Ireland in which the offence is being investigated;
(b) if he arrested him in England or Wales, to take the person arrested to the nearest convenient police station in Scotland or to a police station within a sheriffdom in which the offence is being investigated or to the nearest convenient designated police station in Northern Ireland or to a designated police station in Northern Ireland in which the offence is being investigated;
(c) if he detained him in England or Wales, to take the person detained to either such police station in Scotland as is mentioned in paragraph (b) above, or to the nearest convenient designated police station in England or Wales;
(d) if he arrested him in Northern Ireland, to take the person arrested either to the nearest convenient designated police station in England or Wales or to a designated police station in a police area in England and Wales in which the offence is being investigated or to the nearest convenient police station in Scotland or to a police station within a sheriffdom in which the offence is being investigated;
(e) if he detained him in Northern Ireland, to take the person detained to either such police station in Scotland as is mentioned in paragraph (b) above, or to the nearest convenient designated police station in Northern Ireland;

and to do so as soon as reasonably practicable.

(8) A constable—

(a) arresting a person under subsection (1) or (3) above, may use reasonable force and shall have the powers of search conferred by section 139;

(b) arresting a person under subsection (2) above shall have the same powers and duties, and the person arrested the same rights, as they would have had if the arrest had been in Scotland; and

(c) detaining a person under subsection (2) above shall act in accordance with the provisions applied by subsection (2) (as modified by subsection (6)) of section 138.

(9) In this section—

"arrestable offence" and "designated police station" have the same meaning as in the Police and Criminal Evidence Act 1984 and, in relation to Northern Ireland, have the same meaning as in the Police and Criminal Evidence (Northern Ireland) Order 1989; and

"constable of a police force", in relation to Northern Ireland, means a member of the Royal Ulster Constabulary or the Royal Ulster Constabulary Reserve.

(10) This section shall not prejudice any power of arrest conferred apart from this section.

DEFINITIONS

"arrestable offence": subs. (9) and s.24(1) of the Police and Criminal Evidence Act 1984.
"constable of a police force": subs. (9).
"designated police station": subs. (9) and s.35(4) of the Police and Criminal Evidence Act 1984.
"reasons": s.138(3)(4).

GENERAL NOTE

This section applies where it is reasonably suspected that an offence has been committed in one jurisdiction (England and Wales; Scotland; Northern Ireland) but the suspected offender is now in one of the other jurisdictions. A constable of a police force in the jurisdiction where the offence was committed may now, in certain circumstances, arrest that suspect without a warrant in the jurisdiction where he now is (subss. (1)(2)(3)). Before exercising the powers, the constable must have reasonable grounds for suspecting that the offence has been committed or attempted. The circumstances are, in the case of offences committed in England and Wales and Northern Ireland (subss. (4)(6)): (a) that the suspected offence is an arrestable offence (see below); or (b) the various reasons set out in s.138(3) apply, *q.v. post*. In the case of offences committed in Scotland (subs. (5)) the constable may exercise such powers as would appear to him to be lawful if the suspect had been arrested in Scotland.

Arrestable offence: an offence for which the Police and Criminal Evidence Act 1984 (c. 60), s.24(1) confers a power of summary arrest. The Northern Ireland equivalent is the Police and Criminal Evidence (Northern Ireland) Order 1989 (S.I. 1989 No. 1341 (N.I. 12)), Art. 26.

Subs. (7)

Designated police station: Police and Criminal Evidence Act 1984 (c. 60), s.35: *i.e.* station(s) designated by the chief officer of police for each police area to be used for the purpose of detaining arrested persons which appear to the chief officer concerned to provide enough accommodation for the purpose. For Northern Ireland, see S.I. 1989 No. 1341, above.

Subs. (8)

"Reasonable force": see General Note to s.136, *ante*.
"Powers of search": see s.139, *post*.

Scottish perspective

This extends the powers of s.136 to arrest without warrant, again subject to the same tests and restrictions as would have applied in the jurisdiction in which the alleged offence occurred.

Accordingly, there should be no temptation for police forces to wait until a suspect is in another jurisdiction within the U.K. before making any arrest.

Powers of arrest etc.: supplementary provisions

138.—(1) The following provisions have effect to supplement section 137 ("the principal section").

(2) Where a person is detained under subsection (2) of the principal section, subsections (2) to (7) of section 2 (detention and questioning at police station) and subsections (1) and (3) to (5) of section 3 (right to have someone informed when arrested or detained) of the Criminal Justice (Scotland) Act 1980 and section 28 (prints, samples etc. in criminal investigations) of the Prisoners and Criminal Proceedings (Scotland) Act 1993 shall apply to detention under that subsection of the principal section as they apply to detention under subsection (1) of the said section 2, but with the modifications mentioned in subsection (6) below.

(3) The reasons referred to in subsections (4)(b) and (6)(b) of the principal section are that—

(a) the name of the suspected person is unknown to, and cannot readily be ascertained by, the constable;

(b) the constable has reasonable grounds for doubting whether a name furnished by the suspected person as his name is his real name;

(c) either—

    (i) the suspected person has failed to furnish a satisfactory address for service; or

    (ii) the constable has reasonable grounds for doubting whether an address furnished by the suspected person is a satisfactory address for service;

(d) the constable has reasonable grounds for believing that arrest is necessary to prevent the suspected person—

    (i) causing physical injury to himself or any other person;

    (ii) suffering physical injury;

    (iii) causing loss of or damage to property;

    (iv) committing an offence against public decency; or

    (v) causing an unlawful obstruction of a highway or road; or

(e) the constable has reasonable grounds for believing that arrest is necessary to protect a child or other vulnerable person from the suspected person.

(4) For the purposes of subsection (3) above an address is a satisfactory address for service if it appears to the constable—

(a) that the suspected person will be at it for a sufficiently long period for it to be possible to serve him with process; or

(b) that some other person specified by the suspected person will accept service of process for the suspected person at it.

(5) Nothing in subsection (3)(d) above authorises the arrest of a person under sub-paragraph (iv) of that paragraph except where members of the public going about their normal business cannot reasonably be expected to avoid the person to be arrested.

(6) The following are the modifications of sections 2 and 3 of the Criminal Justice (Scotland) Act 1980 which are referred to in subsection (2) above—

(a) in section 2—

    (i) in subsection (2), the reference to detention being terminated not more than six hours after it begins shall be construed as a reference to its being terminated not more than four hours after the person's arrival at the police station to which he is taken under subsection (7)(c) of the principal section; and

    (ii) in subsections (4) and (7), references to "other premises" shall be disregarded; and

(b) in section 3(1), references to "other premises" shall be disregarded.

GENERAL NOTE

This section provides for the circumstances in which the powers in s.137 may be exercised. Subsection (3) relates to offences committed in England and Wales or Northern Ireland where the arrest without warrant takes place in a jurisdiction which is not the jurisdiction where the offence was committed. It deals in particular with situations where the suspected offence is not an arrestable offence but where the service of a summons is not practicable for the reasons set out in the subsection. The subsection follows the wording in the Police and Criminal Evidence Act 1984, s.25(3) (general arrest conditions).

"Reasonable grounds for doubting" (subs. (3)(b)(c)(ii)); "reasonable grounds for believing": (subs. (3)(d)(e)): these words impose a condition before the powers may be exercised. The reasonable grounds known to the constable must *in fact* exist: it is not sufficient for the constable to *think or suppose* that they exist: see *Nakkuda Ali v. M.F. de S. Jarayatne* C.L.C. 1639, 2388, *per* Lord Radcliffe (giving the judgment of the House of Lords). The question whether such grounds did exist or not is a matter for a court to determine as a matter of fact: *Registrar of Restrictive Trading Agreements v. Smith (W.H.) & Son* [1969] C.L.Y. 3531 *per* Denning L.J.

Subsections (4) and (5) are similar to subss. (4) and (5) of the Police and Criminal Evidence Act 1984 (c. 60), s.25.

Scottish perspective

The most significant difference between the treatment of those arrested or detained outside Scotland under ss.136 or 137 is that contained in subs. (6) of this section. Given that it may take considerable time for a person detained outwith Scotland to be taken even to the nearest convenient police station in Scotland, never mind to a police station in the sheriffdom where the offence is being investigated (s.137(7)(b)(c)(d)), four hours is perhaps a generous allowance. It does, however, reduce the time available for detention if the person is taken to a nearby designated police station in England, or (Northern) Wales or Northern Ireland.

Search powers available on arrests under sections 136 and 137

139.—(1) The following powers are available to a constable in relation to a person arrested under section 136(1), (2)(b) or (3)(a) or 137(1) or (3).

(2) A constable to whom this section applies may search the person if the constable has reasonable grounds for believing that the person may present a danger to himself or others.

(3) Subject to subsections (4) to (6) below, a constable to whom this section applies may—

    (a) search the person for anything—

        (i) which he might use to assist him to escape from lawful custody; or

        (ii) which might be evidence relating to an offence; and

    (b) enter and search any premises in which the person was when, or was immediately before, he was arrested for evidence relating to the offence for which he was arrested.

(4) The power to search conferred by subsection (3) above is only a power to search to the extent that is reasonably required for the purpose of discovering any such thing or any such evidence.

(5) The powers conferred by this section to search a person are not to be construed as authorising a constable to require a person to remove any of his clothing in public other than an outer coat, jacket, headgear, gloves or footwear but they do authorise a search of a person's mouth.

(6) A constable may not search a person in the exercise of the power conferred by subsection (3)(a) above unless he has reasonable grounds for believing that the person to be searched may have concealed on him anything for which a search is permitted under that paragraph.

(7) A constable may not search premises in the exercise of the power conferred by subsection (3)(b) above unless he has reasonable grounds for believing that there is evidence for which a search is permitted under that paragraph.

(8) In so far as the power of search conferred by subsection (3)(b) above relates to premises consisting of two or more separate dwellings, it is limited to a power to search—

(a) any dwelling in which the arrest took place or in which the person arrested was immediately before his arrest; and

(b) any parts of the premises which the occupier of any such dwelling uses in common with the occupiers of any other dwellings comprised in the premises.

(9) A constable searching a person in the exercise of the power conferred by subsection (2) above may seize and retain anything he finds, if he has reasonable grounds for believing that the person searched might use it to cause physical injury to himself or to any other person.

(10) A constable searching a person in the exercise of the power conferred by subsection (3)(a) above may seize and retain anything he finds, other than an item subject to legal privilege, if he has reasonable grounds for believing—

(a) that he might use it to assist him to escape from lawful custody; or

(b) that it is evidence of an offence, or has been obtained in consequence of the commission of an offence.

(11) Nothing in this section shall be taken to affect the power conferred by section 15(3), (4) and (5) of the Prevention of Terrorism (Temporary Provisions) Act 1989.

(12) In this section—

"item subject to legal privilege" has the meaning given to it—

(a) as respects anything in the possession of a person searched in England and Wales, by section 10 of the Police and Criminal Evidence Act 1984;

(b) as respects anything in the possession of a person searched in Scotland, by section 40 of the Criminal Justice (Scotland) Act 1987;

(c) as respects anything in the possession of a person searched in Northern Ireland, by Article 12 of the Police and Criminal Evidence (Northern Ireland) Order 1989;

"premises" includes any place and, in particular, includes—

(a) any vehicle, vessel, aircraft or hovercraft;

(b) any offshore installation; and

(c) any tent or movable structure; and

"offshore installation" has the meaning given to it by section 1 of the Mineral Workings (Offshore Installations) Act 1971.

DEFINITIONS
"item subject to legal privilege": subs. (12).
"offshore installation": subs. (12).
"premises": subs. (12).

GENERAL NOTE
This section defines the powers of search, entry and seizure available to a constable in England and Wales and Northern Ireland in the execution of warrants and to a constable in England and Wales when exercising his powers of arrest in Scotland and Northern Ireland.

Subs. (1)
This subsection applies where a constable has arrested a person:

(a) in Scotland under a warrant issued in England and Wales or Northern Ireland (s.136(1), *ante*); or

(b) in England and Wales under a warrant issued in Northern Ireland (s.136(2)(b), *ante*); or

(c) in Northern Ireland under a warrant issued in England and Wales (s.136(3)(a)).

The subsection also applies where a constable of an England and Wales police force has arrested without warrant a person in Scotland or Northern Ireland for a suspected offence committed in England and Wales (s.136(1)) or a constable of a Northern Ireland police force has arrested without warrant a person in England and Wales or Scotland for a suspected offence committed in Northern Ireland (s.137(3)).

The subsection does not apply to a constable of a Scottish police force seeking to arrest a person in England and Wales or Northern Ireland with or without a warrant for offences committed in Scotland.

N.B. that the section applies only to those *arrested* and not those *detained* and that the constable may act on his own authority. But the provisions of the Police and Criminal Evidence Act 1984 (c. 60), s.117 (the Northern Ireland equivalent is the Police and Criminal Evidence Order (N.I.) Order 1989, (S.I. 1989 No. 134) Art. 88, use of reasonable force by constable in exercise of power, are not repeated here: since these provisions are "self-standing" not an extension of the 1984 Act, it would seem that "reasonable force" cannot be applied.

Search of the person: By subs. (2) (similar to the Police and Criminal Evidence Act 1984 (c. 60), s.32(1) and the Police and Criminal Evidence Order (N.I.) 1989, Art. 34(1)(a)) a constable may search a person if he has reasonable grounds for believing that the person may present a danger to himself or others. See subs. (9) (similar to the Police and Criminal Evidence Act 1984, s.32(8)) for the power to seize and retain anything found which might be used to inflict injury.

By subs. (3)(a) (similar to the Police and Criminal Evidence Act 1984, s.32(2)) the constable may search the person arrested for anything which he might use to escape or which might be evidence of an offence (*note* "an offence" not "the offence for which arrested"; *contrast* with search of premises, below). The powers of search of the person conferred by the section are limited: the arrested person need be required only to remove in public his outer coat, jacket, headgear or gloves (subs. (5), similar to the s.32(4), as amended by s.59 of this Act, *ante*) but *note* that the aforementioned s.32(4), does not refer to "headgear" or "hat".

Searches of arrested persons for aids to escape or evidence of offences may only take place if there are "reasonable grounds for believing" (as to which, see the General Note to s. 138, above) (subs. (6), similar to the Police and Criminal Evidence Act 1984 (c. 60), s.32(5)). But if such a search does take place there is a power to seize and retain the aid to escape or evidence of an offence (subs. (10) similar to the Police and Criminal Evidence Act 1984 (c. 60), s.32(9)). "Items subject to legal privilege" cannot be retained.

Search of premises

The power to enter and search premises (subs. (3)(b) similar to the Police and Criminal Evidence Act 1984, s.32(2)(b), Police and Criminal Evidence (N.I.) Order 1989, Art. 34(2)(b)) for evidence against an arrested person relates only to premises in which he was when arrested or immediately before being arrested. Where the premises are dwellings the power applies only to the dwelling itself and the common parts (*e.g.* the stairs of a block of flats) (subs. (8), similar to the Police and Criminal Evidence Act 1984, s.32(7)). Thus the section would apply to a house out of which a person has just come who is then arrested in the street (*R. v. Beckford (Junior)* [1992] C.L.Y. 802), but presumably not to some other house the address of which is found on his person. The evidence concerned is evidence only of the offence for which he was arrested, not some other offence (*cf.* with Searches of the Person above) and must actually be evidence of that offence, not an object which will assist in the search for evidence (*e.g.* car keys which would enable a car to be searched: *R. v. Churchill* [1990] C.L.Y. 3536a). The constable must have "reasonable grounds for believing" that the evidence is there (subs. (7)) but whether he has that belief is for the jury (*Beckford*, above). *R. v. Badham* [1987] C.L.Y. 707 (a Crown Court case) it was held that the search must flow on the arrest and not occur several hours later; but the reason for that appears to be because the heading to the Police and Criminal Evidence Act 1984 (c. 60), s.32, is "search upon arrest". The heading to this section is not at all the same.

Subs. (11)

Similar to the Police and Criminal Evidence Act 1984 (c. 60), s.32(10). Subsections (3)(4)(5) of s.15 of the Prevention of Terrorism (Temporary Provisions) Act 1989 provide that a constable may stop and search a person for documents or other evidence that he is a person liable to arrest under s.14 of that Act.

Reciprocal powers of arrest

140.—(1) Where a constable of a police force in England and Wales would, in relation to an offence, have power to arrest a person in England or Wales under section 24(6) or (7) or 25 of the Police and Criminal Evidence Act 1984 (arrestable offences and non-arrestable offences in certain circumstances) a constable of a police force in Scotland or in Northern Ireland shall have the like power of arrest in England and Wales.

(2) Where a constable of a police force in Scotland or in Northern Ireland arrests a person in England or Wales by virtue of subsection (1) above—

    (a) the constable shall be subject to requirements to inform the arrested person that he is under arrest and of the grounds for it corresponding to the requirements imposed by section 28 of that Act;

(b) the constable shall be subject to a requirement to take the arrested person to a police station corresponding to the requirement imposed by section 30 of that Act and so also as respects the other related requirements of that section; and

(c) the constable shall have powers to search the arrested person corresponding to the powers conferred by section 32 of that Act.

(3) Where a constable of a police force in Scotland would, in relation to an offence, have power to arrest a person in Scotland, a constable of a police force in England and Wales or in Northern Ireland shall have the like power of arrest in Scotland.

(4) Where a constable of a police force in England or Wales or in Northern Ireland arrests a person in Scotland by virtue of subsection (3) above, the arrested person shall have the same rights and the constable the same powers and duties as they would have were the constable a constable of a police force in Scotland.

(5) Where a constable of a police force in Northern Ireland would, in relation to an offence, have power to arrest a person in Northern Ireland under Article 26(6) or (7) or 27 of the Police and Criminal Evidence (Northern Ireland) Order 1989 (arrestable offences and non-arrestable offences in certain circumstances) a constable of a police force in England and Wales or Scotland shall have the like power of arrest in Northern Ireland.

(6) Where a constable of a police force in England and Wales or in Scotland arrests a person in Northern Ireland by virtue of subsection (5) above—

(a) the constable shall be subject to requirements to inform the arrested person that he is under arrest and of the grounds for it corresponding to the requirements imposed by Article 30 of that Order;

(b) the constable shall be subject to a requirement to take the arrested person to a police station corresponding to the requirement imposed by Article 32 of that Order and so as respects the other related requirements of that Article; and

(c) the constable shall have powers to search the arrested person corresponding to the powers conferred by Article 34 of that Order.

(7) In this section "constable of a police force", in relation to Northern Ireland, means a member of the Royal Ulster Constabulary or the Royal Ulster Constabulary Reserve.

DEFINITIONS
"constable of a police force": subs. (7).

GENERAL NOTE
This section enables a constable from one jurisdiction in the U.K. who is present in another jurisdiction to arrest a person using the police powers of arrest to the local jurisdiction.

Subsection (1) gives a constable of a Scotland or Northern Ireland police force the same power to arrest in England and Wales as a constable of an England and Wales police force. That power is a power to arrest without warrant in respect of an arrestable offence which the constable reasonably suspects the person has committed or is about to commit (Police and Criminal Evidence Act 1984 (c. 60), s.24(6)(7)). It is also a power to arrest without warrant for a non-arrestable offence where the general arrest conditions are satisfied, that is, the constable has reasonable grounds to suspect that the offence has been committed or attempted (or is being committed or attempted) but for reasons similar to those set out in s.138(3), *ante*, service of a summons is impracticable or inappropriate: (Police and Criminal Evidence Act 1984 (c. 60), s.25).

N.B. that the requirements laid upon the constable (to inform the arrested person that he has been arrested and why, and what happens in the case of arrests other than at police stations) and his powers of search are as laid down by English law: subs. (2).

Subsection (3) makes similar provision for arrest in Scotland by a constable of an England and Wales or Northern Ireland police force but *note* that the applicable law here is Scots law.

Subsections (5) and (6) make similar provision for arrest in Northern Ireland by a constable of a Scotland or England and Wales force but *note* that the applicable law is that laid down by

Northern Ireland law, *i.e.* Police and Criminal Evidence (N.I.) Order 1989 (S.I. 1989 No. 1341 (N.I. 12)).

The difference between this section and s.137, *ante* is that this section gives a constable from one U.K. jurisdiction a power of arrest in one of the other U.K. jurisdictions for an offence committed in that other jurisdiction but he must exercise that power according to the law of that jurisdiction. Section 137 also gives a constable from one of the U.K. jurisdictions a power to arrest in one of the other U.K. jurisdictions but the offence must have been committed in the constable's own jurisdiction and the powers of arrest must be exercised according to the law of that jurisdiction.

Scottish perspective

It must be presumed that any police officer seeking to exercise powers accorded by this section will be given the appropriate training in the significantly different rules operating in each of the jurisdictions in relation to powers of arrest.

Aid of one police force by another

141.—(1) The chief officer of police of a police force in England and Wales may, on the application of the chief officer of a police force in Scotland or the chief constable of the Royal Ulster Constabulary in Northern Ireland, provide constables or other assistance for the purpose of enabling the Scottish force or the Royal Ulster Constabulary to meet any special demand on its resources.

(2) The chief officer of a police force in Scotland may, on the application of the chief officer of police of a police force in England and Wales or the chief constable of the Royal Ulster Constabulary in Northern Ireland, provide constables or other assistance for the purpose of enabling the English or Welsh force or the Royal Ulster Constabulary to meet any special demand on its resources.

(3) The chief constable of the Royal Ulster Constabulary in Northern Ireland may, on the application of the chief officer of police of a police force in England and Wales or the chief officer of a police force in Scotland, provide constables or other assistance for the purpose of enabling the English or Welsh force or the Scottish force to meet any special demand on its resources.

(4) If it appears to the Secretary of State to be expedient in the interests of public safety or order that any police force should be reinforced or should receive other assistance for the purpose of enabling it to meet any special demand on its resources, and that satisfactory arrangements under subsection (1), (2) or (3) above cannot be made, or cannot be made in time, he may direct the chief officer of police of any police force in England and Wales, the chief officer of any police force in Scotland or the chief constable of the Royal Ulster Constabulary, as the case may be, to provide such constables or other assistance for that purpose as may be specified in the direction.

(5) While a constable is provided under this section for the assistance of another police force he shall, notwithstanding any enactment,—

(a) be under the direction and control of the chief officer of police of that other force (or, where that other force is a police force in Scotland or the Royal Ulster Constabulary in Northern Ireland, of its chief officer or the chief constable of the Royal Ulster Constabulary respectively); and

(b) have in any place the like powers and privileges as a member of that other force therein as a constable.

(6) The police authority maintaining a police force for which assistance is provided under this section shall pay to the police authority maintaining the force from which that assistance is provided such contribution as may be agreed upon between those authorities or, in default of any such agreement, as may be provided by any agreement subsisting at the time between all police authorities generally, or, in default of such general agreement, as may be determined by the Secretary of State.

(7) Any expression used in the Police Act 1964, the Police (Scotland) Act 1967 or the Police Act (Northern Ireland) 1970 and this section in its application to England and Wales, Scotland and Northern Ireland respectively has the same meaning in this section as in that Act.

(8) In this section "constable of a police force", in relation to Northern Ireland, means a member of the Royal Ulster Constabulary or the Royal Ulster Constabulary Reserve.

DEFINITION
"constable of a police force": subs. (7).

GENERAL NOTE
This section makes provision for the chief officer of police or the chief constable to provide constables or other assistance to a chief officer in any other jurisdiction within the U.K. It also provides the circumstances under which the Secretary of State may direct a chief officer or chief constable within his jurisdiction to provide constables or other assistance within the U.K.

Scottish perspective
This is the most obvious of this set of provisions which could contribute to the creation of a national police force, perhaps initially in relation to specific tasks performed by the police or in responding to particularly serious incidents where existing expertise is thinly spread throughout the U.K.

PART XI

SEXUAL OFFENCES

Rape

Rape of women and men

142. For section 1 of the Sexual Offences Act 1956 (rape of a woman) there shall be substituted the following section—

"Rape of woman or man

1.—(1) It is an offence for a man to rape a woman or another man.

(2) A man commits rape if—

(a) he has sexual intercourse with a person (whether vaginal or anal) who at the time of the intercourse does not consent to it; and

(b) at the time he knows that the person does not consent to the intercourse or is reckless as to whether that person consents to it.

(3) A man also commits rape if he induces a married woman to have sexual intercourse with him by impersonating her husband.

(4) Subsection (2) applies for the purpose of any enactment.".

DEFINITIONS
"rape": s.1 of the Sexual Offences Act 1950 (2)(3) as substituted by this section.

GENERAL NOTE
The effect of this section is to remove the word "unlawful" from the statutory definition of rape as it appeared in the Sexual Offences (Amendment) Act 1976 and to define sexual intercourse to include anal intercourse. Thus rape within marriage and "male rape" become offences. This section was added to the Bill by way of Opposition amendment during its passage through the House of Lords.
(a) Rape within marriage: for several centuries, *i.e.* since the time of Hale, it had been considered that a man could not be guilty of raping his wife. The expression "unlawful sexual intercourse" was taken to mean sexual intercourse outside marriage. However, in *R. v. R.* [1992] 1 A.C. 599 the House of Lords held that a man may be convicted of raping his wife. The Law Commission in its Report, *Rape within Marriage*, (1992), HMSO, HC 167, recommended that the offence of rape should be re-defined by omitting the word "unlawful" from the relevant Acts. Thus, the offence of rape, as defined in s.1(1) of the Sexual Offences (Amendment) Act 1976, is re-defined by this section which is substituted for s.1 of the Sexual Offences Act 1956. Section 1(1) of the 1976 Act ceases to have effect but is largely re-enacted (apart from the word "unlawful") by this section. Subsection (2) removes the word "unlawful" from ss.2(1) and 3(1) of the 1956 Act.

(b) "Male rape": an amended version of this section (introduced by Lord Ponsonby of Shul-brede, *Hansard*, H.L. Vol. 556 col. 1605 *et seq.* was accepted by the Government in the House of Lords. The meaning of *sexual intercourse* is extended to include not only vaginal intercourse but also anal intercourse. Previously, by the Sexual Offences (Amendment) Act 1976 (c. 82), s.7(2), "rape" had been defined as referring to "natural intercourse ... only": see also *R. v. Gaston* [1981] C.L.Y. 522 (where it was held that there was no such offence as attempted rape *per anum*). The effect of the amendments is to make it an offence to commit buggery without consent with either a man or a woman. Thus, the offence of rape can now be committed against a man as well as a woman. The Government spokesman referred to "substantial press coverage of an offence called 'male rape'—that is, the non-consensual buggery of one man by another man." (col. 1607).

By Sched. 10, para. 35, *post*, amending the Sexual Offences (Amendment) Act 1976 (c. 82), s.1(2) (reasonable belief in consent to sexual intercourse being a matter for the jury) applies to trials for rape offences against men as well as against women. As a result of this change in the law, male complainants will have the same protection (under s.2 of the 1976 Act) as females from cross-examination about their sexual history. (Consequential amendments to s.2 of the 1976 Act are made by Sched. 10, para. 35, *post*).

The protection of the anonymity of rape complainants by s.4 of the 1976 Act will now apply in the cases of the new, extended definition of rape as opposed to the narrower definition in ss.1–5 of the 1976 Act. Schedule 10, para. 36, *post*, makes amendments to s.4 of the 1976 Act conse-quent upon the changes to the law made by this section. Schedule 10, para. 26, amends the Theft Act 1968 (c. 60), s.9(2), so that an offence intended by a trespasser which will constitute burglary now includes "raping any person" rather than "raping any woman".

Male rape and buggery

Male rape and buggery

143.—(1) Section 12 of the Sexual Offences Act 1956 (offence of buggery) shall be amended as follows.

(2) In subsection (1), after the words "another person" there shall be inserted the words "otherwise than in the circumstances described in subsec-tion (1A) below".

(3) After subsection (1), there shall be inserted the following subsections—

"(1A) The circumstances referred to in subsection (1) are that the act of buggery takes place in private and both parties have attained the age of eighteen.

(1B) An act of buggery by one man with another shall not be treated as taking place in private if it takes place—

(a) when more than two persons take part or are present; or

(b) in a lavatory to which the public have or are permitted to have access, whether on payment or otherwise.

(1C) In any proceedings against a person for buggery with another person it shall be for the prosecutor to prove that the act of buggery took place otherwise than in private or that one of the parties to it had not attained the age of eighteen.".

DEFINITIONS

"lawful circumstances": subs. (3), amending Sexual Offences Act 1956, s.12.

"private": subs. (3).

GENERAL NOTE

Section 12(1) of the Sexual Offences Act 1956 now reads: "It is an offence for a person to commit buggery with another person *otherwise than in the circumstances described in subsection 1A below* or with an animal." The words in italics were added by subs. (2), above. *The circum-stances described in subs. (1A))* appear in subs. (3) above. The effect of the subsection is that buggery of one person by another is not unlawful provided the act takes place in private and both parties are 18 years of age or over. Previously, such an act between a man and a woman was unlawful, but not if it occurred (with consent) between two men if 21 years of age or over. The new subsections make consensual buggery of a woman by a man now lawful: previously such an act was an offence with a maximum penalty of life imprisonment. A short prison sentence was considered appropriate for this offence: *Dixon* [1994] Crim.L.R. 579 and *R. v. Bush (William*

James) [1990] C.L.Y. 1212. The clause was introduced by Baroness Mallalieu [H.L. Debs. Cols. 74 *et seq.*, June 20, 1626, July 11] and the Government spokesman said: "The Criminal Law Revision Committee called for a change in the law in 1984 ... This is a matter relating to the private sexual activity of consenting adults ... a sensible amendment ..." *Note* that the age of consent is *18*, not 16 as with vaginal sexual intercourse. This is in line with the changes made by s.145, *post.*

Revised penalties for certain sexual offences

Revised penalties for buggery and indecency between men

144.—(1) The following paragraphs of the Second Schedule to the Sexual Offences Act 1956 (which prescribe the punishments for offences of buggery and of indecency between men) shall be amended as follows.

(2) In paragraph 3—

(a) in sub-paragraph (a) (buggery), for the entry in the third column there shall be substituted "If with a person under the age of sixteen or with an animal, life; if the accused is of or over the age of twenty-one and the other person is under the age of eighteen, five years, but otherwise two years."; and

(b) in sub-paragraph (b) (attempted buggery), for the entry in the third column there shall be substituted "If with a person under the age of sixteen or with an animal, life; if the accused is of or over the age of twenty-one and the other person is under the age of eighteen, five years, but otherwise two years.".

(3) In paragraph 16—

(a) in sub-paragraph (a) (indecency between men), for the entry in the third column there shall be substituted "If by a man of or over the age of twenty-one with a man under the age of eighteen, five years; otherwise two years."; and

(b) in sub-paragraph (b) (attempted procurement of commission by a man of an act of gross indecency with another man), for the entry in the third column there shall be substituted "If the attempt is by a man of or over the age of twenty-one to procure a man under the age of eighteen to commit an act of gross indecency with another man, five years; otherwise two years.".

GENERAL NOTE

This section amends Sched. 2 to the Sexual Offences Act 1956 in order to increase the maximum sentence for attempted buggery of a person under 16 to life imprisonment (the same as buggery of such a person). If a person over 21 commits these offences (or indecency between men or attempting to procure an act of gross indecency) with a person under 18, the maximum penalty is five years' imprisonment. In all other cases the maximum for these offences is two years.

Homosexuality

Age at which homosexual acts are lawful

145.—(1) In section 1 of the Sexual Offences Act 1967 (amendment of law relating to homosexual acts in private), for "twenty-one" in both places where it occurs there is substituted "eighteen".

(2) In section 80 of the Criminal Justice (Scotland) Act 1980 (homosexual offences), for "twenty-one" in each place where it occurs there is substituted "eighteen".

(3) In Article 3 of the Homosexual Offences (Northern Ireland) Order 1982 (homosexual acts in private), for "21" in both places where it occurs there is substituted "18".

DEFINITIONS

"homosexual acts": s.1(7) of the Sexual Offences Act 1967.
"private": s.1(2) of the Sexual Offences Act 1967.

GENERAL NOTE

This section reduces to 18 the minimum age at which two men may engage in consensual homosexual acts in private. The clause was first introduced in the Bill in the House of Commons, February 21, 1994, (*Hansard*, H.C. Vol. 238, col. 74 *et seq.*) in a debate initiated by Mrs Edwina Currie M.P. The change in the law has effect throughout the U.K.

Subs. (1)

This subsection relates to England and Wales and amends s.1 of the Sexual Offences Act 1967. *Note* that the changes in the law refer not just to buggery (which is in any case covered by s.143, *ante*) but also to other homosexual acts in private.

A *homosexual act* is defined by the Sexual Offences Act 1967, s.1(7). The subsection provides that a man shall be treated as doing such an act "if, and only if, he commits buggery with another man or commits an act of gross indecency with another man or is a party to the commission by a man of such an act."

Private homosexual acts are not private if "done (a) when more than two persons take part or are present; or (b) in a lavatory to which the public have or are permitted to have access, whether on payment or otherwise" (see the 1967 Act, s.1(2)). As to the meaning of *privacy* the Court of Appeal has approved a direction as follows: "You look at all the surrounding circumstances, the time of night, the nature of the place including such matters as lighting and you consider further the likelihood of a third person coming upon the scene": *R. v. Reakes* [1974] C.L.Y. 751.

Subs. (3)

This subsection makes similar amendments for Northern Ireland. "Homosexual act" is defined in Art. 2 of the 1982 Order. For an act "in private", see Art. 3(2) of the 1982 Order.

Extension of Sexual Offences Act 1967 to the armed forces and merchant navy

146.—(1) Section 1(5) of the Sexual Offences Act 1967 (homosexual acts in the armed forces) is repealed.

(2) In section 80 of the Criminal Justice (Scotland) Act 1980—

(a) subsection (5) (homosexual acts in the armed forces) shall cease to have effect;

(b) in subsection (7)—

(i) after paragraph (b) there shall be inserted the word "or"; and

(ii) paragraph (d) (homosexual acts on merchant ships) and the word "; or" immediately preceding that paragraph shall cease to have effect; and

(c) subsection (8) (interpretation) shall cease to have effect.

(3) Section 2 of the Sexual Offences Act 1967 (homosexual acts on merchant ships) is repealed.

(4) Nothing contained in this section shall prevent a homosexual act (with or without other acts or circumstances) from constituting a ground for discharging a member of Her Majesty's armed forces from the service or dismissing a member of the crew of a United Kingdom merchant ship from his ship or, in the case of a member of Her Majesty's armed forces, where the act occurs in conjunction with other acts or circumstances, from constituting an offence under the Army Act 1955, the Air Force Act 1955 or the Naval Discipline Act 1957.

Expressions used in this subsection and any enactment repealed by this section have the same meaning in this subsection as in that enactment.

DEFINITIONS

"homosexual acts": s.1(7) of the Sexual Offences Act, 1967.

"member of the crew": *ibid.*

"United Kingdom merchant ship": s.2(3) of the Sexual Offences Act 1967, as preserved by subs. (4) of this section.

GENERAL NOTE

This section provides that homosexual acts committed by personnel in the Armed Forces which would not be offences under civilian law will no longer be offences under the Service Discipline Acts. It further provides that homosexual acts committed between merchant seamen on board a U.K. ship which would not be offences if committed by other persons of the same age and in the same circumstances shall not be offences under the law of England and Wales or Scotland: subss. (1) and (2). However, such acts may still constitute offences under the Service Discipline Acts and may lead service personnel to be discharged from the armed forces or merchant seamen to be dismissed from a ship.

Homosexuality on merchant ships and in the armed forces: Northern Ireland

147.—(1) In the Homosexual Offences (Northern Ireland) Order 1982, the following are revoked—
  (a) in article 3(1) (homosexual acts in private), the words "and Article 5 (merchant seamen)"; and
  (b) article 5 (homosexual acts on merchant ships).
  (2) Article 3(4) of the Homosexual Offences (Northern Ireland) Order 1982 (homosexual acts in the armed forces) is revoked.
  (3) Nothing in this section shall prevent a homosexual act (with or without other acts or circumstances) from constituting a ground for discharging a member of Her Majesty's armed forces from the service or dismissing a member of the crew of a United Kingdom merchant ship from his ship or, in the case of a member of Her Majesty's armed forces, where the act occurs in conjunction with other acts or circumstances, from constituting an offence under the Army Act 1955, the Air Force Act 1955 or the Naval Discipline Act 1957.
  Expressions used in this subsection and any enactment repealed by this section have the same meaning in this subsection as in that enactment.

DEFINITIONS
  "homosexual act": Art. 2 of the Homosexual Offences (Northern Ireland) Order 1982 (S.I. 1982 No. 1536 (N.I. 19)).
  "in private": see Art. 3(2), *ibid.*
  "United Kingdom merchant ship": Art. 5(3), *ibid.*

GENERAL NOTE
  This section makes, for Northern Ireland, provision corresponding to that made by cl. 146 for the rest of the U.K.

Amendment of law relating to homosexual acts in Scotland

148. In section 80(6) of the Criminal Justice (Scotland) Act 1980 (which defines "homosexual act" for the purpose of section 80), after "gross indecency" there is inserted "or shameless indecency".

GENERAL NOTE
  Neither "gross indecency" nor "shameless indecency" has been precisely defined in Scots law. This amendment to the Criminal Justice (Scotland) Act 1980 simply removes any doubt that all consensual sexual activity between males over the age of 18 which takes place in private is no longer criminal.

PART XII

MISCELLANEOUS AND GENERAL

The Parole Board

Incorporation of the Parole Board

149. In section 32 of the Criminal Justice Act 1991 (which provides the constitution and basic functions of the Parole Board), for subsection (1), there shall be substituted the following subsection—
  "(1) The Parole Board shall be, by that name, a body corporate and as such shall be constituted in accordance with, and have the functions conferred by, this Part.".

GENERAL NOTE

The effect of this section is "to give the Parole Board full nondepartmental public body status" according to the Minister of State Home Office (*Hansard*, H.C. Vol. 556 col. 1626, July 11, 1994). In an earlier debate, Lord Windlesham (a former chairman of the Parole Board) had introduced an amendment to a like effect. The principle of the amendment was accepted by the Government which then introduced its own version of the new clause. The amendment was required because the 1991 Act had given the Parole Board certain new powers (the responsibility to review and take final decisions on the release of life prisoners serving discretionary sentences of life imprisonment; and the duty to decide whether to release on licence prisoners eligible for parole who are serving sentences of four to less than seven years); and also because of the fact that the local review committees were being phased out. Prior to the 1991 Act the Parole Board was a purely recommendatory body, offering recommendations to the Home Secretary. The changes effected by the 1991 Act resulted in the Board's becoming more of an executive body, and the new status conferred by this section reflects its independence and accountability in decision-making.

Schedule 10, para. 70, *post*, replacing Sched. 5 to the 1991 Act, contains provisions relating to the Parole Board: status and capacity; membership; payments to members; proceedings; staff; financial provisions; authentication of Board's seal; presumption of authenticity of documents issued by the Board; accounts and audit; reports; bail (exclusion in rape and homicide cases); probation officers for offenders subject to secure training orders; secure training orders (cost of supervision by probation officer).

Powers to recall prisoners released on licence

150. In section 50 of the Criminal Justice Act 1991 (power by order to transfer certain functions to the Parole Board) subsection (4) shall cease to have effect and, in subsection (1), for the words "(2) to (4)" there shall be substituted the words "(2) or (3)".

GENERAL NOTE

This section makes changes to the 1991 Act concerning the recall to custody of persons on parole. Under the Act there were two parallel systems: one operated by the Home Secretary and the other by the Parole Board. This led to confusion for the police and probation service when decisions to recall those on parole had to be made. Accordingly, it was agreed that only one system should operate, under the control of the Home Secretary. This section gives effect to that agreement. However, the Parole Board will continue to review decisions to recall those on parole.

Prisons: powers in relation to prisoners, visitors and others

Power to test prisoners for drugs

151.—(1) After section 16 of the Prison Act 1952 there shall be inserted the following section—

"Testing prisoners for drugs

16A.—(1) If an authorisation is in force for the prison, any prison officer may, at the prison, in accordance with prison rules, require any prisoner who is confined in the prison to provide a sample of urine for the purpose of ascertaining whether he has any drug in his body.

(2) If the authorisation so provides, the power conferred by subsection (1) above shall include power to require a prisoner to provide a sample of any other description specified in the authorisation, not being an intimate sample, whether instead of or in addition to a sample of urine.

(3) In this section—

"authorisation" means an authorisation by the governor;

"drug" means any drug which is a controlled drug for the purposes of the Misuse of Drugs Act 1971;

"intimate sample" has the same meaning as in Part V of the Police and Criminal Evidence Act 1984;

"prison officer" includes a prisoner custody officer within the meaning of Part IV of the Criminal Justice Act 1991; and "prison rules" means rules under section 47 of this Act.".

(2) After section 41A of the Prisons (Scotland) Act 1989 there shall be inserted the following section—

"Testing prisoners for drugs

41B.—(1) If an authorisation is in force for the prison, any officer of the prison may, at the prison, in accordance with rules under section 39 of this Act, require any prisoner who is confined in the prison to provide a sample of urine for the purpose of ascertaining whether he has any drug in his body.

(2) If the authorisation so provides, the power conferred by subsection (1) above shall include power to require a prisoner to provide a sample of any other description specified in the authorisation, not being an intimate sample, whether instead of or in addition to a sample of urine.

(3) In this section—

"authorisation" means an authorisation by the governor;

"drug" means any drug which is a controlled drug for the purposes of the Misuse of Drugs Act 1971; and

"intimate sample" means a sample of blood, semen or any other tissue fluid, saliva or pubic hair, or a swab taken from a person's body orifice.".

DEFINITIONS

"authorisation": s.16A of the Prison Act 1952, as inserted by this section.

"drug": s.16A of the Prison Act 1952, as inserted by this section.

"intimate sample": s.16A of the Prison Act 1952, as inserted by this section; Police and Criminal Evidence Act 1984, Pt. V.

"prison officer": s.16A of the Prison Act 1952, as inserted by this section; Criminal Justice Act 1991, Pt. IV.

"prison rules": s.16A of the Prison Act 1952, as inserted by this section.

GENERAL NOTE

Subs. (1)

This subsection inserts a new s.16A in the Prison Act 1952 in order to give prison officers and prisoner custody officers in England and Wales powers, when authorised to do so, to require prisoners to provide samples of urine and other non-intimate samples for drug-testing (subs. (1)). The purpose of the section is to "act as an important deterrent and a powerful signal that drug misuse in prisons is completely unacceptable". There is no requirement that prison governors seek authorisation from the courts in the exercise of their power under the section although the Government will, when establishing policy, take into account their responsibility under the European Convention on Human Rights: Minister of State, Scottish Office (*Hansard*, H.L. Vol. 555, col. 1852).

Subs. (3)

Drug: for the meaning of "controlled drug" see Misuse of Drugs Act 1971 (c. 38), ss.2, 37(1) and Sched. 2.

Intimate sample: see the General Note to s.54, *ante.*

Prison officer includes *prisoner custody officer* as to which see the General Note to s.94, *ante.*

Scottish perspective

Subs. (2)

The provisions for visits, home leaves and placements outside prisons for prisoners in Scotland have, combined with a general increase in popularity of drug abuse, made drugs (including alcohol) much easier to obtain in prisons. The availability of simple tests to detect the presence of forbidden substances in a prisoner's body makes testing attractive to prisons. Testing can not only provide accurate evidence of violation of the rules but can also operate as a deterrent to prisoners and as a means of assuring the wider public that rules are being enforced. Many prisoners are keen on the introduction of testing, to protect themselves against otherwise subjective opinions and to enable them to demonstrate that the trust being placed in them is justified. Drug testing has already been used, on a voluntary basis, in several Scottish prisons and with good results. It would also be a useful process if plans to set up "drug free units" are to be taken forward confidently. Schedule 10, para. 64 extends this power to young offenders institutions and remand centres.

Powers of search by authorised employees in prisons

152.—(1) In the Prison Act 1952, after section 8, there shall be inserted the following section—

"Powers of search by authorised employees

8A.—(1) An authorised employee at a prison shall have the power to search any prisoner for the purpose of ascertaining whether he has any unauthorised property on his person.

(2) An authorised employee searching a prisoner by virtue of this section—

(a) shall not be entitled to require a prisoner to remove any of his clothing other than an outer coat, jacket, headgear, gloves and footwear;

(b) may use reasonable force where necessary; and

(c) may seize and detain any unauthorised property found on the prisoner in the course of the search.

(3) In this section "authorised employee" means an employee of a description for the time being authorised by the governor to exercise the powers conferred by this section.

(4) The governor of a prison shall take such steps as he considers appropriate to notify to prisoners the descriptions of persons who are for the time being authorised to exercise the powers conferred by this section.

(5) In this section "unauthorised property", in relation to a prisoner, means property which the prisoner is not authorised by prison rules or by the governor to have in his possession or, as the case may be, in his possession in a particular part of the prison.".

(2) In the Prisons (Scotland) Act 1989, after section 41, there shall be inserted the following section—

"Powers of search by authorised employees

41A.—(1) An authorised employee at a prison shall have the power to search any prisoner for the purpose of ascertaining whether he has any unauthorised property on his person.

(2) An authorised employee searching a prisoner by virtue of this section—

(a) shall not be entitled to require a prisoner to remove any of his clothing other than an outer coat, jacket, headgear, gloves and footwear;

(b) may use reasonable force where necessary; and

(c) may seize and detain any unauthorised property found on the prisoner in the course of the search.

(3) In this section "authorised employee" means an employee of a description for the time being authorised by the governor to exercise the powers conferred by this section.

(4) The governor of a prison shall take such steps as he considers appropriate to notify to prisoners the descriptions of employees who are for the time being authorised employees.

(5) In this section—

"employee" means an employee (not being an officer of a prison) appointed under section 2(1) of this Act; and

"unauthorised property", in relation to a prisoner, means property which the prisoner is not authorised by rules under section 39 of this Act or by the governor to have in his possession or, as the case may be, in his possession in a particular part of the prison.".

DEFINITIONS

"authorised employee": s.8A(3) of the Prison Act 1952, as inserted by this section.

"unauthorised property": s.8A(5) of the Prison Act 1952, as inserted by this section.

GENERAL NOTE

Subs. (1)

This subsection by inserting a new s.8A in the Prison Act 1952 provides for authorised civilian staff in directly managed prisons in England and Wales to have powers of (non-intimate) search of prisoners.

Note the reference in para. (b) of subs. (2) to the new s.8A to *reasonable force*. It is envisaged that this will protect "authorised employees" (*i.e.* civilian employees) from allegations of mistreatment arising from normal searching procedure. It is *not* envisaged that such employees will be used to search forcibly a prisoner who resists. In Committee in the House of Commons (Standing Committee B, col. 1063, March 1, 1994) the Government spokesman said that "civilian staff would not be able to conduct intimate or strip searches". *Note*, also, that they may not require a prisoner to remove more than his outer clothing: subs. (2)(a) of the new section.

For the powers of prison officers (Prison Act 1952 (c. 52), s.8), see the General Note to s.126, *ante*.

Scottish perspective

Subs. (2)

Existing provision allowed only prison officers to conduct searches on prisoners. With the increasing use of civilian staff as, for example, work shop instructors, teachers *etc* in supervising prisoners, this power is now necessary. The searches which can be authorised to be conducted by civilians cannot include intimate or strip searches (subs. (2)) and the governor of each prison is empowered to decide which categories of staff should be authorised to conduct searches (subs. (3)). The power extends to remand centres and young offenders institutions (Sched. 10, para. 64).

Prohibited articles in Scottish prisons

153.—(1) Section 41 of the Prisons (Scotland) Act 1989 (unlawful introduction of tobacco, etc. into prison) shall be amended as follows.

(2) In subsection (1), for the words from the beginning to "shall be guilty" there shall be substituted—

"(1) Any person who without reasonable excuse brings or introduces, or attempts by any means to bring or introduce, into a prison—

(a) any drug;

(b) any firearm or ammunition;

(c) any offensive weapon;

(d) any article to which section 1 of the Carrying of Knives etc. (Scotland) Act 1993 applies; or

(e) without prejudice to paragraphs (a) to (d) above, any article which is a prohibited article within the meaning of rules under section 39 of this Act,

shall be guilty".

(3) After subsection (2) there shall be inserted the following subsections—

"(2A) Where an officer of a prison has reasonable grounds for suspecting that a person who is in or is seeking to enter a prison has in his possession any article mentioned in paragraphs (a) to (e) of subsection (1) above he shall, without prejudice to any other power of search under this Act, have power to search that person and any article in his possession and to seize and detain any article mentioned in those paragraphs found in the course of the search.

(2B) The power conferred by subsection (2A) above—

(a) shall be exercised in accordance with rules under section 39 of this Act;

(b) shall not be construed as authorising the physical examination of a person's body orifices;

(c) so far as relating to any article mentioned in paragraph (c), (d) or (e) of subsection (1) above (and not falling within paragraph (a) or (b) of that subsection), shall not be construed as authorising an officer of a prison to require a person to remove any of his clothing other than an outer coat, jacket, headgear, gloves and footwear; and

(d) shall include power to use reasonable force where necessary.".

(4) For subsection (3) there shall be substituted the following subsections—

"(3) Where an officer of a prison has reasonable grounds for suspecting that any person has committed or is committing an offence under subsection (1) above he may, for the purpose of facilitating investigation by a constable into the offence, detain that person in any place in the prison in question and may, where necessary, use reasonable force in doing so.

(4) Detention under subsection (3) above shall be terminated not more than six hours after it begins or (if earlier)—

(a) when the person is detained in pursuance of any other enactment or subordinate instrument;

(b) when the person is arrested by a constable; or

(c) where the governor of the prison or a constable investigating the offence concludes that there are no such grounds as are mentioned in subsection (3) above or the officer of the prison concludes that there are no longer such grounds,

and the person detained shall be informed immediately upon the termination of his detention that his detention has been terminated.

(5) Where a person has been released at the termination of a period of detention under subsection (3) above he shall not thereafter be detained under that subsection on the same grounds or on any grounds arising out of the same circumstances.

(6) At the time when an officer of a prison detains a person under subsection (3) above he shall inform the person of his suspicion, of the suspected offence and of the reason for the detention; and there shall be recorded—

(a) the place where and the time when the detention begins;

(b) the suspected offence;

(c) the time when a constable or an officer of the police authority is informed of the suspected offence and the detention;

(d) the time when the person is informed of his rights in terms of subsection (7) below and the identity of the officer of the prison so informing him;

(e) where the person requests such intimation as is specified in subsection (7) below to be sent, the time when such request is—

(i) made; and

(ii) complied with; and

(f) the time when, in accordance with subsection (4) above, the person's detention terminates.

(7) A person who is being detained under subsection (3) above, other than a person in respect of whose detention subsection (8) below applies, shall be entitled to have intimation of his detention and of the place where he is being detained sent without delay to a solicitor and to one other person reasonably named by him and shall be informed of that entitlement when his detention begins.

(8) Where a person who is being detained under subsection (3) above appears to the officer of the prison to be under 16 years of age, the officer of the prison shall send without delay to the person's parent, if known, intimation of the person's detention and of the place where he is being detained; and the parent—

> (a) in a case where there is reasonable cause to suspect that he has been involved in the alleged offence in respect of which the person has been detained, may; and
>
> (b) in any other case, shall,

be permitted access to the person.

(9) The nature and extent of any access permitted under subsection (8) above shall be subject to any restriction essential for the furtherance of the investigation or the well-being of the person.

(10) In this section—

> "drug" means any drug which is a controlled drug for the purposes of the Misuse of Drugs Act 1971;
>
> "firearm" and "ammunition" have the same meanings as in the Firearms Act 1968;
>
> "offensive weapon" has the same meaning as in the Prevention of Crime Act 1953; and
>
> "parent" includes a guardian and any person who has actual custody of a person under 16 years of age.".

GENERAL NOTE

Section 41 of the Prisons (Scotland) Act 1989 specified letters, tobacco and spirits as the major prohibited goods, though it also added "or other article not allowed by rules". This new formulation more accurately reflects the items which pose particular problems, while continuing the catch-all provision in the new s.41(2)(1)(e).

Under existing provisions (the Prisons and Young Offenders Institutions (Scotland) Rules 1994 (S.I. 1994 No. 1931), r. 86) officers were empowered to search visitors only with the consent of the visitor. The only sanction available when the visitor refused to be searched was to refuse admission (r. 86(4)), though the officer could also apprehend a person offending against s.41 (s.41(3)) of the Prisons (Scotland) Act 1989. The new provision gives officers the power to conduct searches in any case where they have reasonable grounds to believe the visitor to be in possession of a prohibited article. The search powers are restricted to "rub down" searches, save in the case of suspected drugs, firearms or ammunition, where a strip search, but not an intimate body search, is allowed.

Officers are also authorised to detain, on reasonable suspicion, any person suspected of bringing in prohibited articles and to continue that detention until the police arrive, or for six hours, whichever is sooner. The same protections available to detainees under s.2 of the Criminal Justice (Scotland) Act 1980 apply and, under Sched. 10, para. 47, the period of detention by prison officers is to count towards the total six hours allowed by s.2.

Harassment, alarm or distress

Offence of causing intentional harassment, alarm or distress

154. In Part I of the Public Order Act 1986 (offences relating to public order), after section 4, there shall be inserted the following section—

"Intentional harassment, alarm or distress

4A.—(1) A person is guilty of an offence if, with intent to cause a person harassment, alarm or distress, he—

> (a) uses threatening, abusive or insulting words or behaviour, or disorderly behaviour, or
>
> (b) displays any writing, sign or other visible representation which is threatening, abusive or insulting,

thereby causing that or another person harassment, alarm or distress.

(2) An offence under this section may be committed in a public or a private place, except that no offence is committed where the words or behaviour are used, or the writing, sign or other visible representation is

displayed, by a person inside a dwelling and the person who is harassed, alarmed or distressed is also inside that or another dwelling.

(3) It is a defence for the accused to prove—

(a) that he was inside a dwelling and had no reason to believe that the words or behaviour used, or the writing, sign or other visible representation displayed, would be heard or seen by a person outside that or any other dwelling, or

(b) that his conduct was reasonable.

(4) A constable may arrest without warrant anyone he reasonably suspects is committing an offence under this section.

(5) A person guilty of an offence under this section is liable on summary conviction to imprisonment for a term not exceeding 6 months or a fine not exceeding level 5 on the standard scale or both.".

GENERAL NOTE

This section inserts a new s.4A into the Public Order Act 1986 and thereby creates a new offence of causing intentional harassment, alarm or distress. The offence created by this section is based on the offence created by s.5 of the 1986 Act (threatening, abusive or insulting words or conduct within the hearing or sight of a person likely to be caused harassment). As in s.5, the offence may be committed in public or private, but not inside a dwelling if the person harassed is also inside the dwelling. However, this section also requires that: (a) the element of intent be proved and (b) that a person actually be caused harassment etc. This section is aimed at serious persistent racial harassment. As a result, it carries a more substantial penalty than s.5. A defendant convicted of an offence under this section is liable to six months' imprisonment and/or a fine of £5,000.

Subsection (3) provides a similar defence to that in s.5(3). This defence must be proved on the balance of probabilities: *R. v. Carr-Briant* [1943] K.B. 607; *D.P.P. v. Clarke; Lewis, O'Connell and O'Keefe* [1992] C.L.Y. 1129; and the question whether the defendant's conduct was reasonable can only be answered by applying an objective test: *D.P.P. v. Clarke, ante.*

Dwelling is defined by the Public Order Act 1986, s.8: "any structure or part of a structure occupied as a person's home or other living accommodation (whether the occupation is separate or shared with others) but does not include any part not so occupied, and for this purpose "structure" includes a tent, caravan, vehicle, vessel or other temporary or movable structure".

Racial hatred: see the General Note to s.155, *post.*

Offence of racially inflammatory publication etc. to be arrestable

Offence of racially inflammatory publication etc. to be arrestable

155.—In section 24(2) of the Police and Criminal Evidence Act 1984 (arrestable offences), after the paragraph (h) inserted by section 166(4) of this Act, there shall be inserted the following paragraph—

"(i) an offence under section 19 of the Public Order Act 1986 (publishing, etc. material intended or likely to stir up racial hatred);".

DEFINITIONS

"publish [and related expressions]": s.29 of the Public Order Act 1986.
"racial hatred": s.17 of the Public Order Act 1986.

GENERAL NOTE

This section amends s.24(2) of the Police and Criminal Evidence Act 1984 to make any offence under s.19 of the Public Order Act 1986 (publication or distribution of written material intended or likely to stir up racial hatred) an arrestable offence. The purpose is to give the police greater powers in investigating such offences. Thus, the police will have the powers of entry, search and seizure conferred by s.32 of the Police and Criminal Evidence Act 1984 in relation to offences under this section.

Racial hatred, under the Public Order Act 1986, s.17, means "hatred against a group of persons in Great Britain defined by reference to colour, race, nationality (including citizenship) or ethnic or national origins".

Prohibition on use of cells from embryos or foetuses

Prohibition on use of cells from embryos or foetuses

156.—(1) The Human Fertilisation and Embryology Act 1990 shall be amended as follows.

(2) After section 3 there shall be inserted the following section—

"Prohibition in connection with germ cells

3A.—(1) No person shall, for the purpose of providing connection with fertility services for any woman, use female germ cells germ cells taken or derived from an embryo or a foetus or use embryos created by using such cells.

(2) In this section—

"female germ cells" means cells of the female germ line and includes such cells at any stage of maturity and accordingly includes eggs; and

"fertility services" means medical, surgical or obstetric services provided for the purpose of assisting women to carry children.".

(3) In section 41(1)(a) (offences under the Act) after the words "section 3(2)" there shall be inserted ", 3A".

DEFINITIONS
"embryo": s.1(1) of the Human Fertilisation and Embryology Act 1990.
"female germ cells": s.3A(2) of the Human Fertilisation and Embryology Act 1990, as inserted by this section.
"fertility services": s.3A(2) of the Human Fertilisation and Embryology Act 1990, as inserted by this section.

GENERAL NOTE
This section inserts s.3A into the Human Fertilisation and Embryology Act 1990 and makes it an offence for a person, for the purpose of providing fertility services for any woman, to use female germ cells (which include immature foetal eggs) taken or derived from an embryo or a foetus or to use embryos created using such cells. The maximum penalty for this offence is 10 years' imprisonment or a fine or both: s.41(1) of the 1990 Act.

The definition of fertility services in the new section is very similar to that of treatment services in the main Act: "medical, surgical or obstetric services provided to the public or a section of the public for the purpose of assisting women to carry children"; see s.2.

Increase in certain penalties

Increase in penalties for certain offences

157.—(1) The enactments specified in column 2 of Part I of Schedule 8 to this Act which relate to the maximum fines for the offences mentioned (and broadly described) in column 1 of that Part of that Schedule shall have effect as if the maximum fine that may be imposed on summary conviction of any offence so mentioned were a fine not exceeding the amount specified in column 4 of that Part of that Schedule instead of a fine of an amount specified in column 3 of that Part of that Schedule.

(2) For the amount of the maximum fine specified in column 3 of Part II of Schedule 8 to this Act that may be imposed under the enactments specified in column 2 of that Part of that Schedule on summary conviction of the offences mentioned (and broadly described) in column 1 of that Part of that Schedule there shall be substituted the amount specified in column 4 of that Part of that Schedule.

(3) For the maximum term of imprisonment specified in column 3 of Part III of Schedule 8 to this Act that may be imposed under the enactments specified in column 2 of that Part of that Schedule on conviction on indictment, or on conviction on indictment or summary conviction, of the offences men-

tioned (and broadly described) in column 1 of that Part of that Schedule there shall be substituted the maximum term of imprisonment specified in column 4 of that Part of that Schedule.

(4) Any reference in column 2 of Part II of Schedule 8 to this Act to a numbered column of Schedule 4 to the Misuse of Drugs Act 1971 is a reference to the column of that number construed with section 25(2)(b) of that Act.

(5) Any reference in column 2 of Part III of Schedule 8 to this Act—

(a) to a numbered column of Schedule 6 to the Firearms Act 1968 is a reference to the column of that number construed with section 51(2) (b) of that Act; or

(b) to a numbered column of Schedule 2 to the Firearms (Northern Ireland) Order 1981 is a reference to the column of that number construed with Article 52(2)(b) of that Order.

(6) Section 143 of the Magistrates' Courts Act 1980 (power of Secretary of State by order to alter sums specified in certain provisions) shall have effect with the insertion, in subsection (2), after paragraph (p), of the following paragraph—

"(q) column 5 or 6 of Schedule 4 to the Misuse of Drugs Act 1971 so far as the column in question relates to the offences under provisions of that Act specified in column 1 of that Schedule in respect of which the maximum fines were increased by Part II of Schedule 8 to the Criminal Justice and Public Order Act 1994.".

(7) Section 289D of the Criminal Procedure (Scotland) Act 1975 (power of Secretary of State by order to alter sums specified in certain provisions of Scots law) shall have effect with the insertion, in subsection (1A), after paragraph (e), of the following paragraph—

"(ee) column 5 or 6 of Schedule 4 to the Misuse of Drugs Act 1971 so far as the column in question relates to the offences under provisions of that Act specified in column I of that Schedule in respect of which the maximum fines were increased by Part II of Schedule 8 to the Criminal Justice and Public Order Act 1994.".

(8) Article 17 of the Fines and Penalties (Northern Ireland) Order 1984 (power of Secretary of State by order to alter sums specified in certain provisions of the law of Northern Ireland) shall have effect with the insertion, in paragraph (2), after sub-paragraph (j) of the following sub-paragraph—

"(k) column 5 or 6 of Schedule 4 to the Misuse of Drugs Act 1971 so far as the column in question relates to the offences under provisions of that Act specified in column 1 of that Schedule in respect of which the maximum fines were increased by Part II of Schedule 8 to the Criminal Justice and Public Order Act 1994.".

(9) Subsections (1), (2) and (3) above do not apply to an offence committed before this section comes into force.

GENERAL NOTE

This section, with Sched. 8, provides for amendments to be made to the Sea Fisheries (Shellfish) Act 1967 and the Misuse of Drugs Act 1971 to increase financial penalties for certain offences. Part II of Sched. 8, *post*, increases the penalties for a number of offences connected with Class C drugs (Misuse of Drugs Act 1971) and one offence connected with Class B drugs (*ibid.*). The purpose of these changes was to uprate the penalties for the possession of certain drugs in order to keep abreast with the uprating which has occurred in other parts of drug law (Standing Committee B, col. 937, February 22, 1994). The Schedule also increases penalties for certain sea-fishery offences (Pt. I) and for certain firearm offences (Pt. III).

Scottish perspective

Increasing maximum penalties for certain offences is a regular part of the process of being seen to be tough on crime. There is little evidence that it ever makes any difference, save by contributing to the general level of inflation in punishment, of which prisons north and south of the border appear to bear the brunt.

Extradition procedures

Extradition procedures

158.—(1) The Extradition Act 1989 shall be amended as follows.

(2) In section 4 (extradition Orders), in subsection (5), for the words "warrant his trial if" there shall be substituted the words "make a case requiring an answer by that person if the proceedings were a summary trial of an information against him and".

(3) In section 7 (extradition request and authority to proceed)—

(a) in subsection (2), in paragraph (b), after the word "evidence" there shall be inserted the words "or, in a case falling within subsection (2A) below, information"; and

(b) after subsection (2), there shall be inserted the following subsection—
"(2A) Where—
(a) the extradition request is made by a foreign state; and
(b) an Order in Council falling within section 4(5) above is in force in relation to that state,
it shall be a sufficient compliance with subsection (2)(b) above to furnish information sufficient to justify the issue of a warrant for his arrest under this Act.".

(4) In section 8 (arrest for purposes of committal)—

(a) in subsection (3) after the word "evidence" there shall be inserted the words "or, in a case falling within subsection (3A) below, information"; and

(b) after subsection (3) there shall be inserted the following subsection—
"(3A) Where—
(a) the extradition request or, where a provisional warrant is applied for, the request for the person's arrest is made by a foreign state; and
(b) an Order in Council falling within section 4(5) above is in force in relation to that state,
it shall be sufficient for the purposes of subsection (3) above to supply such information as would, in the opinion of the person so empowered, justify the issue of a warrant of arrest.".

(5) In section 9 (committal proceedings)—

(a) in subsection (2), for the words from "jurisdiction" to the end there shall be substituted the words "powers, as nearly as may be, including powers to adjourn the case and meanwhile to remand the person arrested under the warrant either in custody or on bail, as if the proceedings were the summary trial of an information against him; and section 16(1)(c) of the Prosecution of Offences Act 1985 (costs on dismissal) shall apply accordingly reading the reference to the dismissal of the information as a reference to the discharge of the person arrested.";

(b) after subsection (2) there shall be inserted the following subsection—
"(2A) If a court of committal in England and Wales exercises its power to adjourn the case it shall on so doing remand the person arrested in custody or on bail.";

(c) in subsection (4), for the words from "warrant the trial" to the end there shall be substituted the words "make a case requiring an answer by the arrested person if the proceedings were the summary trial of an information against him."; and

(d) in subsection (8)(a), for the words from "warrant his trial" to the end, there shall be substituted the words "make a case requiring an answer by that person if the proceedings were the summary trial of an information against him.".

(6) In section 22 (International Convention cases), in subsection (5), for the words from "warrant his trial" to the end, there shall be substituted the words "make a case requiring an answer by that person if the proceedings were the summary trial of an information against him".

(7) In section 35 (interpretation), after subsection (2), there shall be inserted the following subsection—

"(3) For the purposes of the application of this Act by virtue of any Order in Council in force under it or section 2 of the Extradition Act 1870, any reference in this Act to evidence making a case requiring an answer by an accused person shall be taken to indicate a determination of the same question as is indicated by a reference (however expressed) in any such Order (or arrangements embodied or recited in it) to evidence warranting or justifying the committal for trial of an accused person.".

(8) In Schedule 1 (provisions applying to foreign states in respect of which an Order in Council under section 2 of the Extradition Act 1870 is in force—

(a) in paragraph 6(1) (hearing of case), for the words from "hear the case" to the end there shall be substituted the words "have the same powers, as near as may be, including power to adjourn the case and meanwhile to remand the prisoner either in custody or on bail, as if the proceedings were the summary trial of an information against him for an offence committed in England and Wales; and section 16(1)(c) of the Prosecution of Offences Act 1985 (costs on dismissal) shall apply accordingly reading the reference to the dismissal of the information as a reference to the discharge of the prisoner.";

(b) after paragraph 6(1) there shall be inserted the following sub-paragraph—

"(1A) If the metropolitan magistrate exercises his power to adjourn the case he shall on so doing remand the prisoner either in custody or on bail."; and

(c) in paragraph 7(1) (committal or discharge of prisoner), for the words from "justify the committal" to "England or Wales" there shall be substituted the words "make a case requiring an answer by the prisoner if the proceedings were for the trial in England and Wales of an information for the crime,".

DEFINITIONS

"authority to proceed": ss.7(1) and 35(1) of the Extradition Act 1989.
"extradition request": ss.7(1) and 35(1) of the Extradition Act 1989.
"provisional warrant": ss.8(1) and 35(1) of the Extradition Act 1989.

GENERAL NOTE

This section and Sched. 9, para. 37, *post.*, amend the Extradition Act 1989 so as to make special provision for the documentation to be provided in support of extradition requests made by countries in respect of which the requirement to produce prima facie evidence has been removed *i.e.* those countries which adhere to the European Convention on extradition. Countries which adhere to the European Convention on extradition are obliged to send information about the offence in question. According to the Home Office Minister: "the Convention is based on a 'no evidence' approach in recognition of the degree of mutual trust that by ratifying the convention, the contracting states have agreed to place in each other's systems" (Standing Committee B, col. 1296, March 10, 1994). On the other hand, the Extradition Act 1989 required *evidence* sufficient to justify the issue of a warrant. The inconsistency between the requirements of the Act and the terms of the Convention is corrected by this section.

The section also makes a technical change to reflect the move to transfer proceedings in place of committals in magistrates' courts.

Section 7(1) of the Extradition Act 1989 provides that an authority to proceed is an order of the Secretary of State issued in pursuance of an extradition request *i.e.* "a request for the surrender of a person under this Act made (a) by some person recognised by the Secretary of State as a diplomatic or consular representative of a foreign state; or (b) by or on behalf of the Government of a designated country, or the Governor of a colony". Section 8(1) of the Extradition Act 1989 provides that a provisional warrant is a warrant for the arrest of a person issued without an authority to proceed by a metropolitan magistrate (as defined by s.8(2)) or a justice of the peace in any part of the U.K. or, in Scotland, by a sheriff, upon information that the said person is or is believed to be in or on his way to the U.K.

Backing of warrants: Republic of Ireland

159.—(1) The Backing of Warrants (Republic of Ireland) Act 1965 shall be amended as follows.

(2) In section 1 (conditions for endorsement of warrants issued in Republic of Ireland), in subsection (1)(b), after the word "acts" there shall be inserted the words "or on his way to the United Kingdom".

(3) In section 2 (proceedings for delivery of person arrested under endorsed warrant), in subsection (2)(a) (excluded offences) the words from ", or an offence under an enactment" to "control" shall be omitted.

(4) In section 4 (procedure for provisional warrants)—
   (a) in subsection (1)(c), after the word "acts" there shall be inserted the words "or on his way to the United Kingdom";
   (b) in subsection (2), for the words "five days" there shall be substituted the words "seven days"; and
   (c) in subsection (3)(b), for the words "three days" there shall be substituted the words "seven days".

(5) In the Schedule (proceedings before magistrates' court), in paragraph 3, for the words from "and the proceedings" to the end, there shall be substituted the words "as if the proceedings were the summary trial of an information against that person.".

GENERAL NOTE

This section amends the Backing of Warrants (Republic of Ireland) Act 1965 so as to enable action to be taken against persons on their way to the U.K., in addition to those already here; to remove the bar on proceedings in respect of offences relating to taxes, duties or exchange control; to extend the life of provisional arrest warrants from five to seven days; and to extend the maximum period of remand from three to seven days. The reason for these changes is to reflect changes being made by the Irish Government. The section also makes a technical change to reflect the move to transfer proceedings in place of committals in magistrates' courts.

Constabulary powers in United Kingdom waters

Extension of powers, etc., of constables to United Kingdom waters

160.—(1) Section 19 of the Police Act 1964 (area within which a constable's powers and privileges are exercisable) shall be amended as follows—
   (a) in subsection (1), after the words "England and Wales" there shall be inserted the words "and the adjacent United Kingdom waters.";
   (b) in subsection (2), after the words "area for which he is appointed" there shall be inserted the words "and, where the boundary of that area includes the coast, in the adjacent United Kingdom waters"; and
   (c) after subsection (5), there shall be inserted the following subsection—
   "(5A) In this section—
      "powers" includes powers under any enactment, whenever passed or made;
      "United Kingdom waters" means the sea and other waters within the seaward limits of the territorial sea;
   and this section, so far as it relates to powers under any enactment, makes them exercisable throughout those waters whether or not the enactment applies to those waters apart from this provision.".

(2) Section 17 of the Police (Scotland) Act 1967 (general functions and jurisdiction of constables) shall be amended as follows—

(a) in subsection (4), after the word "Scotland" there shall be inserted the words "and (without prejudice to section 1(2) of this Act) the adjacent United Kingdom waters"; and

(b) after subsection (7) there shall be inserted the following subsection—

"(7A) In this section—

"powers" includes powers under any enactment, whenever passed or made;

"United Kingdom waters" means the sea and other waters within the seaward limits of the territorial sea;

and this section, so far as it relates to powers under any enactment, makes them exercisable throughout those waters whether or not the enactment applies to those waters apart from this provision.".

DEFINITIONS

"powers": s.19(5A) of the Police Act 1964, as inserted by this section.
"United Kingdom waters": s.19(5A) of the Police Act 1964, as inserted by this section.

GENERAL NOTE

This section amends s.19 of the Police Act 1964 (jurisdiction of constables) and s.17 of the Police (Scotland) Act 1967 to provide that a constable's powers and privileges are exercisable in U.K. waters. The purpose of the enactment of subs. (1), amending s.19 of the Police Act 1964, is to rectify an anomaly pointed out in a Law Commission report published in 1978. The anomaly was that, although the courts had a common law jurisdiction to try offences committed off-shore within the 12-mile limit, s.19 of the Police Act 1964 extended only to England and Wales and did not go beyond the high-tide mark. The police are now able to be involved in off-shore policing to combat terrorism and drug-running as well as general criminal investigation.

Obtaining computer-held information

Procuring disclosure of, and selling, computer-held personal information

161.—(1) In section 5 of the Data Protection Act 1984 (prohibitions in relation to personal data, including disclosure), after subsection (5), there shall be inserted the following subsections—

"(6) A person who procures the disclosure to him of personal data the disclosure of which to him is in contravention of subsection (2) or (3) above, knowing or having reason to believe that the disclosure constitutes such a contravention, shall be guilty of an offence.

(7) A person who sells personal data shall be guilty of an offence if (in contravention of subsection (6) above) he has procured the disclosure of the data to him.

(8) A person who offers to sell personal data shall be guilty of an offence if (in contravention of subsection (6) above) he has procured or subsequently procures the disclosure of the data to him.

(9) For the purposes of subsection (8) above, an advertisement indicating that personal data are or may be for sale is an offer to sell the data.

(10) For the purposes of subsections (7) and (8) above, "selling", or "offering to sell", in relation to personal data, includes selling, or offering to sell, information extracted from the data.

(11) In determining, for the purposes of subsection (6), (7) or (8) above, whether a disclosure is in contravention of subsection (2) or (3) above, section 34(6)(d) below shall be disregarded.".

(2) In consequence of the amendment made by subsection (1) above—

(a) in subsection (5) of that section, after the word "other" there shall be inserted the word "foregoing"; and

(b) in section 28 (exemptions: crime and taxation), in subsection (3)—
    (i) after the words "section 26(3)(a) above" there shall be inserted the words "or for an offence under section 5(6) above"; and
    (ii) after the words "to make" there shall be inserted the words "or (in the case of section 5(6)) to procure".

DEFINITIONS
  "data": s.1(2) of the Data Protection Act 1984.
  "disclosure": s.1(9) of the Data Protection Act 1984.
  "offering to sell": subss. (9) and (10).
  "personal data": s.1(3) of the Data Protection Act 1984.
  "selling": subs. (10).

GENERAL NOTE
  This section amends s.5 of the Data Protection Act 1984 in order to strengthen the prohibition against the disclosure or selling of computer-held personal information in breach of an entry registered with the Data Protection Registrar. Part II of the Data Protection Act 1984 requires organisations holding such information to register that fact and to include in the entry, details of those to whom the information may be disclosed. It is an offence to hold such information unless an entry has been made; and it is also an offence to disclose such information to a person not detailed in the entry. Subsections (6)–(8) of this section make it an offence (punishable by way of fine) to procure the disclosure of such information in breach of the entry or to sell or offer to sell information so procured. The section is subject to the exemptions in s.28 of the Data Protection Act 1984 relating to personal data held for the prevention and detection of crime, the apprehension and detection of offenders and the collection of taxes.

Scottish perspective
  This is a response to media coverage showing how easy it is to obtain personal data, *e.g.* bank account details, on the payment of fees.

Access to computer material by constables and other enforcement officers

  162.—(1) In section 10 of the Computer Misuse Act 1990 (offence of unauthorised access not to apply to exercise of law enforcement powers), after paragraph (b), there shall be inserted the following words—
    "and nothing designed to indicate a withholding of consent to access to any program or data from persons as enforcement officers shall have effect to make access unauthorised for the purposes of the said section 1(1).
    In this section "enforcement officer" means a constable or other person charged with the duty of investigating offences; and withholding consent from a person "as" an enforcement officer of any description includes the operation, by the person entitled to control access, of rules whereby enforcement officers of that description are, as such, disqualified from membership of a class of persons who are authorised to have access.".
  (2) In section 17(5) of that Act (when access is unauthorised), after paragraph (b), there shall be inserted the following words—
    "but this subsection is subject to section 10.".

DEFINITIONS
  "enforcement officer": s.10 of the Computer Misuse Act 1990, as inserted by this section.

GENERAL NOTE
  This section is designed to prevent an abuse of the Computer Misuse Act 1990 (which was enacted to deal with the "computer hacking"). It amends s.10 of the Computer Misuse Act 1990 in order to enable the police and other enforcement officers to gain access to any program or data. This section makes clear that any notice purporting to prevent a police officer from gaining access unauthorised under the 1990 Act shall not have effect. The Computer Misuse Act 1990, s.1(1) provides that it is an offence to secure unauthorised access to a computer program or data. Section 10(1) of the Act provides that s.1(1) has effect without prejudice to the operation of any enactment relating to powers of inspection search or seizure. In the House of Lords (*Hansard,*

H.L. Vol. 556, col. 136) the Minister of State, Home Office described how it is possible to gain access via the telephone network to "bulletin boards", some of which have been used to convey obscene material, including child pornography and which have built into them a notice purporting to deny access to law enforcement officers and are intended to attract the protection of the Computer Misuse Act 1990. "The police would like to be able to gain access to these systems—in the same way members of the public can—without the fear that they may be committing a criminal offence. This amendment does not give the police special powers to access private computer systems. Members of the public will remain entitled to operate computer systems to which they control access. The amendment simply makes it clear that the computer system's owner cannot invoke the provisions of the Computer Misuse Act 1990 in order to deny access to police officers while allowing access to every other member of the public."

Closed-circuit television by local authorities

Local authority powers to provide closed-circuit television

163.—(1) Without prejudice to any power which they may exercise for those purposes under any other enactment, a local authority may take such of the following steps as they consider will, in relation to their area, promote the prevention of crime or the welfare of the victims of crime—

(a) providing apparatus for recording visual images of events occurring on any land in their area;

(b) providing within their area a telecommunications system which, under Part II of the Telecommunications Act 1984, may be run without a licence;

(c) arranging for the provision of any other description of telecommunications system within their area or between any land in their area and any building occupied by a public authority.

(2) Any power to provide, or to arrange for the provision of, any apparatus includes power to maintain, or operate, or, as the case may be, to arrange for the maintenance or operation of, that apparatus.

(3) Before taking such a step under this section, a local authority shall consult the chief officer of police for the police area in which the step is to be taken.

(4) In this section—

"chief officer of police", in relation to a police area in Scotland, means the chief constable of a police force maintained for that area;

"local authority"—

(a) in England, means a county council or district council;

(b) in Wales, means a county council or county borough council; and

(c) in Scotland, has the meaning given by section 235(1) of the Local Government (Scotland) Act 1973; and

"telecommunications system" has the meaning given in section 4 of the Telecommunications Act 1984 and "licence" means a licence under section 7 of that Act.

(5) Until 1st April 1996, in this section "local authority" means, in Wales, a county council or district council.

DEFINITIONS

"chief officer of police": subs. (4).
"licence": subs. (4).
"local authority": subss. (4)(5).
"telecommunications system": subs. (4).

GENERAL NOTE

The purpose of this section is to make clear the powers available to local councils outside London to enable them to spend money on closed circuit televisions in town centres and other places which are not council property. Before setting up a system local authorities must consult the chief officer of police for the area.

Scottish perspective
Successful experiments with city centre video recording have taken place in several towns and cities throughout Scotland. Initial scepticism that the cameras would only displace crime seems to have been unfounded and towns like Airdrie are reporting significant reductions in crime throughout the area. Funding of such projects has posed some problems and these have not been entirely solved by the involvement of the private sector.

Serious fraud

Extension of powers of Serious Fraud Office and of powers to investigate serious fraud in Scotland

164.—(1) Section 4 of the Criminal Justice (International Co-operation) Act 1990 (obtaining evidence in the United Kingdom for use overseas) shall be amended as follows—
(a) after subsection (2), there shall be inserted the following sub-sections—
"(2A) Except where the evidence is to be obtained as is mentioned in subsection (2B) below, if the Secretary of State is satisfied—
(a) that an offence under the law of the country or territory in question has been committed or that there are reasonable grounds for suspecting that such an offence has been committed; and
(b) that proceedings in respect of that offence have been instituted in that country or territory or that an investigation into that offence is being carried on there,
and it appears to him that the request relates to an offence involving serious or complex fraud, he may, if he thinks fit, refer the request or any part of the request to the Director of the Serious Fraud Office for him to obtain such of the evidence to which the request or part referred relates as may appear to the Director to be appropriate for giving effect to the request or part referred.
(2B) Where the evidence is to be obtained in Scotland, if the Lord Advocate is satisfied as to the matters mentioned in paragraphs (a) and (b) of subsection (2A) above and it appears to him that the request relates to an offence involving serious or complex fraud, he may, if he thinks fit, give a direction under section 51 of the Criminal Justice (Scotland) Act 1987.";
(b) in subsection (3), after the words "subsection (2)" there shall be inserted the words "(2A) or (2B)"; and
(c) in subsection (4), after the words "subsection (2)(a) and (b)" there shall be inserted the words "or (2A)(a) and (b)".
(2) Section 2 of the Criminal Justice Act 1987 (investigative powers of Director of Serious Fraud Office) shall be amended as follows—
(a) in subsection (1), for the words from "the Attorney-General" to "the request" there shall be substituted "an authority entitled to make such a request";
(b) after subsection (1), there shall be inserted the following sub-sections—
"(1A) The authorities entitled to request the Director to exercise his powers under this section are—
(a) the Attorney-General of the Isle of Man, Jersey or Guernsey, acting under legislation corresponding to section 1 of this Act and having effect in the Island whose Attorney-General makes the request; and
(b) the Secretary of State acting under section 4(2A) of the Criminal Justice (International Co-operation) Act 1990, in response to a request received by him from an overseas court, tribunal or authority (an "overseas authority").

(1B) The Director shall not exercise his powers on a request from the Secretary of State acting in response to a request received from an overseas authority within subsection (1A)(b) above unless it appears to the Director on reasonable grounds that the offence in respect of which he has been requested to obtain evidence involves serious or complex fraud.";

(c) after subsection (8), there shall be inserted the following subsections—

"(8A) Any evidence obtained by the Director for use by an overseas authority shall be furnished by him to the Secretary of State for transmission to the overseas authority which requested it.

(8B) If in order to comply with the request of the overseas authority it is necessary for any evidence obtained by the Director to be accompanied by any certificate, affidavit or other verifying document, the Director shall also furnish for transmission such document of that nature as may be specified by the Secretary of State when asking the Director to obtain the evidence.

(8C) Where any evidence obtained by the Director for use by an overseas authority consists of a document the original or a copy shall be transmitted, and where it consists of any other article the article itself or a description, photograph or other representation of it shall be transmitted, as may be necessary in order to comply with the request of the overseas authority."; and

(d) in subsection (18), at the end, there shall be inserted the words "; and "evidence" (in relation to subsections (1A)(b), (8A), (8B) and (8C) above) includes documents and other articles.".

(3) In section 51(1) of the Criminal Justice (Scotland) Act 1987 (investigative powers of Lord Advocate as respects serious or complex fraud), at the end there shall be added "; and he may also give such a direction by virtue of section 4(2B) of the Criminal Justice (International Co-operation) Act 1990 or on a request being made to him by the Attorney-General of the Isle of Man, Jersey or Guernsey acting under legislation corresponding to this section and sections 52 to 54 of this Act.".

(4) In section 52 of the Criminal Justice (Scotland) Act 1987 (investigation by nominated officer—

(a) after subsection (7) there shall be inserted—

"(7A) Any evidence obtained by the Lord Advocate by virtue of section 4(2B) of the Criminal Justice (International Co-operation) Act 1990 shall be furnished by him to the Secretary of State for transmission to the overseas authority in compliance with whose request (in the following subsections referred to as the "relevant request") it was so obtained.

(7B) If, in order to comply with the relevant request it is necessary for that evidence to be accompanied by any certificate, affidavit or other verifying document, the Lord Advocate shall also furnish for transmission such document of that nature as appears to him to be appropriate.

(7C) Where any evidence obtained by virtue of the said section 4(2B) consists of a document, the original or a copy shall be transmitted and where it consists of any other article the article itself or a description, photograph or other representation of it shall be transmitted, as may be necessary in order to comply with the relevant request."; and

(b) in subsection (8), after the definition of "documents" there shall be inserted—

" "evidence", in relation to a relevant request, includes documents and other articles;".

DEFINITIONS
"authority entitled to make such a request": s.2(1A) of the Criminal Justice Act 1987, as inserted by this section.

"documents": s.2(18) of the Criminal Justice Act 1987, see below.

"evidence": s.2(18) of the Criminal Justice Act 1987, as amended by this section; s.4(5) of the Criminal Justice (International Co-operation) Act 1990, see below.

"overseas authority": s.2(1A)(b) of the Criminal Justice Act 1987, as inserted by this section.

GENERAL NOTE

Subs. (1)

This subsection amends s.4 of the Criminal Justice (International Co-operation) Act 1990 so that the Home Secretary may refer a request for evidence relating to serious or complex fraud from a court, tribunal or prosecuting authority outside the U.K., or from an authority appearing to have the function of making such a request, to the Director of the Serious Fraud Office. *Evidence* is defined by s.4(5) of the 1990 Act as including "documents and other articles".

Subs. (2)

Section 2 of the Criminal Justice Act 1987 formerly empowered the Director of the Serious Fraud Office to investigate serious frauds either on his own account (s.1) or at the request of the Att.-Gen. of the Isle of Man, Jersey or Guernsey (s.2(1)). He may now also exercise his powers in response to a request from an overseas court, tribunal or authority if it appears to him that the request relates to an offence involving serious or complex fraud. Any evidence obtained by him for use by the overseas authority shall be dispatched to the Secretary of State for transmission to the requesting overseas authority, together with any required certificates, affidavits or other verifying documents.

Evidence "includes documents and other articles": see s.2(18), added by this section. *Documents* "includes information recorded in any form and in relation to information recorded otherwise than in legible form, references to its production include references to producing a copy of the information in legible form"; s.2(18) of the 1987 Act.

Scottish perspective

New powers are only available in relation to the investigation of serious or complex frauds when proceedings have been instigated or investigations are being carried out in a foreign country.

Copyright and illicit recordings: enforcement of offences

Enforcement of certain offences relating to copyright and illicit recordings

165.—(1) The Copyright, Designs and Patents Act 1988 shall be amended as follows.

(2) After section 107 (offences relating to copyright) there shall be inserted the following section—

"Enforcement by local weights and measures authority

107A.—(1) It is the duty of every local weights and measures authority to enforce within their area the provisions of section 107.

(2) The following provisions of the Trade Descriptions Act 1968 apply in relation to the enforcement of that section by such an authority as in relation to the enforcement of that Act—

section 27 (power to make test purchases),

section 28 (power to enter premises and inspect and seize goods and documents),

section 29 (obstruction of authorised officers), and

section 33 (compensation for loss, &c. of goods seized).

(3) Subsection (1) above does not apply in relation to the enforcement of section 107 in Northern Ireland, but it is the duty of the Department of Economic Development to enforce that section in Northern Ireland.

For that purpose the provisions of the Trade Descriptions Act 1968 specified in subsection (2) apply as if for the references to a local weights and measures authority and any officer of such an authority there were substituted references to that Department and any of its officers.

(4) Any enactment which authorises the disclosure of information for the purpose of facilitating the enforcement of the Trade Descriptions Act 1968 shall apply as if section 107 were contained in that Act and as if the functions of any person in relation to the enforcement of that section were functions under that Act.

(5) Nothing in this section shall be construed as authorising a local weights and measures authority to bring proceedings in Scotland for an offence.".

(3) After section 198 (offences relating to illicit recordings) there shall be inserted the following section—

"Enforcement by local weights and measures authority

198A.—(1) It is the duty of every local weights and measures authority to enforce within their area the provisions of section 198.

(2) The following provisions of the Trade Descriptions Act 1968 apply in relation to the enforcement of that section by such an authority as in relation to the enforcement of that Act—

> section 27 (power to make test purchases),
> section 28 (power to enter premises and inspect and seize goods and documents),
> section 29 (obstruction of authorised officers), and
> section 33 (compensation for loss, &c. of goods seized).

(3) Subsection (1) above does not apply in relation to the enforcement of section 198 in Northern Ireland, but it is the duty of the Department of Economic Development to enforce that section in Northern Ireland.

For that purpose the provisions of the Trade Descriptions Act 1968 specified in subsection (2) apply as if for the references to a local weights and measures authority and any officer of such an authority there were substituted references to that Department and any of its officers.

(4) Any enactment which authorises the disclosure of information for the purpose of facilitating the enforcement of the Trade Descriptions Act 1968 shall apply as if section 198 were contained in that Act and as if the functions of any person in relation to the enforcement of that section were functions under that Act.

(5) Nothing in this section shall be construed as authorising a local weights and measures authority to bring proceedings in Scotland for an offence.".

DEFINITIONS
"copyright": s.1(1) of the Copyright, Designs and Patents Act 1988.
"recording": s.180(2) of the Copyright, Designs and Patents Act 1988.

GENERAL NOTE
This section was introduced to overrule the decision in *Kent County Council v. Price (Ralph Robert)* [1993] C.L.Y. 484 in which the Divisional Court held that the use by a trader of a disclaimer provided a defence to a charge under the Trade Descriptions Act 1968 relating to counterfeit goods brought by trading standards officers. Until then, trading standards officers had relied on the powers they had assumed had been conferred by the Act.

As a result of this section trading standards officers will now be able to take enforcement action against copyright offences under s.107 of the 1988 Act and will also be able to take such action against offences involving illicit recordings of performances (so-called "bootleg copies") under s.198 of the Trade Descriptions Act 1968. (The need to prove the falsity of the trade description will thus be averted.)

Scottish perspective
While the Trading Standards departments in Scotland are to be given these new duties, both the new sections make clear that the remit of the departments in Scotland is not to extend to initiating criminal proceedings. Thus the Departments will be confined to reporting cases to the Procurators Fiscal.

Ticket touts

Sale of tickets by unauthorised persons

166.—(1) It is an offence for an unauthorised person to sell, or offer or expose for sale, a ticket for a designated football match in any public place or place to which the public has access or, in the course of a trade or business, in any other place.

(2) For this purpose—

(a) a person is "unauthorised" unless he is authorised in writing to sell tickets for the match by the home club or by the organisers of the match;

(b) a "ticket" means anything which purports to be a ticket; and

(c) a "designated football match" means a football match, or football match of a description, for the time being designated under section 1(1) of the Football (Offences) Act 1991.

(3) A person guilty of an offence under this section is liable on summary conviction to a fine not exceeding level 5 on the standard scale.

(4) In section 24(2) of the Police and Criminal Evidence Act 1984 (arrestable offences), after the paragraph (g) inserted by section 85(2) of this Act there shall be inserted the following paragraph—

"(h) an offence under section 166 of the Criminal Justice and Public Order Act 1994 (sale of tickets by unauthorised persons);".

(5) Section 32 of the Police and Criminal Evidence Act 1984 (search of persons and premises (including vehicles) upon arrest) shall have effect, in its application in relation to an offence under this section, as if the power conferred on a constable to enter and search any vehicle extended to any vehicle which the constable has reasonable grounds for believing was being used for any purpose connected with the offence.

(6) The Secretary of State may by order made by statutory instrument apply this section, with such modifications as he thinks fit, to such sporting event or category of sporting event for which 6,000 or more tickets are issued for sale as he thinks fit.

(7) An order under subsection (6) above may provide that—

(a) a certificate (a "ticket sale certificate") signed by a duly authorised officer certifying that 6,000 or more tickets were issued for sale for a sporting event is conclusive evidence of that fact;

(b) an officer is duly authorised if he is authorised in writing to sign a ticket sale certificate by the home club or the organisers of the sporting event; and

(c) a document purporting to be a ticket sale certificate shall be received in evidence and deemed to be such a certificate unless the contrary is proved.

(8) Where an order has been made under subsection (6) above, this section also applies, with any modifications made by the order, to any part of the sporting event specified or described in the order, provided that 6,000 or more tickets are issued for sale for the day on which that part of the event takes place.

<small>DEFINITIONS</small>

"designated football match": subs. (2)(c); s.1(1) of the Football (Offences) Act 1991.

"ticket": subs. (2)(b).

"ticket sale certificate": subs. (7)(a).

"unauthorised": subs. (2)(a).

<small>GENERAL NOTE</small>

This section makes it an offence for a person (not authorised in writing to do so) to sell a ticket for a designated football match in public or by way of trade or business. Authority to sell tickets may only be given by the home club or the organisers of the match. A designated football match is, by the Football (Offences) Act 1991, s.1(1) an association football match designated, or of a description designated for the purposes of the 1991 Act by order of the Home Secretary.

The reason why this section applies only to football is one of public order and public safety. The report by Lord Justice Taylor on the Hillsborough disaster identified two problems arising particularly out of ticket touting at football matches: (1) the presence of such touts outside football grounds acted as a focus for disorder since it encouraged those without tickets to travel to the ground hoping to obtain tickets which could sometimes result in unruly behaviour; (2) ticket touts sold tickets on an indiscriminate basis with the result that supporters of one team could find themselves among supporters of another team which could lead to public disorder.

Note that, although *touting* is not specifically defined, the offence as described by subs. (1) is a sufficient definition of touting for the purposes of the section. Subsection (4) makes the offence under this section an arrestable offence. Accordingly, the police have powers to search any vehicle which a constable reasonably believes was being used in connection with the offence *e.g.* the tout's car, used by him to get to football matches: subs. (5). (For comment on "reasonable grounds", see the General Note to s.138, *ante*).

Note that under subss. (6)–(8) the Home Secretary has power to make orders extending the provisions of this section to other sporting events for which 6,000 or more tickets are issued for sale.

Taxi touts

Touting for hire car services

167.—(1) Subject to the following provisions, it is an offence, in a public place, to solicit persons to hire vehicles to carry them as passengers.

(2) Subsection (1) above does not imply that the soliciting must refer to any particular vehicle nor is the mere display of a sign on a vehicle that the vehicle is for hire soliciting within that subsection.

(3) No offence is committed under this section where soliciting persons to hire licensed taxis is permitted by a scheme under section 10 of the Transport Act 1985 (schemes for shared taxis) whether or not supplemented by provision made under section 13 of that Act (modifications of the taxi code).

(4) It is a defence for the accused to show that he was soliciting for passengers for public service vehicles on behalf of the holder of a PSV operator's licence for those vehicles whose authority he had at the time of the alleged offence.

(5) A person guilty of an offence under this section shall be liable on summary conviction to a fine not exceeding level 4 on the standard scale.

(6) In this section—

"public place" includes any highway and any other premises or place to which at the material time the public have or are permitted to have access (whether on payment or otherwise); and

"public service vehicle" and "PSV operator's licence" have the same meaning as in Part II of the Public Passenger Vehicles Act 1981.

(7) In section 24(2) of the Police and Criminal Evidence Act 1984 (arrestable offences), after the paragraph (i) inserted by section 155 of this Act there shall be inserted the following paragraph—

"(j) an offence under section 167 of the Criminal Justice and Public Order Act 1994 (touting for hire car services).".

DEFINITIONS

"public place": subs. (6).
"public service vehicle"; "PSV operator's licence": subs. (6).

GENERAL NOTE

This section makes it an offence to tout car services for hire in public. It was originally introduced in the House of Commons (*Hansard*, H.C. Vol. 241, cols. 154–157), withdrawn and reintroduced in the House of Lords (H.L. Vol. 556, cols. 153–154). It is designed to deal with people who tout for passengers from vehicles operating as unlicensed taxis. The offence is arrestable and carries with it a maximum fine of £2,500. *Touting* is not specifically defined by the section but the offence is sufficiently described in subs. (1). The section is designed to combat two forms of conduct: preying on strangers and tourists in places such as London, especially Heathrow, where excessive charges and aggressive behaviour by the drivers of unlicensed taxis have been a problem; (2) the fact that these unlicensed taxis may not be validly insured.

Public service vehicle and *PSV operator's licence* are defined by the Public Passenger Vehicles Act 1981 as follows:

"public service vehicle: a motor vehicle (other than a tramcar) which (a) being a vehicle adapted to carry more than 8 passengers, is used for carrying passengers for hire or reward; or (b) being a vehicle not so adapted, is used for carrying passengers for hire or reward at separate fares in the course of a business of carrying passengers": s.1(1).

"PSV operator's licence: a PSV operator's licence granted under the provisions of Part II of this Act": s.82(1).

General

Minor and consequential amendments and repeals

168.—(1) The enactments mentioned in Schedule 9 to this Act shall have effect with the amendments there specified (being minor amendments).

(2) The enactments mentioned in Schedule 10 to this Act shall have effect with the amendments there specified (amendments consequential on the foregoing provisions of this Act).

(3) The enactments mentioned in Schedule 11 to this Act (which include enactments which are spent) are repealed or revoked to the extent specified in the third column of that Schedule.

GENERAL NOTE
This section introduces Scheds. 9–11 making minor and consequential amendments and repeals.

Power of Secretary of State to make payments or grants in relation to crime prevention, etc.

169.—(1) The Secretary of State may, with the consent of the Treasury—
(a) make such payments, or
(b) pay such grants, to such persons,
as he considers appropriate in connection with measures intended to prevent crime or reduce the fear of crime.

(2) Any grant under subsection (1)(b) above may be made subject to such conditions as the Secretary of State may, with the agreement of the Treasury, see fit to impose.

(3) Payments under this section shall be made out of money provided by Parliament.

GENERAL NOTE
This section provides statutory authority for the Home Secretary to make payments and pay grants for crime prevention.

Security costs at party conferences

170.—(1) The Secretary of State may, with the consent of the Treasury, pay grants towards expenditure incurred by a qualifying political party, or by a person acting for a qualifying political party, on measures to which this section applies.

(2) This section applies to measures which are—
(a) taken for the protection of persons or property in connection with a conference held in Great Britain for the purposes of the party, and
(b) certified by a chief officer of police as having been appropriate.

(3) A political party is a "qualifying political party" for the purposes of this section if, at the last general election before the expenditure was incurred,—

(a) at least two members of the party were elected to the House of Commons, or

(b) one member of the party was elected to the House of Commons and not less than 150,000 votes were given to candidates who were members of the party.

(4) Payments under this section shall be made out of money provided by Parliament.

DEFINITIONS
"qualifying political party": subs. (3).

GENERAL NOTE
This section provides the Home Secretary with statutory authority for making grants for measures of security at party conferences. Before the enactment of this section, funds had been made available to the main political parties (under the Appropriation Acts) by the Home Secretary using guidelines to determine qualifying areas of expenditure, such as the certification by a chief officer of police that the expenditure was appropriate. These guidelines will continue: Standing Committee B, col. 1037, March 1, 1994.

Expenses etc. under Act

171. There shall be paid out of money provided by Parliament—

(a) any sums required by the Secretary of State for making payments under contracts entered into under or by virtue of sections 2, 3, 7, 11, 96, 99, 100, 102(4), 106(1), 112(1) or 118(3) or paragraph 1 of Schedule 1;

(b) any administrative expenses incurred by the Secretary of State; and

(c) any increase attributable to this Act in the sums payable out of money so provided under any other Act.

GENERAL NOTE
This section provides for expenses under the Act to be met out of money provided by Parliament.

Short title, commencement and extent

172.—(1) This Act may be cited as the Criminal Justice and Public Order Act 1994.

(2) With the exception of section 82 and subject to subsection (4) below, this Act shall come into force on such day as the Secretary of State or, in the case of sections 52 and 53, the Lord Chancellor may appoint by order made by statutory instrument, and different days may be appointed for different provisions or different purposes.

(3) Any order under subsection (2) above may make such transitional provisions and savings as appear to the authority making the order necessary or expedient in connection with any provision brought into force by the order.

(4) The following provisions and their related amendments, repeals and revocations shall come into force on the passing of this Act, namely sections 5 to 15 (and Schedules 1 and 2), 61, 63, 65, 68 to 71, 77 to 80, 81, 83, 90, Chapters I and IV of Part VIII, sections 142 to 148, 150, 158(1), (3) and (4), 166, 167, 171, paragraph 46 of Schedule 9 and this section.

(5) No order shall be made under subsection (6) of section 166 above unless a draft of the order has been laid before, and approved by a resolution of, each House of Parliament.

(6) For the purposes of subsection (4) above

(a) the following are the amendments related to the provisions specified in that subsection, namely, in Schedule 10, paragraphs 26, 35, 36, 59, 60 and 63(1), (3), (4) and (5);

(b) the repeals and revocations related to the provisions specified in that subsection are those specified in the Note at the end of Schedule 11.

(7) Except as regards any provisions applied under section 39 and subject to the following provisions, this Act extends to England and Wales only.

(8) Sections 47(3), 49, 61 to 67, 70, 71, 81, 82, 146(4), 157(1), 163, 169 and 170 also extend to Scotland.

(9) Section 83(1) extends to England and Wales and Northern Ireland.

(10) This section, sections 68, 69, 83(3) to (5), 88 to 92, 136 to 141, 156, 157(2), (3), (4), (5) and (9), 158, 159, 161, 162, 164, 165, 168, 171 and Chapter IV of Part VIII extend to the United Kingdom and sections 158 and 159 also extend to the Channel Islands and the Isle of Man.

(11) Sections 93, 95 and 101(8), so far as relating to the delivery of prisoners to or from premises situated in a part of the British Islands outside England and Wales, extend to that part of those Islands.

(12) Sections 102(1) to (3), 104, 105 and 117, so far as relating to the transfer of prisoners to or from premises situated in a part of the British Islands outside Scotland, extend to that part of those Islands, but otherwise Chapter II of Part VIII extends to Scotland only.

(13) Sections 47(4), 83(2), 84(5) to (7), 87, Part IX, sections 145(2), 146(2), 148, 151(2), 152(2), 153, 157(7) and 160(2) extend to Scotland only.

(14) Sections 118, 120, 121 and 125, so far as relating to the delivery of prisoners to or from premises situated in a part of the British Islands outside Northern Ireland, extend to that part of those islands, but Otherwise Chapter III of Part VIII extends to Northern Ireland only.

(15) Sections 53, 84(8) to (11), 85(4) to (6), 86(2), 145(3), 147 and 157(8) extend to Northern Ireland only.

(16) Where any enactment is amended, repealed or revoked by Schedule 9, 10 or 11 to this Act the amendment, repeal or revocation has the same extent as that enactment; except that Schedules 9 and 11 do not extend to Scotland in so far as they relate to section 17(1) of the Video Recordings Act 1984.

GENERAL NOTE
This section sets out the Act's short title, commencement and territorial extent.

SCHEDULES

Section 12   SCHEDULE 1

ESCORT ARRANGEMENTS: ENGLAND AND WALES

Arrangements for the escort of offenders detained at secure training centres

1.—(1) The Secretary of State may make arrangements for any of the following functions, namely—

(a) the delivery of offenders from one set of relevant premises to another;

(b) the custody of offenders held on the premises of any court (whether or not they would otherwise be in the custody of the court) and their production before the court;

(c) the custody of offenders temporarily held in a secure training centre in the course of delivery from one secure training centre to another; and

(d) the custody of offenders while they are outside a secure training centre for temporary purposes,

to be performed in such cases as may be determined by or under the arrangements by custody officers who are authorised to perform such functions.

(2) In sub-paragraph (1)(a) above, "relevant premises" means a court, secure training centre, police station or hospital.

(3) Arrangements made by the Secretary of State under sub-paragraph (1) above ("escort arrangements") may include entering into contracts with other persons for the provision by them of custody officers.

(4) Any person who, under a warrant or a hospital order or hospital remand is responsible for the performance of any such function as is mentioned in sub-paragraph (1) above shall be

deemed to have complied with the warrant, order or remand if he does all that he reasonably can to secure that the function is performed by a custody officer acting in pursuance of escort arrangements.

(5) In this paragraph—

"hospital" has the same meaning as in the Mental Health Act 1983;

"hospital order" means an order for a person's admission to hospital made under section 37, 38 or 44 of that Act, section 5 of the Criminal Procedure (Insanity) Act 1964 or section 6, 14 or 14A of the Criminal Appeal Act 1968;

"hospital remand" means a remand of a person to hospital under section 35 or 36 of the Mental Health Act 1983;

"warrant" means a warrant of commitment, a warrant of arrest or a warrant under section 46, 47, 48, 50 or 74 of that Act.

Monitoring etc. of escort arrangements

2.—(1) Escort arrangements shall include the appointment of—

(a) an escort monitor, that is to say, a Crown servant whose duty it shall be to keep the arrangements under review and to report on them to the Secretary of State; and

(b) a panel of lay observers whose duty it shall be to inspect the conditions in which offenders are transported or held in pursuance of the arrangements and to make recommendations to the Secretary of State.

(2) It shall also be the duty of an escort monitor to investigate and report to the Secretary of State on any allegations made against custody officers acting in pursuance of escort arrangements.

(3) Any expenses incurred by members of lay panels may be defrayed by the Secretary of State to such extent as he may with the approval of the Treasury determine.

Powers and duties of custody officers acting in pursuance of escort arrangements

3.—(1) A custody officer acting in pursuance of escort arrangements shall have the following powers, namely—

(a) to search in accordance with rules made by the Secretary of State any offender for whose delivery or custody he is responsible in pursuance of the arrangements; and

(b) to search any other person who is in or is seeking to enter any place where any such offender is or is to be held, and any article in the possession of such a person.

(2) The powers conferred by sub-paragraph (1)(b) above to search a person shall not be construed as authorising a custody officer to require a person to remove any of his clothing other than an outer coat, headgear, jacket or gloves.

(3) A custody officer shall have the following duties as respects offenders for whose delivery or custody he is responsible in pursuance of escort arrangements, namely—

(a) to prevent their escape from lawful custody;

(b) to prevent, or detect and report on, the commission or attempted commission by them of other unlawful acts;

(c) to ensure good order and discipline on their part;

(d) to attend to their wellbeing; and

(e) to give effect to any directions as to their treatment which are given by a court,

and the Secretary of State may make rules with respect to the performance by custody officers of their duty under (d) above.

(4) The powers conferred by sub-paragraph (1) above, and the powers arising by virtue of sub-paragraph (3) above, shall include power to use reasonable force where necessary.

(5) The power to make rules under this paragraph shall be exercisable by statutory instrument which shall be subject to annulment in pursuance of a resolution of either House of Parliament.

Interpretation

4. In this Schedule—

"escort arrangements" has the meaning given by paragraph 1 above; and

"offender" means an offender sentenced to secure training under section 1 of this Act.

"secure training centre" includes—

(a) a contracted out secure training centre;

(b) any other place to which an offender may have been committed or transferred under section 2 of this Act.

Section 12   SCHEDULE 2

CERTIFICATION OF CUSTODY OFFICERS: ENGLAND AND WALES

Preliminary

1. In this Schedule—
    "certificate" means a certificate under section 12(3) of this Act;
    "the relevant functions", in relation to a certificate, means the escort functions or custodial
        duties authorised by the certificate.

Issue of certificates

2.—(1) Any person may apply to the Secretary of State for the issue of a certificate in respect
of him.

(2) The Secretary of State shall not issue a certificate on any such application unless he is
satisfied that the applicant—
    (a) is a fit and proper person to perform the relevant functions; and
    (b) has received training to such standard as he may consider appropriate for the perform-
       ance of those functions.

(3) Where the Secretary of State issues a certificate, then, subject to any suspension under
paragraph 3 or revocation under paragraph 4 below, it shall continue in force until such date or
the occurrence of such event as may be specified in the certificate.

(4) A certificate authorising the performance of both escort functions and custodial duties
may specify different dates or events as respects those functions and duties respectively.

Suspension of certificate

3.—(1) This paragraph applies where at any time—
    (a) in the case of a custody officer acting in pursuance of escort arrangements, it appears to
       the escort monitor that the officer is not a fit and proper person to perform escort
       functions;
    (b) in the case of a custody officer performing custodial duties at a contracted out secure
       training centre, it appears to the person in charge of the secure training centre that the
       officer is not a fit and proper person to perform custodial duties; or
    (c) in the case of a custody officer performing contracted out functions at a directly managed
       secure training centre, it appears to the person in charge of that secure training centre that
       the officer is not a fit and proper person to perform custodial duties.

(2) The escort monitor or person in charge may—
    (a) refer the matter to the Secretary of State for a decision under paragraph 4 below; and
    (b) in such circumstances as may be prescribed by regulations made by the Secretary of State,
       suspend the officer's certificate so far as it authorises the performance of escort functions
       or, as the case may be, custodial duties pending that decision.

(3) The power to make regulations under this paragraph shall be exercisable by statutory
instrument which shall be subject to annulment in pursuance of a resolution of either House of
Parliament.

Revocation of certificate

4. Where at any time it appears to the Secretary of State that a custody officer is not a fit and
proper person to perform escort functions or custodial duties, he may revoke that officer's certificate so far as it authorises the performance of those functions or duties.

False statements

5. If any person, for the purpose of obtaining a certificate for himself or for any other person—
    (a) makes a statement which he knows to be false in a material particular; or
    (b) recklessly makes a statement which is false in a material particular,
he shall be liable on summary conviction to a fine not exceeding level 4 on the standard scale.

Section 27   SCHEDULE 3

BAIL: SUPPLEMENTARY PROVISIONS

Bail Act 1976

1. Section 5 of the Bail Act 1976 (supplementary provisions about decisions on bail) shall be
amended as follows—

(a) in subsection (1)(d), after the words "a court" there shall be inserted the words "or constable"; and

(b) after subsection (10), there shall be inserted the following subsection—

"(11) This section is subject, in its application to bail granted by a constable, to section 5A of this Act.".

2. After section 5 of the Bail Act 1976 there shall be inserted the following section—

"Supplementary provisions in cases of police bail

5A.—(1) Section 5 of this Act applies, in relation to bail granted by a custody officer under Part IV of the Police and Criminal Evidence Act 1984 in cases where the normal powers to impose conditions of bail are available to him, subject to the following modifications.

(2) For subsection (3) substitute the following—

"(3) Where a custody officer, in relation to any person,—

(a) imposes conditions in granting bail in criminal proceedings, or

(b) varies any conditions of bail or imposes conditions in respect of bail in criminal proceedings,

the custody officer shall, with a view to enabling that person to consider requesting him or another custody officer, or making an application to a magistrates' court, to vary the conditions, give reasons for imposing or varying the conditions.".

(3) For subsection (4) substitute the following—

"(4) A custody officer who is by virtue of subsection (3) above required to give reasons for his decision shall include a note of those reasons in the custody record and shall give a copy of that note to the person in relation to whom the decision was taken.".

(4) Subsections (5) and (6) shall be omitted.".

Magistrates' Courts Act 1980

3. After section 43A of the Magistrates' Courts Act 1980 there shall be inserted the following section—

"Power to grant bail where police bail has been granted

43B.—(1) Where a custody officer—

(a) grants bail to any person under Part IV of the Police and Criminal Evidence Act 1984 in criminal proceedings and imposes conditions, or

(b) varies, in relation to any person, conditions of bail in criminal proceedings under section 3(8) of the Bail Act 1976,

a magistrates' court may, on application by or on behalf of that person, grant bail or vary the conditions.

(2) On an application under subsection (1) the court, if it grants bail and imposes conditions or if it varies the conditions, may impose more onerous conditions.

(3) On determining an application under subsection (1) the court shall remand the applicant, in custody or on bail in accordance with the determination, and, where the court withholds bail or grants bail the grant of bail made by the custody officer shall lapse.

(4) In this section "bail in criminal proceedings" and "vary" have the same meanings as they have in the Bail Act 1976.".

Section 44	SCHEDULE 4

TRANSFER FOR TRIAL

PART I

PROVISIONS SUBSTITUTED FOR SECTIONS 4 TO 8 OF MAGISTRATES' COURTS ACT 1980

Transfer for trial

Transfer for trial: preliminary

4.—(1) Where—

(a) a person is charged before a magistrates' court with an offence which is triable only on indictment; or

(b) a person is charged before a magistrates' court with an offence triable either way and—

(i) the court has decided that the offence is more suitable for trial on indictment, or

(ii) the accused has not consented to be tried summarily,

the court and the prosecutor shall proceed with a view to transferring the proceedings for the offence to the Crown Court for trial.

(2) Where, under subsection (1) above or any other provision of this Part, a magistrates' court is to proceed with a view to transferring the proceedings for the offence to the Crown Court for trial, sections 5 to 8C below, or such of them as are applicable, shall apply to the proceedings against the accused, unless—

(a) the prosecutor decides to discontinue or withdraw the proceedings;

(b) the Commissioners of Customs and Excise decide, under section 152(a) of the Customs and Excise Management Act 1979, to stay or compound the proceedings;

(c) the court proceeds to try the information summarily under section 25(3) or (7) below; or

(d) a notice of transfer under section 4 of the Criminal Justice Act 1987 or section 53 of the Criminal Justice Act 1991 is served on the court.

(3) The functions of a magistrates' court under sections 5 to 8C below may be discharged by a single justice.

(4) A magistrates' court may, at any stage in the proceedings against the accused, adjourn the proceedings, and if it does so shall remand the accused.

(5) Any reference in this Part to a magistrates' court proceeding with a view to transfer for trial is a reference to the court and the prosecutor proceeding with a view to transferring the case to the Crown Court for trial and any reference to transferring for trial shall be construed accordingly.

Prosecutor's notice of prosecution case

5.—(1) Where this section applies to proceedings against an accused for an offence, the prosecutor shall, within the prescribed period or within such further period as the court may on application by the prosecutor allow, serve on the magistrates' court a notice of his case which complies with subsection (2) below.

(2) The notice of the prosecution case shall—

(a) specify the charge or charges the proceedings on which are, subject to section 6 below, to be transferred for trial;

(b) subject to subsection (5) below, include a set of the documents containing the evidence (including oral evidence) on which the charge or charges is or are based; and

(c) contain such other information (if any) as may be prescribed;

and in this Part a "notice of the prosecution case" means a notice which complies with this subsection.

(3) The accused and any co–accused shall be given an opportunity to oppose in writing within the prescribed period the grant of an extension of time under subsection (1) above.

(4) On serving the notice of the prosecution case on the magistrates' court, the prosecutor shall serve a copy of the notice on the accused, or each of the accused, unless the person to be served cannot be found.

(5) There shall be no requirement on the prosecutor to include in the notice of the prosecution case copies of any documents referred to in the notice as having already been supplied to the court or the accused, as the case may be.

(6) In this section "co-accused", in relation to the accused, means any other person charged in the same proceedings with him.

Application for dismissal

6.—(1) Where a notice of the prosecution case has been given in respect of proceedings before a magistrates' court, the accused, or any of them, may, within the prescribed period, or within such further period as the court may on application allow, make an application in writing to the court ("an application for dismissal") for the charge or, as the case may be, any of the charges to be dismissed.

(2) If an accused makes an application for dismissal he shall, as soon as reasonably practicable after he makes it, send a copy of the application to—

(a) the prosecutor; and

(b) any co-accused.

(3) The prosecutor shall be given an opportunity to oppose the application for dismissal in writing within the prescribed period.

(4) The prosecutor and any co-accused shall be given an opportunity to oppose in writing within the prescribed period the grant of an extension of time under subsection (1) above.

(5) The court shall permit an accused who has no legal representative acting for him to make oral representations to the court when it considers his application for dismissal.

(6) An accused who has a legal representative acting for him and who makes an application for the dismissal of a charge may include in his application a request that, on the

ground of the complexity or difficulty of the case, oral representations of his should be considered by the court in determining the application; and the court shall, if it is satisfied that representations ought, on that ground, to be considered, give leave for them to be made.

(7) The prosecutor shall be given an opportunity to oppose in writing within the prescribed period the giving of leave under subsection (6) above for representations to be made.

(8) If the accused makes the representations permitted under subsection (5) or (6) above, the court shall permit the prosecutor to make oral representations in response.

(9) Except for the purpose of making or hearing the representations allowed by subsection (5), (6) or (8) above, the prosecutor and the accused shall not be entitled to be present when the court considers the application for dismissal.

(10) The court, after considering the written evidence and any oral representations permitted under subsection (5), (6) or (8) above, shall, subject to subsection (11) below, dismiss a charge which is the subject of an application for dismissal if it appears to the court that there is not sufficient evidence against the accused to put him on trial by jury for the offence charged.

(11) Where the evidence discloses an offence other than that charged the court need not dismiss the charge but may amend it or substitute a different offence; and if the court does so the amended or substituted charge shall be treated as the charge the proceedings on which are to be transferred for trial.

(12) If the court permits the accused to make oral representations under subsection (6) above, but the accused does not do so, the court may disregard any document containing or indicating the evidence that he might have given.

(13) Dismissal of the charge, or any of the charges, against the accused shall have the effect of barring any further proceedings on that charge or those charges on the same evidence other than by preferring a voluntary bill of indictment.

(14) In this section "co-accused" has the same meaning as in section 5 above.

Transfer for trial

7.—(1) Where a notice of the prosecution case has been served on a magistrates' court with respect to any proceedings and—
    (a) the prescribed period for an application for dismissal has expired without any such application, or any application for an extension of that time, having been made; or
    (b) an application for dismissal has been made and dismissed, or has succeeded in relation to one or more but not all the charges,
the court shall, within the prescribed period, in the prescribed manner, transfer the proceedings for the trial of the accused on the charges or remaining charges to the Crown Court sitting at a place specified by the court.

(2) In selecting the place of trial, the court shall have regard to—
    (a) the convenience of the defence, the prosecution and the witnesses;
    (b) the expediting of the trial; and
    (c) any direction given by or on behalf of the Lord Chief Justice with the concurrence of the Lord Chancellor under section 75(1) of the Supreme Court Act 1981.

(3) On transferring any proceedings to the Crown Court the magistrates' court making the transfer shall—
    (a) give notice of the transfer and of the place of trial to the prosecutor and to the accused or each of the accused; and
    (b) send to the Crown Court sitting at the place specified by the court a copy of the notice of the prosecution case and of any documents referred to in it as having already been supplied to the magistrates' court on which it was served and (where an application for dismissal has been made) a copy of any other evidence permitted under section 6 above.

Remand

8.—(1) Where an accused has been remanded in custody, on transferring proceedings against him for trial a magistrates' court may—
    (a) order that the accused shall be safely kept in custody until delivered in due course of law; or
    (b) release the accused on bail in accordance with the Bail Act 1976, that is to say, by directing him to appear before the Crown Court for trial.

(2) Where—
    (a) a person's release on bail under subsection (1)(b) above is conditional on his providing one or more sureties; and

(b) in accordance with subsection (3) of section 8 of the Bail Act 1976, the court fixes the amount in which the surety is to be bound with a view to the surety's entering into his recognisance subsequently in accordance with subsections (4) and (5) or (6) of that section,

the court shall in the meantime make an order such as is mentioned in subsection (I)(a) above.

(3) Where the court has ordered that a person be safely kept in custody in accordance with paragraph (a) of subsection (1) above, then, if that person is in custody for no other cause, the court may, at any time before his first appearance before the Crown Court, grant him bail in accordance with the Bail Act 1976 subject to a duty to appear before the Crown Court for trial.

(4) The court may exercise the powers conferred on it by subsection (1) above in relation to the accused without his being brought before it if it is satisfied—

(a) that he has given his written consent to the powers conferred by subsection (1) above being exercised in his absence;

(b) that he had attained the age of 17 years when he gave that consent; and

(c) that he has not withdrawn that consent.

(5) Where proceedings against an accused are transferred for trial after he has been remanded on bail to appear before a magistrates' court on an appointed day, the requirement that he shall so appear shall cease on the transfer of the proceedings unless the magistrates' court transferring the proceedings states that it is to continue.

(6) Where that requirement ceases by virtue of subsection (5) above, it shall be the duty of the accused to appear before the Crown Court at the place specified by the magistrates' court on transferring the proceedings against him for trial or at any place substituted for it by a direction under section 76 of the Supreme Court Act 1981.

(7) If, in a case where the magistrates' court states that the requirement mentioned in subsection (5) above is to continue, the accused appears or is brought before the magistrates' court, the court shall have the powers conferred on a magistrates' court by subsection (1) above and, where the court exercises those powers, subsections (2) and (3) above shall apply as if the powers were exercised under subsection (1) above.

(8) This section is subject to section 4 of the Bail Act 1976, section 41 below, regulations under section 22 of the Prosecution of Offences Act 1985 and section 25 of the Criminal Justice and Public Order Act 1994.

Reporting restrictions

8A.—(1) Except as provided in this section, it shall not be lawful—

(a) to publish in Great Britain a written report of an application for dismissal to a magistrates' court under section 6 above; or

(b) to include in a relevant programme for reception in Great Britain a report of such an application,

if (in either case) the report contains any matter other than matter permitted by this section.

(2) A magistrates' court may, on an application for the purpose made with reference to proceedings on an application for dismissal, order that subsection (1) above shall not apply to reports of those proceedings.

(3) Where in the case of two or more accused one of them objects to the making of an order under subsection (2) above, the magistrates' court shall make the order if, and only if, the court is satisfied, after hearing the representations of the accused, that it is in the interests of justice to do so.

(4) An order under subsection (2) above shall not apply to reports of proceedings under subsection (3) above, but any decision of the court to make or not to make such an order may be contained in reports published or included in a relevant programme before the time authorised by subsection (5) below.

(5) It shall not be unlawful under this section to publish or include in a relevant programme a report of an application for dismissal containing any matter other than matter permitted by subsection (9) below where the application is successful.

(6) Where—

(a) two or more persons are charged in the same proceedings; and

(b) applications for dismissal are made by more than one of them,

subsection (5) above shall have effect as if for the words "the application is" there were substituted the words "all the applications are".

(7) It shall not be unlawful under this section to publish or include in a relevant pro-

gramme a report of an unsuccessful application for dismissal at the conclusion of the trial of the person charged, or of the last of the persons charged to be tried.

(8) Where, at any time during its consideration of an application for dismissal, the court proceeds to try summarily the case of one or more of the accused under section 25(3) or (7) below, while dismissing the application for dismissal of the other accused or one or more of the other accused, it shall not be unlawful under this section to publish or include in a relevant programme as part of a report of the summary trial, after the court determines to proceed as aforesaid, a report of so much of the application for dismissal containing any matter other than matter permitted by subsection (9) below as takes place before the determination.

(9) The following matters may be published or included in a relevant programme without an order under subsection (2) above before the time authorised by subsection (5) or (7) above, that is to say—

  (a) the identity of the magistrates' court and the names of the justices composing it;
  (b) the names, age, home address and occupation of the accused;
  (c) the offence, or offences, or a summary of them, with which the accused is or are charged;
  (d) the names of legal representatives engaged in the proceedings;
  (e) where the proceedings are adjourned, the date and place to which they are adjourned;
  (f) the arrangements as to bail;
  (g) whether legal aid was granted to the accused or any of the accused.

(10) The addresses that may be published or included in a relevant programme under subsection (9) are addresses—

  (a) at any relevant time; and
  (b) at the time of their publication or inclusion in a relevant programme.

(11) If a report is published or included in a relevant programme in contravention of this section, the following persons, that is to say—

  (a) in the case of a publication of a written report as part of a newspaper or periodical, any proprietor, editor or publisher of the newspaper or periodical;
  (b) in the case of a publication of a written report otherwise than as part of a newspaper or periodical, the person who publishes it;
  (c) in the case of the inclusion of a report in a relevant programme, any body corporate which is engaged in providing the service in which the programme is included and any person having functions in relation to the programme corresponding to those of the editor of a newspaper,

shall be liable on summary conviction to a fine not exceeding level 5 on the standard scale.

(12) Proceedings for an offence under this section shall not, in England and Wales, be instituted otherwise than by or with the consent of the Attorney General.

(13) Subsection (1) above shall be in addition to, and not in derogation from, the provisions of any other enactment with respect to the publication of reports of court proceedings.

(14) In this section—

  "publish", in relation to a report, means publish the report, either by itself or as part of a newspaper or periodical, for distribution to the public;
  "relevant programme" means a programme included in a programme service (within the meaning of the Broadcasting Act 1990); and
  "relevant time" means a time when events giving rise to the charges to which the proceedings relate occurred.

Avoidance of delay

8B. Where a notice of the prosecution case has been given in respect of proceedings before a magistrates' court, the court shall, in exercising any of its powers in relation to the proceedings, have regard to the desirability of avoiding prejudice to the welfare of any witness that may be occasioned by unnecessary delay in transferring the proceedings for trial.

Public notice of transfer

8C. Where a magistrates' court transfers proceedings for trial, the clerk of the court shall, within the prescribed period, cause to be displayed in a part of the court house to which the public have access a notice containing the prescribed information.

PART II

CONSEQUENTIAL AMENDMENTS

Preliminary

1. In this Part of this Schedule—
"the 1853 Act" means the Criminal Procedure Act 1853;
"the 1878 Act" means the Territorial Waters Jurisdiction Act 1878;
"the 1883 Act" means the Explosive Substances Act 1883;
"the 1933 Act" means the Administration of Justice (Miscellaneous Provisions) Act 1933;
"the 1948 Act" means the Criminal Justice Act 1948;
"the 1952 Act" means the Prison Act 1952;
"the 1955 Act" means the Army Act 1955;
"the 1957 Act" means the Naval Discipline Act 1957;
"the 1967 Act" means the Criminal Justice Act 1967;
"the 1968 Act" means the Firearms Act 1968;
"the 1969 Act" means the Children and Young Persons Act 1969;
"the 1973 Act" means the Powers of Criminal Courts Act 1973;
"the 1976 Act" means the Bail Act 1976;
"the 1978 Act" means the Interpretation Act 1978;
"the 1979 Act" means the Customs and Excise Management Act 1979;
"the 1980 Act" means the Magistrates' Courts Act 1980;
"the 1981 Act" means the Supreme Court Act 1981;
"the 1982 Act" means the Criminal Justice Act 1982;
"the 1983 Act" means the Mental Health Act 1983;
"the 1984 Act" means the County Courts Act 1984;
"the 1985 Act" means the Prosecution of Offences Act 1985;
"the 1986 Act" means the Agricultural Holdings Act 1986;
"the 1987 Act" means the Criminal Justice Act 1987;
"the 1988 Act" means the Legal Aid Act 1988;
"the 1991 Act" means the Criminal Justice Act 1991; and
"the 1992 Act" means the Sexual Offences (Amendment) Act 1992.

Criminal Procedure Act 1853 (c. 30.)

2. In section 9 of the 1853 Act (bringing up a prisoner to give evidence), for the words "under commitment for trial" there shall be substituted the words "pending his trial in the Crown Court".

Territorial Waters Jurisdiction Act 1878 (c. 73.)

3. In section 4 of the 1878 Act (procedure under that Act), for the words "committal of" there shall be substituted the words "transfer of proceedings against".

Explosive Substances Act 1883 (c. 3.)

4. In section 6(3) of the 1883 Act (inquiry by Attorney-General, and apprehension of absconding witnesses), for the words "committing for trial of" there shall be substituted the words "consideration of an application for dismissal under section 6 of the Magistrates' Courts Act 1980 made by such person for such crime or the transfer for trial of proceedings against".

Children and Young Persons Act 1933 (c. 12.)

5. In section 42 of the Children and Young Persons Act 1933 (deposition of child or young person), for subsection (2)(a) there shall be substituted the following paragraph—
"(a) if the deposition relates to an offence in respect of which proceedings have already been transferred to the Crown Court for trial, to the proper officer of the court to which the proceedings have been transferred; and".

6. In section 56(1) of the Children and Young Persons Act 1933 (powers of courts to remit young offenders to youth court)—
  (a) for the words "the offender was committed" there shall be substituted the words "proceedings against the offender were transferred"; and
  (b) for the words "he was not committed" there shall be substituted the words "proceedings against him were not transferred".

Administration of Justice (Miscellaneous Provisions) Act 1933 (c. 36.)

7.—(1) Section 2 of the 1933 Act (procedure for indictment of offenders) shall be amended as follows.
  (2) In subsection (2)—
  (a) for paragraph (a) there shall be substituted the following paragraph—
    "(a) the proceedings for the offence have been transferred to the Crown Court for trial; or";
  (b) for proviso (i) there shall be substituted the following proviso—
    "(i) where the proceedings for the offence have been transferred to the Crown Court for trial, the bill of indictment against the person charged may include, either in substitution for or in addition to counts charging the offence in respect of which proceedings have been transferred, any counts founded on the evidence contained in the documents sent to the Crown Court by the magistrates' court on transferring the proceedings, being counts which may lawfully be joined in the same indictment;";
  (c) in proviso (iA)—
    (i) for the word "material" there shall be substituted the words "the evidence contained in the documents"; and
    (ii) after the words "person charged" there shall be inserted the words "or which is referred to in those documents as having already been sent to the person charged"; and
  (d) in proviso (ii), for the words "the committal" there shall be substituted the words "charge the proceedings on which were transferred for trial".
  (3) In subsection (3), in proviso (b), for the words from "a person" to "for trial" there shall be substituted the words "proceedings against a person have been transferred for trial and that person".

Criminal Justice Act 1948 (c. 58.)

8.—(1) The 1948 Act shall be amended as follows.
  (2) In section 27(1) (remand and committal of persons aged 17 to 20), for the words "trial or sentence" there shall be substituted the words "sentence or transfers proceedings against him for trial".
  (3) In section 80(1) (interpretation of expressions used in the Act), in the definition of "Court of summary jurisdiction", for the words from "examining" to the end there shall be substituted the words "a magistrates' court proceeding with a view to transfer for trial;".

Prison Act 1952 (c. 52.)

9.—(1) Section 43 of the 1952 Act (remand centres, etc.) shall be amended as follows.
  (2) In subsection (I)(a)—
  (a) the words "trial or" shall be omitted; and
  (b) after the word "sentence" there shall be inserted the words "or are ordered to be safely kept in custody on the transfer of proceedings against them for trial".
  (3) In subsection (2)—
  (a) in paragraph (b)—
    (i) the words "trial or" shall be omitted; and
    (ii) after the word "sentence" there shall be inserted the words "or is ordered to be safely kept in custody on the transfer of proceedings against her for trial"; and
  (b) in paragraph (c)—
    (i) the words "trial or" shall be omitted; and
    (ii) after the word "sentence" there shall be inserted the words "or ordered to be safely kept in custody on the transfer of proceedings against him for trial".
  10. In section 47(5) of the 1952 Act (rules for the management of prisons, remand centres, etc.), for the words "committed in custody" there shall be substituted the words "ordered to be safely kept in custody on the transfer of proceedings against them".

Army Act 1955 (c. 18.)

11. In section 187(4) of the 1955 Act (proceedings against persons suspected of illegal absence)—

(a) for the words from "courts of" to "justices" there shall be substituted the words "magistrates' courts proceeding with a view to transfer for trial"; and
(b) for the words "so acting" there shall be substituted the words "so proceeding".

Air Force Act 1955 (c. 19.)

12. In section 187(4) of the Air Force Act 1955 (proceedings against persons suspected of illegal absence)—
(a) for the words from "courts of" to "justices" there shall be substituted the words "magistrates' courts proceeding with a view to transfer for trial"; and
(b) for the words "so acting" there shall be substituted the words "so proceeding".

Geneva Conventions Act 1957 (c. 52.)

13. In section 5 of the Geneva Conventions Act 1957 (reduction of sentence and custody of protected persons)—
(a) in subsection (1), for the word "committal" there shall be substituted the words "the transfer of the proceedings against him"; and
(b) in subsection (2)—
     (i) for the word "committal" the first time it occurs there shall be substituted the words "the transfer of the proceedings against him"; and
     (ii) for the words "remand or committal order" there shall be substituted the words "court on remanding him or transferring proceedings against him for trial".

Naval Discipline Act 1957 (c. 53.)

14. In section 109(4) of the 1957 Act (proceedings against persons suspected of illegal absence)—
(a) for the words from "1952" to "justices" there shall be substituted the words "1980, that is to say the provisions relating to the constitution and procedure of magistrates' courts proceeding with a view to transfer for trial"; and
(b) for the words "so acting" there shall be substituted the words "so proceeding".

Criminal Justice Act 1967 (c. 80.)

15.—(1) The 1967 Act shall be amended as follows.
(2) In section 9 (general admissibility of written statements), in subsection (1), for the words "committal proceedings" there shall be substituted the words "proceedings under sections 4 to 6 of the Magistrates' Courts Act 1980".
(3) In section 11 (notice of alibi), in subsection (8), in the definition of "the prescribed period", for the words from "the end" to "or" there shall be substituted the words "the transfer of the proceedings to the Crown Court for trial, or".

Criminal Appeal Act 1968 (c. 19.)

16. In section 1(3) of the Criminal Appeal Act 1968 (limitation of right of appeal in case of scheduled offence), for the word "committed" there shall be substituted the words "transferred proceedings against".

Firearms Act 1968 (c. 27.)

17. In paragraph 3(3) of Part II of Schedule 6 to the 1968 Act (trial of certain offences under that Act)—
(a) after the word "If" there shall be inserted the words ", under section 6 of the said Act of 1980,";
(b) for the words from "determines" to "for trial" there shall be substituted the words "dismisses the charge against the accused";
(c) in sub-subparagraph (a), for the words from "inquire" to "justices" there shall be substituted the words "proceed with a view to transferring for trial proceedings for the listed offence";
(d) in sub-subparagraph (b)—

(i) for the words "inquire into" there shall be substituted the words "proceed in respect of"; and

(ii) for the words from "its inquiry" to "justices" there shall be substituted the words "a view to transferring for trial proceedings for that offence".

Theft Act 1968 (c. 60.)

18. In section 28(4) of the Theft Act 1968 (orders for restitution), for the words from ", the depositions" to the end there shall be substituted the words "and, where the proceedings have been transferred to the Crown Court for trial, the documents sent to the Crown Court by the magistrates' court under section 7(3)(b) of the Magistrates' Courts Act 1980.".

Children and Young Persons Act 1969 (c. 54.)

19. In section 23(1) of the 1969 Act (remands and committals to local authority accommodation)—

(a) in paragraph (a), for the words "or commits him for trial or sentence" there shall be substituted the words ", transfers proceedings against him for trial or commits him for sentence"; and

(b) for the words "the remand or committal shall be" there shall be substituted the words "he shall be remanded or committed".

Powers of Criminal Courts Act 1973 (c. 62.)

20. In section 21(2) of the 1973 Act (restriction on imposing sentences of imprisonment, etc., on persons not legally represented)—

(a) for the words "or trial" there shall be substituted the words "or in respect of whom proceedings have been transferred to the Crown Court for trial"; and

(b) after the words "committed him" there shall be inserted the words "or which transferred proceedings against him".

21. In section 32(1)(b) of the 1973 Act (enforcement, etc., of fines imposed and recognisances forfeited by Crown Court)—

(a) the words "tried or" shall be omitted; and

(b) after the words "dealt with" there shall be inserted the words "or which transferred proceedings against him to the Crown Court for trial".

Bail Act 1976 (c. 63.)

22. In section 3 of the 1976 Act (incidents of bail in criminal proceedings)—

(a) in subsection (8) (variation and imposition of bail conditions by court), for the words from "committed" to "trial or" there shall be substituted the words "released a person on bail on transferring proceedings against him to the Crown Court for trial or has committed him on bail to the Crown Court"; and

(b) in subsection (8A), for the words "committed on bail" there shall be substituted the words "released on bail on the transfer of proceedings against him".

23. In section 5 of the 1976 Act (supplementary provisions about decisions on bail)—

(a) in subsection (6)(a)—

(i) for the word "committing" there shall be substituted the words "transferring proceedings against"; and

(ii) after the words "Crown Court" where they occur first, there shall be inserted the words "or has already done so"; and

(b) in subsection (6A)(a), for sub-paragraph (i) there shall be substituted the following sub-paragraph—

"(i) section 4(4) (adjournment when court is proceeding with a view to transfer for trial);".

24. In section 6(6)(b) of the 1976 Act (absconding by person released on bail), for the words from "commits" to "another offence" there shall be substituted the words "transfers proceedings against that person for another offence to the Crown Court for trial".

25. In section 9(3)(b) of the 1976 Act (agreeing to indemnify sureties in criminal proceedings), for the words from "commits" to "another offence" there shall be substituted the words "transfers proceedings against that person for another offence to the Crown Court for trial".

Sexual Offences (Amendment) Act 1976 (c. 82.)

26. In section 3 of the Sexual Offences (Amendment) Act 1976 (application of restrictions on evidence at trials for rape etc. to committal proceedings etc.), for subsection (1) there shall be substituted the following subsection—

"(1) Where a magistrates' court considers an application for dismissal of a charge for a rape offence, then, except with the consent of the court, evidence shall not be adduced and a question shall not be asked at the consideration of the application which, if the proceedings were a trial at which a person is charged as mentioned in subsection (1) of the preceding section and each of the accused in respect of whom the application for dismissal is made were charged at the trial with the offences to which the application relates, could not be adduced or asked without leave in pursuance of that section.".

27. In section 4(6)(c) of the Sexual Offences (Amendment) Act 1976 (anonymity of complainants in rape etc. cases), for the words "commits him for trial on" there shall be substituted the words "transfers proceedings against him for trial for".

Interpretation Act 1978 (c. 30.)

28. In Schedule 1 to the 1978 Act—
(a) in the definition of "Committed for trial", paragraph (a) shall be omitted; and
(b) after the definition of "The Tax Acts" there shall be inserted the following definition—
    " "Transfer for trial" means the transfer of proceedings against an accused to the Crown Court for trial under section 7 of the Magistrates' Courts Act 1980.".

Customs and Excise Management Act 1979 (c. 2.)

29.—(1) The 1979 Act shall be amended as follows.
(2) In section 147 (proceedings for offences under customs and excise Acts), in subsection (2), for the words from the beginning to "justices" there shall be substituted the words "Where, in England or Wales, on an application under section 6 of the Magistrates' Courts Act 1980 for dismissal of a charge under the customs and excise Acts, the court has begun to consider the evidence and any representations permitted under that section,".
(3) In section 155 (persons who may conduct proceedings under customs and excise Acts), in subsection (1), for the words "examining justices" there shall be substituted the words "magistrates' court proceeding with a view to transfer for trial".

Reserve Forces Act 1980 (c. 9.)

30. In paragraph 2(4) of Schedule 5 to the Reserve Forces Act 1980 (proceedings against persons suspected of illegal absence)—
(a) for the words "acting as examining justices" there shall be substituted the words "proceeding with a view to transfer for trial"; and
(b) for the words "so acting" there shall be substituted the words "so proceeding".

Magistrates' Courts Act 1980 (c. 43.)

31.—(1) Section 2 of the 1980 Act (jurisdiction of magistrates' courts) shall be amended as follows.
(2) In subsection (3), for the words from "as examining" to "any offence" there shall be substituted the words "to proceed with a view to transfer for trial where the offence charged was".
(3) In subsection (4), for the words "as examining justices" there shall be substituted the words "to proceed with a view to transfer for trial".
(4) In subsection (5), for the words "as examining justices" there shall be substituted the words "to proceed with a view to transfer for trial".
32. In section 19 of the 1980 Act (court to consider mode of trial of either way offence), in subsection (4), for the words from "to inquire" to the end of the subsection there shall be substituted the words "with a view to transfer for trial.".
33. In section 20 of the 1980 Act (procedure where summary trial appears more suitable), in subsection (3)(b), for the words from "to inquire" to the end there shall be substituted the words "with a view to transfer for trial.".
34. In section 21 of the 1980 Act (procedure where trial on indictment appears more suitable), for the words from "to inquire" to the end there shall be substituted the words "with a view to transfer for trial.".
35.—(1) Section 23 of the 1980 Act (procedure where court proceeds to determine mode of trial in absence of accused) shall be amended as follows.
(2) In subsection (4)(b)—
(a) for the words from "to inquire" to "justices" there shall be substituted the words "with a view to transfer for trial"; and
(b) for the word "hearing" there shall be substituted the word "proceedings".
(3) In subsection (5)—
(a) for the words from "to inquire" to "justices" there shall be substituted the words "with a view to transfer for trial"; and

(b) for the word "hearing" there shall be substituted the word "proceedings".

36.—(1) Section 24 of the 1980 Act (trial of child or young person for indictable offence) shall be amended as follows.

(2) In subsection (1)—

(a) in paragraph (b), for the word "commit" there shall be substituted the words "proceed with a view to transferring the proceedings in relation to"; and

(b) for the words from "commit the accused" to the end there shall be substituted the words "proceed with a view to transferring the proceedings against the accused for trial.".

(3) In subsection (2), for the words from "commits" to "him for trial" there shall be substituted the words "proceeds with a view to transferring for trial the proceedings in relation to a person under the age of 18 years for an offence with which he is charged jointly with a person who has attained that age, the court may also proceed with a view to transferring for trial proceedings against him".

37.—(1) Section 25 of the 1980 Act (court's power to change from summary trial to committal proceedings and vice versa) shall be amended as follows.

(2) In subsection (2)—

(a) for the words from "to inquire" to "justices" there shall be substituted the words "with a view to transfer for trial"; and

(b) for the word "hearing" there shall be substituted the word "proceedings".

(3) For subsection (3) there shall be substituted the following subsection—

"(3) Where on an application for dismissal of a charge under section 6 above the court has begun to consider the evidence and any representations permitted under that section, then, if at any time during its consideration it appears to the court, having regard to any of the evidence or representations, and to the nature of the case, that the offence is after all more suitable for summary trial, the court may—

(a) if the accused is present, after doing as provided in subsection (4) below, ask the accused whether he consents to be tried summarily and, if he so consents, may (subject to subsection (3A) below) proceed to try the information summarily; or

(b) in the absence of the accused—

(i) if the accused's consent to be tried summarily is signified by the person representing him, proceed to try the information summarily; or

(ii) if that consent is not so signified, adjourn the proceedings without remanding the accused, and if it does so, the court shall fix the time and place at which the proceedings are to be resumed and at which the accused is required to appear or be brought before the court in order for the court to proceed as provided in paragraph (a) above.".

(4) In subsection (5), in paragraph (b), for the words from "inquire" to "fall" there shall be substituted the words "consider the evidence and any representations permitted under section 6 above on an application for dismissal of a charge in a case in which, under paragraph (a) or (b) of section 24(1) above, the court is required to proceed with a view to transferring the proceedings to the Crown Court for trial,".

(5) In subsection (6)—

(a) for the words from "to inquire" to "justices" there shall be substituted the words "with a view to transfer for trial"; and

(b) for the word "hearing" there shall be substituted the word "proceedings".

(6) In subsection (7), for the words "the inquiry" there shall be substituted the words "its consideration of the evidence and any representations permitted under section 6 above.".

38. For section 26 of the 1980 Act (power to issue summons in certain circumstances) there shall be substituted the following section—

"Power to issue summons in certain circumstances

26. Where, in the circumstances mentioned in section 23(1)(a) above, the court is not satisfied that there is good cause for proceeding in the absence of the accused, the justice or any of the justices of which the court is composed may issue a summons directed to the accused requiring his presence before the court; and if the accused is not present at the time and place appointed for the proceedings under section 19(1) or 22(1) above, as the case may be, the court may issue a warrant for his arrest.".

39. In section 28 of the 1980 Act (use in summary trial of evidence given in committal proceedings)—

(a) for the words from "inquire" to "justices" there shall be substituted the words "consider the evidence under section 6 above"; and

(b) for the words from "then" to "any" there shall be substituted the words "any oral".

40. In section 29 of the 1980 Act (remission of person under 18 to youth court for trial), in subsection (2)(b)(i), for the words from "to inquire" to "discharges him" there shall be substituted the words "with a view to transfer for trial".

41. In section 42 of the 1980 Act (restriction on justices sitting after dealing with bail), in subsection (2), for the words "committal proceedings" there shall be substituted the words "proceedings before the court on an application for dismissal of a charge under section 6 above.".

42.—(1) Section 97 of the 1980 Act (summons to witness) shall be amended as follows.

(2) In subsection (1)—

(a) the words from "at an inquiry" to "be) or" shall be omitted; and

(b) for the words "such a court" there shall be substituted the words "a magistrates' court for that county, that London commission area or the City (as the case may be)".

(3) After subsection (1) there shall be inserted the following subsection—

"(1A) Where a magistrates' court is proceeding with a view to transferring proceedings against an accused for an offence to the Crown Court for trial, subsection (1) above shall apply in relation to evidence or a document or thing material to the offence subject to the following modifications—

(a) no summons shall be issued by a justice of the peace after the expiry of the period within which a notice of the prosecution case under section 5 above must be served or the service of the notice of the prosecution case, if sooner; and

(b) the summons shall require the person to whom it is directed to attend before the justice issuing it or another justice for that county, that London commission area or the City of London (as the case may be) to have his evidence taken as a deposition or to produce any document or thing.".

(4) In subsection (2)—

(a) after the words "subsection (1)" there shall be inserted the words "or (1A)"; and

(b) after the word "court" there shall be inserted the words "or justice, as the case may be,".

(5) In subsection (2A), after the words "subsection (1)" there shall be inserted the words "or (1A)".

(6) In subsections (3) and (4), after the words "a magistrates' court" or "the court" wherever they occur there shall be inserted the words "or justice, as the case may be,".

43.—(1) Section 128 of the 1980 Act (remand in custody or on bail) shall be amended as follows.

(2) In subsection (1)(b), for the words "inquiring into or" there shall be substituted the words "proceeding with a view to transferring the proceedings against that person for trial or is".

(3) In subsections (1A), (3A), (3C) and (3E), for the words "section 5" there shall be substituted the words "section 4(4)".

(4) In subsection (4)—

(a) for the words from "during an inquiry" to the words "committed by him" there shall be substituted the words "when it is proceeding with a view to transfer for trial"; and

(b) in paragraph (c)—

(i) for the word "hearing" there shall be substituted the word "proceedings"; and

(ii) for the words from "person" to "committed" there shall be substituted the words "proceedings against the person so bailed being transferred".

44. In section 129 of the 1980 Act (further remand), in subsection (4)—

(a) for the words from "commits" to "bail" there shall be substituted the words "transfers for trial proceedings against a person who has been remanded on bail"; and

(b) for the words "so committed" there shall be substituted the words "in respect of whom proceedings have been transferred".

45. In section 130 of the 1980 Act (transfer of remand hearings), in subsection (1), for the words "section 5" there shall be substituted the words "section 4(4)".

46. In section 145(1)(f) of the 1980 Act (rules: supplementary provisions), for the word "committed" there shall be substituted the words "in respect of whom proceedings have been transferred".

47.—(1) Schedule 3 to the 1980 Act (corporations) shall be amended as follows.

(2) In paragraph 1(1), for the words "commit a corporation" there shall be substituted the words ", in the case of a corporation, transfer the proceedings".

(3) In paragraph 2(a), for the words from "a statement" to "to" there shall be substituted the words "an application to dismiss".

(4) In paragraph 6, for the words "inquiry into," there shall be substituted the words "transfer for trial".

48. In paragraph 5 of Schedule 5 to the 1980 Act (transfer of remand hearings), for the words "sections 5" there shall be substituted the words "sections 4(4)".

Criminal Attempts Act 1981 (c. 47.)

49. In section 2(2)(g) of the Criminal Attempts Act 1981 (application of procedural and other provisions to attempts), the words "or committed for trial" shall be omitted.

Contempt of Court Act 1981 (c. 49.)

50. In section 4(3)(b) of the Contempt of Court Act 1981 (contemporary reports of proceedings)—
(a) for the words "committal proceedings" there shall be substituted the words "an application for dismissal under section 6 of the Magistrates' Courts Act 1980"; and
(b) for the words from "subsection (3)" to " 1980" there shall be substituted the words "subsection (5) or (7) of section 8A of that Act".

Supreme Court Act 1981 (c. 54.)

51. In section 76 of the 1981 Act (alteration of place of Crown Court trial)—
(a) in subsection (1), for the words from "varying the decision" to the end there shall be substituted the words "substituting some other place for the place specified in a notice relating to the transfer of the proceedings to the Crown Court or by varying a previous decision of the Crown Court";
(b) in subsection (3), for the words from the beginning to the words "varying the place of trial;" there shall be substituted the following words—
    "If he is dissatisfied with the place of trial—
      (a) the defendant may apply to the Crown Court for a direction, or further direction, varying the place of trial specified in a notice relating to the transfer of the proceedings to the Crown Court or fixed by the Crown Court, or
      (b) the prosecutor may apply to the Crown Court for a direction, or further direction, varying the place of trial specified in a notice given by the magistrates' court under section 7 of the Magistrates' Courts Act 1980 or fixed by the Crown Court;"; and
(c) after subsection (4) there shall be inserted the following subsection—
    "(5) In this section any reference to a notice relating to the transfer of proceedings to the Crown Court is a reference to the notice given by the magistrates' court under section 7 of the Magistrates' Courts Act 1980 or by the prosecutor under section 4 of the Criminal Justice Act 1987 or section 53 of the Criminal Justice Act 1991.".

52.—(1) Section 77 of the 1981 Act (date of Crown Court trial) shall be amended as follows.
(2) In subsection (1), for the words from "a person's committal" to "beginning of the trial" there shall be substituted the words "the transfer of proceedings for trial by the Crown Court and the beginning of the trial;".
(3) In subsection (2)—
(a) for the words preceding paragraph (a) there shall be substituted the words "The trial of a person on charges the proceedings on which have been transferred for trial to the Crown Court—"; and
(b) in paragraph (a), for the words "his consent" there shall be substituted the words "the consent of the person charged".
(4) In subsection (3), for the word "committal" there shall be substituted the word "transfer".
(5) After subsection (3) there shall be inserted the following subsections—
    "(4) Where a notice of the prosecution case has been given in respect of any proceedings, the Crown Court before which the proceedings are to be tried shall, in exercising any of its powers in relation to the proceedings, have regard to the desirability of avoiding prejudice to the welfare of any witness that may be occasioned by unnecessary delay in bringing the proceedings to trial.
    (5) In this section references to the transfer of proceedings for trial are references to a transfer by a magistrates' court under section 7 of the Magistrates' Courts Act 1980 or by the prosecutor under section 4 of the Criminal Justice Act 1987 or section 53 of the Criminal Justice Act 1991 and the date of transfer for trial is the date on which the transfer is effected under the said section 7 or, where the transfer is by the prosecutor, the date specified in his notice of transfer.".

53. In section 80(2) of the 1981 Act (process to compel appearance before Crown Court), for the words from "the person" to "committed" there shall be substituted the words "proceedings against the person charged have not been transferred".

Criminal Justice Act 1982 (c. 48.)

54. In section 1(2) of the 1982 Act (restrictions on custodial sentences for persons under 21)—
(a) the words "trial or" shall be omitted; and

(b) after the word "sentence" there shall be inserted the words "or ordered to be safely kept in custody on the transfer of proceedings against him for trial".

55. In section 3(2) of the 1982 Act (restriction on imposing custodial sentences on persons under 21 not legally represented)—
(a) for the words "or trial" there shall be substituted the words "or in respect of whom proceedings have been transferred to the Crown Court for trial"; and
(b) after the words "committed him" there shall be inserted the words "or transferred proceedings against him".

Mental Health Act 1983 (c. 20.)

56.—(1) Section 52 of the 1983 Act (provisions relating to persons remanded by magistrates' courts) shall be amended as follows.
(2) In subsection (2), for the words from "accused" to "or" there shall be substituted the words "court, on transferring proceedings against the accused to the Crown Court for trial, orders him to be safely kept in custody, or commits the accused in custody to the Crown Court".
(3) In subsection (5), after the words "expired or that" there shall be inserted the words "proceedings against the accused are transferred to the Crown Court for trial or".
(4) In subsection (6), after the word "If" there shall be inserted the words "proceedings against the accused are transferred to the Crown Court for trial or".
(5) In subsection (7)—
(a) for the words from "inquire" to "into" there shall be substituted the words "proceed with a view to transferring for trial proceedings for"; and
(b) for the words from "commit" to "1980" there shall be substituted the words "transfer proceedings against him for trial".

County Courts Act 1984 (c. 28.)

57. In section 57(1) of the 1984 Act (evidence of prisoners), for the words "under committal" there shall be substituted the words "following the transfer of proceedings against him".

Police and Criminal Evidence Act 1984 (c. 60.)

58. In section 62(10)(a) of the Police and Criminal Evidence Act 1984 (power of court to draw inferences from failure of accused to consent to provide intimate sample), for sub-paragraph (i) there shall be substituted the following sub-paragraph—
"(i) whether to grant an application for dismissal made by that person under section 6 of the Magistrates' Courts Act 1980 (application for dismissal of charge in course of proceedings with a view to transfer for trial); or".

Prosecution of Offences Act 1985 (c. 23.)

59. In section 16 of the 1985 Act (defence costs)—
(a) in subsection (1), for paragraph (b) there shall be substituted the following paragraph—
"(b) a magistrates' court determines not to transfer for trial proceedings for an indictable offence;"; and
(b) in subsection (2)(a), for the word "committed" there shall be substituted the words "in respect of which proceedings against him have been transferred".
60. In section 21(6) of the 1985 Act (interpretation, etc.), in paragraph (b), for the words from "the accused" to "but" there shall be substituted the words "proceedings against the accused are transferred to the Crown Court for trial but the accused is".
61. In section 22 of the 1985 Act (time limits for preliminary stages of criminal proceedings), in subsection (11)—
(a) in the definition of "appropriate court", in paragraph (a) for the words from "accused" to "or" there shall be substituted the words "proceedings against the accused have been transferred for trial or the accused has been"; and
(b) in the definition of "custody of the Crown Court", for paragraph (a) there shall be substituted the following paragraph—
"(a) section 8(1) of the Magistrates' Court Act 1980 (remand of accused where court is proceeding with a view to transfer for trial); or".
62. In section 23 of the 1985 Act (discontinuance of proceedings in magistrates' courts), in subsection (2)(b)(i), for the words "accused has been committed" there shall be substituted the words "proceedings against the accused have been transferred".

Agricultural Holdings Act 1986 (c. 5.)

63. In paragraph 12(1) of Schedule 11 to the 1986 Act (procedure on arbitrations under the Act) for the words "under committal" there shall be substituted the words "following the transfer of proceedings against him".

Criminal Justice Act 1987 (c. 38.)

64.—(1) The 1987 Act shall be amended as follows.

(2) In section 4(1) (notices of transfer in serious fraud cases)—

(a) in paragraph (b)(i), for the words from "person" to "trial" there shall be substituted the words "proceedings against the person charged to be transferred for trial"; and

(b) in paragraph (c), for the words from the beginning to "justices" there shall be substituted the words "not later than the time at which the authority would be required to serve a notice of the prosecution case under section 5 of the Magistrates' Courts Act 1980,".

(3) In section 5 (procedure for notices of transfer)—

(a) in subsection (9)(a), for the words "a statement of the evidence" there shall be substituted the words "copies of the documents containing the evidence (including oral evidence)"; and

(b) after subsection (9) there shall be inserted the following subsection—

"(9A) Regulations under subsection (9)(a) above may provide that there shall be no requirement for copies of any documents referred to in the documents sent with the notice of transfer as having already been supplied to accompany the copy of the notice of the transfer.".

(4) In section 6(5) (applications for dismissal), for the words from "a refusal" to the end there shall be substituted the words "the dismissal of a charge or charges against an accused under section 6 of the Magistrates' Courts Act 1980.".

Criminal Justice Act 1988 (c. 33.)

65. In section 40 of the Criminal Justice Act 1988 (power to include counts for certain summary offences in indictment), in subsection (1), for the words from "an examination" to the end, there shall be substituted the words "the documents sent with the copy of a notice of the prosecution case to the Crown Court".

66.—(1) Section 41 of the Criminal Justice Act 1988 shall be amended as follows.

(2) In subsection (1)—

(a) for the words preceding paragraph (a) there shall be substituted the words "Where a magistrates' court transfers to the Crown Court for trial proceedings against a person for an offence triable either way or a number of such offences, it may also transfer to the Crown Court for trial proceedings against a person for any summary offence with which he is charged and which—"; and

(b) for the words from "appears" to "case" there shall be substituted the words "was sent to the person charged with the notice of the transfer of the proceedings".

(3) In subsection (2)—

(a) for the words from "commits" to "indictment" there shall be substituted the words "transfers to the Crown Court for trial proceedings against a person"; and

(b) for the words "who is committed" there shall be substituted the words "in respect of whom proceedings are transferred".

(4) In subsection (4), for the words "committal of" there shall be substituted the words "transfer for trial of proceedings against".

Legal Aid Act 1988 (c. 34.)

67. In section 20 of the 1988 Act (authorities competent to grant criminal legal aid), in subsection (4), after paragraph (a) there shall be inserted the following paragraph—

"(aa) which proceeds with a view to transferring proceedings to the Crown Court for trial,".

68. In section 21 of the 1988 Act (availability of criminal legal aid)—

(a) in subsection (3)(a), for the words from "a person" to "his" there shall be substituted the words "proceedings against a person who is charged with murder are transferred to the Crown Court for trial, for that person's"; and

(b) in subsection (4), for the word "commits" there shall be substituted the words "transfers the proceedings against".

69.—(1) Schedule 3 to the 1988 Act (enforcement of contribution orders) shall be amended as follows.

(2) In paragraph 1(b)—

(a) for the words from "who" to "by a magistrates' court)" there shall be substituted the words "against whom proceedings were transferred for trial or who was committed for sentence"; and

(b) for the words "committed him" there shall be substituted the words "transferred the proceedings against him or committed him for sentence".

(3) In paragraph 9(b), for sub-subparagraph (i) there shall be substituted the following sub-subparagraph—

"(i) in the proceedings against the legally assisted person being transferred to the Crown Court for trial or in the legally assisted person being committed to the Crown Court for sentence, or".

(4) In paragraph 10(2)(b), for sub-subparagraph (i) there shall be substituted the following sub-subparagraph—

"(i) in the proceedings against the legally assisted person being transferred to the Crown Court for trial or in the legally assisted person being committed to the Crown Court for sentence, or".

Coroners Act 1988 (c. 13.)

70. In section 16 of the Coroners Act 1988 (adjournment of inquest)—

(a) in subsection (1)(b), for the words "examining justices" there shall be substituted the words "a magistrates' court which is to proceed with a view to transferring proceedings against that person for trial,"; and

(b) in subsection (8)—

(i) for the words "examining justices" there shall be substituted the words "a magistrates' court considering an application for dismissal under section 6 of the Magistrates' Courts Act 1980"; and

(ii) for the words from "person" to "committed" there shall be substituted the words "proceedings against the person charged are transferred".

71. In section 17 of the Coroners Act 1988 (supplementary provisions applying on adjournment of inquest)—

(a) in subsection (2)—

(i) after the word "Where" there shall be inserted the words "proceedings against"; and

(ii) for the words "is committed" there shall be substituted the words "are transferred"; and

(b) in subsection (3)(b), for the words "that person is committed" there shall be substituted the words "proceedings against that person are transferred".

War Crimes Act 1991 (c. 13.)

72. In the War Crimes Act 1991—

(a) in section 1(4) (introducing the Schedule providing a procedure for use instead of committal proceedings for certain war crimes), the words "England, Wales or" shall be omitted; and

(b) Part I of the Schedule (procedure for use in England and Wales instead of committal proceedings) shall be omitted.

Criminal Justice Act 1991 (c. 53.)

73.—(1) The 1991 Act shall be amended as follows.

(2) In section 53 (notices of transfer in certain cases involving children)—

(a) in subsection (1)(a), for the words from "person" to "trial" there shall be substituted the words "proceedings against the person charged to be transferred for trial"; and

(b) in subsection (2), for the words from "before" to the end, there shall be substituted the words "not later than the time at which the Director would be required to serve a notice of the prosecution case under section 5 of the Magistrates' Courts Act 1980,".

(3) In paragraph 4 of Schedule 6 (procedure for notices of transfer)—

(a) in sub-paragraph (1)(a) for the words "a statement of the evidence" there shall be substituted the words "copies of the documents containing the evidence (including oral evidence)"; and

(b) after sub-paragraph (1) there shall be inserted the following sub-paragraph—

"(1A) Regulations under sub-paragraph (1)(a) above may provide that there shall be no requirement for copies of any documents referred to in the documents sent with the notice of transfer as having already been supplied to accompany the copy of the notice of transfer.".

(4) In paragraph 5 of Schedule 6 (applications for dismissal), in sub-paragraph (7), for the words from "a refusal" to the end there shall be substituted the words "the dismissal of a charge or charges against an accused under section 6 of the Magistrates' Courts Act 1980.".

(5) In paragraph 6 of Schedule 6 (reporting restrictions), in sub-paragraph (8), for the words "sub-paragraphs (5) and (6)" there shall be substituted the words "sub-paragraphs (5) and (7)".

Sexual Offences (Amendment) Act 1992 (c. 34.)

74. In section 6(3)(c) of the 1992 Act, for the words "commits him" there shall be substituted the words "transfers proceedings against him".

Section 45   SCHEDULE 5

MAGISTRATES' COURTS: DEALING WITH CASES WHERE ACCUSED PLEADS GUILTY

Non-appearance of accused: plea of guilty

1. For section 12 of the Magistrates' Courts Act 1980 ("the 1980 Act") there shall be substituted the following section—

"Non-appearance of accused: plea of guilty
      12.—(1) This section shall apply where—
      (a) a summons has been issued requiring a person to appear before a magistrates' court, other than a youth court, to answer to an information for a summary offence, not being—
            (i) an offence for which the accused is liable to be sentenced to be imprisoned for a term exceeding 3 months; or
            (ii) an offence specified in an order made by the Secretary of State by statutory instrument; and
      (b) the clerk of the court is notified by or on behalf of the prosecutor that the documents mentioned in subsection (3) below have been served upon the accused with the summons.
      (2) The reference in subsection (1)(a) above to the issue of a summons requiring a person to appear before a magistrates' court other than a youth court includes a reference to the issue of a summons requiring a person who has attained the age of 16 at the time when it is issued to appear before a youth court.
      (3) The documents referred to in subsection (1)(b) above are—
      (a) a notice containing such statement of the effect of this section as may be prescribed;
      (b) a concise statement in the prescribed form of such facts relating to the charge as will be placed before the court by or on behalf of the prosecutor if the accused pleads guilty without appearing before the court; and
      (c) if any information relating to the accused will or may, in those circumstances, be placed before the court by or on behalf of the prosecutor, a notice containing or describing that information.
      (4) Where the clerk of the court receives a notification in writing purporting to be given by the accused or by a legal representative acting on his behalf that the accused desires to plead guilty without appearing before the court—
      (a) the clerk of the court shall inform the prosecutor of the receipt of the notification; and
      (b) the following provisions of this section shall apply.
      (5) If at the time and place appointed for the trial or adjourned trial of the information—
      (a) the accused does not appear; and
      (b) it is proved to the satisfaction of the court, on oath or in such manner as may be prescribed, that the documents mentioned in subsection (3) above have been served upon the accused with the summons,
      the court may, subject to section 11(3) and (4) above and subsections (6) to (8) below, proceed to hear and dispose of the case in the absence of the accused, whether or not the prosecutor is also absent, in like manner as if both parties had appeared and the accused had pleaded guilty.
      (6) If at any time before the hearing the clerk of the court receives an indication in writing purporting to be given by or on behalf of the accused that he wishes to withdraw the notification—

(a) the clerk of the court shall inform the prosecutor of the withdrawal; and

(b) the court shall deal with the information as if the notification had not been given.

(7) Before accepting the plea of guilty and convicting the accused under subsection (5) above, the court shall cause the following to be read out before the court by the clerk of the court, namely—

(a) the statement of facts served upon the accused with the summons;

(b) any information contained in a notice so served, and any information described in such a notice and produced by or on behalf of the prosecutor;

(c) the notification under subsection (4) above; and

(d) any submission received with the notification which the accused wishes to be brought to the attention of the court with a view to mitigation of sentence.

(8) If the court proceeds under subsection (5) above to hear and dispose of the case in the absence of the accused, the court shall not permit—

(a) any other statement with respect to any facts relating to the offence charged; or

(b) any other information relating to the accused,

to be made or placed before the court by or on behalf of the prosecutor except on a resumption of the trial after an adjournment under section 10(3) above.

(9) If the court decides not to proceed under subsection (5) above to hear and dispose of the case in the absence of the accused, it shall adjourn or further adjourn the trial for the purpose of dealing with the information as if the notification under subsection (4) above had not been given.

(10) In relation to an adjournment on the occasion of the accused's conviction in his absence under subsection (5) above or to an adjournment required by subsection (9) above, the notice required by section 10(2) above shall include notice of the reason for the adjournment.

(11) No notice shall be required by section 10(2) above in relation to an adjournment—

(a) which is for not more than 4 weeks; and

(b) the purpose of which is to enable the court to proceed under subsection (5) above at a later time.

(12) No order shall be made under subsection (I) above unless a draft of the order has been laid before and approved by resolution of each House of Parliament.

(13) Any such document as is mentioned in subsection (3) above may be served in Scotland with a summons which is so served under the Summary Jurisdiction (Process) Act 1881.".

Application of section 12 procedure where accused appears

2. After section 12 of the 1980 Act there shall be inserted the following section—

"Application of section 12 where accused appears

12A.—(1) Where the clerk of the court has received such a notification as is mentioned in subsection (4) of section 12 above but the accused nevertheless appears before the court at the time and place appointed for the trial or adjourned trial, the court may, if he consents, proceed under subsection (5) of that section as if he were absent.

(2) Where the clerk of the court has not received such a notification and the accused appears before the court at that time and place and informs the court that he desires to plead guilty, the court may, if he consents, proceed under section 12(5) above as if he were absent and the clerk had received such a notification.

(3) For the purposes of subsections (1) and (2) above, subsections (6) to (11) of section 12 above shall apply with the modifications mentioned in subsection (4) or, as the case may be, subsection (5) below.

(4) The modifications for the purposes of subsection (1) above are that—

(a) before accepting the plea of guilty and convicting the accused under subsection (5) of section 12 above, the court shall afford the accused an opportunity to make an oral submission with a view to mitigation of sentence; and

(b) where he makes such a submission, subsection (7)(d) of that section shall not apply.

(5) The modifications for the purposes of subsection (2) above are that—

(a) subsection (6) of section 12 above shall apply as if any reference to the notification under subsection (4) of that section were a reference to the consent under subsection (2) above;

(b) subsection (7)(c) and (d) of that section shall not apply; and

(c) before accepting the plea of guilty and convicting the accused under subsection (5) of that section, the court shall afford the accused an opportunity to make an oral submission with a view to mitigation of sentence.".

Consequential amendments

3.—(1) In consequence of the amendments made by paragraphs 1 and 2 above the Magistrates' Courts Act 1980 shall be further amended as follows.

(2) For section 13(4), there shall be substituted the following subsection—

"(4) This section shall not apply to an adjournment on the occasion of the accused's conviction in his absence under subsection (5) of section 12 above or to an adjournment required by subsection (9) of that section.".

(3) In section 13(5), for " 12(2)" there shall be substituted "12(5)".

(4) In section 155(2), for "12(8)" there shall be substituted "12(13)".

Section 114   SCHEDULE 6

CERTIFICATION OF PRISONER CUSTODY OFFICERS: SCOTLAND

Preliminary

1. In this Schedule—

"certificate" means a certificate under section 114 of this Act;

"the relevant functions", in relation to a certificate, means the escort functions or custodial duties authorised by the certificate.

Issue of certificates

2.—(1) The Secretary of State may, on the application of any person, issue a certificate in respect of that person.

(2) The Secretary of State shall not issue a certificate on any such application unless he is satisfied that the applicant—

(a) is a fit and proper person to perform the relevant functions; and

(b) has received training to such standard as he may consider appropriate for the performance of those functions.

(3) Where the Secretary of State issues a certificate, then, subject to any suspension under paragraph 3 or revocation under paragraph 4 below, it shall continue in force until such date or the occurrence of such event as may be specified in the certificate.

(4) A certificate authorising the performance of both escort functions and custodial duties may specify different dates or events as respects those functions and duties respectively.

Suspension of certificate

3.—(1) This paragraph applies where at any time—

(a) in the case of a prisoner custody officer acting in pursuance of prisoner escort arrangements, it appears to the prisoner escort monitor for the area concerned that the officer is not a fit and proper person to perform escort functions;

(b) in the case of a prisoner custody officer performing custodial duties at a contracted out prison, it appears to the controller of that prison that the officer is not a fit and proper person to perform custodial duties; or

(c) in the case of a prisoner custody officer performing contracted out functions at a directly managed prison, it appears to the governor of that prison that the officer is not a fit and proper person to perform custodial duties.

(2) The prisoner escort monitor, controller or governor may—

(a) refer the matter to the Secretary of State for a decision under paragraph 4 below; and

(b) in such circumstances as may be prescribed by prison rules, suspend the officer's certificate so far as it authorises the performance of escort functions or, as the case may be, custodial duties pending that decision.

Revocation of certificate

4. Where at any time (whether on a reference to him under paragraph 3(2)(a) above or otherwise) it appears to the Secretary of State that a prisoner custody officer is not a fit and proper

person to perform escort functions or custodial duties, he may revoke that officer's certificate so far as it authorises the performance of those functions or duties.

False statements

5. If any person, for the purpose of obtaining a certificate for himself or for any other person—
　(a)　makes a statement which he knows to be false in a material particular; or
　(b)　recklessly makes a statement which is false in a material particular,
he shall be guilty of an offence and liable on summary conviction to a fine not exceeding level 4 on the standard scale.

Section 122(2)　　　　　SCHEDULE 7

CERTIFICATION OF PRISONER CUSTODY OFFICERS: NORTHERN IRELAND

Preliminary

1. In this Schedule—
　"certificate" means a certificate under section 122 of this Act;
　"the relevant functions", in relation to a certificate, means the escort functions authorised
　　by the certificate.

Issue of certificates

2.—(1) Any person may apply to the Secretary of State for the issue of a certificate in respect of him.
　(2) The Secretary of State shall not issue a certificate on any such application unless he is satisfied that the applicant—
　(a)　is a fit and proper person to perform the relevant functions; and
　(b)　has received training to such standard as he may consider appropriate for the perform-
　　ance of those functions.
　(3) Where the Secretary of State issues a certificate, then, subject to any suspension under paragraph 3 or revocation under paragraph 4 below, it shall continue in force until such date or the occurrence of such event as may be specified in the certificate.

Suspension of certificate

3.—(1) This paragraph applies where at any time it appears to the prisoner escort monitor for the area concerned, that a prisoner custody officer is not a fit and proper person to perform the escort functions.
　(2) The prisoner escort monitor may—
　(a)　refer the matter to the Secretary of State for a decision under paragraph 4 below; and
　(b)　in such circumstances as may be prescribed by regulations made by the Secretary of State,
　　suspend the officer's certificate so far as it authorises the performance of escort functions.
　(3) The power to make regulations under this paragraph shall be exercisable by statutory instrument which shall be subject to annulment in pursuance of a resolution of either House of Parliament.

Revocation of certificate

4. Where at any time it appears to the Secretary of State that a prisoner custody officer is not a fit and proper person to perform escort functions, he may revoke that officer's certificate so far as it authorises the performance of those functions.

False statements

5. If any person, for the purpose of obtaining a certificate for himself or for any other person—
　(a)　makes a statement which he knows to be false in a material particular; or
　(b)　recklessly makes a statement which is false in a material particular,
he shall be liable on summary conviction to a fine not exceeding level 4 on the standard scale.

Section 157.

SCHEDULE 8

INCREASE IN PENALTIES

PART I

INCREASE OF FINES FOR CERTAIN SEA FISHERIES OFFENCES

(1) *Enactment creating offence*	(2) *Penalty enactment*	(3) *Old maximum fine*	(4) *New maximum fine*
SEA FISHERIES (SHELLFISH) ACT 1967 (c. 83).			
Offences under section 3(3) (dredging etc. for shellfish in contravention of restrictions etc. or without paying toll or royalty).	Section 3(3).	Level 2.	Level 5.
Offences under section 5(7) (obstruction of inspector or other person or refusal or failure to provide information to inspector etc.).	Section 5(7).	Level 3.	Level 5.
Offences under section 7(4) (fishing, dredging etc. in area where right of several fishery conferred or private oyster bed).	Section 7(4).	Level 3.	Level 5.
Offences under section 14(2) (contravention of order prohibiting the deposit or taking of shellfish, or importation of shellfish, or non-compliance with conditions of licences).	Section 14(2).	Level 4.	Level 5.
Offences under section 14(5) (obstruction of inspector).	Section 14(5).	Level 3.	Level 5.
Offences under section 16(1) (selling etc. of oysters between certain dates).	Section 16(1).	Level 1.	Level 4.
Offences under section 17(1) (taking and selling etc. of certain crabs).	Section 17(1).	Level 3.	Level 5.
Offences under section 17(3) (landing and selling etc. of certain lobsters).	Section 17(4).	Level 3.	Level 5.

Part II

Increase of Fines for Certain Misuse of Drugs Offences

(1) Enactment creating offence	(2) Penalty enactment	(3) Old maximum fine	(4) New maximum fine
MISUSE OF DRUGS ACT 1971 (c. 38)			
Offences under section 4(2) committed in relation to Class C drugs (production, or being concerned in the production of, a controlled drug).	Schedule 4, column 6.	£500	£2,500
Offences under section 4(3) committed in relation to Class C drugs (supplying or offering to supply a controlled drug or being concerned in the doing of either activity by another).	Schedule 4, column 6.	£500	£2,500
Offences under section 5(2) committed in relation to Class B drugs (having possession of a controlled drug).	Schedule 4, column 5.	£500	£2,500
Offences under section 5(2) committed in relation to Class C drugs (having possession of a controlled drug).	Schedule 4, column 6.	£200	£1,000
Offences under section 5(3) committed in relation to Class C drugs (having possession of a controlled drug with intent to supply it to another).	Schedule 4, column 6.	£500	£2,500
Offences under section 8 committed in relation to Class C drugs (being the occupier, or concerned in the management, of premises and permitting or suffering certain activities to take place there).	Schedule 4, column 6.	£500	£2,500
Offences under section 12(6) committed in relation to Class C drugs (contravention of direction prohibiting practitioner etc. from possessing, supplying etc. controlled drugs).	Schedule 4, column 6.	£500	£2,500
Offences under section 13(3) committed in relation to Class C drugs (contravention of direction prohibiting practitioner etc. from prescribing, supplying etc. controlled drugs).	Schedule 4, column 6.	£500	£2,500

PART III

INCREASE IN PENALTIES FOR CERTAIN FIREARMS OFFENCES

(1) *Enactment creating offence*	(2) *Penalty enactment*	(3) *Old maximum term of imprisonment*	(4) *New maximum term of imprisonment*
FIREARMS ACT 1988 (c. 27).			
Offences under section 1(1) committed in an aggravated form within the meaning of section 4(4) (possessing etc. shortened shot gun or converted firearm without firearm certificate).	Schedule 6, column 4.	5 years.	7 years.
Offences under section 1(1) in any other case (possessing etc. firearms or ammunition without firearm certificate).	Schedule 6, column 4.	3 years.	5 years.
Offences under section 2(1) (possessing etc. shot gun without shot gun certificate).	Schedule 6, column 4.	3 years.	5 years.
Offences under section 3(1) (trading in firearms without being registered as a firearms dealer).	Schedule 6, column 4.	3 years.	5 years.
Offences under section 3(2) (selling firearms to person without a certificate).	Schedule 6, column 4.	3 years.	5 years.
Offences under section 3(3) (repairing, testing etc. firearm for person without a certificate).	Schedule 6, column 4.	3 years.	5 years.
Offences under section 3(5) (falsifying certificate, etc., with view to acquisition of firearm).	Schedule 6, column 4.	3 years.	5 years.
Offences under section 4(1) (shortening a shot gun).	Schedule 6, column 4.	5 years.	7 years.
Offences under section 4(3) (conversion of firearms).	Schedule 6, column 4.	5 years.	7 years.

(1) Enactment creating offence	(2) Penalty enactment	(3) Old maximum term of imprisonment	(4) New maximum term of imprisonment
Offences under section 5(1) (possessing or distributing prohibited weapons or ammunition).	Schedule 6, column 4.	5 years.	10 years.
Offences under section 5(1A) (possessing or distributing other prohibited weapons).	Schedule 6. column 4.	(a) On summary conviction, 3 months. (b) On conviction on indictment, 2 years.	(a) On summary conviction, 6 months. (b) On conviction on indictment, 10 years.
Offences under section 19 (carrying loaded firearm other than air weapon in public place).	Schedule 6, column 4.	5 years.	7 years.
Offences under section 20(1) (trespassing with firearm other than air weapon in a building).	Schedule 6, column 4.	5 years.	7 years.
Offences under section 21(4) (contravention of provisions denying firearms to ex-prisoners and the like).	Schedule 6, column 4.	3 years.	5 years.
Offences under section 21(5) (supplying firearms to person denied them under section 21).	Schedule 6, column 4.	3 years.	5 years.
Offences under section 42 (failure to comply with instructions in firearm certificate when transferring firearm to person other than registered dealer; failure to report transaction to police).	Schedule 6, column 4.	3 years.	5 years.
FIREARMS (NORTHERN IRELAND) ORDER 1981 (SI 1981/155 (NI 2))			
Offences under Article 3(1) (possessing etc. firearms or ammunition without firearm certificate).	Schedule 2, column 4.	3 years.	5 years.
Offences under Article 4(1) (trading in firearms without being registered as a firearms dealer).	Schedule 2, column 4.	3 years.	5 years.
Offences under Article 4(2) (selling firearms to person without a certificate).	Schedule 2, column 4.	3 years.	5 years.
Offences under Article 4(3) (repairing, testing etc. firearm for person without a certificate).	Schedule 2, column 4.	3 years.	5 years.
Offences under Article 4(4) (falsifying certificate, etc., with view to acquisition of firearm).	Schedule 2, column 4.	3 years.	5 years.

(1) *Enactment creating offence*	(2) *Penalty enactment*	(3) *Old maximum term of imprisonment*	(4) *New maximum term of imprisonment*
Offences under Article 5(1) (shortening a shot gun).	Schedule 2, column 4.	5 years.	7 years.
Offences under Article 5(3) (conversion of firearms).	Schedule 2, column 4.	5 years.	7 years.
Offences under Article 6(1) (possessing or distributing prohibited weapons or ammunition).	Schedule 2, column 4.	5 years.	10 years.
Offences under Article 6(1A) (possessing or distributing other prohibited weapons).	Schedule 2, column 4.	(a) On summary conviction, 3 months. (b) On conviction on indictment, 2 years.	(a) On summary conviction, 6 months. (b) On conviction on indictment, 10 years.
Offences under Article 22(5) (contravention of provisions denying firearms to ex-prisoners and the like).	Schedule 2, column 4.	3 years.	5 years.
Offences under Article 22(7) (supplying firearms to person denied them under Article 22).	Schedule 2, column 4.	3 years.	5 years.
Offences under Article 43 (failure to comply with instructions in firearm certificate when transferring firearm to person other than registered dealer; failure to report transaction to police).	Schedule 2, column 4.	3 years.	5 years.

          SCHEDULE 9

MINOR AMENDMENTS

Poaching: increase in penalties

1.—(1) The Game Act 1831 shall be amended as follows.

(2) In section 30 (trespassing in search or pursuit of game)—

(a) for the words "level 1" there shall be substituted the words "level 3"; and

(b) for the words "level 3" there shall be substituted the words "level 4".

(3) In section 32 (searching for or pursuing game with a gun and using violence, etc.), for the words "level 4" there shall be substituted the words "level 5".

(4) The Game (Scotland) Act 1832 shall be amended as follows.

(5) In section 1 (trespassing in search or pursuit of game)—

(a) for the words "level 1" there shall be substituted the words "level 3"; and

(b) for the words "level 3" there shall be substituted the words "level 4".

(6) In section 1 (penalty for assaults on persons acting under the Act), for the words "level 1" there shall be substituted the words "level 3".

(7) The amendments made by this paragraph shall not apply to offences committed before this paragraph comes into force.

Sexual offences: procurement of women

2. In sections 2(1) and 3(1) of the Sexual Offences Act 1956 (procurement of women to have unlawful sexual intercourse by threats or false pretences), the word "unlawful" shall be omitted.

Electronic transmission of obscene material

3. In section 1(3) of the Obscene Publications Act 1959 (definition of publication for purposes of that Act), in paragraph (b), after the words "projects it" there shall be inserted the words ", or, where the matter is data stored electronically, transmits that data.".

GENERAL NOTE

The amendment to the Obscene Publications Act 1959, made by this paragraph, means that the transmission of electronic data amounts to "publication" for the purposes of the Act. The amendment arises from recommendations made by the Select Committee on Home Affairs inquiry into computer pornography.

Poaching: forfeiture of vehicles

4. After section 4 of the Game Laws (Amendment) Act 1960 there shall be inserted the following section—

"Forfeiture of vehicles

4A.—(1) Where a person is convicted of an offence under section thirty of the Game Act 1831 as one of five or more persons liable under that section and the court is satisfied that any vehicle belonging to him or in his possession or under his control at the relevant time has been used for the purpose of committing or facilitating the commission of the offence, the court may make an order for forfeiture under this subsection in respect of that vehicle.

(2) The court may make an order under subsection (1) above whether or not it also deals with the offender in respect of the offence in any other way and without regard to any restriction on forfeiture in any enactment.

(3) Facilitating the commission of the offence shall be taken for the purposes of subsection (1) above to include the taking of any steps after it has been committed for the purpose of—

(a) avoiding apprehension or detection; or

(b) removing from the land any person or property connected with the offence.

(4) An order under subsection (1) above shall operate to deprive the offender of his rights, if any, in the vehicle to which it relates, and the vehicle shall (if not already in their possession) be taken into the possession of the police.

(5) Where any vehicle has been forfeited under subsection (1) above, a magistrates' court may, on application by a claimant of the vehicle, other than the offender from whom it was forfeited under subsection (1) above, make an order for delivery of the vehicle to the applicant if it appears to the court that he is the owner of the vehicle.

(6) No application shall be made under subsection (5) above by any claimant of the vehicle after the expiration of six months from the date on which an order in respect of the vehicle was made under subsection (1) above.

(7) No such application shall succeed unless the claimant satisfies the court either that he had not consented to the offender having possession of the vehicle or that he did not know, and had no reason to suspect, that the vehicle was likely to be used for a purpose mentioned in subsection (1) above.

(8) An order under subsection (5) above shall not affect the right of any person to take, within the period of six months from the date of an order under subsection (5) above, proceedings for the recovery of the vehicle from the person in possession of it in pursuance of the order, but on the expiration of that period the right shall cease.

(9) The Secretary of State may make regulations for the disposal of vehicles, and for the application of the proceeds of sale of vehicles, forfeited under subsection (1) above where no application by a claimant of the property under subsection (5) above has been made within the period specified in subsection (6) above or no such application has succeeded.

(10) The regulations may also provide for the investment of money and the audit of accounts.

(11) The power to make regulations under subsection (9) above shall be exercisable by statutory instrument which shall be subject to annulment in pursuance of a resolution of either House of Parliament.

(12) In this section, "relevant time", in relation to a person convicted of an offence such as is mentioned in subsection (1) above, means the time when the vehicle was used for the purpose of committing or facilitating the commission of the offence, or the time of the issue of a summons in respect of the offence.".

Magistrates' courts' jurisdiction in cases involving children and young persons

5. In section 18 of the Children and Young Persons Act 1963 (jurisdiction of magistrates' courts in certain cases involving children and young persons)—
   (a) in paragraph (a), for the words "the age of seventeen" there shall be substituted the words "the age of eighteen"; and
   (b) in paragraph (b), for the words "the age of seventeen" there shall be substituted the words "the age of eighteen".

Service of documents by first class post

6.—(1) In section 9(8) of the Criminal Justice Act 1967 (which relates to the service of a written statement to be admitted as evidence in criminal proceedings—
   (a) in paragraph (c), after the word "service" there shall be inserted the words "or by first class post"; and
   (b) in paragraph (d), after the word "service" there shall be inserted the words "or by first class post".

(2) In section 11(7) of the Criminal Justice Act 1967 (which provides for the means by which a notice of alibi may be given), after the word "service" there shall be inserted the words "or by first class post".

(3) In section 1 of the Road Traffic Offenders Act 1988 (which requires warning of prosecution for certain offences to be given), after subsection (1), there shall be inserted the following subsection—

"(1A) A notice required by this section to be served on any person may be served on that person—
   (a) by delivering it to him;
   (b) by addressing it to him and leaving it at his last known address; or
   (c) by sending it by registered post, recorded delivery service or first class post addressed to him at his last known address.".

GENERAL NOTE

This paragraph extends the methods of service of documents (as provided for in the relevant enactments) to include service, not only by registered letter or recorded delivery (as presently provided for), but also by first class post (as provided for in the paragraph).

Transfers of proceedings

7. In section 11 of the Criminal Justice Act 1967 (notice of alibi), in subsection (8)—
   (a) in the definition of "the prescribed period" (as amended by paragraph 2 of Schedule 2 to the Criminal Justice Act 1987), for the words "section 4 of the Criminal Justice Act 1987" there shall be substituted the words "a relevant transfer provision"; and
   (b) after that definition there shall be inserted the following definition—
   " "relevant transfer provision" means—
   (a) section 4 of the Criminal Justice Act 1987; or
   (b) section 53 of the Criminal Justice Act 1991.".

Offences aggravated by possession of firearms

8. In Schedule 1 to the Firearms Act 1968 (which lists the offences to which section 17(2) (possession of firearms when committing or being arrested for specified offences) relates)—
(a) in paragraph 4, after the word "Theft" there shall be inserted the word "robbery"; and
(b) after paragraph 5, there shall be inserted the following paragraphs—
"5A. An offence under section 90(1) of the Criminal Justice Act 1991 (assaulting prisoner custody officer).
5B. An offence under section 13(1) of the Criminal Justice and Public Order Act 1994 (assaulting secure training centre custody officer).".

Notice of proceedings

9. In section 34(2) of the Children and Young Persons Act 1969 (which requires notice of certain proceedings to be given to a probation officer), for the words "the age of seventeen" there shall be substituted the words "the age of eighteen".

Treatment of mental condition of offenders placed on probation

10.—(1) Paragraph 5 of Schedule 1A to the Powers of Criminal Courts Act 1973 (requirement in probation order for treatment of offender's mental condition) shall be amended as follows.
(2) In sub-paragraph (2)—
(a) after the words "such part" there shall be inserted the words "or parts"; and
(b) after the words "medical practitioner" there shall be inserted the words "or a chartered psychologist (or both, for different parts)".
(3) In sub-paragraph (3)(c), after the words "medical practitioner" there shall be inserted the words "or chartered psychologist (or both)".
(4) In sub-paragraphs (6) and (8), after the words "medical practitioner" (wherever they occur) there shall be inserted the words "or chartered psychologist".
(5) In sub-paragraph (10), after the words "In this paragraph" there shall be inserted the words "—
"chartered psychologist" means a person for the time being listed in the British Psychological Society's Register of Chartered Psychologists; and".

GENERAL NOTE
The purpose of this amendment to the Powers of Criminal Courts Act 1973 is to enlarge the categories of those permitted to carry out treatment in these circumstances (previously confined to medical practitioners). The category will now include chartered psychologists (not confined to clinical psychologists, but including forensic and counselling psychologists). Such a person must be properly qualified.

Rehabilitation of offenders placed on probation

11.—(1) In section 5 of the Rehabilitation of Offenders Act 1974 (rehabilitation periods for particular sentences)—
(a) in Table A in subsection (2), in the entry relating to fines or other sentences subject to rehabilitation under that Act, after the words "subsections (3)" there shall be inserted the words ", (4A)".
(b) in subsection (4), the words "or placed on probation," and "or probation order" shall be omitted; and
(c) after subsection (4), there shall be inserted the following subsection—
"(4A) Where in respect of a conviction a person was placed on probation, the rehabilitation period applicable to the sentence shall be—
(a) in the case of a person aged eighteen years or over at the date of his conviction, five years from the date of conviction;
(b) in the case of a person aged under the age of eighteen years at the date of his conviction, two and a half years from the date of conviction or a period beginning with the date of conviction and ending when the probation order ceases or ceased to have effect, whichever is the longer.".
(2) The amendments made by this paragraph shall apply only in relation to persons placed on probation after the date on which this paragraph comes into force.

GENERAL NOTE
The effect of this amendment is to make the period of rehabilitation for those placed on probation (formerly 12 months or the length of the order, if longer) the same as the period for other community sentences or fines, *i.e.* five years.

Transfers of proceedings

12. In section 3 of the Bail Act 1976 (general provisions)—
(a) in subsection (8A) (inserted by paragraph 9 of Schedule 2 to the Criminal Justice Act 1987), for the words "section 4 of the Criminal Justice Act 1987" there shall be substituted the words "a relevant transfer provision"; and
(b) after subsection (9) there shall be inserted the following subsection—
"(10) In subsection (8A) above "relevant transfer provision" means—
(a) section 4 of the Criminal Justice Act 1987, or
(b) section 53 of the Criminal Justice Act 1991.".

Anonymity of victims of certain offences

13. In section 4 of the Sexual Offences (Amendment) Act 1976 (anonymity of victims in rape etc. cases), after subsection (6) there shall be inserted the following subsection—
"(6A) For the purposes of this section, where it is alleged or there is an accusation that an offence of incitement to rape or conspiracy to rape has been committed, the person who is alleged to have been the intended victim of the rape shall be regarded as the alleged victim of the incitement or conspiracy or, in the case of an accusation, as the complainant.".

GENERAL NOTE
This paragraph amends s.4 of the Sexual Offences (Amendment) Act 1976 in order to protect the identity of complainants in cases of incitement and conspiracy to commit rape.

Execution of warrants for non-payment

14.—(1) In section 38A(6) of the Criminal Law Act 1977 (execution of warrants for imprisonment for non-payment of fine), for the words "the age of 17 years" there shall be substituted the words "the age of 18 years".
(2) In section 38B(6) of the Criminal Law Act 1977 (execution of warrants for commitment for non-payment of due sum), for the words "the age of 17 years" there shall be substituted the words "the age of 18 years".

Committals for sentence

15. In section 38 of the Magistrates' Courts Act 1980 (power of magistrates' court to commit offender to Crown Court for sentence), in subsection (2)(b)—
(a) the words from "committed" to "21 years old" shall be omitted; and
(b) for the words "sentence of imprisonment" there shall be substituted the words "custodial sentence".

Conditional or absolute discharge: appeal to Crown Court

16. In section 108(1A) of the Magistrates' Courts Act 1980 (right of appeal to Crown Court in case of conditional or absolute discharge), for the words "Section 13" there shall be substituted the words "Section IC".

Transfers of proceedings

17. In section 76 of the Supreme Court Act 1981 (alteration by Crown Court of place of trial) (as amended by paragraph 10 of Schedule 2 to the Criminal Justice Act 1987)—
(a) in subsection (1), for the words "section 4 of the Criminal Justice Act 1987" there shall be substituted the words "a relevant transfer provision";
(b) in subsection (3), for the words "section 4 of the Criminal Justice Act 1987" there shall be substituted the words "a relevant transfer provision"; and
(c) after subsection (4) there shall be inserted the following subsection—
"(5) In this section "relevant transfer provision" means—
(a) section 4 of the Criminal Justice Act 1987, or
(b) section 53 of the Criminal Justice Act 1991.".

The amendments made by this paragraph shall cease to have effect on the coming into force of the amendments made by paragraph 51 of Schedule 4 to this Act.

Transfers of proceedings

18. In section 77 of the Supreme Court Act 1981 (date of trial) (as amended by paragraph 11 of Schedule 2 to the Criminal Justice Act 1987)—

(a) in subsection (1), for the words "section 4 of the Criminal Justice Act 1987" there shall be substituted the words "a relevant transfer provision";

(b) in subsection (2), after the words "committed by a magistrates' court" there shall be inserted the words "or in respect of whom a notice of transfer under a relevant transfer provision has been given";

(c) in subsection (3), after the words "committal for trial" there shall be inserted the words "or of a notice of transfer"; and

(d) after subsection (3), there shall be inserted the following subsection—

"(4) In this section "relevant transfer provision" means—

(a) section 4 of the Criminal Justice Act 1987, or

(b) section 53 of the Criminal Justice Act 1991.".

The amendments made by this paragraph shall cease to have effect on the coming into force of the amendments made by paragraph 52 of Schedule 4 to this Act.

Transfers of proceedings

19. In section 81 of the Supreme Court Act 1981 (bail by Crown Court)—

(a) in subsection (1)(a) (as amended by paragraph 12 of Schedule 2 to the Criminal Justice Act 1987), for the words "section 4 of the Criminal Justice Act 1987" there shall be substituted the words "a relevant transfer provision"; and

(b) after subsection (6), there shall be inserted the following subsection—

"(7) In subsection (1) above "relevant transfer provision" means—

(a) section 4 of the Criminal Justice Act 1987, or

(b) section 53 of the Criminal Justice Act 1991.".

Electronic transmission of obscene material (Scotland)

20. In section 51(8) of the Civic Government (Scotland) Act 1982, after the words "otherwise reproducing" there shall be inserted the words ", or, where the material is data stored electronically, transmitting that data".

Fines for breach of attendance centre orders or rules

21. In section 19 of the Criminal Justice Act 1982 (breach of attendance centre orders or rules), for the subsection (3A) inserted by section 67(5) of the Criminal Justice Act 1991 there shall be substituted the following subsection—

"(3A) A fine imposed under subsection (3) above shall be deemed, for the purposes of any enactment, to be a sum adjudged to be paid by a conviction.".

Video recordings

22. In section 1 of the Video Recordings Act 1984 (which provides for the interpretation of, among other terms, "video work" and "video recordings")—

(a) in subsection (2), in paragraph (a), the word "or" before the words "magnetic tape" shall be omitted and after those words there shall be inserted the words "or any other device capable of storing data electronically"; and

(b) in subsection (3), the word "or" before the words "magnetic tape" shall be omitted and after those words there shall be inserted the words "or any other device capable of storing data electronically".

GENERAL NOTE

The amendment to the Video Recordings Act 1984, made by this paragraph, means that material stored electronically on media other than magnetic tapes or disks (*e.g.* chips and cartridges) comes within the meaning of video work or recording for the purposes of the Act.

Standard period of validity of search warrants

23. In the following enactments there shall be omitted the words from "within" to "warrant" (which prescribe the period of validity of warrants under those enactments for which section 16(3) of the Police and Criminal Evidence Act 1984 prescribes a standard period of one month), namely—

(a) section 4(2) of the Protection of Children Act 1978; and
(b) section 17(1) of the Video Recordings Act 1984.

GENERAL NOTE

This paragraph extends the standard period of validity of search warrants under the relevant Acts from 14 days to one month.

Transfers of proceedings

24. In section 62(10) of the Police and Criminal Evidence Act 1984 (power of court to draw inferences from failure of accused to consent to provide intimate sample), after paragraph (a) there shall be inserted the following paragraph—
"(aa) a judge, in deciding whether to grant an application made by the accused under—
(i) section 6 of the Criminal Justice Act 1987 (application for dismissal of charge of serious fraud in respect of which notice of transfer has been given under section 4 of that Act); or
(ii) paragraph 5 of Schedule 6 to the Criminal Justice Act 1991 (application for dismissal of charge of violent or sexual offence involving child in respect of which notice of transfer has been given under section 53 of that Act); and".

Transfers of proceedings

25. In section 16 of the Prosecution of Offences Act 1985 (defence costs)—
(a) in subsection (2)(aa) (inserted by paragraph 14 of Schedule 2 to the Criminal Justice Act 1987), for the words "section 4 of the Criminal Justice Act 1987" there shall be substituted the words "a relevant transfer provision"; and
(b) after subsection (11) there shall be inserted the following subsection—
"(12) In subsection (2)(aa) "relevant transfer provision" means—
(a) section 4 of the Criminal Justice Act 1987, or
(b) section 53 of the Criminal Justice Act 1991.".

Award of costs against accused

26. In section 18(5) of the Prosecution of Offences Act 1985 (award of costs against accused), for the words "the age of seventeen" there shall be substituted the words "the age of eighteen".

Transfers of proceedings

27. In section 22 of the Prosecution of Offences Act 1985 (time limits for preliminary stages of criminal proceedings), in subsection (11), in the definition of "custody of the Crown Court", after paragraph (c) (inserted by paragraph 104 of Schedule 15 to the Criminal Justice Act 1988), there shall be inserted the following paragraph, preceded by the word ", or", namely—
"(d) paragraph 2(1)(a) of Schedule 6 to the Criminal Justice Act 1991 (custody after transfer order in certain cases involving children).".

Confiscation orders in drug trafficking cases: variation of sentences

28. In section 1A of the Drug Trafficking Offences Act 1986 (inserted by section 8 of the Criminal Justice Act 1993) (power of court to postpone determinations required before a confiscation order can be made), after subsection (9) there shall be inserted the following subsection—
"(9A) Where the court has sentenced the defendant under subsection (7) above during the specified period it may, after the end of that period, vary the sentence by imposing a fine or making any such order as is mentioned in section 1(5)(b)(ii) or (iii) of this Act so long as it does so within a period corresponding to that allowed by section 47(2) or (3) of the Supreme Court Act 1981 (time allowed for varying a sentence) but beginning with the end of the specified period.".

GENERAL NOTE

This paragraph permits a court to impose a fine or make a forfeiture order in cases where it postpones making a confiscation order.

Transfer of fraud cases

29. In section 4 of the Criminal Justice Act 1987 (transfer of certain fraud cases to Crown Court), in subsection (1)(b)(ii), for the words "seriousness and complexity" there shall be substituted the words "seriousness or complexity".

GENERAL NOTE
The Royal Commission on Criminal Justice (1993, Cm. 2263, para. 7.60) recommended that the Criminal Justice Act 1987 be amended to allow the transfer procedure under the Act to be applied to serious *or* complex cases, rather than serious *and* complex cases, as the Act originally provided. This was because under the old formulation fraud cases (suitable for transfer) had been made subject to full committal proceedings. This paragraph makes the amendment recommended by the Commission.

Fraud cases: preparatory hearings

30. In section 7 of the Criminal Justice Act 1987 (preparatory hearings for certain fraud cases), in subsection (1), for the words "seriousness and complexity" there shall be substituted the words "seriousness or complexity".

Transfers of proceedings

31. In section 25(1) of the Criminal Justice Act 1988 (principle to be followed by court in certain proceedings), in paragraph (a), after head (iii) there shall be inserted the following—
"(iv) on the hearing of an application under paragraph 5 of Schedule 6 to the Criminal Justice Act 1991 (applications for dismissal of charges in certain cases involving children transferred from magistrates' court to Crown Court); or".

Evidence through television links

32. In section 32 of the Criminal Justice Act 1988 (evidence through television links), in subsection (3B) (inserted by section 55(4) of the Criminal Justice Act 1991), for the words "subsection (3) above" there shall be substituted the words "subsection (3A) above".

Competence of children

33. In section 33A of the Criminal Justice Act 1988 (inserted by section 52(1) of the Criminal Justice Act 1991), after subsection (2) there shall be inserted the following subsection—
"(2A) A child's evidence shall be received unless it appears to the court that the child is incapable of giving intelligible testimony.".

GENERAL NOTE
This paragraph amends s.33A of the Criminal Justice Act 1988 in order to make it plain that the competency examination is abolished. This procedure required the court (before the witness gave evidence) to examine the child to ensure that he or she understood the nature of the oath. Now, the child should give evidence and only be stopped if it becomes clear that he or she cannot give an intelligible account. This was the intention of those presenting the legislation to Parliament: Standing Committee B, col. 1026, February 24, 1994. However, if the witness appears incapable of giving intelligible evidence the court has a discretion under the section to exclude his or her evidence. Section 52 of the 1991 Act, as originally drafted, provided that the power of the court to determine that a person is not competent applied to children as it applied to other persons. The purpose of this provision must have been to ensure that the witness could communicate in an intelligible and coherent manner. The amendment enacted in this paragraph makes this purpose clear.
The Advisory Group on Video Evidence recommended in its Report (1989, Home Office, London, known as the "Pigot Report" after the Group's Chairman, His Honour Judge Thomas Pigot, Q.C.) that judges should admonish child witnesses to give a full and truthful account of what occurred in terms suitable to their age and understanding. Such an admonition would ensure that the child understands the importance of the occasion and the particular duty to tell the truth in court. Since the witness will be giving evidence unsworn it is submitted that (despite the abolition of the competency examination) it will still be necessary for the judge to ensure that the child understands these matters.

Reviews of sentencing

34. In section 35 of the Criminal Justice Act 1988 (kinds of case referable for review of sentence)—

(a) in subsection (3), for the words following "case" there shall be substituted the following words—

"—

(a) of a description specified in an order under this section; or

(b) in which sentence is passed on a person—

(i) for an offence triable only on indictment; or

(ii) for an offence of a description specified in an order under this section"; and

(b) in subsection (4), after the word "case", there shall be inserted the words "of a description specified in the order or to any case".

GENERAL NOTE

This paragraph amends s.35 of the 1988 Act in order to make a wider range of cases available for review of sentence. During the Committee stage of the Bill in the House of Commons, the Minister of State at the Home Office said that the sole purpose of this amendment was to extend to cases of serious and complex fraud the power of the Attorney General to refer unduly lenient sentences to the Court of Appeal: Standing Committee B, col. 990, February 24, 1994.

Assaulting prisoner custody officer triable with indictable offence

35. In section 40(3) of the Criminal Justice Act 1988 (summary offences triable with indictable offences), after paragraph (a), there shall be inserted the following paragraphs—

"(aa) an offence under section 90(1) of the Criminal Justice Act 1991 (assaulting a prisoner custody officer);

(ab) an offence under section 13(1) of the Criminal Justice and Public Order Act 1994 (assaulting a secure training centre custody officer)".

Confiscation orders: variation of sentence

36. In section 72A of the Criminal Justice Act 1988 (inserted by section 28 of the Criminal Justice Act 1993) (power of court to postpone determinations required before a confiscation order can be made), after subsection (9) there shall be inserted the following subsection—

"(9A) Where the court has sentenced the defendant under subsection (7) above during the specified period it may, after the end of that period, vary the sentence by imposing a fine or making any such order as is mentioned in section 72(5)(b) or (c) above so long as it does so within a period corresponding to that allowed by section 47(2) or (3) of the Supreme Court Act 1981 (time allowed for varying a sentence) but beginning with the end of the specified period.".

GENERAL NOTE

This paragraph permits the court to impose a fine or make a forfeiture order in cases where it decides to postpone making a confiscation order.

Extradition from the United Kingdom

37.—(1) The Extradition Act 1989 shall be amended as follows.

(2) In section 2(4) (law of, and conduct in, parts or dependencies of foreign States)—

(a) for the words "subsections (1) to (3) above" there shall be substituted the words "this Act, except Schedule 1"; and

(b) at the end there shall be inserted the following paragraph preceded by the word "; but"—

"(d) reference shall be made to the law of the colony or dependency of a foreign state or of a designated Commonwealth country, and not (where different) to the law of the foreign state or Commonwealth country, to determine the level of punishment applicable to conduct in that colony or dependency.".

(3) In section 7 (procedure for making and implementing extradition requests)—

(a) in subsection (1)—

(i) after the word "made" there shall be inserted the words "to the Secretary of State";

(ii) for paragraph (a) there shall be substituted the following paragraph—

"(a) by—

(i) an authority in a foreign state which appears to the Secretary of State to have the function of making extradition requests in that foreign state, or

(ii) some person recognised by the Secretary of State as a diplomatic or consular representative of a foreign state; or" and

(iii) after paragraph (b), there shall be inserted the words—

"and an extradition request may be made by facsimile transmission and an authority to proceed issued without waiting to receive the original";

(b) in subsection (2)—

(i) in paragraph (c), after the word "warrant" there shall be inserted the words "or a duly authenticated copy of a warrant"; and

(ii) in paragraph (d), after the word "certificate" there shall be inserted the words "or a duly authenticated copy of a certificate"; and

(c) after subsection (6), there shall be inserted the following subsection—

"(7) Where an extradition request is made by facsimile transmission this Act (including subsection (2) above) shall have effect as if the foreign documents so sent were the originals used to make the transmission and receivable in evidence accordingly.".

GENERAL NOTE

The purpose of these amendments to the 1989 Act is to simplify extradition proceedings. Subsection (2) provides a power to extradite to the overseas territories of extradition partners. Subsection (3) simplifies the procedure for making extradition requests, allowing the Secretary of State to receive requests through non-diplomatic channels and by means of faxed documents (which will now be admissible in evidence in such proceedings) and authenticated copies of arrest warrants and certificates of conviction.

Remands and committals of young persons to secure accommodation

38. In section 21 of the Children Act 1989 (provision of accommodation for children on remand, etc.), in subsection (2)(c)(i), after the words "on remand" there shall be inserted the words "(within the meaning of the section)".

Non-intimate samples: samples of hair

39. In Article 63 of the Police and Criminal Evidence (Northern Ireland) Order 1989 (regulation of taking of non-intimate samples), at the end, there shall be inserted the following paragraph—

"(10) Where a sample of hair other than pubic hair is to be taken the sample may be taken either by cutting hairs or by plucking hairs with their roots so long as no more are plucked than the person taking the sample reasonably considers to be necessary (in point of quantity or quality) for the purpose of enabling information to be produced by means of analysis used or to be used in relation to the sample.".

GENERAL NOTE

The purpose of this paragraph is to extend to Northern Ireland powers provided for other parts of the U.K. in Part IV of the Act and ensure that RUC officers may take samples of plucked hair with roots for DNA analysis.

Pre-sentence reports

40.—(1) The Criminal Justice Act 1991 shall be amended as follows.

(2) In section 3 (requirement to obtain pre-sentence reports before passing custodial sentences)—

(a) in subsection (2), the words from the beginning to "indictment," shall be omitted;

(b) after subsection (2), there shall be inserted the following subsection—

"(2A) In the case of an offender under the age of eighteen years, save where the offence or any other offence associated with it is triable only on indictment, the court shall not form such an opinion as is mentioned in subsection (2) above or subsection (4A) below unless there exists a previous pre-sentence report obtained in respect of the offender and the court has had regard to the information contained in that report, or, if there is more than one such report, the most recent report.";

(c) in subsection (4)—

(i) the words from "which is" to "applies" shall be omitted;

(ii) for the words "comply with that subsection" there shall be substituted the words "obtain and consider a pre-sentence report before forming an opinion referred to in subsection (1) above"; and

(iii) in paragraph (a), after the word "shall" there shall be inserted the words ", subject to subsection (4A) below,"; and

(d) after subsection (4) there shall be inserted the following subsection—

"(4A) Subsection (4)(a) above does not apply if the court is of the opinion—

(a) that the court below was justified in forming an opinion that it was unnecessary to obtain a pre-sentence report, or

(b) that, although the court below was not justified in forming that opinion, in the circumstances of the case at the time it is before the court, it is unnecessary to obtain a presentence report.".

(3) In section 7 (requirement to obtain pre-sentence reports before passing certain community sentences)—

  (a) in subsection (3), at the beginning, there shall be inserted the words "Subject to subsection (3A) below,";

  (b) after subsection (3), there shall be inserted the following subsections—

    "(3A) Subsection (3) above does not apply if, in the circumstances of the case, the court is of the opinion that it is unnecessary to obtain a pre-sentence report.

    (3B) In the case of an offender under the age of eighteen years, save where the offence or any other offence associated with it is triable only on indictment, the court shall not form such an opinion as is mentioned in subsection (3A) above or subsection (5) below unless there exists a previous pre-sentence report obtained in respect of the offender and the court has had regard to the information contained in that report, or, if there is more than one such report, the most recent report.";

  (c) in subsection (4)—

      (i) for the words "comply with" there shall be substituted the words "obtain and consider a pre-sentence report before forming an opinion referred to in"; and

      (ii) in paragraph (a), after the word "shall" there shall be inserted the words ", subject to subsection (5) below,";

  (d) after subsection (4) there shall be inserted the following subsection—

    "(5) Subsection (4)(a) above does not apply if the court is of the opinion—

    (a) that the court below was justified in forming an opinion that it was unnecessary to obtain a pre-sentence report, or

    (b) that, although the court below was not justified in forming that opinion, in the circumstances of the case at the time it is before the court, it is unnecessary to obtain a pre-sentence report.".

GENERAL NOTE

  This paragraph amends ss.3 and 7 of the Criminal Justice Act 1991 in order to increase the court's discretion to sentence an offender without first obtaining a pre-sentence report. Under the 1991 Act, as originally drafted, sentence could only be passed without a report in the case of an offence triable only on indictment. The statutory obligation to obtain a report is now removed and a report has no longer to be obtained by the court before passing a custodial sentence in a summary case or a case triable either way or before passing a community sentence. The court is no longer bound to obtain a report if it is of the opinion that in all the circumstances it is not necessary to obtain a report. However, the court must obtain a report in relation to a defendant under the age of 18 unless the offence is triable only on indictment or there is a pre-existing report.

  The effect of this change will be to prevent the waste of time and resources which occurred when a court had to obtain a report although it was wholly unnecessary, *e.g.* when passing sentence upon a defendant already serving a prison sentence. In practical terms the position may well revert to what it was before the enactment of the 1991 Act, *i.e.* the court will exercise its discretion whether to obtain a report according to the particular circumstances of the case; and not according to a formula.

Curfew orders

  41. In section 12 of the Criminal Justice Act 1991 (curfew orders) after subsection (4) there shall be inserted the following subsection—

    "(4A) A court shall not make a curfew order unless the court has been notified by the Secretary of State that arrangements for monitoring the offender's whereabouts are available in the area in which the place proposed to be specified in the order is situated and the notice has not been withdrawn.".

GENERAL NOTE

  The amendment to s.12 of the 1991 Act made by this paragraph will enable trials of electronically monitored curfew orders to take place. According to the Home Office the trial areas will be in Manchester, Reading and Norfolk: the trials are to last for nine months and will take place in 1995.

Fines

  42.—(1) Sections 18 and 20 of the Criminal Justice Act 1991 (which relate respectively to the fixing of fines and financial circumstances orders) shall be amended as provided in sub-paragraphs (2) and (3) below.

  (2) In section 18—

(a) for subsection (1), there shall be substituted the following subsection—

"(1) Before fixing the amount of any fine to be imposed on an offender who is an individual, a court shall inquire into his financial circumstances."; and

(b) in subsection (3), after the word "fine" there shall be inserted the words "to be imposed on an offender (whether an individual or other person)".

(3) In section 20, in subsections (1), (1A), (1B), (1C), (2) and (3) for the words "a person" and "any person" there shall be substituted the words "an individual" and "any individual".

(4) In section 57(4) of that Act (application to local authorities of power to order fines to be paid by a parent or guardian), paragraph (b) shall be omitted.

(5) The amendments made by this paragraph apply in relation to offenders convicted (but not sentenced) before the date on which this paragraph comes into force as they apply in relation to offenders convicted after that date.

False statements as to financial circumstances

43. After section 20 of the Criminal Justice Act 1991 there shall be inserted the following section—

"False statements as to financial circumstances

20A.—(1) A person who is charged with an offence who, in furnishing a statement of his financial circumstances in response to an official request—

(a) makes a statement which he knows to be false in a material particular;

(b) recklessly furnishes a statement which is false in a material particular; or

(c) knowingly fails to disclose any material fact,

shall be liable on summary conviction to imprisonment for a term not exceeding three months or a fine not exceeding level 4 on the standard scale or both.

(2) For the purposes of this section an official request is a request which—

(a) is made by the clerk of the magistrates' court or the appropriate officer of the Crown Court, as the case may be; and

(b) is expressed to be made for informing the court, in the event of his being convicted, of his financial circumstances for the purpose of determining the amount of any fine the court may impose.

(3) Proceedings in respect of an offence under this section may, notwithstanding anything in section 127(1) of the 1980 Act (limitation of time), be commenced at any time within two years from the date of the commission of the offence or within six months from its first discovery by the prosecutor, whichever period expires the earlier.".

Effect of previous probation orders and discharges

44.—(1) Section 29 of the Criminal Justice Act 1991 (as substituted by section 66(6) of the Criminal Justice Act 1993) (effect of previous convictions and offending while on bail and treatment of certain orders as sentences and convictions) shall be amended as follows.

(2) In subsection (4), for the words "conditional discharge order" there shall be substituted the words "an order discharging the offender absolutely or conditionally".

(3) After subsection (4) there shall be inserted the following subsections—

"(5) A conditional discharge order made after 30th September 1992 (which, by virtue of section 1A of the Powers of Criminal Courts Act 1973, would otherwise not be a sentence for the purposes of this section) is to be treated as a sentence for those purposes.

(6) A conviction in respect of which an order discharging the offender absolutely or conditionally was made after 30th September 1992 (which, by virtue of section 1C of the Powers of Criminal Courts Act 1973, would otherwise not be a conviction for those purposes) is to be treated as a conviction for those purposes.".

(4) The amendments made by this paragraph shall apply in relation to offenders convicted (but not sentenced) before the date on which this paragraph comes into force as they apply in relation to offenders convicted after that date.

Sexual offences

45.—(1) In section 31(1) of the Criminal Justice Act 1991 (which defines, amongst other expressions, "sexual offence"), for that definition, there shall be substituted the following definition—

" "sexual offence" means any of the following—

(a) an offence under the Sexual Offences Act 1956, other than an offence under section 30, 31 or 33 to 36 of that Act;

(b) an offence under section 128 of the Mental Health Act 1959;

(c) an offence under the Indecency with Children Act 1960;

(d) an offence under section 9 of the Theft Act 1968 of burglary with intent to commit rape;

(e) an offence under section 54 of the Criminal Law Act 1977;

(f) an offence under the Protection of Children Act 1978;

(g) an offence under section 1 of the Criminal Law Act 1977 of conspiracy to commit any of the offences in paragraphs (a) to (f) above;

(h) an offence under section 1 of the Criminal Attempts Act 1981 of attempting to commit any of those offences;

(i) an offence of inciting another to commit any of those offences;".

(2) The amendment made by this paragraph shall apply in relation to offenders convicted (but not sentenced) before the date on which this paragraph comes into force as it applies in relation to offenders convicted after that date.

GENERAL NOTE

The definition of "sexual offence" in s.31(1) of the 1991 Act is replaced by a new section and extended by this paragraph to include, *inter alia*, attempts and conspiracy to commit sexual offences. The result is that the number of offences is widened for which the court is permitted to pass a longer sentence under s.2 of the Act to protect the public from serious harm.

Discretionary life prisoners

46.—(1) In section 34 of the Criminal Justice Act 1991 (duty to release discretionary life prisoners after they have served the relevant part of their sentence and the Parole Board has directed their release)—

(a) in subsection (6), for the words after "sentence" there shall be substituted the following words—

"—

(a) account shall be taken of any corresponding relevant period; but

(b) no account shall be taken of any time during which the prisoner was unlawfully at large within the meaning of section 49 of the Prison Act 1952 ("the 1952 Act")."; and

(b) after that subsection, there shall be inserted the following subsection—

"(6A) In subsection (6)(a) above, "corresponding relevant period" means the period corresponding to the period by which a determinate sentence of imprisonment imposed on the offender would fall to be reduced under section 67 of the Criminal Justice Act 1967 (reduction of sentences to take account of police detention or remands in custody).".

(2) In paragraph 9(2) of Schedule 12 to that Act (application of early release provisions of the Act to existing life prisoners), after paragraph (b) there shall be inserted the following paragraph, preceded by the word "and"—

"(c) in section 34 of this Act, paragraph (a) of subsection (6) and subsection (6A) were omitted.".

GENERAL NOTE

This paragraph amends s.34 of the 1991 Act to provide that time spent in police detention or on remand in custody shall be taken into account when calculating the part of the discretionary life sentence specified by the court to meet the needs of retribution and deterrence.

Committals for sentence

47. In section 40(3) of the Criminal Justice Act 1991 (power of magistrates' court to commit offender convicted of new offence during currency of previous sentence to Crown Court for sentence), in paragraph (b), for the words from "in accordance with" to the end there shall be substituted the words "; and the Crown Court to which he has been so committed may make such an order with regard to him as is mentioned in subsection (2) above.".

Extradited persons: sentence of imprisonment to reflect custody

48.—(1) In section 47 of the Criminal Justice Act 1991 (computation of sentences of imprisonment of persons extradited to United Kingdom), in subsection (4), in the definition of "extradited to the United Kingdom", after paragraph (iv), there shall be inserted the following paragraph, preceded by the word "or"—

"(v) in pursuance of arrangements with a foreign state in respect of which an Order in Council under section 2 of the Extradition Act 1870 is in force;".

(2) In each of sections 218(3) and 431(3) of the Criminal Procedure (Scotland) Act 1975 (corresponding provisions for Scotland), after paragraph (c) there shall be inserted the following paragraph—

"(cc) in pursuance of arrangements with a foreign state in respect of which an Order in Council under section 2 of the Extradition Act 1870 is in force;".

GENERAL NOTE
This paragraph will permit a court, when passing sentence, to take into account any time spent by the defendant in custody when waiting for extradition from abroad.

Transfers of proceedings

49. In section 53 of the Criminal Justice Act 1991 (notices of transfer in certain cases involving children—
   (a) in subsection (1), for the words "served" and "on" there shall be substituted the words "given" and "to";
   (b) in subsection (2), for the word "served" there shall be substituted the word "given";
   (c) in subsection (3), for the word "service" there shall be substituted the word "giving"; and
   (d) in subsection (4), for the word "serve" there shall be substituted the word "give".

Community sentences: binding over of parent or guardian

50. In section 58(2) of the Criminal Justice Act 1991 (power of court to bind over parent or guardian of young offender), at the end, there shall be inserted the following paragraph—
   "Where the court has passed on the relevant minor a community sentence (within the meaning of section 6 above) it may include in the recognisance a provision that the minor's parent or guardian ensure that the minor complies with the requirements of that sentence.".

GENERAL NOTE
   Section 58 of the 1991 Act allows a court (if it thinks it desirable in order to prevent the commission of further offences by a child) to bind over a parent in a sum of up to £1,000 to take proper care of, and exercise proper control over, the child. The amendment to the section, made by this paragraph, will give the court power to add a further requirement to such a recognisance, *i.e.* to ensure that the child complies with any community sentence passed on the child. The purpose is to involve the parent (in appropriate cases) in the child keeping appointments and attending when instructed to do so.

Confiscation orders in terrorist–related activities cases: variation of sentences

51.—(1) In section 48 of the Northern Ireland (Emergency Provisions) Act 1991 (postponed confiscation orders etc.), after subsection (3B) there shall be inserted the following subsection—
   "(3C) Where the court has sentenced the defendant under subsection (2) or (3) above during the specified period it may, after the end of that period, vary the sentence by imposing a fine or making any such order as is mentioned in subsection (5)(b) or (c) below so long as it does so within a period corresponding to that allowed by section 49(2) or (3) of the Judicature (Northern Ireland) Act 1978 (time allowed for varying a sentence) but beginning with the end of the specified period.".
   (2) For the purposes of section 69 of the Northern Ireland (Emergency Provisions) Act 1991 (temporary provisions) the amendment made in that Act by this paragraph shall be treated, as from the time when this paragraph comes into force, as having been continued in force by the order made under subsection (3) of that section which has effect at that time.

Anonymity of victims of certain offences

52.—(1) The Sexual Offences (Amendment) Act 1992 shall be amended as follows.
   (2) In section 2(1) (offences to which the Act applies), after paragraph (e) there shall be inserted the following paragraphs—
   "(f) any conspiracy to commit any of those offences;
   (g) any incitement of another to commit any of those offences.".
   (3) In section 6 (interpretation)—
   (a) after subsection (2) there shall be inserted the following subsection—
   "(2A) For the purposes of this Act, where it is alleged or there is an accusation that an offence of conspiracy or incitement of another to commit an offence mentioned in section 2(1)(a) to (d) has been committed, the person against whom the substantive offence is alleged to have been intended to be committed shall be regarded as the person against whom the conspiracy or incitement is alleged to have been committed.
   In this subsection, "the substantive offence" means the offence to which the alleged conspiracy or incitement related."; and

(b) in subsection (3), after the words "references in" there shall be inserted the words "subsection (2A) and in".

GENERAL NOTE
This paragraph amends the Sexual Offences (Amendment) Act 1992 in order to protect the identity of complainants in cases of incitement and conspiracy to commit the sexual offences which are the subject of the Act.

Application of 1993 Act powers to pre-commencement offences

53. Section 78(6) of the Criminal Justice Act 1993 (application of Act to pre-commencement offences) shall have effect, and be deemed always to have had effect, with the substitution, for the words from "or the powers" to the end, of the words "and, where it confers a power on the court, shall not apply in proceedings instituted before the coming into force of that provision.".

GENERAL NOTE
The purpose of this paragraph is to amend s.78(6) of the 1993 Act to enable the confiscation provisions under the Act to apply only to proceedings commenced after the new provisions come into force.

Section 168(2)   SCHEDULE 10

CONSEQUENTIAL AMENDMENTS

Bail: exclusion in homicide and rape cases

1. In section 2 of the Habeas Corpus Act 1679 (bail for persons released from custody under habeas corpus while awaiting trial), after the words "brought as aforesaid shall" there shall be inserted the words ", subject to section 25 of the Criminal Justice and Public Order Act 1994,".

Evidence of accused in criminal proceedings

2. In section 1 of the Criminal Evidence Act 1898 (competency of accused to give evidence in criminal proceedings), proviso (b) shall be omitted.

Evidence of accused in criminal proceedings

3. In section 1 of the Criminal Evidence Act (Northern Ireland) 1923 (competency of accused to give evidence in criminal proceedings)—
   (a) after the words "Provided as follows:—" there shall be inserted the following proviso—
   "(a) A person so charged shall not be called as a witness in pursuance of this Act except upon his own application;";
   (b) proviso (b) shall be omitted.

Responsibility for fine for breach of requirements of secure training order

4. In section 55(1A) of the Children and Young Persons Act 1933 (power of court to order parent or guardian to pay fine imposed on child or young person), after paragraph (b) there shall be inserted the following paragraph—
   "(c) a court would impose a fine on a child or young person under section 4(3) of the Criminal Justice and Public Order Act 1994 (breach of requirements of supervision under secure training order),".

Bail: exclusion in homicide and rape cases

5. In section 56(3) of the Children and Young Persons Act 1933 (powers of courts remitting young offenders to youth court), after the word "may" there shall be inserted the words ", subject to section 25 of the Criminal Justice and Public Order Act 1994,".

Bail: exclusion in homicide or rape cases

6. In section 37(1) of the Criminal Justice Act 1948 (power of High Court to grant bail on case stated or application for certiorari)—
   (a) in paragraph (b), after the word "may" there shall be inserted the words ", subject to section 25 of the Criminal Justice and Public Order Act 1994,"; and
   (b) in paragraph (d), after the word "may" there shall be inserted the words ", subject to section 25 of the Criminal Justice and Public Order Act 1994,".

Modernisation of "servant" in Prison Act

7. In section 3(1) of the Prison Act 1952 (officers and servants at prisons), for the word "servants" there shall be substituted the words "employ such other persons".

Use of young offender institutions as secure training centres

8. In section 37(4) of the Prison Act 1952 (prisons not deemed closed where used as remand centres etc.), at the end, there shall be inserted the words "or secure training centre".

Young offenders absconding from secure training centres

9.—(1) Section 49 of the Prison Act 1952 (persons unlawfully at large) shall be amended as follows.

(2) In subsection (1), after the words "young offenders institution" there shall be inserted the words "or a secure training centre".

(3) In subsection (2), for the words between "detained in a" and "is unlawfully" there shall be substituted the words "young offenders institution or in a secure training centre".

(4) In subsection (2), in proviso (a), for the words after "prison" there shall be substituted the words "remand centre, young offenders institution or secure training centre".

Bail: exclusion in homicide and rape cases

10. In section 4(2) of the Administration of Justice Act 1960 (power of High Court to grant bail to persons appealing to the House of Lords), after the words "Divisional Court shall" there shall be inserted the words ", subject to section 25 of the Criminal Justice and Public Order Act 1994,".

Young offenders: application of prison rules

11. In section 23(4) of the Criminal Justice Act 1961 (which applies provisions relating to prison rules to other institutions), before the words "and remand centres" there shall be inserted the words "secure training centres".

Young offenders: transfer, supervision and recall within British Islands

12.—(1) Part III of the Criminal Justice Act 1961 (transfer, supervision and recall within British Islands) shall have effect with the following amendments.

(2) In section 29—

(a) in subsection (1), for the words from "youth custody centre" to "young offenders institution" there shall be substituted the words "or institution for young offenders to which this subsection applies";

(b) after subsection (2), there shall be inserted the following subsection—

"(2A) The institutions for young offenders to which subsection (1) above applies are the following: a remand centre, young offenders institution or secure training centre and, in Northern Ireland, a young offenders centre.".

(3) In section 30—

(a) in subsection (3), for the words between "prison" and "in any part" there shall be substituted the words "or institution for young offenders to which this subsection applies";

(b) after subsection (3), there shall be inserted the following subsection—

"(3A) The institutions for young offenders to which subsection (3) above applies are the following: a young offenders institution or secure training centre and, in Northern Ireland, a young offenders centre.".

(4) In section 32, in subsection (2), after paragraph (k), there shall be inserted the following paragraph—

"(l) sections 1 and 3 of the Criminal Justice and Public Order Act 1994.".

(5) In section 38(3), for paragraph (a), there shall be substituted the following paragraph—

"(a) the expression "imprisonment or detention" means imprisonment, custody for life, detention in a young offenders institution or in a secure training centre or detention under an equivalent sentence passed by a court in the Channel Islands or the Isle of Man;".

Payment of damages by police authority

13. In section 48(4) of the Police Act 1964 (payment by police authority of damages awarded against constables), after the words "section 14 of this Act" there shall be inserted the words "or section 141 of the Criminal Justice and Public Order Act 1994".

Cross-border enforcement: extension of protection

14. In section 51 of the Police Act 1964 (assaults on, and obstruction of, constables), after subsection (3), there shall be inserted the following subsection—

"(4) This section also applies to a constable who is a member of a police force maintained in Scotland or Northern Ireland when he is executing a warrant or otherwise acting in England or Wales by virtue of any enactment conferring powers on him in England and Wales.".

Bail: exclusion in homicide and rape cases

15. In section 22(1) of the Criminal Justice Act 1967 (power of High Court to grant bail), after the word "may", there shall be inserted the words ", subject to section 25 of the Criminal Justice and Public Order Act 1994,".

Young offenders: detention under secure training order

16. Section 67 of the Criminal Justice Act 1967 (computation of sentences of imprisonment or detention passed in England and Wales) shall be amended by the insertion in subsection (5), after paragraph (b), of the following paragraph—

"(c) to secure training orders under section 1 of the Criminal Justice and Public Order Act 1994;".

Payment of damages by Scottish police authority

17. In section 39(4) of the Police (Scotland) Act 1967 (payment by police authority of damages awarded against constables), after the words "section 11 of this Act" there shall be inserted the words "or section 141 of the Criminal Justice and Public Order Act 1994".

Assaults on constables etc.

18. In section 41 of the Police (Scotland) Act 1967 (assaults on constables etc.), after subsection (2), there shall be inserted the following subsection—

"(3) This section also applies to a constable who is a member of a police force maintained in England and Wales or in Northern Ireland when he is executing a warrant or otherwise acting in Scotland by virtue of any enactment conferring powers on him in Scotland.".

Bail: exclusion in homicide and rape cases

19. In section 8(2)(a) of the Criminal Appeal Act 1968 (powers of Court of Appeal on retrial), after the words "custody or" there shall be inserted the words ", subject to section 25 of the Criminal Justice and Public Order Act 1994,".

Bail: exclusion in homicide and rape cases

20. In section 11(5) of the Criminal Appeal Act 1968 (powers of Court of Appeal on quashing interim hospital order), after the word "may" there shall be inserted the words ", subject to section 25 of the Criminal Justice and Public Order Act 1994,".

Bail: exclusion in homicide and rape cases

21. In section 16(3)(b) of the Criminal Appeal Act 1968 (powers of Court of Appeal on allowing an appeal against a finding that a person is under a disability), after the word "may" there shall be inserted the words ", subject to section 25 of the Criminal Justice and Public Order Act 1994,".

Bail: exclusion in homicide and rape cases

22. In section 19(1) of the Criminal Appeal Act 1968 (power of Court of Appeal to grant bail), after the word "may", there shall be inserted the words ", subject to section 25 of the Criminal Justice and Public Order Act 1994,".

Bail: exclusion in homicide and rape cases

23. In section 36 of the Criminal Appeal Act 1968 (power of Court of Appeal to grant bail on appeal by defendant), after the word "may" there shall be inserted the words ", subject to section 25 of the Criminal Justice and Public Order Act 1994".

Young offenders: possession of firearms

24.—(1) The Firearms Act 1968 shall be amended as follows.

(2) In section 21 (possession of firearms by persons previously convicted of crime)—

(a) in subsection (2), after the word "Scotland" there shall be inserted the words "or who has been subject to a secure training order"; and

(b) for subsection (2A) there shall be substituted—

"(2A) For the purposes of subsection (2) above, "the date of his release" means—

(a) in the case of a person sentenced to imprisonment with an order under section 47(1) of the Criminal Law Act 1977 (prison sentence partly served and partly suspended), the date on which he completes service of so much of the sentence as was by that order required to be served in prison;

(b) in the case of a person who has been subject to a secure training order—

(i) the date on which he is released from detention under the order;

(ii) the date on which he is released from detention ordered under section 4 of the Criminal Justice and Public Order Act 1994; or

(iii) the date halfway through the total period specified by the court in making the order,

whichever is the later.".

(3) In section 52(1) (forfeiture and disposal of firearms), in paragraph (a), after the word "Scotland" there shall be inserted the words "or is subject to a secure training order".

Cross-border enforcement: extension of protection

25. In section 7 of the Criminal Justice (Miscellaneous Provisions) Act (Northern Ireland) 1968 (assaults on, and obstruction of, constables), after subsection (3), there shall be inserted the following subsection—

"(4) This section also applies to a constable who is a member of a police force maintained in England and Wales or Scotland when he is executing a warrant or otherwise acting in Northern Ireland by virtue of any statutory provision conferring powers on him in Northern Ireland.".

Sexual offences: male rape

26. In section 9(2) of the Theft Act 1968 (offences which if intended by a trespasser constitute burglary), for the words "raping any woman" there shall be substituted the words "raping any person".

Payment of damages by Police Authority for Northern Ireland

27. In section 14(5) of the Police Act (Northern Ireland) 1970 (payment by Police Authority of damages awarded against persons serving with the Royal Ulster Constabulary), for the words "section 19" there shall be substituted the words "section 141 of the Criminal Justice and Public Order Act 1994".

Jury service: penalty for serving when not qualified

28. In section 20(5) of the Juries Act 1974 (offences in connection with jury service), at the end of paragraph (d) there shall be inserted "; or

(e) knowing that he is not qualified for jury service by reason of section 40 of the Criminal Justice and Public Order Act 1994, serves on a jury,".

Custody officers: ineligibility for jury service

29. In Part I of Schedule 1 to the Juries Act 1974, in Group B (ineligibility for jury service of certain persons concerned with the administration of justice), after the entry for prisoner custody officers within the meaning of Part IV of the Criminal Justice Act 1991, there shall be inserted the following entry—

"Custody officers within the meaning of Part I of the Criminal Justice and Public Order Act 1994".

Rehabilitation of offenders subject to secure training orders

30. In section 5(6) of the Rehabilitation of Offenders Act 1974 (rehabilitation periods for particular sentences), after paragraph (c), there shall be inserted the following paragraph, preceded by the word "or"—

"(d) a secure training order under section 1 of the Criminal Justice and Public Order Act 1994;".

Prisoner custody officers: ineligibility for jury service

31. In Schedule 2 to the Juries (Northern Ireland) Order 1974 (exemptions from jury service) in the group headed "Persons connected with the administration of justice", at the end there shall be inserted—

> "Prisoner custody officers within the meaning of section 122(1) of the Criminal Justice and Public Order Act 1994.".

Bail: exclusion in homicide and rape cases

32. In section 4 of the Bail Act 1976 (entitlement to bail), after subsection (7), there shall be inserted the following subsection—

> "(8) This section is subject to section 25 of the Criminal Justice and Public Order Act 1994 (exclusion of bail in cases of homicide and rape).".

Police bail: variation by magistrates

33. In section 4(2) of the Bail Act 1976 (occasions for implementation of right to bail), in paragraph (b), after the words "for bail" there shall be inserted the words "or for a variation of the conditions of bail".

Bail: no right for persons offending while on bail

34. In Part III of Schedule 1 to the Bail Act 1976, in paragraph 2, at the end, there shall be inserted the words "; and so as respects the reference to an offence committed by a person on bail in relation to any period before the coming into force of paragraph 2A of Part 1 of this Schedule.".

Sexual offences: male rape

35.—(1) The Sexual Offences (Amendment) Act 1976 shall be amended as follows.

(2) In section 1(2) (reasonable grounds for belief in consent to intercourse), after the word "woman" there shall be inserted the words "or man".

(3) In section 2(3) (restrictions on evidence at trials for rape etc.), after the word "woman" there shall be inserted the words "or man".

(4) In section 7(2) (interpretation of terms used in the Act—

(a) the words from "references" to "only);" shall be omitted; and

(b) for the words "and section 46 of that Act" there shall be substituted the words "section 46 of the Sexual Offences Act 1956".

Sexual offences: male rape

36.—(1) Section 4 of the Sexual Offences (Amendment) Act 1976 (anonymity of complainants in rape etc. cases) shall be amended as follows.

(2) In subsection (1)—

(a) in paragraph (a)—

> (i) after the word "woman" in both places where it occurs there shall be inserted the words "or man";
>
> (ii) for the words "woman's name nor her address" there shall be substituted the words "name nor the address of the woman or man";
>
> (iii) after the words "of her" there shall be inserted the words "or him";
>
> (iv) for the words "her lifetime" there shall be substituted the words "that person's lifetime"; and
>
> (v) for the words "identify her" there shall be substituted the words "identify that person"; and

(b) in paragraph (b)—

> (i) after the word "woman" there shall be inserted the words "or man"; and
>
> (ii) for the words "her lifetime" there shall be substituted the words "that person's lifetime".

(3) In subsection (5A), after the word "woman" there shall be inserted the words "or man".

(4) In subsection (5B), for the words "woman's peace or comfort" there shall be substituted the words "peace or comfort of the woman or man".

(5) In subsection (6), in the definition of "complainant", after the word "woman" there shall be inserted the words "or man".

Indecent photographs etc.

37.—(1) The Protection of Children Act 1978 shall be amended as follows.

(2) In section 2(3), after the words "proceedings under this Act" there shall be inserted the words "relating to indecent photographs of children".

(3) In section 4—

(a) in subsection (1), after the word "photograph" there shall be inserted the words "or pseudo-photograph"; and

(b) in subsection (2), after the word "photographs" there shall be inserted the words "or pseudo-photographs".

(4) In section 5(2), (5) and (6), after the word "photographs" there shall be inserted the words "or pseudo-photographs".

Indecent photographs etc. (Northern Ireland)

38.—(1) The Protection of Children (Northern Ireland) Order 1978 shall be amended as follows.

(2) In Article 4(1)—

(a) after the word "photograph" there shall be inserted the words "or pseudo-photograph"; and

(b) after the word "photographs" there shall be inserted the words "or pseudo-photographs".

(3) In Article 5(3) and (5), after the word "photographs" there shall be inserted the words "or pseudo-photographs".

(4) In Article 6(1), after the word "photographs" there shall be inserted the words "or pseudo-photographs".

(5) In Article 7(1), after the word "Order" there shall be inserted the words "relating to indecent photographs of children".

Secure training orders: absence of accused

39. In section 11(3) of the Magistrates' Courts Act 1980 (certain sentences and orders not to be made in absence of accused), after the word "make" there shall be inserted the words "a secure training order or".

Procedure for young offenders in cases of grave crimes

40. In section 24(1)(a) of the Magistrates' Courts Act 1980 (exception to summary trial of children or young persons) the words "he has attained the age of 14 and" shall be omitted.

Bail: exclusion in homicide and rape cases

41. In section 29(4)(b) of the Magistrates' Courts Act 1980 (person under 18 remitted to youth court for trial), after the word "may" there shall be inserted the words ", subject to section 25 of the Criminal Justice and Public Order Act 1994,".

Bail: exclusion in homicide and rape cases

42. In section 37(1) of the Magistrates' Courts Act 1980 (committal to Crown Court for sentence), after the word "may" there shall be inserted the words ", subject to section 25 of the Criminal Justice and Public Order Act 1994,".

Police bail

43. In section 43(1) of the Magistrates' Courts Act 1980 (bail under the Police and Criminal Evidence Act 1984), after the words "bail under" there shall be inserted the words "Part IV of".

Bail: exclusion in homicide or rape cases

44. In section 113(1) of the Magistrates' Courts Act 1980 (power of magistrates' court to grant bail on appeal to Crown Court or by way of case stated), after the word "may" there shall be inserted the words ", subject to section 25 of the Criminal Justice and Public Order Act 1994,".

Prisoner custody officers: ineligibility for jury service

45. In Part I of Schedule 1 to the Law Reform (Miscellaneous Provisions) (Scotland) Act 1980 (which makes ineligible for jury service persons connected with the administration of justice), in Group B, after paragraph (o) there shall be inserted the following paragraph—

"(oo) prisoner custody officers within the meaning of section 114(1) of the Criminal Justice and Public Order Act 1994;".

Young offenders: detention in the custody of a constable and others

46. In section 6 of the Imprisonment (Temporary Provisions) Act 1980 (detention in the custody of a constable—
(a) in subsection (1), after the words "remand centre" there shall be inserted the words "secure training centre";
(b) in subsection (2), after the words "remand centre" there shall be inserted the words "secure training centre"; and
(c) after the subsection (3) inserted by section 94 of this Act, there shall be inserted the following subsection—
    "(4) Any reference in this section to a constable includes a reference to a custody officer (within the meaning of section 12 of the Criminal Justice and Public Order Act 1994) acting in pursuance of escort arrangements (within the meaning of Schedule 1 to that Act).".

Detention by constables and officers of a prison etc.: maximum period

47. In section 2 of the Criminal Justice (Scotland) Act 1980 (detention and questioning at police station etc.)—
(a) at the beginning of subsection (3A) there shall be inserted "Subject to subsection (3B) below,"; and
(b) after subsection (3A) there shall be inserted the following subsection—
    "(3B) Subsection (3A) above shall not apply in relation to detention under section 41(3) of the Prisons (Scotland) Act 1989 (detention in relation to introduction etc. into prison of prohibited article), but where a person was detained under section 41(3) immediately prior to his detention under subsection (1) above the period of six hours mentioned in subsection (2) above shall be reduced by the length of that earlier detention.".

Bail: exclusion in homicide and rape cases

48. In section 81(1) of the Supreme Court Act 1981 (power of Crown Court to grant bail), after the word "may", there shall be inserted the words ", subject to section 25 of the Criminal Justice and Public Order Act 1994,".

Young offenders: legal representation

49. In section 3(1) of the Criminal Justice Act 1982 (restriction on certain sentences where offender not legally represented), after paragraph (d) there shall be inserted the following paragraph, preceded by the word "or"—
"(e) make a secure training order,".

Young offenders: early release

50. In section 32 of the Criminal Justice Act 1982 (early release by order of classes of prisoners and other persons), after subsection (7), there shall be inserted the following subsection—
    "(7A) Subsections (1) and (4) above shall apply in relation to secure training centres and persons detained in such centres as they apply, by virtue of section 43(5) of the Prison Act 1952, to young offenders institutions and to persons detained in such institutions.".

Bail: exclusion in homicide and rape cases

51. In section 51(4) of the Mental Health Act 1983 (power of court to remit or release on bail detained person), after the words "above or" there shall be inserted the words ", subject to section 25 of the Criminal Justice and Public Order Act 1994,".

Video recordings

52.—(1) The Video Recordings Act 1984 shall be amended as follows.
(2) In section 13, after subsection (2), there shall be inserted the following subsection—
    "(3) A person guilty of an offence under this section shall be liable, on summary conviction, to a fine not exceeding level 5 on the standard scale.".
(3) For section 15 there shall be substituted the following section—

"Time limit for prosecutions
    15.—(1) No prosecution for an offence under this Act shall be brought after the expiry of the period of three years beginning with the date of the commission of the offence or one year beginning with the date of its discovery by the prosecutor, whichever is earlier.
    (2) In Scotland, the reference in subsection (1) above to the date of discovery by the prosecutor shall be construed as a reference to the date on which evidence sufficient in the opinion of the Lord Advocate to warrant proceedings came to his knowledge.

(3) For the purposes of subsection (2) above—
  (a) a certificate signed by the Lord Advocate or on his behalf and stating the date on which evidence came to his knowledge shall be conclusive evidence of that fact;
  (b) a certificate purporting to be signed as mentioned in paragraph (a) above shall be presumed to be so signed unless the contrary is proved; and
  (c) a prosecution shall be deemed to be brought on the date on which a warrant to apprehend or to cite the accused is granted provided that the warrant is executed without undue delay.".

Interim possession order: power of entry

53. In section 17 of the Police and Criminal Evidence Act 1984 (police powers of entry to effect arrest etc.)—
  (a) in subsection (1)(c), after sub-paragraph (iii), there shall be inserted the following sub-paragraph—
    "(iv) section 76 of the Criminal Justice and Public Order Act 1994 (failure to comply with interim possession order);";
  (b) in subsection (3), after the words "subsection (1)(c)(ii)" there shall be inserted the words "or (iv)".

Bail: exclusion in homicide and rape cases

54. In section 38(1) of the Police and Criminal Evidence Act 1984 (duty of custody officer to release on bail or without bail after charge), after the word "shall" there shall be inserted the words ", subject to section 25 of the Criminal Justice and Public Order Act 1994,".

Searches of persons detained at police stations

55. In section 54(1)(b) of the Police and Criminal Evidence Act 1984 (searches of persons detained at police stations), for the words "under section 47(5) above" there shall be substituted the words ", as a person falling within section 34(7), under section 37 above".

Fingerprinting: speculative searches

56. In section 61 of the Police and Criminal Evidence Act 1984 (which regulates the taking of fingerprints)—
  (a) after subsection (7) there shall be inserted the following subsection—
    "(7A) If a person's fingerprints are taken at a police station, whether with or without the appropriate consent—
      (a) before the fingerprints are taken, an officer shall inform him that they may be the subject of a speculative search; and
      (b) the fact that the person has been informed of this possibility shall be recorded as soon as is practicable after the fingerprints have been taken."; and
  (b) in subsection (8), after the word "them" there shall be inserted the words "and, in the case falling within subsection (7A) above, the fact referred to in paragraph (b) of that subsection".

Intimate samples: speculative searches

57. In section 62 of the Police and Criminal Evidence Act 1984 (which regulates the taking of intimate body samples)—
  (a) after subsection (7) there shall be inserted the following subsection—
    "(7A) If an intimate sample is taken from a person at a police station—
      (a) before the sample is taken, an officer shall inform him that it may be the subject of a speculative search; and
      (b) the fact that the person has been informed of this possibility shall be recorded as soon as practicable after the sample has been taken."; and
  (b) in subsection (8), after the words "subsection (7)" there shall be inserted the words "or (7A)".

Non-intimate samples: speculative searches

58. In section 63 of the Police and Criminal Evidence Act 1984 (which regulates the taking of non-intimate body samples)—
  (a) after the subsection (8A) inserted by section 55 of this Act, there shall be inserted the following subsection—
    "(8B) If a non-intimate sample is taken from a person at a police station, whether with or without the appropriate consent—

(a) before the sample is taken, an officer shall inform him that it may be the subject of a speculative search; and

(b) the fact that the person has been informed of this possibility shall be recorded as soon as practicable after the sample has been taken."; and

(b) in subsection (9), after the words "(8A)" there shall be inserted the words "or (8B)".

Sexual offences: male rape and buggery

59. In Part I of Schedule 5 to the Police and Criminal Evidence Act 1984 (serious arrestable offences mentioned in section 116(2)(a) of that Act), for item 7 (buggery) there shall be substituted—

"7. Buggery with a person under the age of 16.".

Trespassory assemblies

60. In section 15(1) of the Public Order Act 1986 (delegation of functions), for "14" there shall be substituted "14A".

Inferences from accused's silence

61.—(1) The Criminal Evidence (Northern Ireland) Order 1988 shall be amended as follows.

(2) In Article 3(1)(a), after the word "questioned" there shall be inserted the words "under caution".

(3) In Article 4—

(a) in paragraph (1)—

(i) for the words "to (7)" there shall be substituted the words "and (4)";

(ii) in sub-paragraph (b), the words "be called upon to" shall be omitted;

(iii) for the words from "if" onwards there shall be substituted the words ", at the conclusion of the evidence for the prosecution, his legal representative informs the court that the accused will give evidence or, where he is unrepresented, the court ascertains from him that he will give evidence";

(b) for paragraphs (2) and (3) there shall be substituted the following paragraph—

"(2) Where this paragraph applies, the court shall, at the conclusion of the evidence for the prosecution, satisfy itself (in the case of proceedings on indictment conducted with a jury, in the presence of the jury) that the accused is aware that the stage has been reached at which evidence can be given for the defence and that he can, if he wishes, give evidence and that, if he chooses not to give evidence, or having been sworn, without good cause refuses to answer any question, it will be permissible for the court or jury to draw such inferences as appear proper from his failure to give evidence or his refusal, without good cause, to answer any question.";

(c) in paragraph (4)—

(i) at the beginning there shall be inserted the words "Where this paragraph applies,";

(ii) in sub-paragraph (a), for the words "from the refusal as appear proper" there shall be substituted the words "as appear proper from the failure of the accused to give evidence or his refusal, without good cause, to answer any question";

(d) in paragraph (5), for the words "refusal to be sworn" there shall be substituted the words "failure to do so"; and

(e) paragraphs (9) and (10) shall be omitted.

(4) In Article 5(1)(b), for the words "the constable" there shall be substituted the words "that or another constable investigating the case".

(5) In Article 5(2), after sub-paragraph (a), for the word "and" there shall be substituted the following sub-paragraph—

"(aa) a judge, in deciding whether to grant an application made by the accused under Article 5 of the Criminal Justice (Serious Fraud) (Northern Ireland) Order 1988 (application for dismissal of charge where a case of fraud has been transferred from a magistrates' court to the Crown Court under Article 3 of that Order); and".

(6) In Article 5, after paragraph 3, there shall be inserted the following paragraph—

"(3A) This Article applies in relation to officers of customs and excise as it applies in relation to constables.".

(7) In Article 6(1)(b), for the words "the constable" there shall be substituted the words "that or another constable investigating the case".

(8) In Article 6(2), after sub-paragraph (a), for the word "and" there shall be substituted the following sub-paragraph—

"(aa) a judge, in deciding whether to grant an application made by the accused under Article 5 of the Criminal Justice (Serious Fraud) (Northern Ireland) Order 1988 (application for dismissal of charge where a case of fraud has been transferred from a magistrates' court to the Crown Court under Article 3 of that Order); and".

(9) In Article 6, after paragraph 2, there shall be inserted the following paragraph—

"(2A) This Article applies in relation to officers of customs and excise as it applies in relation to constables.".

(10) In Article 6(3), for the words "do so" there shall be substituted the words "comply with the request".

Samples: application to terrorist suspects

62.—(1) The Prevention of Terrorism (Temporary Provisions) Act 1989 shall be amended as provided in sub-paragraphs (2) and (3) below.

(2) In section 15 (provisions supplementary to powers to arrest and detain suspected persons), after subsection (10), there shall be inserted the following subsections—

"(11) Section 62(1) to (11) of the Police and Criminal Evidence Act 1984 (regulation of taking of intimate samples) shall apply to the taking of an intimate sample from a person under subsection (9) above as if—

(a) for subsection (2) there were substituted—

"(2) An officer may only give an authorisation under subsection (1) or (1A) above for the taking of an intimate sample if he is satisfied that it is necessary to do so in order to assist in determining—

(a) whether that person is or has been concerned in the commission, preparation or instigation of acts of terrorism to which section 14 of the Prevention of Terrorism (Temporary Provisions) Act 1989 applies; or

(b) whether he is subject to an exclusion order under that Act;

or if the officer has reasonable grounds for suspecting that person's involvement in an offence under any of the provisions mentioned in subsection (1)(a) of that section and for believing that an intimate sample will tend to confirm or disprove his involvement"; and

(b) in subsection (6), after the word "includes", there were inserted the words "where relevant".

(12) In this section, "intimate sample" has the same meaning as in section 65 of the Police and Criminal Evidence Act 1984.

(13) Section 63(1) to (9) of the Police and Criminal Evidence Act 1984 (regulation of taking of non-intimate samples) shall apply to the taking of a non-intimate sample from a person by a constable under subsection (9) above as if—

(a) for subsection (4) there were substituted—

"(4) An officer may only give an authorisation under subsection (3) above for the taking of a non-intimate sample if he is satisfied that it is necessary to do so in order to assist in determining—

(a) whether that person is or has been concerned in the commission, preparation or instigation of acts of terrorism to which section 14 of the Prevention of Terrorism (Temporary Provisions) Act 1989 applies; or

(b) whether he is subject to an exclusion order under that Act;

or if the officer has reasonable grounds for suspecting that person's involvement in an offence under any of the provisions mentioned in subsection (1)(a) of that section and for believing that a non-intimate sample will tend to confirm or disprove his involvement"; and

(b) in subsection (7), after the word "includes" there were inserted the words "where relevant".

(14) In this section, "non-intimate sample" has the same meaning as in section 65 of the Police and Criminal Evidence Act 1984.".

(3) In Schedule 5, in paragraph 7 (provisions supplementary to powers to detain persons pending examination etc.), after sub-paragraph (6), there shall be inserted the following sub-paragraphs—

"(6A) Section 62(1) to (11) of the Police and Criminal Evidence Act 1984 (regulation of taking of intimate samples) shall apply to the taking of an intimate sample from a person under sub-paragraph (5) above as if—

(a) for subsection (2) there were substituted—

"(2) An officer may only give an authorisation under subsection (1) or (1A) above for the taking of an intimate sample if he is satisfied that it is necessary to do so in order to assist in determining—

(a) whether that person is or has been concerned in the commission, preparation or instigation of acts of terrorism to which paragraph 2 of Schedule

5 to the Prevention of Terrorism (Temporary Provisions) Act 1989 applies; or

(b) whether he is subject to an exclusion order under that Act; or

(c) whether there are grounds for suspecting that he has committed an offence under section 8 of that Act"; and

(b) in subsection (6), after the word "includes", there were inserted the words "where relevant".

(6B) In this paragraph, "intimate sample" has the same meaning as in section 65 of the Police and Criminal Evidence Act 1984.

(6C) Section 63(1) to (9) of the Police and Criminal Evidence Act 1984 (regulation of taking of non-intimate samples) shall apply to the taking of a non-intimate sample from a person by a constable under sub-paragraph (5) above as if—

(a) for subsection (4) there were substituted—

"(4) An officer may only give an authorisation under subsection (3) above for the taking of a non-intimate sample if he is satisfied that it is necessary to do so in order to assist in determining—

(a) whether that person is or has been concerned in the commission, preparation or instigation of acts of terrorism to which paragraph 2 of Schedule 5 to the Prevention of Terrorism (Temporary Provisions) Act 1989 applies;

(b) whether he is subject to an exclusion order under that Act; or

(c) whether there are grounds for suspecting that he has committed an offence under section 8 of that Act"; and

(b) in subsection (7), after the word "includes", there were inserted the words "where relevant".

(6D) In this paragraph, "non-intimate sample" has the same meaning as in section 65 of the Police and Criminal Evidence Act 1984.".

(4) In consequence of the foregoing amendments—

(a) in section 62 of the Police and Criminal Evidence Act 1984 (which regulates the taking of intimate body samples), at the end there shall be inserted the following subsection—

"(12) Nothing in this section, except as provided in section 15(11) and (12) of, and paragraph 7(6A) and (6B) of Schedule 5 to, the Prevention of Terrorism (Temporary Provisions) Act 1989, applies to a person arrested or detained under the terrorism provisions.";

(b) in section 63 of the Police and Criminal Evidence Act 1984 (which regulates the taking of non-intimate body samples), at the end there shall be inserted the following subsection—

"(10) Nothing in this section, except as provided in section 15(13) and (14) of, and paragraph 7(6C) and (6D) of Schedule 5 to, the Prevention of Terrorism (Temporary Provisions) Act 1989, applies to a person arrested or detained under the terrorism provisions."; and

(c) in section 28(2) of the Prevention of Terrorism (Temporary Provisions) Act 1989 (extent), in paragraph (b) (provisions extending only to England and Wales), after the words "section 15(10)" there shall be inserted the words "to (14)" and after the words "paragraph 7(6)" there shall be inserted the words "to (6D)".

(5) For the purposes of section 27 of the Prevention of Terrorism (Temporary Provisions) Act 1989 (temporary provisions), the amendments made by this paragraph shall be treated, as from the time when those amendments come into force, as having been continued in force by the order under subsection (6) of that section which has effect at that time.

Prevention of terrorism: consents for prosecutions etc.

63.—(1) The Prevention of Terrorism (Temporary Provisions) Act 1989 shall be amended as follows.

(2) In section 17(1)(b) (purposes of investigations), for the words "section 21(4) of that Act" there shall be substituted the words "section 28(3) of that Act".

(3) In section 19(1) (consents required for prosecutions), after paragraph (a), there shall be inserted the following paragraph—

"(aa) in England and Wales for an offence under section 13A, 16A or 16B except by or with the consent of the Director of Public Prosecutions;".

(4) In section 28(2) (extent), in paragraph (a) (provisions not extending to Northern Ireland), for the words "and section 15(1)", there shall be substituted the words ", sections 13A and 15(1) and Part IVA".

(5) For the purposes of section 27 (temporary provisions), the amendments made by this paragraph shall be treated, as from the time when those amendments come into force, as having been continued in force by the order under subsection (6) of that section which has effect at that time.

Young offenders: powers to search and to test for drugs

64. In section 19(4) of the Prisons (Scotland) Act 1989 (remand centres and young offenders institutions), for the words "and 41" there shall be substituted the words "41, 41A and 41B".

Non-appearance of accused: plea of guilty

65. In section 20(1A) of the Criminal Justice Act 1991 (power of court to make financial circumstances order in absence of accused where guilty plea notified) for the words "section 12(2)" there shall be substituted the words "section 12(4)".

Young offenders: secure training order a custodial sentence

66. In section 31(1) of the Criminal Justice Act 1991 (which defines, amongst other expressions, "custodial sentence'), in paragraph (b) of that definition, after the words "1982 Act", there shall be inserted the words, "or a secure training order under section 1 of the Criminal Justice and Public Order Act 1994".

Bail: exclusion in homicide and rape cases

67. In section 40(3)(b) of the Criminal Justice Act 1991 (committal for sentence of offender convicted of offence during currency of original sentence), at the beginning, there shall be inserted the words "subject to section 25 of the Criminal Justice and Public Order Act 1994,".

Contracted out prisons: exclusion of search powers

68. In section 87(3) of the Criminal Justice Act 1991 (provisions of Prison Act 1952 not applying to contracted out prisons), after the word "officers)" there shall be inserted the words "and section 8A (powers of search by authorised employees)".

Testing prisoners for drugs: director's function

69. In section 87(4) of the Criminal Justice Act 1991 (certain functions as governor to be functions of director of contracted out prisons), after "13(1)" insert "16A".

The Parole Board

70. For Schedule 5 to the Criminal Justice Act 1991 (supplementary provisions about the Parole Board) there shall be substituted the following Schedule—

"SCHEDULE 5

The Parole Board: Supplementary Provisions

Status and capacity

1.—(1) The Board shall not be regarded as the servant or agent of the Crown or as enjoying any status, immunity or privilege of the Crown; and the Board's property shall not be regarded as property of, or held on behalf of, the Crown.

(2) It shall be within the capacity of the Board as a statutory corporation to do such things and enter into such transactions as are incidental to or conducive to the discharge of its functions under Part II of this Act.

Membership

2.—(1) The Board shall consist of a chairman and not less than four other members appointed by the Secretary of State.

(2) The Board shall include among its members—
(a) a person who holds or has held judicial office;
(b) a registered medical practitioner who is a psychiatrist;
(c) a person appearing to the Secretary of State to have knowledge and experience of the supervision or after-care of discharged prisoners; and
(d) a person appearing to the Secretary of State to have made a study of the causes of delinquency or the treatment of offenders.

(3) A member of the Board—
(a) shall hold and vacate office in accordance with the terms of his appointment;
(b) may resign his office by notice in writing addressed to the Secretary of State;
and a person who ceases to hold office as a member of the Board shall be eligible for re-appointment.

Payments to members

3.—(1) The Board may pay to each member such remuneration and allowances as the Secretary of State may determine.

(2) The Board may pay or make provision for paying to or in respect of any member such sums by way of pension, allowances or gratuities as the Secretary of State may determine.

(3) If a person ceases to be a member otherwise than on the expiry of his term of office and it appears to the Secretary of State that there are special circumstances that make it right that he should receive compensation, the Secretary of State may direct the Board to make to that person a payment of such amount as the Secretary of State may determine.

(4) A determination or direction of the Secretary of State under this paragraph requires the approval of the Treasury.

Proceedings

4.—(1) Subject to the provisions of section 32(5) of this Act, the arrangements relating to meetings of the Board shall be such as the Board may determine.

(2) The arrangements may provide for the discharge, under the general direction of the Board, of any of the Board's functions by a committee or by one or more of the members or employees of the Board.

(3) The validity of the proceedings of the Board shall not be affected by any vacancy among the members or by any defect in the appointment of a member.

Staff

5.—(1) The Board may appoint such number of employees as it may determine.

(2) The remuneration and other conditions of service of the persons appointed under this paragraph shall be determined by the Board.

(3) Any determination under sub-paragraph (1) or (2) shall require the approval of the Secretary of State given with the consent of the Treasury.

(4) The Employers' Liability (Compulsory Insurance) Act 1969 shall not require insurance to be effected by the Board.

6.—(1) Employment with the Board shall be included among the kinds of employment to which a scheme under section 1 of the Superannuation Act 1972 can apply, and accordingly in Schedule 1 to that Act (in which those kinds of employment are listed) at the end of the list of Other Bodies there shall be inserted—
"Parole Board.".

(2) The Board shall pay to the Treasury, at such times as the Treasury may direct, such sums as the Treasury may determine in respect of the increase attributable to this paragraph in the sums payable under the Superannuation Act 1972 out of money provided by Parliament.

Financial provisions

7.—(1) The Secretary of State shall pay to the Board—
(a) any expenses incurred or to be incurred by the Board by virtue of paragraph 3 or 5; and
(b) with the consent of the Treasury, such sums as he thinks fit for enabling the Board to meet other expenses.

(2) Any sums required by the Secretary of State for making payments under sub-paragraph (1) shall be paid out of money provided by Parliament.

Authentication of Board's seal

8. The application of the seal of the Board shall be authenticated by the signature of the Chairman or some other person authorised for the purpose.

Presumption of authenticity of documents issued by Board

9. Any document purporting to be an instrument issued by the Board and to be duly executed under the seal of the Board or to be signed on behalf of the Board shall be received in evidence and shall be deemed to be such an instrument unless the contrary is shown.

Accounts and audit

10.—(1) It shall be the duty of the Board—
(a) to keep proper accounts and proper records in relation to the accounts;

(b) to prepare in respect of each financial year a statement of accounts in such form as the Secretary of State may direct with the approval of the Treasury; and

(c) to send copies of each such statement to the Secretary of State and the Comptroller and Auditor General not later than 31st August next following the end of the financial year to which the statement relates.

(2) The Comptroller and Auditor General shall examine, certify and report on each statement of accounts sent to him by the Board and shall lay a copy of every such statement and of his report before each House of Parliament.

(3) In this paragraph, 'financial year' means the period beginning with the date on which the Board is incorporated and ending with the next following 31st March, and each successive period of twelve months.

Reports

11. The Board shall as soon as practicable after the end of each financial year make to the Secretary of State a report on the performance of its functions during the year; and the Secretary of State shall lay a copy of the report before Parliament.".

Bail: exclusion in homicide and rape cases

71. In Schedule 6 to the Criminal Justice Act 1991 (procedure on notice of transfer in certain cases involving children), in paragraph 2(1), after the word "1976" where it occurs first there shall be inserted the words ", section 25 of the Criminal Justice and Public Order Act 1994".

Probation officers for offenders subject to secure training orders

72. In section 4 of the Probation Service Act 1993 (functions of probation committee)—

(a) in subsection (1), after paragraph (d), there shall be inserted the following paragraph—

"(dd) to make arrangements for the selection, from the probation officers appointed for or assigned to a petty sessions area within their probation area, of an officer to supervise any person subject to supervision by a probation officer under a secure training order (within the meaning of section 1 of the Criminal Justice and Public Order Act 1994) naming as that petty sessions area the petty sessions area within which the person to be supervised resides for the time being;"; and

(b) in subsection (4), for the words "paragraph (c) or (d)" there shall be substituted the words "paragraph (c), (d) or (dd)".

Secure training orders: cost of supervision by probation officer

73. In section 17 of the Probation Service Act 1993 (probation committee expenditure)—

(a) in subsection (1), for the words "and (5)" there shall be substituted the words "(5) and (5A)"; and

(b) after subsection (5) there shall be inserted the following subsection—

"(5A) Nothing in sections 18 or 19 requires there to be paid out of the metropolitan police fund or defrayed by a local authority any expenses of a probation committee which are defrayed by the Secretary of State under section 3(6) of the Criminal Justice and Public Order Act 1994.".

Section 168(3)   SCHEDULE 11

REPEALS

Chapter	Short Title	Extent of repeal
1848 c. 42.	Indictable Offences Act 1848.	Sections 12, 14 and 15.
1898 c. 36.	Criminal Evidence Act 1898.	In section 1, proviso (b).
1923 c. 9 (N.I.).	Criminal Evidence Act (Northern Ireland) 1923.	In section 1, proviso (b).
1925 c. 86.	Criminal Justice Act 1925.	Section 13(3). Section 49(2).
1952 c. 52.	Prison Act 1952.	In section 43(1)(a), the words "trial or". In section 43(1), the word "and" at the end of paragraph (b). In section 43(2)(b) and (c), the words "trial or".

Chapter	Short Title	Extent of repeal
1956 c. 69.	Sexual Offences Act 1956.	In section 2(1), the word "unlawful". Section 2(2). In section 3(1), the word "unlawful". Section 3(2). Section 4(2). Section 22(2). Section 23(2).
1963 c. 37.	Children and Young Persons Act 1963.	In section 57(2), the words "Section 49 of the principal Act and" and "an appeal by case stated or".
1965 c. 45.	Backing of Warrants (Republic of Ireland) Act 1965.	In section 2(2)(a), the words from ", or an offence under an enactment" to "control".
1965 c. 69.	Criminal Procedure (Attendance of Witnesses) Act 1965.	Section 1.
1967 c. 60.	Sexual Offences Act 1967.	In section 1(1), the words "but subject to the provisions of the next following section". Section 1(5). Section 2. Section 3.
1967 c. 77.	Police (Scotland) Act 1967.	Section 18.
1967 c. 80.	Criminal Justice Act 1967.	Section 7. In section 36(1), the definition of "committal proceedings". In section 67(5), the word "and" at the end of paragraph (a).
1968 c. 19.	Criminal Appeal Act 1968.	In Schedule 2, paragraph 1, the words from "section 13(3)" to "but".
1968 c. 52.	Caravan Sites Act 1968.	Sections 6 to 12. In section 16, the definition of "gipsies".
1969 c. 54.	Children and Young Persons Act 1969.	Section 10(1) and (2). In section 57(4), the words "49 and the said sections".
1969 c. 63.	Police Act 1969.	Sections 1, 3, 6 and 7.
1970 c. 9 (N.I.).	Police Act (Northern Ireland) 1970.	Sections 19 and 20.
1972 c. 71.	Criminal Justice Act 1972.	In section 46(1), the following words— "Section 102 of the Magistrates' Courts Act 1980 and"; "which respectively allow"; "committal proceedings and in other"; "and section 106 of the said Act of 1980"; "which punish the making of"; "102 or"; ", as the case may be". Section 46(2).
1973 c. 62.	Powers of Criminal Courts Act 1973.	In section 32(1)(b), the words "tried or".
1974 c. 23.	Juries Act 1974.	In section 10, the words "physical disability or".
1974 c. 53.	Rehabilitation of Offenders Act 1974.	In section 5(4), the words "or placed on probation," and "or probation order".
1976 c. 63.	Bail Act 1976.	Section 1(4). In section 3(6), the words "(but only by a court)".
1976 c. 82.	Sexual Offences (Amendment) Act 1976.	Section 1(1). In section 7(2), the words from "references" to "only);".
1977 c. 45.	Criminal Law Act 1977.	Section 6(3). Section 38.

Chapter	Short Title	Extent of repeal
1978 c. 30.	Interpretation Act 1978.	In Schedule 1, paragraph (a) of the definition of "Committed for trial".
1978 c. 37.	Protection of Children Act 1978.	In section 1(1)(a), the words following "child". In section 4(2), the words from "within" to "warrant".
1980 c. 43.	Magistrates' Courts Act 1980.	In section 22(1), the words "subject to subsection (7) below". In section 24(1)(a) the words "he has attained the age of 14 and". In section 38(2)(b), the words from "committed" to "21 years old". In section 97(1), the words from "at an inquiry" to "be) or". Section 102. Section 103. Section 105. Section 106. Section 145(1)(e). In section 150(1), the definition of "committal proceedings". In Schedule 5, paragraph 2.
1980 c. 62.	Criminal Justice (Scotland) Act 1980.	In section 80, subsection (5); in subsection (7), paragraph (d) and the word "; or" immediately preceding that paragraph; and subsection (8).
1981 c. 47.	Criminal Attempts Act 1981.	In section 2(2)(g), the words "or committed for trial".
1982 c. 48.	Criminal Justice Act 1982.	In section 1(2), the words "trial or". Section 12(6), (7) and, in subsection (11), paragraph (b) and the word "and". Section 67(5). In Schedule 14, paragraph 8.
S.I. 1982/1536 (N.I. 19).	Homosexual Offences (Northern Ireland) Order 1982.	In Article 3, in paragraph (1), the words "and Article 5 (merchant seamen" and paragraph (4). Article 5.
1984 c. 39.	Video Recordings Act 1984.	In section 1, in subsection (2)(a), the word "or" and in subsection (3), the word "or" where it occurs first. In section 17(1), the words from "within" to "warrant".
1984 c. 60.	Police and Criminal Evidence Act 1984.	Section 37(1)(b), together with the word "or" preceding it. Section 47(5). In section 62(10), the words following "proper". In section 118(1), the definition of "intimate search".
1985 c. 23.	Prosecution of Offences Act 1985.	In Schedule 1, paragraph 1.
1986 c. 64.	Public Order Act 1986.	Section 39. In section 42(2), "39".
1987 c. 38.	Criminal Justice Act 1987.	In Schedule 2, paragraphs 10 and 11.
1988 c. 33.	Criminal Justice Act 1988.	In section 25(1)(a)(ii), the word "or". Section 32A(10). In section 34(2), the words from "in relation to" to the end. Section 126. In section 160, in subsection (1), the words from "(meaning" to "16)" and subsection (5).

Chapter	Short Title	Extent of repeal
1988 c. 34.	Legal Aid Act 1988.	In section 20(4)(a), the words "trial or". Section 20(4)(bb). Section 20(5).
S.I. 1988/1987 (N.I. 20).	Criminal Evidence (Northern Ireland) Order 1988.	In Article 4, in paragraph (1)(b) the words "be called upon to" and paragraphs (9) and (10).
1989 c. 45.	Prisons (Scotland) Act 1989.	Section 33.
1989 c. 54.	Children Act 1989.	In Schedule 5, paragraph 7(2)(f). In Schedule 6, paragraph 10(2)(j).
1990 c. 42.	Broadcasting Act 1990.	In Schedule 20, in paragraph 3(2), the words "and 49".
1991 c. 13.	War Crimes Act 1991.	In section 1(4), the words "England, Wales or". Part I of the Schedule.
1991 c. 24.	Northern Ireland (Emergency Provisions) Act 1991.	In Schedule 7, paragraph 5(3)(c).
1991 c. 53.	Criminal Justice Act 1991.	In section 3(2), the words from the beginning to "indictment,". In section 3(4), the words from "which is" to "applies". Section 50(4). Section 52(2). Section 57(4)(b), together with the word "and" preceding it. Section 64.
S.I. 1992/1829.	Parole Board (Transfer of Functions) Order 1992.	In Article 3, the words from "and 39" to "licence)" and the words "and (4)".
1993 c. 24.	Video Recordings Act 1993.	Section 3.
1993 c. 36.	Criminal Justice Act 1993.	Section 67(2).

Note: The repeals that are to come into force on the passing of this Act are the following, namely, the repeals in the Sexual Offences Act 1967, the Caravan Sites Act 1968, the Sexual Offences (Amendment) Act 1976, the Public Order Act 1986, the Criminal Justice (Scotland) Act 1980 and the Homosexual Offences (Northern Ireland) Order 1982.

INDEX

References are to sections and Schedules

AGGRAVATED TRESPASS, *see* TRESPASS
AMENDMENTS,
  consequential, 168(2), Sched. 10
  minor, 168(1), Sched. 9
ARMED FORCES,
  application of rules as to silence of accused,
    39
  homosexual acts, 146–7
ARRESTABLE OFFENCES, 85

BAIL,
  not granted, where, 25
  offences while on, 26
  person on bail not qualified as juror, 40
  police powers,
    arrest for failure to answer to police bail,
      29
    conditional bail, 27, Sched. 3
    detention after charge, 28
    previous conviction, 25
    reconsideration of decision granting, 30
BODY SAMPLES,
  meanings of intimate and non-intimate, 58
  mouth searches, 59
  police powers, 54–6
  retention in certain cases, 57

CAMPERS,
  gipsy sites, repeal of provisions relating to,
    80
  removal of,
    court orders for, 78
    direction by local authority to unauthor-
      ised campers to leave land, 77
  service of notice on, 79
  vehicles of, 77
  see also SQUATTERS; TRESPASS
CHARACTER, IMPUTATIONS ON, 31
CHILDREN'S TESTIMONY: VIDEO RECORDINGS, 50
CIRCUIT JUDGES AS JUDGES OF CRIMINAL DIV-
    ISION OF COURT OF APPEAL, 52
COMMENCEMENT, 172(2)–(6)
COMMITTAL PROCEEDINGS, 44
COMPUTERS, *see* DATA PROTECTION
COPYRIGHT: ENFORCEMENT OF OFFENCES, 165
CORROBORATION,
  abolition of rules, 32
  sexual offences, abolition of requirements,
    33
CRIME PREVENTION GRANTS, 169
CRIMINAL APPEALS,
  circuit judges as judges of criminal division
    of Court of Appeal, 52
  Northern Ireland: expenses, 53

CRIMINAL DAMAGE AS SUMMARY OFFENCE, 46
CROSS-BORDER ENFORCEMENT,
  aid of one police force by another, 141
  arrest powers, 137–8
    reciprocal, 140
  execution of warrants, 136
  search powers, 139
CUSTODIAL SENTENCES FOR YOUNG OFFENDERS,
  life sentences: accommodation, 18
  long-term detention, 16
  maximum length of detention, 17

DATA PROTECTION,
  access to computer material by constables
    and other enforcement officers, 162
  procuring disclosure of, and selling, com-
    puter-held information, 161
DISABLED PERSONS AS JURORS, 41
DRUGS,
  increase in fines for offences, 157, Sched. 8,
    Part II
  power to search prisoners for, 151

EVIDENCE,
  children's testimony: video recordings, 50
  corroboration rules abolished, 32
  imputations on character, 31
  intimidation of witnesses, 51
  silence of accused, *see* SILENCE OF ACCUSED,
    INFERENCES FROM
EXPENSES UNDER THIS ACT, 171
EXTENT, 172(7)–(16)
EXTRADITION PROCEDURES,
  amendments to existing law, 158
  backing of warrants, 159

FINES: RECOVERY FROM INCOME SUPPORT, 47
FINGERPRINTS, 56
FIREARMS OFFENCES,
  increase in penalties, 157, Sched. 8, Part III
FOOTBALL MATCHES: TICKET TOUTS, 166

GERM CELLS, PROHIBITION ON USE OF, 156
GIPSY SITES, 80
GUILTY PLEAS,
  magistrates' courts powers extended, 45
  reduction in sentences, 48

HARASSMENT,
  intentional harassment, alarm or distress:
    offence, 154

HARASSMENT—*cont.*
  racially inflammatory publications, 155
HOMOSEXUALITY, *see* SEXUAL OFFENCES
HUMAN FERTILISATION,
  prohibition on use of cells from embryos or
    foetuses, 156

ILLICIT RECORDINGS,
  enforcement of offences, 165
INTIMIDATION OF WITNESSES, 51

JURIES,
  separation of jury during consideration of
    verdict, 43
  service on,
    disabled persons, 41
    excuse on religious grounds, 42
    person on bail not qualified, 40

MAGISTRATES' COURTS,
  criminal damage as summary offence: rel-
    evant sum, 46
  examining justices: functions abolished, 44,
    Sched. 4
  guilty pleas: extension of procedures, 45,
    Sched. 5
  recovery of fines by deduction from income
    support, 47
  transfer for trial instead of committal pro-
    ceedings, 44, Sched. 4
MANSLAUGHTER, 25
MURDER AND ATTEMPTED MURDER: BAIL, 25
MUSIC, AMPLIFIED, 63

NORTHERN IRELAND,
  expenses in criminal appeals, 53
  homosexual acts on merchant ships and in
    armed forces, 147
  video recordings offences, 91
  see also PRISON SERVICES AND PRISON SERVICE

OBSCENITY,
  arrestable offences, 85
  indecent photographs of children,
    imprisonment as sentence, 86–7
    pseudo-photographs, 84
  obscene offensive or annoying telephone
    calls, 92
  see also VIDEO RECORDINGS OFFENCES

PAROLE BOARD,
  incorporation of, 149
  powers to recall prisoners released on
    licence, 150
  released prisoners: conditions in licence
    (Scotland), 131
PARTY CONFERENCES: SECURITY COSTS, 170
PENALTIES, INCREASE IN, 157, Sched. 8

POLICE POWERS,
  body samples,
    intimate, 54
      meaning of, 58
      mouth searches, 59
    non-intimate, 55
      meaning of, 58
    retention of, 57
  fingerprints and samples: supplementary
    provisions, 56
  stop and search,
    in anticipation of violence, 60
    prevention of terrorism, 81
  United Kingdom waters: extension of con-
    stabulary powers, 160
  see also BAIL; CROSS-BORDER ENFORCEMENT;
    RAVES; TRESPASS OFFENCES
POLITICAL PARTY CONFERENCES: SECURITY
  COSTS, 170
PORNOGRAPHY, *see* OBSCENITY
PREVENTION OF TERRORISM,
  activities and financial resources of terror-
    ists, investigation into, 83
  offences,
    possession of articles for suspected ter-
      rorist purposes, 82
    unlawful collection of information, 82
  stop and search powers, 81
PRISON SERVICES AND PRISON SERVICE,
  employment in Prison Service,
    inducements to withold services or to
      indiscipline, 127
    pay and related conditions, 128
    relevant employment legislation, 126
  England and Wales,
    contracted out functions at directly
      managed prisons, 99
    contracted out prisons,
      powers as to, 96
      prisoners temporarily out of, 98
      temporary attachment of prison offi-
        cers, 97
    drugs: power to test prisoners for, 151
    minor and consequential amendments,
      101
    prisoner escort arrangements, 93
      breaches of discipline by prisoners
        under escort, 95
      custody officers acting in pursuance of:
        powers and duties, 94
    provision of prisons by contractors, 100
    search powers by authorised employees,
      152
  Northern Ireland,
    interpretation, 125
    prisoner custody officers,
      certification, 122, Sched. 7
      protection of, 123
    prisoner escort arrangements,
      breaches of discipline by prisoners
        under escort, 121
      custody officers acting in pursuance of:
        powers and duties, 120
      monitoring of, 119
      provision of, 118

PRISON SERVICES AND PRISON SERVICE—*cont.*
  Northern Ireland—*cont.*
    wrongful disclosure of information, 124
  Scotland,
    contracted out functions, 112
    contracted out prisons,
      breaches of discipline by prisoners
        temporarily out of, 109
      intervention by Secretary of State, 111
      officers of, 107
      powers as to, 106
      prison rules: consequential modifi-
        cations, 110
      prisoner custody officers: powers and
        duties, 108
    interpretation, 117
    minor and consequential amendments,
      116
    prisoner custody officers,
      certification, 114(2), Sched. 6
      general provisions, 114
    prisoner escort arrangements, 102
      breaches of discipline by prisoners
        under escort, 105
      custody officers acting in pursuance of:
        powers and duties, 104
      monitoring of, 103
    prisoners,
      amendments to existing legislation,
        134–5
      children: detention and release, 130
      released: conditions in licence: Parole
        Board recommendations, 131
      supervised release orders: standard
        requirements, 132
      transfer of persons detained by police
        and customs officers, 129
      transferred life prisoners: extension of
        categories, 133
    prohibited articles brought into prisons,
      153
    provision of new prisons, 113
    search powers by authorised employees,
      152
    wrongful disclosure of information, 115
  see also PAROLE BOARD
PUBLIC ORDER, *see* CAMPERS; HARASSMENT;
  RAVES; SQUATTERS; TRESPASS OFFENCES

RACIALLY INFLAMMATORY PUBLICATIONS, 155
RAPE, *see* SEXUAL OFFENCES
RAVES,
  entry and seizure powers, 64
  exempt persons, 63(5), 63(10)
  forfeiture of sound equipment, 66
  interpretation, 63(10)
  licensed entertainment exempt, 63(9)
  meaning of, 63(1)
  offences, 63(6)–(8)
  power to remove persons attending or pre-
    paring for, 63
  power to stop persons from proceeding, 65
  preparation for, 63(2)
REPEALS, 168(3), Sched. 11

SCOTLAND,
  indecent photographs of children: sentence
    of imprisonment, 87
  serious fraud, powers to investigate,
    164(3)–(4)
  see also PRISON SERVICES AND PRISON SERVICE
SEA FISHERIES OFFENCES: INCREASE IN PENAL-
  TIES, 157, Sched. 8, Part I
SEARCHES, *see* BODY SAMPLES: POLICE POWERS
SECURE ACCOMMODATION FOR YOUNG
  OFFENDERS,
  cost of, 21
  extension of kinds of, 19
  management of, 22
  not immediately available, 2(2)
  secure remands, 20
SECURE TRAINING CENTRES, *see* SECURE TRAIN-
  ING ORDERS
SECURE TRAINING ORDERS,
  age limits, 1(1)(a)
    deemed age, 1(9)
    substituted ages, 1(10)
  conditions for making, 1(5)
    court's duty to state that conditions satis-
      fied, 1(7)
  consequential amendments, 5
  custodial sentence, as, 1(6), 2(7)
  imprisonable offence, meaning of, 1(8)
  local authorities' role, 2, 3
  meaning of, 1(2)
  period of detention, 1(3)–(4), 2(3)
  power to make, 1(1)
  secure training centres,
    accommodation not immediately avail-
      able, 2(2)
    contracted out,
      custody officers' powers, 9
      functions at directly managed centres,
        11
      interpretation, 15
      management: intervention by Sec-
        retary of State, 10
      officers, 8
      power to enter into contract, 7
    custody officers,
      certification arrangements, 12(2),
        Sched. 2
      meaning of, 12(3)
      protection of, 13
    detention in, 1(2)
    escort arrangements, 12, Sched. 1
      offences in connection with, 13
    management of, 6
    release on compassionate grounds, 2(6)
    transfer elsewhere, 2(4)
    wrongful disclosure of information relat-
      ing to offenders, 14
  supervision under,
    breach of requirements, 4
    requirements for, 3
SEIZURE,
  cross-border enforcement, 139(9)–(10)
  prohibited articles in Scottish prisons, 153
  raves, 64(4)
    forfeiture of sound equipment, 66

Seizure—*cont.*
  retention and charges for seized property, 67
  trespassing vehicles, 62(1)
Serious Fraud,
  extension of powers of Serious Fraud Office, 164
Sexual Offences,
  corroboration requirements abolished, 33
  homosexuality,
    acts in private: age at which lawful, 145
    armed forces and merchant navy, in, 146–7
  rape,
    bail, 25
    male rape and buggery, 143
    meaning of, 142
    of women and men, 142
    revised penalties, 144
Short Title, 172(1)
Silence of Accused, Inferences from,
  Armed Forces, application of rules to, 39
  facts, failure to mention, when questioned or charged, effect of, 34
  objects, substances or marks, effect of failure or refusal to account for, 36
  presence at particular place, effect of failure or refusal to account for, 37
  trial, effect of silence at, 35
Squatters,
  adverse occupation of residential premises: offence, 73
  displaced residential occupiers requesting trespassers to leave, 73
    special position, of, 72
  interim possession orders,
    false or misleading statements, 75
    trespassing during currency of order, 76
  protected intending occupiers,
    meaning of, 74
    requesting trespassers to leave, 73
    special position of, 72
  see also Campers; Trespass
Stop and Search, see Police Powers
Supervision,
  breach of order, 1(5)(c)(ii)
  breach of requirements, 4
  under secure training order, 3

Taxi Touts, 167
Telephone Calls, 92
Television, Closed Circuit,
  provision by local authorities, 163

Terrorism, see Prevention of Terrorism
Ticket Touts, 166
Trespass,
  aggravated trespass,
    offence, 68
    powers of police to remove trespassers, 69
  power to remove trespassers,
    common land, 61(7)–(8)
    damage or insulting behaviour, 61(1)(a)
    direction to leave, 61
    interpretation, 61(9)
    offence,
      arrest without warrant, 61(5)
      defences, 61(6)
      failure to leave or re-entry after direction, 61(4)
    vehicles on land,
      seizure of, 62
    six or more, 61(1)(b)
  trespassory assemblies,
    prohibition of and offences in connection with, 70
    stopping persons from proceeding to, 71
  see also Campers; Squatters
Trespassory Assemblies, see Trespass

United Kingdom Waters: Constabulary Powers, 160

Video Recordings Offences,
  enforcement by enforcing authorities outside their areas, 91
  increase in penalties, 88
  restriction of exemptions, 89
  suitability, 90
Violence, Serious: Threat of Incidents Involving, 60

Weights and Measures Authority,
  copyright and illicit recordings: enforcement powers, 165

Young Offenders,
  arrest for breaches of conditions of remand, 23
  police detention, 24
  publication of report of cases, 49
  see also Custodial Sentences for Young Offenders; Secure Accommodation for Young Offenders; Secure Training Orders

MARRIAGE ACT 1994

(1994 c. 34)

An Act to amend the Marriage Act 1949 so as to enable civil marriages to be solemnized on premises approved for the purpose by local authorities and so as to provide for further cases in which marriages may be solemnized in registration districts in which neither party to the marriage resides; and for connected purposes.   [3rd November 1994]

PARLIAMENTARY DEBATES

Hansard, H.C. Vol. 245, col. 526; Vol. 246, col. 1327; H.L. Vol. 557, col. 550; Vol. 558, col. 625. The Bill was discussed in Standing Committee C on July 6, 1994.

INTRODUCTION

This Act enables civil marriages to be solemnized on premises approved by local authorities by amending the Marriage Act 1949 (c. 76). The Secretary of State may by regulations make provision for and in connection with the approval by local authorities of premises for the solemnization of marriages. The Schedule makes consequential amendments.

Solemnization of marriages on premises approved by local authorities

1.—(1) In section 26(1) of the Marriage Act 1949 (marriages which may be solemnized on authority of superintendent registrar's certificate) after paragraph (b) there shall be inserted—

"(bb) a marriage on approved premises;".

(2) After section 46 of that Act there shall be inserted—

"Marriages on approved premises

Approval of premises

46A.—(1) The Secretary of State may by regulations make provision for and in connection with the approval by local authorities of premises for the solemnization of marriages in pursuance of section 26(1)(bb) of this Act.

(2) The matters dealt with by the regulations may include—

(a) the kinds of premises in respect of which approvals may be granted;

(b) the procedure to be followed in relation to applications for approval;

(c) the considerations to be taken into account by a local authority in determining whether to approve any premises;

(d) the duration and renewal of approvals;

(e) the conditions that must or may be imposed by a local authority on granting or renewing an approval;

(f) the determination and charging by local authorities of fees in respect of applications for the approval of premises and in respect of the renewal of approvals;

(g) the circumstances in which a local authority must or may revoke an approval;

(h) the review of any decision to refuse an approval or the renewal of an approval, to impose conditions on granting or renewing an approval or to revoke an approval;

(i) the notification to the Registrar General of all approvals granted, renewed or revoked;

    (j) the keeping by local authorities of registers of approved premises;

    (k) the issue by the Registrar General of guidance supplementing the provision made by the regulations.

    (3) In this section "local authority" means a county council, metropolitan district council or London borough council.

    (4) Regulations under this section may make different provision for different cases or circumstances.

    (5) Any regulations under this section shall be made by statutory instrument, subject to annulment in pursuance of a resolution of either House of Parliament.

Solemnization of marriage on approved premises

    46B.—(1) Any marriage on approved premises in pursuance of section 26(1)(bb) of this Act shall be solemnized in the presence of—

    (a) two witnesses, and

    (b) the superintendent registrar and a registrar of the registration district in which the premises are situated.

    (2) Without prejudice to the width of section 46A(2)(e) of this Act, the Secretary of State shall exercise his power to provide for the imposition of conditions as there mentioned so as to secure that members of the public are permitted to attend any marriage solemnized on approved premises in pursuance of section 26(1)(bb) of this Act.

    (3) Each of the persons contracting such a marriage shall make the declaration and use the form of words set out in section 44(3) of this Act in the case of marriages in registered buildings in the presence of a registrar.

    (4) No religious service shall be used at a marriage on approved premises in pursuance of section 26(1)(bb) of this Act."

    (3) The Schedule to this Act contains amendments consequential on those set out above in this section.

Registration districts in which marriages may be solemnized

    2.—(1) In section 35 of the Marriage Act 1949 (marriages in registration district in which neither party resides) after subsection (2) there shall be inserted—

    "(2A) A superintendent registrar may issue a certificate or, if the marriage is to be by licence, a certificate and licence, for the solemnization of a marriage in the office of another superintendent registrar, notwithstanding that the office is not within a registration district in which either of the persons to be married resides.

    (2B) A superintendent registrar may issue a certificate or, if the marriage is to be by licence, a certificate and licence, for the solemnization of a marriage on approved premises, notwithstanding that the premises are not within a registration district in which either of the persons to be married resides."

    (2) For section 36 of that Act (superintendent registrar to issue licences only for marriages to be solemnized in his registration district) there shall be substituted—

"Superintendent registrar not normally to issue licences for marriages in registered buildings outside his district

    36. Subject to section 35 of this Act, a superintendent registrar shall not issue a licence for the solemnization of a marriage in a registered building which is not within his registration district."

Short title and commencement

3.—(1) This Act may be cited as the Marriage Act 1994.

(2) This Act shall come into force on such day as the Secretary of State may appoint by order made by statutory instrument; and different days may be appointed for different purposes.

Section 1   SCHEDULE

APPROVED PREMISES: CONSEQUENTIAL AMENDMENTS

1. The Marriage Act 1949 shall be amended in accordance with paragraphs 2 to 8 below.

2. In section 27(3) (particulars to be stated in a notice of marriage) for "the church or other building in which" there shall be substituted "the church or other building or premises in or on which".

3. In section 49 (void marriages)—

(a) after paragraph (e) there shall be inserted—

"(ee) in the case of a marriage purporting to be in pursuance of section 26(1)(bb) of this Act, on any premises that at the time the marriage is solemnized are not approved premises;",

(b) the word "or" at the end of paragraph (f) and of paragraph (g) shall be omitted, and

(c) after paragraph (g) there shall be inserted—

"(gg) in the case of a marriage on approved premises, in the absence of the superintendent registrar of the registration district in which the premises are situated or in the absence of a registrar of that district; or".

4. In section 50(1) of that Act (person to whom superintendent registrar's certificate to be delivered) after paragraph (c) there shall be inserted—

"(cc) if the marriage is to be solemnized on approved premises, the registrar in whose presence the marriage is to be solemnized;".

5. After section 51(1) (fees of registrars for attending marriages) there shall be inserted—

"(1A) In the case of persons married on approved premises in pursuance of section 26(1)(bb) of this Act—

(a) subsection (1) of this section shall not apply, but

(b) the superintendent registrar in whose presence the persons are married shall be entitled to receive from them a fee of an amount determined in accordance with regulations under section 46A of this Act by the local authority that approved the premises."

6. In section 53 (persons by whom marriages are to be registered) after paragraph (f) there shall be added—

"(g) in the case of a marriage solemnized on approved premises in pursuance of section 26(1)(bb) of this Act, by the registrar in whose presence the marriage is solemnized."

7. In section 75 (offences relating to solemnization of marriages)—

(a) in subsection (2)(a)(ii) after "office" there shall be inserted ", approved premises",

(b) after subsection (2)(a) there shall be inserted—

"(aa) solemnizes a marriage purporting to be in pursuance of section 26(1)(bb) of this Act on premises that are not approved premises;",

(c) after subsection (2)(c) there shall be inserted—

"(cc) solemnizes a marriage on approved premises in pursuance of section 26(1)(bb) of this Act in the absence of a registrar of the district in which the premises are situated;", and

(d) in subsection (3)(d) for "section 26(1)(dd)" there shall be substituted "section 26(1)(bb) or (dd)".

8. In section 78(1) (interpretation) before the definition of "authorised chapel" there shall be inserted—

" "approved premises" means premises approved in accordance with regulations under section 46A of this Act as premises on which marriages may be solemnized in pursuance of section 26(1)(bb) of this Act;".

9. In section 1(1) of the Marriage (Registrar General's Licence) Act 1970 (marriages which may be solemnized by Registrar General's licence) for "elsewhere than at a registered building or the office of a superintendent registrar" there shall be substituted "elsewhere than at a registered building, the office of a superintendent registrar or approved premises".

INDEX

References in roman type are to sections of this Act: references in italic are to sections of the Marriage Act 1949 (as amended)

APPROVED PREMISES,
consequential amendments, 1, Sched.
outside registrar's district, 2, *36*
registers maintained by local authorities,
1(2), *46A(2)(j)*
regulations as to, 1(2), *46A*
solemnization of marriages on, 1(1), *46B*

COMMENCEMENT, 3(2)
CONSEQUENTIAL AMENDMENTS, 1, Sched.

FORM OF WORDS, 1(2), *46B(3)*

LOCAL AUTHORITIES, 1(2), *46(A)*

PUBLIC'S RIGHT TO ATTEND MARRIAGES, 1(2), *46B(2)*

REGISTRATION DISTRICTS, 2, *35(2A)–(2B)*
RELIGIOUS SERVICES, 1(2), *46B(4)*
RESIDENCE OF PARTIES, 2, *35(2B)*

SHORT TITLE, 3(1)
SOLEMNIZATION OF MARRIAGES ON APPROVED
PREMISES,
requirements for, 1(2), *46B*
SUPERINTENDENT REGISTRAR,
certificate of, 1, 2, *35*
presence at marriages, 1(2), *46B(1)(b)*

WITNESSES, 1(2), *46B(1)(A)*

SALE AND SUPPLY OF GOODS ACT 1994*

(1994 c. 35)

ARRANGEMENT OF SECTIONS

Provisions relating to the United Kingdom

SECT.
1. Implied term about quality.
2. Acceptance of goods and opportunity to examine them.
3. Right of partial rejection.

Provisions relating to England and Wales and Northern Ireland

4. Modification of remedies in non-consumer cases.

Provisions relating to Scotland

5. Remedies for breach of contract.
6. Provision equivalent to Part I of Supply of Goods and Services Act 1982.

General

7. Amendments and repeals.
8. Short title, commencement and extent.

SCHEDULES:
Schedule 1—Provision equivalent to Part I of Supply of Goods and Services Act 1982 for Scotland.
Schedule 2—Minor and consequential amendments.
Schedule 3—Repeals.

An Act to amend the law relating to the sale of goods; to make provision as to the terms to be implied in certain agreements for the transfer of property in or the hire of goods, in hire-purchase agreements and on the exchange of goods for trading stamps and as to the remedies for breach of the terms of such agreements; and for connected purposes.   [3rd November 1994]

PARLIAMENTARY DEBATES
Hansard, H.C. Vol. 237, col. 633; Vol. 243, col. 1054; Vol. 245, col. 526; H.L. Vol. 557, cols. 472, 960; Vol. 558, col. 686.
The Bill was discussed in Standing Committee C between March 16–23, 1994.

INTRODUCTION AND GENERAL NOTE
This Act was introduced as a Private Member's Bill sponsored by Mr David Clelland M.P. It implements most of the findings of the English and Scottish Law Commissions contained in their joint Report of May 1987: *The Sale and Supply of Goods* (Law Com. No. 160, Scot. Law Com. No. 104, Cm. 137) (henceforth "the Report"). The Report resulted from a remit dated January 25, 1979, by the then Lord Chancellor, to consider:
(a) whether the undertakings as to the quality and fitness of goods implied under the law relating to the sale of goods, hire-purchase and other contracts for the supply of goods, require amendment;
(b) the circumstances in which a person, to whom goods are supplied under a contract of sale, hire-purchase or other contract for the sale of goods, is entitled, where there has been a breach by the supplier of a term implied by statute, to (i) reject the goods and treat the contract as repudiated, (ii) claim against the supplier a diminution or extinction of the price, or (iii) claim damages against the supplier;
(c) the circumstances in which, by reason of the Sale of Goods Act 1893 (56 & 57 Vict. c. 71), the buyer loses the right to reject the goods;
and also to make recommendations.
It is a reflection of both the length of time that the Law Commissions took to respond, and the delay since the Report, that the 1893 Act has long since been repealed and replaced by the Sale

---

* Annotations by W. H. Thomas, Solicitor, Editor of The Encyclopedia of Consumer Law and W. C. H. Ervine, B.A., LL.B. (Dublin); LL.M. (London).

of Goods Act 1979 (c. 54) ("the 1979 Act"). A Bill, brought in by Mr Martyn Jones in 1989, to implement a report by the National Consumer Council on consumer guarantees had incorporated the three main proposals of the Law Commissions. Because of Government opposition to the suggested method of regulating guarantees that Bill was lost.

The Report proposed that the implied term as to merchantable quality should be redrawn so as to make it clear that it applied to minor defects and covered the durability of goods. For contracts for the sale of goods, it was proposed that there should be a right of partial rejection, and clarification of the circumstances in which the right to reject was lost. The terminology relating to implied terms was to be altered.

Section 1 implements the main proposal in the Report, that the phrase "merchantable quality" should be replaced by words more in tune with current trading conditions. The Report suggested "acceptable quality" but the draughtsman of the Act preferred "satisfactory quality". The section contains a non-exhaustive list of matters to be considered when it has to be decided whether quality meets the test.

Section 2 clarifies the question of acceptance, although it may not go as far as many consumer advocates desire, particularly in the light of the judgment in *Bernstein* v. *Pamson Motors (Golders Green)* [1987] 2 All E.R. 220 (see below).

Section 3 provides that if a buyer has accepted some of a batch of goods he does not lose the right to reject the rest if they do not conform to the contract.

Sections 4 and 5 provide that where a buyer is not acting as a consumer he may not reject goods if the breach is so slight that it would be unreasonable to do so—separate provisions are needed for England and Wales, and for Scotland.

Section 6 introduces Sched. 1 containing, for Scotland, provisions equivalent to Pt. I of the Supply of Goods and Services Act 1982 (c. 29) which, although not substantively changing Scots law, will bring it into line with the rest of the U.K.

Section 7 introduces Sched. 2 which sets out a considerable number of consequential amendments to existing legislation (some of which are reflected in appropriate repeals in Sched. 3).

In the Report in 1987 the Law Commissions drew attention to the fact that the task of putting what they called "patches" into the 1979 Act had proved hard. They said that there were many questions which could be asked to which the Act gave no answer and which no case had then decided. Anyone who specialises in consumer affairs will be familiar with a range of problems which arise daily and to which no sensible answer can be given; not least is the question of how long the right to reject remains alive, how to assess the conflicting interests of retailer and consumer once the curtain has descended—and then to indicate damages acceptable to both sides. It is only where the amount at stake is large that anyone is likely to litigate; virtually all the reported cases involve cars. This means that there is no body of case law to which reference may be made which makes the task of those advising consumers and retailers (and, to a lesser extent, manufacturers) even more difficult.

The problems mentioned by the Law Commissions led them then to conclude that it was doubtful how much further "patching" could continue and that it might be better in future to start with a new Act. There are those who have for many years believed that there was scope for a "Consumer Law Act" which would contain not only the law relating to the sale of goods and supply of services but also spell out what our continental civilian law colleagues call the "law of obligations". It would be very helpful to have a law that stated, in terms, for example; how a contract is made, as many people believe that a telephone conversation ordering goods or asking a plumber to call does not create legally binding relations; the circumstances in which a retailer is required to make a full refund of the price; when a person is entitled to a repair or replacement; and what consequential loss is properly claimable and when. With the increasing amount of E.U. civil legislation affecting consumers, package tour contracts, doorstep selling, distance selling, product safety and unfair contract terms, the argument becomes more and more cogent.

It is also the case that many of these alterations to the 1979 Act (as well as to the Supply of Goods (Implied Terms) Act 1973 (c. 13) ("the 1973 Act") and the Supply of Goods and Services Act 1982 (c. 29) ("the 1982 Act")) apply to commercial contracts for the sale and supply of goods and services which are equally affected by E.U. legal developments as by international conventions. This may make the amended 1979 Act even more unwieldy when trying to balance the interests of consumers (which this Act addresses) and commercial relationships.

Since 1980 there have been four cases about new cars and a short analysis of the way in which the courts considered how the implied terms fitted the given facts of those cases may assist.

In *Wadham Stringer (Clifton)* [1980] RTR 309 the plaintiff's new Princess 2200, bought in February 1978, had a series of faults, some trivial but others more serious, culminating in what he claimed was a major brake problem. He took the car back to the garage each time and the trouble was corrected. In May 1978, despite attempted cures including replacement of the main servo, discs and braking system, the brakes were still knocking, and he finally took legal advice and rejected the car for breach of the conditions in s.14 of the Sale of Goods Act 1979. The plaintiff lost his case. The judge said the technical evidence showed that there was no defect in the brakes although they did knock occasionally. The fact that he had suffered many irritating faults—all of which had been put right—did not entitle him to reject the car. At no time was the issue of "acceptance" discussed, although interestingly the defendants conceded that if there had been a brake problem making the car unroadworthy in May (three months after purchase) he would have been entitled to reject.

In *Rogers* v. *Parish (Scarborough)* [1987] Q.B. 933 the plaintiff bought a new Range Rover and rejected it after six months and 5,500 miles because of defective oil seals, gearbox defects and bodywork problems. The trial judge held against him on the basis that the defects did not make the car unmerchantable, unusable or unfit for any normal purpose, as they were capable of repair and were repaired at no cost to the aggrieved buyer. If the defects recurred and the buyer had lost confidence in the seller's ability to repair them, his remedy was to go to another garage. However, the Court of Appeal was unanimous in allowing the plaintiff's appeal. They referred to the ruling in *Lee* v. *York Coach & Marine* [1977] RTR 35, that the fact that a defect is repairable does not prevent it making goods unmerchantable if it is of a sufficient degree. The defects present in the car when delivered made it unfit for its intended purpose and unmerchantable. Again, curiously, there was no discussion of "acceptance" although the judgment means that even after six months the right to reject may not be lost. The Court of Appeal also concluded that, when looking at "merchantable quality", one would include not only the ability to drive from A to B but doing so "with the appropriate degree of comfort, ease of handling and reliability and, one might add, of pride in the vehicle's outward and interior appearance" depending on the market at which the car is aimed, *per* Mustill L.J. at p. 944, who added that the "buyer is entitled to value for his money".

This case was followed in *Raynham Farm Co.* v. *Symbol Motor Corp., The Times,* January 27, 1987, also involving a Range Rover, and s.13 of the 1979 Act. The car was rejected within 17 days of purchase and after 900 miles because of serious bodywork problems, the car having been badly damaged by fire and rebuilt. The basis of the claim was that the car was not "new" when sold and the judge held that clearly it was not, asking the rhetorical question first posed in *Ashington Piggeries* v. *Hill (Christopher)*, *Hill (Christopher)* v. *Norsildmel* [1972] A.C. 441: "[is] that what the buyer bargained for?" Had the plaintiff known of the actual history of the car he would not have bought it. Even applying the tests about newness laid down in *R.* v. *Ford Motor Co.* [1974] 1 W.L.R. 1220, the judge held that the major work which the car had undergone made it impossible to hold that, at the time it was sold to the plaintiff, it was new.

The legal issues raised in *Bernstein* v. *Pamson Motors (Golders Green)* [1987] 2 All E.R. 220 were never satisfactorily resolved. The plaintiff bought a new Nissan Laurel car at the end of 1984 and on January 3, 1985 after 140 miles and three weeks the engine seized up when he was driving along a motorway. Although it was fully repaired under warranty, the plaintiff had lost confidence in the car and sought to reject for breach of condition in s.14. The plaintiff lost his action, the judge holding that although the defect went far beyond anything which a buyer should be prepared to take on, Mr Bernstein had "accepted" the car. Although s.34 gives a buyer a reasonable time in which to inspect goods to see whether they conform, allowing the engine to be replaced was equivalent to an act of ownership and thus brought the matter within s.35. The plaintiff was only entitled to damages for the cost of petrol, five days without a car and something to make up for his ruined day out, totalling £237.50. Although reference was made to *Bartlett* v. *Marcus (Sidney)* [1965] 1 W.L.R. 1013 (see below) and to the *Raynham Farm* case *supra*, the judge was not referred to any of the other cases about cars where acceptance was a factor.

Mr Bernstein lodged a notice of appeal, but the matter was dropped when he received a full settlement from the garage. It would have been very helpful for all involved in consumer affairs to have had an up-to-date judgment from the Court of Appeal on when acceptance occurs and precludes rejection as it is one of the most commonly asked questions by retailers in all sectors.

There are six cases that deal with second hand cars. *Bartlett* v. *Marcus (Sidney)* [1965] 2 All E.R. 753, C.A., concerned a three-year-old Jaguar with a defective clutch which the plaintiff rejected after four weeks. The court decided, in effect, that as long as a used car could be driven out of the forecourt, the owner was stuck with it unless the defect was exceptional. Lord Denning said that: "a buyer should realise when he buys a second hand car, defects may appear sooner or later . . . even when he buys from a dealer, the most he can require is that it should be reasonably fit for . . . being driven along the road". This view was modified by the same judge in *Crowther* v. *Shannon Motor Co.* [1975] 1 W.L.R. 30. Here an eight-year-old Jaguar, with 82,165 miles on the clock, was driven more than 2,300 miles in the first three weeks with its new owner; it broke down on the M3 with a seized up engine. Both the trial judge and the Appeal Court upheld the plaintiff's claim for rejection, Denning L.J. distinguishing *Bartlett* by saying that if a car does not go for a reasonable time and the engine breaks up, the car was not fit for its purpose when sold.

Further confusion was caused by *Lee* v. *York Coach & Marine* [1977] RTR 35 where an eight-year-old Morris was rejected on the day it was purchased and was described as unsafe to drive by a vehicle examiner. Mrs Lee delayed issuing her summons in the Corby County Court until six months had passed and the Court of Appeal held that she was entitled to damages but only for breach of warranty as, by her delay, she was deemed to have accepted the car.

Two cases concerning used Rolls-Royces followed. In the first, *M & T Hurst Consultants* v. *Grange Motors*, October 16, 1981, Manchester High Court, was two years old, had a smell of petrol in the boot and a rattle. The plaintiff rejected it after three weeks when he had a report saying that the petrol smell was caused by vapour coming back into the car instead of escaping (making it potentially lethal) and the rattle was a badly attached shock absorber mounting. Judgment was awarded to the plaintiff.

In *Keeley* v. *Guy McDonald*, February 1, 1984, London High Court, the plaintiff, after a short period, did not reject but claimed damages for various defects in the engine and gearbox. He won and was awarded damages of the difference between the car's unrepaired value and its value if the implied conditions had not been broken.

Finally, in *Business Application Specialists* v. *Nationwide Credit*, April 18, 1988, C.A., a two-and-a-half-year-old Mercedes with 37,000 miles on the clock was found, after two months and 800 miles, to have excessive oil consumption and loss of power. Independent evidence said that these were unusual, but the cost of putting them right was small in comparison with the cost of the car. The judge said that the car was both fit and merchantable. The Court of Appeal upheld the judgment, repeating Lord Denning's words in *Bartlett*.

N.B. Extracts from the 1979 Act, with the major amendments made by this Act, can be found as an Appendix 1 at the back of the Act.

COMMENCEMENT
The Act will come into force on January 3, 1995.

ABBREVIATIONS
the 1893 Act: the Sale of Goods Act 1893 (c. 71).
the 1973 Act: the Supply of Goods (Implied Terms) Act 1973 (c. 13).
the 1979 Act: the Sale of Goods Act 1979 (c. 54).
the 1982 Act: the Sale of Goods and Services Act 1982 (c. 29).
the 1987 Act: the Consumer Protection Act 1987 (c. 43).

Provisions relating to the United Kingdom

Implied term about quality

1.—(1) In section 14 of the Sale of Goods Act 1979 (implied terms about quality or fitness) for subsection (2) there is substituted—

"(2) Where the seller sells goods in the course of a business, there is an implied term that the goods supplied under the contract are of satisfactory quality.

(2A) For the purposes of this Act, goods are of satisfactory quality if they meet the standard that a reasonable person would regard as satisfactory, taking account of any description of the goods, the price (if relevant) and all the other relevant circumstances.

(2B) For the purposes of this Act, the quality of goods includes their state and condition and the following (among others) are in appropriate cases aspects of the quality of goods—

(a) fitness for all the purposes for which goods of the kind in question are commonly supplied,

(b) appearance and finish,

(c) freedom from minor defects,

(d) safety, and

(e) durability.

(2C) The term implied by subsection (2) above does not extend to any matter making the quality of goods unsatisfactory—

(a) which is specifically drawn to the buyer's attention before the contract is made,

(b) where the buyer examines the goods before the contract is made, which that examination ought to reveal, or

(c) in the case of a contract for sale by sample, which would have been apparent on a reasonable examination of the sample."

(2) In section 15 of that Act (sale by sample) in subsection (2)(c) for "rendering them unmerchantable" there is substituted "making their quality unsatisfactory".

DEFINITIONS
"business": s.61(1) of the 1979 Act.
"buyer": s.61(1) of the 1979 Act.
"condition": s.11(3) of the 1979 Act.
"contract of sale": ss.2(1) and 61(1) of the 1979 Act.
"goods": s.61(1) of the 1979 Act.
"quality": s.14(2B) of the 1979 Act.
"seller": s.61(1) of the 1979 Act.
"warranty": s.61(1) of the 1979 Act.

GENERAL NOTE
This section applies to England and Wales and Scotland and substitutes a reformed definition of the implied terms as to quality for subss. (2) and (6) of s.14 of the 1979 Act and clarifies the relationship between s.14(2) and s.15(2)(c) of that Act. It applies to all contracts for the sale of goods where the seller sells in the course of a business, whether or not the buyer is a consumer or a commercial person, and applies to all kinds of goods. The reform, which replaces "merchantable quality" with "satisfactory quality", is intended to explain more clearly that the implied term (see below) covers all aspects of the goods, including both aesthetic and functional aspects.

Subs. 14(2) of the 1979 Act
The former definition of "merchantable" quality was derived from Victorian cases but although it was suitable at the time the law was codified in what became the Sale of Goods Act 1893 because that process drew heavily on an analysis of both the reported cases (which were all commercial ones) and of commercial usage, it gradually became clear that it was not suitable for all cases. It became necessary for judges to explain what the word "merchantable" meant, which was sometimes defined as meaning that goods had to be fit for their purpose, which rather defeated the object of having two separate implied terms—one for quality in s.14(2) the other for fitness for use in s.14(3). Indeed, looking at the modern reports on cars, there is a judicial blurring of the two which has made life more difficult for the practitioner.

The adjective "satisfactory" was chosen, rather than "acceptable" as proposed by the Law Commissions, for two reasons. First, what might be regarded as acceptable—a new car with a dent in the bodywork goes just as well as one without and is therefore acceptable as a means of transport—might not be satisfactory, because the buyer expects a product which is as near perfect as can be. Secondly, there might well be confusion in the mind of laymen between "acceptable" and "acceptance" (that vital concept dealt with later in both this Act and the 1979 Act).

The word "term" is used here and elsewhere in the amendments to the 1979 Act (and in the Trading Stamps Act 1964 (c. 71) and the 1973 Act) instead of the familiar terminology of "condition" and "warranty". This is because of the different approach to the building blocks of a contract in England and Wales on the one hand, where both words are familiar and have different meanings and where the breach of each gives rise to different consequences, and in Scotland on the other, where they are unknown and where the concept of a "material part" of a contract is preferred. Using "term" enables the same implied terms to apply in both jurisdictions and avoids repetition of similar but not identical language.

Subs. 14(2A) of the 1979 Act
This provides the first part of the new definition in the form of a general test based on the standard expected by a reasonable person to be "satisfactory" taking account of any description, price and other relevant circumstances.

Subs. 14(2B) of the 1979 Act
This contains the second part of the new definition by inserting a non-exhaustive list of factors to be taken into consideration when measuring how satisfactory goods are. The words "state or condition" are taken from the existing definition of "quality" in s.61(1) of the 1979 Act.

Subs. 14(2B)(a) of the 1979 Act
The Law Commissions concluded that goods of a particular description and price should be fit for all their common purposes unless there was an indication to the contrary. If the trader fails to indicate that the goods are not fit for all their common purposes then he may be in breach of the

implied quality term if he sells something commonly supplied for two purposes but which is in fact only fit for one.

Subs. 14(2B)(b), (c) of the 1979 Act

Originally it was intended that these three items, appearance, finish and freedom from minor defects, should be taken together but the Law Commissions finally concluded that "appearance and finish" should be in a separate category from "freedom from minor defects" to avoid any doubt that a minor defect must necessarily be a defect in appearance or finish. While second hand goods might be expected to have blemishes or defects and thus not be breaches of contract, a new car with an oil leak would have a "minor defect" and, even though it could be remedied quickly, the buyer will now have a remedy, unlike the buyer in *Millars of Falkirk* v. *Turpie* [1976] S.L.T. 66.

Subs. 14(2B)(d) of the 1979 Act

This overlaps with the "general safety requirement" contained in Pt. II of the Consumer Protection Act 1987 (c. 43) which places an obligation on the seller (or anyone else in the chain of distribution) to ensure that consumer goods are reasonably safe having regard to all the circumstances. That Act imposes criminal sanctions, although the test of safety in s.10(2) will be a useful rule of thumb when looking at the requirement of safety in the new sale of goods regime. Regard should also be had to the "product safety" liability contained in Pt. I of the 1987 Act.

Subs. 14(2B)(e) of the 1979 Act

The new requirement of durability takes effect at the time of supply and, from the consumer's point of view, is one of the most important reforms. Although the lack of durability will only become apparent at a later stage, it will show that, at the point of sale, the goods were not sufficiently durable.

Subs. 14(2C) of the 1979 Act

There have always been statutory limitations to the implied term of merchantable quality and these are currently set out in the provisos to s.14(2) of the 1979 Act. Paragraphs (2C)(a) and (b) contain those two provisos which limit the availability of the implied quality term in two different situations arising before the contract is made. Defects specifically drawn to the buyer's attention are excluded and defects which would have been revealed by an examination are excluded—but only when the buyer actually did examine them. Paragraph (2C)(c) is an added limitation to sales by sample which makes it clear that the implied quality term does not apply to defects which would have been apparent on a reasonable examination of the sample even if the buyer had not in fact made such an examination.

Section 1(2) amends s.15 of the 1979 Act consequential upon the new para. (2C)(c) above.

Acceptance of goods and opportunity to examine them

2.—(1) In section 35 of the Sale of Goods Act 1979 (acceptance) for the words from "when he intimates" to "(2)" there is substituted—
   "subject to subsection (2) below—
      (a) when he intimates to the seller that he has accepted them, or
      (b) when the goods have been delivered to him and he does any act in relation to them which is inconsistent with the ownership of the seller.
   (2) Where goods are delivered to the buyer, and he has not previously examined them, he is not deemed to have accepted them under subsection (1) above until he has had a reasonable opportunity of examining them for the purpose—
      (a) of ascertaining whether they are in conformity with the contract, and
      (b) in the case of a contract for sale by sample, of comparing the bulk with the sample.
   (3) Where the buyer deals as consumer or (in Scotland) the contract of sale is a consumer contract, the buyer cannot lose his right to rely on subsection (2) above by agreement, waiver or otherwise.
   (4) The buyer is also deemed to have accepted the goods when after the lapse of a reasonable time he retains the goods without intimating to the seller that he has rejected them.

(5) The questions that are material in determining for the purposes of subsection (4) above whether a reasonable time has elapsed include whether the buyer has had a reasonable opportunity of examining the goods for the purpose mentioned in subsection (2) above.

(6) The buyer is not by virtue of this section deemed to have accepted the goods merely because—

    (a) he asks for, or agrees to, their repair by or under an arrangement with the seller, or

    (b) the goods are delivered to another under a sub-sale or other disposition.

(7) Where the contract is for the sale of goods making one or more commercial units, a buyer accepting any goods included in a unit is deemed to have accepted all the goods making the unit; and in this subsection "commercial unit" means a unit division of which would materially impair the value of the goods or the character of the unit.

    (8)".

(2) In section 34 of that Act (buyer to have opportunity to examine goods)—

    (a) the words from the beginning to "(2)" are repealed; and

    (b) at the end of that section there is inserted "and, in the case of a contract for sale by sample, of comparing the bulk with the sample."

DEFINITIONS

"buyer": s.61(1) of the 1979 Act.
"commercial unit": s.35(7) of the 1979 Act (as inserted).
"consumer contract": s.61(1) of the 1979 Act (as inserted).
"deals as consumer": s.61(5A) of the 1979 Act (as inserted).
"delivery": s.61(1) of the 1979 Act.
"goods": s.61(1) of the 1979 Act.
"seller": s.61(1) of the 1979 Act.

GENERAL NOTE

This section applies to England and Wales and Scotland. It changes the operation of ss.34 and 35 of the 1979 Act and reorganises their contents to make the relationship clearer.

Under the existing law, the moment when goods are "accepted" is of crucial importance, especially to consumers. Once it has passed, the right to reject the goods, cancel the contract and recover the price paid is lost for ever. As no one knows when the point of acceptance is reached because the 1979 Act refers only to a "reasonable time" and judgments speak of different periods of time (three weeks in *Bernstein* v. *Pamson Motors, supra*; six months in *Rogers* v. *Parish, supra*), there remains a great deal of uncertainty. Added to that, the present law "deems" acceptance when a buyer does something which "is inconsistent with the ownership of the seller". This would include having goods repaired or invoking a manufacturer's guarantee—both of which are steps which any reasonable consumer would regard as sensible and not a reason, should the defect prove incapable of being put right, to deprive him of his right to reject. Experience has also shown that many consumers do not want to reject the goods; they want to keep them once they have been repaired, adjusted or made to conform.

In addition, the 1979 Act "deems" acceptance when the buyer intimates that he has accepted the goods and, to this end, many buyers are asked to sign "acceptance notes", "delivery notes" or "receipts" which the seller may use to prove that the right to reject had been lost—even though the buyer might genuinely and reasonably believe that he was merely signing a piece of paper to show that the goods had been delivered to the right place at the right time.

When the Law Commissions first consulted they proposed that a consumer should not, by signing an acceptance note, lose the right to reject unless he had actually had a reasonable opportunity of examining the goods. Although this was originally intended only to benefit consumers, the new wording extends this to all buyers and covers all types of intimation. No contracting out is permitted in consumer transactions.

Subs. 35(1) of the 1979 Act

This contains the first two circumstances in which a buyer is deemed to have accepted goods: (a) intimation and (b) an inconsistent act after delivery. There is nothing new here.

Subs. 35(2) of the 1979 Act

This subsection places in a more logical order the right of examination and the consequences where a reasonable opportunity to do so is not provided. It repeats the situation in s.34(1) of the 1979 Act; in addition there is added the right, in a sale by sample, to compare the bulk with the sample (the 1994 Act repeals s.15(2)(b) of the 1979 Act).

Despite the changes made by the Act, there still remain considerable areas of uncertainty masked by the familiar use of "reasonable". If one buys a camera in the summer sales intending to give it as a Christmas present, and keeps it in the original box unopened for several months, will one be regarded as having had a "reasonable time" to examine the camera for conformity in the intervening six months and therefore have lost the right to reject? Similarly with a pair of ski-boots bought at the end of the season and kept, unused, for 10 or 11 months. In Standing Committee C, col. 37, on March 16, 1994 it was claimed that in this situation a court would consider the period of non-use irrelevant. With respect to the opinion there expressed, the decision in *Bernstein* v. *Pamson Motors, supra,* raises serious doubts about how the judicial mind might approach this issue.

Subs. 35(3) of the 1979 Act

In order to prevent consumers being prejudiced by signing any acceptance note or other document containing terms which might tend to mean that they had accepted the goods, this subsection provides that the right to examine cannot be lost by contracting out, waiver, estoppel or personal bar. There is no similar provision in commercial situations.

Subss. 35(4) and (5) of the 1979 Act

This repeats the third, and most common, situation for deemed acceptance; where the buyer does nothing and time passes. At some point it will be too late for rejection. When that arrives is a matter for the courts. Subsection (5) makes it clear that whether a reasonable opportunity for examination was available should be taken into account when judging whether a reasonable time has elapsed.

Subs. 35(6) of the 1979 Act

Consumers and their advisers are given considerable help by the insertion of two new qualifications for the circumstances in which acceptance is deemed. Paragraph (6)(a) means that the perfectly normal step of asking for a repair by the seller does not of itself amount to an act inconsistent with the ownership of the seller; para. (6)(b) specifies that a sub-sale "or other disposition" (like a gift) does not amount to acceptance. It will also enable a retailer, who was required by a consumer to take back defective goods, to pursue his claim against the supplier without being held to have accepted the goods because of the effluxion of time or the sale.

Subs. 35(7) of the 1979 Act

The Law Commissions thought it wrong that a buyer might be able to reject part of the goods and keep the rest. They believed that the buyer should not be allowed to break down the goods in order to reject something less than the whole. They gave examples; a buyer who accepted part only of a set (a single volume of an encyclopedia sold as a set) would be deemed to have accepted the whole; a buyer who accepted one shoe of a pair would be deemed to have accepted the pair (but this was not to prevent the purchase of one of a number of identical items, if each was in fact a self-contained unit).

Section 2(2) makes consequential amendments to s.34 of the 1979 Act.

Right of partial rejection

3.—(1) After section 35 of the Sale of Goods Act 1979 there is inserted the following section—

> **"Right of partial rejection**
> 35A.—(1) If the buyer—
> (a) has the right to reject the goods by reason of a breach on the part of the seller that affects some or all of them, but
> (b) accepts some of the goods, including, where there are any goods unaffected by the breach, all such goods,
> he does not by accepting them lose his right to reject the rest.
> (2) In the case of a buyer having the right to reject an instalment of goods, subsection (1) above applies as if references to the goods were references to the goods comprised in the instalment.

(3) For the purposes of subsection (1) above, goods are affected by a breach if by reason of the breach they are not in conformity with the contract.

(4) This section applies unless a contrary intention appears in, or is to be implied from, the contract."

(2) At the beginning of section 11(4) of that Act (effect of accepting goods) there is inserted "Subject to section 35A below".

(3) Section 30(4) of that Act (rejection of goods not within contract description) is repealed.

<small>DEFINITIONS</small>
"buyer": s.61(1) of the 1979 Act.
"goods": s.61(1) of the 1979 Act.
"seller": s.61(1) of the 1979 Act.

<small>GENERAL NOTE</small>
This section applies to England and Wales and Scotland and inserts s.35A into the 1979 Act, containing a right of partial rejection. Under the existing law, s.30(4) of the 1979 Act gives a buyer a right of partial rejection when the seller delivers goods which were ordered mixed with other goods not within the contract. The buyer may accept the goods in conformity and reject the rest or reject everything. If he had accepted some of the goods, he would be treated as having accepted all (including those outside the contract). The right to reject only applied when the unwanted goods were of a different description, and not merely when they were defective.

Now, unless the parties to a contract otherwise agree, the section gives the buyer a general right of partial rejection where some of the goods delivered do not conform to the contract, for whatever reason, not merely failure to correspond with description. This extends the existing rules about the delivery of the wrong quantity of goods (see general note to s.4 below).

Subsection 35A(1) specifies the circumstances in which the right of partial rejection arises. So long as the buyer has not accepted the goods (and so lost the right to reject), the effect of this subsection is that he may:
(a) accept all the conforming goods and reject all the non-conforming goods; or
(b) accept all the conforming goods and some of those which do not conform, and reject the rest; or
(c) reject all the goods; or
(d) keep all the goods;
(e) keep most of the goods but reject only the most defective.

For example, if one bought 100 tiles and found that, on delivery, 40 were cracked, one will now be able to retain the 60 and reject the 40 or retain the 60 and some of the 40 (for use where cut tiles are needed) and reject the rest; but the right to reject the 100 is not lost.

Subsection 35A(2) provides that where a buyer has the right to reject an instalment of goods, the same right of partial rejection will apply to the goods in the instalment.

Subsection 35A(3) makes it clear that the expression "affected by the breach" in subs. 35A(1) means that the goods are not in conformity with the contract.

Subsection 35A(4) permits contracting-out (in consumer contracts as in commercial ones) either expressly or by implication.

Subsection (2) of this section adds a qualification to s.11(4) of the 1979 Act. That section, which applies to England and Wales only, enacts that once goods have been accepted, the right to reject is lost and what would before acceptance have been a claim for breach of condition has to be treated as one for breach of warranty. The buyer has to retain the goods, notwithstanding the defects and his claim is limited to damages.

Subsection (3) repeals s.30(4) of the 1979 Act.

Provisions relating to England and Wales and Northern Ireland

Modification of remedies in non-consumer cases

4.—(1) After section 15 of the Sale of Goods Act 1979 there is inserted the following—

"Miscellaneous

Modification of remedies for breach of condition in non-consumer cases
15A.—(1) Where in the case of a contract of sale—
(a) the buyer would, apart from this subsection, have the right to

reject goods by reason of a breach on the part of the seller of a term implied by section 13, 14 or 15 above, but

(b) the breach is so slight that it would be unreasonable for him to reject them,

then, if the buyer does not deal as consumer, the breach is not to be treated as a breach of condition but may be treated as a breach of warranty.

(2) This section applies unless a contrary intention appears in, or is to be implied from, the contract.

(3) It is for the seller to show that a breach fell within subsection (1)(b) above.

(4) This section does not apply to Scotland."

(2) In section 30 of that Act (delivery of shortfall or excess) after subsection (2) there is inserted—

"(2A) A buyer who does not deal as consumer may not—

(a) where the seller delivers a quantity of goods less than he contracted to sell, reject the goods under subsection (1) above, or

(b) where the seller delivers a quantity of goods larger than he contracted to sell, reject the whole under subsection (2) above,

if the shortfall or, as the case may be, excess is so slight that it would be unreasonable for him to do so.

(2B) It is for the seller to show that a shortfall or excess fell within subsection (2A) above.

(2C) Subsections (2A) and (2B) above do not apply to Scotland."

DEFINITIONS
"buyer": s.61(1) of the 1979 Act.
"contract of sale": s.2(. . and s.61(1) of the 1979 Act.
"deal as consumer": s.61 (5A) of the 1979 Act (as inserted).
"goods": s.61(1) of the 19/1 Act.
"warranty": s.61(1) of the 1979 Act.

GENERAL NOTE
This section, which applies only to England and Wales, amends the 1979 Act in two ways which modify the right of rejection in non-consumer cases.

First, subs. (1) inserts s.15A into the 1979 Act. Subsection 15A(1) provides that, where a breach is so slight as to make rejection unreasonable, a non-consumer buyer will have to treat it as a breach of warranty, and claim damages, and not as a breach of condition. This provision will apply unless an intention to the contrary appears in the contract or by implication. Subsection 15A(3) places the onus for showing that the breach was so slight on the seller.

Secondly, subs. (2) inserts subss. 30(2A), (2B) and (2C) into of the 1979 Act. This extends the principle of preventing unreasonable rejection to cases where the wrong quantity is delivered. In non-consumer contracts, rejection of the whole will not be allowed where the excess or shortfall was so slight that it would be unreasonable; but there is a right to reject the excess, however slight. The onus of proof of the slightness of the shortfall or excess lies on the seller.

Provisions relating to Scotland

Remedies for breach of contract

5.—(1) After section 15A of the Sale of Goods Act 1979, which is inserted by section 4(1) above, there is inserted the following section—

"Remedies for breach of contract as respects Scotland
15B.—(1) Where in a contract of sale the seller is in breach of any term of the contract (express or implied), the buyer shall be entitled—

   (a) to claim damages, and

   (b) if the breach is material, to reject any goods delivered under the contract and treat it as repudiated.

   (2) Where a contract of sale is a consumer contract, then, for the purposes of subsection (1)(b) above, breach by the seller of any term (express or implied)—

   (a) as to the quality of the goods or their fitness for a purpose,

   (b) if the goods are, or are to be, sold by description, that the goods will correspond with the description,

   (c) if the goods are, or are to be, sold by reference to a sample, that the bulk will correspond with the sample in quality,

shall be deemed to be a material breach.

   (3) This section applies to Scotland only."

   (2) In section 30 of that Act (delivery of shortfall or excess) before subsection (3) there is inserted—

   "(2D) Where the seller delivers a quantity of goods—

   (a) less than he contracted to sell, the buyer shall not be entitled to reject the goods under subsection (1) above,

   (b) larger than he contracted to sell, the buyer shall not be entitled to reject the whole under subsection (2) above,

unless the shortfall or excess is material.

   (2E) Subsection (2D) above applies to Scotland only."

   (3) After section 53 of that Act there is inserted the following section—

"Measure of damages as respects Scotland

   53A.—(1) The measure of damages for the seller's breach of contract is the estimated loss directly and naturally resulting, in the ordinary course of events, from the breach.

   (2) Where the seller's breach consists of the delivery of goods which are not of the quality required by the contract and the buyer retains the goods, such loss as aforesaid is prima facie the difference between the value of the goods at the time of delivery to the buyer and the value they would have had if they had fulfilled the contract.

   (3) This section applies to Scotland only."

DEFINITIONS

"buyer": s.61(1) of the 1979 Act.
"consumer contract": s.25(1) of the Unfair Contract Terms Act 1977
"contract of sale": ss.2(1) and 61(1) of the 1979 Act
"goods": s.61(1) of the 1979 Act
"seller": s.61(1) of the 1979 Act.

GENERAL NOTE

This section applies only to Scotland and implements several recommendations of the report. It inserts ss.15B and 53A into the 1979 Act as well as inserting subs. (2D) into s.30 of that Act.

Subs. (1)

This subsection inserts s.15B into the 1979 Act setting out the buyer's basic remedies of damages and treating the contract as repudiated. Earlier attempts to take account of the different approach of Scots law to breach of contract were not successful and have led to uncertainty. The inappropriate English terms "condition" and "warranty" were used and in s.11(5) of the 1979 Act an unsatisfactory attempt was made to take account of the Scottish differences. To understand fully how this section operates it is necessary to realise that the various terms implied in contracts of sale by ss.12 to 15 of the 1979 Act will no longer be described as "conditions" or "warranties", merely "implied terms". The new s.14 of the 1979 Act is drafted in this way (see s.1(1) of the 1994 Act) and the other implied terms are amended in similar fashion by Sched. 2, para. 5. Section 11(5) of the 1979 Act is repealed by the same Schedule.

Section s.15B(1) sets out the buyer's basic remedies in terminology directly relevant to Scots law. Material breach is the basis for the right to treat the contract as repudiated and to reject the goods.

Section s.15B(2) makes it clear that in consumer contracts the implied terms relating to quality, fitness for a purpose, correspondence with description of the goods, or that the bulk will correspond with a sample in quality, give rise to material breaches entitling the buyer to treat the contract as repudiated and reject the goods. Dicta in *Millars of Falkirk* v. *Turpie* [1976] S.L.T. (Notes) 66 had raised doubts as to whether this was the effect of s.11(5) of the 1979 Act.

"Consumer contract" is given the same meaning as in s.25(1) of the Unfair Contract Terms Act 1977 (c. 50) as a result of Sched. 2, para. 3(9)(a)(i).

Subs. (2)

This subsection inserts subs. (2D) into s.30 of the 1979 Act which deals with the rules on wrong quantity. The effect of the provision is that a buyer will not be entitled to reject all the goods where the wrong quantity has been delivered, unless the shortfall or excess is material. The Law Commissions' report points out that materiality will depend on the circumstances. As they observe in para. 6.21 of the report, in some cases even a slight shortfall would be material; in others it would be wholly immaterial, and should not justify rejection of the whole of the goods.

Subs. (3)

This subsection inserts s.53A into the 1979 Act which applies only to Scotland. This is a further consequence of the policy of using terminology appropriate to Scots law. Section 53 of the 1979 Act is disapplied to Scotland by Sched. 2, para. 3(7).

Provision equivalent to Part I of Supply of Goods and Services Act 1982

6. Schedule 1 to this Act shall have effect for the purpose of making provision equivalent to Part I of the Supply of Goods and Services Act 1982 for Scotland.

GENERAL NOTE

When the Supply of Goods and Services Act 1982 (c. 29) ("the 1982 Act") was enacted no part of it applied to Scotland. In Pt. 7 of the report, the Scottish Law Commission recommended that Pt. I should be extended, with the necessary modifications, to Scotland. The appropriate provisions are set out in Sched. 1 to this Act; see the general note thereto.

General

Amendments and repeals

7.—(1) Schedule 2 to this Act (which makes minor and consequential amendments of the Sale of Goods Act 1979 and the Uniform Laws on International Sales Act 1967, and makes amendments of enactments relating to the supply of goods corresponding to the amendments of that Act of 1979 made by this Act) shall have effect.

(2) The enactments mentioned in Schedule 3 to this Act are repealed to the extent specified in column 3 of that Schedule.

GENERAL NOTE

This section is self-explanatory. Annotations to the consequential amendments set out in Sched. 2 appear at the end of that Schedule.

Short title, commencement and extent

8.—(1) This Act may be cited as the Sale and Supply of Goods Act 1994.

(2) This Act shall come into force at the end of the period of two months beginning with the day on which it is passed.

(3) This Act has effect in relation to contracts of sale of goods, hire purchase agreements, contracts for the transfer of goods, contracts for the hire of goods and redemptions of trading stamps for goods (as the case may be) made after this Act comes into force.

(4) This Act extends to Northern Ireland.

GENERAL NOTE

This Act comes into force on January 3, 1995. Subsection (3) provides that contracts for the sale or supply of goods made before the commencement date are not affected by the new provisions.

SCHEDULES

Section 6   SCHEDULE 1

PROVISION EQUIVALENT TO PART I OF SUPPLY OF GOODS AND SERVICES ACT 1982 FOR SCOTLAND

1. After Part I of the Supply of Goods and Services Act 1982 there is inserted the following Part—

"PART IA

SUPPLY OF GOODS AS RESPECTS SCOTLAND

Contracts for the transfer of property in goods

The contracts concerned

11A.—(1) In this Act in its application to Scotland a "contract for the transfer of goods" means a contract under which one person transfers or agrees to transfer to another the property in goods, other than an excepted contract.

(2) For the purposes of this section an excepted contract means any of the following—

(a) a contract of sale of goods;

(b) a hire-purchase agreement;

(c) a contract under which the property in goods is (or is to be) transferred in exchange for trading stamps on their redemption;

(d) a transfer or agreement to transfer for which there is no consideration;

(e) a contract intended to operate by way of mortgage, pledge, charge or other security.

(3) For the purposes of this Act in its application to Scotland a contract is a contract for the transfer of goods whether or not services are also provided or to be provided under the contract, and (subject to subsection (2) above) whatever is the nature of the consideration for the transfer or agreement to transfer.

Implied terms about title, etc.

11B.—(1) In a contract for the transfer of goods, other than one to which subsection (3) below applies, there is an implied term on the part of the transferor that in the case of a transfer of the property in the goods he has a right to transfer the property and in the case of an agreement to transfer the property in the goods he will have such a right at the time when the property is to be transferred.

(2) In a contract for the transfer of goods, other than one to which subsection (3) below applies, there is also an implied term that—

(a) the goods are free, and will remain free until the time when the property is to be transferred, from any charge or encumbrance not disclosed or known to the transferee before the contract is made, and

(b) the transferee will enjoy quiet possession of the goods except so far as it may be disturbed by the owner or other person entitled to the benefit of any charge or encumbrance so disclosed or known.

(3) This subsection applies to a contract for the transfer of goods in the case ·of which there appears from the contract or is to be inferred from its circumstances an intention that the transferor should transfer only such title as he or a third person may have.

(4) In a contract to which subsection (3) above applies there is an implied term that all charges or encumbrances known to the transferor and not known to the transferee have been disclosed to the transferee before the contract is made.

(5) In a contract to which subsection (3) above applies there is also an implied term that none of the following will disturb the transferee's quiet possession of the goods, namely—

(a) the transferor;

(b) in a case where the parties to the contract intend that the transferor should transfer only such title as a third person may have, that person;

(c) anyone claiming through or under the transferor or that third person otherwise than under a charge or encumbrance disclosed or known to the transferee before the contract is made.

(6) In section 21 of the 1977 Act after subsection (3) there is inserted the following subsection—

"(3A) Notwithstanding anything in the foregoing provisions of this section, any term of a contract which purports to exclude or restrict liability for breach of the obligations arising under section 11B of the Supply of Goods and Services Act 1982 (implied terms about title, freedom from encumbrances and quiet possession in certain contracts for the transfer of property in goods) shall be void."

Implied terms where transfer is by description

11C.—(1) This section applies where, under a contract for the transfer of goods, the transferor transfers or agrees to transfer the property in the goods by description.

(2) In such a case there is an implied term that the goods will correspond with the description.

(3) If the transferor transfers or agrees to transfer the property in the goods by reference to a sample as well as by description it is not sufficient that the bulk of the goods corresponds with the sample if the goods do not also correspond with the description.

(4) A contract is not prevented from falling within subsection (1) above by reason only that, being exposed for supply, the goods are selected by the transferee.

Implied terms about quality or fitness

11D.—(1) Except as provided by this section and section 11E below and subject to the provisions of any other enactment, there is no implied term about the quality or fitness for any particular purpose of goods supplied under a contract for the transfer of goods.

(2) Where, under such a contract, the transferor transfers the property in goods in the course of a business, there is an implied term that the goods supplied under the contract are of satisfactory quality.

(3) For the purposes of this section and section 11E below, goods are of satisfactory quality if they meet the standard that a reasonable person would regard as satisfactory, taking account of any description of the goods, the price (if relevant) and all the other relevant circumstances.

(4) The term implied by subsection (2) above does not extend to any matter making the quality of goods unsatisfactory—

(a) which is specifically drawn to the transferee's attention before the contract is made,

(b) where the transferee examines the goods before the contract is made, which that examination ought to reveal, or

(c) where the property in the goods is, or is to be, transferred by reference to a sample, which would have been apparent on a reasonable examination of the sample.

(5) Subsection (6) below applies where, under a contract for the transfer of goods, the transferor transfers the property in goods in the course of a business and the transferee, expressly or by implication, makes known—

(a) to the transferor, or

(b) where the consideration or part of the consideration for the transfer is a sum payable by instalments and the goods were previously sold by a credit-broker to the transferor, to that credit-broker,

any particular purpose for which the goods are being acquired.

(6) In that case there is (subject to subsection (7) below) an implied term that the goods supplied under the contract are reasonably fit for the purpose, whether or not that is a purpose for which such goods are commonly supplied.

(7) Subsection (6) above does not apply where the circumstances show that the transferee does not rely, or that it is unreasonable for him to rely, on the skill or judgment of the transferor or credit-broker.

(8) An implied term about quality or fitness for a particular purpose may be annexed by usage to a contract for the transfer of goods.

(9) The preceding provisions of this section apply to a transfer by a person who in the course of a business is acting as agent for another as they apply to a transfer by a principal in the course of a business, except where that other is not transferring in the course of a busi-

ness and either the transferee knows that fact or reasonable steps are taken to bring it to the transferee's notice before the contract concerned is made.

Implied terms where transfer is by sample

11E.—(1) This section applies where, under a contract for the transfer of goods, the transferor transfers or agrees to transfer the property in the goods by reference to a sample.

(2) In such a case there is an implied term—

(a) that the bulk will correspond with the sample in quality;

(b) that the transferee will have a reasonable opportunity of comparing the bulk with the sample; and

(c) that the goods will be free from any defect, making their quality unsatisfactory, which would not be apparent on reasonable examination of the sample.

(3) For the purposes of this section a transferor transfers or agrees to transfer the property in goods by reference to a sample where there is an express or implied term to that effect in the contract concerned.

Remedies for breach of contract

11F.—(1) Where in a contract for the transfer of goods a transferor is in breach of any term of the contract (express or implied), the other party to the contract (in this section referred to as "the transferee") shall be entitled—

(a) to claim damages; and

(b) if the breach is material, to reject any goods delivered under the contract and treat it as repudiated.

(2) Where a contract for the transfer of goods is a consumer contract and the transferee is the consumer, then, for the purposes of subsection (1)(b) above, breach by the transferor of any term (express or implied)—

(a) as to the quality of the goods or their fitness for a purpose;

(b) if the goods are, or are to be, transferred by description, that the goods will correspond with the description;

(c) if the goods are, or are to be, transferred by reference to a sample, that the bulk will correspond with the sample in quality,

shall be deemed to be a material breach.

(3) In subsection (2) above, "consumer contract" has the same meaning as in section 25(1) of the 1977 Act; and for the purposes of that subsection the onus of proving that a contract is not to be regarded as a consumer contract shall lie on the transferor.

Contracts for the hire of goods

The contracts concerned

11G.—(1) In this Act in its application to Scotland a "contract for the hire of goods" means a contract under which one person ("the supplier") hires or agrees to hire goods to another, other than an excepted contract.

(2) For the purposes of this section, an excepted contract means any of the following—

(a) a hire-purchase agreement;

(b) a contract under which goods are (or are to be) hired in exchange for trading stamps on their redemption.

(3) For the purposes of this Act in its application to Scotland a contract is a contract for the hire of goods whether or not services are also provided or to be provided under the contract, and (subject to subsection (2) above) whatever is the nature of the consideration for the hire or agreement to hire.

Implied terms about right to transfer possession etc.

11H.—(1) In a contract for the hire of goods there is an implied term on the part of the supplier that—

(a) in the case of a hire, he has a right to transfer possession of the goods by way of hire for the period of the hire; and

(b) in the case of an agreement to hire, he will have such a right at the time of commencement of the period of the hire.

(2) In a contract for the hire of goods there is also an implied term that the person to whom the goods are hired will enjoy quiet possession of the goods for the period of the hire except so far as the possession may be disturbed by the owner or other person entitled to the benefit of any charge or encumbrance disclosed or known to the person to whom the goods are hired before the contract is made.

(3) The preceding provisions of this section do not affect the right of the supplier to repossess the goods under an express or implied term of the contract.

Implied terms where hire is by description

11I.—(1) This section applies where, under a contract for the hire of goods, the supplier hires or agrees to hire the goods by description.

(2) In such a case there is an implied term that the goods will correspond with the description.

(3) If under the contract the supplier hires or agrees to hire the goods by reference to a sample as well as by description it is not sufficient that the bulk of the goods corresponds with the sample if the goods do not also correspond with the description.

(4) A contract is not prevented from falling within subsection (1) above by reason only that, being exposed for supply, the goods are selected by the person to whom the goods are hired.

Implied terms about quality or fitness

11J.—(1) Except as provided by this section and section 11K below and subject to the provisions of any other enactment, there is no implied term about the quality or fitness for any particular purpose of goods hired under a contract for the hire of goods.

(2) Where, under such a contract, the supplier hires goods in the course of a business, there is an implied term that the goods supplied under the contract are of satisfactory quality.

(3) For the purposes of this section and section 11K below, goods are of satisfactory quality if they meet the standard that a reasonable person would regard as satisfactory, taking account of any description of the goods, the consideration for the hire (if relevant) and all the other relevant circumstances.

(4) The term implied by subsection (2) above does not extend to any matter making the quality of goods unsatisfactory—

(a) which is specifically drawn to the attention of the person to whom the goods are hired before the contract is made, or

(b) where that person examines the goods before the contract is made, which that examination ought to reveal; or

(c) where the goods are hired by reference to a sample, which would have been apparent on reasonable examination of the sample.

(5) Subsection (6) below applies where, under a contract for the hire of goods, the supplier hires goods in the course of a business and the person to whom the goods are hired, expressly or by implication, makes known—

(a) to the supplier in the course of negotiations conducted by him in relation to the making of the contract; or

(b) to a credit-broker in the course of negotiations conducted by that broker in relation to goods sold by him to the supplier before forming the subject matter of the contract,

any particular purpose for which the goods are being hired.

(6) In that case there is (subject to subsection (7) below) an implied term that the goods supplied under the contract are reasonably fit for that purpose, whether or not that is a purpose for which such goods are commonly supplied.

(7) Subsection (6) above does not apply where the circumstances show that the person to whom the goods are hired does not rely, or that it is unreasonable for him to rely, on the skill or judgment of the hirer or credit-broker.

(8) An implied term about quality or fitness for a particular purpose may be annexed by usage to a contract for the hire of goods.

(9) The preceding provisions of this section apply to a hire by a person who in the course of a business is acting as agent for another as they apply to a hire by a principal in the course of a business, except where that other is not hiring in the course of a business and either the person to whom the goods are hired knows that fact or reasonable steps are taken to bring it to that person's notice before the contract concerned is made.

Implied terms where hire is by sample

11K.—(1) This section applies where, under a contract for the hire of goods, the supplier hires or agrees to hire the goods by reference to a sample.

(2) In such a case there is an implied term—

(a) that the bulk will correspond with the sample in quality; and

(b) that the person to whom the goods are hired will have a reasonable opportunity of comparing the bulk with the sample; and

(c) that the goods will be free from any defect, making their quality unsatisfactory, which would not be apparent on reasonable examination of the sample.

(3) For the purposes of this section a supplier hires or agrees to hire goods by reference to a sample where there is an express or implied term to that effect in the contract concerned.

Exclusion of implied terms, etc.

Exclusion of implied terms etc.
11L.—(1) Where a right, duty or liability would arise under a contract for the transfer of goods or a contract for the hire of goods by implication of law, it may (subject to subsection (2) below and the 1977 Act) be negatived or varied by express agreement, or by the course of dealing between the parties, or by such usage as binds both parties to the contract.

(2) An express term does not negative a term implied by the preceding provisions of this Part of this Act unless inconsistent with it.

(3) Nothing in the preceding provisions of this Part of this Act prejudices the operation of any other enactment or any rule of law whereby any term (other than one relating to quality or fitness) is to be implied in a contract for the transfer of goods or a contract for the hire of goods."

2. In section 18(1) of that Act—
(a) in paragraph (b) of the definition of "credit-brokerage" after "bailment" there is inserted "or as regards Scotland the hire";
(b) in the definition of "goods"—
    (i) for "include all personal chattels (including" there is substituted "includes all personal chattels, other than things in action and money, and as regards Scotland all corporeal moveables; and in particular "goods" includes";
    (ii) for "or bailment" there is substituted "bailment or hire";
    (iii) "), other than things in action and money" is omitted.

3. In section 18(2) of that Act after "assignment" there is inserted "assignation".

4. In section 20(6) of that Act after "Act" there is inserted "except Part IA, which extends only to Scotland" and for "but not" there is substituted "and Parts I and II do not extend".

DEFINITIONS
"businesses": s.18(1) of the 1982 Act.
"contract for the transfer of goods": s.11A(1) of the 1982 Act.
"credit-broker": s.18(1) of the 1982 Act.
"goods": s.18(1) of the 1982 Act as amended by Sched. 1, para. 2(6).
"hire-purchase agreement": s.18(1) of the 1982 Act.
"property": s.18(1) of the 1982 Act.
"quality": s.18(3) of the 1982 Act as inserted by Sched. 2, para. 6(10).
"transferee": s.18(1) of the 1982 Act.
"transferor": s.18(1) of the 1982 Act.

GENERAL NOTE
This Schedule inserts Pt. IA into the 1982 Act, providing, with the necessary modifications, an equivalent to the provisions in Pt. I which have operated since January 1983 in England and Wales. The main modifications that are necessary are the elimination of the references to the English terms "conditions" and "warranties" and the redrafting of the provisions on hire, to avoid the use of the English concept of bailment. Paragraph 2 of the Schedule amends s.18 of the 1982 Act, which is the interpretation section. Paragraph 3 contains an amendment to take account of Scottish terminology. Paragraph 4 makes minor amendments to the 1982 Act consequent upon the addition of Pt. IA.

Part IA of the 1982 Act
Paragraph 1, setting out Pt. IA of the 1982 Act, can be divided into three sets of sections. Section 11A defines "contracts for the transfer of goods", and, in ss.11B to 11F, the terms to be implied therein and the remedies for their breach are set out.

Section 11G defines a contract for the hire of goods and ss.11H to 11K set out the terms to be implied in such contracts. In the case of contracts for the hire of goods there are no statutory provisions relating to remedies for breach. The Scottish Law Commission (see para. 4.34 of the report) concluded that the common law remedies were satisfactory. Finally, s.11L deals with exclusion of liability.

The effect of the insertion of Pt. IA is that a regime similar to that providing implied terms in contracts of sale is now provided for contracts of hire, barter, trading-in and various contracts where goods are exchanged for coupons, tokens, vouchers or labels. An advantage is that uncertainty is removed from the law in relation to trading-in and hire. It was not clear whether trading-in involved a contract of sale or was barter. See T.B. Smith, *Exchange or Sale?* (1974) 48

Tulane L.R. 1029 where various approaches are discussed, and *Sneddon* v. *Durant* [1982] S.L.T. (Sh.Ct.) 39 where a contract involving the trade-in of a car was held to be a sale. In relation to the terms to be implied in such contracts and the remedies for their breach the classification no longer matters. It may still be important for other aspects of a transaction such as passing of the property and risk. For a recent case where such an issue arose in relation to barter, see *O'Neill* v. *Chief Constable of Strathclyde* [1994] S.C.L.R. 253.

In the case of hire there has been doubt over whether there is any implied warranty against latent defects and over the scope of any implied warranty as to fitness for purpose. Part IA resolves these doubts.

In relation to barter the legislation differs from the common law to some degree. The Scots common law of barter and of sale were essentially the same and terms were implied that goods should conform to any description applied to them and be priceworthy. In so far as priceworthiness differs from the concept of satisfactory quality, the legislation alters the law relating to barter. As far as remedies are concerned it certainly does. At common law the only remedy for breach of the implied terms was rejection and rescission of the contract. It was not possible to retain the goods and claim a diminution of the price; see *Urquart* v. *Wylie* [1953] S.L.T. (Sh. Ct.) 87. On the other hand, where the defect was latent the remedy was rather wider than under the 1979 Act in that damages could still be obtained where the defect was not discovered for some time. See the authorities cited in footnote 92 on p.17 of the report. Under this Part the remedies of damages and rejection are available. As the provisions on acceptance in the 1979 Act do not apply the common law rule permitting damages for latent defects still applies.

s.11A

Subsection 1 provides that contracts analogous to sale under which the property in goods is transferred or agreed to be transferred are subject to this Part with certain exceptions.

Subsection 2 sets out the contracts which are not within the definition of a "contract for the transfer of goods". The first three have in common the fact that separate legislation provides similar implied terms. The relevant legislation is, in the case of sale, the 1979 Act, ss.12 to 15, for hire-purchase, the Supply of Goods (Implied Terms) Act 1973 (c. 13), ss.8 to 12, and the Trading Stamps Act 1964 (c. 71), s.4. Subsection (2)(d) excludes gifts. It is quite understandable that genuine gifts, especially those between private individuals, should be outside the ambit of the legislation. However, difficult questions may arise in relation to the "free gifts" associated with sales promotions. The difficulties of classifying such transactions were clearly displayed in the speeches of the House of Lords in *Esso Petroleum* v. *Customs and Excise Commissioners* [1976] 1 W.L.R. 1. From those speeches it would seem that the "gift" might be classified as a sale in some cases and thus subject to the 1979 Act, or some other kind of contract and so subject to this Act. It would appear from para. 7.3 of the report that the Scottish Law Commission take this view. Subsection (2)(e) adopts an exclusion similar to that in s.62(4) of the 1979 Act.

Subsection (3) clarifies the law in relation to contracts involving the transfer of goods and the provision of services in that it makes clear that the provision of services does not take it outside the definition of a contract for the transfer of goods. Such a provision was necessary because there is considerable doubt over the legal categorisation of what, in England, is known as a contract for work and materials relating to such common transactions as having a car serviced or repaired or central heating installed. For a discussion of the background see *The Laws of Scotland: the Stair Memorial Encyclopaedia*, Vol. 6, para. 66.

s.11B

This section is closely modelled on s.12 of the 1979 Act with some changes such as the substitution of "transferor" for "seller" and "transferee" for "buyer".

Subsection (6) adds subs. (3A) to the Unfair Contract Terms Act 1977 providing that any term of a contract purporting to exclude or restrict the implied terms about title contained in this section shall be void.

s.11C

This section is modelled on s.13 of the 1979 Act. By virtue of s.21(1)(a) of the Unfair Contract Terms Act 1977 the liability arising under this section cannot be excluded or restricted by reference to any contract term in a consumer contract. In other cases it may be excluded or restricted in so far as fair and reasonable.

s.11D

This section is modelled on s.14 of the 1979 Act as amended by this Act. It should be noted that the definition of the term "satisfactory quality" is inserted in a convoluted way. Subsection (3) sets out the general definition of this term. Unlike the new version of s.14 of the 1979 Act, this is not followed by a subsection setting out the factors to be taken into account in assessing satisfactory quality. Instead, these factors are set out in Sched. 2, para. 6(10) which sets out the minor and consequential amendments to the 1982 Act. On the meaning of "satisfactory quality" see the annotation to s.1, above.

By virtue of s.21(1)(a) of the Unfair Contract Terms Act 1977 the liability arising under this section cannot be excluded or restricted by reference to any contract term in a consumer contract. In other cases it may be excluded or restricted in so far as fair and reasonable.

s.11E

This section implies in contracts for the transfer of goods, terms identical to those implied in contracts of sale by s.15 of the 1979 Act. By virtue of s.21(1)(a) of the Unfair Contract Terms Act 1977 the liability arising under this section cannot be excluded or restricted by reference to any contract term in a consumer contract. In other cases it may be excluded or restricted in so far as fair and reasonable.

s.11F

The Scottish Law Commission in para. 4.33 of the report recommended that the same remedies should be available in relation to other contracts for the supply of goods as are applied to contracts of sale. In relation to the contracts for the transfer of goods as defined by s.11A(1) this is achieved by this section. The effect of the reform is succinctly set out in para. 4.33 of the report as follows:

"...on the supplier's breach the person supplied with the goods would always be entitled to damages for any loss even if he retained defective goods (thus changing the common law rule) and would also, if the breach were material, be entitled to reject the goods and treat the contract as repudiated. In consumer contracts, breach of any of the implied terms relating to quality, fitness for purpose, description, or sample (and of any of the express terms on the same matters) would be deemed to be material, as in sale. With non-consumer contracts the buyer would have to establish a material breach to be entitled to reject the goods and treat the contract as repudiated ... The consequences of rejecting the goods and treating the contract as repudiated would, as in the case of sale and as in the case of these other contracts at present, be governed by common law. So would the loss of the right to reject".

Even in the case of consumer contracts, the implied term about title is not deemed to be material. However, as the Law Commissions observe in the report (footnote 24 on p.42), in practically all cases it would be material. They cite, as a rare case where it might not be, a situation where the defect in the seller's title is cured almost immediately after the relevant time.

Subsection (3) applies the definition of "consumer contract" set out in s.25(1) of the Unfair Contract Terms Act 1977 to this section and also provides, as does that Act, that the onus of proving that a contract is not a consumer contract is on the person transferring the goods.

s.11G

The Scottish Law Commission in Part 7 of its report, noted that it: "was clearly undesirable that there should be doubt and uncertainty about the implied terms in a contract of hire". Sections 11H to 11K remove such doubts by providing statutorily implied terms. This section defines a contract of hire for the purposes of the Act in terms which place it in the category of *locatio conductio rei*, the letting to hire of a thing, as opposed to the other contracts of location. Excluded are contracts of hire-purchase and transactions involving trading stamps where similar terms are implied by the Supply of Goods (Implied Terms) Act 1973 and the Trading Stamps Act 1964 respectively. A wide range of contracts with various names such as "contract hire", "rental lease", "finance lease" or "equipment lease" will be covered. The essential feature is that the supplier gives possession of the goods to another. This means that some transactions, popularly referred to as hire, will not fall within this part of the Act because they are not, in law, contracts of hire. Examples would be the "hire" of a coach and driver by a club to go on an outing or, in a commercial context, the "hiring" by a building contractor of a crane and its driver. In neither case does the customer have possession of the goods though they may have the benefit of them. These contracts are contracts for services.

Subsection (3) makes clear that a contract is still one of hire despite the fact that services are provided, and that the nature of the consideration for the hire is immaterial to determining its nature. This establishes that a transaction where hire is combined with the provision of services as, for example, where the supplier of equipment undertakes to keep it serviced and repaired, is still a contract of hire. The hire element will be subject to this Act while the services will be subject to the common law relating to services.

s.11H

This section implements the recommendation of the Scottish Law Commission that there should be implied terms that the supplier has the right to transfer possession of goods by way of hire and that the person to whom the goods are hired will have quiet possession. Subsection (3) makes it clear that these provisions do not affect any right which the supplier may have to repossess the goods. By virtue of s.21(1)(b) of the Unfair Contract Terms Act 1977 these terms may be excluded or restricted by means of a contractual term if it is fair and reasonable.

s.11I

This section follows the model of the 1979 Act in implying terms that the goods hired should correspond with their description and, where appropriate, with any sample. By virtue of s.21(1) (a) of the Unfair Contract Terms Act 1977 the liability arising under this section cannot be excluded or restricted by reference to any contract term in a consumer contract. In other cases it may be excluded or restricted in so far as is fair and reasonable.

s.11J

This section is modelled on s.14 of the 1979 Act as amended by this Act. It should be noted that the definition of the term "satisfactory quality" is achieved in a convoluted way. Subsection (3) sets out the general definition of this term. Unlike the new version of s.14 of the 1979 Act this is not followed by a subsection setting out the factors to be taken into account in assessing satisfactory quality. Instead, these factors are set out in Sched. 2, para. 6(10) which sets out the minor and consequential amendments to the 1982 Act. On the meaning of "satisfactory quality" see the annotation to s.1, above.

By virtue of s.21(1)(a) of the Unfair Contract Terms Act 1977 the liability arising under this section cannot be excluded or restricted by reference to any contract term in a consumer contract. In other cases it may be excluded or restricted in so far as is fair and reasonable.

s.11K

This section implements the Scottish Law Commission's recommendations about the terms to be implied when goods are hired by reference to a sample. Once again the 1979 Act model is followed. By virtue of s.21(1)(a) of the Unfair Contract Terms Act 1977 the liability arising under this section cannot be excluded or restricted by reference to any contract term in a consumer contract. In other cases it may be excluded or restricted in so far as is fair and reasonable.

Section 7   SCHEDULE 2

MINOR AND CONSEQUENTIAL AMENDMENTS

The Trading Stamps Act 1964 (c. 71)

1.—(1) Section 4 of the Trading Stamps Act 1964 (terms to be implied on redemption of trading stamps) is amended as follows.

(2) In subsection 1(a) and (b) for "warranty" there is substituted "term" and for subsection (1)(c) there is substituted—

"(c) an implied term that the goods are of satisfactory quality."

(3) For subsections (2) and (3) there is substituted—

"(2) For the purposes of paragraph (c) of subsection (1) of this section, goods are of satisfactory quality if they meet the standard that a reasonable person would regard as satisfactory, taking account of any description of the goods and all the other relevant circumstances.

(2A) For the purposes of that paragraph, the quality of goods includes their state and condition and the following (among others) are in appropriate cases aspects of the quality of goods—

(a) fitness for all the purposes for which goods of the kind in question are commonly supplied,

(b) appearance and finish,

(c) freedom from minor defects,

(d) safety, and

(e) durability.

(2B) The term implied by that paragraph does not extend to any matter making the quality of goods unsatisfactory—

(a) which is specifically drawn to the attention of the person obtaining the goods before or at the time of redemption, or

(b) where that person examines the goods before or at the time of redemption, which that examination ought to reveal.

(3) As regards England and Wales, the terms implied by subsection (1) of this section are warranties."

The Trading Stamps Act (Northern Ireland) 1965 (c. 6 (N.I.))

2.—(1) Section 4 of the Trading Stamps Act (Northern Ireland) 1965 (warranties to be implied on redemption of trading stamps) is amended as follows.

(2) For subsection (1)(c) there is substituted—

"(c) an implied warranty that the goods are of satisfactory quality."

(3) For subsection (2) there is substituted—

"(2) For the purposes of paragraph (c) of subsection (1), goods are of satisfactory quality if they meet the standard that a reasonable person would regard as satisfactory, taking account of any description of the goods and all the other relevant circumstances.

(3) For the purposes of that paragraph, the quality of goods includes their state and condition and the following (among others) are in appropriate cases aspects of the quality of goods—

(a) fitness for all the purposes for which goods of the kind in question are commonly supplied,

(b) appearance and finish,

(c) freedom from minor defects,

(d) safety, and

(e) durability.

(4) The warranty implied by that paragraph does not extend to any matter making the quality of goods unsatisfactory—

(a) which is specifically drawn to the attention of the person obtaining the goods before or at the time of redemption, or

(b) where that person examines the goods before or at the time of redemption, which that examination ought to reveal."

The Uniform Laws on International Sales Act 1967 (c. 45)

3. In section 1 of the Uniform Laws on International Sales Act 1967 (application of Uniform Law on the International Sale of Goods) in subsection (4)(c) for "12 to 15" there is substituted "12 to 15B".

The Supply of Goods (Implied Terms) Act 1973 (c. 13)

4.—(1) The Supply of Goods (Implied Terms) Act 1973 is amended as follows.

(2) In section 8 (implied terms as to title)—

(a) for "condition" (in subsection (1)(a)) and for "warranty" (in subsections (1)(b), (2)(a) and (2)(b)) there is substituted "term"; and

(b) at the end of that section there is inserted—

"(3) As regards England and Wales and Northern Ireland, the term implied by subsection (1)(a) above is a condition and the terms implied by subsections (1)(b), (2)(a) and (2)(b) above are warranties."

(3) In section 9 (bailing or hiring by description)—

(a) in subsection (1) for "condition" there is substituted "term"; and

(b) after that subsection there is inserted—

"(1A) As regards England and Wales and Northern Ireland, the term implied by subsection (1) above is a condition."

(4) In section 10 (implied undertakings as to quality or fitness)—

(a) for subsection (2) there is substituted—

"(2) Where the creditor bails or hires goods under a hire purchase agreement in the course of a business, there is an implied term that the goods supplied under the agreement are of satisfactory quality.

(2A) For the purposes of this Act, goods are of satisfactory quality if they meet the standard that a reasonable person would regard as satisfactory, taking account of any description of the goods, the price (if relevant) and all the other relevant circumstances.

(2B) For the purposes of this Act, the quality of goods includes their state and condition and the following (among others) are in appropriate cases aspects of the quality of goods—

(a) fitness for all the purposes for which goods of the kind in question are commonly supplied,

(b) appearance and finish,

(c) freedom from minor defects,

(d) safety, and

(e) durability.

(2C) The term implied by subsection (2) above does not extend to any matter making the quality of goods unsatisfactory—

(a) which is specifically drawn to the attention of the person to whom the goods are bailed or hired before the agreement is made,

(b) where that person examines the goods before the agreement is made, which that examination ought to reveal, or

(c) where the goods are bailed or hired by reference to a sample, which would have been apparent on a reasonable examination of the sample";

(b) for "condition or warranty" (in subsections (1) and (4)) and for "condition" (in subsection (3)) there is substituted "term"; and

(c) after subsection (6) there is inserted—

"(7) As regards England and Wales and Northern Ireland, the terms implied by subsections (2) and (3) above are conditions."

(5) In section 11 (samples)—

(a) at the beginning there is inserted "(1)";

(b) for "condition" there is substituted "term";

(c) in paragraph (c) for "rendering them unmerchantable" there is substituted "making their quality unsatisfactory"; and

(d) at the end there is inserted—

"(2) As regards England and Wales and Northern Ireland, the term implied by subsection (1) above is a condition."

(6) After that section there is inserted the following section—

"Modification of remedies for breach of statutory condition in non-consumer cases

11A.—(1) Where in the case of a hire purchase agreement—

(a) the person to whom goods are bailed would, apart from this subsection, have the right to reject them by reason of a breach on the part of the creditor of a term implied by section 9, 10 or 11(1)(a) or (c) above, but

(b) the breach is so slight that it would be unreasonable for him to reject them,

then, if the person to whom the goods are bailed does not deal as consumer, the breach is not to be treated as a breach of condition but may be treated as a breach of warranty.

(2) This section applies unless a contrary intention appears in, or is to be implied from, the agreement.

(3) It is for the creditor to show—

(a) that a breach fell within subsection (1)(b) above, and

(b) that the person to whom the goods were bailed did not deal as consumer.

(4) The references in this section to dealing as consumer are to be construed in accordance with Part I of the Unfair Contract Terms Act 1977.

(5) This section does not apply to Scotland."

(7) For section 12 (exclusion of implied terms and conditions) there is substituted the following section—

"Exclusion of implied terms

12. An express term does not negative a term implied by this Act unless inconsistent with it."

(8) After section 12 there is inserted the following section—

"Remedies for breach of hire-purchase agreement as respects Scotland

12A.—(1) Where in a hire-purchase agreement the creditor is in breach of any term of the agreement (express or implied), the person to whom the goods are hired shall be entitled—

(a) to claim damages, and

(b) if the breach is material, to reject any goods delivered under the agreement and treat it as repudiated.

(2) Where a hire-purchase agreement is a consumer contract, then, for the purposes of subsection (1) above, breach by the creditor of any term (express or implied)—

(a) as to the quality of the goods or their fitness for a purpose,

(b) if the goods are, or are to be, hired by description, that the goods will correspond with the description,

(c) if the goods are, or are to be, hired by reference to a sample, that the bulk will correspond with the sample in quality,
shall be deemed to be a material breach.

(3) In subsection (2) above "consumer contract" has the same meaning as in section 25(1)
of the Unfair Contract Terms Act 1977; and for the purposes of that subsection the onus of
proving that a hire-purchase agreement is not to be regarded as a consumer contract shall
lie on the creditor.

(4) This section applies to Scotland only."

(9) In section 15 (supplementary)—

(a) in subsection (1), the words from ""condition" and "warranty"" to "material to the
agreement" are omitted;

(b) subsection (2) is omitted; and

(c) in subsection (4), for "condition or warranty" there is substituted "term".

The Sale of Goods Act 1979 (c. 54)

5.—(1) The Sale of Goods Act 1979 is amended as follows.

(2) In section 11 (when condition to be treated as warranty)—

(a) for subsection (1) there is substituted—
"(1) This section does not apply to Scotland."; and

(b) subsection (5) is omitted.

(3) In section 12 (implied terms about title etc.)—

(a) for "condition" (in subsection (1)) and for "warranty" (in subsections (2), (4) and (5))
there is substituted "term"; and

(b) after subsection (5) there is inserted—
"(5A) As regards England and Wales and Northern Ireland, the term implied by subsection (1) above is a condition and the terms implied by subsections (2), (4) and (5) above are
warranties."

(4) In section 13 (sale by description)—

(a) in subsection (1) for "condition" there is substituted "term"; and

(b) after that subsection there is inserted—
"(1A) As regards England and Wales and Northern Ireland, the term implied by subsection (1) above is a condition."

(5) In section 14 (implied terms about quality or fitness)—

(a) for "condition or warranty" (in subsections (1) and (4)) and for "condition" (in subsection
(3)) there is substituted "term"; and

(b) for subsection (6) there is substituted—
"(6) As regards England and Wales and Northern Ireland, the terms implied by subsections (2) and (3) above are conditions."

(6) In section 15 (sale by sample)—

(a) in subsection (2), for "condition" there is substituted "term" and paragraph (b) is omitted;
and

(b) for subsection (3) there is substituted—
"(3) As regards England and Wales and Northern Ireland, the term implied by subsection (2) above is a condition."

(7) In section 53 (remedy for breach of warranty) for subsection (5) there is substituted—
"(5) This section does not apply to Scotland."

(8) In section 55 (exclusion of implied terms) in subsection (2) for "condition or warranty" (in
both places) there is substituted "term".

(9) In section 61 (interpretation)—

(a) in subsection (1)—

(i) after the definition of "buyer" there is inserted—
""consumer contract" has the same meaning as in section 25(1) of the Unfair Contract Terms Act 1977; and for the purposes of this Act the onus of proving that a
contract is not to be regarded as a consumer contract shall lie on the seller"; and

(ii) the definition of "quality" is omitted;

(b) subsection (2) is omitted; and

(c) after subsection (5) there is inserted—
"(5A) References in this Act to dealing as consumer are to be construed in accordance
with Part I of the Unfair Contract Terms Act 1977; and, for the purposes of this Act, it is for
a seller claiming that a buyer does not deal as consumer to show that he does not."

(10) For the heading "*Conditions and warranties*" that precedes sections 10 to 14 there is
substituted the heading "*Implied terms etc.*".

The Supply of Goods and Services Act 1982 (c. 29)

6.—(1) The Supply of Goods and Services Act 1982 is amended as follows.

(2) In section 1 (the contracts concerned), in subsections (1) and (3) after "Act" there is inserted "in its application to England and Wales and Northern Ireland".

(3) In section 4 (contracts for transfer: quality or fitness) for subsections (2) and (3) there is substituted—

"(2) Where, under such a contract, the transferor transfers the property in goods in the course of a business, there is an implied condition that the goods supplied under the contract are of satisfactory quality.

(2A) For the purposes of this section and section 5 below, goods are of satisfactory quality if they meet the standard that a reasonable person would regard as satisfactory, taking account of any description of the goods, the price (if relevant) and all the other relevant circumstances.

(3) The condition implied by subsection (2) above does not extend to any matter making the quality of goods unsatisfactory—

(a) which is specifically drawn to the transferee's attention before the contract is made,

(b) where the transferee examines the goods before the contract is made, which that examination ought to reveal, or

(c) where the property in the goods is transferred by reference to a sample, which would have been apparent on a reasonable examination of the sample.";

and subsection (9) is omitted.

(4) In section 5 (transfer by sample)—

(a) in subsection (2)(c), for "rendering them unmerchantable" there is substituted "making their quality unsatisfactory"; and

(b) subsection (3) is omitted.

(5) After section 5 there is inserted the following section—

"**Modification of remedies for breach of statutory condition in non-consumer cases**

5A.—(1) Where in the case of a contract for the transfer of goods—

(a) the transferee would, apart from this subsection, have the right to treat the contract as repudiated by reason of a breach on the part of the transferor of a term implied by section 3, 4 or 5(2)(a) or (c) above, but

(b) the breach is so slight that it would be unreasonable for him to do so,

then, if the transferee does not deal as consumer, the breach is not to be treated as a breach of condition but may be treated as a breach of warranty.

(2) This section applies unless a contrary intention appears in, or is to be implied from, the contract.

(3) It is for the transferor to show that a breach fell within subsection (1)(b) above."

(6) In section 6 (the contracts concerned) in subsections (1) and (3) after "Act" there is inserted "in its application to England and Wales and Northern Ireland".

(7) In section 9 (contracts for hire: quality or fitness) for subsections (2) and (3) there is substituted—

"(2) Where, under such a contract, the bailor bails goods in the course of a business, there is an implied condition that the goods supplied under the contract are of satisfactory quality.

(2A) For the purposes of this section and section 10 below, goods are of satisfactory quality if they meet the standard that a reasonable person would regard as satisfactory, taking account of any description of the goods, the consideration for the bailment (if relevant) and all the other relevant circumstances.

(3) The condition implied by subsection (2) above does not extend to any matter making the quality of goods unsatisfactory—

(a) which is specifically drawn to the bailee's attention before the contract is made,

(b) where the bailee examines the goods before the contract is made, which that examination ought to reveal, or

(c) where the goods are bailed by reference to a sample, which would have been apparent on a reasonable examination of the sample.";

and subsection (9) is omitted.

(8) In section 10 (hire by sample)—

(a) in subsection (2)(c), for "rendering them unmerchantable" there is substituted "making their quality unsatisfactory"; and

(b) subsection (3) is omitted.

(9) After section 10 there is inserted the following section—

"**Modification of remedies for breach of statutory condition in non-consumer cases**

10A.—(1) Where in the case of a contract for the hire of goods—

(a) the bailee would, apart from this subsection, have the right to treat the contract as repudiated by reason of a breach on the part of the bailor of a term implied by section 8, 9 or 10(2)(a) or (c) above, but

(b) the breach is so slight that it would be unreasonable for him to do so,

then, if the bailee does not deal as consumer, the breach is not to be treated as a breach of condition but may be treated as a breach of warranty.

(2) This section applies unless a contrary intention appears in, or is to be implied from, the contract.

(3) It is for the bailor to show that a breach fell within subsection (1)(b) above."

(10) In section 18 (interpretation) in subsection (1) the definition of "quality" is omitted and at the end of that section there is inserted—

"(3) For the purposes of this Act, the quality of goods includes their state and condition and the following (among others) are in appropriate cases aspects of the quality of goods—

(a) fitness for all the purposes for which goods of the kind in question are commonly supplied,

(b) appearance and finish,

(c) freedom from minor defects,

(d) safety, and

(e) durability.

(4) References in this Act to dealing as consumer are to be construed in accordance with Part I of the Unfair Contract Terms Act 1977; and, for the purposes of this Act, it is for the transferor or bailor claiming that the transferee or bailee does not deal as consumer to show that he does not."

GENERAL NOTE

This Schedule replaces the words "condition" and "warranty" with the neutral word "term" in most existing legislation which is concerned with the sale of goods:

(a) the Trading Stamps Act 1964 (c. 71);

(b) the Trading Stamps Act (Northern Ireland) 1965 (c. 6 (N.I.));

(c) the Uniform Laws on International Sales Act 1967 (c. 45);

(d) the Supply of Goods (Implied Terms) Act 1973 (c. 13);

(e) the Sale of Goods Act 1979 (c. 54); and

(f) the Supply of Goods and Services Act 1982 (c. 29).

In the 1964 Act, the 1965 Act, the 1973 Act and the 1982 Act it substitutes new sections containing the revised implied quality terms. In the 1967 Act there are substituted new section numbers to take account of the new sections 15A and 15B inserted in the 1979 Act. In the 1979 Act minor amendments are made to give effect to this Act and new definitions are added to s.61(1) and by s.61(5A).

Para. 4(8)

This subparagraph inserts s.12A into the Supply of Goods (Implied Terms) Act 1973 which applies to Scotland. It is another example of the implementation of the policy advocated by the Scottish Law Commission, of providing a regime of remedies which is both consistent across the range of contracts for the supply of goods and which uses the appropriate Scottish terminology.

Section 7   SCHEDULE 3

REPEALS

Chapter	Short title	Extent of repeal
1973 c. 13.	The Supply of Goods (Implied Terms) Act 1973.	In section 15, in subsection (1), the words from ""condition" and "warranty"" to "material to the agreement" and subsection (2).
1979 c. 54.	The Sale of Goods Act 1979.	Section 11(5). Section 15(2)(b). Section 30(4). In section 34, the words from the beginning to "(2)". In section 61, in subsection (1) the definition of "quality" and subsection (2).

Chapter	Short title	Extent of repeal
1982 c. 29.	The Supply of Goods and Services Act 1982.	Section 4(9). Section 5(3). Section 9(9). Section 10(3). Section 17(1). In section 18(1), the definition of "quality" and in the definition of "goods" the words "), other than things in action and money".

APPENDIX

TEXT OF SECTIONS 11 TO 15B, 30, 34 TO 35A AND 53A OF THE SALE OF GOODS ACT 1979 (c. 54) AS AMENDED BY THE SALE AND SUPPLY OF GOODS ACT 1994 (c. 35)

When condition to be treated as warranty

11.—(1) **This section does not apply to Scotland.**

[(1) *Subsections (2) to (4) and (7) below do not apply to Scotland and subsection (5) below applies only to Scotland.*]

(2) Where a contract of sale is subject to a condition to be fulfilled by the seller, the buyer may waive the condition, or may elect to treat the breach of the condition as a breach of warranty and not as a ground for treating the contract as repudiated.

(3) Whether a stipulation in a contract of sale is a condition, the breach of which may give rise to a right to treat the contract as repudiated, or a warranty, the breach of which may give rise to a claim for damages but not to a right to reject the goods and treat the contract as repudiated, depends in each case on the construction of the contract; and a stipulation may be a condition, though called a warranty in the contract.

(4) **Subject to section 35A below,** where a contract of sale is not severable and the buyer has accepted the goods or part of them, the breach of a condition to be fulfilled by the seller can only be treated as a breach of warranty, and not as a ground for rejecting the goods and treating the contract as repudiated, unless there is an express or implied term of the contract to that effect.

[(5) *In Scotland, failure by the seller to perform any material part of a contract of sale is a breach of contract, which entitles the buyer either within a reasonable time after delivery to reject the goods and treat the contract as repudiated, or to return the goods and treat the failure to perform such material part as a breach which may give rise to a claim for compensation or damages.*]

(6) Nothing in this section affects a condition or warranty whose fulfilment is excused by law by reason of impossibility or otherwise.

(7) Paragraph 2 of Schedule 1 below applies in relation to a contract made before 22 April 1967 or (in the application of this Act to Northern Ireland) 28 July 1967.

AMENDMENTS

Sched. 2 to the 1994 Act substituted subs. (1) and repealed subs. (5).

Section 3(2) of the 1994 Act inserted the words in subs. (4).

Implied terms about title, etc.

12.—(1) In a contract of sale, other than one to which subsection (3) below applies, there is an implied **term** [*condition*] on the part of the seller that in the case of a sale he has the right to sell the goods, and in the case of an agreement to sell he will have such a right at the time when the property is to pass.

(2) In a contract of sale, other than one to which subsection (3) below applies, there is also an implied **term** [*warranty*] that—

(a) the goods are free, and will remain free until the time when the property is to pass, from any charge or encumbrance not disclosed or known to the buyer before the contract is made, and

(b) the buyer will enjoy quiet possession of the goods except so far as it may be disturbed by the owner or other person entitled to the benefit of any charge or encumbrance so disclosed or known.

(3) This subsection applies to a contract of sale in the case of which there appears from the contract or is to be inferred from its circumstances an intention that the seller should transfer only such title as he or a third person may have.

(4) In a contract to which subsection (3) above applies there is an implied **term** [*warranty*] that all charges or encumbrances known to the seller and not known to the buyer have been disclosed to the buyer before the contract is made.

(5) In a contract to which subsection (3) above applies there is also an implied **term** [*warranty*] that none of the following will disturb the buyer's quiet possession of the goods, namely—

(a) the seller;

(b) in a case where the parties to the contract intend that the seller should transfer only such title as a third person may have, that person;

(c) anyone claiming through or under the seller or that third person otherwise than under a charge or encumbrance disclosed or known to the buyer before the contract is made.

N.B. All text in bold type is amendment, substitution or insertion and all text in italic type is repealed material.

(5A) As regards England and Wales and Northern Ireland, the term implied by subsection (1) above is a condition and the terms implied by subsections (2), (4) and (5) above are warranties.

(6) Paragraph 3 of Schedule 1 below applies in relation to a contract made before 18 May 1973.

AMENDMENTS

Changes to this section were made by Sched. 2 to the 1994 Act.

Sale by description

13.—(1) Where there is a contract for the sale of goods by description, there is an implied **term** [*condition*] that the goods will correspond with the description.

(1A) As regards England and Wales and Northern Ireland, the term implied by subsection (1) above is a condition.

(2) If the sale is by sample as well as by description it is not sufficient that the bulk of the goods corresponds with the sample if the goods do not also correspond with the description.

(3) A sale of goods is not prevented from being a sale by description by reason only that, being exposed for sale or hire, they are selected by the buyer.

(4) Paragraph 4 of Schedule 1 below applies in relation to a contract made before 18 May 1973.

AMENDMENTS

Changes to this section were made by Sched. 2 to the 1994 Act.

Implied terms about quality or fitness

14.—(1) Except as provided by this section and section 15 below and subject to any other enactment, there is no implied **term** [*condition or warranty*] about the quality or fitness for any particular purpose of goods supplied under a contract of sale.

(2) Where the seller sells goods in the course of a business, there is an implied term that the goods supplied under the contract are of satisfactory quality.

(2A) For the purposes of this Act, goods are of satisfactory quality if they meet the standard that a reasonable person would regard as satisfactory, taking account of any description of the goods, the price (if relevant) and all the other relevant circumstances.

(2B) For the purposes of this Act, the quality of goods includes their state and condition and the following (among others) are in appropriate cases aspects of the quality of goods—

    (a) fitness for all the purposes for which goods of the kind in question are commonly supplied,

    (b) appearance and finish,

    (c) freedom from minor defects,

    (d) safety, and

    (e) durability.

(2C) The term implied by subsection (2) above does not extend to any matter making the quality of goods unsatisfactory—

    (a) which is specifically drawn to the buyer's attention before the contract is made,

    (b) where the buyer examines the goods before the contract is made, which that examination ought to reveal, or

    (c) in the case of a contract for sale by sample, which would have been apparent on a reasonable examination of the sample.

    [*(2) Where the seller sells goods in the course of a business, there is an implied condition that the goods supplied under the contract are of merchantable quality, except that there is no such condition—*

        (a) as regards defects specifically drawn to the buyer's attention before the contract is made; or

        (b) if the buyer examines the goods before the contract is made, as regards defects which that examination ought to reveal.]

(3) Where the seller sells goods in the course of a business and the buyer, expressly or by implication, makes known—

    (a) to the seller, or

    (b) where the purchase price or part of it is payable by instalments and the goods were previously sold by a credit-broker to the seller, to that credit-broker,

any particular purpose for which the goods are being bought, there is an implied **term** [*condition*] that the goods supplied under the contract are reasonably fit for that purpose, whether or not that is a purpose for which such goods are commonly supplied, except where the circumstances show that the buyer does not rely, or that it is unreasonable for him to rely, on the skill or judgment of the seller or credit-broker.

(4) An implied **term** [*condition or warranty*] about quality or fitness for a particular purpose may be annexed to a contract of sale by usage.

(5) The preceding provisions of this section apply to a sale by a person who in the course of a business is acting as agent for another as they apply to a sale by a principal in the course of a

business, except where that other is not selling in the course of a business and either the buyer knows that fact or reasonable steps are taken to bring it to the notice of the buyer before the contract is made.

(6) As regards England and Wales and Northern Ireland, the terms implied by subsections (2) and (3) above are conditions.

[*(6) Goods of any kind are of merchantable quality within the meaning of subsection (2) above if they are as fit for the purpose or purposes for which goods of that kind are commonly bought as it is reasonable to expect having regard to any description applied to them, the price (if relevant) and all the other relevant circumstances.*]

(7) Paragraph 5 of Schedule 1 below applies in relation to a contract made on or after 18 May 1973 and before the appointed day, and paragraph 6 in relation to one made before 18 May 1973.

(8) In subsection (7) above and paragraph 5 of Schedule 1 below references to the appointed day are to the day appointed for the purposes of those provisions by an order of the Secretary of State made by statutory instrument.

AMENDMENTS

Section 1 of the 1994 Act substituted subs. (2) and inserted subss. (2A), (2B) and (2C).

Sched. 2 to the 1994 Act substituted the word "term" in subss (1), (3) and (4) and substituted subs. (6).

Sale by sample

15.—(1) A contract of sale is a contract for sale by sample where there is an express or implied term to that effect in the contract.

(2) In the case of a contract for sale by sample there is an implied **term** [*condition*]—

(a) that the bulk will correspond with the sample in quality;

  [*(b) that the buyer will have a reasonable opportunity of comparing the bulk with the sample;*]

(c) that the goods will be free from any defect, **making their quality unsatisfactory** [*rendering them unmerchantable*], which would not be apparent on a reasonable examination of the sample.

(3) As regards England and Wales and Northern Ireland, the term implied by subsection (2) above is a condition.

  [*(3) In subsection (2)(e) above "unmerchantable" is to be construed in accordance with section 14(6) above.*]

(4) Paragraph 7 of Schedule 1 below applies in relation to a contract made before 18 May 1973.

AMENDMENTS

Section 1 of the 1994 Act substituted the words in para. (2)(c).

All other changes were made by Sched. 2 of the 1994 Act.

Modification of remedies for breach of condition in non-consumer cases

15A.—**(1) Where in the case of a contract of sale—**

(a) the buyer would, apart from this subsection, have the right to reject goods by reason of a breach on the part of the seller of a term implied by section 13, 14 or 15 above, but

(b) the breach is so slight that it would be unreasonable for him to reject them,

then, if the buyer does not deal as consumer, the breach is not to be treated as a breach of condition but may be treated as a breach of warranty.

(2) This section applies unless a contrary intention appears in, or is to be implied from, the contract.

(3) It is for the seller to show that a breach fell within subsection (1)(b) above.

(4) This section does not apply to Scotland.

AMENDMENTS

This section was inserted by s.4(1) of the 1994 Act.

Remedies for breach of contract as respects Scotland

15B.—**(1) Where in a contract of sale the seller is in breach of any term of the contract (express or implied), the buyer shall be entitled—**

(a) to claim damages, and

(b) if the breach is material, to reject any goods delivered under the contract and treat it as repudiated.

(2) Where a contract of sale is a consumer contract, then, for the purposes of subsection (1)(b) above, breach by the seller of any term (express or implied)—

(a) as to the quality of the goods or their fitness for a purpose,

(b) **if the goods are, or are to be, sold by description, that the goods will correspond with the description,**

(c) **if the goods are, or are to be, sold by reference to a sample, that the bulk will correspond with the sample in quality,**

shall be deemed to be a material breach.

(3) This section applies to Scotland only.

AMENDMENTS

This section was inserted by s.5(1) of the 1994 Act.

Delivery of wrong quantity

30.—(1) Where the seller delivers to the buyer a quantity of goods less than he contracted to sell, the buyer may reject them, but if the buyer accepts the goods so delivered he must pay for them at the contract rate.

(2) Where the seller delivers to the buyer a quantity of goods larger than he contracted to sell, the buyer may accept the goods included in the contract and reject the rest, or he may reject the whole.

(2A) A buyer who does not deal as consumer may not—

(a) where the seller delivers a quantity of goods less than he contracted to sell, reject the goods under subsection (1) above, or

(b) where the seller delivers a quantity of goods larger than he contracted to sell, reject the whole under subsection (2) above,

if the shortfall or, as the case may be, excess is so slight that it would be unreasonable for him to do so.

(2B) It is for the seller to show that a shortfall or excess fell within subsection (2A) above.

2(C) Subsections (2A) and (2B) above do not apply to Scotland.

(2D) Where the seller delivers a quantity of goods—

(a) less than he contracted to sell, the buyer shall not be entitled to reject the goods under subsection (1) above,

(b) larger than he contracted to sell, the buyer shall not be entitled to reject the whole under subsection (2) above,

unless the shortfall or excess is material.

(2E) Subsection (2D) above applies to Scotland only.

(3) Where the seller delivers to the buyer a quantity of goods larger than he contracted to sell and the buyer accepts the whole of the goods so delivered he must pay for them at the contract rate.

[*(4) Where the seller delivers to the buyer the goods he contracted to sell mixed with goods of a different description not included in the contract, the buyer may accept the goods which are in accordance with the contract and reject the rest, or he may reject the whole.*]

(5) This section is subject to any usage of trade, special agreement, or course of dealing between the parties.

AMENDMENTS

Subss. (2A), (2B) and (2C) were inserted by s.4(2) of the 1994 Act.

Subss. (2D) and (2E) were inserted by s.5(2) of the 1994 Act.

Subs. (4) was repealed by s.3(3) of the 1994 Act.

Buyer's right of examining the goods

34. [*(1) Where goods are delivered to the buyer, and he has not previously examined them, he is not deemed to have accepted them until he has had a reasonable opportunity of examining them for the purpose of ascertaining whether they are in conformity with the contract.*

(2)]

Unless otherwise agreed, when the seller tenders delivery of goods to the buyer, he is bound on request to afford the buyer a reasonable opportunity of examining the goods for the purpose of ascertaining whether they are in conformity with the contract **and, in the case of a contract for sale by sample, of comparing the bulk with the sample.**

AMENDMENTS

Changes to this section were made by s.2(2) of the 1994 Act.

Acceptance

35.—(1) The buyer is deemed to have accepted the goods [*when he intimates to the seller that he has accepted them, or (except where section 34 above otherwise provides) when the goods have been delivered to him and he does any act in relation to them which is inconsistent with the own-*

ership of the seller or when after the lapse of a reasonable time he retains the goods without intimating to the seller that he has rejected them.

(2)]

subject to subsection (2) below—

(a) when he intimates to the seller that he has accepted them, or

(b) when the goods have been delivered to him and he does any act in relation to them which is inconsistent with the ownership of the seller.

(2) Where goods are delivered to the buyer, and he has not previously examined them, he is not deemed to have accepted them under subsection (1) above until he has had a reasonable opportunity of examining them for the purpose—

(a) of ascertaining whether they are in conformity with the contract and,

(b) in the case of a contract for sale by sample, of comparing the bulk with the sample.

(3) Where the buyer deals as consumer or (in Scotland) the contract of sale is a consumer contract, the buyer cannot lose his right to rely on subsection (2) above by agreement, waiver or otherwise.

(4) The buyer is also deemed to have accepted the goods when after the lapse of a reasonable time he retains the goods without intimating to the seller that he has rejected them.

(5) The questions that are material in determining for the purposes of subsection (4) above whether a reasonable time has elapsed include whether the buyer has had a reasonable opportunity of examining the goods for the purpose mentioned in subsection (2) above.

(6) The buyer is not by virtue of this section deemed to have accepted the goods merely because—

(a) he asks for, or agrees to, their repair by or under an arrangement with the seller, or

(b) the goods are delivered to another under a sub-sale or other disposition.

(7) Where the contract is for the sale of goods making one or more commercial units, a buyer accepting any goods included in a unit is deemed to have accepted all the goods making the unit; and in this subsection "commercial unit" means a unit division of which would materially impair the value of the goods or the character of the unit.

(8) Paragraph 10 of Schedule 1 below applies in relation to a contract made before 22 April 1967 or (in the application of this Act to Northern Ireland) 28 July 1967.

AMENDMENTS

Changes to this section were made by s.2(1) of the 1994 Act.

Right of partial rejection

35A.—(1) If the buyer—

(a) has the right to reject the goods by reason of a breach on the part of the seller that affects some or all of them, but

(b) accepts some of the goods, including, where there are any goods unaffected by the breach, all such goods,

he does not by accepting them lose his right to reject the rest.

(2) In the case of a buyer having the right to reject an instalment of goods, subsection (1) above applies as if references to the goods were references to the goods comprised in the instalment.

(3) For the purposes of subsection (1) above, goods are affected by a breach if by reasons of the breach they are not in conformity with the contract.

(4) This section applies unless a contrary intention appears in, or is to be implied from, the contract.

AMENDMENTS

This section was inserted by s.3(1) of the 1994 Act.

Measure of damages as respects Scotland

53A.—(1) The measure of damages for the seller's breach of contract is the estimated loss directly and naturally resulting, in the ordinary course of events, from the breach.

(2) Where the seller's breach consists of the delivery of goods which are not of the quality required by the contract and the buyer retains the goods, such loss as aforesaid is prima facie the difference between the value of the goods at the time of delivery to the buyer and the value they would have had if they had fulfilled the contract.

(3) This section applies to Scotland only.

AMENDMENTS

This section was inserted by s.5(3) of the 1994 Act.

INDEX

References are to sections and Schedules

ACCEPTANCE OF GOODS, 2
AMENDMENTS, 7(1), Sched. 2

BREACH OF CONTRACT (SCOTLAND), 5

COMMENCEMENT, 8(2)
CONTRACTS COVERED BY ACT, 8(3)

ENGLAND AND WALES AND NORTHERN IRELAND
    PROVISIONS, 4
EXAMINATION OF GOODS, 2(2)
EXCESS, 4, 5
EXTENT, 8(4)

IMPLIED TERM ABOUT QUALITY, 1

MEASURE OF DAMAGES (SCOTLAND), 5

NON-CONSUMER CASES, 4

PARTIAL REJECTION OF GOODS, 3

QUALITY, IMPLIED TERM ABOUT, 1

REMEDIES,
    for breach of contract (Scotland), 5
    modification of, 4
REPEALS, 7(2), Sched. 3

SCOTLAND PROVISIONS, 5–6
SHORT TITLE, 8(1)
SHORTFALL, 4, 5
SUPPLY OF GOODS AND SERVICES ACT 1982,
    Scottish provisions, 6, Sched. 1

UNITED KINGDOM PROVISIONS, 1–3

WARRANTY, BREACH OF, 4

LAW OF PROPERTY (MISCELLANEOUS PROVISIONS) ACT 1994*

(1994 c. 36)

ARRANGEMENT OF SECTIONS

PART I

IMPLIED COVENANTS FOR TITLE

The covenants

SECT.
1. Covenants to be implied on a disposition of property.
2. Right to dispose and further assurance.
3. Charges, incumbrances and third party rights.
4. Validity of lease.
5. Discharge of obligations where property subject to rentcharge or leasehold land.

Effect of covenants

6. No liability under covenants in certain cases.
7. Annexation of benefit of covenants.
8. Supplementary provisions.
9. Modifications of statutory forms.

Transitional provisions

10. General saving for covenants in old form.
11. Covenants in old form implied in certain cases.
12. Covenants in new form to be implied in other cases.
13. Application of transitional provisions in relation to options.

PART II

MATTERS ARISING IN CONNECTION WITH DEATH

14. Vesting of estate in case of intestacy or lack of executors.
15. Registration of land charges after death.
16. Concurrence of personal representatives in dealings with interests in land.
17. Notices affecting land: absence of knowledge of intended recipient's death.
18. Notices affecting land: service on personal representatives before filing of grant.
19. Functions of Public Trustee in relation to notices, etc.

PART III

GENERAL PROVISIONS

20. Crown application.
21. Consequential amendments and repeals.
22. Extent.
23. Commencement.
24. Short title.

SCHEDULES:
    Schedule 1—Consequential amendments.
    Schedule 2—Repeals.

An Act to provide for new covenants for title to be implied on dispositions of property; to amend the law with respect to certain matters arising in connection with the death of the owner of property; and for connected purposes. [3rd November 1994]

PARLIAMENTARY DEBATES
    Hansard, H.L. Vol. 554, cols. 1269, 1344; Vol. 556, cols. 68, 657; H.C. Vol. 247, col. 280; Vol. 248, col. 151.
    The Bill was discussed in Special Standing Committee between May 11 and June 7, 1994; in Public Bill Committee on June 7, 1994 and in Standing Committee A on October 19, 1994.

* Annotations by Sidney Ross, Barrister, Middle Temple and Lincoln's Inn.

INTRODUCTION AND GENERAL NOTE

The aim of the reforms effected by Pt. I of this Act is to achieve adequate protection for the purchaser by providing guarantees which are given by, and enforceable against, the vendor, and which are expressed in terms of what the purchaser might reasonably expect. The words by means of which the covenants are implied describe the type of guarantee, not the capacity of the vendor, and the covenants implied by the guarantees are no longer qualified.

It will be seen that there is no covenant implied by the Act which corresponds to the covenant for quiet enjoyment. This is a deliberate omission. In the case of freehold property and disposals of existing leases it has no part to play in guaranteeing title, and the matters against which it affords protection could be better dealt with by appropriate restrictive covenants. Where a lease is granted, it can, and often does, include such an express covenant, so there is no need for it to be implied by statute.

Part II of the Act, although expressed to deal with matters arising in connection with death, does not affect the general law of administration of estates, but introduces specific provisions which are intended to be of practical assistance to those required to deal with the consequences of the death of a landowner.

PART I

IMPLIED COVENANTS FOR TITLE

The covenants

Covenants to be implied on a disposition of property

1.—(1) In an instrument effecting or purporting to effect a disposition of property there shall be implied on the part of the person making the disposition, whether or not the disposition is for valuable consideration, such of the covenants specified in sections 2 to 5 as are applicable to the disposition.

(2) Of those sections—

(a) sections 2, 3(1) and (2), 4 and 5 apply where dispositions are expressed to be made with full title guarantee; and

(b) sections 2, 3(3), 4 and 5 apply where dispositions are expressed to be made with limited title guarantee.

(3) Sections 2 to 4 have effect subject to section 6 (no liability under covenants in certain cases); and sections 2 to 5 have effect subject to section 8(1) (limitation or extension of covenants by instrument effecting the disposition).

(4) In this Part—

"disposition" includes the creation of a term of years;

"instrument" includes an instrument which is not a deed; and

"property" includes a thing in action, and any interest in real or personal property.

DEFINITIONS

"disposition": s.1(4).

"instrument": s.1(4).

"property": s.1(4).

GENERAL NOTE

This section enunciates the principle that covenants shall be implied in any instrument effecting or purporting to effect a disposition of property, and distinguishes between dispositions expressed to be made with full or limited title guarantee. It also provides for the exclusion, limitation or extension of liability under the covenants in certain cases defined by other sections of the Act.

Right to dispose and further assurance

2.—(1) If the disposition is expressed to be made with full title guarantee or with limited title guarantee there shall be implied the following covenants—

(a) that the person making the disposition has the right (with the concurrence of any other person conveying the property) to dispose of the property as he purports to, and

(b) that that person will at his own cost do all that he reasonably can to give the person to whom he disposes of the property the title he purports to give.

(2) The latter obligation includes—

(a) in relation to a disposition of an interest in land the title to which is registered, doing all that he reasonably can to ensure that the person to whom the disposition is made is entitled to be registered as proprietor with at least the class of title registered immediately before the disposition; and

(b) in relation to a disposition of an interest in land the title to which is required to be registered by virtue of the disposition, giving all reasonable assistance fully to establish to the satisfaction of the Chief Land Registrar the right of the person to whom the disposition is made to registration as proprietor.

(3) In the case of a disposition of an existing legal interest in land, the following presumptions apply, subject to the terms of the instrument, in ascertaining for the purposes of the covenants implied by this section what the person making the disposition purports to dispose of—

(a) where the title to the interest is registered, it shall be presumed that the disposition is of the whole of that interest;

(b) where the title to the interest is not registered, then—

(i) if it appears from the instrument that the interest is a leasehold interest, it shall be presumed that the disposition is of the property for the unexpired portion of the term of years created by the lease; and

(ii) in any other case, it shall be presumed that what is disposed of is the fee simple.

DEFINITIONS
  "disposition": s.1(4).
  "instrument": s.1(4).
  "property": s.1(4).

GENERAL NOTE
  This section sets out the two covenants (the right to dispose of the property and further assurance) that are implied whichever type of guarantee is given, and provides for certain obligations to be performed where the disposition is either of an interest in land the title to which is registered (see subs. (2)(a)) or of an interest in land the title to which is required to be registered by virtue of the disposition (see subs. (2)(b)). Presumptions in relation to dispositions of existing legal interests in land are dealt with in subs. (3).

Charges, incumbrances and third party rights

3.—(1) If the disposition is expressed to be made with full title guarantee there shall be implied a covenant that the person making the disposition is disposing of the property free—

(a) from all charges and incumbrances (whether monetary or not), and

(b) from all other rights exercisable by third parties,

other than any charges, incumbrances or rights which that person does not and could not reasonably be expected to know about.

(2) In its application to charges, incumbrances and other third party rights subsection (1) extends to liabilities imposed and rights conferred by or under any enactment, except to the extent that such liabilities and rights are, by reason of—

(a) being, at the time of the disposition, only potential liabilities and rights in relation to the property, or

(b) being liabilities and rights imposed or conferred in relation to property generally,

not such as to constitute defects in title.

(3) If the disposition is expressed to be made with limited title guarantee there shall be implied a covenant that the person making the disposition has not since the last disposition for value—

(a) charged or incumbered the property by means of any charge or incumbrance which subsists at the time when the disposition is made, or granted third party rights in relation to the property which so subsist, or

(b) suffered the property to be so charged or incumbered or subjected to any such rights,

and that he is not aware that anyone else has done so since the last disposition for value.

DEFINITIONS
   "disposition": s.1(4).
   "property": s.1(4).

GENERAL NOTE
This section is concerned with the covenant for freedom from incumbrances, which is implied only when the disposition is with full title guarantee. It is drawn more widely than the covenant in Pt. I of Sched. 2 to the Law of Property Act 1925 (c. 20), with the intent that it should cover both financial claims and rights such as easements.

Validity of lease

4.—(1) Where the disposition is of leasehold land and is expressed to be made with full title guarantee or with limited title guarantee, the following covenants shall also be implied—

(a) that the lease is subsisting at the time of the disposition, and

(b) that there is no subsisting breach of a condition or tenant's obligation, and nothing which at that time would render the lease liable to forfeiture.

(2) If the disposition is the grant of an underlease, the references to "the lease" in subsection (1) are references to the lease out of which the underlease is created.

DEFINITIONS
   "disposition": s.1(4).

GENERAL NOTE
This section applies to dispositions of leasehold land, whether with full or limited title guarantee. Subsection (1) sets out the implied covenants, which are to the effect that there is a valid and subsisting lease which is not liable to forfeiture. The combined effect of the definition of "disposition" in s.1(4) and the words "If the disposition is *the grant of an underlease*" [emphasis added] in s.4(2) gives rise to a problem, in that unless "disposition" can be construed so as to include a contract to grant an underlease, equitable underleases are outside the ambit of s.4(2).

By s.1(4), "disposition" includes a term of years, and must be taken to include an equitable lease. Equitable leases include contracts to grant underleases, or informal underleases which are treated as if they were contracts to grant underleases; see *Walsh* v. *Lonsdale* (1882) 21 Ch.D. 9 and *Parker* v. *Taswell* (1858) 2 De G & J 559. However, the word "grant" imports the actual creation of a term, and that excludes a mere agreement to create a term; see *City and Permanent Building Society* v. *Miller* [1952] Ch. 840, C.A., *per* Jenkins L.J. at p. 853. It therefore appears that, in the present state of the law, the word "disposition" cannot be construed so as to bring equitable underleases within s.4(2).

Discharge of obligations where property subject to rentcharge or leasehold land

5.—(1) Where the disposition is a mortgage of property subject to a rentcharge, or of leasehold land, and is expressed to be made with full title guarantee or with limited title guarantee, the following covenants shall also be implied.

(2) If the property is subject to a rentcharge, there shall be implied a covenant that the mortgagor will fully and promptly observe and perform all the obligations under the instrument creating the rentcharge that are for the time being enforceable with respect to the property by the owner of the rentcharge in his capacity as such.

(3) If the property is leasehold land, there shall be implied a covenant that the mortgagor will fully and promptly observe and perform all the obligations under the lease subject to the mortgage that are for the time being imposed on him in his capacity as tenant under the lease.

(4) In this section "mortgage" includes charge, and "mortgagor" shall be construed accordingly.

DEFINITIONS
  "disposition": s.1(4).
  "instrument": s.1(4).
  "mortgage": s.5(4).
  "mortgagor": s.5(4).
  "property": s.1(4).

GENERAL NOTE
This section implies covenants on the part of a mortgagor of land which is subject to a rentcharge (see subs. (2)), or of leasehold land (see subs. (3)), and applies to dispositions with either full or limited title guarantee. The mortgagee's security is reinforced by the mortgagor's covenant that he will fully and promptly observe and perform the obligations under the instrument creating the rentcharge or, as the case may be, the lease which is subject to the mortgage.

Effect of covenants

No liability under covenants in certain cases

6.—(1) The person making the disposition is not liable under the covenants implied by virtue of—

  (a) section 2(1)(a) (right to dispose),
  (b) section 3 (charges, incumbrances and third party rights), or
  (c) section 4 (validity of lease),

in respect of any particular matter to which the disposition is expressly made subject.

(2) Furthermore that person is not liable under any of those covenants for anything (not falling within subsection (1))—

  (a) which at the time of the disposition is within the actual knowledge, or
  (b) which is a necessary consequence of facts that are then within the actual knowledge,

of the person to whom the disposition is made.

(3) For this purpose section 198 of the Law of Property Act 1925 (deemed notice by virtue of registration) shall be disregarded.

DEFINITIONS
  "disposition": s.1(4).

GENERAL NOTE
This section excludes liability under the implied covenants in ss.2(1)(a), 3 and 4 in two ways. Subsection (1) provides for exclusion in respect of any particular matter to which the disposition is expressly made subject. Subsection (2) excludes the disponor's liability in respect of anything which does not fall within subs. (1) and which at the time of the disposition is within the actual knowledge, or which is a necessary consequence of facts which are at that time within the actual knowledge, of the disponee. Some concern was expressed as to the meaning and effect of the word "facts" in subs. (2)(b); see the official report of the Public Bill Committee, H.L., cols. 17–18, June 7, 1994. Subsection (3) provides that s.198 of the Law of Property Act 1925 shall be disregarded for that purpose.

Annexation of benefit of covenants

7. The benefit of a covenant implied by virtue of this Part shall be annexed and incident to, and shall go with, the estate or interest of the person to whom the disposition is made, and shall be capable of being enforced by every person in whom that estate or interest is (in whole or in part) for the time being vested.

DEFINITIONS
  "disposition": s.1(4).

GENERAL NOTE
  This section, which provides for annexation of the benefit of implied covenants to the estate or interest of the disponee, was the subject of considerable debate, since the Law Commission had recommended that the benefit of the covenants should not run with the land. See the official report of the Public Bill Committee, H.L., cols. 9–12, June 7, 1994 and *Hansard*, H.L. Vol. 556, cols. 69–71.

Supplementary provisions

8.—(1) The operation of any covenant implied in an instrument by virtue of this Part may be limited or extended by a term of that instrument.

(2) Sections 81 and 83 of the Law of Property Act 1925 (effect of covenant with two or more jointly; construction of implied covenants) apply to a covenant implied by virtue of this Part as they apply to a covenant implied by virtue of that Act.

(3) Where in an instrument effecting or purporting to effect a disposition of property a person is expressed to direct the disposition, this Part applies to him as if he were the person making the disposition.

(4) This Part has effect—

(a) where "gyda gwarant teitl llawn" is used instead of "with full title guarantee", and

(b) where "gyda gwarant teitl cyfyngedig" is used instead of "with limited title guarantee",

as it has effect where the English words are used.

DEFINITIONS
  "disposition": s.1(4).
  "instrument": s.1(4).

GENERAL NOTE
  This section contains supplementary provisions. By s.1(3), ss.2 to 5 have effect subject to subs. (1) of this section, which enables the operation of any implied covenant to be extended or limited by the terms of the instrument. Where a covenant implied by the Act is in favour of two or more persons, subs. (2) gives the benefit of the covenant to the survivor or survivors of them. Subsection (3) puts a person who is expressed to direct a disposition in the same position as if he were actually making the disposition. Subsection (4) permits the use of the Welsh language equivalents of "with full title guarantee" and "with limited title guarantee".

Modifications of statutory forms

9.—(1) Where a form set out in an enactment, or in an instrument made under an enactment, includes words which (in an appropriate case) would have resulted in the implication of a covenant by virtue of section 76 of the Law of Property Act 1925, the form shall be taken to authorise instead the use of the words "with full title guarantee" or "with limited title guarantee" or their Welsh equivalent given in section 8(4).

(2) This applies in particular to the forms set out in Schedule 1 to the Settled Land Act 1925 and Schedules 4 and 5 to the Law of Property Act 1925.

DEFINITIONS
  "instrument": s.1(4).

GENERAL NOTE
  This section provides for the modification of statutory forms, in particular those set out in Sched. 1 to the Settled Land Act 1925 (c. 18) and Scheds. 4 and 5 to the Law of Property Act 1925, so as to allow the use of words which imply covenants under this Act.

Transitional provisions

General saving for covenants in old form

10.—(1) Except as provided by section 11 below (cases in which covenants in old form implied on disposition after commencement), the following provisions, namely—

(a) section 76 of the Law of Property Act 1925, and

(b) section 24(1)(a) of the Land Registration Act 1925,

are repealed as regards dispositions of property made after the commencement of this Part.

(2) The repeal of those provisions by this Act accordingly does not affect the enforcement of a covenant implied by virtue of either of them on a disposition before the commencement of this Part.

DEFINITIONS
"disposition": s.1(4).
"property": s.1(4).

GENERAL NOTE
This section is the first of four sections which make transitional provisions. It is a general saving for covenants implied by virtue of s.76 of the Law of Property Act 1925 (c. 20) or s.24(1) of the Land Registration Act 1925 (c. 21) on a disposition before the commencement of Pt. I of this Act.

Covenants in old form implied in certain cases

11.—(1) Section 76 of the Law of Property Act 1925 applies in relation to a disposition of property made after the commencement of this Part in pursuance of a contract entered into before commencement where—

(a) the contract contains a term providing for a disposition to which that section would have applied if the disposition had been made before commencement, and

(b) the existence of the contract and of that term is apparent on the face of the instrument effecting the disposition,

unless there has been an intervening disposition of the property expressed, in accordance with this Part, to be made with full title guarantee.

(2) Section 24(1)(a) of the Land Registration Act 1925 applies in relation to a disposition of a leasehold interest in land made after the commencement of this Part in pursuance of a contract entered into before commencement where—

(a) the covenant specified in that provision would have been implied on the disposition if it had been made before commencement, and

(b) the existence of the contract is apparent on the face of the instrument effecting the disposition,

unless there has been an intervening disposition of the leasehold interest expressed, in accordance with this Part, to be made with full title guarantee.

(3) In subsections (1) and (2) an "intervening disposition" means a disposition after the commencement of this Part to, or to a predecessor in title of, the person by whom the disposition in question is made.

(4) Where in order for subsection (1) or (2) to apply it is necessary for certain matters to be apparent on the face of the instrument effecting the disposition, the contract shall be deemed to contain an implied term that they should so appear.

DEFINITIONS
"disposition": s.1(4).
"instrument": s.1(4).
"intervening disposition": s.11(3).

GENERAL NOTE
This section deals with two types of disposition where a contract for the disposition had been entered into before the commencement of Pt. I of the Act and no intervening disposition (as defined in subs. (3)) expressed to be with full title guarantee has been made. Subsection (1) applies to the case where the terms of the contract require a disposition into which covenants would be implied by virtue of s.76 of the Law of Property Act 1925. Subsection (2) applies where a contract for the disposition of registered leasehold land would have resulted in a transfer into which covenants would have been implied by s.24(1) of the Land Registration Act 1925. In each case there is a proviso that the old law will apply if certain matters are apparent on the face of the instrument, and subs. (4) is a deeming provision relating to those matters.

Covenants in new form to be implied in other cases

12.—(1) This section applies to a contract for the disposition of property entered into before the commencement of this Part where the disposition is made after commencement and section 11 (cases in which covenants in old form to be implied) does not apply because there has been an intervening disposition expressed, in accordance with this Part, to be with full title guarantee.

(2) A contract which contains a term that the person making the disposition shall do so as beneficial owner shall be construed as requiring that person to do so by an instrument expressed to be made with full title guarantee.

(3) A contract which contains a term that the person making the disposition shall do so—

(a) as settlor, or

(b) as trustee or mortgagee or personal representative,

shall be construed as requiring that person to do so by an instrument expressed to be made with limited title guarantee.

(4) A contract for the disposition of a leasehold interest in land entered into at a date when the title to the leasehold interest was registered shall be construed as requiring the person making the disposition for which it provides to do so by an instrument expressed to be made with full title guarantee.

(5) Where this section applies and the contract provides that any of the covenants to be implied by virtue of section 76 of the Law of Property Act 1925 or section 24(1)(a) of the Land Registration Act 1925 shall be implied in a modified form, the contract shall be construed as requiring a corresponding modification of the covenants implied by virtue of this Part.

DEFINITIONS
"disposition": s.1(4).
"instrument": s.1(4).
"intervening disposition": s.11(3).
"property": s.1(4).

GENERAL NOTE
This section implies covenants in the new form where there has been a contract for a disposition before the commencement of Pt. I of the Act but s.11 does not apply because there has been an intervening disposition expressed to be with full title guarantee. Subsections (2) and (3) regulate the position where a contract requires the disponor to dispose of the property in a specified capacity. Subsection (4) provides for certain dispositions of leasehold interests in land to be made by an instrument expressed to be made with full title guarantee. Subsection (5) deals with contractual requirements to modify covenants implied by virtue of s.76 of the Law of Property Act 1925 or s.24(1) of the Land Registration Act 1925.

Application of transitional provisions in relation to options

13. For the purposes of sections 11 and 12 (transitional provisions: implication of covenants in old form in certain cases and new form in others) as they apply in relation to a disposition of property in accordance with an option granted before the commencement of this Part and exercised after commencement, the contract for the disposition shall be deemed to have been entered into on the grant of the option.

DEFINITIONS
"disposition": s.1(4).
"property": s.1(4).

GENERAL NOTE

This section deals with the application of the transitional provisions in relation to options.

PART II

MATTERS ARISING IN CONNECTION WITH DEATH

Vesting of estate in case of intestacy or lack of executors

14.—(1) For section 9 of the Administration of Estates Act 1925 (vesting of estate of intestate between death and grant of administration) substitute—

"**Vesting of estate in Public Trustee where intestacy or lack of executors**
9.—(1) Where a person dies intestate, his real and personal estate shall vest in the Public Trustee until the grant of administration.
(2) Where a testator dies and—
(a) at the time of his death there is no executor with power to obtain probate of the will, or
(b) at any time before probate of the will is granted there ceases to be any executor with power to obtain probate,
the real and personal estate of which he disposes by the will shall vest in the Public Trustee until the grant of representation.
(3) The vesting of real or personal estate in the Public Trustee by virtue of this section does not confer on him any beneficial interest in, or impose on him any duty, obligation or liability in respect of, the property."
(2) Any real or personal estate of a person dying before the commencement of this section shall, if it is property to which this subsection applies, vest in the Public Trustee on the commencement of this section.
(3) Subsection (2) above applies to any property—
(a) if it was vested in the Probate Judge under section 9 of the Administration of Estates Act 1925 immediately before the commencement of this section, or
(b) if it was not so vested but as at commencement there has been no grant of representation in respect of it and there is no executor with power to obtain such a grant.
(4) Any property vesting in the Public Trustee by virtue of subsection (2) above shall—
(a) if the deceased died intestate, be treated as vesting in the Public Trustee under section 9(1) of the Administration of Estates Act 1925 (as substituted by subsection (1) above); and
(b) otherwise be treated as vesting in the Public Trustee under section 9(2) of that Act (as so substituted).
(5) Anything done by or in relation to the Probate Judge with respect to property vested in him as mentioned in subsection (3)(a) above shall be treated as having been done by or in relation to the Public Trustee.
(6) So far as may be necessary in consequence of the transfer to the Public Trustee of the functions of the Probate Judge under section 9 of the Administration of Estates Act 1925, any reference in an enactment or instrument to the Probate Judge shall be construed as a reference to the Public Trustee.

DEFINITIONS
"instrument": s.1(4).
"property": s.1(4).

GENERAL NOTE

Subsection (1) amends the Administration of Estates Act 1925 (c. 23) by substituting a new s.9 for that Act, which provides for the vesting of property in the Public Trustee where either the deceased died intestate (s.9(1), as substituted) or he died testate and there is no executor or, before the grant of probate, there ceases to be any executor able to obtain probate (s.9(2), as substituted). Subsection (2) provides for property of a person who dies before the commencement of the subsection to vest in the Public Trustee if it is property to which the subsection applies, for which see subs. (3). Subsection (4) provides for such property to be treated as vested in the Public Trustee by virtue of the substituted s.9 of the Administration of Estates Act 1925. Subsections (5) and (6) put the Public Trustee in the place of the Probate Judge for certain purposes.

Registration of land charges after death

15.—(1) The Land Charges Act 1972 is amended as follows.

(2) In section 3 (registration of land charges), after subsection (1) (registration in name of estate owner), insert—

　　"(1A) Where a person has died and a land charge created before his death would apart from his death have been registered in his name, it shall be so registered notwithstanding his death."

(3) In section 5 (register of pending actions), after subsection (4) (entry in name of person whose estate or interest is intended to be affected), insert—

　　"(4A) Where a person has died and a pending land action would apart from his death have been registered in his name, it shall be so registered notwithstanding his death."

(4) In section 6 (register of writs and orders affecting land), after subsection (2) (entry in name of estate owner or other person whose land is affected), insert—

　　"(2A) Where a person has died and any such writ or order as is mentioned in subsection (1)(a) or (b) above would apart from his death have been registered in his name, it shall be so registered notwithstanding his death."

(5) The amendments made by this section do not apply where the application for registration was made before the commencement of this section, but without prejudice to a person's right to make a new application after commencement.

GENERAL NOTE

This section amends the Land Charges Act 1972 (c. 61) so as to enable land charges created before the death of a person (subs. (1), amending s.3 of the 1972 Act), pending land actions which would have been registered but for his death (subs. (2), amending s.5) and writs and orders which would have been registered in the name of an estate owner but for his death (subs. (3), amending s.6) to be registered notwithstanding his death.

Concurrence of personal representatives in dealings with interests in land

16.—(1) In section 2(2) of the Administration of Estates Act 1925 (concurrence of all personal representatives required for conveyance of real estate)—

(a) after "a conveyance of real estate devolving under this Part of this Act" insert "or a contract for such a conveyance";

(b) omit the words ", save as otherwise provided as respects trust estates including settled land," (which are unnecessary); and

(c) after "any conveyance of the real estate" insert "or contract for such a conveyance".

(2) Section 2(2) of the Administration of Estates Act 1925 as amended by subsection (1) above (concurrence of all personal representatives required for conveyance of real estate or contract for such conveyance) applies in relation to an interest under a trust for sale of land as in relation to real estate.

(3) The amendments made by subsection (1) apply to contracts made after the commencement of this section; and subsection (2) applies to contracts made after the commencement of this section and to conveyances so made otherwise than in pursuance of a contract made before commencement.

GENERAL NOTE

This section amends s.2(2) of the Administration of Estates Act 1925 so as to require, in a case where there are two or more personal representatives, the concurrence of all of them in any contract to convey real estate or any interest arising under a trust for sale of land.

Notices affecting land: absence of knowledge of intended recipient's death

17.—(1) Service of a notice affecting land which would be effective but for the death of the intended recipient is effective despite his death if the person serving the notice has no reason to believe that he has died.

(2) Where the person serving a notice affecting land has no reason to believe that the intended recipient has died, the proper address for the purposes of section 7 of the Interpretation Act 1978 (service of documents by post) shall be what would be the proper address apart from his death.

(3) The above provisions do not apply to a notice authorised or required to be served for the purposes of proceedings before—

(a) any court,

(b) any tribunal specified in Schedule 1 to the Tribunals and Inquiries Act 1992 (tribunals within general supervision of Council on Tribunals), or

(c) the Chief Land Registrar or any district registrar or assistant district registrar;

but this is without prejudice to the power to make provision in relation to such proceedings by rules of court, procedural rules within the meaning of section 8 of the Tribunals and Inquiries Act 1992 or rules under section 144 of the Land Registration Act 1925.

GENERAL NOTE

This section provides that service of a notice affecting land which would have been effective but for the death of the intended recipient shall be effective notwithstanding his death if the person serving the notice has no reason to believe that he has died (subs. (1)). Subsection (2) specifies the proper address for service in those circumstances, and subs. (3) creates certain exceptions to subs. (1).

Notices affecting land: service on personal representatives before filing of grant

18.—(1) A notice affecting land which would have been authorised or required to be served on a person but for his death shall be sufficiently served before a grant of representation has been filed if—

(a) it is addressed to "The Personal Representatives of" the deceased (naming him) and left at or sent by post to his last known place of residence or business in the United Kingdom, and

(b) a copy of it, similarly addressed, is served on the Public Trustee.

(2) The reference in subsection (1) to the filing of a grant of representation is to the filing at the Principal Registry of the Family Division of the High Court of a copy of a grant of representation in respect of the deceased's estate or, as the case may be, the part of his estate which includes the land in question.

(3) The method of service provided for by this section is not available where provision is made—

(a) by or under any enactment, or

(b) by an agreement in writing,

requiring a different method of service, or expressly prohibiting the method of service provided for by this section, in the circumstances.

GENERAL NOTE
This section deals with the circumstances in which a notice which would have been required or authorised to be served on a person is sufficiently served before a grant of representation has been filed; see subss. (1) and (2). Subsection (3) creates certain exceptions to sub. (1).

Functions of Public Trustee in relation to notices, etc.

19.—(1) The Public Trustee may give directions as to the office or offices at which documents may be served on him—

  (a) by virtue of section 9 of the Administration of Estates Act 1925 (as substituted by section 14(1) above), or

  (b) in pursuance of section 18(1)(b) above (service on Public Trustee of copy of certain notices affecting land);

and he shall publish such directions in such manner as he considers appropriate.

  (2) The Lord Chancellor may by regulations make provision with respect to the functions of the Public Trustee in relation to such documents; and the regulations may make different provision in relation to different descriptions of document or different circumstances.

  (3) The regulations may, in particular, make provision requiring the Public Trustee—

  (a) to keep such documents for a specified period and thereafter to keep a copy or record of their contents in such form as may be specified;

  (b) to keep such documents, copies and records available for inspection at such reasonable hours as may be specified; and

  (c) to supply copies to any person on request.

In this subsection "specified" means specified by or under the regulations.

  (4) Regulations under this section shall be made by statutory instrument which shall be subject to annulment in pursuance of a resolution of either House of Parliament.

  (5) The following provisions of the Public Trustee Act 1906, namely—

  (a) section 8(5) (payment of expenses out of money provided by Parliament), and

  (b) section 9(1), (3) and (4) (provisions as to fees),

apply in relation to the functions of the Public Trustee in relation to documents to which this section applies as in relation to his functions under that Act.

GENERAL NOTE
This section makes provision for the Public Trustee to direct how notices shall be served on him (subs. (1)) and for the Lord Chancellor to make regulations concerning the functions of the Public Trustee (subss. (2) to (4)). Provision is made for the Public Trustee to charge fees (subs. (5)).

PART III

GENERAL PROVISIONS

Crown application

20. This Act binds the Crown.

Consequential amendments and repeals

21.—(1) The enactments specified in Schedule 1 are amended in accordance with that Schedule, the amendments being consequential on the provisions of this Act.

  (2) The enactments specified in Schedule 2 are repealed to the extent specified.

(3) In the case of section 76 of the Law of Property Act 1925 and section 24(1)(a) of the Land Registration Act 1925, those provisions are repealed in accordance with section 10(1) above (general saving for covenants in old form).

(4) The amendments consequential on Part I of this Act (namely those in paragraphs 1, 2, 3, 5, 7, 9 and 12 of Schedule 1) shall not have effect in relation to any disposition of property to which, by virtue of section 10(1) or 11 above (transitional provisions), section 76 of the Law of Property Act 1925 or section 24(1)(a) of the Land Registration Act 1925 continues to apply.

Extent

22.—(1) The provisions of this Act extend to England and Wales.

(2) In addition—

(a) the provisions of Schedules 1 and 2 (consequential amendments and repeals) extend to Scotland so far as they relate to enactments which so extend; and

(b) the provisions of Schedule 1 extend to Northern Ireland so far as they relate to enactments which so extend.

Commencement

23.—(1) The provisions of this Act come into force on such day as the Lord Chancellor may appoint by order made by statutory instrument.

(2) Different days may be appointed for different provisions and for different purposes.

Short title

24. This Act may be cited as the Law of Property (Miscellaneous Provisions) Act 1994.

SCHEDULES

Section 21(1)   SCHEDULE 1

CONSEQUENTIAL AMENDMENTS

Law of Property Act 1925 (c. 20)

1. In section 77(1) of the Law of Property Act 1925 (implied covenants in conveyances subject to rents), for "the last preceding section" substitute "Part I of the Law of Property (Miscellaneous Provisions) Act 1994".

Land Registration Act 1925 (c. 21)

2. In section 38(2) of the Land Registration Act 1925 (effect of implied covenants in dispositions of registered land), after "the Law of Property Act 1925" insert "or Part I of the Law of Property (Miscellaneous Provisions) Act 1994".

Law of Property (Joint Tenants) Act 1964 (c. 63)

3. In section 1(1) of the Law of Property (Joint Tenants) Act 1964 (assumptions on sale of land by survivor of joint tenants), omit the words "he conveys as beneficial owner or".

Land Commission Act 1967 (c. 1)

4.—(1) In Part II of Schedule 12 to the Land Commission Act 1967 (betterment levy: effect of death etc. on liability), paragraph 10 (provisions as to intestacy) is amended as follows.

(2) In sub-paragraph (1)—

(a) for "the Probate Judge", in each place where the words occur, substitute "the Public Trustee"; and

(b) for "letters of administration of that person's estate are granted" substitute "a grant of representation is made in respect of that person's estate".

(3) Omit sub-paragraph (2) (definition of "the Probate Judge").

Leasehold Reform Act 1967 (c. 88)

5.—(1) In section 10 of the Leasehold Reform Act 1967 (rights to be conveyed to tenant on enfranchisement), in subsection (1) omit the words from "nor to enter into any covenant for title" to the end, and after that subsection insert—

"(1A) The landlord shall not be required to enter into any covenant for title beyond those implied under Part I of the Law of Property (Miscellaneous Provisions) Act 1994 in a case where a disposition is expressed to be made with limited title guarantee; and in the absence of agreement to the contrary he shall be entitled to be indemnified by the tenant in respect of any costs incurred by him in complying with the covenant implied by virtue of section 2(1)(b) of that Act (covenant for further assurance)."

(2) In section 15 of that Act (terms of tenancy to be granted on extension), for subsection (9) substitute—

"(9) In granting the new tenancy, the landlord shall not be bound to enter into any covenant for title beyond—

(a) those implied from the grant, and

(b) those implied under Part I of the Law of Property (Miscellaneous Provisions) Act 1994 in a case where a disposition in expressed to be made with limited title guarantee, but not including (in the case of a sub-tenancy) the covenant in section 4(1)(b) of that Act (compliance with terms of lease);

and in the absence of agreement to the contrary the landlord shall be entitled to be indemnified by the tenant in respect of any costs incurred by him in complying with the covenant implied by virtue of section 2(1)(b) of that Act (covenant for further assurance).

(9A) A person entering into any covenant required of him as landlord (under subsection (9) or otherwise) shall be entitled to limit his personal liability to breaches of that covenant for which he is responsible."

(3) In Schedule 1 to that Act (enfranchisement or extension by sub-tenants), in paragraph 7(1)(a), after "that tenancy" insert ", and the reference in subsection (1A) of that section to the covenants for title implied under Part I of the Law of Property (Miscellaneous Provisions) Act 1994 shall be read as excluding the covenant in section 4(1)(b) of that Act (compliance with terms of lease)".

Consumer Credit Act 1974 (c. 39)

6. In section 176 of the Consumer Credit Act 1974 (service of documents), for subsection (7) (service not to be effected on Probate Judge) substitute—

"(7) The following enactments shall not be construed as authorising service on the Public Trustee (in England and Wales) or the Probate Judge (in Northern Ireland) of any document which is to be served under this Act—

section 9 of the Administration of Estates Act 1925;

section 3 of the Administration of Estates Act (Northern Ireland) 1955."

Rentcharges Act 1977 (c. 30)

7. In section 11(2) of the Rentcharges Act 1977 (additional covenants relating to rentcharge deemed included and implied in conveyance), for "section 76 of the Law of Property Act 1925" substitute "Part I of the Law of Property (Miscellaneous Provisions) Act 1994".

Rent Act 1977 (c. 42)

8. In Part I of Schedule 2 to the Rent Act 1977 (provisions for determining application of resident landlord exemption), in paragraph 1 (periods to be disregarded in ascertaining whether landlord resident at all times since grant of tenancy), in sub-paragraph (c)(iii) (period during which interest of landlord vested in Probate Judge), for "the Probate Judge, within the meaning of that Act" substitute "the Probate Judge or the Public Trustee".

Housing Act 1985 (c. 68)

9.—(1) Schedule 6 to the Housing Act 1985 (conveyance of freehold or grant of lease in pursuance of right to buy) is amended as follows.

(2) In Part I (common provisions), after paragraph 4 insert—

"4A. The conveyance or grant shall be expressed to be made by the landlord with full title guarantee (thereby implying the covenants for title specified in Part I of the Law of Property (Miscellaneous Provisions) Act 1994)."

(3) In paragraph 5, for "covenants" substitute "other covenants".

(4) In Part II (conveyance of freehold), omit paragraph 10.

Financial Services Act 1986 (c. 60)

10. In section 45(1) of the Financial Services Act 1986 (miscellaneous exemptions from regulation of investment business), in paragraph (a) for "the President of the Family Division of the High Court" substitute "the Public Trustee".

Housing Act 1988 (c. 50)

11. In Part III of Schedule 1 to the Housing Act 1988 (provisions for determining application of resident landlord exemption), in paragraph 17 (periods to be disregarded in ascertaining whether landlord resident at all times since grant of tenancy), in sub-paragraph (c)(ii) (period during which interest of landlord vested in Probate Judge), for "the Probate Judge, within the meaning of that Act" substitute "the Probate Judge or the Public Trustee".

Leasehold Reform, Housing and Urban Development Act 1993 (c. 28)

12.—(1) In section 34 of the Leasehold Reform, Housing and Urban Development Act 1993 (conveyance to nominee purchaser), in subsection (9) after second "conveyed" add ", and with the reference to the covenants for title implied under Part I of the Law of Property (Miscellaneous Provisions) Act 1994 being read as excluding the covenant in section 4(1)(b) of that Act (compliance with terms of lease)".

(2) In section 57 of that Act (terms on which new lease is to be granted), for subsection (8) substitute—

"(8) In granting the new lease the landlord shall not be bound to enter into any covenant for title beyond—

(a) those implied from the grant, and

(b) those implied under Part I of the Law of Property (Miscellaneous Provisions) Act 1994 in a case where a disposition is expressed to be made with limited title guarantee, but not including (in the case of an underlease) the covenant in section 4(1)(b) of that Act (compliance with terms of lease);

and in the absence of agreement to the contrary the landlord shall be entitled to be indemnified by the tenant in respect of any costs incurred by him in complying with the covenant implied by virtue of section 2(1)(b) of that Act (covenant for further assurance).

(8A) A person entering into any covenant required of him as landlord (under subsection (8) or otherwise) shall be entitled to limit his personal liability to breaches of that covenant for which he is responsible."

(3) In Schedule 7 to that Act (conveyance to nominee purchaser on enfranchisement), for paragraph 2(2)(b) substitute—

"(b) to enter into any covenant for title beyond those implied under Part I of the Law of Property (Miscellaneous Provisions) Act 1994 in a case where a disposition is expressed to be made with limited title guarantee;

and in the absence of agreement to the contrary the freeholder shall be entitled to be indemnified by the nominee purchaser in respect of any costs incurred by him in complying with the covenant implied by virtue of section 2(1)(b) of that Act (covenant for further assurance)."

(4) In Schedule 9 to that Act (grant of leases back to former freeholder) after paragraph 9 insert—

"Covenants for title

9A. The lessor shall not be bound to enter into any covenant for title beyond—

(a) those implied from the grant, and

(b) those implied under Part I of the Law of Property (Miscellaneous Provisions) Act 1994 in a case where a disposition is expressed to be made with limited title guarantee."

Section 21(2)   SCHEDULE 2

REPEALS

Chapter	Short title	Extent of repeal
15 & 16 Geo. 5 c. 20.	Law of Property Act 1925.	Section 76. In Schedule 2, Parts I to VI.
15 & 16 Geo. 5 c. 21.	Land Registration Act 1925.	Section 24(1)(a).
15 & 16 Geo. 5 c. 23.	Administration of Estates Act 1925.	In section 2(2), the words ", save as otherwise provided as respects trust estates including settled land,". Section 36(3). In section 55(1), paragraph (xv).
1964 c. 63.	Law of Property (Joint Tenants) Act 1964.	In section 1(1), the words "he conveys as beneficial owner or".
1967 c. 1.	Land Commission Act 1967.	In Schedule 12, paragraph 10(2).
1967 c. 88.	Leasehold Reform Act 1967.	In section 10(1), from the words "nor to enter into any covenant for title" to the end.
1970 c. 31.	Administration of Justice Act 1970.	In Schedule 2, paragraph 5.
1985 c. 6.	Companies Act 1985.	Section 209(10)(d).
1985 c. 68.	Housing Act 1985.	In Schedule 6, paragraph 10.

INDEX

References are to sections and Schedules

BENEFICIAL OWNER, 12(2)

CHARGES,
  implied covenant as to, 3
  see also MORTGAGES
COMMENCEMENT, 23
CONSEQUENTIAL AMENDMENTS, 21(1), Sched. 1
CROWN BOUND BY ACT, 20

DEATH,
  concurrence of personal representatives in dealings with interest in land, 16
  intestacy or lack of executors,
    vesting of estate in Public Trustee, 14
  notices affecting land,
    absence of knowledge of intended recipient's death, 17
    Public Trustee's functions, 19
    service on personal representatives before filing of grant, 18
  registration of land charges after, 15
DISPOSITION,
  meaning of, 1(4)

EXECUTORS, *see* DEATH
EXPRESS TERMS EXCLUDING LIABILITY, 6
EXTENT, 22

FULL TITLE GUARANTEE,
  dispositions with, 1(2)(a)
  statutory forms, modification of, 9
  Welsh terms, 8(4)

IMPLIED COVENANTS,
  annexation of benefit of, 7
  charges, incumbrances and third party rights, 3
  directed dispositions, 8(3)
  effect of, 6–9
  enforcement of, 7
  extension by express term, 8(1)
  further assurance, 2
  joint covenantors, 8(2)
  limitation by express term, 8(1)
  mortgages, in, 5
  no liability cases, 6
  on disposition of property, 1
  rentcharges, 5
  right to dispose, 2
  statutory forms, modification of, 9

IMPLIED COVENANTS—*cont.*
  transitional provisions,
    new form covenants implied in certain cases, 12
    old form covenants implied in certain cases, 11
    options, 13
    saving for covenants in old form, 10
  validity of lease, 4
INCUMBRANCES, 3
INSTRUMENT,
  meaning of, 1(4)
INTESTACY, *see* DEATH

LAND CHARGES,
  registration after death, 15
LEASEHOLD LAND,
  implied covenants,
    mortgagor to observe obligations under lease, 5
    validity of lease, 4
    transitional provisions, 11(2), 12(4)
LIMITED TITLE GUARANTEE,
  dispositions with, 1(2)(b)

MORTGAGES,
  subject to rentcharge, 5

OPTIONS, 13

PERSONAL REPRESENTATIVES, *see* DEATH
PROPERTY,
  meaning of, 1(4)
PUBLIC TRUSTEE,
  functions in relation to notices, 19
  vesting of estate in, 14

REPEALS, 21(2)–(4), Sched. 2

SHORT TITLE, 24
STATUTORY FORMS, MODIFICATION OF, 9

THIRD PARTY RIGHTS, 3
TRANSITIONAL PROVISIONS, 10–13

WELSH DISPOSITIONARY TERMS, 8(4)

DRUG TRAFFICKING ACT 1994*

(1994 c. 37)

ARRANGEMENT OF SECTIONS

PART I

CONFISCATION ORDERS

Introductory

SECT.
1. Meaning of "drug trafficking" and "drug trafficking offence".

Confiscation orders

2. Confiscation orders.
3. Postponed determinations.
4. Assessing the proceeds of drug trafficking.
5. Amount to be recovered under confiscation order.
6. Meaning of "amount that might be realised" and "realisable property".
7. Value of property etc.
8. Gifts caught by this Act.
9. Application of procedure for enforcing fines.
10. Interest on sums unpaid under confiscation orders.

Statements etc in connection with confiscation orders

11. Statements relating to drug trafficking.
12. Provision of information by defendant.

Further proceedings in connection with confiscation orders

13. Reconsideration of case where court has not proceeded under section 2.
14. Re-assessment of whether defendant has benefited from drug trafficking.
15. Revised assessment of proceeds of drug trafficking.
16. Increase in realisable property.
17. Inadequacy of realisable property.
18. Compensation.

Confiscation orders where defendant has absconded or died

19. Powers of High Court where defendant has absconded or died.
20. Effect of conviction where High Court has acted under section 19.
21. Variation of confiscation orders made by virtue of section 19.
22. Compensation etc where absconder is acquitted.
23. Power to discharge confiscation order and order compensation where absconder returns.
24. Provisions supplementary to sections 21, 22 and 23.

Restraint orders and charging orders

25. Cases in which restraint orders and charging orders may be made.
26. Restraint orders.
27. Charging orders in respect of land, securities etc.
28. Charging orders: supplementary provisions.

Realisation of property

29. Realisation of property.
30. Application of proceeds of realisation and other sums.

Exercise of powers for the realisation of property

31. Exercise by High Court, county court or receiver of powers for the realisation of property.

Insolvency of defendants etc.

32. Bankruptcy of defendant etc.

---

* Annotations by Rudi F. Fortson, LL.B. (Lond.) of the Middle Temple, Barrister.

33. Sequestration in Scotland of defendant etc.
34. Winding up of company holding realisable property.

Protection for insolvency officers etc.

35. Insolvency officers dealing with property subject to restraint order.
36. Receivers: supplementary provisions.

Enforcement of orders made outside England and Wales

37. Recognition and enforcement of orders and functions under Part I of the Criminal Justice (Scotland) Act 1987.
38. Enforcement of Northern Ireland orders.
39. Enforcement of external confiscation orders.
40. Registration of external confiscation orders.

Interpretation

41. Interpretation of Part I.

PART II

DRUG TRAFFICKING MONEY IMPORTED OR EXPORTED IN CASH

42. Seizure and detention.
43. Forfeiture.
44. Appeal against forfeiture order made by a magistrates' court.
45. Appeal against forfeiture order made by sheriff.
46. Rules of court.
47. Receipts.
48. Interpretation of Part II.

PART III

OFFENCES IN CONNECTION WITH PROCEEDS OF DRUG TRAFFICKING

49. Concealing or transferring proceeds of drug trafficking.
50. Assisting another person to retain the benefit of drug trafficking.
51. Acquisition, possession or use of proceeds of drug trafficking.
52. Failure to disclose knowledge or suspicion of money laundering.
53. Tipping-off.
54. Penalties.

PART IV

MISCELLANEOUS AND SUPPLEMENTAL

Investigations into drug trafficking

55. Order to make material available.
56. Authority for search.
57. Provisions supplementary to sections 55 and 56.
58. Offence of prejudicing investigation.
59. Disclosure of information held by government departments.

Prosecution of offences etc.

60. Prosecution by order of the Commissioners of Customs and Excise.
61. Extension of certain offences to Crown servants and exemptions for regulators etc.

Interpretation of Act

62. Meaning of "property" and related expressions.
63. General interpretation.
64. Index of defined expressions.

Supplemental

65. Consequential amendments and modifications of other Acts.
66. Transitional provisions and savings.

67. Repeals etc.
68. Extent.
69. Short title and commencement.

    Schedules:
        Schedule 1—Consequential amendments.
        Schedule 2—Transitional provisions etc.
        Schedule 3—Repeals.

An Act to consolidate the Drug Trafficking Offences Act 1986 and certain provisions of the Criminal Justice (International Co-operation) Act 1990 relating to drug trafficking.   [3rd November 1994]

Parliamentary Debates
   Hansard, H.L. Vol. 555, col. 1440; Vol. 556, cols. 992, 1516; Vol. 557, col. 10; H.C. Vol. 248, col. 319.

Introduction and General Note

On July 8, 1986, by virtue of the Drug Trafficking Offences Act 1986 (c. 32) (the 1986 Act), Parliament introduced sweeping and radical changes in the law to enable the courts to recover the proceeds of drug trafficking. Sections 1(3), 2(1), 24, 34, 38 and 40 came into force on September 30, 1986 (see the Drug Trafficking Offences Act 1986 (Commencement No. 1) Order 1986 (S.I. 1986 No. 1488) (C. 53)), followed by sections 27 to 29, 31 and 33 (in force on December 30, 1986) and the remainder on January 12, 1987; see the Drug Trafficking Offences Act 1986 (Commencement No. 3) Order 1986 (S.I. 1986 No. 2145 (C. 85)).

The 1986 Act has since been amended by the Criminal Justice (Scotland) Act 1987 (c. 62), the Land Registration Act 1988 (c. 3), the Criminal Justice Act 1988 (c. 33), the Criminal Justice (International Co-operation) Act 1990 (c. 5) and the Criminal Justice Act 1993 (c. 36), Pt. II (the 1993 Act).

Why the 1994 Act was enacted

On February 9, 1995, the European Court of Human Rights upheld a complaint, in the case of Welch, that confiscation orders made under the Drug Trafficking Offences Act 1986 (c. 32) prior to that Act coming into force on January 12, 1987, were in contravention of Art. 7 of the European Convention of Human Rights which provides: "*Nor shall a heavier penalty be imposed than the one that was applicable at the time the criminal offence was committed*". Crucial to this decision was the vexed question as to whether confiscation orders are penal in nature, or merely a reparative remedy, but for present purposes, the point to note is that the relevant date (for the purposes of applying the 1986 Act) is the date the offence was committed. This may have important consequences so far as the Drug Trafficking Act 1994 is concerned which came into force on February 3, 1995. That Act applies to defendants *charged* with a drug trafficking offence (or against whom proceedings have been instituted for such an offence) *after* that date (see s.66). In other words, the relevant date is the date on which the defendant was charged – not the date the offence was actually committed. Although described in the Preamble as an "act to consolidate the Drug Trafficking Offences Act 1986 and certain provisions of the Criminal Justice (International Co-operation) Act 1990 . . .", the 1994 Act radically overhauls the way in which drug trafficking confiscation proceedings are to be investigated and conducted, and it strengthens the court's powers of enforcement in respect of the gathering and furnishing of information (relevant to confiscation proceedings) as well as ensuring the satisfaction (in full) of amounts payable under a confiscation order. We should ask ourselves therefore, in the light of the decision of the European Court of Human Rights, whether s.66 of the 1994 Act in contravention of Art. 7? On one view, the 1994 Act includes provisions which are now more favourable to the defendant (*e.g.* that the court now has a discretion whether to embark upon a drug trafficking enquiry) but there are unquestionably other provisions which are deliberately intended to be more draconian in their effect than was the case under the 1986 Act. The mandatory application of the statutory assumptions under s.4 is one example and the application of the civil standard of proof (s.2(8)) is another. For the purpose of making any of the statutory assumptions, it is of course true to say that the effect of an assumption once made, and not rebutted, is likely to be the same whether the standard of proof is phrased in terms of the civil or the criminal standard of proof but this is not necessarily so; see the result in *R.* v. *Enwezor* (1991) 93 Cr.App.R. 233. It is true also that the court need not make an assumption under s.4 if to do so would give rise to a "serious risk of injustice in the defendant's case" (s.4(4)(b)) but this is not the same thing as vesting a discretion in the court as to whether an assumption may be made or not. Furthermore, the mere fact that determinations are made by applying the civil standard of proof does not invariably mean that a confiscation order is not penal in nature. As the European Court indicated, it is necessary to look behind appearances.

Ironically, s.66 of the 1994 Act was the product of further reflection by the Government as to the effect of s.78(6) of the 1993 Act (which never came into force). By s.78(6) of the 1993 Act, an offence *committed* before the coming into force of Pts. II, III or IV of the 1993 Act, would have meant that the old law would have been applicable even if the defendant had been charged or convicted of that offence many years after its commission. Thus, an offender, who fled the jurisdiction in 1990 and who was not charged and convicted of a drug trafficking offence until the year 2005, could have expected the court (under s.78(6) of the 1993 Act) to deal with him under the old law. This is probably exactly what Parliament intended should happen in the interests of fairness to the accused. However, as David Thomas has pointed out (see "The Criminal Justice Act 1993", [1994] Crim.L.R. 100), one effect of s.78(6) of the 1993 Act would have been that two sets of rules would have run in parallel for many years causing confusion where, for example, the indictment includes two counts, one of which relates to an offence before the relevant date and the other after that date. To avoid this result, Parliament enacted s.66 of the 1994 Act which makes the date on which an accused is *charged* (or against whom proceedings have been instituted) the relevant date for the purposes of the Act.

Part II of the 1993 Act was designed radically to reform the 1986 Act but the only provisions which actually came into force were:

(i) s.16, on February 15, 1994 (acquisition, possession or use of proceeds of drug trafficking) introducing s.23A into the 1986 Act – now s.51 of this Act;

(ii) s.17, on February 15, 1994 which inserted corresponding provisions in s.42 of the Criminal Justice (Scotland) Act 1987;

(iii) s.18, on April 1, 1994 (offences in connection with drug money laundering) which inserted s.26B (now s.52 of this Act) and s.26C (now s.53 of this Act) into the 1986 Act;

(iv) s.19 which, on April 1, 1994, inserted similar provisions found in s.18 into s.43 of the Criminal Justice (Scotland) Act 1987;

(v) s.26, which on April 1, 1994, inserted s.31(2A) into the 1986 Act (disclosure of information etc. received in privileged circumstances) and which is now subs. (3) of s.58 of this Act.

According to a Home Office Circular (19/1994) the implementation of Pts. II to IV of the 1993 Act was proving to be more problematical than anticipated and implementation was intended to be deferred until the summer of 1994. However, it would seem that no sooner had the ink of the 1993 Act dried, than the Government decided the time had come to consolidate various statutory powers and controls in relation to the proceeds of drug trafficking and, perhaps, the proceeds of other areas of criminal conduct as well. Although no detailed explanation has officially been given by the Government for legislating in this fashion, it is not difficult to imagine what the reasons must have been. When, on October 22, 1992, the Criminal Justice Bill came before Parliament, it consisted of six parts and a total of 48 clauses but, by the date of Royal Assent (July 27, 1993) the Bill had expanded to seven parts with a total of 79 clauses. At a late stage in the Bill's progress through Parliament, substantial amendments were made to the Northern Ireland (Emergency Provisions) Act 1991 (c. 24) and the Prevention of Terrorism (Temporary Provisions) Act 1989 (c. 4). Many of those provisions were included broadly to align the confiscation provisions, relating to the financing of terrorism, with the 1986 Act (as it was to have been similarly amended by the 1993 Act, Pt. II). Money laundering offences relating to "criminal conduct" – that is to say, other than drug trafficking (see s.93A(7) of the CJA 1988 and s.29 of the 1993 Act) – were added by Pt. III of the 1993 Act to the provisions of the Criminal Justice Act 1988, and again, those particular offences would have corresponded to offences under the 1986 Act (as amended by the 1993 Act, Pt. II). What is often overlooked is that it is not just the courts which have powers of forfeiture and confiscation: some powers are vested in the hands of particular law enforcement agencies, most notably the Commissioners of Customs and Excise (see s.148 of the Customs and Excise Management Act 1979 (c. 2)) albeit subject to the courts performing a supervisory role. It follows that powers of forfeiture or confiscation are now to be found in an array of enactments and statutory instruments depending on (i) the agency or court seeking to exercise any of those powers, (ii) the relevant territorial jurisdiction of the agency or court in question, and (iii) the nature of the criminal activities complained of. Not surprisingly, this confusing state of affairs has prompted calls for the introduction of a single comprehensive model and a code which could be applied throughout Britain (or even overseas): see the (Standing Committee B, col. 114, June 8, 1993, *per* Mr David Trimble.) The call for codification has also been supported by Lord Colville of Culross who, in relation to the current legislation, has said that the:

"Northern Ireland (Emergency Provisions) Act 1991 applies throughout the U.K.; the courts will have to be prepared to exercise powers under the Drug Trafficking Offences Act 1986, the Criminal Justice Act 1988, Prevention of Terrorism (Temporary Provisions) Act 1989, Northern Ireland (Emergency Provisions) Act 1991, and the Criminal Justice Act 1993. Not only do some of the powers overlap, but the codes are different in detail, as can be seen in Northern Ireland where the first two Acts mentioned above had their confiscation powers enacted by Order in Council. There is the additional dimension of the extension of these provisions to the Isle of Man, Jersey and Guernsey, which can be done to some, but not to a complete degree, by the U.K. government under Prevention of Terrorism (Temporary Provisions) Act 1989, s.28 (3) and Northern Ireland (Emergency Provisions) Act 1991, s.71(3). However, it can also be done by legislation in Tynwald; at the moment the Isle of Man is ahead of the field in that their Prevention of Terrorism Act 1990 has valuable provisions for reciprocal enforcement. In the Channel Islands, negotiations are still proceeding as to the extent of legislation to be presented to the respective States. It cannot be easy for any of them to keep up with the flow of legislative changes on the financial front and it is particularly important that they should be up-to-date in light of the facilities which would otherwise be available to terrorists in these off-shore market places. A U.K. codification would give them the opportunity to legislate on the basis of a single, comprehensive model".

Of all of these important measures, it is the drug trafficking legislation which is both the most draconian and the most likely to be encountered by criminal law practitioners. It is therefore particularly important that the law in this area should be comprehensive and comprehensible. The first objective would certainly not have been attainable had Pt. II of the 1993 Act come into force. It seems that the Government reflected on observations made by Lord Colville (and others) who called for codification, and hence the Drug Trafficking Bill was introduced in the Lords on May 25, 1994. Unfortunately the Government, for reasons which are not entirely clear, kept the idea of introducing a consolidating Bill something of a secret until the Drug Trafficking Bill was on the point of being introduced into the House of Lords. One reason for this may be that the Government was uncertain as to whether there was going to be sufficient time to see the Bill through Parliament given that the Police and Magistrates' Courts Bill and the Criminal Justice and Public Order Bill were already under detailed and protracted scrutiny. There may also have been some doubt as to whether the Drug Trafficking Bill was an appropriate consolidating measure; it may have been better to try to consolidate (or to codify) a range of other statutory provisions, or even to go further and introduce other measures in the fight against money-laundering.

When the 1993 Act was passed, a flurry of contributions quickly followed from commentators who anticipated that much of the Act would be brought into force by April 1, 1994, at the latest. This expectation was heightened when many provisions of the 1993 Act did come into force within that time-scale and the Money Laundering Regulations 1993 (S.I. 1993 No. 1933) came into force on April 1, 1994. It therefore seemed logical to expect all or most of Pt. II of the Act to be brought into force at the same time and clearly the Home Office were mindful of this. Nevertheless, the delay gave the Government the opportunity to look again at the measures enacted in the 1993 Act.

The 1994 Act – a consolidatory measure

It must be emphasised that the 1994 Act is a consolidating measure but it will be seen that Parliament has taken the opportunity to rectify (and to modify) certain aspects of the previous legislation including Pt. II of the 1993 Act. Most of these changes are matters of drafting form, but there are also some significant changes in substance to the working of the new provisions. For example, by s.78(6) of the 1993 Act, an offence committed before the coming into force of Pts. II, III or IV of the 1993 Act, would have meant that the old law would have applied even if the defendant had been charged or convicted of that offence many years after its commission so that two sets of rules would need to be kept in mind, and applied, by the courts for a very long time – if not indefinitely. Thus, an offender who fled the jurisdiction in 1990 and who was not convicted of a drug trafficking offence until the year 2005 could have expected the court (under s.78(6) of the 1993 Act) to deal with him under the old law. No doubt part of the thinking behind s.78(6) was to protect the interests of a defendant whose prosecution and/or trial was delayed through no fault of his or her own. On the other hand, as David Thomas has pointed out (see *"The Criminal Justice Act 1993"* [1994] Crim.L.R. 100), s.78(6) was probably enacted in deference to the principle against retroactive criminal legislation, but two sets of rules could cause confusion where, for example, the indictment includes two counts, one of which relates to an offence before the relevant date and the other after that date. To avoid this result, Parliament enacted s.66 of the 1994 Act which makes the date an accused is *charged* (or against whom proceedings have been instituted) the relevant date for the purposes of this Act.

A second significant charge relates to s.3(10) of this Act which provides:

"Where the court has sentenced the defendant under subsection (7) above during the specified period it may, after the end of that period, vary the sentence by imposing a fine or making any such order as is mentioned in section 2(5)(b)(ii) or (iii) of this Act, so long as it does so within a period corresponding to that allowed by section 47(2) or (3) of the Supreme Court Act 1981 (time allowed for varying a sentence) but beginning with the end of the specified period".

Under the new scheme, introduced by this Act, it will now be possible for the courts to postpone the drug trafficking enquiry for a period of up to six months after the date of conviction (or longer in exceptional cases) but the court may nevertheless proceed to sentence the defendant during the "specified period" (see s.3(7)). However, the court cannot at that stage fine the defendant or make any monetary order against him or make any order under s.27 of the Misuse of Drugs Act 1971 (c. 38) (the 1971 Act) or s.43 of the Powers of Criminal Courts Act 1973 (c. 62). What would happen if, two months after sentence, the court decides to make a nominal order (or to make a confiscation order reflecting the full amount of the defendant's benefit from drug trafficking) but the court then wishes to fine the offender? Is the court debarred from so doing? Without s.3(10) (the equivalent of which did not appear in the 1993 Act) it is possible that the courts would have held that s.3(7) of this Act merely empowers the court to proceed to sentence but (because a confiscation order is a sentence) the process of sentencing, before the Crown Court, is not complete until the end of the "specified period" under s.3 of the Act. However, to put the matter beyond doubt, the Lord Chancellor moved (by way of amendment) what is now s.3(10) and said:

"This amendment and Amendment No. 2 [repealing sched. 9, para. 26 of the Criminal Justice and Public Order Act 1994] are necessary to bring into the consolidation an amendment made to the Criminal Justice and Public Order Bill during its Committee stage in your Lordship's House. That amends section 1A of the Drug Trafficking Offences Act 1986, to remove a practical difficulty which may prevent the court from passing certain kinds of sentences on a defendant after it has decided to exercise its power under section 1A to postpone making a determination under section 1 as to whether a defendant has benefited from drug trafficking or as to whether a defendant has benefited from drug trafficking or as to the amount to be recovered from him, so that further information can be obtained. The Joint Committee on Consolidation Bills was informed that the Government would move amendments in the same terms to this consolidation Bill.

The second amendment to the third schedule is, as I have said, a consequential amendment to repeal the amending provision in the Criminal Justice and Public Order Bill which will be spent when the consolidation comes into force" (*Hansard*, H.L. Vol. 556, col. 992).

This Act repeals and re-enacts most of the 1986 Act except for s.24(6) (early release provisions); s.32 (authorisation of delay in notifying arrest, the Police and Criminal Evidence Act 1984 (c. 60), s.65, as amended by sched. 1, para. 8 of this Act); s.34 (inserting s.9A into the Misuse of Drugs Act 1971); s.40(1), (3)–(5) (short title, commencement and extent). The Act also consolidates Pt. III of the Criminal Justice (International Co-operation) Act 1990 (c. 5) (drug trafficking money imported or exported in cash) as well as s.14 (concealing or transferring the proceeds of drug trafficking) in so far as s.14 of the 1990 Act applied to England and Wales (see s.68(7) of this Act) and a number of smaller amendments to ss.15(1), 15(3), 23A (except Scotland), 30(2) and (3), 31(2), and sched. 4, para. 4 of the 1990 Act.

Most of Pt. II of the 1993 Act is repealed (and re-enacted in this Act) except for ss.17 and 19 (Scotland) and ss.20, 22, 24 and 26 insofar as those provisions relate to Scotland. Schedule 9, para. 28 of the Criminal Justice and Public Order Act 1994 is now redundant (see s.3(10)) and is thus repealed by s.67, Sched. 3 of this Act.

It will therefore be appreciated that this Act (which largely extends to England and Wales only (see s.68) is not a codifying measure on the scale, or of the type, advocated by Lord Colville (see above).

Although codification of the laws of forfeiture and confiscation is an obvious and laudable objective, its attainment is improbable in the foreseeable future not least because major political and ideological differences exist (both domestically and internationally) as to the viability and validity of employing a variety of measures and devices designed to strip offenders of their ill-gotten gains. Much of what is now being done, so far as drug trafficking and money laundering is concerned, is bound up with international obligations and agreements but the methods adopted by the courts to confiscate assets differs considerably between nations.

The Home Office Working Group in their Report on the Drug Trafficking Offences Act 1986 (May 1991) found that the 1986 Act had worked "reasonably well" (see para. 1) but they made a number of recommendations which were given statutory force by ss.7 to 15 (inclusive) of Pt. II of the 1993 Act but which are now re-enacted in this Act.

By the end of 1992 some £35 million had been ordered to be confiscated under the 1986 Act and by May 1992 £15 million had actually been realised or was subject to receivership (see *Hansard*, H.L. Vol. 539, col. 1383).

The rationale of confiscation

It is important to realise that the Act does not merely tinker with existing law but radically overhauls the way in which drug trafficking confiscation proceedings are to be investigated and conducted, and strengthens the court's powers of enforcement in respect of the gathering and furnishing of information (relevant to confiscation proceedings) as well as ensuring the satisfaction (in full) of amounts payable under a confiscation order.

Previously, the courts were equipped only with the statutory powers of forfeiture, the making of "deprivation" orders or "criminal bankruptcy" orders, and/or the imposition of fines. Save for criminal bankruptcy orders these powers continue to exist, but they are very limited in scope. Thus, by s.27 of the 1971 Act, only those assets which directly relate to an offence committed by the accused, under that Act, may be forfeited: see *R. v. Morgan* [1977] Crim.L.R. 488, C.A. Choses in action and intangibles are not usually capable of being forfeited: see *R. v. Khan*; *R. v. Crawley* [1982] 1 W.L.R. 1405, C.A. Drug profits, originally received by the accused but then transferred to a third party, could not be seized. It was to meet such weaknesses in the law that the 1986 Act was enacted following recommendations contained in the Home Affairs Committee Fifth Report "Misuse of Hard Drugs Interim Report" (H.C. 399, (1985)) which had approved the American policy of giving the court "draconian powers" to strip drug dealers of assets acquired during the course of their drug dealing even where their connection with drug trafficking offences was merely "probable".

This seemingly straightforward but important statement of policy conceals the extent of the power required to enforce it. Three points should thus be noted. First, the policy stems from the scale and nature of the illicit drug trade, often involving more than one jurisdiction and the laundering of substantial sums of money at home and abroad affecting a number of institutions or corporate bodies, many of whom may be totally innocent parties. Secondly, the policy is intended to "remove the profit motive by allowing the confiscation of all the trafficker's proceeds from drug trafficking, following conviction" (*per* Secretary of State, Home Office, *Hansard*, H.C. Vol. 222, col. 866). Thirdly, the policy is also intended to ensure that drug trafficking profits cannot be re-cycled to fund further drug trafficking (*ibid.*). Fourth, the thinking behind the policy would seem to be that in order to achieve the last-mentioned objective, the confiscation of assets in circumstances where their connection with drug-trafficking is merely probable is justified. Fifth, a connection that need only be "probable" suggests the application of a civil standard of proof in confiscation proceedings: see Art. 7 of the Vienna Convention 1988. Sixth, the stripping of drug assets accrued during the course of the dealer's drug dealing involves tracing assets throughout his career. Seventh, the gleaning of information and "intelligence" is an essential pre-requisite of enforcement.

Some of these aforementioned points either cut across or challenge traditional principles, and rules of procedure in the context of criminal proceedings. Nowhere has this been more apparent in respect of the Drug Trafficking Offences Act 1986 (as originally drafted) than the application of the burden and standard of proof: see *R. v. Dickens* [1990] 2 Q.B. 102; *R. v. Redbourne* [1992] 1 W.L.R. 1182 and *R. v. Rose* [1993] 1 W.L.R. 844; and "Making statutory assumptions under the Drug Trafficking Offences Act", *Archbold News*, Issue No. 5; May 28, 1993; see now s.2(8) replacing s.1(7A) of the Drug Trafficking Offences Act 1986 inserted by s.7(2) of the 1993 Act.

It has been argued that the jurisprudential justification for the approach adopted in the Drug Trafficking Offences Act 1986 is that confiscation proceedings are not penal in nature but essentially civil or reparative consequent upon a conviction of a "drug trafficking offence" in accordance with traditional principles. This is examined more fully below (and see Lord Ackner, *Hansard*, H.L. Vol. 540, cols. 744 and 749). Note that the existing legislation has to be viewed alongside an international campaign to tackle international crime of which fraud (hence Pt. I), drug trafficking and terrorism are of the greatest concern.

Originally only Pts. II and III were included in the Criminal Justice Bill 1993 following the Home Office Working Group's recommendations (see the Reports of the Drug Trafficking Offences Act 1986 (May 1991) and the Criminal Justice Act 1988 (November 1992). However, Parliament took the opportunity (albeit at a late stage of the Bill's passage through both Houses of Parliament) to widen the scope of the legislation by including new offences in relation to money laundering. These include failing to disclose to a constable knowledge or suspicion of drug money laundering activities (s.52 of this Act, formerly s.18 of the 1993 Act) and "tipping off" another about a current or proposed drug money laundering investigation (s.53 of this Act, formerly s.19 of the 1993 Act). The provisions of Pts. I and III of this Act resemble various measures enacted by Pts. III and IV of the 1993 Act (*i.e.* amending the Criminal Justice Act 1988 and the Northern Ireland (Emergency Provisions) Act 1991 in respect of the financing of terrorism).

Note also the E.C. Council Directive 91/308/EEC following the Council of Europe Convention on Laundering, Tracing, Seizure and Confiscation of Proceeds of Crime. Note also s.26 of the 1986 Act (as amended) and the Drug Trafficking Offences Act (Designated Countries and Territories) Order 1990 (S.I. 1990 No. 1199) (as amended by S.I. 1991 No. 1465). Orders made in Scotland under the Criminal Justice (Scotland) Act 1987 may now be enforced in England and Wales: see the Drug Trafficking Offences Act (Enforcement in England and Wales) Order 1988 (S.I. 1988 No. 593).

In contrast with American law, the British model remains less draconian (notwithstanding representations made by American law enforcement agencies to the British Government) but the trend is clearly in favour of the American approach. The U.S.A. has been developing powerful anti-money laundering laws over the last 20 years. The Bank Secrecy Act 1970 (U.S.) applies to financial institutions and businesses which accept large sums of cash. A "financial institution" is very broadly defined: see *U.S. v. Rigdon* (1989) 874 F.2d 774 and *U.S. v. Clines* (1992) 958 F.2d 578. The Bank Secrecy Act 1970 requires businesses and individuals to submit Currency Transaction Reports (CTRs) as well as various reports of currency instruments, foreign bank accounts, and cash payments over U.S. $10,000 in a trade or business. Businesses and their employees may be required to lodge Criminal Referral Forms (CRFs) in respect of any "known or suspected criminal violation ... committed against [or through] a bank" used to facilitate a criminal transaction. Failure to file a CRF may result in so-called civil penalties being assessed against the institution, its officers or employees. Data and intelligence gleaned from these records are collated on a database utilised by FINCEN (Financial Crimes Enforcement Network). The Anti-Abuse Act 1988 (U.S.) includes a requirement upon the Secretary to the Treasury to negotiate with other countries to ensure that they have adequate records on international currency transactions, which might be taken as a requirement for mandatory reporting along United States lines. The question as to what happens to all this information is a matter of growing concern and debate. The Money Laundering Control Act (1986) (U.S.), creates a number of offences in respect of the knowing participation by any person in transactions with persons who derive their money from specified unlawful activities, *e.g.* drug trafficking. Forfeiture, under U.S. legislation, is permitted under the Bank Secrecy Act 1970, the Money Laundering Control Act 1986 (U.S.), the Comprehensive Drug Abuse Prevention and Control Act, the Controlled Substances Act, the Racketeer-Influenced and Corrupt Organisations (RICO) and the Continuing Criminal Enterprise statutes.

Of particular interest are two concepts in American law. First, some statutory provisions enjoy a reduced standard of proof requiring the government to prove only a "probable" cause to believe "that a substantial connection exists between the property to be forfeited" and the act which contravenes the statute: *U.S. v. Four Million Dollars* (1985) 762 F.2d 895 (1985). Secondly, there is the "Relation-Back Doctrine" which is based on the fiction that illegally obtained property vests in the government at the time of the offence.

Notwithstanding the above, the Drug Trafficking Offences Act 1986 has been appropriately described as a "draconian" piece of legislation and was intended to be so: see *R. v. Dickens* (1990) 91 Cr.App.R. 164, *per* Lord Lane C.J. at 167; *R. v. Comiskey* (1990) 12 Cr.App.R.(S.) 562, *per* Tucker J. at 568; *R. v. Smith (Ian)* (1989) 89 Cr.App.R. 253; *per* Lord Lane C.J. at 238, and *R. v. Robson (Steven Kenneth)* (1991) 92 Cr.App.R. 1. The 1994 Act has the potential for being a thoroughly fierce piece of legislation but it also has enough scope to allow the courts to restrain its application and thus to modify its impact. Thus, by s.2(8) of the Act, the standard of proof required to determine whether a person has benefited from drug trafficking, or the amount to be recovered under a confiscation order, is now to be the civil standard of proof. The significance, of whether the relevant standard (under the 1986 Act) should be the criminal standard or not, was particularly relevant in the context of the court's power under the 1986 Act to make any of the statutory assumptions if it was appropriate to do so: see *R. v. Enwezor* (1991) 93 Cr.App.R. 233, *R. v. Redbourne* [1992] 1 W.L.R. 1182 and *Rose* [1993] 1 W.L.R. 844.

However, unlike the 1986 Act, the court is not obliged to embark upon a drug trafficking enquiry where a defendant falls to be sentenced for a drug trafficking offence (see s.2(1) of this Act) but once it does do so then (unlike the 1986 Act) it is obliged to make what are now called the "required assumptions" (s.4(2)) unless to make any of the statutory assumptions set out in s.4(3) of this Act is either (i) shown to be incorrect in the defendant's case (s.4(4)(a)) or "the court is satisfied that there would be a serious risk of injustice in the defendant's case if the assumptions were to be made" (s.4(4)(b)). It will be interesting to see how the courts use these provisions in practice. Would the existence of a reasonable doubt as to the correctness of any of the prosecution's allegations (notwithstanding s.2(8)) be sufficient to create "a serious risk of injustice" so as to entitle a court not to make one of the "required assumptions" by virtue of s.4(4)(b)? And what does a "serious risk" mean in the context of this Act? If it means that the assumption is probably incorrect then there would arguably be no need for s.4(4)(b) at all because no doubt s.4(4)(a) would be discharged by the defendant to the civil standard of proof. If "serious risk" means a real or substantial doubt then when does a reasoned doubt (reasonable doubt?) not create a serious risk of injustice?

It will also be of interest to monitor the extent to which the courts adapt the provisions of this Act for purposes which are not specifically catered for under the Act. For example, a defendant who co-operates with a law enforcement agency could not, under the old law, invite the prosecutor and the court not to embark upon confiscation proceedings in exchange for co-operating with the authorities but, under s.2 of the Act, such a result seems possible: see *R. v. Atkinson* (*Michael Frederick*) (1993) 14 Cr.App.R.(S.) 182 and *R. v. Finch* [1992] Crim.L.R. 901. Would that be a permissible use of the machinery under the Act in the eyes of the court?

Confiscation: – penal or reparation?
The answer to this question is not of mere academic interest: it explains how the legislation has developed and explains some of the difficulties of construction which have arisen. The answer was also of criminal importance to the decision of the European Court of Human Rights in *Welch*, February 9, 1995, *supra*. On one view, the 1986 Act was intended to be primarily punitive in nature and thus was to be construed as a penal statute. The alternative view was that the Act was always intended to be reparative or compensatory in nature (society being the victim) and thus the legislation was to be construed and applied in accordance with the less restrictive rules of evidence and procedure found in civil law. Not surprisingly, those competing views have been voiced, most notably, in connection with the standard of proof applicable to those matters which the prosecution are required to prove under the 1986 Act: see *R. v. Dickens* [1990] 2 Q.B. 102; *R. v. Enwezor* (1991) 93 Cr.App.R. 233; *R. v. Redbourne* [1992] 1 W.L.R. 1182. However, if the 1986 Act was only reparative (being civil in nature) and not penal, then several consequences arguably follow:
 (i) the appropriate standard of proof is the civil standard;
 (ii) evidence may be adduced and received in accordance with civil law principles. This is particularly relevant in respect of the admission of hearsay evidence and documentation (*e.g.* are transcripts admissible?);
 (iii) the appropriate court is a court of civil jurisdiction;
 (iv) the making of a confiscation order is not a penal order and therefore should not be regarded as a "sentence" for the purposes of an appeal to the Court of Appeal (Criminal Division): by contrast, see *R. v. Johnson* [1991] 2 Q.B. 249 and *R. v. Hayden* [1975] 1 W.L.R. 852 at p. 854G;
 (v) legal aid should be granted under a Civil Legal Aid Order;
 (vi) if the 1986 Act is not penal then a court is not constrained to resolve an ambiguity in favour "of the defendant": see *R. v. Chapman, The Times*, November 18, 1991.
The view that confiscation under the 1986 and 1994 Acts is reparative appears to be gaining ground – at least within law enforcement circles. It is strongly advocated by the Home Office, the Central Confiscation Unit and, indeed, by the Government (see *Hansard*, H.L. Vol. 539, col. 1347; Vol. 540, cols. 1469, 1483).
On the other hand, although the making of a confiscation order follows a conviction for a "drug trafficking offence" (s.2(1)), nevertheless the amount assessed to represent (and to be recovered as) his proceeds of drug trafficking need not derive from the offence for which he was convicted at all. This is because the defendant's benefit may include proceeds received as a result of drug trafficking carried on by him or "by another" – anywhere in the world (ss.2(2), (3), 4(1), 5(1)). The court may include payments received or made by the defendant which have no connection with the offence before the court but, if any of the assumptions are made within the terms of s.4(2) and (5), then they will be assumed to be in connection with drug trafficking carried on by the defendant himself. Unlike civil judgments, unpaid confiscation orders carrying severe terms of imprisonment in default of payment (depending on the sum outstanding). Lord Lane C.J. in *R. v. Dickens* [1990] 2 Q.B. 102 seems to have regarded the 1986 Act as being penal in nature and therefore the burden was held to be on the prosecution to prove (to the criminal standard of proof) that the defendant has benefited from drug trafficking and the amount of such benefit (*cf.* the *obiter dictum* of Leggatt L.J. in *Re Thomas* [1992] 4 All E.R. 814 at p. 819).
By contrast, confiscation under the Criminal Justice Act 1988 depends on the prosecution proving that the benefit received by the defendant derived from an offence proved (or admitted) to have been committed by him (s.71 and see s.71(4)). The burden of proving the fact that a benefit had been received, and the amount of the benefit, is on the prosecution – without the assistance of statutory assumptions such as those to be found in s.4 of the 1994 Act.
When the 1993 Act was being debated as a Bill, both Houses were divided as to whether confiscation proceedings were "civil" in nature. The Minister of State for the Home Office emphasised that the application of a civil standard of proof was always the Government's intention but that the 1986 Act did not make that intention sufficiently clear resulting in the courts applying a criminal standard of proof at certain stages of the proceedings (see *R. v. Dickens* [1990] 2 Q.B. 102 and *Hansard*, H.L. Vol. 539, cols. 1350, 1383). Lord Ackner and Lord Bright-

man supported the view that the civil standard should apply (see *Hansard*, H.L. Vol. 520, cols. 1471, 1472) while Lord Williams of Mostyn (see *Hansard*, H.L. Vol. 540, col. 741) pointed out that confiscation of assets involved a finding that the defendant had benefited from drug trafficking – a criminal activity. This issue is further developed below in respect of s.2(8) of the 1994 Act.

The European Court of Human Rights: Welch v. *United Kingdom*
   On February 9, 1995, the European Court of Human Rights upheld a complaint, in the case of *Welch*, that confiscation orders made under the Drug Trafficking Offences Act 1986 (c. 32) prior to that Act coming into force on January 12, 1987, was in contravention of Art. 7 of the European Convention of Human Rights which provides: "*Nor shall a heavier penalty be imposed than the one that was applicable at the time the criminal offence was committed*". In order to succeed the applicant had to show that the confiscation order was a "penalty" and it seems to have been the British Government's case that the 1986 Act is essentially reparative in nature following the conviction for a drug trafficking offence. This argument is not new and, indeed, in *R.* v. *Redbourne* (1993) 96 Cr.App.R. 201 the prosecution conceded that if the 1986 Act is penal then it would be in breach of its international obligations including Art. 7(1) of the European Convention of Human Rights (but see *Re T.* (1993) 96 Cr.App.R. 194, Leggatt LJ. at p. 200). Various apsects of the 1986 legislation may indeed be civil in nature (e.g. the making of restraint order, disclosure orders, etc.) but a confiscation order is quite clearly penal in character and the European Court unanimously so held for the following reasons. First, the court may make assumptions under s.2(3) of the Act, that property held or transferred to the defendant within the relevant period represents the proceeds of his drug trafficking. Secondly, by seeking to confiscate the proceeds (and not just the profits of drug trafficking) irrespective of whether there had been any personal enrichment (see *R.* v. *Simons* (1994) 98 Cr.App.R. 100), the order went beyond the notions of reparation and prevention into the realm of punishment. Thirdly, the Act by conferring such broad powers of confiscation on the courts is also pursuing the aim of punishing the offender and that the aims of prevention and reparation may be seen as constituent elements of the very notion of punishment. Fourthly, the judge was also empowered to determine the amount of imprisonment to be served in default of payment. However, the European Court went on to accept the proposition that the judge has a discretion, in fixing the amount of the order, to take into consideration the degree of culpability of the accused, however, this is a proposition of questionable validity although mitigation may be affected by the findings of a drug trafficking enquiry: see *R.* v. *McNulty* [1994] Crim.L.R. 385.

The Scottish approach
   Most of the provisions of the Drug Trafficking Offences Act 1986 do not apply to Scotland: see s.40. A Bill to recover the proceeds of drug trafficking was considered by the Scottish Grand Committee and the First Scottish Standing Committee in 1987. In May of that year, the Criminal Justice (Scotland) Act 1987 (c. 41) received Royal Assent. The Scottish model is also draconian but, unlike the Crown Court in England, the power of the High Court of Justiciary to make a confiscation order is discretionary. The court is not obliged to embark upon an investigation as to the extent of an accused's proceeds of drug trafficking every time the accused is convicted of a drug trafficking offence. Indeed the High Court of Justiciary can only exercise its discretion upon the application of the prosecutor who must make his application prior to sentence or before any part of it has been pronounced (see the Criminal Justice (Scotland) Act 1987, s.1(1)). The Government's view was that relatively few orders will be made in Scotland each year and this view is certainly being confirmed in practice. One merit of the Scottish model is the considerable saving of court time in cases where it is obvious from the outset that the defendant has no assets capable of being realised and where, after investigation by the court, a nil confiscation order is the only realistic order which the court can make. There is also force in the argument that the courts should be primarily concerned with serious cases of drug trafficking and this was one of the reasons why s.1 of the Drug Trafficking Offences Act 1986 has been repealed in favour of s.2(1) of this Act.
   In England, even a solitary incident at the lowest end of the gravity scale was sufficient to trigger proceedings under the Drug Trafficking Offences Act 1986.
   English courts remain obliged to make an order (if they can) for the total amount which the court assesses to be the value of the defendant's proceeds of drug trafficking (or the value of the accused's realisable property plus the value of the gifts caught by the 1986 Act). In Scotland such a figure represents not a mandatory amount to be confiscated, but the maximum sum, which the High Court of Justiciary may confiscate. The overriding task of the High Court (if it makes an order) is to require the defendant to pay "such amount as the Court considers appropriate" (s.1(1) of the Criminal Justice (Scotland) Act 1987 (c. 41)) which does not exceed that ceiling. The discretionary power of the court to determine an "appropriate" amount enables the court to

arrive at a decision which does not deprive the defendant of all his assets with the consequential hardship which may descend upon innocent third parties.

The broad approach in England and Wales

Three points should be borne in mind whenever the court embarks upon a drug trafficking enquiry. First, what is to be confiscated are the proceeds of drug trafficking and not merely drug profits. A trafficker who receives £1,000 for the sale of a drug cannot seek to deduct the expenses he incurred in buying and transporting it: *R. v. Smith (Ian)* [1989] 1 W.L.R. 765. Broadly speaking his gross receipts are his proceeds. Secondly, the value of a confiscation order will not always signify the extent to which the defendant himself has been engaged in drug trafficking because the 1986 Act catches all drug proceeds received by the defendant whether as a result of his drug trafficking or another's: see *R. v. Smith (Ian)* [1989] 1 W.L.R. 765, and *R. v. Comiskey* (1991) 93 Cr.App.R. 227 (and note s.4(1)(a) and s.2(3) of the 1994 Act). Thirdly, it is irrelevant whether the drug trafficking in question took place within the jurisdiction of the courts of the U.K., or abroad subject to a "corresponding law": see s.1(1), 1(2), 1(4) of the 1994 Act.

The method by which a court may assess the value of the proceeds of drug trafficking was one of the most controversial features of the 1986 Act and more so in the light of Pt. I of the 1994 Act. There will often be cases where an accused can be shown to have received property over a period of years but there exists little or no evidence to prove that the property represents the proceeds of drug trafficking. Accordingly, the 1994 Act creates a number of far-reaching assumptions which the court is obliged to make unless the statutory exceptions apply. Inevitably, in complicated and hotly contested confiscation proceedings, much court time will be spent tracing funds and ascertaining their origin.

The Previous and the Present Position

(i) *The court's discretion to embark upon a confiscation hearing*

Whenever a defendant appeared before the Crown Court to be sentenced in respect of one or more "drug trafficking offences", the court was obliged to embark upon a drug trafficking enquiry in every case. This is no longer the case. By s.2(1) of the 1994 Act, the court need only embark upon confiscation proceedings if it is asked to do so by the prosecutor or when (even if not asked) the court considers that it is appropriate for it to proceed under the Act. Note that although s.2(1)(a) requires the prosecutor to "ask" that the court proceeds under s.2, in fact this courtesy belies the reality: once "asked" the court is obliged to embark upon a 1994 Act enquiry. No doubt most prosecutors will be sensible in their approach to such enquiries – but it is not clear what control (even in costs) the court has over decisions taken by prosecutors who compel a court to proceed under s.2 even if the court believes the exercise is inappropriate. The 1994 Act does not expressly cater for cases where the prosecution ask the court to proceed in circumstances where it is manifestly inappropriate for them to make that request: the most obvious example is where the defendant clearly has no realisable assets (beyond the clothes he is wearing in the dock) and there is no material before the court to suggest that any such assets are likely to be available in the foreseeable future. It remains to be seen whether the courts will seek to penalise a wasteful enquiry, initiated by the prosecutor, in costs, notwithstanding the terms of s.2(1)(a) which might entitle the prosecution to argue that they were merely exercising their statutory power.

(ii) *Making determinations under the 1994 Act*

There are three determinations which the court is likely to make under the Act:
(1) If the court decides to embark on confiscation proceedings it must first decide whether there is a benefit received by the defendant:
    (a) Formerly, the persuasive burden was on the prosecution to prove this issue to the criminal law standard of proof: see *R. v. Dickens* [1990] 2 Q.B. 102; *R. v. Enwezor* (1991) 93 Cr.App.R. 233. The persuasive burden remains on the prosecution but to the civil standard (see *s.2(8)* of the 1994 Act). Accordingly, *Dickens* and *Enwezor* are over-ruled on this point.
    (b) The court was empowered (but not obliged) to make any of the statutory assumptions contained in s.2(2) and (3) of the 1986 Act. The burden of rebuttal was on the defendant: see *Dickens* and *Enwezor*, above, and *R. v. Redbourne* [1992] 1 W.L.R. 1182. The court must now make the "required assumption" unless the statutory exceptions apply (see s.4(2)–(5) of the 1994 Act).
(2) If question (1) is answered affirmatively, then the court proceeds to assess the value of the proceeds of drug trafficking received by him (s.5(1) of the 1994 Act) but whereas, under the old law, the court could make a nil order, or no order (different courts seem to have had differing views about whether they should make a nil order or no order) now the court

is required to make a confiscation order for at least a "nominal amount" (s.5(3)(b)). Accordingly, if the court wishes to make, literally, no order, then unless the prosecutor has asked the court to proceed under s.2 of the 1994 Act, the court should not embark upon confiscation proceedings at all.

(3) What is the amount that might be realised under a confiscation order? The following points should be noted in determination of the amount to be recovered:

    (a) The value of the defendant's proceeds represents *prima facie* the "amount to be recovered" under a confiscation order: s.5(1);

    (b) The persuasive burden remains on the prosecution but now only to the civil standard of proof (s.2(8));

    (c) Under the 1994 Act, the "required assumptions" must be made unless the statutory exceptions apply (s.4(2)–(5)).

    (d) The court can be asked (or decide of its volition) to assess the "amount that may be realised" under s.5(3) as defined by s.6(1), being the total value of realisable property held by the defendant plus the total value of gifts made by him and caught by the Act: ss.5(3), 6(1) and 8.

    (e) Previously, if the defendant satisfied the court on a balance of probabilities that the "amount that might be realised" was less than the "amount to be recovered" then the court confiscated the lesser amount: see s.4(3) of the 1986 Act. See *R. v. Ilsemann* (1990) 12 Cr.App.R.(S.) 398; *R. v. Comiskey* (1991) 93 Cr.App.R. 227; and *R. v. Carroll* (1992) 13 Cr.App.R.(S.) 99. The judge issued a certificate recording that finding of fact: s.4(2) of the 1986 Act.

        This remains the position under the new procedure by virtue of s.5(3) and s.5(2) but the 1994 Act, like its predecessor, says nothing about the incidence of proof, presumably because the position is likely to be regarded as covered by authority: *e.g. Ilsemann* and *Comiskey* above.

    (f) If the defendant fails to discharge the burden on him, or failed to raise the issue at all, then the court may make a confiscation order for the full amount determined under steps (1) and (2) above: but see *Comiskey* (above) and *R. v. Keston* (1990) 12 Cr.App.R.(S.) 93 (wrongly referred to as "*Preston*" in [1990] Crim.L.R. 528). The law remains unchanged.

(iii) *Enforcement of confiscation orders as fines*

The court treats the confiscation order as a fine and imposes a sentence of imprisonment in default: s.9. Unlike the old law (under the 1986 Act) even if the defendant serves a sentence of imprisonment in default, the court under s.9(5) may still proceed to enforce payment of the confiscation order and see the commentary to s.9 below.

(iv) *Variation or discharge*

In a proper case, the court may vary or discharge the confiscation order. The powers of the court in this regard have been substantially widened and strengthened under the 1994 Act, thus:

    (a) formerly only a defendant could vary an order under s.14 of the 1986 Act (now s.7 of the 1994 Act), but now a receiver appointed under ss.26 or 29 of the 1994 Act may also apply under s.17(1) to vary or to discharge the confiscation order;

    (b) third parties may now make representations to the court: see s.17(5);

    (c) a court now has power to: make a confiscation order where, the evidence did not, originally, justify the making of such an order: s.13(2); re-assess whether the defendant has benefited from drug trafficking: s.14; revise its assessment of the value of the defendant's proceeds of drug trafficking: s.15;

    (d) the court also has power to increase the amount which a defendant may be ordered to pay under a confiscation order: s.16 (which re-enacts s.16 of the Criminal Justice (International Co-operation) Act 1990).

        The Court of Appeal has advised judges to state the relevant findings at each stage of the proceedings, *per* Neill L.J. in *R. v. Johnson* [1991] 2 Q.B. 249 at p. 260.

(iv) *Confiscating assets of the absconder or the deceased*

The High Court now has the power, by virtue of ss.19–24 of the 1994 Act, to make a confiscation order in the case of a defendant (charged with a drug trafficking offence) who absconds for a period of two years – whether convicted or not – and a power of confiscation in the case of a defendant who is convicted of a drug trafficking offence but who dies before the Crown Court can make a confiscation order. For these purposes, no statutory assumptions may be made pursuant to s.4(2) of the Act (see s.19(6)(a)) and, in the case of an absconder, the court shall not make a confiscation order unless it is satisfied that the prosecutor has taken reasonable steps to contact him (s.19(6)(c)). The court may also hear representations from third parties who are "likely to be affected by the making of a confiscation order by the court" (s.19(6)(d)). If the High Court decides not to make a confiscation order in respect of an absconder, the prosecution are not entitled to re-open the matter under s.14 of the 1994 Act if they come into possession of evidence which had not been considered by the court until the absconder returns: see s.19(9). Similarly, the High Court has no power to revise any assessment of the absconder's proceeds of drug trafficking whilst he remains an absconder: see ss.15 and 19(10). The defendant who ceases to be an absconder may apply for a variation of a confiscation order made under s.19 within a period of six years from the date the order was made: see s.21.

(v) *Receivers; charging orders and compensation*

Upon the making of a confiscation order, the prosecution may ask the High Court to appoint a receiver to realise assets that are held either by the defendant, or by persons to whom the defendant has directly or indirectly made a "gift" for the purposes of the Act: see ss.6 and 29. Property realised by the receiver may then be applied towards satisfying the order: see ss.30 and 31. Special rules will apply in the case of any person (not just the defendant) who is adjudged to be bankrupt but who nevertheless holds "realisable property": see ss.32 and 33. Special rules also apply to companies which are in the process of being wound up but which possess realisable property: s.34.

In order to avoid the risk that a defendant may be tempted to dispose of his assets before a court can confiscate them, the High Court is empowered, upon the application of the prosecutor, to grant a restraint order prohibiting any person from dealing with "realisable property" except as directed by the court: ss.25 and 26. Furthermore, a receiver may be appointed to take possession of any realisable property and to manage or to deal otherwise with that property: s.26(7).

It is desirable, in cases where a confiscation order has not yet been made, to register a charge on the property to secure the payment of moneys to the Crown. The 1994 Act provides the necessary machinery for doing so by virtue of s.27 (see, formerly, s.9 of the 1986 Act). Accordingly, the High Court may, upon the application of the prosecutor, grant a charging order (*ex parte* if necessary) and may appoint a Receiver to take possession of the property: s.29.

Where a defendant is aggrieved that the prosecution has detrimentally meddled in his financial affairs, and proceedings do not result in a conviction for a drug trafficking offence, he may apply to the High Court for an order of compensation to be paid to him: ss.18 and 22. For the purposes of s.18 these must be "serious default" on the part of a person concerned in the investigation or prosecution of the offence in question resulting in the loss but "the court shall not order compensation to be paid in any case where it appears to the court that the proceedings would have been instituted or continued even if the serious default had not occurred" (see s.18(3); formerly para. 12 to Sched. 5, Criminal Justice Act 1988 amending s.19 of the 1986 Act.) It is no longer necessary to show that the loss is "substantial". The "amount of compensation … shall be such as the High Court thinks just in all the circumstances of the case": s.18(4).

Is a confiscation order a sentence?

Nothing in this Act alters the existing law in this regard.

Section 9 of the Criminal Appeal Act 1968 states that a person "may appeal to the Court of Appeal against any sentence … passed on him for the offence". At first sight, a confiscation order is not passed on the defendant in respect of the offence, or offences, for which he appeared before the court. It is not a penalty but an order of deprivation. By s.50(1) a sentence includes "any order made by a court when dealing with an offender". In *Johnson* (above), the Court of Appeal held that despite the wording of s.2(4) and (5) of the 1986 Act a confiscation order does form part of the sentence because, the powers of the High Court in relation to a confiscation order can only be exercised where the order is not subject to appeal: see now s.29(1)(c) and s.41(8) of the 1994 Act. Confiscation orders can be made by the Criminal Division of the Court of Appeal: see this Act, s.9(6); and there was support in the words of Lord Widgery C.J. in *R. v. Hayden* [1975] 1 W.L.R. 852 at p. 854G, when he said that an order for costs comes within the definition of "sentence" in s.50(1) of the Criminal Appeal Act 1968 because "it is an order which is contingent upon there having been a conviction and it is contingent on the person by whom the payment is to be made, having been convicted in that why". In Scotland the matter is put beyond doubt by s.1(4) of the Criminal Justice (Scotland) Act 1987.

However s.2(5)(c) states that the court should "leave the order out of account in determining the appropriate sentence or other manner of dealing with the defendant". The sentiments expressed in s.2(5)(c) are consistent with the general principles of sentencing in that an accused is entitled to be sentenced on the basis of what is proved or admitted (to the criminal standard of proof) in respect of the offences for which he falls to be sentenced: see *R. v. Ayensu and Ayensu* (1982) 4 Cr.App.R.(S.) 248; *R. v. Ralf* (1989) 11 Cr.App.R.(S.) 121; *R. v. Reeves (R.J.)* (1983) 5

Cr.App.R.(S.) 292; *R. v. Bragason* [1988] Crim.L.R. 778; and the provisions of the Criminal Justice Act 1991 which tend to support that approach.

In *R. v. Harper* (1989) 11 Cr.App.R.(S.) 240, the Court of Appeal seems to have encroached on this principle in holding that the sentencer may pay some regard to the evidence placed before him under the 1986 Act if it rebuts an assertion made in mitigation, *e.g.* that the offence represented an isolated incident. In *R. v. Saunders* (1991) 92 Cr.App.R. 6, Hutchison J. said (at p. 10):

" ... it would be absurd to say that if in the course of the Drug Trafficking Offences Act investigation the defendant, for example, admitted extensive drug trafficking, the sentencing judge should entirely disregard that in determining the appropriate sentence. He could and should take it into account in the manner indicated a moment ago".

The Court of Appeal in *Saunders* made two other important observations. The first is that the sentencer should be careful not to take into account factual matters of which the sentencer had not been satisfied beyond reasonable doubt, and this presumably remains the law notwithstanding s.2(8) of the 1994 Act: but see *R. v. McNulty* (1994) 15 Cr.App.R.(S.) 606 and read the commentary to that case [1994] Crim.L.R. 385, 386. The second point is that the sentencer should not use the assumptions (under s.2(3) of the 1986 Act) to make a finding "adverse to the defendant in the realm of sentencing which he would not have made applying the ordinary burden of proof" (*per* Hutchison J. at p. 10): and see *R. v. Callan* (1994) 98 Cr.App.R. 467. Presumably, this remains the law notwithstanding s.4(2)–(5) of the 1994 Act.

In Scotland under the Criminal Justice (Scotland) Act 1987 (c. 41) the court is not obliged to sentence at the conclusion of the inquiry. Instead, the court may sentence the offender without delay and deal with the matter of confiscation at an adjourned date no more than six months after the date of conviction: s.2(1) of the Criminal Justice (Scotland) Act 1987.

Delaying sentencing

Previously, when the court intended to make a confiscation order, it had to determine the amount to be recovered from the defendant before sentencing him (s.1(4) of the 1986 Act). Furthermore, the court was obliged to take account of the order before imposing a fine (s.1(5)(b)(i)), or before making an order under s.27 of the 1971 Act (forfeiture orders) or s.43 of the Powers of the Criminal Courts Act 1973 (c. 62) (as amended) (deprivation orders): see the 1986 Act, s.1(5)(b)(ii) and (iii).

Since a court was debarred from proceeding to sentence until the court had gone through the procedural steps under that Act, this often meant that sentence was adjourned for a considerable period of time in order to enable the parties to prepare and to present evidence and arguments in pursuance of the 1986 Act inquiry. Occasionally that inquiry is so complicated and protracted that the proceedings take longer to hear than the contested criminal trial itself. In *R. v. Smith (Ian)* [1989] 1 W.L.R. 765, the appellant was convicted on January 26, 1988 but sentence, and the making of a confiscation order in the sum of £14,000, was not imposed until May 6, after a three-day hearing. In *R. v. Robson* (1991) 92 Cr.App.R. 1 there was a delay of some four months between conviction and sentence. It was difficult to see what justification there was for the mandatory position which then existed under the 1986 Act. One explanation was that the legislature considered that the court should not be in a position to sentence until all factual matters had been resolved, but this supposes that the sentencer would be entitled to have regard to the evidence placed before him under the 1986 Act.

Now, under the 1994 Act the court need not wait until a determination is made of the amount which may be recovered under a confiscation order before sentencing the defendant: see s.3(7) of the 1994 Act. Moreover, the court is not prevented from imposing a fine, or making an order under s.27 of the 1971 Act or s.43 of the Powers of Criminal Courts Act 1973, or any other monetary order, merely because a confiscation order is made beyond the 28-day period when the defendant was first sentenced for the offence before the court: see s.3(10).

Persons to whom s.2 of the 1994 Act applies

Confiscation orders may only be made against persons who appear before the Crown Court to be sentenced in respect of one or more "drug trafficking offences", a classification which, by s.1(3) of the 1994 Act, means:

"(a) an offence under section 4(2) or (3) or 5(3) of the Misuse of Drugs Act 1971 (production, supply and possession for supply of controlled drugs);

(b) an offence under section 20 of that Act (assisting in or inducing commission outside United Kingdom of offence punishable under a corresponding law);

(c) an offence under—

(i) section 50(2) or (3) of the Customs and Excise Management Act 1979 (improper importation),

(ii) section 68(2) of that Act (exportation), or

(iii) section 170 of that Act (fraudulent evasion),
in connection with a prohibition or restriction on importation or exportation having effect by virtue of section 3 of the Misuse of Drugs Act 1971;
(d) an offence under section 12 of the Criminal Justice (International Co-operation) Act 1990 (manufacture or supply of substance specified in Schedule 2 to that Act);
(e) an offence under section 19 of that Act (using ship for illicit traffic in controlled drugs);
(f) an offence under section 49, 50 or 51 of this Act or section 14 of the Criminal Justice (International Co-operation) Act 1990 (which makes, in relation to Scotland and Northern Ireland, provision corresponding to section 49 of this Act);
(g) an offence under section 1 of the Criminal Law Act 1977 of conspiracy to commit any of the offences in paragraphs (a) to (f) above;
(h) an offence under section 1 of the Criminal Attempts Act 1981 of attempting to commit any of those offences; and
(i) an offence of inciting another person to commit any of those offences, whether under section 19 of the Misuse of Drugs Act 1971 or at common law;
and includes aiding, abetting, counselling or procuring the commission of any of the offences in paragraphs (a) to (f) above".

The content of s.1(3) of the 1994 Act broadly follows s.38(1) of the 1986 Act as amended by the Criminal Justice (International Co-operation) Act 1990, sched. 4, para. 4(4) and by s.24(9) of the 1993 Act.

Jurisdiction

Only the Crown Court is empowered to make a confiscation order under s.2. Although the section applies in cases where the defendant is committed by the magistrates' court to the Crown Court for sentence pursuant to s.38 of the Magistrates' Courts Act 1980, it does not apply to juveniles who are committed to the Crown Court with a view to being sentenced to youth custody under s.37 of the Magistrates' Courts Act 1980 (as amended by the Criminal Justice Act 1991) or where the powers of the court are limited to dealing with the defendant in a way in which a magistrates' court might have dealt with him in connection with the offence charged: (see the 1994 Act, s.2(7)(b)). Accordingly, s.2 does not apply to defendants who appeal to the Crown Court against their conviction and/or sentence in the magistrates' court. Furthermore, s.2 has no application where a defendant has been "previously … sentenced or otherwise dealt with in respect of his conviction for the offence or … any of the offences concerned": s.2(1). Section 2 therefore does not apply to persons who are in breach of a community service order or a suspended sentence of imprisonment.

Making a confiscation order

Once the court has decided to embark upon a drug trafficking enquiry the court must go on to determine whether the defendant has benefited from drug trafficking (s.2(2)), and if he has, to determine the amount to be recovered (see ss.2(4) and 5). Realistically, each element must be examined in the context of the other, since an amount can only be recovered if it represents a benefit of drug-trafficking, and vice versa (and see *R. v. Simons* (1994) 98 Cr.App.R. 100).

By s.3 of the 1994 Act, the court will now be entitled to postpone the determination of the question of benefit or the amount to be recovered under a confiscation order where the defendant has appealed his conviction or where the court requires further information. Maximum periods are stipulated by the relevant provisions under s.3 of the 1994 Act. Whether a determination has been postponed or not, the court is now equipped with far more extensive powers, than was the case under the 1986 Act, to require both the prosecution and the defendant to furnish information which the court considers relevant in connection with any of the determinations to be made under the Act: see ss.11 and 12. If the defendant fails, without reasonable excuse, to provide the information sought by the court, then the court may draw such inferences from that failure as it considers appropriate: see s.12(5). It is not apparent from this provision to what extent negligent default on the part of the defendant's legal advisers could nevertheless bind the defendant.

Accordingly, one cannot divorce the method by which the court must determine whether the defendant has benefited from drug-trafficking, from the procedure laid down in the Act for assessing the value of the defendant's proceeds of that trade.

Section 2(4) (formerly, s.1(4) of the 1986 Act as amended by the 1993 Act) provides that:
"If the court determines that he has so benefited, the court shall, *before sentencing or otherwise dealing with him in respect of the offence or, as the case may be, any of the offences concerned,* determine in accordance with section 4 of this Act the amount to be recovered in his case by virtue of this section" [emphasis added].

The italicised words should be omitted if, but only if, the court proceeds under ss.13 or 14 or 15 of the 1994 Act, or where determinations under s.2 have been postponed for the purpose of obtaining further information (see ss. 3 and 3(8)).

When one therefore looks at s.5(1), the "amount to be recovered" is to be equated with "the amount the Crown Court assesses to be the value of the defendant's proceeds of drug trafficking".

There will often be cases where an accused no longer holds capital and/or savings to that extent. The Act does not seek to make him bankrupt in those circumstances but, by s.5(3), the "amount to be recovered" shall be the amount that can be "realised".

Determination of "benefit"

The court must first determine whether the defendant has "benefited" from drug trafficking. If it is obvious that the defendant has obtained no benefit then nothing is to be gained by expending court time and money proceeding any further. The legislature may have originally contemplated that cases in which there was no discernible benefit would be weeded out speedily and expeditiously. Frequently the prosecution indicates to the court, upon conviction, that the defendant has received no benefit and the court is invited to make a nil confiscation order. In the author's experience the Customs and Excise often take a sensible, realistic and robust view in this regard.

In *R. v. Dickens* (1990) 2 Q.B. 102, Lord Lane C.J. appears to have had this approach in mind when he said at p. 106:

" ... the judge has to make a preliminary assessment as to whether it is or is likely to be a 'benefit' case or not. No doubt the evidence from the trial, if there has been one, or from a recital of the facts if there has been a plea, will be enough for him to form such a preliminary assessment".

This approach did not always find favour with the judiciary on the grounds that it was for the court to determine in every case whether the accused had benefited from drug trafficking or not and this the court could only do if it was fully informed of the defendant's financial affairs during the relevant period.

The Home Office Working Group (1991) was unanimously in favour of the continuation of mandatory confiscation orders (para. 2.5) but suggested that the way in which the court determines whether to invoke the assumptions should be reformed. They considered that one approach would be to provide that

"once an individual had been convicted of drug trafficking, the court should be *required to assume* that all property appearing to it to be in his possession (or which appears to have passed through his hands over the last six years etc.) represents the proceeds of drug trafficking. *Only the application of the prosecutor could relieve the court from the requirement to make these assumptions although the court would retain the discretion to make the assumptions if it wished, even if the prosecutor recommended against.* Once the assumptions had been made, it would be up to the defendant to seek to persuade the court that the assumptions were inappropriate, either in regard to the whole of his property or specific items of it" (emphasis added; para. 2.6).

However, notwithstanding the view of the Home Office Working Group, it is plain that the amendments made by the 1993 Act and re-enacted in the 1994 Act do not give effect to their proposals in either paras.2.5 or 2.6. The prosecutor has a limited discretion by virtue of s.2(1) as to whether to ask the court to proceed under the Act but the prosecutor has no power to apply to "relieve the court from the requirements to make [the] assumptions ... .": see s.4(2). Furthermore, the effect of s.2(1) is exactly the opposite of the mandatory system for making confiscation orders recommended by the Home Office Working Group.

The Working Party also recommended that the Drug Trafficking Offences Act 1986 should be amended "to ensure that the court would make the assumptions in all cases, unless satisfied, from arguments produced by the defendant or any other information available to it, either during the trial or otherwise, that it would be inappropriate to do so. An example of this would be where the case was of such a minor nature that the procedure would not, in the judge's view, be warranted. The judge would, of course, not apply the assumptions where it was obvious that they were incorrect. Where the court concluded that the assumptions should not be applied, it would be required to state its reasons and those reasons would be subject to challenge in a higher court" (para. 2.8). However, the recommendations of the Working Party do not seem to have been accepted on this point because the making of assumptions are now mandatory (see s.4(2)) except in respect of two circumstances neither of which appear to be broad enough to entitle a judge not to make any of the assumptions merely because the procedure would not, in the judge's view, be warranted.

Thus, the court must make the assumptions unless (i) the assumption in question is shown to be incorrect in the defendant's case (s.4(4)(a)), or (ii) the court is satisfied that there would be a serious risk of injustice in his case if the assumption were to be made; s.4(4)(b). Note the phrase "serious risk". It could, perhaps, be argued that one of the considerations which the court would be entitled to take into account, when deciding whether to embark upon on enquiry under s.2(1), is the appropriateness of making any of the assumptions under the Act for the reasons given, *inter alia*, by the Working Group (para. 2.8, above). It is not clear whether such an approach would be contrary to the intention of the Legislature. The parliamentary debates provide little assistance on this point and it would have been a simple matter for the draughtsman to have included in s.4 a provision not dissimilar to that found in s.2(1). The statutory exceptions in s.4(4) are not free of difficulty. Who raises an issue under s.4(4)(a) or (b)? Would any risk of injustice (which is not merely fanciful) be regarded by the courts as a "serious" one given the consequences that will flow from the making of an assumption? Even if the reasons stated for not applying the assumptions under s.4 of the 1994 Act are erroneous, that does not seem to entitle the prosecution to apply for re-assessment under s.14 of this Act nor is it clear that the prosecutor would be entitled to seek judicial review of a judge's decision in the light of his stated reasons.

Under the Scottish legislation, the High Court is not required, as a first step, to determine whether the defendant has benefited from drug trafficking. This is because the making of a confiscation order is in any event discretionary. The High Court is swiftly directed to assess the value of the defendant's proceeds of drug trafficking in accordance with s.3 of the Criminal Justice (Scotland) Act 1987.

Definition of benefit

The Phrase "benefited from drug trafficking" is a term which falls to be construed in accordance with s.2(3) (above), and see s.1(1) and (2) of the 1994 Act. A benefit continues to have the following features:

   (i) it must be a payment or other reward;

   (ii) it must be received by a person;

   (iii) the payment must be received in connection with drug trafficking;

   (iv) the drug trafficking must have been carried on by the recipient or another;

   (v) the recipient knew that the payment or reward was made "in connection with drug trafficking": *R. v. Richards* [1992] 2 All E.R. 573.

Quantifying the defendant's proceeds of drug trafficking

The second step is for the court to assess the value of the defendant's proceeds of drug trafficking. Note the word "value." What has to be recovered *prima facie* is the value of the defendant's proceeds of drug trafficking (s.5) and not necessarily the value of tangible assets known to exist in the hands of the defendant.

The initial calculation involves aggregating all gross receipts received in connection with drug trafficking and then revaluing the total amount if necessary under s.7(2) to reflect inflation, profitable investment or market fluctuation. The severity of that calculation may be mitigated by the provisions of s.5(3), which provide that the amount to be recovered under the confiscation order is the amount that might be realised if that amount is less than the value of the defendant's proceeds of drug trafficking. The court is concerned with "proceeds", not profit, and therefore the expense involved in buying, selling, transporting or distributing the drug is irrelevant and the court can make no deduction in respect of drug proceeds reinvested in another purchase of drugs: see *R. v. Smith (Ian)* [1989] 1 W.L.R. 765; *R. v. McDonald* (1990) 12 Cr.App.R.(S.) 457 and *R. v. Comiskey* (1991) 93 Cr.App.R. 227.

A "payment" or "other reward" may be cash but it may also be a benefit in kind, *e.g.* an airline ticket: see *R. v. Osei* [1988] Crim.L.R. 775. A payment or reward may also be a "gift", a chose in action or another intangible: see s.62(1) of this Act. It does not matter when the payment or reward was received by the defendant. There is no time limit as to how far back the prosecution may scan. Thus, payments made before the commencement of the Act are included. The payment must actually be received by the defendant; presumably an offer to advance a payment or reward cannot be taken into account; and similarly a payment which has been misdirected, (*i.e.* forwarded to another individual in error) cannot feature in the calculation. It does not matter whether the payment is in connection with the defendant's drug trafficking or someone else's: see s.4(1)(a).

The practical effect of s.4(1) may be summarised as follows. If the prosecution can prove that a payment or reward was received by the defendant at any time, and if it can be proved to be connected with drug trafficking, then such a payment represents the "proceeds" of drug-trafficking for the purposes of the Act. Obviously, there will be many occasions when the prosecution cannot prove the link between a payment and a drug-trafficking offence – however suspicious the circumstances of its receipt may seem. Parliament therefore requires the court to make certain "assumptions" concerning the origin of property received by the accused in the circumstances set out in s.4(3), and the court may take into account any statement tendered by the prosecution as to any matters relevant "to the assessment of the value" of the defendant's proceeds of drug trafficking: s.11(1).

Although the 1994 Act provides that a defendant may also tender a statement to the Crown Court (s.11(9)) it seems that the contents of that statement should be confined to matters relevant to determining "the amount that might be realised" rather than the value of any payments or rewards received by him; assessing the statement is to be conclusive of the matters of which it relates within the terms of s.11(9).

Evidential considerations. The defendant is of course entitled to call evidence during the hearing and he may seek an adjournment for that purpose: see *R. v. Nicholson* (1990) 12 Cr.App.R.(S.) 58, and *R. v. Jenkins* (1990) 12 Cr.App.R.(S.) 582. If the defendant fails to keep proper records, but he has acquired and spent large sums of money (the origin of which he is not able to explain), then he runs the risk that the court will make findings adverse to him on the basis of the statutory assumptions under s.4(2)–(5): see *R. v. Small* (*Michael*) (1989) 88 Cr.App.R. 184.

Joint beneficiaries. Where two or more defendants have been engaged in a joint enterprise to commit a drug trafficking offence but one defendant is shown to have received more payments during the relevant period than the other, the court must determine the total value of the benefits received jointly and then determine the value of the benefit received by each of the defendants. In the absence of any evidence on the point, the sentencer may (but is not obliged) to assume that the defendants shared equally: see *R. v. Porter* (*Jeremy*) [1990] 1 W.L.R. 1260, but contrast that decision with *R. v. Chrastny* (*No. 2*) [1991] 1 W.L.R. 1381. There is nothing in the 1993 Act which alters the previous position.

Assets held abroad. By s.62(2) (formerly s.38(3) of the 1986 Act), the 1994 Act applies to property whether it is situated in England and Wales or elsewhere: *R. v. Hopes* (1989) 11 Cr.App.R.(S.) 38. The Act applies to all unlawful drug trafficking ventures wherever they are carried out and the Act applies in respect of property held by the defendant anywhere in the world (see s.62(2) of the 1994 Act). The burden will therefore rest on the defendant to liquidate his assets or face the alternative of serving a consecutive sentence in default.

The approach adopted in *Hopes* appears to have differed from that in *R. v. Bragason* (1988) Crim.L.R. 778 where the court assessed B's proceeds of drug trafficking at £15,000 but certified that the amount which might be realised from the assets which he held "in the jurisdiction" as nil. It is not clear whether the sentencer thought that it was necessary to assess the value of assets held by the defendant in England and Wales but, if he did, he was clearly in error (see also s.62(3)).

Some ramifications of section 4(2)–(5). Even if a defendant is convicted of supplying drugs over a very short period of time, the court is required to assume that all property transferred to the defendant over the preceding six years (prior to the moment when proceedings were instituted against him) was a payment or reward made in connection with drug trafficking carried on by the defendant and moreover, that any expenditure made by the defendant over that period came out of the proceeds of drug trafficking. Where property is proved to have been received by an accused and where there is no evidence at all to suggest that when he received it, the accused (or the transferor) were engaged in drug trafficking, then such a lack of evidence may of itself be the best evidence to show that the "assumptions", which the court can make under s.4(4)(a), are incorrect.

Assessing the amount that might be realised

What is to be recovered by the court, under a confiscation order, is the amount which the Crown Court assesses to be the value of the defendant's proceeds of drug trafficking: s.5(1). This figure represents the ideal.

However, the reality of the situation will often be that the defendant only has assets for a value which is lower than the amount which the court assesses to be the value of the defendant's proceeds of drug trafficking. The court may therefore reduce the value of the confiscation order and recover the lesser amount or a "nominal amount" (*per* s.5(3)), but only within the terms of ss.5(3), 6(1) and 6(2). The circumstances in which the court can confiscate a lesser amount are very limited and the following points should be borne in mind.

First, there exists no provision under the 1994 Act for reducing the amount on grounds of personal hardship. Accordingly, no reduction can be made on the basis that the only realisable asset held by the defendant is the matrimonial home (but see *R. v. Keston* (1990) 12

Cr.App.R.(S.) 93 where a contrary impression is given). On the other hand, it remains to be seen whether (by virtue of s.2(1) decisions taken by prosecutors and by the courts not to proceed under the 1994 Act are influenced by considerations of hardship.

Secondly, the court must confiscate the full amount (being the defendant's proceeds of drug trafficking) unless it is satisfied that the lesser amount represents the "amount that might be realised" under s.5(3). In those circumstances the court must make an order for the lesser amount. There is no half-way house.

"The amount that might be realised" is defined by s.6(1). It is not the same thing as "realisable property" which is separately defined by s.6(2). In the majority of cases the practical effect is that the "amount that might be realised" under s.5 will be the value of the "realisable property," but this need not necessarily be so: see *R. v. Carroll* (1992) 13 Cr.App.R.(S.) 99.

Thirdly, any "realisable property" which forms part of the determination of the "amount that might be realised" under ss.6(1) and 4(3) need not, of itself, have been acquired with the proceeds of drug trafficking because the definition of "realisable property" in s.6(2) includes legitimately acquired property: *R. v. Chrastny (No. 2)* [1991] 1 W.L.R. 1381.

Fourthly, the burden will normally be on the defendant to satisfy the court of the matters referred to in s.5(3), but it would seem that in appropriate cases the court may, of its own volition, make a determination under that subsection: see *R. v. Keston* (1990) 12 Cr.App.R.(S.) 93; *R. v. Comiskey* (1991) 93 Cr.App.R. 227; *R. v. Ilsemann* (1990) 12 Cr.App.R.(S.) 398 and *R. v. Carroll* (1992) 13 Cr.App.R.(S.) 99. The court is not obliged to determine the extent of the defendant's realisable assets in every case where the court proposes to make a confiscation order. This is because the Act places the burden on the defendant to satisfy the order or serve a consecutive sentence of imprisonment in default of payment: see *R. v. Ilsemann* (1990) 12 Cr.App.R. (S.) 398.

The criteria. Section 5(3) provides:
"If the court is satisfied that the amount that might be realised at the time the confiscation order is made [*(or) a 'determination is made'*] is less than the amount the court assesses to be the value of his proceeds of drug trafficking, the amount to be recovered in the defendant's case under the confiscation order shall be
  (a) the amount appearing to the court to be the amount that might be so realised, or
  (b) a nominal amount, where it appears to the court (on the information available to it at the time) that the amount that might be realised is nil".
Note: the words in italics have been inserted into s.5(3) merely for ease of reference. Where the court revises its assessment of the defendant's proceeds of drug trafficking (under the provisions of s.15 of the 1994 Act) then s.5(3) shall have effect as if for "confiscation order is made" there were substituted "determination is made": see s.15(9)(b).

Definition of "realisable property". Section 6(2) provides:
"In this Act, 'realisable property' means, subject to subsection (2) below—
  (a) any property held by the defendant; and
  (b) any property held by a person to whom the defendant has directly or indirectly made a gift caught by this Act".
"Realisable property" therefore includes property held by the defendant (s.6(2)(a)) but also gifts caught by the Act which are held by any person (s.6(2)(b)); and see *R. v. Walbrook and Glasgow* [1994] Crim.L.R. 613. Powers of the High Court are exercisable over "realisable property": see ss.26, 27 and 29.

Definition of the "amount that might be realised". Section 6(1) (formerly 5(3) of the 1986 Act, as amended) provides:
"For the purposes of this Act the amount that might be realised at the time a confiscation order is made against the defendant is:
  (a) the total of the values at that time of all the realisable property held by the defendant less
  (b) where there are obligations having priority at that time the total amounts payable in pursuance of such obligations,
  together with the total of the values at that time of all gifts caught by this Act".
Note: if the court revises its assessment of the defendant's proceeds of drug trafficking (under s.15 of the 1994 Act) then s.6(1) shall have effect as if for "a confiscation order is made" there were substituted the words "of the determination": see s.15(9)(c).

Section 6(1) is concerned with values not limited to the value of realisable property. The draftsmen did not refer to "realisable property" in s.5 and this omission is deliberate. The Act contemplates a situation in which the defendant made gifts "caught" by the Act (as defined by s.8(1), formerly, s.5(9) of the 1986 Act), the value of which may be assessed for the purposes of ss.6(1) and 5, but which fall outside the strict definition of "realisable property" as set out in s.6(2).

In *R. v. Dickens* [1990] 2 Q.B. 102, the Court of Appeal referred to the fact that "realisable property" and "amount that might be realised" were separately defined under the Act and meant two very different things. Lord Lane C.J. said (at p. 111):

" ... the phrase 'realisable property' does not appear in section 4 of the Drug Trafficking Offences Act 1986 and in particular does not appear in section 4(3). If Parliament had wished the confiscation order to be confined to the defendant's 'realisable property' as defined by section 5(1), then it would undoubtedly have said so in section 4(3), which it did not. We have no doubt that that was deliberate and was designed to ensure that drug traffickers could not protect the assets they had acquired through drug trafficking by 'giving' those assets to others".

Accordingly, the judge was entitled to look at the value of the gift made by D to his wife. That gift was caught by the Act (s.5(9) of the 1986 Act – now s.8(1)) and its value fell within the definition of "the amount that might be realised" (now s.6(2) of this Act) for the purposes of what is now s.5(3) of this Act (formerly s.4(3)). The fact that the gift to the wife could no longer physically be realised was irrelevant.

Who raises the issue under s.5(3) of the DTA? In theory the court need only make two determinations before making a confiscation order. First, whether the defendant has benefited from drug trafficking and secondly, to assess the value of the defendant's proceeds of drug trafficking. In practice, the court will often need to go on and assess the amount that might actually be realised under s.5(3) of this Act. However, the opening words, "If the court is satisfied ... " pose the question as to whether the court, of its own motion, should initiate the third stage or whether it is the defendant who must take the initiative and satisfy the court on a balance of probabilities that a lesser amount should be confiscated. In *R. v. Johnson* [1991] 2 Q.B. 249, Neill L.J. said (at p. 259):

"It is only necessary to make a calculation in accordance with section 4(3) of the 1986 Act (now s.5(3) of the 1994 Act) if it appears that the amount that might be realised at the time that the confiscation order is made is less than the amount the court assesses to be the value of the defendant's proceeds of drug trafficking. In the present case it is accepted on behalf of the appellant that her proceeds were not less than £1,300".

Those last few words imply that it is for the defendant to initiate a determination under s.5(3). However, *R. v. Keston* (1990) 12 Cr.App.R.(S.) 93 can be read as implying that in every case the court should determine "the amount that might be realised" under s.5(3). However, the judgment does not, in terms, go that far and such a statement would be at variance with *R. v. Johnson* [1991] 2 Q.B. 249; *R. v. Comiskey* (1991) 93 Cr.App.R. 227; *R. v. Ilsemann* (1990) 12 Cr.App.R. (S.) 398 and *R. v. Carroll* (1992) 13 Cr.App.R.(S.) 99.

In *R. v. Dickens* [1990] 2 Q.B. 102 the Court of Appeal did remark that determining the "amount that might be realised" may overlap with the determination of the defendant's proceeds of drug trafficking.

In *Comiskey* (above), Tucker J. asked whether there was anything to cause the judge to be satisfied that the amount that might be realised was less than the value of the defendant's proceeds of drug trafficking in circumstances where the appellant did not give evidence during the 1986 Act enquiry or call evidence.

The burden is certainly not on the Crown to satisfy the court under s.5(3), but the mere fact that the defendant is normally in a better position to shoulder the burden does not therefore preclude the court, of its own motion, following the steps in s.5(3): see the judgment of Tucker J. in *Comiskey* (at p. 567).

The authorities decided under the 1986 Act are still relevant for these purposes and therefore seem to show that either the defendant or the court may take the initiative to make a determination under ss.5(3) and 6(2). Each case depends on its own facts. What has not been conclusively decided is whether the defendant carries merely an evidential burden under s.5(3) or whether he must go on and discharge the persuasive burden as well.

Evidential or persuasive burden under s.5(3) of the DTA? This is not a straightforward issue: see Fortson, *Law on the Misuse of Drugs and Drug Trafficking Offences,* (1992); 2 ed., at para. 12–84. Given that the "amount to be recovered" under s.5(3) is the "amount that might be realised", it follows that any question as to the standard of proof is to be resolved by s.2(8) of this Act. Arguably s.2(8) does not go far enough to make it plain whether the defendant always carries the persuasive burden but, in practice, the net effect is that the defendant will generally have the task of discharging not only the evidential burden but also the persuasive burden because, in reality, how else is he to satisfy the court of the relevant matters in s.5(3)? On first principles, evidence of any witness (including therefore a defendant) which is unchallenged, is to be accepted as representing the truth of the matter testified on pain of punishment for perjury if the evidence subsequently transpires to be false. In *R. v. Johnson* [1991] 2 Q.B. 249, the Court of Appeal seems to have followed this approach: see *R. v. McDonald* (1990) 12 Cr.App.R.(S.) 457.

The approach suggested above would result in little or no prejudice to the prosecution because where the court makes a confiscation order and later discovers that assets are available to the court which were originally unknown, then the court may vary the order under s.47 of the Supreme Court Act 1981 (c. 54) within the relevant time limit: see *R. v. Miller* (1991) 92 Cr.App.R. 191 and the provisions of the Criminal Justice (International Co-operation) Act 1990 (c. 5), s.16 now re-enacted as s.16 of this Act.

Quantifying the amount that might be realised. The "amount that might be realised" is defined by s.6(1) of the 1994 Act (formerly, 5(3) of the 1986 Act, as amended):
"For the purposes of this Act the amount that might be realised at the time a confiscation order is made against the defendant is—
(a) the total of the values at that time of all the realisable property held by the defendant, less
(b) where there are obligations having priority at that time the total amounts payable in pursuance of such obligations,
together with the total of the values at that time of all gifts caught by this Act".
Note: if the court revises its assessment of the defendant's proceeds of drug trafficking (under s.15 of the 1994 Act) then s.6(1) shall have effect as if for "a confiscation order is made" there were substituted the words "of the determination": see s.15(9)(c).

The calculation therefore involves the sum of the value of "realisable property" (defined by s.6(2)) plus the value of gifts caught by the Act (see s.8(1): formerly s.5(9)) but excluding the total value of payments made in pursuance of obligations "having priority". Such obligations are specified in s.6(4) of the 1994 Act (formerly, s.5(7) of the 1986 Act as amended by s.12 of the 1993 Act) as follows:
"For the purposes of subsection (1) above, an obligation has priority at any time if it is an obligation of the defendant
(a) to pay an amount due in respect of a fine, or other order of a court, imposed or made on conviction of any offence, where the fine was imposed or order made before the confiscation order [*(or) "determination"*], or
(b) to pay any sum which would be included among the preferential debts (within the meaning given by section 386 of the Insolvency Act 1986) in the defendant's bankruptcy commencing on the date of the confiscation order or winding up under an order of the court made on that date".
Note: the italicised words within the square brackets have been added to s.6(4)(a) for ease of reference. Where a court revises its assessment of the value of the defendant's proceeds of drug trafficking under s.15 of the 1994 Act, ss.5(2), 6(4) and s.11(9)(a) are to be read as if for the words "confiscation order" there were substituted "determination": see s.15(9).

"Obligations having priority": ss.6(1) and 6(4). See *R. v. McDonald* (1990) 12 Cr.App.R.(S.) 457.

Valuation and re-valuations. Provisions dealing with the revaluation of property and gifts to take account of changes in the value of money, successful investment and so on, are to be found in s.7(1), s.7(2) and s.7(3) (formerly, ss.5(4), 5(5) and 5(6) of the 1986 Act).

The obvious importance of putting before the court up-to-date and accurate information regarding values and expenses cannot be too strongly emphasised if a fair order is to be made: *R. v. Lemmon* (1992) 13 Cr.App.R.(S.) 66.

It is not necessary that the assets must be proved to be the proceeds of drug trafficking for the purposes of ss.5(3) and 6(1) except in the case of gifts made more than six years prior to the institution of proceedings against him (see s.6(2)(b)): see *R. v. Chrastny (No. 2)* [1991] 1 W.L.R. 1385 and see *R. v. Chapman, The Times,* November 18, 1991.

Establishing an interest in property. Realisable property also includes a beneficial interest created under a resulting or constructive trust: see *R. v. Robson* (1991) 92 Cr.App.R. 1; see also *Eves v. Eves* [1975] 1 W.L.R. 1338 and *Grant v. Edwards* [1986] Ch. 638. In both of those latter cases the court concluded that a beneficial interest was conferred in circumstances where the beneficiary had acted to her detriment. Accordingly, in *Robson,* the court reduced the confiscation order to £1,490.

Value of the drugs. There is already clear authority for the proposition that proceeds which have been invested in buying drugs, which have then been sold and the proceeds of that sale rolled over into yet another purchase of drugs, all count towards the determination of the benefit received: see *R. v. Smith* [1989] 1 W.L.R. 765 and *R. v. Butler* [1993] Crim.L.R. 320.

Actual value of property. There is authority for the proposition that the combined effect of ss.6(1) and 6(2) is to suggest that what the court has to have regard to in determining the "amount that might be realised" is the actual property held by the defendant or by a person to whom he has given it: *R. v. Comiskey* (1990) 12 Cr.App.R.(S.) 562 at p. 568.

ABBREVIATIONS

The 1971 Act: the Misuse of Drugs Act 1971 (c. 38)
The 1973 Act: the Powers of the Criminal Courts Act 1973 (c. 62)
The 1986 Act: the Drug Trafficking Offences Act 1986 (c. 32)
The 1993 Act: the Criminal Justice Act 1993 (c. 36)
The CJA 1988: the Criminal Justice Act 1988 (c. 33)

PART I

CONFISCATION ORDERS

Introductory

Meaning of "drug trafficking" and "drug trafficking offence"

1.—(1) In this Act "drug trafficking" means, subject to subsection (2) below, doing or being concerned in any of the following, whether in England and Wales or elsewhere—

(a) producing or supplying a controlled drug where the production or supply contravenes section 4(1) of the Misuse of Drugs Act 1971 or a corresponding law;

(b) transporting or storing a controlled drug where possession of the drug contravenes section 5(1) of that Act or a corresponding law;

(c) importing or exporting a controlled drug where the importation or exportation is prohibited by section 3(1) of that Act or a corresponding law;

(d) manufacturing or supplying a scheduled substance within the meaning of section 12 of the Criminal Justice (International Co-operation) Act 1990 where the manufacture or supply is an offence under that section or would be such an offence if it took place in England and Wales;

(e) using any ship for illicit traffic in controlled drugs in circumstances which amount to the commission of an offence under section 19 of that Act;

(f) conduct which is an offence under section 49 of this Act or which would be such an offence if it took place in England and Wales;

(g) acquiring, having possession of or using property in circumstances which amount to the commission of an offence under section 51 of this Act or which would amount to such an offence if it took place in England and Wales.

(2) "Drug trafficking" also includes a person doing the following, whether in England and Wales or elsewhere, that is to say, entering into or being otherwise concerned in an arrangement whereby—

(a) the retention or control by or on behalf of another person of the other person's proceeds of drug trafficking is facilitated; or

(b) the proceeds of drug trafficking by another person are used to secure that funds are placed at the other person's disposal or are used for the other person's benefit to acquire property by way of investment.

(3) In this Act "drug trafficking offence" means any of the following—

(a) an offence under section 4(2) or (3) or 5(3) of the Misuse of Drugs Act 1971 (production, supply and possession for supply of controlled drugs);

(b) an offence under section 20 of that Act (assisting in or inducing commission outside United Kingdom of offence punishable under a corresponding law);

(c) an offence under—

(i) section 50(2) or (3) of the Customs and Excise Management Act 1979 (improper importation),

(ii) section 68(2) of that Act (exportation), or

(iii) section 170 of that Act (fraudulent evasion),

in connection with a prohibition or restriction on importation or exportation having effect by virtue of section 3 of the Misuse of Drugs Act 1971;

(d) an offence under section 12 of the Criminal Justice (International Co-operation) Act 1990 (manufacture or supply of substance specified in Schedule 2 to that Act);

(e) an offence under section 19 of that Act (using ship for illicit traffic in controlled drugs);

(f) an offence under section 49, 50 or 51 of this Act or section 14 of the Criminal Justice (International Co-operation) Act 1990 (which makes, in relation to Scotland and Northern Ireland, provision corresponding to section 49 of this Act);

(g) an offence under section 1 of the Criminal Law Act 1977 of conspiracy to commit any of the offences in paragraphs (a) to (f) above;

(h) an offence under section 1 of the Criminal Attempts Act 1981 of attempting to commit any of those offences; and

(i) an offence of inciting another person to commit any of those offences, whether under section 19 of the Misuse of Drugs Act 1971 or at common law;

and includes aiding, abetting, counselling or procuring the commission of any of the offences in paragraphs (a) to (f) above.

(4) In this section "corresponding law" has the same meaning as in the Misuse of Drugs Act 1971.

(5) For the purposes of the application of Part II of this Act in Scotland and Northern Ireland, "drug trafficking" shall be construed in accordance with section 48(2) of this Act.

DEFINITIONS
"corresponding law": s.1(4).
"drug trafficking": s.1(1), (2), (5).
"drug trafficking offence": s.1(3).

GENERAL NOTE
In one sense it was a logical step to put the definition of these crucial expressions in the first section of the Act, but whereas the 1986 Act had only one definition section (s.38), this Act has split up the old s.38 into what is now ss.1, 41, 48, 62, 63 and 64 (s.64 helpfully provides an expanded index of defined expressions). The definition of a "confiscation order" does not form part of any interpretation section (although it is listed in the index of defined expressions, s.64) but the term is separately defined in s.2(9) of the Act. Many practitioners might be assisted by a table of sections under the 1986 Act (and other enactments) showing their corresponding provisions under this Act.

Confiscation orders

Confiscation orders

2.—(1) Subject to subsection (7) below, where a defendant appears before the Crown Court to be sentenced in respect of one or more drug trafficking offences (and has not previously been sentenced or otherwise dealt with in respect of his conviction for the offence or, as the case may be, any of the offences concerned), then—

(a) if the prosecutor asks the court to proceed under this section, or

(b) if the court considers that, even though the prosecutor has not asked it to do so, it is appropriate for it to proceed under this section,
it shall act as follows.

(2) The court shall first determine whether the defendant has benefited from drug trafficking.

(3) For the purposes of this Act, a person has benefited from drug trafficking if he has at any time (whether before or after the commencement of this Act) received any payment or other reward in connection with drug trafficking carried on by him or another person.

(4) If the court determines that the defendant has so benefited, the court shall, before sentencing or otherwise dealing with him in respect of the offence or, as the case may be, any of the offences concerned, determine in accordance with section 5 of this Act the amount to be recovered in his case by virtue of this section.

(5) The court shall then, in respect of the offence or offences concerned—
(a) order the defendant to pay that amount;
(b) take account of the order before—
　　(i) imposing any fine on him;
　　(ii) making any order involving any payment by him; or
　　(iii) making any order under section 27 of the Misuse of Drugs Act 1971 (forfeiture orders) or section 43 of the Powers of Criminal Courts Act 1973 (deprivation orders); and
(c) subject to paragraph (b) above, leave the order out of account in determining the appropriate sentence or other manner of dealing with him.

(6) No enactment restricting the power of a court dealing with an offender in a particular way from dealing with him also in any other way shall by reason only of the making of an order under this section restrict the Crown Court from dealing with an offender in any way the court considers appropriate in respect of a drug trafficking offence.

(7) Subsection (1) above does not apply in relation to any offence for which a defendant appears before the Crown Court to be sentenced if—
(a) he has been committed to the Crown Court for sentence in respect of that offence under section 37(1) of the Magistrates' Courts Act 1980 (committal to Crown Court with a view to sentence of detention in a young offender institution); or
(b) the powers of the court (apart from this section) to deal with him in respect of that offence are limited to dealing with him in any way in which a magistrates' court might have dealt with him in respect of the offence.

(8) The standard of proof required to determine any question arising under this Act as to—
(a) whether a person has benefited from drug trafficking, or
(b) the amount to be recovered in his case by virtue of this section, shall be that applicable in civil proceedings.

(9) In this Act "confiscation order" means an order under this section and includes, in particular, such an order made by virtue of section 13, 14 or 19 of this Act.

DEFINITIONS
　"benefited from drug trafficking": s.2(3).
　"confiscation order": s.2(9).
　"defendant": s.63(1).
　"drug trafficking offence": s.1.

GENERAL NOTE

Subs. (1)

Section 2(1) of the Act represents the combined effect of s.1(1) of the 1986 Act as amended by s.7(1) of the 1993 Act.

Under the 1986 Act, whenever a defendant appeared before the Crown Court to be sentenced in respect of one or more "drug trafficking offences", the court was obliged to embark upon a drug trafficking enquiry in every case. This is no longer the case. By s.2(1) of the Act, the court need only embark upon confiscation proceedings if it is asked to do so by the prosecutor or when (even if not asked) the court considers that it is appropriate for it to proceed under the Act.

The purpose of this provision (which originally appeared as s.7 of the 1993 Act amending s.1(1) of the 1986 Act) was described by the then Secretary of State for the Home Deprtment (Kenneth Clarke):

"[the provision] relieves the court from following the confiscation procedures . . . each time that it convicts a drug trafficker. Confiscation will take place only when notice is served on the court by the prosecutor, or at the court's discretion. This will filter out those cases in which there is obviously little or no benefit, or no realisable property. This does not mean that we are softening our approach to drug traffickers. The minor cases that do not attract a confiscation hearing under the new arrangements will continue to be dealt with severely by means of fines and forfeiture orders, as well as by imprisonment." (*Hansard*, H.C. Vol. 222, col. 866).

Note that although s.2(1)(a) requires the prosecutor to "ask" that the court proceed under s.2, in fact this courtesy belies the reality: once "asked" the court is obliged to embark upon an enquiry. No doubt most prosecutors will be sensible in their approach to such enquiries – but it is not clear what control (even in costs) the court has over decisions taken by prosecutors who compel a court to proceed under s.2 even if the court believes the exercise is inappropriate.

The making of a confiscation order follows a conviction for a "drug trafficking offence" (s.2(1)), nevertheless the amount assessed to represent (and to be recovered as) his proceeds of drug trafficking need not derive from the offence for which he was convicted at all. This is because the defendant's benefit may include proceeds received as a result of drug trafficking carried on by him or "by another" – anywhere in the world: ss.2(2), (3), 4(1), 5(1). The court may include payments received or made by the defendant which have no connection with the offence before the court but, if any of the assumptions are made within the terms of s.4(2) to (5), then they will be assumed to be in connection with drug trafficking carried on by the defendant himself. In addition, it should be noted that the terms of s.2(1) of the Act may now give prosecutors and the courts greater scope to reward those defendants, who assist the law enforcement agencies, by not invoking the provisions of that section. In *R. v. Atkinson* (1993) 14 Cr.App.R.(S.) 182 and *R. v. Finch* [1992] Crim.L.R. 901, it was held that a defendant who agrees a "section 3 statement" (now see s.11), or a schedule of assets, with the prosecution does not prevent the court making up its own mind and confiscating a higher figure. This was because the court was obliged to follow the steps set out in the 1986 Act as originally drafted so that where (for example) a defendant gave considerable assistance to law enforcement agencies, he could not be "rewarded" by way of a "concession" made by the prosecution not to confiscate assets under a confiscation order which would result in the loss of his home or prized motor vehicle. The court was bound to confiscate such assets if it could. However, the effect of s.2(1) is to leave that possibility open although, clearly, the court has the final say by virtue of what is now s.2(1)(b) of the Act.

Subss. (2) and (3)

These provisions correspond to the old s.1(2) and (3) of the 1986 Act. Note that the making of a confiscation order involves three separate determinations: (i) has the defendant benefited from drug trafficking? A single payment or reward, received in connection with drug trafficking carried on by the defendant or by another, is sufficient to lead the court to the next stage; (ii) what is the "value of the defendant's proceeds of drug trafficking" (s.5(1))?; and (iii) what is the "amount to be recovered" under a confiscation order? *Prima facie*, this figure will be the same as the value of the defendant's proceeds of drug trafficking (s.5(1)) unless the "amount that might be realised at the time the confiscation order is made is less" than the value of the defendant's proceeds of drug trafficking (s.5(3)). Note the assumptions which the court can make under s.4(2)–(5) of the Act. The final determination, (*i.e.* of the amount to be recovered from the defendant), should normally be made before sentencing the defendant (s.2(4)) unless further information is required by the court in order to make any of the determinations under the Act (see s.3(1), (7)–(9)).

Subs. (4)

Note the commentary to subss. (2) and (3) above. This provision corresponds to s.1(4) of the 1986 Act but the words "before sentencing" to "offences concerned" should be treated as being omitted if the court is exercising powers (which were not originally part of the 1986 Act) under s.13 (see s.13(7)), s.14 (note s.14(4)) and s.15 (note s.15(4)), *i.e.* cases where the court had not proceeded under s.2, or where the court wishes to re-assess whether the defendant has benefited from drug trafficking, or to revise its assessment of the value of the defendant's proceeds of drug trafficking. The same words in s.2(4) should similarly be omitted if the court postpones a determination under s.3: see s.3(8).

Subs. (5)

This provision corresponds to s.1(5) of the 1986 Act. Note that criminal bankruptcy orders under s.39 of the Powers of Criminal Courts Act 1973 (c. 62) were repealed by the Criminal Justice Act 1988.

Subss. (6) and (7)

These provisions correspond to s.1(6) and (7) of the 1986 Act.

Subs. (8)

Note the commentary, above, in respect of the standard of proof.

The effect of s.2(8) is to overrule the decisions of *R. v. Dickens* [1990] 2 Q.B. 102 and *R. v. Enwezor* (1991) 93 Cr.App.R. 233 insofar as they held that the criminal standard of proof applied at any stage of the proceedings (*Hansard*, H.L. Vol. 539, col. 1383).

The Home Office Working Group in their Report on the Drug Trafficking Offences Act 1986 (1991) recommended that the civil standard of proof was the appropriate one. This seems to have been the Government's intention when the Drug Trafficking Offences Bill was introduced into the House of Lords. Lord Glenarthur (in proposing what became s.2 of the 1986 Act; now see s.4 of this Act) said:

"The burden will remain on the prosecution, in the usual way, to prove beyond reasonable doubt that the defendant is guilty of the offence of which he is charged. Once a person has been convicted of a drug trafficking offence however, the onus *may* be placed on him to show which, if any, of his assets were *legitimately acquired* ... Such information is, however, very clearly within the knowledge of the offender ..." *Hansard*, H.L. Vol. 472, col. 92. (emphasis added).

This approach was permitted by "Article 7 of the Vienna Convention 1988 which provides that "Each Party may consider ensuring that the onus of proof be reversed regarding the lawful origin of alleged proceeds or other property liable to confiscation, to the extent that such action is consistent with the principles of its domestic law and with the nature of the judicial and other proceedings".

The views of the Working Group are in marked contrast to the Home Affairs Committee who (in their 7th Report, *Drug Trafficking and Related Serious Crime* (1989)), accepted that a shift to the civil standard of proof would represent a "far reaching change in English criminal law" and required further evidence of its necessity. The National Drugs Intelligence Co-ordinator did not "appear to favour this solution" (para. 8.2). The Home Office Affairs Committee recommended that the Home Office set up a Working Group whose membership consisted of representatives from the Home Office, H.M. Customs and Excise, the National Drugs Intelligence Unit, the Crown Prosecution Service and members representing the Association of Chief Police Officers. The views of the Criminal Bar Association were sought by the Home Office upon publication of the 1991 Report. For their part, the Criminal Bar Association expressed disquiet at such a shift. The views of other interested parties and bodies were also sought by the Home Office. It is apparent that at least one judge endorsed the recommendation of the Working Group that the civil standard should apply to decide the benefit, and the amount of the benefit, and that the court should make the assumptions in all cases unless they are rebutted by the defendant (Standing Committee B, June 8 1993, col. 79). It is not clear to what extent this represented the views of the majority of the judiciary.

Although the application of the criminal standard of proof was not welcomed by the Government, or by the law enforcement agencies, it is difficult to test objectively (rather than merely by anecdotal accounts) whether the criminal standard has in practice made the task of confiscating drug profits more difficult. Certainly, the result in *R. v. Enwezor* (1991) 93 Cr.App.R. 233 would have been different if the civil standard had been upheld but, in the majority of cases, the task of the prosecution was "considerably lightened" by the assumption which the court previously had a discretion to make (see Lord Lane C.J. in *R. v. Dickens* [1990] 2 Q.B. 102). That task would now be lightened still further given the mandatory effect of s.4(2)–(5) of this Act. Note that an assumption made under s.4(3) of the 1994 Act proceeds on the basis that the payment or expenditure was made in connection with drug trafficking carried on by the defendant and by no one else. The making of an assumption results in a grave finding of fact and thus, given both the consequences of such a finding, as well as the stigma which it inevitably attracts, it is conceivable that the courts will require a high degree of probability in any event.

As Lord Ackner pointed out during the debates in respect of Pt. II of the 1993 Act, proof on the civil standard varies in its weight according to what has to be proved (*Hansard*, H.L. Vol. 540, col. 1472) and see the judgment of Denning L.J. in *Bater v. Bater* [1951] P. 35, at pp. 36–37, and see *Blyth v. Blyth* (*No. 2*) [1966] A.C. 643.

A proposed amendment to the Criminal Justice Bill, substituting the phrase "a balance of probabilities" in place of "the civil standard", was withdrawn (*Hansard*, H.L. Vol. 540, col. 1474).

Note that the "amount to be recovered" is a term of art employed in s.2(4) and s.5(3) of this Act. That term is to be distinguished from the "amount that might be realised" which is another term of art – employed in ss.5(3) and 6(1). Given that the "amount to be recovered" could be assessed to be the "amount that might be realised" it follows that any question as to the standard of proof applicable to an assessment under s.5(3) is the civil standard by virtue of s.2(8).

Postponed determinations

3.—(1) Where the Crown Court is acting under section 2 of this Act but considers that it requires further information before—

    (a) determining whether the defendant has benefited from drug trafficking, or

    (b) determining the amount to be recovered in his case by virtue of that section,

it may, for the purpose of enabling that information to be obtained, postpone making the determination for such period as it may specify.

(2) More than one postponement may be made under subsection (1) above in relation to the same case.

(3) Unless it is satisfied that there are exceptional circumstances, the court shall not specify a period under subsection (1) above which—

    (a) by itself, or

    (b) where there have been one or more previous postponements under subsection (1) above or (4) below, when taken together with the earlier specified period or periods,

exceeds six months beginning with the date of conviction.

(4) Where the defendant appeals against his conviction, the court may, on that account—

    (a) postpone making either or both of the determinations mentioned in subsection (1) above for such period as it may specify; or

    (b) where it has already exercised its powers under this section to postpone, extend the specified period.

(5) A postponement or extension under subsection (1) or (4) above may be made—

    (a) on application by the defendant or the prosecutor; or

    (b) by the court of its own motion.

(6) Unless the court is satisfied that there are exceptional circumstances, any postponement or extension under subsection (4) above shall not exceed the period ending three months after the date on which the appeal is determined or otherwise disposed of.

(7) Where the court exercises its power under subsection (1) or (4) above, it may nevertheless proceed to sentence, or otherwise deal with, the defendant in respect of the relevant offence or any of the relevant offences.

(8) Where the court has so proceeded, section 2 of this Act shall have effect as if—

    (a) in subsection (4), the words "before sentencing or otherwise dealing with him in respect of the offence or, as the case may be, any of the offences concerned" were omitted; and

    (b) in subsection (5)(c), after "determining" there were inserted "in relation to any offence in respect of which he has not been sentenced or otherwise dealt with".

(9) In sentencing, or otherwise dealing with, the defendant in respect of the relevant offence or any of the relevant offences at any time during the specified period, the court shall not—

(a) impose any fine on him; or

(b) make any such order as is mentioned in section 2(5)(b)(ii) or (iii) of this Act.

(10) Where the court has sentenced the defendant under subsection (7) above during the specified period it may, after the end of that period, vary the sentence by imposing a fine or making any such order as is mentioned in section 2(5)(b)(ii) or (iii) of this Act, so long as it does so within a period corresponding to that allowed by section 47(2) or (3) of the Supreme Court Act 1981 (time allowed for varying a sentence) but beginning with the end of the specified period.

(11) In this section—

"the date of conviction" means—

(a) the date on which the defendant was convicted; or

(b) where he appeared to be sentenced in respect of more than one conviction, and those convictions were not all on the same date, the date of the latest of those convictions; and

"the relevant offence" means the drug trafficking offence in respect of which the defendant appears (as mentioned in section 2(1) of this Act) before the court;

and references to an appeal include references to an application under section 111 of the Magistrates' Courts Act 1980 (statement of case by magistrates' court).

DEFINITIONS

"benefited from drug trafficking": s.2(3).
"date of conviction": s.3(11).
"drug trafficking": s.1.
"relevant offence": s.3(11).

GENERAL NOTE

Previously the court was bound to determine the amount to be recovered under a confiscation order (and to make such an order if possible) before proceeding to sentence. This frequently led to long delays between conviction and sentence, but the inevitable desire to keep the delay to a minimum occasionally resulted in further assets being revealed after the confiscation was made. Lengthy and costly Drug Trafficking Offences Act 1986 enquiries were also futile if the relevant conviction was quashed on appeal. Accordingly, by s.3 the court may now postpone the determination of the question of benefit or the amount to be recovered under a confiscation order where the defendant has appealed his conviction or where the court requires further information. Maximum periods are imposed by the relevant provisions.

Subss. (2) and (4)

In statutorily prescribed circumstances the period of postponement may be extended. The court may proceed to sentence the defendant notwithstanding a period of postponement or extension: subs. (7).

Subss. (1)–(7)

The power to postpone or grant an extension of time (even where the defendant appeals against his conviction) rests with the Crown Court. Unless there are "exceptional circumstances" the period of postponement may be for any period not exceeding six months and the court may order one or several postponements providing the total period does not exceed six months from the date of conviction: see subss. (3) and (11). Where the defendant is convicted on more than one indictment (*e.g.* as a result of separate committals or separate trials ordered on severance of an indictment) the period of postponement runs from the last conviction for a drug trafficking offence (see subs. (11) and Standing Committee B, May 27, 1993, col. 62). This applies whether or not the convictions occurred at the same or different Crown Courts (*ibid.*).

Subss. (9) and (10)

Subsections (9) and (10) follow the amendments made to the 1986 Act by s.8 of the 1993 Act but after that Act was passed the Government clearly reflected on sentencing difficulties that might arise if a court proceeded to sentence an offender under s.3(7) but, at the end of the "specified period", regarded itself as debarred from dealing with him in one of the ways mentioned in s.2(5)(b) merely because the "specified period" ended more than 28 days after sentence was originally passed. The courts might well have construed s.3(7) as meaning that the process of sentencing *commences* on the date of conviction (see s.3(11)(b)) but is not concluded until after any determination is made under s.2 of this Act. However, on July 4, 1994, the Lord Chancellor moved by Amendment what is now s.3(10), and he gave the following explanation in the House of Lords.

"This amendment and Amendment No. 2 [repealing sched. 9, para. 26 of the Criminal Justice and Public Order Act 1994] are necessary to bring into the consolidation an amendment made to the Criminal Justice and Public Order Bill during its Committee stage in your Lordship's House. That amends Section 1A of the Drug Trafficking Offences Act 1986, to remove a practical difficulty which may prevent the court from passing certain kinds of sentences on a defendant after it has decided to exercise its power under Section 1A to postpone making a determination under Section 1 as to whether a defendant has benefited from drug trafficking or as to the amount to be recovered from him, so that further information can be obtained. The Joint Committee on Consolidation Bills was informed that the Government would move amendments in the same terms to this consolidation Bill.

The second amendment to the third schedule is, as I have said, a consequential amendment to repeal the amending provision in the Criminal Justice and Public Order Bill which will be spent when the consolidation comes into force" (*Hansard*, H.L. Vol. 556, col. 992).

Subs. (11)

Where the defendant appeals against a conviction the court may, for that reason alone, postpone a determination (as above). Where the period of six months has expired, the period may be further extended (s.3(4)(b)), but once the appeal is heard the Crown Court must proceed with the Drug Trafficking Act enquiry within three months unless there are "exceptional circumstances" justifying a longer period. It is not easy to predict instances which the court could properly treat as "exceptional" but it is foreseeable that a lack of court time may be held to be one such exception: consider *R. v. Norwich Crown Court, ex p. Cox* (1993) 97 Cr.App.R. 145 and *R. v. Governor of Winchester Prison, ex p. Roddie* [1991] 1 W.L.R. 303.

Assessing the proceeds of drug trafficking

4.—(1) For the purposes of this Act—

(a) any payments or other rewards received by a person at any time (whether before or after the commencement of this Act) in connection with drug trafficking carried on by him or another person are his proceeds of drug trafficking; and

(b) the value of his proceeds of drug trafficking is the aggregate of the values of the payments or other rewards.

(2) Subject to subsections (4) and (5) below, the Crown Court shall, for the purpose—

(a) of determining whether the defendant has benefited from drug trafficking, and

(b) if he has, of assessing the value of his proceeds of drug trafficking,
make the required assumptions.

(3) The required assumptions are—

(a) that any property appearing to the court—

(i) to have been held by the defendant at any time since his conviction, or

(ii) to have been transferred to him at any time since the beginning of the period of six years ending when the proceedings were instituted against him,

was received by him, at the earliest time at which he appears to the court to have held it, as a payment or reward in connection with drug trafficking carried on by him;

(b) that any expenditure of his since the beginning of that period was met out of payments received by him in connection with drug trafficking carried on by him; and

(c) that, for the purpose of valuing any property received or assumed to have been received by him at any time as such a reward, he received the property free of any other interests in it.

(4) The court shall not make any required assumption in relation to any particular property or expenditure if—

(a) that assumption is shown to be incorrect in the defendant's case; or

(b) the court is satisfied that there would be a serious risk of injustice in the defendant's case if the assumption were to be made;

and where, by virtue of this subsection, the court does not make one or more of the required assumptions, it shall state its reasons.

(5) Subsection (2) above does not apply if the only drug trafficking offence in respect of which the defendant appears before the court to be sentenced is an offence under section 49, 50 or 51 of this Act.

(6) For the purpose of assessing the value of the defendant's proceeds of drug trafficking in a case where a confiscation order has previously been made against him, the court shall leave out of account any of his proceeds of drug trafficking that are shown to the court to have been taken into account in determining the amount to be recovered under that order.

(7) References in subsection (6) above to a confiscation order include a reference to a confiscation order within the meaning of—

(a) the Drug Trafficking Offences Act 1986; or

(b) Part I of the Criminal Justice (Scotland) Act 1987.

(8) For the purposes of the application of Part II of this Act in Scotland and Northern Ireland, the expression "proceeds of drug trafficking" shall be construed in accordance with section 48(2) of this Act.

DEFINITIONS
"benefited from drug trafficking": s.2(3).
"drug trafficking": ss.1(1)(2), 48(2).
"proceeds of drug trafficking": ss.4(1)(a)(8), 48(2).

GENERAL NOTE

Subs. (1)
This provision re-enacts s.2(1) of the 1986 Act. Note that the court is concerned with "proceeds" not merely profit. Note also that the defendant's proceeds may relate to the drug activities of the defendant or to those of others, whether carried out in England and Wales or elsewhere.

Subss. (2), (3) and (5)
Under the 1986 Act, s.2, the courts had a discretion whether to involve any of the statutory assumptions mentioned in s.2 (now s.4(3)) or not. The Government intended by s.9 of the 1993 Act to remove the discretionary aspect of making any of the statutory assumptions, but that section was never brought into force. The substance of s.9 of the 1993 Act has, however, been re-enacted in s.4(2)–(4). Note that s.4(2) does not apply if the only "drug trafficking offence" (see s.1(3)) in respect of which the defendant appears before the court to be sentenced is (for want of a better term) a money-laundering offence under ss.40, 50 or 51 of this Act. It is important to remember that the offences under ss.40, 50 and 51 are strictly speaking "drug trafficking offences" but they are not, it would seem, regarded as being of a type which deserve the application of the draconian measures found in s.4(2)–(4). This approach is consistent with the law as it stood under the 1986 Act: see s.2(4) and s.24 of that Act, s.14 and Sched. 4, para. 4(2) of the Criminal Justice (International Co-operation) Act 1990 (c. 5) and s.16 of the 1993 Act.

Section 4(2) does not apply where a defendant has absconded or died and the High Court is being asked to exercise any of its powers under s.19 of this Act: see s.19(6)(a).

The assumptions. If the court makes any of the assumptions specified in s.4 then (as is apparent from the wording of s.4(2)), it will be made on the basis that the defendant has received a payment or reward in connection with drug-trafficking carried on by him and by no-one else.

Previously, the court had a discretion whether or not to invoke any of the statutory assumptions but the Drug Trafficking Offences Act 1986, as originally drafted, did not indicate the circumstances in which it was appropriate to apply them. See *R. v. Redbourne* [1992] 1 W.L.R. 1182, *R. v. Rose* [1993] 1 W.L.R. 844, *Making Statutory Assumptions Under the Drug Trafficking Offences Act* (R. Fortson, *Archbold News*, Issue No. 5, May 28, 1993) and the Report of the Home Office Working Group on the Drug Trafficking Offences Act 1986 (1991) at para. 2.6.

By virtue of subs. (4) the trial judge should not make any of the assumptions specified in subs. (3) if "any of the assumptions are shown to be incorrect in the defendant's case", or if "the court is satisfied that there would be a serious risk of injustice in his case if the assumptions were to be made": subs. (4)(b).

Shown to be incorrect. Subsection (4)(a) follows the wording of s.2(2) of the 1986 Act. In *R. v. Dickens* [1990] 2 Q.B. 102, it was held that the burden of proving an assumption to be incorrect falls on the defendant. With this proposition the Home Office Working Group appears to have no quarrel (see para. 2.8 and para. 2.10(iv)).

One reading of subs. (4)(a) suggests that the burden need not necessarily be on the defendant if the words "is the defendant's case" are to be treated as being synonymous in meaning with the words "in the case against the defendant". It would have been very easy for the draftsman simply to have used the words "shown to be incorrect by the defendant". If the evidence in the case – no matter who adduces it – shows an assumption to be incorrect, then the court may not make it.

In para. 2.10(iv) of their Report, the Home Office Working Group suggested that the onus should be on the defendant to rebut the assumption, but (somewhat inconsistently) they also suggested that the court need not make the assumption if "for any other reason" it would not be appropriate to do so (para. 2.10(ii)).

In *R. v. Johnson* [1991] 2 Q.B. 249 the appellant received a cheque for £6,750 which had been credited to her account. A few days later the bank debited the account on the basis that the cheque was dishonoured on presentation. The court was entitled to make the assumption that the appellant received a payment in connection with drug trafficking but the cheque was plainly of no value as it was dishonoured, and thus the assumption (if made) would be shown to be incorrect by proof (whoever adduced the evidence) that the cheque had no value. Again, a motor car was bought by the appellant for £6,000 of which £5,600 was obtained by way of a loan from a finance house. The judge was entitled to make the assumption, *prima facie*, that she held the car and received it as a payment or reward in connection with drug trafficking carried on by her. However, there was no evidence that the money from the finance company was tainted and so the assumption would again be shown to be incorrect in the defendant's case.

Serious risk of injustice. As the 1986 Act was originally drafted, once the court had decided to invoke any of the statutory assumptions, the only statutory justification for not relying upon them was the possibility that "any of the assumptions are shown to be incorrect in the defendant's case": s.2(2) of the 1986 Act. This limb remains by virtue of subs. (4)(a) but a second reason is now included in subs. (4)(b), namely the risk of serious injustices.

Would any risk of injustice (which is not merely fanciful) be regarded by the courts as a "serious" one given the consequences that will flow from the making of an assumption? Even if the reasons stated for not applying the assumptions under subs. (4)(b) are erroneous, that does not seem to entitle the prosecution to apply for re-assessment under s.13, nor is it clear that the prosecutor would be entitled to seek judicial review of a judge's decision in the light of his stated reasons.

Weight attaching to an assumption

In *R. v. Redbourne* [1992] 1 W.L.R. 1182 the Court of Appeal also considered what effect the making of an assumption would have if it was not rebutted by or on behalf of the defendant. The short answer is that an assumed fact must be treated as being true. There would be little point in making an assumption if such a result were not to follow. The point is reinforced by the wording of subs. (4)(a) which includes a proviso in respect of the converse case where an assumption is shown to be "incorrect" in the defendant's case.

Although it was not expressly stated by the 1986 Act, there is clear authority for the proposition that the prosecution has the task of proving both the fact that the defendant has benefited from drug trafficking and the extent of that benefit: see *R. v. Dickens* [1990] 2 Q.B. 102 and *R. v. Enwezor* (1991) 93 Cr.App.R. 233. The 1994 Act does not alter the earlier position as to the incidence of proof but the standard of proof is now on a balance of probabilities: s.2(8).

The following example demonstrates the relevant principles now to be applied. Suppose D is shown to have received a payment of £1,000 one year prior to proceedings being instituted against him for a drug trafficking offence. The burden rests on the prosecution to prove to the civil standard, that D received it in connection with drug trafficking carried on by him or another (s.4(1)) and that he therefore benefited to the sum of £1,000: s.2(3). Assuming there was no direct evidence that D received the money in connection with drug trafficking (but the prosecution can show that D was unemployed at the material time with no known sources of legitimate income) then the judge is entitled to find as a fact that the sum was "transferred to [the defendant]" during the relevant period (s.2(3)(a)(ii)) and that accordingly he "held it" at that moment (see s.62(5)(b) (formerly s.38(10)) and s.62(5)(a) (formerly s. 38(7))). That fact alone is enough to enable the court to make the assumption under s.4(3)(a)(ii). Accordingly, the judge must assume that the sum was "received" by the defendant as a payment or reward in connection with drug trafficking carried on by the defendant (s.4(3)(a)(ii)).

In *Enwezor* (above) the judge made a confiscation order of £20,000. A total of £11,000 had been paid into a building society account in the name of the appellant's sister. The appellant contended that the payments were made by various people coming from Nigeria and not (as alleged) by himself. The trial judge ruled that the payments into the account were gifts caught by the Act which represented the proceeds of drug trafficking and that the appellant had benefited by that amount. The judge said "it is plain from the general tenor and working of the Act that the ordinary criminal burden and standard of proof is not applicable". He accordingly made his determination on the basis of the civil standard of proof. The judge added that "if the criminal standard of proof had applied I would not have found … against him". It was held, on appeal, that the judge was entitled to rely on the assumptions under s.2(2) and (3) of the 1986 Act (see now s.4(2)–(5)) but that the correct standard of proof was the criminal standard and that since the judge would have reached a different conclusion on that basis the appeal would be allowed. In the light of s.2(8) the result in *Enwezor* would now be different.

Section 4 should be read in conjunction with s.2(8) (standard of proof). Once again Members of Parliament sought clarification and evidence that amendments to what was then s.2 of the 1986 Act were necessary (Standing Committee B, May 27, 1993, col. 66). However, the Home Office did not maintain statistics on the number of cases in which assumptions had not been applied but the Minister of State for the Home Office referred to a "wealth of anecdotal evidence" that the previous provisions were unsatisfactory. The reasoning appears to have been that in cases where the prosecution cannot determine whether property passing through the defendant's hands was legitimately acquired or not, then the prosecution can progress no further because there is no obligation on the offender to account for such property given that s.11(8) specifically does not require the defendant to admit any allegation that property referred to in the statement represents the proceeds of drug trafficking. The 1994 Act, by s.12(2), empowers the court to order the defendant to give it such information as may be specified in the order and if the defendant fails, without reasonable excuse, to comply with that order then the court may draw such inference "as it considers appropriate" (s.12(5)). If it is permissible to ask the defendant whether or not he admits that the property represents the proceeds of drug trafficking then it would seem to be open to the court (in appropriate cases) to draw an adverse inference if he fails to answer the question. Arguably, s.12(5) is more "open-ended" than s.11(8) and thus the two provisions would not actually be in conflict. The reason for making assumptions mandatory would thus seem to be designed (in part) to lever the defendant into disclosing the origin of the property received by him – a lever which is then extended by s.12(2) and (5).

Subs. (6)

This provision substantially re-enacts s.2(4) of the 1986 Act. It is clearly designed to protect a defendant from having the proceeds which formed part of one confiscation order being, again, taken into account for the purpose of another confiscation order, *e.g.* where the defendant commits a subsequent drug trafficking offence. There is, however, one important qualification to this principle which appears in s.15(8) of this Act. Under s.15(1) and (2), the court may revise its assessment of the value of the defendant's proceeds of drug trafficking if there is evidence that satisfies the court that the real value of those proceeds is higher than was thought to be the case at the time the original confiscation order was made. Obviously, the purpose of s.15 would be defeated if a defendant could pray in aid s.4(6) and thus s.15(8) ensures that the sums (which were properly taken into account when the confiscation order under review was made) are taken into account for the purposes of s.15. Note that similar considerations apply where a defendant ceases to be an absconder and applies for a variation of the amount of a confiscation order made in his absence: see s.21(4) below.

Amount to be recovered under confiscation order

5.—(1) Subject to subsection (3) below, the amount to be recovered in the defendant's case under the confiscation order shall be the amount the Crown Court assesses to be the value of the defendant's proceeds of drug trafficking.

(2) If the court is satisfied as to any matter relevant for determining the amount that might be realised at the time the confiscation order is made (whether by reason of the acceptance of an allegation made in a statement given under section 11 of this Act or made in the giving of information under section 12 of this Act, or otherwise) the court may issue a certificate giving the court's opinion as to the matters concerned, and shall do so if satisfied as mentioned in subsection (3) below.

(3) If the court is satisfied that the amount that might be realised at the time the confiscation order is made is less than the amount the court assesses to be the value of his proceeds of drug trafficking, the amount to be recovered in the defendant's case under the confiscation order shall be—

    (a) the amount appearing to the court to be the amount that might be so realised; or

    (b) a nominal amount, where it appears to the court (on the information available to it at the time) that the amount that might be so realised is nil.

DEFINITIONS

"amount that might be realised": s.6(1).
"amount to be recovered": s.5(1).
"confiscation order": s.2(9).
"proceeds of drug trafficking": s.4(1)(a).

GENERAL NOTE

Subss. (1) and (2)

These provisions broadly re-enact s.4(1) and (2) of the 1986 Act. Section 5(2) appears in slightly amended form to that which existed as s.4(2) to reflect the amended provisions of s.3 of the 1986 Act (now ss.11 and 12 of this Act).

Subs. (3)

In the ordinary way the amount to be recovered is the amount the court assesses to be the defendant's proceeds of drug trafficking. Usually, the defendant will not be able to pay the full amount and thus the court will realistically look to confiscate the "amount that might be realised". Frequently that figure is nil. Originally, when the Drug Trafficking Offences Act 1986 was enacted, the prosecution could not apply to vary the order if assets held by the defendant (at the time the order was made) subsequently came to light or the value had subsequently increased. This was remedied by s.16 of the Criminal Justice (International Co-operation) Act 1990 (c. 5), now s.16 of this Act. However, it will be seen that s.16 of this Act (like its predecessor) only applies where the defendant is ordered to pay "an amount" by way of a confiscation order (albeit that the amount is less than the value of his proceeds of drug trafficking). It frequently happened that courts made "nil" confiscation orders under the 1986 Act (or even "no order") but it would be straining the English language to say that "nil" is nevertheless an "amount" for the purposes of s.16. Accordingly, assets that had been hidden at the time the "nil" confiscation order was made, but which subsequently surfaced, escaped the effect of s.16 of the Criminal Justice (International Co-operation) Act 1990. To defeat that abuse, s.5(3)(b) (originally enacted as s.7(3)(1) of the 1993 Act) now requires the court to make a confiscation order for at least a "nominal amount".

Meaning of "amount that might be realised" and "realisable property"

6.—(1) For the purposes of this Act the amount that might be realised at the time a confiscation order is made against the defendant is—

    (a) the total of the values at that time of all the realisable property held by the defendant, less

    (b) where there are obligations having priority at that time, the total amount payable in pursuance of such obligations,

together with the total of the values at that time of all gifts caught by this Act.

(2) In this Act "realisable property" means, subject to subsection (3) below—

(a) any property held by the defendant; and

(b) any property held by a person to whom the defendant has directly or indirectly made a gift caught by this Act.

(3) Property is not realisable property if there is in force in respect of it an order under any of the following enactments, namely—

(a) section 27 of the Misuse of Drugs Act 1971 (forfeiture orders);

(b) section 43 of the Powers of Criminal Courts Act 1973 (deprivation orders);

(c) section 223 or 436 of the Criminal Procedure (Scotland) Act 1975 (forfeiture of property);

(d) section 13(2), (3) or (4) of the Prevention of Terrorism (Temporary Provisions) Act 1989 (forfeiture orders).

(4) For the purposes of subsection (1) above, an obligation has priority at any time if it is an obligation of the defendant—

(a) to pay an amount due in respect of a fine, or other order of a court, imposed or made on conviction of an offence, where the fine was imposed or the order was made before the confiscation order; or

(b) to pay any sum which would be included among the preferential debts (within the meaning given by section 386 of the Insolvency Act 1986) in the defendant's bankruptcy commencing on the date of the confiscation order or winding up under an order of the court made on that date.

DEFINITIONS

"amount that might be realised": s.6(1).

"confiscation order": s.2(9).

"defendant": s.63(1).

"gift caught by this Act": s.8(1).

"obligations having priority": s.6(1).

"realisable property": s.6(2).

GENERAL NOTE

These provisions re-enact s.5(3) (now s.6(1)), s.5(1) (now s.6(2)), s.5(2) (now s.6(3)) and s.5(7) (now s.6(4)) of the 1986 Act. The operation of these provisions has been explained in the introduction to Pt. I of this Act, above. Note that the "amount that might be realised" and "realisable property" are two different terms of art and two different arithmetic determinations. Thus, when s.5(3) refers to the "amount that might be so realised" it is referring to s.6(1) *not* to s.6(2) and (3).

Value of property etc.

7.—(1) Subject to the following provisions of this section and to section 8 of this Act, for the purposes of this Act the value of property (other than cash) in relation to any person holding the property is the market value of the property, except that, where any other person holds an interest in the property, the value is—

(a) the market value of the first-mentioned person's beneficial interest in the property, less

(b) the amount required to discharge any incumbrance (other than a charging order) on that interest.

(2) Subject to section 8(2) of this Act, references in this Act to the value at any time (referred to in subsection (3) below as "the material time") of a gift caught by this Act or of any payment or reward are references to—

(a) the value of the gift, payment or reward to the recipient when he received it, adjusted to take account of subsequent changes in the value of money, or

(b) where subsection (3) below applies, the value there mentioned, whichever is the greater.

(3) Subject to section 8(2) of this Act, if at the material time the recipient holds—

(a) the property which he received (not being cash), or

(b) property which, in whole or in part, directly or indirectly represents in his hands the property which he received,

the value referred to in subsection (2)(b) above is the value to him at the material time of the property mentioned in paragraph (a) above or, as the case may be, of the property mentioned in paragraph (b) above so far as it so represents the property which he received, but disregarding in either case any charging order.

(4) References in this section to a charging order include a reference to a charging order within the meaning of the Drug Trafficking Offences Act 1986.

DEFINITIONS
"charging order": s.27(2).
"person holding property": s.62(5)(a).
"property": s.62(1).
"value of gift": s.7(2).
"value of property": s.7(1).

GENERAL NOTE
Subject to one or two minor drafting modifications, s.7(1) re-enacts s.5(4) of the 1986 Act; s.7(2) and (3) re-enact s.5(5) and (6) of that Act.

Gifts caught by this Act

8.—(1) A gift (including a gift made before the commencement of this Act) is caught by this Act if—

(a) it was made by the defendant at any time since the beginning of the period of six years ending when the proceedings were instituted against him; or

(b) it was made by the defendant at any time and was a gift of property—

(i) received by the defendant in connection with drug trafficking carried on by him or another person; or

(ii) which in whole or in part directly or indirectly represented in the defendant's hands property received by him in that connection.

(2) For the purposes of this Act—

(a) the circumstances in which the defendant is to be treated as making a gift include those where he transfers property to another person directly or indirectly for a consideration the value of which is significantly less than the value of the consideration provided by the defendant; and

(b) in those circumstances, the provisions of subsection (1) above and of section 7 of this Act shall apply as if the defendant had made a gift of such share in the property as bears to the whole property the same proportion as the difference between the values referred to in paragraph (a) above bears to the value of the consideration provided by the defendant.

DEFINITIONS
"defendant": s.63(1).
"drug trafficking": s.1(1).
"gift of property": s.8(1).

"institution of proceedings": s.41(2).

GENERAL NOTE
Section 8(1) re-enacts s.5(9) of the 1986 Act while s.8(2) re-enacts s.5(1) of that Act.

Subs. (2)
Where a defendant pays £1,500 for a rare vase which he then sells to another for £500 the defendant has thus made a gift which is caught by the Act: see s.8(2)(a). The difference between the price paid by the defendant and then received by him is £1,000 and thus the value of the share of the gift is 2:1 (see subs. (2)(b)). This ratio is important for the purposes of s.7(2) of the Act because the appropriate value of the gift is its adjusted value to take account of any changes in the value of money: see s.7(2)(a). Thus, if the vase (by the date of determination under s.2) was worth £3,000 then the value of the gift would be £2,000.

Application of procedure for enforcing fines

9.—(1) Where the Crown Court orders the defendant to pay any amount under section 2 of this Act, sections 31(1) to (3C) and 32(1) and (2) of the Powers of Criminal Courts Act 1973 (powers of Crown Court in relation to fines and enforcement of Crown Court fines) shall have effect as if that amount were a fine imposed on him by the Crown Court.

(2) Where—

(a) a warrant of commitment is issued for a default in payment of an amount ordered to be paid under section 2 of this Act in respect of an offence or offences, and

(b) at the time the warrant is issued, the defendant is liable to serve a term of custody in respect of the offence or offences,

the term of imprisonment or of detention under section 9 of the Criminal Justice Act 1982 (detention of persons aged 18 to 20 for default) to be served in default of payment of the amount shall not begin to run until after the term mentioned in paragraph (b) above.

(3) The reference in subsection (2) above to the term of custody which the defendant is liable to serve in respect of the offence or offences is a reference to the term of imprisonment, detention in a young offender institution, or detention under section 4 of the 1982 Act which he is liable to serve in respect of the offence or offences; and for the purposes of this subsection—

(a) consecutive terms and terms which are wholly or partly concurrent shall be treated as a single term; and

(b) there shall be disregarded—

(i) any sentence suspended under section 22(1) of the 1973 Act (power to suspend sentence of imprisonment) which has not taken effect at the time the warrant is issued;

(ii) in the case of a sentence of imprisonment passed with an order under section 47(1) of the Criminal Law Act 1977 (sentences of imprisonment partly served and partly suspended) any part of the sentence which the defendant has not at that time been required to serve in prison; and

(iii) any term of imprisonment or detention fixed under section 31(2) of the 1973 Act (term to be served in default of payment of fine etc) for which a warrant of commitment has not been issued at that time.

(4) In the application of Part III of the Magistrates' Courts Act 1980 to amounts payable under confiscation orders—

(a) such an amount is not a sum adjudged to be paid by a conviction for the purposes of section 81 (enforcement of fines imposed on young offenders), or a fine for the purposes of section 85 (remission of fines), of that Act; and

    (b) in section 87 of that Act (enforcement by High Court or county court), subsection (3) shall be omitted.

    (5) Where the defendant serves a term of imprisonment or detention in default of paying any amount due under a confiscation order, his serving that term does not prevent the confiscation order from continuing to have effect, so far as any other method of enforcement is concerned.

    (6) This section applies in relation to confiscation orders made by—

    (a) the criminal division of the Court of Appeal, or

    (b) the House of Lords on appeal from that division,

as it applies in relation to confiscation orders made by the Crown Court, and the last reference in subsection (1) above to the Crown Court shall be construed accordingly.

DEFINITIONS
    "confiscation order": s.2(9).
    "defendant": s.63(1).

GENERAL NOTE
    The procedure for the enforcement of a confiscation order is basically to treat the making of the order as a fine which can thus be enforced in a like manner. Except for subs. (5), the new provisions broadly follow those in the 1986 Act, s.6. The court which makes the confiscation order must specify a term of imprisonment to be imposed in default. These are of course maximum terms of imprisonment and in the event of commitment for default of payment, it must be served consecutively to any sentence of imprisonment (or detention) imposed for the drug trafficking offence itself: see subs. (2). Commitment to prison is a measure of last resort but unlike a fine (or indeed a confiscation order under the old law) the defaulter can no longer serve a term of imprisonment in default of payment and expect to be released from his obligations to satisfy the confiscation order. This is the result of subs. (5) (originally inserted into the 1986 Act by s.13 of the 1993 Act but which did not come into force). The plain purpose of the 1986 Act was that a person convicted of a drug trafficking offence should be deprived of his proceeds of drug trafficking by way of a confiscation order to the extent that he was in possession of adequate resources to satisfy the order. Any magistrate (who issues a warrant of commitment) should therefore consider all other methods of enforcing payment prior to the issue of the warrant: see *R. v. Harrow Justices, ex p. D.P.P.* [1991] 1 W.L.R. 395.

    Under the 1986 Act, the practical consequences flowing from the defendant's commitment to prison were three-fold. First, the period to be served in default relieved the defendant of the requirement to satisfy that proportion of the order which remained outstanding. The defendant therefore effectively "served" his way out of paying the order and so defeated the primary purpose of the Act. Secondly, a warrant, once issued, cannot be withdrawn by the magistrates' court: see *R. v. Newport Pagnell Justices, ex p. Smith* (1988) 152 J.P. 475. Thirdly, proceedings for the purposes of the 1986 Act were "concluded" upon the defendant serving a term of imprisonment in default of payment: s.38(12) as amended by Sched. 5, para. 16 of the Criminal Justice Act 1988. Although this result must have been part of the Government's strategy at the time, it was quickly criticised as enabling drug traffickers to keep their ill-gotten gains for purposes lawful or unlawful.

    Following the Seventh Report of the Home Office Affairs Committee *Drug Trafficking and Related Serious Crime* (1989), the Home Office Working Group (1991) expressed concern that trafficking could obstruct the satisfaction of a confiscation order by shifting funds. Once he had served a term of imprisonment in default, his property would not be liable to confiscation wherever it was situated. The Group therefore recommended that a term of imprisonment served in default should not expunge what ought to be regarded as a "debt" (para. 3.11). Accordingly, what is now subs. (5) has been introduced into the legislation to give effect to that proposal (derived from s.13(1) of the 1993 Act which inserted s.6(7) into the 1986 Act).

    Section 38(12) of the 1986 Act has now been replaced by s.41 of this Act. Powers conferred on the High Court in respect of the making of a restraint or charging order, or the realisation of property by the appointment of a receiver, are only exercisable where proceedings are not concluded: see ss.25–31 and 41(3), below.

    Even where monies had actually been taken from the defendant at the time of his arrest, it was a mandatory requirement of s.6 of the 1986 Act that a term of imprisonment be imposed in default of payment of the sums confiscated: see *R. v. Popple* (1993) 14 Cr.App.R.(S.) 60. This is because Customs and Excise officers, for example, did not have power to pay money in satisfaction of a confiscation order without first obtaining the defendant's consent or applying to a magistrates' court for a distress warrant.

By s.9(2) of the 1994 Act, a term of imprisonment (or detention), ordered to be served in default of payment, shall run after the defendant has served any sentences of imprisonment which were imposed in respect of the offences for which he appeared at the Crown Court.

Since confiscation orders are enforced as fines imposed on defendants by the Crown Court, the 1994 Act (like its predecessor) employs the machinery created by the Powers of Criminal Courts Act 1973 (c. 62) and the Magistrates' Courts Act 1980 (c. 43) for the collection of sums due under confiscation orders. Thus by s.31 of the 1973 Act, the Crown Court may allow time for the payment of the amount due or it may direct payment by instalment but it must fix a term of imprisonment in default of payment (s.31(2) of the 1973 Act). Prior to the 1986 Act, the maximum term of imprisonment in default was 12 months for an amount exceeding £10,000 (s.31(3A) of the 1973 Act) but the 1986 Act contemplated that the magistrates' courts would be collecting and enforcing confiscation orders for amounts in excess of £1 million (see s.32 of the 1973 Act). Section 6 of the 1986 Act therefore amended the table of default terms of imprisonment in s.31(3A) of the 1973 Act so that an amount exceeding £1 million carries a maximum term in default of payment of 10 years' imprisonment. Although there exists a line of cases in which the Court of Appeal have held that the term off imprisonment imposed for an offence, plus any term imposed in default term of payment of a fine, should not constitute an excessive sentence when viewed globally (see *R. v. Michel and others* (1984) 6 Cr.App.R.(S.) 379 and *R. v. Chatt* (1984) 6 Cr.App.R.(S) 75) nevertheless it seems that different considerations apply where the court is concerned with terms imposed in default of the payment of a confiscation order because the purpose of the default term is to encourage or to coerce payment of the sum due under the order; see *R. v. Garner and others* (1985), 7 Cr.App.R.(S) 285. In any event, the table of default terms of imprisonment in s.31(3A) of the 1973 Act are maximum terms only and, in the ordinary way, the court would be likely to determine that the appropriate term would fall between the maximum of the band being considered and the maximum of the band immediately below but much would depend on the facts of the case: see *R. v. Szrajber*, 15 Cr.App.R.(S) 821.

Interest on sums unpaid under confiscation orders

10.—(1) If any sum required to be paid by a person under a confiscation order is not paid when it is required to be paid (whether forthwith on the making of the order or at a time specified under section 31(1) of the Powers of Criminal Courts Act 1973) that person shall be liable to pay interest on that sum for the period for which it remains unpaid; and the amount of the interest shall for the purposes of enforcement be treated as part of the amount to be recovered from him under the confiscation order.

(2) The Crown Court may, on the application of the prosecutor, increase the term of imprisonment or detention fixed in respect of the confiscation order under subsection (2) of section 31 of the 1973 Act (as it has effect by virtue of section 9 of this Act) if the effect of subsection (1) above is to increase the maximum period applicable in relation to the order under subsection (3A) of that section.

(3) The rate of interest under subsection (1) above shall be that for the time being applying to a civil judgment debt under section 17 of the Judgments Act 1838.

DEFINITIONS
"confiscation order": s.2(9).

GENERAL NOTE
This provision was first introduced into the drug trafficking legislation by s.15 of the Criminal Justice (International Co-operation) Act 1990 (c. 5) so as to empower a court to take out of the hands of the drug trafficker interest which had accrued on monies held by a person under an unpaid confiscation order. The 1986 Act did not specifically cater for this problem and neither did the Criminal Justice (Scotland) Act 1987. Accordingly, s.15 of the 1990 Act was introduced to fill that deficiency in the law. Section 10 of the 1994 Act reproduces s.15 of the 1990 Act insofar as it applies to England and Wales. Section 15 of the 1990 Act still applies in Scotland: see Sched. 3, below.

Note that s.10 does not permit the Crown Court to increase the value of the confiscation order to take account of interest due. It merely treats the interest as if it were part of the amount to be recovered under the confiscation order, *i.e.* "for the purposes of enforcement": subs. (1). Section

10 is needed because the same result could not be achieved under ss.13, 14 or 15 and it would be inappropriate to involve the s.16 procedure: indeed it would be impossible to do so in cases where no order was made under s.5(3).

Statements etc in connection with confiscation orders

Statements relating to drug trafficking

11.—(1) Where the prosecutor asks the court to proceed under section 2 of this Act he shall give the court, within such period as it may direct, a statement of matters which he considers relevant in connection with—

    (a) determining whether the defendant has benefited from drug trafficking; or

    (b) assessing the value of his proceeds of drug trafficking.

(2) In this section such a statement is referred to as a "prosecutor's statement".

(3) Where the court proceeds under section 2 of this Act without the prosecutor having asked it to do so, it may require him to give it a prosecutor's statement, within such period as it may direct.

(4) Where the prosecutor has given a prosecutor's statement—

    (a) he may at any time give the court a further such statement; and

    (b) the court may at any time require him to give it a further such statement, within such period as it may direct.

(5) Where any prosecutor's statement has been given and the court is satisfied that a copy of the statement has been served on the defendant, it may require the defendant—

    (a) to indicate to it, within such period as it may direct, the extent to which he accepts each allegation in the statement; and

    (b) so far as he does not accept any such allegation, to give particulars of any matters on which he proposes to rely.

(6) Where the court has given a direction under this section it may at any time vary it by giving a further direction.

(7) Where the defendant accepts to any extent any allegation in any prosecutor's statement, the court may, for the purposes of—

    (a) determining whether the defendant has benefited from drug trafficking, or

    (b) assessing the value of his proceeds of drug trafficking,

treat his acceptance as conclusive of the matters to which it relates.

(8) If the defendant fails in any respect to comply with a requirement under subsection (5) above he may be treated for the purposes of this section as accepting every allegation in the prosecutor's statement in question apart from—

    (a) any allegation in respect of which he has complied with the requirement; and

    (b) any allegation that he has benefited from drug trafficking or that any payment or other reward was received by him in connection with drug trafficking carried on by him or another person.

(9) Where—

    (a) there is given to the Crown Court by the defendant a statement as to any matters relevant to determining the amount that might be realised at the time the confiscation order is made, and

    (b) the prosecutor accepts to any extent any allegation in the statement,

the court may, for the purposes of that determination, treat the acceptance by the prosecutor as conclusive of the matters to which it relates.

(10) An allegation may be accepted, or particulars of any matter may be given, for the purposes of this section in such manner as may be prescribed by rules of court or as the court may direct.

(11) No acceptance by the defendant under this section that any payment or other reward was received by him in connection with drug trafficking carried on by him or another person shall be admissible in evidence in any proceedings for an offence.

DEFINITIONS
"benefited from drug trafficking": s.2(3).
"defendant": s.63(1).
"drug trafficking": s.1(1).
"prosecutor's statement": s.11.
"value of proceeds of drug trafficking": s.4(1)(b).

GENERAL NOTE

Evidence
The judge is entitled to rely on the evidence given during the trial of the drug trafficking offence. The prosecution is not obliged to call or recall that evidence again during the drug trafficking investigation: see *R. v. Jenkins* (1990) 12 Cr.App.R.(S.) 582 but see *Rose* (1993) Cr.App.R. 257. The prosecution may rely on and call evidence in respect of any statement or notice served by them in accordance with s.3 of the 1986 Act. As the Court of Appeal in *R. v. Comiskey* (1991) 93 Cr.App.R. 227 remarked:
"Section 3 of the Act provides convenient and effective machinery for ascertaining matters relevant to the courts' determination of the amount to be paid under a confiscation order. It is very desirable that those responsible for the prosecution of offences should make full use of this".
The court also pointed out the desirability, in appropriate cases, of inviting the defendant to indicate to what extent he accepts the Crown's allegations or, if he does not do so, to indicate any matters he proposes to rely on (see now s.11(5)). Previously, a statement made out of court by a person not called as a witness could not be admitted, except in accordance with established principles of admissibility at common law or under statute: see *R. v. Chrastny (No. 2)* [1991] 1 W.L.R. 1381.
It may be for this reason that allegations accepted or matters indicated for the purposes of s.3 which formerly could be presented either orally "before the court", or in writing in accordance with the Crown Court Rules (*i.e.* the old s.5(5)), may now be presented in such fashion as "the court may direct", see s.11(10).
Putting the relevant party to "strict proof" of their case will often result in the contents of any statement tendered to the other side not being admitted for a variety of reasons, *e.g.* the statement infringes the hearsay rule. Where, for example, a prosecutor is in possession of information alleging that on certain dates valuable property was given to the accused, he may seek to embody those allegations in a statement which he can then serve on the defence by way of s.9 of the Criminal Justice Act 1967 (c. 80), in the hope that the statement will be accepted. In fact, if put to strict proof, the prosecutor might find that he cannot prove the contents at all.
Under the 1994 Act the procedure for the provision of information has been strengthened. The procedure applies not only to the usual situation where the court proceeds under s.2, following a conviction for a drug trafficking offence, but also where the court is asked to proceed under s.2 when it originally declined to do so (s.13(11)); or where the court is asked to re-assess whether the defendant has benefited from drug trafficking (s.14(8)); or where the court revises its assessment of the proceeds of any trafficking (s.15(3)); or where the defendant has died or absconded (s.19(6)(b)).
Where a prosecutor does not serve a "prosecutor's statement", the court may order him to serve one (s.11(3)).
This section asks the court to adopt an inquisitorial role. The defendant may therefore be asked to state those matters (if any) which he proposes to rely on to refute an allegation contained in the statement tendered. The penalty, for a failure to comply with s.11, is set out in subs. (8). He may thus be treated as accepting every allegation in the prosecutor's statement in question apart from those stated in subs. (8).
Although it is obvious, from the wording of subs. (8)(b), that the legislature was not prepared to go so far as to say that a defendant's non-compliance with the requirements of subs. (5) should be construed as an admission either that he benefited from drug trafficking, or that any payment or reward received by him represents the proceeds of that activity, the reality of the situation is that once the prosecution has established that the defendant has received property, it is open to the court to see if it may assume that the payment was received in connection with drug trafficking by virtue of s.4(2)–(5).

Provision of information by defendant

12.—(1) This section applies where—

(a) the prosecutor has asked the court to proceed under section 2 of this Act; or

(b) no such request has been made but the court is nevertheless proceeding, or considering whether to proceed, under section 2.

(2) For the purpose of obtaining information to assist it in carrying out its functions, the court may at any time order the defendant to give it such information as may be specified in the order.

(3) An order under subsection (2) above may require all, or any specified part, of the required information to be given to the court in such manner, and before such date, as may be specified in the order.

(4) Crown Court Rules may make provision as to the maximum or minimum period that may be allowed under subsection (3) above.

(5) If the defendant fails, without reasonable excuse, to comply with any order under this section, the court may draw such inference from that failure as it considers appropriate.

(6) Where the prosecutor accepts to any extent any allegation made by the defendant in giving to the court information required by an order under this section, the court may treat that acceptance as conclusive of the matters to which it relates.

(7) For the purposes of this section, an allegation may be accepted in such manner as may be prescribed by Crown Court Rules or as the court may direct.

DEFINITIONS
"defendant": s.63(1).

GENERAL NOTE
This was originally introduced into the drug trafficking legislation by s.10(5) of the 1993 Act but it was never actually brought into force. It is a measure which is likely to have a considerable impact on the way confiscation determinations proceed under the Act. Restraint orders often include an order against the defendant to provide information disclosing the existence of all assets held by the defendant or by persons likely to be affected by the order. Such a disclosure order is usually followed by a clause granting the defendant limited protection from the material being used as evidence adduced by the prosecution in the proceedings pending against him. To what extent this section is similarly used remains to be seen, and no doubt the courts will be called upon to provide guidance as to grounds which do, or do not, amount to a "reasonable excuse" for a failure to comply with an order under it (see subs. (5)).

Further proceedings in connection with confiscation orders

Reconsideration of case where court has not proceeded under section 2

13.—(1) This section applies where the defendant has appeared before the Crown Court to be sentenced in respect of one or more drug trafficking offences but the court has not proceeded under section 2 of this Act.

(2) If the prosecutor has evidence—

(a) which was not available to him when the defendant appeared to be sentenced (and accordingly was not considered by the court), but

(b) which the prosecutor believes would have led the court to determine that the defendant had benefited from drug trafficking if—

(i) the prosecutor had asked the court to proceed under section 2 of this Act, and

(ii) the evidence had been considered by the court,

he may apply to the Crown Court for it to consider the evidence.

(3) The court shall proceed under section 2 of this Act if, having considered the evidence, it is satisfied that it is appropriate to do so.

(4) In considering whether it is appropriate to proceed under that section, the court shall have regard to all the circumstances of the case.

(5) Where, having decided to proceed under that section, the court proposes to make a confiscation order against the defendant, it shall order the payment of such amount as it thinks just in all the circumstances of the case.

(6) In considering the circumstances of any case the court shall have regard, in particular, to the amount of any fine or fines imposed on the defendant in respect of the offence or offences in question.

(7) Where the court is proceeding under section 2 of this Act by virtue of this section, subsection (4) of that section shall have effect as if the words "before sentencing or otherwise dealing with him in respect of the offence or, as the case may be, any of the offences concerned" were omitted.

(8) The court may take into account any payment or other reward received by the defendant on or after the date of conviction, but only if the prosecutor shows that it was received by the defendant in connection with drug trafficking carried on by the defendant or another person on or before that date.

(9) In considering under this section any evidence which relates to any payment or reward to which subsection (8) above applies, the court shall not make the assumptions which would otherwise be required by section 4 of this Act.

(10) No application shall be entertained by the court under this section if it is made after the end of the period of six years beginning with the date of conviction.

(11) Sections 11 and 12 of this Act shall apply where the prosecutor makes an application under this section as they apply where the prosecutor asks the court to proceed under section 2 of this Act.

(12) In this section "the date of conviction" means—

(a) the date on which the defendant was convicted; or

(b) where he appeared to be sentenced in respect of more than one conviction, and those convictions were not all on the same date, the date of the latest of those convictions.

DEFINITIONS
"confiscation order": s.2(9).
"date of conviction": s.13(12).
"defendant": s.63(1).
"drug trafficking": s.1(1)(2).
"drug trafficking offence": s.1(3).

GENERAL NOTE

Further proceedings in connection with confiscation orders
As originally drafted, the 1986 Act allowed a defendant to apply for a downward variation of the confiscation order but it did not give the court a power to vary or to re-assess the amount to be recovered under a confiscation order if assets (or evidence relevant to determinations made under the Act) come to light after the making of an order. Reform, in this area, has been piecemeal which aggravates an already confused and difficult area of the law.

There are three determinations which a court will normally make if it embarks upon a drug trafficking enquiry under s.2 of the 1994 Act. First, whether the defendant has benefited from drug trafficking at all. Secondly, the amount which represents the total proceeds of the defendant's drug trafficking. Thirdly, the "amount that might be realised" under what is now s.5(3) and s.6(2) of this Act.

The Criminal Justice (International Co-operation) Act 1990 (c. 5) amended the law in respect of the third determination but it did not touch the first two determinations (and see para. 4.1 of the Working Group Report (1991)).

Reforms introduced by ss.13, 14 and 15 address the problems associated with the first two determinations.

(a) Section 13 empowers the Crown Court to embark upon a drug trafficking enquiry when it had earlier declined to do so. This provision is particularly significant given that by s.2(1) a court may not be asked by the prosecutor to proceed under s.2 in every case.

(b) By s.14, the court, which did embark upon an enquiry but nevertheless concluded that there was no benefit received by the defendant, can now reassess that determination if new evidence becomes available.

(c) By s.15, the court may re-assess the value of the defendant's proceeds of drug trafficking if new evidence comes to light. Prosecutors will be anxious to keep this figure under review because it represents the maximum that can be recovered under a confiscation order. Accordingly, where the prosecutor successfully applies to the Crown Court for an increased confiscation order on the basis that there were more realisable assets in existence than at first known (*i.e.* under s.16 below, formerly s.16 of the Criminal Justice (International Co-operation) Act 1990) it follows that the new order cannot exceed the amount originally determined to be the value of the defendant's proceeds of drug trafficking.

Common to each of these new provisions is a six-year time-limit which runs from the date of the defendant's last conviction for a drug trafficking offence in respect of which he appeared before the Crown Court to be sentenced at the time the confiscation order was made.

These provisions have been attacked as "hounding" a man who has been convicted (*Hansard*, H.L. Vol. 539, col. 1357) and it is perhaps to this end that s.13(4) was enacted but even where a court is required to make a determination under s.14 or s.15, the court is not entitled to rely on any of the statutory assumptions under s.2 (and similarly in respect of s.13). Furthermore, both under s.13 and s.15 the court appears to be entitled to mitigate the amount to be confiscated as is "just in all the circumstances" (see s.13(5) and s.15(12)).

Under this provision the court may be asked, by the prosecutor, to embark upon a drug trafficking enquiry if evidence was not previously available to him which he believes would have led the court to conclude that the defendant had benefited from drug trafficking. Under s.2(1), the court is not obliged to proceed under the 1994 Act and this could be for a number of reasons (including tactical ones) in circumstances where the prosecutor did have compelling evidence at the time the defendant was due to be sentenced but the prosecution decided not to rely on it. If the prosecutor subsequently changes direction, he can only go back to the Crown Court if he has something else which was not available to him originally. A safeguard (if one were needed) is provided by subss. (3) and (4) so that the court is entitled to have regard to "all the circumstances of the case" before concluding that it would be "appropriate" to proceed under s.2: see subs. (3).

If the court relies on payments received by the defendant on or after the date of conviction then the prosecution must prove (to the civil standard: see s.2(8)) that (a) he received the payment; (b) he received it in connection with drug trafficking carried on by him or by another; and (c) the drug trafficking activity occurred before the date of conviction: see subs. (8) and (12). Presumably the reasoning behind this approach is that the conviction should be seen as marking the end of the defendant's drug trafficking career, for confiscation purposes, and that the use of the assumptions is justified where payments are received up and until the moment of conviction.

Where a determination is made under s.2(4), the court is only obliged to order a payment that is "just" in all the circumstances. The court is required to have "regard" (but not necessarily to leave out of account) any fine paid by the defendant (subs. (6)) and presumably other financial or forfeiture orders as well.

Re-assessment of whether defendant has benefited from drug trafficking

14.—(1) This section applies where the court has made a determination under section 2(2) of this Act ("the section 2(2) determination") that the defendant has not benefited from drug trafficking.

(2) If the prosecutor has evidence—

(a) which was not considered by the court in making the section 2(2) determination, but

(b) which the prosecutor believes would have led the court to determine that the defendant had benefited from drug trafficking if it had been considered by the court,

he may apply to the Crown Court for it to consider that evidence.

(3) If, having considered the evidence, the court is satisfied that it would have determined that the defendant had benefited from drug trafficking if that evidence had been available to it, the court—

(a) shall make—

(i) a fresh determination under subsection (2) of section 2 of this Act; and

(ii) a determination under subsection (4) of that section of the amount to be recovered by virtue of that section; and

(b) may make an order under that section.

(4) Where the court is proceeding under section 2 of this Act by virtue of this section, subsection (4) of that section shall have effect as if the words

"before sentencing or otherwise dealing with him in respect of the offence or, as the case may be, any of the offences concerned" were omitted.

(5) The court may take into account any payment or other reward received by the defendant on or after the date of the section 2(2) determination, but only if the prosecutor shows that it was received by the defendant in connection with drug trafficking carried on by the defendant or another person on or before that date.

(6) In considering under this section any evidence which relates to any payment or reward to which subsection (5) above applies, the court shall not make the assumptions which would otherwise be required by section 4 of this Act.

(7) No application shall be entertained by the court under this section if it is made after the end of the period of six years beginning with the date of conviction; and in this subsection "the date of conviction" has the same meaning as in section 13 of this Act.

(8) Sections 11 and 12 of this Act shall apply where the prosecutor makes an application under this section as they apply where the prosecutor asks the court to proceed under section 2 of this Act.

DEFINITIONS
    "confiscation order": s.2(9).
    "date of conviction": s.13(12).
    "defendant": s.63(1).
    "drug trafficking": s.1(1)(2).
    "drug trafficking offence": s.1(3).

GENERAL NOTE
    By subs. (2), the court appears to be required to form an opinion based on hindsight—*i.e.* that it "would have" determined that the defendant had benefited from drug trafficking if the evidence which ultimately came to light had been available to it. Payments received by the defendant after the date on which the court originally concluded he received no benefit may be taken into account, but the prosecution will not be able to rely on the statutory assumptions.

Revised assessment of proceeds of drug trafficking

15.—(1) This section applies where the court has made a determination under subsection (4) of section 2 of this Act of the amount to be recovered in a particular case by virtue of that section ("the current section 2(4) determination").

(2) Where the prosecutor is of the opinion that the real value of the defendant's proceeds of drug trafficking was greater than their assessed value, the prosecutor may apply to the Crown Court for the evidence on which the prosecutor has formed his opinion to be considered by the court.

(3) Sections 11 and 12 of this Act shall apply where the prosecutor makes such an application as they apply where the prosecutor asks the court to proceed under section 2 of this Act, but subject (in the case of section 11) to subsection (9)(a) below.

(4) If, having considered the evidence, the court is satisfied that the real value of the defendant's proceeds of drug trafficking is greater than their assessed value (whether because the real value at the time of the current section 2(4) determination was higher than was thought or because the value of the proceeds in question has subsequently increased), the court shall make a fresh determination under subsection (4) of section 2 of this Act of the amount to be recovered by virtue of that section.

(5) In subsections (2) and (4) above—
    "assessed value" means the value of the defendant's proceeds of drug trafficking as assessed by the court in accordance with section 5(1) of this Act; and

"real value" means the value of the defendant's proceeds of drug trafficking which took place—
    (a) in the period by reference to which the current section 2(4)
determination was made; or
    (b) in any earlier period.

(6) Where the court is proceeding under section 2 of this Act by virtue of
this section, subsection (4) of that section shall have effect as if the words
"before sentencing or otherwise dealing with him in respect of the offence or,
as the case may be, any of the offences concerned" were omitted.

(7) Any determination under section 2(4) of this Act by virtue of this section shall be by reference to the amount that might be realised at the time
when the determination is made.

(8) In the case of any determination under section 2(4) of this Act by virtue
of this section, section 4(6) of this Act shall not apply in relation to any of the
defendant's proceeds of drug trafficking taken into account in respect of the
current section 2(4) determination.

(9) In relation to any such determination by virtue of this section—

(a) sections 5(2), 6(4) and 11(9)(a) of this Act shall have effect as if for
"confiscation order" there were substituted "determination";

(b) section 5(3) shall have effect as if for "confiscation order is made"
there were substituted "determination is made"; and

(c) section 6(1) of this Act shall have effect as if for "a confiscation order is
made against the defendant" there were substituted "of the
determination".

(10) The court may take into account any payment or other reward
received by the defendant on or after the date of the current section 2(4)
determination, but only if the prosecutor shows that it was received by the
defendant in connection with drug trafficking carried on by the defendant or
another person on or before that date.

(11) In considering under this section any evidence which relates to any
payment or reward to which subsection (10) above applies, the court shall not
make the assumptions which would otherwise be required by section 4 of this
Act.

(12) If, as a result of making the fresh determination required by subsection (4) above, the amount to be recovered exceeds the amount set by the
current section 2(4) determination, the court may substitute for the amount
to be recovered under the confiscation order which was made by reference to
the current section 2(4) determination such greater amount as it thinks just in
all the circumstances of the case.

(13) Where the court varies a confiscation order under subsection (12)
above it shall substitute for the term of imprisonment or of detention fixed
under section 31(2) of the Powers of Criminal Courts Act 1973 in respect of
the amount to be recovered under the order a longer term determined in
accordance with that section (as it has effect by virtue of section 9 of this Act)
in respect of the greater amount substituted under subsection (12) above.

(14) Subsection (13) above shall apply only if the effect of the substitution
is to increase the maximum period applicable in relation to the order under
section 31(3A) of the 1973 Act.

(15) No application shall be entertained by the court under this section if it
is made after the end of the period of six years beginning with the date of
conviction; and in this subsection "the date of conviction" has the same
meaning as in section 13 of this Act.

DEFINITIONS
    "confiscation order": s.2(9).
    "date of conviction": s.13(12).
    "defendant": s.63(1).
    "drug trafficking": s.1(1)(2).

"drug trafficking offence": s.1(3).

GENERAL NOTE

There appears to be a difference of scope in the ambit of these provisions when subs. (2) (formerly, s.5C(2) of the 1986 Act inserted by s.12 of the 1993 Act) is read in contrast with subs. (4). Subsection (2) seems to look to the "real value" as it should have been assessed at the time the order was made but the conclusion which the court is actually entitled to make under subs. (4), includes any increased value of the proceeds in question. Be that as it may, the governing provision is subs. (4). The court therefore looks at the current value of the proceeds (which were ascertained by the date the confiscation order was originally made: see subs. (4)), plus any payments received by the defendant on, or after, that date which were the fruits of drug trafficking carried on by the defendant or another before that moment (subs. (10)). The prosecution cannot rely on the statutory assumptions (subs. (11)). However, the "amount to be recovered", under a fresh confiscation order, is *prima facie* the "amount that might be realised" (see ss. 5(3), 6(2) and 15(7)). It follows that if the defendant's finances have improved by the date of the subsequent determination, it is the higher figure which is relevant. Given that the court is being asked to make a fresh confiscation order it follows that section 4(6) must be disregarded and that is what s.15(8) is designed to achieve. Even if, *prima facie*, the "amount to be recovered" (being the "amount that might be realised") is greater than it was originally assessed to be, nevertheless, the court need only order such greater amount as it thinks just in all the circumstances of the case.

Increase in realisable property

16.—(1) This section applies where, by virtue of section 5(3) of this Act, the amount which a person is ordered to pay by a confiscation order is less than the amount assessed to be the value of his proceeds of drug trafficking.

(2) If, on an application made in accordance with subsection (3) below, the High Court is satisfied that the amount that might be realised in the case of the person in question is greater than the amount taken into account in making the confiscation order (whether it was greater than was thought when the order was made or has subsequently increased) the court shall issue a certificate to that effect, giving the court's reasons.

(3) An application under subsection (2) above may be made either by the prosecutor or by a receiver appointed in relation to the realisable property of the person in question under section 26 or 29 of this Act or in pursuance of a charging order.

(4) Where a certificate has been issued under subsection (2) above the prosecutor may apply to the Crown Court for an increase in the amount to be recovered under the confiscation order; and on that application the court may—

(a) substitute for that amount such amount (not exceeding the amount assessed as the value referred to in subsection (1) above) as appears to the court to be appropriate having regard to the amount now shown to be realisable; and

(b) increase the term of imprisonment or detention fixed in respect of the confiscation order under subsection (2) of section 31 of the Powers of Criminal Courts Act 1973 (as it has effect by virtue of section 9 of this Act) if the effect of the substitution is to increase the maximum period applicable in relation to the order under subsection (3A) of that section.

DEFINITIONS

"amount to be recovered": s.5(1).
"charging order": s.27(2).
"confiscation order": s.2(9).
"drug trafficking": s.1(1)(2).

GENERAL NOTE

By an ingenious route, the prosecution in *R. v. Miller* (1991) 92 Cr.App.R. 191 successfully applied for a variation of the order by invoking the provisions of s.47 of the Supreme Court Act 1981 (c. 54) in circumstances where further assets, held by the defendant at the time the order was made, were discovered. This route might not be appropriate in all cases and, in any event, the procedure is subject to time-limits (normally 28 days): see also *R. v. Onwuka* (1992) 95 Cr.App.R. 47.

In 1990, Parliament enacted the Criminal Justice (International Co-operation) Act 1990 (c. 5) and took the opportunity to amend the law. Parliament did not, technically speaking, amend the 1986 Act itself but, by s.16 of the 1990 Act, the prosecution became entitled to apply for a variation in the limited circumstances specified in s.16 as it then appeared (see now s.16, above):

"(1) This section has effect where by virtue of section 4(3) of the Drug Trafficking Offences Act 1986 (insufficient realisable property) [now s. 5(3)], the amount which a person is ordered to pay by a confiscation order is less than the amount assessed to be the value of his proceeds of drug trafficking.

(2) If, on an application made in accordance with subsection (3) below, the High Court is satisfied that the amount that might be realised in the case of the person in question is greater than the amount taken into account in making the confiscation order (whether it was greater than was thought when the order was made or has subsequently increased) the court shall issue a certificate to that effect, giving the court's reasons.

(3) An application under subsection (2) above may be made either by the prosecutor or by a receiver appointed under the said Act of 1986 in relation to the realisable property of the person in question.

(4) Where a certificate has been issued under subsection (2) above the prosecutor may apply to the Crown Court for an increase in the amount to be recovered under the confiscation order; and on that application the court may—

(a) substitute for that amount such amount (not exceeding the amount assessed as the value referred to in subsection (1) above) as appears to the court to be appropriate having regard to the amount now shown to be realisable; and

(b) increase the term of imprisonment or detention fixed in respect of the confiscation order under subsection (2) of section 31 of the Powers of Criminal Courts Act 1973 (imprisonment in default of payment) if the effect of the substitution is to increase the maximum period applicable in relation to the order under subsection (3A) of that section."

Note that the terms of imprisonment in default are maximum terms: see *R. v. Szrajber*, 15 Cr.App.R.(S.) 821.

Similar amendments were made to Scottish law by s.17 of the 1990 Act (see s.1(1)(b) of the Criminal Justice (Scotland) Act 1987 (c. 41)).

Section 16 of the Criminal Justice (International Co-operation) Act 1990 (c. 5) is now repealed (see s.67, Sched. 3, below) and substantially re-enacted in this section.

It will be seen from the wording of this section that the High Court is itself empowered to vary the order. It can do no more than certify that the facts set out in subs. (2) exist and leave it to the Crown Court to substitute an amount that is "appropriate" (subs. (4)(a)) and to increase the default period accordingly (subs. (4)(b)).

Note that this section does not apply to property which comes into the possession of the defendant after the order is made. Furthermore, an application made under this section is subject to a ceiling, namely, the amount which the Crown Court assessed to be the proceeds of the defendant's drug trafficking. That figure will often be calculated on the basis of what was believed to be the defendant's financial position, over the relevant period, at the time the original order was made. The Home Office Working Group on Confiscation suggests that the Crown Court should be empowered to make a fresh order on the basis of a reassessment of the extent of the defendant's benefit.

Under both s.17 (formerly s.14 of the 1986 Act) and s.16 it is necessary to go to the High Court first and not straight to the Crown Court. It is not clear why the legislature thought this route to be desirable or necessary. An initial reaction is that the provisions were intended to confer upon the High Court a supervisory role and thus safeguard the interests of persons likely to be affected by a successful application, but the terms of ss.16 and 17 impose a mandatory obligation on the High Court to issue a certificate upon making the requisite findings of fact for the purposes of ss.16(2) and 17. Neither of these two sections gives any indication or guidance as to the burden or standard of proof.

Inadequacy of realisable property

17.—(1) If, on an application made in respect of a confiscation order by—

(a) the defendant, or

(b) a receiver appointed under section 26 or 29 of this Act or in pursuance of a charging order,

the High Court is satisfied that the realisable property is inadequate for the payment of any amount remaining to be recovered under the confiscation order, the court shall issue a certificate to that effect, giving the court's reasons.

(2) For the purposes of subsection (1) above—

(a) in the case of realisable property held by a person who has been adjudged bankrupt or whose estate has been sequestrated the court shall take into account the extent to which any property held by him may be distributed among creditors; and

(b) the court may disregard any inadequacy in the realisable property which appears to the court to be attributable wholly or partly to anything done by the defendant for the purpose of preserving any property held by a person to whom the defendant had directly or indirectly made a gift caught by this Act from any risk of realisation under this Act.

(3) Where a certificate has been issued under subsection (1) above, the person who applied for it may apply to the Crown Court for the amount to be recovered under the confiscation order to be reduced.

(4) The Crown Court shall, on an application under subsection (3) above—

(a) substitute for the amount to be recovered under the order such lesser amount as the court thinks just in all the circumstances of the case; and

(b) substitute for the term of imprisonment or of detention fixed under subsection (2) of section 31 of the Powers of Criminal Courts Act 1973 in respect of the amount to be recovered under the order a shorter term determined in accordance with that section (as it has effect by virtue of section 9 of this Act) in respect of the lesser amount.

(5) Rules of court may make provision—

(a) for the giving of notice of any application under this section; and

(b) for any person appearing to the court to be likely to be affected by any exercise of its powers under this section to be given an opportunity to make representations to the court.

<small>DEFINITIONS</small>
"amount to be recovered": s.5(1).
"defendant": s.63(1).
"realisable property": s.6(2).

<small>GENERAL NOTE</small>

Variation by a defendant or by a receiver
Formerly under s.14 it was limited to the defendant alone to apply for a variation of a confiscation order made under the 1986 Act. Two major changes have been introduced into this section, s.17. First, the application may be made either by the defendant or by a receiver appointed under s.26 or s.29, below. Secondly, subs. (5) now addresses the concern expressed by members of the judiciary (among others) in respect of the interests of third parties who seemed (under the 1986 Act as originally drafted) not to have any *locus standi* in confiscation proceedings before the Crown Court. By contrast, third party representation was always expressly catered for in the 1986 Act in respect of High Court proceedings where property was sought to be realised by a receiver (see s.11(8) of the 1986 Act, now s.29(8)). Since 1988, third parties have had a right to apply to vary or to discharge a charging order: s.9(8) of the 1986 Act, Sched. 5 of the Criminal Justice Act 1988, and see now s.27(8), below.

Variation by the defendant
A variation of a confiscation order is to be carefully distinguished from an appeal against the making of an order. Where a defendant complains that the court erred in the determination of the order, *e.g.* in the assessment of his proceeds of drug trafficking, then his appropriate course is to appeal against the making of the order because such an order is a sentence for the purposes of ss.9 and 11 of the Criminal Appeal Act 1968, see *R. v. Johnson* [1991] 2 Q.B. 249.

However, a variation of a confiscation order under this Act is confined to a reduction in the amount of the order in cases where the defendant's realisable property is inadequate to satisfy the making of an order.

Note that the High Court can do no more than issue a certificate and give its reasons for so doing. It cannot vary the order under this section. Clearly if the defendant has been adjudged bankrupt then the court must take into account the extent to which his property will be distributed amongst his creditors. The court must also guard against the manipulative defendant who has taken steps to prevent the court seizing his assets: see subs. (2).

By subs. (3), where a certificate has been issued under subs. (1), the person who applied for it "may apply to the Crown Court for the amount to be recovered under the order to be reduced". The powers of the Crown Court are set out in subs. (4).

It would seem that the Crown Court is obliged to substitute a lesser amount although the actual figure is entirely a matter for the court to decide. Even if the High Court were to quantify the amount by which the realisable property is inadequate to satisfy the order, the Crown Court is not obliged to that extent but must substitute a lesser amount "as the court thinks just in all the circumstances of the case": subs. (4)(a).

Nothing in s.17 requires the prosecution to be put on notice of an application under that section which, may therefore be made *ex parte*. However, it is difficult to imagine many applications proceeding on that basis and it is submitted that the appropriate course is for the prosecutor to be notified.

Compensation

18.—(1) If proceedings are instituted against a person for any drug trafficking offence or offences and either—
  (a) the proceedings do not result in his conviction for any drug trafficking offence, or
  (b) he is convicted of one or more drug trafficking offences but—
        (i) the conviction or convictions concerned are quashed, or
        (ii) he is pardoned by Her Majesty in respect of the conviction or convictions concerned,
the High Court may, on an application by a person who held property which was realisable property, order compensation to be paid to the applicant if, having regard to all the circumstances, it considers it appropriate to make such an order.

(2) The High Court shall not order compensation to be paid in any case unless the court is satisfied—
  (a) that there has been some serious default on the part of a person concerned in the investigation or prosecution of the offence or offences concerned, being a person mentioned in subsection (5) below; and
  (b) that the applicant has suffered loss in consequence of anything done in relation to the property by or in pursuance of—
        (i) an order of the High Court or a county court under sections 26 to 29 of this Act; or
        (ii) an order of the Court of Session under section 11 (as applied by subsection (6) of that section), 27 or 28 of the Criminal Justice (Scotland) Act 1987 (inhibition and arrestment of property affected by restraint order and recognition and enforcement of orders under this Act).

(3) The High Court shall not order compensation to be paid in any case where it appears to the court that the proceedings would have been instituted or continued even if the serious default had not occurred.

(4) The amount of compensation to be paid under this section shall be such as the High Court thinks just in all the circumstances of the case.

(5) Compensation payable under this section shall be paid—
  (a) where the person in default was, or was acting as, a member of a police force, out of the police fund out of which the expenses of that police force are met;
  (b) where the person in default was a member of the Crown Prosecution Service or was acting on behalf of the service, by the Director of Public Prosecutions; and

(c) where the person in default was an officer within the meaning of the Customs and Excise Management Act 1979, by the Commissioners of Customs and Excise.

DEFINITIONS
"drug trafficking offences": s.1(3).
"proceedings are instituted": s.41(2).
"realisable property": s.6(2).

GENERAL NOTE
These provisions substantially re-enact s.19 of the 1986 Act as amended by the Criminal Justice Act 1988, sched. 5, para. 12(b) and (d), the Criminal Justice (Scotland) Act 1987, s.45(7)(d) and the 1993 Act, s.24(2).

Confiscation orders where defendant has absconded or died

Powers of High Court where defendant has absconded or died

19.—(1) Subsection (2) below applies where a person has been convicted of one or more drug trafficking offences.

(2) If the prosecutor asks it to proceed under this section, the High Court may exercise the powers of the Crown Court under this Act to make a confiscation order against the defendant if satisfied that the defendant has died or absconded.

(3) Subsection (4) below applies where proceedings for one or more drug trafficking offences have been instituted against a person but have not been concluded.

(4) If the prosecutor asks it to proceed under this section, the High Court may exercise the powers of the Crown Court under this Act to make a confiscation order against the defendant if satisfied that the defendant has absconded.

(5) The power conferred by subsection (4) above may not be exercised at any time before the end of the period of two years beginning with the date which is, in the opinion of the court, the date on which the defendant absconded.

(6) In any proceedings on an application under this section—
(a) section 4(2) of this Act shall not apply;
(b) section 11 of this Act shall apply as it applies where the prosecutor asks the court to proceed under section 2 of this Act, but with the omission of subsections (5), (7) and (8);
(c) the court shall not make a confiscation order against a person who has absconded unless it is satisfied that the prosecutor has taken reasonable steps to contact him; and
(d) any person appearing to the court to be likely to be affected by the making of a confiscation order by the court shall be entitled to appear before the court and make representations.

(7) Subject to subsection (8) below, section 9 of this Act applies in relation to confiscation orders made by the High Court by virtue of this section as it applies in relation to confiscation orders made by the Crown Court and, for that purpose, references to the Crown Court in the provisions of the 1973 Act referred to in subsection (1) of that section (except in section 32(1)(b) of that Act) shall be construed as references to the High Court.

(8) Where the High Court makes a confiscation order by virtue of this section in relation to a defendant who has died, section 9(1) of this Act shall be read as referring only to sections 31(1) and 32(1) of the 1973 Act.

(9) Where the High Court—
(a) has been asked to proceed under this section in relation to a defendant who has absconded, but

(b) has decided not to make a confiscation order against him,
section 14 of this Act shall not apply at any time while he remains an
absconder.

(10) Where a confiscation order has been made in relation to any defendant by virtue of this section, section 15 of this Act shall not apply at any time while he is an absconder.

DEFINITIONS
"confiscation order": s.2(9).
"defendant": s.63(1).
"drug trafficking offence": s.1(1).
"proceedings ... concluded": s.41(3).

GENERAL NOTE
As the law stood, where a defendant either died or absconded before a confiscation order was made, the court was powerless to make a confiscation order. An indication of the sort of problems that can arise where a defendant absconds was demonstrated in *R. v. Chrastny (No. 2)* [1991] 1 W.L.R. 1385. In that case the court had to determine whether property held jointly between husband and wife (both of whom had been jointly charged with a drug trafficking offence) was "realisable" for the purposes of s.4(3) of the 1986 Act (now s.5(3), above), in circumstances where the wife had been convicted but where the husband had absconded. The court answered that question affirmatively. If the husband were to be apprehended, tried and convicted then the court could not include, in any confiscation order against him, property realised to satisfy the order payable by his wife because the property was no longer under his control: *per* Glidewell L.J. at p. 1394. The Home Office Working Group on Confiscation identified three situations to which different considerations may apply but which originally fell outside the ambit of the 1986 Act namely (1) death after conviction but before a confiscation order is made, (2) the defendant absconds after conviction but before the order is made, and (3) the defendant either dies or absconds before conviction.

The High Court now has power, by virtue of ss.19–24 of the 1994 Act, to make a confiscation order in the case of the defendant (charged with a drug trafficking offence) who absconds for a period of two years – whether convicted or not – and a power of confiscation in the case of a defendant who is convicted of a drug trafficking offence but who dies before the Crown Court can make a confiscation order. For these purposes, no statutory assumptions may be made pursuant to s.4(2) of the Act (see s.19(6)(a)) and, in the case of an absconder, the court shall not make a confiscation order unless it is satisfied that the prosecutor has taken reasonable steps to contact him (s.19(6)(c)). The court may also hear representations from third parties who are "likely to be affected by the making of a confiscation order by the court" (s.19(6)(d)). If the High Court decides not to make a confiscation order in respect of an absconder, the prosecution are not entitled to re-open the matter under s.14 of the 1994 Act if they come into possession of evidence which had not been considered by the court until the absconder returns: s.19(9). Similarly, the High Court has no power to revise any assessment of the absconder's proceeds of drug trafficking whilst he remains an absconder: see ss.15 and 19(10). The defendant who ceases to be an absconder may apply for a variation of a confiscation order made under s.19 within a period of six years from the date the order was made: see s.21.

Death or absconding after conviction
The Working Group, in their Report on the Drug Trafficking Offences Act 1986 (1991), saw no reason to distinguish between the two cases (in principle) and thought that it should be possible to make confiscation orders in each case (para. 5.6). The 1994 Act broadly follows that approach. When reading s.19, it is important to group subss. (1) and (2) together, and to read subss. (3) and (4) together. The reason is that subss. (1) and (2) apply to defendants who have been convicted of a drug trafficking offence but where the defendant has either died or absconded. By contrast, subss. (3) and (4) only relate to defendants who have absconded prior to conviction. They have no application to defendants who have died before they were able to appear for the trial.

Whichever category is appropriate, it is only the High Court (exercising the powers of the Crown Court) which can make a confiscation order under this section.

Where a defendant absconds, whether convicted (s.19(1)) or not (s.19(3)), the High Court cannot be asked by the prosecutor to make a confiscation order under s.19 until at least two years after the date on which the defendant absconded: see subs. (5).

It is not clear what the position would be if a defendant inexplicably went "missing" *e.g.* after a boating trip in mysterious circumstances pending the 1986 Act enquiry but after conviction.

Would the court treat him as having "absconded" or must the court wait seven years until he could be presumed dead? Note the obligation imposed on the prosecution by subs. (6). Note that the statutory assumptions do not apply: subs. (6)(a).

Where an absconder returns, the High Court may cancel the confiscation order if there has been undue delay on the part of the prosecution in pursuing proceedings under s.19(4) of the 1994 Act: see s.23(2). This provision codifies s.19B(1)–(3) of the 1986 Act inserted by s.15 of the 1993 Act.

Defendant dies or absconds before conviction
The Working Group sought views as to whether the courts should be empowered to commence proceedings against persons who died or absconded prior to conviction (para. 5.9) but Parliament clearly took the view that it would be too drastic a step to extend the provisions of s.19 to those who died and who could never answer the indictment which they faced.

Where an absconder is acquitted (whether in his absence or otherwise), the court by which the defendant was acquitted (*e.g.* the Crown Court) may cancel the confiscation order: s.22(1) and (2), and the defendant may apply for compensation if he has suffered loss as is just in all the circumstances of the case: s.22.

Note the power of the High Court to vary confiscation orders upon the application of the defendant, which was made under s.19: see s.21.

Effect of conviction where High Court has acted under section 19

20.—(1) Where, in the case of any defendant, the High Court has made a confiscation order by virtue of section 19 of this Act, the Crown Court shall, in respect of the offence or, as the case may be, any of the offences concerned—
  (a) take account of the order before—
        (i) imposing any fine on the defendant;
       (ii) making any order involving any payment by him; or
     (iii) making any order under section 27 of the Misuse of Drugs Act 1971 (forfeiture orders) or section 43 of the Powers of Criminal Courts Act 1973 (deprivation orders); and
  (b) subject to paragraph (a) above, leave the order out of account in determining the appropriate sentence or other manner of dealing with him.
(2) Where the High Court has made a confiscation order by virtue of section 19 of this Act and the defendant subsequently appears before the Crown Court to be sentenced in respect of one or more of the offences concerned, section 2(1) of this Act shall not apply so far as his appearance is in respect of that offence or those offences.

DEFINITIONS
  "defendant": s.63(1).
  "confiscation order": s.2(9).

GENERAL NOTE
  See General Note to s.19, above.

Variation of confiscation orders made by virtue of section 19

21.—(1) This section applies where—
  (a) the High Court has made a confiscation order by virtue of section 19(4) of this Act, and
  (b) the defendant has ceased to be an absconder.
(2) If the defendant alleges that—
  (a) the value of his proceeds of drug trafficking in the period by reference to which the determination in question was made (the "original value"), or
  (b) the amount that might have been realised at the time the confiscation order was made,

was less than the amount ordered to be paid under the confiscation order, he may apply to the High Court for it to consider his evidence.

(3) If, having considered that evidence, the court is satisfied that the defendant's allegation is correct, it—

(a) shall make a fresh determination under subsection (4) of section 2 of this Act; and

(b) may, if it considers it just in all the circumstances, vary the amount to be recovered under the confiscation order.

(4) In the case of any determination under section 2 of this Act by virtue of this section, section 4(6) of this Act shall not apply in relation to any of the defendant's proceeds of drug trafficking taken into account in determining the original value.

(5) Where the court varies a confiscation order under this section—

(a) it shall substitute for the term of imprisonment or of detention fixed under section 31(2) of the Powers of Criminal Courts Act 1973 in respect of the amount to be recovered under the order a shorter term determined in accordance with that section (as it has effect by virtue of section 19 of this Act) in respect of the lesser amount; and

(b) on the application of a person who held property which was realisable property, it may order compensation to be paid to the applicant in accordance with section 24 of this Act if—

(i) it is satisfied that the applicant has suffered loss as a result of the making of the confiscation order; and

(ii) having regard to all the circumstances of the case, the court considers it to be appropriate.

(6) No application shall be entertained by the court under this section if it is made after the end of the period of six years beginning with the date on which the confiscation order was made.

DEFINITIONS

"confiscation order": s.2(9).
"defendant": s.63(1).
"drug trafficking offence": s.1(1).
"proceedings ... concluded": s.41(3).

GENERAL NOTE

This section re-enacts s.19C of the 1986 Act, inserted by s.15 of the 1993 Act. That provision never came into force. Section 21 is designed to enable the defendant who has ceased to be an absconder to apply to the High Court for a downward variation of a confiscation order which was made in his absence. The burden will be on the defendant to satisfy the court of the correctness of his case that either the value of his proceeds of drug trafficking, or the amount that was capable of being realised, was less than the amount ordered to be paid under a confiscation order. Even if the defendant succeeds in establishing that the amount ordered by the court was too high, the High Court is not obliged to vary the order but may do so if it is "just in all the circumstances" to do so: see subs.21(3).

Note that defendants must comply with a time limit of six years within which to make an application under this section.

Compensation etc. where absconder is acquitted

22.—(1) This section applies where—

(a) the High Court has made a confiscation order by virtue of section 19(4) of this Act, and

(b) the defendant is subsequently tried for the offence or offences concerned and acquitted on all counts.

(2) The court by which the defendant is acquitted shall cancel the confiscation order.

(3) The High Court may, on the application of a person who held property which was realisable property, order compensation to be paid to the appli-

cant in accordance with section 24 of this Act if it is satisfied that the applicant has suffered loss as a result of the making of the confiscation order.

DEFINITIONS
"confiscation order": s.2(9).
"defendant": s.63(1).

GENERAL NOTE
The defendant must prove that he has suffered loss and any claim for compensation must be made within the framework of s.24 of the Act.

Power to discharge confiscation order and order compensation where absconder returns

23.—(1) This section applies where—
(a) the High Court has made a confiscation order by virtue of section 19(4) of this Act in relation to an absconder;
(b) the defendant has ceased to be an absconder; and
(c) section 22 of this Act does not apply.
(2) The High Court may, on the application of the defendant, cancel the confiscation order if it is satisfied that—
(a) there has been undue delay in continuing the proceedings in respect of which the power under section 19(4) of this Act was exercised; or
(b) the prosecutor does not intend to proceed with the prosecution.
(3) Where the High Court cancels a confiscation order under this section it may, on the application of a person who held property which was realisable property, order compensation to be paid to the applicant in accordance with section 24 of this Act if it is satisfied that the applicant has suffered loss as a result of the making of the confiscation order.

DEFINITIONS
"confiscation order": s.2(9).
"defendant": s.63(1).

GENERAL NOTE
See the General Note to s.19, above.

Provisions supplementary to sections 21, 22 and 23

24.—(1) Where the High Court orders compensation to be paid under section 21, 22 or 23 of this Act, the amount of that compensation shall be such as the court considers just in all the circumstances of the case.
(2) Rules of court may make provision—
(a) for the giving of notice of any application under section 21, 22 or 23 of this Act; and
(b) for any person appearing to the court to be likely to be affected by any exercise of its powers under any of those sections to be given an opportunity to make representations to the court.
(3) Any payment of compensation under any of those sections shall be made by the Lord Chancellor.
(4) Where the court cancels a confiscation order under section 22 or 23 of this Act it may make such consequential or incidental order as it considers appropriate in connection with the cancellation.

DEFINITIONS
"compensation": ss.21(5)(b), 22, 23(3).
"confiscation order": s.2(9).

Restraint orders and charging orders

Cases in which restraint orders and charging orders may be made

25.—(1) The powers conferred on the High Court by sections 26(1) and 27(1) of this Act are exercisable where—

(a) proceedings have been instituted in England and Wales against the defendant for a drug trafficking offence or an application has been made by the prosecutor in respect of the defendant under section 13, 14, 15, 16 or 19 of this Act;

(b) the proceedings have not, or the application has not, been concluded; and

(c) the court is satisfied that there is reasonable cause to believe—

(i) in the case of an application under section 15 or 16 of this Act, that the court will be satisfied as mentioned in section 15(4) or, as the case may be, 16(2) of this Act; or

(ii) in any other case, that the defendant has benefited from drug trafficking.

(2) The court shall not exercise those powers by virtue of subsection (1) above if it is satisfied—

(a) that there has been undue delay in continuing the proceedings or application in question; or

(b) that the prosecutor does not intend to proceed.

(3) The powers mentioned in subsection (1) above are also exercisable where—

(a) the court is satisfied that, whether by the laying of an information or otherwise, a person is to be charged with a drug trafficking offence or that an application of a kind mentioned in subsection (1)(a) above is to be made in respect of the defendant; and

(b) the court is also satisfied as mentioned in subsection (1)(c) above.

(4) For the purposes of sections 26 and 27 of this Act, at any time when those powers are exercisable before proceedings have been instituted—

(a) references in this Act to the defendant shall be construed as references to the person referred to in subsection (3)(a) above;

(b) references in this Act to the prosecutor shall be construed as references to the person who the High Court is satisfied is to have the conduct of the proposed proceedings; and

(c) references in this Act to realisable property shall be construed as if, immediately before that time, proceedings had been instituted against the person referred to in subsection (3)(a) above for a drug trafficking offence.

(5) Where the court has made an order under section 26(1) or 27(1) of this Act by virtue of subsection (3) above, the court shall discharge the order if proceedings in respect of the offence are not instituted, whether by the laying of an information or otherwise, or (as the case may be) if the application is not made, within such time as the court considers reasonable.

DEFINITIONS
"defendant": s.63(1).
"proceedings ... concluded": s.41(3).
"proceedings ... instituted": s.41(2).

GENERAL NOTE
As originally drafted the circumstances in which proceedings for a drug trafficking offence were to be treated as "concluded" were relatively straight-forward because the machinery for varying a confiscation was limited only to an application made by the defendant under s.14 (s.38(12) of the 1986 Act).

Not only will proceedings now *not* be concluded upon serving a sentence in default of payment (s.9(5), above) but the ability of the prosecution to seek a re-determination of issues under s.2, above, over a period of six years from the date of the relevant conviction or determination (see ss.13, 14 and 15, above) means that the machinery necessary to enforce the satisfaction of the order had to be re-defined. Thus: (a) the powers of the High Court in which restraint and charging orders may be made under ss.26(1) and 27(1) are extended to applications brought by the prosecutor under s.16 (defendant who has died or absconded) and ss.13, 14 and 15 (re-determination under s.2); (b) the same powers exist even if any such applications are to be made (subs. (3) as amended) subject to the safeguards set out in subs. (5); (c) restraint orders under s.26 may be varied or discharged: s.26(5); (d) similarly, changing orders may be varied or discharged: s.27(7); (e) powers under s.29 may be exercised where an order is not satisfied; and (f) the circumstances in respect of proceedings for "drug trafficking offences", which can be said to be "concluded", are re-defined: s.41(3).

Restraint orders

26.—(1) The High Court may by order (in this Act referred to as a "restraint order") prohibit any person from dealing with any realisable property, subject to such conditions and exceptions as may be specified in the order.

(2) A restraint order may apply—

(a) to all realisable property held by a specified person, whether the property is described in the order or not; and

(b) to realisable property held by a specified person, being property transferred to him after the making of the order.

(3) This section shall not have effect in relation to any property for the time being subject to a charge under section 27 of this Act or section 9 of the Drug Trafficking Offences Act 1986.

(4) A restraint order—

(a) may be made only on an application by the prosecutor;

(b) may be made on an ex parte application to a judge in chambers; and

(c) shall provide for notice to be given to persons affected by the order.

(5) A restraint order—

(a) may be discharged or varied in relation to any property; and

(b) shall be discharged on the conclusion of the proceedings or of the application in question.

(6) An application for the discharge or variation of a restraint order may be made by any person affected by it.

(7) Where the High Court has made a restraint order, the High Court or a county court—

(a) may at any time appoint a receiver—

(i) to take possession of any realisable property, and

(ii) in accordance with the court's directions, to manage or otherwise deal with any property in respect of which he is appointed, subject to such exceptions and conditions as may be specified by the court; and

(b) may require any person having possession of property in respect of which a receiver is appointed under this section to give possession of it to the receiver.

(8) For the purposes of this section, dealing with property held by any person includes (without prejudice to the generality of that expression)—

(a) where a debt is owed to that person, making a payment to any person in reduction of the amount of the debt; and

(b) removing the property from Great Britain.

(9) Where a restraint order has been made a constable may seize any realisable property for the purpose of preventing its removal from Great Britain.

(10) In subsection (9) above, the reference to a restraint order includes a reference to a restraint order within the meaning of Part I of the Criminal Justice (Scotland) Act 1987, and in relation to such an order "realisable property" has the same meaning as in that Part.

(11) Property seized under subsection (9) above shall be dealt with in accordance with the directions of the court which made the order.

(12) The Land Charges Act 1972 and the Land Registration Act 1925 shall apply—

(a) in relation to restraint orders, as they apply in relation to orders affecting land made by the court for the purpose of enforcing judgments or recognisances; and

(b) in relation to applications for restraint orders, as they apply in relation to other pending land actions.

(13) The prosecutor shall be treated for the purposes of section 57 of the Land Registration Act 1925 (inhibitions) as a person interested in relation to any registered land to which a restraint order or an application for such an order relates.

DEFINITIONS
"property": s.62(1).
"realisable property": s.6(2).
"restraint order": s.26(1).

GENERAL NOTE
This section substantially reproduces s.8 of the 1986 Act as amended by the Criminal Justice Act 1988, Sched. 5 and (so far as subs. (7) is concerned) by s.24(1) of the 1993 Act. Where the court makes a restraint order it may discharge that order if proceedings for the offence are not instituted, or if an application for a restraint order is not made within a reasonable time: s.25(5), above. Compensation may be paid if "a person who held property which was realisable property" (see s.18(1)) has suffered loss in consequence of an order under s.26 of the Act: see s.18(2), above.

Charging orders in respect of land, securities etc.

27.—(1) The High Court may make a charging order on realisable property for securing the payment to the Crown—

(a) where a confiscation order has not been made, of an amount equal to the value from time to time of the property charged; and

(b) where a confiscation order has been made, of an amount not exceeding the amount payable under the confiscation order.

(2) For the purposes of this Act a charging order is an order made under this section imposing on any such realisable property as may be specified in the order a charge for securing the payment of money to the Crown.

(3) A charging order—

(a) may be made only on an application by the prosecutor;

(b) may be made on an ex parte application to a judge in chambers;

(c) shall provide for notice to be given to persons affected by the order; and

(d) may be made subject to such conditions as the court thinks fit including, without prejudice to the generality of this paragraph, such conditions as it thinks fit as to the time when the charge is to become effective.

(4) Subject to subsection (6) below, a charge may be imposed by a charging order only on—

(a) any interest in realisable property which is an interest held beneficially by the defendant or by a person to whom the defendant has directly or indirectly made a gift caught by this Act and is an interest—

(i) in any asset of a kind mentioned in subsection (5) below; or

(ii) under any trust; or

(b) any interest in realisable property held by a person as trustee of a trust ("the relevant trust") if the interest is in such an asset or is an interest under another trust and a charge may by virtue of paragraph (a) above be imposed by a charging order on the whole beneficial interest under the relevant trust.

(5) The assets referred to in subsection (4) above are—

(a) land in England and Wales; or

(b) securities of any of the following kinds—
   (i) government stock;
   (ii) stock of any body (other than a building society) incorporated within England and Wales;
   (iii) stock of any body incorporated outside England and Wales or of any country or territory outside the United Kingdom, being stock registered in a register kept at any place within England and Wales;
   (iv) units of any unit trust in respect of which a register of the unit holders is kept at any place within England and Wales.

(6) In any case where a charge is imposed by a charging order on any interest in an asset of a kind mentioned in subsection (5)(b) above, the court may provide for the charge to extend to any interest or dividend payable in respect of the asset.

(7) In relation to a charging order, the court—
(a) may make an order discharging or varying it; and
(b) shall make an order discharging it—
   (i) on the conclusion of the proceedings or of the application in question; or
   (ii) on payment into court of the amount payment of which is secured by the charge.

(8) An application for the discharge or variation of a charging order may be made by any person affected by it.

(9) In this section "building society", "dividend", "government stock", "stock" and "unit trust" have the same meaning as in the Charging Orders Act 1979.

DEFINITIONS
"building society": Charging Order Act 1979, s.27(a).
"charging order": s.27(2).
"confiscation order": s.2(9).
"interest in realisable property": s.62(3).
"realisable property": s.6(2).
"relevant trust": s.27(4)(b).

GENERAL NOTE
   This section re-enacts much of s.9 of the 1986 Act as amended by s.13(7) of the 1993 Act (in respect of subs. (7)), and Sched. 5 to the Criminal Justice Act 1988. Where the court makes a charging order it may discharge that order if proceedings for the offence are not instituted, or if an application for a restraint order is not made within a reasonable time: s.25(5). Compensation may be paid if "a person who held property which was realisable property" (see s.18(1)) has suffered loss in consequence of an order under s.27 of the Act: s.18(2), above.

Charging orders: supplementary provisions

28.—(1) The Land Charges Act 1972 and the Land Registration Act 1925 shall apply in relation to charging orders as they apply in relation to orders or writs made or issued for the purpose of enforcing judgments.

(2) Where a charging order has been registered under section 6 of the Land Charges Act 1972, subsection (4) of that section (effect of non-registration of writs and orders registrable under that section) shall not apply to an order appointing a receiver made in pursuance of the charging order.

(3) Subject to any provision made under section 29 of this Act or by rules of court, a charge imposed by a charging order shall have the like effect and shall be enforceable in the same courts and in the same manner as an equitable charge created by the person holding the beneficial interest or, as the case may be, the trustees by writing under their hand.

(4) Where a charging order has been protected by an entry registered under the Land Charges Act 1972 or the Land Registration Act 1925, an

order under section 27(7) of this Act discharging the charging order may direct that the entry be cancelled.

(5) The Secretary of State may by order made by statutory instrument amend section 27 of this Act by adding to or removing from the kinds of asset for the time being referred to there any asset of a kind which in his opinion ought to be so added or removed.

(6) An order under subsection (5) above shall be subject to annulment in pursuance of a resolution of either House of Parliament.

DEFINITIONS
"beneficial interest": s.62(4)(b).
"charging order": s.27(2).
"interest": s.62(3).
"Secretary of State": Interpretation Act 1978, s.5.

GENERAL NOTE
This section reproduces s.10(2)–(6) of the 1986 Act. The Secretary of State for these purposes is the Secretary of State for the Home Office.

Realisation of property

Realisation of property

29.—(1) Where a confiscation order—
(a) has been made under this Act,
(b) is not satisfied, and
(c) is not subject to appeal,
the High Court or a county court may, on an application by the prosecutor, exercise the powers conferred by subsections (2) to (6) below.

(2) The court may appoint a receiver in respect of realisable property.

(3) The court may empower a receiver appointed under subsection (2) above, under section 26 of this Act or in pursuance of a charging order—
(a) to enforce any charge imposed under section 27 of this Act on realisable property or on interest or dividends payable in respect of such property; and
(b) in relation to any realisable property other than property for the time being subject to a charge under section 27 of this Act, to take possession of the property subject to such conditions or exceptions as may be specified by the court.

(4) The court may order any person having possession of realisable property to give possession of it to any such receiver.

(5) The court may empower any such receiver to realise any realisable property in such manner as the court may direct.

(6) The court may—
(a) order any person holding an interest in realisable property to make to the receiver such payment as it may direct in respect of any beneficial interest held by the defendant or, as the case may be, the recipient of a gift caught by this Act; and
(b) on the payment being made, by order transfer, grant or extinguish any interest in the property.

(7) Subsections (4) to (6) above do not apply to property for the time being subject to a charge under section 27 of this Act or section 9 of the Drug Trafficking Offences Act 1986.

(8) The court shall not in respect of any property exercise the powers conferred by subsection (3)(a), (5) or (6) above unless a reasonable opportunity has been given for persons holding any interest in the property to make representations to the court.

DEFINITIONS
"charging order": s.27.
"confiscation order": s.2(9).
"interest", in relation to property: s.62(3).
"property": s.62(1).
"property ... held": s.62(5)(a).
"property ... transferred": s.62(5)(b).
"realisable property": s.6(2).

GENERAL NOTE

Appointment and powers of a receiver
In summary, once a confiscation order has been made which is not subject to appeal and which has not been satisfied, the High Court may, on the application of the prosecutor, appoint a receiver to realise any realisable property (subs. (5)) with a view to satisfying the confiscation order (s.31(2)) and to apply the property so realised on the defendant's behalf towards the satisfaction of the order (s.30(1)). A reasonable opportunity must be given for persons holding any interest in the property to make representations to the court (subs. (8)). Sums remaining in the hands of the receiver after the satisfaction of a confiscation order must be distributed among the holders of property in such proportions as the court shall direct (s.30(3)). The material powers conferred on a receiver are set out in this section (formerly, s.11 of the 1986 Act, as amended by s.13(8) of the 1993 Act).
Note that by subs. (1)(c), a receiver cannot be appointed if the order is subject to appeal.
Again, by subs. (1)(b), a receiver can only be appointed if the confiscation order "is not satisfied". By s.41(3) (formerly, s.38(12) of the 1986 Act) proceedings in England and Wales for an offence are concluded on the occurrence of one of the events set out in that section.
The powers of the High Court or the receiver must be exercised within the framework set out in s.31.

Application of proceeds of realisation and other sums

30.—(1) The following sums in the hands of a receiver appointed under section 26 or 29 of this Act or in pursuance of a charging order, that is—
   (a) the proceeds of the enforcement of any charge imposed under section 27 of this Act,
   (b) the proceeds of the realisation, other than by the enforcement of such a charge, of any property under section 26 or 29 of this Act, and
   (c) any other sums, being property held by the defendant,
shall be applied, subject to subsection (2) below, on the defendant's behalf towards the satisfaction of the confiscation order.
  (2) Before any such sums are so applied they shall be applied—
   (a) first, in payment of such expenses incurred by a person acting as an insolvency practitioner as are payable under section 35(3) of this Act; and
   (b) second, in making such payments (if any) as the High Court or a county court may direct.
  (3) If, after the amount payable under the confiscation order has been fully paid, any such sums remain in the hands of such a receiver as is mentioned in subsection (1) above, the receiver shall distribute those sums—
   (a) among such of those who held property which has been realised under this Act, and
   (b) in such proportions,
as the High Court or a county court may direct after giving a reasonable opportunity for such persons to make representations to the court.
  (4) The receipt of any sum by a justices' clerk on account of an amount payable under a confiscation order shall reduce the amount so payable, but the justices' clerk shall apply the money received for the purposes specified in this section and in the order so specified.
  (5) The justices' clerk shall first pay any expenses incurred by a person acting as an insolvency practitioner and payable under section 35(3) of this Act but not already paid under subsection (2) above.

(6) If the money was paid to the justices' clerk by a receiver appointed under section 26 or 29 of this Act or in pursuance of a charging order the justices' clerk shall next pay the receiver's remuneration and expenses.

(7) After making—

(a) any payment required by subsection (5) above, and

(b) in a case to which subsection (6) above applies, any payment required by that subsection,

the justices' clerk shall reimburse any amount paid under section 36(2) of this Act.

(8) Any balance in the hands of the justices' clerk after he has made all payments required by the preceding provisions of this section shall be treated for the purposes of section 61 of the Justices of the Peace Act 1979 (application of fines, etc.) as if it were a fine imposed by a magistrates' court.

(9) In this section "justices' clerk" has the same meaning as in the Justices of the Peace Act 1979.

DEFINITIONS
  "charging order": s.27(2).
  "confiscation order": s.2(9).
  "defendant": s.63(1).
  "justice's clerk": s.30(9).

GENERAL NOTE
By subs. (1), what was s.12(1) of the 1986 Act has been reorganised into the form which now appears, but the overall effect of this section is to consolidate the provisions of s.12 of the 1986 Act as amended by sched. 5, of the Criminal Justice Act 1988.

Exercise of powers for the realisation of property

Exercise by High Court, county court or receiver of powers for the realisation of property

31.—(1) The following provisions apply to the powers conferred—

(a) on the High Court or a county court by sections 26 to 30 of this Act; or

(b) on a receiver appointed under section 26 or 29 of this Act or in pursuance of a charging order.

(2) Subject to the following provisions of this section, the powers shall be exercised with a view to making available for satisfying the confiscation order or, as the case may be, any confiscation order that may be made in the defendant's case, the value for the time being of realisable property held by any person, by means of the realisation of such property.

(3) In the case of realisable property held by a person to whom the defendant has directly or indirectly made a gift caught by this Act, the powers shall be exercised with a view to realising no more than the value for the time being of the gift.

(4) The powers shall be exercised with a view to allowing any person other than the defendant or the recipient of any such gift to retain or recover the value of any property held by him.

(5) In exercising the powers, no account shall be taken of any obligations of the defendant or of the recipient of any such gift which conflict with the obligation to satisfy the confiscation order.

(6) An order may be made or other action taken in respect of a debt owed by the Crown.

DEFINITIONS
  "charging order": s.27.
  "confiscation order": s.2(9).
  "gift": s.8(2).
  "interest", in relation to property: s.62(3).
  "obligations having priority": s.6(4).

"property": s.62(1).
"realisable property": s.6(2).

GENERAL NOTE
This section largely reproduces s.13 of the 1986 Act.

Insolvency of defendants etc.

Bankruptcy of defendant etc.

32.—(1) Where a person who holds realisable property is adjudged bankrupt—
  (a) property for the time being subject to a restraint order made before the order adjudging him bankrupt, and
  (b) any proceeds of property realised by virtue of section 26(7) or 29(5) or (6) of this Act for the time being in the hands of a receiver appointed under section 26 or 29 of this Act,
is excluded from the bankrupt's estate for the purposes of Part IX of the Insolvency Act 1986 ("the 1986 Act").
  (2) Where a person has been adjudged bankrupt, the powers conferred on the High Court or a county court by sections 26 to 30 of this Act or on a receiver so appointed shall not be exercised in relation to—
  (a) property for the time being comprised in the bankrupt's estate for the purposes of Part IX of the 1986 Act;
  (b) property in respect of which his trustee in bankruptcy may (without leave of the court) serve a notice under section 307, 308 or 308A of that Act (after-acquired property and tools, clothes etc. exceeding value of reasonable replacement, and certain tenancies); and
  (c) property which is to be applied for the benefit of creditors of the bankrupt by virtue of a condition imposed under section 280(2)(c) of that Act;
but nothing in that Act shall be taken as restricting, or enabling the restriction of, the exercise of those powers.
  (3) Subsection (2) above does not affect the enforcement of a charging order—
  (a) made before the order adjudging the person bankrupt; or
  (b) on property which was subject to a restraint order when the order adjudging him bankrupt was made.
  (4) Where, in the case of a debtor, an interim receiver stands appointed under section 286 of the 1986 Act and any property of the debtor is subject to a restraint order, the powers conferred on the receiver by virtue of that Act do not apply to property for the time being subject to the restraint order.
  (5) Where a person is adjudged bankrupt and has directly or indirectly made a gift caught by this Act—
  (a) no order shall be made under section 339 or 423 of the 1986 Act (avoidance of certain transactions), in respect of the making of the gift, at any time when—
      (i) proceedings for a drug trafficking offence have been instituted against him and have not been concluded;
      (ii) an application has been made in respect of the defendant under section 13, 14, 15, 16 or 19 of this Act and has not been concluded; or
      (iii) property of the person to whom the gift was made is subject to a restraint order or charging order; and
  (b) any order made under section 339 or 423 after the conclusion of the proceedings or of the application shall take into account any realisation under this Act of property held by the person to whom the gift was made.

DEFINITIONS
"charging order": s.27.
"confiscation order": s.2(9).
"defendant": s.63(1).
"gift": s.8(2).
"gift caught by the Act": s.8(1).
"proceedings concluded": s.41(3).
"proceedings instituted": s.41(2).
"property": s.62(1).
"realisable property": s.6(2).
"restraint order": s.26.

Sequestration in Scotland of defendant etc.

33.—(1) Where the estate of a person who holds realisable property is sequestrated—

(a) property for the time being subject to a restraint order made before the award of sequestration, and

(b) any proceeds of property realised by virtue of section 26(7) or 29(5) or (6) of this Act for the time being in the hands of a receiver appointed under section 26 or 29 of this Act,

is excluded from the debtor's estate for the purposes of the Bankruptcy (Scotland) Act 1985 ("the 1985 Act").

(2) Where an award of sequestration has been made, the powers conferred on the High Court or a county court by sections 26 to 30 of this Act or on a receiver so appointed shall not be exercised in relation to—

(a) property comprised in the whole estate of the debtor within the meaning of section 31(8) of the 1985 Act; and

(b) any income of the debtor which has been ordered, under section 32(2) of that Act, to be paid to the permanent trustee or any estate which, under section 31(10) or 32(6) of that Act, vests in the permanent trustee;

and it shall not be competent to submit a claim in relation to the confiscation order to the permanent trustee in accordance with section 48 of that Act.

(3) Nothing in the 1985 Act shall be taken as restricting, or enabling the restriction of, the exercise of the powers mentioned in subsection (2) above.

(4) Subsection (2) above does not affect the enforcement of a charging order—

(a) made before the award of sequestration; or

(b) on property which was subject to a restraint order when the award of sequestration was made.

(5) Where, during the period before sequestration is awarded—

(a) an interim trustee stands appointed under section 2(5) of the 1985 Act, and

(b) any property in the debtor's estate is subject to a restraint order,

the powers conferred on the trustee by virtue of that Act do not apply to property for the time being subject to the restraint order.

(6) Where the estate of a person is sequestrated and he has directly or indirectly made a gift caught by this Act—

(a) no decree shall be granted under section 34 or 36 of the 1985 Act (gratuitous alienations and unfair preferences), in respect of the making of the gift, at any time when—

(i) proceedings for a drug trafficking offence have been instituted against him and have not been concluded;

(ii) an application has been made in respect of the defendant under section 13, 14, 15, 16 or 19 of this Act and has not been concluded; or

(iii) property of the person to whom the gift was made is subject to a restraint order or charging order; and

(b) any decree made under section 34 or 36 after the conclusion of the proceedings or of the application shall take into account any realisation under this Act of property held by the person to whom the gift was made.

(7) In any case in which, notwithstanding the coming into force of the 1985 Act, the Bankruptcy (Scotland) Act 1913 applies to a sequestration, subsection (2) above shall have effect as if for paragraphs (a) and (b) there were substituted—

"(a) property comprised in the whole property of the debtor which vests in the trustee under section 97 of the Bankruptcy (Scotland) Act 1913; and

(b) any income of the bankrupt which has been ordered under subsection (2) of section 98 of that Act to be paid to the trustee, or any estate which, under subsection (1) of that section, vests in the trustee;"

and subsection (3) above shall have effect as if for the reference in that subsection to the 1985 Act there were substituted a reference to the Act of 1913.

DEFINITIONS
  "charging order": s.27.
  "confiscation order": s.2(9).
  "defendant": s.63(1).
  "gift": s.8(2).
  "gift caught by the Act": s.8(1).
  "proceedings concluded": s.41(3).
  "proceedings instituted": s.41(2).
  "property": s.62(1).
  "realisable property": s.6(2).
  "restraint order": s.26.

Winding up of company holding realisable property

34.—(1) Where realisable property is held by a company and an order for the winding up of the company has been made or a resolution has been passed by the company for the voluntary winding up of the company, the functions of the liquidator (or any provisional liquidator) shall not be exercisable in relation to—

(a) property for the time being subject to a restraint order made before the relevant time; and

(b) any proceeds of property realised by virtue of section 26(7) or 29(5) or (6) of this Act for the time being in the hands of a receiver appointed under section 26 or 29 of this Act.

(2) Where, in the case of a company, such an order has been made or such a resolution has been passed, the powers conferred on the High Court or a county court by sections 26 to 30 of this Act or on a receiver so appointed shall not be exercised in relation to any realisable property held by the company in relation to which the functions of the liquidator are exercisable—

(a) so as to inhibit him from exercising those functions for the purpose of distributing any property held by the company to the company's creditors; or

(b) so as to prevent the payment out of any property of expenses (including the remuneration of the liquidator or any provisional liquidator) properly incurred in the winding up in respect of the property;

but nothing in the Insolvency Act 1986 shall be taken as restricting, or enabling the restriction of, the exercise of those powers.

(3) Subsection (2) above does not affect the enforcement of a charging order made before the relevant time or on property which was subject to a restraint order at the relevant time.

(4) In this section—
   "company" means any company which may be wound up under the Insolvency Act 1986; and
   "the relevant time" means—
>   (a) where no order for the winding up of the company has been made, the time of the passing of the resolution for voluntary winding up;
>   (b) where—
>>   (i) such an order has been made, but
>>   (ii) before the presentation of the petition for the winding up of the company by the court, such a resolution had been passed by the company,
>   the time of the passing of the resolution; and
>   (c) in any other case where such an order has been made, the time of the making of the order.

DEFINITIONS
   "company": s.34(4).
   "defendant": s.63(1).
   "property": s.62(1).
   "realisable property": s.6(2).
   "relevant time": s.34(4).
   "restraint order": s.26.

Protection for insolvency officers etc.

Insolvency officers dealing with property subject to restraint order

35.—(1) Without prejudice to the generality of any enactment contained in the Insolvency Act 1986 or in any other Act, where—
   (a) any person acting as an insolvency practitioner seizes or disposes of any property in relation to which his functions are not exercisable because it is for the time being subject to a restraint order, and
   (b) at the time of the seizure or disposal he believes, and has reasonable grounds for believing, that he is entitled (whether in pursuance of an order of the court or otherwise) to seize or dispose of that property,
he shall not be liable to any person in respect of any loss or damage resulting from the seizure or disposal except in so far as the loss or damage is caused by his negligence in so acting.

(2) A person acting as an insolvency practitioner shall, in the circumstances mentioned in subsection (1)(a) and (b) above, have a lien on the property, or the proceeds of its sale, for such of his expenses as were incurred in connection with the liquidation, bankruptcy or other proceedings in relation to which the seizure or disposal purported to take place and for so much of his remuneration as may reasonably be assigned for his acting in connection with those proceedings.

(3) Where a person acting as an insolvency practitioner—
   (a) incurs expenses in respect of such property as is mentioned in paragraph (a) of subsection (1) above and in so doing does not know and has no reasonable grounds to believe that the property is for the time being subject to a restraint order, or
   (b) incurs expenses other than expenses in respect of such property as is so mentioned, being expenses which, but for the effect of a restraint order, might have been met by taking possession of and realising the property,
that person shall be entitled (whether or not he has seized or disposed of that property so as to have a lien under subsection (2) above) to payment of those expenses under section 30(2) or (5) of this Act.

(4) In this Act the expression "acting as an insolvency practitioner" shall be construed in accordance with section 388 of the Insolvency Act 1986 (interpretation) except that for the purposes of such construction—

(a) the reference in subsection (2)(a) of that section to a permanent or interim trustee in sequestration shall be taken to include a reference to a trustee in sequestration; and

(b) subsection (5) of that section (which includes provision to the effect that nothing in the section is to apply to anything done by the official receiver) shall be disregarded;

and the expression shall also comprehend the official receiver acting as receiver or manager of the property.

DEFINITIONS

"acting as an insolvency practitioner": s.35(4).

GENERAL NOTE

This largely reproduces s.17A of the 1986 Act as inserted into that Act by sched. 5 of the Criminal Justice Act 1988.

Receivers: supplementary provisions

36.—(1) Where a receiver appointed under section 26 or 29 of this Act or in pursuance of a charging order—

(a) takes any action in relation to property which is not realisable property, being action which he would be entitled to take if it were such property, and

(b) believes, and has reasonable grounds for believing, that he is entitled to take that action in relation to that property,

he shall not be liable to any person in respect of any loss or damage resulting from his action except in so far as the loss or damage is caused by his negligence.

(2) Any amount due in respect of the remuneration and expenses of a receiver so appointed shall, if no sum is available to be applied in payment of it under section 30(6) of this Act, be paid by the prosecutor or, in a case where proceedings for a drug trafficking offence are not instituted, by the person on whose application the receiver was appointed.

Enforcement of orders made outside England and Wales

Recognition and enforcement of orders and functions under Part I of the Criminal Justice (Scotland) Act 1987

37.—(1) Her Majesty may by Order in Council make such provision as Her Majesty considers expedient for the purpose—

(a) of enabling property in England and Wales which is realisable property for the purposes of Part I of the Criminal Justice (Scotland) Act 1987 to be used or realised for the payment of any amount payable under a confiscation order made under that Part of that Act; and

(b) of securing that, where no confiscation order has been made under that Part of that Act, property in England and Wales which is realisable property for the purposes of that Part of that Act is available, in the event that such an order is so made, to be used or realised for the payment of any amount payable under it.

(2) Without prejudice to the generality of the power conferred by subsection (1) above, an Order in Council under this section may—

(a) provide that, subject to any specified conditions—

(i) the functions of a person appointed under section 13 of the Criminal Justice (Scotland) Act 1987, and

(ii) such descriptions of orders made under or for the purposes of Part I of that Act as may be specified,

shall have effect in the law of England and Wales;

(b) make provision—

(i) for the registration in the High Court of such descriptions of orders made under or for the purposes of that Part of that Act as may be specified; and

(ii) for the High Court to have, in relation to the enforcement of orders made under or for the purposes of that Part of that Act which are so registered, such powers as may be specified; and

(c) make provision as to the proof in England and Wales of orders made under or for the purposes of that Part of that Act.

(3) In subsection (2) above "specified" means specified in an Order in Council under this section.

(4) An Order in Council under this section may amend or apply, with or without modifications, any enactment.

(5) An Order in Council under this section may contain such incidental, consequential and transitional provisions as Her Majesty considers expedient.

(6) An Order in Council under this section shall be subject to annulment in pursuance of a resolution of either House of Parliament.

DEFINITIONS
"charging order": s.27.
"confiscation order": s.2(9).
"defendant": s.63(1).
"property": s.62(1).
"specified": s.37(3).

Enforcement of Northern Ireland orders

38.—(1) Her Majesty may by Order in Council provide that, for the purposes of sections 17 and 25 to 36 of this Act, this Act shall have effect as if—

(a) references to confiscation orders included a reference to orders made by courts in Northern Ireland which appear to Her Majesty to correspond to confiscation orders;

(b) references to drug trafficking offences included a reference to any offence under the law of Northern Ireland (not being a drug trafficking offence) which appears to Her Majesty to correspond to such an offence;

(c) references to proceedings in England and Wales or to the institution or conclusion in England and Wales of proceedings included a reference to proceedings in Northern Ireland or to the institution or conclusion in Northern Ireland of proceedings, as the case may be; and

(d) the references to the laying of an information in section 25(3) and (5) of this Act included references to making a complaint under Article 20 of the Magistrates' Courts (Northern Ireland) Order 1981.

(2) An Order in Council under this section may provide for those sections to have effect, in relation to anything done or to be done in Northern Ireland, subject to such further modifications as may be specified in the order.

(3) An Order in Council under this section may contain such incidental, consequential and transitional provisions as Her Majesty considers expedient.

(4) An Order in Council under this section may, in particular, provide for section 18 of the Civil Jurisdiction and Judgments Act 1982 (enforcement of United Kingdom judgments in other parts of the United Kingdom) not to apply in relation to such orders as may be prescribed by the Order.

(5) An Order in Council under this section shall be subject to annulment in pursuance of a resolution of either House of Parliament.

DEFINITIONS
"confiscation order": s.2(9).
"defendant": s.63(1).
"drug trafficking offence": s.1(3).
"proceedings concluded": s.41(3).
"proceedings instituted": s.41(2).

Enforcement of external confiscation orders

39.—(1) Her Majesty may by Order in Council—
  (a) direct in relation to a country or territory outside the United Kingdom designated by the Order (a "designated country") that, subject to such modifications as may be specified, the relevant provisions of this Act shall apply to external confiscation orders and to proceedings which have been or are to be instituted in the designated country and may result in an external confiscation order being made there;
  (b) make—
        (i) such provision in connection with the taking of action in the designated country with a view to satisfying a confiscation order,
        (ii) such provision as to evidence or proof of any matter for the purposes of this section and section 40 of this Act, and
        (iii) such incidental, consequential and transitional provision,
      as appears to Her Majesty to be expedient; and
  (c) (without prejudice to the generality of this subsection) direct that, in such circumstances as may be specified, proceeds which arise out of action taken in the designated country with a view to satisfying a con- fiscation order shall be treated as reducing the amount payable under the order to such extent as may be specified.

(2) In this section "external confiscation order" means an order made by a court in a designated country for the purpose of recovering, or recovering the value of, payments or other rewards received in connection with drug trafficking.

(3) An Order in Council under this section may make different provision for different cases or classes of case.

(4) The power to make an Order in Council under this section includes power to modify the relevant provisions of this Act in such a way as to confer power on a person to exercise a discretion.

(5) An Order in Council under this section shall be subject to annulment in pursuance of a resolution of either House of Parliament.

(6) For the purposes of this section, "the relevant provisions of this Act" are this Part, except sections 10 and 16, and Part IV.

DEFINITIONS
"confiscation order": s.2(9).
"defendant": s.63(1).
"external confiscation order": s.39(2).
"proceedings concluded": s.41(3).
"proceedings instituted": s.41(2).
"relevant provisions of this Act": s.39(6).

Registration of external confiscation orders

40.—(1) On an application made by or on behalf of the Government of a designated country, the High Court may register an external confiscation order made there if—
  (a) it is satisfied that at the time of registration the order is in force and not subject to appeal;

(b) it is satisfied, where the person against whom the order is made did not appear in the proceedings, that he received notice of the proceedings in sufficient time to enable him to defend them; and

(c) it is of the opinion that enforcing the order in England and Wales would not be contrary to the interests of justice.

(2) In subsection (1) above "appeal" includes—

(a) any proceedings by way of discharging or setting aside a judgment; and

(b) an application for a new trial or a stay of execution.

(3) The High Court shall cancel the registration of an external confiscation order if it appears to the court that the order has been satisfied by payment of the amount due under it.

(4) In this section "designated country" and "external confiscation order" have the same meaning as in section 39 of this Act.

Interpretation

Interpretation of Part I

41.—(1) This section shall have effect for the interpretation of this Part.

(2) Proceedings for an offence are instituted—

(a) when a justice of the peace issues a summons or warrant under section 1 of the Magistrates' Courts Act 1980 (issue of summons to, or warrant for arrest of, accused) in respect of the offence;

(b) when a person is charged with the offence after being taken into custody without a warrant;

(c) when a bill of indictment is preferred under section 2 of the Administration of Justice (Miscellaneous Provisions) Act 1933 in a case falling within paragraph (b) of subsection (2) of that section (preferment by direction of the criminal division of the Court of Appeal or by direction, or with the consent, of a High Court judge);

and where the application of this subsection would result in there being more than one time for the institution of proceedings, they shall be taken to have been instituted at the earliest of those times.

(3) Proceedings for a drug trafficking offence are concluded—

(a) when the defendant is acquitted on all counts;

(b) if he is convicted on one or more counts, but the court decides not to make a confiscation order against him, when it makes that decision; or

(c) if a confiscation order is made against him in those proceedings, when the order is satisfied.

(4) An application under section 13, 14 or 19 of this Act is concluded—

(a) if the court decides not to make a confiscation order against the defendant, when it makes that decision; or

(b) if a confiscation order is made against him as a result of that application, when the order is satisfied.

(5) An application under section 15 or 16 of this Act is concluded—

(a) if the court decides not to vary the confiscation order in question, when it makes that decision; or

(b) if the court varies the confiscation order as a result of the application, when the order is satisfied.

(6) A confiscation order is satisfied when no amount is due under it.

(7) For the purposes of this section as it applies to sections 32 and 33 of this Act, a confiscation order is also satisfied when the defendant in respect of whom it was made has served a term of imprisonment or detention in default of payment of the amount due under the order.

(8) An order is subject to appeal until (disregarding any power of a court to grant leave to appeal out of time) there is no further possibility of an appeal on which the order could be varied or set aside.

PART II

GENERAL NOTE

In recent years it has been the experience of the Customs and Excise that large sums of cash are being exported from and imported into the U.K. There currently exist no exchange control regulations in this country so that cash imported may be changed into foreign currency which is then exported. Neither the officers of Customs and Excise, nor the police, have any powers to seize the cash to investigate its origins if there are reasonable grounds for suspecting that the cash directly or indirectly represents the proceeds of someone's drug trafficking. As a result of complaints expressed in evidence by American and British law enforcement officers to the Home Affairs Select Committee (see the 7th Report 1989, Vol. I, para. 87) Parliament enacted Pt. III of the Criminal Justice (International Co-operation) Act 1990 (c. 5), ss.25–29 now ss.42, 43, 46, 47 and 48 of this Act.

The Metropolitan Police also complained that the abolition of exchange controls has been exploited by drug traffickers (see para. 87 of the 7th Report). The Home Affairs Committee has therefore recommended that the law be changed to: (i) require anyone importing or exporting cash over a limit set by H.M. Customs to declare it; (ii) make illegal the import or export of proceeds of drug trafficking or other serious crimes and; (iii) allow customs officers to retain cash entering or leaving the country which they know or suspect arises from the proceeds of such crime.

This approach has found favour with the Customs and Excise with the consequent assumption of the powers which may be required by Art. 5 of the 1988 Vienna Convention (see para. 88 of the 7th Report). These recommendations have not become law. Section 42 of this Act (formerly s.25 of the Criminal Justice (International Co-operation) Act 1990) is limited to the cash suspected to represent a person's proceeds of drug trafficking but not where it may relate to other criminal acts. It is debatable whether the Home Affairs Committee's original proposals would run contrary to existing laws concerning the free movement of capital and the E.C. Capital Liberalisation Directive. The Home Affairs Committee has suggested that requiring a declaration of cash over a pre-set limit would not require primary legislation but could be achieved by an order issued under s.1 of the Import, Export and Customs Powers (Defence) Act 1939 (c. 69).

The effect of Pt. II is draconian. The general scheme is as follows. Where a customs officer, or a constable, has reasonable grounds for suspecting that the "cash" imported or exported (being £10,000 or more) directly or indirectly represents the proceeds of drug trafficking, the officer may seize that cash (s.42(1), formerly s.25(1) of the Criminal Justice (International Co-operation) Act 1990) and detain it for up to 48 hours without the need to make any application to a court. After 48 hours, the officer must either return the cash or apply to a justice of the peace (or in Scotland the sheriff) for an order permitting its continued detention on the grounds set out in s.42(2). The order cannot endure longer than three months (s.25(3)), but further orders can be made by the court provided the total period of detention does not exceed two years from the date of the first order (s.25(3)). It should be noted that these powers may be exercised even if no criminal proceedings have been instituted (or even contemplated) against any person for a drug trafficking offence in connection with the money seized. Where proceedings are instituted (s.42(7), formerly s.25(6) of the 1990 Act), or where application is made to forfeit the money on the basis that it represents drug proceeds (s.43(1), formerly s.26(1) of the 1990 Act), the cash is not to be released until the relevant proceedings have been concluded (and so overrides the two-year restriction set out in s.42(3)). If forfeiture is applied for, the prosecutor need only prove that the cash represents the proceeds of drug trafficking to the civil standard. This was at variance with the position under the 1986 Act: see *R. v. Dickens* [1991] 2 Q.B. 102 and *R. v. Enwezor* (1991) 93 Cr.App.R. 233, but see now s.2(8), above.

The person from whom the cash was seized, or any person on whose behalf the cash was being exported or imported, may apply to the magistrates' court (or in Scotland the sheriff) for the money to be released on the basis that there are no grounds for its detention, or its detention is not justified (s.42(6), formerly s.25(5) of the 1990 Act). Clearly in this instance the burden is on the applicant (presumably to the civil standard).

Notice may be required to be given, made by rules of court, to persons affected by the order (s.46(1), formerly s.28(1) of the 1990 Act).

The money must be held in an interest-bearing account (payable to the Crown if forfeited or to the person entitled to possession if released), unless the money was released within 48 hours of its seizure: s.42(8), formerly s.27 of the 1990 Act.

It should be noted that "exported" has an extended meaning and includes cash "being brought to any place in the United Kingdom for the purpose of being exported": s.48(1), formerly s.29(1) of the 1990 Act.

DRUG TRAFFICKING MONEY IMPORTED OR EXPORTED IN CASH

Seizure and detention

42.—(1) A customs officer or constable may seize and, in accordance with this section, detain any cash which is being imported into or exported from the United Kingdom if—

(a) its amount is not less than the prescribed sum; and

(b) he has reasonable grounds for suspecting that it directly or indirectly represents any person's proceeds of drug trafficking, or is intended by any person for use in drug trafficking.

(2) Cash seized by virtue of this section shall not be detained for more than 48 hours unless its continued detention is authorised by an order made by a justice of the peace or in Scotland the sheriff; and no such order shall be made unless the justice or, as the case may be, the sheriff is satisfied—

(a) that there are reasonable grounds for the suspicion mentioned in subsection (1) above; and

(b) that continued detention of the cash is justified while its origin or derivation is further investigated or consideration is given to the institution (whether in the United Kingdom or elsewhere) of criminal proceedings against any person for an offence with which the cash is connected.

(3) Any order under subsection (2) above shall authorise the continued detention of the cash to which it relates for such period, not exceeding three months beginning with the date of the order, as may be specified in the order; and a magistrates' court or in Scotland the sheriff, if satisfied as to the matters mentioned in that subsection, may thereafter from time to time by order authorise the further detention of the cash but so that—

(a) no period of detention specified in such an order shall exceed three months beginning with the date of the order; and

(b) the total period of detention shall not exceed two years from the date of the order under subsection (2) above.

(4) Any order under subsection (2) above shall provide for notice to be given to persons affected by the order.

(5) Any application for an order under subsection (2) or (3) above shall be made—

(a) by the Commissioners of Customs and Excise or a constable if made to a justice or magistrates' court; and

(b) by a procurator fiscal if made to the sheriff.

(6) At any time while cash is detained by virtue of the preceding provisions of this section—

(a) a magistrates' court or in Scotland the sheriff may direct its release if satisfied—

(i) on an application made by the person from whom it was seized or a person by or on whose behalf it was being imported or exported, that there are no, or are no longer any, such grounds for its detention as are mentioned in subsection (2) above; or

(ii) on an application made by any other person, that detention of the cash is not for that or any other reason justified; and

(b) a customs officer or constable, or in Scotland a procurator fiscal, may release the cash if satisfied that its detention is no longer justified, but shall first notify the justice, magistrates' court or sheriff under whose order it is being detained.

(7) If at a time when any cash is being detained by virtue of the preceding provisions of this section—

(a) an application for its forfeiture is made under section 43 of this Act, or

(b) proceedings are instituted (whether in the United Kingdom or elsewhere) against any person for an offence with which the cash is connected, the cash shall not be released until any proceedings pursuant to the application or, as the case may be, the proceedings for that offence have been concluded.

(8) Cash seized under this section and detained for more than 48 hours shall, unless required as evidence of an offence, be held in an interest-bearing account and the interest accruing on any such cash shall be added to that cash on its forfeiture or release.

DEFINITIONS
"cash": s.48(1).
"constable": s.63(1).
"customs officer": s.48(1).
"drug trafficking": s.1(1)(2); Criminal Justice (Scotland) Act 1987, Pt. I.
"exported": s.48(1).
"prescribed sum": s.48(3).
"proceeds of drug trafficking": Criminal Justice (Scotland) Act 1987, Pt. I (Scotland only).

GENERAL NOTE
See the General Note to Pt. II, above.

Forfeiture

43.—(1) A magistrates' court or in Scotland the sheriff may order the forfeiture of any cash which has been seized under section 42 of this Act if satisfied, on an application made while the cash is detained under that section, that the cash directly or indirectly represents any person's proceeds of drug trafficking, or is intended by any person for use in drug trafficking.

(2) Any application for an order under this section shall be made—
 (a) by the Commissioners of Customs and Excise or a constable if made to a magistrates' court; and
 (b) by a procurator fiscal if made to the sheriff.

(3) The standard of proof in proceedings on an application under this section shall be that applicable to civil proceedings; and an order may be made under this section whether or not proceedings are brought against any person for an offence with which the cash in question is connected.

(4) Proceedings on an application under this section to the sheriff shall be civil proceedings.

DEFINITIONS
"cash": s.48(1).
"constable": s.63(1).
"customs officer": s.48(1).
"drug trafficking": s.1(1)(2); Criminal Justice (Scotland) Act 1987, Pt. I.
"exported": s.48(1).
"proceeds of drug trafficking": Criminal Justice (Scotland) Act 1987, Pt. I (Scotland only).

GENERAL NOTE
See the General Note to Pt. II, above.

Appeal against forfeiture order made by a magistrates' court

44.—(1) This section applies where an order for the forfeiture of cash ("the forfeiture order") is made under section 43 of this Act by a magistrates' court.

(2) Any party to the proceedings in which the forfeiture order is made (other than the applicant for the order) may, before the end of the period of 30 days beginning with the date on which it is made, appeal to the Crown Court or, in Northern Ireland, to a county court.

(3) An appeal under this section shall be by way of a rehearing.

(4) On an application made by the appellant to a magistrates' court at any time, that court may order the release of so much of the cash to which the forfeiture order relates as it considers appropriate to enable him to meet his legal expenses in connection with the appeal.

(5) The court hearing an appeal under this section may make such order as it considers appropriate.

(6) If it upholds the appeal, the court may order the release of the cash, or (as the case may be) the remaining cash, together with any accrued interest.

(7) Subsection (3) of section 43 of this Act applies in relation to a rehearing on an appeal under this section as it applies to proceedings under that section.

DEFINITIONS
  "cash": s.48(1).
  "forfeiture order": s.44(1).

GENERAL NOTE
  This section was originally inserted into s.26 of the Criminal Justice (International Co-operation) Act 1990 (c. 5) by s.25 of the 1993 Act. See the General Note to Pt. II, above.

Appeal against forfeiture order made by sheriff

45. Any party to proceedings in which an order for the forfeiture of cash is made by the sheriff under section 43 of this Act may appeal against the order to the Court of Session.

Rules of court

46.—(1) Provision may be made by rules of court with respect to applications or appeals to any court under this Part, for the giving of notice of such applications or appeals to persons affected, for the joinder, or in Scotland sisting, of such persons as parties and generally with respect to the procedure under those sections before any court.

(2) Subsection (1) above is without prejudice to the generality of any existing power to make rules.

Receipts

47.—(1) Any money representing cash forfeited under this Part or accrued interest thereon shall be paid into the Consolidated Fund.

(2) Subsection (1) above does not apply—

(a) where an appeal is made under section 44 or 45 of this Act, before the appeal is determined or otherwise disposed of; and

(b) in any other case—

  (i) where the forfeiture was ordered by a magistrates' court, before the end of the period of 30 days mentioned in section 44(2) of this Act; or

  (ii) where the forfeiture was ordered by the sheriff, before the end of any period within which, in accordance with rules of court, an appeal under section 45 of this Act must be made.

Interpretation of Part II

48.—(1) In this Part—

  "cash" includes coins and notes in any currency;

  "customs officer" means an officer commissioned by the Commissioners of Customs and Excise under section 6(3) of the Customs and Excise Management Act 1979; and

  "exported", in relation to any cash, includes its being brought to any place in the United Kingdom for the purpose of being exported.

(2) In the application of this Part in Scotland and Northern Ireland, "drug trafficking" and "the proceeds of drug trafficking"—
- (a) as respects Scotland, have the same meaning as in Part I of the Criminal Justice (Scotland) Act 1987; and
- (b) as respects Northern Ireland, have the same meaning as in the Criminal Justice (Confiscation) (Northern Ireland) Order 1990.

(3) In section 42 of this Act "the prescribed sum" means such sum in sterling as may for the time being be prescribed for the purposes of that section by an order made by the Secretary of State by statutory instrument subject to annulment in pursuance of a resolution of either House of Parliament; and in determining under that section whether an amount of currency other than sterling is not less than the prescribed sum that amount shall be converted at the prevailing rate of exchange.

(4) For the avoidance of doubt it is hereby declared that notwithstanding sections 8 and 9 of the Isle of Man Act 1979 references in this Part to importation into or export from the United Kingdom include references to importation into the United Kingdom from the Isle of Man and exportation from the United Kingdom to the Isle of Man.

Part III

INTRODUCTION
In 1989 the National Drugs Intelligence Co-ordinator informed the Home Affairs Committee on Drug Trafficking and Related Serious Crime that at least £1,800 million (derived from drug trafficking) was circulating in the U.K. The amount of money being laundered is now thought to be as high as £57 million a year from drug sales in America and Europe alone. Despite the 1986 Act, the U.K. continues to be a major centre for money laundering. In the same year, the Home Office told the Committee that the 1986 Act has promoted drug traffickers to adopt greater sophistication in their efforts to launder the proceeds, so that money laundering is "probably the most organised aspect of drug trafficking": see the Home Affairs Committee 7th Report (1989). The Home Office indicated that although the evidence of links between organised crime and drug trafficking was largely anecdotal "there is an undoubted link between the two". The link is said to be evident between the drugs trade and the financing of wars and terrorism but usually the link is much more basic and symptomatic of general criminal activity committed by drug traffickers. There is much in the 1993 Act and now this Act, which represents the views and the concerns of the legislature when the Drug Trafficking Offences Bill was being debated. It is plain from the Official Reports that Parliament regarded the 1986 Act as marking only the first step in the fight against organised crime and not solely against drug trafficking. The extent to which other areas of the law in 1986 required reform (*e.g.* extradition, banking and international co-operation in respect of the gathering and calling of evidence) meant that the 1986 Act could not embrace every activity that was either linked (or akin) to drug trafficking and money-laundering. Parliament was also mindful that the Criminal Justice Bill (now the Criminal Justice Act 1988) was being drafted but had to be considered by Parliament. Lord Harris of Greenwich explained the problem when he said

"... [I]t is an illusion to imagine that drug trafficking can be treated as an isolated crime ... we are confronted with the existence of highly sophisticated criminal syndicates. The operators move effectively from one form of serious crime to another; from drug trafficking to armed robbery, from counterfeit currency operations to large-scale fraud and then back again to drug trafficking" (*Hansard*, H.L. Vol. 474, col. 1115).

The object of money laundering is to transfer the proceeds of crime through the financial sector so that it re-emerges back into legitimate commercial or financial concerns controlled or directed by the participants in the criminal enterprise. The methods by which proceeds are concealed are as varied as ingenuity permits, ranging from the setting up of so-called "paper trails" (designed to "lose" the proceeds in a diverse and confusing "maze" of translations) to the use of various shields – whether jurisdictional or rooted in privilege and confidentiality.

Organised crime exploits the three elements of business, supply, demand and profit, and the law enforcement agencies (while traditionally deployed to tackle the first two elements) are devoting more resources to tackling the profit element for two reasons; (a) funds removed from circulation cannot be re-used to finance further criminal enterprises, and (b) it removes the incentive to commit crime.

Given that drug trafficking and money laundering operate on an international scale, many of the provisions of the 1986 Act (and subsequent legislation) are the product of diplomatic efforts and rooted in several Treaties, Conventions, Bi-lateral Agreements and (now) European Directives: see the *European Convention on Mutual Assistance 1957* (which the U.K. was not able to ratify until the enactment of the Criminal Justice (International Co-operation) Act 1990); the *United Nations Convention Against Illicit Traffic In Narcotic Drugs and Psychotropic Substances 1988* (the Vienna Convention, ratified by the U.K. in 1991); the *Council of Europe Convention on Laundering, Search, Seizure and Confiscation of the Proceeds of Crime 1990* (yet to be ratified by the U.K.). See also the European Council Directive (91/308/EEC) and the Drug Trafficking Offences Act (Designated Countries and Territories) Order 1990 (S.I. 1990 No. 1199) (as amended by S.I. 1991 No. 1465). Orders made in Scotland under the Criminal Justice (Scotland) Act 1987 may now be enforced in England and Wales: see the Drug Trafficking Offences Act (Enforcement in England and Wales) Order 1988 (S.I. 1988 No. 593).

The Financial Action Task Force (FATF) made a number of radical proposals in 1990 which went beyond those agreed at the 1988 United Nations Convention. FATF recommended that member states should address their money laundering provisions to various major crimes and not just drug trafficking. It also suggested that rules of secrecy or confidentiality held by various financial institutions should be qualified so as to permit suspicious transactions to be reported to the authorities.

These proposals were already in Parliament's mind in 1986 (see *Hansard*, H.L. Vol. 474, col. 1094); and s.50 of this Act (formerly s.24 of the 1986 Act) makes it an offence to assist another to retain the benefit of drug trafficking in circumstances where the defendant knew or even suspected that the assisted person has benefited from drug trafficking. Section 50 does not impose an obligation to disclose a suspicion but where a person or body (*e.g.* a bank) discloses suspicions to the authorities he will have the protections afforded to him by s.50(3) (*e.g.* against breach of contract) and he may continue to act for the person under suspicion (*e.g.* without closing his bank account) within the limits set out in s.50(3) (see also the Wilton Park Paper 65, 1993, HMSO).

For over 20 years, the United States of America has been developing powerful anti-money laundering laws both by way of its legislation and at common law. The Bank Secrecy Act 1970 (U.S.) applies to financial institutions and businesses which accept large sums of cash. A "financial institution" is very broadly defined: See *U.S. v. Rigdon* (1989) 874 F.2d 774 and *U.S. v. Clines* (1992) 958 F.2d 578. The BSA requires businesses and individuals to submit Currency Transaction Reports (CTRs) as well as various reports of currency instruments, foreign bank accounts, and cash payments over 10,000 U.S. dollars in a trade or business. Businesses and their employees may be required to lodge Criminal Referral Forms (CRFs) in respect of any "known or suspected criminal violation ... committed against [or through] a bank" used to facilitate a criminal transaction. Failure to file a CRF may result in so-called civil penalties being assessed against the institution, its officers or employees. Data and intelligence gleaned from these records are collated on a database utilised by FINCEN (Financial Crimes Enforcement Network). The Anti-Abuse Act 1988 includes a requirement upon the Secretary to the Treasury to negotiate with other countries to ensure that they have adequate records on international currency transactions, which might be taken as a requirement for mandatory reporting along United States lines.

The Money Laundering Control Act (1986) (U.S.) creates a number of offences in respect of the knowing participation by any person in transactions with persons who derive their money from specified unlawful activities, *e.g.* drug trafficking.

Forfeiture, under U.S. legislation, is permitted under the Bank Secrecy Act 1970 (U.S.), the Money Laundering Control Act 1986 (U.S.), the Comprehensive Drug Abuse Prevention and Control Act, the Controlled Substances Act, the Racketeer-Influenced and Corrupt Organisations (RICO) and the Continuing Criminal Enterprise statutes. Of particular interest here are two concepts. First, some statutory provisions enjoy a reduced standard of proof requiring the government to prove only a "probable" cause to believe "that a substantial connection exists between the property to be forfeited" and the act which contravenes the statute: see *U.S. v. Four Million Dollars* (1985) 762 F.2d 895 (1985). Secondly, there is the "Relation-Back Doctrine" which is based on the fiction that illegally obtained property vests in the government at the time of the offence.

Developments in the U.S. have to some extent been mirrored elsewhere as a large number of countries have collaborated to combat drug trafficking and money laundering. These two activities now have to be seen in the context of each other.

The American model was considered by the House of Lords in 1986 (*Hansard*, H.L. Vol. 474, col. 1112) when it was pointed out that American law was not confined to drug trafficking. The British Government was not then prepared to move in the direction of the American model although the then Parliamentary Under-Secretary had indicated that "there might be movement in the future" (*Hansard, ibid*).

Significantly, Art. 5(1) of the Vienna Convention 1988 provides that each party is to adopt such measures as may be necessary to enable confiscation of "... (a) the proceeds derived from offences established in accordance with article 3, paragraph 1, or property the value of which corresponds to that of such proceeds ..." while Art. 5(3) requires each party to empower its courts to order that bank, financial or commercial records be made available or seized. Provision for the reversal of the burden of proof is made by Art. 7: "each Party may consider ensuring that the onus of proof be reversed regarding the lawful origin of alleged proceeds or other property liable to confiscation, to the extent that such action is consistent with the principles of its domestic law and with the nature of the judicial and other proceedings".

Article 3 of the 1988 Convention also requires member states to make the concealment or disguising of the proceeds of drug trafficking an offence without reference (as appeared in s.24 of the 1986 Act) to "facilitating" or "assisting" the drug trafficker. Article 3 also requires the creation of an offence of handling the proceeds of drug trafficking.

Accordingly, the Home Affairs Committee in their Seventh Report (Vol I, session 1988–89) recommended that English law be amended so that the U.K. could ratify Art. 3.

The U.S. authorities made representations to the Home Affairs Committee that the U.K. should introduce money laundering measures similar to those already operating in the U.S. The 1994 Act suggests that the Government are moving in that direction but the severity of American law should not be underestimated both in terms of the draconian effect of their law and the vigorous way it is enforced with very heavy penalties for non-compliance: see also the European Council Directive 91/308/EEC (O.J. L166/77).

Offences relevant to Pt. III & Pt. IV of the 1994 Act
    The relevant offences are now:
    (a) Assisting another to retain the benefit of drug trafficking "knowing or suspecting" that the assisted person is a drug trafficker or someone who has benefited from drug trafficking: s.50, formerly s.24 of the 1986 Act;
    (b) Prejudicing investigations: s.58, formerly s.31 of the 1986 Act;
    (c) Concealing, disguising, transferring or removing the proceeds of drug trafficking; the offence being committed by the trafficker himself: s.49(1), formerly s.14 of the Criminal Justice (International Co-operation) Act 1990;
    (d) Concealing, disguising, transferring or removing the proceeds of drug trafficking; the offence being committed by another who assists any person to avoid prosecution for a drug trafficking offence or the making or enforcement of a confiscation order: s.49(2);
    (e) Acquisition, possession or use of proceeds of drug trafficking: s.51 of the 1994 Act (formerly s.23A of the 1986 Act inserted by s.16 of the 1993 Act);
    (f) Failing to disclose knowledge of suspicion of money laundering: s.52;
    (g) Disclosing information to another which is likely to prejudice an investigation or proposed investigation: s.53.

OFFENCES IN CONNECTION WITH PROCEEDS OF DRUG TRAFFICKING

Concealing or transferring proceeds of drug trafficking

49.—(1) A person is guilty of an offence if he—
    (a) conceals or disguises any property which is, or in whole or in part directly or indirectly represents, his proceeds of drug trafficking, or
    (b) converts or transfers that property or removes it from the jurisdiction, for the purpose of avoiding prosecution for a drug trafficking offence or the making or enforcement in his case of a confiscation order.

(2) A person is guilty of an offence if, knowing or having reasonable grounds to suspect that any property is, or in whole or in part directly or indirectly represents, another person's proceeds of drug trafficking, he—
    (a) conceals or disguises that property, or
    (b) converts or transfers that property or removes it from the jurisdiction, for the purpose of assisting any person to avoid prosecution for a drug trafficking offence or the making or enforcement of a confiscation order.

(3) In subsections (1)(a) and (2)(a) above the references to concealing or disguising any property include references to concealing or disguising its

nature, source, location, disposition, movement or ownership or any rights with respect to it.

GENERAL NOTE

Several sets of offences were created in s.14 of the Criminal Justice (International Co-operation) Act 1990 (c. 5) to give legislative effect to the provisions of Art. 3 of the 1988 Vienna Convention against Illicit Traffic in Narcotic Drugs and Psychotropic Substances. By s.14(1)(a) of the 1990 Act, it was made an offence to conceal or to disguise property which represented the proceeds of drug trafficking. This offence has been retained and is now to be found in subs. (1)(a). The second offence was that of converting, transferring or removing such property: s.14 (1)(b) of the 1990 Act. This offence is re-enacted in subs. (1)(b). Note that both of these offences relate to the activities of the drug trafficker himself.

By contrast, s.14(2) of the 1990 Act created similar offences but these relate to the same activities committed by a person other than the trafficker himself. These offences have also been re-enacted as subs. (2).

The third offence under s.14(3) of the 1990 Act was aimed at those who receive gifts knowing or having reasonable grounds to suspect that the gift represented the proceeds of another's drug trafficking. However, the 1993 Act inserted s.23A into the 1986 Act which made it an offence knowingly to acquire, use or to be in possession of the proceeds of drug trafficking (now re-enacted in s.51, below) and thus s.14(3) of the 1990 Act was repealed by Sched. 6, Pt. I of the 1993 Act.

Offences under ss.49, 50 and 51 are "drug trafficking offences". However, none of these offences entitle the courts to make any of the "assumptions" under s.4(2), above: see s.4(5). This is to preserve the distinction between money-laundering offences and more serious drug trafficking offences (see the Home Secretary, *Hansard*, H.L. Vol. 514, col. 902).

A conviction for an offence under ss.49, 50 or 51 puts the offender in the category of prisoners in respect of whom the Secretary of State has no power of early release (see s.65 and para. 7 to Sch. 1 of the 1994 Act and see the 1990 Act, s.31(1) and Sched. 4, para. 3 amending Pt. II of Sched. 1 to the Criminal Justice Act 1982 (c. 48), and the Home Secretary, *Hansard*, H.L. Vol. 514, col. 902).

Assisting another person to retain the benefit of drug trafficking

50.—(1) Subject to subsection (3) below, a person is guilty of an offence if he enters into or is otherwise concerned in an arrangement whereby—

    (a) the retention or control by or on behalf of another person (call him "A") of A's proceeds of drug trafficking is facilitated (whether by concealment, removal from the jurisdiction, transfer to nominees or otherwise), or

    (b) A's proceeds of drug trafficking—

        (i) are used to secure that funds are placed at A's disposal, or

        (ii) are used for A's benefit to acquire property by way of investment,

and he knows or suspects that A is a person who carries on or has carried on drug trafficking or has benefited from drug trafficking.

(2) In this section, references to any person's proceeds of drug trafficking include a reference to any property which in whole or in part directly or indirectly represented in his hands his proceeds of drug trafficking.

(3) Where a person discloses to a constable a suspicion or belief that any funds or investments are derived from or used in connection with drug trafficking, or discloses to a constable any matter on which such a suspicion or belief is based—

    (a) the disclosure shall not be treated as a breach of any restriction upon the disclosure of information imposed by statute or otherwise; and

    (b) if he does any act in contravention of subsection (1) above and the disclosure relates to the arrangement concerned, he does not commit an offence under this section if—

        (i) the disclosure is made before he does the act concerned and the act is done with the consent of the constable; or

        (ii) the disclosure is made after he does the act, but is made on his initiative and as soon as it is reasonable for him to make it.

(4) In proceedings against a person for an offence under this section, it is a defence to prove—

(a) that he did not know or suspect that the arrangement related to any person's proceeds of drug trafficking;

(b) that he did not know or suspect that by the arrangement the retention or control by or on behalf of A of any property was facilitated or, as the case may be, that by the arrangement any property was used as mentioned in subsection (1)(b) above; or

(c) that—

     (i) he intended to disclose to a constable such a suspicion, belief or matter as is mentioned in subsection (3) above in relation to the arrangement, but

     (ii) there is reasonable excuse for his failure to make any such disclosure in the manner mentioned in paragraph (b)(i) or (ii) of that subsection.

(5) In the case of a person who was in employment at the time in question, subsections (3) and (4) above shall have effect in relation to disclosures, and intended disclosures, to the appropriate person in accordance with the procedure established by his employer for the making of such disclosures as they have effect in relation to disclosures, and intended disclosures, to a constable.

GENERAL NOTE

Section 50 (formerly s.24 of the 1986 Act) makes it an offence for another to assist a drug trafficker to retain the benefit of the latter's drug trafficking. Section 49 (formerly s.14(1) of the 1990 Act) makes the drug trafficker himself guilty of an offence if he attempts to avoid the events referred to in s.49.

Acquisition, possession or use of proceeds of drug trafficking

51.—(1) A person is guilty of an offence if, knowing that any property is, or in whole or in part directly or indirectly represents, another person's proceeds of drug trafficking, he acquires or uses that property or has possession of it.

(2) It is a defence to a charge of committing an offence under this section that the person charged acquired or used the property or had possession of it for adequate consideration.

(3) For the purposes of subsection (2) above—

(a) a person acquires property for inadequate consideration if the value of the consideration is significantly less than the value of the property; and

(b) a person uses or has possession of property for inadequate consideration if the value of the consideration is significantly less than the value of his use or possession of the property.

(4) The provision for any person of services or goods which are of assistance to him in drug trafficking shall not be treated as consideration for the purposes of subsection (2) above.

(5) Where a person discloses to a constable a suspicion or belief that any property is, or in whole or in part directly or indirectly represents, another person's proceeds of drug trafficking, or discloses to a constable any matter on which such a suspicion or belief is based—

(a) the disclosure shall not be treated as a breach of any restriction upon the disclosure of information imposed by statute or otherwise; and

(b) if he does any act in relation to the property in contravention of subsection (1) above, he does not commit an offence under this section if—

     (i) the disclosure is made before he does the act concerned and the act is done with the consent of the constable; or

(ii) the disclosure is made after he does the act, but is made on his initiative and as soon as it is reasonable for him to make it.

(6) For the purposes of this section, having possession of any property shall be taken to be doing an act in relation to it.

(7) In proceedings against a person for an offence under this section, it is a defence to prove that—

(a) he intended to disclose to a constable such a suspicion, belief or matter as is mentioned in subsection (5) above, but

(b) there is reasonable excuse for his failure to make any such disclosure in the manner mentioned in paragraph (b)(i) or (ii) of that subsection.

(8) In the case of a person who was in employment at the time in question, subsections (5) and (7) above shall have effect in relation to disclosures, and intended disclosures, to the appropriate person in accordance with the procedure established by his employer for the making of such disclosures as they have effect in relation to disclosures, and intended disclosures, to a constable.

(9) No constable or other person shall be guilty of an offence under this section in respect of anything done by him in the course of acting in connection with the enforcement, or intended enforcement, of any provision of this Act or of any other enactment relating to drug trafficking or the proceeds of drug trafficking.

DEFINITIONS

"drug trafficking": s.1(1).
"inadequate consideration": s.51.
"possession": s.51(6); Criminal Justice (Scotland) Act 1987, s.42A(6).
"proceeds of drug trafficking": s.4(1)(a).
"property": s.62(1).

GENERAL NOTE

This section should be read and compared with s.14(3) of the Criminal Justice (International Co-operation) Act 1990 (c. 5) since both were drafted to deal with property coming into the hands of another which represents in whole, or in part, directly or indirectly, the proceeds of drug trafficking. The offence under s.14(3) of the 1990 Act was narrower in the sense that it was confined to property which had been "acquired", presumably in the sense that the recipient acquired an interest in the property or was held by the recipient on more than a merely temporary or short-terms basis. By contrast, this section includes any acquisition, but the section also includes the possession or use of that property. Presumably, the defendant (in order to be in possession) must know that he has it (see *Warner v. Metropolitan Police Commissioner* [1969] 2 A.C. 256) and this seems to be supported by s.51(6) which appears to define possession in terms of "doing an act in relation to" the property. This may mean no more than that a person exercises control over the property in question.

An essential exemption is given by subs. (9) to persons who deal with the property in connection with the investigation, detection or judicial process relating to drug trafficking matters by virtue of any enactment.

On the other hand, this section is narrower than s.14(3) of the 1990 Act in terms of the *mens rea* required to be proved. Under s.14(3) it was enough if a defendant acquired property "knowing or having reasonable grounds to suspect" its drug trafficking origins. The objective element does not appear in s.51 and what is required is actual knowledge; suspicion is not enough.

Subs. (1)

This provision is very widely drawn. It is not clear whether legal advisers (whether prosecuting or defending) are included in this provision.

Subss. (2) and (3)

Under s.14(3) of the 1990 Act the burden was on the prosecution to prove that the defendant acquired the property for "no or inadequate consideration" but this last ingredient is omitted from s.51. Instead, the burden is cast on to the defendant to prove that he provided "adequate consideration". Presumably, it will be for the jury to decide whether the consideration provided is in fact "adequate" having regard to subs. (3) but it is likely that it will fall to the courts to decide what that phrase means. Subsection (3) provides two instances where consideration is "inadequate" but is subs. (3) a closed category? If a person pays an excessive price for the property is the consideration to be regarded as being "adequate"? By s.62(1) "property" includes money. If services are provided in consideration for a substantial sum of drug money, how is it to be determined that the value of the service was not worth what was claimed or charged? (see *Hansard*, H.C. Vol. 222, col. 907, Sir Ivan Lawrence Q.C.). In the majority of cases, issues as to value may be resolved with expert help.

The upshot of s.51 seems to be that it will be lawful to use a drug trafficker's villa or motor vehicle providing an adequate sum is paid for it – but it will be an offence if he pays too little or nothing. It seems that knowledge of the origins of the property will not taint the consideration nor will it negate the defence.

Subs. (4)

This provision is designed to achieve the same result as s.14(5) of the 1990 Act. The provisions of s.51 are designed to exclude persons who provide goods or services to another so long as the goods or services supplied were not of "assistance to him in drug trafficking". If the goods or services are of assistance to him then subs. (4) creates a fiction and deems the supply not to be adequate consideration. Subsection (4) is intended to protect trades-people who are paid for goods and services from the proceeds of drug trafficking (see Standing Committee B, June 8, 1993, col. 93). It is not clear whether the defendant must know or intend that the goods or services supplied "are of assistance to him in drug trafficking" for the purposes of subs. (4).

Subss. (5) and (7)

This follows the model provided by s.24(3) of the 1986 Act; and see Sched. 7 to the Prevention of Terrorism (Temporary Provisions) Act 1989 (c. 4). Subsections (5) and (7) are designed to protect persons (particularly those employed in the financial sector) from any action for breach of contract, confidence or a duty arising out of their obligations to their clients.

Both subs. (5) and s.50(3) refer to the disclosure of "suspicions". There would seem to be two reasons why disclosure based on "suspicion" is said to be irrelevant. First, disclosure based on any higher standard would present individuals with a difficult issue of fact to resolve. How much information do they need to satisfy themselves before they could (or are required to) disclose a belief? (see *Hansard*, H.L. Vol. 474, col. 1114). Secondly, law enforcement agencies act on suspicion and accordingly a lot of intelligence could be lost if all that could be disclosed were beliefs. The Government consider that it would be "up to the policemen, the professionals, the investigators to decide whether or not [the suspicion] was true" (*per* Earl Ferrers, *Hansard*, H.L. Vol. 540, col. 753).

Subsection (7) follows the model in s.50(4)(c), above (formerly s.24(4)(c) of the 1986 Act).

Failure to disclose knowledge or suspicion of money laundering

52.—(1) A person is guilty of an offence if—

(a) he knows or suspects that another person is engaged in drug money laundering,

(b) the information, or other matter, on which that knowledge or suspicion is based came to his attention in the course of his trade, profession, business or employment, and

(c) he does not disclose the information or other matter to a constable as soon as is reasonably practicable after it comes to his attention.

(2) Subsection (1) above does not make it an offence for a professional legal adviser to fail to disclose any information or other matter which has come to him in privileged circumstances.

(3) It is a defence to a charge of committing an offence under this section that the person charged had a reasonable excuse for not disclosing the information or other matter in question.

(4) Where a person discloses to a constable—

(a) his suspicion or belief that another person is engaged in drug money laundering, or

(b) any information or other matter on which that suspicion or belief is based,

the disclosure shall not be treated as a breach of any restriction imposed by statute or otherwise.

(5) Without prejudice to subsection (3) or (4) above, in the case of a person who was in employment at the time in question, it is a defence to a charge of committing an offence under this section that he disclosed the information or

other matter in question to the appropriate person in accordance with the procedure established by his employer for the making of such disclosures.

(6) A disclosure to which subsection (5) above applies shall not be treated as a breach of any restriction imposed by statute or otherwise.

(7) In this section "drug money laundering" means doing any act—

(a) which constitutes an offence under section 49, 50 or 51 of this Act; or

(b) in the case of an act done otherwise than in England and Wales, which would constitute such an offence if done in England and Wales;

and for the purposes of this subsection, having possession of any property shall be taken to be doing an act in relation to it.

(8) For the purposes of this section, any information or other matter comes to a professional legal adviser in privileged circumstances if it is communicated, or given, to him—

(a) by, or by a representative of, a client of his in connection with the giving by the adviser of legal advice to the client;

(b) by, or by a representative of, a person seeking legal advice from the adviser; or

(c) by any person—

(i) in contemplation of, or in connection with, legal proceedings; and

(ii) for the purpose of those proceedings.

(9) No information or other matter shall be treated as coming to a professional legal adviser in privileged circumstances if it is communicated or given with a view to furthering any criminal purpose.

DEFINITIONS

"drug money laundering": s.52(7).

"privileged circumstances": s.52(8)(9).

GENERAL NOTE

This section creates an offence new to English law. Although s.50 and s.51 both include provisions to protect those who disclose their suspicions concerning drug trafficking carried on by another, in neither provision is there an actual obligation to make a disclosure. By contrast, s.52 makes it an offence to fail to disclose to a constable (or to an "appropriate person": see subs. (5)) as soon as reasonably practicable, knowledge or even a suspicion that a person is engaged in drug money laundering, where that knowledge or suspicion is gained in the course of a person's employment. Protection is afforded to legal advisers who give legal advice on a "privileged occasion" as defined by subs. (8) but not if information is received or given to further "any criminal purpose" – not just drug trafficking (subs. (1)).

The history of this offence has its roots in American law (see the General Note to s.51, above). When the 1986 Act was being debated as a Bill, Lord Denning moved an amendment (No. 30, subsequently withdrawn; see *Hansard*, H.L. Vol. 472, col. 1185) which proposed that the Secretary of State be empowered to draw up a scheme requiring banks and financial institutions to report to various authorities any deposit of, or a transaction in, currency exceeding a certain sum. This, in turn, was modelled on the American Bank Secrecy Act reported.

Following publication of the Guidance Notes on Money Laundering for Banks and Building Societies, on December 10, 1990, the number of suspicious transactions reported amounted to some 12,000 cases without mandatory legislation (*Hansard*, H.L. Vol. 539, cols.1373, 1385). The Home Affairs Committee had previously expressed concern that financial institutions would adopt an approach that was too passive and which would require the Government to "take the initiative" (para. 8 of their Seventh Report, 1988–89). In the light of agreements reached by the Council of Europe Convention on Laundering, Tracing, Seizure and Confiscation of Proceeds of Crime (1990) and the Council Directive 91/308/EEC, s.52 was enacted.

By Art. 6 of that Directive, member states are required to ensure that credit and financial institutions, their directors and employees co-operate fully with the authorities by informing them of "any fact which might be an indication of money laundering". By Art. 7 such institutions are required to "refrain from carrying out transactions which they know or suspect to be related to money laundering until they have appraised the authorities".

By Art. 9 a disclosure in good faith to the authorities "shall not constitute a breach of any restriction on disclosure of information imposed by contract or by any legislative, regulatory or administrative provision". The provisions of that Directive are to extend in whole, or in part, to professions and various undertakings "likely to be used for money laundering purposes": Art. 12.

Section 52 is not, by itself, as extensive in its scope as the Directive permits since it is limited to drug money laundering only. The reasons for including a mere suspicion in this provision are essentially the same as those relevant to s.51: see the General Note to that section.

Tipping-off

53.—(1) A person is guilty of an offence if—

(a) he knows or suspects that a constable is acting, or is proposing to act, in connection with an investigation which is being, or is about to be, conducted into drug money laundering, and

(b) he discloses to any other person information or any other matter which is likely to prejudice that investigation or proposed investigation.

(2) A person is guilty of an offence if—

(a) he knows or suspects that a disclosure has been made to a constable under section 50, 51 or 52 of this Act ("the disclosure"), and

(b) he discloses to any other person information or any other matter which is likely to prejudice any investigation which might be conducted following the disclosure.

(3) A person is guilty of an offence if—

(a) he knows or suspects that a disclosure of a kind mentioned in section 50(5), 51(8) or 52(5) of this Act ("the disclosure") has been made, and

(b) he discloses to any person information or any other matter which is likely to prejudice any investigation which might be conducted following the disclosure.

(4) Nothing in subsections (1) to (3) above makes it an offence for a professional legal adviser to disclose any information or other matter—

(a) to, or to a representative of, a client of his in connection with the giving by the adviser of legal advice to the client; or

(b) to any person—

(i) in contemplation of, or in connection with, legal proceedings; and

(ii) for the purpose of those proceedings.

(5) Subsection (4) above does not apply in relation to any information or other matter which is disclosed with a view to furthering any criminal purpose.

(6) In proceedings against a person for an offence under subsection (1), (2) or (3) above, it is a defence to prove that he did not know or suspect that the disclosure was likely to be prejudicial in the way mentioned in that subsection.

(7) No constable or other person shall be guilty of an offence under this section in respect of anything done by him in the course of acting in connection with the enforcement, or intended enforcement, of any provision of this Act or of any other enactment relating to drug trafficking or the proceeds of drug trafficking.

(8) In this section "drug money laundering" has the same meaning as in section 52 of this Act.

DEFINITIONS

"drug money laundering": s.52(7).
"privileged circumstances": s.52(8)(9).

GENERAL NOTE

This section creates three offences. First, it is an offence for a defendant who knows or suspects that an investigation into drug money laundering is being conducted (or is about to be) to divulge that fact, or other information, which is likely to prejudice such an investigation: subs. (1). Secondly, if a disclosure of a suspicion (or information) has been lawfully disclosed to a constable (*e.g.* by a bank) under s.51, s.50 or s.52 then it is an offence to disclose to another information which is likely to prejudice an investigation which might be conducted on the basis of the original disclosure: subs. (2). The third offence is similar to that created by subs. (2), but involves the original disclosure being made to an "appropriate person" (*e.g.* an employer).

There is an exemption in the case of legal advisers (within the terms of subss. (4) and (5)).

It is a defence to each of the three offences if the defendant proves that he did not know or suspect that the disclosure was likely to be prejudicial: subs. (6).

Penalties

54.—(1) A person guilty of an offence under section 49, 50 or 51 of this Act shall be liable—

(a) on summary conviction, to imprisonment for a term not exceeding six months or to a fine not exceeding the statutory maximum or to both; and

(b) on conviction on indictment, to imprisonment for a term not exceeding fourteen years or to a fine or to both.

(2) A person guilty of an offence under section 52 or 53 of this Act shall be liable—

(a) on summary conviction, to imprisonment for a term not exceeding six months or to a fine not exceeding the statutory maximum or to both; or

(b) on conviction on indictment, to imprisonment for a term not exceeding five years or to a fine or to both.

PART IV

MISCELLANEOUS AND SUPPLEMENTAL

Investigations into drug trafficking

Order to make material available

55.—(1) A constable may, for the purpose of an investigation into drug trafficking, apply to a Circuit judge for an order under subsection (2) below in relation to particular material or material of a particular description.

(2) If on such an application the judge is satisfied that the conditions in subsection (4) below are fulfilled, he may make an order that the person who appears to him to be in possession of the material to which the application relates shall—

(a) produce it to a constable for him to take away, or

(b) give a constable access to it,

within such period as the order may specify.

This subsection has effect subject to section 59(11) of this Act.

(3) The period to be specified in an order under subsection (2) above shall be seven days unless it appears to the judge that a longer or shorter period would be appropriate in the particular circumstances of the application.

(4) The conditions referred to in subsection (2) above are—

(a) that there are reasonable grounds for suspecting that a specified person has carried on or has benefited from drug trafficking;

(b) that there are reasonable grounds for suspecting that the material to which the application relates—

(i) is likely to be of substantial value (whether by itself or together with other material) to the investigation for the purpose of which the application is made; and

(ii) does not consist of or include items subject to legal privilege or excluded material; and

(c) that there are reasonable grounds for believing that it is in the public interest, having regard—

          (i) to the benefit likely to accrue to the investigation if the material is obtained, and
          (ii) to the circumstances under which the person in possession of the material holds it,
that the material should be produced or that access to it should be given.

(5) Where the judge makes an order under subsection (2)(b) above in relation to material on any premises he may, on the application of a constable, order any person who appears to him to be entitled to grant entry to the premises to allow a constable to enter the premises to obtain access to the material.

(6) An application under subsection (1) or (5) above may be made ex parte to a judge in chambers.

(7) Provision may be made by Crown Court Rules as to—

(a) the discharge and variation of orders under this section; and

(b) proceedings relating to such orders.

(8) An order of a Circuit judge under this section shall have effect as if it were an order of the Crown Court.

(9) Where the material to which an application under subsection (1) above relates consists of information contained in a computer—

(a) an order under subsection (2)(a) above shall have effect as an order to produce the material in a form in which it can be taken away and in which it is visible and legible; and

(b) an order under subsection (2)(b) above shall have effect as an order to give access to the material in a form in which it is visible and legible.

(10) An order under subsection (2) above—

(a) shall not confer any right to production of, or access to, items subject to legal privilege or excluded material;

(b) shall have effect notwithstanding any obligation as to secrecy or other restriction upon the disclosure of information imposed by statute or otherwise; and

(c) may be made in relation to material in the possession of an authorised government department;

and in this subsection "authorised government department" means a government department which is an authorised department for the purposes of the Crown Proceedings Act 1947.

<small>DEFINITIONS</small>
   "authorised government department": s.55(10).
   "constable": s.63(1).
   "excluded material": s.57 and s.11 of the Police and Criminal Evidence Act 1984.
   "items subject to legal privilege": s.57 and s.10 of the Police and Criminal Evidence Act 1984.
   "premises": s.57 and s.23 of the Police and Criminal Evidence Act 1984.

Authority for search

56.—(1) A constable may, for the purpose of an investigation into drug trafficking, apply to a Circuit judge for a warrant under this section in relation to specified premises.

(2) On such application the judge may issue a warrant authorising a constable to enter and search the premises if the judge is satisfied—

(a) that an order made under section 55 of this Act in relation to material on the premises has not been complied with;

(b) that the conditions in subsection (3) below are fulfilled; or

(c) that the conditions in subsection (4) below are fulfilled.

(3) The conditions referred to in subsection (2)(b) above are—

(a) that there are reasonable grounds for suspecting that a specified person has carried on or has benefited from drug trafficking;

(b) that the conditions in subsection (4)(b) and (c) of section 55 of this Act are fulfilled in relation to any material on the premises; and

(c) that it would not be appropriate to make an order under that section in relation to the material because—

(i) it is not practicable to communicate with any person entitled to produce the material;

(ii) it is not practicable to communicate with any person entitled to grant access to the material or entitled to grant entry to the premises on which the material is situated; or

(iii) the investigation for the purpose of which the application is made might be seriously prejudiced unless a constable could secure immediate access to the material.

(4) The conditions referred to in subsection (2)(c) above are—

(a) that there are reasonable grounds for suspecting that a specified person has carried on or has benefited from drug trafficking;

(b) that there are reasonable grounds for suspecting that there is on the premises material relating to the specified person or to drug trafficking which is likely to be of substantial value (whether by itself or together with other material) to the investigation for the purpose of which the application is made, but that the material cannot at the time of the application be particularised; and

(c) that—

(i) it is not practicable to communicate with any person entitled to grant entry to the premises;

(ii) entry to the premises will not be granted unless a warrant is produced; or

(iii) the investigation for the purpose of which the application is made might be seriously prejudiced unless a constable arriving at the premises could secure immediate entry to them.

(5) Where a constable has entered premises in the execution of a warrant issued under this section, he may seize and retain any material, other than items subject to legal privilege and excluded material, which is likely to be of substantial value (whether by itself or together with other material) to the investigation for the purpose of which the warrant was issued.

DEFINITIONS

"authorised government department": s.55(10).

"constable": s.63(1).

"excluded material": s.57 and s.11 of the Police and Criminal Evidence Act 1984.

"items subject to legal privilege": s.57 and s.10 of the Police and Criminal Evidence Act 1984.

"premises": s.57 and s.23 of the Police and Criminal Evidence Act 1984.

Provisions supplementary to sections 55 and 56

57.—(1) For the purposes of sections 21 and 22 of the Police and Criminal Evidence Act 1984 (access to, and copying and retention of, seized material)—

(a) an investigation into drug trafficking shall be treated as if it were an investigation of or in connection with an offence; and

(b) material produced in pursuance of an order under section 55(2)(a) of this Act shall be treated as if it were material seized by a constable.

(2) In sections 55 and 56 of this Act "excluded material", "items subject to legal privilege" and "premises" have the same meaning as in the 1984 Act.

Offence of prejudicing investigation

58.—(1) Where, in relation to an investigation into drug trafficking—

(a) an order under section 55 of this Act has been made or has been applied for and has not been refused, or

(b) a warrant under section 56 of this Act has been issued,

a person is guilty of an offence if, knowing or suspecting that the investigation is taking place, he makes any disclosure which is likely to prejudice the investigation.

(2) In proceedings against a person for an offence under this section, it is a defence to prove—

(a) that he did not know or suspect that the disclosure was likely to prejudice the investigation; or

(b) that he had lawful authority or reasonable excuse for making the disclosure.

(3) Nothing in subsection (1) above makes it an offence for a professional legal adviser to disclose any information or other matter—

(a) to, or to a representative of, a client of his in connection with the giving by the adviser of legal advice to the client; or

(b) to any person—

(i) in contemplation of, or in connection with, legal proceedings; and

(ii) for the purpose of those proceedings.

(4) Subsection (3) above does not apply in relation to any information or other matter which is disclosed with a view to furthering any criminal purpose.

(5) A person guilty of an offence under this section shall be liable—

(a) on summary conviction, to imprisonment for a term not exceeding six months or to a fine not exceeding the statutory maximum or to both; and

(b) on conviction on indictment, to imprisonment for a term not exceeding five years or to a fine or to both.

GENERAL NOTE

Section 31(1) of the 1986 Act provided:

"Where, in relation to an investigation into drug trafficking, an order under section 27 of this Act has been made or has been applied for and has not been refused or a warrant under section 28 of this Act has been issued, a person who, knowing or suspecting that the investigation is taking place, makes any disclosure which is likely to prejudice the investigation is guilty of an offence".

It will be seen that s.58 broadly re-enacts s.31(1) of the 1986 Act. Section 58(3) was originally inserted into s.31 by s.26 of the 1993 Act. Section 55, above, is concerned with the making of material available to a constable or an officer of customs and excise relevant to an investigation into drug trafficking.

An offence under s.58 can only be committed if an order under s.55 has been made or applied for, or a warrant (authorising a search) has been issued under s.56. The prosecution must prove that the accused knew or suspected that the investigation was taking place, but it is not necessary for the prosecution to prove either that he knew or suspected that any of the steps mentioned in subs. (1) had in fact been taken, or that he knew or suspected that the disclosure was likely to prejudice the investigation.

Disclosure of information held by government departments

59.—(1) Subject to subsection (4) below, the High Court may on an application by the prosecutor order any material mentioned in subsection (3) below which is in the possession of an authorised government department to be produced to the court within such period as the court may specify.

(2) The power to make an order under subsection (1) above is exercisable if—

(a) the powers conferred on the court by sections 26(1) and 27(1) of this Act are exercisable by virtue of subsection (1) of section 25 of this Act; or

(b) those powers are exercisable by virtue of subsection (3) of that section and the court has made a restraint or charging order which has not been discharged;

but where the power to make an order under subsection (1) above is exercisable by virtue only of paragraph (b) above, subsection (4) of section 25 of this Act shall apply for the purposes of this section as it applies for the purposes of sections 26 and 27 of this Act.

(3) The material referred to in subsection (1) above is any material which—

(a) has been submitted to an officer of an authorised government department by the defendant or by a person who has at any time held property which was realisable property;

(b) has been made by an officer of an authorised government department in relation to the defendant or such a person; or

(c) is correspondence which passed between an officer of an authorised government department and the defendant or such a person;

and an order under that subsection may require the production of all such material or of a particular description of such material, being material in the possession of the department concerned.

(4) An order under subsection (1) above shall not require the production of any material unless it appears to the High Court that the material is likely to contain information that would facilitate the exercise of the powers conferred on the court by sections 26 to 29 of this Act or on a receiver appointed under section 26 or 29 of this Act or in pursuance of a charging order.

(5) The court may by order authorise the disclosure to such a receiver of any material produced under subsection (1) above or any part of such material; but the court shall not make an order under this subsection unless a reasonable opportunity has been given for an officer of the department to make representations to the court.

(6) Material disclosed in pursuance of an order under subsection (5) above may, subject to any conditions contained in the order, be further disclosed for the purposes of the functions under any provision of this Act, apart from section 16, of the receiver or the Crown Court.

(7) The court may by order authorise the disclosure to a person mentioned in subsection (8) below of any material produced under subsection (1) above or any part of such material; but the court shall not make an order under this subsection unless—

(a) a reasonable opportunity has been given for an officer of the department to make representations to the court; and

(b) it appears to the court that the material is likely to be of substantial value in exercising functions relating to drug trafficking.

(8) The persons referred to in subsection (7) above are—

(a) any member of a police force;

(b) any member of the Crown Prosecution Service; and

(c) any officer within the meaning of the Customs and Excise Management Act 1979.

(9) Material disclosed in pursuance of an order under subsection (7) above may, subject to any conditions contained in the order, be further disclosed for the purposes of functions relating to drug trafficking.

(10) Material may be produced or disclosed in pursuance of this section notwithstanding any obligation as to secrecy or other restriction upon the disclosure of information imposed by statute or otherwise.

(11) An order under subsection (1) above and, in the case of material in the possession of an authorised government department, an order under section 55(2) of this Act may require any officer of the department (whether named in the order or not) who may for the time being be in possession of the material concerned to comply with it, and such an order shall be served as if the proceedings were civil proceedings against the department.

(12) The person on whom such an order is served—

(a) shall take all reasonable steps to bring it to the attention of the officer concerned; and

(b) if the order is not brought to that officer's attention within the period referred to in subsection (1) above, shall report the reasons for the failure to the court;

and it shall also be the duty of any other officer of the department in receipt of the order to take such steps as are mentioned in paragraph (a) above.

(13) In this section "authorised government department" means a government department which is an authorised department for the purposes of the Crown Proceedings Act 1947.

DEFINITIONS
"authorised government department": s.55(10).
"charging order": s.27.
"constable": s.63(1).
"material": s.59(3).
"premises": s.57 and s.23 of the Police and Criminal Evidence Act 1984.

Prosecution of offences etc

Prosecution by order of the Commissioners of Customs and Excise

60.—(1) Proceedings for a specified offence may be instituted by order of the Commissioners of Customs and Excise ("the Commissioners").

(2) Any proceedings for a specified offence which are so instituted shall be commenced in the name of an officer.

(3) In the case of the death, removal, discharge or absence of the officer in whose name any proceedings for a specified offence were commenced, those proceedings may be continued by another officer.

(4) Where the Commissioners investigate, or propose to investigate, any matter with a view to determining—

(a) whether there are grounds for believing that a specified offence has been committed, or

(b) whether a person should be prosecuted for a specified offence,

that matter shall be treated as an assigned matter within the meaning of the Customs and Excise Management Act 1979.

(5) Nothing in this section shall be taken—

(a) to prevent any person (including any officer) who has power to arrest, detain or prosecute any person for a specified offence from doing so; or

(b) to prevent a court from proceeding to deal with a person brought before it following his arrest by an officer for a specified offence, even though the proceedings have not been instituted by an order made under subsection (1) above.

(6) In this section—

"officer" means a person commissioned by the Commissioners; and

"specified offence" means—

(a) an offence under Part III or section 58 of this Act;

(b) attempting to commit, conspiracy to commit or incitement to commit any such offence; or

(c) any other offence of a kind prescribed in regulations made by the Secretary of State for the purposes of this section;

and references to the institution of proceedings for an offence shall be construed in accordance with section 41(2) of this Act.

(7) The power to make regulations under subsection (6) above shall be exercisable by statutory instrument.

(8) Any such instrument shall be subject to annulment in pursuance of a resolution of either House of Parliament.

DEFINITIONS
"Commissioners": s.60(1) and s.1(1) of the Customs and Excise Management Act 1979.
"officer": s.60(6).
"specified offence": s.60.

Extension of certain offences to Crown servants and exemptions for regulators etc.

61.—(1) The Secretary of State may by regulations provide that, in such circumstances as may be prescribed, sections 49(2), 50 to 53 and 58 of this Act shall apply to such persons in the public service of the Crown, or such categories of person in that service, as may be prescribed.

(2) Section 52 of this Act shall not apply—

(a) to any person designated by regulations made by the Secretary of State for the purposes of this paragraph; or

(b) in such circumstances as may be prescribed, to any person who falls within such category of person as may be prescribed for the purposes of this paragraph.

(3) The Secretary of State may designate for the purposes of paragraph (a) of subsection (2) above any person appearing to him to be performing regulatory, supervisory, investigative or registration functions.

(4) The categories of person prescribed by the Secretary of State for the purposes of paragraph (b) of subsection (2) above shall be such categories of person connected with the performance by any designated person of regulatory, supervisory, investigative or registration functions as he considers it appropriate to prescribe.

(5) In this section—

"the Crown" includes the Crown in right of Her Majesty's Government in Northern Ireland; and

"prescribed" means prescribed by regulations made by the Secretary of State.

(6) Any power to make regulations under this section shall be exercisable by statutory instrument.

(7) Any such instrument shall be subject to annulment in pursuance of a resolution of either House of Parliament.

Interpretation of Act

Meaning of "property" and related expressions

62.—(1) In this Act "property" includes money and all other property, real or personal, heritable or moveable, including things in action and other intangible or incorporeal property.

(2) This Act applies to property whether it is situated in England and Wales or elsewhere.

(3) In this Act "interest", in relation to property, includes right.

(4) In this Act—

(a) references to property held by a person include a reference to property vested in his trustee in bankruptcy, permanent or interim trustee within the meaning of the Bankruptcy (Scotland) Act 1985 or liquidator; and

(b) references to an interest held by a person beneficially in property include a reference to an interest which would be held by him beneficially if the property were not so vested.

(5) For the purposes of this Act—

(a) property is held by any person if he holds any interest in it; and
(b) property is transferred by one person to another if the first person transfers or grants to the other any interest in the property.

General interpretation

63.—(1) In this Act—
"constable" includes a person commissioned by the Commissioners of Customs and Excise under section 6(3) of the Customs and Excise Management Act 1979;
"defendant" means a person against whom proceedings have been instituted (within the meaning given in section 41(2) of this Act) for a drug trafficking offence (whether or not he has been convicted);
"modifications" includes additions, alterations and omissions.
(2) In this Act references to anything received in connection with drug trafficking include a reference to anything received both in that connection and in some other connection.
(3) Subject to section 66(2) and (6) of this Act—
(a) any reference in this Act to an offence includes a reference to an offence committed before the commencement of this Act; and
(b) any reference in this Act to "drug trafficking" includes a reference to drug trafficking carried out before the commencement of this Act.

Index of defined expressions

64. In this Act the expressions listed below are defined by, or otherwise fall to be construed in accordance with, the provisions of this Act indicated below—

acting as an insolvency practitioner	section 35(4)
amount that might be realised	section 6(1)
amount to be recovered	section 5(1)
benefited from drug trafficking	section 2(3)
charging order	section 27(2)
conclusion of an application	
—under section 13, 14 or 19	section 41(4)
—under section 15 or 16	section 41(5)
conclusion of proceedings for a drug	
trafficking offence	section 41(3)
confiscation order	section 2(9)
constable	section 63(1)
defendant	section 63(1)
drug trafficking	
—generally	section 1(1) and (2)
—for the application of Part II in	
Scotland and Northern Ireland	section 48(2)
drug trafficking offence	section 1(3)
gift caught by this Act	section 8(1)
"held", in relation to property	section 62(5)(a)
institution of proceedings for an offence	section 41(2)
"interest", in relation to property	section 62(3)
making a gift	section 8(2)
modifications	section 63(1)
proceeds of drug trafficking	
—generally	section 4(1)(a)
—for the application of Part II in	
Scotland and Northern Ireland	section 48(2)
property	section 62(1)
realisable property	section 6(2)
restraint order	section 26(1)

"satisfied", in relation to a confiscation order	section 41(6) and (7)
"subject to appeal", in relation to an order	section 41(8)
"transferred" in relation to property	section 62(5)(b)
value of gift, payment or reward	section 7(2)
value of proceeds of drug trafficking	section 4(1)(b)
value of property	section 7(1).

Supplemental

Consequential amendments and modifications of other Acts

65.—(1) The enactments mentioned in Schedule 1 to this Act shall have effect subject to the amendments there specified (being amendments consequential upon the provisions of this Act).

(2) In section 1(2)(a) of the Rehabilitation of Offenders Act 1974 (failure to pay fines etc. not to prevent person becoming rehabilitated) the reference to a fine or other sum adjudged to be paid by or imposed on a conviction does not include a reference to an amount payable under a confiscation order.

(3) Section 281(4) of the Insolvency Act 1986 (discharge of bankrupt not to release him from liabilities in respect of fines, etc.) shall have effect as if the reference to a fine included a reference to a confiscation order.

(4) Section 55(2) of the Bankruptcy (Scotland) Act 1985 (discharge of debtor not to release him from liabilities in respect of fines etc.) shall have effect as if the reference to a fine included a reference to a confiscation order.

Transitional provisions and savings

66.—(1) The transitional provisions and savings set out in Schedule 2 to this Act shall have effect.

(2) Part I and section 59 of this Act shall not apply—

(a) in relation to any proceedings for, or in respect of, an offence if the person accused (or, as the case may be, convicted) of that offence was charged with the offence (whether by the laying of an information or otherwise) before the date on which this Act comes into force, or

(b) in relation to any proceedings not within paragraph (a) above instituted before that date,

and references in this subsection to proceedings include a reference to any order made by a court in the proceedings.

(3) Accordingly (and without prejudice to section 16 of the Interpretation Act 1978), the relevant enactments and any instrument made under any of those enactments shall continue to apply in relation to any proceedings within subsection (2)(a) or (b) above (and, in particular, in relation to any confiscation order, within the meaning of the Drug Trafficking Offences Act 1986, made in any such proceedings) as if this Act had not been passed.

(4) In subsection (3) above "the relevant enactments" are—

(a) the enactments reproduced in Part I and section 59 of this Act,

(b) any other enactment reproduced by this Act, so far as applicable in relation to any of the enactments reproduced in that Part or that section, and

(c) any enactment amended by this Act,

but do not include any enactment which, immediately before the date on which this Act comes into force, had not come into force.

(5) Subsection (2) above is without prejudice to section 4(7), 7(4), 26(3) or 29(7) of this Act.

(6) Nothing in section 19(3) or (4) of this Act shall apply to any proceedings—

(a) for an offence committed before the commencement of this Act; or

(b) for one or more offences, any one of which was so committed.

Repeals etc.

67.—(1) The enactments mentioned in Schedule 3 to this Act are repealed to the extent specified in the third column of that Schedule.

(2) Paragraph 9 of Schedule 2 to the Criminal Justice (Confiscation) (Northern Ireland) Order 1990 (which amends section 29(1) of the Criminal Justice (International Co-operation) Act 1990) is hereby revoked.

Extent

68.—(1) Subject to the following provisions of this section, this Act extends to England and Wales only.

(2) The following provisions of this Act also extend to Scotland—
 (a) section 11(11);
 (b) sections 32 to 35 and 36(1);
 (c) Part II;
 (d) section 59(10) to (13);
 (e) this section;
 (f) section 69;
 (g) sections 1, 41, 62, 63, 64, 65(1), 66 and 67(1), so far as they relate to provisions which extend to Scotland; and
 (h) Schedule 2.

(3) The following provisions of this Act also extend to Northern Ireland—
 (a) Part II;
 (b) this section;
 (c) section 69;
 (d) sections 63, 64, 65(1), 66 and 67(1), so far as they relate to provisions which extend to Northern Ireland; and
 (e) Schedule 2.

(4) Section 67(2) of this Act extends to Northern Ireland only.

(5) The modifications of other enactments specified in section 65(2) to (4) of this Act, and the amendments specified in Schedule 1 to this Act, have the same extent as the enactments to which they relate.

(6) Subject to subsection (7) below, the repeals contained in Schedule 3 to this Act have the same extent as the provisions to which they relate.

(7) The repeals of—
 (a) sections 14 and 23A of the Criminal Justice (International Co-operation) Act 1990, and
 (b) paragraph 5 of Schedule 4 to the Criminal Justice Act 1993,
extend to England and Wales only.

Short title and commencement

69.—(1) This Act may be cited as the Drug Trafficking Act 1994.

(2) This Act comes into force at the end of the period of three months beginning with the day on which it is passed.

SCHEDULES

Section 65   SCHEDULE 1

CONSEQUENTIAL AMENDMENTS

Land Registration Act 1925 (c. 21)

1. In section 49 of the Land Registration Act 1925 (protection of certain interests etc by notice) in subsection (1)(g), the words "the Drug Trafficking Offences Act 1986 or" shall be

omitted, and after the words "the Criminal Justice Act 1988" there shall be inserted the words "or the Drug Trafficking Act 1994".

Criminal Appeal Act 1968 (c. 19)

2. In section 50 of the Criminal Appeal Act 1968 (meaning of "sentence"), in subsection (1), as amended by paragraph 1 of Schedule 5 to the Criminal Justice Act 1993—
   (a) in paragraph (d), for the words "Drug Trafficking Offences Act 1986" there shall be substituted the words "Drug Trafficking Act 1994"; and
   (b) in paragraph (g), for the words "section 4A of the Act of 1986" there shall be substituted the words "section 19 of the Act of 1994".

Misuse of Drugs Act 1971 (c. 38)

3. In section 21 of the Misuse of Drugs Act 1971 (offences by corporations), after the word "1990" there shall be inserted the words "or section 49 of the Drug Trafficking Act 1994".
4. In section 23 of that Act (power to search and obtain evidence), in subsection (3A)—
   (a) after the word "1990" there shall be inserted the words "or section 49 of the Drug Trafficking Act 1994"; and
   (b) after the words "that Act" there shall be inserted the words "of 1990".
5. In section 27 of that Act (forfeiture of things relating to certain offences), in subsection (1), for the words "section 38(1) of the Drug Trafficking Offences Act 1986" there shall be substituted the words "section 1(3) of the Drug Trafficking Act 1994".

Civil Jurisdiction and Judgments Act 1982 (c. 27)

6. In section 18 of the Civil Jurisdiction and Judgments Act 1982 (enforcement of United Kingdom judgments in other parts of the United Kingdom) the following shall be substituted for subsection (4A)—
   "(4A) This section does not apply as respects—
   (a) the enforcement in Scotland of orders made by the High Court or a county court in England and Wales under or for the purposes of Part VI of the Criminal Justice Act 1988 or the Drug Trafficking Act 1994 (confiscation of the proceeds of certain offences or of drug trafficking); or
   (b) the enforcement in England and Wales of orders made by the Court of Session under or for the purposes of Part I of the Criminal Justice (Scotland) Act 1987 (confiscation of the proceeds of drug trafficking)."

Criminal Justice Act 1982 (c. 48)

7. In Part II of Schedule 1 to the Criminal Justice Act 1982 (persons convicted of offences under certain enactments not eligible for early release), at the end there shall be added—

"DRUG TRAFFICKING ACT 1994

Section 49 (concealing or transferring the proceeds of drug trafficking).
Section 50 (assisting another person to retain the benefit of drug trafficking).
Section 51 (acquisition, possession or use of proceeds of drug trafficking)."

Police and Criminal Evidence Act 1984 (c. 60)

8. In section 65 of the Police and Criminal Evidence Act 1984 (provisions supplementary to Part V), for the words "Drug Trafficking Offences Act 1986", in both places where they occur, there shall be substituted the words "Drug Trafficking Act 1994".
9. In section 116 of that Act (meaning of "serious arrestable offence"), in subsection (2), paragraph (aa) shall be omitted and at the end there shall be added "and
   (c) any of the offences mentioned in paragraphs (a) to (f) of section 1(3) of the Drug Trafficking Act 1994."

Bankruptcy (Scotland) Act 1985 (c. 66)

10.—(1) In section 5 of the Bankruptcy (Scotland) Act 1985 (sequestration of the estate of a living or deceased debtor), in subsection (4), for the words "section 1(8) of the Drug Trafficking

Offences Act 1986" there shall be substituted the words "section 2(9) of the Drug Trafficking Act 1994".

(2) In section 7(1) of that Act (constitution of apparent insolvency)—

(a) in the definition of "charging order", the words "by section 9(2) of the Drug Trafficking Offences Act 1986 or" shall be omitted, and after the word "1988" there shall be inserted the words "or by section 27(2) of the Drug Trafficking Act 1994";

(b) in the definition of "confiscation order", for the words "section 1(8) of the said Act of 1986" there shall be substituted the words "section 2(9) of the said Act of 1994"; and

(c) in the definition of "restraint order", for the words "section 8 of the said Act of 1986" there shall be substituted the words "section 26 of the said Act of 1994".

Drug Trafficking Offences Act 1986 (c. 32)

11. In section 40 of the Drug Trafficking Offences Act 1986 (extent), for subsection (4) there shall be substituted—

"(4) Section 34 of this Act and, so far as it relates to that section, this section, extend also to Scotland."

Criminal Justice (Scotland) Act 1987 (c. 41)

12. In section 3 of the Criminal Justice (Scotland) Act 1987 (assessment of the proceeds of drug trafficking), for paragraph (a) of subsection (4) there shall be substituted—

"(a) section 2 of the Drug Trafficking Act 1994; or".

13. In section 7 of that Act (application of provisions relating to fines to enforcement of confiscation orders), in subsection (2), in the entry relating to section 403 of the Criminal Procedure (Scotland) Act 1975, for the words "Drug Trafficking Offences Act 1986" there shall be substituted the words "Drug Trafficking Act 1994".

14. In section 10 of that Act (seizure of property subject to restraint order), in subsection (1), for the words "Drug Trafficking Offences Act 1986" there shall be substituted the words "Drug Trafficking Act 1994".

15. In section 11 of that Act (inhibition and arrestment of property affected by restraint order or interdict under section 12 of that Act), in subsection (6) (which applies section 11 of that Act, with modifications, to certain orders under section 8 of the Drug Trafficking Offences Act 1986)—

(a) for the words "section 8 of the Drug Trafficking Offences Act 1986" there shall be substituted the words "section 26 of the Drug Trafficking Act 1994";

(b) in paragraph (a)—

(i) for the words "subsection (2) of section 7" there shall be substituted the words "subsection (3) of section 25"; and

(ii) for the words "subsection (3)(b)" there shall be substituted the words "subsection (4)(b)";

(c) in paragraph (b)—

(i) for the words "section 5" there shall be substituted the words "section 6"; and

(ii) for the words "subsection (2) of the said section 7" there shall be substituted the words "subsection (3) of the said section 25";

(d) in the subsection (3A) set out in paragraph (g), for the words "section 13 of the Drug Trafficking Offences Act 1986" there shall be substituted the words "section 31 of the Drug Trafficking Act 1994"; and

(e) in sub-paragraph (ii) of paragraph (h), for the words " "section 8, 11 or 12 of the said Act of 1986" " there shall be substituted the words " "section 26, 29 or 30 of the said Act of 1994" ".

16. In section 23 of that Act (exercise of powers by Court of Session or administrator), in subsection (7)—

(a) for the words "section 13 of the Drug Trafficking Offences Act 1986" there shall be substituted the words "section 31 of the Drug Trafficking Act 1994"; and

(b) for the words "section 13", in the second place where they occur, there shall be substituted the words "section 31".

17. In section 26 of that Act (compensation), in subsection (2)(b), for the words "section 24A of the Drug Trafficking Offences Act 1986", there shall be substituted the words "section 37 of the Drug Trafficking Act 1994".

18.—(1) Section 27 of that Act (recognition and enforcement of orders under the Drug Trafficking Offences Act 1986) shall be amended as set out in this paragraph.

(2) In subsection (2), for the words "section 8, 11 or 12 of the Drug Trafficking Offences Act 1986" there shall be substituted the words "section 26, 29 or 30 of the Drug Trafficking Act 1994".

(3) In subsection (4), for the words "section 11(3)(a) of the said Act of 1986" there shall be substituted the words "section 29(3)(a) of the said Act of 1994".

(4) In subsection (5)—

(a) in paragraph (a), for the words "section 8,11, 12 or 30 of the said Act of 1986" there shall be substituted the words "section 26, 29, 30 or 59 of the said Act of 1994"; and

(b) in paragraph (c), for the words "section 8, 11 or 12" there shall be substituted the words "section 26, 29 or 30".

(5) In subsection (6)—

(a) for the words "section 8 of the said Act of 1986" there shall be substituted the words "section 26 of the said Act of 1994"; and

(b) for the words "section 7(4)" there shall be substituted the words "section 25(5)".

(6) In subsection (8), for the words "section 11(6) of the said Act of 1986" there shall be substituted the words "section 29(6) of the said Act of 1994".

19.—(1) Section 28 of that Act (provisions supplementary to section 27 of that Act) shall be amended as set out in this paragraph.

(2) In subsection (4), for the words "Drug Trafficking Offences Act 1986" there shall be substituted the words "Drug Trafficking Act 1994".

(3) In subsection (5)(b), for the words "section 8, 11 or 12 of the said Act of 1986" there shall be substituted the words "section 26, 29 or 30 of the said Act of 1994".

(4) In subsection (6) for the words "Drug Trafficking Offences Act 1986" there shall be substituted the words "Drug Trafficking Act 1994".

20. In section 35 of that Act (winding up of company holding realisable property), in subsection (4), for the words "section 1 of the Drug Trafficking Offences Act 1986" there shall be substituted the words "section 2 of the Drug Trafficking Act 1994".

Criminal Justice Act 1988 (c. 33)

21. In section 71 of the Criminal Justice Act 1988 (confiscation orders), in subsection (9) (meaning of certain expressions used in Part VI of that Act), in paragraph (b), for the words "Drug Trafficking Offences Act 1986" there shall be substituted the words "Drug Trafficking Act 1994".

22. In section 151 of that Act (Customs and Excise power of arrest), in subsection (5), for the words "section 38(1) of the Drug Trafficking Offences Act 1986 other than an offence under section 24" there shall be substituted the words "section 1(3) of the Drug Trafficking Act 1994 other than an offence under section 50".

Extradition Act 1989 (c. 33)

23. In section 22(4) of the Extradition Act 1989 (offences in relation to which provision applying that Act may be made under that section), in sub-paragraph (i) of paragraph (h), for the words "Drug Trafficking Offences Act 1986; and" there shall be substituted the words "Drug Trafficking Act 1994;".

24. In Schedule 1 to that Act (provisions deriving from the Extradition Act 1870 etc), in paragraph 15 (certain acts deemed to be offences committed within the jurisdiction of foreign state), in sub-paragraph (j), for the words "Drug Trafficking Offences Act 1986;" there shall be substituted the words "Drug Trafficking Act 1994;".

Criminal Justice (International Co-operation) Act 1990 (c. 5)

25. In section 9(6) of the Criminal Justice (International Co-operation) Act 1990 (offences in connection with which power to make provision for the enforcement in the United Kingdom of foreign forfeiture etc orders may be exercised), for the words "section 38(1) of the Drug Trafficking Offences Act 1986" there shall be substituted the words "section 1(3) of the Drug Trafficking Act 1994".

26. In section 13(6) of that Act (purposes for which information obtained pursuant to regulations under that section may be disclosed), for the words "Drug Trafficking Offences Act 1986" there shall be substituted the words "Drug Trafficking Act 1994".

27.—(1) Section 15 of that Act (interest on sums unpaid under confiscation orders) shall be amended as set out in sub-paragraphs (2) to (4) below.

(2) In subsection (1), the words "under section 31(1) of the Powers of Criminal Courts Act 1973 or" shall be omitted.

(3) The following shall be substituted for subsection (2)—

"(2) The sheriff may, on the application of the prosecutor, increase the term of imprisonment or detention fixed in respect of the confiscation order under section 396(2) of the said

Act of 1975 (imprisonment in default of payment) if the effect of subsection (1) above is to increase the maximum period applicable in relation to the order under section 407(1A) of the said Act of 1975."

(4) In subsection (3), the words from "shall be that" to "Scotland" shall be omitted.

28. In section 24 of that Act (interpretation of Part II), in subsection (2), for the words "Drug Trafficking Offences Act 1986" there shall be substituted the words "Drug Trafficking Act 1994".

29. In section 32(4) of that Act (which provides that Her Majesty may by Order in Council direct that that Act shall extend to the Channel Islands, the Isle of Man or any colony), after the words "this Act" there shall be inserted the words "and those provisions of the Drug Trafficking Act 1994 which re-enact provisions of this Act".

Criminal Justice Act 1993 (c. 36)

30.—(1) Section 79 of the Criminal Justice Act 1993 shall be amended as set out in this paragraph.

(2) In subsection (2) (provisions extending to the United Kingdom), the references to section 25 and to paragraph 5 of Schedule 4 shall be omitted.

(3) In subsection (3) (provisions extending to Great Britain only), the words "13(9) to (11)," and "24(2), (3) and (7) to (10)," shall be omitted.

(4) In subsection (5) (provisions extending to Scotland and Northern Ireland only) after the word "34(2)" there shall be inserted the words "and paragraph 5 of Schedule 4".

Section 66   SCHEDULE 2

TRANSITIONAL PROVISIONS ETC

General transitional provisions and savings

1. Anything done or having effect as if done (including the making of subordinate legislation) under or for the purposes of any provision repealed or revoked by this Act has effect as if done under or for the purposes of any corresponding provision of this Act.

2. Any reference (express or implied) in this Act or any other enactment, or in any instrument or document, to a provision of this Act is (so far as the context permits) to be read as being or (according to the context) including in relation to times, circumstances and purposes before the commencement of this Act a reference to the corresponding provision repealed or revoked by this Act.

3. Any reference (express or implied) in any enactment, or in any instrument or document, to a provision repealed or revoked by this Act is (so far as the context permits) to be read as being or (according to the context) including in relation to times, circumstances and purposes after the commencement of this Act a reference to the corresponding provision of this Act.

4. Paragraphs 1 to 3 above—
(a) have effect in place of section 17(2) of the Interpretation Act 1978 (but are without prejudice to any other provision of that Act); and
(b) are subject to section 66(2) to (6) of this Act.

Provision in relation to section 32 of this Act

5. In any case in which a petition in bankruptcy was presented, or a receiving order or adjudication in bankruptcy was made, before 29 December 1986 (the date on which the Insolvency Act 1986 came into force), section 32 of this Act has effect with the following modifications—
(a) for references to the bankrupt's estate for the purposes of Part IX of that Act there are substituted references to the property of the bankrupt for the purposes of the Bankruptcy Act 1914;
(b) for references to the Act of 1986 and sections 280(2)(c), 286, 339 and 423 of that Act there are respectively substituted references to the Act of 1914 and to sections 26(2), 8, 27 and 42 of that Act;
(c) the references in subsection (4) to an interim receiver appointed as there mentioned include, where a receiving order has been made, a reference to the receiver constituted by virtue of section 7 of the Act of 1914; and
(d) subsection (2)(b) is omitted.

Provision in relation to section 34 of this Act

6. In any case in which a winding up of a company commenced, or is treated as having commenced, before 29 December 1986 (the date on which the Insolvency Act 1986 came into force), section 34 of this Act has effect with the substitution for references to the Insolvency Act 1986 of references to the Companies Act 1985.

Provision in relation to Part II of this Act

7. Nothing in sections 43(4), 44 or 45 of this Act shall apply to an order made before the coming into force of this Act under section 26 of the Criminal Justice (International Co-operation) Act 1990.

Provision in relation to section 21(3) of the Criminal Justice Act 1993

8. The repeal by this Act of subsection (2) of section 21 of the Criminal Justice Act 1993 (which substitutes a new subsection for section 24A(6) of the Drug Trafficking Offences Act 1986) shall not affect the operation of paragraphs (c) to (h) of subsection (3) of that section (which provides for the same subsection as is set out in subsection (2) to be substituted for certain other enactments).

Provision in relation to section 26(1) of the Criminal Justice Act 1993

9. The repeal by this Act of subsection (1) of section 26 of the Criminal Justice Act 1993 (which inserts subsections (2A) and (2B) into section 31 of the Drug Trafficking Offences Act 1986 shall not affect the operation of subsection (2) of that section (which provides for the same subsections to be inserted into section 42 of the Criminal Justice (Scotland) Act 1987).

Provision in relation to Schedule 4 to the Criminal Justice Act 1993

10. The repeal by this Act of paragraph 1 of Schedule 4 to the Criminal Justice Act 1993 (which inserts a section 36B into the Drug Trafficking Offences Act 1986) shall not affect the operation of the remaining provisions of that Schedule (which provide for a modified version of that section to be inserted into certain other Acts).

Further transitional provision

11. The Secretary of State may by order made by statutory instrument, in connection with the coming into force of any provision of this Act in so far as it reproduces the effect of any provision of the Criminal Justice Act 1993, make such further transitional provision or savings as he considers appropriate.

Section 67   SCHEDULE 3

REPEALS

Chapter	Short title	Extent of repeal
1925 c. 21.	The Land Registration Act 1925.	In section 49(1)(g), the words "the Drug Trafficking Offences Act 1986 or".
1984 c. 60.	The Police and Criminal Evidence Act 1984.	Section 116(2)(aa).
1985 c. 66.	The Bankruptcy (Scotland) Act 1985.	In section 7(1), in the definition of "charging order", the words "by section 9(2) of the Drug Trafficking Offences Act 1986 or".
1986 c. 32.	The Drug Trafficking Offences Act 1986.	The whole Act, except sections 24(6), 32, 34, and 40(1) and (3) to (5).
1987 c. 41.	The Criminal Justice (Scotland) Act 1987.	Section 31. Section 45(3) and (7).

Chapter	Short title	Extent of repeal
1988 c. 33.	The Criminal Justice Act 1988.	Section 103(1). In Schedule 5, Part I.
1988 c. 50.	The Housing Act 1988.	In Schedule 17, paragraphs 71 and 72.
1990 c. 5.	The Criminal Justice (International Co-operation) Act 1990.	Section 14. In section 15, in subsection (1), the words "under section 31(1) of the Powers of Criminal Courts Act 1973 or", and in subsection (3) the words from "shall be that" to "Scotland". Section 16. Section 23A. Sections 25 to 29. Section 30(2) and (3). Section 31(2). In Schedule 4, paragraph 4.
1993 c. 36.	The Criminal Justice Act 1993.	Sections 7 to 16. Section 18. Section 20(1). Section 21(2) and (3)(a) and (b). Section 22(1). Section 24(1) to (11). Section 25. Section 26(1). Section 78(7). In section 79, in subsection (2), the references to section 25 and to paragraph 5 of Schedule 4; and in subsection (3), the words "13(9) to (11)," and "24(2), (3) and (7) to (10),". In Schedule 4, paragraphs 1 and 5. In Schedule 5, paragraphs 5 and 6.
1994 c. 33.	The Criminal Justice and Public Order Act 1994.	In Schedule 9, paragraph 28.

TABLE OF DERIVATIONS

Notes:

1. This Table shows the derivation of the provisions of the Act.
2. The following abbreviations are used in the table:—

1986 = Drug Trafficking Offences Act 1986 (c. 32)
1987 = Criminal Justice (Scotland) Act 1987 (c. 41)
1988 = Criminal Justice Act 1988 (c. 33)
1990 = Criminal Justice (International Co-operation) Act 1990 (c. 5)
1993 = Criminal Justice Act 1993 (c. 36)

Provision	Derivation
1(1), (2)	1986 s.38(1) "drug trafficking"; 1990 Sch. 4, para. 4(3); 1993 s.24(8)
(3)	1986 s.38(1) "drug trafficking offence"; 1990 Sch. 4, para. 4(4); 1993 s.24(9)
(4)	1986 s.38(1) "corresponding law"
(5)	Drafting
2(1)	1986 s.1(1); 1993 s.7(1)
(2) to (6)	1986 s.1(2) to (6)
(7)	1986 s.1(7); 1988 Sch. 8, para. 2
(8)	1986 s.1(7A); 1993 s.7(2)
(9)	1986 s.38(1) "confiscation order"; 1993 Sch. 5, para. 6 (part)

Provision	Derivation
3(1) to (9)	1986 s.1A(1) to (9); 1993 s.8 (part)
(10)	1986 s.1A(9A); Criminal Justice and Public Order Act 1994 (c.33) Sch. 9, para. 28
(11)	1986 s.1A(10), (11); 1993 s.8 (part)
4(1)	1986 s.2(1); 1990 s.29(1) (part)
(2)	1986 s.2(2); 1993 s.9(2)
(3)	1986 s.2(3); 1993 s.9(4)
(4)	1986 s.2(2A), (2B); 1993 s.9(3)
(5)	1986 s.2(4); 1990 Sch. 4, para. 4(2); 1993 s.16(2)
(6)	1986 s.2(5) (part)
(7)	1986 s.2(5) (part); 1987 s.45(7)(a); drafting
(8)	Drafting
5(1), (2)	1986 s.4(1), (2)
(3)	1986 s.4(3); 1993 s.7(3)
6(1)	1986 s.5(3)
(2)	1986 s.5(1)
(3)	1986 s.5(2); Prevention of Terrorism (Temporary Provisions) Act 1989 (c.4) Sch. 8, para. 7
(4)	1986 s.5(7)
7(1) to (3)	1986 s.5(4) to (6)
(4)	Drafting
8	1986 s.5(9), (10)
9(1), (2)	1986 s.6(1), (2)
(3)	1986 s.6(3); 1988 Sch. 8, para. 2
(4)	1986 s.6(4)
(5)	1986 s.6(7); 1993 s.13(1)
(6)	1986 s.6(6) (part)
10	1990 s.15 (part)
11(1)	1986 s.3(1) (part); 1993 s.10(2) (part)
(2) to (7)	1986 s.3(1A) to (2); 1993 s.10(2) (part)
(8)	1986 s.3(3); 1993 s.10(3), Sch. 5, para. 5
(9)	1986 s.3(4)
(10)	1986 s.3(5); 1993 s.10(4)
(11)	1986 s.3(6)
12(1)	1986 s.3A(1) (part); 1993 s.10(5) (part)
(2) to (7)	1986 s.3A(2) to (7); 1993 s.10(5) (part)
13(1) to (10)	1986 s.5A(1) to (10); 1993 s.12 (part)
(11)	1986 ss.3(1) (part), 3A(1) (part); 1993 s.10(2) (part), (5) (part)
(12)	1986 s.5A(11); 1993 s.12 (part)
14(1) to (6)	1986 s.5B(1) to (6); 1993 s.12 (part)
(7)	1986 s.5B(8); 1993 s.12 (part); drafting
(8)	1986 ss.3(1) (part), 3A(1) (part); 1993 s.10(2) (part), (5) (part)
15(1), (2)	1986 s.5C(1), (2); 1993 s.12 (part)
(3)	1986 ss.3(1) (part), 3A(1) (part); 1993 s.10(2) (part), (5) (part)
(4)	1986 s.5C(4); 1993 s.12 (part)
(5)	1986 s.5C(3); 1993 s.12 (part)
(6) to (14)	1986 s.5C(5) to (13); 1993 s.12 (part)
(15)	1986 s.5C(15); 1993 s.12 (part); drafting
16	1990 s.16
17(1)	1986 s.14(1); 1993 s.11(2)
(2)	1986 s.14(2)

Provision	Derivation
(3)	1986 s.14(3); 1993 s.11(3)
(4)	1986 s.14(4)
(5)	1986 s.14(5); 1993 s.11(4)
18(1)	1986 s.19(1); 1988 Sch. 5, para. 12(b)
(2)	1986 s.19(2); 1987 s.45(7)(d); 1993 s.24(2) (part)
(3)	1986 s.19(2A); 1988 Sch. 5, para. 12(d)
(4), (5)	1986 s.19(3), (4)
19(1) to (5)	1986 s.4A(1) to (5); 1993 s.14(1) (part)
(6)	1986 ss.3(1) (part), 4A(6); 1993 ss.10(2) (part), 14(1) (part)
(7)	1986 s.6(6) (part); 1993 s.14(2); drafting
(8)	1986 s.6(8); 1993 s.14(3)
(9)	1986 s.5B(7); 1993 s.12 (part)
(10)	1986 s.5C(14); 1993 s.12 (part)
20	1986 s.4B; 1993 s.14(1) (part)
21	1986 s.19C(1) to (5), (9); 1993 s.15 (part)
22	1986 s.19A(1) to (3); 1993 s.15 (part)
23	1986 s.19B(1) to (3); 1993 s.15 (part)
24(1)	1986 ss.19A(4), 19B(4), 19C(6); 1993 s.15 (part)
(2)	1986 ss.19A(5), 19B(5), 19C(7); 1993 s.15 (part)
(3)	1986 ss.19A(6), 19B(6), 19C(8); 1993 s.15 (part)
(4)	1986 ss.19A(7), 19B(7); 1993 s.15 (part)
25(1)	1986 s.7(1); 1993 s.13(3)
(2)	1986 s.7(6); 1993 s.13(5) (part)
(3)	1986 s.7(2); 1993 s.13(4)
(4)	1986 s.7(3)
(5)	1986 s.7(4), (5); 1988 Sch. 5, para. 2(b); 1993 s.13(5) (part)
26(1), (2)	1986 s.8(1), (2)
(3)	1986 s.8(3); drafting
(4)	1986 s.8(4)
(5)	1986 s.8(5); 1993 s.13(6)
(6)	1986 s.8(5A); 1988 Sch. 5, para. 3(1)
(7)	1986 s.8(6); 1993 s.24(1)
(8)	1986 s.8(7)
(9)	1986 s.8(8) (part); 1987 s.45(7)(b)(i) (part)
(10)	1986 s.8(8) (part); 1987 s.45(7)(b)(i) (part)
(11)	1986 s.8(9); 1987 s.45(7)(b)(ii)
(12), (13)	1986 s.8(10), (11); 1988 Sch. 5, para. 3(2)
27(1), (2)	1986 s.9(1), (2)
(3)	1986 s.9(3); 1988 Sch. 5, para. 4(1)
(4) to (6)	1986 s.9(4) to (6)
(7)	1986 s.9(7); 1993 s.13(7)
(8)	1986 s.9(8); 1988 Sch. 5, para. 4(2)
(9)	1986 s.10(7)
28	1986 s.10(2) to (6)
29(1)	1986 s.11(1); 1993 s.13(8)
(2) to (6)	1986 s.11(2) to (6)
(7)	1986 s.11(7); drafting
(8)	1986 s.11(8)
30(1)	1986 s.12(1) (part)
(2)	1986 s.12(1) (part); 1988 Sch. 5, para. 6(2); 1993 s.24(2) (part)

Provision	Derivation
(3)	1986 s.12(2); 1993 s.24(2) (part)
(4) to (9)	1986 s.12(3) to (7); 1988 Sch. 5, para. 6(3)
31(1)	1986 s.13(1); 1993 s.24(2) (part)
(2) to (4)	1986 s.13(2) to (4)
(5)	1986 s.13(6)
(6)	1986 s.13(5)
32(1)	1986 s.15(1)
(2)	1986 s.15(2), (3); Housing Act 1988 (c.50) Sch. 17, para. 71; 1993 s.24(2) (part)
(3), (4)	1986 s.15(4), (5)
(5)	1986 s.15(6); 1993 s.13(9)
33(1)	1986 s.16(1)
(2)	1986 s.16(2); 1987 s.45(7)(c)(i); 1988 Sch. 5, para. 8(2); Housing Act 1988 (c. 50) Sch. 17, para. 72; 1993 s.24(2) (part).
(3), (4)	1986 s.16(3), (4)
(5)	1986 s.16(5); 1988 Sch. 5, para. 8(3); Interpretation Act 1978 (c. 30) s.17(2)
(6)	1986 s.16(6); 1993 s.13(10)
(7)	1986 s.16(7)
34(1)	1986 s.17(1)
(2)	1986 s.17(2), (3); 1993 s.24(2) (part)
(3), (4)	1986 s.17(4), (5)
35(1), (2)	1986 s.17A(1); 1988 Sch. 5, para. 10 (part)
(3)	1986 s.17A(2); 1988 Sch. 5, para. 10 (part); 1993 s.24(3)
(4)	1986 s.17A(3); 1988 Sch. 5, para. 10 (part)
36(1)	1986 s.18(1)
(2)	1986 s.18(2); 1993 s.24(4)
37(1) to (5)	1986 s.24A(1) to (5); 1987 s.31 (part)
(6)	1986 s.24A(6); 1987 s.31 (part); 1993 s.21(2)
38(1)	1986 s.25(1); 1988 Sch. 5, para. 14(1); 1993 s.22(1) (part)
(2), (3)	1986 s.25(2), (3)
(4)	1986 s.25(3A); 1993 s.22(1) (part)
(5)	1986 s.25(4); 1993 s.21(3)(a)
39(1) to (4)	1986 s.26(1), (2) (part), (3), (4); 1988 Sch. 5, para. 15 (part)
(5)	1986 s.26(5); 1993 s.21(3)(b)
(6)	Drafting
40(1) to (3)	1986 s.26A; 1988 Sch. 5, para. 15 (part)
(4)	Drafting
41(1)	Drafting
(2)	1986 s.38(11)
(3) to (7)	1986 s.38(12) to (12D); 1993 s.13(11)
(8)	1986 s.38(13); 1988 Sch. 5, para. 16
42(1) to (3)	1990 s.25(1) to (3)
(4)	1990 s.28(1)
(5) to (7)	1990 s.25(4) to (6)
(8)	1990 s.27
43(1) to (3)	1990 s.26(1) to (3)
(4)	1990 s.26(4); 1993 s.25(3)
44	1990 s.26A; 1993 s.25(1) (part)
45	1990 s.26B; 1993 s.25(1) (part)

Provision	Derivation
46(1)	1990 s.28(2); 1993 s.25(4)
(2)	1990 s.28(3)
47(1)	1990 s.30(2)
(2)	1990 s.30(3); 1993 s.25(5)
48(1)	1990 s.29(1) (part)
(2)	1990 s.29(1) (part); Criminal Justice (Confiscation) (Northern Ireland) Order 1990, S.I. 1990/2588 (N.I. 17), Sch. 2, para. 9
(3), (4)	1990 s.29(2), (3)
49(1), (2)	1990 s.14(1), (2) (part)
(3)	1990 s.14(4) (part)
50(1), (2)	1986 s.24(1), (2)
(3)	1986 s.24(3); 1993 s.18(2)
(4)	1986 s.24(4)
(5)	1986 s.24(4A); 1993 s.18(3)
51	1986 s.23A(1) to (8), (10); 1993 s.16(1) (part)
52(1) to (6)	1986 s.26B(1) to (6); 1993 s.18(1) (part)
(7)	1986 s.26B(7), (8); 1993 s.18(1) (part)
(8), (9)	1986 s.26B(9), (10); 1993 s.18(1) (part)
53(1) to (6)	1986 s.26C(1) to (6); 1993 s.18(1) (part)
(7)	1986 s.26C(9); 1993 s.18(1) (part)
(8)	1986 s.26C(7); 1993 s.18(1) (part)
54(1)	1986 ss.23A(9), 24(5); 1990 s.14(6); 1993 s.16(1) (part)
(2)	1986 ss.26B(11), 26C(8); 1993 s.18(1) (part)
55(1) to (5)	1986 s.27(1) to (5)
(6)	1986 s.27(10); 1993 s.24(5) (part)
(7), (8)	1986 s.27(6), (7)
(9)	1986 s.27(8); 1993 s.24(5) (part)
(10)	1986 ss.27(9), 38(1) "authorised government department"
56	1986 s.28
57	1986 s.29
58(1), (2)	1986 s.31(1), (2)
(3), (4)	1986 s.31(2A), (2B); 1993 s.26(1)
(5)	1986 s.31(3)
59(1) to (12)	1986 s.30
(13)	1986 s.38(1) "authorised government department"
60	1986 s.36A; 1993 s.20(1)
61	1986 s.36B; 1990 s.23A (part); 1993 Sch. 4, paras. 1, 5 (part)
62(1)	1986 s.38(1) "property"
(2)	1986 s.38(3)
(3)	1986 s.38(1) "interest"
(4)	1986 s.38(8), (9)
(5)	1986 s.38(7), (10)
63(1)	"constable": 1986 s.38(1) "constable". "defendant": 1986 s.38(1) "defendant"; 1993 Sch. 5, para. 6 (part). "modifications": 1986 s.26(2) "modifications"; 1988 Sch. 5, para. 15 (part)
(2)	1986 s.38(5)
(3)	1986 s.38(4) (part); drafting
64	1986 s.38(2); drafting
65(1)	Drafting
(2)	1986 s.39(3)
(3), (4)	1986 s.39(5), (6)
66 to 69	Drafting

TABLE OF DESTINATIONS

INTERPRETATION ACT 1978
c.30

1978	**1994**
s.17(2).	s.33(5)

DRUG TRAFFICKING OFFENCES ACT 1986
c.32

1986	**1994**	**1986**	**1994**	**1986**	**1994**
s.1(1).	s.2(1)	s.8(2).	26(2)	s.19(2A).	18(3)
(2)–(6).	2(2)–(6)	(3).	26(3)	(3), (4). . . .	18(4), (5)
(7).	2(7)	(4).	26(4)	19A(1)–(3). . .	22
(7A).	2(8)	(5).	26(5)	(4).	24(1)
1A(1)–(9). . .	3(1)–(9)	(5A).	26(6)	(5).	24(2)
(9A).	3(10)	(6).	26(7)	(6).	24(3)
(10), (11).	3(11)	(7).	26(8)	(7).	24(4)
2(1).	4(1)	(8) (part). . .	26(9), (10)	19B(1)–(3) . .	23
(2).	4(2)	(9).	26(11)	(4).	24(1)
(2A).	4(4)	(10).	26(12)	(5).	24(2)
(3).	4(3)	(11).	26(13)	(6).	24(3)
(4).	4(5)	9(1), (2). . . .	27(1), (2)	(7).	24(4)
(5) (part). . .	4(6), (7)	(3).	27(3)	19C(1)–(5) . .	21
3(1) (part). . .	11(1), 13(1),	(4)–(6). . . .	27(4)–(6)	(6).	24(1)
	14(8), 15(3),	(7).	27(7)	(7).	24(2)
	19(6)	(8).	27(8)	(8).	24(3)
(1A)–(2). . .	11(2)–(7)	10(2), (3). . . .	28	(9).	21
(3).	11(8)	(4).	11(10), 28	23A(1)–(8). .	51
(4).	11(9)	(5), (6). . . .	28	(9).	54(1)
(6).	11(11)	(7).	27(9)	(10). . . .	51
3A(1) (part).	12(1), 13(1),	11(1).	29(1)	24(1), (2). . . .	50(1), (2)
	14(8), 15(3)	(2)–(6). . . .	29(2)–(6)	(3).	50(3)
(2)–(7). . .	12(2)–(7)	(7).	29(7)	(4).	50(4)
4(1).	5(1)	(8).	29(8)	(4A).	50(5)
(2).	5(2)	12(1) (part) .	30(1), (2)	(5).	54(1)
(3).	5(3)	(2).	30(3)	24A(1)–(5). .	37(1)–(5)
4A(1)–(5). . .	19(1)–(5)	(3)–(7). . .	30(4)–(9)	(6).	37(6)
(6).	19(6)	13(1).	31(1)	25(1).	38(1)
4B.	20	(2)–(4). . .	31(2)–(4)	(2), (3). . . .	38(2), (3)
5(1).	6(2)	(5).	31(6)	(3A).	38(4)
(2).	6(3)	(6).	31(5)	(4).	38(5)
(3).	6(1)	(7).	27(7)	26(1).	39(1)
(4)–(6). . . .	7(1)–(3)	14(1).	17(1)	(2) (part) .	39(2)
(7).	6(4)	(2).	17(2)	(2).	63(1)
(9).	8	(3).	17(3)	(3).	39(3)
(10).	8	(4).	17(4)	(4).	39(4)
5A(1)–(10). .	13(1)–(10)	(5).	17(5)	(5).	39(5)
(11).	13(12)	15(1).	32(1)	26A	40(1)–(3)
5B(1)–(6). . .	14(1)–(6)	(2).	32(2)	26B(1)–(6) . .	52(1)–(6)
(7).	19(9)	(3).	32(2)	(7), (8) . .	52(7)
(8).	14(7)	(4), (5). . . .	32(3), (4)	(9), (10). .	52(8), (9)
5C(1), (2) . . .	15(1), (2)	(6).	32(5)	(11).	54(2)
(3).	15(4), (5)	16(1).	33(1)	26C(1)–(6) . .	53(1)–(6)
(4).	15(4)	(2).	33(2)	(7).	53(8)
(5)–(13) . .	15(6)–(14)	(3), (4). . . .	33(3), (4)	(8).	54(2)
(14).	19(10)	(5).	33(5)	(9).	53(7)
(15).	15(15)	(6).	33(6)	27(1)–(5). . . .	55(1)–(5)
6(1).	9(1)	(7).	33(7)	(6), (7). . . .	55(7), (8)
(2).	9(2)	17(1).	34(1)	(8).	55(9)
(3).	9(3)	(2).	34(2)	(9).	55(10)
(4).	9(4)	(3).	34(2)	(10)	55(6)
(6) (part). . .	9(6), 19(7)	(4), (5). . . .	34(3), (4)	28	56
(7).	9(5)	17A(1).	35(1), (2)	29	57
7(1).	25(1)	(2).	35(3)	30	59(1)–(2)
(2).	25(3)	(3).	35(4)	31(1), (2). . . .	58(1), (2)
(3).	25(4)	18(1).	36(1)	(2A), (2B)	58(3), (4)
(4).	25(5)	(2).	36(2)	(3).	58(5)
(5).	25(5)	19(1).	18(1)	36A	60
(6).	25(2)	(2).	18(2)	36B.	61
8(1).	26(1)				

TABLE OF DESTINATIONS

1986	1994	1986	1994	1986	1994
s.38(1)........	1(1)–(4), 2(9), 55(10), 59(13), 62(1), 62(3), 63(1)	s.38(4) (part) .	63(3)	s.38(11)	41(2)
		(5)........	63(2)	(12)–(12D)	41(3)–(7)
		(7)........	62(5)	(13)	41(8)
		(8)........	62(4)	39(3)........	65(2)
(2)........	64	(9)........	62(4)	(5), (6)....	65(3), (4)
(3)........	62(2)	(10)	62(5)		

CRIMINAL JUSTICE (SCOTLAND) ACT 1987
c.41

1987	1994
s.31 (part)	s.37(1)–(5), (6)
45(7)(a).....	4(7)
(b)(i) (part)	26(9), (10)
(ii)..	26(11)
(c)(i)...	33(2)
(d).....	18(2)

HOUSING ACT 1988
c.50

1988	1994
Sched. 17,	
para. 71	s.32(2)
para. 72	33(2)

CRIMINAL JUSTICE ACT 1988
c.33

1988	1994	1988	1994	1988	1994
Sched. 5,		Sched. 5—cont.		Sched. 5—cont.	
para. 2(b) ..	s.25(5)	para. 8(3)...	33(5)	para. 15	
para. 3(1)...	26(6)	para. 10		(part)....	39(1)–(4), 40(1)–(3), 63(1)
para. 3(2)...	26(12), (13)	(part)....	35(1), (2), (3), (4)		
para. 4(1)...	27(3)				
para. 4(2)...	27(8)	para. 12(b) .	18(1)	para. 16	41(8)
para. 6(2)...	30(2)	para. 12(d) .	18(3)	Sched. 8,	
para. 6(3)...	30(4)–(9)	para. 14(1) .	38(1)	para. 2	2(7), 9(3)
para. 8(2)...	33(2)				

PREVENTION OF TERRORISM (TEMPORARY PROVISIONS) ACT 1989
c.4

1989	1994
Sched. 8,	
para. 7	s.6(3)

CRIMINAL JUSTICE (INTERNATIONAL CO-OPERATION) ACT 1990
c.5

1990	1994	1990	1994	1990	1994
s.14(1), (2)		s.25(6)........	42(7)	s.29(1) (part) .	4(1), 48(1), 48(2)
(part)......	s.49(1), (2)	26(1)–(3)....	43(1)–(3)		
(4) (part) .	49(3)	(4)........	43(4)	(2), (3)....	48(3), (4)
(6)........	54(1)	26A	44	30(2)........	47(1)
15 (part)	10	26B	45	(3)........	47(2)
16	16	27	42(8)	Sched. 4,	
23A (part) ..	61	28(1)........	42(4)	para. 4(2)...	4(5)
25(1)–(3)....	42(1)–(3)	(2)........	46(1)	para. 4(3)...	1(1), (2)
(4)........	42(5)	(3)........	46(2)	para. 4(4)...	1(3)
(5)........	42(6), 47(2)				

37–104

TABLE OF DESTINATIONS

CRIMINAL JUSTICE ACT 1993
c.36

1993	1994	1993	1994	1993	1994
s.7(1)........	s.2(1)	s.13(3).......	25(1)	s.21(3)(a).....	38(5)
(2).........	2(8)	(4).......	25(3)	(b).....	39(5)
(3).........	5(3)	(5) (part) .	25(2), (5)	22(1) (part) .	38(1), (4)
8 (part)	3(1)–(9), (11)	(6).......	26(5)	24(1)........	26(7)
9(2).........	4(2)	(8).......	29(1)	(2) (part) .	18(2), 30(2),
(3).........	4(4)	(9).......	32(5)		(3), 31(1),
(4).........	4(3)	(10)	33(6)		32(2), 33(2),
10(2) (part) .	11(1), 11(2)–	(11)	41(3)–(7)		34(2)
	(7), 13(11),	14(1) (part) .	19(1)–(5), (6),	(3)........	35(3)
	14(8), 15(8)		20	(4)........	36(2)
(3).......	11(8)	(2).......	19(7)	(5) (part) .	55(6), (9)
(5) (part) .	12(1), (2)–(7),	15 (part)	21, 22, 23,	(8)........	1(1), (2)
	13(11), 14(8),		24(1), (2), (3),	(9)........	1(3)
	15(3)		(4)	25(1) (part) .	44, 45
11(2)........	17(1)	16(1) (part) .	51, 54(1)	(3)........	43(4)
(3)........	17(3)	(2).......	4(5)	(4)........	46(1)
(4)........	17(5)	18(1) (part) .	52(1)–(6), (7),	26(1)........	58(3), (4)
12 (part)	13(1)–(10),		(8), (9), 53(1)–	Sched. 4,	
	(12), 14(1)–		(6), (7), (8),	paras. 1, 5	
	(6), (7), 15(1),		54(2)	(part)....	61
	(2), (4), (5),	(2).......	50(3)	Sched. 5,	
	(6)–(14), (15),	(3).......	50(5)	para. 5	11(8)
	19(9), (10)	21(2).......	37(6)	para. 6	
13(1)........	9(5)			(part)....	2(9), 63(1)

CRIMINAL JUSTICE AND PUBLIC ORDER ACT 1994
c.33

1994	1994
Sched. 9,	
para. 28	s.3(10)

CRIMINAL JUSTICE (CONFISCATION) (NORTHERN IRELAND) ORDER 1990
(S.I. No. 2588) (N.I. 17)

1990	1994
Sched. 2,	
para. 9	s.48(2)

INDEX

References are to sections and Schedules

ABSCONDED DEFENDANT, *see* CONFISCATION
  ORDERS

BENEFITING FROM DRUG TRAFFICKING,
  determination of, 2(2)–(4)
  re-assessment of whether defendant has
    benefited, 14

COMMENCEMENT, 69(2)
COMPENSATION, 18
CONFISCATION ORDERS,
  "amount that might be realised", 6
  amount to be recovered, 5
  assessing proceeds of trafficking, 4
  charging orders,
    application for, 27(2)
    powers of court, 25
    property charged, 27
    registration under Land Charges Acts, 28
  court's powers, 2
  defendant absconded or dead,
    powers of court to make order, 19
      compensation where absconder
        acquitted, 22–24
      conviction, effect of, 20
      return of absconder, 23
      variation, 21
  enforcement of those made outside
    England and Wales,
    external orders,
      enforcement of, 39
      registration of, 40
    Northern Ireland orders, 38
    Scottish orders, 37
  fines, application of procedure for enforc-
    ing, 9
  further proceedings in connection with,
    compensation, 18
    inadequacy of realisable property, 17
    re-assessment of whether defendant has
      benefited, 14
    reconsideration of case, 13
    revised assessment of proceeds, 15
  gifts caught by this Act, 8
  insolvency of defendants,
    court's powers, 32
    protection of insolvency officers, 35
    receivers,
      actions of, 36(1)
      remuneration and expenses, 36(2)
    sequestration in Scotland, 33
    winding up of company holding realis-
      able property, 34
  interest on sums unpaid under, 10

CONFISCATION ORDERS—*cont.*
  interpretation, 41
  modifications of other Acts, 65(2)–(4)
  postponed determinations, 3
  realisation of property,
    application of proceeds, 30
    exercise of powers, 31
    powers of court, 29
    "property" defined, 62
    "realisable property" defined, 6
  restraint orders,
    effect of, 26
    powers of court, 25
  statements in connection with,
    information by defendant, provision of,
      12
    relating to drug trafficking, 11
  value of property, 7
CONSEQUENTIAL AMENDMENTS, 65, Sched. 1
CROWN SERVANTS, 61

DEAD DEFENDANT, *see* CONFISCATION ORDERS
DRUG TRAFFICKING,
  meaning of term, 1(1)–(2)
  offences, 1; *see also* OFFENCES

EXTENT, 68

INFORMATION, *see* INVESTIGATIONS INTO DRUG
  TRAFFICKING; OFFENCES
INSOLVENCY, *see* CONFISCATION ORDERS
INTERPRETATION,
  general, 63
  index of defined expressions, 64
  "property" and related expressions, 62
INVESTIGATIONS INTO DRUG TRAFFICKING,
  authority for search, 56
  information held by government depart-
    ments: disclosure, 59
  order to make information available, 55
  under PACE 1984, 57
  prejudicing: offence, 58
  seized material, 57(b)

MONEY IMPORTED OR EXPORTED IN CASH,
  forfeiture,
    appeals against,
      magistrates' court orders, 44
      sheriff's orders, 45
    orders for, 43
    receipts, 47
    rules of court, 46
  interpretation, 48
  seizure and detention, 42

MONEY LAUNDERING, 52

OFFENCES,
    under existing law, 1(3)
    prosecution of,
        Commissioners of Customs and Excise,
            order of, 60
        Crown servants, 61
    under this Act,
        acquisition, possession or use of pro-
            ceeds, 51
        assisting another to retain benefit, 50
        concealing or transferring proceeds, 49
        failure to disclose knowledge or sus-
            picion of money laundering, 52
        penalties, 54
        prejudicing investigation, 58
        tipping-off, 53

PROCEEDS OF TRAFFICKING,
    assessment, 4
    offences, *see* OFFENCES
    revised assessment, 15
PROSECUTION OF OFFENCES, *see* OFFENCES

REPEALS, 67, Sched. 3

SAVINGS, 66(2)–(5)
SHORT TITLE, 69(1)

TIPPING-OFF, 53
TRANSITIONAL PROVISIONS, 66(1), Sched. 2

EUROPEAN UNION (ACCESSIONS) ACT 1994

(1994 c. 38)

An Act to amend the definition of "the Treaties" and "the Community Treaties" in section 1(2) of the European Communities Act 1972 so as to include the treaty concerning the accession of the Kingdom of Norway, the Republic of Austria, the Republic of Finland and the Kingdom of Sweden to the European Union; and to approve that treaty for the purposes of section 6 of the European Parliamentary Elections Act 1978.

[3rd November 1994]

PARLIAMENTARY DEBATES
Hansard, H.C. Vol. 246, cols. 658, 1044; H.L. Vol. 557, col. 521; Vol. 558, cols. 408, 771.

INTRODUCTION
This Act makes amendments to s.1(2) of the European Communities Act 1972 (c. 68), extending the definitions of "the treaties" and "the Community treaties" and approves the treaty concerning the accession of the Kingdom of Norway, the Republic of Austria, the Republic of Finland and the Kingdom of Sweden to the European Union for certain purposes.

Extended meaning of "the Treaties" and "the Community Treaties"

1. In section 1(2) of the European Communities Act 1972, in the definition of "the Treaties" and "the Community Treaties", after paragraph (m) there shall be inserted the words "and

    (n) the treaty concerning the accession of the Kingdom of Norway, the Republic of Austria, the Republic of Finland and the Kingdom of Sweden to the European Union, signed at Corfu on 24th June 1994;".

Powers of European Parliament

2. For the purposes of section 6 of the European Parliamentary Elections Act 1978 the treaty concerning the accession of the Kingdom of Norway, the Republic of Austria, the Republic of Finland and the Kingdom of Sweden to the European Union, signed at Corfu on 24th June 1994, is approved.

Short title

3. This Act may be cited as the European Union (Accessions) Act 1994.

INDEX

References are to sections

AUSTRIA, 1, 2

COMMUNITY TREATIES,
  extended meaning, 1

EUROPEAN PARLIAMENT,
  powers, 2

FINLAND, 1, 2

NORWAY, 1, 2

PARLIAMENTARY ELECTIONS, 2

SHORT TITLE, 3
SWEDEN, 1, 2

TREATIES,
  extended meaning, 1

LOCAL GOVERNMENT ETC. (SCOTLAND) ACT 1994*

(1994 c. 39)

ARRANGEMENT OF SECTIONS

PART I

LOCAL GOVERNMENT REORGANISATION

CHAPTER 1

LOCAL GOVERNMENT AREAS, AUTHORITIES AND ELECTIONS

SECT.
1. Local government areas in Scotland.
2. Constitution of councils.
3. Orkney, Shetland and Western Isles.
4. Convener and depute convener.
5. Elections and term of office of councillors.
6. Date of elections.
7. Establishment of new local authorities and supplementary provisions.

CHAPTER 2

STAFF

8. Transfer of employees.
9. Effect of section 8 on contracts of employment.
10. Continuity of employment.
11. Remuneration of employees of local authorities.
12. Staff commission.
13. Compensation for loss of office or diminution of emoluments.
14. Employment by new authorities.

CHAPTER 3

PROPERTY

15. Transfer of property.
16. Property held on trust.
17. Educational endowments.
18. Residuary bodies.
19. Property commission.

CHAPTER 4

GENERAL

20. Joint committees and joint boards.
21. Application of section 211 of the 1973 Act to joint boards.
22. Community councils.
23. Duty to prepare decentralisation schemes.

CHAPTER 5

FINANCE

Transitional provisions

24. Transitional provisions: finance.
25. Financing of new authorities prior to 1st April 1996.

Valuation and rating

26. Valuation lists.
27. Valuation areas and authorities and appointment of assessors etc.

*Annotations by CMG Himsworth, Faculty of Law, University of Edinburgh.

28. Valuation rolls.
29. Valuation appeal panels and committees.
30. Rating authorities.

CHAPTER 6

FUNCTIONS

Education

31. Education.
32. Co-operation between education authorities.

Planning

33. Structure plans.

Police

34. Reorganisation of police areas.
35. Amalgamation schemes.

Fire services

36. Fire services.

Rivers

37. River purification boards.

Roads

38. Roads.
39. Roads authority for boundary bridges.

Public transport

40. Establishment etc. of Strathclyde Passenger Transport Authority.
41. Amendment of section 13 of Transport Act 1968.

Traffic

42. Power to secure management of traffic control system.
43. Guidance as to exercise of traffic powers.
44. Restriction on order-making powers of existing authorities.

Social work

45. Chief social work officer.

CHAPTER 7

MISCELLANEOUS

46. Licensing boards.
47. Proceedings in district courts: transitional provisions.

48. Amendment of District Courts (Scotland) Act 1975.
49. Justices of the peace.
50. Stipendiary magistrates.
51. Registration of births, deaths and marriages.
52. Tweed Fisheries Commissioners.
53. Records held by local authorities.
54. Use, acquisition and disposal of records.
55. Restriction on disposal of assets and entering into contracts by existing authorities.
56. Duty of existing authorities and assessors to provide information to new authorities.
57. Power and duty of existing local authorities to assist new authorities.
58. Further provision as to discharge of functions by authorities.
59. Local Acts and instruments.
60. Applications to sheriff in cases of difficulty.
61. Interpretation of Part I.

PART II

WATER AND SEWERAGE REORGANISATION

New water and sewerage authorities

62. New water and sewerage authorities.
63. Alteration of water areas and sewerage areas.
64. Maps of areas.
65. General duties of Secretary of State and of new authorities.
66. Codes of practice for new water and sewerage authorities.

Protection of customers' interests etc.

67. Scottish Water and Sewerage Customers Council.
68. Functions of Customers Council.
69. Power of Customers Council to require information.
70. Annual reports by, and information from, Customers Council.
71. Funding of Customers Council.
72. References to Monopolies and Mergers Commission.

Environmental protection

73. Duty of new authorities as respects Natural Heritage Area or area of special interest.

Charges

74. Charges for services provided.
75. Maximum charges for services provided with help of new authority.
76. Charges schemes.
77. Publication of summary of charges scheme.
78. Liability of occupiers etc. for charges.
79. Collection of charges by local authority.
80. Power to demand and recover charges not to affect duty to maintain domestic water supply etc.
81. Reduced charges.
82. Arrears of charges: restrictions on voting.

Finances of new authorities

83. Duties and powers relating to finance.
84. Financing and borrowing.
85. Guarantees.
86. Directions as to payment and investment.
87. Accounts.
88. Audit of accounts.

Subsidiary powers of new authorities

89. Subsidiary powers of new authorities.

Dissolution of Central Scotland Water Development Board

90. Dissolution of Central Scotland Water Development Board.

Transfer of property, rights and liabilities to new authorities

91. Transfer of property, rights and liabilities to new authorities.
92. Transfer schemes: general.

93. Preparations for transfer of functions etc. to new authorities.
94. Power to require provision of information and assistance as respects transfer schemes.
95. Supplementary provision as to transfer schemes.
96. Transfer schemes: exemption from stamp duty and stamp duty reserve tax.

Transfer etc. of staff

97. Staff: application of Chapter 2 of Part I etc.

Land transactions

98. Acquisition of land by agreement.
99. Compulsory acquisition of land.
100. Disposal of land.

Amendment of Sewerage (Scotland) Act 1968

101. Authorisation of construction of certain private sewers etc.
102. Emptying of septic tanks.
103. Register as respects trade effluents.
104. Disapplication of restrictions on disclosure of information.

Further amendment of Water (Scotland) Act 1980

105. Restriction on references to Secretary of State of questions regarding water supply.
106. Removal of restriction on supply of water to premises outwith water authority's limits of supply.
107. Supply of water for use outwith Scotland.
108. Further provision as regards removal of restrictions on supply of water outwith limits of supply.
109. Right of objection to proposed laying of mains.
110. Vesting of certain supply pipes.
111. Duty of water authority to keep map showing water mains etc.
112. Simplification of provisions as respects opting for water supply by meter.
113. Actings of Secretary of State on default of water authority.
114. Publication and provision of information as respects quality of private supplies of water.
115. Regulations as to certain procedures.

Miscellaneous provisions as respects new authorities

116. Power of Secretary of State to give directions to new authorities.
117. Directions in the interests of national security.
118. Provision of information, etc.
119. Records held by new authorities.
120. Duty of new authorities to collaborate.
121. Power of new authorities to promote or oppose private legislation.
122. Supply of goods and services to new authorities by local authorities.
123. Power to require local authorities and assessors to supply information to new authorities.

Other miscellaneous provisions

124. Cancellation of obligation to contribute towards certain expenses incurred as respects sewerage, or disposal of sewage, in rural localities.

General

125. Interpretation of Part II.
126. Orders under Part II.

PART III

THE PRINCIPAL REPORTER AND THE SCOTTISH CHILDREN'S REPORTER ADMINISTRATION

The Principal Reporter

127. The Principal Reporter.

The Scottish Children's Reporter Administration

128. The Scottish Children's Reporter Administration.
129. Appeal against dismissal of Principal Reporter and other officers.

Additional functions of the Principal Reporter

130. Annual report of Principal Reporter.
131. Delegation of Principal Reporter's functions.

Functions of the Administration

132. Duty of Administration to provide accommodation etc. for children's hearings.
133. Ancillary powers of Administration.
134. Directions by the Secretary of State.

Finance of the Administration

135. Government grants to the Administration.

Reports, accounts etc. of the Administration

136. Reports, accounts etc. of the Administration.

General and supplemental

137. Staff: application of Chapter 2 of Part I.
138. Property etc.: application of Chapter 3 of Part I.

PART IV

MISCELLANEOUS

Social work

139. Report by local authority for purpose of investigation preliminary to children's hearing.

Voluntary organisations

140. Power of local authorities to provide assistance to voluntary organisations.

Byelaws

141. Byelaws under section 121 of Civic Government (Scotland) Act 1982.

Polling districts

142. Organisation of polling districts.

Education

143. Self-governing schools: certain proposals under Education (Scotland) Act 1980.
144. Denominational schools: proposals under section 22D of Education (Scotland) Act 1980.
145. Provision of school transport and other facilities.

Roads

146. Definition of "road".
147. Provisions consequential on making of special road order.
148. Toll orders.
149. Road works register.
150. Traffic signs.

Valuation and rating

151. Exclusion from valuation roll of shootings, deer forests, fishings and fish counters.
152. Amendment of definition of "lands and heritages".
153. Power of Secretary of State to prescribe amount of non-domestic rate.
154. Rating of unoccupied lands and heritages.
155. Rating of lands and heritages partly unoccupied for a short time.
156. Remission of rates on account of hardship.
157. Certain orders relating to valuation not to be treated as hybrid.
158. Grants in respect of certain rate rebates.
159. Rating of enterprise zone.
160. Further provision as to valuation by formula.
161. Power of Secretary of State to combine and divide lands and heritages.
162. Abolition of Scottish Valuation Advisory Council.

Amendment of Transport Act 1968

163. Guarantees by Strathclyde Passenger Transport Authority.

Finance

164. Calculation of limits on spending.

165. Powers of authorities to borrow and lend money.
166. Grants in relation to ethnic minorities.
167. Special grants.
168. Direct Labour Organisation/Direct Services Organisation Accounts.
169. Statements of support services costs.

Resources

170. Effective use of resources.

Economic development

171. Functions to include promotion of economic development.

Tourism

172. Duty of Secretary of State to establish area tourist boards.
173. Power of Secretary of State to amend and revoke schemes.
174. Power of local authority to submit amending schemes to Secretary of State.
175. Provision of assistance to boards by old authorities.
176. Powers to carry on tourism-related activities.

PART V

GENERAL AND SUPPLEMENTARY

General

177. Parliamentary disqualification.
178. Financial provisions.
179. Savings.

Supplementary

180. Minor and consequential amendments and repeals.
181. Consequential and supplementary provisions.
182. Further transitional provisions.
183. Interpretation and amendment of statutory references.
184. Short title, commencement and extent.

SCHEDULES:
    Schedule 1—New local government areas.
        Part I—New areas.
        Part II—Provisions as to boundaries.
    Schedule 2—Establishment of new local authorities.
    Schedule 3—Residuary bodies.
    Schedule 4—Amendments of the 1972 Act.
    Schedule 5—Strathclyde Passenger Transport Authority.
        Part I—The Authority.
        Part II—Matters which may be dealt with by order under section 40.
    Schedule 6—Entry relating to new Scottish local authority to be inserted in Schedule 1 to the Tweed Fisheries Act 1969.
    Schedule 7—Constitution and proceedings etc. of a new water and sewerage authority.
    Schedule 8—Water and sewerage areas.
    Schedule 9—Constitution and proceedings etc. of the Scottish Water and Sewerage Customers Council.
    Schedule 10—Recovery by diligence of charges payable to a collecting authority by virtue of section 79.
    Schedule 11—Water and sewerage transfer schemes.
    Schedule 12—Status, constitution and proceedings of the Scottish Children's Reporter Administration.
    Schedule 13—Minor and consequential amendments.
    Schedule 14—Repeals.

An Act to make provision with respect to local government and the functions of local authorities; to make amendments in relation to local government finance, local authority accounts and the records of local authorities; to establish a Strathclyde Passenger Transport Authority for the purposes of the Transport Act 1968; to provide for the establishment of new water and sewerage authorities; to provide for the establishment of a council to represent the interests of customers and potential customers of those new authorities; to provide for the vesting in those new authorities of the property, rights and liabilities of the Central Scotland Water Development Board and of such property, rights and liabilities of regional and islands councils as those councils have as water authorities, as providers of sewerage and in relation to dealing with the contents of sewers; to provide for the dissolution of that Board; to cancel certain obligations to contribute towards expenses which have been incurred by local authorities in making provision for sewerage or disposal of sewage in rural localities; to create an office of Principal Reporter and transfer to him the functions of reporters to children's hearings; to establish a body to facilitate the performance by the Principal Reporter of his functions; to amend the Social Work (Scotland) Act 1968 in relation to children's hearings; to amend the procedure for making byelaws under section 121 of the Civic Government (Scotland) Act 1982; to transfer to local authorities responsibility for fixing and reviewing polling districts and polling places in Parliamentary elections; to amend section 21 of the Self-Governing Schools etc. (Scotland) Act 1989; to amend the law relating to roads and the placing of traffic signs on roads; to make amendments in relation to valuation and rating; to abolish the Scottish Valuation Advisory Council; to empower the Strathclyde Passenger Transport Authority to guarantee certain obligations; to empower local authorities to make grants to ethnic minorities; to confer on local authorities the function of promoting economic development; to provide for the establishment of area tourist boards; to make amendments in relation to lieutenancies; all as respects Scotland; and for connected purposes.   [3rd November 1994]

PARLIAMENTARY DEBATES
Hansard, H.C. Vol. 235, cols. 533, 641; Vol. 243, cols. 691, 819; Vol. 244, col. 212; Vol. 248, cols. 1416, 1469; H.L. Vol. 555, cols. 1324, 1588; Vol. 556, cols. 657, 1820, 1845, 1895, 1935, 1972, 1996, 2044; Vol. 557, cols. 397, 418, 593, 901; Vol. 558, cols. 211, 643.
    The Bill was discussed in Scottish Standing Committee between February 1 and April 21, 1994.

INTRODUCTION AND GENERAL NOTE
    Although the main purpose of this Act is to make provision for the reorganisation of local government in Scotland with effect from April 1996, it is also the vehicle for a number of other administrative changes. The "etc." of the Act's short title is an abbreviation of nearly a page taken up by the long title (described in debate as longer than many whole Acts – *Hansard*, H.L. Vol. 555, col. 1365) in cataloguing the contents of the Act.
    Local government reorganisation itself is dealt with in Pt. I of the Act – the new areas and authorities (Chap. 1); staff (Chap. 2); property (Chap. 3); general provisions (Chap. 4); finance (including changes affecting valuation and rating) (Chap. 5); provisions affecting specific functions (Chap. 6); miscellaneous (Chap. 7). Schedules 1–6 to the Act make supplementary provision in these areas.
    Part II of the Act makes provision for the major reorganisation of water and sewerage services in Scotland – also due to take effect in April 1996. The three new authorities and a Customers Council are created and related provision is made. See also Scheds. 7–11.
    Part III of the Act (and Sched. 12) makes provision for the new office of Principal Reporter (to exercise powers under the Social Work (Scotland) Act 1968 (c. 49) and the Criminal Procedure (Scotland) Act 1975 (c. 21)) to head the Scottish Children's Reporter Administration. Part IV of the Act contains a number of further miscellaneous provisions, and Pt. V with Scheds. 13 and 14 (amendments and repeals) contains general and supplementary sections.

COMMENCEMENT

As provided by s.184(2), with the exception of s.163 (Guarantees by Strathclyde Passenger Transport Authority), the Act is to come into force on days appointed by the Secretary of State. A first commencement order (Local Government etc. (Scotland) Act 1994 (Commencement No. 1) Order 1994 (S.I. 1994 No. 2850) (C. 63)) brought into force, with effect from November 8, 1994, ss.1, 5, 7, 12, 57, 61, 97(6), 125, 137(1), 157, 177(1) and (3), 178, 181(1), (2), (8) and (9), 183(1) and 184 and Scheds. 1 and 2. The order also brought into force, from January 4, 1995, all remaining sections between 8 and 17 and then ss.24, 34, 38, 40, 44, 47, 49, 50, 51(3), 60, 97 (remainder), 101, 104, 113–115, 124, 126, 137 (remainder), 141, 143, 146–151, 165–167, 170, 172, 173, 175, 179, 182, Sched. 5 and certain of the amendments and repeals in Scheds. 13–14. The order was also used to modify, under s.182(2), certain provisions in the Sewerage (Scotland) Act 1968 (c. 47) and the Control of Pollution Act 1974 (c. 40) by substituting the word "local" for "sewerage". A second commencement order – The Local Government etc. (Scotland) Act 1994 (Commencement No. 2) Order 1994 (S.I. 1994 No. 3150 (C. 74)) – brought into force on December 31, 1994, Sched. 13, para. 176(1) and (19)(b), and s.180(1) so far as it relates to those provisions; on January 4, 1995, ss.153, 160, 161, certain repeals in Sched. 14 and s.180(2) so far as it relates to those repeals; on April 1, 1995, ss.152, 154, 155, 156, 158, 159, 162(1), Sched. 13, paras. 57, 60(4), 67(1)(2)(5) and 100(2)(4)(5), certain repeals in Sched. 14 and s.180 so far as it applies to those Schedules.

ABBREVIATIONS

The 1973 Act: The Local Government (Scotland) Act 1973 (c. 65).
The 1975 Act: The Local Government (Scotland) Act 1975 (c. 30).

PART I

LOCAL GOVERNMENT REORGANISATION

GENERAL NOTE

The structure of local government in Scotland has been comprehensively reorganised twice in the course of the twentieth century. On the first occasion, in May 1930 under the terms of the Local Government (Scotland) Act 1929 (c. 25), the powers of the county councils (originally created under the Local Government (Scotland) Act 1889 (c. 50)) and of the town councils of burghs were consolidated, and the separate district committees (highways and public health), parish councils, district boards of control (mental health), distress committees (public assistance) and education authorities were abolished. A pattern of district councils with powers delegated to them by county councils was also set up but the districts were never given significant responsibilities. The 1929 Act was repealed and replaced (but without modification of the structure of local government) by the Local Government (Scotland) Act 1947 (c. 43), some of whose provisions still survive.

By the 1960s it was widely felt that the structure which had by then served for over 30 years was becoming inadequate to the task. There was a number of complaints whose seriousness varied according to the viewpoint of the observer but all pointed in the direction of reform. In the central belt, in particular, local authorities were too small to undertake the planning and infrastructural functions necessary for the economic development then hoped for. The cities, Glasgow in particular, were quite unable to solve the housing and other social problems within their own boundaries. Across Scotland, there were too many authorities.

In 1966 the Government responded by setting up the Royal Commission chaired by Lord Wheatley to inquire into and report on the structure of local government in Scotland. A parallel Royal Commission for England was established under Lord Redcliffe-Maud.

The Wheatley Commission took evidence and deliberated until 1969 and their Report (Cmnd. 4150) which appeared in that year was very influential in determining the form of reorganisation which was to follow. Moreover, it has retained significance as a benchmark for the measurement of quality of procedures of inquiry and evaluation, and for its powerful endorsement of the status and function of the system of local authorities it recommended. The Wheatley Report was widely cited in the debates prior to and during the Parliamentary stages of the 1994 Act.

The Wheatley Commission opened their Report by saying that "[s]omething is seriously wrong with local government in Scotland. It is not that local authorities have broken down, or that services have stopped functioning. The trouble is not so obvious as that. It is rather that the local government system as a whole is not working properly – it is not doing the job that it ought to be doing. At the root of the trouble is the present structure of local government." The very large number of authorities of five different types produced a system which was no longer rational in terms of boundaries of authorities, and the allocation and co-ordination of functions. The cure was to be found in the adoption of four basic objectives for local government:

(1) *Power*. Local government to play a more important, responsible and positive part in the running of the country;
(2) *Effectiveness*. Local authorities to be adequately equipped in terms of resources to provide services in the most satisfactory manner;
(3) *Local Democracy*. The system must involve the exercise of power through elected representatives who are locally accountable; and
(4) *Local Involvement*. Local people should be involved as much as possible in the process of reaching decisions.

To give effect to these objectives, it was necessary to match the functions of local government in terms of the demands each made on size of population and resources for its effective performance and, on the other hand, the communities identifiable in the country and capable of sustaining authorities of appropriate sizes. The demands of the different types of function quickly ruled out a single tier of all-purpose authorities and pointed instead towards a two-tier system based on:

(a) the regional level of community (Wheatley identified seven such regions) to which would be given the major strategic services including structure planning, roads and transportation, water, sewerage, education, social work and housing, and
(b) the shire level of community (at which 37 districts were identified) to which the more "local" services of building control, environmental health, development control and some licensing functions would be given.

All the main recommendations of the Wheatley Commission were accepted not only by the Labour Government of the time but also by the Conservative Government elected into office in 1970 and it was substantially the Wheatley recommendations which were enacted in the 1973 Act to take effect on May 16, 1975. There were some departures from Wheatley. The number of regions had risen to nine (*i.e.* to include new regions in Fife and the Borders) and the number of districts to 53. More importantly, the three islands areas of Orkney, Shetland, and the Western Isles were taken out of the Highland Region and were each given their own all-purpose islands council (with amalgamations for the police, fire, and valuation functions). The broad division of functions between mainland regions and districts recommended by Wheatley was retained save that housing became a district function.

The structure established by the 1973 Act has remained largely in place, with only small boundary adjustments. Some amendments were made to the distribution of functions, following the recommendations of the Stodart Committee (Cmnd. 8115, 1981), by the Local Government and Planning (Scotland) Act 1982 (c. 43). At the time of the Local Government (Scotland) Act 1978 (c. 4), it was assumed that one of the first projects of the proposed new Assembly would have been the reform of local government – probably involving the adoption of a single-tier system – but the devolution referendum and the repeal of the 1978 Act brought such speculation to an end.

When the idea of a single-tier system next returned to the reform agenda, it did so under the greatly changed political circumstances of the 1990s reflected in the consultations which preceded the 1994 Act. In June 1991, the Scottish Office issued the first consultative document entitled *The Structure of Local Government in Scotland: The Case for Change/Principles of the New System*. (The document was discussed in the Scottish Grand Committee on June 18 and 20, 1991.) In short this paper explained why the Government thought there should be a move from two-tier local government to a single-tier system. It claimed that two-tier government led to confusion in the public mind; that some of the regional authorities were too large and too remote; that there was duplication and waste despite the rationalisations implemented after the Stodart Report; and that there was delay and friction in relations between authorities. Changes in central government policy towards local government were now designed to increase consumer choice of services; to give consumers a greater role in determining how services should be delivered; to encourage authorities to consider alternative methods of service delivery; and to work in partnership with others in the public and private sectors and with individuals. In particular, the Government pointed to such initiatives as the creation of school boards; self-governing status for schools; the promotion of home ownership and the rights of tenants; the deregulation and privatisation of transport services; the impact of compulsory competitive tendering; the developing role of Scottish Enterprise, Scottish Homes and Local Enterprise Companies; and the increasing emphasis placed on value for money in local government, strong financial management and public accountability.

In the Government's view, the problems of the two-tier system, coupled with the demands placed on authorities required to perform a function greatly changed since the days of the

Wheatley Report, constituted an argument for the adoption of a single-tier system. Wheatley had considered the single-tier option but had rejected it for reasons the Government believed to be no longer valid. They did not offer, at this stage, any detailed views on which functions should remain with local authorities (beyond pointing out the increasing effect of competitive tendering, the transition of authorities from providers to enablers, and the already-announced removal of further education from local authority control). Nor were there proposals as to how large-scale and specialised functions such as policing, fire services, water and sewerage might be discharged. There would be further consultation on management systems. Views were invited, however, on issues arising from the adoption of a single-tier system based on principles including: adherence to the democratic tradition; the need to reflect, in the choice of units, local loyalties and traditions and physical and social characteristics – but without the need for all units to be of uniform size; and the need for cost-effective, efficient and accountable authorities.

The 1991 document was duly followed in 1992 by *The Structure of Local Government in Scotland: Shaping the New Councils*. This reconfirmed the Government's commitment to unitary authorities and the general principles which would underpin the new system. The paper consisted mostly of a quite detailed treatment, on a function by function basis, of how services would be administered by the proposed unitary authorities (including discussion of the various forms of joint arrangements which might be required), followed by illustrations of how Scotland might be divided into areas compatible with a 24 unit structure, a 35 and a 51 unit structure. A further short section on the financial implications of reorganisation attracted enormous controversy. The management consultants Touche Ross had produced a report on probable costs – both transitional and long-term – demonstrating substantial savings of between £43 million and £548 million over a five year period, depending on the form of reorganisation adopted. The challenge to the Touche Ross figures was carried forward into the Parliamentary debates on the 1994 Act where it was argued (*e.g.* at First Scottish Standing Committee, col. 43) that costs of as much as £720 million (a COSLA estimate) might be involved.

The White Paper containing the Government's final proposals, *Shaping the Future – The New Councils* (Cm. 2267, July 1993), followed a second debate on local government reform in the Scottish Grand Committee on February 1, 1993. The White Paper stated the Government's commitment to a new structure of 28 local authorities, 25 of which would replace the nine regional and 53 district councils, leaving the three islands councils intact. The new authorities would be elected as "shadow" authorities on a convenient day in 1995 and take over full control on April 1, 1996.

The paper contained further proposals on the future of individual services (on which see the annotations of the relevant sections of the Act); heralded the formation of the centralised administration of the Children's Reporter service (see now Pt. III of the Act); and formally adopted the plan for reallocating the water and sewerage services, at present provided by the regional and islands councils, to three public water authorities. This had earlier been the subject of a consultation paper issued in 1992 *Investing for our Future* (see Pt. II of the Act).

Another issue addressed in *Shaping the Future* was internal management, the subject of an earlier consultation paper *The Internal Management of Local Authorities in Scotland* (March 1993). This was an interesting document which recalled that, between the publication of the Wheatley Report and its implementation, a committee had advised on the management structures to be adopted by the new authorities. The Paterson Report's recommendations (*e.g.* that authorities have a policy and resources committee and a smaller number of service committees) had been widely adopted. Now, however, local authorities were again looking to changes in management arrangements, some of which might require statutory change.

The 1993 consultation paper, following work done by a working party representative of local authorities and central government, first examined the existing committee-based system of administration in comparison with alternative models including a "council manager system" (an appointed chief executive with separately conferred statutory powers), a system based on a "directly-elected provost" (similar to the strong mayor model in the US), a "cabinet model", and a model involving increased powers to delegate decision-taking to individual councillors (an issue earlier investigated by the Widdicombe Committee – *The Conduct of Local Authority Business* Cmnd. 9797 (1986)). The paper then went on to discuss whether, if the existing committee system were broadly retained, there should be changes, such as the relaxation of the requirements to have specific committees and specific officers for education and social work. Another focus was "statutory obstacles to joint arrangements" between authorities given the probable need for the greater use of such arrangements in a unitary system and there were proposals for change in relation to joint boards and also contracting arrangements between authorities (especially those affected by the Local Authorities (Goods and Services) Act 1970). Views were also invited on councillor numbers, electoral arrangements, the eligibility of council employees to stand for election to council membership and councillors' allowances.

Many of these issues were reported in *Shaping the Future* as still being under consideration but the Government had already decided to adhere broadly to the existing committee-based system of internal management.

Other matters addressed by the White Paper included the consequences of reorganisation for other bodies and organisations including the lieutenancies, the voluntary sector, sheriffdoms, health boards, local enterprise companies and community councils; and transitional matters including the need for a Staff Commission, the "shadow" authorities, the probable need for "residuary bodies" and the effects of reorganisation on compulsory competitive tendering.

On the question of financing the new authorities the Government considered that no significant change would be required. The council tax would continue to be the basis of local taxation and support from Aggregate External Finance (revenue support grant, specific grants and non-domestic rate income) would also continue, as would the Government's power to cap council tax levels and its controls over capital spending under s.94 of the 1973 Act. The White Paper also returned to the vexed question of the financial implications of reorganisation itself. Acknowledging that there would be an "ongoing debate on costs" the Government claimed that there was the potential to make "significant savings" under a single-tier structure. With 28 councils, a saving in the range from £110 million – £330 million over five years (probably £200 million) should be possible. Transitional costs were estimated at between £120 million and £196 million – which should, therefore, be recoverable within five years out of the predicted savings.

As a result of the changes made in Pt. I of the Act (and to a lesser extent in Pt. IV), the statute book is left in a distinctly non user-friendly condition. The Acts which implemented the last reorganisation, the 1973 Act and the 1975 Act, still survive, though very heavily amended now by later legislation including this Act, and even parts of the Local Government (Scotland) Act 1947 and other pre-1973 legislation (mainly of a financial character) also remain on the statute book in truncated form. The area cries out for consolidation.

CHAPTER 1

LOCAL GOVERNMENT AREAS, AUTHORITIES AND ELECTIONS

Local government areas in Scotland

1.—(1) Scotland shall, in accordance with the provisions of this Part of this Act, have local government areas for the administration of local government on and after 1st April 1996.

(2) Scotland shall be divided into the local government areas named in column I of Part I of Schedule 1 to this Act, and those areas shall comprise the areas described in column 2 of Part I.

(3) On 1st April 1996—

(a) all local government areas existing immediately before that date which are regions or districts; and

(b) all regional and district councils,

shall cease to exist.

(4) Part II of Schedule 1 (provisions as to boundaries) shall have effect.

GENERAL NOTE

This section, by incorporating the contents of Sched. 1, gives effect to the principal purpose of the Act, the reorganisation of the structure of local government in Scotland with effect from April 1, 1996. The 32 new local government areas are identified and named (Sched. 1, Pt. I) and all the existing local authority areas which are, in terms of the 1973 Act regions or districts, together with the regional and district councils, are abolished from the same date.

There are 32 new areas which, it will be noticed, is four more than the number proposed in *Shaping the Future – the New Councils*, discussed above in the General Note on Part I. As originally introduced into the Commons, the Bill did provide for the 28 areas first suggested (subject, however, to certain minor adjustments affecting the boundaries between South Lanarkshire and Glasgow; the City of Dundee; and certain boundaries in Lothian) but, at a fairly early stage, (*e.g.* *Hansard*, H.C. Vol. 235, col. 540) the Government indicated some willingness to be flexible in the matter of the number of authorities and their boundaries. Thus, in the House of Commons Committee stage, the topics for debate included:

• the division of territory between the two originally proposed areas of Aberdeenshire, Angus and Mearns, which led to adjustments including the removal of Mearns to Aberdeenshire (and the consequent change of name) (First Scottish Standing Committee, col. 192);

- an attempt to alter Dundee's boundaries in relation to areas including Monifieth and Invergowrie which resulted in small adjustments (*ibid.*, col. 216);
- Helensburgh's inclusion in Argyll and Bute and the transfer of Luss from Dumbarton (*ibid.* cols. 249, 250);
- the addition of East Ayrshire to join North and South Ayrshire (*ibid.* col. 266);
- the removal of Berwickshire from a combination with East Lothian to rejoin the Borders and the restructuring of the originally proposed Lothians (*i.e.* West and Mid) to produce a combined East and Mid and separate West Lothian (*ibid.* col. 282) (the *separate* East Lothian and Mid Lothian areas were subsequently agreed at the House of Commons Report stage – see *Hansard*, H.C. Vol. 243, col. 894);
- the highly controversial proposal to create a new area of Clackmannan (First Scottish Standing Committee, col. 285 *et seq.*) – a proposal subsequently agreed at Report stage (*Hansard*, H.C. Vol. 243, col. 894), thus producing the smallest new authority in population terms (about 48,000);
- a proposal (later dropped) to create a new Clydesdale area (First Scottish Standing Committee, col. 316 *et seq.*);
- a proposal for a Cumbernauld and Kilsyth area, also withdrawn (*ibid.* col. 331);
- an attempt to divide Fife (in a manner similar to the division of Ayrshire) to produce a separate Dunfermline (*ibid.*, col. 366); and
- a successful move to extract Inverclyde from West Renfrewshire to create another new area (*ibid.*, col. 385).

By the end of the Commons Committee stage the number of proposed authorities had risen from 28 to 30 (with the addition of East Ayrshire and Inverclyde), rising to 32 by the end of Commons Report stage (with the addition of Clackmannan and the splitting of East and Mid Lothian already referred to). Although the new local government map stayed almost completely stable in debate thereafter (some technical adjustments to the Schedule were made at the Lords Committee stage – *Hansard*, H.L. Vol. 557, cols. 917–920 – affecting the boundary between Dundee and Angus), this did not prevent many of the old battles and some new ones being fought in the Lords Committee, (*Hansard*, H.L. Vol. 556, cols. 691–768, 1820–1829) and again at Report Stage (*Hansard*, H.L. Vol. 557, cols. 917–958) and Third Reading (*Hansard*, H.L. Vol. 558, cols. 667–671). New areas for debate opened up, in particular, on the question of whether to divide the Highland Region into two new local government areas instead of one.

Debate on how the country should be divided also provided the opportunity for discussion of a wide range of related issues including *e.g.* the subsequent review of boundaries by the local government boundary commission (see *e.g. Hansard*, H.L. Vol. 556, col. 689). Amendments made to the 1973 Act by Sched. 13, para. 92(2)–(4) and (67) accelerate that review process. An initial review must take place as soon as possible after reorganisation (the 1973 Act, s.16). Other issues discussed included the alleged inevitability and undesirability of a more widespread use of joint boards and other systems of joint working between authorities (see *e.g. Hansard*, H.L. Vol. 556, cols. 708–710 and see notes on s.20) and the general viability of the small authorities, especially Clackmannan; arrangements for the division of areas into electoral wards (see also s.5); and, from a party political point of view, allegations that the new map was being drawn, in some areas, along lines which smacked of electoral gerrymandering (see *e.g. Hansard*, H.C. Vol. 235, col. 550 – "the most crudely and shamelessly gerrymandering map of local government that Britain has seen this Century" (George Robertson MP) – for one example among many).

Debate on s.1 and Sched. 1 was also used as the vehicle for proposing a delay in implementation of the reorganisation to *e.g.* 1997 (see *Hansard*, H.L. Vol. 557, cols. 912–917) or 1998 or 2000 (First Scottish Standing Committee, col. 131) on the grounds that the timetable would be too tight; and also to debate the merits of a Scottish Assembly, whether as the body to oversee local government reform or to become the top tier of local government (see especially *Hansard*, H.L. Vol. 556, cols. 657–668 and Vol. 557, col. 901).

One interesting feature of the debates on the Bill in the Lords was the extent of participation by peers who had a close involvement in the last reorganisation in 1975, in the reforms made to the system since then and in the actual work of local government at present. Thus, amongst others, Lord Stodart, Baroness Carnegy, Lord Ewing, and Lord Minto (Convener, Borders Regional Council) all contributed to the Second Reading Debate.

Subs. (1)

As to what constitutes "Scotland" for these purposes, the Rockall Act 1972 placed Rockall in Scotland and, at that time, in the District of Harris in the County of Inverness. It continues, therefore, to be within the Western Isles area.

The "areas" established by this subsection (and then named and described in accordance with subs. (2)) are never given a generic name. They are not, for instance, counties (as before 1975), or regions or districts (from 1975 to 1996), but simply "areas".

It should, however, be noted that, under s.23 of the 1973 Act (a new version of which is substituted by Sched. 13, para. 92(5)), a local authority may resolve (by a majority of two-thirds at a special meeting) to change the name of its area. This has been welcomed as a possible opportunity for the adoption of *e.g.* "county" (see *Hansard*, H.L. Vol. 555, col. 1375).

Subs. (2)
It will be noticed that some of the area descriptions in Column 2 of Pt. I of Sched. 1 have achieved a degree of complexity. In some measure, this simply reflects the difficulties inevitable in a process of drawing lines where they have not existed before. It was also, however, a feature seized upon by those who have alleged that electoral gerrymandering has been involved (see above).

Subs. (3)
While the areas which are regions and districts and the councils for such areas are abolished on April 1, 1996, the islands areas and councils will remain – although renamed in accordance with s.3(1).

Subs. (4)
Part II of Sched. 1 provides for the mering (*i.e.* defining on a map) of the boundaries of the new areas by the Ordnance Survey and for the definitions of certain terms used in Pt. I

Constitution of councils

2.—(1) For every local government area there shall be a council consisting of a convener and councillors.

(2) Subject to any provision of this Act, the council for each local government area shall on and after 1st April 1996 have all the functions exercised immediately before that date in relation to their area by any existing regional, islands or district council.

(3) The council for each local government area shall be a body corporate by the name "The Council" with the addition of the name of the particular area, and shall have a common seal.

DEFINITIONS
"local government area": s.1.

GENERAL NOTE
This section constitutes the council for every area defined by s.1 and, very importantly, allocates to each new council from April 1, 1996 the functions previously allocated to existing councils in its area – subject to other provisions in the Act.

A council constituted under this section becomes a "local authority" for the purposes of the 1973 Act – see the 1973 Act, s.235(1) as amended by s.180(1) and para. 92(66) of Sched. 13 to this Act, and also s.183(2) of this Act which, subject to other specific provisions, ensures that references in other legislation to a "local authority" within the meaning of the 1973 Act and the Local Government (Scotland) Act 1947 are to be construed as references to a council under this section. Section 61 of this Act provides that expressions used in Pt. I of the Act as well as the 1973 Act have the same meaning as in the 1973 Act. Thus, where "local authority" is used, as in ss.53 and 54, it means a "council" constituted under this section. But note also that "local authority" has an extended meaning in ss.58 and 59 and that there are a number of other terms used in Pt. I. In particular, note an "existing local authority" (general definition in s.61, though with a modified definition in, *inter alia*, ss.8, 9 and 59), a "new authority" (separately defined in many sections but not in s.7), "authority" (*i.e.* including an existing and a new authority) and, in s.44, a "successor authority". See also the note on s.3(1).

Subs. (1)
The number of councillors for each council is determined by reference to the number of electoral wards in its area (see s.5) and the council consists of the councillors and the convener, a term adopted to replace "chairman" in the 1973 Act and amended from "chairman" at House of Commons Report stage (*Hansard*, H.C. Vol. 243, col. 895), following debate in Committee (First Scottish Standing Committee, cols. 393–397). For the election of the convener, see s.4.

Though the Act is silent on the matter, the council is presumably nevertheless duly constituted as a council, even before the convener's election.

Subs. (2)

In general, councils inherit the functions of existing councils in their areas but different provision is made for some functions – see, above all, Pt. II of the Act for water and sewerage functions and Pt. III for the children's reporter functions.

Subs. (3)

The councils become, as councils have in the past, bodies corporate, *i.e.* legal personae with an existence separate from the councillors themselves. For the authentication of documents by seal, see s.193 of the 1973 Act. This subsection gives each council an initial name – simply "The Council" with the addition (presumably before the word "Council") of the name of the area, as listed in Sched. 1. Partly because those areas themselves are not given a generic name (see s.1), there may be a wish on the part of some councils to give themselves a new name. This may be done under the new s.23 of the 1973 Act substituted by Sched. 13, para. 92(5) to this Act, though there are certain procedural requirements including the need for a specially convened meeting and a two-thirds majority at the meeting.

Orkney, Shetland and Western Isles

3.—(1) The islands councils of Orkney, Shetland and the Western Isles shall continue to exist as bodies corporate but, on and after 1st April 1996—
  (a) they shall be known as "Orkney Islands Council", "Shetland Islands Council" and "Western Isles Council"; and
  (b) their areas shall be known as "Orkney Islands", "Shetland Islands" and "Western Isles",
respectively.

(2) The islands councils consisting of the councillors elected for the islands areas of Orkney, Shetland and the Western Isles at the ordinary election held in 1994 shall continue as councils until the second ordinary election of councillors for the new councils held under section 5 of this Act.

DEFINITIONS
  "council": s.2.

GENERAL NOTE

This section provides for the continued existence of the three islands councils but, from April 1, 1996, with amended titles. It avoids the need for the election of a "shadow" authority on April 6, 1995 (see s.5(2)). In debate, it was argued that confusion might arise as a result of separating the content of s.3 from s.2 and their merger was urged (First Scottish Standing Committee, cols. 397–398).

Subs. (1)

This subsection continues the three islands councils in existence after April 1, 1996 but with the name of the Western Isles Islands Council contracted to "Western Isles Council". The names of their areas are also shortened by losing the word "area" from each. It seems to be an oddity about the terminology used in this Act that it is the names of the *areas* rather than of the actual councils which are used in many subsequent sections (see ss.8(7), 9(5), 11(10), 12(8), 13(7), 16(9), 17(14) and 19(7)) to describe "authorities" constituted under s.2. But see s.44(5) where the formula "councils for Orkney Islands etc." is used.

Subs. (2)

The islands councils will continue as councils until the "second ordinary elections" for the new councils to be held in 1999. See note on s.5(3) for when the first ordinary elections for the islands should take place.

Convener and depute convener

4.—(1) The council of each local government area shall elect a convener from among the councillors.

(2) A council may elect a member of the council to be depute convener.

(3) Subject to the provisions of this section and of Schedule 2 to this Act, the standing orders of a council may make provision for—

   (a) the duration of the term of office (which may not extend beyond the next ordinary election of the council); and
   (b) the procedure for early removal from office,
of the convener and depute convener.

   (4) The election of the convener shall be the first business transacted at the first meeting of the council held after an ordinary election of councillors and at that meeting, until the convener is elected, the returning officer or, failing him, such councillor as may be selected by the meeting shall preside.

   (5) A person holding the office of convener or depute convener shall be eligible for re-election but shall cease to hold office upon ceasing to be a councillor.

   (6) On a casual vacancy occurring in the office of convener, an election to fill the vacancy shall be held as soon as practicable by the council at a meeting of the council the notice of which specifies the filling of the vacancy as an item of business, and the depute convener or, failing him, a councillor selected by the meeting shall preside.

   (7) The convener of each of the councils of the cities of Aberdeen, Dundee, Edinburgh and Glasgow shall, with effect from 1st April 1996, be known by the title of "Lord Provost", and the convener of each other council shall be known by such title as that council may decide:
       Provided that no such other council may, without the consent of the Secretary of State, decide that their convener shall be known by the title of "Lord Provost".

   (8) A council may pay the convener and depute convener, for the purpose of enabling each of them to meet the expenses of his office, such allowance as the council think reasonable.

DEFINITIONS
   "council": s.2.
   "local government area": s.1.

GENERAL NOTE
   Section 2(1) of the Act provides that a council is to consist of its "convener and councillors". Replacing ss.3 and 3A of the 1973 Act, this section, read with Sched. 2 to the Act and Sched. 7 (as amended) to the 1973 Act, provides for the election, term of office, title and expenses of the convener and, if the council decides to have one, a depute convener.

Subss. (1) and (2)
   These make outline provision for the elections. For further detail, see subs. (4) and Sched. 2 to this Act and Sched. 7 (as amended) to the 1973 Act.

Subs. (3)
   This contains an important change from the 1973 Act provisions. Standing orders of a council may provide for the terms of office of the convener and depute convener to be for a period ending before the next ordinary council elections – so allowing greater flexibility in the matter – and for early removal. It should be noted that Sched. 2, para. 7 provides for the offices of convener and depute convener elected after the council elections of April 1995 to terminate at the first council meeting on or after April 1, 1996, by which time a council would have had the opportunity to make standing orders governing conveners' terms of office.

Subs. (4)
   This subsection should be read with paras. 4 and 5 of Sched. 2 to this Act and para. 5 of Sched. 7 (as amended) to the 1973 Act. If there is an "equality of votes" in the matter of appointment of a council member to "any particular office", the difficulty is to be resolved not by the second or casting vote of the person presiding but the "decision shall be by lot". This subsection was amended significantly at the House of Lords Report stage (*Hansard*, H.L. Vol. 557, cols. 969–971), following concerns expressed earlier, to add the important proviso concerning the use of the title "Lord Provost". As matters now stand, the four main cities will have to use the title "Lord Provost" for their conveners, as at present. Other councils will have a choice but would require the Secretary of State's consent to use "Lord Provost". In debate, the Minister of State indicated that a positive decision would be made only on proof of an historical title and in consul-

tation with the Lord Lyon, if appropriate (*ibid.*, col. 969). The principal suggested possible claimant was Perth.

Subs. (8)

Expenses paid under this section do not disqualify (as paid office or employment) for the purposes of election to or membership of an authority (see the 1973 Act, s.31 as amended).

Elections and term of office of councillors

5.—(1) Councillors for each local government area shall be elected by the local government electors for that area in accordance with this Part of this Act and the Representation of the People Act 1983.

(2) Notwithstanding the provisions of section 43 of that Act of 1983 (day of ordinary local elections in Scotland), the first ordinary election of councillors for each council other than the councils of Orkney Islands, Shetland Islands and Western Isles shall take place on 6th April 1995.

(3) The second ordinary election of councillors shall take place in 1999, and ordinary elections shall take place every third year thereafter.

(4) Councillors shall retire on the day of the ordinary election next following the date on which they were elected.

(5) Each local government area shall be divided into electoral wards, and each such ward shall return one councillor.

(6) There shall be a separate election for each electoral ward.

DEFINITIONS
"council": s.2.
"local government area": s.1.

GENERAL NOTE
Much of the election law applicable to the new councils is contained, as before, in the Representation of the People Act 1983 (c. 2) and the relevant continuing provisions of the 1973 Act – see especially ss.29–37 of the 1973 Act. Replacing ss.4 and 5 of the 1973 Act, however, this section provides for elections in general, the initial elections, and for the occurrence of elections (once every three years from 1999). The three-year cycle replaces the existing four-year cycle – following consultation in *The Internal Management of Local Authorities in Scotland* (1993). Some efforts were made during the Bill's Parliamentary passage to establish a four-year cycle, said to be preferred by many in local government at present (see, *e.g. Hansard*, H.L. Vol. 557, cols. 971–977). The Minister of State said there was no absolutely right answer (*ibid.*, col. 975) but that the Government preferred a three-year cycle. It was not persuaded that authorities could not move quickly towards implementing their programmes within the three-year period. Councillors elected in 1995 (*i.e.* all except in the islands) to "shadow authorities" will stay in office until 1999.

Subs. (1)

Rules concerning qualification for election are not altered by the Act. The opportunity was, however, taken in debates on the Bill to try to make changes and, in particular, to lift the ban on council employees standing for election to their employer council, especially because the move to unitary authorities will, under existing rules, deny membership to many thousands of employees in their own area. These attempts were, however, resisted by the Government on the same grounds of conflict of interest which the Montgomery Committee (on local government in the islands) found persuasive in 1984; (see, *e.g. Hansard*, H.L. Vol. 557, cols. 977–983).

Subs. (2)

Because the islands are not affected by the structural changes (see s.3) the councillors elected in those three areas in 1994 will serve right through until 1999 (but see note on subs. (3)). The "normal" date for ordinary elections is determined by the 1983 Act, s.43 (see s.6 below). Elections to the other new authorities will take place on April 6, 1995 which imposes quite an abrupt timetable from the date of Royal Assent – a timetable which even the new chairman of the Staff Commission was quoted as calling "dangerously tight" (see *e.g. Hansard*, H.C. Vol. 248, col. 1423). The Government's view was that it was no shorter than in 1973–1974 and was manageable. For the period from April 1995 to March 1996 the new councils operate as "shadow" authorities, *i.e.* lacking statutory responsibility for service provision but with the obligation to make plans (including appointment of staff) for April 1996. For other provisions affecting this transitional phase see, *e.g.* ss.14, 25, 55–57.

See also the Local Government (Transitional Election Arrangements) (Scotland) Order 1994 (S.I. 1994 No. 3255).

Subs. (3)

This establishes the three-year election cycle from 1999. Presumably subss. (2) and (3), read with s.3(2), do ensure the holding of elections in the islands in 1999 – although it may seem strange for those authorities to hold what are only ever described as second ordinary elections without the holding of any first ordinary elections in those areas.

Subss. (5) and (6)

Directions are to be made by the Secretary of State to divide areas into wards – see Sched. 2, para. 1. One almost inevitable consequence of a reorganisation in the direction of a single tier of authorities is that the total number of councillors in Scotland will be greatly reduced. It was claimed in debate that, whereas there would be only 1200 elected councillors, there will be about 5000 appointed quango members (*Hansard*, H.C. Vol. 244, col. 255). This led to an attempt to raise the minimum number of councillors to 1680 (*Hansard*, H.L. Vol. 556, cols. 1868–1872). Although final decisions were yet to be made, the Government indicated in debate that the initial ward boundaries would be based mainly on existing district wards but on regional divisions in Borders, Dumfries and Galloway, and Fife (*Hansard*, H.L. Vol. 557, col. 986). It has, however, since been announced (and directions were issued on November 8, 1994) that the electoral wards to be used will be the existing district council wards in almost all areas. The principal exception is in the Highlands area where that would have produced 132 councillors; there will instead be 72. There will be 1161 wards in all in mainland Scotland, to which may be added the 84 seats in the islands to produce a total number of councillors across Scotland (shadow authorities plus islands) of 1245.

Date of elections

6. For subsection (1) of section 43 of the Representation of the People Act 1983 (day of ordinary local elections in Scotland) substitute—

"(1) In every year in which ordinary elections of councillors for local government areas in Scotland are held, the day of election is—
　(a) the first Thursday in May; or
　(b) such other day as may be fixed by the Secretary of State by order made by statutory instrument not later than 1st February in the year preceding the year or, in the case of an order affecting more than one year, the first year in which the order is to take effect.

(1A) An order made under subsection (1)(b) above shall be subject to annulment in pursuance of a resolution of either House of Parliament.".

Definitions

"local government area": s.1.

General Note

At present, s.43(1) of the Representation of the People Act 1983 requires ordinary local elections to be held on the first Thursday in May. Sometimes this day has proved to be inappropriate but changing it requires primary legislation – as in 1986 (see the Representation of the People Act 1985 (c. 50), s.18). This section enables a change to be made instead by order – but the statutory instrument must be made at least 15 months earlier, *i.e.* by February 1 in the preceding year – "no Government could decide on a whim to alter an election date. Moreover the new date of election could not be postponed indefinitely, it must be in the same year" (First Scottish Standing Committee, col. 469). The new subs. (1A) to be inserted into s.43 of the 1983 Act was added at the Commons Report stage (*Hansard*, H.C. Vol. 243, col. 895).

Establishment of new local authorities and supplementary provisions

7.—(1) Schedule 2 to this Act shall have effect with respect to the establishment of the new local authorities, the suspension of elections of existing authorities and related matters.

(2) This Part of this Act shall have effect, in relation to such establishment, subject to the provisions of that Schedule.

(3) Schedule 2 shall not apply in relation to the councils of Orkney Islands, Shetland Islands and Western Isles.

DEFINITIONS
"existing authorities": s.61.

GENERAL NOTE
Some of the provisions of Sched. 2 which are incorporated by this section have already been referred to in the notes on ss.4 and 5. The Schedule provides for:
(1) The first elections of councillors (including directions as to wards – see s.5) and the appointment of returning officers. Somewhat controversially it is to be officers appointed by existing *regions* who will be the returning officers in April 1995.
(2) The stipulation (by interpretation of s.29 of the 1973 Act) that, for the purposes of enabling candidates to satisfy the "local connection" conditions of that section, the new local authority areas are deemed to have existed for at least 12 months.
(3) Provision for first meetings.
(4) The suspension of ordinary (casual) by-elections to existing authorities after November 16, 1994, with vacancies to be filled instead by election by an authority itself.
(5) Elections of conveners and depute conveners after April 1, 1996.

CHAPTER 2

STAFF

Transfer of employees

8.—(1) Subject to the provisions of this section, the Secretary of State may by order make provision with respect to—
(a) the transfer of employees from an existing local authority to a new authority with effect from 1st April 1996; and
(b) any matters arising out of or related to such transfer.
(2) An order under this section may, without prejudice to the generality of subsection (1)(a) above—
(a) make provision as to the new authority to which groups of employees, or particular employees, are to be transferred;
(b) prescribe a general rule or rules by which the transfer of employees, or of specified groups of employees, can be determined.
(3) Each regional and district council shall, in accordance with the provisions of an order made under this section, prepare a scheme in relation to the transfer under or by virtue of this Act of their employees.
(4) No scheme under subsection (3) above shall be made without the consent of the new authority or authorities, or of the new water and sewerage authority or authorities (within the meaning of Part II of this Act), to whom the employees concerned are to be transferred or, failing such consent, without the consent of the Secretary of State.
(5) The Secretary of State shall by order under this section provide for the transfer of all fire and police personnel employed by an existing local authority for the purposes of a fire brigade or police force to the new authority which will, after 1st April 1996, have responsibility as respects that brigade or force.
(6) An order under this section shall be made by statutory instrument subject to annulment in pursuance of a resolution of either House of Parliament.
(7) In this section—
"existing local authority" includes a joint committee and a joint board but does not, subject to any other provision of this Act, include an islands authority;

"fire personnel" means any persons employed by an existing local authority for the sole purpose of assisting a fire brigade maintained by that authority;

"new authority" means any of the authorities constituted under section 2 of this Act (other than Orkney Islands, Shetland Islands or Western Isles), a residuary body and a joint board; and

"police personnel" means any persons employed by virtue of section 9 of the Police (Scotland) Act 1967 (employees other than constables).

DEFINITIONS
"existing local authority": subs. (7).
"fire personnel": subs. (7).
"joint board": s.61; s.235(1) of the 1973 Act.
"joint committee": s.61; s.235(1) of the 1973 Act.
"new authority": subs. (7).
"police personnel": subs. (7).
"residuary body": ss.18 and 183.

GENERAL NOTE
This is the first of a group (Chap. 2) of important sections relating to the staffing consequences of local government reorganisation. Along with the provisions in Chap. 2 itself, account should also be taken of s.34 (continued existence of police forces), s.36 (continued existence of fire brigades), s.97 (transfer of staff to new water and sewerage authorities), and s.137 (transfer of staff to the Scottish Children's Reporter Administration).

The main purpose of s.8 itself is not to provide detailed rules for the transfer of staff from existing to new authorities, but to enable the Secretary of State to make such provision by order (subs. (1)). This may be done by identifying the new authority to which groups of employees are to be transferred and the prescription of a general rule or rules by which the transfer of employees can be determined (subs. (2)).

In debates (*e.g. Hansard*, H.L. Vol. 556, cols. 1895–1906; H.L. Vol. 557, cols. 987–997), this section attracted wide discussion of how employees' interests might best be protected. This included attempts to ensure that an order under the section would provide that *all* existing employees should transfer to a new one, as well as attempts to make explicit the application of the E.C. Acquired Rights Directive (EC Council Directive 77/187) and the Transfer of Undertakings (Protection of Employment) ("TUPE") Regulations 1981 (S.I. 1981 No. 1794). In brief, the Government's response was that it would be to the advantage of neither employees nor authorities to make transfer mandatory. To the extent that they were relevant to this situation the "TUPE" regulations would apply, whether or not express reference to them was made in the Act.

The "existing local authorities" and "new authorities" to which the section relates do not include the islands authorities which, in terms of s.3(1) continue to exist. However, these definitions are adapted when the rules relating to staff are applied to the new water and sewerage authorities and the Reporter Administration by ss.97 and 137.

Subsection (3) (which was inserted at the Commons Report stage col. 896) provides that an order under the section must enable existing authorities to prepare schemes for the transfer of their own employees. The schemes must be consented to by the relevant new authorities or, failing their consent, by the Secretary of State (subs. (4)).

Subsection (5) was also added at the Commons Report stage col. 896 and requires the Secretary of State to provide, by transfer order, for the non-uniformed staff from existing police and fire authorities (including the joint boards) to the relevant new authorities.

Effect of section 8 on contracts of employment

9.—(1) This section applies to any person transferred from an existing local authority to a new authority under or by virtue of an order under section 8 of this Act.

(2) The contract of employment between such a person (the "employee") and his present employer shall not be terminated by the abolition of that employer but shall have effect from 1st April 1996 (the "transfer date") as if originally made between the employee and such new authority (his "new employer") as may be specified in relation to him in an order made under section 8 of this Act.

(3) Without prejudice to subsection (2) above

(a) all the present employer's rights, powers, duties and liabilities under or in connection with a contract to which that subsection applies shall by virtue of this section be transferred on the transfer date to the new employer; and

(b) anything done before the transfer date by or in relation to the present employer in respect of that contract or the employee shall be deemed after that date to have been done by or in relation to the new employer.

(4) Subsections (2) and (3) above are without prejudice to any right of an employee to terminate his contract of employment if a substantial change is made to his detriment in his terms and conditions of employment, but no such right shall arise by reason only of the change of employer effected by section 8 of this Act.

(5) In this section—

"existing local authority" includes a joint committee and a joint board but does not, subject to any other provision of this Act, include an islands authority; and

"new authority" means any of the authorities constituted under section 2 of this Act (other than Orkney Islands, Shetland Islands or Western Isles), a residuary body and a joint board.

DEFINITIONS

"employee": subs. (2).
"existing local authority": subs. (5).
"joint board": s.61; s.235(1) of the 1973 Act.
"joint committee": s.61; s.235(1) of the 1973 Act.
"new authority": subs. (5).
"new employer": subs. (2).
"residuary body": s.183 and s.18.
"transfer date": subs. (2).

GENERAL NOTE

This section addresses the position of the individual employee transferred from an existing to a new authority by virtue of an order under s.8, by ensuring that the contract of employment does not terminate, but continues as if originally made between the employee and the new authority (subs. (2)). As was made clear (*e.g. Hansard*, H.L. Vol. 556, col. 1901 and Vol. 557, col. 992), even if an order were not made in respect of particular employees of an existing authority under s.8, the position of most of them would be assured under the Transfer of Undertakings (Protection of Employment) Regulations 1981 (S.I. 1981 No. 1794) (the TUPE Regulations). The section does not effect the rights conferred by the Regulations but it makes quite clear the position of those employees transferred under s.8.

Subsection (3) expands on the effect of ensuring continuity of the contract of employment. It effects the transfer of the rights, duties, etc. from one employer to the other whilst also preserving the effect of things done under the contract by the existing employer prior to the transfer date of April 1, 1996. Subsection (4), however, confirms that the continuity of the contract is without prejudice to any rights the employee may have to terminate the contract on the grounds of substantial detrimental change to the terms and conditions – but the transfer under s.8 does not in itself give rise to such a right to terminate.

As with s.8, this section does not normally apply to the islands authorities but may do so in relation to transfers to the new water and sewerage authorities and the Children's Reporter Administration.

Continuity of employment

10.—(1) This section applies to a person who at any time after the passing of this Act ceases to be employed by an existing local authority (his "former employer") if—

(a) the termination of his employment is attributable, directly or indirectly, to any provision made by or under this Act;

(b) he is subsequently employed by another person (his "new employer"); and

(c) by virtue of section 84 of the Employment Protection (Consolidation) Act 1978 (renewal or re-engagement) that subsequent employment precludes his receiving any redundancy payment under Pt. VI of that Act.

(2) Where this section applies to a person, Schedule 13 to the said Act of 1978 (computation of a period of employment for the purposes of that Act) shall have effect in relation to that person as if it included the following provisions, that is to say—

(a) the period of employment of that person with his former employer shall count as a period of employment with his new employer; and

(b) the change of employer shall not break the continuity of the period of employment.

(3) Where this section applies to a person, the period of his employment with his former employer shall count as a period of employment with his new employer for the purposes of any provision of his contract of employment with his new employer which depends on his length of service with that employer.

(4) In this section "existing local authority" includes a joint committee and a joint board but does not, subject to any other provision of this Act, include an islands authority.

DEFINITIONS
"existing local authority": subs. (4).
"former employer": subs. (1).
"joint board": s.61; s.235(1) of the 1973 Act.
"joint committee": s.61; s.235(1) of the 1973 Act.
"new employer": subs. (1).

GENERAL NOTE
This section is intended to preserve the continuity of employment of an employee of an existing local authority:

(1) who is not transferred under s.8 (and who therefore does not receive the benefits of s.9);

(2) whose employment is terminated in circumstances "attributable directly or indirectly, to any provision made by or under this Act";

(3) who is subsequently re-employed; and

(4) who is not entitled to receive any redundancy payment under Pt. VI of the Employment Protection (Consolidation) Act 1978 (c. 44) by reason of s.84 of that Act.

That section precludes a redundancy payment where both the former and new employers are listed in the Redundancy Payments (Local Government) (Modification) Order 1983 (S.I. 1983 No. 1160) – the list currently includes existing local authorities and will be extended to include the new authorities – and where, for example, re-employment takes place within four weeks. Those who will benefit from this provision will include those who are recruited to a new authority from an existing authority during the shadow year (see First Scottish Standing Committee, cols. 530–531).

The section does not guarantee employees the same terms and conditions as they previously enjoyed. What it does, however, is to provide that, for the purposes of Sched. 13 to the Employment Protection (Consolidation) Act 1978 (periods of employment to qualify for entitlement to, *e.g.* maternity leave and protection against unfair dismissal), the period of employment with the existing (old) authority will count as if a period of employment with the new authority, and as if there were no break in the continuity of employment (subs. (2)).

The Redundancy Payments (Local Government) (Modification) Order 1983 itself gives the same protection as far as any eventual entitlement to redundancy payments is concerned and all those protections are further supplemented by subs. (3) which ensures that, for the purposes of any provision of the new contract of employment, the period of employment with the former employer will count.

As with ss.8 and 9, the provisions of this section are extended to apply to employees subsequently employed by a new water and sewerage authority (s.97) or the Children's Reporter Administration (s.137) hence the option offered by subs. (4) to include an islands authority where needed.

Remuneration of employees of local authorities

11.—(1) For the purposes of this section the Secretary of State may, after consulting such associations of local authorities as appear to him to be appropriate—

(a) designate such existing body as he considers appropriate; or

(b) by order made by statutory instrument establish a new body,

(in this section referred to, in either case, as "the advisory body") to consider any increase made or proposed to be made by an authority in the remuneration of any of their employees.

(2) An order under subsection (1)(b) above—

(a) may make provision as to the constitution and membership of the body established;

(b) may include provision as to the employment of staff and the remuneration and superannuation of the members and staff of the body; and

(c) shall be subject to annulment in pursuance of a resolution of either House of Parliament.

(3) For the purpose of enabling them to carry out their functions under this section, the advisory body shall consult and seek information from authorities and, if requested to do so by the advisory body, the Secretary of State may give a direction to any such authority requiring them to furnish to the advisory body such information as may be specified in the direction relating to the remuneration and other terms and conditions of employment of such employees of the authority as may be so specified.

(4) If it appears to the advisory body that an authority have fixed or propose to fix for any employee or class of employee of theirs a rate of remuneration which, having regard to any recommended levels of remuneration formulated on a national basis by representatives of local authorities and employees of local authorities, is greater than that which the advisory body consider appropriate for that employee or class of employees, they shall notify the authority concerned and recommend to them the rate of remuneration which should be paid to the employee or class of employees concerned.

(5) If it appears to the advisory body that an authority to whom they have made a recommendation under subsection (4) above are not complying with that recommendation, then, after giving notice in writing to the authority concerned of their intention to do so, they may refer the matter to the Secretary of State; and on such a reference the Secretary of State, after consultation with such associations of local authorities and of employees of local authorities as he considers appropriate in relation to the employee or class of employees concerned, may give a direction to that authority requiring them, with effect from such date as may be specified in the direction (not being earlier than the date on which notice was given to them by the advisory body), to pay such employee or class of employees of theirs as was the subject of the recommendation and as may be so specified remuneration at the rate recommended by the advisory body under subsection (4) above and specified in the direction.

(6) An authority to whom a direction is given under subsection (3) or subsection (5) above shall comply with the direction.

(7) If at any time in the period of three months beginning on 1st April 1996 it appears to the advisory body that the remuneration paid at any time before that date to any employee or class of employees of an existing local authority was such that, if that authority had not ceased to exist, the advisory body would have made a recommendation to the authority under subsection (4) above or, having made such a recommendation before that date, would have referred the matter to the Secretary of State under subsection (5) above, they shall notify the Secretary of State and report to him the rate of remuneration which in their opinion should have been paid to the employee or class of employees concerned immediately before 1st April 1996 or such earlier date

as may be specified in the report, being the date on which the employee or employees ceased to be employed by the local authority concerned.

(8) On receiving a report under subsection (7) above the Secretary of State may, after such consultation as is specified in subsection (5) above, by order made by statutory instrument provide that, for the purposes of the provisions of this Act, or of any regulations made under section 24 of the Superannuation Act 1972 (compensation for loss of office etc.), relating to transfer of officers and compensation for loss of office, the employee or class of employees to whom the report relates and who are specified in the order shall be deemed to have been receiving, immediately before 1st April 1996 or such earlier date as may be specified in the report, remuneration at the rate stated in the report and specified in the order.

(9) An order made under subsection (8) above shall be subject to annulment in pursuance of a resolution of either House of Parliament.

(10) In this section—

"authority" means an existing local authority and a new authority;

"existing local authority" includes a joint committee and a joint board but does not include an islands authority; and

"new authority" means any of the authorities constituted under section 2 of this Act (other than Orkney Islands, Shetland Islands and Western Isles) and a joint board.

(11) The Secretary of State may not give a direction under subsection (5) above nor make an order under subsection (8) above after 31st March 1997.

DEFINITIONS

"advisory body": subs. (1).

"authority": subs. (10).

"existing local authority": subs. (10).

"joint board": s.61; s.235(1) of the 1973 Act.

"joint committee": s.61; s.235(1) of the 1973 Act.

"new authority": subs. (10).

GENERAL NOTE

One of the concerns the Government has expressed about the process of reorganisation is its possible cost and, in particular, the risk that salary costs may rise sharply. This section meets that concern by conferring powers on the Secretary of State to restrict levels of remuneration. Similar powers were available at the time of the 1975 reorganisation – see s.221 of the 1973 Act.

The mechanism adopted involves setting up an "advisory body" (whether a body already in existence or specially established) "to consider any increase made or proposed to be made by an authority in the remuneration of any of their employees" (subs. (1)).

The section contains two main procedures which may be triggered by the advisory body. The first is where, in relation to an authority (either existing or new), the body considers that a rate of remuneration (fixed or proposed) is higher than it considers appropriate. It may then recommend an appropriate level and, if that is not complied with, refer the non-compliance to the Secretary of State who may issue a direction with which the authority must comply (subss. (4)–(6)) The second procedure focuses on the first three months of reorganisation, *i.e.* from April 1, 1996, and provides the opportunity for the advisory body to commence (or carry forward) the above procedure in respect of a local authority which ceased to exist at reorganisation. In that event, the Secretary of State may, by statutory instrument, provide that, for the purposes of this Act and regulations under s.24 of the Superannuation Act 1972, the employees concerned are deemed to have been receiving remuneration at the level stated in the advisory body's report.

By subs. (11), the Secretary of State's powers to issue a direction or make an order cease after March 31, 1997, *i.e.* a year after reorganisation. In terms of ss.97 and 137, the powers under this section may be applied to local authorities (including, in this case, islands authorities) and to the new water and sewerage authorities and the Children's Reporter Administration respectively.

Subsection (9) achieved some notoriety as its addition to the Bill was the sole amendment made during the whole of the House of Lords Committee stage (see *Hansard*, H.L. Vol. 556, cols. 1906–1907). The amendment's origins were acknowledged to lie in a report of the Delegated Powers Scrutiny Committee which had suggested that an order-making power such as that conferred by subs. (8) should be subject to the negative resolution procedure.

Staff commission

12.—(1) The Secretary of State shall, after such consultation, whether before or after the passing of this Act, as he thinks fit, by order establish a staff commission for the purpose of carrying out such functions in relation to the staff and staffing of authorities as he may consider appropriate.

(2) Without prejudice to the generality of subsection (1) above, an order under this section may confer on the staff commission the functions of—

(a) considering and keeping under review the arrangements for the recruitment of staff by new authorities and for the transfer in consequence of this Act or of any instrument made under it of staff employed by existing local authorities which cease to exist by virtue of Chapter 1 of this Part of this Act;

(b) considering such staffing problems arising out of, in consequence of or in connection with any provision of or instrument made under this Act as may be referred to them by the Secretary of State or by any authority;

(c) advising the Secretary of State as to the steps necessary to safeguard the interests of such staff; and

(d) advising authorities, either by the commission or by persons nominated by them.

(3) An order under this section may make provision as to the constitution and membership of the commission, the appointment and removal from office by the Secretary of State of the chairman and members of the commission, the employment of staff and the remuneration and superannuation of the members and staff of the commission.

(4) The Secretary of State may give directions—

(a) to the staff commission as to—
    (i) the carrying out by them of their functions; and
    (ii) their procedure;

(b) to any authority with respect to the furnishing by them of information requested by the commission; and

(c) to any authority with respect to—
    (i) the implementation by them of any advice given by, or by persons nominated by, the commission; and
    (ii) the payment by them of any expenses incurred by the commission in doing anything requested by them.

(5) Any expenses incurred by the staff commission and not recovered by them from an authority shall be paid by the Secretary of State out of money provided by Parliament.

(6) The Secretary of State may by order provide for the winding up of the commission and the disposal of their assets.

(7) An order under this section shall be made by statutory instrument subject to annulment in pursuance of a resolution of either House of Parliament.

(8) In this section—

"authority" means an existing local authority and a new authority;

"existing local authority" includes a joint committee and a joint board but does not, except as may be provided by any other provision of this Act, include an islands authority; and

"new authority" means any of the authorities constituted under section 2 of this Act (other than Orkney Islands, Shetland Islands or Western Isles), a residuary body and a joint board.

DEFINITIONS
"authority": subs. (8).
"existing local authority": subs. (8).
"joint board": s.61; s.235(1) of the 1973 Act.
"joint committee": s.61; s.235(1) of the 1973 Act.

"new authority": subs. (8).
"residuary body": ss.18 and 183.

GENERAL NOTE

This section provides for the Secretary of State to establish a staff commission by order made by statutory instrument (subss. (1) and (7)). The purposes of the commission will be specified in the order but may include the functions of review and advice (to both the Secretary of State, and the existing and new authorities) on the matters stated in subs. (2). Subsection (3) provides for the constitution of the commission and remuneration for members and staff. Subsection (4) gives important powers to the Secretary of State to give directions to the commission and also to local authorities (including directions to pay the expenses of the commission).

Unlike the case of the property commission which may be established under s.19, there is a statutory obligation on the Government to establish a staff commission. It was created in embryo, as a Staff Advisory Committee under the chairmanship of Mr Robert Peggie, as the Bill was passing through Parliament. The commission was formally established by order on November 25, 1994 (see the Local Government Staff Commission (Scotland) Order 1994 (S.I. 1994 No. 2958)).

In debate, much attention was focused on suggestions that the Secretary of State's powers of control over the Commission were too wide, and on the consequent loss of necessary independence for the Commission itself (see First Scottish Standing Committee, cols. 550–573).

As with other provisions in this Chapter, this section is extended by ss.97 and 137 to the staffing consequences of establishing the new water and sewerage authorities and the Children's Reporter Administration respectively.

Compensation for loss of office or diminution of emoluments

13.—(1) This section applies to any person who at any time after the passing of this Act is in the service of—

(a) an existing local authority;

(b) a new authority; or

(c) a residuary body,

and who suffers loss of employment or diminution of emoluments which is attributable to any provision made by, under or by virtue of this Act.

(2) Where the Secretary of State makes provision by regulations under section 24 of the Superannuation Act 1972 (compensation for loss of office etc.) in relation to compensation in respect of any such loss or diminution as is referred to in subsection (1) above, such compensation shall be paid only in accordance with those regulations; and accordingly none of the bodies mentioned in subsection (1) above shall pay any such compensation under any other statutory provision, by virtue of any provision in a contract, or otherwise.

(3) Subsection (2) above shall not preclude the making of any payment to which a person is entitled by virtue of contractual rights acquired by him on or before 9th December 1993.

(4) Regulations under the said section 24 shall not provide compensation for a person to whom this section applies in respect of any such loss or diminution as is mentioned in subsection (1) above so far as attributable to the termination (without prejudice to the provision of compensation where the said loss or diminution is attributable otherwise than to such termination) on or before 1st April 1996 of a contract made after 9th December 1993 which provides for the employment of that person for a fixed term extending beyond 1st April 1996.

(5) For the purpose of determining under subsections (5) or (6) of section 82 (general exclusions from right to redundancy payment) or section 84(3) (renewal of contract or re-engagement) of the Employment Protection (Consolidation) Act 1978—

(a) whether the provisions of a new contract offered to a person employed by any such body as is mentioned in subsection (1) above differ from the corresponding provisions of his previous contract; and

(b) whether employment under the new contract is suitable in relation to that person, there shall be treated as forming part of the remuneration payable under the new contract any compensation to which that person is or, if he accepted the offer, would be entitled in accordance with this section.

(6) Except as provided in subsection (5) above nothing in this section shall be construed as affecting any entitlement to a redundancy payment under Part VI of the said Act of 1978 or to any payment by virtue of any provision of the Superannuation Act 1972 other than the said section 24.

(7) In this section—

"existing local authority" includes a joint committee and a joint board but does not, except as may be provided by any other provision of this Act, include an islands authority; and

"new authority" means any of the authorities constituted under section 2 of this Act (other than Orkney Islands, Shetland Islands or Western Isles) and a joint board.

DEFINITIONS

"existing local authority": subs. (7).
"joint board": s.61; s.235(1) of the 1973 Act.
"joint committee": s.61; s.235(1) of the 1973 Act.
"new authority": subs. (7).
"residuary body": ss.18 and 183.

GENERAL NOTE

The purpose of this section is to provide that the powers available to the Secretary of State under s.24 of the Superannuation Act 1972 (c. 11) to provide compensation for loss of employment *etc.* attributable to reorganisation, will operate as a ceiling on the payment of such compensation. To avoid what the Government regarded as invidious differences between levels of compensation payable across the country, payments of compensation at levels higher than those prescribed are outlawed (subs. (2)). The only exception is where a contractual right to the payment of a higher level of compensation was acquired prior to December 9, 1993 – the date of publication of the Local Government etc. (Scotland) Bill (subs. (3)). In similar vein, however, no compensation will be payable to a person who entered into a short term contract of employment after December 9, 1993 which is terminated (by reason of reorganisation) on or before April 1, 1996 (subs. (4)).

Subsection (5) seeks to ensure that where an employee is offered compensation for accepting a new (local authority) job on terms less favourable than his or her previous post, then such compensation will be taken into account in relation to certain issues (identified in the references to ss.82 and 84 of the Employment Protection (Consolidation) Act 1978 and paras. (a) and (b) of subs. (5)) under employment legislation. Subsection (6) ensures that, subs. (5) apart, normal entitlements to redundancy payments are not affected by this section.

As with other provisions in this Chapter, this section is extended by ss.97 and 137 to apply to staff moving to the new water and sewerage authorities and the Children's Reporter Administration respectively.

Employment by new authorities

14.—(1) If a new authority enter into a contract of employment with a person who has received or is entitled to receive a redundancy payment under Part VI of the Employment Protection (Consolidation) Act 1978—

(a) by reason of his dismissal at any time—

(i) after the passing of this Act by a regional or district council; or

(ii) after the passing of this Act and before 1st April 1996 by a joint committee or a joint board; or

(b) by reason of his having been employed, immediately before 1st April 1996, by such a council, committee or board under a contract of employment which would have continued but for the abolition of such councils, committees or boards on that date and who is not transferred to a new authority by virtue of an order under section 8 of this Act, the authority shall, if the Secretary of State so directs, pay to him, or to such person as he may direct, an amount equal to the redundancy payment.

(2) The Secretary of State shall not give a direction under subsection (1) above in respect of the employment of any person by a new authority if the authority satisfy him—

(a) that they could not reasonably have made that person an offer of employment on the terms and conditions of the contract first mentioned in that subsection which, if accepted by him, would have precluded his entitlement to the redundancy payment; or

(b) that the authority made such an offer but that the person concerned acted reasonably in refusing it; or

(c) that he could reasonably have refused such an offer if it had been made by the authority.

(3) In any case in which an amount is payable by a new authority under subsection (1) above there shall also be payable by them to the Secretary of State or to such person as he may direct an amount equal to any compensation under the regulations referred to in section 13(2) of this Act which has been paid or is payable to the person concerned before the time when he enters into the contract.

(4) In this section "new authority" means any of the authorities constituted under section 2 of this Act and a joint board.

DEFINITIONS
"joint board": s.61; s.235(1) of the 1973 Act.
"joint committee": s.61; s.235(1) of the 1973 Act.
"new authority": subs. (4).

GENERAL NOTE
This section is designed to enable the Secretary of State to direct in appropriate circumstances that where a person has been employed by a new authority, having earlier been dismissed by an old authority and become entitled to redundancy and other compensation payments, an amount equal to those payments must be paid to the Secretary of State himself or to some other person (which might be a residuary body). The idea is that this should operate as a deterrent to authorities (and individuals) who might otherwise seek to use the reorganisation process *both* to create an obligation to make redundancy payments *and* to re-employ the person concerned. *Bona fide* exceptions to the operation of this deterrent are listed in subs. (2).

CHAPTER 3

PROPERTY

Transfer of property

15.—(1) Subject to subsection (5) below, the Secretary of State may by order provide that any property vested in one or more existing local authorities immediately before 1st April 1996 shall on that date be transferred to and vest in such new authority or authorities as may be specified in or determined under the order.

(2) An order under this section may include provision for the transfer of all rights, liabilities and obligations of an existing local authority on 1st April 1996 to such new authority or authorities as may be specified in or determined under the order.

(3) An order under this section may make different provision in relation to—

(a) different items or categories of property;

(b) different, or different categories of, rights, liabilities or obligations; and

(c) different authorities.

(4) The power to transfer property conferred by this section includes power to transfer property which is held by an existing local authority as part

of the common good, but such property may not be transferred to a residuary body and, in administering such property, any authority to which it is transferred shall—

    (a) except in the case of the councils for Aberdeen, Dundee, Edinburgh and Glasgow, have regard to the interests of the inhabitants of the area to which the common good related prior to 16th May 1975; and

    (b) in the case of the councils for Aberdeen, Dundee, Edinburgh and Glasgow, have regard to the interests of all the inhabitants of their areas.

(5) This section does not apply to any property which is transferred under or by virtue of section 16, 17 or 91 of this Act.

(6) Orders under this section shall be made by statutory instrument, and a statutory instrument containing an order under this section shall be subject to annulment in pursuance of a resolution of either House of Parliament.

(7) For the purposes of this section—

    "existing local authority" includes a joint committee and a joint board but does not, subject to any other provision of this Act, include an islands authority;

    "new authority" means any of the authorities constituted under section 2 of this Act, and includes a joint board and a residuary body; and

    "property" includes any records held by, or in the custody of, an existing local authority.

DEFINITIONS

    "existing local authority": subs. (7).
    "joint board": s.61; s.235(1) of the 1973 Act.
    "joint committee": s.61; s.235(1) of the 1973 Act.
    "new authority": subs. (7).
    "property": subs. (7).
    "records": s.61.
    "residuary body": s.183(1); s.18.

GENERAL NOTE

This section makes general provision for the transfer of property from existing local authorities to new authorities on April 1, 1996. It does *not* apply to property transferred by virtue of s.16 (trusts), s.17 (educational endowments) or s.91 (new water authorities). It is applied, however, to property transfers in connection with the Principal Reporter system (s.138).

The principal power is given by subs. (1) to the Secretary of State to vest property by order (subs. (6)) which may include provisions stipulated in subss. (2) and (3). Although this is not made mandatory, it may be expected that the order-making power would be used following consultation with the Property Commission if one is established under s.19.

It should be observed that, in this section, a "new authority", to which the property of an "existing authority" may be transferred, is defined to include any "residuary body" which may be established under s.18. For an explanation of the function of such a body, see the notes on that section.

Subsection (4) makes special provision in relation to property held as part of the common good, and operates as a successor to s.222(2) and (3) of the 1973 Act. The normal result of a property transfer from one authority to another on reorganisation is to place the property at the disposal of the new authority to be used, subject to the normal constraints of the law, for the benefit of any part of the area of that authority and its people. It was, however, felt appropriate at the time of the 1975 reorganisation to provide that the funds and other property deriving from the common good of burghs, which were to be transferred to the relevant district and islands councils, should be used by those councils for the benefit of the inhabitants of the area of those burghs (*i.e.* "of the area to which the common good related prior to 16 May, 1975"). There was an exception in the case of the four major cities where it was felt more appropriate to permit the use of the common good over the whole of the area of the new district councils. The same formula is retained in this section. Property from the common good cannot be transferred to a residuary body.

Notice that property to be transferred may include "records" (subs. (7)). For the duties of authorities in relation to these and other records, see ss.53 and 54.

In general debate on the section, the opportunity was taken to discuss difficult questions of the transfer of office property and the issue of whether or not (by reference to Buchan and Midlothian) council offices should be in the council's own area (First Scottish Standing Committee, cols. 581–582).

Property held on trust

16.—(1) All property held on trust immediately before 1st April 1996 by—

(a) an existing local authority; or

(b) a councillor and the proper officer or a specified officer of such an authority,

shall on that day be transferred to and vest (subject to the same trust) in the appropriate new authority.

(2) The authority in whom property is vested by virtue of subsection (1) above shall nominate a sufficient number of their councillors to act as trustees of that property and in so doing shall have regard to the terms of the trust deed; and where the property is held immediately before 1st April 1996 by the persons mentioned in subsection (1)(b) above, the authority shall nominate the proper officer as one of the trustees.

(3) All property held on trust immediately before 1st April 1996 by a specified officer of an existing local authority shall on that date be transferred to and vest (subject to the same trust) in the proper officer of the appropriate new authority.

(4) Where, immediately before 1st April 1996, property is held on trust by the holder of an office, whether as a councillor, the proper officer or a specified officer, connected with an existing local authority or authorities and any other person, the appropriate new authority or authorities shall, on the application of the trustees, nominate a sufficient number of their councillors to act in place of such holder and in so doing shall have regard to the terms of the trust deed and, where the terms of the trust deed so require, the said authority or authorities shall nominate their proper officer or the proper officer of one of them as one of the trustees.

(5) Where the area of the existing local authority in which, or in any councillor or officer of which, any trust property is vested falls entirely within the area of a new authority, that new authority is the appropriate new authority for the purposes of this section.

(6) Where the area of the existing local authority in which, or in any councillor or officer of which, any trust property is vested falls within the area of two or more new authorities, those authorities may agree in writing as to which of them is or are the appropriate new authority or authorities for the purposes of this section; and such agreement shall be conclusive as to the vesting of the property in one or more of those new authorities.

(7) Where the authorities mentioned in subsection (6) above cannot reach agreement as to the vesting of any trust property any of them may refer the matter to the Secretary of State, who may give a direction as to which is the appropriate authority or, as the case may be, which are the appropriate authorities; and a direction by the Secretary of State under this subsection shall be conclusive as to the vesting of the trust property in the new authority or authorities concerned.

(8) An agreement under subsection (6) above and a direction under subsection (7) above may relate to trust property generally, or to particular items, types or classes of such property, or to trust property situated in a particular part of an authority's area.

(9) In this section—

"existing local authority" includes a joint committee and a joint board but does not include an islands authority; and

"new authority" includes any of the authorities constituted under section 2 of this Act (other than Orkney Islands, Shetland Islands or Western Isles) and a joint board.

(10) This section shall not apply to property which is subject to section 17 of this Act.

Definitions
"existing local authority": subs. (9).
"joint board": s.61; s.235(1) of the 1973 Act.
"joint committee": s.61; s.235(1) of the 1973 Act.
"new authority": subs. (9).

General Note
Section 15 enacts the general rules for the transfer of property from existing to new local authorities at local government reorganisation on April 1, 1996. By virtue, however, of s.15(5) that section does not apply to property held on trust which, subject to the exception of educational endowments (dealt with by s.17), is transferred under the terms of this section.

The main rule is as stated in subs. (1) – property held on trust by either an existing local authority, or by a councillor and property officer, or by a specified officer, is transferred to and vests (subject to the trust) in the appropriate new authority. Subsection (2) then instructs the new authority on the nomination of equivalent new trustees.

Subsection (3) makes special provision for any trust where property is held by a "specified officer" (*i.e.* a holder of a named office which, in cases such as directors of education and social work, will cease to exist as such after April 1, 1996 (see ss.31 and 45)). Such property passes to the "proper officer" of the new authority (*i.e.* an officer appointed for the purpose by the authority (s.235(3) of the 1973 Act)). Subsection (4) provides for new authorities to nominate appropriate new trustees (on the application of the trustees).

It should be noted that the section does not (by virtue of the definitions of authorities in subs. (9)) apply to islands authorities where transfer is presumably deemed to be unnecessary. It is not completely clear how transfers under *e.g.* subs. (3) may take place in the islands.

Identification of the "appropriate" (successor) authority is in terms of subss. (5)–(8). The main rule identifies the authority by reference to the area in which the trust property entirely lies (subs. (5)). If the trust property does not fall entirely within the area of one new authority, there is provision for agreement (subs. (6)) or direction by the Secretary of State (subs. (7)) – in either case subject to subs. (8).

Educational endowments

17.—(1) Where, immediately before 1st April 1996, educational endowments are to any extent vested in an existing local authority, the Secretary of State may by order make schemes providing for such endowments, on that date, to be transferred to and vest to the same extent in such new authority or authorities as may be specified in or determined under the scheme.

(2) A scheme made under this section may provide for educational endowments, to the extent that they are vested by virtue of his office in the holder of an office connected with an existing local authority or in a person nominated by such an authority, to be transferred to and vest in a person holding an office in, or nominated by, such new authority or authorities as may be specified in or determined under the scheme.

(3) A scheme under this section may provide for powers with respect to an educational endowment which are vested in an existing local authority or, by virtue of his office, in the holder of an office connected with such an authority or in a person nominated by such an authority, to be transferred to and vest in such new authority or authorities or, as the case may be, in a person holding office connected with, or nominated by, such an authority, as may be specified in or determined under the scheme.

(4) A scheme under this section may provide for any rights to be paid money out of an educational endowment which are vested in an existing local authority to be transferred to and vest in such new authority or authorities as may be specified in or determined under the scheme.

(5) The Secretary of State may require any existing local authority to provide him, in such form as he may specify, with their proposals for the transfer, in accordance with the provisions of this section, of any such educational endowments, powers or rights as are mentioned in subsections (1), (2), (3) or (4) above.

(6) Subject to subsection (7) below, a scheme under this section may make such provision in relation to an educational endowment as the Secretary of State considers appropriate and, without prejudice to the generality of the foregoing, may include provision for—

(a) amending or revoking the governing instrument of an endowment;

(b) grouping, amalgamating, combining or dividing any endowments;

(c) the purposes to which, and the conditions under which, any such endowments may be applied;

(d) incorporating or establishing new governing bodies, or dissolving, combining or uniting any governing bodies;

(e) the powers of the governing body of any endowment.

(7) In exercising his powers under subsection (6) above, the Secretary of State shall make no more changes with respect to any endowment than appear to him to be necessary or expedient in consequence of the alteration of local government areas effected by this Part of this Act.

(8) Schemes under this section may make different provision in relation to different endowments or categories of endowment, different provision in respect of different items or categories of property, rights, liabilities and obligations, and different provision in respect of different authorities.

(9) Subject to the provisions of the governing instrument of an educational endowment (including such an instrument made or amended by a scheme under this section), where, as the result of the election of a new authority occurring after 1st April 1996, it is necessary for a person to be nominated by the authority or by a committee thereof to be vested (to any extent) with the endowment, in terms of subsection (2) above, or to be vested with any power, in terms of subsection (3) above, that person shall be so nominated at the first meeting of the authority or committee held after it has been elected or appointed; and in such a case the person who (to the said extent) was last vested with the endowment or, as the case may be, who was last vested with the power, before the meeting shall continue therein until the date of the meeting.

(10) Section 19 of this Act applies in relation to educational endowments as it applies in relation to the property referred to in that section.

(11) An order under this section shall be made by statutory instrument subject to annulment in pursuance of a resolution of either House of Parliament.

(12) Expressions used in this section and in Part VI of the Education (Scotland) Act 1980 have the same meaning in this section as in that Part.

(13) Nothing in this section shall affect any other power to reorganise any educational endowment or otherwise to alter the provisions of any trust.

(14) In this section—

"authority" includes an existing local authority and a new authority;

"existing local authority" includes a joint committee and a joint board but does not include an islands authority; and

"new authority" means any of the authorities constituted under section 2 of this Act (other than Orkney Islands, Shetland Islands or Western Isles) and a joint board.

DEFINITIONS

"authority": subs. (14).

"existing local authority": subs. (14).

"joint board": s.61; s.235(1) of the 1973 Act.

"joint committee": s.61; s.235(1) of the 1973 Act.

"new authority": subs. (14).

GENERAL NOTE

Excluded from the effect of the more general provisions for the transfer of property from existing to new authorities contained in ss.15–16 are educational endowments. These are the subject matter of s.17 which makes provision for their transfer (save in relation to the islands authorities – subs. (14)), and requires this to be done in schemes made by order of the Secretary of State (subss. (1) and (11)). For an attempt to exclude the Secretary of State from making provision contrary to the wishes of affected authorities, see *Hansard*, H.L. Vol. 556, col. 1917.

Such schemes may make provision for the transfer and vesting of endowments themselves (subs. (2)), powers with respect to an endowment (subs. (3)) and rights to be paid money out of an endowment (subs. (4)). A scheme may include the provisions specified in subs. (6) (*i.e.* amending governing instruments etc.), but subject to the restriction in subs. (7) that changes must be only such as appear to the Secretary of State necessary or expedient in consequence of reorganisation. Schemes may make different provision in relation to different endowments etc. (subs. (8)). Subsection (5) gives the Secretary of State the power to require existing authorities to provide him with their own proposals for transfer.

Subsection (9) makes provision for the situation *after* April 1, 1996 where a new authority (or a committee) must make a nomination (under a governing instrument of an endowment – whether or not amended by a scheme under this section) of a person to be vested with an endowment (or a power in relation to endowment).

Subsection (10) applies to this section the provisions of s.19, *i.e.* relating to the Property Commission, if one is established. Subsection (12) applies to this section the meanings given to expressions used in Pt. VI of the Education (Scotland) Act 1980 (c. 44). For those, reference should, in particular, be made to s.122 of that Act where *e.g.* "educational endowment", "governing body" and "governing instrument" are defined.

Residuary bodies

18.—(1) The Secretary of State may by order establish one or more bodies, to be known as "residuary bodies", for the purpose of—
   (a) taking over and exercising such functions with respect to such property, rights and liabilities as may be transferred under section 15 of this Act; and
   (b) exercising such other functions, including, without prejudice to the generality of the foregoing, any functions which may be conferred on a property commission under section 19 of this Act,
as he may so prescribe.

(2) An order under this section may apply to a residuary body, with such modifications as may be specified, any enactment which applies to a local authority in Scotland.

(3) The Secretary of State may give directions to a residuary body as to—
   (a) the carrying out by them of any of their functions; and
   (b) the exercise by them of any of the powers conferred on them by or under this section.

(4) The Secretary of State may require a residuary body to make payments of such amounts, and at such times, as he may specify to a local authority or a joint board.

(5) The Secretary of State may require any local authority in the area in which a residuary body operates to meet such proportion of their expenses as he may determine.

(6) Any expenses incurred by a residuary body shall, in so far as they are not otherwise met, be paid by the Secretary of State out of money provided by Parliament.

(7) The Secretary of State may direct a residuary body to prepare, within such time as he may specify in the direction, a scheme for their winding up and for the disposal of their property, rights and liabilities.

(8) Subject to subsection (9) below, where a residuary body have prepared a scheme such as is mentioned in subsection (7) above, the Secretary of State may by order give effect to that scheme, subject to any modifications he considers appropriate, and any such order may—
   (a) include provision for the disposal, whether by transfer or otherwise, of the body's property; and
   (b) contain such supplementary and transitional provision as the Secretary of State thinks necessary or expedient.

(9) Where a residuary body is wound up in accordance with an order under subsection (8) above sections 8, 9, 10 and 13 of this Act shall apply, with any necessary modifications, to the staff of the residuary body as they apply to the staff of an existing local authority.

(10) Schedule 3 to this Act has effect in relation to residuary bodies.

(11) An order under this section shall be made by statutory instrument subject to annulment in pursuance of a resolution of either House of Parliament.

DEFINITIONS
"existing local authority": s.61.
"joint board": s.61; s.235(1) of the 1973 Act.

GENERAL NOTE
It will be noted that one possible beneficiary of an order transferring property under s.15 of the Act is a "residuary body" (s.15(7)). This section (and Sched. 3) provides for the establishment of such bodies and their functions.

The device of the residuary body was first used in British local government practice at the time of the abolition of the Greater London Council and the English metropolitan counties under the Local Government Act 1985 (c. 51). Under that Act, as will be the case in Scotland in 1996, a larger number of small authorities succeeded to the property rights and liabilities of their bigger predecessors. The idea is that, if this appears appropriate, specialised bodies should be given transitional responsibility for the winding-up of the affairs of the old authorities (as well as assuming the functions of the property commission to be established under s.19) rather than burdening the new authorities in their early years with these difficult and technical tasks.

The setting up of any residuary body will be done by order of the Secretary of State (subss. (1) and (11)), and he may give directions as to the carrying out of its functions. Such directions may include the preparation of a scheme to wind up its affairs (subss. (3) and (7)), following which the Secretary of State may give effect to the scheme (modified if appropriate) and dispose of the body's property.

In debate a number of issues were raised on provisions in s.18 and Sched. 3 (*Hansard*, H.L. Vol. 556, cols. 1925–1928). Although conceding that a residuary body should have a good knowledge of the authorities with which it worked and appointments would be made very much in agreement with them, the Government argued the bodies should not consist entirely of local authority members. Residuary bodies would not, however, be set up in opposition to local government but as a facilitator (see also First Scottish Standing Committee, cols. 597–617).

Property commission

19.—(1) Subject to subsection (2) below and after such consultation, whether before or after the passing of this Act, as he considers appropriate, the Secretary of State may by order establish a property commission for the purpose of—

    (a) advising authorities on matters relating to property to be transferred from existing local authorities to new authorities;

    (b) advising the Secretary of State on the general principles on which such property should be transferred; and

    (c) carrying out such other functions in relation to the transfer of property as may be specified in the order,

and for the purposes of this section "property" includes property held on trust to which section 16 of this Act applies.

(2) An order under this section may make provision as to the constitution and membership of the commission, the appointment and removal from office by the Secretary of State of the chairman and members of the commission, the employment of staff and the remuneration and superannuation of the members and staff of the commission.

(3) The Secretary of State may give directions—

    (a) to the commission as to the carrying out by them of their functions;

(b) as to the area or areas in which the commission are to carry out their functions;

(c) as to the procedure to be followed by the commission;

(d) for the supplying of information to the commission by any authority; and

(e) to any authority—

(i) as to the implementation of advice given to them by the commission; and

(ii) as to the payment by them of any expenses incurred by the commission in doing anything requested of them by that authority.

(4) The Secretary of State may by order provide for the winding up of the commission and the disposal of their assets.

(5) Any expenses incurred by the property commission and not recovered by them from an authority shall be paid by the Secretary of State out of money provided by Parliament.

(6) An order under this section shall be made by statutory instrument subject to annulment in pursuance of a resolution of either House of Parliament.

(7) In this section—

"authority" includes an existing local authority and a new authority;

"existing local authority" includes a joint committee and a joint board but does not include an islands authority; and

"new authority" means any of the authorities constituted under section 2 of this Act (other than Orkney Islands, Shetland Islands and Western Isles) and a joint board.

DEFINITIONS

"authority": subs. (7).
"existing local authority": subs. (7).
"joint board": s.61; s.235(1) of the 1973 Act.
"joint committee": s.61; s.235(1) of the 1973 Act.
"new authority": subs. (7).

GENERAL NOTE

This section provides the Secretary of State with the power (but not, in contrast with the 1973 Act, the duty) to establish a Property Commission with the mainly advisory functions set out in subs. (1). Although the content of the section was amended during its passage through the Commons to ensure greater specificity in the contents of any order establishing a Property Commission, the Government made it clear that a decision on whether or not a commission would be required would be left until a later stage. By the House of Lords Report stage it was still unclear whether a Property Commission would be established. A decision would be taken "in the coming months" (*Hansard*, H.L. Vol. 558, col. 313). It was thought that the property consequences of the 1996 reorganisation might be much less complex than those associated with that in 1975. It would, in general, be easier to consolidate property holdings in the hands of unitary authorities than to divide property between regions and districts.

If any residuary body is established under s.18, it may be given the functions of a Property Commission.

The setting up of a commission would be by order made by the Secretary of State following consultation (which may have taken place before or after the passing of the Act) (subss. (1) and (6)).

CHAPTER 4

GENERAL

Joint committees and joint boards

20. After section 62 of the 1973 Act (standing orders, etc.) there shall be inserted—

"**Incorporation of joint committees**

62A.—(1) Where—

(a) arrangements are made (whether under this Act or any other enactment) for two or more local authorities (in this Part of this Act referred to as "the relevant authorities") to discharge any of their functions, or any functions in any area, jointly;

(b) the relevant authorities have—

(i) appointed, or propose to appoint, a joint committee to discharge those functions; and

(ii) advertised their proposals in accordance with subsection (2) below; and

(c) application is made, in writing, to the Secretary of State by the relevant authorities for the incorporation of that joint committee (or proposed joint committee) as a joint board to carry out those functions,

the Secretary of State may by order establish a joint board in accordance with this section to discharge those functions.

(2) Before applying to the Secretary of State under subsection (1)(c) above, the relevant authorities shall place in at least one daily newspaper circulating in their areas an advertisement—

(a) giving brief details of what they propose to do;

(b) giving an address to which representations about the proposal may be sent; and

(c) fixing a date, being not less than 8 weeks after the date on which the advertisement appears, within which representations may be made,

and they shall include with their application evidence that an advertisement has been placed.

(3) Where any representations are timeously made in response to an advertisement placed in accordance with subsection (2) above, the relevant authorities shall consider them and shall include with their application a statement that they have done so.

(4) An order under subsection (1) above shall delegate to the joint board such of the functions of the relevant authorities as may be specified in the order and may include provision with respect to—

(a) the constitution and proceedings of the joint board;

(b) matters relating to the membership of the joint board;

(c) the transfer to the joint board of any property, rights and liabilities of the relevant authorities;

(d) the transfer to the joint board of any staff of the relevant authorities;

(e) the supply of services or facilities by the relevant authorities to the joint board,

and may, without prejudice to the generality of paragraphs (a) to (e) above, apply (with or without modifications) any of the provisions of Part V of this Act to a joint board as those provisions apply to a joint committee.

(5) A joint board established under this section shall be a body corporate and shall have a common seal.

(6) An order under subsection (1) above shall be in terms agreed by the relevant authorities.

(7) An instrument containing an order under this section shall be subject to annulment in pursuance of a resolution of either House of Parliament.

Power of Secretary of State to establish joint boards

62B.—(1) Where the Secretary of State considers—

(a) that any functions, or any functions in any area, of the relevant authorities should be discharged jointly by those authorities; and

(b) that arrangements, or satisfactory arrangements, for the joint discharge of those functions—

(i) have not been made by the relevant authorities; or
(ii) have ceased to be in operation,
he may, after consulting the relevant authorities, by order establish a joint board in accordance with this section.

(2) Subsections (4) and (5) of section 62A of this Act shall apply to a joint board established under this section as they apply to a joint board established under that section with the substitution of a reference to subsection (1) of this section for the reference to subsection (1) of that section.

(3) No order shall be made under subsection (1) above unless a draft of the instrument containing the order has been laid before, and approved by resolution of, each House of Parliament.

Further provisions relating to joint boards
62C.—(1) Where a joint board has been established by order under section 62A or 62B of this Act, the Secretary of State may by order provide—
(a) for excluding any functions, or any functions in any area, from those specified in the order establishing that joint board; and
(b) for the dissolution of the joint board.

(2) An order shall not be made under subsection (1) above unless the Secretary of State has consulted the relevant authorities.

(3) An instrument containing an order under this section shall be subject to annulment in pursuance of a resolution of either House of Parliament.

(4) The power to make an order under this section or section 62A or 62B of this Act shall include power to make such transitional, incidental, supplemental or consequential provision as the Secretary of State thinks necessary or expedient.

(5) An order under this section or section 62A or 62B of this Act may, for the purpose of making such provision as is mentioned in subsection (4) above—
(a) apply with or without modifications;
(b) extend, exclude or amend; or
(c) repeal or revoke with or without savings,
any enactment or any instrument made under any enactment.".

DEFINITIONS
"1973 Act": s.183(1).
"enactment": s.61; s.235(1) of the 1973 Act.
"joint board": s.61; s.235(1) of the 1973 Act.
"joint committee": s.61; s.235(1) of the 1973 Act.
"local authority": s.61; s.235(1) of the 1973 Act, as amended by Sched. 13.
"relevant authorities": s.62A(1) of the 1973 Act, as inserted by s.20.

GENERAL NOTE
One of the general advantages claimed for the new structure of single-tier authorities is that both the councils themselves and members of the public will benefit from the improved accountability and efficiency deriving from having only one council per local government area. In *Shaping the Future – The New Councils* (1993), the Government also acknowledged, however, that delivery of services by joint arrangements with other authorities, already used to some extent in the two-tier system, might be expected to expand.

The Government did not propose to extend the compulsory use of joint arrangements. Those already in place for police and fire services, the Passenger Transport Executive in and around Glasgow, and the assessor service, would remain but otherwise councils would, in general, choose whether to adopt joint arrangements.

Two statutory changes would, however, be put in place. One would be to provide greater flexibility in setting up joint *boards* (*i.e.* with separate legal personality) without the need for special primary legislation in each case, instead of simply appointing a joint committee under existing powers in the 1973 Act. In future joint boards would be set up by order of the Secretary of State on a request, from two or more authorities, which he considers to be reasonable. This power is provided by the new s.62A inserted into the 1973 Act by this section.

The other change would be to allow the Secretary of State to intervene to set up a joint board where he thought an existing level of service was unsatisfactory and could be improved by such joint arrangements. This power is provided in the new s.62B also inserted by this section. The new s.62C makes certain supplementary provision in relation to joint boards established under ss.62A and 62B.

In debates on the Bill, opposition to the increased use of joint arrangements between the new councils was voiced at many points. It was part of the argument against establishing a larger number of smaller authorities in the first place and it was also part of the argument raised in relation to specific functions and the quality of service delivery in future. Many of the attacks came, however, in relation to s.20 itself (see *e.g.* First Scottish Standing Committee, cols. 644–667). There would, it was argued, be confusion in the public mind and a loss of democratic accountability.

The new s.62A of the 1973 Act
The principal power to establish joint committees is contained in s.56(5) of the 1973 Act and it is where such a committee has been established or proposed that application can now be made in writing to the Secretary of State to incorporate a joint board. Although the White Paper referred to the need for the Secretary of State to think that the authorities' request was "reasonable", that criterion is not made explicit. Subsection (2) (with related consequential amendments) was inserted at the House of Lords Report stage following commitments given in Committee and imposes substantial additional requirements of prior publicity before application is made to the Secretary of State (*Hansard*, H.L. Vol. 558, cols. 215–218).

The provisions of s.62A should be read in conjunction with those in s.62C including the powers of the Secretary of State to exclude functions, dissolve a board or make "supplemental" provision.

The new s.62B of the 1973 Act
This contains the Secretary of State's power to intervene and, after consultation, establish a joint board on his own initiative. Such an order is made subject to an affirmative resolution, which reflects the seriousness of this power to impose a joint board. In debate, the hope was expressed that it might never need to be used. It was, however, also emphasised that "the services involved would continue to be run by the local authorities concerned" (*Hansard*, H.L. Vol. 558, col. 216). The Secretary of State would not appoint a board's members nor be involved in decisions taken. It was suggested that the reserve power to create a compulsory joint board might be used if, following the abolition of the regions, the standard of service delivered in the trading standards or public analyst functions was inadequate.

It should be noted that, whilst this section incorporates the provisions of subss. (4) and (5) of s.62A, subs. (6), requiring the terms of an order to be agreed by the authorities, is not so incorporated.

The new s.62C of the 1973 Act
This section enables the Secretary of State, having already his powers under ss.62A or 62B to create a joint board, to exclude functions from that board, or to dissolve the joint board. Subsections (4) and (5) of this section permit the making of supplemental provisions in orders under ss.62A or 62B or 62C, which may include amendment or repeal of Acts of Parliament.

Application of section 211 of the 1973 Act to joint boards

21. In section 211 of the 1973 Act (provisions for default of local authority), after subsection (4) insert—
    "(5) The provisions of this section shall apply to a joint board as they apply to a local authority.".

DEFINITIONS
    "1973 Act": s.183(1).
    "joint board": s.61; s.235(1) of the 1973 Act.
    "local authority": s.61; s.235(1) of the 1973 Act, as amended by Sched. 13.

GENERAL NOTE
    Section 211 of the 1973 Act gives the Secretary of State various powers (including inquiry, order and enforcement action in the Court of Session) to compel action by a local authority

where it is believed to be in default. This amendment applies the same rules to joint boards (including those which may be established under the new provisions enacted under s.20).

Community councils

22.—(1) Subject to subsection (2) below, schemes for the establishment of community councils made and approved under section 52 of the 1973 Act, including any such schemes as amended by virtue of section 53 of that Act, which are effective immediately before 1st April 1996 shall continue to have effect in respect of the area, or part of an area, to which they apply on and after that date.

(2) Without prejudice to their duty under section 53 of the 1973 Act, on and after 1st April 1996, a local authority may revoke a scheme (or an amended scheme) such as is mentioned in subsection (1) above in so far as it relates to their area and make a new scheme in accordance with this section.

(3) Where a local authority propose to make a new scheme such as is mentioned in subsection (2) above—

(a) they shall give public notice of their intention to revoke the existing scheme and make a new scheme for the establishment of community councils, and any such notice shall invite the public, within a period of not less than eight weeks from the date of the notice, to make suggestions as to the areas and composition of the community councils;

(b) after considering suggestions made under paragraph (a) above, the local authority shall prepare and give public notice of a draft scheme which shall contain—

(i) a map showing the boundaries of the proposed areas of community councils and their populations, and the boundaries of any area for which the local authority consider a community council to be unnecessary;

(ii) where a local authority consider that a community council is unnecessary for any area, a statement of their reasons for arriving at that conclusion;

(iii) provisions relating to qualifications of electors, elections or other voting arrangements, composition, meetings, financing and accounts of community councils;

(iv) provisions concerning the procedures to be adopted by which the community councils on the one hand and the local and public authorities with responsibilities in the areas of the community councils on the other will keep each other informed on matters of mutual interest; and

(v) such other information as, in the opinion of the local authority, will help the public to make a reasonable appraisal of the scheme;

(c) the notice mentioned in paragraph (b) above shall invite the public, within a period of not less than eight weeks from the date of the notice, to make representations to the local authority as respects the draft scheme;

(d) after considering any representations made under paragraph (c) above, the local authority may, after giving public notice of the amendments to the proposals and a further invitation to make representations, amend the draft scheme to take account of those representations and adopt it;

(e) the local authority shall give public notice of the scheme in its adopted form together with public notice of such a scheme as it applies to each proposed area, by exhibition in that area, and any such notice shall contain an invitation to electors in the area concerned to apply in writing to the authority for the establishment of a community council in accordance with the scheme.

DEFINITIONS
  "1973 Act": s.183(1).
  "local authority": s.61; s.235(1) of the 1973 Act, as amended by Sched. 13.

GENERAL NOTE

  One of the more significant innovations made by the 1973 Act was the introduction, on the recommendation of the Wheatley Commission, of community councils. The point of community councils was not to provide a third tier of local government but for each council "to ascertain, co-ordinate and express to the local authorities for its area, and to public authorities, the views of the community which it represents, in relation to matters for which those authorities are responsible, and to take such action in the interests of that community as appears to it to be expedient and practicable" (s.51(2) of the 1973 Act).

  As the Government said in their consultation paper *Shaping the New Councils* (1992), "community councils vary widely" – in terms of the size of population they represent, levels of funding and degrees and types of activity. The Government decided to retain the councils after reorganisation but also to consider strengthening their representational role in relation to the planning and licensing functions of local authorities.

  This section maintains existing community council schemes but gives the new local authorities the opportunity to revoke any scheme affecting their area and then to make a new scheme. Unlike the original schemes after the 1975 reorganisation, this may be done without the involvement of the Secretary of State. Provision is made for initial representations from the public followed by more detailed consultation on a draft scheme before its adoption.

  As mentioned in debate (First Scottish Standing Committee, col. 672), the changes made by this section will be accompanied by a strengthening of community councils' rights to consultation on planning matters. Community councils are also required to be consulted in relation to the new decentralisation schemes (s.23(4)).

Duty to prepare decentralisation schemes

  23.—(1) Every council shall have a duty to prepare a draft decentralisation scheme for their area in accordance with this section.

  (2) A draft decentralisation scheme shall contain a council's proposals for the administration of their functions within the whole area of the council and shall specify the date or dates by which such a draft scheme shall be implemented and, without prejudice to the generality of the foregoing, may include provision as to—

  (a) arrangements for the holding of meetings of the council (or any committee or sub-committee of the council) at particular places within the area of the council;

  (b) the establishment of committees for particular areas and the delegation to those committees (under section 56 of the 1973 Act) of specified functions of the council;

  (c) the location of offices of the council within the council's area, the staffing of such offices and the delegation to members of staff (under the said section 56) of specified functions;

  (d) the provision of facilities at particular places within the area of the council where advice may be obtained on services provided by the council.

  (3) Every council shall, before 1st April 1997, give public notice of the fact that they have prepared a draft decentralisation scheme and of the places within their area where copies of the draft scheme may be inspected, and any such notice shall invite the public, within a period of not less than eight weeks from the date of the notice, to make to the council representations as regards the draft scheme.

  (4) Every council shall, during the period mentioned in subsection (3) above, consult the community councils within their area about the draft scheme.

  (5) After considering any representations made under subsection (3) or (4) above, the council may amend the draft scheme (whether to take account of those representations or otherwise) and shall adopt the scheme.

(6) After the scheme has been adopted, the council shall—

(a) send a copy of the scheme in its adopted form to the Secretary of State; and

(b) give public notice of such scheme.

(7) Where a scheme has been adopted, it shall be the duty of the council concerned to implement the scheme by the date or dates specified in the scheme.

(8) A council may amend a scheme adopted under this section or revoke and replace such a scheme but the amended scheme or, as the case may be, new scheme shall be adopted in accordance with the provisions of this section, subject to such modifications as are necessary.

(9) The Secretary of State may, after consulting such associations of local authorities and such other persons as appear to him to be appropriate, issue guidance with respect to the form and content of decentralisation schemes.

(10) A council shall take account of any guidance issued under subsection (9) above.

DEFINITIONS

"1973 Act": s.183(1).

"local authority": s.61; s.235(1) of the 1973 Act, as amended by Sched. 13.

GENERAL NOTE

In *Shaping the Future – The New Councils* (Cm. 2267, 1993) the Government declared that one of its "main objectives in reorganising local government has been to make it more accessible and accountable to local people" (para. 3.5). Simply to have a single-tier system would, it thought, go a long way towards this but it wanted to give councils additional encouragement "to seek the views of their electors and respond to their concerns". Thus, councils would be required to devise and publish, by April 1, 1997, plans showing how they will devolve responsibility in their organisations, use local offices to make services accessible and establish new arrangements for consulting and involving local communities. There would be central guidance but schemes would not require the approval of the Secretary of State.

This section is intended to give effect to these aims. The adoption of a decentralisation scheme is a process under the control of a council, subject to the obligations to consult (subss. (3) and (4)), and to take account of the Secretary of State's guidance (subss. (9) and (10)). However, the council *must* adopt the scheme (subs. (5)), although the precise timetable for adoption is not laid down, and it *must* implement the scheme by the date it specifies. Presumably to fail to do so would render the council vulnerable to default action by the Secretary of State (under s.211 of the 1973 Act), to judicial review, or perhaps to the attentions of the local ombudsman.

Defending the Government's proposals for decentralisation, the Minister of State in the House of Lords described the issue as "a cornerstone of the new structure of local government in Scotland" but that, given the diversity of size and nature of the new authorities, it was "important not to be over-prescriptive in terms of specifying what should or should not be included in . . . schemes" (*Hansard*, H.L. Vol. 558, cols. 221–222). Although perhaps appropriate in relation to Fife or Highlands, there should not, for instance, be any general requirement that decision-making be formally delegated.

The section had earlier attracted a long and wide-ranging debate at the Commons Committee Stage (First Scottish Standing Committee, cols. 677–773). Scottish Office guidance on the process was promised (*ibid.*, cols. 756 and 767). There was an interesting attempt (resisted on technical grounds) to exempt "decentralised committees" from the provisions of s.15 of the Local Government and Housing Act 1989 (c. 42) (duty to allocate seats to political groups) – a section which has not yet been brought into effect in Scotland (see *ibid.*, cols. 772–773).

CHAPTER 5

FINANCE

Transitional provisions

Transitional provisions: finance

24. After section 94 of the 1992 Act insert—

"Transitional provisions

94A.—(1) The Secretary of State may, after consulting such associations of local authorities as appear to him to be appropriate, specify in a report, as regards the financial year 1996–97 and any local authority, the amount which in his opinion should be used as the basis of comparison for the purposes of paragraph 1(1) of Schedule 7 to this Act.

(2) A report under this section—

(a) shall contain such explanation as the Secretary of State considers desirable of the calculation by him of the amount mentioned in subsection (1) above; and

(b) shall be laid before the House of Commons.

(3) A report under this section may relate to two or more authorities and may be amended by a subsequent report under this section.

(4) If a report under this section is approved by resolution of the House of Commons, paragraph 1(1) of Schedule 7 to this Act shall have effect, as regards the financial year 1996–97 and any authority to which the report relates, as if the amount mentioned in subsection (1) above were the basis of comparison there referred to.

(5) This section shall not apply in relation to Orkney Islands, Shetland Islands and Western Isles.".

DEFINITIONS
"local authority": s.61; s.235(1) of the 1973 Act, as amended by Sched. 13.

GENERAL NOTE
Section 94 of and Sched. 7 to the Local Government Finance Act 1992 (c. 14) give the Secretary of State the power to propose a reduction in the level of council tax (*i.e.* cap the council tax) of a local authority where he considers either that its planned expenditure is excessive or that there has been an excessive increase as compared with the previous year. In *Shaping the Future – The New Councils* (Cm. 2267, 1993) the Government made clear its intention that in order to avoid "a surge in spending by local government" and to protect local tax payers at the time or reorganisation, the power to cap would be retained.

One transitional consequence of this is the need for a specific power to establish the baseline figures with which proposed spending by authorities (except the islands authorities) in 1996–1997 will be compared for the purposes of assessing whether an "increase" in spending is excessive. The means for doing this (by report approved by the House of Commons) is provided by this section.

In debate, an attempt was made to suspend the availability of capping powers in 1996–1997 to ensure that the full transitional costs of reorganisation could be financed but the Government insisted that the powers were essential (*Hansard*, H.L. Vol. 556, cols. 1935–1938). There had earlier been a long debate on the section at the Commons Committee Stage (First Scottish Standing Committee, cols. 774–815). The opportunity was used to revisit issues relating to the whole cost of reorganisation.

Financing of new authorities prior to 1st April 1996

25.—(1) The Secretary of State may with the consent of the Treasury make grants of such amounts, and subject to such conditions, to local authorities as he considers appropriate.

(2) A local authority may with the consent of the Secretary of State (who shall in turn seek the consent of the Treasury) borrow by way of temporary loan or overdraft from a bank or otherwise any sums which they may tempor-

arily require for the purpose of defraying expenses (including the payment of sums due by them to meet the expenses of other authorities) pending the receipt of revenues receivable by them after 1st April 1996.

(3) Grants made under this section shall be made out of money provided by Parliament.

(4) In this section "local authority" means any of the local authorities the members of which are to be elected, in accordance with section 5 of this Act, on 6th April 1995.

DEFINITIONS
"local authority": subs. (4).

GENERAL NOTE
Transitional provision is made by this section to enable the Secretary of State to make grants (subs. (1)) to the authorities to be elected on April 6, 1995 (*i.e.* the "shadow authorities" and not, therefore, including the islands councils). Although this is not specified in the section (and indeed subs. (1) is not drafted to include any cut-off date), this will be to enable initial provision for staff appointments and necessary planning, in advance of April 1, 1996. Similarly, the same authorities are given powers to borrow, subject to the consent of the Secretary of State, pending the commencement of full funding arrangements from the same date.

In the Lords it was stated that it had yet to be decided whether one or other method of funding would be used (or both in combination). Discussions with C.O.S.L.A. were taking place. (*Hansard*, H.L. Vol. 558, col. 228.)

Valuation and rating

Valuation lists

26.—(1) Subject to the provisions of this section, the local assessor for each new local authority area shall compile for the council for that area, from the existing valuation lists, a valuation list as at 1st April 1996.

(2) The provisions of section 84 of the 1992 Act (compilation and maintenance of valuation lists) shall apply, with any necessary modifications, to a valuation list compiled under subsection (1) above as they apply to a valuation list compiled under that section.

(3) As soon as reasonably practicable after compiling a valuation list under subsection (1) above, the local assessor shall send a copy of the list to the council for whose area the list was compiled; and the council shall, as soon as reasonably practicable, deposit it at their principal office.

(4) Subsection (1) above does not apply to the local assessors for the councils of the Borders, Dumfries and Galloway, Fife, Highland, Orkney Islands, Shetland Islands or Western Isles.

(5) In this section—

"existing valuation lists" means the lists maintained under the said section 84 of the 1992 Act on the day on which this section comes into force in relation to the area of any regional council whose area includes any part of the area of the new authority; and

"valuation list" has the same meaning as in the 1992 Act.

(6) A local assessor shall compile a list under this section by extrapolating from the existing valuation lists and, accordingly, except to the extent that valuation may be required to be carried out under any provision of the 1992 Act, shall not carry out any valuation of property for the purposes of a list compiled under this section.

DEFINITIONS
"1992 Act": s.61.
"council": s.2.
"existing valuation list": subs. (5).
"valuation list": subs. (5).

GENERAL NOTE
    Essential to the administration of the system of local finance based on the council tax, which is to continue after reorganisation, is the preparation by the "local assessor" of a "valuation list" for each local government area. The "local assessor" is, by s.84(10) of the Local Government Finance Act 1992, defined as the "assessor" appointed for valuation for rating purposes but, although the two offices are combined in the same person, functions in relation to the council tax (as under this section) are quite distinct from the valuation for rating functions (as under s.27 of this Act). A slight terminological oddity in this section (and s.27) is the use of "local authority area" instead of "local government area" as in s.1.
    The general law on the council tax is contained in Pt. II of the Local Government Finance Act 1992 and reference should be made to that Act for a detailed account. Under s.84 of that Act, valuation lists have already been prepared and are in operation for existing local authority areas. Because the areas identified in subs. (4) will continue to operate within existing boundaries, no new valuation lists will be required. In other areas, however, subs. (1) requires each local assessor to prepare a new valuation list as at April 1, 1996. This operation is to be done "from the existing valuation lists" (subs. (1)) or "by extrapolating from the existing valuation lists" (subs. (4)). No new valuation of property is required. A copy of the new list must be sent to the council for whose area it was compiled.

Valuation areas and authorities and appointment of assessors etc.

    27.—(1) Each local authority area shall be a valuation area, and the council of each area shall be the valuation authority for that area; and on and after 1st April 1996 the valuation authorities constituted under this section shall have and exercise in relation to valuation the powers exercisable by valuation authorities immediately prior to that date.
    (2) Every valuation authority shall, in accordance with the provisions of this section, appoint an assessor and such number of depute assessors as the authority may consider necessary for the purposes of the Valuation Acts; and any assessor or depute assessor appointed under the 1973 Act by a regional or islands council and holding office immediately before 1st April 1996 shall cease to hold office on that date.
    (3) The Secretary of State shall by order prescribe the qualifications required to be possessed by any person appointed to the office of assessor or depute assessor and, except as otherwise provided in such an order, a person shall not be appointed as assessor or depute assessor unless he possesses the qualifications so prescribed.
    (4) A depute assessor appointed under this section shall have and may exercise all the functions of an assessor so appointed.
    (5) An assessor or depute assessor appointed under this section shall hold office on such reasonable terms and conditions, including conditions as to remuneration, as the authority appointing him think fit.
    (6) An assessor or depute assessor appointed under this section shall hold office during the pleasure of the valuation authority but shall not be removed from office (or required to resign as an alternative thereto) except—
        (a) by a resolution of the authority passed by not less than two-thirds of the members present at a meeting of the authority the notice of which specifies as an item of business the consideration of the removal from office of the assessor or his being required to resign; and
        (b) with the consent of the Secretary of State,
and before deciding whether or not to give such consent the Secretary of State shall give the authority and the assessor an opportunity of being heard by a person appointed by the Secretary of State.
    (7) If it appears to the Secretary of State that any functions, or any functions in any area, of two or more valuation authorities should be discharged jointly by those authorities, he may by order establish a joint board in accordance with this section.
    (8) An order under this section shall delegate to the joint board such of the

functions of the valuation authorities concerned under the Valuation Acts as may be specified in the order and may include such incidental, consequential and supplemental provision as the Secretary of State considers necessary or expedient for bringing the order into operation and for giving full effect thereto.

(9) Without prejudice to the generality of subsection (8) above, an order under this section may include provision with respect to—

(a) the constitution and proceedings of the joint board;

(b) matters relating to the membership of the joint board;

(c) the transfer to the joint board of any property, rights and liabilities of the authorities concerned;

(d) the transfer to the joint board of any staff of the authorities concerned;

(e) the supply of services or facilities by the authorities concerned to the joint board; and

(f) the dissolution of the joint board,

and may, without prejudice to the generality of paragraphs (a) to (f) above, apply (with or without modifications) any of the provisions of Part V of the 1973 Act to a joint board established under this section as those provisions apply to a joint committee.

(10) A joint board established under this section shall be a body corporate and shall have a common seal.

(11) An order under this section shall be made by statutory instrument subject to annulment in pursuance of a resolution of either House of Parliament.

(12) Any reference in any enactment to a valuation authority shall, where any function to which that enactment relates is for the time being exercised by a joint board established under this section, include any such joint board.

DEFINITIONS

"1973 Act": s.183(1).

"joint board": s.61; s.235(1) of the 1973 Act.

"joint committee": s.61; s.235(1) of the 1973 Act.

"the Valuation Acts": s.183(1).

"valuation area": subs. (1).

"valuation authority": subs. (1).

GENERAL NOTE

In addition to this section, note the provisions in Sched. 14 which repeal s.1 of the Valuation and Rating (Scotland) Act 1956 (c. 60) (which dealt with the appointment of assessors) and s.116 of the 1973 Act (valuation areas, assessors, etc.).

This section replaces those earlier provisions and establishes each (new) local authority area (or "local government area" – see the note to s.26) as a valuation area. The council, subject to subss. (7)–(12) under which joint boards may be established, becomes the valuation authority with the powers previously enjoyed by existing authorities (subs. (1)). At present, although there are a total of 12 regional and islands councils, there are, as a result of compulsory amalgamations, only 10 valuation authorities (and assessors). *Shaping the Future – The New Councils* (Cm. 2267, 1993) made it clear that, as part of a strategy of seeking a harmonised approach to valuation both within Scotland and in comparison with England and Wales, the number of authorities and assessors should not increase above 10, and the powers to create joint boards will be used to achieve this. In debate, it was stated that precise boundaries for the resulting combined areas had not yet been decided and the Government was still consulting on this. In response to questions, the Minister confirmed that, although the practice of combining the roles of assessor and of electoral registration officer had worked well and was expected to continue, there was no intention to make the combination mandatory by statute (First Scottish Standing Committee, cols. 890–891).

Valuation authorities do not themselves have substantive responsibilities for the valuation process. Instead their main function is to appoint the assessor (who also becomes the "local assessor" for council tax purposes – see s.26) and depute assessors, whose task is to make up valuation rolls (on which see also s.28), and to perform all the other functions imposed by valuation legislation. For a detailed account, see *Armour* on *Valuation for Rating* (5th ed., by J.J. Clyde and J.A.D. Hope).

The provisions relating to these appointments (subss. (2)–(6)) are drawn from existing rules in the Valuation and Rating (Scotland) Act 1956 and the 1973 Act – including the power of the Secretary of State to prescribe qualifications (subs. (3) – for existing rules see the Local Government (Qualification of Assessors) (Scotland) Regulations 1956 (S.I. 1956 No. 1594), and the protection of tenure of assessors and deputes (subs. (6)). It was stated in debate (First Scottish Standing Committee, col. 889) that the Government had no current intention to vary the present qualifications which had served the system well since 1956. There had been a review in the 1980s but a change had not been considered appropriate. Under subs. (2), existing assessors appointed by regional and islands councils cease to hold office at April 1, 1996. However, it may be queried whether this unambiguously includes those assessors appointed not by a single regional or islands council but by joint committees acting for councils in combination; see the Valuation (Combination of Councils) (Scotland) (No. 2) Order 1974 (S.I. 1974 No. 1565).

Valuation rolls

28.—(1) Subject to the provisions of this section, the assessor for each valuation area shall make up for the valuation authority for that area, from the existing valuation rolls, a valuation roll as at 1st April 1996.

(2) Subsection (1) above does not apply to the assessors for the councils of the Borders, Dumfries and Galloway, Fife, Highland, Orkney Islands, Shetland Islands or Western Isles.

(3) In this section "existing valuation rolls" means the rolls made up under subsection (1) of section 1 of the 1975 Act (valuation roll and revaluation) and in force by virtue of subsection (2) of that section on the day on which this section comes into force in relation to the area of any existing valuation authority whose area includes any part of the area of the new valuation authority.

(4) Valuation rolls made up under this section shall be made up in the form prescribed for the purposes of section 1 of the 1975 Act; and subsections (4) and (5) of that section shall apply to such rolls as they apply to valuation rolls made up under subsection (1) of that section.

(5) An assessor shall make up a valuation roll under this section by extrapolating from the existing valuation rolls, and accordingly, except to the extent that alteration of the valuation roll may be required to be carried out under section 2 of the 1975 Act (alteration to valuation roll in force), shall not make any alteration of the entries in the roll for the purposes of a roll made up under this section.

DEFINITIONS
  "1975 Act": s.183(1).
  "existing valuation rolls": subs. (3).
  "valuation area": s.27.
  "valuation authority": s.27.

GENERAL NOTE
  This section is intended to achieve in relation to the rating valuation roll what s.26 does for the preparation of council tax valuation lists to accommodate the creation of the new valuation areas. With the exception of the assessors for the seven councils identified in subs. (2) (*i.e.* those whose areas are unaffected by reorganisation), assessors must make up a valuation roll as at April 1, 1996. This is a process to be based on "existing valuation rolls" as explained in subs. (3) and, therefore, by "extrapolation" but without alteration (subs. (5)).
  Subsection (4) applies to the duties under this section the terms of s.1 of the 1975 Act and especially subss. (4) and (5) of that section. These ensure that assessors provide copies of the roll to rating authorities and that those authorities make the rolls open to public inspection.

Valuation appeal panels and committees

29.—(1) With effect from 1st April 1996—
  (a) valuation appeal panels and valuation appeal committees shall be constituted for each valuation area, in accordance with the provisions of this section and with regulations made by the Secretary of State, for the purpose of hearing and determining appeals and complaints—

      (i) under the Valuation Acts; and
      (ii) under sections 81(1) and 87(6) of the 1992 Act (council tax appeals); and

  (b) every local valuation panel and valuation appeal committee constituted under section 4 of the 1975 Act shall cease to exist, and that section shall cease to have effect.

(2) A valuation appeal committee shall consist of members of a valuation appeal panel, and members of such a panel shall be appointed by the sheriff principal after such consultation as he thinks fit.

(3) Regulations under this section may make provision—

  (a) for one valuation appeal panel to be appointed to serve two or more valuation areas;

  (b) as to—
      (i) the qualifications of members of a valuation appeal panel, and of any secretary or assistant secretary to be appointed to such a panel;
      (ii) the maximum and minimum number of members of any such panel; and
      (iii) the termination of the appointment of such members;

  (c) with respect to the appointment of—
      (i) one of those members as chairman of the panel;
      (ii) such number of deputy chairmen as the sheriff principal considers appropriate; and
      (iii) a secretary and, if the sheriff principal considers it necessary, an assistant secretary or assistant secretaries of the panel;

  (d) as to—
      (i) the number of valuation appeal committees to be formed from a valuation appeal panel;
      (ii) the maximum and minimum number of members of such a committee; and
      (iii) the manner in which members of a valuation appeal committee are to be selected from a valuation appeal panel;

  (e) as to the terms and conditions of employment (including remuneration and allowances) of any secretary or assistant secretary of a valuation appeal panel;

  (f) as to the payment to members of a valuation appeal panel and a valuation appeal committee of such allowances as the Secretary of State may determine;

  (g) as to the defraying of any expenses incurred by a valuation appeal panel or committee; and

  (h) for any other matter which appears to the Secretary of State to be necessary, expedient or appropriate for the purpose of the administration of valuation appeal panels and committees,

and regulations under this section may make different provision in respect of different valuation appeal areas or different valuation panels.

(4) All members of a valuation appeal panel shall reside or be engaged in business or be employed in the valuation area or areas for which the panel is responsible; and no person appointed as the secretary or an assistant secretary of a panel shall be an officer of a local authority or shall by himself or by any partner or assistant appear before a valuation appeal committee for that area.

(5) A valuation authority may pay reasonable subscriptions, whether annually or otherwise, to the funds of any association of members or officers of valuation appeal panels or valuation appeal committees formed for the purpose of consultation as to the common interests of those panels or committees and the discussion of matters relating to valuation.

(6) The provisions of the Valuation Acts with regard to appeals and complaints shall, with any necessary modifications, apply to a committee consti-

tuted under this section in like manner as they applied before 1st April 1996 to a committee constituted under the 1975 Act.

(7) Where the area served by a valuation appeal panel is situated in more than one sheriffdom, its members shall be appointed by the sheriff principal for such one of those sheriffdoms as the Secretary of State may direct.

(8) Regulations under this section shall be made by statutory instrument which shall be subject to annulment in pursuance of a resolution of either House of Parliament.

DEFINITIONS
"1975 Act": s.183(1).
"1992 Act": s.61.
"the Valuation Acts": s.183(1).
"valuation area": s.27.
"valuation authority": s.27.

GENERAL NOTE
This section should be read with Sched. 14 which repeals s.4 of the 1975 Act, which constituted local valuation panels and valuation appeal committees. The section establishes the rules for the new panels and committees from April 1, 1996. The function of the committees is, as explained in subs. (1), to hear and determine valuation (for rating) appeals and council tax appeals. Panels (and committees) are to be established in accordance with regulations made by the Secretary of State (subss. (1), (3) and (8)), and members of panels are to be appointed by the sheriff principal (subs. (2), subject to subs. (7)).

Although this section abandons the concept of the "model scheme" as the means of prescribing rules in this area, the Secretary of State's powers appear to remain much as they were under the 1975 Act. Subsections (4) and (5) substantially repeat the terms of subss. (6) and (7) of s.4 of the 1975 Act.

Rating authorities

30. The rating authority for any local government area shall be the local authority for that area and, in this Act and in any other enactment (whether passed or made before or after the passing of this Act), the expression "rating authority" shall be construed in accordance with this section.

DEFINITIONS
"enactment": s.61; s.235(1) of the 1973 Act.
"local government area": s.1.

GENERAL NOTE
Under the two-tier system of local government it has been the regional (and islands) councils which, as "rating authorities", have had the responsibility for levying rates. Under the new system, all the unitary authorities become "rating authorities". The responsibilities are now confined to "non-domestic rates" and are subject to the Secretary of State's powers to prescribe particular levels of rate poundage under s.7A (and eventually s.7B) of the 1975 Act, both as inserted by s.110 of the Local Government Finance Act 1992. They are set out, *inter alia*, in Pt. XI of the Local Government (Scotland) Act 1947 and Pt. I of the 1975 Act (both as much amended).

CHAPTER 6

FUNCTIONS

Education

Education

31. For section 124 of the 1973 Act (education committees) there shall be substituted—

"Membership of committees appointed by education authorities

124.—(1) Where an education authority appoint a committee whose purposes include—

(a) advising the authority on any matter relating to the discharge of their functions as education authority; or

(b) discharging any of those functions of the authority on their behalf,

the members of such committee shall, notwithstanding the provisions of section 57(3) and (4)(a) of this Act, be appointed in accordance with this section.

(2) Subject to the provisions of section 59 of this Act, an education authority who appoint a committee such as is mentioned in subsection (1) above shall secure that—

(a) at least half of the persons appointed by them to be members of such committee are members of the authority; and

(b) the persons appointed by them to be members of such committee shall include the three persons mentioned in subsection (4) below.

(3) Subject to the provisions of subsection (2) above, an education authority may appoint persons who are not members of the authority to be members of a committee such as is mentioned in subsection (1) above.

(4) The three persons mentioned in subsection (2)(b) above (who shall not be members of the education authority appointing such committee) are—

(a) one representative of the Church of Scotland, nominated in such manner as may be determined by the General Assembly of the Church;

(b) in the case of the education authority for each area other than Orkney Islands, Shetland Islands and Western Isles, one representative of the Roman Catholic Church, nominated in such manner as may be determined by the Scottish Hierarchy of the Church; and

(c) one person or, in the case of the education authorities for Orkney Islands, Shetland Islands and Western Isles, two persons, in the selection of whom the authority shall have regard (taking account of the representation of churches under paragraphs (a) and (b) above) to the comparative strength within their area of all the churches and denominational bodies having duly constituted charges or other regularly appointed places of worship there.

(5) Where two or more authorities appoint a joint committee whose purposes include discharging any of the functions of those authorities as education authorities on their behalf, section 57(3) of this Act shall apply to such a joint committee as if for the words "two-thirds" there were substituted the words "one-half".".

DEFINITIONS

"1973 Act": s.183(1).

"education authority": s.61; s.235(1) of the 1973 Act; s.135(1) of the Education (Scotland) Act 1980, as amended by para. 118(9) of Sched. 13 to this Act.

"joint committee": s.61; s.235(1) of the 1973 Act.

GENERAL NOTE

This is one of a number of provisions affecting the education service – see also s.32, ss.143–145, and amendments (Sched. 13, para. 118) and repeals (Sched. 14) affecting the Education (Scotland) Act 1980.

This section substitutes a new s.124 in the 1973 Act. Along with the repeal of s.127 of and Sched. 10 to the 1973 Act by Sched. 14 of this Act, it effects two main changes in relation to "education committees". In the first place, the new councils will not, from April 1, 1996, be formally required to establish a committee by that name at all. The new s.124 inserted by this section applies only where an authority appoints a committee whose purposes *include* those set out in subs. (1). This change attracted great controversy when debated in Parliament (see *e.g.* First Scottish Standing Committee, col. 900 *et seq.*) – as did a similar change affecting social work committees. It accompanied the abolition of the *obligation* to have a Director of Education. The Government's justification was, however, that these changes would afford greater flexibility for authorities in the management of their affairs (see *The Internal Management of Local Authorities in Scotland* (1993) Ch. 3). It would also facilitate the setting up of joint arrangements between authorities.

Where a committee with educational responsibilities is set up, however, it is the Government's wish to retain certain of the special features affecting their composition. In particular, at least half the members must also be members of the authority (the general rule in relation to other committees is "at least two-thirds"; see s.57(3) of the 1973 Act), and there must be the religious representation required by the new subs. (4).

However, the second major change introduced, also the cause of great controversy in Parliament (see *e.g. Hansard*, H.L. Vol. 556, cols. 1939–41), was the removal of the long-standing obligation to appoint two of the authority's teachers to the committee. This feature of education committees had been the subject of discussion for many years (see *e.g.* Widdicombe Report (Cmnd. 9797, paras. 5.104–5.106)). The Government's view was that it had become an anomaly. However, the power (as opposed to the duty) to appoint teachers has been retained. Thus para. 92(29) of Sched. 13 substitutes a new s.126 in the 1973 Act which provides that, notwithstanding s.59 of that Act (which disqualifies from membership of committees and sub-committees any employees of the authority), a person is not disqualified from being a member of an education committee (or sub-committee or joint committee), by reason of being a teacher in an educational establishment managed by the authority. Read together, the terms of the two sections now impose no limit on the number of teachers who may be appointed to an education committee.

As already mentioned, the abolition of the statutory requirement to establish an education committee is accompanied by the abolition of the requirement to appoint a Director of Education. This is achieved by the repeal (by Sched. 13, para. 118(4) and Sched. 14 to this Act) of s.78 of the Education (Scotland) Act 1980. It will be noted, by contrast, that the Government's commitment to abolish the office of Director of Social Work was replaced by the intention to create a "chief social work officer" – see s.45 and the debates referred to there. The case for a statutory education officer was not, however, made out (*Hansard*, H.L. Vol. 556, col. 1943 and Vol. 558, col. 260). Existing directors of education were not required to be professionally qualified; there was less need for the identification of a single officer responsible for specific statutory duties; in contrast with *e.g.* urgent admissions to secure accommodation, there was no express statutory identification of the need for a specific officer. Not all were persuaded by these arguments and, for an attempt to reinstate a statutory director of education, see the House of Lords Third Reading debate at *Hansard*, H.L. Vol. 558, col. 659. (For earlier debate, see also First Scottish Standing Committee, col. 957.)

Co-operation between education authorities

32.—(1) Section 23 of the Education (Scotland) Act 1980 (provision by education authority for education of pupils belonging to areas of other authorities) shall be amended in accordance with this section.

(2) After subsection (1) there shall be inserted—

"(1A) Without prejudice to any other provision of this Act, for the purposes of their duty under section 1 of this Act an education authority shall have power to make arrangements with another education authority (in this subsection referred to as a "provider authority") for the provision of school education or further education for any pupils belonging to the area of the authority in a school or educational establishment under the management of the provider authority.

(1B) Arrangements made under this Act by an education authority for the placing of children in schools may include provision to give effect to any arrangements made under subsection (1A) above.

(1C) Where the arrangements for the placing of children in schools subsisting before the establishment of new local government areas under Part I of the Local Government etc. (Scotland) Act 1994 lead, as a consequence of such establishment, to school education for pupils belonging to the area of one education authority being provided at schools or educational establishments under the management of another education authority, nothing in this Act shall prevent such arrangements from continuing until they are changed by an education authority in accordance with this Act.".

(3) After subsection (3) there shall be inserted—

"(3A) Where an education authority's arrangements for the placing of children in schools under their management give any priority to siblings of pupils attending such schools, those arrangements shall not discriminate between siblings belonging to the area of that education authority and siblings belonging to the area of another education authority.".

DEFINITIONS

"education authority": s.61; s.235(1) of the 1973 Act; s.135(1) of the Education (Scotland) Act 1980, as amended by para. 118(9) of Sched. 13 to this Act.
"local government area": s.1.

GENERAL NOTE

During the Parliamentary debates, the restructuring of local government gave rise to a number of concerns over educational service provision, including attempts to insert a new duty to provide nursery education (*e.g.* at *Hansard*, H.L. Vol. 558, col. 231); to improve provision for those with special educational needs (*e.g. Hansard*, H.L. Vol. 556, col. 1945); and efforts to strengthen school library services in respect of which undertakings were given by the Government to make new regulations following consultation (*Hansard*, H.L. Vol. 556, col. 1949). Another major concern was that of access to schools following alterations in local authority boundaries affecting *e.g.* arrangements between secondary schools cut off from their "feeder" primaries, and the particular consequences for children in the same family where one child was already admitted to a secondary school and a younger sibling might risk being denied access because of boundary changes (see First Scottish Standing Committee, 22nd sitting). Section 23 of the Education (Scotland) Act 1980 made general provision for inter-authority education and it is amended by this section.

The new subs. (1A) clarifies and reinforces the power of an education authority to fulfil its general duty to secure educational provision under s.1 of the 1980 Act by using the services of another "provider authority", not only for the benefit of occasional pupils (as might be inferred from s.23 as it originally operated) but also for the benefit of more substantial numbers of pupils. The new subs. (1B) enables such arrangements (under subs. (1A)) to be given effect to under arrangements for the placing of children in schools under s.28B of the 1980 Act – the choice of school provisions.

Arrangements for the placing of children in schools can be formally changed under the terms of s.22A of the 1980 Act and the Education (Publication and Consultation Etc.) (Scotland) Regulations 1981 (S.I. 1981 No. 1558) but, until any such change is made in an area affected by local government reorganisation (*i.e.* with some schools of a former authority in one new area and some in another), the new subs. (1C) is designed to ensure that existing placing arrangements can continue to operate.

The amendment made by the addition of the new subs. (3A) is in similar vein and is intended to give the same benefit of "sibling priority" rules to siblings belonging to the area of another authority (*i.e.* particularly a different "new" authority as a result of changes made by local government reorganisation), as to siblings in the authority's own area.

Planning

Structure plans

33.—(1) After section 4 of the 1972 Act insert—

"Structure plans

4A.—(1) The Secretary of State may by order designate areas ("structure plan areas") in respect of which planning authorities are to prepare structure plans.

(2) The district of every planning authority in Scotland shall be included in a structure plan area.

(3) A structure plan area may extend to the district of more than one planning authority, and may extend to only part of the district of a planning authority.

(4) Where a structure plan area extends to the district of more than one planning authority, the planning authorities concerned shall jointly

carry out the functions conferred upon them under sections 4, 5, 6, 6A and 8 of this Act in accordance with such arrangements as they may agree for that purpose under sections 56 (discharge of functions by local authorities), 57 (appointment of committees) and 58 (expenses of joint committees) of the Local Government (Scotland) Act 1973.

(5) An order under this section shall be made by statutory instrument subject to annulment in pursuance of a resolution of either House of Parliament.".

(2) Schedule 4 to this Act, which makes further amendments to the 1972 Act, shall have effect.

DEFINITIONS
"1972 Act": s.61.
"joint committee": s.61; s.235(1) of the 1973 Act.
"planning authority": s.61; s.172 of the 1973 Act, as substituted by Sched. 13.
"structure plan area": new s.4A(1).

GENERAL NOTE
One of the criticisms levelled at the reforms leading to a relatively large number of unitary authorities has been that the carrying out of certain functions will become less effective. One such function is that of the making of "structure" plans – *i.e.* the upper-tier of the system of development plans originally enacted in 1969, but not implemented until the 1975 reorganisation, where the new regional (and islands) councils were given this responsibility. For Parliamentary debate, see *e.g.* First Scottish Standing Committee, col. 1070 *et seq.* and H.L. Vol. 556, col. 1950 and Vol. 558, cols. 245–250.

As predicted in paras. 3.18–3.20 of *The New Councils* (Cm. 2267, 1993), the Government's response to the problem is in terms of this new s.4A inserted into the Town and Country Planning (Scotland) Act 1972 (c. 52). The Secretary of State is given the power to designate by order "structure plan areas" which may extend into the area of more than one planning authority, or which may include only a part of such an area. The new subs. (4) provides for any resulting need for joint arrangements between authorities, which may be made under ss.56–58 of the 1973 Act. Although this is not spelled out in the new s.4A itself, another possibility is that the Secretary of State's powers under s.62B of the 1973 Act (inserted by s.20 of this Act) might be used to insist on the creation of a joint board, where agreement on the matter cannot be reached by the authorities concerned (*Hansard*, H.L. Vol. 558, col. 248). The whole question of how joint arrangements may be organised is further addressed in amendments made to the Town and Country Planning (Scotland) Act 1972 by Sched. 4 to this Act. In particular, the new s.5, as substituted by Sched. 4, para. 3, provides that, where an order has been made under the new s.4A, a structure plan for the new area must be submitted for the Secretary of State's approval. It also provides that, where the new area extends to the districts of more than one planning authority and those authorities cannot agree on a joint structure plan, the authorities must submit alternative proposals (with reasons). This obligation is, however, specifically stated (s.5(1B)) to be without prejudice to s.15 of the Town and Country Planning (Scotland) Act 1972 (default powers of the Secretary of State) and s.62B of the 1973 Act (see s.20 of this Act). Further consequential amendments to the Town and Country Planning (Scotland) Act 1972 made by Sched. 4 include provision for "adequate publicity" for alternative proposals (new s.6(1A)); an additional requirement to consult other affected authorities (new s.6A); a new power for authorities to act jointly in making local plans (new s.9(1A)); and new default powers for the Secretary of State to require one authority to perform functions jointly on behalf of itself and one or more other planning authorities (new s.15(2A)).

An attempt to introduce a requirement to establish joint arrangements for the management of regional or country parks was rejected in the Lords (*Hansard*, H.L. Vol. 556, cols. 1999–2000).

Police

Reorganisation of police areas

34. After section 21 of the Police (Scotland) Act 1967 there shall be inserted the following section—

"Reorganisation of police areas

21B.—(1) Subject to the provisions of this section, the police forces established and maintained for existing police areas in Scotland under this Act immediately prior to 1st April 1996 shall continue in existence on and after that date in accordance with the provisions of this section.

(2) The police forces for the existing police areas of Fife and Dumfries and Galloway shall be the police forces for the new police areas of the same names.

(3) The Secretary of State shall, before 1st April 1996, by order make amalgamation schemes amalgamating the police areas mentioned in the second column of the table below into the combined police areas mentioned in the first column of that table, and the police forces for the existing police areas shown in brackets in the first column shall be the police forces for the new combined police areas.

TABLE

Combined area	Police areas comprised
Northern (Northern).	Highland, Western Isles, Orkney Islands, Shetland Islands.
Grampian (Grampian).	Aberdeenshire, Moray, City of Aberdeen.
Tayside (Tayside).	Perthshire and Kinross, Angus, City of Dundee.
Central Scotland (Central Scotland).	Stirling, Clackmannan, Falkirk.
Lothian and Borders (Lothian and Borders).	City of Edinburgh, East Lothian, Midlothian, West Lothian, the Borders.
Strathclyde (Strathclyde).	Argyll and Bute, Dumbarton and Clydebank, City of Glasgow, East Dunbartonshire, Inverclyde, North Lanarkshire, South Lanarkshire, Renfrewshire, East Renfrewshire, East Ayrshire, North Ayrshire, South Ayrshire.

(4) Subject to section 19A of this Act, an amalgamation scheme made under this section may contain such provision as the Secretary of State considers necessary or appropriate for the purposes of the scheme including, without prejudice to the generality of the foregoing, any provision which is required to be made, or which may be made, in an amalgamation scheme made by virtue of section 19 of this Act.

(5) Before making an amalgamation scheme under this section the Secretary of State shall—

(a) consult such police authorities as appear to him to be affected by the scheme; and

(b) where any such authority submit objections to the scheme, inform that authority in writing whether he accepts the objections and, if he does not, why he does not.

(6) The schemes made by an order under this section shall not take effect before 1st April 1996, except in relation to—

(a) the constitution of joint police boards; and

(b) the carrying out by those boards of any functions necessary to bring the schemes into operation on that date.

(7) An order under this section shall be made by statutory instrument subject to annulment in pursuance of a resolution of either House of Parliament.".

DEFINITIONS
"police area": s.50 of the Police (Scotland) Act 1967.
"police authority": s.50 of the Police (Scotland) Act 1967.
"police force": s.50 of the Police (Scotland) Act 1967.

GENERAL NOTE
The Government made clear in *The New Councils* (Cm. 2267, 1993) that it was its intention that, although the local authority structure would change radically on April 1, 1996, the structure of the existing eight police forces should remain in place (para. 3.12). This inevitably required that amalgamations of the police areas would have to take place, with joint boards created as the new police authorities.

In the event, two police areas (mentioned in the new s.21B(2) inserted into the Police (Scotland) Act 1967 (c. 77) (by this section) – Fife and Dumfries and Galloway – survive as continuing new areas. The other six areas are to be created in the manner indicated in the table in subs. (3). Two combined areas will be in areas already covered by joint arrangements, but the Lothian and Borders authority will need in future to represent five new councils and, in the area of the Northern force, the joint board will be reconstituted out of the four new councils for the same area.

The necessary amalgamation schemes are to be made under subs. (3), by statutory instrument (subs. (7)), and subject to the consultation required by subs. (5). The schemes may have limited effect prior to April 1, 1996, as indicated in subs. (6). Section 19 of the Police (Scotland) Act 1967 referred to in subs. (4) is the section under which ordinary amalgamation schemes may be made. A new s.19A is inserted by para. 71(6) of Sched. 13 to this Act and provides that joint police boards established under the Police (Scotland) Act 1967 "shall be incorporated with a common seal and have power to hold land and to borrow money".

It should be noted that, in addition to the amendments made to the Police (Scotland) Act 1967 by this section, by s.35, and by Sched. 13, para. 71, important changes have also been made by Pt. II of the Police and Magistrates' Courts Act 1994 (c. 29). The latter are concerned principally with the establishment of police forces and *e.g.* dismissals and complaints, but also include the conferring of new powers on the Secretary of State to give directions to a police authority following an adverse report by inspectors of (s.54 of the Police and Magistrates' Courts Act 1994 inserting a new s.26A into the Police (Scotland) Act 1967), and permitting police authorities to delegate functions to the chief constable (s.64 amending s.63 of the 1973 Act).

Amalgamation schemes

35. For section 20 of the Police (Scotland) Act 1967 there shall be substituted the following section—

"Power of Secretary of State to make amalgamation schemes

20.—(1) If it appears to the Secretary of State that it is expedient in the interests of efficiency to make an amalgamation scheme for any police areas, he may, in accordance with the provisions of this section, make such amalgamation schemes, containing such provisions, as he considers appropriate.

(2) Without prejudice to the generality of subsection (1) above, but subject to section 19A of this Act, an amalgamation scheme under this section may provide—

(a) for the amalgamation of any two or more police areas into a combined area;

(b) for the alteration of an existing combined area by the addition to or deletion from it of any police area;

(c) for the establishment or re-establishment and maintenance of police forces for any police area or combined area resulting from the scheme;

(d) for the dissolution and winding up of any joint police board constituted under a pre-existing amalgamation scheme, or for the reconstitution of any such board;

(e) for the transfer or retransfer to such police forces as may be determined by the scheme of constables affected by the scheme;

(f) for the transfer or retransfer to such authorities as may be determined by the scheme of any officers, property, rights or liabilities affected by the scheme;

(g) for the doing of anything which is required to be done, or which may be done, in an amalgamation scheme made under section 19 of this Act; and

(h) for any other matters incidental to or consequential on the provisions of the scheme.

(3) Before making a scheme under this section which contains provision such as is mentioned in subsection (2)(a) or (b) above the Secretary of State shall—

(a) consult such police authorities as appear to him to be affected by the scheme; and

(b) where any such authority submit objections to the scheme, inform that authority in writing whether he accepts the objections and, if he does not, why he does not.

(4) A scheme under this section shall be contained in an order made by statutory instrument subject to annulment in pursuance of a resolution of either House of Parliament.".

DEFINITIONS

"police area": s.50 of the Police (Scotland) Act 1967.
"police authority": s.50 of the Police (Scotland) Act 1967.
"police force": s.50 of the Police (Scotland) Act 1967.

GENERAL NOTE

The new s.20 of the Police (Scotland) Act 1967 substituted by this section gives wider powers to the Secretary of State in respect of "amalgamation schemes". He is no longer confined to situations in which police authorities for the relevant areas have failed to submit a satisfactory scheme of their own under s.19 of the Police (Scotland) Act 1967. Nor is he restricted, in making a scheme, merely to the combination of two or more existing areas, but he may now seek to achieve any of the other purposes listed in subs. (2) of the new section.

The new s.19(A) (referred to in s.20(2)) is inserted by para. 71(6) of Sched. 13 to the Act, and requires that any joint police board established by a scheme be incorporated with a common seal etc.

Fire services

Fire services

36. For section 147 of the 1973 Act (fire services) there shall be substituted—

"**Fire services**

147.—(1) Subject to the provisions of this section, the fire brigades maintained in Scotland for the purposes of the Fire Services Acts 1947 to 1959 by fire authorities or, where administration schemes have been made, joint committees for combined areas immediately before 1st April 1996 shall continue in existence on and after that date.

(2) Subject to the provisions of the Fire Services Act 1947, the fire authority for the purposes of the Fire Services Acts 1947 to 1959 shall, until 31st March 1996, continue to be a regional or islands council and thereafter shall be a local authority.

(3) The fire brigades for the existing fire authorities of Fife and Dumfries and Galloway shall be the fire brigades for the new fire authorities of the same names.

(4) The Secretary of State shall, before 1st April 1996, by order make schemes (hereafter referred to as "administration schemes") for the local government areas comprised in each of the combined areas set out in the Table at the end of this subsection for the provision in the combined area of the services required by section 1 of the Fire Services Act 1947; and the fire brigades for the existing areas shown in brackets in the first column shall be the fire brigades for the new combined areas.

TABLE

Combined area	Local government areas comprised
Central (Central Region).	Clackmannan, Falkirk, Stirling.
North Eastern (Grampian Region).	Aberdeenshire, City of Aberdeen, Moray.
Northern (Northern).	Highland, Orkney Islands, Shetland Islands, Western Isles.
South Eastern (South Eastern).	East Lothian, Midlothian, West Lothian, the Borders, City of Edinburgh.
Mid and South Western (Strathclyde Region).	Argyll and Bute, City of Glasgow, Dumbarton and Clydebank, East Dunbartonshire, Inverclyde, East Renfrewshire, East Ayrshire, North Ayrshire, South Ayrshire, North Lanarkshire, South Lanarkshire, Renfrewshire.
Mid Eastern (Tayside Region).	Angus, City of Dundee, Perthshire and Kinross.

(5) Subject to subsection (6) below, an administration scheme made under this section may contain such provision as the Secretary of State considers necessary or appropriate for the purposes of the scheme including, without prejudice to the generality of the foregoing, any provision which is required to be made, or which may be made, in an administration scheme under section 36 of the Fire Services Act 1947.

(6) An administration scheme made under this section shall provide for the incorporation of the joint board with a common seal and shall confer on such a board power to hold land and to borrow money.

(7) Before making an administration scheme under this section the Secretary of State shall—

(a) consult such fire authorities as appear to him to be affected by the scheme; and

(b) where any such authority submit objections to the scheme, inform that authority in writing whether he accepts the objections and, if he does not, why he does not.

(8) An administration scheme made under this section shall not take effect before 1st April 1996, except so far as it relates to—

(a) the constitution of the joint board for fire services; and

(b) the performance by that board of functions necessary for bringing the scheme into full operation on that date.

(9) A statutory instrument containing an order under this section shall be subject to annulment in pursuance of a resolution of either House of Parliament.".

DEFINITIONS

"1973 Act": s.183(1).

"administration scheme": new s.147(4).

"fire authority": s.38 of the Fire Services Act 1947.

"joint board": s.61; s.235(1) of the 1973 Act.

GENERAL NOTE

As with the police service (see s.34), the Government's view in *Shaping the Future – The New Councils* (Cm. 2267, 1993) was that the same number of fire brigades would continue to operate after reorganisation. This is provided for by subs. (1) of the new s.147 inserted by this section into the 1973 Act.

The retention of the eight brigades requires, however, that, with the creation (by subs. (2)) of the new councils as fire authorities from April 1, 1996, there is a need for amalgamation arrangements by "administration schemes" in all areas except the two council areas mentioned in subs. (3). Subsections (4)–(8) and (10) are concerned with the making of such schemes for the combined areas listed in the table in subs. (4), subject to requirements of consultation etc. (subs. (7)), to take effect from April 1, 1996 (subject to the limited exceptions in subs. (8)).

Substantial amendments to s.36 of the Fire Services Act 1947 (c. 41) are made by para. 27(3) of Sched. 13. These include revised rules for the making of administration and establishment schemes.

Rivers

River purification boards

37.—(1) Without prejudice to subsection (3) of section 135A of the 1973 Act (transitional provision in variation orders), a variation order under the said section 135A may include provision for the termination of appointment on 31st March 1996 of those members of the board appointed by regional or district councils.

(2) Each council constituted under section 2 of this Act shall, by no later than 31st March 1996, determine which members of that council shall be appointed with effect from 1st April 1996, in accordance with a variation order including such provision as is mentioned in subsection (1) above, to be members of the river purification board or boards within whose area the council lies.

GENERAL NOTE
Local government reorganisation from April 1, 1996 necessitates the alteration of the composition of river purification boards. This section empowers the Secretary of State to make provision in variation orders to terminate the appointment of members from regional and district councils; and to require new councils to determine their own appointments by March 31, 1996.

In addition, note the corresponding amendments made to ss.135–135A of the 1973 Act by para. 92(34) and (35) of Sched. 13. These amendments, most importantly, reconstitute the membership of river purification boards as one half from members of relevant local authorities and one half from members appointed by the Secretary of State (instead of one third from regional councils, one third from districts and one third appointed by the Secretary of State); see First Scottish Standing Committee, cols. 1201–1202. The section was described as an "insurance policy": the expectation is that it will not be necessary, should legislation to establish a Scottish Environmental Protection Agency (which would take over the responsibilities of the river purification authorities) be implemented by April 1996.

Roads

Roads

38.—(1) The Roads (Scotland) Act 1984 shall be amended in accordance with this section.

(2) After section 12 there shall be inserted the following sections—

"Transitory provisions

Transitional power of Secretary of State as respects existing roads
12A.—(1) Without prejudice to section 5 of this Act, where the Secretary of State considers that it is necessary or expedient as a result of, or in connection with, the establishment of new local government areas on 1st April 1996—
   (a) that any existing road should become a trunk road; or
   (b) that any trunk road should cease to be a trunk road,
he may by order direct that the road shall become a trunk road or, as the case may be, shall cease to be a trunk road, as from such date as may be specified in that regard in the order.

(2) Where an order under this section directs that a road shall cease to be a trunk road, it may also direct that—

(a) as from the date specified in that regard in the order, the local roads authority for the area shall become the roads authority for the road; and

(b) the authority shall enter the road in their list of public roads.

(3) An order under this section may relate to one or more roads.

Transitional power of Secretary of State as respects proposed roads

12B.—(1) Without prejudice to section 5 of this Act, where the Secretary of State considers that it is necessary or expedient as a result of, or in connection with, the establishment of new local government areas on 1st April 1996—

(a) that any proposed road—

(i) to be constructed by the local roads authority; and

(ii) in respect of which all necessary planning permission has been granted or is deemed to have been granted,

should become a trunk road; or

(b) that any proposed road—

(i) to be constructed by the Secretary of State as a trunk road; and

(ii) in relation to which an order has been made under section 5 of this Act,

should not become a trunk road,

he may by order direct that the proposed road shall or, as the case may be, shall not become a trunk road.

(2) Where an order is made in respect of a proposed road as mentioned in subsection (1)(a) above—

(a) subject to subsection (6) below, the Secretary of State may, for the purposes of the construction of that road, do any thing which he would have been entitled to do if an order under section 12 of this Act (in this section referred to as a "section 12 order") had been made in relation to that road; and

(b) where an environmental statement has been published in respect of the project, the Secretary of State shall not be required to publish a further environmental statement,

but otherwise the Secretary of State shall in all respects be in the same position in relation to that proposed road as the local roads authority would have been if such order had not been made.

(3) Where an order is made in respect of a proposed road as mentioned in subsection (1)(b) above—

(a) the local roads authority may proceed with construction of the said road as if all necessary planning permission had been granted;

(b) the section 12 order made in relation to that road shall apply as if—

(i) the local roads authority were the roads authority referred to in such order; and

(ii) all necessary planning permission has been granted; and

(c) where an environmental statement has been published in respect of the project, the local roads authority shall not be required to publish a further environmental statement.

(4) Where an order under this section directs that a proposed road shall not become a trunk road, it may also direct that—

(a) as from the date specified in that regard in the order, the local roads authority for the area shall become the roads authority for the proposed road; and

(b) on such date as may be specified in that regard in the order, the authority shall enter the road in their list of public roads.

(5) An order under this section may relate to one or more proposed roads.

(6) The Secretary of State shall not by virtue of this section be empowered—

(a) to stop up a road as mentioned in section 12(1)(a)(i) of this Act; or

(b) to do anything mentioned in paragraphs (a) and (b) of section 70 of this Act except where the local roads authority have been so authorised under a section 12 order; and where such an order has been made, the Secretary of State may do anything he would have been authorised to do if the order had been made by him.

(7) In this section and in section 12C of this Act "planning permission" means permission under Part III of the Town and Country Planning (Scotland) Act 1972.

Transitional power of Secretary of State as respects special road schemes

12C.—(1) Where the Secretary of State considers that it is necessary or expedient as a result of, or in connection with, the establishment of new local government areas on 1st April 1996 that—

(a) a special road which the Secretary of State is authorised to provide by virtue of a scheme under section 7 of this Act (a "section 7 scheme") should be provided by a local roads authority; or

(b) a special road which a local roads authority is authorised to provide by virtue of a section 7 scheme which has been confirmed by the Secretary of State should be provided by the Secretary of State,

he may by order direct that the local roads authority or, as the case may be, the Secretary of State shall be authorised to provide such special road; and the section 7 schemes relating to those special roads shall (notwithstanding their terms) be deemed to authorise the provision of such special roads by the local roads authority and the Secretary of State respectively.

(2) Where an order is made in respect of a special road as mentioned in subsection (1)(a) above—

(a) where the Secretary of State has made an order under section 9 of this Act (a "section 9 order") in relation to that special road, the local roads authority may treat that order as if it were an order made by them and confirmed by the Secretary of State;

(b) any necessary planning permission (whether relating to the special road or the doing of anything authorised by virtue of the section 9 order) shall be deemed to have been granted to the local roads authority; and

(c) where an environmental statement has been published in respect of the project, the local roads authority shall not be required to publish a further environmental statement.

(3) Where an order is made in respect of a special road as mentioned in subsection (1)(b) above—

(a) if the local roads authority have made a section 9 order which has been confirmed by the Secretary of State, the Secretary of State may treat that section 9 order as if it were an order made by him; and

(b) where an environmental statement has been published in respect of the project, the Secretary of State shall not be required to publish a further environmental statement,

but otherwise the Secretary of State shall in all respects be in the same position in relation to that special road as the local roads authority would have been if such order had not been made.

Application of section 112 to orders under sections 12A, 12B, 12C and 12E

12D. The provisions of section 112 of this Act shall apply, subject to such modifications as the Secretary of State may by order specify, to roads, proposed roads and special roads such as may be mentioned in orders made under sections 12A, 12B, 12C and 12E of this Act as they apply to roads mentioned in the said section 112.

Further power of Secretary of State as respects proposed roads and special road schemes

12E.—(1) Where the Secretary of State considers that it is necessary or expedient as a result of, or in connection with, the establishment of new local government areas on 1st April 1996 that any proposed road to be constructed by a local roads authority should become a trunk road, but the condition mentioned in subsection (1)(a)(ii) of section 12B of this Act is not satisfied in relation to such proposed road, he may, notwithstanding the provisions of that subsection, by order direct that the proposed road shall become a trunk road.

(2) The provisions of paragraphs (a) and (b) of section 12B(2) of this Act shall apply where an order is made under subsection (1) above as they apply where an order is made under subsection (1)(a) of that section.

(3) Where the Secretary of State considers that it is necessary or expedient as a result of, or in connection with, the establishment of new local government areas on 1st April 1996 that a special road in respect of which a section 7 scheme has been made by a local roads authority but not confirmed by the Secretary of State should be provided by him, he may, notwithstanding the provisions of subsection (1)(b) of section 12C of this Act, by order, direct that he shall be authorised to provide such special road by virtue of such scheme.

(4) The provisions of paragraphs (a) and (b) of section 12C(3) of this Act shall apply where an order is made under subsection (3) above as they apply where an order is made under subsection (1)(b) of that section.

(5) An order under subsection (1) or (3) above may include provision specifying the extent to which compliance before the making of that order with any statutory requirement in relation to the proposed road or, as the case may be, special road shall be deemed to satisfy for all purposes any statutory requirement which the Secretary of State would, apart from such provision, have been required to comply with in relation to that proposed road or special road.

(6) As from the date of an order under subsection (1) or (3) above, the proposed road or, as the case may be, special road shall be deemed always to have been a proposed road to be constructed by the Secretary of State or a special road which the Secretary of State is authorised to provide.

Further provisions as to orders

12F. An order under section 12A, 12B, 12C, 12D or 12E of this Act may not be made so as to take effect more than 3 years after 1st April 1996.".

(3) In section 112 (transfer of property and liabilities on road becoming or ceasing to be a trunk road)—

(a) in subsection (1), after paragraph (c) there shall be inserted the following paragraph—

"(d) any property such as is mentioned in subsection (1A) below";

(b) after subsection (1) there shall be inserted the following subsections—

"(1A) The property mentioned in paragraph (d) of subsection (1) above is property which—
> (a) was, immediately before the operative date, vested in the former roads authority for the purposes of their functions in relation to more than one road (including the road mentioned in that subsection); and
> (b) is specified in an order made by the Secretary of State.

(1B) Where any property is transferred to and vests in the Secretary of State as mentioned in subsection (1)(d) above, he shall make arrangements with the former roads authority as respects the use of that property; and any dispute between the Secretary of State and the former roads authority as to any arrangements made under this subsection shall be determined in like manner as any dispute such as is mentioned in subsection (7) below."; and

(c) in subsection (2), for the words "subsection (1)" there shall be substituted the words "subsections (1) and (1A)".

(4) In section 143(2)(a)(ii) (orders subject to negative resolution), after "section 8" there shall be inserted ", 12A, 12B, 12C, 12D, 12E".

DEFINITIONS
"local roads authority": s.151 of the Roads (Scotland) Act 1984.
"public road": s.151 of the Roads (Scotland) Act 1984.
"roads authority": s.151 of the Roads (Scotland) Act 1984, as amended by Sched. 13, para. 135.
"special road": s.151 of the Roads (Scotland) Act 1984.
"trunk road": s.151 of the Roads (Scotland) Act 1984.

GENERAL NOTE
This section should be read together with the amendments made to the Roads (Scotland) Act 1984 by para. 135 of Sched. 13. After reorganisation, the new councils become roads authorities.

Although this was not a necessary consequence of reorganisation, the Government made it clear in *Shaping the Future – The New Councils* (Cm. 2267, 1993) that it wished to take the opportunity to rationalise the responsibility for roads throughout Scotland and, in particular, the line between local authority roads and the trunk roads administered by the Scottish Office. Central to this would be the elimination of the distinction between the primary route network – the motorways (special roads) and routes marked with green signs – and the trunk road network. All the primary routes would become trunk roads, following a review "to ensure that signing, trunking and detrunking proposals are consistent with the new council boundaries and a basic system of national through routes". All remaining public roads would be local roads (*ibid.*, paras. 3.15–3.16).

The new ss.12A–12F inserted into the Roads (Scotland) Act 1984, together with the amendments made to s.112 of the same Act, provide order-making powers for the Secretary of State (with supplemental powers) to enable him to make the different categories of adjustment in the status of roads, both existing and proposed. The Secretary of State's existing power in s.5 of the Roads (Scotland) Act 1984 to trunk and detrunk roads is appropriate for use only in relation to individual roads.

The new s.12A
This provides a general power to trunk or detrunk existing roads – as a result of or in connection with the reorganisation.

The new s.12B
This makes similar provision to that contained in the new s.12A in relation to *proposed* roads, but with the supplementary protection of the position of the "acquiring" body (subss. (2) and (3)), *e.g.* in relation to planning permission and environmental statements.

The new s.12C
This makes similar provision in relation to special roads (motorways).

The new s.12D
This should be read together with the amendments made to s.112 of the Roads (Scotland) Act 1984 (c. 54) by s.38(3). Section 112 relates to the necessary transfer of property and liabilities on a road becoming or ceasing to be a trunk road.

The new s.12E

This confers further powers on the Secretary of State in cases where the planning permission requirement of a road or the confirmation of a special road scheme is not satisfied.

The new s.12F

All orders referred to above must take effect within three years from April 1, 1996.

Roads authority for boundary bridges

39. After section 81 of the Roads (Scotland) Act 1984 there shall be inserted—

"Roads authority for boundary bridges

81A.—(1) This section applies where a public road is carried by a bridge over a waterway and the bridge lies partly in the areas of two local roads authorities.

(2) Where this section applies, the authorities concerned may make arrangements as to—

(a) which of them shall be the roads authority in relation to that bridge;

(b) the performance by such roads authority in relation to the bridge of any of the roads functions of the other authority; and

(c) the making of contributions by that other authority to the roads authority in respect of expenditure incurred in the performance of those functions.

(3) Where arrangements are not made as mentioned in subsection (2) above, the Secretary of State may, on the application of one of the roads authorities concerned, make a determination in respect of the matters mentioned in paragraphs (a) to (c) of that subsection.

(4) A determination of the Secretary of State under subsection (3) above shall be binding.".

DEFINITIONS

"local roads authority": s.151 of the Roads (Scotland) Act 1984.

"public road": s.151 of the Roads (Scotland) Act 1984.

"roads authority": s.151 of the Roads (Scotland) Act 1984, as amended by Sched. 13, para. 135.

GENERAL NOTE

This section, by inserting a new s.81A in the Roads (Scotland) Act 1984, addresses the problems about responsibilities (including financial responsibilities) for bridges over waterways and lying partly in the areas of two local roads authorities. The problems were expected to increase as a result of the proliferation of new roads authorities from April 1996. The new s.81A enables the two authorities to make arrangements in relation to the matters set out in subs. (2), subject to the possible alternative of the regulation of these matters by determination of the Secretary of State under subss. (3) and (4).

Public transport

Establishment etc. of Strathclyde Passenger Transport Authority

40.—(1) With effect from 1st April 1996 there shall be a Passenger Transport Authority to be known as the Strathclyde Passenger Transport Authority (in this section referred to as "the Authority") for the Strathclyde Passenger Transport Area for the purposes of Part II of the Transport Act 1968.

(2) On 1st April 1996 all of the functions, staff, property, rights, liabilities and obligations of Strathclyde Regional Council as Passenger Transport Authority shall be transferred to and vest in the Authority.

(3) Section 9 of this Act shall apply to any person transferred to the Authority under this section as if any reference in that section to a new authority included a reference to the Authority.

(4) The Secretary of State may by order—
(a) designate the passenger transport area of the Authority; and
(b) make provision for the constitution and membership of the Authority in accordance with the provisions of Schedule 5 to this Act.

(5) Without prejudice to the provisions of the said Schedule 5, an order under subsection (4) above shall include—
(a) such provision with respect to any of the matters referred to in that Schedule; and
(b) such supplementary, incidental and consequential provision,
as the Secretary of State considers necessary or expedient.

(6) Before making an order under subsection (4) above the Secretary of State shall consult such persons or bodies as he thinks fit.

(7) The following provisions of the 1973 Act shall apply, subject to any necessary modifications, with respect to the Authority as they apply with respect to a local authority or, in the case of section 106(2), a body, that is to say—
(a) section 95 (financial administration);
(b) section 96 (accounts and audit);
(c) section 97 (Commission for Local Authority Accounts in Scotland);
(d) section 97A (studies for improving economy etc. in services);
(e) section 97B (furnishing of information and documents to Commission);
(f) section 98 (expenses and accounts of Commission);
(g) section 99 (general duties of auditors);
(h) section 100 (auditor's right of access to documents);
(i) section 101 (right of interested person to inspect and object to accounts: completion of audit);
(j) section 102 (reports to Commission by Controller of Audit);
(k) section 103 (action by Commission on reports by Controller of Audit);
(l) section 104 (action by Secretary of State on recommendation by Commission under section 103(3));
(m) section 105 (regulations as to accounts); and
(n) section 106(2) (accounts of officer to be audited in certain circumstances).

(8) The Secretary of State may by order vary the passenger transport area of the Authority.

(9) An order under this section shall be made by statutory instrument subject to annulment in pursuance of a resolution of either House of Parliament.

(10) Schedule 5 to this Act (which makes provision for the constitution, proceedings etc. of the Authority) shall have effect.

DEFINITIONS
"1973 Act": s.183(1).
"the Authority": subs. (1).

GENERAL NOTE
This section should be read together with s.41, as well as the amendments made to the Transport Act 1968 (c. 73) by para. 80 of Sched. 13, and the minor repeals affecting the same Act made by Sched. 14.

The Transport Act 1968 established new arrangements for public transport provision in defined urban areas involving the setting up of Passenger Transport Authorities (PTAs) and Passenger Transport Executives (PTEs). In Scotland, one such area was designated, namely the Greater Glasgow area. Originally, a separately constituted Greater Glasgow PTA (with corresponding PTE) was established, but the Strathclyde Regional Council took over as PTA in 1975.

Now, the abolition of the Strathclyde Regional Council after March 31, 1996 requires the setting up of a new Strathclyde PTA. This section (together with Sched. 5) makes the necessary provision. It will be seen that, in very large measure, the rules are left to be made by delegated legislation in orders to be made under subss. (4)–(6). A few rules *are* laid down in advance including the requirement (Sched. 5, para. 2) that the Authority's membership be drawn from the councils of the constituent local authority areas (to be prescribed), but the actual numbers involved will be settled by delegated legislation – as will the long list of "matters" listed in Part II of the Schedule. Subsection (7) applies to the Authority the specified financial administration and audit provisions of the 1973 Act.

In debate, this section provided the opportunity for extended discussion of other matters relating to public transport, including the availability of concessionary fare schemes, after reorganisation; see First Scottish Standing Committee, (26th sitting).

Amendment of section 13 of Transport Act 1968

41. For section 13 of the Transport Act 1968 (grants to the Executive) there shall be substituted—

"Grants and payments

13.—(1) Any expenditure of the Strathclyde Passenger Transport Authority shall, in so far as not otherwise met, be met by the local authorities whose areas lie wholly or partly within the area of the Authority in such proportions as the authorities may agree.

(2) Where—

(a) the authorities mentioned in subsection (1) above cannot reach agreement as to the proportions in which the expenditure of the Authority shall be met by them and the Authority make an application to the Secretary of State for resolution of the matter; or

(b) it appears to the Secretary of State that those authorities are unable to reach such agreement,

the Secretary of State shall determine the proportions in which such expenditure shall be met by those authorities.

(3) The Authority shall have power to make grants to the Executive for any purpose.".

DEFINITIONS

"the Executive": s.9 of Transport Act 1968.

GENERAL NOTE

This section is consequential upon s.40 which creates a newly constituted Strathclyde Passenger Transport Authority to take over from Strathclyde Regional Council on April 1, 1996. The substituted s.13 of the Transport Act 1968 puts joint responsibility on the local authorities in the area (with power to the Secretary of State to intervene if necessary under subs. (2)) to fund the PTA, which in turn funds the PTE (subs. (3)).

Traffic

Power to secure management of traffic control system

42.—(1) Where the Secretary of State considers that—

(a) for the purposes of securing the expeditious, convenient and safe movement of vehicular and other traffic (including pedestrians), a system of traffic control should extend across the roads of two or more traffic authorities; and

(b) the authorities for those roads have not made satisfactory joint arrangements for the exercise of such of their functions under the Road Traffic Regulation Act 1984 as are necessary to secure the provision and management of such a system of traffic control,

he may make an order under this section.

(2) An order under this section may transfer to the Secretary of State such functions of those authorities under that Act as he considers necessary to enable him to secure the provision and management of such a system.

(3) The Secretary of State may enter into arrangements with such an authority for the carrying out by that authority on his behalf of the functions mentioned in subsection (2) above.

(4) Any expenses reasonably incurred by the Secretary of State in exercising the functions transferred by an order under this section may be recovered

by him from the traffic authorities from which the functions were transferred in such proportions—

    (a) as may be agreed between the authorities; or

    (b) where there is no agreement, as may be determined by him.

    (5) In this section—

      "road" has the same meaning as in the Roads (Scotland) Act 1984; and

      "traffic authority" has the meaning given by section 121A of the Road Traffic Regulation Act 1984.

Definitions

  "road": subs. (5).

  "traffic authority": subs. (5).

General Note

  This section should be read together with ss.43 and 44, as well as para. 134 of Sched. 13 (which makes a number of minor amendments to the Road Traffic Regulation Act 1984 (c. 27) consequential upon local government reorganisation).

  The general functions of traffic authorities for the purposes of the Road Traffic Regulation Act 1984 are those mentioned in subs. (1)(a). The section anticipates that, on local government reorganisation from April 1, 1996 and the transfer of traffic responsibilities to a much larger number of authorities, there will be a heightened need for the making of satisfactory joint arrangements between authorities to secure a system of traffic control and, failing such arrangements, for the intervention of the Secretary of State.

  Thus, the Secretary of State is empowered, under the conditions mentioned in subs. (1), to make an order transferring functions to himself (subs. (2)), subject to reallocating the functions to a local authority (subs. (3)), and with provision for him to recover expenses reasonably incurred from the relevant authorities (subs. (4)).

Guidance as to exercise of traffic powers

    43.—(1) For the purpose of ensuring that the exercise by an authority of any of the powers mentioned in subsections (2) and (3) below does not have an adverse effect on the expeditious, convenient and safe movement of vehicular and other traffic (including pedestrians)—

    (a) on the roads of any other authority; or

    (b) on the national system of routes for through traffic in Scotland,

the Secretary of State may issue guidance to an authority as to the exercise of those powers.

    (2) The powers referred to in subsection (1) above are the powers of an authority to make, vary or revoke orders under or by virtue of any of the following sections of the Road Traffic Regulation Act 1984, that is to say—

    (a) section 1 (traffic regulation orders);

    (b) section 9 (experimental traffic orders);

    (c) section 19 (orders concerning public service vehicles);

    (d) section 32 (provision of parking places by authorities);

    (e) section 35 (orders as to use of parking places);

    (f) section 37 (orders relating to general scheme of traffic control);

    (g) section 38 (orders as to use of parking places as bus or coach stations);

    (h) section 45 (orders designating paying parking places);

    (i) section 46 (further orders regulating paying parking places);

    (j) section 49 (designation orders and designated parking places);

    (k) section 53 (designation orders);

    (l) section 82(2) (directions concerning restricted roads); and

    (m) section 84 (speed limits on certain roads).

    (3) The powers referred to in subsection (1) above are the powers of an authority under sections 36 (construction of road humps) and 39A (construction of traffic calming works) of the Roads (Scotland) Act 1984.

    (4) Before issuing guidance under this section the Secretary of State shall consult the Common Services Agency for the Scottish Health Service in respect of the provision by them of an ambulance service by virtue of the

National Health Service (Functions of the Common Services Agency) (Scotland) Order 1974 and—

(a) the chief constables of the police forces maintained;

(b) the fire authorities (within the meaning of the Fire Services Act 1947); and

(c) the authorities,

for the areas to which the guidance relates.

(5) Without prejudice to his power to make regulations under paragraph 21 of Schedule 9 to the Road Traffic Regulation Act 1984 or, as the case may be, section 39B(1) of the Roads (Scotland) Act 1984, the Secretary of State may by regulations make provision as to the procedures to be followed by authorities in relation to the guidance.

(6) An authority shall, before exercising any power mentioned in subsections (2) and (3) above, and subject to any regulations made under subsection (5) above—

(a) have regard to any guidance issued to them under this section;

(b) consider whether the proposed exercise of such power would be likely to have an effect on the expeditious, convenient and safe movement of vehicular and other traffic (including pedestrians)—

(i) on a road in the area of any other authority; or

(ii) on a road in the national system of routes for through traffic in Scotland; and

(c) if the proposed exercise would, in their opinion, have such an effect, consult—

(i) in the case of a road such as is mentioned in paragraph (b)(i) of this subsection, the other authority; or

(ii) in the case of a road such as is mentioned in paragraph (b)(ii) of this subsection, the Secretary of State.

(7) Where an authority take any action which, in the opinion of the Secretary of State—

(a) is contrary to any guidance issued to the authority under this section; and

(b) has or is likely to have an adverse effect on either of the matters referred to in paragraphs (a) and (b) of subsection (1) above,

the Secretary of State may, after consulting the authority, direct the authority to take such steps within a period specified by him as may be necessary to conform with that guidance.

(8) If, in the opinion of the Secretary of State, an authority have failed to comply with a direction under subsection (7) above, he may exercise any of their powers for the purpose of giving effect to the direction; and any expenses reasonably incurred by him in doing so shall be recoverable by him from that authority.

(9) The power to make regulations under this section shall be exercisable by statutory instrument subject to annulment in pursuance of a resolution of either House of Parliament.

(10) In this section—

"authority" means—

(a) in relation to the exercise of the powers mentioned in subsection (2) above, a traffic authority (within the meaning of the Road Traffic Regulation Act 1984); and

(b) in relation to the exercise of the powers mentioned in subsection (3) above, a roads authority (within the meaning of the Roads (Scotland) Act 1984); and

"road" has the same meaning as in the Roads (Scotland) Act 1984.

DEFINITIONS

"authority": subs. (10).

"road": subs. (10).

GENERAL NOTE

Like s.42, this section is passed in anticipation that the larger number of smaller traffic authorities after local government reorganisation in April 1996 may require greater central supervision to ensure satisfactory service provision. It gives the Secretary of State new powers to issue "guidance" (subs. (1)) on the use of the powers listed in subs. (2) (powers under the Road Traffic Regulation Act 1984 – road traffic regulation orders etc.) and subs. (3) (powers under the Roads (Scotland) Act 1984 – road humps and traffic calming). The powers are to be exercised after consultation with the Common Services Agency (on ambulances), and the chief constables, fire authorities, and local (traffic and roads) authorities, for the relevant areas (subs. (4)).

Thereafter, an authority must "have regard to the guidance" and, as required by subs. (6), consult with other authorities or the Secretary of State, before exercising the listed powers. Then, most stringently, the Secretary of State is given powers to *direct* observance of the guidances (subs. (7)) and, in the event of non-compliance, to take the default action (with the right to recover his expenses) in subs. (8).

Restriction on order-making powers of existing authorities

44.—(1) Where a regional council propose to make an order such as is mentioned in subsection (2) below and the order—

(a) will come into effect after such date as the Secretary of State may by order made by statutory instrument prescribe; and

(b) will continue in effect after 31st March 1996,

they shall, before making the order, seek the consent of the successor authority.

(2) The orders referred to in subsection (1) above are any orders made under the following provisions of the Road Traffic Regulation Act 1984—

(a) section 1 (traffic regulation orders);
(b) section 9 (experimental traffic orders);
(c) section 14 (temporary traffic orders);
(d) section 32 (provision of parking places by authorities);
(e) section 35 (orders relating to use of parking places);
(f) section 37 (orders as to general scheme of traffic control);
(g) section 45 (orders designating paying parking places);
(h) section 46 (further orders regulating paying parking places); and
(i) section 84 (speed limits on certain roads).

(3) Where a successor authority refuse their consent to a proposed order to which this section applies the regional council shall not make the order without having obtained the consent of the Secretary of State.

(4) Where—

(a) a regional council have sought the consent of a successor authority to the making of a proposed order to which this section applies; and

(b) the successor authority have failed, within 6 weeks of such consent being sought, to consent,

the successor authority shall be deemed to have given such consent.

(5) In this section "successor authority" means any council constituted under section 2 of this Act (other than the councils for Orkney Islands, Shetland Islands and Western Isles) in whose area the proposed order will have effect.

DEFINITIONS

"successor authority": subs. (5).

GENERAL NOTE

This section resembles s.55 in its underlying purpose, in that it is designed to prevent a regional council, as an (outgoing) traffic authority, from making an order under the Road Traffic Regulation Act 1984 (which would come into effect after a prescribed date and continue in effect following reorganisation after March 31, 1996) without first seeking the consent of the "successor authority" (subs. (5)) in whose area the order would have effect or, if that consent is denied, without the consent of the Secretary of State (subs. (3)). Failure on the part of a successor authority to grant its consent (or presumably the absence of a refusal of consent) within six weeks of the regional council's approach produces a deemed consent (subs. (4)).

Social work

Chief social work officer

45.—For section 3 of the Social Work (Scotland) Act 1968 (director of social work), there shall be substituted the following section—

"Chief social work officer

3.—(1) For the purposes of their functions under this Act and the enactments mentioned in section 5(1B) of this Act, a local authority shall appoint an officer to be known as the chief social work officer.

(2) The qualifications of the chief social work officer shall be such as may be prescribed by the Secretary of State.".

DEFINITIONS

"local authority": ss.1(2) and 94 of the Social Work (Scotland) Act 1968, as amended by Sched. 13, para. 76(2).

GENERAL NOTE

This section was inserted as a new clause at Lords Report stage (see *Hansard*, H.L. Vol. 558, cols. 254–260), following an undertaking given at Committee stage (*Hansard*, H.L. Vol. 556, col. 2015). Originally, it had been the Government's intention that, in the interests of the administrative flexibility sought in the consultation paper *The Internal Management of Local Authorities in Scotland* (1993), the formal requirement that local authorities should appoint someone to the named offices of Director of Social Work and Director of Education, should be removed. Appropriate amendments to the Social Work (Scotland) Act 1968 and the Education (Scotland) Act 1980 were included in the Bill. The commitment to abolish the office of Director of Education was carried out and s.78 of the Education (Scotland) Act 1980 was repealed by this Act (see General Note to s.31).

In relation to Directors of Social Work, however, the Government offered a compromise in the shape of the requirement contained in this section that a "chief social work officer", holding prescribed qualifications, should be appointed by each authority. Some authorities might continue to designate this person as Director of Social Work but this would not be compulsory and administrative flexibility would, therefore, continue to be available.

The change was made in the light of representations made about the special character of social work services and the need for a qualified professional to be responsible for them. Vulnerable groups dependent on the community care and child care services would be reassured, as would the courts and children's panels. The human rights issues involved were considered to be very important. Progress on the implementation of community care and establishing national standards for social work services would be maintained.

In addition to including the provision enabling the Secretary of State to prescribe professional qualifications, the substituted s.3 of the Social Work (Scotland) Act 1968 requires that the officer be appointed "for the purposes of" the existing functions, under that Act and those new functions listed in s.5(1B), as inserted by Sched. 13, para. 76(3). These cover a wide range, but probably the most important are powers under, *e.g.* s.44(6) (direction as to transfer of child), of the Social Work (Scotland) Act 1968 and powers under s.58A(3), s.58B(3) and s.58E(1) of the same Act (all three of which relate to the provision of secure accommodation for children and were powers added by the Health and Social Services Adjudication Act 1983 (c. 41)). In all these cases, exceptionally in local government practice, powers were vested directly in the Director of Social Work and now pass to the new chief social work officer. Until the amendments were made substituting the new office for the old, the Bill had provided simply for the powers to pass to an officer nominated by the authority. For continuing suspicions that the abolition of the office of Director would lead to a down-grading of social work services, see the debate on the Lords' Amendments in the Commons at *Hansard*, H.C. Vol. 248, cols. 1443–1464.

CHAPTER 7

MISCELLANEOUS

Licensing boards

46.—(1) A council may determine whether their area shall be divided into licensing divisions for the purposes of the Licensing (Scotland) Act 1976.

(2) Where a determination is made under this section, the council shall forthwith notify the Secretary of State of such determination and cause notice thereof to be published in two successive weeks in one or more newspapers circulating in the area.

(3) Every council shall, by no later than 31st March 1996, elect the members of the licensing board for—

(a) their area; or

(b) where a determination has been made under this section, each licensing division of their area.

(4) Any thing done by any licensing board for any area before 1st April 1996 shall, to the extent that it has effect before that date, have effect after that date as if it had been done by the licensing board for that area (or, as the case may be, the licensing board whose area falls wholly or partly within that area) on that date.

(5) In this section "council" means a council constituted under section 2 of this Act.

DEFINITIONS
    "council": subs. (5); s.2.

GENERAL NOTE
    This section should be read together with the relevant amendments to, and repeals of, s.1 of the Licensing (Scotland) Act 1976 (c. 66) (see Sched. 13, para. 106, and Sched. 14). Licensing responsibilities are at present discharged by boards (appointed from district and islands councils) responsible for the area of the council or for a division thereof. This section ensures that the new councils acquire the power of election to the boards (which must continue to consist of not less than one quarter of a council's members, and in no case less than 5 members, under s.1(4) of the Licensing (Scotland) Act 1976), as well as the power to divide their areas into divisions (formerly s.1(3) of that Act). Such a division is to be carried out in accordance with subss. (1) and (2).

Proceedings in district courts: transitional provisions

47. Where proceedings were instituted before 1st April 1996 in any district court and those proceedings have not been completed by that date, then, for the purpose of enabling those proceedings to be continued on and after that date, and for preserving in other respects the continuity of the administration of justice—

(a) the district court having jurisdiction on and after that date in the area where the proceedings were instituted shall be treated as succeeding to, and being the same court as, the district court in which the proceedings were instituted, and any verdict, sentence, order, complaint, notice, citation, warrant, or other proceedings or document shall have effect accordingly; and

(b) the clerk of the district court in which the proceedings were instituted shall transfer all records, productions and documents relating to those proceedings to the clerk of the district court treated as succeeding to that court.

GENERAL NOTE
    This section should be read together with s.48, and para. 96 of Sched. 13 which makes amendments to the District Courts (Scotland) Act 1975 (c. 20), including provision for a "local authority" for the purposes of that Act to become a council under the 1994 Act (instead of a district or islands council). This section makes necessary transitional provision for new district courts to continue business commenced in the predecessor courts, including the transfer of records by clerks of the two courts.

Amendment of District Courts (Scotland) Act 1975

48. In section 2 of the District Courts (Scotland) Act 1975 (district of, and exercise of jurisdiction by, district court), after subsection (1) there shall be inserted the following subsection—

"(1A) In determining where and when a district court should sit, a local authority shall have regard to the desirability of minimising the expense and inconvenience occasioned to those directly involved, whether as parties or witnesses, in the proceedings before the court.".

DEFINITIONS

"local authority": s.26 of the District Courts (Scotland) Act 1975, as amended by Sched. 13, para. 96 (5).

GENERAL NOTE

See also s.47 and the amendments and repeals referred to in the General Note to that section.

This section, by amendment of the District Courts (Scotland) Act 1975, takes account of the fact that the commission areas for new district courts may be larger than existing ones, and requires the new councils to have regard to minimising the expense and inconvenience to parties and witnesses in deciding where and when courts should sit.

An interesting debate prompted by this section related to the gradual erosion of local authority income from fines imposed by district courts. As explained by the Lord Advocate (*Hansard*, H.L. Vol. 558, col. 268) Scottish authorities are, in contrast with the position in England, permitted to retain some of the income from fines: 100 per cent in the case of common law offences but only 10 per cent for statutory offences. The shift to an emphasis on prosecution of the latter type of offence does affect local authority income.

Justices of the peace

49.—(1) Any person holding office as justice of the peace for any commission area by virtue of the provisions of section 9(2) or 10(3) of the District Courts (Scotland) Act 1975 immediately before 1st April 1996 shall, on and after that date, hold office as justice of the peace for the commission area in which he resides on that date.

(2) Any person holding office as justice of the peace for any commission area on and after 1st April 1996 by virtue of the provisions of subsection (1) above shall hold that office as if appointed in accordance with the said section 9(2).

(3) Where the Secretary of State is satisfied in all the circumstances that it is expedient that any such person as is mentioned in subsection (1) above should hold that office for another commission area, he may so direct; and any such direction shall have effect, and shall be treated for the purposes of the said Act of 1975, as an instrument appointing that person in accordance with the said section 9(2) to hold office for such commission area as is mentioned in the direction.

DEFINITIONS

"commission area": s.26 of the District Courts (Scotland) Act 1975, as amended by Sched. 13, para. 96(5).

"justice of the peace": s.26 of the District Courts (Scotland) Act 1975.

GENERAL NOTE

This section makes necessary provision for the continuation in office after April 1, 1996 of justices of the peace holding office under s.9(2) or s.10(3) of the District Courts (Scotland) Act 1975 (but *not ex officio* justices appointed under s.11 of that Act). Normally the person will, under subs. (1), hold office for the commission area in which he resides but this can be varied by direction of the Secretary of State under subs. (3). See also s.50 (stipendiary magistrates).

Stipendiary magistrates

50.—(1) Any person who holds office as stipendiary magistrate for any area immediately before 1st April 1996 shall, on that date, become a stipendiary magistrate in the district court having jurisdiction in that area and shall be deemed in all respects to have been appointed by virtue of section 5(1) of the District Courts (Scotland) Act 1975.

(2) The provisions of sections 8, 9 and 10 of this Act shall apply, subject to any necessary modifications, to the transfer of stipendiary magistrates on 1st April 1996.

GENERAL NOTE

This section ensures that persons already holding office as stipendiary magistrates prior to April 1, 1996 will continue to do so thereafter. Subsection (2) applies to the transfer of stipendiary magistrates the provisions (with the loose qualification "subject to any necessary modifications") in ss.8–10 in the Act, which enable the Secretary of State to transfer by order employees of existing local authorities to new authorities, and which provide for continuity of employment thereafter. See also ss.48–49 in relation to district courts and justices of the peace.

Registration of births, deaths and marriages

51.—(1) The Registration of Births, Deaths and Marriages (Scotland) Act 1965 shall be amended in accordance with the provisions of this section.

(2) For section 5(3) (registration districts and registration authorities) there shall be substituted the following subsection—

"(3) For each registration district there shall be a local registration authority which shall be the local authority in whose area the registration office or the principal premises of that office are, immediately before the commencement of section 51 of the Local Government etc. (Scotland) Act 1994, situated.".

(3) In section 8 (registration offices)—

(a) in subsection (1), after the words "registration office" there shall be inserted the words "which may comprise principal premises and such subordinate premises as they may, with the approval of the Registrar General, consider appropriate"; and

(b) at the end there shall be inserted the following subsection—

"(6) References in this Act to the registration office shall, unless the context otherwise requires, be construed as including all the premises provided and maintained by a local registration authority as parts of the registration office.".

(4) In section 15 (information concerning finding of infant children)—

(a) in subsections (1) and (3), for the words "director of social work" there shall be substituted "chief social work officer"; and

(b) subsection (4) shall cease to have effect.

(5) In section 56(1) (interpretation), after the definition of "function" there shall be inserted the following definition—

" "local authority" means a council constituted under section 2 of the Local Government etc. (Scotland) Act 1994;".

DEFINITIONS

"local authority": s.56(1) of the Registration of Births, Deaths and Marriages (Scotland) Act 1965, as inserted by subs. (5).

"local registration authority": s.5 of the Registration of Births, Deaths and Marriages (Scotland) Act 1965.

"registration district": s.5 of the Registration of Births, Deaths and Marriages (Scotland) Act 1965.

GENERAL NOTE

The effect of this section is to transfer responsibilities under the Registration of Births, Deaths and Marriages (Scotland) Act 1965 (c. 49) by the amendment made to s.56(1) of that Act by subs. (5), from regional and islands councils to the new councils. The section also identifies (by the amendment made by subs. (2)) the appropriate authority for each "registration district" (the boundaries of which are not affected by local government reorganisation but which may be adjusted later under that Act) as the authority in whose area "the registration office or the principal premises of that office" are situated. In subs. (3) the opportunity is taken to clarify, by amendment of s.8 of that Act, that "registration office" in that Act, as amended, refers not only to the "principal premises" in the registration district (which will, as explained above, identify the successor registration authority) but also subordinate premises. Subsection (4) takes account of the substitution by s.45 of the Act of a new s.3 of the Social Work (Scotland) Act 1968, replacing the office of "director of social work" with that of "chief social work officer".

Tweed Fisheries Commissioners

52.—(1) On 1st April 1996 each person holding office as representative commissioner appointed by any of the district councils of Berwickshire, Roxburgh, Ettrick and Lauderdale or Tweeddale under the Tweed Fisheries Act 1969 shall go out of office.

(2) The function of appointing representatives formerly appointed by the councils mentioned in subsection (1) above shall be transferred to the new council for the Borders.

(3) In Schedule 1 to the said Act of 1969, for the entries relating to the district councils of Berwickshire, Roxburgh, Ettrick and Lauderdale and Tweeddale there shall be substituted the entry relating to the Borders Council set out in Schedule 6 to this Act.

GENERAL NOTE

This section (read together with Sched. 6 to the Act) provides a revised composition of the River Tweed Council – the Tweed Fisheries Commissioners – to take account of the replacement of the district councils mentioned in subs. (1) by the new Borders Council and give to the latter Council (in subs. (2) "the new council for the Borders") the function of appointing the local authority representatives on the River Tweed Council.

Records held by local authorities

53.—(1) A local authority shall, in accordance with the provisions of this section, make proper arrangements for the preservation and management of any records which have been—

(a) transferred to and vested in them by virtue of an order under section 15 of this Act;

(b) created or acquired by them in the exercise of any of their functions; or

(c) otherwise placed in their custody,

and shall, before putting any such arrangements into effect, or making any material change to such arrangements, consult the Keeper of the Records of Scotland, and have regard to any comments which he may make on the proposed arrangements or changes.

(2) A local authority may dispose of any records which they do not consider to be worthy of preservation.

(3) Before entering into any arrangements to which section 58 of this Act or section 56 of the 1973 Act (arrangements for discharge of functions by local authorities) applies with regard to the preservation and management of any records, a local authority shall consult the Keeper.

(4) Where a local authority hold records relating to the property or functions of any other local authority, that other authority shall, subject to any arrangements made under section 58 of this Act or section 56 of the 1973 Act by the two authorities—

(a) be entitled to free access to, and copies of, any such records; and

(b) pay to the local authority holding the records such proportion of the costs incurred by that authority in preserving and managing the records—

(i) as the authorities may agree; or

(ii) as may, failing such agreement, be determined by the Secretary of State.

(5) The Keeper shall be entitled to free access to any records held by a local authority.

(6) For the purposes of this section and section 54 of this Act "records" includes charters, deeds, minutes, accounts and other documents, and any other records, of whatever form and in whatever medium, which convey information, but does not include records which are the property of the Registrar General of Births, Deaths and Marriages for Scotland.

DEFINITIONS
  "1973 Act": s.183(1).
  "records": subs. (6).

GENERAL NOTE
  This section should be read in conjunction with s.54.
  One of the issues raised in para. 33.3 of *Shaping the New Councils* (1992) and paras. 3.40–3.42
of *Shaping the Future – The New Councils* (Cm. 2267, 1993) was that of building on the progress
made by a number of local authorities towards the creation of local archives of their own records.
The principal duty imposed on existing authorities is contained in s.200 of the 1973 Act and this is
replaced, in relation to the new councils, by this section and s.54 (see note to s.54 for the survival
of the duties in s.200 in relation to river purification boards).
  Subsection (1) imposes the principal duty to "make proper arrangements for the preservation
and management" of records. See s.15 for the general procedures for the vesting of the property
(in this case, the records) of existing authorities in the new councils from April 1, 1996. An
innovation is the obligation (see also subs. (3)) to consult the Keeper of the Records of Scotland
(and have regard to his comments), before putting arrangements into effect. Subsection (3)
recognises the general power of a council to arrange for the discharge of a function by, *inter alia*,
another authority but requires consultation with the Keeper before this is done. Subsections (4)
and (5) provide for access to records by one authority whose records are held by another (but
with an obligation to contribute to the cost of preservation, etc.) or held by the Keeper.
  The section prompted debate in which concern was expressed about the loss in recent years of
local records of historical importance, and the need for an improved service organised by larger
numbers of professional archivists (*Hansard*, H.L. Vol. 558, cols. 269–271).

Use, acquisition and disposal of records

54.—(1) A local authority may do anything which appears to them to be
appropriate for the purpose of enabling proper use to be made of their
records and, without prejudice to the generality of the foregoing, may—
  (a) make provision for enabling persons, with or without charge and sub-
      ject to such conditions as the authority may determine, to inspect the
      records and to make or obtain copies thereof;
  (b) prepare, or procure or assist in the preparation of, indices and guides
      to and calendars and summaries of the records;
  (c) publish, or procure or assist in the publication of, the records or any
      index or guide to or calendar or summary of the records;
  (d) hold exhibitions of the records and arrange for the delivery of
      explanatory lectures, with or without charging for admission to such
      exhibitions or lectures;
  (e) direct that the records be temporarily entrusted to other persons for
      exhibition or study.
  (2) Nothing in subsection (1) above shall be taken as authorising the doing
of any act which infringes copyright or contravenes conditions subject to
which records are under the control of an authority.
  (3) A local authority may—
  (a) acquire by way of purchase records which, or (in the case of a collec-
      tion) the majority of which, appear to the authority to be of general or
      local interest;
  (b) accept the gift of records which or, in the case of a collection, the
      majority of which appear to the authority to be of general or local
      interest.
  (4) A local authority may accept the deposit of records—
  (a) authorised to be deposited with it by any enactment; and
  (b) which appear to the authority to be of general or local interest.
  (5) In section 200 of the 1973 Act (records)—
  (a) subsections (1) to (6), (8), (9) and (11)(b) shall cease to have effect;
      and
  (b) in subsections (7) and (10)—
          (i) for the word "local", in each place where it occurs, there shall
      be substituted the words "river purification"; and

(ii) for the word "authority", in each place where it occurs, there shall be substituted the word "board".

DEFINITIONS
"1973 Act": s.183(1).
"enactment": s.61; s.235 of the 1973 Act.
"records": s.53(6).

GENERAL NOTE
See also s.53.

This section expands on the duties of local authorities in relation to their records formerly contained in s.200 of the 1973 Act and extended by s.53. The principal powers (reflecting provision already made by s.1 of the Local Government (Records) Act 1962 (c. 56) for England and Wales) are contained in subs. (1), while subss. (3) and (4) make explicit provision for the acquisition of records by purchase or gift. The principal effect of subs. (5) is to repeal most of s.200 of the 1973 Act but to retain the duties in subss. (7) and (10) of that section in relation only to river purification boards – to which ss.53 and 54 of this Act do not apply.

Restriction on disposal of assets and entering into contracts by existing authorities

55.—(1) On and after the relevant date, an existing authority shall not, without the consent of the relevant successor authority or, in a case to which subsection (9) below applies, the Secretary of State—
   (a) without prejudice to section 74 of the 1973 Act (disposal of land), dispose of any land for a consideration exceeding £250,000; or
   (b) enter into any of the contracts mentioned in subsection (2) below.
(2) The contracts referred to in subsection (1)(b) above are—
   (a) contracts—
         (i) in terms of which the authority incurs a liability to meet capital expenses within the meaning of section 94 of the 1973 Act (capital expenses); and
         (ii) where the consideration exceeds £2,500,000; and
   (b) contracts, other than contracts such as are mentioned in subparagraph (a)(i) above—
         (i) the period of which purports to extend beyond 31st March 1996 or is capable of being so extended; and
         (ii) where the consideration exceeds £250,000.
(3) The relevant date for the purposes of this section is such date as the Secretary of State may by order made by statutory instrument determine; and different such dates may be so determined in respect of any of the successor authorities mentioned in subsections (4) to (8) below or, in a case to which subsection (9) below applies, the Secretary of State.
(4) Subject to subsections (5) to (8) below, the relevant successor authority in relation to any proposed disposal or contract by a regional or district council is—
   (a) in relation to any disposal of land, the new local authority within whose area the land will be situated; and
   (b) in relation to any other contracts, any new local authority whose area will include the whole or any part of the area of the existing local authority.
(5) The relevant successor authority in relation to any proposed disposal of relevant property (within the meaning assigned by paragraph (b) of section 91(1) of this Act) or proposed contract in so far as it relates to functions mentioned in that paragraph is, in the case of—
   (a) Lothian, Borders, Fife or Central Region, the East of Scotland Water Authority;

(b) Strathclyde or Dumfries and Galloway Region, the West of Scotland Water Authority; and

(c) Tayside, Highland or Grampian Region or an Islands Area, the North of Scotland Water Authority.

(6) The relevant successor authority in relation to any proposed disposal or contract by the Central Scotland Water Development Board is the East of Scotland Water Authority.

(7) The relevant successor authority in relation to any proposed disposal or contract by a police authority or, where an amalgamation scheme has been made, a joint committee for any existing police area is—

(a) in the case of each of Fife and Dumfries and Galloway, the police authority for the new police area of the same name; and

(b) in the case of each of the police authorities or, as the case may be, joint committees for the areas or combined areas shown in brackets in the first column of the Table in section 21B(3) of the Police (Scotland) Act 1967 (reorganisation of police areas), the joint board for the corresponding combined area shown in that column.

(8) The relevant successor authority in relation to any proposed disposal or contract by a fire authority or, where an administration scheme has been made, a joint committee, is—

(a) in the case of each of Fife and Dumfries and Galloway, the fire authority for the new area of the same name; and

(b) in the case of each of the fire authorities or, as the case may be, joint committees for the areas or combined areas shown in brackets in the first column of the Table in section 147(4) of the 1973 Act (fire services), the joint board for the corresponding combined area shown in that column.

(9) Where—

(a) a disposal of land such as is mentioned in subsection (1)(a) above is of land held or acquired by the authority for the construction or improvement of any road; or

(b) a contract such as is mentioned in subsection (2) above is for works for the construction or improvement of any road; and

(c) where, in either case, the Secretary of State has given notice to the authority concerned of his intention to make an order under section 12A(1)(a), 12B(1)(a), 12C(1)(b), 12E(1) or 12E(3) of the Roads (Scotland) Act 1984 directing that a road or proposed road should become a trunk road or that he should be authorised to provide a special road,

the consent required shall, in either case, be that of the Secretary of State.

(10) The requirement to seek consent imposed by this section shall not apply to—

(a) any disposal of land in respect of which the consent of the Secretary of State is required under section 12(7) of the Housing (Scotland) Act 1987; and

(b) any contract entered into by an existing authority in or in connection with the exercise of the power conferred on them by section 24 of the Local Government Act 1988 (power to provide financial assistance for privately let housing accommodation).

(11) This section applies to any granting of an option to require an existing authority to make a disposal of land or enter into a contract which would require the consent of a successor authority or the Secretary of State as it applies to such a disposal or contract.

(12) In this section "existing authority" means a regional or district council, the Central Scotland Water Development Board, any police authority or joint committee for a police force established under the Police (Scotland) Act 1967, any fire authority or joint committee for a fire brigade established

in Scotland under the Fire Services Act 1947 and, for the purposes of the matters mentioned in subsection (5) above, includes an islands council.

DEFINITIONS
  "1973 Act": s.183(1).
  "existing authority": subs. (12).
  "road": s.151 of the Roads (Scotland) Act 1984.
  "special road": s.151 of the Roads (Scotland) Act 1984.
  "trunk road": s.151 of the Roads (Scotland) Act 1984.

GENERAL NOTE
  This section is one of many in the Act which are concerned with the transition from existing to new authorities, and in this case recognises the interest which a "successor authority" will have in major transactions (disposal of land for a consideration exceeding £250,000, or contracts which are valued at over £2.5 million if involving capital liability or, if not, at over £250,000, or contracts having effect beyond March 31, 1996) entered into by existing authorities. The consent of the successor authority or, in the case of a contract defined by subs. (9), the Secretary of State, is required on or after the "relevant date", which is to be prescribed by statutory instrument (subs. (3)). By virtue of subs. (10), certain housing sales or transfers are exempted from the need for shadow authority consent. It was explained by the Lord Advocate when para. (b) of subs. (10) was inserted at House of Lords Report stage, that one of the primary motivations for existing authorities to undertake housing stock transfers was the prospect of securing a capital receipt, and that this should not be frustrated by a shadow authority for political reasons or to secure a receipt for itself (*Hansard*, H.L. Vol. 558, col. 272, where amendments raising other transitional problems of property transfer were also discussed).
  The existing "authorities" (which can include, where the "successor authority" is the North of Scotland Water Authority, an islands council) are defined in subs. (12), and the "successor authorities" identified by reference to the functions they perform are defined in subss. (4)–(8).

Duty of existing authorities and assessors to provide information to new authorities

56.—(1) Subject to the provisions of this section, existing local authorities and assessors shall provide new authorities with such information as the latter may reasonably require for the purpose of carrying out, whether before or after 1st April 1996, any of their functions.

(2) A new authority may not require information to be provided from any existing authority or assessor whose area does not correspond, at least in part, with the area of the new authority.

(3) An assessor shall not be required under subsection (1) above to provide any information to a new authority which he is not required to provide to an existing authority.

(4) In this section—
  "assessor" means an assessor appointed under section 116 of the 1973 Act (appointment of assessors);
  "existing local authority" includes a joint committee and a joint board; and
  "new authority" means any of the authorities constituted under section 2 of this Act, and includes a joint board.

DEFINITIONS
  "1973 Act": s.183(1).
  "assessor": subs. (4).
  "existing local authority": subs. (4).
  "new authority": subs. (4).

GENERAL NOTE
  Another transitional need of the new shadow councils is access to information which is held by existing authorities and by assessors, and which the new councils "may reasonably require for the purpose of carrying out" their functions, whether before or after April 1, 1996. The obligation to provide such information is imposed by this section, subject to the restrictions contained in subss. (2) and (3).

Power and duty of existing local authorities to assist new authorities

57.—(1) An existing local authority may do anything which in their opinion is appropriate for the purpose of—

(a) facilitating the transfer of their functions, staff and assets to a new authority; or

(b) facilitating the carrying out by a new authority of their functions on and after 1st April 1996.

(2) Without prejudice to the generality of subsection (1) above, existing local authorities having functions in relation to any part of the area of a new authority may establish, or the Secretary of State may require them to establish, a committee in the area of that new authority to consider any matter which it is expedient they should consider in order to ensure the effective operation of that authority on and after 1st April 1996.

(3) Existing local authorities may establish, or the Secretary of State may direct them to establish, a committee in relation to the areas of any group of new authorities to consider any matter which it is expedient they should consider in order to ensure the effective operation of those authorities on and after 1st April 1996.

(4) A committee established under subsection (2) or (3) above shall consist of such number of representatives of the authorities by whom it is established as may be agreed between them or, in default of such agreement, as may be determined by the Secretary of State.

(5) The Secretary of State may direct an existing local authority to do anything which in his opinion is appropriate for the purpose of putting a new authority in a position to carry out their functions with effect from 1st April 1996.

(6) A direction under subsection (5) above—

(a) may be made subject to such conditions (for example, as to payment by the new authority) as may be specified in it; and

(b) shall be complied with by the authority to which it is made.

(7) Any expenses incurred by a committee established under subsection (2) or (3) above shall be defrayed by the authorities by whom the committee was established in such proportions respectively as may be agreed amongst or between them or, in default of agreement, as may be determined by the Secretary of State.

(8) In this section—

"existing local authority" includes a joint committee and a joint board; and

"new authority" means any of the authorities constituted under section 2 of this Act, and includes a joint board.

DEFINITIONS
  "existing local authority": subs. (8).
  "joint board": s.61; s.235(1) of the 1973 Act.
  "joint committee": s.61; s.235(1) of the 1973 Act.
  "new authority": subs. (8).

GENERAL NOTE
  In further reinforcement of the need for existing authorities to assist the transition to reorganised local government (a process which in *Shaping the Future – the New Councils* (Cm. 2267, 1993) the Government envisaged involving working groups of existing and new authorities), this section gives the necessary statutory powers to the existing authorities. The general power is provided in subs. (1) and this is supplemented by powers to establish a committee in relation to the area of a new authority or group of authorities (which committee may also be *required* by Secretary of State) (subss. (2) and (3)). Any such committee is to consist of numbers of representatives of authorities as are agreed by them or, in default, by determination of the Secretary of

State (subs. (4)). In addition, the Secretary of State has a more general power to direct existing authorities to do things in order to assist the transition, as provided by subs. (5).

Further provision as to discharge of functions by authorities

58.—(1) Subject to the provisions of this section, a local authority (a "contracting authority") may agree with any other local authority (a "supplying authority") that the supplying authority shall carry out for the contracting authority any activity or service which the contracting authority are required to, or may legitimately, carry out.

(2) An agreement under this section—

(a) may provide for activities or services to be carried out by two or more authorities jointly; and

(b) may include such terms as to payment as the authorities concerned consider appropriate.

(3) Anything requiring to be done by a supplying authority under an agreement under this section shall be treated as one of their statutory functions.

(4) The Secretary of State may by regulations make such provision as he thinks fit in relation to the exercise by local authorities of the power conferred by this section and, without prejudice to the generality of the foregoing, such regulations may include provision—

(a) prohibiting or restricting to such extent as may be prescribed the use of the power in relation to such activities or services, or such class or classes of activities or services, as may be so prescribed;

(b) specifying, either generally or in relation to such activities or services, or such classes of activities or services, as may be so prescribed, which authorities may enter into agreements under this section.

(5) This section is without prejudice to any other power under or by virtue of which a local authority may arrange for the carrying out of any of their activities or services by another authority.

(6) A statutory instrument containing regulations under this section shall be subject to annulment in pursuance of a resolution of either House of Parliament.

(7) For the purposes of this section "local authority" includes a residuary body and a joint board.

DEFINITIONS
  "contracting authority": subs. (1).
  "joint board": s.61; s.235(1) of the 1973 Act.
  "local authority": subs. (7).
  "residuary body": s.183(1); s.18.
  "supplying authority": subs. (1).

GENERAL NOTE
  One of the Government's expectations expressed in *Shaping the Future – The New Councils* (Cm. 2267, 1993) was that new authorities would "have to consider, to a greater extent than in the past, the possibilities of providing services or parts of services in conjunction with other authorities" (para. 3.2). One consequence is the provision for joint boards in s.20. Another was to provide "a flexible legal framework which enables local authorities to choose from a wide range of providers including, in most instances, other local authorities".
  This section (which has a parallel in s.25 of the Local Government (Wales) Act 1994 (c. 19)) supplements existing powers in the Local Authorities (Goods and Services) Act 1970 and enables a local authority (a "contracting authority") to agree with another (a "supplying authority") that the latter would carry out an activity or service for the former (subs. (1)). See also s.56 of the 1973 Act. It must be an activity or service the contracting authority is required to, or may "legitimately" (a curious choice of word in this context), carry out.

Quite separately there should be noted the new powers conferred on ministers by ss.70–71 of the Deregulation and Contracting Out Act 1994 (c. 40) under which, with some qualifications and exceptions, a minister may by order provide that functions, which may be delegated by an authority to an officer under s.56 of the 1973 Act, may be exercised (with the agreement of a local authority) by some other person or employees of that person.

Subs. (2)
Arrangements may be made for two or more supplying authorities to act jointly.

Subs. (3)
What is undertaken by a supplying authority is to be "treated as one of their statutory functions", which is a little difficult to understand in the absence of some specification of the sense in which, or the purpose for which, the thing done is to be treated as one of an authority's functions. A similar formula is used in s.25(6) of the Local Government (Wales) Act 1994 – although it is there prefaced by the words "As respects the exercise of any of their other statutory powers...". Presumably the subsection at least ensures that s.69 (subsidiary powers) and ss.70 and 71 (acquisition of land) of the 1973 Act are applied to these functions.

Subs. (4)
This subsection enables the Secretary of State to restrict, or otherwise specify, the extent of the use of the powers under this section. This power has a specific intended use, namely to exclude work subject to compulsory competitive tendering "given that there is a clear private sector market for such work" (*Hansard*, H.L. Vol. 556, col. 2024).

Subs. (5)
This provision prompted discussion of the additional need to provide for joint service delivery agencies set up by two or more authorities (*Hansard*, H.L. Vol. 556, col. 2025). That was rejected but it was pointed out that authorities do have a wide range of options for provision "through a joint committee, by a lead authority, by an in-house team or by purchase of services from the private or voluntary sectors" (*ibid.*).

Local Acts and instruments

59.—(1) Subject to subsection (2) below, any local statutory provision to which this section applies and which is not continued in force by any other provision of this Part of this Act shall—

    (a) notwithstanding the changes of administrative areas and local authorities effected by or under this Part of this Act and, in the case of an instrument made under any enactment, notwithstanding the repeal of that enactment, continue to apply on and after 1st April 1996 to, but only to, the area, things or persons to which or to whom it applies before that date;

    (b) have effect subject to any necessary modifications and to the modifications made by subsection (3) below;

but the continuation by this subsection of an instrument made under any enactment shall not be construed as prejudicing any power to vary or revoke the instrument which is exercisable apart from this subsection.

    (2) Subsection (1) above shall have effect subject to the provisions of—

    (a) subsection (6) below;

    (b) this Part of this Act;

    (c) any Act passed after this Act and before 1st April 1996; and

    (d) any order made under—

        (i) section 181 of this Act; or

        (ii) the following provisions of this section.

    (3) Any local statutory provision to which this section applies and which relates to functions exercisable by an existing local authority of any description by virtue of any public general enactment shall have effect as if for any reference to the authority by whom the functions are exercised immediately before 1st April 1996 there were substituted a reference to the authority by whom those functions are exercisable on and after that date.

    (4) Subsection (3) above shall not come into force until 1st April 1996 and shall have effect subject to any provision to the contrary made by, or by any

instrument made under, this Part of this Act and, without prejudice to the foregoing, the Secretary of State may by order provide for the exercise of functions conferred by any local statutory provision to which this section applies and exclude the operation of that subsection where it would otherwise conflict with any provision of the order.

(5) Where any local statutory provision is continued in force in any area by subsection (1) above or is amended or modified in its application to any area by an order under section 181 of this Act, the Secretary of State may by that order, or in the case of a provision continued as aforesaid, by an order under this subsection—

    (a) extend the provision throughout the new local government area in which it is continued in force;

    (b) provide that that provision as so continued, amended, modified or extended shall have effect in that area to the exclusion of any enactment for corresponding purposes, including any enactment contained in or applied by this Act;

    (c) make such modifications of any such enactment in its application to that area as will secure that the enactment will operate harmoniously with the said provision in that area;

    (d) repeal or revoke any local statutory provision to which this section applies and which appears to the Secretary of State to have become spent, obsolete or unnecessary or to have been substantially superseded by any enactment or instrument which applies or may be applied to the area, persons or things to which or to whom that provision applies;

    (e) transfer to any local authority appearing to the Secretary of State to be appropriate any functions of an existing local authority under a local statutory provision to which this section applies which are not to become functions of some other authority under any provisions of this Act except section 181 of this Act and this section, or under any other instrument made under this Act, being functions exercisable by any existing local authority abolished by this Act;

    (f) without prejudice to paragraph (e) above, make such modifications of any local statutory provision to which this section applies in its application to any new local government area as appear to the Secretary of State to be expedient.

(6) All local statutory provisions to which this subsection applies shall cease to have effect on 31st December 1999, but the Secretary of State may—

    (a) by order exempt any such provision from the foregoing provision of this subsection;

    (b) from time to time by order postpone the date on which any local statutory provision applying to the whole or part of any local government area is to cease to have effect under this subsection.

(7) An order under this section shall be made by statutory instrument subject to annulment in pursuance of a resolution of either House of Parliament.

(8) This section applies to any local statutory provision in force immediately before 1st April 1996 and not expressly repealed or revoked by this Act, and subsection (6) above applies to the following local statutory provisions—

    (a) a provision of a local Act, the Bill for which was promoted by a local authority;

    (b) a provision of an Act confirming a provisional order made on the application of a local authority;

    (c) a provision of an order made on such an application which was subject to special parliamentary procedure;

    (d) any byelaw; and

    (e) any management rule made under section 112 of the Civic Government (Scotland) Act 1982 (management rules),

not being a provision relating to a statutory undertaking.

(9) In this section—

"existing local authority" means a regional or district council;

"local authority" means an existing local authority, a joint committee, an authority constituted under section 2 of this Act, a joint board and a residuary body; and, for the purposes of subsection (6) above, includes any local authority in existence prior to 16th May 1975;

"local statutory provision" includes—

    (a) a provision of a public general Act passed with respect only to the whole or part of an existing local government area;

    (b) a provision of an instrument made under such a public general Act;

    (c) an instrument in the nature of a local statutory provision made under any other public general Act;

    (d) a provision of a local Act or a provision of an instrument made under any such Act;

    (e) a provision of an Act confirming a provisional order;

    (f) a provision of an order which was subject to special parliamentary procedure;

    (g) any byelaw; and

    (h) any management rule made under section 112 of the Civic Government (Scotland) Act 1982 (management rules),

but does not include any enactment or instrument in so far as that enactment or instrument relates to functions mentioned in section 91(1)(b) of this Act nor any order under section 6 of the 1975 Act; and

"statutory undertaking" means any railway, light railway, tramway, road transport, water transport, canal, inland navigation, ferry, dock, harbour, pier or lighthouse undertaking, any market undertaking or any undertaking for the supply of electricity, gas, hydraulic power or district heating.

DEFINITIONS

"enactment": s.61; s.235(1) of the 1973 Act.
"existing local authority": subs. (9).
"joint board": s.61; s.235(1) of the 1973 Act.
"joint committee": s.61; s.235(1) of the 1973 Act.
"local authority": subs. (9).
"local statutory provision": subs. (9).
"residuary body": s.183(1); s.18.
"statutory undertaking": subs. (9).

GENERAL NOTE

Just as in the case of the 1975 reorganisation, one matter of at least technical difficulty is the question of what happens to rules of local application, whose present scope and extent are defined by reference to local government areas which are being replaced by others. This section defines such rules as "local statutory provisions" (subs. (9)) and continues them in force, notwithstanding the changes of administrative areas and local authorities, after April 1, 1996 but applying "only to, the area, things or persons of which or to whom" they previously applied (subs. (1)).

This general rule is subject to the following qualifications:

(a) the continued application of local statutory provisions as above is subject to subs. (6) (see below), to other provisions in Pt. I of this Act, to other Acts passed after this Act but before April 1, 1996 (but query where passed after April 1, 1996), and to any order made under this section (see below) or made under s.181 (consequential and supplementary provisions) of the Act;

(b) the application of the provisions is "subject to any necessary modifications" (although it is not clear what these might be) (subs. (1)(b)); and also to

(c) other modifications needed to accommodate the changes of functions from existing to new authorities on April 1, 1996 (subs. (3)), but subject again to orders made by the Secretary of State adjusting that position (subs. (4));

(d) all provisions continued in force under subs. (1) (whether or not with their effect modified under s.181) are subject to wide powers of the Secretary of State to extend, modify, repeal, revoke, etc., their effect (subs. (5));

(e) all the local statutory provisions continued in force as above and falling within the categories defined in subs. (8) (which narrows the wider definition in subs. (9) for this purpose to include only *provision made or promoted by a local authority*) cease to have effect on December 31, 1999 – but subject again to the power of the Secretary of State by order to exempt certain orders or postpone the date of repeal (subs. (6)). An assurance was given that requests made to the Secretary of State for exemption from repeal on December 31, 1999 "will be considered sympathetically" (*Hansard*, H.L. Vol. 556, col. 2028). There may be a question about how subs. (6) will be applied in relation to "local statutory provisions" in the existing islands areas. By subs. (8), as mentioned, the scope of subs. (6) is confined to Acts, byelaws, etc., made or promoted by a "local authority", defined in subs. (9) as, in the first place, an "existing local authority" – meaning only a regional or district council and not, therefore, including an islands council. Measures made or promoted by an islands council do not fall to be repealed on December 31, 1999. This is logical (as is the general non-application of the section to the islands) because there is not the same problem there of succession to the areas of different existing authorities. However, subs. (9) does extend the definition (for the purposes of subs. (6)) of a local authority to include a pre-1975 authority. This seems, technically, a little odd because the phrase "local authority" is not used in subs. (6). If, however, subs. (9) is to be given meaning by applying it to subs. (8), then, in turn, the repeals made by subs. (6) might be taken to include pre-1975 legislation in the islands, including, importantly, the Orkney County Council and Zetland County Council Acts 1974 (for debate, see First Scottish Standing Committee, cols. 1419–1422).

Quite separately, the scope of the repeals effected by subs. (6) is narrowed to exclude provisions relating to statutory undertakings (subss. (8) and (9)).

Applications to sheriff in cases of difficulty

60. Sections 231 (applications to sheriff in cases of difficulty) and 232 (applications to court) of the 1973 Act shall apply in relation to a difficulty arising in the carrying out of this Part of this Act as they apply in relation to a difficulty arising in the carrying out of that Act.

DEFINITIONS
"1973 Act": s.183(1).

GENERAL NOTE
This section extends ss.231 and 232 of the 1973 Act to difficulties "arising in the carrying out of this Part of this Act" (*i.e.* not to "difficulties" which might arise under any of the later Parts of the Act). Sections 231 and 232 (whose origins lie in legislation going back to the Burgh Police (Scotland) Act 1892 (c. 55) and the Town Councils (Scotland) Act 1900 (c. 49)) give a wide power for an application to be made to the sheriff (with further possible appeal by application to the sheriff principal and appeal to the Court of Session) by a local authority, or any seven local electors or a returning officer, in the case of a difficulty arising in carrying the Act into effect, a procedural question, or a question about elections, and where there is no other provision made for determining the question.

Interpretation of Part I

61. In this Part of this Act, unless the context otherwise requires—
"existing local authority" means a regional, islands or district council;
"records" shall be construed in accordance with section 53 of this Act;
"the 1972 Act" means the Town and Country Planning (Scotland) Act 1972;
"the 1992 Act" means the Local Government Finance Act 1992,
and expressions used in this Part of this Act and in the 1973 Act shall have the same meanings in this Part as in that Act.

DEFINITIONS
"1973 Act": s.183(1).

GENERAL NOTE
As already pointed out in the note to s.2, this interpretation section performs the important function of applying to expressions used in both Pt. I of this Act and in the 1973 Act the meanings given to them by that Act. As also already mentioned, the term "existing local authority" is redefined in some sections in the Part.

PART II

WATER AND SEWERAGE REORGANISATION

GENERAL NOTE

Water supply and sewerage services have, since the reorganisation of 1975, been the responsibility of the regional and islands councils, although the financing of the services has been placed on a rather different basis from that applicable to other services. When the community charge (poll tax) was introduced in 1989, a separate community water charge was made for domestic water supplies, whilst a water rate continued to be levied on non-domestic premises. Similar systems of separate charging for water were later introduced when the change to the council tax was made in 1993. For sewerage services, a separate non-domestic sewerage rate was introduced from 1993, whilst charges for domestic services were included within general council tax payments (Local Government Finance Act 1992, Sched. 11).

In the general consultation papers issued prior to the 1994 Act a more substantial separation of water and sewerage from other local services was anticipated. In *The Case for Change* (June 1991), it was suggested that "the provision of water and sewerage services might best be handled by organisations separate from the new unitary authorities" (para. 23). In *Shaping the New Councils* (October 1992), there was reference to some of the special problems involved in the adoption of increasingly sophisticated water and sewerage systems, the high capital investment required, and the need for separate consideration to be given to these issues (para. 21).

This came in the form of a consultation paper, *Water and Sewerage in Scotland: Investing for Our Future*, issued in November 1992. This paper spelled out more fully the case for careful consideration of the future of the two services – to ensure high quality, low cost to the consumer, and the safeguarding of the environment, especially by meeting E.C. standards on water quality, bathing water and waste water treatment. Administratively, the options offered by the paper were to:

(a) place the services with the new unitary local authorities;

(b) create joint boards of the new unitary authorities;

(c) create a "lead authority" structure under which one local authority would be given service responsibility for both its own and surrounding areas;

(d) set up separate appointed water authorities;

(e) create a national water authority;

(f) establish joint local authority/private sector schemes;

(g) set up one or more public limited companies; and

(h) create a franchising system – *i.e.* an alternative route towards placing the services in the private sector by placing the service operation in the hands of private franchisees.

In the event, the Government's choice, following consultation, was to adopt option (d). In *Shaping the Future – The New Councils* (Cm. 2267, 1993), it proposed the establishment of three new water authorities – "Public ownership of the authorities can be combined with a major role for the private sector in providing and financing much of the essential and large capital investment programme needed over the next decade…" (para. 3.22). The authorities would be subject to appropriate regulations and financial controls and would be required to set charges at levels necessary to recover costs in full. Charges would inevitably rise to ensure the achievement of the ambitious investment programmes that were necessary. Also required, in line with the Citizen's Charter, was a "separate and independent representation for consumers' interests".

The outcome is this Part of the 1994 Act, the main purpose of which is to establish the three new water authorities (East, West, and North of Scotland) with responsibilities for water and sewerage in their areas and, amongst other things, establishes the new Customers Council. Substantial amendments are made to the Water (Scotland) Act 1980 (c. 45) and the Sewerage (Scotland) Act 1968 (c. 47).

The reorganisation of water and sewerage services under Part II of the Act was as bitterly opposed in Parliament as the general local government reorganisation under Part I. Although the Government's final choice was in favour of three new public authorities rather than outright privatisation, there were:

(a) continuing allegations that the eventual aim was privatisation (the Prime Minister had appeared to favour this solution – a point recalled, *e.g.* at *Hansard*, H.C. Vol. 243, col. 703 (referring to the Prime Minister's speech at *Hansard*, H.C. Vol. 220, col. 783)). Although the Government may successfully have rejected any claims that its intention was to privatise the industry for the time being, that position is complicated by the increasing emphasis it has given to applying to water and sewerage services in Scotland the policies being pursued under the Private Finance Initiative. (See *Breaking New Ground: towards a new partnership between the public and private sectors* (1993)). In brief, the theory underlying this Initiative is that it should stimulate efficiency, improved services, and fresh flows of investment from private sector sources in areas where full-scale privatisation is less appropriate, *i.e.* especially where costs cannot be met in full from charges on users. Instead, the half-way house of a contribution of private service provision and investment is contemplated. Flagship projects in *Breaking New Ground* are the new Skye Bridge, and the proposed new Forth Road Bridge. Also included in the Scottish Office sector of the programme, however, is the proposal that, although water and sewerage services will remain in the public sector, the demands for investment to meet, *inter alia*, new E.C. water quality standards, require a private sector contribution of around $1 billion. The mechanism to be used (initially by existing local authorities and then by the three new water authorities) is Build, Own, Operate (B.O.O.) schemes. Under these, private sector companies are expected to provide services to the authorities in return for payment. One consequence of this is that certain existing provisions in the Water (Scotland) Act 1980 and the Sewerage (Scotland) Act 1968 require adjustment, and this is the purpose of several of the provisions in this Part of the Act. See, *e.g.* ss.98–99, 101 and 182;

(b) denunciations of the transfer of responsibility for the services from elected local authorities to government appointed quangos. The opportunity was taken in debate to try to reinstate local authority (or other democratic) control into the provision of these services. See, *inter alia, Hansard*, H.C. Vol. 243, cols. 694 *et seq.*, and *Hansard*, H.L. Vol. 556, cols. 2044–2061, Vol. 558, cols. 280–290, and cols. 646–659. At certain points, it was claimed that members of the new quangos *would* be democratically accountable (First Scottish Standing Committee, col. 1538) because they would be responsible through the Secretary of State to Parliament. A number of assurances were given by the Government (see *Hansard*, H.L. Vol. 556, col. 2058) that appointments to the new authorities would include a "significant number of councillors", but that there would also be a need for many other people with "professional, business and financial" expertise;

(c) concerns about the level of service to be provided to consumers, and the prices to be charged. Some reliance was placed in debate upon the results of an opinion poll, conducted by the Strathclyde Regional Council, on the question "Do you agree with the Government's proposal for the future of water and sewerage services?" On a "turnout" of 71.5 per cent, it was found that 97.2 per cent (or 1,194,000) replied that they did not (see, *e.g.* First Scottish Standing Committee, 30th sitting and *Hansard*, H.L. Vol. 556, col. 2046).

New water and sewerage authorities

New water and sewerage authorities

62.—(1) There shall be established—

(a) a body, to be known as the East of Scotland Water Authority, which, as from 1st April 1996, shall be—
    (i) the water authority for the eastern water area; and
    (ii) the sewerage authority for the eastern sewerage area;

(b) a body, to be known as the West of Scotland Water Authority, which, as from that date, shall be—
    (i) the water authority for the western water area; and
    (ii) the sewerage authority for the western sewerage area; and

(c) a body, to be known as the North of Scotland Water Authority, which, as from that date, shall be—
    (i) the water authority for the northern water area; and
    (ii) the sewerage authority for the northern sewerage area;

but any reference in any enactment, including this Act, to water authorities generally, shall not be taken to include a reference to any of the above bodies as sewerage authority.

(2) Schedule 7 to this Act shall have effect with respect to the constitution and proceedings of, and other matters relating to, each of the bodies established by subsection (1) above (those bodies being, in this Act, collectively referred to as the "new water and sewerage authorities").

(3) The water areas and sewerage areas mentioned in subsection (1) above and in column 1 of Schedule 8 to this Act comprise the areas for the time being respectively described in column 2 of that Schedule.

GENERAL NOTE
This section, together with Scheds. 7 and 8, contitutes the three new water and sewerage authorities, and defines their areas. These provisions should be read together with Sched. 13, para. 119(2), as well as the relevant provisions in Sched. 14 which repeal ss.3–5 of the Water (Scotland) Act 1980 (which established regional and islands councils as water authorities – subject to some redefinition of the areas of their responsibilities). Note also the amendments made to s.1 of the Sewerage (Scotland) Act 1968 by para. 75(2) of Sched. 13; and the parallel amendments, made to s.109 of the Water (Scotland) Act 1980 by para. 119(53) of Sched. 13 and to s.59(1) of the Sewerage (Scotland) Act 1980 by para. 75(28) of Sched. 13, which require that the terms "water authority" and "sewerage authority" respectively be "construed in accordance with section 62 of the Local Government etc. (Scotland) Act 1994".

Subject to the other provisions of this Part of the Act and to the other amendments made to the two Acts referred to above, the broad effect is to transfer to the three bodies established by s.62(1) all the water and sewerage responsibilities discharged, until March 31, 1996, by the regional and islands councils. See also s.90 for the dissolution of the Central Scotland Water Development Board. It will be noted that the section names each body a "Water Authority"; establishes each as the water authority for a defined water area, and the sewerage authority for a defined sewerage area; and then explains that all are to be "collectively referred to" in the Act as the "new water and sewerage authorities" – a slightly odd drafting technique because, although the plural terminology is retained in the interpretation section (s.125), many references in this Part of the Act are to a (singular) new water and sewerage authority.

In Sched. 7, each is simply referred to as an "authority" and the Schedule goes on to set out rules (standard for a quango of this type) concerning, *inter alia*, appointment to membership of authorities (between seven and eleven plus its chief executive), chairmen and deputy chairmen, remuneration, etc., staff (on which see also s.97), and proceedings.

The water and sewerage areas defined in subs. (3) and Sched. 8 are also the subject of s.63 (alteration) and s.64 (maps). It will be noted from column 2 of Sched. 8 that the areas are initially defined by reference to the areas of existing regions and islands areas, but subject to the combination with the Eastern Areas of "added areas" – thus also producing Water Areas which are not coterminous with Sewerage Areas except in the Northern Areas.

Alteration of water areas and sewerage areas

63.—(1) Subject to subsection (4) below, the Secretary of State may from time to time by order amend column 2 of Schedule 8 to this Act so as to alter water areas or sewerage areas of the new water and sewerage authorities.

(2) A statutory instrument containing an order under this section shall be subject to annulment in pursuance of a resolution of either House of Parliament.

(3) An order under this section may include such incidental, supplementary and consequential provisions as the Secretary of State may consider necessary or expedient for the purposes of the order.

(4) Before making an order under this section the Secretary of State shall prepare a draft of the order, shall consult with every new water and sewerage authority whose area would be altered by the order and with the Customers Council and shall publish in the Edinburgh Gazette, and in one or more local newspapers circulating in the geographical area affected by the order, a notice—

(a) stating the general effect of the order;
(b) specifying the places where copies of the draft order, and of any maps relating to it, may be inspected, free of charge and at all reasonable times, during a period of not less than twenty-eight days which begins with the date on which the notice is so published; and
(c) stating that any person affected by the order may within that period, by intimation in writing to the Secretary of State, object to the proposed making of the order.

(5) The Secretary of State shall serve a copy of a notice published under subsection (4) above on every body which he has, in accordance with that subsection, consulted.

(6) The Secretary of State shall have regard to any objection made by virtue of subsection (4)(c) above and timeously received; and he may then pro-

ceed to make the order, either in the form of the draft order or as amended by him.

(7) For the purposes of subsection (6) above, an objection is timeously received if received by the end of the specified period of not less than twenty-eight days which begins with the latest date on which is published an issue of the Edinburgh Gazette, or of a local newspaper, in which the notice mentioned in subsection (4) above appears by virtue of that subsection.

DEFINITIONS
  "Customers Council": s.125.
  "new water and sewerage authorities": s.125.

GENERAL NOTE
  The original water areas and sewerage areas, with effect from April 1, 1996, are defined by s.62 and Sched. 8, but this section permits the Secretary of State to adjust those areas by amending column 2 of Sched. 8 by order made by statutory instrument (subss. (1)–(3)), subject to the obligations to consult affected authorities and others as specified in subss. (4)–(7).

Maps of areas

64.—(1) The Secretary of State shall, as soon as is practicable after—
  (a) the coming into force of section 62(3) of, and Schedule 8 to, this Act, send to each of the new water and sewerage authorities a map of their water area and of their sewerage area, both as described in column 2 of that Schedule;
  (b) making an order under section 63 of this Act altering water areas or sewerage areas, send to each of the new water and sewerage authorities of the areas altered a map of their water area, or as the case may be their sewerage area, as so altered.

(2) Any map which is sent to an authority under subsection (1) above shall, until superseded by a map subsequently sent under that subsection, be kept at the principal office of the authority; and the authority shall provide reasonable facilities for inspection of the map by any person and shall permit a copy of it, or of an extract of it, to be taken by a person on his paying such reasonable amount as the authority may determine.

DEFINITIONS
  "new water and sewerage authorities": s.125.

GENERAL NOTE
  This section requires the Secretary of State to issue to the new authorities maps of their (two) areas (and, if they are amended, maps of the amended areas), which are to be made available by the authorities for public inspection.

General duties of Secretary of State and of new authorities

65.—(1) For section 1 of the 1980 Act (which imposes on the Secretary of State certain duties as respects water conservation and supply) there shall be substituted—

"General duties of Secretary of State and of water authorities
  1. It shall be the duty of the Secretary of State and of the water authorities when exercising their respective functions or powers under or by virtue of this Act—

   (a) to promote the conservation and effective use of the water
resources of, and the provision of adequate water supplies
throughout, Scotland; and

   (b) to secure the collection, preparation, publication and dissemination of information and statistics relating to such resources and
supplies.".

(2) It shall be the duty of the Secretary of State and of the new water and
sewerage authorities when exercising their respective functions or powers
under or by virtue of this Act, the 1968 Act or the 1980 Act—

   (a) to have regard to the interests of every person who is a customer or
potential customer of any such authority and especially of such of
those persons as—

      (i) are likely, by reason of some persistent medical condition or
of family circumstances, to require to have a much greater supply of
water, or to make much greater use of facilities for the disposal of
sewage, than might ordinarily have been expected; or

      (ii) are ordinarily resident in some rural part of Scotland;

   (b) to further, so far as may be consistent with the purposes of any enactment relating to their respective functions (whether or not functions
under or by virtue of this Act, the 1968 Act or the 1980 Act)—

      (i) the conservation and enhancement of natural beauty and the
conservation of flora and fauna; and

      (ii) the conservation of geological or physiographical features of
special interest;

   (c) to have regard to the desirability of preserving for the public any freedom of access (including access for recreational purposes) to areas of
forest, woodland, mountains, moor, bog, cliff, foreshore, loch or reser-
voir and to other places of natural beauty; and

   (d) to have regard to the desirability of protecting and conserving—

      (i) buildings;

      (ii) sites; and

      (iii) objects,

of archaeological, architectural or historic interest and of maintaining
the availability to the public of any facility for visiting or inspecting any
such building, site or object.

DEFINITIONS
   "1968 Act": s.125.
   "1980 Act": s.125.
   "new water and sewerage authorities": s.125.

GENERAL NOTE
   Many detailed amendments to the functions of water and sewerage authorities, as they are
transferred from regional and islands councils to the three new authorities, are made in amendments to the Water (Scotland) Act 1980 and the Sewerage (Scotland) Act 1968 by later sections
of, and Sched. 13, to this Act.
   This section, however, makes a number of more general amendments by the recasting of s.1 of
the Water (Scotland)Act 1980, with the imposition of new general duties on both the Secretary
of State and the new authorities in respect of both branches of their activities.

Subs. (1)
   The former s.1. of the Water (Scotland) Act 1980 was confined to the imposition of duties on
the Secretary of State but was, otherwise, in substantively similar terms to the new s.1 – save that
the obligation to appoint an advisory committee is now omitted.

Subs. (2)
   The proposed shifting of responsibility of water and sewerage from elected local councils to
the three new quangos produced many concerns about the policies likely to be adopted by the
new authorities in relation to their customers and the environment. Such concerns (see also s.66)
were fully expressed in the Parliamentary debates on the Bill; see, *e.g.* First Scottish Standing
Committee, 35th sitting, at which Government amendments, including the clause which has

become s.73, were discussed. Also introduced at that stage were amendments to this subsection including the clauses protective of residents in a "rural part of Scotland" and (in para. (c)) of "access for recreational purposes".

Codes of practice for new water and sewerage authorities

66.—(1) A new water and sewerage authority shall draft a code of practice which shall make provision—
  (a) as to their standards of performance in providing services to their customers;
  (b) for procedures for dealing with complaints by their customers or their potential or former customers;
  (c) as respects the circumstances in which they will pay compensation if or in so far as those standards are not attained; and
  (d) as respects such matters as are incidental to the provision made under paragraphs (a) to (c) above;
and the code may include such supplemental provisions as appear to the authority to be appropriate.

(2) A code drafted by an authority under subsection (1) above shall be sent by them to the Customers Council no later than the date on which they first, under subsection (4)(a) of section 76 of this Act, send a draft charges scheme to the Council; and subsections (4) to (6) of the said section 76 shall apply as respects any such draft code of practice as they apply to any such draft charges scheme.

(3) The authority shall endeavour to comply with their code of practice as for the time being approved by virtue of this section; but contravention of that code shall not of itself give rise to any criminal or civil liability.

(4) Subject to subsection (1) above, the authority may from time to time—
  (a) vary; or
  (b) revoke and replace,
their code of practice as so approved; and the varied or new code shall be sent forthwith by them in draft to the Customers Council.

(5) Subsections (4) to (6) of section 76 of this Act shall apply as respects a draft sent under subsection (4) above as they apply, by virtue of subsection (2) above, to a draft sent under the said subsection (2).

(6) The authority shall take such steps as appear to them appropriate to inform customers and potential or former customers of the contents for the time being of their code approved by virtue of this section.

DEFINITIONS
  "Customers Council": s.125.
  "new water and sewerage authorities": s.125.

GENERAL NOTE
  This section was added at Committee stage in the Commons (for debate, see First Scottish Standing Committee, col. 1713), and is intended to particularise the general obligations owed by the new water and sewerage authorities to their customers set out in s.65(2)(a). It imposes a duty upon each authority to adopt a code of practice providing for the matters referred to in subs. (1)(a)–(d), a code with which the authority must "endeavour to comply" but where contravention will not in itself give rise to any criminal or civil liability (subs. (3)).
  The procedure for the adoption of the code is by the preparation of a draft (subs. (1)), and is regulated by subs. (2) which incorporates the same procedures for approval by the Customers Council (see s.67) or, failing the Council, the Secretary of State, as must be adopted for "charges schemes" under s.76(4)–(6). Subsections (4) and (5) authorise the variation and/or revocation and replacement of a code of practice, subject to a similar system of approval by the Customers Council. Under subs. (6), authorities are required to take appropriate steps to inform customers and potential customers of the content of their codes of practice.

Protection of customers' interests etc.

Scottish Water and Sewerage Customers Council

67.—(1) There shall be established a body to be known as the Scottish Water and Sewerage Customers Council (in this Part of this Act referred to as "the Customers Council") for the purpose of representing the interests of customers and potential or former customers of the new water and sewerage authorities.

(2) Schedule 9 to this Act shall have effect with respect to the constitution and proceedings of, and other matters relating to, the Customers Council.

DEFINITIONS
"new water and sewerage authorities": s.125.

GENERAL NOTE
This section (together with Sched. 9, and ss.68–71) makes provision for the establishment and functions of the Scottish Water and Sewerage Customers Council. See s.177(2) for disqualification of members of the Council from membership of the House of Commons.

As explained in *Shaping the Future – The New Councils* (Cm. 2267, 1993), in the light of the move to the new water and sewerage authorities, the inevitability of rising charges to fund new investment programmes, and "in line with the principles of the Citizen's Charter, there will be a clear need to establish separate and independent representation for consumers' interest" (para. 3.23). The outcome is the Customers Council. In debate (First Scottish Standing Committee, cols. 1720–22), it was promised that the Council would be operational before April 1996, with a target of spring or summer 1995.

Schedule 9 contains some fairly standard form provisions for the constitution and proceedings of the Customers Council but points of interest include:
Para. 3 This requires the Secretary of State, when making appointments to the Council, to choose people not only with relevant knowledge or experience but also representative of domestic (defined in para. 4) and non-domestic customers – both actual and potential – and specifically including those from rural areas (para. 3(a), by reference to s.65(2)(a)(ii)).
Para. 4 This requires the Council to establish three committees – one for the area of each of the three new authorities.
Para. 11 This requires at least one meeting per year of those committees to be "open to all members of the public".

Functions of Customers Council

68.—(1) For the purpose mentioned in section 67(1) of this Act, the Customers Council shall—
  (a) keep under review all matters appearing to it to affect the interests of customers or potential or former customers of the new water and sewerage authorities;
  (b) consult each authority about such of those matters as appear to affect the interests of the customers or potential or former customers of that authority; and
  (c) make such representations as it considers appropriate to those authorities, or as the case may be to that authority, about any such matter.

(2) The Customers Council shall investigate any complaint made to it by a customer or potential or former customer of a new water and sewerage authority, as respects a function of that authority (whether as water authority or as sewerage authority), unless it appears to the Council that the complaint is vexatious or frivolous.

(3) Without prejudice to subsection (1)(c) above, where the Customers Council considers it appropriate to do so in connection with a complaint investigated by it under subsection (2) above, it shall make representations on behalf of the complainer to the authority in question about any matter—

(a) to which the complaint relates; or

(b) which appears to the Council to be relevant to the subject matter of the complaint.

(4) The Customers Council shall advise the Secretary of State on any matter which appears to the Council, or to him, to relate to—

(a) the standard of service provided by a new water and sewerage authority to their customers; or

(b) the manner in which any such authority conduct their relations with their customers or potential or former customers.

(5) The Customers Council shall have power to do anything which is calculated to facilitate, or is incidental or conducive to, the performance of any of its functions under this Act; and without prejudice to that generality, or to section 70(2) of this Act, may make such arrangements as it thinks fit to inform customers and potential or former customers of the new water and sewerage authorities about matters affecting, or likely to affect, their interests.

DEFINITIONS

"Customers Council": s.125.

"new water and sewerage authorities": s.125.

GENERAL NOTE

This section defines the principal functions of the Customers Council. It should be read together with ss.69–71, with s.66 (codes of practice), and with s.76 (charges schemes).

The purpose of the Council (s.67(1)) is to represent the interests of customers and potential customers of the three new water and sewerage authorities and subs. (1) of this section sets out the main functions of reviewing, consulting and making representations. Under subss. (2) and (3) the Council is required to investigate complaints and, where appropriate, make representations to authorities in relation to them, and the Council is also required (subs. (4)) to advise the Secretary of State on matters relating to standards of service and relations between the authorities and their customers. Incidental powers under subs. (5) include the power to provide information to customers (over and above the reporting function under s.70).

Power of Customers Council to require information

69. A new water and sewerage authority shall, on being requested to do so by the Customers Council, supply the Council with such information held by them as it may reasonably seek in the exercise of its functions under this Act; but where the authority and the Council cannot agree as to whether the information is sought reasonably, either of them may refer the matter to the Secretary of State, whose determination in that regard shall be final.

DEFINITIONS

"Customers Council": s.125.

"new water and sewerage authorities": s.125.

GENERAL NOTE

If the Customers Council is to be successful, it must have reasonable access to information held by the three water and sewerage authorities. The power to request such information (subject to the resolution of any dispute by the Secretary of State) is provided by this section.

Annual reports by, and information from, Customers Council

70.—(1) Without prejudice to subsection (3) below, the Customers Council shall, as soon as practicable after the end of each financial year, make to the Secretary of State a report on its activities during that financial year; but no such report shall be required in respect of any financial year ending before 31st March 1997.

(2) The Customers Council shall arrange for the report to be published in such manner as it considers appropriate.

(3) The Customers Council shall furnish the Secretary of State with such information regarding the exercise, or proposed exercise, of its functions under this Act as he may from time to time require.

DEFINITIONS
"Customers Council": s.125.
"financial year": s.125.

GENERAL NOTE
This section requires the Customers Council to report annually to the Secretary of State; publish the reports; and supply information required by the Secretary of State.

Funding of Customers Council

71.—(1) The Secretary of State may, to such extent as may be approved by the Treasury, defray or contribute towards the expenses of the Customers Council.

(2) Any sums required by the Secretary of State for the purposes of subsection (1) above shall be paid out of money provided by Parliament.

(3) A new water and sewerage authority shall contribute towards the expenses of the Customers Council by making payments of such amounts, and at such times, to the Council as the Secretary of State may direct.

DEFINITIONS
"Customers Council": s.125.
"new water and sewerage authorities": s.125.

GENERAL NOTE
The Customers Council is to be funded by grants from the Secretary of State, and contributions from the water and sewerage authorities in amounts directed by the Secretary of State.

References to Monopolies and Mergers Commission

72. In section 11(3) of the Competition Act 1980 (entities as respects which references may be made to the Monopolies and Mergers Commission), after paragraph (c) there shall be inserted the following paragraph—
"(cc) the new water and sewerage authorities, within the meaning of the Local Government etc. (Scotland) Act 1994;".

DEFINITIONS
"new water and sewerage authorities": s.125.

GENERAL NOTE
The amendment made to s.11(3) of the Competition Act 1980 (c. 21) by this section designates the three new water and sewerage authorities as bodies in respect of which references may be made to the Monopolies and Mergers Commission (*i.e.* in relation to alleged abuse of monopoly power).

In debate (First Scottish Standing Committee, cols. 1750–1755) this section was taken as an opportunity to discuss whether the new authorities should be subject to the Parliamentary or Local Ombudsman. The Government's view was that their role was commercial and that they were not a part of local government.

Environmental protection

Duty of new authorities as respects Natural Heritage Area or area of special interest

73.—(1) Where an area of land ("the relevant land")—
 (a) has been designated under section 6(2) of the Natural Heritage (Scotland) Act 1991 ("the 1991 Act") as a Natural Heritage Area; or
 (b) is, in the opinion of Scottish Natural Heritage ("the environmental authority"), of special interest by reason of its flora, fauna or geological or physiographical features,
and the environmental authority consider that it may at any time be affected by schemes, works, operations or activities of a new water and sewerage authority ("the relevant authority"), the environmental authority shall by written notice advise the relevant authority that they so consider; but they shall forthwith notify the relevant authority of any cancellation or variation, under section 6(7) of the 1991 Act, of the designation or if they cease to be of the opinion mentioned in paragraph (b) above.

 (2) Where the relevant authority intend to carry out any scheme, work, operation or activity which appears to them likely to, as the case may be—
 (a) prejudice significantly the value of the relevant land, or any part of it, as a Natural Heritage Area (the designation mentioned in subsection (1)(a) above not having been cancelled or so varied as no longer to apply to the part in question); or
 (b) destroy or damage any of the flora, fauna or features, by reference to which the environmental authority formulated their opinion under subsection (1)(b) above as respects the special interest of the relevant land (notification of their ceasing to be of that opinion not having been given),
the relevant authority shall consult with the environmental authority before commencing the scheme, work, operation or activity.

 (3) Subsection (2) above shall not apply in relation to anything done by the relevant authority in an emergency if particulars of what is done and of the emergency are notified by them to the environmental authority as soon as is practicable after the thing is done.

 (4) Any expression not defined in this Act but used both in this section and in the 1991 Act, shall be construed in accordance with that Act.

DEFINITIONS
 "1991 Act": subs. (1).
 "environmental authority": subs. (1).
 "new water and sewerage authorities": s.125.
 "relevant authority": subs. (1).
 "relevant land": subs. (1).

GENERAL NOTE
 Section 65(2) imposes some general environmental duties on both the Secretary of State and the new water and sewerage authorities, but this section (added at Committee stage in the Commons) imposes certain additional responsibilities. It concerns those situations where either a Natural Heritage Area has been designated on an area of "relevant land", or where the land is in the opinion of Scottish Natural Heritage "of special interest by reason of its flora, fauna, or geological or physiographical features". This last formula derives from that used in s.28 of the Wildlife and Countryside Act 1981 (c. 69) to defined areas of land of special (scientific) interest – commonly "sites of special scientific interest" or "SSSIs". A peculiarity of that legislation is that

such sites are not "designated" but come into existence through the "opinion" of Scottish Natural Heritage – which is then obliged to communicate its "opinion" by notification to the planning authority, owners/occupiers, and the Secretary of State. It is thus again the "opinion" of Scottish Natural Heritage which may trigger activity under this section.

Scottish Natural Heritage, as the "environmental authority", must give written notice to a new water and sewerage authority if it considers that such an area of land "may at any time be affected by schemes, works, operations or activities" of that authority (subs. (1)). Then, if the conditions mentioned ("prejudice significantly" the land or "destroy or damage" its features) are satisfied, the water and sewerage authority must (except in the "emergency" circumstances mentioned in subs. (3)) consult with Scottish Natural Heritage before commencing the works, etc. There is no obligation on the authority to desist from undertaking the works, however Scottish Natural Heritage responds.

Charges

Charges for services provided

74.—(1) Subject to the provisions of this Part of this Act and of sections 9A and 47 of the 1980 Act (no charge for water in certain cases), the powers of a new water and sewerage authority shall include power—

(a) to fix charges for any services provided in the course of carrying out their functions; and

(b) to demand and recover charges fixed under this section from any person to whom they provide services.

(2) The powers conferred by subsection (1) above shall be exercisable—

(a) by or in accordance with a charges scheme under section 76 of this Act; or

(b) by or in accordance with an agreement with the person to be charged.

(3) Subject to the provisions of this Part of this Act, a new water and sewerage authority may fix charges under this section by reference to such matters, and may adopt such methods and principles for the calculation and imposition of the charges, as appear to them to be appropriate.

(4) Nothing in this Part of this Act shall entitle a new water and sewerage authority to fix, demand or recover a charge for—

(a) under subsection (2) of section 6 of the 1980 Act (duty to provide water supply), taking pipes; or

(b) under subsection (2)(a) of section 1 of the 1968 Act (duty to provide sewerage), taking public sewers,

to the point or points mentioned in the subsection in question.

(5) A new water and sewerage authority exercising their powers under subsection (1) above by entering into such agreements as are mentioned in subsection (2)(b) above shall endeavour to ensure that no undue preference is shown, and that there is no undue discrimination, in determining the conditions of those agreements.

(6) Nothing in subsections (1) to (3) above or in any charges scheme under section 76 of this Act shall affect any power of a new water and sewerage authority to fix charges under any power conferred otherwise than under or by virtue of this Part of this Act.

DEFINITIONS

"1968 Act": s.125.
"1980 Act": s.125.
"charges scheme": s.125.
"new water and sewerage authorities": s.125.

GENERAL NOTE

This section, together with ss.75–82 (and, in supplementation of s.79, Sched. 10), provides the rules according to which the new water and sewerage authorities must charge for their services.

These provisions replace those contained in Sched. 11 to the Local Government Finance Act 1992 (repealed by Sched. 14), according to which the regional and islands councils charge for their water and sewerage services until March 31, 1996. Those charges were, in brief, for water: direct charges for metered supplies, a council water charge (for domestic consumers), and a non-domestic water rate; for sewerage: a proportion of the council tax, and a non-domestic sewerage rate.

This section itself confers the general power on authorities to charge for their services, subject to other provisions in the Act. Most importantly, the powers under subs. (1) are to be exercised in accordance with a charges scheme (s.76), or in accordance with an agreement with the person charged (subs. (2)).

No charge may be made in the two circumstances referred to in subs. (1) – s.9A of the Water (Scotland) Act 1980 relates to water for fire-fighting and s.47 of that Act to situations where water had to be supplied free prior to May 16, 1949. Nor may charges be made for the provision of pipes under s.6(2) of that Act, or, for public sewers under s.1(2)(a) of the Sewerage (Scotland) Act 1968 to the statutorily defined points. Otherwise authorities have the freedom conferred by subs. (3) (still subject to the need for a charges scheme or agreement) to fix charges by reference to such matters, methods and principles as appear appropriate, subject to the qualification in subs. (5) which requires that, where charges are based on agreement, an authority must "endeavour to ensure that no undue preference is shown, and that there is no undue discrimination, in determining the conditions of those agreements". This strange language (taken from Sched. 5 to the Abolition of Domestic Rates Etc. (Scotland) Act 1987 (c. 47) and the Local Government Finance Act 1992) was discussed in Parliamentary debates at First Scottish Standing Committee, cols. 1755–58, where subs. (5) (reflecting the wording already used in s.76(7)) was added. The minister explained that, although the obligation not to discriminate should apply to charges schemes and to charges fixed by agreement, it would not be appropriate to extend that obligation to charges for trade effluent fixed under the Sewerage (Scotland) Act 1968.

Authorities are free from the constraints in this section if a power to charge is separately conferred by legislation other than in this Part of the Act (subs. (6)).

Maximum charges for services provided with help of new authority

75.—(1) The Secretary of State may from time to time by order fix maximum charges which a person who is not a new water and sewerage authority may recover from another such person in respect of the supply of water to, the provision of sewerage to, or the disposal of sewage for that other person with the help of services provided by any such authority.

(2) For the purposes of this section, water is supplied to, sewerage provided to, or sewage disposed of for a person with the help of services provided by an authority if—

(a) a facility for that person to have access to a supply of water provided by the authority, as water authority, in pipes, or to make use of sewerage which is, or facilities for the disposal of sewage which are, provided by the authority as sewerage authority, is made available to that person otherwise than by the authority;

(b) that person is provided with a supply of water in pipes by a person to whom the water is supplied, directly or indirectly, by the authority as water authority; or

(c) that person is provided with sewerage, or with facilities for the disposal of sewage, by a person who, for the purposes of providing the sewerage or facilities, makes use of sewerage or of such facilities provided, directly or indirectly, by the authority as sewerage authority.

(3) An order under this section may make different provision in relation to different persons, circumstances or localities and may fix a maximum charge either by specifying the maximum amount of the charge or by specifying a method of calculating that amount.

(4) Where a person pays a charge in respect of anything to which an order under this section relates and the amount paid exceeds the maximum charge fixed by the order, the amount of the excess shall be recoverable by that person from the person to whom he paid the charge.

(5) A statutory instrument containing an order under this section shall be subject to annulment in pursuance of a resolution of either House of Parliament.

DEFINITIONS

"new water and sewerage authorities": s.125.

GENERAL NOTE

This section was described as a protection against profiteering (First Scottish Standing Committee, col. 1760). It seeks to prevent someone, who has had the "help of services" provided by a water and sewerage authority at prices regulated under this Act, from making an excessive profit by selling on a service to another person (*e.g.* the proprietor of a static caravan park passing on charges to residents). The circumstances aimed at are identified in subs. (2), and the mechanism of control is for the Secretary of State to make an order fixing maximum charges (subss. (1), (3) and (5)), with any amount paid over and above such a maximum becoming recoverable from the payee (subs. (4)).

Charges schemes

76.—(1) A new water and sewerage authority may, in accordance with this section, make a scheme (in this Part of this Act referred to as a "charges scheme") which (either or both)—

(a) fixes the charges to be paid for any relevant services provided by them;

(b) makes provision with respect to the times and methods of payment of the charges fixed by the scheme.

(2) Services are relevant for the purposes of subsection (1)(a) above if they are provided by the authority in the course of carrying out their functions and are not services as respects which conditions as to payment may be imposed under section 29(3)(j) of the 1968 Act (conditions relating to the reception, treatment and disposal of trade effluent).

(3) A charges scheme may—

(a) make different provision for different cases, or classes of case, including different provision in relation to different circumstances or localities;

(b) contain supplemental, consequential and transitional provisions for the purposes of the scheme;

(c) revoke or amend a previous charges scheme.

(4) A charges scheme shall not come into force before—

(a) it has been sent in draft to, and approved by, the Customers Council, such approval being to the scheme having effect either—

    (i) without modifications; or

    (ii) with such modifications as, after consulting with and obtaining the agreement of the authority, the Council thinks fit to make; or

(b) where the Council is not prepared to give approval under paragraph (a) above, or cannot obtain the agreement of the authority to some or all of the modifications which it would make under sub-paragraph (ii) of that paragraph, the draft (with any modifications to it which may have been agreed between the Council and the authority) has been sent by the Council to, and approved by, the Secretary of State, such approval being to the scheme having effect either—

    (i) without modifications (or further modifications); or

    (ii) with such modifications as, after consulting with the Council and the authority, he thinks fit to make,

and the scheme shall have effect accordingly.

(5) Where three months have elapsed since the Customers Council has received a charges scheme in draft by virtue of paragraph (a) of subsection

(4) above and the Council has neither given approval under that paragraph nor sent the draft to the Secretary of State under paragraph (b) of that subsection, the new water and sewerage authority which made the scheme may require the Council so to send it to him.

(6) Where, under—

(a) paragraph (a) of subsection (4) above, the Customers Council gives approval to a charges scheme it shall send a copy of the scheme as so approved to the Secretary of State;

(b) paragraph (b) of that subsection, the Secretary of State gives approval to such a scheme he shall send a copy of the scheme as so approved to the Council.

(7) A new water and sewerage authority in making a charges scheme, and the Customers Council and the Secretary of State in considering whether to give approval to such a scheme, shall endeavour to ensure that no undue preference is shown, and that there is no undue discrimination, in the fixing of charges.

(8) Nothing in any charges scheme shall affect any power of a new water and sewerage authority to enter into such an agreement with any person in any particular case as determines the charges to be made for the services provided to that person by them.

DEFINITIONS
"Customers Council": s.125.
"new water and sewerage authorities": s.125.
"relevant services": subs. (2).

GENERAL NOTE
This section, s.78 (which imposes liability to pay charges under schemes on occupiers) and s.79 (collection of charges by local authorities) are the core provisions in the new system of charges for water and sewerage services.

Charges are required to be determined in accordance with schemes. Although the formula in subs. (1) is the permissive "may", there is a clear obligation on water and sewerage authorities to make a scheme. Section 83(1) requires authorities to ensure that "their revenue is not less than sufficient to meet their total outgoings", and s.74(1) and (2) permit charges to be imposed only under a charges scheme or by agreement.

A charges scheme has to relate to "relevant services" (subs. (1)(a)), which are defined in subs. (2) to include all the functions of an authority, with the exception of the services mentioned in s.29(3)(j) of the Sewerage (Scotland) Act 1968, which relates to charges made for the reception of trade effluent.

The scheme may make provision as specified in subs. (3), but the main emphasis in the section is on procedures imposed on authorities for the protection of their customers (or potential customers). In accordance with the terms of subss. (4)–(6), the authority must obtain the approval of the Customers Council (see ss.67–71) to a draft of the scheme before it comes into force or, failing approval of the Council (which may be conditional on modifications agreed with the authority), the approval of the Secretary of State (with or without modifications). In addition, subs. (7), in language echoing that used in s.74(5), requires that authorities, the Customers Council, and the Secretary of State, must endeavour to avoid undue preference or discrimination. Meanwhile subs. (8), in its reference to the power to charge separately from a charges scheme by agreement, reinforces s.74(2)(b).

Publication of summary of charges scheme

77. A new water and sewerage authority shall, on a charges scheme made by them being approved under section 76(4) of this Act—

(a) provide, at such offices of the authority, and at such other places, as the authority think fit, reasonable facilities—

(i) for inspection of the scheme by any person; and

(ii) for any person to take a copy of the scheme, or of an extract of it, on his paying such reasonable amount as the authority may determine; and

(b) advertise those facilities, and publish such summary of the scheme as appears to them to be appropriate, in at least one newspaper circulating in their water and sewerage areas.

DEFINITIONS
"charges scheme": s.125.
"new water and sewerage authorities": s.125.

GENERAL NOTE
This section requires that a water and sewerage authority makes available its approved charges scheme for public inspection, and publishes a summary of the scheme in at least one newspaper circulating in its areas.

Liability of occupiers etc. for charges

78.—(1) Subject to the following provisions of this section and except in so far as provision to the contrary is made by any agreement to which a new water and sewerage authority are a party—

(a) supplies of water provided by them shall be treated for the purposes of this Part of this Act as services provided to the occupier for the time being of any premises supplied; and

(b) the provision of sewerage, and the disposal of sewage, provided by them shall be treated for such purposes as provision to, or as disposal for, the occupier for the time being of any premises which—

　　(i) are drained by a sewer or drain connecting, either directly or through an intermediate sewer or drain, with such a public sewer of the authority as is provided for foul water or surface water or both; or

　　(ii) are premises the occupier of which has, in respect of the premises, the benefit of facilities which drain to a sewer or drain so connecting;

and such supply of water, provision of sewerage or disposal of sewage are referred to in subsection (2) below as "relevant services".

(2) Subject to subsection (3) below, charges which, under the preceding provisions of this Part of this Act, are fixed in relation to any premises by reference to volume may be imposed so that a person remains liable, in relation to those premises, to pay charges for relevant services provided by a new water and sewerage authority after the person has ceased to be occupier of the premises.

(3) A person shall not be liable by virtue of subsection (2) above for any charges fixed in relation to any premises by a new water and sewerage authority except where—

(a) he fails to inform the authority of the ending of his occupation of the premises at least two working days before he ceases to occupy them; and

(b) the charges are in respect of a period ending no later than with the first relevant day.

(4) In paragraph (b) of subsection (3) above, "the first relevant day" means whichever of the following first occurs after the person ceases to occupy the premises—

(a) where the person informs the authority of the ending of his occupation (but not timeously), the twenty–eighth day after informing the authority;

(b) any day on which any meter would normally have been read in order for the amount of the charges to be determined;

(c) any day on which any other person informs the authority that he has become the new occupier of the premises.

(5) In subsection (3)(a) above, reference to two working days is to a period of forty-eight hours calculated after disregarding any time falling on—

(a) a Saturday or Sunday;

(b) Christmas Day or Good Friday; or
(c) a day which is a bank holiday in Scotland under the Banking and Financial Dealings Act 1971.

(6) In the application of this section to services which are the subject of a determination under section 79(1)(a) of this Act, references in subsection (1) above to the occupier of premises shall be construed as references to the person liable under or by virtue of sections 75 to 77 of the Local Government Finance Act 1992 to pay council tax in respect of the premises ("council tax" being construed in accordance with section 70(1) of that Act).

DEFINITIONS
"first relevant day": subs. (4).
"new water and sewerage authorities": s.125.
"relevant services": subs. (1).

GENERAL NOTE
Provision for liability to pay for water and sewerage services until March 31, 1996 was mainly contained in the Local Government Finance Act 1992. In most respects carrying forward provisions introduced in 1989 with the community charge by the Abolition of Domestic Rates Etc. (Scotland) Act 1987, Sched. 11 to the 1992 Act established the forms of charging (by rates and otherwise) referred to in the notes to s.74.

Now this section (read together with s.79) seeks to simplify this position with effect from April 1, 1996. The general aim appears to be that the "occupier" shall be the person liable to pay charges for services provided although (a) this is not categorically stated in the section; and (b), apart from the particular circumstances (which may, in practice, cover most situations) identified in subs. (6), there is no general definition of "occupier" offered by the section.

Subsection (1) does, however, provide that, subject to agreement to the contrary, the delivery of water and sewerage services is to be treated as being to the occupier. Subsections (2)–(5) make detailed provision to the effect that, where a charge is fixed in relation to any premises by reference to (metered) volume, liability to pay may continue (see subs. (3)) even though the person may have ceased to be occupier.

Subsection (6) needs to be read together with s.79(1)(a) which provides for local authorities (as "collecting authorities") to become responsible for the collection of charges from dwellings. In that event, the liable "occupier" is the person already liable under the Local Government Finance Act 1992 to pay the council tax.

Collection of charges by local authority

79.—(1) The Secretary of State may by order determine—
(a) that as respects services provided, within a financial year specified in the order, by a new water and sewerage authority (in this section referred to as the "providing authority") to dwellings within the area of a local authority (in this section and in Schedule 10 to this Act referred to as the "collecting authority"), or within such part of that area as may be so specified, the collecting authority and not the providing authority shall demand and recover charges (other than charges in respect of a supply of water taken by meter) payable for those services under a charges scheme; and
(b) that the collecting authority shall, at such intervals as may be so specified, make such payments to the providing authority (to whom no other amount shall be payable under the charges scheme for the services provided) as may be so specified or as may be determined in accordance with the provisions of the order.

(2) A statutory instrument containing an order under subsection (1) above shall be subject to annulment in pursuance of a resolution of either House of Parliament.

(3) An order under subsection (1) above may include provision as to—
(a) forms and procedures which the collecting authority shall adopt in demanding payment;

  (b) circumstances in which a customer of the providing authority who is aggrieved by a decision or calculation of the collecting authority may appeal—

          (i) except in a case specified by virtue of sub-paragraph (ii) below, to a valuation appeal committee (constituted under section 29 of this Act); or

          (ii) in a case which the order may specify, to a body constituted under the order (or under a previous such order) to consider appeals as respects any such case;

  (c) procedures to be followed in any appeal by virtue of paragraph (b) above;

  (d) the provision, for the purposes of this section, of information by the providing authority to the collecting authority; or

  (e) the keeping by the collecting authority of accounts and records as respects their functions by virtue of this section and the exhibition of, or of copies of, such accounts and records to the providing authority.

(4) Schedule 10 to this Act shall apply as respects the recovery by diligence of charges payable to a collecting authority by virtue of the foregoing provisions of this section.

(5) In subsection (1)(a) above, "dwelling" has the same meaning as in Part II of the Local Government Finance Act 1992.

DEFINITIONS

"charges scheme": s.125.
"collecting authority": subs. (1).
"dwelling": subs. (5).
"financial year": s.125.
"local authority": s.125.
"new water and sewerage authorities": s.125.
"providing authority": subs. (1).

GENERAL NOTE

For other principal provisions relating to charging see ss.74–78 above (as read with s.83).

This section enables the Secretary of State to provide by order that, for collection purposes, the responsibilities of the water and sewerage authority ("providing authority") should pass to the relevant local authority (as "collecting authority") in respect of services provided to "dwellings". The collecting authority would be required to account to the providing authority by making payments as provided for in the order. The incorporation of the definition of "dwelling" from the Local Government Finance Act 1992 (subs. (5)) ensures that these provisions for collection by local authorities (as read with s.78(6) which redefines the "occupier" for the purposes of liability), bring the procedures for collection of both charges for water and sewerage, and for the council tax, into the same collection regime. This matching of the two regimes may be carried forward further by such other provisions in the order as may be made under subs. (3) – including, in the ordinary case, the reference of appeals (subject to subs. (3)(b)(ii)) to the newly reconstituted valuation appeal committees. It is not clear which other bodies are contemplated for other appeals. In general debate on this section, it was made clear (*Hansard*, H.L. Vol. 556, cols. 2070–2071) that the Government definitely intended that local authorities should act as collecting authorities. An order in respect of 1996–97 was to be brought forward after Royal Assent. In the early years, the new water authorities would not have in place an easy and efficient form of allocation. The local authorities would, therefore, collect charges for domestic (unmetered) water and domestic sewerage; water authorities would collect from non-domestic consumers and for metered water. One effect of the changes from April 1, 1996 would be that the cost of domestic sewerage services would transfer from council tax bills to the bills issued on behalf of the water authorities.

Schedule 10 makes provision for diligences available for the recovery of charges by a collecting authority including, most importantly, the summary warrant procedure. In parliamentary debate, much attention was given to questions of the enforcement of payment and, in particular, the possibility that the threat of cutting off supplies of water might be used for this purpose. See also the General Note to s.80 below.

Power to demand and recover charges not to affect duty to maintain domestic water supply etc.

80. Subsections (1)(b) of section 74 and (1), (3) and (4) of section 79 of this Act are without prejudice to the duties of a new water and sewerage authority under section 6 of the 1980 Act (which include the duty to maintain a supply of wholesome water provided to meet a requirement for domestic purposes) or to the entitlements of any person under section 12 or 13 of the 1968 Act (which include the entitlement of an occupier of premises to drain into public sewers to which the drains or private sewers of the owner of the premises are connected).

DEFINITIONS
"1968 Act": s.125.
"1980 Act": s.125.
"new water and sewerage authorities": s.125.

GENERAL NOTE
This section was introduced at Committee stage in the Commons (First Scottish Standing Committee, cols. 2014–2017) to try to make clear – something which the Government had argued was clear in the first case – that the powers contained in the Act to recover payment for services did not include the sanction of disconnection of domestic water and sewerage supplies and services. This is done by reinforcing the position that the powers of recovery, etc., are "without prejudice" to the duties to maintain the services under the Sewerage (Scotland) Act 1968 and the Water (Scotland) Act 1980.

Reduced charges

81.—(1) The Secretary of State may make regulations as regards any case where—
    (a) a person is, under a charges scheme, liable to pay an amount to a new water and sewerage authority or to a local authority; and
    (b) conditions prescribed in the regulations are fulfilled.
    (2) The regulations may provide that the amount the person is liable to pay shall be an amount which—
    (a) is less than the amount it would be but for the regulations; and
    (b) is determined in accordance with rules prescribed in the regulations.
    (3) The conditions mentioned in subsection (1)(b) above, and the rules referred to in subsection (2)(b) above, may be prescribed by reference to such factors as the Secretary of State thinks fit.
    (4) The power to make regulations under this section shall be exercisable by statutory instrument, which shall be subject to annulment in pursuance of a resolution of either House of Parliament.

DEFINITIONS
"charges scheme": s.125.
"local authority": s.125.
"new water and sewerage authorities": s.125.

GENERAL NOTE
This section enables the Secretary of State to make provision by regulations for the reduction of charges to categories of persons stipulated in the regulations. In debate, it was intimated by Government that there was no intention to use the powers under this section to introduce means-tested reductions in charges. The section might, however, be used to introduce transitional reduction schemes if that appeared appropriate (*Hansard*, H.L. Vol. 556, cols. 2070–71).

Arrears of charges: restrictions on voting

82.—(1) This section applies at any time to a member of a local authority, or a member of a committee of a local authority or of a joint committee of two or more local authorities (including in either case a subcommittee), if at that time a charge payable by virtue of section 79(1) of this Act has become payable by him and has remained unpaid for at least two months.

(2) Subject to subsection (4) below, if a member to whom this section applies is present at a meeting of the authority or committee at which any matter concerning how the authority are to exercise such functions as they have by virtue of section 79 of this Act is a subject of consideration, he shall, at the meeting and as soon as practicable after its commencement, disclose the fact that this section applies to him and shall not vote on any question with respect to the matter.

(3) If a person fails to comply with subsection (2) above, he shall be guilty of an offence, and shall for each such offence be liable on summary conviction to a fine not exceeding level 3 on the standard scale, unless he proves that he did not know—

(a) that this section applied to him at the time of the meeting; or

(b) that the matter in question was a subject of consideration at the meeting.

(4) Subsections (1) to (3) of section 41 of the 1973 Act (removal or exclusion of disability) shall apply in relation to, and to any disability imposed by, this section as they apply in relation to, and to any disability imposed by, section 38 of that Act (provisions as to disability of members of authorities from voting).

(5) In subsection (1) above "joint committee" has the meaning given by section 235(1) of the 1973 Act.

DEFINITIONS

"1973 Act": s.183(1).

"joint committee": subs. (5); s.235(1) of the 1973 Act.

"local authority": s.125.

GENERAL NOTE

This section extends to their responsibilities for collection of charges under s.79(1), restrictions on voting similar to those which apply already (by virtue of the Local Government Finance Act 1992, s.112) in relation to the council tax, council water charge (and residually the community charge), and which affect local authority members (or members of committees and joint committees) who are two months or more in arrears with payments. Subsection (2) requires disclosure of the arrears, and prohibits voting with respect to a matter relating to collection under s.79, subject to the criminal penalties imposed by subs. (3).

In subs. (4), the provisions incorporated from s.41 of the 1973 Act enable the Secretary of State to remove a disability from voting, where the number of members of an authority so disabled would be so great a proportion as to impede business, or in any other case where the disability should be removed in the interests of the inhabitants of the area.

Finances of new authorities

Duties and powers relating to finance

83.—(1) It shall be the duty of a new water and sewerage authority so to discharge their functions as to secure that, taking one year with another, their revenue is not less than sufficient to meet their total outgoings.

(2) The Secretary of State may, with the approval of the Treasury, by order direct that a new water and sewerage authority shall discharge their functions, during any period specified in the direction, with a view to securing that they achieve in respect of that period a rate of return on the value of their net assets (as for the time being defined for the purposes of this section by the Secretary of State) which is not less than such rate as the Secretary of State specifies in the direction as the rate of return which he considers it is reasonable for the authority in question to achieve; but a statutory instrument containing any order made under this subsection shall be subject to annulment in pursuance of a resolution of either House of Parliament.

(3) After consultation with a new water and sewerage authority, the Secretary of State may, with the approval of the Treasury, determine that the authority shall (in addition to or in place of a duty imposed by virtue of subsection (2) above but without prejudice to the duty imposed by subsection (1)

above) be subject to a specified duty of a financial nature; and different determinations may be so made in relation to different authorities and to different functions and activities of an authority.

(4) Where a duty specified in a determination under subsection (3) above is in place of a duty imposed by virtue of subsection (2) above, the determination shall be by order.

(5) A determination under subsection (3) above may—

(a) relate to a period beginning before the date on which it is made;

(b) contain incidental or supplemental provisions;

(c) be varied (by order where the determination was by order) by a subsequent determination under that subsection.

(6) An order made by virtue of subsection (4) above shall not be made unless a draft of the order has been laid before, and approved by resolution of, each House of Parliament.

(7) It shall be the duty of a new water and sewerage authority to secure that their charges make a proper contribution to their duties, as respect financial matters, under this Part of this Act, taking into account—

(a) the authority's present circumstances and future prospects; and

(b) any duty imposed on them by virtue of subsection (2) or (3) above.

DEFINITIONS

"new water and sewerage authorities": s.125.

GENERAL NOTE

This section is the first in a group concerned with the general financial arrangements of the new water and sewerage authorities. It contains two principal elements. The first (in subs. (1)) is a general duty upon each authority to ensure that their revenue (on which see ss.74–81 (charges) and s.84 (grants)) is "not less than sufficient to meet their total outgoings". This obligation is subject to the formula "taking one year with another". Such a formula has been used in a number of earlier statutes in relation to the financial regimes of public bodies. In a recent English case it was described as "not a term of legal art; it is borrowed from accountancy and means no more ... than that the council is not confined to the current or coming year in quantifying the costs which it is going to recover ..." (*R.* v. *Tower Hamlets Health Authority, ex p. Tower Hamlets Combined Traders Association* July 19, 1993, unreported).

The second main element is the set of rules contained in subss. (2)–(6), according to which the Secretary of State may by order prescribe specific target rates of return on their net assets, which the authorities, in addition to meeting their obligations under subs. (1), must achieve (subs. (2)). In addition to *or* in place of that obligation, the Secretary of State may determine that an authority "be subject to a specified duty of a financial nature" (subs. (3)). Subsection (5) adds certain formal parameters to these determinations. Under subs. (4) it is laid down that where a direction is made "*in place of* a duty imposed by virtue of subs. (2)" (*i.e.* not where it is simply in addition), the direction must be made by order (and see subs. (6)).

Financing and borrowing

84.—(1) The Secretary of State may—

(a) out of money provided by Parliament and subject to such conditions as he thinks fit to impose, make payment under this paragraph (except for the purpose mentioned in paragraph (b) below), by way of grant to a new water and sewerage authority—

(i) in respect of the exercise of their functions; and

(ii) in respect of their administrative expenses;

(b) out of money so provided, make payment under this paragraph by way of grant to such an authority for the purpose of meeting, or alleviating, any loss they may sustain—

(i) by reason of their complying with a direction given under section 117 of this Act; or

(ii) by virtue of regulations made under section 81 of this Act,

of such sums as he may, with the consent of the Treasury, determine.

(2) Subject to subsection (7) below, for the purpose of the exercise of any of their functions, a new water and sewerage authority—

(a) may, subject to such conditions as, with the consent of the Treasury, the Secretary of State thinks fit to impose, borrow from him, and he may lend to them, sums of such amounts as he may, with such consent, determine; and

(b) may, with the consent of the Secretary of State given with the approval of the Treasury, borrow money, whether in sterling or otherwise, from any other person or body, whether in the United Kingdom or elsewhere.

(3) Where a body (whether the Board or a local authority) whose property, rights and liabilities are to be transferred to a new water and sewerage authority under a transfer scheme, is liable to repay an amount borrowed, sums lent to the new water and sewerage authority under paragraph (a) of subsection (2) above may, without prejudice to the generality of that paragraph, include sums to be paid by them to the body for the purpose of enabling the body, before the transfer date, to make such repayment; and a body who receive an amount from a new water and sewerage authority by virtue of this subsection shall, in accordance with any direction to them under this subsection by the Secretary of State, use the amount for that purpose.

(4) Any loans made in pursuance of subsection (2)(a) above shall be repaid to the Secretary of State at such times and by such methods, and interest on the loans shall be paid to him at such times and at such rates, as he may from time to time, with the consent of the Treasury, direct.

(5) The Treasury may issue, out of the National Loans Fund, to the Secretary of State such sums as are necessary to enable him to make loans in pursuance of subsection (2)(a) above; and any sums received by him in pursuance of subsection (4) above shall be paid into that fund.

(6) It shall be the duty of the Secretary of State, as respects each financial year—

(a) to prepare, in such form and manner as the Treasury may direct, an account of sums issued to the Secretary of State in pursuance of subsection (5) above, of any sums required to be paid into the National Loans Fund in pursuance of that subsection and of the disposal by him of the respective sums; and

(b) to send a copy of the account to the Comptroller and Auditor General not later than the end of the month of November next following that financial year;

and the Comptroller and Auditor General shall examine, certify and report on the account and shall lay copies of it, and of his report on it, before each House of Parliament.

(7) The aggregate amount outstanding, otherwise than by way of interest, in respect of—

(a) all lending to the new water and sewerage authorities under subsection (2) above; and

(b) all amounts borrowed which those authorities are liable to repay by virtue of section 91(1) of this Act,

shall not exceed £3,000 million, or such greater sum not exceeding £4,500 million as the Secretary of State may, with the consent of the Treasury, by order specify.

(8) An order made under subsection (7) above shall not be made unless a draft of the order has been laid before, and approved by resolution of, the Commons House of Parliament.

DEFINITIONS
"Board": s.125.
"local authority": s.125.
"new water and sewerage authorities": s.125.
"transfer date": s.125.
"transfer scheme": s.125.

GENERAL NOTE
This section contains the principal powers available to the Secretary of State which enable him to give different forms of financial assistance to the new water and sewerage authorities. Note also the power to give guarantees in s.85 below. This section confers the power to make grants and the power to lend to the authorities. Because of the significance of the connection between these powers and the probable level of charges to consumers, this section attracted much debate. There were, in particular, some comparisons drawn between Scotland and England where, at the time of water privatisation in that country a "green dowry" was given to the new water companies in the shape of a writing-off of debts. It was, however, explained that this would be inappropriate in Scotland. There was no privatisation and so no green dowry (First Scottish Standing Committee, cols. 1818–1821).

Subsection (1) enables the Secretary of State, subject to the consent of the Treasury, to make grants for the normal operational purposes mentioned in para. (a), and also to alleviate the cost to authorities of meeting the requirements of directions given in the interests of national security under s.117, or the cost of reductions in charges under s.81 (para. (b)).

Subsection (2) enables authorities to borrow from the Secretary of State and, with his consent, from other sources (whether in the U.K. or otherwise), with special provision made in subs. (3) for borrowing by authorities from the Secretary of State of sums necessary to pay to a local authority (or the Central Scotland Water Development Board) any sum owed by the latter at the time that property, rights and liabilities are transferred to a new authority under a transfer scheme (see s.91). Subsections (4), (5) and (6) make provision incidental to the main lending power in subs. (2)(a), especially in relation to contributions from the National Loans Fund (and accounting arrangements therefor) to fund loans made by the Secretary of State.

Subsections (7) and (8) impose a limit (subject to amendment by order requiring affirmative resolution in the House of Commons) of £3,000 million on the total combined capital debt of the three new authorities, *i.e.* arising out of loans under subs. (2) and amounts repayable as a result of debts transferred under s.91(1) at the time the authorities are inaugurated.

Guarantees

85.—(1) The Secretary of State may, with the consent of the Treasury, guarantee, in such manner and on such conditions as he thinks fit, the repayment of the principal of, the payment of interest on, and the discharge of any other financial obligation in connection with, any sums which a new water and sewerage authority borrow from a person other than the Secretary of State.

(2) Immediately after a guarantee is given under this section, the Secretary of State shall lay a statement of the guarantee before each House of Parliament; and where any sum is issued for fulfilling a guarantee so given, he shall lay before each House of Parliament a statement relating to that sum, as soon as possible after the end of each financial year, beginning with that in which the sum is issued and ending with that in which all liability in respect of the principal of the sum and in respect of interest on it is finally discharged.

(3) Any sums required by the Secretary of State for fulfilling a guarantee under this section shall be charged on and issued out of the Consolidated Fund.

(4) If any sums are issued by the Secretary of State in fulfilment of a guarantee given by him under this section the authority in question shall make to him, at such times and in such manner as, with the consent of the Treasury, he may from time to time direct, payments of such amounts as, with such consent, he may so direct in or towards repayment of the sums so issued and payments of interest, at such rate as, with such consent, he may so direct, on the amount outstanding for the time being in respect of sums so issued.

DEFINITIONS
"financial year": s.125.
"new water and sewerage authorities": s.125.

GENERAL NOTE
This section supplements s.84 by enabling the Secretary of State to guarantee loans made to the new water or sewerage authorities by persons other than the Secretary of State (see s.84(2)(b)). Such a guarantee must be reported to Parliament (as must any payment in fulfilment

of the guarantee) (subs. (2)); any such payments must be charged to the Consolidated Fund (subs. (3)); and arrangements made for their recovery from the authority concerned (subs. (4)). The purpose of the guarantees would be to assist the authorities to seek the most advantageous loans.

Directions as to payment and investment

86. The Secretary of State may from time to time, after consultation with a new water and sewerage authority, direct them—

(a) to pay to him, on a date specified in the direction, such sum as may be so specified, being a sum not required; or

(b) to invest, in such manner as may be so specified, such sum as may be so specified, being a sum not immediately required,

for the exercise of their functions nor apart from this section payable under or by virtue of any provision of this Act.

DEFINITIONS
"new water and sewerage authorities": s.125.

GENERAL NOTE
This section (in a form common to other public bodies – but very oddly and misleadingly laid out in the final two lines) gives powers to the Secretary of State to require, after consultation, surplus funds of a new authority either to be paid to him or to be invested in a manner specified.

Accounts

87.—(1) It shall be the duty of a new water and sewerage authority—

(a) to keep proper accounts and proper records in relation to the accounts; and

(b) to prepare in respect of each financial year a statement of accounts giving a true and fair view of the state of affairs and the income and expenditure of the authority in question.

(2) Every statement of accounts prepared by an authority in accordance with this section shall comply with any requirement which the Secretary of State has, with the consent of the Treasury, notified in writing to the authority and which relates to—

(a) the information to be contained in the statement;

(b) the manner in which that information is to be presented; or

(c) the methods and principles according to which the statement is to be prepared.

(3) In this Part of this Act "financial year" means any period of twelve months ending with, and including, the last day of March.

DEFINITIONS
"new water and sewerage authorities": s.125.
"financial year": s.125; subs. (3).

GENERAL NOTE
This section requires each new water and sewerage authority to keep proper accounts and prepare a financial statement. See s.88 below for auditing of the accounts. The power in subs. (2) of the Secretary of State to issue requirements as to the statements will enable him to impose a degree of uniformity between the three authorities.

Audit of accounts

88.—(1) The accounts of a new water and sewerage authority shall be audited by auditors appointed for each financial year by the Secretary of State.

(2) A person shall not be eligible for appointment for the purposes of subsection (1) above unless he is eligible for appointment as a company auditor under section 25 of the Companies Act 1989.

(3) A copy of any accounts of an authority which are audited under subsection (1) above and of the report made on those accounts by the auditors shall

be sent to the Secretary of State as soon as reasonably practicable after the report is received by the authority; and the Secretary of State shall lay a copy of any accounts or report sent to him under this subsection before Parliament.

(4) In this section "accounts", in relation to an authority, includes any statement under section 87 of this Act.

DEFINITIONS
    "accounts": subs. (4).
    "financial year": s.125.
    "new water and sewerage authorities": s.125.

GENERAL NOTE
    This section enables the Secretary of State to ensure the audit of the accounts of the three new water and sewerage authorities by an auditor (qualified under s.25 of the Companies Act 1989 (c. 40)) appointed by him. A copy of the audited accounts must be laid before Parliament.

Subsidiary powers of new authorities

Subsidiary powers of new authorities

    89.—(1) A new water and sewerage authority may—
    (a) commission or support (whether by financial means or otherwise) research which in their opinion is relevant to, or directly related to, any of their functions; or
    (b) themselves initiate and carry out research which in their opinion is directly related to any of their functions.

    (2) With the consent of the Secretary of State, a new water and sewerage authority—
    (a) may form or promote, or join with any other person in forming or promoting, a company (within the meaning of the Companies Act 1985);
    (b) may (whether in Scotland or elsewhere) provide advice and assistance to any person as respects any matter in which they have skill and experience.

    (3) Without prejudice to any powers exercisable apart from this subsection but subject to the provisions of this Act and of the 1968 and 1980 Acts, a new water and sewerage authority shall have power to do anything (whether in Scotland or elsewhere) which is calculated to facilitate, or is conducive or incidental to, the discharge of any of their functions.

DEFINITIONS
    "1968 Act": s.125.
    "1980 Act": s.125.
    "new water and sewerage authorities": s.125.

GENERAL NOTE
    This section confers additional powers on the water and sewerage authorities, in supplementation of the general duties imposed by s.65, the additional powers deriving from the Sewerage (Scotland) Act 1968 and the Water (Scotland) Act 1980, both as amended.

Subs. (1)
    Formerly, local authorities as sewerage authorities could, under s.40 of the Sewerage (Scotland) Act 1968, undertake or commission relevant research. That section is repealed by Sched. 14 to the Act, but replaced by this subsection giving the new authorities similar powers in relation to both their sewerage and water functions.

Subs. (2)
    This empowers the new authorities to form companies etc., and to provide advice and assistance. This might include consultancy and laboratory services (see First Scottish Standing Committee, col. 1827).

Subs. (3)

This gives authorities the standard subsidiary powers (comparable to s.69 of the 1973 Act for local authorities) routinely given to statutory bodies to do things incidental etc., to their main functions. It was stressed that, because this was *not* a privatisation, the new authorities would not have the trading freedoms given to the private sector bodies in England (*ibid.*, col. 1827).

Dissolution of Central Scotland Water Development Board

Dissolution of Central Scotland Water Development Board

90.—(1) The Central Scotland Water Development Board shall be dissolved on 1st April 1996.

(2) Notwithstanding the repeal by this Act of paragraph (c) of section 106(1) of the 1973 Act (application of certain provisions of that Act to bodies other than local authorities etc.), the provisions applied by virtue of that paragraph to the Board shall, as respects the financial year ending on 31st March 1996, continue to apply after that date in relation to the Board; but anything which shall or may be done or enjoyed, or any access, inspection or copying which shall or may be allowed, under or by virtue of any of those provisions or of section 118 of that Act (financial returns) by, or by an officer of, the Board shall, or as the case may be may, after that date, be done, enjoyed or allowed by, or by an officer of, the East of Scotland Water Authority in place of the Board or of an officer of the Board.

DEFINITIONS

"1973 Act": s.183(1).
"Board": s.125.
"financial year": s.125.

GENERAL NOTE

Section 80 of the Water (Scotland) Act 1980 continued in existence the Central Scotland Water Development Board (it had been established under s.3 of the Water (Scotland) Act 1967 (c. 78)), with the functions (reconfirmed by s.81 of the Water (Scotland) Act 1980) originally transferred to it on May 16, 1968 (under s.4 of the Water (Scotland) Act 1967 (c. 78)) from earlier joint water boards, and with an area comprising "the limits of supply as water authorities of the Tayside, Fife, Lothian, Central and Strathclyde regional councils". The Board's principal function was to develop new sources for the supply of water in bulk to the constituent authorities. It operated two water supply schemes, Loch Lomond and Loch Turret (including the hydro-electric power station in Glen Turret); see *Investing in our Future* paras. 1.6 and 1.11.

Subs. (1)

The creation of the new water and sewerage authorities from April 1, 1996 makes the Central Board no longer necessary and it is abolished from that date. Sections 80 and 81 of the Water (Scotland) Act 1980 are repealed, as is the remainder of Pt. VIII of that Act under which other Water Development Boards might have been (but never were) created.

Subs. (2)

Section 106(1)(c) extends to water development boards (*i.e.* in practice the Central Board) the provisions in ss.93–105 of the 1973 Act which relate to the funds, capital expenses, and the auditing of accounts of local authorities. Despite the repeal of this paragraph by Sched. 14 to this Act, the provisions will continue to apply in relation to the accounts, etc., of the Board for the financial year to March 31, 1996, but with responsibilities transferred from the Board to the East of Scotland Water Authority and its officials.

Transfer of property, rights and liabilities to new authorities

Transfer of property, rights and liabilities to new authorities

91.—(1) Subject to subsections (8) and (9) below, and to section 95 of this Act, on 1st April 1996 (in this Part of this Act referred to as "the transfer date") all property, rights and liabilities to which—

(a) the Central Scotland Water Development Board (in this Part of this Act referred to as "the Board") are entitled or subject immediately before that date; and

(b) the regional and islands councils, in the exercise of their functions under any enactment in relation to water supply, to the provision of sewerage and to their dealing with the contents of sewers, are so entitled or subject (in this section referred to as their "relevant" property, rights and liabilities),

shall, by virtue of this subsection, transfer to and vest in the new water and sewerage authorities and be allocated as between those authorities in accordance with such schemes as are mentioned in subsection (2) below.

(2) Subject to subsections (5) and (7) below, on or before such date as the Secretary of State may direct (in this section referred to as the "scheme submission date"), the Board and each of the regional and islands councils shall make and submit to him a scheme for the transfer under subsection (1) above of—

(a) the Board's; or
(b) as the case may be, the council's relevant,

property, rights and liabilities (any such scheme so made, or made by the Secretary of State under subsection (8) below, being in the following provisions of this Part of this Act referred to as a "transfer scheme").

(3) The transfer scheme submitted by the Board shall, subject to section 95 of this Act, provide for all their property, rights and liabilities to be transferred to, and apportioned between, the new water and sewerage authorities in accordance with such guidance as may be given to the Board by the Secretary of State under this subsection.

(4) The transfer scheme submitted by a regional or islands council shall, subject to subsection (5) below and to section 95 of this Act, provide in the case of—

(a) Lothian, Borders, Fife or Central Region, for all their relevant property, rights and liabilities to be transferred to the East of Scotland Water Authority;
(b) Strathclyde or Dumfries and Galloway Region, for all their relevant property, rights and liabilities to be transferred to the West of Scotland Water Authority;
(c) Highland or Grampian Region or an Islands Area, for all their relevant property, rights and liabilities to be transferred to the North of Scotland Water Authority; and
(d) Tayside Region—
    (i) for all their relevant property, rights and liabilities except such as they are entitled or subject to in the exercise of functions in relation to the provision of sewerage, or dealing with the contents of sewers, in the first added area (within the meaning of Schedule 8 to this Act), to be transferred to the North of Scotland Water Authority; and
    (ii) for the property, rights and liabilities excepted by subparagraph (i) above to be transferred to the East of Scotland Water Authority.

(5) In preparing a transfer scheme for the purposes of subsection (1) above a council shall take into account any advice given by the Secretary of State as to the provisions he regards as appropriate for inclusion in the scheme (and in particular, but without prejudice to that generality, as to the description of relevant property, rights and liabilities it is in his view appropriate to transfer to the new water and sewerage authority or authorities in question).

(6) The Secretary of State, after such consultation with the Board or, as the case may be, with the council which prepared the transfer scheme, as he thinks fit, may—

(a) approve the scheme, either with or without modifications; or
(b) refuse to approve it,

and a transfer scheme approved under this subsection shall come into force on the transfer date.

(7) Before the scheme submission date the Secretary of State may give notice to the Board, or as the case may be to a council, that on the basis of such information as has (or has not) been submitted to him by the body in question, he considers it unlikely that the body will be in a position, by that date, to submit a transfer scheme to him in conformity with subsections (2) to (4), or as the case may be (5), above; and a body to which such notice is given need not comply (and shall take no further steps to comply) with subsection (2) above.

(8) If—

(a) the Secretary of State has given notice to the Board or to a council under subsection (7) above;

(b) the Board or council do not submit a transfer scheme under subsection (2) above; or

(c) the Board or council submit a transfer scheme which (either or both)—

    (i) has not been prepared in accordance with the provisions of this Part of this Act; or

    (ii) could not reasonably be approved by the Secretary of State even after the exercise by him, as extensively as he considers appropriate, of his powers of modification under subsection (6)(a) above,

he may, in respect of the property, rights and liabilities of the Board or as the case may be of the relevant property, rights and liabilities of the council in question, himself make a transfer scheme to take effect on the transfer date.

(9) There shall not transfer or vest by virtue of subsection (1) above—

(a) any right as respects—

    (i) a charge or rate mentioned in sub–paragraphs (a) to (c) of paragraph 1 of Schedule 11 to the Local Government Finance Act 1992 (charges or rate out of which expenditure incurred by local authority in meeting requisition under Part IV or VIII of the 1980 Act, or in the exercise of functions in relation to water supply, to be met);

    (ii) a community charge or community water charge (within the meaning of the Abolition of Domestic Rates Etc. (Scotland) Act 1987) or council tax (within the meaning of Part II of the said Act of 1992); or

    (iii) a non-domestic sewerage rate (whether levied under paragraph 19 of Schedule 5 to the said Act of 1987 or under paragraph 20 of the said Schedule 11); or

(b) any right or liability arising under a contract of employment.

(10) Where the Secretary of State makes a transfer scheme under subsection (8) above, he may recover his reasonable expenses in so doing, or such proportion of those expenses as he thinks fit—

(a) before the transfer date, from the Board or as the case may be from the council in question; or

(b) on or after the transfer date, from the authority to which property, rights and liabilities of the council have transferred by virtue of paragraph (a), (b), (c) or as the case may be (d)(i) of subsection (4) above or, in the case of the Board, from the authority mentioned in the said paragraph (a),

by such means as appear to him to be appropriate; and without prejudice to the generality of this subsection those means may include, as respects a council, setting off the expenses payable by them against revenue support grant or non-domestic rate income payable by him to them under paragraph 3 of Schedule 12 to the Local Government Finance Act 1992.

DEFINITIONS
"Board": subs. (1); s.125.
"new water and sewerage authorities": s.125.

"relevant property rights and liabilities": subs. (1).
"scheme submission date": subs. (2).
"transfer scheme": subs. (2); s.125.

GENERAL NOTE
This section is the first of a group concerned with the property and other consequences of the transfer of water and sewerage functions from regional and islands councils (and the Central Scotland Water Development Board) to the new water and sewerage authorities on April 1, 1996. Although the staffing consequences of the transfer are dealt with (in s.97) by adopting the provisions earlier in the Act relating to local government reorganisation itself, the property consequences attract separate sections. (For the property consequences of setting up the Children's Reporter Administration, see s.138.) See also ss.92–96 for further provisions relating to transfer schemes.

The general provision that "property rights and liabilities" (not including the rates, charges and employment rights mentioned in subs. (9)) will transfer from the Board and the relevant existing local authorities to the new water and sewerage authorities is made in subs. (1). This is done by means of schemes, prepared by the existing councils in the manner indicated in subs. (4), and by the Board subject to the guidance mentioned in subs. (3). The schemes must be submitted to the Secretary of State by a date ("scheme submission date") directed by him (subs. (2)), but subject to the power of the Secretary of State to relax that requirement (subs. (7)). The preparation of the schemes is subject to the obligation to take account of any advice given by the Secretary of State under subs. (5), and is also subject to s.95 which incorporates the extensive further provisions of Sched. 11.

After the submission of a scheme to the Secretary of State, it is for him to approve it, with or without modifications, or to refuse to do so. If it is approved, then it takes effect on April 1, 1996, the transfer date. If, however, it is not approved, and could not reasonably be approved even if modified or if any of the other circumstances mentioned in subs. (8) arises, the Secretary of State may himself make a scheme to take effect on the transfer date, and may recover his reasonable expenses for doing so from either an existing authority or a new authority in accordance with subs. (10) *i.e.* in the case of an existing council, by means of including a set-off against payment of grant or non-domestic rate income.

Transfer schemes: general

92.—(1) A transfer scheme may—
(a) define the property, rights and liabilities to be transferred to the transferee—
 (i) by specifying the property, rights and liabilities in question;
 (ii) by specifying all the property, rights and liabilities referable to a particular part of the transferor's functions; or
 (iii) partly in the one way and partly in the other;
(b) provide that any rights or liabilities specified, or described, in the scheme shall be enforceable by or against either the transferor's successor or the transferee or by or against both the successor and the transferee;
(c) impose on the successor or the transferee an obligation to enter into such written agreements with, or execute such other instruments in favour of, as the case may be, the transferee or the successor or such other person as may be specified in the scheme;
(d) make appropriate supplemental, incidental, consequential or transitional provision.

(2) An obligation imposed by a provision included in a transfer scheme by virtue of paragraph (c) of subsection (1) above shall be enforceable by civil proceedings by the successor or the transferee or the other person for an interdict or for any other appropriate remedy.

(3) A transaction of any description which is effected in pursuance of any such provision as is mentioned in subsection (2) above—
(a) shall have effect subject to any enactment which provides for transactions of that description to be registered in a statutory register; and
(b) subject to paragraph (a) above, shall be binding on all other persons notwithstanding that the transaction would, apart from this subsection, have required the consent or concurrence of any other person.

(4) A right of pre-emption, right of irritancy or similar right affecting land (including, without prejudice to the generality of the expression "similar right", any right under a clause providing for return or reversion in specified circumstances) shall not operate or become exercisable as a result of any transfer of land—

(a) by virtue of a transfer scheme;

(b) by or under an agreement or instrument made or executed pursuant to any provision of Schedule 11 to this Act or pursuant to any directions given, or requirement imposed, under that Schedule; or

(c) pursuant to an obligation imposed by a provision included in a transfer scheme by virtue of paragraph (c) of subsection (1) above;

and, without prejudice to paragraph 8 of that Schedule, any such right shall accordingly have effect in the case of any such transfer as if the transferee in relation to that transfer were the same person in law as the transferor and as if no transfer of the land had taken place.

(5) Subsection (4) above shall have effect in relation to—

(a) the grant or creation of an estate or interest in, or right over, land; or

(b) the doing of any other thing in relation to land,

as it has effect in relation to a transfer of land; and any reference in that subsection or in the following provisions of this section to the transferor or the transferee shall be construed accordingly.

(6) In any case where any such right as is mentioned in subsection (4) above would, apart from that subsection, have operated in favour of, or become exercisable by, a person, but the circumstances are such that, in consequence of the operation of that subsection, the right cannot subsequently operate in favour of that person or, as the case may be, become exercisable by him, such compensation as may be just shall be paid to him by the transferor, the transferor's successor or the transferee (or, in so far as the particular application of these provisions admits, by any two or by all of them) in respect of the extinguishment of the right.

(7) Any dispute as to whether any, and (if so) how much, compensation is payable under subsection (6) above, or as to the person to whom or authority by whom it shall be paid, shall be referred to and determined by an arbiter appointed by the Lord President of the Court of Session.

(8) Subject to subsection (10) below, if it appears to the regional council, or as the case may be to the islands council or the Board, that a person is, or may be, entitled to compensation under subsection (6) above—

(a) they shall by written notice inform the person that he is, or may be, so entitled and shall invite him to make such representations as he wishes to them within fourteen days after the date of issue of the notice; or

(b) where they do not know (either or both)—

    (i) the name of the person concerned;

    (ii) his address,

they shall publish, in such manner as they consider appropriate, a notice containing information about the interest affected and inviting any person who thinks that he is, or may be, entitled to compensation in respect of the interest to make such representations as he wishes to them by a date which they shall specify in the notice, being a date not less than twenty-eight days after the date of publication.

(9) Any reference in this Part of this Act to a transferor's successor is inapplicable where the transferor is the Board and is otherwise to be construed as a reference to the council for any local government area named in column 1 of Schedule 1 to this Act which is wholly or partly conterminous with the area of the transferor.

(10) Where the last of the fourteen days after the date of issue of a notice under paragraph (a) of subsection (8) above falls on or after the transfer date, or the date specified in a notice published under paragraph (b) of that subsection so falls, and the representations are invited by—

(a) a transferor other than the Board, the notice shall direct that any such representations be made to the transferor or, on or after that date, to the transferor's successor;

(b) the Board, the notice shall direct that any such representations be made to the Board or, on or after that date, to a specified transferee of the Board (the transferee in question being that which appears to the Board to be the most appropriate in the circumstances).

DEFINITIONS
"Board": s.125.
"transfer scheme": s.125.

GENERAL NOTE
This section provides further rules which are to apply to the transfer schemes to be made under s.91, and which seek to ensure that schemes properly specify the "property, rights and liabilities" to be transferred, and that rights and obligations arising under the schemes are enforceable.

Thus subs. (1) imposes the duty to define the property, rights and liabilities in accordance with para. (a); to provide that rights or liabilities specified or described in a scheme are enforceable by or against the transferor's successor (*i.e.* a new local authority and, therefore, inapplicable where the transferor is the Board; see subs. (9)), or the transferee (the new water and sewerage authority), or against both of them (para. (b)); to impose on either the successor or the transferee an obligation to enter into written agreements with (or execute instruments in favour of) the other or another specified person (para. (c)); and to make incidental, etc., provision (para. (d)).

Subsections (2) and (3) take forward the arrangements required to be made under para. (c). Subsection (2) requires that the obligation to enter into written agreements, etc., be enforceable by civil proceedings for interdict or other appropriate remedy. Subsection (3) requires that transactions, effected in pursuance of such obligations contained in a transfer scheme, be subject to statutory requirements of registration, and further provides that they should be binding on "all other persons" notwithstanding that the consent (or concurrence) of another person would otherwise have been required.

Subsections (4)–(8) and (10) are aimed at ensuring that for certain purposes, in relation to rights affecting land, the transfer from old to new authority is deemed *not* to have occurred, *e.g.* a right of pre-emption does not fall to be exercised if land is transferred under a scheme, if transferred by virtue of Sched. 11, or by virtue of an obligation imposed under subs. (1)(c) (subss. (4)–(5). However, if a right, made inoperable by subs. (4), therefore cannot ever be exercised, then "such compensation as may be just" is payable (subs. (6)), subject, in the case of a dispute, to arbitration in accordance with subs. (7). Some of the more difficult situations which might conceivably arise were discussed by the Lord Advocate (*Hansard*, H.L. Vol. 556, col. 2076). In such a case, notice to the person entitled to compensation, or publicity (if the person, or address, is unknown), is required under subss. (8) and (10).

Preparations for transfer of functions etc. to new authorities

93.—(1) Subject to the provisions of this Act, a regional or islands council or the Board may do anything which is calculated to facilitate, or is conducive or incidental to, the prospective transfer—

(a) of their property, rights and liabilities which is provided for in section 91(1) of this Act; or

(b) of their rights and liabilities under contracts of employment which is provided for by virtue of section 97 of this Act.

(2) All the regional or islands councils whose areas fall, wholly or partly, within either or both of the areas mentioned in—

(a) paragraph (a) of subsection (1) of section 62 of this Act may jointly establish, or be required by the Secretary of State jointly to establish, a committee to consider any matter which it is expedient should be considered before 1st April 1996 in order to ensure the effective operation of the East of Scotland Water Authority thereafter;

(b) paragraph (b), or as the case may be paragraph (c), of that subsection, may so establish or be required by the Secretary of State so to establish, a committee to consider as respects, respectively, the West of Scotland Water Authority or the North of Scotland Water Authority any such matter as a committee established under paragraph (a) above is to consider as respects the East of Scotland Water Authority.

(3) A committee established under subsection (2) above shall consist of such number (and respective numbers) of representatives of the councils by whom it is established as may be agreed between the councils or, in default of agreement, as may be determined by the Secretary of State.

(4) Any expenses incurred by a committee established under subsection (2) above shall be defrayed by the councils by whom the committee was established in such proportions respectively as may be agreed between them or, in default of agreement, as may be determined by the Secretary of State.

DEFINITIONS
"Board": s.125.

GENERAL NOTE
This section anticipates that the regional and islands councils (and the Central Scotland Water Development Board) will need to undertake a number of tasks incidental to their obligations to transfer both "property, rights and liabilities" (s.91(1)), and employment rights and liabilities (s.97), to the new water and sewerage authorities. The power to do this is provided in subs. (1).

Subsection (2) (supplemented by subss. (3) and (4)) enables existing local authorities (or, if the Secretary of State so decides, requires them) to establish three joint committees "to consider any matter which it is expedient should be considered before April 1, 1996" in order to ensure the effective operation of the water and sewerage authorities thereafter. The three joint committees are to be drawn from the regional and islands councils whose areas overlap with the water or sewerage areas of the new authorities. Subsections (3) and (4) provide for membership of the committees (by agreement of the councils or, in default, by determination of the Secretary of State), and for the defraying of their expenses (similarly).

Power to require provision of information and assistance as respects transfer schemes

94.—(1) The Secretary of State may direct the Board or any regional or islands council to furnish him, within such period as he may specify (being a period of not less than twenty-one days from the giving of the direction), with such information and assistance as he may require for the purposes of, or in connection with, his functions under section 91 of this Act.

(2) Without prejudice to the generality of subsection (1) above, the assistance mentioned in that subsection includes allowing a person who is authorised for the purposes of this section by the Secretary of State (and who need not be an officer of the Secretary of State) access to land or premises of the Board, or as the case may be of the council, at such reasonable times as that person may request.

(3) For the purposes of subsection (2) above—
(a) the period of not less than twenty-one days mentioned in subsection (1) above shall be the period by the end of which access must be allowed if requested in accordance with subsection (2); and
(b) a consecutive following period shall be specified in the direction under subsection (1) above, during which requests by the person for access (which may include access at the reasonable times for the whole or any part of so much of that period as for the time being remains) shall continue to be allowed.

DEFINITIONS
"Board": s.125.

GENERAL NOTE
The purpose of this section is to give the Secretary of State access to information, and assistance (including access to land and premises) from regional and islands councils and the Central Scotland Water Development Board, in connection with his functions under s.91 in relation to transfer schemes. Such information, etc., may be required within a period of not less than 21 days (with that rule adapted in the case of requests for access to land or premises – see subs. (3)).

Supplementary provision as to transfer schemes

95. Schedule 11 to this Act shall apply to transfers under this Part of this Act.

GENERAL NOTE
    This section applies the provisions of Sched. 11 to transfers (*i.e.* of property rights and liabilities) under this Part of the Act. That Schedule makes detailed rules in supplementation of s.92 and provides, *inter alia*, for the allocation of property, etc., where questions arise as to the proper division between the relevant new water and sewerage authority and a successor local authority, where property was attributable in part to a water or sewerage function and in part to a function passing to the local authority. Further provisions relate to the variation of transfers by agreement; certain restrictions on subsequent dealings in land; the construction of agreements, etc.; and the effects on third parties.

Transfer schemes: exemption from stamp duty and stamp duty reserve tax

96.—(1) Stamp duty shall not be chargeable on a transfer scheme or, subject to subsection (2) below, on any instrument which is certified to the Commissioners of Inland Revenue by the Secretary of State as having been made in pursuance of such a scheme.

    (2) No instrument which is certified as mentioned in subsection (1) above shall be taken to be duly stamped unless—

    (a) it is stamped with the duty to which it would but for that subsection be liable; or

    (b) it has, in accordance with section 12 of the Stamp Act 1891, been stamped with a particular stamp denoting that it is not chargeable with that duty or that it is duly stamped.

    (3) Stamp duty shall not be chargeable on any instrument which is made for the purposes of Schedule 11 to this Act.

    (4) No agreement made for the purposes of, or for purposes connected with, a transfer scheme shall give rise to a charge to stamp duty reserve tax; and no agreement which is made in pursuance of the said Schedule 11 shall give rise to such a charge.

DEFINITIONS
    "transfer scheme": s.125.

GENERAL NOTE
    This section is designed to ensure that neither a transfer scheme nor an instrument made pursuant to a scheme or to Sched. 11, shall be subject to stamp duty. Nor shall agreements connected with a transfer scheme be subject to stamp duty reserve tax.

Transfer etc. of staff

Staff: application of Chapter 2 of Part I etc.

97.—(1) In consequence of, or in connection with, the transfer and vesting effected by virtue of section 91(1) of this Act, the Secretary of State may by order under section 8(1) of this Act make provision in relation to the transfer of staff from the Board and from the regional and islands councils to the new water and sewerage authorities; and, subject to subsection (2) below, sections 8 and 9 of this Act shall apply as respects any such transfer as those sections apply to the transfer of staff from an existing local authority (however defined in those sections) to a new authority (however so defined).

    (2) Subsections (3) and (4) of section 8 of this Act shall apply as respects such employees of the Board or of an islands council as are transferred to a new water and sewerage authority as those subsections apply as respects employees of a regional council who are so transferred (subsection (6) of that section applying to an order made by virtue of this subsection as that subsection applies to an order made by virtue of subsection (1) above).

(3) Section 10 of this Act shall apply as respects persons ceasing to be employed by the Board or by an islands council and being employed by a new water and sewerage authority as that section applies as respects persons ceasing to be employed by an existing local authority (as defined in that section) and being employed by another person (whether or not a new water and sewerage authority).

(4) The advisory body designated, or as the case may be established, under section 11 of this Act shall carry out such functions in relation to the employees of the Board and, in so far as wholly or mainly employed in the exercise of such functions as are mentioned in section 91(1)(b) of this Act, of the islands authorities as the advisory body have, under section 11, in relation to employees of existing local authorities (as defined in subsection (10) of section 11); and, subject to subsection (5) below, subsections (3) to (8) and (11) of section 11 shall apply accordingly.

(5) As applied by subsection (4) above—

(a) subsections (3) to (6) of section 11 of this Act shall be construed as if references to an authority (unqualified by the word "local") were references to the Board or to an islands council; and

(b) subsection (7) of that section shall be construed as if—

(i) the reference to an authority not having ceased to exist were a reference to the Board not having ceased to exist or to an islands authority not having ceased to have such functions as are mentioned in section 91(1)(b) of this Act; and

(ii) the references to "an existing authority", "the authority" and "the local authority concerned" shall be construed as references to the Board or to an islands council.

(6) The staff commission established under section 12 of this Act shall carry out such functions in relation to the employees of the Board and, in so far as wholly or mainly employed in the exercise of such functions as are mentioned in section 91(1)(b) of this Act, of the islands authorities as the commission have, under or by virtue of section 12, in relation to staff transferred from an existing local authority (as defined in subsection (8) of section 12) to a new authority (as so defined).

(7) This subsection applies to any person who, at any time after the passing of this Act, is in the service—

(a) of the Board or, in so far as wholly or mainly employed in the exercise of such functions as are mentioned in section 91(1)(b) of this Act, of an islands council; or

(b) of a new water and sewerage authority,

and who suffers loss of employment or diminution of emoluments which is attributable to any provision made by, under or by virtue of this Part, or Part V, of this Act.

(8) Subsections (2) to (6) of section 13 of this Act shall apply as respects a person to whom subsection (7) above applies as they apply as respects a person to whom that section applies.

DEFINITIONS
"Board": s.125.
"new water and sewerage authorities": s.125.

GENERAL NOTE
Chapter 2 of Pt. I of the Act makes provision for many of the staffing consequences of the reorganisation of local government to take effect from April 1, 1996. Since the islands areas are largely unaffected by the reorganisation, the islands authorities are excluded from the arrangements made. This section adopts and adapts the provisions of Chap. 2 of Pt. I to the staffing consequences of the transfer of local authority responsibilities (including in this case those of the islands councils) for water and sewerage (and also the responsibility of the Central Scotland

Water Development Board), not to successor local authorities, but to the new water and sewerage authorities. For the equivalent application of the provisions to the setting up of the Children's Reporter Administration, see s.137.

For the content of the rules so adapted for application to the new authorities, see the notes on ss.8–13. Section 14 (also in the same Chapter and which seeks to restrict certain payments by the new local authorities) does not apply to the water and sewerage authorities. It should be noted that s.93(1) of the Act enables regional and islands councils to do anything incidental to the prospective transfer of their rights and liabilities under contracts of employment.

Land transactions

Acquisition of land by agreement

98.—(1) A new water and sewerage authority may under this subsection, for the purposes of any of their functions under this or any other enactment or for the purpose of there being provided, by some person other than themselves—

(a) a supply of water to the public; or

(b) a system, to which the public shall have access, of drains, sewers or sewage treatment works,

acquire by agreement any land (other than water rights) whether situated inside or outside their water area or sewerage area.

(2) In relation to any acquisition of land under subsection (1) above, the Lands Clauses Acts (except in so far as they relate to acquisition other than by agreement and to access to the special Act and except sections 120 to 125 of the Lands Clauses Consolidation (Scotland) Act 1845), and—

(a) in a case where the acquisition is in relation to the authority's functions as sewerage authority or for the purpose of the provision of a system such as is mentioned in paragraph (b) of that subsection, sections 6 and 70 to 78 of the Railways Clauses Consolidation (Scotland) Act 1845 (as originally enacted and not as amended by section 15 of the Mines (Working Facilities and Support) Act 1923); and

(b) in any other case, the said section 6 and Part IV of Schedule 4 to the 1980 Act,

are hereby incorporated with this section; and, in construing those Acts for the purposes of that subsection, this section shall be deemed to be the special Act and the authority shall be deemed to be the promoters of the undertaking or company as the case may require.

DEFINITIONS
"1980 Act": s.125.
"new water and sewerage authorities": s.125.

GENERAL NOTE
This section gives the new water and sewerage authorities the power to acquire land by agreement (see s.99 for compulsory acquisition). It replaces s.15 of the Water (Scotland) Act 1980 which is repealed by this Act. Although subs. (1) enables acquisitions outside their areas, the operation of the Act extends to Scotland only (s.184(4)).

It will be noted that subs. (1) authorises the acquisition of land, not only for the provision of a water or sewerage service by the authority itself, but also for its provision by "some person other than themselves". This enables the use of the section for B.O.O. schemes under the Private Finance Initiative; see the General Note to Pt. II. For the equivalent extension of the powers of existing local authorities on a transitional basis, see s.182. Subsection (2) applies to this power the provisions of the Lands Clauses Acts, and other existing legislation relating to the payment of compensation on land acquisition.

Compulsory acquisition of land

99.—(1) Without prejudice to the provisions of any order under section 17 of the 1980 Act (acquisition of water rights) and subject to section 18 of that Act (authorisation of compulsory acquisition of land necessary for purposes of order under section 17), a new water and sewerage authority may, for any of the purposes mentioned in subsection (1) of section 98 of this Act, be authorised by the Secretary of State to purchase compulsorily under this subsection such land as may, under that subsection, be acquired by them by agreement.

(2) A new water and sewerage authority are a statutory undertaker for the purposes of subsection (1)(b) of section 120 of the Local Government, Planning and Land Act 1980 (persons to whose compulsory acquisition of an interest in land the Acquisition of Land (Authorisation Procedure) (Scotland) Act 1947 in certain circumstances applies) not only (by virtue of the definition of "statutory undertaker" in subsection (3)(a) of that section) in respect of their functions as water authority but also in respect of their functions as sewerage authority.

(3) A new water and sewerage authority may be authorised by the Secretary of State to purchase compulsorily, or may acquire by agreement, land for giving in exchange for such land as is mentioned in section 1(2)(b) of the said Act of 1947.

DEFINITIONS
"1980 Act": s.125.
"new water and sewerage authorities": s.125.

GENERAL NOTE
See s.98 above for the acquisition of land by agreement by new water and sewerage authorities, for purposes including the provision of water or sewerage services by a person other than an authority itself in relation to B.O.O. schemes.

This section provides the powers for compulsory acquisition, with the authority of the Secretary of State. By providing that the new authorities are "statutory undertakers" for the purposes of s.120 of the Local Government, Planning and Land Act 1980 (c. 65) in respect of both water and sewerage functions, the powers and procedures of the Acquisition of Land (Authorisation Procedure) (Scotland) Act 1947) (c. 42) are applied to them (subs. 2)). Subsection (3) gives the authorities the power to acquire land to be given in exchange for land forming part of a common or open space or held "inalienably" by the National Trust for Scotland.

Disposal of land

100.—(1) Subject to subsection (2) below, a new water and sewerage authority may dispose of land held by them in any manner, to whomsoever and for whatever purpose they wish.

(2) Except with the consent of the Secretary of State, a new water and sewerage authority shall not dispose of land under subsection (1) above for a consideration less than the best that could reasonably be expected to be obtained on the open market.

DEFINITIONS
"new water and sewerage authorities": s.125.

GENERAL NOTE
This section gives to new water and sewerage authorities a wide power to dispose of land, subject to the "best consideration" qualification in subs. (2).

Amendment of Sewerage (Scotland) Act 1968

Authorisation of construction of certain private sewers etc.

101. The following section shall be inserted after section 3 of the 1968 Act—

"Authorisation of construction of certain private sewers etc.

3A.—(1) Without prejudice to their powers under section 3 of this Act (including any power to authorise the construction, on their behalf, of a public sewer), a sewerage authority may authorise a person to con-

struct, within their area but whether or not connecting with their sewers
or sewage treatment works, a sewer—

    (a) in, under or over any road, or under any cellar or vault below any
       road; or

    (b) in, on or over any land which does not form part of a road and is
       not land as respects which he is owner, lessee or occupier,

but where authorisation is so given, subsection (2) of section 3 of this Act
shall apply in respect of the person and the construction proposed as
that subsection applies in respect of a sewerage authority and works proposed by them under subsection (1) of that section.

    (2) The sewerage authority—

    (a) in giving authorisation to a person under subsection (1) above; or

    (b) as respects any sewer (not being a sewer constructed by or on
       behalf of the authority) whose construction by a person does not
       require such authorisation,

may, in a case where the proposed sewer will connect with their sewers
or sewage treatment works, determine (and by written notice advise the
person) that all, or a part which they shall specify in the notice, of the
sewer constructed shall not vest in them through the operation of section 16(1)(c) of this Act and shall instead vest in him; but notwithstanding the determination the sewerage authority may on such terms and
conditions as they think fit, then or at some later time enter into an
agreement under which the sewer, or as the case may be the part, shall
vest in them.".

Definitions
  "1968 Act": s.125.
  "public sewer": s.59(1) of the Sewerage (Scotland) Act 1968.
  "sewerage treatment works": s.59(1) of the Sewerage (Scotland) Act 1968.
  "sewer": s.59(1) of the Sewerage (Scotland) Act 1968.
  "sewerage authority": s.59(1) of the Sewerage (Scotland) Act 1968, as amended by Sched. 13.

General Note
  Section 3 of the Sewerage (Scotland) Act 1968 gives powers to sewerage authorities to construct public sewers within or outwith their areas, subject to procedural safeguards for owners
and occupiers of land in subs. (2). This requires, *inter alia*, application to the sheriff for decision if
the consent of an affected owner or occupier is not forthcoming.
  This section inserts a new s.3A of that Act which permits other "private" persons (see the
B.O.O. schemes discussed in the General Note to Pt. II) to construct a sewer, provided it is with
the authorisation of the sewerage authority (which authorisation may only be given to construction *within* the area of the authority). The new private sewer need not connect with a public
sewer. The new s.3A(2) enables the authority to leave ownership of some or all of the new sewer
in the hands of the person constructing the sewer, subject to the possibility of its acquisition by
agreement at a later date.

Emptying of septic tanks

    102. For section 10 of the 1968 Act (whereby local authorities are under a
duty to empty septic tanks only where they have passed a resolution electing
to do so) there shall be substituted—

    "Emptying of septic tanks
      10.—(1) It shall be the duty of a sewerage authority to empty a septic
tank serving premises in their area on their being requested to do so by
the owner or occupier of the premises; but that duty is subject to subsection (2) below and as respects any particular septic tank—

(a) to its being reasonably practicable to empty the tank; and
(b) to all proper charges for their doing so being timeously paid.

(2) The duty does not extend to septic tanks which receive trade effluent; but the authority may, at the request of an owner or occupier of
premises served by any such septic tank, agree to empty it on such conditions as to payment or otherwise as they think fit.

(3) If any question arises under this section as to whether emptying is
reasonably practicable or as to whether a septic tank receives trade
effluent, it shall be determined summarily by the sheriff, whose decision
in the matter shall be final.

(4) For the purposes of subsection (1) above, a charge is proper if fixed
in accordance with, and timeously paid if paid in accordance with, a
charges scheme (within the meaning of Part II of the Local Government
etc. (Scotland) Act 1994).".

DEFINITIONS
"1968 Act": s.125.
"charges scheme": s.125.
"occupier": s.59(1) of the Sewerage (Scotland) Act 1968.
"owner": s.59(1) of the Sewerage (Scotland) Act 1968.
"sewerage authority": s.59(1) of the Sewerage (Scotland) Act 1968.
"trade effluent": s.59(1) of the Sewerage (Scotland) Act 1968.

GENERAL NOTE
This section, containing a reformulated duty to empty septic tanks, attracted debate in which
it was noted that, at present, all authorities empty septic tanks from time to time without charge –
with the exception of Tayside which makes a small charge (see First Scottish Standing Committee, col. 1837).

The substituted s.10 of the Sewerage (Scotland) Act 1968 removes the need for a resolution of
the sewerage authority (a resolution no longer being appropriate as the function moves from
local authority to quango) but, more importantly, imposes a general duty on the new authorities
to empty septic tanks. That obligation is, however, subject to the qualifications contained in subs.
(1) (reasonably practicable and charges timeously paid), subs. (2) (trade effluent), and subs. (3)
(questions concerning these issues, as under the original s.10, referred to the sheriff).

Register as respects trade effluents

103. The following sections shall be inserted after section 37 of the 1968
Act—

"Register for purposes of Part II
37A.—(1) A sewerage authority shall maintain a register for the purposes of this Part of this Act.

(2) The authority shall enter in the register—
(a) such particulars as may be prescribed—
(i) of any consent, affecting their area and for the time being
extant, given (whether before or after the coming into force of
this section) under this Part of this Act; and
(ii) of any agreement, affecting their area and for the time
being extant, entered into (whether before or after the coming
into force of this section) under section 37 of this Act; and
(b) such particulars of other matters relative to their functions under
this Part of this Act as may be prescribed.

(3) It shall be the duty of a sewerage authority—
(a) to secure that the register maintained by them in pursuance of
subsection (1) above is, after such date as may be prescribed,
open to inspection by the public free of charge at all reasonable
hours; and

(b) to afford members of the public reasonable facilities for obtaining from them, on payment of reasonable charges, copies of entries in the register.

(4) In subsections (2) and (3) above, "prescribed" means prescribed by the Secretary of State by regulations made under this subsection by statutory instrument.

(5) An instrument containing regulations under subsection (4) above shall be subject to annulment in pursuance of a resolution of either House of Parliament.

Exclusion from register of information affecting national security

37B.—(1) No information shall be included in a register maintained under section 37A of this Act if and so long as, in the opinion of the Secretary of State, the inclusion in the register of that information, or of information of that description, would be contrary to the interests of national security.

(2) The Secretary of State may, for the purposes of subsection (1) above, give to a sewerage authority directions—

(a) specifying information, or descriptions of information, to be excluded from the register; or

(b) specifying descriptions of information to be referred to him for his determination;

and no information referred to him in pursuance of paragraph (b) above shall be included in the register until he determines that it should be so included.

(3) The sewerage authority shall notify the Secretary of State of any information they exclude from the register in pursuance of directions under subsection (2) above.

(4) A person may, as respects any information which (but for this section) might be included in the register but which he believes may be information whose inclusion would be contrary to the interests of national security, by notice so inform the Secretary of State, specifying the information and indicating its apparent nature; and if the person does so—

(a) he shall advise the sewerage authority that he has given such notice; and

(b) no information in respect of which such advice has been given shall be included in the register until the Secretary of State has determined that it should be so included.".

DEFINITIONS

"1968 Act": s.125.

"sewerage authority": s.59(1) of the Sewerage (Scotland) Act 1968.

GENERAL NOTE

The insertion by this section of new ss.37A and 37B into the Sewerage (Scotland) Act 1968 is intended to impose on sewerage authorities an obligation to maintain a public register of consents for discharges to sewers under Pt. II of the Act. The new obligation parallels the existing obligations imposed on river purification authorities to maintain a register of consents to discharge to surface waters (see the Control of Pollution Act 1974, s.41 (as substituted by the Water Act 1989)). The detailed rules governing the new registers will be contained in regulations to be made by the Secretary of State.

The new s.37B requires the exclusion from the register, of information made the subject of a direction from the Secretary of State, on the grounds that inclusion of the information (or of a certain description of information) would be "contrary to the interests of national security". This is similar to s.42(1)(b) of the Control of Pollution Act 1974 ("contrary to the public interest") and there is also a parallel in s.21 of the Environmental Protection Act 1990 (c. 43).

Disapplication of restrictions on disclosure of information

104. In section 50 of the 1968 Act (which imposes restrictions on the disclosure of information obtained under or by virtue of that Act)—
  (a) in subsection (2), after paragraph (a) there shall be inserted—
      "(aa) in prescribed circumstances or for prescribed purposes; or"; and
  (b) after subsection (3) there shall be added—
      "(4) In paragraph (aa) of subsection (2) above, "prescribed" means prescribed by the Secretary of State by regulations made under this subsection by statutory instrument.
      (5) An instrument containing regulations under subsection (4) above shall be subject to annulment in pursuance of a resolution of either House of Parliament.
      (6) Subsections (1) and (2) above are subject to regulation 3(7) of the Environmental Information Regulations 1992 (which disapplies restrictions on disclosure if in pursuance of the regulations).".

DEFINITIONS
"1968 Act": s.125.

GENERAL NOTE
  Section 50 of the Sewerage (Scotland) Act 1968 restricts the disclosure of information obtained by sewerage authorities. The amendments made to s.50 by this section: (a) authorise the Secretary of State to prescribe exceptions to the general restrictions on disclosure, and (b) make explicit that the restrictions must be read subject to the Environmental Information Regulations 1992 (SI 1992 No. 3240), which disapply restrictions on disclosure in accordance with the regulations.

Further amendment of Water (Scotland) Act 1980

Restriction on references to Secretary of State of questions regarding water supply

105. In section 9(4) of the 1980 Act (which provides that questions as to the terms and conditions on which water is supplied etc. are to be referred to the Secretary of State in the absence of agreement), after the word "supplied" there shall be inserted "(not being a question as respects charges for the water which is to be supplied)".

DEFINITIONS
"1980 Act": s.125.

GENERAL NOTE
  Sections 74–77 of this Act make provision for the new water and sewerage authorities to fix charges and, in particular, to do so in accordance with charging schemes. These have to be approved by the Customers Council or, failing that, the Secretary of State. The amendment made to s.9(4) of the Water (Scotland) Act 1980 by this section recognises the existence of that new regime by removing the possibility of a separate appeal to the Secretary of State on the matter of charging for supply for non-domestic purposes. The amended section continues to provide for an appeal on other matters.

Removal of restriction on supply of water to premises outwith water authority's limits of supply

106. For section 12 of the 1980 Act (which provides for a water authority giving a supply of water to premises situated outwith their limits of supply if the water authority within whose limits the premises are situated consents) there shall be substituted—

"Supply of water to premises outwith limits of supply
  12. Where premises are situated outwith the limits of supply of a water authority, the authority may, after informing the water authority within

whose limits of supply the premises are situated, give a supply of water to the premises.".

DEFINITIONS
"1980 Act": s.125.
"water authority": s.109(1) of the Water (Scotland) Act 1980, as amended by Sched. 13.

GENERAL NOTE
This section substitutes a new s.12 of the Water (Scotland) Act 1980 which now permits the supply of water by one authority in the area of another, but without the need for the latter's consent, as was previously required. The second authority need now only be informed.

Supply of water for use outwith Scotland

107. The following section shall be inserted after section 13 of the 1980 Act—

"Supply of water for use outwith Scotland

13A.—(1) A water authority may, if for the time being they are satisfied that such supplies of water as are available to them are likely to be more than sufficient to enable them to fulfil their duties as respects the supply of water to premises in Scotland, enter into an agreement with any other person to give him, on such terms and conditions as they think fit and whether or not in bulk, a supply of water for use outwith Scotland.

(2) For the purposes of laying any pipes or installing any apparatus connected therewith, being pipes or apparatus required for giving a supply of water in pursuance of an agreement entered into under subsection (1) above, a water authority may exercise, either within or outwith their limits of supply, the like powers with respect to laying mains or breaking open roads as are exercisable by them under this Act for the purposes of laying mains, but subject to the like conditions and obligations.".

DEFINITIONS
"1980 Act": s.125.
"water authority": s.109(1) of the Water (Scotland) Act 1980, as amended by Sched. 13.

GENERAL NOTE
This is a section which attracted much interest in debate (see, in particular, First Scottish Standing Committee, cols. 1838–1843). By inserting a new s.13A into the Water (Scotland) Act 1980, it gives a new power to water authorities to agree, subject to the condition that they have more than sufficient water for supply in Scotland, to supply water outwith Scotland, whether or not in bulk. Assurances were given that water would be sold in this way only if it were genuinely surplus to requirements.
Ancillary powers are provided in subs. (2). These (laying mains or breaking open roads) may be exercised "either within or outwith their limits of supply". Although the new section refers to the exercise of powers outwith Scotland, this Act (and the Water (Scotland) Act 1980) have effect only in Scotland, and it was confirmed in debate that the infrastructural powers of any of the three water authorities would stop abruptly at the border.

Further provision as regards removal of restrictions on supply of water outwith limits of supply

108. For section 21 of the 1980 Act (which provides powers for the purposes of a water authority providing the whole or part of their limits of supply with a supply of water) there shall be substituted—

"Power to carry out works

21. Without prejudice to any other powers which they may have, a water authority may, for the purposes of providing a supply of water under this Act and subject to its provisions—
    (a) construct, alter, acquire by purchase, lease or otherwise, or renew or maintain, waterworks;

    (b) so acquire any undertaking belonging to persons, other than a water authority, who are supplying or are authorised to supply water;

    (c) so acquire premises to be used for the purposes of the authority and maintain such premises;

    (d) contract with any person for a supply by him of water in bulk or otherwise; or

    (e) erect and maintain a house for the use of a person employed by them for the purposes of their undertaking.".

DEFINITIONS

"1980 Act": s.125.
"premises": s.109(1) of the Water (Scotland) Act 1980.
"water authority": s.109(1) of the Water (Scotland) Act 1980, as amended by Sched. 13.

GENERAL NOTE

This section substitutes a new s.21 in the Water (Scotland) Act 1980. The change made is that it removes the restriction in the existing section confining the power to carry out works to an authority's limits of supply, except with the consent of the other authorities affected. The removal of the restriction is necessary in the light of the amendments made by ss.106 and 107.

Right of objection to proposed laying of mains

109. In section 23 of the 1980 Act (power to lay mains), after subsection (1) there shall be inserted—

"(1A) If within two months after the service of a notice under subsection (1)(b) above the owner or occupier objects to the water authority about the proposed works (and that objection is not withdrawn), the authority shall not proceed to lay the main but shall refer the matter by summary application to the sheriff, who may—

    (a) grant consent to the proposed works, either unconditionally or subject to such terms and conditions as he thinks just; or

    (b) withhold his consent;

and the decision of the sheriff on the matter shall be final.".

DEFINITIONS

"1980 Act": s.125.
"occupier": s.109(1) of the Water (Scotland) Act 1980.
"owner": s.109(1) of the Water (Scotland) Act 1980.
"premises": s.109(1) of the Water (Scotland) Act 1980.
"water authority": s.109(1) of the Water (Scotland) Act 1980, as amended by Sched. 13.

GENERAL NOTE

This section, by inserting a new subs. (1A) into s.23 of the Water (Scotland) Act 1980, and thus providing a new means of recourse to the sheriff where an owner or occupier of land objects to the laying of mains, brings s.23 into line with the equivalent provision in relation to the construction of sewers – see s.3(2) of the Sewerage (Scotland) Act 1968.

Vesting of certain supply pipes

110. In section 24 of the 1980 Act (which makes provision as regards communication and supply pipes)—

    (a) in subsection (4)—

        (i) after the word "road" there shall be inserted "and is not, by virtue of any of subsections (5) to (8) below, vested in them"; and

        (ii) at the end there shall be added "and to the terms and conditions of any such agreement as is mentioned in subsection (8) below"; and

    (b) after subsection (4) there shall be added—

"(5) Where the laying of a supply pipe is completed after such day as the Secretary of State may under this subsection by order appoint, so much of that pipe as may lie between a communication pipe with which it connects and the curtilage of the premises supplied shall, on such completion, vest in the water authority in whom is vested the communication pipe as shall any apparatus used wholly or mainly in connection with that supply pipe; and a supply pipe in so far as so lying is, together with any apparatus so used in connection with it, referred to in the following provisions of this section as a "relevant supply pipe".

(6) Subject to subsection (7) below, on such day as the Secretary of State may by order appoint, a relevant supply pipe which is not then vested in any water authority (and whose laying is complete) shall vest in the water authority in whom the communication pipe is vested.

(7) Subsection (6) above shall have no effect in relation to any relevant supply pipe in respect of which notice is both given and not withdrawn, within the period of three months before the day appointed under that subsection—

(a) to the water authority in question by the person (or as the case may be any one of the persons) in whom the pipe is, or will immediately before that day be, vested stating that he does not wish the pipe to vest in the water authority under that subsection; or

(b) to such person (or as the case may be persons) by the water authority stating that the pipe is inappropriate for the purpose of supplying water to the premises, whether by reason of its state of repair or otherwise,

but at any time after the appointed day the person, or as the case may be persons, in whom the pipe is vested may by notice specify a day on which he desires (or they desire) that the pipe shall vest in the authority and if the pipe is on that specified day appropriate for the purpose of supplying water to the premises it shall vest accordingly.

(8) If a relevant supply pipe does not vest in a water authority by virtue of subsection (6) or (7) above, the pipe may nevertheless vest by agreement in the authority—

(a) on such terms and conditions; and

(b) as from such day after the appointed day,

as the person (or persons) and the water authority consider appropriate.

(9) The water authority shall, at their own expense, carry out any necessary work of maintenance, repair or renewal of relevant supply pipes vested in them by virtue of any of subsections (5) to (7) above; but this subsection is without prejudice to the terms and conditions of any such agreement as is mentioned in subsection (8) above.

(10) Any dispute arising under subsection (7) above as to whether—

(a) a notice under paragraph (b) of that subsection should be withdrawn as unjustified;

(b) apparatus is used wholly or mainly in connection with a supply pipe; or

(c) on a specified day a relevant supply pipe is appropriate for the purpose of supplying water to the premises,

shall be referred by the person or persons in whom the pipe is vested to the Secretary of State, who may determine the dispute himself or, if he thinks fit, refer it for determination by arbitration.".

Definitions

"1980 Act": s.125.

"premises": s.109(1) of the Water (Scotland) Act 1980.

"relevant supply pipe": new subs. (5).

"water authority": s.109(1) of the Water (Scotland) Act 1980, as amended by Sched. 13.

General Note

This section makes amendments to s.24 of the Water (Scotland) Act 1980 which are intended to bring a greater part of the pipe system used for the supply of water into the ownership of the water authorities, thus enabling them to have more control over the condition of the system and reduce leakages, and so forth.

This is to be done by enabling the Secretary of State to set two appointed days. The first may be set under the new s.24(5) and from that date forward all *new* supply piping from a "communication pipe" to the curtilage of premises supplied shall vest in the water authority.

Then, by the second appointed day set under subs. (6) (but subject to the qualifications in subs. (7)–(10)), such *existing* piping shall similarly vest. There is, however, provision under subs. (7) for the owner of the pipe to dissent from this arrangement (by notice given within three months before the appointed day) but that, in turn, may be withdrawn and the pipe vest provided it is "appropriate for the purpose" (subs. (7)). In any event, the pipe may vest in the water authority by agreement (subs. (8)). Similarly the authority itself may, by notice, reject the vesting on the appointed day if the pipe is "inappropriate", whether by reason of its state of repair or otherwise. Disputes as to matters including the appropriateness of the pipe go to the Secretary of State under subs. (10). Normally the vesting of a pipe in the water authority carries with it the duty to maintain, repair, etc., at the authority's expense, but an agreement under subs. (8) (*i.e.* one under which the authority might be accepting a pipe in disrepair) may provide otherwise (subs. (9)).

Duty of water authority to keep map showing water mains etc.

111. The following section shall be inserted after section 24 of the 1980 Act—

> **"Keeping of map showing water mains, etc.**
> 24A.—(1) A water authority shall keep deposited at their principal office a map showing and distinguishing so far as is reasonably practicable all water mains, communication pipes and supply pipes which are vested in them by virtue of this Act or of Part II of the Local Government etc. (Scotland) Act 1994; and the authority shall provide reasonable facilities at that office for inspection of the map by any person and shall permit a copy of the map, or of an extract of it, to be taken by a person on his paying such reasonable amount as.the authority may determine.
>
> (2) A water authority shall keep deposited at such of their offices, other than their principal office, as they consider appropriate, a copy relevant to the office in question of part of the map mentioned in subsection (1) above; and the authority shall provide the like facilities and permission in relation to the copy part, at the office at which that copy is deposited, as, under subsection (1) above, they do in relation to the map mentioned in that subsection at their principal office.
>
> (3) For the purposes of subsection (2) above, a copy is relevant to an office if it is of such part of the map mentioned in subsection (1) above as appears to the water authority to be appropriate having regard to the geographical location of that office.".

Definitions

"1980 Act": s.125.

"water authority": s.109(1) of the Water (Scotland) Act 1980, as amended by Sched. 13.

General Note

Under s.11 of the Sewerage (Scotland) Act 1968, a sewerage authority is required to keep a map showing public sewers on deposit and available for inspection. That section is substantially amended by Sched. 13, para. 75(8). This section now brings into line the authorities' obligations as water authorities by inserting a new s.24A into the Water (Scotland) Act 1980.

Simplification of provisions as respects opting for water supply by meter

112. For section 41A of the 1980 Act (which makes provision as respects the supply of water by meter) there shall be substituted—

> "**Supply of water by meter**
>
> 41A. The occupier of premises to which water is supplied shall have the option, provided that he has (if he is not himself the owner of the premises) the consent of the owner, of taking the supply by meter; but the exercise of that option shall be conditional upon—
>
> (a) the payment by the occupier of any reasonable charges made by the authority under section 35 of this Act; and
>
> (b) the acceptance by him of such reasonable terms and conditions as may be published by the water authority under section 55(1) of this Act,
>
> and any question as to whether any such charges or terms and conditions are reasonable shall, in default of agreement, be referred to the Secretary of State who may determine it himself or, if he thinks fit, refer it to arbitration.".

DEFINITIONS
"1980 Act": s.125.
"occupier": s.109(1) of the Water (Scotland) Act 1980.
"owner": s.109(1) of the Water (Scotland) Act 1980.
"premises": s.109(1) of the Water (Scotland) Act 1980.

GENERAL NOTE
Section 41A of the Water (Scotland) Act 1980, which provided the option of a metered water supply, was inserted by the Local Government Finance Act 1992, and thus appeared in a form complicated by the need to express the right to such a metered supply by reference to the rules for liability to council tax or rates. This section now substitutes a new version of s.41A in simplified form.

Actings of Secretary of State on default of water authority

113. In section 76E(4) of the 1980 Act (which provides for enforcement, by default order, of requirements as to quality of water unless the Secretary of State is satisfied that failures complained of were of a trivial nature or that certain undertakings given are being complied with), in paragraph (a)—

(a) the words after "of", where it first occurs, shall be sub-paragraph (i) of the paragraph; and

(b) after that sub-paragraph there shall be added—
   "; or
   (ii) are not continuing and are unlikely to recur;".

DEFINITIONS
"1980 Act": s.125.

GENERAL NOTE
This section makes a small adjustment to s.76E of the Water (Scotland) Act 1980 (inserted by Sched. 22 to the Water Act 1989), and thus modifies the Secretary of State's obligations to take enforcement action if a water authority defaults in its duty to maintain water quality. Already he need not intervene if the failures are trivial, etc.; in addition, he need not now act in circumstances where failures "are not continuing and are unlikely to recur".

Publication and provision of information as respects quality of private supplies of water

114. In section 76F of the 1980 Act (general functions of local authorities in relation to water quality), after subsection (6) there shall be added—

"(7) The Secretary of State may by regulations require a local authority—

(a) to publish information about the quality of private supplies of water for domestic or food production purposes to any premises in their area; and

(b) to provide information to prescribed persons about the quality of water so supplied.

(8) Regulations under subsection (7) above—

(a) shall prescribe both the information which is to be published or provided in pursuance of the regulations and the manner and circumstances in which it is to be published or provided;

(b) may require the provision of information by a local authority to any person to be free of charge or may authorise it to be subject to the payment by that person to the authority of a prescribed charge; and

(c) may impose such other conditions on the provision of information by a local authority to any person as may be prescribed.".

DEFINITIONS
"1980 Act": s.125.

GENERAL NOTE
The amendments made by this section to s.76F of the Water (Scotland) Act 1980 (inserted by Sched. 22 to the Water Act 1989) are intended to impose (by regulations made by the Secretary of State) on *local* authorities, in relation to *private* supplies of water (for domestic or food production purposes), similar obligations to publish information about water quality as apply to *water* authorities in relation to *public* supplies.

Schedule 13, para. 119 makes a number of other amendments to Pt. VIA of the Water (Scotland) Act 1980, one of which is to delete the definition of "local authority" – a term also used in other parts of that Act, as amended. The resulting lack of a definition may be curious but will, presumably, not be the cause of confusion.

Regulations as to certain procedures

115. In section 101 of the 1980 Act (provisions as to regulations), after subsection (1A) there shall be added—

"(1B) The Secretary of State may by regulations make provision as to—

(a) the manner in which and the time within which a question or dispute may be referred (other than by him for determination by arbitration), or a request may be made, in pursuance of section 6(3), 9(4) or 24(10) of this Act and as to the procedure for dealing with any such reference or request; and

(b) the manner in which, subject to sections 76G and 76H of this Act, written representation or objection may be made, submitted or withdrawn under subsection (2) of the said section 76H.".

DEFINITIONS
"1980 Act": s.125.

GENERAL NOTE
Section 101 of the Water (Scotland) Act 1980 enables the Secretary of State to make regulations for various purposes. This section inserts a new subs. (1B), under which he may regulate the procedures governing reference to him of issues under s.6(3) (duty to provide supply), s.9(4) (non-domestic supply) and s.24(10) (inserted by s.110 of this Act and relating to vesting of supply pipes); and representations and objections under s.76H (water quality). The intention is to use the regulations to cut down delays in the procedures.

Miscellaneous provisions as respects new authorities

Power of Secretary of State to give directions to new authorities

116.—(1) Subject to subsection (2) below, the Secretary of State may under this subsection give a new water and sewerage authority directions of a general or specific character (but not such directions as may be given under section 117 of this Act) as to the exercise of the authority's functions; and it shall be the duty of the authority to comply with those directions.

(2) Before giving an authority directions under subsection (1) above, the Secretary of State shall consult the authority.

DEFINITIONS
    "new water and sewerage authorities": s.125.

GENERAL NOTE
    This section gives a general power (for a more specific and more swingeing power exercisable in the interests of national security, see s.117) to the Secretary of State, to give directions (which may be general or specific in character) to a new water and sewerage authority "as to the exercise of the authority's functions". Unlike a direction under s.117, a direction under this section may not supplant those functions. An authority must be consulted beforehand but, when made, the directions are binding and the authority must comply with them.

Directions in the interests of national security

117.—(1) The Secretary of State may, after consultation with a new water and sewerage authority, give the authority such directions of a general character as appear to him requisite or expedient—

(a) in the interests of national security; or
(b) for the purpose of mitigating the effects of any civil emergency which may occur.

(2) If it appears to the Secretary of State to be requisite or expedient to do so in the national interest or for the purpose of mitigating the effects of any civil emergency which has occurred or may occur, he may, after consultation with a new water and sewerage authority, give the authority a direction requiring that they do, or as the case may be do not do, a particular thing specified in the direction.

(3) A new water and sewerage authority, notwithstanding any other duty imposed on them by, under or by virtue of this or any other Act, shall comply with any direction given to them under this section by the Secretary of State.

(4) The Secretary of State shall lay before each House of Parliament a copy of a direction given under this section unless he is of the opinion that disclosure of the direction is against the interests of national security.

(5) A person shall not disclose, or be required on any basis whatsoever to disclose, anything done by virtue of this section if the Secretary of State is of the opinion that disclosure of the thing would be against the interests of national security and has notified him of that opinion.

(6) A person who, in contravention of subsection (5) above, discloses anything shall be guilty of an offence and liable, on conviction on indictment, to imprisonment for a term not exceeding two years or to a fine or to both.

(7) In subsections (1) and (2) above, "civil emergency" means a natural disaster or other emergency which in the opinion of the Secretary of State is, or may be, likely—

(a) so to disrupt water supplies, the provision of sewerage or disposal of sewage in; or
(b) to involve such destruction of, or damage to, life or property in,
any area as seriously and adversely to affect all the inhabitants of the area, or a substantial number of them, whether by depriving them of any of the essentials of life or otherwise.

DEFINITIONS
    "civil emergency": subs. (7).
    "new water and sewerage authorities": s.125.

GENERAL NOTE
    See s.116 for the Secretary of State's general power to give directions to the new water and sewerage authorities. This section gives a much stronger power, in that compliance by an auth-

ority is required "notwithstanding any other duty imposed on them" (subs. (3)), but this is so only in the circumstances (in the interests of national security, mitigation of civil emergency) referred to in subss. (1) and (2).

Subsection (2) requires "consultation" with the authority concerned. Note that subss. (5) and (6) forbid the disclosure by any person of anything done under the section by the Secretary of State, if he is of the opinion it would be against the interests of national security and the person is notified; a ban which could conceivably affect those "consulted" under subs. (2). Subsection (4) requires Parliament to be informed of a direction, again unless, in the Secretary of State's opinion, national security requires otherwise. Local authorities have certain existing powers in relation to emergencies and disasters. The relevant provision (s.84 of the 1973 Act) is amended by Sched. 13, para. 92(2).

Provision of information, etc.

118.—(1) A new water and sewerage authority shall provide the Secretary of State with such information relating to the exercise (and proposed exercise) of their functions as he may from time to time require, and for that purpose shall—
  (a) permit any person authorised to do so by the Secretary of State to inspect and make copies of their accounts, books, documents or papers; and
  (b) provide that person with such explanations in relation to the things inspected as the person may reasonably require.

(2) As respects, and as soon as possible after the end of, each financial year, a new water and sewerage authority shall make to the Secretary of State a report on the exercise of their powers, and the performance of their functions.

(3) The Secretary of State shall lay before each House of Parliament a copy of each report received by him under subsection (2) above.

DEFINITIONS
  "new water and sewerage authorities": s.125.

GENERAL NOTE
  This section imposes standard form obligations on the new water and sewerage authorities to supply information to the Secretary of State, and to make annual reports, which are to be laid before Parliament.

Records held by new authorities

119.—(1) Subject to subsection (3) below—
  (a) this section applies to all records (in whatever form or medium)—
        (i) transferred to and vested in a new water and sewerage authority by virtue of section 91(1) of this Act;
        (ii) created or acquired by them in the exercise of any of their functions; or
        (iii) otherwise in their keeping;
  (b) the authority shall ensure that the records, other than such as are mentioned in paragraph (c) below, are preserved and managed in accordance with such arrangements as the authority, after consulting the Keeper of the Records of Scotland, shall put into effect;
  (c) records which, in the opinion of the authority, are not worthy of preservation may be disposed of by them;
  (d) the authority may from time to time revise the arrangements mentioned in paragraph (b) above but before making any material change to those arrangements shall consult the Keeper; and

(e) the authority—

(i) shall secure that the Keeper has at all reasonable hours, unrestricted access to the records preserved by them;

(ii) may afford members of the public, free of charge or on payment of reasonable charges, facilities for inspecting, and for obtaining copies or extracts from, those records.

(2) Nothing in subsection (1)(e)(ii) above permits infringement of copyright or contravention of conditions subject to which records are in the keeping of the authority.

(3) In so far as any provision of, or inserted or amended by, this Part of this Act, being a provision which relates to records of a specific kind, is (but for this subsection) inconsistent with subsection (1) above, that subsection is subject to the provision in question.

DEFINITIONS
"new water and sewerage authorities": s.125.

GENERAL NOTE
This section imposes obligations on the new water and sewerage authorities to ensure the preservation and management of their records. It was inserted during the Commons Committee stage (cols. 2009–10). The parallel sections which impose similar duties on the new local authorities are ss.53 and 54, although it may be noted that they do comprise a very much fuller code – including *e.g.* at s.53(6) a definition of "records". Another difference is that, whilst s.15 specifically defines "property" to include records, s.91 does not.

Duty of new authorities to collaborate

120.—(1) The new water and sewerage authorities shall, in matters of common interest which relate to the performance of their functions, consult together and collaborate with each other.

(2) Where a new water and sewerage authority propose to investigate a potential new source of water supply they shall, as soon as is practicable, give to any other such authority likely to be interested, notice of the proposal so that such consultation as is required in relation to the proposal by subsection (1) above may then begin.

DEFINITIONS
"new water and sewerage authorities": s.125.

GENERAL NOTE
Insofar as it relates to water functions (which, in subs. (2), it does exclusively), this section, requiring consultation and collaboration between authorities, replicates s.83 of the Water (Scotland) Act 1980. That section is repealed by Sched. 14, and the general obligation is extended to both the water and sewerage functions.

Power of new authorities to promote or oppose private legislation

121.—(1) A new water and sewerage authority may, where they are satisfied that it is expedient to do so—

(a) with the consent of the Secretary of State, petition for the issue of a provisional order under the Private Legislation Procedure (Scotland) Act 1936; or

(b) oppose any private legislation in Parliament.

(2) The consent mentioned in paragraph (a) of subsection (1) above shall be withheld if the Secretary of State considers that the powers sought by the order petitioned for could be obtained by means of an order under the 1980 Act or, as the case may be, under the 1968 Act.

(3) An application for the consent so mentioned shall be accompanied by a concise summary of the purposes of the order petitioned for.

(4) In paragraph (b) of subsection (1) above, "private legislation in Parliament" includes—

(a) a provisional order and a Confirmation Bill relating to such an order; and

(b) any local or personal Bill.

DEFINITIONS
"new water and sewerage authorities": s.125.

GENERAL NOTE
Section 82 of the 1973 Act gave local authorities the power to promote (under the Private Legislation Procedure (Scotland) Act 1936 (c. 52) or oppose private legislation. Under s.92 of the Water (Scotland) Act 1980 (now repealed by Sched. 14), similar powers were given to the Central Scotland Water Development Board. Subject to the qualifications contained in subss. (2) and (3), the powers to promote and oppose private legislation are extended to the new water and sewerage authorities. What seems to be missing from the powers conferred is the power to promote a local Bill in substitution of a provisional order, if that is required under s.2 of the Private Legislation Procedure (Scotland) Act 1936 (*cf.* s.82 of the 1973 Act).

Supply of goods and services to new authorities by local authorities

122. The powers conferred by section 1 of the Local Authorities (Goods and Services) Act 1970 (supply of goods and services by local authorities to public bodies) shall be exercisable by a local authority as if the new water and sewerage authorities were public bodies within the meaning of that section.

DEFINITIONS
"local authority": s.125.
"new water and sewerage authorities": s.125.

GENERAL NOTE
The Local Authorities (Goods and Services) Act 1970 (c. 39) permits a local authority to agree with "any public body within the meaning of this section" (s.1 of that Act) to supply various categories of goods and services. "Public body" means a local authority, or some other body specified in an order under s.1(5) and now, by virtue of this section, a new water and sewerage authority.

Power to require local authorities and assessors to supply information to new authorities

123.—(1) The Secretary of State may, by regulations made by statutory instrument subject to annulment in pursuance of a resolution of either House of Parliament, require a local authority or an assessor to furnish relevant information (whether in documentary form or in such other form as he may specify) to a new water and sewerage authority.

(2) For the purposes of subsection (1) above, information is relevant if, being information held—

(a) by the local authority in connection with their—

(i) setting, levying or collecting council tax or council water charges (within the meaning of Part II of the Local Government Finance Act 1992) or the non-domestic water rate or non-domestic sewerage rate (as defined in paragraphs (c) and (d) of section 99(2) of that Act before the repeal of those paragraphs by this Act); or

(ii) levying or collecting the non-domestic rate (as for the time being defined in section 37(1) of the 1975 Act); or

(b) as the case may be, by the assessor in connection with his functions under any enactment,

its possession by the new water and sewerage authority would, in the opinion of the Secretary of State, be likely to assist that authority to make a charges scheme or to collect, or arrange to have collected, such charges as may be fixed by a charges scheme made by them.

(3) In the application of subsections (1) and (2) above to any requirement to furnish information imposed—

(a) before 1st April 1996, "local authority" means a regional or islands council and "assessor" an assessor appointed under section 116(2) or (5) of the 1973 Act; and

(b) on or after that date—

> (i) "local authority" means a council constituted under section 2 of this Act or a residuary body; and
>
> (ii) "assessor" shall be construed in accordance with section 27 of this Act.

(4) Without prejudice to the generality of subsections (1) and (2) above, in those subsections "information" includes a copy of the whole, or of any part of, a valuation roll or valuation list.

DEFINITIONS
  "assessor": subs. (3).
  "information": subs. (4).
  "local authority": subs. (3).
  "new water and sewerage authorities": s.125.

GENERAL NOTE
Earlier sections in the Act (see especially ss.74–79), and provisions in Sched. 10, provide for the powers of the new water and sewerage authorities "to make a charges scheme or to collect, or arrange to have collected, such charges as may be fixed" (subs. (2)). This section recognises that, in order to carry out those functions, the authorities will require "relevant information" held by local authorities and rating assessors, and gives the Secretary of State the power to make regulations according to which local authorities and assessors will be required to furnish such information to the water authorities.

To be "relevant" for those purposes, the information must fall into one or other of categories (a) and (b) in subs. (2). In particular, in the case of information to be obtained from a local authority, the authority must hold that information in its capacity as the authority responsible for the setting, levying or collecting of council tax, non-domestic water rates or non-domestic sewerage rates; or for the levying or collecting (but not setting, because that is now the Secretary of State's function) of non-domestic rates.

Because the information will need to be first available to the new authorities in advance of April 1, 1996 and, therefore, during the final period of the old local authorities (and to be available to the assessor whilst still appointed under the 1973 Act), provision is made in subs. (3) for the regulations to apply to both the old and new regimes.

One terminological point which the section does not appear to make completely clear is that, although in subs. (2) (and also in subs. (4)) it is clear that the council tax as well as non-domestic rating functions are involved, council tax valuations and the preparation of "valuation lists" are functions not of the "assessor" appointed under the 1973 Act (and now the 1994 Act), but of the "local assessor", an office created by s.84(10) of the Local Government Finance Act 1992 (as substituted by Sched. 13, para. 176(6)).

Other miscellaneous provisions

Cancellation of obligation to contribute towards certain expenses incurred as respects sewerage, or disposal of sewage, in rural localities

124. Any contribution which the Secretary of State undertook, before 1st April 1986, to make towards such expenses as are mentioned in section 1(1)(b) of the Rural Water Supplies and Sewerage Act 1944 (expenses incurred by a local authority in making adequate provision for the sewerage, or the disposal of the sewage, of a rural locality), and which, though payable on or after that date has not been paid, shall cease to be exigible.

GENERAL NOTE
Schedule 14 to the Act repeals what little that remains of the Rural Water Supplies and Sewerage Act 1944 (c. 26), but s.1(1)(b) of that Act (referred to in this section and which concerned the expenses incurred by local authorities also referred to) was repealed by the Local Authority (Grants) (Termination) (Scotland) Order 1986 (S.I. 1986 No. 672). Following that repeal, however, and the absorption of contributions into the then rate support grant, the obligation on the Secretary of State to make separate contributions was not formally ended. This section terminates that obligation.

General

Interpretation of Part II

125. In this Part of this Act—

"the Board" means the Central Scotland Water Development Board;

"charges scheme" has the meaning given by section 76(1);

"the Customers Council" means the Scottish Water and Sewerage Customers Council (provision for the establishment of which is made by section 67(1));

"financial year" has the meaning given by section 87(3);

"local authority" means, subject to section 123(3), a council constituted under section 2;

"the new water and sewerage authorities" has the meaning given by section 62(2);

"the 1968 Act" means the Sewerage (Scotland) Act 1968;

"the 1980 Act" means the Water (Scotland) Act 1980;

"successor" shall be construed in accordance with section 92(9);

"transfer date" has the meaning given by subsection (1) of section 91 and "transfer scheme" the meaning given by subsection (2) of that section.

GENERAL NOTE

This section provides interpretations of a number of the words and phrases used in Pt. II of the Act. The curiosity of defining the new water and sewerage authorities in the plural has already been noted (see note to s.62). Although the Sewerage (Scotland) Act 1968 and the Water (Scotland) Act 1980 are "defined", there is no general incorporation into this Part of the Act of meanings given by those Acts to specific terms. Thus, in s.78 for instance, terms such as "sewer", "drain", etc., remain undefined.

Orders under Part II

126. Any power to make an order under this Part of this Act is exercisable by statutory instrument.

GENERAL NOTE

It seems that most order-making powers are already individually identified as to be made by statutory instrument. One that is not, perhaps uniquely, is the power in s.84(7).

PART III

THE PRINCIPAL REPORTER AND THE SCOTTISH CHILDREN'S REPORTER ADMINISTRATION

GENERAL NOTE

Although general social work responsibilities will pass directly from the regional councils to the new councils (but with changed arrangements for their administration – see s.45 above), the Government had, at an early stage, acknowledged that special arrangements would be necessary in relation to some aspects of the system of children's panels and children's hearings. In the consultation paper *Shaping the New Councils* (October 1992) it was assumed that, whilst oversight of the panel system could pass to the single tier authorities, it would be necessary, if a structure of 35 or more authorities were established, to set up arrangements for smaller authorities to combine together to provide the Reporter service, in order to ensure that departments were of sufficient size to operate effectively. However, by the time of the White Paper *Shaping the Future – The New Councils* (Cm. 2267, July 1993), Government thinking had shifted from local combinations of Reporters' departments towards a nationally operated Reporter service. It "proposed to set up a new body responsible for providing the Reporter service to children's hearings throughout Scotland. The board of this new body will be responsible for the management of the service but not for professional decisions which will remain with reporters, who will be responsible to a Chief Reporter .... The new arrangements will be designed to continue the key elements of independent decision making by reporters and close links with children's hearings" (para. 3.11). The changes were not received without objection in Parliament. In particular, Tam Dalyell MP was anxious about the effects that this "nationalisation" of the Reporter service would have upon the distinctive balance maintained at present in Scotland between the different elements of child care law and the children's hearing system. It posed many questions about the effectiveness and accountability of the services offered (see First Scottish Standing Committee, cols. 1867–1871).

The Principal Reporter

The Principal Reporter

127.—(1) There shall be an officer, to be known as the "Principal Reporter", to whom there are hereby transferred the functions under the Social Work (Scotland) Act 1968 (hereafter referred to in this Part of this Act as "the 1968 Act") and the Criminal Procedure (Scotland) Act 1975 of reporters appointed under subsection (1) of section 36 of the 1968 Act, which subsection shall cease to have effect.

(2) The first appointment to the office of Principal Reporter shall be made by the Secretary of State on such terms and conditions as he may, with the approval of the Treasury, determine.

DEFINITIONS
    "1968 Act": subs. (1).
    "Principal Reporter": subs. (1).

GENERAL NOTE
    As explained in the General Note on Pt. III of the Act, the functions which are, until March 31, 1996, vested in reporters to children's hearings appointed by regional and islands councils under s.36(1) of the Social Work (Scotland) Act 1968, will be transferred thereafter to a single officer with jurisdiction throughout Scotland to be known as the "Principal Reporter". This section makes provision for that officer. Subsequent sections make related provision including, most importantly, for the setting up of the "Scottish Children's Reporter Administration", which will be the agency which will "facilitate" the work of the Principal Reporter and which will make appointments to that office, after the first which is to be made by the Secretary of State under s.127(2).
    The main functions of reporters transferred to the Principal Reporter are those conferred by Pt. III of the Social Work (Scotland) Act 1968, and include the power to investigate the circumstances of children referred on grounds of need for compulsory measures of care and, where appropriate, to arrange children's hearings and to process cases through subsequent judicial proceedings. Other functions are conferred by the Criminal Procedure (Scotland) Act 1975 under which a child may be referred by a court to a reporter, either where the child has committed an offence, or where a sexual offence has been committed against the child.
    Some of the debate on this section has been mentioned in the General Note on Pt. III as a whole. The centralising of the Reporter service was not uncontroversial. One point which the Government sought to clarify was that, although the Reporter service was being radically altered, there was no intention to centralise the arrangements for children's panels. These would still be "part and parcel of the arrangements that exist at the moment" (*Hansard*, H.L. Vol. 557, col. 399). Although some fears had been expressed, it was hoped that recruitment to panels might improve when local authorities covered smaller areas from April 1996 (*ibid.*, col. 401).

The Scottish Children's Reporter Administration

The Scottish Children's Reporter Administration

128.—(1) There shall be a body, to be known as the "Scottish Children's Reporter Administration" (hereinafter in this Act referred to as the "Administration").

(2) The Principal Reporter shall be the chief officer of the Administration.

(3) The general purpose of the Administration shall be to facilitate the performance by the Principal Reporter of his functions under the 1968 Act and the Criminal Procedure (Scotland) Act 1975.

(4) Appointments to the office of Principal Reporter subsequent to the first such appointment shall be made by the Administration with the consent

of the Secretary of State on such terms and conditions as it may, with the approval of the Secretary of State given with the consent of the Treasury, determine.

(5) The Administration shall have such other officers as are necessary in order to assist the Principal Reporter; they shall, subject to section 137 of this Act, be appointed by the Administration on such terms as it may, with the approval of the Secretary of State given with the consent of the Treasury, determine.

(6) Schedule 12 to this Act (which provides as to the status, constitution and proceedings of the Administration and other matters relating to it) shall have effect.

(7) The Administration shall be responsible for the management of its officers, including their discipline and removal from office and their deployment throughout Scotland for the purposes of performing their duties.

(8) Nothing in this section or any other provision of this Act shall be taken as authorising the Administration to direct or guide the Principal Reporter in the performance of his functions under the 1968 Act and the Criminal Procedure (Scotland) Act 1975.

DEFINITIONS
"1968 Act": s.127(1).
"Administration": subs. (1).
"Principal Reporter": s.127(1).

GENERAL NOTE
This section (read together with Sched. 12 – see subs. (6)) creates the agency (the "Scottish Children's Reporter Administration") of which the Principal Reporter (see s.127) is to be the chief officer (subs. (2)). The general purpose of the Administration is as stated in subs. (3), with more specific purposes relating to appointments (especially of the Principal Reporter with the approval of the Secretary of State, after the first appointment), and other staff matters in subss. (4), (5) and (7). All of the above provisions are subject to subs. (8), which is designed to leave the Principal Reporter free to exercise his or her statutory judgment in professional matters without direction or guidance from the Administration; thus creating a relationship similar to that between a chief constable and police authority. The Minister of State thought that subs. (8) contained "a separation and an independence of quite crucial importance. We want to leave the principal reporter within the system in Scotland in a position where he can exercise his important professional decision-making independent of any interference" (see *Hansard*, H.L. Vol. 557, col. 403). Notice also the employment protection given to the Principal Reporter by the appeal mechanism in s.129.

Schedule 12 makes detailed provision for the Administration, including rules on membership (between five and eight, including the Principal Reporter), and the terms of appointment of members, chairmen and deputy chairmen, remuneration, proceedings, and so forth.

Appeal against dismissal of Principal Reporter and other officers

129.—(1) If dismissed by the Administration, the Principal Reporter or any prescribed officer of the Administration may appeal to the Secretary of State against the dismissal.

(2) An officer may be prescribed for the purposes of this section by reference to a class thereof so prescribed.

(3) In an appeal under this section the Administration shall be the respondent.

(4) The—
(a) procedure in relation to an appeal under this section;
(b) effect of the making of such an appeal;
(c) powers of the Secretary of State to dispose of such an appeal (including powers to make directions as to liability for expenses); and
(d) effect of the exercise of such powers
shall be as prescribed.

(5) In this section, "prescribed" means prescribed by regulations made by the Secretary of State.

(6) Regulations under this section shall be made by statutory instrument subject to annulment in pursuance of a resolution of either House of Parliament.

DEFINITIONS
"Administration": s.128(1).
"prescribed": subs. (5).
"Principal Reporter": s.127(1).

GENERAL NOTE
The notes on ss.127–128 explain the general position of the Principal Reporter in relation to the Administration. Section 128(7) gives power to the Administration to dismiss its officers, but this section seeks to give some employment protection, and consequently some independence, to the Principal Reporter, by giving him or her a right of appeal to the Secretary of State – a right which may be extended to other prescribed officers (subss. (1), (2), (5)). Procedures, etc., are required to be prescribed under subs. (4).

Additional functions of the Principal Reporter

Annual report of Principal Reporter

130.—(1) The Principal Reporter shall—
(a) as soon as possible after the 31st March following upon the coming into force of this section make a report to the Administration on the exercise and performance to that date of—
    (i) his functions under the 1968 Act and the Criminal Procedure (Scotland) Act 1975; and
    (ii) such functions as it has delegated to him under this Act; and
(b) make similar reports as to each subsequent period of twelve months ending on 31st March as soon as possible after the end of that period.
(2) If the date on which this section comes into force falls on a day after 30th September and before 31st March, the first report by the Principal Reporter under this section shall be for the period ending with the next succeeding 31st March.

DEFINITIONS
"1968 Act": s.127(1).
"Administration": s.128(1).
"Principal Reporter": s.127(1).

GENERAL NOTE
This section requires the Principal Reporter to make an annual report to the Administration in accordance with the timetable set by the section. It should be noted that the report must include reference to functions delegated to the Principal Reporter by the Administration (see Sched. 12, para. 12), and include matters delegated by the Principal Reporter to other officers under s.131. The Reporter's report is not required to be published and is to be distinguished from the Administration's annual report to the Secretary of State under s.136.

Delegation of Principal Reporter's functions

131.—(1) The Principal Reporter may delegate functions (other than that of making reports under section 130 of this Act) to other officers of the Administration.
(2) In performing any function delegated to him under subsection (1) above, an officer shall comply with any instructions or guidance given by the Principal Reporter.
(3) Any delegation made under subsection (1) above or instruction or guidance given for the purposes of subsection (2) above may be—
(a) to all officers, or to a class or classes of officer specified in the delegation, instruction or, as the case may be, guidance or to an individual officer so specified;
(b) of a general or specific character,

and may be varied or revoked by a subsequent delegation so made or a subsequent instruction or, as the case may be, subsequent guidance so given.

DEFINITIONS
    "Administration": s.128(1).
    "Principal Reporter": s.127(1).

GENERAL NOTE
    The Principal Reporter is permitted to delegate functions (including, presumably, functions already delegated to him or her by the Administration under Sched. 12, para. 12) to other officers who will be distributed throughout Scotland, subject to the restrictions referred to in subss. (1) and (2). Although the section does not expressly require that the delegation (or the instructions and guidance referred to in subs. (2)) be in writing, this may probably be inferred from the language used, *e.g.* "specified".

Functions of the Administration

Duty of Administration to provide accommodation etc. for children's hearings

132.—(1) The Administration shall provide suitable accommodation and facilities for children's hearings under section 34 of the 1968 Act.

(2) Accommodation and facilities provided under subsection (1) above shall be provided for each local government area (but may be sited in another) and shall be dissociated from criminal courts and police stations.

DEFINITIONS
    "1968 Act": s.127(1).
    "Administration": s.128(1).

GENERAL NOTE
    At present, s.34(3) of the Social Work (Scotland) Act 1968 requires local authorities to provide "suitable accommodation and facilities dissociated from criminal courts and police stations" for children's hearings. That subsection is repealed by Sched. 14 and replaced by this section which transfers the same obligations to the Administration.

Ancillary powers of Administration

133. The Administration shall have power to do all such things as are incidental or conducive to the achievement of its general purpose and the performance of its functions, including power to acquire, hold and dispose of land or any interest in or right over land.

DEFINITIONS
    "Administration": s.128(1).

GENERAL NOTE
    For the "general purpose" of the Administration, see s.128(3). Its functions include those referred to in ss.128, 132 and 136. This section confers ancillary powers (*cf.* in relation to local authorities, s.69 of the 1973 Act). It should be noted that the transfer of property from local authorities is effected by s.138.

Directions by the Secretary of State

134.—(1) The Secretary of State may give the Administration directions of a general or specific character with regard to the achievement of its general purpose and discharge of its functions, and the Administration shall comply with any such directions.

(2) A direction given under this section may be varied or revoked by a subsequent direction so given.

DEFINITIONS
"Administration": s.128(1).

GENERAL NOTE
This section, giving power to the Secretary of State to give directions to the Administration, should be read alongside the more specific powers of the Secretary of State contained in ss.127, 128, 129, 135, 136 and Sched. 12. He is not authorised to instruct the Principal Reporter in the exercise of his or her duties.

Finance of the Administration

Government grants to the Administration

135.—(1) The Secretary of State may, with the approval of the Treasury, make to the Administration grants of such amounts as he thinks fit.

(2) A grant under this section may be made subject to such conditions as the Secretary of State may, with the approval of the Treasury, determine.

DEFINITIONS
"Administration": s.128(1).

GENERAL NOTE
This section enables the Secretary of State to make financial provision for the Administration by means of grants.

Reports, accounts etc. of the Administration

Reports, accounts etc. of the Administration

136.—(1) The Administration shall—
(a) furnish the Secretary of State with such returns, accounts and other information with respect to its property and activities or proposed activities as he may, from time to time, require;
(b) afford him facilities for the verification of information so furnished; and
(c) for the purpose of such verification, permit any person authorised in that behalf by the Secretary of State to inspect and make copies of the accounts, books, documents or papers of the Administration and to give that person such explanation of anything he is entitled to inspect as he may reasonably require.

(2) The Administration shall—
(a) as soon as possible after the 31st March following upon the coming into force of section 128 of this Act make a report to the Secretary of State on the exercise and performance of its functions to that date incorporating in that report a copy of so much of the report made to it by the Principal Reporter as to that period as was made under section 130(1)(a)(i) of this Act; and
(b) make a similar report to him as to each subsequent period of twelve months ending on 31st March as soon as possible after the end of such period,

and a copy of every such report shall be laid before each House of Parliament by the Secretary of State:

Provided that if the date upon which the said section 128 comes into force falls on a day after 30th September and before 31st March, the first report of the Administration under this section shall be for the period ending with the next succeeding 31st March.

(3) The Administration shall keep proper accounts and other records, and shall prepare for each financial year a statement of account in such form as the Secretary of State with the approval of the Treasury may direct and shall submit those statements of account to the Secretary of State at such time as he may with the approval of the Treasury direct.

(4) The Secretary of State shall, on or before the 30th November in any year, transmit to the Comptroller and Auditor General the statement of account of the Administration for the financial year last ended.

(5) The Comptroller and Auditor General shall examine and certify the statements of account transmitted to him under subsection (4) above, and shall lay copies of them together with his report thereon before each House of Parliament.

(6) In this section "financial year" means the period beginning with the date upon which section 128 of this Act comes into force and ending with the 31st March following that date and each period of twelve months thereafter:

Provided that if the date upon which the said section 128 comes into force falls on a day after 30th September and before 31st March, the first financial year of the Administration shall end with the next succeeding 31st March.

DEFINITIONS
"Administration": s.128(1).
"financial year": subs. (6).

GENERAL NOTE
This section makes standard provision for the supply of reports and accounts by a non-departmental body. Although subjected to scrutiny by the Comptroller and Auditor General (subss. (4) and (5)), nothing in the Act puts the Administration within the jurisdiction of the Ombudsman.

General and supplemental

Staff: application of Chapter 2 of Part I

137.—(1) Sections 8 (except subsections (3) and (4)), 9 and 12 of this Act shall apply also in relation to the transfer to the Administration of officers appointed under subsection (1) of section 36 of the 1968 Act and staff provided in pursuance of subsection (6) of that section with the following modifications—

(a) references to an existing local authority shall include references to an islands council and references to a new authority shall be construed as references to the Administration; and

(b) the reference in section 12(2)(a) to authorities which cease to exist by virtue of Chapter 1 of Part I of this Act shall include a reference to authorities which cease to have functions under section 36(1) and (6) of the 1968 Act.

(2) Section 10 of this Act shall, with the modification specified in subsection (3) below, apply in relation to persons ceasing to be officers appointed or staff provided as mentioned in subsection (1) above and being subsequently employed by the Administration as it applies in relation to persons ceasing to be employed by an existing local authority and being subsequently employed by another person.

(3) The modification referred to in subsection (2) above is that references in section 10 of this Act to an existing local authority shall include references to an islands council.

(4) Section 11 of this Act shall apply also in relation to the remuneration of officers appointed and staff provided as mentioned in subsection (1) above with the following modifications—

(a) references to an authority shall be construed as references only to an existing local authority and references to an existing local authority shall include references to an islands council;

(b) the reference in subsection (5) to the Secretary of State consulting associations of local authorities and employees of local authorities shall include a reference to the Secretary of State consulting the Administration; and

(c) the reference in subsection (7) to an authority not having ceased to exist shall include a reference to an authority not having ceased to have functions under section 36(1) and (6) of the 1968 Act.

(5) Section 13 of this Act shall apply in relation to officers appointed or staff provided as mentioned in subsection (1) above with the modification that references in that section to an existing local authority shall include references to an islands council.

DEFINITIONS
"1968 Act": s.127(1).
"Administration": s.128(1).

GENERAL NOTE
This section applies to the Administration an amended version of Chap. 2 of Pt. I of the Act, in order to provide for the transfer of staff from existing local authorities, including, in this case, islands councils which are not for the most part affected by staff transfer matters (but see also s.97 in relation to transfers to the new water and sewerage authorities). See notes on ss.8–13.

Property etc.: application of Chapter 3 of Part I

138.—(1) Chapter 3 of Part I of this Act shall, with the modifications specified in subsection (2) below, apply in relation to the transfer to the Principal Reporter or the Administration of the property, rights, liabilities and obligations of reporters appointed under section 36(1) of the 1968 Act and such property, rights, liabilities and obligations as a local authority for the purpose of that Act has for the purposes of—

(a) their functions under section 34(3) of that Act (duty to provide suitable accommodation and facilities for children's hearings); or

(b) providing accommodation and facilities for, or otherwise facilitating or supporting the performance of the functions of, reporters appointed under subsection (1) of section 36 of the 1968 Act or staff provided in pursuance of subsection (6) of that section.

(2) The modifications referred to in subsection (1) above are as follows—

(a) references in Chapter 3 of Part I of this Act to existing local authorities shall include references to reporters appointed under section 36(1) of the 1968 Act and to islands councils; and

(b) references in that Chapter to new local authorities shall include references to the Principal Reporter and to the Administration.

DEFINITIONS
"1968 Act": s.127(1).
"Administration": s.128(1).
"Principal Reporter": s.127(1).

GENERAL NOTE
In a manner similar to that adopted in relation to staff in s.137, this section applies to the Principal Reporter and the Administration, in modified form, the provisions of Chap. 3 of Pt. I which relate to the transfer of property. The section seems to leave unclear the division between the Principal Reporter and the Administration, of the "property, rights, liabilities and obligations transferred".

PART IV

MISCELLANEOUS

Social work

Report by local authority for purpose of investigation preliminary to children's hearing

139.—(1) In section 38 of the Social Work (Scotland) Act 1968 (initial investigation of cases by the reporter), after subsection (1), there shall be inserted—

"(1A) For the purposes of making any initial investigation under subsection (1) above, the Principal Reporter may request from the local authority a report on the child and his social background and it shall be the duty of the authority to supply the report which may contain information from any such person as the Principal Reporter or the local authority may think fit.

(1B) A report requested under subsection (1A) above may contain information additional to that given by the local authority under section 37(1A)(b) of this Act.".

(2) In section 39 of that Act (action on initial investigation), after subsection (4), there shall be inserted the following subsection—

"(4A) A report requested under subsection (4) above may contain information additional to that given in a report under section 38(1A) of this Act.".

DEFINITIONS

"local authority": s.94 of the Social Work (Scotland) Act 1968.
"Principal Reporter": s.36(5A) of the Social Work (Scotland) Act 1968, as inserted by Sched. 13; s.127(1).

GENERAL NOTE

The primary purpose of this amendment to ss.38 and 39 of the Social Work (Scotland) Act 1968 is to enable the new Principal Reporter (see Pt. III of the Act) to require local authorities to supply to the Reporter a report on a child and his or her social background, at the stage when the Reporter is making "initial investigations" into the case. This report may contain information additional to any already supplied under s.37(1A)(b) of the Social Work (Scotland) Act 1968. That section refers to information which may be supplied (following enquiries if necessary) by a local authority.

Voluntary organisations

Power of local authorities to provide assistance to voluntary organisations

140. In section 88 of the 1973 Act (provision of information etc. on matters relating to functions of local authority), after subsection (2) there shall be inserted—

"(3) A local authority may assist voluntary organisations to provide for individuals—
(a) information and advice concerning those individuals' rights and obligations; and
(b) assistance, either by the making or receiving of communications or by providing representation to or before any person or body, in asserting those rights or fulfilling those obligations.".

DEFINITIONS

"1973 Act": s.183(1).

GENERAL NOTE

This section was added to the Bill at Commons Report stage (*Hansard*, H.C. Vol. 243, cols. 691–2) following proposals made by Citizens Advice Scotland. A similar amendment had earlier been made to the equivalent section in England and Wales (s.142 of the Local Government Act 1972 (c. 70)) by the Local Government and Housing Act 1989 (c. 42). The new section gives a specific power to local authorities to assist voluntary organisations in order to provide for individuals information and advice concerning their rights and obligations, and assistance by making or receiving communications or by providing representation before a "person or body".

Byelaws

Byelaws under section 121 of Civic Government (Scotland) Act 1982

141. In section 121 of the Civic Government (Scotland) Act 1982 (control of the seashore, adjacent waters and inland waters)—
(a) in subsection (5), for paragraph (b) there shall be substituted—
　　"(b)　the local authority have given notice in writing of their proposal to make byelaws to each person having a proprietorial interest such as is mentioned, in relation to the byelaws, in paragraph (a) above whose identity has been ascertained as mentioned in the said paragraph (a);";
(b) in subsection (6) the words from "and of" to "that proposal" shall cease to have effect; and
(c) in subsection (7)—
　　　　(i) the words from "but the" to "his consent"; and
　　　　(ii) the word "nevertheless",
　　shall cease to have effect.

DEFINITIONS
"local authority": s.133 of the Civic Government (Scotland) Act 1982, as amended by Sched. 13.

GENERAL NOTE
Section 121 of the Civic Government (Scotland) Act 1982 (c. 45) gives district and islands councils the power to make byelaws for a variety of purposes connected with the control of the seashore (and its adjacent waters) and of inland waters. The procedural requirements laid down for the making of any such byelaws are, however, quite rigorous and, at present, include the need to make enquiries reasonably necessary to ascertain the existence and identity of all persons having a proprietorial interest in the seashore, etc., and then, with only limited exceptions, to obtain their consent. The effect of the amendment now made to s.121 is to require that such persons are given notice in writing of the proposal to make byelaws, but to remove the need for their consent.

In debate, the changes were, in particular, related to the controversy surrounding the need for byelaws affecting Loch Lomond (*Hansard*, H.L. Vol. 557, cols. 411–413) where single proprietors had held up the process. The principle of the new rules was said to be welcomed by the Scottish Landowners' Federation. It was pointed out that individual landowners, with others, would be protected by the consultative arrangements and by the need for confirmation of byelaws by the Secretary of State.

Polling districts

Organisations of polling districts

142.—(1) Section 18 of the Representation of the People Act 1983 (polling districts and places at parliamentary elections) shall be amended in accordance with this section.
(2) In subsection (3)—
(a) for the words from "returning officer's" to "places", where it first occurs, there shall be substituted the words "duty of every local authority to divide their area into polling districts for the purpose of parliamentary elections for so much of any constituency as is situated in their area and to designate the polling places for those polling districts";

(b) in paragraph (a)—
      (i) for the words "returning officer" there shall be substituted the words "local authority";
      (ii) for the words "the constituency" there shall be substituted the words "so much of the constituency as falls within their area"; and
      (iii) for the word "he" there shall be substituted the words "the local authority";
and

(c) in paragraph (b), for the words from the beginning to "constituency", where it last occurs, there shall be substituted the words "each electoral ward, within the meaning of section 5 of the Local Government etc. (Scotland) Act 1994, which is wholly or partly within so much of any constituency as falls within their area".

(3) In subsection (5)—

(a) the words "any interested authority or" and "(or in Scotland, the returning officer)" shall cease to have effect;

(b) the words "or returning officer", in both places where they occur, shall cease to have effect; and

(c) in the definition of "interested authority", sub-paragraph (iii) shall cease to have effect.

(4) In subsection (6), the words "or returning officer" shall cease to have effect.

GENERAL NOTE
   This section should be read together with para. 130 of Sched. 13 which makes a number of small amendments to the Representation of the People Act 1983 consequential upon local government reorganisation.
   The important change made by this section is, by amendment of s.18(3) of that Act, to shift the responsibility for reviewing polling arrangements for parliamentary elections from the returning officer (designated for this purpose, at present by regional councils but then exercising statutory responsibilities in his or her own right) to the local authority itself. This has the effect of removing the present anomalous situation in which the funding of the returning officer's functions is formally left unprovided for. Regional councils have no statutory responsibility for the cost of these functions, but this will obviously change with the reallocation of the functions themselves. The section was added as a new clause at Commons Committee stage (see First Scottish Standing Committee, col. 2012).
   The related (transitional) question of who should serve as returning officers at the 1995 elections is dealt with in Sched. 2, para. 2.

Education

Self-governing schools: certain proposals under Education (Scotland) Act 1980

143. For subsection (1) of section 21 of the Self-Governing Schools etc. (Scotland) Act 1989 (effect of pending procedure for acquisition of self-governing status on certain proposals for that school) there shall be substituted—
   "(1) Subject to section 14(2) of this Act, where a proposal to do any thing to a school, being a proposal to which this section applies—
      (a) is published under section 22A of the 1980 Act (consultation on certain changes in educational matters), but before a decision is reached on the proposal the education authority receive written notice such as is mentioned in subsection (6) of section 13 of this Act, either of a first resolution or of a request, as regards that school, they shall not decide on the proposal;

(b) is submitted under section 22B, 22C or 22D of the 1980 Act (consent for certain changes in educational matters or for certain changes affecting denominational schools), but before the Secretary of State consents to the proposal the education authority receive such notice as is mentioned in paragraph (a) above as regards that school, the consent cannot validly be given,

unless and until one of the conditions specified in section 24(2) of this Act is satisfied as regards that school.

(1A) This section applies to a proposal—

(a) to discontinue the school; or

(b) to do any one of such other things to the school as the Secretary of State may by order prescribe.".

DEFINITIONS
"1980 Act": s.80 of the Self-Governing Schools etc. (Scotland) Act 1989.
"denomination school": s.80 of the Self-Governing Schools etc. (Scotland) Act 1989.
"education authority": s.80 of the Self-Governing Schools etc. (Scotland) Act 1989.

GENERAL NOTE
The purpose of this section is to reverse the effect of *Hughes* v. *Strathclyde Regional Council* 1994 S.L.T. 915; 1994 S.C.L.R. 49, by substituting new subss. (1) and (1A) in place of the existing s.21(1) of the Self-Governing Schools etc. (Scotland) Act 1989 (c. 39).

The general point of that subsection was to suspend progress on certain proposals affecting a school (notably to close it), while procedures for changing the school to self-governing status (by balloting of parents) are pending. However, the effect of *Hughes* v. *Strathclyde Regional Council* (above) had been that commencing such procedures in relation to one school might be enough to require the suspension of a proposal to close *another* school, thus enabling (contrary to the principal purpose of the Act) those opposed to the closure of one school deliberately to engineer a "self-governing" ballot at a nearby school, and thus ensure the suspension of the closure procedures meantime.

The substituted subs. (1) now makes clear (in both paras. (a) and (b)) that the two sets of procedures must relate to the *same* school. The new subs. (1A) limits the type of proposal affecting the school (which would be suspended pending a ballot, etc.), to a proposal:

(a) to discontinue the school, and

(b) to do other prescribed things to the school.

The Government has indicated that the list of prescribed things would encompass proposals for "essential changes to characteristics" at the balloting school (see First Scottish Standing Committee, col. 1904).

Denominational schools: proposals under section 22D of Education (Scotland) Act 1980

144. In section 22D of the Education (Scotland) Act 1980 (further provisions relating to denominational schools)—

(a) in subsection (2)(a), for the word "the" there shall be substituted "an";

(b) in subsection (2)(c)—

    (i) for the words "the education authority", where they first occur, there shall be substituted "any education authority affected by it";

    (ii) in sub-paragraph (i), for the words "the result" there shall be substituted "any of the results"; and

    (iii) in subparagraph (ii), after the word "authority", there shall be inserted "submitting the proposal under subsection (1) above"; and

(c) for subsections (3) and (4) there shall be substituted the following subsection—

"(3) The results referred to in subsection (2)(c)(i) above are—

(a) a significant deterioration for pupils belonging to the area of the education authority submitting the proposal under subsection (1) above; or

(b) a significant deterioration for pupils belonging to the area of any other education authority; or

(c) where neither paragraph (a) nor paragraph (b) above applies, such a deterioration for pupils as mentioned in the said paragraph (a) and pupils belonging to the area of another education authority as, taken together, amounts to a significant deterioration,

in the provision, distribution or availability of school education in schools of the kind referred to in subsection (2)(a) above compared with such provision, distribution or availability in other public schools.".

DEFINITIONS
"education authority": s.135 of the Education (Scotland) Act 1980.
"pupil": s.135 of the Education (Scotland) Act 1980.
"school": s.135 of the Education (Scotland) Act 1980.

GENERAL NOTE
The purpose of the existing s.22D of the Education (Scotland) Act 1980 (c. 44) (inserted by s.6 of the Education (Scotland) Act 1981 (c. 58)) is to ensure that proposals by education authorities to do certain things to a denominational school (including discontinuing the school, amalgamating it with another, changing its site or changing its admission arrangements) which are opposed by the denominational body concerned (in the case of a Roman Catholic School, the Scottish Hierarchy of the Church), require the consent of the Secretary of State.

The principal amendment made to the section is the substitution of a new s.22D(3) which seeks to ensure that the effect of local government reorganisation on April 1, 1996, when the larger number of education authority areas will mean an increased likelihood that proposals affecting denominational schools in one area will affect pupils from other areas as well, will be taken account of in the operation of the section's protective mechanisms. The "significant deterioration" for pupils now relates to pupils of the area of the authority making the proposal, pupils of another area, or the two in combination.

Provision of school transport and other facilities

145.—(1) The Education (Scotland) Act 1980 shall be amended in accordance with this section.

(2) In section 50(3) (power of education authority to provide transport and other facilities in exceptional circumstances)—

(a) in paragraph (a)—

(i) after the word "with", where it first occurs, there shall be inserted "—

(i) "; and

(ii) after the word "Act" there shall be inserted "—

(ii) any arrangements made by them under section 23(1A) of this Act; or

(iii) the arrangements subsisting before the establishment of new local government areas under Part I of the Local Government etc. (Scotland) Act 1994 and continuing by virtue of section 23(1C) of this Act"; and

(b) in paragraph (b), after the word "them" there shall be inserted "or another education authority".

(3) In section 51 (provision of transport and other facilities)—

(a) in subsection (2A)—

(i) in paragraph (a)—

(A) after the word "with" there shall be inserted "—

(i)"; and

(B) after the word "Act" there shall be inserted—

"(ii) any arrangements made by them under section 23(1A) of this Act; or

(iii) the arrangements subsisting before the establishment of new local government areas under Part I of the Local Government etc. (Scotland) Act 1994 and continuing by virtue of section 23(1C) of this Act"; and

(ii) in paragraph (b), after the word "them" there shall be inserted "or another education authority"; and

(b) after subsection (2AC) there shall be inserted the following subsection—

"(2AD) Without prejudice to the generality of subsection (1) above, the duty imposed by that subsection applies in cases where a pupil attends a school or educational establishment under the management of another education authority—

(a) in accordance with any arrangements made by them under section 23(1A) of this Act;

(b) in accordance with the arrangements subsisting before the establishment of new local government areas under Part I of the Local Government etc. (Scotland) Act 1994 and continuing by virtue of section 23(1C) of this Act; or

(c) if at the time when the pupil was placed in that school or educational establishment it was under the management of the education authority for the area to which the pupil belonged, and is under the management of another education authority as a consequence of the establishment of such new local government areas.".

DEFINITIONS
"education authority": s.135(1) of the Education (Scotland) Act 1980.
"educational establishment": s.135(1) of the Education (Scotland) Act 1980.
"school": s.135(1) of the Education (Scotland) Act 1980.

GENERAL NOTE
The general purpose of this section is to clarify the extent of the duties and powers of education authorities, principally in relation to the provision of school transport in the light of reorganisation from April 1, 1996, and the prospect that increasing numbers of pupils may attend schools in the areas of other authorities. The section should be read in the light of the amendments made to s.23 of the Education (Scotland) Act 1980 by s.32 of this Act.

Probably the most important amendments made by the section are those in subs. (3) affecting s.51 of the Education (Scotland) Act 1980. It is under that section (as amended by s.2 of the Education (Scotland) Act 1981) that an authority has a *duty* to provide free transport arrangements for pupils beyond "walking distance" from their "designated" school, and a *power* to provide such transport for pupils attending school by virtue of a placing request. The amendments in subs. (3)(a) are intended to ensure that the *duty* to provide transport will apply where a pupil is placed at a school of another authority by virtue of s.23(1A) or s.23(1C) of that Act, or by virtue of the school being in another area after reorganisation.

Roads

Definition of "road"

146. In section 151 of the Roads (Scotland) Act 1984 (interpretation), after subsection (1) there shall be inserted the following subsection—

"(1A) A way to which the public has access (by whatever means and whether subject to a toll or not) which passes over a bridge constructed in pursuance of powers conferred by, or by an order made under or confirmed by, a private Act shall, for the purposes of the definition of "road" in subsection (1) above, be treated as if there were a public right of passage over it.".

DEFINITIONS
"road": s.154(1) of the Roads (Scotland) Act 1984.

GENERAL NOTE
The new subsection inserted by this section into s.151 of the Roads (Scotland) Act 1984 is intended to ensure (or remove any previous existing doubt) that a road (a "way") over a bridge provided under Private Act powers and subject to a toll (the existing examples are the Forth and

Tay road bridges) is definitely a "road" – defined by s.151 (1) of that Act (as amended by the New Roads and Street Works Act 1991 (c. 22)) as a "way ... over which there is a public right of passage". For an explanation in the Parliamentary debates see *Hansard*, H.L. Vol. 557, cols. 427–429.

Provisions consequential on making of special road order

147. After section 113 of the Roads (Scotland) Act 1984 there shall be inserted the following section—

> **"Dissolution of certain bodies in consequence of order under section 9**
> 113A.—(1) Where—
> (a) an order under section 9 of this Act transfers to a special road authority a road for the management and maintenance of which a body other than a roads authority was, prior to the coming into force of the order, responsible under any enactment; and
> (b) the functions of that body relate solely to that road,
> the Secretary of State may by order (in this section referred to as a "dissolution order") dissolve the body.
>
> (2) A dissolution order may transfer or provide for the transfer to—
> (a) the special road authority referred to in subsection (1)(a) above; or
> (b) such other person as the Secretary of State considers appropriate, of such of the property, rights and liabilities of the body dissolved by the order as the Secretary of State considers appropriate.
>
> (3) A dissolution order may make provision in connection with the transfer of staff employed by or for the purposes of the body.
>
> (4) Without prejudice to the generality of subsection (2) above, a dissolution order may make provision regarding liability for the payment of any pensions, allowances or gratuities which would otherwise have been the responsibility of the body.
>
> (5) A dissolution order may make incidental provision as to the interests, rights and liabilities of third parties with respect to property, rights and liabilities transferred by the order.
>
> (6) In subsection (5) above the reference to third parties is a reference to persons other than the body and the persons referred to in subsection (2)(a) and (b) above.
>
> (7) A dissolution order may repeal or amend—
> (a) any enactment in a private Act; and
> (b) any provision of an order made under or confirmed by a private Act,
> which, in consequence of the making of the order, is no longer required or, as the case may be, requires to be amended.".

DEFINITIONS
"dissolution order": new subs. (1).
"roads authority": s.151 of the Roads (Scotland) Act 1984.
"special road authority": s.151 of the Roads (Scotland) Act 1984.

GENERAL NOTE
The machinery is already in place for bringing existing roads into a "special road scheme" – see s.9 of the Roads (Scotland) Act 1984. This section inserts a new section in that Act which provides for the situation arising where responsibility for such an existing road is not in the hands of a roads authority (local authority or the Secretary of State), but another body (*e.g.* the joint boards responsible for the Forth and Tay bridges) whose function would disappear if the road were taken into a scheme. The Secretary of State is given the power to dissolve the body by means of a dissolution order (subs. (1)), which may provide for the various matters listed in the section, including (under subs. (7)) the repeal or amendment of a private Act. The order-making procedure is regulated by s.143 of that Act (as amended by the New Roads and Street Works Act 1991 and Sched. 13, para. 135(9) to this Act). Orders under the new section are to be by statutory instrument subject to the negative resolution procedure.

Toll orders

148.—(1) In paragraph 14D(1) of Schedule 1 to the Roads (Scotland) Act 1984 (procedure for making and confirming toll orders), at the end of paragraph (a) (and before the word "and" immediately following it) there shall be inserted the following paragraph—

"(aa) that existing road is free of toll,".

(2) In section 27 of the New Roads and Street Works Act 1991 (toll orders), after subsection (9) there shall be inserted the following subsection—

"(9A) On the date when a toll order comes into force any provision of any enactment (other than an enactment contained in this Act) which confers a power or imposes a duty to charge tolls for the use of all or part of any road to which the toll order relates shall cease to have effect.".

DEFINITIONS

"toll order": s.27(1) of the New Roads and Street Works Act 1991.

GENERAL NOTE

Existing provisions in the Roads (Scotland) Act 1984, as amended by the New Roads and Street Works Act 1991, and provisions in that Act itself require that, where an existing public road is taken into a special road scheme and a toll is imposed, the toll order must be subject to special parliamentary procedure. The amendment made by this section to para. 14D(1) of Sched. 1 to the Roads (Scotland) Act 1984 (inserted by the New Roads and Street Works Act 1991) makes that procedure necessary only if the existing road is itself free from any toll. If it is already subject to a toll the special parliamentary procedure will not be required.

The amendment to s.27 of the New Roads and Street Works Act 1991 ensures that, in the same circumstances, the making of the new toll order will displace the old power (or duty) to impose a toll.

Road works register

149. In section 112 of the New Roads and Street Works Act 1991 (road works register)—

(a) in subsection (4), for the words from "of road" to "section" there shall be substituted the words "under this section of such road works authorities as he may specify";

(b) after subsection (4) there shall be inserted the following subsection—

"(4A) Before making any arrangements under subsection (4) the Secretary of State shall consult—

(a) any road works authority having duties under this section which he intends not to specify for the purposes of the arrangements; and

(b) any undertaker (other than a person having permission under section 109 to execute road works) having apparatus in a road for which such road works authority is responsible."; and

(c) in subsection (5), after the word—

(i) "require" there shall be inserted the word "the"; and

(ii) "authorities" there shall be inserted the words "so specified".

DEFINITIONS

"road": s.107(1) of the New Roads and Street Works Act 1991.
"road works authority": s.108(1) of the New Roads and Street Works Act 1991.
"undertaker" s.107(4) of the New Roads and Street Works Act 1991.

GENERAL NOTE

This section was inserted as a new clause at House of Lords Report stage. It was explained (*Hansard*, H.L. Vol. 558, col. 253) that the amendments it makes to s.112 of the New Roads and Street Works Act 1991 enable the Secretary of State to limit the scope of the centrally maintained register of notifications given by utilities to road works authorities of their wish to place apparatus in the road. The Secretary of State may, subject to the consultative procedure laid down, exclude named authorities. The islands councils have expressed the wish not to use the central register.

Traffic signs

150.—(1) Notwithstanding the provisions of section 67 of the Road Traffic Regulation Act 1984 (persons empowered to place traffic signs on road in emergency etc.), the Secretary of State may, with the consent of the chief officer of police for the area concerned as respects a road or any structure on a road, place on that road, or on any structure on that road, traffic signs (of any size, colour and type prescribed or authorised under section 64 of the said Act of 1984), indicating prohibitions, restrictions or requirements relating to vehicular traffic, as may be necessary or expedient to prevent or mitigate congestion or obstruction of traffic, or danger to or from traffic, in consequence of extraordinary circumstances; and the power to place signs conferred by this subsection shall include power to maintain a sign for a period of 7 days or less from the time when it was placed, but no longer.

(2) Section 36 of the Road Traffic Act 1988 (drivers to comply with traffic signs) shall apply to signs placed in the exercise of the power conferred by subsection (1) above.

(3) In this section—

"road" has the meaning given by section 151(1) of the Roads (Scotland) Act 1984; and

"traffic sign" has the meaning given by section 64(1) of the Road Traffic Regulation Act 1984.

DEFINITIONS

"road": subs. (3); s.151(1) of the Roads (Scotland) Act 1984.
"traffic sign": subs. (3); s.64(1) of the Road Traffic Regulation Act 1984.

GENERAL NOTE

Under s.67 of the Road Traffic Regulation Act 1984, the power to place (mandatory) traffic signs (with which, by s.36 of the Road Traffic Act 1988 (c. 52), drivers must comply) is given to the police. This section now extends, in similar terms, and requiring the consent of the chief constable for the area, the same power to the Secretary of State.

Valuation and rating

Exclusion from valuation roll of shootings, deer forests, fishings and fish counters

151.—(1) On and after 1st April 1995 no shootings, deer forests, fishings or fish counters shall be entered in the valuation roll.

(2) Nothing in subsection (1) above shall affect any right of a district salmon fishery board (within the meaning of section 40(1) of the Salmon Act 1986) to require the assessor to value and enter any rights of salmon fishing in the valuation roll for the purposes of fishery assessments only.

(3) For the purposes of this section—

"fish counter" means any weir or other structure in inland waters primarily used for the purpose of counting fish; and

"inland waters" has the same meaning as in section 24(1) of the Salmon and Freshwater Fisheries (Protection) (Scotland) Act 1951.

DEFINITIONS

"fish counter": subs. (3).
"inland waters": subs. (3); s.24(1) of the Salmon and Freshwater Fisheries (Protection) (Scotland) Act 1951 (c. 26).

GENERAL NOTE

This section exempts with effect from *April 1, 1995* (an abruptness complained about in the Parliamentary debates, see *Hansard*, H.L. Vol. 555, col. 1391), shootings, fishings, etc., from rating in that, from that date, they are not to be entered in the valuation roll. It should be read together with Sched. 14, which repeals the Sporting Lands Rating (Scotland) Act 1886 (c. 15).

The effect of the section is to bring the law on the rating of sporting rights in Scotland much closer to that in England – a feature, as explained by the Lord Advocate, common to many of the provisions now contained in ss.151–162 of the Act (see *Hansard*, H.L. Vol. 557, cols. 431–432). He went on to explain, in response to concerns expressed, that, although the new rule would, in removing the inequality of liability between England and Wales and Scotland, produce a loss of revenue in the non-domestic rating pool (less than £2 million), this would not be disadvantageous to local authorities who would be reimbursed from other sources.

A district salmon fishery board is defined, by s.40(1) of the Salmon Act 1986 (c. 62), to be the committee of an association of proprietors of salmon fisheries within the meaning of s.14 of the same Act.

Amendment of definition of "lands and heritages"

152.—(1) The Lands Valuation (Scotland) Act 1854 shall be amended as follows.

(2) In section 42 (interpretation), in the definition of "lands and heritages", for the words from "all machinery fixed" to the end of the first proviso substitute the words "such class or classes of plant or machinery in or on any lands and heritages as may be prescribed by the Secretary of State by regulations".

(3) After section 42 add—

"**Regulations**

43.—(1) Regulations under section 42 of this Act may, if made so as to take effect other than at the beginning of a year of revaluation (within the meaning of the Local Government (Scotland) Act 1975), provide for the revaluation of any lands and heritages affected by the regulations.

(2) The power to make regulations under the said section 42 shall be exercisable by statutory instrument.

(3) Any statutory instrument containing regulations made under the said section 42 shall be subject to annulment in pursuance of a resolution of either House of Parliament.".

DEFINITIONS
"year of revaluation": s.37(1) of the 1975 Act.

GENERAL NOTE
The amendments made by this section to the Lands Valuation (Scotland) Act 1854 (c. 91) implement many of the recommendations of the Wood Committee on *The Rating of Plant and Machinery* (Cm. 2170, 1993), which were designed to enable a harmonisation of valuation of plant and machinery within the United Kingdom.

The amendment to s.42 of that Act, giving power to the Secretary of State to determine by order which forms of plant and machinery shall be rateable, will enable a definitive listing of the items subject to rating. Subsection (3), by inserting the new s.43, provides for the order-making power to be exercised by statutory instrument subject to annulment, and (in s.43(1)) for any change made between years of revaluation to be accompanied by an appropriate revaluation of the affected lands and heritages.

Power of Secretary of State to prescribe amount of non-domestic rate

153—(1) For any financial year, the Secretary of State may by regulations prescribe that the amount payable as non-domestic rate in respect of any lands and heritages shall be such amount as may be determined in accordance with prescribed rules.

(2) Rules prescribed under this section may be framed by reference to such factors as the Secretary of State thinks fit and such factors may, without prejudice to that generality, include the circumstances of persons by whom rates are payable.

(3) Regulations under this section may make different provision in relation to different areas and different classes of lands and heritages and, without prejudice to that generality, may make different provision in relation to lands and heritages whose rateable value exceeds, and those whose rateable value does not exceed, a prescribed figure.

(4) Where regulations under this section apply in relation to any lands and heritages or class of lands and heritages, the non-domestic rate for the finan-

cial year to which the regulations relate shall be levied in respect of such lands and heritages, or class of lands and heritages, in accordance with the regulations.

(5) The power to make regulations under this section shall be exercisable by statutory instrument.

(6) Any instrument containing regulations under this section shall be subject to annulment in pursuance of a resolution of either House of Parliament.

GENERAL NOTE

This section is another designed to enable harmonisation of the law and practice of non-domestic rating between Scotland, and England and Wales. It does so by giving the Secretary of State substantial powers to prescribe by regulations rules to determine the *actual amount payable* in respect of different lands and heritages. These new powers are in addition to those existing powers under ss.7A and 7B of the 1975 Act (as inserted by s.110 of the Local Government Finance Act 1992) to prescribe the level of rates in different areas and, ultimately, uniformly across Scotland. The rules which can be made under the new powers may take account of a variety of considerations including (subs. (2)) "the circumstances of persons by whom rates are payable".

Although the underlying purpose of the section may be fairly clear, it does appear to incorporate some drafting difficulties, not the least of which is the failure to incorporate the section into existing codes, perhaps most appropriately in this case the 1975 Act. Apart from anything else, this appears to leave important phrases such as "financial year" and "non-domestic rate" undefined. A point not made clear within the section is whether the "prescribed rules" (subss. (1) and (2)) are to be incorporated into the "regulations" (subss. (1) and (3)–(6)). If not, the rules will not be subject to the requirements of statutory instrument procedure such as publication and printing.

Rating of unoccupied lands and heritages

154. For section 24 of the Local Government (Scotland) Act 1966 (liability to be rated in respect of certain unoccupied property) substitute—

"Unoccupied lands and heritages

24.—(1) Subject to subsection (2) below, no rates shall be payable in respect of lands and heritages which are unoccupied.

(2) The Secretary of State may by regulations prescribe a class or classes of lands and heritages such as are mentioned in subsection (1) above for which the rates payable shall be the rates mentioned in subsection (3) below.

(3) A person entitled to possession of lands and heritages which fall within a class prescribed by regulations under this section shall be liable to pay a rate equal to one half of the amount of the non-domestic rate which would have been payable if such lands and heritages had been occupied; and the enactments relating to rating shall apply with any necessary modifications as if the lands and heritages were occupied by that person.

(4) Where any lands and heritages fall within a class prescribed by regulations under subsection (2) above, such lands and heritages shall be treated for the purposes of section 4 of the Local Government (Financial Provisions etc.) (Scotland) Act 1962 as if they are being used for the purpose for which they were used when they were last occupied.

(5) Any statutory instrument containing regulations made under this section shall be subject to annulment in pursuance of a resolution of either House of Parliament.".

GENERAL NOTE

This section should be read together with s.155 (rating of lands and heritages partly unoccupied for a short time), and with the repeals in Sched. 14 of ss.243, 243A, 243B and 244 of the Local Government (Scotland) Act 1947 (c. 43), and of parts of s.25 of, and Sched. 3 to, the Local Government (Scotland) Act 1966 (c. 51).

Like the previous three sections, the purpose of the section is to enable greater harmonisation of rating law and practice between Scotland and England and Wales. At present, s.243(2) of the

Local Government (Scotland) Act 1947 makes general provision for the remission of rates on lands and heritages unoccupied and unfurnished for at least three months, but this has to be read subject to the existing s.24 of the Local Government (Scotland) Act 1966, which permits a rating authority to levy rates on a "person entitled to possession" of unoccupied property who allows the property to remain unoccupied for over six months (see also s.25 of that Act and Sched. 3).

The new s.24 of the Local Government (Scotland) Act 1966 inserted by this section creates a general exemption from rates for unoccupied (on which see the new s.24B, inserted by s.155 below) property, without need for a qualifying period of three months, but subject to the power of the Secretary of State to prescribe classes of unoccupied lands and heritages which are to be liable to rates levied at half the ordinary amount, subject to other forms of mandatory or discretionary relief. Any such relief is to be based on the purpose for which the lands and heritages were used when last occupied, if relevant to the reduction and remission of rates payable by charities (s.4 of the Local Government (Financial Provisions, etc.) (Scotland) Act 1962 (c. 9)).

See now the Non-Domestic Rating (Unoccupied Property) (Scotland) Regulations 1994 (S.I. 1994 No. 3200).

Rating of lands and heritages partly unoccupied for a short time

155. After section 24 of the Local Government (Scotland) Act 1966 insert—

"Lands and heritages partly unoccupied for a short time

24A.—(1) If it appears to the rating authority that part of any lands and heritages included in the valuation roll is unoccupied but will remain so for a short time only, the authority may request the assessor to apportion the rateable value between the occupied and unoccupied parts and on being thus requested the assessor shall apportion the rateable value accordingly.

(2) As from whichever is the later of the following—

(a) the date on which lands and heritages the rateable value of which has been apportioned under subsection (1) above became partly occupied;

(b) the commencement of the financial year in which the request under that subsection relating to those lands and heritages was made,

until whichever of the events specified in subsection (3) below first occurs, the value apportioned to the occupied part of the lands and heritages shall, subject to subsection (4) below, be treated for rating purposes as if it were the rateable value ascribed to the lands and heritages in the valuation roll.

(3) The events mentioned in subsection (2) above are—

(a) the reoccupation of any of the unoccupied part;

(b) the end of the financial year in which the request was made;

(c) a further apportionment of the value of the lands and heritages taking effect under subsection (1) above;

(d) the lands and heritages to which the apportionment relates becoming completely unoccupied.

(4) Where any lands and heritages fall within such class or classes of lands and heritages as may be prescribed by the Secretary of State by regulations, the value to be treated for rating purposes as if it were the rateable value ascribed to the lands and heritages in the valuation roll shall be the sum of—

(a) the value apportioned to the occupied part of the lands and heritages; and

(b) one half of the value apportioned to the unoccupied part of the lands and heritages.

(5) Notwithstanding paragraph (b) of subsection (3) above, if it appears to the rating authority that the part of the lands and heritages which was unoccupied at the date of an apportionment of the rateable value thereof under subsection (1) above has continued after the end of the financial year referred to in that paragraph to be unoccupied but will remain so for a short time only, the authority may direct that the

apportionment shall continue to have effect for the next financial year; and subsections (2), (3)(a), (c) and (d) and (4) above shall have effect in relation to that year accordingly.

(6) Any statutory instrument containing regulations made under this section shall be subject to annulment in pursuance of a resolution of either House of Parliament.

(7) In this section "financial year" has the meaning assigned to it by section 96(5) of the Local Government (Scotland) Act 1973.

Certain lands and heritages to be treated as unoccupied

24B.—(1) For the purposes of section 24 of this Act, to lands and heritages shall be treated as unoccupied if, apart from this section, they would fall to be treated as occupied by reason only of there being kept on the lands and heritages plant, machinery or equipment—

    (a) which was last used on the lands and heritages when they were last in use; or

    (b) which is intended for use on the lands and heritages.

(2) Subsection (1) above applies to the unoccupied part of lands and heritages for the purposes of section 24A of this Act as it applies to unoccupied lands and heritages for the purposes of the said section 24.".

DEFINITIONS

"financial year": subs. (7); s.96(5) of the 1973 Act.
"rating authority": s.30.

GENERAL NOTE

This section should be read in conjunction with s.154, and with the repeals referred to in the notes on that section.

By inserting the new s.24A into the Local Government (Scotland) Act 1966, this section again enables harmonisation, by providing for a rating authority to request the assessor to take account of lands and heritages which are *partly* unoccupied, by apportioning the total value between the occupied and unoccupied parts and attributing a raised value to the occupied part – subject, as in the new s.24 above, to the prescription by the Secretary of State of certain properties in respect of which a half value may be attributed to the unoccupied portion (subs. (4)). The period during which such an arrangement can subsist is determined by reference to subss. (2) and (3), and subject to continuation under subs. (5) (but what is not clear is the meaning of "a short time only" – a phrase retained from s.243A of the Local Government (Scotland) Act 1947 in subss. (1) and (5) – see *Armour on Valuation for Rating* para. 14–09).

On s.24B, see s.154 above, substituting a new s.24 in the Local Government (Scotland) Act 1966 and see the Non-Domestic Rating (Unoccupied Property) (Scotland) Regulations 1994 (S.I. 1994 No. 3200).

Remission of rates on account of hardship

156. After section 25 of the Local Government (Scotland) Act 1966 insert—

"Exemption from payment of rates

Remission of rates on account of hardship

25A. Every rating authority may, on the application of any person liable to pay any rate levied by the authority, remit payment (in whole or in part) of the rate if the authority are satisfied that—

    (a) the person would sustain hardship if the authority did not do so; and

(b) it is reasonable for the authority to do so, having regard to the interests of persons liable to pay council tax set by them.".

DEFINITIONS
"rating authority": s.30.

GENERAL NOTE
This is another harmonisation provision (see, for England and Wales, s.49 of the Local Government Finance Act 1988 (c. 41)) and one which, in replacing s.244 of the Local Government (Scotland) Act 1947, substitutes a test of "hardship" for one of "poverty or inability to pay" in a rating authority's power to remit rates, a test which relates better to the financial condition of many non-domestic ratepayers rather than the householder for whom the original formula was devised.

The obligation for the rating authority to have regard, when considering an application for remission, to the interests of council tax payers derives from the English legislation. Although non-domestic rates have largely ceased to be a "local" tax and, therefore, general rate income does not, in the ordinary way, directly affect the bills of council tax payers, the cost of remission under this section will be borne to the extent of 25 per cent by the local authority (and 75 per cent by central government); see Sched. 12, para. 10 to the Local Government Finance Act 1992 and regulations made thereunder.

Certain orders relating to valuation not to be treated as hybrid

157. In section 6 of the 1975 Act (valuation by formula of certain lands and heritages), after subsection (7) add—

"(8) An order under this section shall, if apart from the provisions of this subsection it would be treated for the purposes of the standing orders of the Lords House of Parliament as a hybrid instrument, proceed in that House as if it were not such an instrument.".

DEFINITIONS
"1975 Act": s 183(1).

GENERAL NOTE
This section makes a technical adjustment (mirroring s.143(11) of the Local Government Finance Act 1988 in respect of similar powers in relation to England and Wales) to ensure that an order made under s.6 of the 1975 Act (the power to value by formula which has been used for industries such as telecommunications, electricity, gas and harbours) shall not be treated as a hybrid instrument for the purpose of the standing orders of the House of Lords. Under the standing orders, such orders may be petitioned against, with petitions heard by the Hybrid Instruments Committee.

Grants in respect of certain rate rebates

158. In section 69 of the Local Government, Planning and Land Act 1980 (grants in respect of rebates under the Rating (Disabled Persons) Act 1978)—

(a) after subsection (1) insert—

"(1A) Subject to subsection (1B) below, no grant shall be paid to any authority in respect of any rebates granted by that authority on or after 1st April 1995.

(1B) A grant shall be payable to any authority granting rebates under the said Act of 1978 in respect of non-domestic water and sewerage rates for the year beginning with 1st April 1995."; and

(b) after subsection (2) insert—

"(2A) Subsections (1A) and (1B) above extend to Scotland only.".

GENERAL NOTE
This section removes (by amendment of s.69 of the Local Government, Planning and Land Act 1980 (c. 65)) the obligation on the Secretary of State to pay a specific grant to authorities which allow a rating rebate under the Rating (Disabled Persons) Act 1978 (c. 40) after April 1, 1995 – except in the case of rebates from non-domestic water and sewerage rates (due, by virtue of the provisions in Pt. II of this Act, to cease from April 1, 1996). The cost of such rebates can be

taken account of in the general revenue support grant made to authorities under Sched. 12 to the Local Government Finance Act 1992.

Rating of enterprise zone

159.—(1) Schedule 32 to the Local Government, Planning and Land Act 1980 shall be amended in accordance with this section.

(2) In paragraph 33(2)(meaning of exempt lands and heritages for purpose of paragraph 33)—

(a) paragraph (a) shall cease to have effect; and

(b) for paragraph (b) substitute—

"(b) the rateable values of the lands and heritages are prescribed under or determined by virtue of an order under section 6 of the Local Government (Scotland) Act 1975 (valuation by formula of certain lands and heritages),".

(3) In paragraph 34 (grants to compensate rating authorities for loss of revenue)—

(a) in sub-paragraph (1)—

(i) at the beginning insert the words "For the financial year 1995–96,"; and

(ii) after "revenue" insert the words "in respect of the non-domestic sewerage rate".

DEFINITIONS
"rating authority": s.30.

GENERAL NOTE
The purpose of this section is, by amendments made to Sched. 32 to the Local Government, Planning and Land Act 1980, to change the basis on which local authorities are compensated for loss of revenue from rates in enterprise zones. At present the Secretary of State must compensate them directly. In 1995–1996 this arrangement will apply only (and for the last time) to sewerage rates. Compensation for loss of non-domestic rate income from 1995–1996 will be made available through revenue support grant.

Further provision as to valuation by formula

160. In section 6 of the 1975 Act (valuation by formula of certain lands and heritages), after subsection (5) there shall be inserted the following subsection—

"(5A) An order under this section may provide that the assessor for any specified valuation area shall carry out such functions in relation to the operation of a formula as may be specified in the order, notwithstanding that such functions may include the valuation of lands and heritages in another valuation area.".

DEFINITIONS
"1975 Act": s.183(1).
"assessor": s.27.
"valuation area": s.27.

GENERAL NOTE
The "formula" referred to in the new subs. (5A) inserted into s.6 of the 1975 Act is a formula which the Secretary of State may prescribe for the valuation of certain types of property, *i.e.* industries including electricity, gas, water, railways, telecommunications, and docks and harbours. The Government's intention is to move from a practice of making annual formula orders to a five-yearly system to be implemented by one (local) assessor on a national basis, somewhat similar to the model of the former Assessor of Public Undertakings (Scotland). Such a practice will require the chosen assessor to have jurisdiction outwith his or her own valuation area, and this is authorised by the new subs. (5A).

Power of Secretary of State to combine and divide lands and heritages

161. After section 6 of the Valuation and Rating (Scotland) Act 1956 there shall be inserted the following section—

"Power of Secretary of State to combine and divide lands and heritages

6A.—(1) The Secretary of State may by order provide that, for all purposes of the Valuation Acts—

(a) lands and heritages specified in the order which would, apart from the order, be treated as justifying separate entries in the valuation roll shall be treated as justifying only one such entry; and

(b) lands and heritages so specified which would, apart from the order, be treated as justifying only one entry in the valuation roll shall be treated as justifying separate entries,

and an order under paragraph (b) above shall specify which parts of the lands and heritages concerned are to be treated as justifying separate entries.

(2) An order under this section shall be made by statutory instrument subject to annulment in pursuance of a resolution of either House of Parliament.".

DEFINITIONS

"Valuation Acts": s.183(1).

GENERAL NOTE

In the ordinary law and practice of valuation for rating, the question of what constitutes the proper unit of valuation – the *unum quid* – warranting a separate entry in the roll, often raises complex issues around which has developed a large amount of case law (see *Armour's Valuation for Rating*, Chap. 6). In relation to certain formula-valued industries however, the order made by the Secretary of State may provide for the inclusion of many lands and heritages (which would otherwise have required separate entries) as a single entry in the roll.

This new s.6A in the Valuation and Rating (Scotland) Act 1956 will enable the Secretary of State to order that specified lands and heritages be treated as justifying either single or separate entries. This power may be used to facilitate the return to conventional valuation of companies and undertakings providing a networked service. Like some other valuation provisions, this section is intended to produce a harmonisation of rules north and south of the Border.

Abolition of Scottish Valuation Advisory Council

162.—(1) The Scottish Valuation Advisory Council constituted under section 3 of the Valuation and Rating (Scotland) Act 1956 ("the 1956 Act") shall cease to exist immediately before 1st April 1996.

(2) In the 1956 Act—

(a) section 3; and

(b) in section 43(1) (interpretation), the definition of "Advisory Council", shall cease to have effect.

DEFINITIONS

"1956 Act": subs. (1).

GENERAL NOTE

The setting up of the Scottish Valuation Advisory Council was one of the recommendations of the Sorn Report on Valuation and Rating (Cmd. 9244, 1954) and was intended, in particular, to assist in the process of implementing the major changes in valuation practice introduced by the Valuation and Rating (Scotland) Act 1956 (see *Armour's Valuation for Rating*, para. 1–18). It is now the Government's view, however, that advice needed on valuation practice and reforms is as well obtained from the assessors' professional body, the Scottish Assessors Association, and other representative organisations. The Council is, therefore, to be abolished from March 31, 1996. The relevant references in that Act are removed by this section.

Amendment of Transport Act 1968

Guarantees by Strathclyde Passenger Transport Authority

163. After section 13 of the Transport Act 1968 there shall be inserted the following section—

"Guarantees by Authority
    13A. The Authority may guarantee any obligation entered into by the Executive with the approval of the Authority.".

DEFINITIONS
    "Authority": s.9 of the Transport Act 1968.
    "Executive": s.9 of the Transport Act 1968.

GENERAL NOTE
    This new s.13A in the Transport Act 1968 (c. 73) will enable the existing Strathclyde Passenger Transport Authority (and the successor authority – see s.40 above) to guarantee obligations entered into by the Passenger Transport Executive.

Finance

Calculation of limits on spending

164.—(1) Section 83 of the 1973 Act (power of local authorities to incur expenditure not otherwise authorised) shall be amended in accordance with this section. (2) In subsection (1)—
    (a) after the words "in the interests of" there shall be inserted the words "and will bring direct benefit to";
    (b) after the words "incur any expenditure" there shall be inserted "(a)"; and
    (c) at the end there shall be added the words—
        "nor
        (b) unless the direct benefit accruing to their area or any part of it or to all or some of the inhabitants of their area will be commensurate with the expenditure to be incurred.".
(3) Subsection (3A) shall cease to have effect.
(4) For subsection (4) substitute—
        "(4) The expenditure of a local authority under this section in any financial year shall not exceed the amount produced by multiplying—
        (a) £3.80, or such other sum as may from time to time be specified in an order made by the Secretary of State; by
        (b) the relevant population of the authority's area.
        (4AA) For the purposes of subsection (4)(b) above the relevant population of a local authority's area shall be determined in accordance with regulations made by the Secretary of State.".
(5) For subsections (5) and (6) substitute—
        "(5) A statutory instrument containing an order or regulations made under this section shall be subject to annulment in pursuance of a resolution of either House of Parliament.".

DEFINITIONS
    "1973 Act": s.183(1).
    "local authority": s.235(1) of the 1973 Act, as amended by Sched. 13.

GENERAL NOTE
    Section 83 of the 1973 Act is sometimes described as the statutory provision which comes nearest to giving Scottish local authorities a form of "general competence" – a power to do things of their own choice for which no more specific provision is made elsewhere. The principal power is to "incur expenditure which in their opinion is in the interests of their area or any part of it or all or some of its inhabitants", but this is subject to certain financial and other restrictions. The s.83 power will continue to apply to the new authorities from April 1996 but with the amendments made by this section.

Subs. (2)
    These amendments narrow the scope of s.83 of the 1973 Act (in the same way that the equivalent provision has already been narrowed in England and Wales – see, s.137 of the Local Government Act 1972, as amended by s.36 of the Local Government and Housing Act 1989) by

requiring that not only should the expenditure be "in the interests of" the area etc., but that it should also "bring direct benefit to" the area or inhabitants, and that the "direct benefit" should be "commensurate with the expenditure to be incurred". The effect of the amendment will probably be to close a gap exposed in *Commission for Local Authority Accounts v. Grampian Regional Council* 1994 S.L.T. 1185 in which the First Division held expenditure by the Council under s.83, which was used to fund contributions to the Scottish Constitutional Convention and the Campaign for a Scottish Assembly, to be lawful.

Subs. (3)

This simply removes subs. (3A) of s.83 which governed the relationship between a regional and a district council in their use of the s.83 powers – rules which will no longer be necessary after April 1, 1996.

Subs. (4)

The most important restriction on the s.83 power is that an upper financial limit is imposed on the annual expenditure of each authority under the section. In the original version of the section, this limit was expressed by reference to the rate income of the authority, and the maximum annual expenditure was fixed at the product of a rate of 2p in the pound. When domestic rates were abolished in 1989, that maximum amount was frozen at the product of a rate of 2p in the last financial year of domestic rating *i.e.* 1988–89. That amount could have been varied by order but from 1996 this reference back to the 1988–89 figures would have been meaningless in relation to the new councils. Instead a completely different method of calculation has been devised and the maximum expenditure will now become £3.80 per head of population in the authority's area – to be calculated in turn under regulations to be made by the Secretary of State. An attempt was made at the House of Lords Report stage to raise the figure of £3.80 to £11.80, based on an assumption that, at present, the total amount of "discretionary expenditure" available to Scottish authorities is £57.9 million. The Government's response was, however, that existing expenditure was, in fact, much lower (£13 million in 1991–1992), and that the new rules (based on £3.80 per head) would permit up to £19.5 million, which would be more than adequate (*Hansard*, H.L. Vol. 558, cols. 307–309).

Subs. (5)

This change is technical and merely condenses the contents of two former subsections into one, and dispenses with the need to permit orders under the section to make different provision for different descriptions of authority.

Powers of authorities to borrow and lend money

165.—(1) The Secretary of State may by regulations made with the consent of the Treasury make provision with respect to the powers of authorities—

(a) to borrow and lend money; and

(b) to establish and operate loans funds.

(2) Regulations under this section may make different provision in respect of different authorities and may include such incidental, supplemental and consequential provision as the Secretary of State considers appropriate.

(3) Without prejudice to the generality of the powers conferred by subsections (1) and (2) above, regulations under this section may—

(a) specify the purposes for which an authority may borrow money;

(b) place limits on amounts which an authority may borrow;

(c) specify the means by which an authority may borrow;

(d) make provision for—

(i) the means by which money borrowed by an authority may be secured; and

(ii) the protection of persons borrowing from an authority;

(e) specify from whom an authority may borrow or to whom they may lend;

(f) specify the terms on which an authority may lend;

(g) make provision as to what assets and liabilities may be paid or transferred into or out of a loans fund and on what terms;

(h) provide for investigations to be carried out at the instance of the Secretary of State into the administration of a loans fund;

(i) place requirements on an authority to obtain such consent as may be prescribed before taking prescribed actions; and

(j) where an authority have failed to comply with the regulations, provide for the Secretary of State to apply to the Court of Session for an order ordaining compliance, and for the court to grant such an application if they think fit.

(4) Where it appears to the Secretary of State to be necessary or expedient, in the light of any regulations made under this section; to amend any reference in any enactment, whether passed before or after the coming into force of this section—

(a) to a loans fund; or

(b) to any provision in Schedule 3 to the 1975 Act,

he may by regulations make such amendment.

(5) Regulations under this section shall be made by statutory instrument, but shall not be made unless a draft of any such statutory instrument has been laid before and approved by resolution of each House of Parliament.

(6) For the purposes of this section "authority" means a local authority, a joint board, a river purification board or the Strathclyde Passenger Transport Authority.

DEFINITIONS
"1975 Act": s.183(1).
"authority": subs. (6).

GENERAL NOTE
Under the present law, s.69 (subsidiary powers) of the 1973 Act confers upon local authorities the power to borrow or lend money – "a local authority shall have the power to do any thing (whether or not involving the expenditure, borrowing or lending of money or the acquisition or disposal of any property or rights) which is calculated to facilitate, or is conducive or incidental to, the discharge of any of their functions". More detailed rules are then contained in s.16 of, and Sched. 3, to the 1975 Act. Paragraph 1(1) of Sched. 3 provides that "without prejudice to s.69 of the Act of 1973", a local authority may borrow for a number of prescribed purposes.

This new provision in s.165 is intended to give the Secretary of State wide powers to make regulations governing borrowing and lending by authorities (as defined in subs. (6)) which will amend and amplify existing rules.

Grants in relation to ethnic minorities

166. For section 11 of the Local Government (Scotland) Act 1966 substitute—

"Grants for certain expenditure in relation to ethnic minorities

11.—(1) Subject to the provisions of this section, the Secretary of State may pay to local authorities which in his opinion are required to make special provision in the exercise of any of their functions in consequence of the presence within their area of persons belonging to ethnic minorities whose language or customs differ from those of the rest of the community, grants of such amounts as he may, with the consent of the Treasury, determine on account of expenditure in respect of the employment of staff.

(2) No grant shall be paid under this section in respect of expenditure incurred before 1st April 1993.".

DEFINITIONS
"local authority": s.46(1) of the Local Government (Scotland) Act 1966, as amended by Sched. 13.

GENERAL NOTE
By replacing the existing s.11 of the Local Government (Scotland) Act 1966, this section is intended to widen the scope of the Secretary of State's powers to make grants in relation to

ethnic minorities, in a way similar to that achieved for the law of England and Wales by the Local Government (Amendment) Act 1993 (c. 27).

The main limitation contained in the old version of s.11 was that, instead of the current reference to "the presence within their area of persons belonging to ethnic minorities whose language or customs differ", etc., the section required "the presence within their areas of substantial numbers of immigrants from the Commonwealth whose language or customs differ", etc.

Special grants

167. After section 108 of the Local Government Finance Act 1992 insert—

"Special grants
108A.—(1) The Secretary of State may, with the consent of the Treasury, pay a grant (in this section referred to as a "special grant") in accordance with this section to a local authority.

(2) Where the Secretary of State proposes to make a special grant to one authority he shall, before making the grant, make a determination stating—
(a) the authority to which the grant is to be paid;
(b) the purpose for which the grant is to be paid; and
(c) the amount of the grant which is to be paid or the manner in which that amount is to be calculated.

(3) Where the Secretary of State proposes to make special grants to more than one authority he shall, before making the grants, make a determination stating—
(a) to which authorities they are to be paid;
(b) the purpose for which they are to be paid; and
(c) either—
    (i) the amount which he proposes to pay to each authority or the manner in which the amount is to be calculated; or
    (ii) the total amount which he proposes to distribute among the authorities and the basis upon which he proposes to distribute that amount.

(4) A determination under subsection (2) or (3) above shall be made with the consent of the Treasury and shall be specified in a report (to be called a special grant report) which shall contain such explanation of the main features of the determination as the Secretary of State considers to be desirable.

(5) A special grant report shall be laid before the House of Commons and, as soon as is reasonably practicable thereafter, the Secretary of State shall send a copy of it to any authority to which he proposes to make a special grant in accordance with the determination.

(6) No special grant shall be paid unless the special grant report containing the determination relating to the grant has been approved by a resolution of the House of Commons.

(7) A special grant report may specify conditions which the Secretary of State may with the consent of the Treasury impose on the payment of, or of any instalment of, any special grant to which the report relates; and the conditions may—
(a) require the provision of returns or other information before a payment is made to the authority concerned; or
(b) relate to the use of the amount paid, or to the repayment in specified circumstances of all or part of the amount paid.

(8) Without prejudice to compliance with any conditions imposed as mentioned in subsection (7) above, a special grant shall be paid at such time or in instalments of such amounts and at such times as the Secretary of State may, with the consent of the Treasury, determine.".

DEFINITIONS
"local authority": s.99 of the Local Government Finance Act 1992, as amended by Sched. 13.
"special grant": new subs. (1).

GENERAL NOTE
This section provides a potentially highly significant new power to the Secretary of State to pay a "special grant" to a local authority or to a number of local authorities. Hitherto, grants to local authorities have taken the form of revenue support grant (distributed to authorities as a whole according to formula), specific grants paid in support of particular services (including, most importantly at present, the police grant), and allocations from non-domestic rate income (distributed with revenue support grant on a formula basis).

This section provides a completely free-standing power enabling the Secretary of State to make individual grants to local authorities of his choice and for whatever purpose. The only constraints are (a) Treasury consent, and (b) the need for prior approval by the House of Commons of a "special grant report" (subss. (4)–(7)), which is required to contain only "such explanation of the main features of the determination [*i.e.* the decision to make the grant, naming the authority or authorities, the purpose of the grant, and its amount] *as the Secretary of State considers to be desirable*". One possible use for these special grant powers which was discussed in debates was to give assistance to the voluntary sector (about which considerable concern was expressed and on which see also s.140) by making "ring- fenced" grants for this purpose to local authorities under this section. That would, however, raise "complex administrative issues" (see *Hansard*, H.L. Vol. 556, col. 1924).

Direct Labour Organisation/Direct Services Organisation Accounts

168.—(1) After section 15 of the 1975 Act there shall be inserted the following section—

"Direct Labour Organisation/Direct Services Organisation Accounts

15A.—(1) A local authority may establish, in, accordance with the provisions of this section, Direct Labour Organisation/Direct Services Organisation Funds (to be known as "DLO/DSO funds") for the purpose of dealing with surpluses and deficits which may occur in respect of—

    (a) any revenue account kept by the authority under section 10(1) (accounts relating to construction or maintenance work) of the Local Government, Planning and Land Act 1980; or

    (b) any account kept by the authority under section 9(2) (accounts) of the Local Government Act 1988.

(2) Any interest earned on money transferred to a reserve fund established under subsection (1) above may be credited to that fund.

(3) Any surplus credited to a fund established under subsection (1) above and which is, in the opinion of the authority, not required for the purpose of dealing with deficits in any such fund, may be transferred by them to the general fund maintained by them under section 93 of the Act of 1973 (general fund).

(4) This section is without prejudice to any specific limitation imposed by or under any enactment as to the manner in which money may be paid into or out of any specific account.".

(2) Paragraphs 22(1)(c) and 24A of Schedule 3 to the 1975 Act shall cease to have effect.

DEFINITIONS
"1975 Act": s.183(1).
"local authority": s.235(1) of the 1973 Act; s.37(2) of the 1975 Act.

GENERAL NOTE
Under existing rules (to be repealed by subs. (2) of this section), local authorities can create DLO (Direct Labour Organisation) reserve funds into which DLO surpluses can be paid and to which deficits can be charged. This section replaces those provisions and makes changes necessary to remove difficulties encountered in practice, by providing in subs. (2) and (3) of the new s.15A of the 1975 Act a power:

(a) to credit to a DLO/DSO fund any interest earned on the fund; and
(b) to transfer certain surpluses from a DLO/DSO fund to the authority's general fund (established under s.93 of the 1973 Act).

Statements of support services costs

169.—(1) The Secretary of State may by regulations require any authority defined for the purposes of section 1(1) of the Local Government Act 1988 ("the 1988 Act") to publish a statement, to be known as a statement of support services costs (hereinafter referred to as a "statement"), of the cost to the authority of each of the activities to which this section applies.
(2) This section applies to—
(a) any activity which is a defined activity within the meaning of section 2(2) of the 1988 Act;
(b) any other prescribed activity.
(3) A statement shall—
(a) show the cost to the authority of the activity to which it applies, whether or not that activity, or any part of it, is carried out by employees of the authority; and
(b) show how that cost is allocated amongst the public services provided by the authority.
(4) A statement shall—
(a) be in such form;
(b) be published on or by reference to such date;
(c) contain such information;
(d) be made available for inspection by the public in such manner; and
(e) be supplied to the public on such terms as to payment,
as may be prescribed, and different provision may be made in relation to the matters mentioned above in relation to different authorities.
(5) Such of the information contained in the statement as may be prescribed shall be included within the annual abstract of accounts (or any equivalent to such an abstract) produced by an authority.
(6) For the purposes of this section the cost of any activity shall be calculated in such manner and by reference to such factors as may be prescribed.
(7). In this section—
"activity", where it is an activity such as is mentioned in—
(a) subsection (2)(a) above, has the meaning given to it by or under the 1988 Act; and
(b) subsection (2)(b) above, has such meaning as may be prescribed;
"prescribed" means prescribed in regulations under this section; and
"public services" means such services provided by the authority as may be prescribed.
(8) Regulations under this section shall be made by statutory instrument subject to annulment in pursuance of a resolution of either House of Parliament.

DEFINITIONS
"1988 Act": subs. (1).
"activity": subs. (7).
"prescribed": subs. (7).
"public services": subs. (7).

GENERAL NOTE
This section is introduced as a consequence of the growth of compulsory competitive tendering ("CCT") in relation to local authorities and, in particular, the impending extension of CCT to cover many of the corporate and professional (including legal) services provided within authorities. In response to the need to identify the separate cost of each such support service activity, the section enables the Secretary of State to require authorities, defined for CCT purposes under the Local Government Act 1988 (c. 9), to include within their annual abstract of

accounts a "statement of support services costs" in respect of each activity defined under s.2(2) of that Act and any other prescribed activity. The required content of the statement is specified in subs. (3), and its form is to be prescribed under subs. (4). Subsection (4) was substantially revised and subs. (5) added at the House of Lords Report stage (see *Hansard*, H.L. Vol. 558, col. 309).

Resources

Effective use of resources

170. After section 122 of the 1973 Act there shall be inserted the following section—

"Duty of local authority to use resources efficiently

122A. It shall be duty of each local authority to make proper arrangements for securing economy, efficiency and effectiveness in their use of resources.".

DEFINITIONS
"1973 Act": s.183(1).
"local authority": s.235(1) of the 1973 Act, as amended by Sched. 13.

GENERAL NOTE
There has been a change in the functions of the Commission for Local Authority Accounts in Scotland (from December 1, 1994, the Accounts Commission for Scotland, by virtue of para. 2 of Sched. 7 to the National Health Service and Community Care Act 1990 (c. 19), and National Health Service and Community Care Act 1990 (Commencement No. 11) (Scotland) Order 1994 (S.I. 1994 No. 2658)) and in the function of its auditors, since it originally assumed responsibility for the scrutiny of local authority accounts in 1975. A statutory concern originally largely confined to the lawfulness of spending in terms of ss.99 and 102 of the 1973 Act was expanded by the Local Government Act 1988, which inserted s.97A and amended s.99 of the 1973 Act to give the Commission and its auditors the responsibility of examining local authority performance against the criteria of "economy, efficiency and effectiveness". This concern for "value for money" rather than legality has been further heightened by the promulgation of the *Citizen's Charter* in 1991.

One change which was never made expressly until the passing of this section – perhaps because it was assumed that it was implicit in the other changes – was any formal adjustment to local authority powers to ensure that the duty to use resources efficiently was recognised. That duty is now imposed on all authorities.

Economic development

Functions to include promotion of economic development

171. After section 171 of the 1973 Act there shall be inserted—

"PART XVIIIA

ECONOMIC DEVELOPMENT

Functions to include promotion of economic development

171A.—(1) Subject to section 171B of this Act, the functions of a local authority shall include the taking of such steps as they may from time to time consider appropriate for promoting the economic development of their area.

(2) Subject to the said section 171B, and without prejudice to any other provision made by or under this, Act, those steps may include participation in and the encouragement of, and provision of financial and other assistance for—

　(a) the setting up or expansion of any commercial, industrial or public undertaking—

　　　(i) which is to be or is situated in the authority's area; or

(ii) the setting up or expansion of which appears likely to increase the opportunities for employment of persons living in that area; and

(b) the creation or protection of opportunities for employment with any such undertaking or with any commercial, industrial or public undertaking, opportunities for employment with which have been or appear likely to be made available to persons living in that area.

(3) For the purposes of this section, the cases in which a local authority shall be treated as providing financial assistance to any person shall include the cases where they do or agree to do any of the following, that is to say—

(a) make a grant to that person;

(b) make a loan to that person or provide him with any further form of credit;

(c) guarantee the performance of any of that person's obligations;

(d) indemnify that person in respect of any liability, loss or damage;

(e) invest in that person's undertaking, in the case of a body corporate, by acquiring share or loan capital in that body or otherwise;

(f) provide that person with any property, services or other financial benefit (including the remission in whole or in part of any liability or obligation) for no consideration or for a consideration which is less than the best that could reasonably be obtained;

(g) join with any other person in doing anything falling within paragraphs (a) to (f) above.

(4) The power conferred on a local authority under subsection (1) above includes power for such authority to engage in activities outside their area for the purpose of promoting the economic development of their area.

(5) Where, in any financial year, a local authority propose to engage in activities such as are mentioned in subsection (4) above outside the United Kingdom, they shall, before the beginning of that financial year—

(a) prepare a document setting out their proposals for engagement in such activities; and

(b) submit that document to the Secretary of State for approval.

(6) Where the Secretary of State approves the proposals set out in any document submitted under subsection (5) above, he may make his approval subject to such conditions as he considers necessary or expedient.

(7) At any time during the financial year to which a document such as is mentioned in subsection (5) above relates—

(a) a local authority may submit to the Secretary of State amendments of the proposals contained in that document; and

(b) subsection (6) above shall apply in relation to those amendments as it applies in relation to proposals submitted in pursuance of subsection (5) above.

(8) The exercise by a local authority of any of their powers under this section shall be subject to the provisions of section 90 of this Act.

Restrictions on promotion of economic development

171B.—(1) The powers of a local authority by virtue of section 171A above, and their powers by virtue of any of the other provisions of this or any other enactment, shall not include power, for the promotion of the economic development of their area, to take any such steps as may be specified or described for the purposes of this section in regulations made by the Secretary of State.

(2) Without prejudice to the generality of subsection (1) above, the Secretary of State may by regulations impose such conditions (including conditions requiring consultation by the local authority of such persons as may be prescribed), and such other restrictions, as may be specified in or determined under the regulations on the exercise, for the purpose of promoting the economic development of their area, of any power of a local authority by virtue of the said section 171A or any other enactment.

(3) The Secretary of State may by order impose such a financial limit as may be specified in or determined under the order on expenditure which—

(a) is, or is of a description, so specified or determined; and

(b) is, by virtue of section 171A above or a provision of this or any other enactment, incurred in any financial year for the purpose of promoting the economic development of their area by a local authority so specified or determined.

(4) A statutory instrument containing regulations under subsection (1) or (2) above or an order under subsection (3) above shall be subject to annulment in pursuance of a resolution of either House of Parliament.

(5) Regulations under subsection (1) or (2) above may contain such incidental provision and such supplemental, consequential and transitional provision in connection with their other provisions as the Secretary of State considers appropriate.

Exercise of certain powers to be subject to provisions of sections 171A and 171B

171C. The exercise by a local authority of any power which they have—

(a) under section 7 of the Local Government (Development and Finance) (Scotland) Act 1964 (power to make advances for erection of buildings);

(b) under section 102 (power to acquire compulsorily certain land) or 109 (power to acquire certain land by agreement) of the Town and Country Planning (Scotland) Act 1972; or

(c) under section 70, 74 or 78 of this Act,

is subject to the provisions of sections 171A and 171B of this Act.".

DEFINITIONS
"1973 Act": s.183(1).
"local authority": s.235(1) of the 1973 Act, as amended by Sched. 13.

GENERAL NOTE
   This section should be read together with the provisions in Sched. 14 which repeal ss.154A and 154B of the 1973 Act. Those sections were inserted into that Act by the Local Government and Planning (Scotland) Act 1982 (c. 43), and gave powers of "industrial promotion" to local authorities. Also repealed are subss. (2A) and (2B) of s.83 of the 1973 Act, which enabled that section to be used for the purpose of giving assistance to commercial and industrial undertakings.
   This section now replaces ss.154A and 154B with powers to promote "economic development", contained in the new ss.171A, 171B and 171C inserted into the 1973 Act. The principal powers are in s.171A, but these must be exercised subject to restrictions to be imposed by the Secretary of State under s.171B. Section 171C requires that certain existing related powers be exercised subject to those two sections.

New s.171A
   The principal power conferred by this section (subject to s.171B) is to take steps which involve "participation in and the encouragement of, and provision of financial and other assistance" for setting up or expanding a commercial, industrial or public undertaking, and creating or protecting opportunities for employment (subs. (2)). The forms of financial assistance concerned may include those spelled out in subs. (3). Subsections (4)–(7) relate to the use of the general power

to promote the economic development of an authority's area by engaging in activities outside their area and, in particular, outwith the U.K. (for which, approval of their plans by the Secretary of State is required). Section 90 of the 1973 Act, referred to in subs. (8), concerns powers to carry on tourism-related activities and is newly substituted by s.176 of this Act.

New s.171B

It is by means of regulations under this section that the Secretary of State may exercise control over the manner in which a local authority may exercise powers for the promotion of economic development, whether under s.171A or otherwise. It was indicated in debate (see *Hansard*, H.L. Vol. 557, cols. 441–442) that the powers in s.171B would be used to impose two conditions on the use of s.171A:

(1) A requirement that local authorities consult other parties, particularly local enterprise companies and chambers of commerce, before taking action on economic development plans; and

(2) A requirement that authorities supply details of whatever economic development activities they carry out.

Regulations on these matters would come into force at reorganisation. No other requirements were envisaged.

New s.171C

The powers referred to in para. (c) relate to acquisition of land by agreement (s.70), disposal of land (s.74), and the erection of buildings (s.78).

Although the general purpose of this section must be to confine the exercise of powers under the statutes listed in paras. (a), (b) and (c) within the parameters imposed by the new ss.171A and 171B, it is not wholly obvious how the powers are to be exercised in all respects, nor how, in some cases, the powers are affected by making their exercise subject to ss.171A and 171B.

Tourism

Duty of Secretary of State to establish area tourist boards

172.—(1) The Secretary of State shall, in accordance with the provisions of this section and not later than 1st April 1996, by order make schemes for the establishment for such areas as may be specified in the order of area tourist boards (hereafter referred to as "boards").

(2) The principal function of a board shall be to carry on activities relating to tourism.

(3) A scheme under this section shall—

(a) make provision for the constitution of a board;

(b) specify the area for which the board is established;

(c) provide that the board shall be a body corporate with a common seal;

(d) provide that the Secretary of State shall appoint the first members of the board and, from among those members, the first members of the controlling body of the board; and thereafter the members of such controlling body shall be appointed by the board;

(e) contain provision stating that it shall not, without the express or general consent given in writing of the Secretary of State (or such body as he may direct the board to consult), carry on activities relating to the promotion of tourism outside the United Kingdom; and

(f) make, where applicable and to such extent as the Secretary of State considers appropriate, transitional provision such as is mentioned in subsection (5) below.

(4) A scheme under this section may—

(a) for the purposes of enabling a board to carry on its principal function, confer additional functions and powers on a board, including power to hold property and to employ staff;

(b) subject to the provisions of this section, provide who may be appointed to be members of the board;

(c) make provision for the payment of remuneration, allowances, pensions and gratuities to members of the board;

(d) subject to the provisions of this section and such conditions as may be specified in the scheme, enable a board to form or acquire a company;

(e) make provision for the board to regulate its own procedure;
(f) make provision for the board to appoint committees (including committees composed of persons who are not members of the board) and for the payment to persons appointed to such committees of such remuneration and allowances as the board may determine;
(g) make provision enabling the board to delegate any of its duties to any of its members who or committees which are authorised (generally or specifically) for the purpose;
(h) make provision as to the method of authentication of documents by the board; and
(i) make provision for such other matters as the Secretary of State thinks fit.

(5) The transitional provision mentioned in paragraph (f) of subsection (3) above is provision for—
(a) the revocation of any scheme made under section 90A of the 1973 Act (schemes for formation of area tourist organisations etc.) by an islands or district council whose area lies wholly or partly within the area of the proposed board;
(b) the winding up and dissolution of any area tourist organisation (whether a body corporate or not) formed by or for the purposes of any scheme made under the said section 90A;
(c) the transfer of any staff of any such area tourist organisation to such board established under this section as may be specified in the order; and
(d) the transfer to and, with effect from the date on which the scheme under this section takes effect, vesting in such board or boards established under this section as may be specified in the order of such property, rights and liabilities of any such tourist organisation as may be so specified.

(6) The number of persons representative of a local authority appointed as members of the controlling body of a board (in this section referred to as "local authority members") shall not exceed the number of subscribing members appointed as members of such a controlling body; and where local authority members are appointed the total number of voting rights accorded to them shall not exceed the total number of voting rights accorded to subscribing members.

(7) For the purposes of subsection (6) above, a subscribing member is a member of a board who—
(a) is such member of the board by reason of his—
(i) being resident, or carrying on business, in the area of the board; and
(ii) carrying on, or having an interest in, activities relating to tourism in the area of the board; and
(b) pays a membership subscription to the board,
and includes, where the subscribing member is a body corporate, a person representative of that body corporate.

(8) A board shall not—
(a) be regarded as a servant or agent of the Crown;
(b) have any status, immunity or privilege of the Crown; or
(c) be exempt from any tax, duty, rate, levy or other charge whatsoever, whether general or local,
and its property shall not be regarded as property of, or held on behalf of, the Crown.

(9) A board shall not—
(a) form or promote, or join with any other person in forming or promoting, any body corporate (including a company (within the meaning of the Companies Act 1985)); or
(b) acquire the majority of the voting rights in such a body corporate,

unless the constitution of any such body corporate contains a provision stating that it shall not, without the express or general consent given in writing of the Secretary of State (or such body as he may direct the board to consult), carry on activities relating to the promotion of tourism outside the United Kingdom.

(10) Before making a scheme under this section the Secretary of State shall consult—

(a) the Scottish Tourist Board; and

(b) any—

(i) district or islands council; and

(ii) new local authority,

whose area lies wholly or partly within the area of the proposed board.

(11) A scheme made by an order under this section shall not take effect before 1st April 1996 except in relation to—

(a) the constitution of a board;

(b) the carrying out by that board of any functions necessary to bring the scheme into operation on that date; and

(c) the winding up of an existing board.

(12) An order under this section shall be made by statutory instrument subject to annulment in pursuance of a resolution of either House of Parliament.

(13) In this section and in sections 173 and 174 of this Act "new local authority" means a council constituted under section 2 of this Act.

DEFINITIONS

"1973 Act": s.183(1).

"board": subs. (1).

"local authority member": subs. (6).

"new local authority": subs. (13).

GENERAL NOTE

This group of sections (ss.172–176) concerns tourism-related functions to be carried out, with full effect from April 1, 1996, by local authorities (under powers contained in a new s.90 of the 1973 Act substituted by s.176), and by a new system of area tourist boards to be established by the Secretary of State under s.172 (subject to amendment etc. under ss.173–175). Note also the repeal by Sched. 14 of s.90A of the 1973 Act.

The background to the changes made by these sections was explained in debate in Parliament (see *Hansard*, H.L. Vol. 557, cols. 443–449). The old s.90 of the 1973 Act (as amended by s.11 of the Local Government and Planning (Scotland) Act 1982) gave various powers to local authorities (islands and district councils) to promote tourism in their areas, including, with the consent of the Secretary of State or the Scottish Confederation of Tourism, promotion abroad; as well as powers to provide and improve tourist facilities. Regional councils may contribute financially to the efforts of district councils and other bodies. Section 90A of the 1973 Act (inserted by the 1982 Act and now repealed by Sched. 14) gave powers to district and islands councils to draw up schemes for the formation of local tourist organisations.

However, the pattern of area tourist boards which emerged was uneven and, following a review of the position, the Government announced a change of direction, designed to remove duplication of effort and a rationalisation of promotional activity.

The principal outcome is contained in this section, with the new duty on the Secretary of State himself to make schemes establishing area tourist boards. For the Government's rejection of the idea that the "shadow" authorities might do this, see *Hansard*, H.L. Vol. 557, col. 446. Although not formally required by the section itself, the intention is that the areas specified in the schemes (subs. (1)) will cover the whole of Scotland. In the debate referred to there was some discussion of boards for particular areas, *e.g.* Argyll.

A scheme constituting an area tourist board must fulfil the requirements specified in subs. (3), including provision as to membership of the board (subs. (3)(a)), and its "controlling body" (not defined). Subsection (3)(a) should be read in conjunction with subss. (4)(b), (6) and (7). The scheme must provide for the Secretary of State to appoint all the first members of the board, although the Act appears silent on who is to appoint to the board thereafter. Subsection (4) does, however, permit rules in the scheme as to whom may be appointed. The Secretary of State also makes initial appointments, from those members, to the "controlling body", but appointments to that body are thereafter for the board, subject to the rules in subss. (6)–(7) which are designed to ensure that local authority representation on the controlling body shall not exceed, either in terms of numbers or voting rights, that of the "subscribing members" (as defined in subs. (7)). For discussion of local authority representation, see *ibid.*, col. 448. See also First Scottish Standing Committee, cols. 1964–1970 when subss. (6) and (7) were inserted. The scheme must also make any appropriate transitional provision, including the winding up of tourist organisations formed under s.90A of the 1973 Act (subss. (3)(f) and (5)).

Other powers which may be included in a scheme are set out in subs. (4), including the power of a board to form or acquire a company. However, note the restrictions imposed on any such company in relation to activities outwith the U.K. (subs. (9)). This reflects the general requirement that a board may carry on its own activities outwith the U.K. only if it has the written consent of the Secretary of State. Requirements to consult affected parties (including local authorities, both old and new), and restrictions on the implementation of a scheme prior to April 1, 1996 are imposed by subss. (10) and (11) respectively.

Power of Secretary of State to amend and revoke schemes

173.—(1) The Secretary of State may by order amend or revoke a scheme made under section 172 of this Act and the provisions of the said section 172 shall, so far as applicable, have effect in relation to any such amending or revoking scheme, subject to any necessary modifications and to the provisions of this section.

(2) Without prejudice to the generality of the provisions of subsection (1) above, provision may be made in an amending or revoking scheme—

(a) for altering the area for which a board (hereafter referred to as the "original board") is constituted under the scheme, whether or not that board is dissolved by virtue of the subsequent scheme;

(b) for the dissolution and winding up of an original board;

(c) for the transfer to such board as may be specified in the subsequent scheme of staff employed by the original board;

(d) for the transfer to and, with effect from the date on which the subsequent scheme takes effect, vesting in such board or boards as may be specified in that scheme of such property, rights and liabilities of the original board as may be so specified;

(e) for any other matters incidental to or consequential on the provisions of such scheme.

(3) The power conferred on the Secretary of State by subsection (1) above may be exercised in relation to an amending or revoking scheme made or, as the case may be, approved by order under this section or section 174 of this Act.

(4) Before making a scheme under this section the Secretary of State shall consult—

(a) the bodies mentioned in section 172(10)(a) and (b)(ii) of this Act; and

(b) where the subsequent scheme alters the area of the original board, any new local authority whose area lies wholly or partly within such altered area.

(5) An order under this section shall be made by statutory instrument; and such instrument shall, where it contains provision such as is mentioned in subsection (2)(a) above, be subject to annulment in pursuance of a resolution of either House of Parliament.

DEFINITIONS
"new local authority": s.172(13).
"original board": subs. (2).

GENERAL NOTE
This section is one of a group (ss.172–176) concerned with the promotion of tourism. See the General Note on s.172.

Sections 173 and 174 make provision for the amendment or revocation of a scheme made under s.172. Section 173 provides for such amendment or revocation on the initiative of the Secretary of State but, although it precedes s.174, it must be anticipated that the procedure in s.174, which is initiated by one or more (new) local authorities whose own areas lie within the area of a tourist board (but then requires the Secretary of State's approval), will be the standard form of amendment. Section 173 is better regarded, from this point of view, as providing a default power.

The section permits the Secretary of State to make a scheme (subject to the terms of s.172 so far as applicable) making amendments etc. to the first scheme, including such provisions as those listed in subs. (2). There must be consultation as stipulated in subs. (4), and subs. (3) ensures that the amending power can be used not only in relation to an "original" scheme but also to amend a scheme made earlier under this section or under s.174, *i.e.* successive amendments may be made. As with orders made under s.172, an order made under this section is to be made by statutory instrument, but is subject to the negative resolution procedure only if the scheme would "alter the area for which a board is constituted" (see subss. (5) and (2)(a)).

Power of local authority to submit amending schemes to Secretary of State

174.—(1) A new local authority whose area lies wholly or partly within the area of a board established by virtue of a scheme made under section 172 or 173 of this Act may, together with any other such authority whose area lies wholly or partly within the area of that board, submit to the Secretary of State for his approval a scheme for the amendment or revocation of such a scheme.

(2) The provisions of sections 172 and 173 of this Act shall, so far as applicable, have effect in relation to an amending or revoking scheme made under this section subject to any necessary modifications and to the provisions of this section. (3) Before making an amending or revoking scheme under this section, the authority or authorities concerned shall consult the Scottish Tourist Board.

(4) The power conferred on new local authorities by subsection (1) above may be exercised in relation to an amending or revoking scheme approved by order under this section.

(5) The Secretary of State may by order approve any scheme submitted to him under this section.

(6) An order under this section shall be made by statutory instrument; and such instrument shall, where it contains provision such as is mentioned in section 173(2)(a) of this Act, be subject to annulment in pursuance of a resolution of either House of Parliament.

DEFINITIONS
"new local authority": s.172(13).

GENERAL NOTE
See the notes on ss.172 and 173. This section provides the procedure for amendment of a tourist board scheme, on the initiative of a (new) local authority in the area, whether or not in combination with another such authority (subs. (1)). There is provision for consultation with the Scottish Tourist Board (though no formal requirement of consultation with any other local authority in the area) (subs. (3)). The power may be used to amend or revoke a scheme already affected by procedures under this section or s.173 (subs. (4)), and the scheme proposed by the local authority/ies must be approved by the Secretary of State by order (subss. (5)–(6)).

Provision of assistance to boards by old authorities

175. District, islands and regional councils may provide financial and other assistance to any area tourist board established by a scheme made under section 172 of this Act whose area lies wholly or partly within the areas of such councils in respect of anything done in pursuance of subsection (11) of that section before 1st April 1996.

GENERAL NOTE
General provision for local authority promotion of tourism with effect from April 1, 1996 is contained in the new s.90 of the 1973 Act inserted by s.176. This section, however, makes short-

term provision for any of the "old" local authorities to give financial or other assistance to area tourist boards in their own areas in the period to March 31, 1996. Under s.172(11) the boards are given very limited transitional powers exercisable during that period.

Powers to carry on tourism-related activities

176. For section 90 of the 1973 Act there shall be substituted the following section—

"Powers of local authority to carry on tourism-related activities

90.—(1) A local authority may—

(a) provide, or encourage any other person to provide, facilities for leisure, conferences, trade fairs and exhibitions or improve, or encourage any other person to improve, any existing facilities for those purposes;

(b) promote, by advertisement or otherwise, facilities provided by that local authority (whether such facilities are owned by the authority or otherwise);

(c) organise, or assist others in the organisation of, and promote, by advertisement or otherwise, conferences, trade fairs and exhibitions;

(d) participate in the area tourist board whose area includes the area of that authority.

(2) Subject to subsection (3) below, a local authority shall not have power to—

(a) encourage persons, by advertisement or otherwise (and whether inside or outside the United Kingdom)—

(i) to visit their area for purposes relating to leisure; or

(ii) to hold conferences, trade fairs or exhibitions within their area;

(b) provide information about accommodation and facilities and services relating to leisure in their area or provide a booking service for such accommodation, to persons visiting their area;

(c) carry on such other activities relating to those mentioned in paragraphs (a) and (b) above as the Secretary of State may by regulations specify.

(3) A local authority shall have power to do any of the things mentioned in paragraphs (a) to (c) of subsection (2) above—

(a) in so far as it is necessary to do any of those things for the purposes of carrying on the activities mentioned in paragraphs (a) and (b) of subsection (1) above; or

(b) where the Secretary of State has given his prior consent (subject to such conditions as he considers necessary or expedient) in writing.

(4) A local authority shall not, for the purposes of carrying on activities relating to tourism other than—

(a) those such as are mentioned in paragraphs (a) to (d) of subsection (1) above; or

(b) by virtue of subsection (3) above, those such as are mentioned in subsection (2) above,

form, acquire or join with any person or body corporate.

(5) Without prejudice to subsection (1) above, a local authority may contribute towards expenses incurred by any person—

(a) doing anything mentioned in paragraph (a) of that subsection; or

(b) organising and holding a conference, trade fair or exhibition.

(6) A local authority may appoint officers for the purposes of enabling the authority to carry out any of their powers under this section; and

section 65 of this Act shall apply in relation to any officers appointed under this subsection subject to the following modifications—

    (a) references to "another local authority" shall be construed as if they were references to an area tourist board; and

    (b) in subsection (2), the words from "but" to the end shall be omitted.

(7) A statutory instrument containing regulations under subsection (2)(c) above shall be subject to annulment in pursuance of a resolution of either House of Parliament.

(8) In this section—

    (a) "area tourist board" means a board established by virtue of an order made or, as the case may be, approved under section 172, 173 or 174 of the Local Government etc. (Scotland) Act 1994;

    (b) "participate" means participation in any one or more of the following ways—

        (i) a local authority or any person representative of a local authority being a member of the area tourist board whose area includes the area of that authority;

        (ii) provision by a local authority to such a board of financial assistance for the purposes of the board's carrying out activities relating to tourism;

        (iii) provision by a local authority to such a board of staff; and

    (c) section 171A(3) of this Act shall apply to this section with the substitution for any references to a person of references to an area tourist board.".

DEFINITIONS

"1973 Act": s.183(1).
"area tourist board": new subs. (8).
"local authority": s.235(1) of the 1973 Act, as amended by Sched. 13.
"participate": new subs. (8).

GENERAL NOTE

This section should be read together with ss.172–175. See, in particular, the General Note on s.172 where, *inter alia*, it is explained that a new s.90 of the 1973 Act is to be substituted by this section. The new section gives revised powers to local authorities to undertake tourism-related activities, which take account of the lead role to be taken by area tourist boards from April 1, 1996.

Thus the principal powers are given by the new subs. (1). These include functions they may themselves perform, but para. (d) permits them to "participate" in the local area tourist board. The term to "participate" is explained in subs. (8)(b) and there defined to include giving to the board "financial assistance", which is, in turn, to be understood, by virtue of subs. (8)(c), to include those categories of assistance listed in the new s.171A(3) of the 1973 Act inserted by s.171 of this Act.

Other powers positively conferred on local authorities are those contained in subs. (5) (contributions towards expenses of other persons for certain activities) and subs. (6), which allows the appointment of staff but, by applying s.65 of the 1973 Act, permits an authority to enter into an agreement with an area tourist board to place its staff at the disposal of the board.

In recognition of the priority to be given to the tourist boards, however, the powers given to local authorities are circumscribed in the terms laid down in subss. (2)–(4). Subject to the exceptions specified in subs. (3), a local authority may not undertake those promotional functions listed in subs. (2) (encouraging visitors, providing information, etc.), to which others may be added in regulations made by the Secretary of State. Subsection (4) restricts the purposes for which local authorities may carry on tourist-related functions through other persons or bodies corporate.

It will be noted that, just as the Secretary of State may, by regulations, extend the categories of activities prohibited to local authorities (subs. 2(c)), he is also specifically empowered to permit (by prior consent given in writing) certain activities which are (or might be) forbidden to local authorities.

PART V

GENERAL AND SUPPLEMENTARY

General

Parliamentary disqualification

177.—(1) Schedule 1 to the House of Commons Disqualification Act 1975 shall be amended as mentioned in subsections (2) and (3) below.

(2) In Part II (bodies of which all members are disqualified for membership of the House of Commons), there shall be inserted at the appropriate places the following entries—

"The East of Scotland Water Authority.";
"The North of Scotland Water Authority.";
"The Scottish Children's Reporter Administration.";
"The Scottish Water and Sewerage Customers Council or any committee established by that council under paragraph 10(1) of Schedule 9 to the Local Government etc. (Scotland) Act 1994."; and
"The West of Scotland Water Authority.".

(3) In Part III (other disqualifying offices) there shall be inserted at the appropriate places the following entries—

"Any member of the staff commission established by virtue of section 12 of the Local Government etc. (Scotland) Act 1994.";
"Any member of a residuary body established by virtue of section 18 of the Local Government etc. (Scotland) Act 1994 who is in receipt of remuneration."; and
"Any member of the property commission established by virtue of section 19 of the Local Government etc. (Scotland) Act 1994.".

GENERAL NOTE
   Schedule 1 to the House of Commons Disqualification Act 1975 (c. 24) lists the various bodies, membership of which disqualifies a person from being a member of the House of Commons and the other "disqualifying offices". This section adds to the disqualified list the members of the Water Authorities and other bodies created by this Act.

Financial provisions

178.—(1) There shall be paid out of money provided by Parliament—
  (a) any expenses of the Secretary of State incurred in consequence of the provisions (other than section 84(5)) of this Act; and
  (b) any increase attributable to this Act in the sums payable out of money so provided under any other enactment.

(2) There shall be paid out of the National Loans Fund any sums issued to the Secretary of State under section 84(5) of this Act.

(3) There shall be paid into—
  (a) the National Loans Fund any sums paid to the Secretary of State under section 84(5) of this Act; and
  (b) the Consolidated Fund any sums paid to the Secretary of State in consequence of any other provision of this Act.

GENERAL NOTE
   This section gives formal authority for the payment, out of funds provided by Parliament (and via the National Loans Fund in respect of loans to the new water authorities under s.84(5)), of the expenses to be incurred by the Secretary of State; and for payments to the National Loans Fund and the Consolidated Fund of sums paid to the Secretary of State.

Savings

179.—(1) The repeal by this Act of—
  (a) sections 65, 66 and 67;

(b) the words from "; and section 65" to the end in section 76H(8); and
(c) the words ", save in sections 64 to 67," in the definition of "owner" in
    section 109(1),
of the 1980 Act, shall not affect the operation of the said sections 65, 66 and 67
as respects—
   (i)   any charging order made before 1st April 1996 under subsection (1) or
        (3) of section 65 (including any charging order so made by virtue of the
        said section 76H(8));
  (ii)   any order made before that date under subsection (2) of section 66; or
 (iii)   any right conferred by those sections to recover expenditure provided
        that the expenditure was incurred before that date.
(2) The repeal by this Act of the said section 65 shall not affect that section's application, under subsection (4) of section 75 of the Agricultural
Holdings (Scotland) Act 1991, to such charging orders as are mentioned in
subsection (2) or (3) of the said section 75.
(3) The repeal by this Act—
(a) of section 47 of the 1968 Act shall not affect the operation of that sec-
    tion as respects—
    (i) any charging order made before 1st April 1996 under subsec-
        tion (1) of that section; or
    (ii) any right conferred by that section to recover expenditure
        provided that the expenditure was incurred before that date;
(b) of the said sections 65, 66 and 67 shall not affect those sections' appli-
    cation, under subsection (2) or (3) of the said section 47, to such charg-
    ing orders as are mentioned in sub-paragraph (i) of paragraph (a)
    above or, as the case may be, for the purpose of the right of recovery
    mentioned in sub-paragraph (ii) of that paragraph.
(4) Without prejudice to subsection (4) of section 72 of the 1980 Act (certain byelaws to cease to have effect at expiration of a specific period unless
extended), or to that subsection as it applies by virtue of section 63(10) of the
Countryside (Scotland) Act 1967 (byelaws as respects recreational use of
waterway or land), a byelaw made by the Board or by any other transferor as
water authority, or having effect, immediately before the transfer date, as if
so made by virtue of section 73(3) of the 1980 Act (power of Secretary of
State to require making of byelaws), shall on and after that date have effect,
though only within the area in which it had effect immediately before that
date, as if made by the transferee as water authority, with any reference in the
byelaws to the transferor being construed, in so far as the context admits, as a
reference to the transferee.
(5) In subsection (4) above, "transferor" and "transferee" mean the transferor and transferee in a transfer scheme; and for the purposes of that subsection the transferee where the transferor is the Board shall be taken to be the
East of Scotland Water Authority only.
(6) Section 125 of this Act applies for the interpretation of subsections (1)
to (5) above as that section applies for the interpretation of Part II of this Act.

DEFINITIONS
  "1968 Act": subs. (6); s.125.
  "1980 Act": subs. (6); s.125.
  "transfer scheme": subs. (6); s.125.
  "transferee": subs. (5).
  "transferor": subs. (5).

GENERAL NOTE
  This section makes provision for the saving of the effect of certain charging orders made under
sections of the Water (Scotland) Act 1980, the Agricultural Holdings (Scotland) Act 1991
(c. 55), and the Sewerage (Scotland) Act 1968, which are repealed by this Act, where it is

necessary for the successor water authorities to be able to rely on the orders to recover expenditure incurred before April 1, 1996 (subss. (1)–(3)). Similarly the effect of certain water authority byelaws is preserved, as if made by the new authorities, but only in relation to the areas to which they formerly applied (subss. (4)–(5)).

Supplementary

Minor and consequential amendments and repeals

180.—(1) Schedule 13 to this Act, which contains minor amendments and amendments consequential upon the provisions of this Act, shall have effect.

(2) The enactments mentioned in Schedule 14 to this Act (which include spent provisions) are hereby repealed to the extent specified in the third column of that Schedule.

GENERAL NOTE

Most of the amendments and repeals in Scheds. 13 and 14 are indeed "minor and consequential". In particular most of the provisions in Sched. 13 are "translations" to take account of the new authorities from April 1996.

Consequential and supplementary provisions

181.—(1) The Secretary of State may at any time, whether before or after 1st April 1996, by order make such incidental, consequential, transitional or supplementary provisions as may appear to him to be necessary or expedient—

(a) for the general or any particular purposes of this Act or in consequence of any of the provisions thereof or for giving full effect thereto; or

(b) in consequence of such of the provisions of this Act or of any other Act passed in the same session as this Act as apply to any area or authority affected by this Act,

and nothing in any other provision of this Act shall be construed as prejudicing the generality of this subsection.

(2) An order under this section may—

(a) make provision, in the case of any body, person, funds or matter affected by this Act, for the transition from the provisions of any enactment to the provisions of this Act, but nothing in such an order shall be inconsistent with any provision of this Act;

(b) in relation to the period prior to 1st April 1996, and subject to such modifications as the Secretary of State thinks necessary or expedient, apply to the new authorities any enactment relating to a local authority in Scotland;

(c) apply, with or without modifications, or amend, repeal or revoke (with or without savings) any provision of an Act passed before this Act or in the same Session, or an instrument made under such an Act before 1st April 1996; or

(d) make savings, or additional savings, from the effect of any repeal made by this Act.

(3) Subject to subsection (6) below, anything done or treated by virtue of any enactment as having been done by or to or in relation to an existing local authority in connection with the discharge of any of their functions shall, as from 1st April 1996, be treated as having been done by, to or in relation to the new authority by whom those functions become exercisable on and after that date by virtue of this Act; and any such thing shall as from that date have effect as if any reference therein to a specified existing local authority by whom those functions were exercisable before that date were a reference to the new authority by whom those functions become exercisable.

(4) Without prejudice to the generality of subsection (3) above, the things to which it refers include—

(a) any agreement, instrument, decision, designation, determination, declaration or order made or treated as having been made by an existing local authority;

(b) any notice or direction given or treated as given by or to such an authority;

(c) any licence, certificate, permission, consent, approval, refusal, exemption, dispensation or relaxation granted or treated as granted by or to such an authority;

(d) any application, request, proposal or objection made or treated as made by or to such an authority;

(e) any fee paid to or by such an authority;

(f) any condition or requirement imposed or treated as imposed by or on such an authority;

(g) any proceedings instituted by or against any such authority; or

(h) any appeal allowed by or in favour of or against such an authority.

(5) If there is any doubt as to the identity of the new authority to whom any particular functions are so transferred, that authority shall be taken to be such as may be specified in a direction given by the Secretary of State.

(6) Subsection (3) above is without prejudice to any express provision made by, or by any instrument or transfer scheme made under, this Act, but has effect subject to any provision to the contrary so made and in particular may be excluded from applying, either wholly or to any specified extent, in any particular case by an order made by the Secretary of State.

(7) Section 25 of the 1973 Act (transitional agreements as to property and finance) shall apply for the purposes of Parts I and V of this Act as if any reference to an order under Part II of that Act included a reference to any provision of Part I of this Act or to any provision of any instrument made under Part I or this Part of this Act, but any agreement made by virtue of this subsection may only be made by new authorities and after 31st March 1996.

(8) An order under this section shall be made by statutory instrument subject to annulment in pursuance of a resolution of either House of Parliament.

(9) In this section—

"existing local authority" includes a joint committee and a joint board and a reporter appointed under section 36(1) of the Social Work (Scotland) Act 1968;

"joint committee" and "joint board" have the meanings given by section 235(1) of the 1973 Act; and

"new authority" means—

(a) any of the authorities constituted under section 2 of this Act;

(b) a joint committee and a joint board;

(c) a residuary body;

(d) the Strathclyde Passenger Transport Authority;

(e) a new water and sewerage authority within the meaning of Part II of this Act;

(f) the Principal Reporter; and

(g) the Scottish Children's Reporter Administration.

DEFINITIONS

"1973 Act": s.183(1).
"existing local authority": subs. (9).
"joint board": subs. (9).
"joint committee": subs. (9).
"new authority": subs. (9).

GENERAL NOTE

This section enables the making of certain "consequential and supplementary provisions". They fall into three groups:

Subss. (1), (2) and (8)

These give power to the Secretary of State to make, by order made by statutory instrument, any incidental, consequential, etc., provisions for the general purposes laid down in subs. (1) and the further purposes (including the power to amend or revoke Acts of Parliament) in subs. (2).

Subss. (3)–(6)

These make provision (subject to subs. (6)) to ensure the continuity of effect of things done and obligations entered into (including those listed in subs. (4)) by local authorities before April 1, 1996 as if they were done or entered into by new authorities, *e.g.* contracts will bind successor authorities; those authorities will take continuing responsibility for actions being investigated by the local ombudsman. Doubts as to which is a successor, *i.e.* "new authority" (see subs. (9)) are to be resolved by directions given by the Secretary of State (subs. (5)).

Subs. (7)

Section 25 of the 1973 Act provides for agreements as to property and finance to be made between authorities following boundary reviews, or, failing agreement, for reference to an arbiter. This subsection extends the provisions of that section to circumstances affected by the provisions of Part I of this Act, or by a provision under an instrument made under Part I *OR* Part V of this Act.

Further transitional provisions

182.—(1) Until 1st April 1996—

(a) section 70 of the 1973 Act (acquisition of land by agreement) shall have effect as if, in subsection (1), after paragraph (b) there were inserted ", or

    (c) there being provided by some person other than themselves a system, to which the public shall have access, of drains, sewers or sewage treatment works,";

(b) section 71 of the 1973 Act (acquisition of land compulsorily) shall have effect as if, in subsection (1), after "enactment" there were inserted "or of there being provided by some person other than themselves a system, to which the public shall have access, of drains, sewers or sewage treatment works"; and

(c) section 15 of the Water (Scotland) Act 1980 (power to acquire land) shall have effect as if, at the end of each of subsections (1) and (3), there were added "or for the purpose of there being provided by some person other than themselves a supply of water to the public".

(2) If the Secretary of State provides, by order under section 184(2) of this Act, that any provision of Part II of (or of Schedule 13 to) this Act which—

(a) amends section 1, 16, 21(1), 22, 23 or 48 of the Sewerage (Scotland) Act 1968 or section 32 of the Control of Pollution Act 1974; or

(b) adds to the said Act of 1968 a new section 3A or 16A or to section 20 of that Act a new subsection (5),

shall come into force before 1st April 1996, he may provide in the order that the section amended, or as the case may be the section or subsection added, shall until that date apply as if modified in such manner as he shall specify in the order; the modifications being such as appear to him to be requisite having regard to the fact that some other provision of that Part (or that Schedule) is not for the time being in effect.

DEFINITIONS

"1973 Act": s.183(1).

GENERAL NOTE

This section was added as a new clause at the House of Lords Report stage to make further transitional provisions. As explained by the Minister of State (see *Hansard*, H.L. Vol. 558, col.

298) it enables existing local authorities to make use of the Private Finance Initiative provisions. See the notes to ss.98 and 101.

Subs. (1)

This is designed to ensure that the three powers of local authority land acquisition which are specified may be used, in the period up to April 1, 1996, by a local authority to anticipate the role of one of the new water and sewerage authorities. The latter assume their own responsibilities from that date, and will have the power under s.98 to acquire land for the provision by some other person of, *inter alia*, a supply of water to the public.

Subs. (2)

This subsection makes wider provision for the possibility that the Private Finance Initiative powers may be, in advance of the creation of the new water and sewerage authorities, conferred on existing local authorities (by the amendments made principally to the Sewerage (Scotland) Act 1968), by allowing the powers to be conferred in modified terms. For an initial use of this power in the Local Government etc. (Scotland) Act 1994 (Commencement No. 1) Order 1994 (S.I. 1994 No. 2850), see note on Commencement.

Interpretation and amendment of statutory references

183.—(1) In this Act, unless the context otherwise requires—
"residuary body" shall be construed in accordance with section 18 of this
Act;
"the Valuation Acts" means the Lands Valuation (Scotland) Act 1854,
the Acts amending that Act and any other enactment relating to
valuation;
"the 1973 Act" means the Local Government (Scotland) Act 1973; and
"the 1975 Act" means the Local Government (Scotland) Act 1975.
(2) Subject to section 59 of this Act and to any particular amendment of any enactment made by or under this Act—
(a) any reference in any enactment to a local authority within the meaning
of the 1973 Act (whether expressed as a reference to such an authority,
or to a regional, islands or district council, or otherwise); or
(b) any reference in any enactment to a local authority within the meaning
of the Local Government (Scotland) Act 1947 ("the 1947 Act") which,
by virtue of paragraph 1(2) of Schedule 27 to the 1973 Act, falls to be
construed as a reference to a local authority within the meaning of the
1973 Act,
shall be construed as a reference to a council constituted under section 2 of this Act.
(3) For the purpose of translating any reference, however expressed, in any enactment to a local authority within the meaning of either the 1973 Act or the 1947 Act to a reference to a council constituted under section 2 of this Act, the Secretary of State may by order made by statutory instrument make such amendments to any such enactment as he considers necessary or expedient.
(4) Subject to any particular amendment of any enactment made by this Act, any reference in any enactment to—
(a) the director of education shall in relation to any purpose be construed
as a reference to the officer appointed by a local authority for that
purpose;
(b) the director of social work shall be construed as a reference to the chief
social work officer.
(5) Any reference in any enactment, other than the Social Work (Scotland) Act 1968 or the Criminal Procedure (Scotland) Act 1975 (in respect of which Acts particular provision is made in Schedule 13 to this Act), to a reporter appointed under section 36(1) of the former Act shall be construed as a reference to the Principal Reporter.

(6) In this section "enactment" means any enactment or instrument made under an enactment, whether passed or made before or after the coming into force of this section; but does not include this Act or any instrument made under this Act.

DEFINITIONS
"1947 Act": subs. (2).
"1973 Act": subs. (1).
"1975 Act": subs. (1).
"enactment": subs. (6).
"residuary body": subs. (1).
"the Valuation Acts": subs. (1).

GENERAL NOTE
This is a general interpretation section which also makes some general amendments to earlier or future enactments (as interpreted by subs. (6)).

Subs. (1)
There are other interpretation sections at s.61 and s.125.
The term "Valuation Acts" is used in ss.27 and 29 of the Act and, as inserted into the Valuation and Rating (Scotland) Act 1956, in s.161.

Subs. (2)
This makes general provision to ensure that legislation which refers to local authorities within the meaning of the 1973 Act (*i.e.* the regional, district and islands councils established by that Act) or of the Local Government (Scotland) Act 1947 (as defined by para. 1(2) of Sched. 27 to the 1973 Act) is construed as referring to a council constituted by s.2 of the 1994 Act. It should be noted that many of the amendments made to the 1973 Act by Sched. 13 to this Act substitute the terminology of "local authority" for the different categories of council created by the 1973 Act and, in particular, that (by para. 92(66) of Sched. 13) the definition of "local authority" in the 1973 Act is amended to mean a council constituted under s.2 of the 1994 Act.

Subs. (3)
In the light of all the amendments made by Sched. 13 to the Act, many of which update references in existing legislation to local authorities, and in the light too of subs. (2) of this section, the power of amendment in this subsection must be viewed as one of last resort. The terminology of "translating" references appears to be new to the statute book and may lead to speculation as to its meaning and thus the scope of the power.

Subs. (4)
The obligation on councils to appoint an officer by the name of Director of Education (under s.78 of the Education (Scotland) Act 1980) is repealed by Sched. 13, para. 118(4) and Sched. 14. This subsection provides that any statutory reference to such an office appointed for any purpose is to be interpreted as an officer appointed for that purpose. See the note on s.31. On the other hand, the change made by s.45 (from Director of Social Work to Chief Social Work Officer) requires a different form of translation.

Subs. (5)
This is designed to ensure that, with the exception of the Social Work (Scotland) Act 1968, and the Criminal Procedure (Scotland) Act 1975 for which specific provision is made, a reference to a (children's panel) reporter is to be construed as a reference to the Principal Reporter created by s.127 of the Act.

Short title, commencement and extent

184.—(1) This Act may be cited as the Local Government etc. (Scotland) Act 1994.

(2) This Act, except section 163, shall come into force on such day as the Secretary of State may by order made by statutory instrument appoint, and different days may be appointed for different purposes.

(3) An order under subsection (2) above may contain such transitional provisions and savings as appear to the Secretary of State to be necessary or expedient in connection with the provisions brought into force.

(4) This Act shall extend to Scotland only.

GENERAL NOTE
Apart from s.163 (Guarantees by Strathclyde Passenger Transport Authority) which came into effect at Royal Assent, the Act is to be brought into effect by order. See the note on Commencement in the introductory section of the annotations. On subs. (4) and the restriction of the scope of the Act to Scotland, see the note on s.107.

SCHEDULES

Section 1(2) and (4)   SCHEDULE 1

NEW LOCAL GOVERNMENT AREAS

PART I

New areas

New local government area	Comprising area of
City of Aberdeen.	Aberdeen District Council.
Aberdeenshire.	Banff and Buchan District Council; Gordon District Council; Kincardine and Deeside District Council.
Angus.	Angus District Council; Tayside electoral divisions 30 (Monifieth) and 31 (Sidlaw) (except first, polling district PDB; secondly, that part of polling district PDC lying to the east and south of a line commencing at the junction of unnamed roads at grid reference NO 3297 3106; then running northwest to the crossroads at Mains of Fowlis at grid reference NO 3247 3239; then running northeastward along the unnamed road between Mains of Fowlis and Liff to the western curtilage of the property known as Cater-Milly at grid reference NO 3300 3276; then running southward and eastward along the western and southern curtilages of the said property to the field boundary at grid reference NO 3308 3259; then continuing southeastward along the said field boundary and across the Liff Burn to the eastern perimeter of the woodland known as Gray Den at grid reference NO 3332 3239; then running north and east along the path running along the said eastern perimeter of Gray Den to its junction with the unnamed track between Liff and Mains of Gray at grid reference NO 3336 3273; then running north to the junction of the said track and the southern curtilage of the property known as Gray Cottage; then running northeastward along the southern curtilages of Gray Cottage, Learsmonth House, Woodend Cottages and No. 31 Church Road to the southern edge of Church Road where it runs between Liff and the Royal Dundee Liff Hospital then running eastward along the continuation of the said road past the northern perimeter of the said Hospital to the road junction at grid refer-

New local government area	Comprising area of
	ence NO 3537 3276; thirdly, that part of polling district ADA lying to the east and south of a line commencing at a point on the A923 road at grid reference NO 3560 3378; then running north along the eastern curtilage of No. 100 Coupar Angus Road and northwestwards along the northern curtilages of Nos. 100 to 122 Coupar Angus Road to the eastern perimeter of Blairfield Road; then northwards along the said eastern perimeter to the field boundary at grid reference NO 3533 3436; then northeastwards along the said field boundary to its junction with Templeton Road at grid reference NO 3577 3455; fourthly, that part of polling district ADC lying to the east and south of a line commencing at grid reference NO 3660 3474 then running northward to the northwest corner of Baldragon Wood at grid reference NO 3658 3496; then running eastward along the northern perimeter of the said wood and continuing along the field boundary to grid reference NO 3725 3491; fifthly, those parts of polling districts ADE and ADF lying to the east and south of a line commencing on the southern boundary of polling district ADE on the A90 road at grid reference NO 4166 3458; then running northwards along the said A90 road to its intersection with Emmock Road at grid reference NO 4180 3508 then running southeastwards along the said Emmock Road to its junction with the unnamed road leading to South Powrie and Barns of Wedderburn then eastwards along the said unnamed road as far as the northwestern curtilage of Barns of Wedderburn at grid reference NO 4347 3469; then running southwestwards and southeastwards along the northwestern and southwestern perimeter of the said property to the point where it meets the unnamed road leading to Fintry at grid reference NO 4347 3458; then running southwestwards along the said unnamed road to the road junction at grid reference NO 4345 3452; and sixthly, those parts of polling districts EDN, EDQ, PDA, WED, WEE, WEF and WEG lying within its boundary).
Argyll and Bute.	Argyll and Bute District Council; Strathclyde electoral division 7 (Helensburgh) and, in Strathclyde electoral division 8 (Vale of Leven), polling district DB77 and that part of polling district DB78 lying north of a line commencing at grid reference NS 3464 8256; then running northeastwards to the field corner at grid reference NS 3469 8264; then southeastwards to the field junction at grid reference NS 3608 8198; then northeastwards to the field

New local government area	Comprising area of
	junction at grid reference NS 3658 8242; then northwestwards to the junction of the field boundary and an unnamed burn at grid reference NS 3613 8269; then generally northeastwards along the course of the said burn to where it meets Loch Lomond at grid reference NS 3743 8336; then due northeastwards from that point to the eastern boundary of the said polling district in Loch Lomond.
East Ayrshire.	Kilmarnock and Loudoun District Council and Cumnock and Doon Valley District Council.
North Ayrshire.	Cunninghame District Council.
South Ayrshire.	Kyle and Carrick District Council.
The Borders.	Borders Regional Council.
Clackmannan.	Clackmannan District Council.
Dumbarton and Clydebank.	Clydebank District Council; Strathclyde electoral divisions 6 (Dumbarton) and 8 (Vale of Leven) (except the areas of the said electoral division 8 included in Argyll and Bute).
Dumfries and Galloway.	Dumfries and Galloway Regional Council.
East Dunbartonshire.	Bearsden and Milngavie District Council; Strathclyde electoral divisions 43 (Kirkintilloch), 44 (Strathkelvin North), 45 (Bishopbriggs) and the South Lenzie/Waterside district ward in Strathclyde electoral division 46 (Chryston).
City of Dundee.	City of Dundee District Council (except Tayside electoral division 30 (Monifieth) and those parts of 31 (Sidlaw) which are in Angus or Perthshire and Kinross).
City of Edinburgh.	City of Edinburgh District Council.
Falkirk.	Falkirk District Council.
Fife.	Fife Regional Council.
City of Glasgow.	City of Glasgow District Council except Strathclyde electoral divisions 37 (Rutherglen/Fernhill), 38 (Cambuslang/Halfway) and, in 35 (King's Park/Toryglen), polling districts RU03, RU04, RU09 and RU18.
Highland.	Highland Regional Council.
Inverclyde.	Inverclyde District Council.
North Lanarkshire.	Cumbernauld and Kilsyth, Motherwell and Monklands District Councils; Strathclyde electoral division 46 (Chryston) (except South Lenzie/Waterside district ward).
South Lanarkshire.	Clydesdale, Hamilton and East Kilbride District Councils; Strathclyde electoral divisions 37 (Rutherglen/Fernhill), 38 (Cambuslang/Halfway) and, in 35 (King's Park/Toryglen), polling districts RU03, RU04, RU09 and RU18.
East Lothian.	East Lothian District Council.
Midlothian.	Midlothian District Council.
West Lothian.	West Lothian District Council.
Moray.	Moray District Council.
Orkney Islands.	Orkney Islands Council.
Perthshire and Kinross.	Perth and Kinross District Council and, in Tayside electoral division 31 (Sidlaw), polling district PDB and that part of polling district PDA

New local government area	Comprising area of
	lying to the south of a line commencing at a point adjacent to Starr Inn Farm at grid reference NO 3309 3051 on the A90 road; then running eastward along the said road to the junction at grid reference NO 3462 3079.
East Renfrewshire.	Eastwood District Council; Strathclyde electoral division 79 (Barrhead).
Renfrewshire.	Renfrew District Council (except Strathclyde electoral division 79 (Barrhead)).
Shetland Islands.	Shetland Islands Council.
Stirling.	Stirling District Council.
Western Isles.	Western Isles Islands Council.

PART II

Provisions as to boundaries

1. The boundaries of the new local government areas shall be mered by Ordnance Survey.
2. In this Schedule—
    "electoral division" means an electoral division for regional council elections as at 5th May 1994;
    "polling district" means a polling district for regional council elections as at 1st December 1993; and
    "ward" means a ward for district council elections as at 7th May 1992.

Section 7(1)   SCHEDULE 2

ESTABLISHMENT OF NEW LOCAL AUTHORITIES

First elections of councillors

1.—(1) For the purpose of any election of councillors held before the relevant year of election, every local government area shall be divided into such electoral wards as may be specified in a direction made by the Secretary of State after carrying out, either before or after the passing of this Act, such consultation as he considers appropriate.

(2) In this paragraph "relevant year of election" means, in relation to a local government area, the first year of ordinary election of councillors for that area occurring after the making of an order constituting the new electoral wards of that local government area in consequence of a review under Schedule 5 to the 1973 Act.

(3) A direction under this paragraph may contain such incidental, consequential, transitional or supplementary provision as the Secretary of State may consider to be appropriate.

2.—(1) Notwithstanding the provisions of section 41(1) (returning officer to be an officer of the council) of the Representation of the People Act 1983 ("the 1983 Act"), at the elections of councillors to be held on 6th April 1995, the returning officer shall be an officer appointed by such regional or district council as the Secretary of State may direct.

(2) Section 42(5) (expenses of election) of the 1983 Act shall not apply to any such election, but all expenditure properly incurred by a returning officer or other officer shall be paid in the first instance by the council by whom the returning officer was appointed and shall be defrayed by the existing authorities concerned in such proportions as may be agreed between them or, failing such agreement, by such of them, and in such proportions, as may be determined by the Secretary of State.

(3) In this paragraph "existing authorities" means the authorities all or part of whose area is included in the area of the new authority whose council is being elected.

Qualification for membership

3. For the purposes of section 29 of the 1973 Act, in its application to a candidate for membership of a new local authority, the new local authority areas shall be treated as having been established not less than twelve months before the day of his nomination as such a candidate.

First meetings of new councils

4.—(1) The first meeting of each new council shall be held within twenty-one days immediately following the day of election.

(2) The first meeting shall be convened by a person designated for that purpose by the Secretary of State, and shall be held at such place as that person may appoint.

(3) The notice of the meeting required by paragraph 2(1) of Schedule 7 to the 1973 Act shall, in the case of the first meeting, be published at the place where the meeting is to be held, and the summons to attend the meeting required by that paragraph shall be signed by the person designated as mentioned in sub-paragraph (2) above.

5.—(1) Until the completion of the election of a convener at the first meeting of a new council, the returning officer appointed as mentioned in paragraph 2 above, or failing him any such councillor as may be selected by the councillors meeting together, shall exercise any functions falling to be exercised by the convener of the council, but the person so acting as convener shall not be entitled to vote unless he is a councillor for the new area.

(2) At the first meeting of a new council the person designated as mentioned in paragraph 4(2) above shall exercise any functions falling to be exercised by the proper officer of the new council in relation to the meeting.

(3) The standing orders for the regulation of the proceedings and business of an existing authority, designated by the Secretary of State, shall apply at the first meeting of a new council.

Suspension of elections

6. No election of councillors of an existing local authority shall be held on or after 16th November 1994, except an election to fill a casual vacancy where the date of the election has been fixed in accordance with section 37(1) of the 1973 Act before 16th November 1994; and on and after that date any such casual vacancy shall be filled by the authority themselves electing a person to fill that vacancy.

Election of convener and depute convener after 1st April 1996

7.—(1) The term of office of the convener and any depute convener elected to a council following the ordinary election on 6th April 1995 shall terminate on the day of the first meeting of the council held on or after 1st April 1996.

(2) At that meeting the election of a convener shall be the first business.

(3) The retiring convener shall be eligible for re-election, but shall in any event preside until a convener has been elected.

Section 18(10)　　　　　　SCHEDULE 3

Residuary Bodies

Incorporation

1. A residuary body shall—
(a) be a body corporate; and
(b) have a common seal.

Status

2. A residuary body shall not be regarded as acting on behalf of the Crown and neither that body nor its members, officers or servants shall be regarded as Crown servants.

Membership

3.—(1) Subject to the provisions of this paragraph, every member of a residuary body shall hold and vacate his office in accordance with the terms of his appointment.

(2) A residuary body shall consist of not less than three and not more than seven members appointed by the Secretary of State; and the Secretary of State shall appoint one of those members to be chairman and may appoint another to be deputy chairman of that body.

(3) The Secretary of State may by order alter either of the numbers specified in sub-paragraph (2) above.

(4) Any member may resign by notice in writing to the Secretary of State, and the chairman or deputy chairman may by a like notice resign his office as such.

(5) The Secretary of State may remove a member from office if satisfied that the member—
(a) has had his estate sequestrated, has made any arrangement with his creditors, has been adjudged bankrupt or has granted a trust deed or a composition contract for his creditors;
(b) is incapacitated by physical or mental illness;
(c) has been absent from meetings of the body for a period of three months otherwise than for a reason approved by the body; or

(d) is in the opinion of the Secretary of State otherwise unable or unfit to discharge the functions of a member.

(6) If the chairman or deputy chairman ceases to be a member he shall also cease to be chairman or deputy chairman.

(7) An order under this paragraph shall be made by statutory instrument subject to annulment by resolution of either House of Parliament.

4. The Secretary of State shall satisfy himself—

(a) before he appoints a person under paragraph 3(2) above, that the person has no financial or other interest likely to affect prejudicially performance as a member of the residuary body in question;

(b) from time to time, that each person so appointed continues, and has continued, to have no such interest.

5. A person in respect of whom the Secretary of State requires to be satisfied as is mentioned in paragraph 4(b) above shall, whenever requested by the Secretary of State to do so, furnish the Secretary of State with such information as the Secretary of State may consider necessary for the purposes of that requirement.

Remuneration etc. of members

6.—(1) A residuary body shall pay to each member such remuneration and allowances (if any) as the Secretary of State may with the consent of the Treasury determine.

(2) As regards any member of a residuary body in whose case the Secretary of State may so determine, the body shall pay or make provision for the payment of such sums by way of pension, allowances and gratuities to or in respect of him as the Secretary of State may with the consent of the Treasury determine.

(3) Where a person ceases to be a member of a residuary body otherwise than on the expiration of his term of office and it appears to the Secretary of State that there are special circumstances which make it right for him to receive compensation, the body shall pay as compensation to that person such amount as the Secretary of State may with the consent of the Treasury determine.

(4) Where an employee of a residuary body becomes a member of that body and immediately before becoming a member was by reference to his employment by that body participating in a superannuation scheme, the body may make provision for him to continue to participate in that scheme, on terms and conditions determined by the body with the consent of the Secretary of State, as if his service as a member were service as an employee; and such scheme shall have effect subject to any provision made under this sub-paragraph.

Staff

7. A residuary body may appoint, on such terms and conditions as they may, with the approval of the Secretary of State given with the consent of the Treasury, determine such employees as they think fit.

8.—(1) A residuary body shall, in the case of such of their employees or former employees as they may, with the approval of the Secretary of State given with the consent of the Treasury, determine—

(a) pay such pensions, allowances or gratuities to or in respect of those employees;

(b) make such payments towards provision of such pensions, allowances or gratuities; or

(c) provide and maintain such schemes (whether contributory or not) for the payment of such pensions allowances or gratuities,

as they may, with the approval of the Secretary of State given with the consent of the Treasury, determine.

(2) The reference in sub-paragraph (1) above to pensions, allowances or gratuities in respect of employees of a residuary body includes a reference to pensions, allowances or gratuities by way of compensation to or in respect of any such employee who suffers loss of office or employment.

Proceedings

9.—(1) A member of a residuary body who is directly or indirectly interested in—

(a) a contract made or proposed to be made by them; or

(b) any other matter whatsoever which falls to be considered by them,

shall as soon as is practicable disclose the nature of his interest at a meeting of the body; and the disclosure shall be recorded in the minutes of the meeting.

(2) In the case mentioned in—

(a) head (a) of sub-paragraph (1) above, the member shall not take part in any deliberation or decision of the body with respect to the contract;

(b) head (b) of that sub-paragraph, the member shall not take part in any deliberation or decision of the body with respect to the matter if the body decide that the interest in question might affect prejudicially his consideration of the matter.

(3) For the purposes of this paragraph, a notice to the effect that a person is a member of a specified body corporate or firm and is to be regarded as interested in any contract which is made with the body corporate or firm after the date of the notice, and in any other matter whatsoever concerning the body corporate or firm which falls to be considered after that date, shall if given at a meeting of the residuary body be a sufficient disclosure of the person's interest to the body.

(4) For the purposes of this paragraph, disclosure at a meeting may be made without the attendance in person of the member in question provided that he takes reasonable steps to ensure that the matter disclosed is raised and taken into consideration at the meeting.

10.—(1) A residuary body shall regulate its own proceedings.

(2) The validity of any proceedings of a residuary body shall not be affected by any vacancy among its members or by any defect in the appointment of any of its members, or by any failure to comply with any requirement of paragraph 9 above.

11.—(1) For a purpose other than is mentioned in sub-paragraph (2) below, a document is validly executed by a residuary body if signed on behalf of that body by their chairman, or by another of their members, or by a person authorised to sign the document on their behalf.

(2) For the purposes of any enactment or rule of law relating to the authentication of documents, a document is validly executed by a residuary body if subscribed on behalf of the body by being executed in accordance with the provisions of sub-paragraph (1) above.

(3) A document which bears to have been executed by a residuary body in accordance with sub-paragraph (2) above shall, in relation to such execution, be a probative document if—

(a) the subscription of the document bears to have been attested by at least one witness; or

(b) the document bears to be sealed with the seal of the body.

Delegation

12.—(1) Anything authorised or required by or under any enactment to be done by a residuary body may be done by any committee formed by them which, or by any of its members or officers who, is authorised (generally or specifically) for the purpose by the body.

(2) Nothing in sub-paragraph (1) above shall prevent a residuary body from doing anything that a committee, member or officer has been authorised to do.

Acquisition and disposal of land

13.—(1) A residuary body may with the consent of the Secretary of State acquire by agreement any land required by it for carrying out its functions.

(2) A residuary body may dispose of any land held by it in such manner as it wishes and shall dispose of any land held by it which is not required by it for carrying out its functions.

Borrowing and lending

14. A residuary body may, subject to any directions by the Secretary of State, borrow and lend money for the purpose of carrying out any of their functions.

Provision of services

15.—(1) A residuary body may by agreement with any relevant new authority, and on such terms as to payment or otherwise as the parties consider appropriate, provide that authority with professional or technical services.

(2) In this paragraph "relevant new authority", in relation to a residuary body, means a new authority exercising functions in the area for which that body is established.

Provision of information by councils

16. A local authority shall, on request, supply a residuary body with such information as the body may reasonably require from that authority for the purpose of carrying out their functions.

Reports and information

17.—(1) A residuary body shall publish an annual report on the discharge of its functions.

(2) A residuary body shall send to the Secretary of State a copy of any report made by it under sub-paragraph (1) above and the Secretary of State shall lay copies of it before each House of Parliament.

(3) A residuary body shall furnish the Secretary of State with such information relating to the discharge of its functions as he may require, and for that purpose shall permit any person author-

ised by him to inspect and make copies of any accounts or other documents of the body and shall afford such explanation of them as that person or the Secretary of State may require.

Supervision by Commissioner for Local Administration in Scotland

18. A residuary body established under this Act shall be included among the authorities to which Part II of the 1975 Act applies.

Section 33(2)   SCHEDULE 4

Amendments of the 1972 Act

1. The 1972 Act shall be amended in accordance with this Schedule.
2. In section 4 (survey of planning districts)
(a) for subsection (1) substitute—
"(1) It shall be the duty of the planning authority to keep under review the matters which may be expected to affect the development of their district or the planning of its development.";
(b) for subsection (2) substitute—
"(2) A planning authority may, if they think fit, institute a fresh survey, examining the matters referred to in subsection (1) above, of the whole or any part of their district, and references in subsection (3) of this section to the district of a planning authority shall be construed as including any part of that district which is the subject of a survey under this subsection.".
3. In section 5 (preparation of structure plans), for subsection (1) substitute—
"(1) Where, as a result of the making of an order under section 4A of this Act, the area in respect of which a planning authority are obliged (whether acting alone or jointly with another authority or authorities) to prepare a structure plan is different from the area in respect of which a structure plan is for the time being in force, they shall prepare and submit to the Secretary of State for his approval a structure plan for their district complying with the provisions of subsection (3) below, together with a copy of the report of any survey which they have carried out under section 4(2) of this Act.
(1A) The Secretary of State may direct a planning authority to carry out their duty under subsection (1) above within a specified period from the direction, and any planning authority to whom such a direction is made shall comply with it.
(1B) Where a structure plan area extends to the district of more than one planning authority, and the authorities concerned are unable to agree on a joint structure plan for that area, then, without prejudice to the Secretary of State's powers under section 15 of this Act and section 62B (power of Secretary of State to establish joint boards) of the Local Government (Scotland) Act 1973 each authority concerned may include in the plan submitted to the Secretary of State alternative proposals in respect of particular matters.
(1C) Where authorities submit alternative proposals under subsection (1B) above, such proposals shall be accompanied by a statement of the reasoning behind the proposals.
(1D) The provisions of section 8(2) of this Act shall apply in relation to structure plans submitted to the Secretary of State under this section as they apply in relation to the submission of alterations to structure plans submitted to him under that section.".
4. In section 6 (publicity in connection with preparation of structure plans), after subsection (1) insert—
"(1A) Where authorities submit alternative proposals in relation to particular matters to the Secretary of State under section 5(1 B) of this Act, their duty under subsection (1) above is to secure that adequate publicity is given in each of their districts to all the matters which either or any of them propose to include in the plan.".
5. After section 6 insert—

"Consultation with other planning authorities
6A. Before submitting a structure plan or proposals for alteration thereof to the Secretary of State, a planning authority shall consult every other planning authority who are likely to be affected by the plan or proposals.".
6. In section 7 (approval or rejection of structure plan by Secretary of State), in subsection (1), after "structure plan" insert "(including any alternative proposals included in the plan by virtue of section 5(1B) of this Act)".
7. In section 9 (preparation of local plans), before subsection (3) insert—
"(1A) Every planning authority shall prepare local plans for all parts of their district, and two or more planning authorities may make a joint local plan extending to parts of each of their districts.".
8. In section 15 (default powers of the Secretary of State)

(a) in subsection (1)—

      (i) in paragraph (a) the words ", after holding a local inquiry or other hearing," shall cease to have effect; and

      (ii) for the words "carry out the survey" substitute "carry out a survey in accordance with the provisions of section 4 of this Act"; and

(b) after subsection (2) insert—

"(2A) Where under subsection (1) of this section the Secretary of State has power to do anything which should have been done by a planning authority acting jointly with another planning authority or authorities, he may, if he thinks fit, authorise one of those authorities to do that thing on behalf of both or all of them.".

9. In section 17 (meaning of "development plan"), at the end insert—

"(5) For the avoidance of doubt it is provided that, notwithstanding—

(a) any changes made to local government areas by the Local Government etc. (Scotland) Act 1994; and

(b) any alterations to structure plan areas made by orders under section 4A of this Act,

the structure plans and local plans made prior to the coming into force of the provisions mentioned in paragraphs (a) and (b) above shall remain in force until replaced by new plans made under or by virtue of those provisions.".

10. For subsection (3) of section 102 (compulsory acquisition of land) substitute—

"(3) Before giving an authorisation under subsection (2) of this section, the Secretary of State shall consult the local authority within whose area the land is situated.".

11. For subsection (9) of section 201 (orders extinguishing right to use vehicles on highway) substitute—

"(9) The competent authorities for the purposes of this section are local authorities, and a competent authority shall not make an order under subsection (2) or (8) of this section, if they are not the roads authority, without obtaining the consent of that authority.".

12. For subsection (5) of section 202 (provision of amenity for highway reserved to pedestrians) substitute—

"(5) The competent authorities for the purposes of this section are local authorities, and a competent authority shall not exercise any powers conferred by this section, if they are not the roads authority, without obtaining the consent of that authority.".

13. In section 242(1) (contributions by local authorities and statutory undertakers)—

(a) for the words from "any", where it first occurs, to "may" substitute "any local authority may"; and

(b) for the words from "of the", where they thirdly occur, to the end substitute "of the area of the local authority".

14. In section 243 (acquisition of property in certain circumstances), for the words "regional, islands or district council" substitute "local authority".

15. In section 275(1) (interpretation), for the definition of "local authority" substitute—

" "local authority" means a council constituted under section 2 of the Local Government etc. (Scotland) Act 1994;".

Section 40(10)   SCHEDULE 5

STRATHCLYDE PASSENGER TRANSPORT AUTHORITY

PART I

The Authority

1. In this Schedule "council" means a council constituted under section 2 of this Act.

2. The Authority shall consist of such number of members appointed respectively by such of the councils of constituent local authority areas, or by such two or more of the councils acting jointly, from among their own members as may be specified in an order made under section 40 of this Act.

3. The chairman of the Authority shall be such one of their number as the members of the Authority may appoint.

4. A person may be appointed as a member of the Authority under paragraph 2 above only if he is a member of the council or one of the councils by whom he is so appointed; and no person who is for the time being a member, officer or employee of the Strathclyde Passenger Transport

Executive or who is for the time being an employee of a subsidiary of that Executive shall be appointed as a member of the Authority, and any person appointed to be a member of the Authority who subsequently becomes a member, officer or employee of that Executive or such a subsidiary shall forthwith vacate his membership of the Authority.

5. A person who at the date of his appointment as a member of the Authority was a member of the council or one of the councils by whom he was so appointed but who subsequently ceases to be a member of that council shall upon so ceasing also vacate office as a member of the Authority.

6. If at any time not less than three months after the coming into force of the order under section 40 of this Act providing for the constitution of the Authority, or after a vacancy has arisen among the members of the Authority which falls to be filled by an appointment made under paragraph 2 above, the initial appointment of any member of the Authority falling to be made under that order or, as the case may be, an appointment to fill that vacancy, has not been made, the Secretary of State, after consultation with the council or councils by whom the appointment falls to be made, may make the appointment on their behalf.

PART II

Matters which may be dealt with by order under section 40

1. The incorporation of the Authority.

2. The appointment in accordance with Part I of this Schedule of members of the Authority.

3. The terms on which and period for which the members of the Authority are to hold office, and the vacation of office by those members.

4. The payment of allowances to, or to any class of, members of the Authority, and the payment of remuneration to the chairman of the Authority.

5. The proceedings of the Authority.

6. The establishment by the Authority of committees and the composition of those committees, including the establishment of advisory committees consisting wholly or partly of persons who are not members of the Authority.

7. The delegation of functions by the Authority to a committee or to the chairman of the Authority.

8. The authentication of documents of the Authority and provision for the treatment of such documents as sufficient evidence of such facts as may be specified by the order.

9. The appointment by the Authority of officers and staff and the payment of remuneration and allowances to any officers and staff appointed by the Authority.

10. Provision as to the superannuation of officers and staff of the Authority.

11. The provision of accommodation for the Authority by the Authority or by the Strathclyde Passenger Transport Executive.

12. Provision applying, with or without modifications, to the Authority or to persons who are or have been members or officers of the Authority any enactment or instrument made under an enactment relating, as the case may be, to, or to persons who are or have been members of, or officers of local authorities or local authorities of a particular description.

13. The making of reports and the furnishing of information by the Authority to the Secretary of State.

14. Any particular matters to be dealt with in the annual report of the Authority under section 16 of the Transport Act 1968.

15. Provision for the council or councils by whom a member of the Authority is appointed to appoint also a deputy to act in that member's place at any meeting of the Authority from which that member is absent, and for applying in relation to any such deputy, with or without modifications, any provision with respect to members of the Authority made by the said Act of 1968 or by the order.

16. Provision, as respects any period before the Authority appoint or are provided with their own officers, for the discharge of functions of officers of the Authority (including the convening of the first meeting of the Authority) by such officers of such of the councils of constituent areas as may be determined in accordance with the order.

Section 52(3)   SCHEDULE 6

ENTRY RELATING TO NEW SCOTTISH LOCAL AUTHORITY TO BE INSERTED IN SCHEDULE 1 TO THE TWEED
FISHERIES ACT 1969

Local authority	Number of representatives	Part of local authority area represented	Number of representatives for each Part	Number of representatives of associations and clubs
1	*2*	*3*	*4*	*5*
"The Borders Council.	34	Former Burgh of Coldstream.	2	1
		Former Burgh of Duns.	2	1
		Former Burgh of Eyemouth.	2	1
		Remainder of the area of the former District of Berwickshire.	3	2
		Former Burgh of Jedburgh.	2	1
		Former Burgh of Kelso.	2	1
		Former Burgh of Hawick.	2	1
		Remainder of the area of the former District of Roxburgh.	3	2
		Former Burgh of Selkirk.	2	1
		Former Burgh of Lauder.	2	1
		Former Burgh of Galashiels.	2	1
		Former Burgh of Melrose.	2	1
		Remainder of the area of the former District of Ettrick and Lauderdale.	3	2
		Former Burgh of Peebles.	2	1
		Former Burgh of Innerleithen.	2	1
		Remainder of the former District of Tweeddale."	1	

Section 62(2)   SCHEDULE 7

CONSTITUTION AND PROCEEDINGS ETC. OF A NEW WATER AND SEWERAGE AUTHORITY

Incorporation

1. A new water and sewerage authority (in this Schedule referred to as an "authority") shall—
(a) be a body corporate; and
(b) have a common seal.

Status

2. An authority shall not—
(a) be regarded as a servant or agent of the Crown;
(b) have any status, immunity or privilege of the Crown;
(c) be exempt from any tax, duty, rate, levy or other charge whatsoever, whether general or local,
and the property of an authority shall not be regarded as property of, or held on behalf of, the Crown.

Membership

3. The members of an authority shall be—
(a) not fewer than seven, nor more than eleven, persons appointed under this sub-paragraph by the Secretary of State from persons who appear to him to have knowledge or experience relevant to the discharge of the functions of the authority; and
(b) the person who is for the time being the chief executive of the authority.
4. The Secretary of State shall satisfy himself—
(a) before he appoints a person under paragraph 3(a) above, that the person has no financial or other interest likely to affect prejudicially performance as a member of the authority in question;
(b) from time to time, that each person so appointed continues, and has continued, to have no such interest.
5. A person in respect of whom the Secretary of State requires to be satisfied as is mentioned in paragraph 4(b) above shall, whenever requested by the Secretary of State to do so, furnish the Secretary of State with such information as the Secretary of State may consider necessary for the purposes of that requirement.
6. Subject to paragraphs 7 and 8 below, each member of an authority other than their chief executive—
(a) shall hold and vacate office in accordance with the terms of the instrument under which he is appointed a member;
(b) may, by written notice to the Secretary of State, resign membership; and
(c) after ceasing to hold office shall be eligible for reappointment to the authority.
7. The Secretary of State may remove a member, other than the chief executive, of an authority from office if satisfied that the member—
(a) has had his estate sequestrated, has been adjudged bankrupt, has made an arrangement with his creditors, or has granted a trust deed for his creditors or a composition contract;
(b) is incapacitated by physical or mental illness;
(c) has been absent from meetings of the authority in question for a period longer than three consecutive months without the permission of the authority; or
(d) is otherwise unable or unfit to discharge his functions as a member or is unsuitable to continue as a member.

Chairmen and deputy chairmen

8.—(1) The Secretary of State shall appoint one of the members of an authority, other than their chief executive, to be their chairman and, after consulting the chairman, may appoint any one of the members to be deputy chairman; and a chairman, or as the case may be deputy chairman, shall hold and vacate the office in question in accordance with the terms of the instrument under which he is appointed to that office.

(2) A member of the authority may resign as chairman or deputy chairman by written notice to the Secretary of State; but a chairman or deputy chairman who ceases to be a member of the authority (whether or not on giving notice under paragraph 6(b) above) ceases to be their chairman or deputy chairman.

(3) Where a member of an authority becomes, or ceases to be, the chairman or deputy chairman of the authority, the Secretary of State may vary the terms of the instrument under which he is appointed a member so as to alter the date on which office as a member is to be vacated.

Remuneration, allowances and pensions

9.—(1) An authority shall pay to their chairman, deputy chairman and members, other than the chief executive—

(a) such remuneration as the Secretary of State may, with the approval of the Treasury, determine; and

(b) such reasonable allowances as may be so determined in respect of expenses properly incurred in the performance (as chairman, deputy chairman or as the case may be members) of duties.

(2) Where a person (other than a chief executive) ceases to be a member of an authority otherwise than on the expiry of his term of office and it appears to the Secretary of State that there are special circumstances which might make it right for the person to receive compensation, the Secretary of State may, with the approval of the Treasury, direct the authority to pay to the person such amount as the Secretary of State may, with such approval, determine.

10. The Secretary of State may, with the consent of the Treasury, determine that in respect of any office held by a person as chairman, deputy chairman or member (other than the chief executive) of an authority, the authority in question shall pay—

(a) such pension, allowance or gratuity to, or in respect of, that person on his retirement or death;

(b) such contribution or other payment towards provision for such pension, allowance or gratuity,

as may be so determined.

Staff

11. The Secretary of State shall, after consultation with an authority's chairman or chairman designate (if there is a person holding, or as the case may be designated to hold, that office) make the first appointment of their chief executive on such terms and conditions as the Secretary of State may, with the consent of the Treasury, determine; and the authority may, with the approval of the Secretary of State, make subsequent appointments to the office of chief executive on such terms and conditions as they may with the approval of the Secretary of State, given with the consent of the Treasury, determine.

12.—(1) Subject to any provision made by virtue of Chapter 2 of Part I of this Act, an authority may appoint on such terms and conditions as they may with the approval of the Secretary of State, given with the consent of the Treasury, determine, such other employees as they consider appropriate.

(2) An authority shall, as regards such of their employees as they may with the approval of the Secretary of State, given with the consent of the Treasury, determine, make such arrangements as they consider appropriate for providing, to or in respect of those employees, pensions, allowances or gratuities; and such arrangements may include the establishment and administration, by the authority or otherwise, of one or more pension schemes.

(3) The reference in sub-paragraph (2) above to the provision of pensions, allowances or gratuities includes a reference to their provision by way of compensation for loss of office or employment or loss or diminution of emoluments.

(4) If a person employed by an authority becomes a member of the authority and was by virtue of that employment a participant in a pension scheme administered by the authority for the benefit of their employees, the authority may determine that his service as a member shall be treated for the purposes of the scheme as service as an employee whether or not any benefits are to be payable to or in respect of him by virtue of paragraph 10 above; but if the authority do so determine, then any discretion as to the benefits payable to or in respect of the person which the scheme confers on them shall be exercisable only with the consent of the Secretary of State given with the approval of the Treasury.

Committees

13. The authority may establish committees for or in connection with the discharge of such of their functions, or the exercise of such of their powers, as the authority may determine.

Proceedings

14. The quorum of an authority, and the arrangements for their meetings, shall be such as the authority in question may determine.

15.—(1) A member of an authority who is directly or indirectly interested in—

(a) a contract made or proposed to be made by them; or

(b) any other matter whatsoever which falls to be considered by them,

shall as soon as is practicable disclose the nature of his interest at a meeting of the authority; and the disclosure shall be recorded in the minutes of the meeting.

(2) In the case mentioned in—

(a) head (a) of sub-paragraph (1) above, the member shall not take part in any deliberation or decision of the authority with respect to the contract;

(b) head (b) of that sub-paragraph, the member shall not take part in any deliberation or decision of the authority with respect to the matter if the authority decide that the interest in question might affect prejudicially his consideration of the matter.

(3) For the purposes of this paragraph, a notice to the effect that a person is a member of a specified body corporate or firm and is to be regarded as interested in any contract which is made with the body corporate or firm after the date of the notice, and in any other matter whatsoever concerning the body corporate or firm which falls to be considered after that date, shall if given at a meeting of the authority be a sufficient disclosure of the person's interest to the authority.

(4) For the purposes of this paragraph, disclosure at a meeting may be made without the attendance in person of the member in question provided that he takes reasonable steps to ensure that the matter disclosed is raised and taken into consideration at the meeting.

16. The validity of any proceedings of an authority shall not be affected by any vacancy among the members of the authority, or by any defect in the appointment of a member, or by any failure to comply with any requirement of paragraph 15 above.

17.—(1) For a purpose other than is mentioned in sub-paragraph (2) below, a document is validly executed by an authority if signed on behalf of that authority by their chief executive, or by another of their members, or by a person authorised to sign the document on their behalf.

(2) For the purposes of any enactment or rule of law relating to the authentication of documents, a document is validly executed by an authority if subscribed on behalf of the authority by being executed in accordance with the provisions of sub-paragraph (1) above.

(3) A document which bears to have been executed by an authority in accordance with sub-paragraph (2) above shall, in relation to such execution, be a probative document if—

(a) the subscription of the document bears to have been attested by at least one witness; or

(b) the document bears to be sealed with the seal of the authority.

Delegation of powers

18.—(1) Anything authorised or required by or under any enactment to be done by the authority may be done by any of their committees which, or by any of their members or officers who, are authorised (whether generally or specially) for the purpose by them.

(2) Nothing in sub-paragraph (1) above shall prevent the authority from doing anything that a committee, member or officer has been authorised to do.

Section 62(3)   SCHEDULE 8

WATER AND SEWERAGE AREAS

Water or Sewerage Area	Area by reference to existing or former administrative areas
Eastern Water Area	Lothian Region. Borders Region. Fife Region. Central Region. The former county of Kinross (in this Schedule referred to as the first added area). That part of the former counties of Stirling and Dunbarton which on 16th May 1975 lay within both Strathclyde Region and the region of the former Mid-Scotland Water Board (such part being in this Schedule referred to as the second added area). That part of Stirling District and Central Region situated at Craigmaddie Loch which on 1st April 1977 was transferred to Strathkelvin District and Strathclyde Region (such part being in this Schedule referred to as the third added area).
Eastern Sewerage Area	Lothian Region. Borders Region.

Water or Sewerage Area	Area by reference to existing or former administrative areas
	Fife Region.
	Central Region.
	The first added area.
Western Water Area	Strathclyde Region except the second and third added areas.
	Dumfries and Galloway Region.
Western Sewerage Area	Strathclyde Region.
	Dumfries and Galloway Region.
Northern Water Area	Highland Region.
	Grampian Region.
	Tayside Region except the first added area.
	The Islands Areas.
Northern Sewerage Area	Highland Region.
	Grampian Region.
	Tayside Region except the first added area.
	The Islands Areas.

Section 67(2)   SCHEDULE 9

CONSTITUTION AND PROCEEDINGS ETC. OF THE SCOTTISH WATER AND SEWERAGE CUSTOMERS COUNCIL

Incorporation

1. The Customers Council shall be a body corporate.

Status

2. The Customers Council shall not be regarded as a servant or agent of the Crown and shall not have any status, immunity or privilege of the Crown.

Membership

3. The members of the Customers Council shall be not fewer than eight, nor more than twelve, persons appointed under this paragraph by the Secretary of State from persons who appear to him to have knowledge or experience relevant to the discharge of the functions of the Council but who are not members or employees of any of the new water and sewerage authorities; so however that he shall seek to ensure that the appointees include persons appropriate to represent, both as respects domestic and as respects non-domestic services, the interests of, respectively—

  (a) customers and potential customers such as are mentioned in section 65(2)(a)(ii) of this Act; and

  (b) other customers and potential customers.

4. For the purposes of paragraph 3 above, services are domestic if provided to dwellings ("dwelling" having the same meaning as in Part II of the Local Government Finance Act 1992) and are otherwise non-domestic.

5. The Secretary of State shall appoint one of the members of the Customers Council to be its chairman and another of them to be its deputy chairman.

6. A member of the Customers Council shall hold and vacate office in accordance with the terms of the instrument appointing him and shall, on ceasing to hold office, be eligible for reappointment; but his membership shall terminate forthwith on his becoming a member or employee of any of the new water and sewerage authorities.

Members' remuneration, pensions and allowances

7.—(1) The Customers Council shall pay to its chairman, deputy chairman and members—

  (a) such remuneration as the Secretary of State may, with the approval of the Treasury, determine; and

  (b) such reasonable allowances as may be so determined in respect of expenses properly incurred in the performance (as chairman, deputy chairman or as the case may be members) of duties.

(2) Where a person ceases to be a member of the Customers Council otherwise than on the expiry of his term of office and it appears to the Secretary of State that there are special circumstances which might make it right for the person to receive compensation, the Secretary of State may, with the approval of the Treasury, direct the Council to pay to the person such amount as the Secretary of State may, with such approval, determine.

8. The Secretary of State may, with the consent of the Treasury, determine that in respect of any office held by a person as chairman, deputy chairman or member of the Customers Council, the Council shall pay—

(a) such pension, allowance or gratuity to, or in respect of, that person on his retirement or death;

(b) such contribution or other payment towards provision for such pension, allowance or gratuity,

as may be so determined.

Staff

9.—(1) The Customers Council may appoint on such terms and conditions as it may with the approval of the Secretary of State, given with the consent of the Treasury, determine, such employees as it considers appropriate.

(2) The Customers Council shall not appoint a person to act as its principal officer except after consultation with the Secretary of State.

(3) The Council shall, as regards such of its employees as it may with the approval of the Secretary of State, given with the consent of the Treasury, determine, make such arrangements as it considers appropriate for providing, to or in respect of those employees, pensions, allowances or gratuities; and such arrangements may include the establishment and administration, by the Council or otherwise, of one or more pension schemes.

(4) The reference in sub-paragraph (3) above to the provision of pensions, allowances or gratuities includes a reference to their provision by way of compensation for loss of office or employment or loss or diminution of emoluments.

(5) If a person employed by the Customers Council becomes a member of the Council and was by virtue of that employment a participant in a pension scheme administered by the Council for the benefit of its employees, the Council may determine that his service as a member shall be treated for the purposes of the scheme as service as an employee whether or not any benefits are to be payable to or in respect of him by virtue of paragraph 8 above; but if the Council does so determine, then any discretion as to the benefits payable to or in respect of the person which the scheme confers on the Council shall be exercisable only with the consent of the Secretary of State given with the approval of the Treasury.

Committees

10.—(1) For or in connection with the discharge of such of its functions, or the exercise of such of its powers, as the Customers Council may determine, it shall establish three committees, the first for the eastern water area and the eastern sewerage area, the second for the western water area and the western sewerage area and the third for the northern water area and the northern sewerage area.

(2) Each committee shall consist of—

(a) a chairman, appointed by the Customers Council, with the approval of the Secretary of State, from the members of the Council; and

(b) not fewer than seven, nor more than eleven, members appointed by the Council from persons who are neither members nor employees of the Council or of a new water and sewerage authority, so however that the Council shall seek to ensure, as respects its appointments under this paragraph, that which the Secretary of State is required to seek to ensure as respects his appointments under paragraph 3 (as read with paragraph 4) of this Schedule.

(3) The terms on which a person appointed under sub-paragraph (2)(b) above shall hold office shall be determined by the Customers Council but his membership of the committee in question shall terminate forthwith on his becoming a member or an employee of any of the new water and sewerage authorities or a member or employee of the Council.

(4) The Customers Council may pay to a person appointed under sub-paragraph (2)(b) above (in respect of his activities as committee member) travelling and other allowances in accordance with such arrangements as may be determined by the Secretary of State with the approval of the Treasury.

Public Committee Meetings

11. In every financial year, at least one meeting of each committee established under paragraph 10 above shall be open to all members of the public.

Section 79(4)   SCHEDULE 10

RECOVERY BY DILIGENCE OF CHARGES PAYABLE TO A COLLECTING AUTHORITY BY VIRTUE OF SECTION 79

1.—(1) This Schedule applies to any sum which has become payable to a collecting authority by virtue of section 79 of this Act and has not been paid.

(2) References in sub-paragraph (1) above to a sum which has become payable and has not been paid include references to a sum forming part of a larger sum which has become payable and the other part of which has been paid.

2.—(1) Subject to sub-paragraphs (4) and (5) below, any sum to which this Schedule applies may be recovered by the collecting authority by diligence—

(a) authorised by a summary warrant granted under sub-paragraph (2) below; or

(b) in pursuance of a decree granted in an action of payment.

(2) The sheriff, on an application by the authority which is accompanied by a certificate from them containing such particulars as may be prescribed by the Secretary of State by regulations, shall grant a summary warrant in a form provided for by Act of Sederunt authorising the recovery, by way of any of the diligences mentioned in sub-paragraph (3) below, of the amount of the sum remaining due and unpaid along with a surcharge of 10 per cent. of that amount.

(3) The diligences referred to in sub-paragraph (2) above are—

(a) a poinding and sale in accordance with Schedule 5 to the Debtors (Scotland) Act 1987;

(b) an earnings arrestment;

(c) an arrestment and action of forthcoming or sale.

(4) It shall be incompetent for the sheriff to grant a summary warrant under sub-paragraph (2) above in respect of any sum to which this Schedule applies if an action has already been raised for the recovery of that sum; and, without prejudice to sub-paragraph (5) below, on the raising of an action for the recovery of any such sum, any existing summary warrant, in so far as it relates to the recovery of that sum, shall cease to have effect.

(5) It shall be incompetent to raise an action in Scotland for the recovery of any sum to which this Schedule applies if, in pursuance of a summary warrant, any of the diligences mentioned in sub-paragraph (3) above for the recovery of that sum has been executed.

(6) The Secretary of State may by order substitute another percentage for the percentage which is for the time being mentioned in sub-paragraph (2) above.

(7) The power to make regulations under sub-paragraph (2) above shall be exercisable by statutory instrument which shall be subject to annulment in pursuance of a resolution of either House of Parliament; and a statutory instrument containing an order made under sub-paragraph (6) above shall be so subject.

3. No misnomer or inaccurate description of any person or place, or mistake or informality, in any notice or other document or communication relating to a demand for, or the recovery of, charges payable to the collecting authority by virtue of section 79 of this Act or in any proceedings for the payment of such charges shall prejudice such recovery.

4.—(1) Subject to sub-paragraph (2) below, and without prejudice to paragraphs 25 to 34 of Schedule 5 to the Debtors (Scotland) Act 1987, the sheriff officer's fees, together with the outlays necessarily incurred by him, in connection with the execution of a summary warrant under paragraph 2 above shall be chargeable against the debtor.

(2) No fees shall be chargeable by the sheriff officer against the debtor for collecting, and accounting to the collecting authority for, the sums paid to him by the debtor in satisfaction of an amount owing to the authority by way of charges payable to them by virtue of section 79 of this Act.

Section 95   SCHEDULE 11

WATER AND SEWERAGE TRANSFER SCHEMES

Allocation of property, rights and liabilities

1.—(1) The provisions of this paragraph and of paragraphs 2 and 3(1) below shall have effect where a transfer to which this Schedule applies is a transfer of property, rights and liabilities of a regional or islands council and the question of allocation of the property, rights and liabilities as between the regional council's successor, or the islands council, and the transferee arises.

(2) Any property, right or liability referable partly to the functions of the council which are transferred and partly to the functions which are retained for the regional council's successor, or the islands council, shall (where the nature of the property, right or liability permits) be divided or apportioned between the successor, or council, and the transferee in such proportions as may be appropriate; and, where any estate or interest in land falls to be so divided, any rent payable by or to any party in respect of that land and any feu-duty, stipend or other outgoing running with the land or right shall be divided or apportioned correspondingly.

(3) Any property, right or liability referable as mentioned in sub-paragraph (2) above but the nature of which does not permit its division or apportionment as so mentioned, shall be transferred to the transferee or retained for the regional council's successor, or the islands council, according to—

    (a) in the case of an estate or interest in land, whether on the transfer date the successor, or islands council, or the transferee appears to be in greater need of the security afforded by that estate or interest or, where neither appears to be in greater need of that security, whether as from that date the successor, or islands council, or the transferee appears likely to make use of the land to the greater extent;

    (b) in the case of any other property or any right or liability, whether as from the transfer date the successor, or islands council, or the transferee appears likely to make use of the property, or as the case may be to be affected by the right or liability, to the greater extent,

subject (in either case) to such arrangements for the protection of the other of them as may be agreed between them.

2.—(1) It shall be the duty of the council (or as the case may be the council's successor) and the transferee, whether before or after the transfer date, so far as it is practicable to arrive at such written agreements and to execute such other instruments as are necessary or expedient to identify or define the property, rights and liabilities transferred to the transferee or retained for the successor, or islands council, and as will—

    (a) afford to the successor, or islands council, and the transferee as against one another such rights and safeguards as they may require for the proper discharge of their respective functions; and

    (b) make as from such date, not being earlier than the transfer date, as may be specified in the agreement or instrument such clarification and modifications of the division of the council's property, rights and liabilities as will best serve the proper discharge of the respective functions of the successor, or the islands council, and the transferee.

(2) Any such agreement shall provide so far as it is expedient—

    (a) for the granting of leases and for the creation of other liabilities and rights over land whether amounting in law to interests in land or not, and whether involving the surrender of any existing interest or the creation of a new interest or not;

    (b) for the granting of indemnities in connection with the severance of leases and other matters; and

    (c) for responsibility for registration of any matter in any statutory register.

(3) If the council (or as the case may be the successor) or the transferee represent to the Secretary of State, or if it appears to the Secretary of State without such a representation, that it is unlikely in the case of any matter on which agreement is required under sub-paragraph (1) above that such agreement will be reached, the Secretary of State may, whether before or after the transfer date, give a direction determining that matter and may include in the direction any provision which might have been included in an agreement under sub-paragraph (1) above; and any property, rights or liabilities required by the direction to be transferred to the transferee shall accordingly be regarded as having been transferred to, and vested in, the transferee by virtue of the scheme (but not until the date of the direction if that is after the transfer date).

Variation of transfers by agreement

3.—(1) At any time before the end of the period of twelve months beginning with the transfer date, the regional council's successor, or the islands council, and the transferee may, with the approval of the Secretary of State, agree in writing that—

    (a) as from such date as may be specified in or determined under the agreement, and

    (b) in such circumstances (if any) as may be so specified,

there shall be transferred from the transferee to, and vested in, the successor, or the islands council, any property, rights and liabilities specified in the agreement.

(2) Subject to sub-paragraph (3) below, in the case of an agreement under sub-paragraph (1) above, the property, rights and liabilities in question shall on the date of the coming into force of the agreement be transferred, and by virtue of the agreement vest, in accordance with the agreement.

(3) The following provisions of this Schedule shall have effect as if—

(a) any reference to a transfer to which this Schedule applies included a reference to a transfer effected in pursuance of an agreement under sub-paragraph (1) above;

(b) any reference to a transaction effected in pursuance of paragraph 2(1) above or of a direction under paragraph 2(3) above included a reference to such an agreement; and

(c) any reference to a vesting by virtue of a transfer scheme included a reference to a vesting by virtue of such an agreement.

Right to production of documents of title

4. Where, on any transfer to which this Schedule applies, a regional council's successor or an islands council is entitled to retain possession of any document relating in part to the title to, or to the management of, any land or other property transferred from the council in question, subsections (1) and (2) of section 16 of the Land Registration (Scotland) Act 1979 (omission of certain clauses in deeds) shall have effect in relation to the transfer as if the transfer had been effected by deed and as if from each of those subsections the words "unless specially qualified" were omitted.

Certificate of vesting

5.—(1) In the case of any transfer to which this Schedule applies, a joint certificate by or on behalf of the transferor (or the transferor's successor) and the transferee that—

(a) any property specified in the certificate;

(b) any such interest in or right over any such property as may be so specified; or

(c) any right or liability so specified,

is, by virtue of this Act, vested in such one of them as may be so specified, or was at a date so specified thus vested, shall be conclusive evidence for all purposes of that fact.

(2) If on the expiration of one month after a request from either the transferor (or the successor) or the transferee for the preparation of such a joint certificate as respects any property, interest, right or liability they have failed to agree on the terms of the certificate, they shall refer the matter to the Secretary of State and issue the certificate in such terms as he may direct.

Restrictions on dealing with certain land

6.—(1) If, as regards a transfer to which this Schedule applies from an islands or regional council, the Secretary of State is satisfied on the representation of the regional council's successor, or the islands council, or the transferee—

(a) that, in consequence of the transfer, different interests in land, whether the same or different land, are held by the successor or islands council and by the transferee; and

(b) that the circumstances are such that this paragraph should have effect,

the Secretary of State may direct that this paragraph shall apply to such of that land as may be specified in the direction.

(2) While the direction mentioned in sub-paragraph (1) above remains in force—

(a) neither the successor, or islands council, nor the transferee shall dispose of any interest to which they may respectively be entitled in any of the specified land, except with the consent of the Secretary of State;

(b) if, in connection with any proposal to dispose of any interest of either the successor (or council) or the transferee in any of the specified land, it appears to the Secretary of State to be necessary or expedient for the protection of either of them, he may—

(i) require either the successor (or council) or the transferee to dispose of any interest to which they may be entitled in any of the specified land to such person and in such manner as may be specified in the requirement;

(ii) require either the successor (or council) or the transferee to acquire from the other any interest in any of the specified land to which that other is entitled; or

(iii) consent to the proposed disposal subject to compliance with such conditions as the Secretary of State may see fit to impose.

(3) A person other than the successor (or islands council) or the transferee dealing with, or with a person claiming under, either the successor (or council) or the transferee shall not be concerned—

(a) to see or enquire whether this paragraph applies, or has applied, in relation to any land to which the dealing relates; or

(b) as to whether the provisions of this paragraph have been complied with in connection with that, or any other, dealing with that land;

and no transaction between persons other than the successor (or council) and the transferee shall be invalid by reason only of a failure to comply with those provisions.

Construction of agreements, statutory provisions and documents

7.—(1) This paragraph applies where, in the case of any transfer to which this Schedule applies, any rights or liabilities transferred are rights or liabilities under an agreement, whether in writing or not, to which the transferor was a party immediately before the transfer date and whether or not the agreement was of such a nature that rights and liabilities under it could be assigned by the transferor.

(2) So far as relating to property, rights or liabilities transferred to the transferee, the agreement shall have effect on and after the transfer date as if—

(a) the transferee had been the party to it;

(b) for any reference (whether express or implied and, if express, however worded) to the transferor there were substituted, as respects anything falling to be done on or after the transfer date, a reference to the transferee;

(c) any reference (whether express or implied and, if express, however worded) to a person employed by, or engaged in the functions of, the transferor and holding a specified office or serving in a specified capacity were, as respects anything falling to be done on or after the transfer date, a reference to such a person as the transferee may appoint or, in default of appointment, to a person employed by, or engaged in the functions of, the transferee who corresponds as nearly as may be to the first-mentioned person;

(d) any reference in general terms (however worded) to persons employed by, persons engaged in the functions of, or agents of, the transferor were, as respects anything to be done on or after the transfer date, a reference to persons employed by, persons engaged in the functions of, or agents of, the transferee.

8.—(1) Except as otherwise provided in any provision of this Part of this Act (whether expressly or by necessary implication), paragraph 7 above shall, so far as applicable, apply in relation to—

(a) any statutory provision,

(b) any provision of an agreement to which the transferor was not a party, and

(c) any provision of a document other than an agreement,

if and in so far as the provision in question relates to any of the transferred property, rights and liabilities, as it applies in relation to an agreement to which the transferor was a party.

(2) In relation to any such statutory or other provision as is mentioned in sub-paragraph (1) above, references in sub-paragraph (2)(b), (c) and (d) of paragraph 7 above to the transferor and to any persons employed by, persons engaged in the functions of, or agents of, the transferor include references made by means of a general reference to a class of persons of which the transferor is one, though not specifically referred to.

9.—(1) The transferee under a transfer to which this Schedule applies and any other person shall, as from the transfer date, have the same rights, powers and remedies (and in particular the same rights and powers as to the taking or resisting of legal proceedings or the making or resisting of applications to any authority) for ascertaining, perfecting or enforcing any right or liability vested in the transferee by virtue of the scheme as they would have had if that right or liability had at all times been a right or liability of the transferee.

(2) Any legal proceedings, or applications to any authority, pending on the transfer date by or against the transferor, in so far as they relate—

(a) to any property, right or liability vested in the transferee by virtue of the scheme, or

(b) to any agreement or enactment relating to any such property, right or liability,

shall be continued by or against the transferee to the exclusion of the transferor or the transferor's successor.

(3) This paragraph is without prejudice to the generality of the provisions of paragraphs 7 and 8 above.

10. The provisions of paragraphs 7 to 9 above shall have effect for the interpretation of agreements, statutory provisions and other instruments subject to the context, and shall not apply where the context otherwise requires.

Third parties affected by vesting provisions

11.—(1) Without prejudice to the provisions of paragraphs 7 to 10 above, any transaction effected between the council (or the council's successor) and the transferee in pursuance of paragraph 2(1) above or of à direction under paragraph 2(3) above shall be binding on all other persons, and notwithstanding that it would, apart from this sub-paragraph, have required the consent or concurrence of any other person.

(2) It shall be the duty of the council (or successor) and the transferee, if they effect any transaction in pursuance of paragraph 2(1) above or of a direction under paragraph 2(3) above, to notify any person who has rights or liabilities which thereby become enforceable as to part by or against the regional council's successor, or the islands council, and as to part by or against the transferee; and if, within twenty-eight days of being notified, such a person applies to the Secretary of State and satisfies him that the transaction operated unfairly against him, the Secretary of State may give such directions to the successor, or the islands council, and the transferee as appear to him appropriate for varying the transaction.

(3) As respects a transfer to which this Schedule applies which is a transfer of property, rights and liabilities of a regional or islands council, if in consequence of the transfer or of anything done in pursuance of the provisions of this Schedule—

(a) the rights or liabilities of any person other than the regional council's successor, or the islands council, and the transferee which are enforceable against or by the successor, or council, become enforceable as to part against or by the successor, or council, and as to part against or by the transferee, and

(b) the value of any property or interest of that person is thereby diminished,

such compensation as may be just shall be paid to that person by the successor (or council), the transferee or both.

(4) Subject to sub-paragraph (5) below, if it appears to the regional or islands council that a person is, or may be, entitled to compensation under sub-paragraph (3) above—

(a) they shall by written notice inform the person that he is, or may be, so entitled and shall invite him to make such representations as he wishes to them within fourteen days after the date of issue of the notice; or

(b) where they do not know (either or both)—

(i) the name of the person concerned;

(ii) his address,

they shall publish, in such manner as they consider appropriate, a notice containing information about the interest affected and inviting any person who thinks that he is, or may be, entitled to compensation in respect of the interest to make such representations as he wishes to them by a date which they shall specify in the notice, being a date not less than twenty-eight days after the date of publication.

(5) Where the last of the fourteen days after the date of issue of a notice under head (a) of sub-paragraph (4) above falls on or after the transfer date, or the date specified in a notice published under head (b) of that sub-paragraph so falls, the notice shall direct that the representations be made to the transferor or, on or after that date, to the transferor's successor.

(6) Any dispute as to whether any, and (if so) how much, compensation is payable under sub-paragraph (3) above, or as to the person to or by whom it shall be paid, shall be referred to and determined by an arbiter appointed by the Lord President of the Court of Session.

(7) If, in the case of any transfer to which this Schedule applies, it appears to the court, at any stage in any court proceedings to which the transferor (or successor) or the transferee and a person other than the transferor (or successor) or the transferee are parties, that the issues in the proceedings—

(a) depend on the identification or definition of any of the property, rights or liabilities transferred which the transferor (or successor) and the transferee have not yet effected, or

(b) raise a question of construction of the relevant provisions of this Act which would not arise if the transferor (or successor) and the transferee constituted a single person,

the court may, if it thinks fit on the application of a party to the proceedings other than the transferor (or the successor) or the transferee, hear and determine the proceedings on the footing that such one of the transferor (or successor) and the transferee as is party to the proceedings represents and is answerable for the other of them, and that the transferor (or successor) and the transferee constitute a single person; and any judgment or order given by the court shall bind both the transferor (or successor) and the transferee accordingly.

(8) In the case of any transfer to which this Schedule applies, it shall be the duty of the transferor (or successor) and the transferee to keep one another informed of any case where either of them may be prejudiced by virtue of sub-paragraph (7) above; and if it is claimed by either the transferor (or successor) or the transferee there has been such prejudice and that the other of them ought to indemnify or make a repayment on that account but that there has been unreasonable failure to meet that claim, whichever of them so claims may refer the matter to the Secretary of State for determination by him.

Interpretation

12. In this Schedule—

"islands council" shall, as the context may require, be construed either as a reference to the islands council of Orkney, Shetland or the Western Isles as the council in question exist or existed before 1st April 1996 or as a reference to Orkney Islands Council, Shetland Islands Council or Western Isles Council;

"statutory provision" means a provision, whether of a general or of a special nature, contained in, or in any document made or issued under, any Act and irrespective of whether the Act itself is of a general or of a special nature; and

"successor" shall be construed in accordance with section 92(9) of this Act.

Section 128(6)   SCHEDULE 12

STATUS, CONSTITUTION AND PROCEEDINGS OF THE SCOTTISH CHILDREN'S REPORTER ADMINISTRATION

Status

1. The Administration shall be a body corporate and shall have a common seal.

2. The Administration shall not—
   (a) be regarded as a servant or agent of the Crown;
   (b) have any status, immunity or privilege of the Crown;
   (c) be exempt from any tax, duty, rate, levy or other charge whatsoever whether general or local,

and its property shall not be regarded as property of, or held on behalf of, the Crown.

Membership

3.—(1) The members of the Administration shall be not fewer than five, nor more than eight, persons one of whom shall be the Principal Reporter; the others shall be appointed by the Secretary of State under this paragraph.

(2) The persons appointed under this paragraph to be members of the Administration shall be persons appearing to the Secretary of State to have knowledge or experience relevant to the general purpose of the Administration or to the functions of the Principal Reporter.

(3) The Secretary of State may, by order, substitute another number for that specified in sub-paragraph (1) above as the maximum number of members of the Administration .

(4) An order under sub-paragraph (3) above shall be made by statutory instrument subject to annulment in pursuance of a resolution of either House of Parliament.

4.—(1) The Secretary of State shall satisfy himself—
   (a) before he appoints a person to be a member of the Administration under paragraph 3 above that the person will have no such financial or other interest as is likely to affect prejudicially the performance of his functions as a member; and
   (b) from time to time that each person so appointed continues, and has continued, to have no such interest.

(2) A person in respect of whom the Secretary of State requires to be satisfied as is mentioned in sub-paragraph (1)(b) above shall, whenever requested by the Secretary of State to do so, furnish the Secretary of State with such information as the Secretary of State may consider necessary for the purposes of fulfilling that requirement.

5. Subject to paragraphs 6 and 7 below, each member of the Administration appointed under paragraph 3 above—
   (a) shall hold and vacate office in accordance with the terms of his appointment;
   (b) may, by notice in writing to the Secretary of State, resign his membership; and
   (c) after ceasing to hold office shall be eligible for reappointment as a member.

6. The Secretary of State may remove from office a member of the Administration appointed under paragraph 3 above if he is satisfied that the member—
   (a) has had his estate sequestrated, has made an arrangement with his creditors, has been adjudged bankrupt or has granted a trust deed for his creditors or a composition contract;
   (b) is incapacitated by physical or mental illness;
   (c) has been absent from meetings of the Administration for a period longer than three months without the permission of the Administration; or
   (d) is otherwise unable or unfit to discharge his functions as a member or is unsuitable to continue as a member.

Chairman and deputy chairman

7.—(1) The Secretary of State shall appoint one of the members of the Administration appointed under paragraph 3 above to be chairman and, after consulting the chairman, shall appoint another of those members to be deputy chairman.

(2) The chairman and deputy chairman shall hold and vacate office in terms of their respective appointments.

(3) A member of the Administration who is chairman or deputy chairman may resign his office by notice in writing to the Secretary of State; and if the chairman or deputy chairman

ceases to be a member of the Administration (whether or not on giving notice under paragraph 5(b) above) he shall cease to be its chairman or, as the case may be, deputy chairman.

(4) Where a member of the Administration becomes, or ceases to be, chairman or deputy chairman, the Secretary of State may vary the terms of his appointment as a member so as to alter the date on which his office as a member is to be vacated.

Remuneration and allowances

8.—(1) The Administration shall—
(a) pay to its members appointed under paragraph 3 above such allowances (if any) and remuneration; and
(b) as regards any such member or former such member determined for the purposes of this paragraph by the Secretary of State, pay such pension, allowance or gratuity to or in respect of him, or make such payments towards the provision of such pension, allowance or gratuity,

as the Secretary of State may, with the approval of the Treasury, determine.

(2) If a person appointed under paragraph 3 above ceases to be a member of the Administration, and it appears to the Secretary of State that there are special circumstances which make it right that he should receive compensation, the Secretary of State may require the Administration to pay to that person a sum of such amount as the Secretary of State may, with the approval of the Treasury, determine.

9.—(1) The Administration shall, in the case of such of its officers or former officers as it may, with the approval of the Secretary of State given with the consent of the Treasury, determine—
(a) pay such pensions, allowances or gratuities to or in respect of those officers;
(b) make such payments towards provision of such pensions, allowances or gratuities; or
(c) provide and maintain such schemes (whether contributory or not) for the payment of such pensions, allowances or gratuities,

as it may, with such approval given with such consent, determine.

(2) The reference in sub-paragraph (1) above to pensions, allowances or gratuities in respect of officers of the Administration includes a reference to pensions, allowances or gratuities by way of compensation to or in respect of any such officer who suffers loss of office.

(3) If an officer of the Administration becomes a member and was by reference to his office a participant in a pension scheme established and administered by it for the benefit of its officers—
(a) the Administration may determine that his service as a member shall be treated for the purposes of the scheme as service as an officer whether or not any benefits are to be payable to or in respect of him by virtue of paragraph 8 above; but
(b) if the Administration determines as aforesaid, any discretion as to the benefits payable to or in respect of him which the scheme confers on the Administration shall be exercised only with the approval of the Secretary of State given with the consent of the Treasury.

Proceedings

10.—(1) The Administration may regulate its own procedure.

(2) The power conferred by sub-paragraph (1) above extends to making provision in relation to the quorum for the meetings of the Administration and the meetings of any committee established by it.

(3) The proceedings of the Administration and of any committee established by it shall not be invalidated by any vacancy amongst its members or the members of such committee or by any defect in the appointment of such member.

Committees

11.—(1) The Administration may appoint persons who are not members of it to be members of any committee established by it.

(2) No committee established by the Administration shall consist entirely of persons who are not members of the Administration.

(3) The Administration shall pay to a person appointed to such a committee such remuneration and allowances (if any) as the Secretary of State may, with the consent of the Treasury, determine.

(4) The Administration may regulate the procedure of any committee established by it and any such committee shall comply with any directions given to it by the Administration.

Delegation of powers

12.—(1) Anything authorised or required by or under any enactment to be done by the Administration may, subject to sub-paragraph (3) below, be done by any of its committees which, or by any of its members or officers who, is authorised (generally or specifically) for the purpose by the Administration.

(2) Nothing in sub-paragraph (1) above shall prevent the Administration from doing anything that a committee, member or officer has been authorised to do.

(3) Sub-paragraph (1) above does not extend to the duties of the Administration under section 136 of this Act.

Documents

13.—(1) For any purpose other than those mentioned in sub-paragraph (2) below, a document is validly executed by the Administration if it is signed on its behalf by a member or by the Principal Reporter or by an officer authorised to sign the document on its behalf.

(2) For the purposes of any enactment or rule of law relating to the authentication of documents, a document is validly executed by the Administration if it is subscribed on its behalf by being executed in accordance with the provisions of sub-paragraph (1) above.

(3) A document which bears to have been executed by the Administration in accordance with sub-paragraph (2) above shall, in relation to such execution, be a probative document if—

(a) the subscription of the document bears to have been attested by at least one witness; or

(b) the document bears to be sealed with the seal of the Administration.

Section 180(1)   SCHEDULE 13

Minor and Consequential Amendments

The Riotous Assemblies (Scotland) Act 1822 (c. 33)

1. In section 10 of the Riotous Assemblies (Scotland) Act 1822 (compensation for damage to buildings caused by acts of riotous assemblies etc.), for "regional or islands council" substitute "council (being a council constituted under section 2 of the Local Government etc. (Scotland) Act 1994)".

The Harbours, Docks and Piers Clauses Act 1847 (c. 27)

2.—(1) The Harbours, Docks and Piers Clauses Act 1847 shall be amended in accordance with this paragraph.

(2) In section 7 (deposit of sheriff's certificate of correction), for "regional or islands council" substitute "council (being a council constituted under section 2 of the Local Government etc. (Scotland) Act 1994)".

(3) In section 8 (plans to be deposited before works may begin), for "of any region or islands area" substitute "for any local government area (within the meaning of the Local Government etc. (Scotland) Act 1994)".

The Burial Grounds (Scotland) Act 1855 (c. 68)

3.—(1) The Burial Grounds (Scotland) Act 1855 shall be amended in accordance with this paragraph.

(2) In each of sections 4 (proceedings on complaint of danger to health), 9 (meeting of board to be convened where requisitioned) and 10 (provision of suitable burial grounds by board after closure, etc.), for "ratepayers", wherever it occurs, substitute "persons (being ratepayers or persons liable to pay council tax)".

(3) In section 10 (provision of suitable burial grounds by board after closure, etc.), the words "any of the Lords Ordinary of" and the words "And provided also, that no land shall be so designated nearer than one hundred yards to any dwelling house without the consent in writing of the owner of such dwelling house;" shall cease to have effect.

(4) In section 11 (consents for new burial grounds), the words from "but no ground" to the end shall cease to have effect.

The Explosives Act 1875 (c. 17)

4.—(1) The Explosives Act 1875 shall be amended in accordance with this paragraph.

(2) In section 110 (local authority), in paragraph 1, for "regional or islands council" substitute "council constituted under section 2 of the Local Government etc. (Scotland) Act 1994".

(3) In section 111 (expenses of local authority), in paragraph (a), for "regional or general rate" substitute "non-domestic rate or the council tax".

The Public Libraries Consolidation (Scotland) Act 1887 (c. 42)

5. For section 2 of the Public Libraries Consolidation (Scotland) Act 1887 (interpretation) substitute—

"**Interpretation**
2. In this Act, except where the context otherwise requires, "library authority" and "museum and art gallery authority", for the purposes of this Act, mean a council constituted under section 2 of the Local Government etc. (Scotland) Act 1994; and "area", in relation to such an authority, shall be construed accordingly.".

The Allotments (Scotland) Act 1892 (c. 54)

6. In section 16 of the Allotments (Scotland) Act 1892 (definitions), in the definition of "local authority", for "an islands or a district council" substitute "a council constituted under section 2 of the Local Government etc. (Scotland) Act 1994".

The Merchant Shipping Act 1894 (c. 60)

7. In section 668 of the Merchant Shipping Act 1894 (Commissioners of Northern Lighthouses)—
   (a) in subsection (1)(b), for the words from "chairmen" to "councils" substitute "conveners of the councils for Highland and Argyll and Bute";
   (b) in subsection (3), for the words from "chairman" to "area" substitute "convener of any council whose area includes"; and
   (c) after subsection (5) insert—
       "(6) In this section "council" means a council constituted under section 2 of the Local Government etc. (Scotland) Act 1994.".

The Light Railways Act 1896 (c. 48)

8. In section 26 of the Light Railways Act 1896 (application to Scotland), in subsection (2), for "regional, islands or district council" substitute "council constituted under section 2 of the Local Government etc. (Scotland) Act 1994".

The Public Health (Scotland) Act 1897 (c. 38)

9. In section 12 of the Public Health (Scotland) Act 1897 (local authorities for the purposes of the Act), for "The islands or district council" substitute "A council constituted under section 2 of the Local Government etc. (Scotland) Act 1994".

The Census Act 1920 (c. 41)

10. In section 9 of the Census Act 1920 (application to Scotland), for subsection (2) substitute—
    "(2) "local authority" means a council constituted under section 2 of the Local Government etc. (Scotland) Act 1994.".

The Celluloid and Cinematograph Film Act 1922 (c. 35)

11. In section 10(1) of the Celluloid and Cinematograph Film Act 1922 (application to Scotland), in the definition of "Local authority", for the words from "the" to the end substitute "a council constituted under section 2 of the Local Government etc. (Scotland) Act 1994.".

The Allotments (Scotland) Act 1922 (c.52)

12. In section 19(1) of the Allotments (Scotland) Act 1922 (interpretation), for "an island or a district council" substitute "a council constituted under section 2 of the Local Government etc. (Scotland) Act 1994".

The Performing Animals (Regulation) Act 1925 (c. 38)

13. In section 6(a) of the Performing Animals (Regulation) Act 1925 (definition of "local authority" in application of Act to Scotland), for "an islands or district council" substitute "a council constituted under section 2 of the Local Government etc. (Scotland) Act 1994".

The Agricultural Produce (Grading and Marking) Act 1928 (c. 19)

14. In section 8 of the Agricultural Produce (Grading and Marking) Act 1928 (application to Scotland), for the words from "region" to "county" substitute "council constituted under section 2 of the Local Government etc. (Scotland) Act 1994 shall be substituted for references to a council of a county".

The Petroleum (Consolidation) Act 1928 (c. 32)

15. In section 24 of the Petroleum (Consolidation) Act 1928 (application to Scotland), for subsection (1) substitute—
    "(1) for paragraphs (a) and (c) of section 2(1) of this Act there shall be substituted the words "a council constituted under section 2 of the Local Government etc. (Scotland) Act 1994".".

The Local Government (Scotland) Act 1929 (c. 25)

16. In section 29 of the Local Government (Scotland) Act 1929 (power of councils to expend money on public health propaganda), for "regional, islands or district council" substitute "council constituted under section 2 of the Local Government etc. (Scotland) Act 1994".

The Road Traffic Act 1930 (c. 43)

17.—(1) The Road Traffic Act 1930 shall be amended in accordance with this paragraph.
    (2) In section 108(1) (interpretation), in the definition of "district", for "a region or islands area" substitute "the area of a council constituted under section 2 of the Local Government etc. (Scotland) Act 1994".
    (3) In section 109(a) (definition of "local authority" in application of the Act to Scotland), for "a regional or islands council" substitute "a council constituted under section 2 of the Local Government etc. (Scotland) Act 1994".
    (4) In section 119(3) (special provisions as to Scotland), for the words from "A" to "shall" substitute "A local roads authority shall".

The Church of Scotland (Property and Endowments) (Amendment) Act 1933 (c. 44)

18. In section 2(2) of the Church of Scotland (Property and Endowments) (Amendment) Act 1933 (transfer of certain churchyards), for the words from "of the" to "which" substitute "constituted under section 2 of the Local Government etc. (Scotland) Act 1994 within whose area".

The Private Legislation Procedure (Scotland) Act 1936 (c. 52)

19. In section 11(6) of the Private Legislation Procedure (Scotland) Act 1936 (powers of councils under Act), for "regional, islands or district council" substitute "council constituted under section 2 of the Local Government etc. (Scotland) Act 1994".

The Harbours, Piers and Ferries (Scotland) Act 1937 (c. 28)

20. In section 31(1) of the Harbours, Piers and Ferries (Scotland) Act 1937 (interpretation), for "regional or islands council" substitute "council constituted under section 2 of the Local Government etc. (Scotland) Act 1994".

The Children and Young Persons (Scotland) Act 1937 (c. 37)

21. In section 110(1) of the Children and Young Persons (Scotland) Act 1937 (interpretation), for "regional or islands council" substitute "council constituted under section 2 of the Local Government etc. (Scotland) Act 1994".

The Public Records (Scotland) Act 1937 (c. 43)

22.—(1) The Public Records (Scotland) Act 1937 shall be amended in accordance with this paragraph.
    (2) In section 5 (transfer of records to Keeper)—
    (a) for subsection (2) substitute—
        "(2) Notwithstanding anything contained in any enactment, it shall be lawful for any local authority or any statutory body corporate in Scotland, with the consent of the Keeper, to transmit such of their records as relate exclusively or mainly to Scotland to the Keeper for custody.
        (2A) For the purposes of this section, "statutory body corporate" means any body corporate established by or under a statute relating to Scotland other than such bodies, or such

classes of such bodies, as may be specified by the Secretary of State in an order made by statutory instrument.

(2B) Nothing in subsection (2) above shall apply to any burgh register of sasines or to any book or public record relating thereto.".

(3) In subsection (1) of section 14 (interpretation), after the definition of "court records" insert—

"the expression "local authority" means an authority constituted under section 2 of the Local Government etc. (Scotland) Act 1994, and includes a joint board and a joint committee;

the expression "statutory body corporate" shall be construed in accordance with section 5(2A) above.".

The Methylated Spirits (Sale by Retail) (Scotland) Act 1937 (c. 48)

23. In section 6 of the Methylated Spirits (Sale by Retail) (Scotland) Act 1937 (interpretation), in the definition of "local authority", for "an islands or district council" substitute "a council constituted under section 2 of the Local Government etc. (Scotland) Act 1994".

The Civil Defence Act 1939 (c. 31)

24. In section 62(1A) of the Civil Defence Act 1939 (power of local authority to appropriate lands and buildings for purposes of civil defence etc.), in paragraph (b), for "regional, islands or district council" substitute "council constituted under section 2 of the Local Government etc. (Scotland) Act 1994".

The Land Drainage (Scotland) Act 1941 (c. 13)

25. In section 7(1) of the Land Drainage (Scotland) Act 1941 (interpretation), in the definition of "rating authority", for the words from "like" to "1929" substitute "meaning assigned to it by section 30 of the Local Government etc. (Scotland) Act 1994".

The Public Health (Scotland) Act 1945 (c. 15)

26. In section 1(8) of the Public Health (Scotland) Act 1945 (local authorities for purposes of enforcement etc. of certain regulations), in the definition of "local authority", for "an islands or district council" substitute "a council constituted under section 2 of the Local Government etc. (Scotland) Act 1994".

The Fire Services Act 1947 (c. 41)

27.—(1) The Fire Services Act 1947 shall be amended in accordance with this paragraph.
(2) In section 15(2) (use of water for fire-fighting purposes)—
(a) at the beginning insert "Without prejudice to section 9A of the Water (Scotland) Act 1980 (prohibition on any charge for water taken to extinguish fires etc.) and"; and
(b) the proviso shall cease to have effect.
(3) In section 36 (application of the Act to Scotland)—
(a) in subsection (2)—
(i) the words "and thirty-six" and "and twenty-three" shall cease to have effect; and
(ii) for the words "joint committee" there shall be substituted the words "joint board";
(b) subsection (3) shall cease to have effect;
(c) after subsection (3) insert—
"(3A) If it appears to any two or more fire authorities that it is expedient that their areas should be combined for fire-fighting purposes, they may submit to the Secretary of State a scheme in that behalf (in this section referred to as an "administration scheme") and the Secretary of State may by order approve any such scheme submitted to him.
(3B) A scheme under subsection (3A) above shall make provision with respect to the matters mentioned in paragraphs (c) and (d) of subsection (8A) below.
(3C) The power to make an order under subsection (3A) above shall be exercisable by statutory instrument subject to annulment in pursuance of a resolution of either House of Parliament.";
(d) in subsection (4)
(i) for paragraph (a) substitute—
"(a) the dis-establishment of the fire brigades maintained by the several fire authorities, the establishment and maintenance of a combined fire brigade for the combined area, and the appointment, subject to any regu-

lations made under this Act, of a firemaster of that combined brigade;"; and

(ii) for the words "joint committee", in each place where they occur, there shall be substituted the words "joint board";

(e) in subsection (5), for the words "joint committee", in each place where they occur, there shall be substituted the words "joint board";

(f) after subsection (5) insert—

"(5A) Not later than 3 months before the date on which a scheme approved under subsection (3A) above or, as the case may be, made under subsection (8)(b) below is intended to come into effect, every fire authority in respect of whose area or combined area such a scheme has been approved or made shall prepare and submit to the Secretary of State for his approval an establishment scheme for their area or combined area under section 19 of this Act, and the Secretary of State may approve the scheme as submitted to him or subject to such modifications as he may direct.";

(g) subsection (6) shall cease to have effect;

(h) for subsection (7) substitute—

"(7) Where an administration scheme has been approved under subsection (3A) above, the fire authorities affected by it may amend or revoke that scheme by a subsequent scheme submitted to the Secretary of State by them jointly and the Secretary of State may by order approve any such subsequent scheme submitted to him.

(7A) A subsequent scheme under subsection (7) above may make provision with respect to any of the matters for which provision is required to be made, or may be made, by virtue of subsections (4), (5), (8)(b) and (8A) of this section.

(7B) The power to make an order under subsection (7) above shall be exercisable by statutory instrument subject to annulment in pursuance of a resolution of either House of Parliament.";

(i) for subsection (8) substitute—

"(8) The Secretary of State may by order—

(a) vary or revoke an administration scheme;

(b) make a new administration scheme which includes provision—

(i) for the division of the original combined area into any two or more areas, being either areas of fire authorities comprised in such combined area or new combined areas constituted by such scheme;

(ii) for the inclusion in the combined area of any additional areas,

and such an order may make provision with respect to any of the matters for which provision is required to be made, or may be made, by virtue of subsections (4), (5) and (8A) of this section.

(8A) An order under subsection (8) above may make provision with respect to any of the following matters—

(a) the transfer or retransfer to such fire brigade as may be determined by the order of the members of any fire brigade affected by the order;

(b) the transfer or retransfer to such fire authorities as may be determined by the order of any officers, property, rights or liabilities of any fire authority affected by the order;

(c) the payment, by such fire authority and subject to such provisions as may be determined by the order, of compensation to officers employed by any fire authority affected by the order who in consequence of it or of anything done under it suffer direct pecuniary loss by reason of the determination of their appointments or the diminution of their emoluments;

(d) in the case of any person who having immediately before the coming into operation of the order been the firemaster of any fire brigade affected by the order does not on the coming into operation of the order become the firemaster of any fire brigade established in consequence of the order, for the payment, in lieu of compensation under paragraph (c) above, of a pension, gratuity or allowance of such amount, subject to such conditions and by such fire authority as may be specified in the order; and

(e) any other matters incidental to or consequential on any provision contained in the order.

(8B) Before making an order under subsection (8) above which contains provision that two or more local government areas should form a combined area for the provision in the combined area of the services mentioned in section 1 of this Act, the Secretary of State shall—

(a) consult such fire authorities as appear to him to be affected by the order; and

(b) where any such authority submit objections to the order, inform that authority in writing whether he accepts the objections and, if he does not, why he does not.

(8C) The power to make an order under subsection (8) above shall be exercisable by statutory instrument subject to annulment in pursuance of a resolution of either House of Parliament.";

(j) for subsection (9) substitute—

"(9) An order made by the Secretary of State under this section shall provide for the incorporation of a joint board with a common seal and shall confer on such a board power to hold land and to borrow money.";

(k) in subsection (10)—

(i) for the words "joint committee" substitute "joint board"; and

(ii) after "this section" insert "or section 147(4) of the Local Government (Scotland) Act 1973";

(l) in subsection (11)—

(i) for the words "joint committee" substitute "joint board"; and

(ii) after "this section" insert "or section 147(4) of the Local Government (Scotland) Act 1973";

(m) in subsection (13)—

(i) for the words "joint committee", in both places where they occur, substitute "joint board"; and

(ii) for the words from "councils" to "comprised" substitute "councils constituted under section 2 of the Local Government etc. (Scotland) Act 1994 whose area is comprised";

(n) for subsection (15) substitute—

"(15) For section 4 of this Act there shall be substituted the following section—

"4. Subject to the provisions of this Act, with effect from 1st April 1996 the fire authority shall be a council constituted under section 2 of the Local Government etc. (Scotland) Act 1994.".";

(o) in subsection (16)—

(i) for the words from "council" to "comprised" substitute "council constituted under section 2 of the Local Government etc. (Scotland) Act 1994 whose area is comprised"; and

(ii) for the words "joint committee", in both places where they occur, substitute "joint board";

(p) after subsection (16) there shall be inserted—

"(16A) In section 19—

(a) for subsection (3) there shall be substituted the following subsection—

"(3) Every fire authority shall, on such dates as the Secretary of State may by regulations prescribe, notify him of the establishment scheme in force in their area on such dates as he may so prescribe."; and

(b) after subsection (8) there shall be inserted—

"(8A) Regulations made under subsection (3) above shall be made by statutory instrument; and such an instrument shall be subject to annulment in pursuance of a resolution of either House of Parliament."; and

(q) in subsection (20)—

(i) for the words "joint committee" there shall be substituted the words "joint board"; and

(ii) after "this section" insert "or section 147(4) of the Local Government (Scotland) Act 1973".

(4) In section 38(1) (interpretation), in the definition of "combined area", after "Act" insert "or section 147 of the Local Government (Scotland) Act 1973".

The Acquisition of Land (Authorisation Procedure) (Scotland) Act 1947 (c. 42)

28. In section 7(1) of the Acquisition of Land (Authorisation Procedure) (Scotland) Act 1947 (interpretation), in the definition of "local authority", for the words from "any" to the end substitute "any council constituted under section 2 of the Local Government etc. (Scotland) Act 1994".

The Civil Defence Act 1948 (c. 5)

29.—(1) The Civil Defence Act 1948 shall be amended in accordance with this paragraph.

(2) After section 4 insert—

"Joint exercise of functions

4A.—(1) Where—

(a) by virtue of any enactment any of the functions of a local authority are exercised by that authority jointly with one or more other local authorities or by a joint board or joint committee; and

(b) by virtue of this Act, an obligation is imposed, or a power conferred, on a local authority in respect of any of these functions,

to the extent that such obligation or, as the case may be, power has a connection with such functions, such obligation shall be performed, or power exercised, by the authorities jointly or, as the case may be, by the joint board or joint committee; and any thing which may, by virtue of this Act, be done by, to or in respect of a local authority may be done by, to or in respect of two or more such authorities or such joint board or joint committee.

(2) In this section "joint board" and "joint committee" have the meanings given by section 235(1) of the Local Government (Scotland) Act 1973.

(3) This section extends to Scotland only.".

(3) In section 9(1) (interpretation), in the definition of "local authority", for the words "a regional, islands or district council" substitute "a council constituted under section 2 of the Local Government etc. (Scotland) Act 1994".

The Local Government Act 1948 (c. 26)

30. In section 145(2) of the Local Government (Scotland) Act 1948 (application of Act to Scotland), in the definition of "local authority", for "regional, islands or district council" substitute "council constituted under section 2 of the Local Government etc. (Scotland) Act 1994".

The National Assistance Act 1948 (c. 29)

31.—(1) The National Assistance Act 1948 shall be amended in accordance with this paragraph.

(2) In section 33(1) (local authorities for the purposes of Part III), for the words "regional or islands council" substitute "council constituted under section 2 of the Local Government etc. (Scotland) Act 1994".

(3) In section 47(12) (appropriate authorities for purposes of section), for the words "the councils of regions and islands areas" substitute "councils constituted under section 2 of the Local Government etc. (Scotland) Act 1994".

(4) In section 48(4) (councils having duty to provide temporary protection for property of certain persons), for the words from "of the region" to "of which" substitute "constituted under section 2 of the Local Government etc. (Scotland) Act 1994 within whose area".

(5) In section 50(2) (authorities having duty in respect of burial or cremation of the dead), for "islands and district councils" substitute "councils constituted under section 2 of the Local Government etc. (Scotland) Act 1994".

(6) In section 65(e) (meaning of "local authority" in application of Act to Scotland), for the words "regional or islands council" substitute "council constituted under section 2 of the Local Government etc. (Scotland) Act 1994".

The Coast Protection Act 1949 (c. 74)

32.—(1) The Coast Protection Act 1949 shall be amended in accordance with this paragraph.

(2) In section 1 (coast protection authorities), for subsection (1) substitute—

"(1) A council constituted under section 2 of the Local Government etc. (Scotland) Act 1994 any part of whose area adjoins the sea shall be the coast protection authority for that area.".

(3) In section 20(5) (contributions towards expenses of coast protection), the words "or the council of a district in Scotland" shall cease to have effect.

(4) In section 22(2) (power to use for incidental purposes land acquired for coast protection), for "the council of a region or islands area" substitute "a council constituted under section 2 of the Local Government etc. (Scotland) Act 1994".

(5) In section 45(1) (service of notices and other documents), for "the council of a region, islands area or district" substitute "a council constituted under section 2 of the Local Government etc. (Scotland) Act 1994".

(6) In the First Schedule (procedure for making orders and provisions as to the validity of orders), in paragraph 8(b)—

(a) after "and to", where it first occurs, insert "a council of"; and
(b) for the words "region, islands area or district" substitute "council constituted under section 2 of the Local Government etc. (Scotland) Act 1994".

The National Parks and Access to the Countryside Act 1949 (c. 97)

33. In section 99(2) of the National Parks and Access to the Countryside Act 1949 (contributions by local authorities), for "regional, islands or district council" substitute "council constituted under section 2 of the Local Government etc. (Scotland) Act 1994".

The Shops Act 1950 (c. 28)

34. In section 73(4) of the Shops Act 1950 (local authorities), for the words from "means" to the end substitute "means a council constituted under section 2 of the Local Government etc. (Scotland) Act 1994".

The Allotments (Scotland) Act 1950 (c. 38)

35.—(1) The Allotments (Scotland) Act 1950 shall be amended in accordance with this paragraph.
(2) In section 9(a) (restriction of obligations to provide allotments), for "the council of an islands area or a district" substitute "a local authority".
(3) In section 13(1)(b) (interpretation), for "an islands council or district council" substitute "a council constituted under section 2 of the Local Government etc. (Scotland) Act 1994".

The Pet Animals Act 1951 (c. 35)

36. In section 7(3) of the Pet Animals Act 1951 (interpretation), for "the council of any islands area or district" substitute "a council constituted under section 2 of the Local Government etc. (Scotland) Act 1994".

The Rag Flock and Other Filling Materials Act 1951 (c. 63)

37. In section 36(3) of the Rag Flock and Other Filling Materials Act 1951 (application of the Act to Scotland), for "an islands or district council" substitute "a council constituted under section 2 of the Local Government etc. (Scotland) Act 1994".

The Rivers (Prevention of Pollution) (Scotland) Act 1951 (c. 66)

38.—(1) The Rivers (Prevention of Pollution) (Scotland) Act 1951 shall be amended in accordance with this paragraph.
(2) In section 6 (financial provisions), for "councils of the regions" substitute "local authorities".
(3) In section 12 (power of river purification board to appoint agents, etc.)—
(a) for subsection (1) substitute—
   "(1) Subject to the provisions of their administrative scheme prepared in pursuance of an order under section 135(5) and (6)(b) of the Local Government (Scotland) Act 1973, a river purification board may, on such terms and conditions as they may agree with the local authority concerned, appoint any local authority whose area is comprised wholly or partly in the river purification board area to act as the agents of the river purification board to carry out any function vested in the board and exercisable within the area of that local authority; and, subject to the terms of the appointment, the local authority so acting as agent may act through any of their committees or sub-committees.";
(b) in subsection (2), after "made)" insert "(or are successors to an authority who have made)"; and
(c) in subsection (4), for "county or town council" substitute "local authority".
(4) In section 13(1) (application of local government enactments) in the subsection to be substituted for subsection (13) for "council of each region and district" substitute "local authority".
(5) In section 16(1) (annual reports of river purification boards), for the words from "the council" to "district" substitute "every local authority whose area".
(6) In section 17(2) (river purification authorities), for "islands councils" substitute "the councils for Orkney Islands, Shetland Islands and Western Isles".
(7) In section 19(2B) (legal proceedings in respect of public sewers)—
(a) for "local authority" substitute "public"; and
(b) for "by whom the sewer is maintained" substitute "in whom the sewer is vested ("public sewer" and "sewerage authority" being construed in accordance with, respectively, sec-

tion 59(1) of the Sewerage (Scotland) Act 1968 and section 62 of the Local Government etc. (Scotland) Act 1994).".

(8) In section 35(1) (interpretation)—

(a) for the definition of "local authority" substitute—

" "local authority" means a council constituted under section 2 of the Local Government etc. (Scotland) Act 1994";

(b) after the definition of "river purification board area" insert—

" "sewerage authority" shall be construed in accordance with section 62 of the Local Government etc. (Scotland) Act 1994;"; and

(c) in paragraph (b) of the definition of "stream", for "local" substitute "sewerage".

The Hypnotism Act 1952 (c. 46)

39. In section 2(4)(b) of the Hypnotism Act 1952 (meaning of "controlling authority"), for "islands or district council" substitute "council constituted under section 2 of the Local Government etc. (Scotland) Act 1994".

The Post Office Act 1953 (c. 36)

40. In section 51(5)(a) of the Post Office Act 1953 (power of local authority to contribute towards new post office etc.)—

(a) for "an islands area or a district" substitute "a local government area"; and

(b) after "thereof", where secondly occurring, insert "(constituted under section 2 of the Local Government etc. (Scotland) Act 1994)".

The Emergency Laws (Miscellaneous Provisions) Act 1953 (c. 47)

41. In section 5(6)(b) of the Emergency Laws (Miscellaneous Provisions) Act 1953 (power of local authorities as respects letting of certain land), for "an islands or district council" substitute "a council constituted under section 2 of the Local Government etc. (Scotland) Act 1994".

The Long Leases (Scotland) Act 1954 (c. 49)

42. In section 4(3) of the Long Leases (Scotland) Act 1954 (refusal of grant of feu right on ground of public interest), for "regional, islands or district council" substitute "council constituted under section 2 of the Local Government etc. (Scotland) Act 1994".

The Transport Charges &c. (Miscellaneous Provisions) Act 1954 (c. 64)

43. In section 6(1)(c) of the Transport Charges &c. (Miscellaneous Provisions) Act 1954 (revision of charges by independent harbour undertakings etc.), for the words from "a Passenger" to "combination" substitute "the Strathclyde Passenger Transport Executive or a council constituted under section 2 of the Local Government etc. (Scotland) Act 1994".

The Army Act 1955 (c. 18)

44.—(1) The Army Act 1955 shall be amended in accordance with this paragraph.

(2) In section 214(5) (application of the Act to Scotland), for "regional, islands or district council" substitute "council constituted under section 2 of the Local Government etc. (Scotland) Act 1994".

(3) In Schedule 5A (powers of court on trial of civilian), in paragraph 2(1), in the definition of "local authority in Scotland", for "regional or islands council" substitute "council constituted under section 2 of the Local Government etc. (Scotland) Act 1994".

The Air Force Act 1955 (c. 19)

45.—(1) The Air Force Act 1955 shall be amended in accordance with this paragraph.

(2) In section 212(5) (application of the Act to Scotland), for "regional, islands or district council" substitute "council constituted under section 2 of the Local Government etc. (Scotland) Act 1994".

(3) In Schedule 5A (powers of court on trial of civilian), in paragraph 2(1), in the definition of "local authority in Scotland", for "regional or islands council" substitute "council constituted under section 2 of the Local Government etc. (Scotland) Act 1994".

The Valuation and Rating (Scotland) Act 1956 (c. 60)

46. In section 43(1) (interpretation) of the Valuation and Rating (Scotland) Act 1956, in the definition of "valuation authority", for the words "section one of this Act" substitute "section 27 of the Local Government etc. (Scotland) Act 1994".

The Naval Discipline Act 1957 (c. 53)

47. In Schedule 4A to the Naval Discipline Act 1957 (powers of court on trial of civilian), in paragraph 2(1), in the definition of "local authority in Scotland", for "regional or islands council" substitute "council constituted under section 2 of the Local Government etc. (Scotland) Act 1994".

The Land Drainage (Scotland) Act 1958 (c. 24)

48. In Schedule 1 to the Land Drainage (Scotland) Act 1958 (procedure for making, varying or revoking certain orders etc.), in paragraph 1, in the definition of "local authority", for "regional, islands or district council" substitute "council constituted under section 2 of the Local Government etc. (Scotland) Act 1994".

The Disabled Persons (Employment) Act 1958 (c. 33)

49. In section 3(5) of the Disabled Persons (Employment) Act 1958 (provision of sheltered employment by local authorities), for "the council of a region or islands area" substitute "a council constituted under section 2 of the Local Government etc. (Scotland) Act 1994".

The Matrimonial Proceedings (Children) Act 1958 (c. 40)

50.—(1) The Matrimonial Proceedings (Children) Act 1958 shall be amended in accordance with this paragraph.
(2) In section 10(2) (committal of child to local authority), for the words from "of the region" to "which" substitute "(constituted under section 2 of the Local Government etc. (Scotland) Act 1994) in whose area".
(3) In section 12(2) (supervision of child by local authority), for "the council of a region or islands area" substitute "a council constituted under section 2 of the Local Government etc. (Scotland) Act 1994".

The Trading Representations (Disabled Persons) Act 1958 (c. 49)

51. In section 1(5) of the Trading Representations (Disabled Persons) Act 1958 (sellers of goods for blind persons etc.), for "regional, islands or district council" substitute "council constituted under section 2 of the Local Government etc. (Scotland) Act 1994".

The Building (Scotland) Act 1959 (c. 24)

52. In section 29(1) of the Building (Scotland) Act 1959 (interpretation), in the definition of "local authority", for the words from "the", where it first occurs, to the end substitute "a council constituted under section 2 of the Local Government etc. (Scotland) Act 1994".

The Deer (Scotland) Act 1959 (c. 40)

53.—(1) The Deer (Scotland) Act 1959 shall be amended in accordance with this paragraph.
(2) In section 25A (licences to deal in venison)—
(a) in subsection (1) for "An islands or district" substitute "A";
(b) in subsection (2) the words "islands and district" shall cease to have effect; and
(c) in subsections (4) and (5) the words "islands or district" shall cease to have effect.
(3) In section 25D(8) (offences), the words "islands or district" shall cease to have effect.
(4) In section 25F (interpretation of Part IIIA), immediately before the definition of "deer" insert—
" "council" means a council constituted under section 2 of the Local Government etc. (Scotland) Act 1994;".

The Caravan Sites and Control of Development Act 1960 (c. 62)

54. In section 24 of the Caravan Sites and Control of Development Act 1960 (power of local authorities to provide sites for caravans)—
(a) in subsection (8), for the words from "an islands" to the end substitute "a council constituted under section 2 of the Local Government etc. (Scotland) Act 1994."; and
(b) subsection (8A) shall cease to have effect.

The Factories Act 1961 (c. 34)

55. In section 176(1) of the Factories Act 1961 (general interpretation), in the definition of "district council", for the words from "Scotland," to the end substitute "Scotland, a council constituted under section 2 of the Local Government etc. (Scotland) Act 1994".

The Flood Prevention (Scotland) Act 1961 (c. 41)

56.—(1) The Flood Prevention (Scotland) Act 1961 shall be amended in accordance with this paragraph.

(2) In section 1 (purposes for which powers of local authorities under the Act are exercisable), for subsection (2) substitute—

"(2) This section applies to all councils constituted under section 2 of the Local Government etc. (Scotland) Act 1994, and in this Act any reference to a local authority is a reference to a council to whom this section applies.".

(3) In section 4(2) (flood prevention schemes), the words "(whether a different authority from the local authority or not)" shall cease to have effect.

(4) Section 12(2) (appropriations where local authority are sewerage or water authority) shall cease to have effect.

(5) In section 15(1) (interpretation)—
(a) after the definition of "sewer" insert—
     " "sewerage authority" shall be construed in accordance with section 62 of the Local Government etc. (Scotland) Act 1994;"; and
(b) after the definition of "statutory undertakers" and "statutory undertaking" insert—
     " "water authority" shall be construed in accordance with section 62 of the Local Government etc. (Scotland) Act 1994;".

The Local Government (Financial Provisions etc.) (Scotland) Act 1962 (c. 9)

57. In subsection (5) of section 4 of the Local Government (Financial Provisions etc.) (Scotland) Act 1962 (reduction and remission of rates payable by charities etc.), for "section two hundred and forty-four of the Act of 1947" substitute "section 25A of the Local Government (Scotland) Act 1966".

The Education (Scotland) Act 1962 (c. 47)

58. In section 145(16) of the Education (Scotland) Act 1962 (general definitions), for "regional or islands council" substitute "council constituted under section 2 of the Local Government etc. (Scotland) Act 1994".

The Betting, Gaming and Lotteries Act 1963 (c. 2)

59.—(1) The Betting, Gaming and Lotteries Act 1963 shall be amended in accordance with this paragraph.

(2) In Schedule 1 (bookmaker's permits, betting agency permits and betting office licences), in paragraph 2, in the definition of "appropriate local authority", in paragraph (b), for sub-paragraphs (i) and (ii) substitute "the council constituted under section 2 of the Local Government etc. (Scotland) Act 1994 within whose area the relevant premises are, or are to be, situated;".

(3) In Schedule 2 (registered pool promoters), in paragraph 1(1)(b), for "the council of an islands area or district" substitute "a council constituted under section 2 of the Local Government etc. (Scotland) Act 1994.".

(4) In Schedule 3 (licensing of tracks for betting)—
(a) in paragraph 5(2)—
     (i) in head (b)(i), for the words from "of" to "which" substitute "constituted under section 2 of the Local Government etc. (Scotland) Act 1994 within whose area";
     (ii) in head (b)(ii), for the words from "general" to "authority", where it secondly occurs, substitute "planning authority"; and
     (iii) for the words from " "general" to "them" substitute " "planning authority" has the meaning given"; and
(b) for paragraph 6(3) substitute—
     "(3) The authorities referred to in sub-paragraph (1)(e) of this paragraph are—
     (a) the planning authority for any area which includes the track or any part thereof;
     (b) any local authority whose area adjoins any area which includes the track or any part thereof,
     where that authority are not the licensing authority.
     In this sub-paragraph, the expression "local authority" means a council constituted under section 2 of the Local Government etc. (Scotland) Act 1994.".

The Local Government (Financial Provisions) (Scotland) Act 1963 (c. 12)

60.—(1) The Local Government (Financial Provisions) (Scotland) Act 1963 shall be amended in accordance with this paragraph.

(2) For subsection (4) of section 7 (apportionment) substitute—

"(4) The assessor for each valuation area shall, not later than the date prescribed by order under section 13 of the Act of 1956 in the year preceding any year of revaluation, estimate the rateable valuation in that year of revaluation of that area, and shall send certified copies of the estimate so made to the rating authority for that area and to the Secretary of State.".

(3) In section 15 (comparison with other lands and heritages)—

(a) in subsection (1B)—

(i) for the words from the beginning to "General Rate Act 1967" substitute "The rateable value ascribed in the non-domestic rating list maintained under the Local Government Finance Act 1988";

(ii) after "England and Wales" insert "such as is mentioned in paragraph 2(1) of Schedule 6 to that Act"; and

(iii) for the words "net annual", where they secondly occur, substitute "rateable";

(b) after subsection (1B) insert—

"(1BA) The rateable value ascribed in the non-domestic rating list maintained under the Local Government Finance Act 1988 to a hereditament in England and Wales such as is mentioned in paragraph 2(1A) of Schedule 6 to that Act shall, for the purposes of subsections (1) and (1A) above, be treated as equal to the rent which, assuming such a letting of the hereditament as is required to be assumed for the purposes of subsection (1B) above, would reasonably be attributable to the non-domestic use of property.

(1BB) The rateable value ascribed in the non-domestic rating list maintained under the Local Government Finance Act 1988 to a hereditament in England and Wales such as is mentioned in paragraph 2(1B) of Schedule 6 to that Act shall, for the purposes of subsections (1) and (1A) above, be treated as equal to the rent which, assuming such a letting of the hereditament as is required to be assumed for the purposes of subsection (1B) above, would, as regards the part of the hereditament which is not exempt from local non-domestic rating, be reasonably attributable to the non-domestic use of property.";

(c) in subsection (1C)(b)—

(i) after "(1B)" insert ", (1BA) or (1BB)"; and

(ii) for "that subsection" substitute "the said subsection (1B), (1BA) or (1BB)"; and

(d) in subsection (2), for the words "section 4 of the Local Government (Scotland) Act 1975" substitute "section 29 of the Local Government etc. (Scotland) Act 1994".

(4) For section 18 (lands and heritages not deemed to be occupied if subject to tenancy etc.) substitute—

"Definition of "occupier"

18. Notwithstanding anything in the definition of "occupier" in subsection (1) of section 379 of the Act of 1947, lands and heritages shall not be deemed for the purposes of section 24 of the Local Government (Scotland) Act 1966 to be occupied as respects the year 1994–95 or any subsequent year by reason only that they are subject to a tenancy or sub-tenancy.".

(5) In section 26(2) (interpretation), in the definition of "local authority", for the words "regional, islands or district council" substitute "council constituted under section 2 of the Local Government etc. (Scotland) Act 1994".

The Animal Boarding Establishments Act 1963 (c. 43)

61. In section 5(2) of the Animal Boarding Establishments Act 1963 (interpretation), in the definition of "local authority", for "the council of any islands area or district" substitute "a council constituted under section 2 of the Local Government etc. (Scotland) Act 1994".

The Public Works Loans Act 1964 (c. 9)

62. After subsection (4) of section 6 (re-borrowing powers of public authorities) of the Public Works Loans Act 1964 insert—

"(5) This section does not apply to local authorities constituted under section 2 of the Local Government etc. (Scotland) Act 1994 or to joint boards in Scotland.".

The Harbours Act 1964 (c. 40)

63. In Schedule 3 to the Harbours Act 1964 (procedure for making harbour revision and empowerment orders), in paragraph 3(ba), for "regional, islands or district council" substitute "council constituted under section 2 of the Local Government etc. (Scotland) Act 1994".

The Riding Establishments Act 1964 (c. 70)

64. In section 6(4) of the Riding Establishments Act 1964 (interpretation), in the definition of "local authority" for "the council of any islands area or district" substitute "a council constituted under section 2 of the Local Government etc. (Scotland) Act 1994".

The Local Government (Development and Finance) (Scotland) Act 1964 (c. 67)

65. In section 16(1) of the Local Government (Development and Finance) (Scotland) Act 1964 (interpretation), in the definition of "local authority", for "regional, islands or district council" substitute "council constituted under section 2 of the Local Government etc. (Scotland) Act 1994".

The Gas Act 1965 (c. 36)

66.—(1) The Gas Act 1965 shall be amended in accordance with this paragraph.

(2) In section 28(1) (interpretation of Part II), in the definition of "local authority", for "regional, islands or district council" substitute "council constituted under section 2 of the Local Government etc. (Scotland) Act 1994".

(3) In paragraph 11(c) of Schedule 6 (interpretation), for "means a regional or islands council" substitute "shall be construed in accordance with section 62 of the Local Government etc. (Scotland) Act 1994".

The Local Government (Scotland) Act 1966 (c. 51)

67.—(1) The Local Government (Scotland) Act 1966 shall be amended in accordance with this paragraph.

(2) In section 25(1) (Schedule 3 to have effect), the words "the determination of rateable values," shall cease to have effect.

(3) In section 44(1) (game licences), for "islands and district councils" substitute "local authorities".

(4) In section 46(1) (interpretation)—

(a) in the definition of "local authority", for "regional, islands or district council" substitute "council constituted under section 2 of the Local Government etc. (Scotland) Act 1994"; and

(b) for the definition of "rating authority" substitute—
" "rating authority" has the meaning assigned to it by section 30 of the Local Government etc. (Scotland) Act 1994;".

(5) In paragraph 8 of Schedule 3 (rating of unoccupied property), for the words "have ceased" substitute the words "has ceased".

The Plant Health Act 1967 (c. 8)

68. For subsection (3) of section 5 of the Plant Health Act 1967 (execution of Act by local authorities) substitute—
"(3) The local authorities for the purposes of this Act shall be the councils constituted under section 2 of the Local Government etc. (Scotland) Act 1994".

The Forestry Act 1967 (c. 10)

69. In section 40(2)(c)(ii) of the Forestry Act 1967 (compulsory purchase of land), for "regional, islands or district council" substitute "council constituted under section 2 of the Local Government etc. (Scotland) Act 1994".

The Slaughter of Poultry Act 1967 (c. 24)

70. In section 8 of the Slaughter of Poultry Act 1967 (interpretation), in the definition of "local authority", for "an islands or district council" substitute "a council constituted under section 2 of the Local Government etc. (Scotland) Act 1994".

The Police (Scotland) Act 1967 (c. 77)

71.—(1) The Police (Scotland) Act 1967 shall be amended in accordance with this paragraph.

(2) In section 1(1) (police areas), for the words "for every region and for every islands area" substitute "for every local government area".

(3) In section 2(1) (police authorities and their functions), for the words from the beginning to "police authority" substitute "For every police area the council constituted under section 2 of the Local Government etc. (Scotland) Act 1994 shall be the police authority".

(4) In section 18 (execution of warrants in borders)—

(a) for the words "regions", in each place where it occurs, substitute "areas";

(b) for the word "region", in each place where it occurs, substitute "area"; and

(c) for "Borders" in both places where it occurs, substitute "Lothian and Borders".

(5) In section 19 (amalgamation schemes)—

(a) in subsections (2), (3), (4), (6), (7) and (9), for the words "joint police committee", in each place where they occur, substitute "joint police board";

(b) in subsection (3), for "committee", where it secondly and thirdly occurs, substitute "board";

(c) subsection (5) shall cease to have effect; and

(d) after subsection (9) insert—

"(10) An order under this section shall be made by statutory instrument subject to annulment in pursuance of a resolution of either House of Parliament.".

(6) After section 19 insert—

"Incorporation of joint police boards

19A. Every amalgamation scheme made under this Act shall include provision that any joint police board established by the scheme shall be incorporated with a common seal and have power to hold land and to borrow money.".

(7) In section 21 (amendment of amalgamation schemes)—

(a) in subsection (1), for the words from the beginning to "section 20 of this Act" substitute—

"(1) An amalgamation scheme may be amended or revoked—

(a) in the case of a scheme made under section 19 of this Act, by a subsequent scheme made under that section or under section 20 of this Act; and

(b) in the case of a scheme made under section 20 or 21B of this Act, by a subsequent scheme made under section 20 of this Act,";

(b) in subsection (2)(a), at the end insert "or for the creation of any new combination of police areas;";

(c) in subsection (2)(c) and (e), for the words "joint police committee", in both places where they occur, substitute "joint police board"; and

(d) in subsection (2)(c), for the words "such committee" substitute "such police board".

(8) In section 22(1) and (2), for the words "joint police committee", in each place where they occur, substitute "joint police board".

(9) In section 23(6), for the words "joint police committee" substitute "joint police board".

(10) In section 26A(2) (power to give directions to police authority after adverse report), for the words "joint police committee" substitute "joint police board".

(11) In section 26B (police efficiency: allocation of funds), for the words "joint police committee" substitute "joint police board".

(12) In section 26C (duty of compliance), for the words "joint police committee" substitute "joint police board".

(13) In section 32 (police grant)—

(a) in subsection (1), for the words "joint police committees" substitute "joint police boards"; and

(b) in subsection (2), for the words—

(i) "joint police committee" substitute "joint police board"; and

(ii) "committee" substitute "board".

(14) In section 32A(1) (grants for expenditure on safeguarding national security), for the words "joint police committee" substitute "joint police board".

(15) In section 36(5) (common services), for the words "joint police committee" and "committee" substitute "joint police board" and "board" respectively.

(16) In section 51(1) (interpretation)—

(a) in the definition of "amalgamation scheme", for the words "21A" substitute "21B"; and

(b) for the definition of "constituent authority" substitute—

" "constituent authority" means a police authority whose area is included in a combined area by virtue of an amalgamation scheme;".

(17) In paragraph 4 of Schedule 2, for the words "joint police committee" substitute "joint police board".

The Countryside (Scotland) Act 1967 (c. 86)

72.—(1) The Countryside (Scotland) Act 1967 shall be amended in accordance with this paragraph.

(2) In section 46(2) (repair and maintenance of public rights of way), after "being a" insert "public".

(3) In section 48A (regional parks)—

(a) in subsection (2)—

(i) for "Regional councils" substitute "Local authorities";

(ii) for "region", where it first occurs, substitute "area";

        (iii) for "council" substitute "authority";

        (iv) after "into" insert "the area of";

        (v) for "region", where it secondly occurs, substitute "local authority"; and

        (vi) for "regional councils" substitute "authorities"; and

  (b) in subsection (4)(c), for "council or councils" substitute "local authority or authorities".

  (4) In section 49 (camping and caravan sites), subsection (5) shall cease to have effect.

  (5) In section 50(3) (provision of accommodation, meals etc.), for the words from "means" to the end substitute "includes a planning authority".

  (6) In section 54(5) (byelaws), for the words from "means" to the end substitute "includes a planning authority".

  (7) In section 63 (provision of recreational facilities by water authorities)—

  (a) in subsection (1), for "local water authority within the meaning of the Water (Scotland) Act 1980" substitute "water authority"; and

  (b) in subsection (11), the words from "and any reference" to the end shall cease to have effect.

  (8) In section 65(5) (authorities which may appoint rangers as respects waterways etc.)—

  (a) paragraph (c);

  (b) in paragraph (f), the words "within the meaning of section 109(1) of the Water (Scotland) Act 1980"; and

  (c) paragraph (g),

shall cease to have effect.

  (9) In section 78(1) (interpretation)—

  (a) in the definition of "local authority", for "regional, islands or district council" substitute "council constituted under section 2 of the Local Government etc. (Scotland) Act 1994"; and

  (b) after the definition of "statutory undertakers" and "statutory undertakings" insert—

      " "water authority" shall be construed in accordance with section 62 of the Local Government etc. (Scotland) Act 1994;".

The New Towns (Scotland) Act 1968 (c. 16)

  73.—(1) The New Towns (Scotland) Act 1968 shall be amended in accordance with this paragraph.

  (2) In section 1A(1)(b) (reduction of designated areas), for "any regional council, district council and islands council" substitute "the local authority".

  (3) In section 35(2) (power of development corporation to transfer their undertakings)—

  (a) for the words from "council of" to "which" substitute "local authority in whose area"; and

  (b) for "council", where it secondly occurs, substitute "local authority".

  (4) In section 36(2)(b) (winding up of development corporation), for the words from "council" to "which" substitute "local authority in whose area".

  (5) In section 47(1) (interpretation), in the definition of "local authority", for "regional, islands or district council" substitute "council constituted under section 2 of the Local Government etc. (Scotland) Act 1994".

  (6) In paragraph 2 of Schedule 1 (procedure for designating site of new town), for the words from "council" to "district in which" substitute "local authority in whose area".

The Health Services and Public Health Act 1968 (c. 46)

  74.—(1) The Health Services and Public Health Act 1968 shall be amended in accordance with this paragraph.

  (2) In section 63(2)(c) (activities in respect of which instruction may be provided etc.), for the words from "or", where it fourthly occurs, to the end substitute "or a council constituted under section 2 of the Local Government etc. (Scotland) Act 1994".

  (3) In section 65(6) (financial and other assistance by local authorities to certain voluntary organisations)—

  (a) in substituted subsection (2A)—

      (i) for "district and islands council" substitute "local authority"; and

      (ii) for "council", where it secondly and thirdly occurs, substitute "local authority"; and

  (b) in substituted subsection (2B)(a), for "regional or islands council" substitute "council constituted under section 2 of the Local Government etc. (Scotland) Act 1994".

The Sewerage (Scotland) Act 1968 (c. 47)

  75.—(1) The Sewerage (Scotland) Act 1968 shall be amended in accordance with this paragraph.

(2) In section 1 (duty of local authority to provide for sewerage in their area)—

(a) in subsection (1), for "every local authority" substitute "each of the sewerage authorities";

(b) for subsection (2) substitute—

"(2) Without prejudice to the generality of subsection (1) above—

(a) a sewerage authority shall, subject to paragraph (b) below, take their public sewers to such point or points as will enable the owners of premises which are to be served by the sewers to connect their drains or private sewers with the public sewers at reasonable cost;

(b) where the sewerage authority have agreed with some other person (in this section referred to as the "private provider") that he will take a private sewer to such point or points as will enable owners to make such connection as is mentioned in paragraph (a) above, that paragraph shall not apply while the agreement subsists.";

(c) in subsection (3), for "local" substitute "sewerage";

(d) in subsection (4)—

(i) for "public sewers" substitute "a public sewer, or under an agreement such as is mentioned in paragraph (b) of subsection (2) above the private sewer of a private provider,";

(ii) for "local authority concerned" substitute "sewerage authority, or as the case may be private provider, concerned"; and

(iii) for "local authority", where those words secondly occur, substitute "authority or private provider"; and

(e) after subsection (4) add—

"(5) The Secretary of State may by regulations make provision as respects the procedure to be followed as respects a request under subsection (4) above.

(6) The power to make regulations under subsection (5) above shall be exercisable by statutory instrument which shall be subject to annulment in pursuance of a resolution of either House of Parliament.".

(3) In section 2 (maintenance of public sewers and other works)—

(a) for "every local authority" substitute "each of the sewerage authorities"; and

(b) after "this Act" insert "or of Part II of the Local Government etc. (Scotland) Act 1994".

(4) In section 3 (construction etc. of public sewers and public sewage treatment works)—

(a) in each of subsections (1), (2) and (4), for "local", in each place it occurs, substitute "sewerage"; and

(b) in subsection (3), after "notices"—

(i) where it secondly occurs, insert "served by a sewerage authority"; and

(ii) where it thirdly occurs, insert "served by a local authority".

(5) In section 4 (power of local authority to close or alter public sewers etc.)—

(a) for "local" substitute "sewerage"; and

(b) after "this Act" insert "or of Part II of the Local Government etc. (Scotland) Act 1994".

(6) In each of sections 6 (functions outwith area of local authority), 8(1) (agreements as to provision of sewers etc. for new premises) and 9 (loan of temporary sanitary conveniences), for "local", wherever it occurs, substitute "sewerage".

(7) In section 7 (agreements between local authorities and the Secretary of State as respects provision, management, maintenance or use of sewers or drains to take water from surface of trunk road etc.)—

(a) in subsection (1)—

(i) for "the Secretary of State" substitute "a roads authority";

(ii) for "local" substitute "sewerage"; and

(iii) for "trunk roads" substitute "a road";

(b) in subsection (2)—

(i) for "the Secretary of State" substitute "a roads authority"; and

(ii) for "local", in both places where it occurs, substitute "sewerage";

(c) in subsection (3)—

(i) for "The Secretary of State or a local" substitute "A roads authority or a sewerage" and

(ii) for "local", where it secondly occurs, substitute "sewerage"; and

(d) at the end add—

"(3A) In the foregoing provisions of this section, "roads authority" has the same meaning as in the Roads (Scotland) Act 1984.".

(8) In section 11 (keeping of map showing public sewers etc.)—

(a) for subsection (1) substitute—

"(1) A sewerage authority shall keep deposited at their principal office a map showing and distinguishing so far as is reasonably practicable all sewers, drains and sewage treatment works which are vested in them by virtue of this Act or of Part II of the Local Government etc. (Scotland) Act 1994 or in respect of which they have made a determination under section 3A(2) of this Act; and the authority shall provide reasonable facilities at that office for inspection of the map by any person and shall permit a copy of the map, or of an extract of it, to be taken by a person on his paying such reasonable amount as the authority may determine.";

(b) in subsection (2), for "local" substitute "sewerage"; and

(c) at the end add—

"(3) A sewerage authority shall keep deposited at such of their offices, other than their principal office, as they consider appropriate, a copy relevant to the office in question of part of the map mentioned in subsection (1) above; and the authority shall provide the like facilities and permission in relation to the copy part, at the office at which that copy is deposited, as, under subsection (1) above, they do in relation to the map mentioned in that subsection at their principal office.

(4) For the purposes of subsection (3) above, a copy is relevant to an office if it is of such part of the map mentioned in subsection (1) above as appears to the sewerage authority to be appropriate having regard to the geographical location of that office.".

(9) In each of sections 12(1), (3), (4), (6), (7) and (8) (rights of owners and occupiers to connect with and drain into public sewers etc.), for "local", wherever it occurs, substitute "sewerage".

(10) In section 13 (rights of owners and occupiers to connect with and drain into public sewers etc. of other authority)—

(a) in each of subsections (1) and (2), for "local", wherever it occurs, substitute "sewerage"; and

(b) in paragraph (a) of the proviso to subsection (1), after "effect to the" insert "sewerage".

(11) In section 14 (direction by local authority as to manner of construction of works)—

(a) in subsection (1), for "the local" substitute "a sewerage";

(b) in each of subsections (2), (4) and (6), for "local" substitute "sewerage".

(12) In section 15 (owner or occupier to remedy defects in drains and other works)—

(a) in subsection (1)—

   (i) after "local authority" insert "or a sewerage authority";

   (ii) after "vested in the" insert "sewerage"; and

   (iii) for "they" substitute "the authority in question";

(b) in subsection (3), for "local authority"—

   (i) where those words first occur, substitute "authority which served the notice"; and

   (ii) where they occur in the proviso, substitute "authority in question"; and

(c) in subsection (4)—

   (i) for the words from "the medical" to "local authority" substitute "a local authority or a sewerage authority that immediate action is required to remedy a defect"; and

   (ii) in paragraph (c), after "authority" insert "which served the notice".

(13) In section 16 (vesting of sewers and other works)—

(a) in subsection (1)—

   (i) for the words from the beginning to "vest in them" substitute "There shall vest in a sewerage authority"; and

   (ii) for paragraph (c) substitute—

      "(c) subject to any determination notified under subsection (2) of section 3A of this Act, all private sewers connecting with their sewers or sewage treatment works;

      (cc) where they enter into an agreement under subsection (2) of the said section 3A or under subsection (2) of section 16A of this Act (and subject to the terms of that agreement), all private sewers, or as the case may be parts of sewers, to which the agreement relates;";

(b) in subsection (2), for "the commencement of this section shall vest in the local" substitute "1st April 1996 shall vest in the sewerage"; and

(c) in subsection (3), for "local" substitute "sewerage".

(14) After section 16 insert—

"Vesting of certain private sewers

16A.—(1) Subject to any agreement entered into under subsection (2) below, there shall vest in a person authorised, under subsection (1) of section 3A of this Act, by a sewerage authority to construct a sewer not connecting with their sewers or sewage treatment works the sewer constructed; and any sewer vested in a person by this subsection or by a determination under subsection (2) of that section shall be his property and he solely responsible for its management, maintenance and renewal.

(2) Notwithstanding subsection (1) above, the sewerage authority may, on such terms and conditions as they think fit, at any time enter into an agreement under which the sewer, or any part of it, shall vest in them.".

(15) In each of sections 17(1), (2), (3) and (4) (taking over of private sewage treatment works), 24(1) and (2) (right to discharge into public sewers), 25 (meaning of new discharge), 26 (new discharge only with consent), 27(1) and (4)(a) (procedure on application for consent to new discharge), 28(1) (time to dispose of application), 29(1) (decision on application), 30(1) (intimation of decision), 31 (appeal against refusals and conditions), 32(1) and (2) (review of consents, conditions and refusals), 33(2) (disputes as to meaning of "existing discharge"), 34 (right to continue existing discharge), 35 (furnishing of information), 36(1) and (2) (review of continuation of existing discharge) and 37(1), (3), (4) and (6) (agreements as respects trade premises), for "local", wherever it occurs, substitute "sewerage".

(16) Section 18 (expenses of local authorities and dissolution of drainage districts) shall cease to have effect.

(17) In section 20 (compensation for loss etc, resulting from exercise of powers under Part I)—
(a) in subsection (1), for "local" substitute "sewerage";
(b) in subsection (3), for "12" substitute "24";
(c) in subsection (4), for "local" in both places where it occurs substitute "sewerage"; and
(d) at the end add—
    "(5) The foregoing provisions of this section shall apply to a person constructing a sewer by virtue of having been authorised to do so under section 3A(1), as they would apply to a sewerage authority constructing a sewer under section 3(1), of this Act.".

(18) In section 21(1) (buildings not to interfere with sewers)—
(a) for "local" substitute "sewerage";
(b) after "erected" insert "or embankment constructed"; and
(c) at the end add "or in respect of which they have made a determination under section 3A(2) of this Act".

(19) In section 22 (protection for statutory undertakers)—
(a) in each of subsections (1) and (3), for "local" substitute "sewerage"; and
(b) after subsection (2) insert—
    "(2A) The foregoing provisions of this section shall apply to a person constructing a sewer by virtue of having been authorised to do so under section 3A(1), as they would apply to a sewerage authority constructing a sewer under section 3(1), of this Act.".

(20) In section 23 (restriction on working minerals), for the words from "any public" to the end substitute "—
(a) any public sewers, public sewage treatment works or public drains; and
(b) any sewers, sewage treatment works or drains not vested in a sewerage authority but forming (or forming part of) any such system as is mentioned in section 98(1)(b) of the Local Government etc. (Scotland) Act 1994,
to which they do not already apply, with the substitution—
    (i) for references to the railway, of references to the sewers, works or drains; and
    (ii) for references to the company, of references to the sewerage authority, or as the case may be to the person other than a sewerage authority, in whom the sewers, works or drains are vested.".

(21) In section 38 (power to extend certain provisions to certain effluents), in each of subsections (1) and (3), for "local" substitute "sewerage".

(22) In each of sections 39 (right to sewage), 41 (breaking open of roads, etc.), 42 (execution of works for authorities by other persons), 44 (power to require information as to ownership etc. of premises) and 45(1) (production of plans and furnishing of information), for "local", wherever it occurs, substitute "sewerage".

(23) Sections 40 (powers of local authorities as to research and publicity) and 47 (recovery of expenses by local authority) shall cease to have effect.

(24) In section 48 (powers of entry)—
(a) in subsection (1)—
    (i) for "an authorised officer of a local authority" substitute "any person duly authorised by a sewerage authority (whether or not an employee of the authority and whether such authorisation is special or general)";
    (ii) in paragraph (d), at the end add "or which may be authorised by them under section 3A of this Act";
    (iii) after paragraph (d) insert—
        "(dd) inspecting, maintaining, repairing, cleansing, emptying, ventilating or renewing any sewer which is not a public sewer but forms part of any such system as is mentioned in section 98(1)(b) of the Local Government etc. (Scotland) Act 1994;"; and

(iv) in paragraph (f), for the words from "the sewers" to the end substitute "—
    (i) public sewers or public sewage treatment works; or
    (ii) sewers or sewage treatment works not vested in a sewerage authority but
forming (or forming part of) any such system as is mentioned in the said section
98(1)(b).";
(b) in subsection (3)—
    (i) for "entering" substitute "entry is made"; and
    (ii) for "local authority" substitute "the authorised person, or the sewerage authority on his behalf,"; and
(c) in subsection (10), for "local authority" substitute "person who carried it out".
(25) In section 51 (procedure on appeal to Secretary of State)—
(a) in each of subsections (2) and (4), for "local" substitute "sewerage"; and
(b) after subsection (6) add—
    "(7) The Secretary of State may by regulations make further provision as respects the
procedure to be followed in any such appeal.
    (8) The power to make regulations under subsection (7) above shall be exercisable by
statutory instrument, which shall be subject to annulment in pursuance of a resolution of
either House of Parliament.".
(26) Section 52 (exemption from stamp duties) shall cease to have effect.
(27) In each of sections 53 (notices etc. to be in writing) and 55(2) (application of the Act to
Crown premises), for "local" substitute "sewerage".
(28) In section 59(1) (interpretation)—
(a) after the definition of "appointed day" insert—
    " "area", in relation to a sewerage authority, shall be construed in accordance with
    section 62 of the Local Government etc. (Scotland) Act 1994;";
(b) the definitions of "authorised officer" and "local authority" shall cease to have effect;
(c) in the definition of "private sewage treatment works", for "local" substitute "sewerage";
(d) in the definition of "public drain", at the end add "or a sewerage authority";
(e) in each of the definitions of "public sewage treatment works" and "public sewer", for
"local" substitute "sewerage";
(f) after the definition of "sewer" insert—
    " "sewerage authority" shall be construed in accordance with section 62 of the Local
    Government etc. (Scotland) Act 1994;"; and
(g) the definition of "trunk road" shall cease to have effect.

The Social Work (Scotland) Act 1968 (c. 49)

76.—(1) The Social Work (Scotland) Act 1968 shall be amended in accordance with this
paragraph.
(2) In section 1(2) (local authorities for the administration of the Act), for the words "regional
and islands councils" substitute the words "councils constituted under section 2 of the Local
Government etc. (Scotland) Act 1994".
(3) In section 5 (powers of Secretary of State)—
(a) in subsection (1A) for the words "section 2(2) of this Act" there shall be substituted the
words "subsection (1B) below"; and
(b) after subsection (1A) there shall be added—
    "(1B) The enactments referred to in subsection (1A) above are—
    (a) this Act as read with sections 1 and 2(1) of the Chronically Sick and Disabled Persons
    Act 1970 and the Disabled Persons (Services, Consultation and Representation) Act
    1986;
    (b) Part IV of the Children and Young Persons (Scotland) Act 1937;
    (c) section 22(2) to (5A), (7) and (8), section 26(2) to (4) and sections 43, 45, 47 and 48 of
    the National Assistance Act 1948;
    (d) the Disabled Persons (Employment) Act 1958;
    (e) sections 10 to 12 of the Matrimonial Proceedings (Children) Act 1958, and sections
    11 and 12 of the Guardianship Act 1973;
    (f) sections 23, 24, 297 and 329 of the Criminal Procedure (Scotland) Act 1975;
    (g) the Children Act 1975;
    (h) the Adoption Act 1976;
    (i) the Adoption (Scotland) Act 1978;
    (j) sections 21 to 23 of the Health and Social Services and Social Security Adjudications
    Act 1983;
    (k) the Mental Health (Scotland) Act 1984;
    (l) the Foster Children (Scotland) Act 1984;
    (m) sections 38(b) and 235 of the Housing (Scotland) Act 1987;

(n) the Access to Personal Files Act 1987; and

(o) section 19 and Part X of the Children Act 1989."; and

(c) in subsection (2), for paragraph (c) there shall be substituted—

"(c) the performance of the functions of local authorities under any of the enactments mentioned in paragraphs (b), (d), (e), (g), (h), (i), (l) and (o) of subsection (1B) above".

(4) In section 5A(3) (local authority plans for community care services)—

(a) paragraph (b) shall cease to have effect; and

(b) in paragraph (c), for "section 2(2)" substitute "5(1B)".

(5) In section 5B(1) (complaints procedure), for "referred to in section 2(2)" substitute "mentioned in section 5(1B)".

(6) In section 6A (inquiries), for "section 2(2)" substitute "section 5(1B)".

(7) In section 10(1) (making of grants and loans for social work), for the words from "enactments" to "of this Act" substitute "mentioned in paragraphs (b), (d), (e), (g), (h), (i) and (l) of section 5(1B) of this Act".

(8) In section 20A(1) (powers of local authority in course of review of child in care) for "their reporter" substitute "the Principal Reporter".

(9) In section 27(3)(c) (content of probation, community service and supervised attendance scheme etc.), for the words from "the social" to the end substitute "a committee or sub-committee of such authorities".

(10) In section 33(3) (publication of list of members of children's panels), for "offices of the director of social work" substitute "principal offices".

(11) In section 34, subsection (3) (duty of local authority to provide suitable accommodation and facilities for children's hearings) shall cease to have effect.

(12) In section 36 (the reporter)—

(a) subsection (4) shall cease to have effect;

(b) for subsection (5) substitute—

"(5) A reporter shall not, except with the consent of the Scottish Children's Reporter Administration, be employed by a local authority.";

(c) after subsection (5) insert—

"(5A) In subsections (2) and (5) above, "reporter" means the Principal Reporter or any officer of the Scottish Children's Reporter Administration to whom there is delegated, under section 131 (1) of the Local Government etc. (Scotland) Act 1994 any function of the Principal Reporter under this Part of this Act or under the Criminal Procedure (Scotland) Act 1975.";

(d) subsection (6) shall cease to have effect; and

(e) in subsection (8), for "duties of the reporter" substitute "functions of the Principal Reporter under this Act and under the Criminal Procedure (Scotland) Act 1975".

(13) In section 36A (power of reporters to conduct proceedings before sheriff)—

(a) in paragraph (a), for the words from "officers", where first occurring, to "solicitors" substitute the words "the reporter, whether or not he is an advocate or solicitor";

(b) in paragraph (b), for "officer" substitute "reporter"; and

(c) at the end add the following—

"In this section, "reporter" has the same meaning as it has in subsections (2) and (5) of section 36 of this Act.".

(14) In section 38 (initial investigation of cases)—

(a) in subsection (1) for "a reporter"; and

(b) in subsection (2) for "the appropriate reporter",

substitute "the Principal Reporter".

(15) In section 44(6) (direction as to transfer of child where disposal other than by discharge of referral), for "a director of social work" substitute "the chief social work officer".

(16) In section 47(1) (duration and variation of supervision requirements) for "their reporter" substitute "the Principal Reporter".

(17) In section 50(1) (appeal from sheriff to Court of Session) for "a reporter" substitute "the Principal Reporter".

(18) In section 54 (transfer of case to another children's hearing), in subsection (1), for the words from "with" to "for a" substitute the words "for the other".

(19) In section 58A(3) (residence in secure accommodation) for "director of social work" substitute "chief social work officer".

(20) In section 58B(3) (order placing child in secure accommodation) for "director of social work" substitute "chief social work officer".

(21) In section 58E(1) (warrants to detain in secure accommodation) for "director of social work" substitute "chief social work officer".

(22) In section 73 (supervision of children moving to Scotland from England and Wales or Northern Ireland), in subsection (1), in paragraph (b), for the words from "reporter" to the end substitute "Principal Reporter".

(23) In section 75(1) (duties of reporter where parent of child subject to certain orders moves to Scotland), for the words from "reporter of the local authority" to "residing" substitute "Principal Reporter".

(24) In section 76(2) (procedure in children's hearing and courts)—

(a) for "a reporter" substitute "the Principal Reporter"; and

(b) the words "to which the case stands referred" shall cease to have effect.

(25) In Schedule 3 (children's panels)—

(a) in paragraph 3—

    (i) at the beginning insert "Subject to paragraph 5B below,"; and

    (ii) sub-paragraph (i) and, in sub-paragraph (ii), the words "in any other case," shall cease to have effect;

(b) after paragraph 5A insert—

    "5B.—(1) Two or more local authorities may, for the purpose of discharging the function imposed on them by paragraph 3 above, make arrangements to form a Children's Panel Advisory Committee for their areas (hereafter referred to as a "joint advisory committee").

    (2) A joint advisory committee shall not be formed in pursuance of arrangements made under sub-paragraph (1) above unless the authorities concerned have obtained the consent in writing of the Secretary of State.

    (3) The Secretary of State may give a direction, in any case where a joint advisory committee has not been formed, to two or more local authorities requiring them to form a joint advisory committee; and the local authorities shall comply with any such direction.

    (4) The provisions of this Schedule shall apply, subject to any necessary modifications, to a joint advisory committee as they apply to a Children's Panel Advisory Committee formed under the said paragraph 3."; and

(c) in paragraph 7, for "may" substitute "shall".

(26) For "reporter", wherever occurring, substitute "Principal Reporter".

(27) Sub-paragraph (26) above does not affect any of the particular amendments made by this paragraph.

The Theatres Act 1968 (c. 54)

77. In section 18(1) of the Theatres Act 1968 (interpretation), for "the islands or district council" substitute "a council constituted under section 2 of the Local Government etc. (Scotland) Act 1994".

The Gaming Act 1968 (c. 65)

78.—(1) The Gaming Act 1968 shall be amended in accordance with this paragraph.

(2) In section 44(3) (local authority not to maintain or contribute to premises licensed under Part II), for "regional council, islands council or district council" substitute "council constituted under section 2 of the Local Government etc. (Scotland) Act 1994".

(3) In Schedule 2 (grant, renewal, cancellation and transfer of licences), in paragraph 2(2), in the definition of "the appropriate local authority", for from the word "(i)" to "district" substitute "the council constituted under section 2 of the Local Government etc. (Scotland) Act 1994".

(4) In Schedule 9 (permits under section 34), in paragraph 1(d), for the words "of the islands area or district in which" substitute "constituted under section 2 of the Local Government etc. (Scotland) Act 1994 in whose area".

The Medicines Act 1968 (c. 67)

79. In section 109 of the Medicines Act 1968 (enforcement in Scotland)—

(a) in subsection (2)(d), for the words from "regional" to the end substitute "council constituted under section 2 of the Local Government etc. (Scotland) Act 1994 and the area of such a council"; and

(b) in subsection (2A), for "an islands or district council" substitute "a council constituted under section 2 of the Local Government etc. (Scotland) Act 1994".

The Transport Act 1968 (c. 73)

80.—(1) The Transport Act 1968 shall be amended in accordance with this paragraph.

(2) In section 9(1) (Passenger Transport Areas, Authorities and Executives)—

(a) in paragraph (a), for sub-paragraph (ii) substitute—

"(ii) in Scotland, such area to be known as the Strathclyde Passenger Transport Area as the Minister may designate for the purposes of section 40 of the Local Government etc. (Scotland) Act 1994;";

(b) in paragraph (b), for sub-paragraph (ii) substitute—

"(ii) in relation to the Strathclyde Passenger Transport Area, the Strathclyde Passenger Transport Authority"; and

(c) in paragraph (c)—

(i) after "be" insert—

"(i) in England and Wales";

and

(ii) after "passenger transport area", where secondly occurring, insert "and

(ii) in Scotland, the Strathclyde Passenger Transport Executive".

(3) In section 9A(9)(b) (general functions of Passenger Transport Authorities and Executives), the words "regional or islands" shall cease to have effect.

(4) In section 9B(1)(a) (consultation and publicity with respect to policies as to services), for "regional council" substitute "council (constituted under section 2 of the Local Government etc. (Scotland) Act 1994)".

(5) In section 10(6) (application of Part I of Harbours, Piers and Ferries (Scotland) Act 1937 to Executive), for the words from "that area" to "that region" substitute "the Executive were within the meaning of that Act a local authority for that area".

(6) In section 34 (assistance for rural bus or ferry service)—

(a) in subsection (2) for the words from "regional" to "jointly" substitute "council or two or more councils acting jointly";

(b) in subsection (3), for "any of the councils aforesaid" substitute "a council";

(c) in subsection (4)—

(i) for "regional or islands councils" substitute "a council"; and

(ii) for "such a" substitute "that"; and

(d) after subsection (4) insert—

"(5) In this section "council" means a council constituted under section 2 of the Local Government etc. (Scotland) Act 1994.".

(7) In section 56 (assistance by Secretary of State or local authority towards capital expenditure on public transport facilities)—

(a) in subsection (2B), in the definition of "relevant local authority", in paragraph (c), for "regional or islands council" substitute "council constituted under section 2 of the Local Government etc. (Scotland) Act 1994";

(b) in subsection (4)(b), the words "regional or islands" shall cease to have effect; and

(c) in subsection (6)(d), for "regional or islands council" substitute "council constituted under section 2 of the Local Government etc. (Scotland) Act 1994".

(8) In section 63(6) (objections to grant of operators' licences), in the definition of "local authority", in paragraph (b), for "regional, islands or district council" substitute "council constituted under section 2 of the Local Government etc. (Scotland) Act 1994".

(9) Section 115(3) (as substituted by paragraph 19 of Schedule 18 to the 1973 Act) shall cease to have effect and after subsection (3) of section 115 (interpretation of Part VII) insert—

"(3A) In sections 109, 112, 113 and 114 of this Act, "local authority" means, as respects Scotland, a council constituted under section 2 of the Local Government etc. (Scotland) Act 1994".

(10) In section 123(2) (power of certain authorities to contribute to cost of barriers etc. at level crossings), for "county council and a town council" substitute "council constituted under section 2 of the Local Government etc. (Scotland) Act 1994".

(11) In section 124(4) (Board's obligations at level crossings with certain roads), for the words from "Scotland" to "council" substitute "Scotland, a council constituted under section 2 of the Local Government etc. (Scotland) Act 1994".

(12) In Schedule 5 (Passenger Transport Authorities and Executives), in Part II, in paragraph 2—

(a) for "regional council", where it first occurs, substitute "council (constituted under section 2 of the Local Government etc. (Scotland) Act 1994)"; and

(b) for "the regional", where secondly occurring, substitute "such".

The Mines and Quarries (Tips) Act 1969 (c. 10)

81. In section 11(3)(b) of the Mines and Quarries (Tips) Act 1969 (meaning of "local authority" for purposes of Part II), for the words from "general" to "1973" substitute "a council constituted under section 2 of the Local Government etc. (Scotland) Act 1994".

The Post Office Act 1969 (c. 48)

82. In section 86(1) of the Post Office Act 1969 (interpretation of Part III), in the definition of "local authority", in paragraph (b), for "regional, islands or district council" substitute "council constituted under section 2 of the Local Government etc. (Scotland) Act 1994".

The Employers' Liability (Compulsory Insurance) Act 1969 (c. 57)

83. In section 3(2)(b) of the Employers' Liability (Compulsory Insurance) Act 1969 (authorities exempted from insurance)—
   (a) for the words from "a", where it thirdly occurs, to "in", where it secondly occurs, substitute "a council constituted under section 2 of the Local Government etc. (Scotland) Act 1994 in"; and
   (b) after "such council" insert "the Strathclyde Passenger Transport Authority".

The Local Authorities (Goods and Services) Act 1970 (c. 39)

84. In section 1(4) of the Local Authorities (Goods and Services) Act 1970 (supply of goods and services by local authorities), in the definition of "local authority"—
   (a) for "regional, islands or district council" substitute "council constituted under section 2 of the Local Government etc. (Scotland) Act 1994"; and
   (b) for "those" substitute "two or more such councils".

The Agriculture Act 1970 (c. 40)

85.—(1) The Agriculture Act 1970 shall be amended in accordance with this paragraph.
   (2) For subsection (2) of section 67 (enforcement authorities and appointment of inspectors and analysts) substitute—
      "(2) In Scotland it shall be the duty of every council constituted under section 2 of the Local Government etc. (Scotland) Act 1994 to enforce this Part of this Act within their area.".
   (3) In section 92 (provision of flood warning systems)—
   (a) in subsection (1), for the words "an islands council", where they first occur, substitute "the council (constituted under section 2 of the Local Government etc. (Scotland) Act 1994) for Orkney Islands, Shetland Islands or Western Isles";
   (b) in the proviso to subsection (1)—
         (i) in paragraph (ia), for the words "by an islands council" substitute "any of those councils"; and
         (ii) for the words from "region" to "within which" substitute "local authority within whose area"; and
   (c) in subsection (2)(b), for "regional or district council" substitute "council constituted under section 2 of the Local Government etc. (Scotland) Act 1994 and "area", in relation to such an authority, shall be construed in accordance with the provisions of Part 1 of that Act".
   (4) In section 94 (arrangements with other bodies), for the words "islands council"—
   (a) where they first occur, substitute "any of the councils mentioned in subsection 92(1) of this Act"; and
   (b) in each of the other places where they occur, substitute "such council".

The Chronically Sick and Disabled Persons Act 1970 (c. 44)

86. In section 21(8) of the Chronically Sick and Disabled Persons Act 1970 (badges for display on motor vehicles used by disabled persons), for the words from "the council", where they thirdly occur, to "Scotland" substitute ", in relation to Scotland, a council constituted under section 2 of the Local Government etc. (Scotland) Act 1994".

The Fire Precautions Act 1971 (c. 40)

87. In section 43(1) of the Fire Precautions Act 1971, in the definition of "local authority", in paragraph (b), for "islands or district council" substitute "council for a local government area".

The Town and Country Planning (Amendment) Act 1972 (c. 42)

88. In section 10C(11) of the Town and Country Planning (Amendment) Act 1972 (grants for repair of buildings in town schemes), for "regional, islands or district council" substitute "council constituted under section 2 of the Local Government etc. (Scotland) Act 1994".

The Poisons Act 1972 (c. 66)

89. In section 11(2) of the Poisons Act 1972 (interpretation), in the definition of "local authority", in paragraph (b), for "the council of a region or islands area" substitute "a council constituted under section 2 of the Local Government etc. (Scotland) Act 1994".

The Employment Agencies Act 1973 (c. 35)

90. In section 13(1) of the Employment Agencies Act 1973 (interpretation), for "regional, islands or district council" substitute "council constituted under section 2 of the Local Government etc. (Scotland) Act 1994".

The Breeding of Dogs Act 1973 (c. 60)

91. In section 5(2) of the Breeding of Dogs Act 1973 (interpretation), in the definition of "local authority", for "an islands or district council" substitute "a council constituted under section 2 of the Local Government etc. (Scotland) Act 1994".

The Local Government (Scotland) Act 1973 (c. 65)

92.—(1) The 1973 Act shall be amended in accordance with this paragraph.

(2) In section 14(1) (duty of the Boundary Commission to review local government areas), for—

(a) "ten", in both places where it occurs, substitute "eight";

(b) "fifteen", in both places where it occurs, substitute "twelve"; and

(c) "16th May 1975" substitute "1st April 1996".

(3) In section 16(2) (duty of the Boundary Commission to review electoral arrangements), for—

(a) "ten", in both places where it occurs, substitute "eight";

(b) "fifteen", in both places where it occurs, substitute "twelve"; and

(c) "initial" substitute "first".

(4) For section 20 (initial review of areas and electoral arrangements) substitute—

"First review of electoral arrangements

20. Schedule 5 to this Act shall have effect with respect to the first review of electoral arrangements for local government areas after 1st April 1996.".

(5) For section 23 (change of name of local government area) substitute—

"Change of name of local government area

23.—(1) The council of a local government area may, by a resolution passed by not less than two-thirds of the members voting thereon at a meeting of the council specially convened for the purpose with notice of the object, change the name of the area.

(2) Notice of any change of name made under this section—

(a) shall be sent by the council concerned to the Secretary of State, to the Director General of the Ordnance Survey and to the Registrar General of Births, Deaths and Marriages for Scotland; and

(b) shall be published in such manner as the Secretary of State may direct.

(3) A change of name made in pursuance of this section shall not affect any rights or obligations of any council, authority or person, or render defective any legal proceedings; and any legal proceedings may be commenced or continued as if there had been no change of name.".

(6) In section 24(5) (provision which may be included in orders under Part II)—

(a) in each of paragraphs (c) and (d), for "areas", wherever it occurs, substitute "wards"; and

(b) in paragraph (f)—

(i) the words "regional, islands or district" shall cease to have effect; and

(ii) for "area" substitute "ward".

(7) In section 28 (supplementary provision to Part II)—

(a) in subsection (1)—

(i) in the definition of "electoral arrangements", for "areas" and, where it fourthly occurs, "area" substitute "wards" and "ward" respectively; and

(ii) for the definition of "local government area" substitute—

" "local government area" means the area of a local authority;"; and
(b) in subsection (2), for the words "this Act", where they thirdly occur, substitute "the Local Government etc. (Scotland) Act 1994.".
(8) In section 31 (disqualification for nomination etc.)—
(a) for the words "chairman or vice-chairman", in both places where they occur, substitute "convener or depute convener";
(b) after subsection (3) insert—
"(3A) A person who is for the time being an officer or employee of the Strathclyde Passenger Transport Authority or an employee of a subsidiary of that Authority shall be disqualified for being appointed or for being a member of the Strathclyde Passenger Transport Authority."; and
(c) subsection (4) shall cease to have effect.
(9) In section 38 (disability of members from voting etc.), in subsection (4) for the words "chairman or vice-chairman" substitute "convener or depute convener".
(10) In section 47 (allowances for attending conferences and meetings)—
(a) in subsection (4), the words ", other than a water development board within the meaning of the Water (Scotland) Act 1980,"; and
(b) subsection (5),
shall cease to have effect.
(11) In section 50B (access to agenda and connected reports), in subsection (4)(b), for the word "chairman" substitute "convener".
(12) In section 50K(2)(b) (interpretation), for "the enactment" substitute "either of the enactments".
(13) In section 55 (assistance to community councils), for "islands and district councils" substitute "councils for local government areas".
(14) In section 56 (arrangements for discharge of functions by local authorities)—
(a) in subsection (6), paragraphs (a) and (c) shall cease to have effect; and
(b) in subsection (9)—
(i) in paragraph (b), for "21 and 21A" substitute "and 21";
(ii) paragraph (c) shall cease to have effect; and
(iii) for paragraph (d) substitute—
"(d) paragraph 3 (Children's Panel Advisory Committees) and paragraph 5B (joint advisory committees) of Schedule 3 to the Social Work (Scotland) Act 1968;".
(15) In section 63 (application of Part V to police authorities)—
(a) in subsection (2) the words "or a district council" shall cease to have effect;
(b) in subsection (3), after paragraph (b) insert—
"(c) sections 62A to 62C.";
(c) in subsections (4) and (5), for the words "joint police committee", in each place where they occur, substitute "joint police board";
(d) in subsection (5)(a), the words "or district council" shall cease to have effect; and
(e) in subsection (5)(b) for the word "committee" substitute "board".
(16) After section 63 insert—

"Sections 62A to 62C not to apply to fire authority
63A. Sections 62A to 62C of this Act shall not apply to a local authority in relation to their functions as a fire authority.".
(17) In section 64(5) (excepted enactments for purposes of section 64(4))—
(a) paragraphs (c) and (f) shall cease to have effect; and
(b) in paragraph (e), for "directors of social work" substitute "chief social work officers".
(18) In section 67 (members of authorities not to be appointed as officers), for the words "chairman or vice-chairman" substitute "convener or depute convener".
(19) In section 83 (power of local authorities to incur expenditure for certain purposes)—
(a) subsections (2A) and (2B) shall cease to have effect; and
(b) in subsection (3)(c), for the words "chairman of a regional, islands or district council, a chairman" substitute "convener of a local authority, a convener".
(20) In section 84 (powers of local authorities with respect to emergencies), subsection (2) shall cease to have effect.
(21) In section 87 (research and the collection of information)—
(a) in subsection (1)—
(i) for "council" substitute "local authority"; and
(ii) the words "any other local authority in the area," shall cease to have effect;
(b) in subsection (2)—

(i) for "a council" substitute "a local authority";

(ii) for the words from "council or" to "the council", where they first occur, substitute "local authority"; and

(iii) the words from "and where" to the end shall cease to have effect; and

(c) subsection (3) shall cease to have effect.

(22) In section 92(2) (meanings of certain expressions for purposes of section), in the definition of "securities", for the words from "has" to the end substitute "means—

(a) investments falling within any of paragraphs 1 to 6 of Schedule 1 to the Financial Services Act 1986 or, so far as relevant to any of those paragraphs, paragraph 11 of that Schedule; or

(b) rights (whether actual or contingent) in respect of money lent to, or deposited with, any society registered under the Industrial and Provident Societies Act 1965 or any building society within the meaning of the Building Societies Act 1986.".

(23) In section 93 (general fund), for subsection (2)(b) substitute—

"(b) which relate to the common good of the council;".

(24) In section 94 (capital expenses), for subsection (1A) substitute—

"(1A) The provisions of this section shall apply to the Strathclyde Passenger Transport Authority as they apply to a local authority; and the giving of approval by the Strathclyde Passenger Transport Authority to any proposal for expenditure referred to in section 15(1) (c) of the Transport Act 1968 shall be deemed for the purposes of this section to be an incurring of liability by the Authority to meet capital expenses.".

(25) In section 100 (auditor's right of access to documents)—

(a) after subsection (1A) insert—

"(1B) Without prejudice to subsection (1) above, the auditor shall be entitled to require any officer, former officer, member or former member of an authority or body whose accounts are required to be audited in accordance with this Part of this Act to give him such information or explanation as he thinks necessary for the purposes of the audit and, if he thinks it necessary, to require any of the persons mentioned above to attend before him in person to give the information or explanation.";

(b) in subsection (2), for "subsection (1)" substitute "subsections (1) and (1B)"; and

(c) in subsection (3)—

(i) after "(1)" insert "or (1B)"; and

(ii) the words from "and to an additional fine" to the end shall cease to have effect.

(26) In subsection (3) of section 102 (reports to Commission by Controller of Audit), for the words "the audit" substitute "any matter arising out of the auditing".

(27) In section 103 (action by Commission for local authority accounts), for subsection (6)(b) substitute—

"(b) may require the attendance of members or officers, or former members or officers, of any local authority to give oral evidence to the Commission; and

(c) may pay to any person attending a hearing under this section such expenses as they think fit.".

(28) For section 123 (education authorities) substitute—

"Education authorities

123. The education authority for the purposes of the Education (Scotland) Act 1980 and any other enactment conferring functions on the education authority shall be a local authority.".

(29) For section 126 (disqualification for membership of education committees etc.) substitute—

"Disqualification for membership of committees appointed by education authorities

126. Notwithstanding the provisions of section 59 of this Act, a person shall not, by reason of his being a teacher employed in an educational establishment under the management of an education authority, be disqualified for being a member of—

(a) a committee such as is mentioned in subsection (1) of section 124 of this Act;

(b) a joint committee of two or more authorities whose purposes include either of those mentioned in paragraphs (a) and (b) of that subsection; or

(c) any sub-committee of such a committee or joint committee.".

(30) In section 128 (educational endowments), in Table B, in subsection (2), for the words "Chairman of council" substitute "Convener of council".

(31) In section 130 (housing)—

(a) in subsection (1), for "an islands or a district council" substitute "a council constituted under section 2 of the Local Government etc. (Scotland) Act 1994"; and

    (b) for subsection (2) substitute—

      "(2) Before any local authority exercise outwith their area any power under Part I of the Housing (Scotland) Act 1987 (provision of housing accommodation) the authority shall give notice of their intention to do so to the local authority in whose area they propose to exercise the power, but failure to give any such notice shall not invalidate the exercise of the power.".

  (32) In section 133 (roads), subsection (1) shall cease to have effect.

  (33) Section 134(1) (building) shall cease to have effect.

  (34) In section 135 (prevention of river pollution)—

    (a) in subsection (2), for "islands councils" substitute "the councils for Orkney Islands, Shetland Islands and Western Isles";

    (b) in subsection (3), for "islands areas" substitute "the areas mentioned in subsection (2) above";

    (c) in subsection (5)—

        (i) in paragraph (a), the words from "not" to the end shall cease to have effect; and

        (ii) for paragraph (b) substitute—

        "(b) that one half of the members of the board shall be appointed from among their members by such of the councils wholly or partly within the area of the board and in such proportions as may be so specified; and that one half of the members of the board shall be appointed by the Secretary of State, after consultation with such bodies as he thinks fit, to represent the interests of persons concerned with the carrying on of agriculture, fisheries or industry in the board's area or any other interests which, in the opinion of the Secretary of State, should be represented on the board,";

    (d) in subsection (6)(d), the word "regional" shall cease to have effect;

    (e) in subsection (7)—

        (i) for from "16th May 1975" to "burghs" substitute "1st April 1996, regional and district councils"; and

        (ii) for from "Schedule 7" to the end of that subsection substitute "subsections (4) to (7) of section 63 of the Local Government etc. (Scotland) Act 1994 (alteration of water areas and sewerage areas) shall apply to the making of such an order as they apply to the making of an order under that section subject to such modifications as may be necessary";

    (f) after subsection (7) insert—

      "(7A) An order under this section shall be made by statutory instrument subject to annulment in pursuance of a resolution of either House of Parliament."; and

    (g) in subsection (9), for from "water development" to "1980" substitute "joint board all the members of which, other than any ex officio members, are appointed by one or more local authorities".

  (35) In section 135A(2) (variation of composition of river purification boards), for paragraphs (b) and (c) substitute—

    "(b) that one half of the members of the board shall be appointed from among their members by such of the councils wholly or partly within the area of the board and in such proportions as may be so specified;".

  (36) Section 137(1) (flood prevention) shall cease to have effect.

  (37) Section 138(1) (coast protection) shall cease to have effect.

  (38) Section 140 (allotments) shall cease to have effect.

  (39) Section 142 (public health) shall cease to have effect.

  (40) Sections 143 (transfer of functions under 1968 Act) and 148(1) (transfer of functions of regional water boards to water authorities) shall cease to have effect.

  (41) In section 145 (Ordnance Survey)—

    (a) in subsection (2)—

        (i) for "regional, islands or district council" substitute "local authority"; and

        (ii) for "council", where it secondly occurs, substitute "authority";

    (b) in subsection (4), for "regional, islands or district council, as the case may be", in both places where it occurs, substitute "local authority"; and

    (c) in subsection (5), for the words from "a region" to "may be" substitute "the area of a local authority".

  (42) In section 146(5) (police), for the words "regions" and "region", in each place where either occurs, substitute respectively "areas" and "area".

  (43) For section 150 (public transport) substitute—

"Schedule 18 to continue to have effect

    150. Schedule 18 to this Act (amendment of certain enactments relating to transport) shall continue to have effect.".

(44) In section 153 (ferries)—
(a) in subsection (1)—
    (i) for "local authorities" substitute "regional or islands councils"; and
    (ii) the words "regional or islands" shall cease to have effect;
(b) in subsection (2)—
    (i) the words "regional or islands" shall cease to have effect; and
    (ii) the word "such", wherever it occurs, shall cease to have effect;
(c) in subsection (3)—
    (i) the words "regional or islands" shall cease to have effect; and
    (ii) the word "such", where it first occurs, shall cease to have effect; and
(d) in subsection (5), after "this section" insert "—
    "council" means a council constituted under section 2 of the Local Government etc.
    (Scotland) Act 1994; and".
(45) In section 154 (piers and harbours)—
(a) in subsection (1)—
    (i) the words "Subject to subsection (3A) below" shall cease to have effect;
    (ii) for "local authorities" substitute "regional, islands or district councils";
    (iii) for "those authorities" substitute "regional, islands or district councils"; and
    (iv) the words "regional or islands" shall cease to have effect;
(b) in subsection (2), the word "regional", in both places where it occurs, shall cease to have effect;
(c) in subsection (3), the words—
    (i) "regional or islands"; and
    (ii) "such",
shall cease to have effect;
(d) subsections (3A) and (3B) shall cease to have effect; and
(e) in subsection (7), after "this section" insert "—
    "council" means a council constituted under section 2 of the Local Government etc.
    (Scotland) Act 1994; and".
(46) Section 155(1) (district council for purposes of Factories Act 1961) shall cease to have effect.
(47) Section 156(1) (local authority responsible for enforcing provisions of Offices, Shops and Railway Premises Act 1963) shall cease to have effect.
(48) Section 157 (local authority responsible for enforcing provisions of Shops Act 1950) shall cease to have effect.
(49) Section 159 (local authority not subject to requirements of Employers' Liability (Compulsory Insurance) Act 1969) shall cease to have effect.
(50) In section 163 (public libraries, museums and art galleries)—
(a) subsection (1);
(b) in subsection (2), the words "as aforesaid"; and
(c) subsection (3),
shall cease to have effect.
(51) Section 168 (census) shall cease to have effect.
(52) In section 169(1) (functions in relation to burial grounds etc.)—
(a) for "councils", where it first occurs, substitute "islands or district councils"; and
(b) for "islands or district councils" substitute "councils constituted under section 2 of the Local Government etc. (Scotland) Act 1994".
(53) In section 170(1) (war memorials), for "islands or district council" substitute "local authority within the meaning of this Act".
(54) In section 170A(5) (application of certain provisions of the 1980 Act to pipes and works for conveying heat etc.)—
(a) paragraph (a) shall cease to have effect; and
(b) for paragraphs (c) and (d) substitute—
    "and
    (c) for any reference to a water authority there were substituted a reference to the local authority in question, whether acting alone or jointly with some other person.".
(55) In section 170B(2) (provisions supplementary to section 170A)—
(a) the words "or water development boards" where they first occur shall cease to have effect; and
(b) for the words "water authorities or water development boards" substitute "a water authority".
(56) Section 171(1) and (2) (local authority for the purposes of certain enactments) shall cease to have effect.

(57) For section 172 (planning authorities) substitute—

"Planning authorities
172.—(1) The planning authority for the purposes of the Act of 1972 and this Part of this Act shall be a local authority, and the district of the planning authority shall be the area of the local authority.
(2) In the term "local planning authority", wherever it occurs in any enactment or instrument made under or by virtue of an enactment, the word "local" shall be omitted.
(3) In any enactment or instrument made under or by virtue of an enactment, a reference to a planning authority shall, unless otherwise provided, or unless the context otherwise requires, be construed as a reference to a local authority.
(4) In this Part of this Act "the Act of 1972" means the Town and Country Planning (Scotland) Act 1972.".
(58) For section 188 (miscellaneous licensing, registration and related matters) substitute—

"Part III of Schedule 24 to continue to have effect
188. Part III of Schedule 24 to this Act (miscellaneous licensing, registration and related matters) shall continue to have effect.".
(59) In section 190 (service of legal proceedings), for the word "chairman", in both places where it occurs, substitute "convener".
(60) For subsection (1) of section 194 (execution of deeds by local authority) substitute—
"(1) For a purpose other than is mentioned in subsection (1A) below, a document is validly executed by a local authority if signed on behalf of that authority by their proper officer.
(1A) For the purposes of any enactment or rule of law relating to the authentication of documents, a document is validly executed by a local authority if subscribed on behalf of the authority by being executed in accordance with the provisions of subsection (1) above.
(1B) A document which bears to have been executed by a local authority in accordance with subsection (1A) above shall, in relation to such execution, be a probative document if—
(a) the subscription of the document bears to have been attested by at least one witness; or
(b) the document bears to be sealed with the seal of the authority.".
(61) In section 201(1) (byelaws for good rule and government), for the words from "the region" to "be" substitute "their area".
(62) In section 202 (procedure, etc., for byelaws), subsection (13) shall cease to have effect.
(63) In section 206 (admission of honorary freemen)—
(a) in subsection (1)—
(i) for "An islands or district council" substitute "A local authority";
(ii) for "council" substitute "authority"; and
(iii) for "the islands area or district", in both places where it occurs, substitute "their area"; and
(b) in subsection (2), for "islands or district council" substitute "local authority".
(64) Section 226 (transitional provision for joint boards existing before 16th May 1975) shall cease to have effect.
(65) Section 230 (transitional establishment of committees of local authorities) shall cease to have effect.
(66) In section 235(1) (interpretation)—
(a) the definitions of "area", "college council", "school council" and "education committee" shall cease to have effect;
(b) for the definition of "electoral area" substitute—
" "electoral ward" shall be construed in accordance with section 5 of the Local Government etc. (Scotland) Act 1994;";
(c) for the definition of "local authority" substitute—
" "local authority" means a council constituted under section 2 of the Local Government etc. (Scotland) Act 1994;"; and
(d) in the definition of "rating authority", for the words from "has" to "Act" substitute "shall be construed in accordance with section 30 of the Local Government etc. (Scotland) Act 1994.".
(67) For Schedule 5 (initial review of local government areas and electoral arrangements) substitute—

SCHEDULE 5

1. As soon as practicable after 1st April 1996 the Boundary Commission shall—
(a) review the electoral arrangements for all local government areas for the purpose of considering future electoral arrangements for those areas; and
(b) formulate proposals for those arrangements.
2. The provisions of Part II of this Act shall apply to a review under paragraph 1 above as they apply to a review under section 16 of this Act except that section 17 of this Act shall have effect as if it required—
(a) the Boundary Commission to submit a report on any review before such date as the Secretary of State may direct; and
(b) the Secretary of State to make an order under the said section 17 giving effect to the proposals of the Commission under the said paragraph 1 (whether as submitted to him or with modifications).".
(68) For heads (a) to (c) of paragraph 1(2) of Schedule 6 (electoral arrangements) substitute ", the number of local government electors shall be, as nearly as may be, the same in every electoral ward of that local government area.".
(69) In Schedule 7 (meetings and proceedings of local authorities)—
(a) in paragraphs 1(4), 3(1), 3(2) and 3(3), for the word "chairman" substitute "convener";
(b) in paragraphs 3(2) and (3), for the words "vice-chairman" substitute "depute convener"; and
(c) in paragraph 5(1), after "such orders" insert "or to the procedure for early removal from office of the convener or depute convener".
(70) In paragraph 4(1) of Schedule 8 (provision as to Commission for local authority accounts), after "Commission" where it first occurs insert ", including any hearing under section 103 of this Act,".
(71) Schedule 13 (amendments of the Rent (Scotland) Act 1971) shall cease to have effect.
(72) Schedule 14 (amendments of enactments relating to roads) shall cease to have effect.
(73) In Schedule 17, in paragraph 1(1)(a) (general construction of certain references), the words "or to a constituent board" and "or to a constituent water authority" shall cease to have effect.
(74) Schedule 22 (planning functions) shall cease to have effect.

The Health and Safety at Work etc. Act 1974 (c. 37)

93.—(1) The Health and Safety at Work etc. Act 1974 shall be amended in accordance with this paragraph.
(2) In section 28 (restrictions on disclosure of information)—
(a) in subsection (3)(c)(ii), for "water authority or water development board who is authorised by that Authority, undertaker, authority or board" substitute "sewerage authority or water authority who is authorised by that authority or undertaker"; and
(b) in subsection (5)(b), for "a water authority, a river purification board or a water development board" substitute "a sewerage authority, a water authority or a river purification board".
(3) In section 53(1) (interpretation), in the definition of "local authority", in paragraph (b), for the words from "regional" to "county council" substitute "council constituted under section 2 of the Local Government etc. (Scotland) Act 1994".

The Consumer Credit Act 1974 (c. 39)

94. In section 189(1) of the Consumer Credit Act 1974 (interpretation), in the definition of "local authority", for "regional, islands or district council" substitute "council constituted under section 2 of the Local Government etc. (Scotland) Act 1994".

The Control of Pollution Act 1974 (c. 40)

95.—(1) The Control of Pollution Act 1974 shall be amended in accordance with this paragraph.
(2) In section 32 (control of discharges of trade and sewage effluent etc.)—
(a) in subsection (1), for "(5)" substitute "(5A)";
(b) for subsection (2) substitute—

"(2) Where any sewage effluent is discharged as mentioned in paragraph (a) of subsection (1) above from any sewer or works—

(a) vested in a sewerage authority; or

(b) vested in a person other than a sewerage authority and forming (or forming part of) a system provided by him such as is mentioned in section 98(1)(b) of the Local Government etc. (Scotland) Act 1994,

and the authority, or as the case may be person, did not cause or knowingly permit the discharge but was bound to receive into the sewer or works, either unconditionally or subject to conditions which were observed, matter included in the discharge, the authority or person shall be deemed for the purposes of that subsection to have caused the discharge.";

(c) in subsection (5), for "local", in both places where it occurs, substitute "sewerage";

(d) after subsection (5) insert—

"(5A) A person in whom any such sewer or works as is described in subsection (2)(b) above is vested (such person being in this subsection referred to as a "relevant person") shall not be guilty of an offence by virtue of subsection (1) of this section by reason only of the fact that a discharge from the sewer or works contravenes conditions of a consent relating to the discharge if—

(a) the contravention is attributable to a discharge which another person caused or permitted to be made into the sewer or works; and

(b) the relevant person either was not bound to receive the discharge into the sewer or works or was bound to receive it there subject to conditions but the conditions were not observed; and

(c) the relevant person could not reasonably have been expected to prevent the discharge into the sewer or works;

and another person shall not be guilty of such an offence in consequence of a discharge which he caused or permitted to be made into a sewer or works vested in a relevant person if the relevant person was bound to receive the discharge there either unconditionally or subject to conditions which were observed."; and

(e) subsection (6) shall cease to have effect.

(3) In section 36 (provisions supplementary to sections 34 and 35)—

(a) in subsection (1)(b) after "area"—

(i) where it first occurs, insert ", and to each water authority within whose limits of supply,"; and

(ii) where it secondly occurs, insert ", or within whose limits of supply,"; and

(b) in subsection (2), for "regional or district council" substitute "council constituted under section 2 of the Local Government etc. (Scotland) Act 1994".

(4) In section 55 (discharges by islands councils)—

(a) in subsection (1), for "an islands council in its area" substitute "the councils for Orkney Islands, Shetland Islands and Western Isles in their areas"; and

(b) in subsection (2), for "islands councils" substitute "the councils for the areas mentioned in that subsection".

(5) In section 56 (interpretation of Part II)—

(a) for the definition of "sewage effluent" substitute—

" "sewage effluent" includes any effluent from sewage disposal, or sewerage, works vested in a sewerage authority;

"sewerage authority" shall be construed in accordance with section 62 of the Local Government etc. (Scotland) Act 1994;"; and

(b) for the definition of "water authority" substitute—

" "water authority" shall be construed in accordance with section 62 of the Local Government etc. (Scotland) Act 1994;".

(6) In section 62(2)(a) (certain exemptions as respects offences relating to noise), after "water authority" insert "("water authority" being construed in accordance with section 62 of the Local Government etc. (Scotland) Act 1994)".

(7) In section 73(1) (interpretation), in the definition of "local authority", in paragraph (b), for "an islands or district council" substitute "a council constituted under section 2 of the Local Government etc. (Scotland) Act 1994".

(8) In section 98 (interpretation of Part V), in the definition of "relevant authority", in paragraph (b), for ", an islands council or a district council" substitute "or a council constituted under section 2 of the Local Government etc. (Scotland) Act 1994".

(9) In section 106(2) (application to Scotland), for the words from the beginning to "is a reference" substitute "In this Act any reference to a river purification authority is".

(10) In Schedule 1A (orders designating nitrate sensitive areas: Scotland), in paragraph 8, for "regional, islands or district council" substitute "council constituted under section 2 of the Local Government etc. (Scotland) Act 1994".

The District Courts (Scotland) Act 1975 (c. 20)

96.—(1) The District Courts (Scotland) Act 1975 shall be amended in accordance with this paragraph.

(2) In section 1A(4) (further provisions as to establishment and disestablishment of district courts), for "district or islands council" substitute "local authority".

(3) Section 7(3) (officer of regional council may act as clerk of district court) shall cease to have effect.

(4) In subsection (1) of section 12 (disqualification in certain cases of justices who are members of local authorities), for "Local Government (Scotland) Act 1973" substitute "Local Government etc. (Scotland) Act 1994".

(5) In section 26 (interpretation), for the definition of—

(a) "commission area" substitute—

" "commission area" means the area of a local authority;"; and

(b) "local authority" substitute—

" "local authority" means a council constituted under section 2 of the Local Government etc. (Scotland) Act 1994".

The Criminal Procedure (Scotland) Act 1975 (c. 21)

97.—(1) The Criminal Procedure (Scotland) Act 1975 shall be amended in accordance with this paragraph.

(2) In—

(a) sections 168 and 364 (power of court, in respect of certain offences, to refer child to reporter), for the words "reporter of the local authority in whose area the child resides" wherever they occur; and

(b) sections 173(1)(a) and (b) and (3) and 372(1)(a) and (b) and (3) and 373 (reference and remit of children's and young persons' cases by courts to children's hearings), for the words "reporter of the local authority", wherever they occur,

substitute the words "Principal Reporter".

(3) In each of sections 186(1)(b) and (c) and 387(1)(b) and (c) (persons who may give information on oath as respects failure to comply with probation order), for "director of social work", wherever it occurs, substitute "chief social work officer".

(4) In section 296(3) (action to be taken where child detained by police) for the words from "reporter" to "detained" where the latter word second occurs substitute the words "Principal Reporter".

(5) In section 413(3) (detention of children), in the definition of "the appropriate local authority", in each of paragraphs (a) and (b), for "regional or islands council" substitute "local authority".

(6) In section 462 (interpretation) the definition of "reporter" shall cease to have effect.

(7) In Schedule 5 (discharge and amendment of probation orders), in paragraph 2(4)(b)—

(a) for "director of social work" substitute "chief social work officer"; and

(b) for "director", where it secondly and thirdly occurs, substitute "chief social work officer".

(8) For the word "reporter", wherever occurring, substitute the words "Principal Reporter".

(9) Sub-paragraph (8) above does not affect any of the particular amendments made by this paragraph.

The Reservoirs Act 1975 (c. 23)

98. In section 2(1) of the Reservoirs Act 1975 (local authorities for purposes of the Act), for "regional and islands councils" substitute "councils constituted under section 2 of the Local Government etc. (Scotland) Act 1994".

The House of Commons Disqualification Act 1975 (c. 24)

99. In Part IV of Schedule 1 to the House of Commons Disqualification Act 1975 (offices disqualifying for particular constituencies)—

(a) in the entry relating to Her Majesty's Lord-Lieutenant or Lieutenant for a region in Scotland—

(i) for the words "a region" substitute "an area"; and

(ii) for the words from "such part" to "Majesty" substitute "the area";

(b) the entry relating to Her Majesty's Lord-Lieutenant or Lieutenant for an islands area in Scotland shall cease to have effect; and

(c) in the entry relating to Her Majesty's Lord-Lieutenant or Lieutenant for the district of the city of Aberdeen, Dundee, Edinburgh, or Glasgow—

(i) the words "the district of" shall cease to have effect; and

(ii) for "district" substitute "city".

The Local Government (Scotland) Act 1975 (c. 30)

100.—(1) The 1975 Act shall be amended in accordance with this paragraph.

(2) In section 2(1)(e) (alterations to valuation roll which is in force)—

(a) after "consequence of" insert "—
    (i)"; and

(b) after "1970" insert "or
    (ii) the making of regulations under section 42 of the Lands Valuation (Scotland) Act 1854;".

(3) In section 7A (provisions as to setting of non-domestic rates)—

(a) for subsection (2) substitute—

"(2) Non-domestic rates shall be levied by each rating authority in respect of lands and heritages in their area—

  (a) in accordance with section 7 of this Act; or
  (b) where the lands and heritages fall within a class of lands and heritages prescribed under section 153 of the Local Government etc. (Scotland) Act 1994, in accordance with those regulations."; and

(b) subsection (3) shall cease to have effect.

(4) For subsection (2) of section 7B (provisions as to setting of non-domestic rates) substitute—

"(2) Non-domestic rates shall be levied by each rating authority in respect of lands and heritages in their area—

  (a) in accordance with section 7 of this Act; or
  (b) where the lands and heritages fall within a class of lands and heritages prescribed under section 153 of the Local Government etc. (Scotland) Act 1994, in accordance with those regulations.".

(5) In subsection (4) of section 8 (payment of rates by instalments), for from "the ground" to "1947" substitute "account of hardship under section 25A of the Local Government (Scotland) Act 1966".

(6) In section 23 (authorities subject to investigation by the Commissioner for Local Government in Scotland)—

(a) in subsection (1)—

    (i) after paragraph (e) insert—
    "(ee) a residuary body established under section 18 of the Local Government etc. (Scotland) Act 1994;";

and

    (ii) after paragraph (i) insert—
    "(j) the Strathclyde Passenger Transport Authority".; and

(b) in subsection (2)—

    (i) for paragraph (a) substitute—
    "(a) any joint board constituted by an administration scheme under section 36 of the Fire Services Act 1947 or section 147 of the Act of 1973";

    (ii) in paragraph (b), for "committee" substitute "board";

    (iii) paragraph (c) shall cease to have effect; and

    (iv) in paragraph (d), for the words from "of Schedule" to "Act of" substitute ", or joint advisory committee formed under paragraph 5B, of Schedule 3 to the Social Work (Scotland) Act".

(7) In subsection (2) of section 28 (reports on investigations), for the word "chairman" substitute "convener".

(8) In section 37(1) (interpretation), in the definition of "material change of circumstances", for the word "for" substitute "the members of which are drawn from the valuation appeal panel serving".

(9) In Schedule 3 (borrowing and lending by local authorities)—

(a) for paragraph 8(3) substitute—

"(3) Sub-paragraphs (1) and (2) above shall not apply in the case of money borrowed for the purpose of the common good, nor shall the security created by those sub–paragraphs include the common good or the revenues thereof.";

(b) in paragraphs 12(1), 13(1), 13(2) and 14, for "16th May 1975", in each place where it occurs, substitute "1st April 1996";

(c) after paragraph 12(1) insert—

"(1A) Sub-paragraph (1) above, so far as it relates to the establishment of a loans fund, does not apply to the councils of Orkney Islands, Shetland Islands and Western Isles, whose loans funds will continue in existence.";

(d) for paragraph 12(2) substitute—

"(2) A loans fund shall not apply to money borrowed for the common good.";

(e) in paragraph 13(1), for the words "section 128 of the Act of 1973 or which is referred to in section 222(2) or 223 of that Act" substitute "section 17 of the Local Government etc. (Scotland) Act 1994 or which is referred to in section 15(5) or 16 of that Act";

(f) in paragraph 22—

(i) in sub-paragraph (1), after head (b) insert—

"(ba) an insurance fund, to be used for the following purposes, namely—

(i) where the authority could have insured against a risk but have not done so, defraying any loss or damage suffered, or expenses incurred, by the authority as a consequence of that risk;

(ii) paying premiums on a policy of insurance against a risk."; and

(ii) in sub-paragraph (2), after "repair fund" insert "or the insurance fund".

(g) in paragraph 24(1), after "repair fund" insert ", or an insurance fund,";

(h) in paragraph 28—

(i) in sub-paragraph (1), after "money," insert "the Strathclyde Passenger Transport Authority"; and

(ii) in sub-paragraph (2), for the words from "Schedule to" to the end insert—

"(a) the aforesaid boards, either generally or to any particular board or class of board; and

(b) the Strathclyde Passenger Transport Authority";

(i) for paragraph 30 substitute—

"30. Nothing in this Schedule shall affect the power of a council having a common good to borrow on the security of the common good or any loan secured thereon."; and

(j) for paragraph 31 substitute—

"31. In this Schedule, unless the context otherwise requires—

"statutory borrowing power" means any power to borrow money conferred on a local authority by or under any enactment, but does not include the power of a council to borrow for the purposes of the common good; and

"trustee securities" means any security in which trustees are for the time being authorised by law to invest trust money.".

The Guard Dogs Act 1975 (c. 50)

101. In section 7 of the Guard Dogs Act 1975 (interpretation), in the definition of "local authority", for "an islands council or a district council" substitute "a council constituted under section 2 of the Local Government etc. (Scotland) Act 1994".

The Safety of Sports Grounds Act 1975 (c. 52)

102. In section 17(1) of the Safety of Sports Grounds Act 1975 (interpretation), in the definition of "local authority", in paragraph (d), for "regional or islands council" substitute "council constituted under section 2 of the Local Government etc. (Scotland) Act 1994".

The Children Act 1975 (c. 72)

103. In section 99(1) of the Children Act 1975 (inquiries in Scotland)—

(a) in paragraph (b), for the words from "paragraphs" to "2(2)" substitute "paragraphs (b), (e), (g), (h), (i), (l) and (o) of section 5(1B)";

(b) the word "or" immediately preceding paragraph (e) shall cease to have effect; and

(c) after paragraph (e) insert "; or

(f) the functions of the Principal Reporter under Part III of the Local Government etc. (Scotland) Act 1994.".

The Lotteries and Amusements Act 1976 (c. 32)

104.—(1) The Lotteries and Amusements Act 1976 shall be amended in accordance with this paragraph.

(2) In section 23(1) (interpretation), in the definition of "local authority", in paragraph (c), for "regional council, an islands council and a district council" substitute "council constituted under section 2 of the Local Government etc. (Scotland) Act 1994".

(3) In Schedule 1 (registration of societies), in paragraph 1(2)(c), for "an islands or district council" substitute "a council constituted under section 2 of the Local Government etc. (Scotland) Act 1994".

(4) In Schedule 3 (permits for commercial provision of amusements with prizes), in paragraph 1(2), in the definition of "local authority", in paragraph (c), for "an islands council and a district

council" substitute "a council constituted under section 2 of the Local Government etc. (Scotland) Act 1994".

The Dangerous Wild Animals Act 1976 (c. 38)

105. In section 7(4) of the Dangerous Wild Animals Act 1976 (interpretation), in the definition of "local authority", for "an islands council or a district council" substitute "a council constituted under section 2 of the Local Government etc. (Scotland) Act 1994".

The Licensing (Scotland) Act 1976 (c. 66)

106.—(1) The Licensing (Scotland) Act 1976 shall be amended in accordance with this paragraph.

(2) In section 1 (licensing boards)—

(a) in subsection (2)(a) for the words—
> (i) "each district and islands area" substitute "the area of each council"; and
> (ii) "subsection (3) below" substitute "section 46(1) of the Local Government etc. (Scotland) Act 1994";

(b) subsection (3) shall cease to have effect;

(c) in subsection (4), the words "district or islands" shall cease to have effect;

(d) in subsection (5)—
> (i) for the words "a district or islands area" substitute "the area of a council"; and
> (ii) the words "or electoral division" shall cease to have effect;

(e) for subsections (6) and (7) substitute—

"(6) On 1st April 1996, the members of a licensing board shall be—
> (a) for an area or, as the case may be, a licensing division of an area which was, immediately before that date, an islands area, the members in office immediately before that date; and
> (b) for any other area or, as the case may be licensing division of such area, the members elected by the council for the area in pursuance of section 46 of the Local Government etc. (Scotland) Act 1994.

(7) Subsequent elections of the members of a licensing board for any area or, as the case may be, a licensing division of such area shall be held—
> (a) except in so far as paragraph (b) below otherwise provides, at the first meeting of the council held after each ordinary election of that council which takes place after 1st April 1996; and
> (b) where a determination under subsection (3) above is made, either—
>> (i) at the meeting at which the determination is made; or
>> (ii) at the first meeting of the council held after such meeting as is mentioned in sub-paragraph (i) above.";

(f) in subsection (8), for the words from "with" to "above" substitute "on 1st April 1996"; and

(g) in subsection (9)—
> (i) for the word "authority", where it first occurs, substitute "council"; and
> (ii) for the words "the council of that authority" substitute "that council".

(3) In section 3(2) (expenses of members of licensing boards), the words "of the district or islands area" shall cease to have effect.

(4) In section 5(8) (council to provide accommodation etc. for licensing board), the words "district or islands" shall cease to have effect.

(5) In section 7 (clerk of licensing boards)—

(a) in subsection (1), the words "district and islands"; and

(b) subsection (2),

shall cease to have effect.

(6) In section 23(7) (meaning of "appropriate authority" for certain purposes), for the words from "in", where it secondly occurs, to the end substitute "the appropriate authority is the council".

(7) In section 105 (procedure on application for grant or renewal of certificate of registration)—

(a) in subsection (2)(b), for the words from "of" to "which" substitute "within whose area"; and

(b) in subsection (3)(c), after "1973" insert "or section 22 of the Local Government etc. (Scotland) Act 1994".

(8) In section 120(6) (consequences of conviction for sale or supply of liquor in unregistered club), for the words from "district" to "in which" substitute "council within whose area".

(9) In section 139(1) (interpretation), after the definition of "contravene" insert—
" "council" means a council constituted under section 2 of the Local Government etc. (Scotland) Act 1994; and references to the area of a council shall be construed accordingly;".

The Supplementary Benefits Act 1976 (c. 71)

107.—(1) Schedule 5 to the Supplementary Benefits Act 1976 (re-establishment courses and resettlement units) shall be amended in accordance with this paragraph.

(2) In paragraph 2(2) (Secretary of State may require councils to exercise functions of providing and maintaining resettlement units)—
(a) the words—
    (i) "and of";
    (ii) ", regions, islands areas"; and
    (iii) "and", where it thirdly occurs,
shall cease to have effect; and
(b) after "of London" insert "and any council constituted under section 2 of the Local Government etc. (Scotland) Act 1994".

(3) In paragraph 4(2) (local authorities to whom grants may be paid for certain purposes)—
(a) the words—
    (i) ", a region, an islands area"; and
    (ii) "or", where it secondly occurs,
shall cease to have effect; and
(b) after "of London" insert "or a council constituted under section 2 of the Local Government etc. (Scotland) Act 1994".

The Race Relations Act 1976 (c. 74.)

108. In section 71 of the Race Relations Act 1976 (local authorities: general statutory duty), the existing wording shall become subsection (1) of that section and after that subsection there shall be added—
"(2) In this section, "local authority", in relation to Scotland, means a council constituted under section 2 of the Local Government etc. (Scotland) Act 1994 ("the 1994 Act") and includes—
(a) a joint board and a joint committee within the meaning of the Local Government (Scotland) Act 1973;
(b) the staff commission established by virtue of section 12 of the 1994 Act;
(c) a water and sewerage authority within the meaning of the 1994 Act; and
(d) the Strathclyde Passenger Transport Authority.".

The Refuse Disposal (Amenity) Act 1978 (c. 3)

109. In section 11(1) of the Refuse Disposal (Amenity) Act 1978 (interpretation), in the definition of "local authority", in paragraph (b), for "an islands or district council" substitute "a council constituted under section 2 of the Local Government etc. (Scotland) Act 1994".

The European Parliamentary Elections Act 1978 (c. 10)

110.—(1) The European Parliamentary Elections Act 1978 shall be amended in accordance with this paragraph.

(2) In Schedule 1 (simple majority system (for Great Britain) with S T V (for Northern Ireland)), in paragraph 4—
(a) in sub-paragraph (2), for the words "region or islands", in each place where they occur, substitute "local government"; and
(b) in sub-paragraph (5)(b), for "a region, islands area or district" substitute "the area of a council constituted under section 2 of the Local Government etc. (Scotland) Act 1994".

(3) In Schedule 2 (European Parliamentary constituencies in Great Britain), in paragraph 5A(4), in the definition of "local authority", in paragraph (b), for "the council of a region, islands area or district" substitute "a council constituted under section 2 of the Local Government etc. (Scotland) Act 1994".

The Adoption (Scotland) Act 1978 (c. 28)

111.—(1) The Adoption (Scotland) Act 1978 shall be amended in accordance with this paragraph.

(2) In section 2 (local authorities' social work), for the words from "which stand" to "committee" substitute the words "under any of the enactments mentioned in subsection (1B) of

section 5 of the Social Work (Scotland) Act 1968 (power of Secretary of State to issue directions to local authorities in respect of their functions under certain enactments)".

(3) In section 65(1) (interpretation), in the definition of "local authority", for "regional or islands council" substitute "council constituted under section 2 of the Local Government etc. (Scotland) Act 1994".

The National Health Service (Scotland) Act 1978 (c. 29)

112.—(1) The National Health Service (Scotland) Act 1978 shall be amended in accordance with this paragraph.

(2) In section 16A (power to make payments towards expenditure on community services), in subsection (1)—

   (a) in paragraph (a), for the words from "relating" to the end substitute "under any of the enactments mentioned in section 5(1B) of the Social Work (Scotland) Act 1968 (power of Secretary of State to issue directions to local authorities in respect of their functions under certain enactments), other than section 3 of the Disabled Persons (Employment) Act 1958;";

   (b) in paragraph (b), the words "of a regional or islands council's" shall cease to have effect;

   (c) in paragraph (c), the words "of a district or islands council's" shall cease to have effect; and

   (d) in paragraph (d), the words "of a regional or islands council's" shall cease to have effect.

(3) In section 108(1) (interpretation), in the definition of "local authority", for "regional, islands or district council" substitute "council constituted under section 2 of the Local Government etc. (Scotland) Act 1994".

The Community Service by Offenders (Scotland) Act 1978 (c. 49)

113.—(1) The Community Service by Offenders (Scotland) Act 1978 shall be amended in accordance with this paragraph.

(2) In section 2(3)(b) (persons to whom copy of community service order to be sent), for "director of social work" substitute "chief social work officer".

(3) In section 12(1) (interpretation), in the definition of "local authority", for "regional or islands council" substitute "council constituted under section 2 of the Local Government etc. (Scotland) Act 1994".

The Inner Urban Areas Act 1978 (c. 50)

114.—(1) The Inner Urban Areas Act 1978 shall be amended in accordance with this paragraph.

(2) In section 1(2) (meaning of "designated district authority"), the words "or region" shall cease to have effect.

(3) In section 2(1) (loans for acquisition of land etc.), the words "or region" in both places where they occur, shall cease to have effect.

(4) In section 7(1)(a) (power to enter into arrangements), the words "or region" shall cease to have effect.

The Bail etc. (Scotland) Act 1980 (c. 4)

115. In section 10(3) of the Bail etc. (Scotland) Act 1980 (sittings of district courts), for "district or islands council" substitute "local authority".

The Reserve Forces Act 1980 (c. 9)

116.—(1) The Reserve Forces Act 1980 shall be amended in accordance with this paragraph.

(2) In section 131 (lieutenancies in Scotland)—

   (a) for subsection (1) substitute—

      "(1) Her Majesty—

      (a) shall appoint a lord-lieutenant for each area of Scotland; and

      (b) may appoint lieutenants for each area of Scotland.

      (1A) For the purposes of the provisions of this Act relating to lieutenancies, Her Majesty—

      (a) shall by Order in Council divide Scotland into such areas as She thinks fit; and

      (b) may in such an Order make such provision with respect to deputy lieutenants as is mentioned in subsection (1B) below.

      (1B) Where an Order in Council is made under subsection (1A) above, any deputy lieutenant holding office immediately before the date on which the Order is made shall (without prejudice to any power of removal or directing removal from any office) continue to hold office on and after that date as deputy lieutenant of the area or city in which he resides or of such other area or city as may be specified in the Order.";

(b) in subsection (2)—
   (i) the words "the district of" shall cease to have effect; and
   (ii) for "such district" substitute "such city";

(c) subsections (3) and (4) shall cease to have effect; and

(d) in subsection (5)—
   (i) for "region" substitute "area"; and
   (ii) the words "the districts of" shall cease to have effect.

(3) In subsection (5) of section 133 (deputy lieutenants), for "the regional or general rate" substitute "the non-domestic rate or the council tax".

(4) In subsection (1) of section 156 (interpretation), immediately before the definition of "home defence service" insert—

" "area", in the application to Scotland of the provisions of this Act relating to the lieutenancies, shall be construed in accordance with section 131(1A) of this Act;".

(5) In paragraph 3 of Schedule 7 (schemes for the establishment of associations), for "region" and "regions" wherever they occur, substitute "local government area" and "local government areas" respectively.

(6) For paragraph 14(2) of Schedule 8 (saving and transitional provisions) substitute—

"(2) Subject to any power of removal or of directing removal from any office, where, immediately before the date on which paragraph 116 of Schedule 13 to the Local Government etc. (Scotland) Act 1994 comes into force—

(a) any lord-lieutenant or lieutenant held office in Scotland, Her Majesty may by Order in Council provide that he shall continue to hold office on and after that date as lord-lieutenant or lieutenant respectively for such area as may be specified in the Order;

(b) any deputy lieutenant held office in Scotland, he shall continue to hold office on and after that date as deputy lieutenant for the area or city in which he resides or such other area or city as may be specified by the Secretary of State in an order made under this paragraph.".

The Slaughter of Animals (Scotland) Act 1980 (c. 13)

117. In section 22 of the Slaughter of Animals (Scotland) Act 1980 (interpretation), in the definition of "local authority", for "an islands or district council" substitute "a council constituted under section 2 of the Local Government etc. (Scotland) Act 1994".

The Education (Scotland) Act 1980 (c. 44)

118.—(1) The Education (Scotland Act 1980 shall be amended in accordance with this paragraph.

(2) In section 4 (duty of education authorities to provide psychological service), the words "regional or island authority" shall cease to have effect.

(3) In section 6 (social activities etc.)—

(a) in subsection (2)—
   (i) the letter "(a)"; and
   (ii) paragraph (b),
  shall cease to have effect; and

(b) subsection (3) shall cease to have effect.

(4) Section 78 (appointment of director of education) shall cease to have effect.

(5) In section 86 (admissibility of documents)—

(a) in paragraph (a), the words from "or" to "authority"; and

(b) in paragraph (e), the words "or by the director of education",

shall cease to have effect.

(6) In subsection (3A) of section 112 (reorganisation schemes), for "Schedule 10 to" substitute "Section 56 of".

(7) In section 122 (interpretation of Part VI), in the definition of "governing instrument", after the words "provisional order", where they first appear, insert "or made under section 17 of the Local Government etc. (Scotland) Act 1994,".

(8) In subsection (3) of section 129 (establishment of Board to conduct examinations, etc.), for "directors of education" substitute "persons employed by education authorities in an administrative capacity as respects the discharge of their education functions".

(9) In subsection (1) of section 135 (interpretation), in the definition of "education authority", for the words "regional or islands council" substitute "council constituted under section 2 of the Local Government etc. (Scotland) Act 1994".

(10) In Schedule A1 (appeal committees)—

(a) in paragraph 3—

(i) in sub-paragraph (a), for the words "the education committee of the authority" there shall be substituted the words "any committee appointed by the authority whose purposes include advising the authority on any matter relating to the discharge of any of their functions as education authority or discharging any of those functions on behalf of such authority";

(ii) in sub-paragraph (b), for the words "the education committee of the authority" there shall be substituted the words "any such committee"; and

(iii) for the words from "as" to "adviser", where it thirdly occurs, there shall be substituted the words "in an administrative or advisory capacity as respects the discharge of their education functions.";

(b) in paragraph 4, for the words "the education committee of the authority" there shall be substituted the words "any committee such as is mentioned in paragraph 3 above"; and

(c) in paragraph 5, for the words "the education committee of the authority" there shall be substituted the words "any committee such as is mentioned in paragraph 3 above".

The Water (Scotland) Act 1980 (c. 45)

119.—(1) The 1980 Act shall be amended in accordance with this paragraph.

(2) Sections 3 to 5 (water authorities and their areas, alterations of limits of supply and maps of such limits) shall cease to have effect.

(3) In section 6(3) (questions arising as respects water authority's duty to provide supply of wholesome water)—

(a) for "10 or more local government electors in the limits of supply of the water authority" substitute "any person aggrieved"; and

(b) for "consulting the authority" substitute "consultation with that person and with the water authority concerned".

(4) In section 9A (prohibition on any charge for water taken to extinguish fires etc.)—

(a) for the words from the beginning to "49" substitute "Notwithstanding anything in section 9";

(b) the existing words as so amended shall be subsection (1) of the section; and

(c) after that subsection add—

"(2) Subsection (1) above shall not have the effect, where any water is used or made available for any of the purposes mentioned in paragraph (a) or (b) of that subsection, of requiring a reduction in the charges imposed in respect of the provision for other purposes of the supply from which the water is taken.".

(5) In section 10 (compensation for damage resulting from exercise of powers)—

(a) in subsection (1)—

(i) for "district council" substitute "local authority"; and

(ii) the words "or water development board" shall cease to have effect;

(b) in subsection (1A)—

(i) the words "onto agricultural land or forestry land" and "or as the case may be water development board's" shall cease to have effect; and

(ii) after "communication" insert "or supply";

(c) in subsection (3), for "12" substitute "24";

(d) in subsection (5)(e), for "26 of the said Act of 1950" substitute "141 of the said Act of 1991"; and

(e) subsection (6) shall cease to have effect.

(6) In section 11 (power of Secretary of State on default of water authority or water development board—

(a) in subsection (1)—

(i) in paragraph (a), the words "or a water development board"; and

(ii) in paragraph (b), the words "or board";

(b) in subsection (2), the words "or board";

(c) in subsection (3), the words "or board" wherever they occur;

(d) in subsection (4), the words "or board" wherever they occur and "or "the transferee board" "; and

(e) in subsections (5) to (7), the words "or board" wherever they occur, shall cease to have effect.

(7) In section 13 (supply of water in bulk)—

(a) in subsection (1), the words "or water development board", in both places where they occur, "or board", in both places where they occur, and "or area" shall cease to have effect;

(b) in subsection (2), the words "or water development board", "or board" wherever they occur, "or area" and "or boards" shall cease to have effect;

(c) in subsection (3)—

(i) the words "or water development board" and "or area, as the case may be," shall cease to have effect; and

(ii) for "streets" substitute "roads"; and

(d) in subsection (6), the words "or water development board" shall cease to have effect.

(8) Section 15 (power to acquire land), shall cease to have effect.

(9) In section 16 (power to survey land and search for water)—

(a) in subsection (1) the words "or water development board"; and

(b) in each of subsections (2), (3) and (8), the words "or board" wherever they occur, shall cease to have effect.

(10) In section 17 (acquisition of water rights)—

(a) in subsection (1), the words "or water development board";

(b) in subsection (2), the words "or water development board" and "or board";

(c) in subsection (3), the words "or water development board" and, in both places where they occur, "or board"; and

(d) in subsection (4), the words "or water development board",

shall cease to have effect.

(11) In section 18(1) (compulsory acquisition of land for water works)—

(a) the words "or board", in both places where they occur, shall cease to have effect; and

(b) for "15" substitute " 99 of the Local Government etc. (Scotland) Act 1994".

(12) Section 20 (power to hold and dispose of land), shall cease to have effect.

(13) In section 22 (power to break open roads), the words "or water development board" shall cease to have effect.

(14) In section 23 (power to lay mains)—

(a) in subsection (1), the words "or water development board" shall cease to have effect;

(b) in subsection (2), the words "or board" shall cease to have effect;

(c) in subsection (3)—

(i) the words "or water development board" shall cease to have effect; and

(ii) for "street" substitute "road"; and

(d) in subsection (4), for "(1)" substitute "(1)(a)".

(15) In section 25 (power to provide public wells)—

(a) in subsection (1)—

(i) for "district council" substitute "local authority"; and

(ii) for "district", where it secondly occurs, substitute "area"; and

(b) in subsection (2)—

(i) for "An islands or district council" substitute "A local authority";

(ii) the words "or district", where they secondly occur, shall cease to have effect;

(iii) after "but" insert "where the Secretary of State is the roads authority";

(iv) for "the district council" substitute "the local authority"; and

(v) for "the roads authority's" substitute "his".

(16) In section 26 (power to close, or restrict use of, wells)—

(a) for "district council" substitute "local authority"; and

(b) in paragraph (a), for "district" substitute "area".

(17) In section 27 (power to close, or restrict use of water from, polluted source)—

(a) in subsection (1)—

(i) for "an islands or district council" substitute "a local authority";

(ii) the words "or district", where they secondly occur, shall cease to have effect; and

(iii) for "the council" substitute "they"; and

(b) in subsection (2), for "council" substitute "local authority"; and

(c) in subsection (3)—

(i) for "council", where that word first occurs, substitute "local authority"; and

(ii) for "the council", where those words secondly and thirdly occur, in each case substitute "them".

(18) In section 28 (water works code)—

(a) in subsection (1), the words "or a water development board"; and

(b) in subsection (2), the words "or water development board", shall cease to have effect.

(19) In section 29 (applications of enactments by order)—

(a) in subsection (2), the words "or water development board"; and

(b) in subsection (3), the words "or board",

shall cease to have effect.

(20) Section 30 (exemption from stamp duty) shall cease to have effect.

(21) In section 32 (power of water undertakers to supply water to water authorities)—

(a) in subsection (1)(b), the words "subject to subsection (2),"; and

(b) subsection (2),

shall cease to have effect.

(22) In section 33 (temporary discharge of water into watercourses)—

(a) in subsection (1), the words "or water development board", "or their area, as the case may be" and "or board";

(b) in subsection (3), the words "or water development board" in both places where they occur; and

(c) in each of subsections (4), (6)(b), (7) to (9) and (11), the words "or board" wherever they occur,

shall cease to have effect.

(23) Section 35(4) (charge for water fittings) shall cease to have effect.

(24) In section 38(1) (entry to premises), the words "or water development board" and, in each of paragraphs (a), (c) and (d), "or board", shall cease to have effect.

(25) Sections 40 (non-domestic water rate) and 41 (levy of non-domestic water rate) shall cease to have effect.

(26) Sections 42 (levy of non-domestic water rate on water works etc.), 43 (levy of non-domestic water rate on shootings and fishings) and 46 (transport hereditaments) shall cease to have effect.

(27) In section 47 (provision as regards certain pre-existing obligations etc.)—

(a) for subsection (1) substitute—

"(1) Subject to section 41A of this Act, no charge shall be fixed, demanded or recovered for a supply of water to premises to which a water authority were, immediately before 16th May 1949, by virtue of any enactment or agreement, under an obligation to provide such a supply free of charge.";

(b) in subsection (2)—

(i) for "leviable in any area specified in the local enactment" substitute ", for a period specified in that enactment, leviable in any area so specified";

(ii) for "specified therein" substitute "so specified"; and

(iii) for the words from "the non-domestic water rate" to the end of the proviso substitute—

"any charge payable in the area in question for a supply of water in any period commencing after 31st March 1996 (the "transfer date" for the purposes of Part II of the Local Government etc. (Scotland) Act 1994 and of this subsection) shall, during the period so specified, bear the same proportion to the charge which (but for this subsection) would be payable for that supply under a charges scheme, as the non-domestic water rate payable there as at the transfer date by virtue of the local enactment and of this subsection (as it had effect on the transfer date) bore to the non-domestic water rate which would otherwise have been payable.";

(c) in subsection (3)—

(i) for the words from the beginning to "such a supply" substitute—

"Where, by virtue of any enactment or agreement in force immediately before 16th May 1949, a water authority were under an obligation to provide a supply of water to any premises"; and

(ii) the word "and", where it first occurs, shall cease to have effect; and

(d) for subsection (7) substitute—

"(7) Nothing in subsection (1) shall be construed as continuing any exemption, and nothing in subsection (3) as continuing any advantage, where under the enactment or agreement in question the obligation which gives rise to the exemption or advantage ceases to exist.".

(28) Sections 48 (levying of, and exemption from, rates) and 49 (payment for supplies by meter) shall cease to have effect.

(29) In section 54 (register of meter to be evidence)—

(a) subsection (2); and

(b) in subsection (3)(b), the words from "and in the case" to the end,

shall cease to have effect.

(30) In section 55 (terms and conditions on which water supplied)—
(a) in subsection (1), after "conditions" insert ", other than as respects charges,"; and
(b) in subsection (4), after "at the" insert "principal".
(31) In section 58 (termination of right to supply of water on special terms)—
(a) in subsection (3), for the words from "under section 49" to "may be," substitute "for a supply of water";
(b) in subsection (4), for "district council" substitute "local authority";
(c) in subsection (6), the words "or the district of a district council" and "or by that district council" shall cease to have effect; and
(d) subsection (8) shall cease to have effect.
(32) Sections 60 (requisitions) and 61 (calculation of amount to be requisitioned) shall cease to have effect.
(33) In section 63 (provision of water supply to new buildings and houses)—
(a) after subsection (1) insert—
    "(1A) In determining adequacy for the purposes of subsection (1), the local authority shall consult, and have regard to the views of, the water authority within whose limits of supply the building is being erected.";
(b) in subsection (5), after "section," insert "except section (1A),"; and
(c) subsection (6) shall cease to have effect.
(34) Sections 64 to 67 (provisions as respects duty of house owners to provide supply of wholesome water for domestic purposes, execution of works on failure to do so, recovery of expenses of such execution and limitation of liability for such expenses) shall cease to have effect.
(35) In section 68 (agreements as to drainage)—
(a) in subsection (1)—
    (i) the words "or water development board" and (both in the subsection and its proviso) "or board" shall cease to have effect; and
    (ii) in paragraph (b), for "regional, islands or district council" substitute "local authority"; and
(b) subsection (3) shall cease to have effect.
(36) In section 69(1) (power to restrict use of hosepipes)—
(a) for "within the meaning of section 117(1) of the Road Traffic Act 1960" substitute "as defined in section 1 of the Public Passenger Vehicles Act 1981"; and
(b) for "within the meaning of section 196 of the Road Traffic Act 1972" substitute "as defined in section 192(1) of the Road Traffic Act 1988".
(37) In section 70 (byelaws for preventing misuse of water)—
(a) in subsection (1), the words "or water development board";
(b) in subsection (2), the words "or board"; and
(c) in subsection (4), the words "or water development board; and
(d) in the proviso to subsection (4), the words ", or as the case may be the Board,",
shall cease to have effect.
(38) In section 71 (byelaws for preventing pollution of water)—
(a) in subsection (1), the words "or water development board" shall cease to have effect;
(b) in subsection (2), for "authority or board" substitute "water authority";
(c) in subsection (3)—
    (i) for "authority or board" substitute "water authority"; and
    (ii) for "regional, islands or district council", in both places where those words occur, substitute "local authority";
(d) in subsection (4), for "authority or board" and "regional, islands or district council" in each case substitute "local authority";
(e) in subsection (5)—
    (i) for "authorities or boards", where those words first occur, substitute "water authorities"; and
    (ii) the words "or board" and, where they secondly occur, "or boards", shall cease to have effect; and
(f) in subsection (6), the words "or boards" shall cease to have effect.
(39) In section 72(2) (duty to enforce byelaws), the words "and water development board" shall cease to have effect.
(40) In section 73 (power of Secretary of State to require the making of byelaws)—
(a) in subsection (1), the words "or water development board" and "or board"; and
(b) in each of subsections (2) and (3), the words "or board" wherever they occur,
shall cease to have effect.
(41) In section 76 (acquisition of land for protection of water)—
(a) in subsection (1)—

(i) after "Act" insert ", or of the Local Government etc. (Scotland) Act 1994,"

(ii) the words "or water development board" and "or board" shall cease to have effect; and

(iii) after "undertaking" insert "or functions";

(b) in subsection (2), the words "or water development board" and (wherever they occur, both in the subsection and its proviso) "or board" shall cease to have effect;

(c) in subsection (3), the words "or water development board", "or their area" and "or board" shall cease to have effect; and

(d) in the proviso to subsection (3), the words "or board" and "or the area of that board", shall cease to have effect.

(42) In section 76F(5) (supplementary regulations in relation to water quality)—

(a) at the beginning insert "Without prejudice to subsection (7) below,"; and

(b) after "supplementing the" insert "foregoing".

(43) In section 76H (effect, confirmation and variation of notice under section 76G)—

(a) in subsection (5), for the words from "may" to the end substitute—

"—(a) may, except where the case is one to which paragraph (b) below applies, take that step themselves in accordance with any applicable provision having effect by virtue of section 76I below; and

(b) may, in a case to which this paragraph applies, take that step themselves and for that purpose exercise the powers which a water authority may, under this Act, exercise for the purpose of their water undertaking.";

(b) after subsection (5) insert—

"(5A) Paragraph (b) of subsection (5) above applies to any case where the local authority are satisfied that the failure arose because the person was unable on reasonable terms to acquire any necessary rights—

(a) to take water from a suitable source;

(b) to lay pipes through any land not belonging to him; or

(c) to do any other work."; and

(c) in subsection (8), the words from "; and section 65" to the end shall cease to have effect.

(44) In section 76I (incidental powers of local authorities)—

(a) in subsection (1), for "subsection (5)" substitute "subsections (5) and (6)";

(b) in subsection (2), at the beginning insert "Subject to subsection (6) below,"; and

(c) after subsection (5) add—

"(6) The foregoing provisions of this section do not apply as respects, but are without prejudice to the exercise of, a power conferred by section 76H(5)(b) above.".

(45) In section 76J(1) (regulations as to standards of wholesomeness), for "Part" substitute "Act".

(46) In section 76L(1) (interpretation of Part VIA), the definitions of "local authority" and "wholesome" shall cease to have effect.

(47) Sections 80 to 92 (provisions as regards water development boards) shall cease to have effect.

(48) In section 100 (power to make orders), for subsection (2) substitute—

"(2) Before making, on his own initiative, an order under section 107 the Secretary of State shall consult all water authorities whose limits of supply would be affected by the order.".

(49) In section 103 (requirement for notices to be in writing)—

(a) for "regional, island or district council" substitute "local authority";

(b) the words "or water development board", in both places where they occur, shall cease to have effect; and

(c) for "regional, islands or district council" substitute "local authority".

(50) In section 104(1) (appeal against decision of sheriff on any application under the Act), after "Act" insert "(other than an application under section 23(1A))".

(51) In section 106(4) (recording of awards in arbitration etc.), for "the said Acts" substitute "this Act".

(52) In section 107 (repeal, amendment and adaptation of local enactments)—

(a) in subsection (1)(b), the words "or a water development board" and "or board"; and

(b) in subsection (5), the words "or a water development board",

shall cease to have effect.

(53) In section 109 (interpretation)—

(a) in subsection (1)—

(i) the definitions of "the 1992 Act", "apportionment scheme", "apportionment note", "Central Board", "constituent water authority", "contributing authority", "council water charge", "net annual value" and "part residential subjects" shall cease to have effect;

(ii) after the definition of "agricultural lands and heritages" insert—

" "area", in relation to a water authority, shall be construed in accordance with section 62 of the Local Government etc. (Scotland) Act 1994;";

(iii) for the definition of "limits of supply" substitute—

" "limits of supply", in relation to a water authority, means the area of the water authority (as construed in accordance with section 62 of the Local Government etc. (Scotland) Act 1994);";

(iv) in the definition of "owner", the words ", save in sections 64 to 67," shall cease to have effect;

(v) for the definition of "water authority" substitute—

" "water authority" shall be construed in accordance with section 62 of the Local Government etc. (Scotland) Act 1994;"; and

(vi) at the end add—

" "wholesome" and cognate expressions shall be construed subject to the provisions of any regulations made under section 76J"; and

(b) in subsection (3), the words "and water development board" shall cease to have effect.

(54) In Schedule 1 (procedure for making orders and making and confirming bylaws)—

(a) in paragraph 2—

(i) in sub-paragraph (i), for "regional council, district council and water development board" substitute "and local authority"; and

(ii) in sub-paragraph (ii), for the words from "where the river" to the end substitute "on the river purification authority within whose area the stream affected is situated".

(b) in paragraph 3, the words "and the area of the water development board" shall cease to have effect;

(c) in paragraph 11—

(i) for "regional council, district council and water development board" substitute "and local authority"; and

(ii) the words "where the river purification authority are not the same authority as the water authority" shall cease to have effect;

(d) in paragraph 12, the words "and the area of the board" shall cease to have effect;

(e) in paragraph 13, the words "not exceeding 10 pence" shall cease to have effect;

(f) in paragraph 14, the words "or board" shall cease to have effect;

(g) in paragraph 17, the words "or board" and "or boards" shall cease to have effect;

(h) in paragraph 19—

(i) the words "or water development board", in both places where they occur and "or area" shall cease to have effect;

(ii) for "regional council, district council and water development board" substitute "and local authority"; and

(iii) for the words from "and any" to "and to" substitute "any navigation authority exercising jurisdiction in relation to any watercourse from which water is proposed to be taken under the rights to be acquired, the river purification authority within whose area the stream is situated and any";

(i) in paragraph 20, the words "or water development board" shall cease to have effect;

(j) in paragraph 23, the words "or board" and "or boards" shall cease to have effect;

(k) in each of paragraphs 24, 26 and 27, the words "or water development board" shall cease to have effect;

(l) in paragraph 25(b), for "council of every region or district" substitute "local authority for any area";

(m) in paragraph 30, the words "or water development board" and "or board" shall cease to have effect; and

(n) in paragraph 31—

(i) for "the proper" substitute "a duly authorised"; and

(ii) the words "or board", in both places where they occur, shall cease to have effect.

(55) In Schedule 2 (orders authorising compulsory acquisition of land), in each of paragraphs 4 and 6, the words "or water development board" wherever they occur shall cease to have effect.

(56) In Schedule 3 (provisions as to breaking open roads and laying communication and supply pipes)—

(a) in paragraph 1, the words "and water development board", "within their limits of supply or area" and from "and outside" to "removing mains" where they secondly occur, shall cease to have effect;

(b) in paragraph 2(2), the words "or board", in both places where they occur, shall cease to have effect;

(c) in paragraph 4(1), the words "within their limits of supply" and "within the said limits" shall cease to have effect;
(d) in paragraph 5—
    (i) the words "within the limits of supply" shall cease to have effect; and
    (ii) for the words "the authority", where they first occur, substitute "any water authority"; and
(e) paragraph 8 shall cease to have effect.
(57) In Schedule 4 (provisions to be incorporated in orders relating to water undertakings)—
(a) in section 24(2)—
    (i) for "regional islands or district council or roads" substitute "local"; and
    (ii) at the end add "or, in relation to roads for which the Secretary of State is roads authority, between the Secretary of State and the undertakers";
(b) in section 40, for "24" substitute "48"; and
(c) in section 46, for "clerk of the local authority of every district" substitute "local authority for every area".
(58) Schedules 7 (procedure for making certain orders) and 8 (further provisions as regards water development boards) shall cease to have effect.

The Local Government, Planning and Land Act 1980 (c. 65)

120.—(1) The Local Government, Planning and Land Act 1980 shall be amended in accordance with this paragraph.
(2) In section 2(1) (duty of authorities to publish information)—
(a) in paragraph (g), for "regional, islands or district council" substitute "council constituted under section 2 of the Local Government etc. (Scotland) Act 1994";
(b) in paragraph (h)—
    (i) for "committee" substitute "board"; and
    (ii) after "that Act" insert "or section 147 of the Local Government (Scotland) Act 1973"; and
(c) in paragraph (k)—
    (i) for"committee" substitute "board"; and
    (ii) for "or 21A" substitute ", 20 or 21B".
(3) In section 8(1) (meaning of "functional work"), in paragraph (b)(iv), for "regional, islands or district council" substitute "council constituted under section 2 of the Local Government etc. (Scotland) Act 1994".
(4) In section 20(1) (interpretation of Part III), in the definition of "local authority", in paragraph (b), for "regional, islands or district council" substitute "council constituted under section 2 of the Local Government etc. (Scotland) Act 1994".
(5) In section 120(3) (compulsory acquisition: exclusion of special parliamentary procedure), in the definition of "local authority", in paragraph (c), for "regional, islands or district council" substitute "council constituted under section 2 of the Local Government etc. (Scotland) Act 1994".
(6) In section 148 (planning control)—
(a) in subsection (1), for the words from "regional" to "areas" substitute "planning authority within whose area"; and
(b) in subsection (2), the words "exercising district planning functions" shall cease to have effect.
(7) In section 165(9)(b) (power to transfer undertaking), for "a regional council and a district council" substitute "any council constituted under section 2 of the Local Government etc. (Scotland) Act 1994 other than the councils for Orkney Islands, Shetland Islands and Western Isles".

The Public Passenger Vehicles Act 1981 (c. 14)

121.—(1) The Public Passenger Vehicles Act 1981 shall be amended in accordance with this paragraph.
(2) In section 5(3) (publication of information by traffic commissioners), in paragraph (b), for "regional or islands council" substitute "council constituted under section 2 of the Local Government etc. (Scotland) Act 1994".
(3) In section 14A(4)(b) (objections to application for PSV operator's licence), for "regional or islands council" substitute "council constituted under section 2 of the Local Government etc. (Scotland) Act 1994".
(4) In section 82(1) (interpretation), in the definition of "local authority", in paragraph (b), for "regional, islands or district council" substitute "council constituted under section 2 of the Local Government etc. (Scotland) Act 1994".

(5) In Schedule 1 (public service vehicles: conditions affecting status or classification), in paragraph 2(2)(b), for "regional or islands council" substitute "council constituted under section 2 of the Local Government etc. (Scotland) Act 1994".

The Animal Health Act 1981 (c. 22)

122. In section 50(3) of the Animal Health Act 1981 (local authorities for purposes of Act), for "regional or islands council" substitute "council constituted under section 2 of the Local Government etc. (Scotland) Act 1994".

The Finance Act 1981 (c. 35)

123. In section 107(3)(b) of the Finance Act 1981 (sale of houses at discount by local authorities etc.), for "regional, district or islands council" substitute "council constituted under section 2 of the Local Government etc. (Scotland) Act 1994".

The Zoo Licensing Act 1981 (c. 37)

124. In section 1(3)(b) of the Zoo Licensing Act 1981 (licensing of zoos by local authorities), for "islands councils and district councils" substitute "councils constituted under section 2 of the Local Government etc. (Scotland) Act 1994".

The Wildlife and Countryside Act 1981 (c. 69)

125.—(1) The Wildlife and Countryside Act 1981 shall be amended in accordance with this paragraph.
(2) In section 27(1) (interpretation of Part I), in the definition of "local authority", in paragraph (b), for "regional, islands or district council" substitute "council constituted under section 2 of the Local Government etc. (Scotland) Act 1994".
(3) In section 36(7) (marine nature reserves), in the definition of "local authority", in paragraph (b), for "regional council, an islands council or a district council" substitute "council constituted under section 2 of the Local Government etc. (Scotland) Act 1994".

The Civil Aviation Act 1982 (c. 16)

126.—(1) The Civil Aviation Act 1982 shall be amended in accordance with this paragraph.
(2) In section 30 (provision of aerodromes and facilities at aerodromes by local authorities)—
 (a) in subsection (1)—
  (i) the words ", other than a district council in Scotland,"; and
  (ii) the words from "and a" to "above",
  shall cease to have effect; and
 (b) in subsection (2), the words ", other than a district council in Scotland," shall cease to have effect.
(3) In section 36(4)(b) (meaning of "relevant authority" for purposes of section), for "islands or district council" substitute "council constituted under section 2 of the Local Government etc. (Scotland) Act 1994".
(4) In section 88(10) (application and interpretation of section), the words ", other than a district council in Scotland," shall cease to have effect.
(5) In section 105(1) (general interpretation), in the definition of "local authority", in paragraph (b), for "regional, islands or district council" substitute "council constituted under section 2 of the Local Government etc. (Scotland) Act 1994".

The Stock Transfer Act 1982 (c. 41)

127. In Schedule 1 to the Stock Transfer Act 1982 (specified securities), in paragraph 7(2), for head (b) substitute—
 "(b) any council constituted under section 2 of the Local Government etc. (Scotland) Act 1994".

The Local Government and Planning (Scotland) Act 1982 (c. 43)

128.—(1) The Local Government and Planning (Scotland) Act 1982 shall be amended in accordance with this paragraph.
(2) For section 9 (re-allocation of responsibility for certain local authority functions relating to the countryside) substitute—

"Part II of Schedule 1 to continue to have effect
 9. Part II of Schedule 1 to this Act (amendment of certain enactments relating to the countryside) shall continue to have effect."

(3) In section 14 (islands or district council's duties in relation to the provision of recreational, sporting, cultural and social facilities and activities)—
(a) in subsection (1), for "an islands or district council" substitute "a local authority";
(b) in subsection (2), the words "regional or islands council as" shall cease to have effect; and
(c) after that subsection add—
    "(3) In subsection (2) above, "water authority" shall be construed in accordance with section 62 of the Local Government etc. (Scotland) Act 1994.".
(4) In section 15(2) (local authority's powers in relation to provision of recreational, sporting etc. facilities), for "An islands or district council" substitute "A local authority".
(5) In section 16 (provisions supplementary to section 15)—
(a) in subsection (1)—
    (i) for "an islands or district council" substitute "a local authority";
    (ii) for paragraph (b) substitute—
    "(b) maintain a body for the promotion of a recreational, sporting, cultural or social activity;"; and
    (iii) in each of paragraphs (c), (g)(ii) and (k)(ii), for "council", wherever it occurs, substitute "authority"; and
(b) in subsection (2)—
    (i) for "an islands or district council" substitute "a local authority"; and
    (ii) in paragraph (a), for "council" substitute "authority".
(6) For section 17 (power of regional council to contribute towards provision of recreational etc. facilities) substitute—

"Power of local authority to contribute towards provision of cultural activities and facilities
    17.—(1) A local authority may contribute by way of grant or loan towards the expenses of any organisation or body which, in the opinion of the authority, provides or promotes the provision of cultural activities or facilities whether inside or outside the area of the local authority concerned.
    (2) Without prejudice to the generality of subsection (1) above, the power conferred by that subsection includes power to make such contribution as will support or promote music, theatre, dance, opera, visual art or other art forms and museums and galleries.".
(7) In section 18 (byelaws in relation to recreational, sporting etc. activities)—
(a) in subsection (1)—
    (i) for "an islands or district council" substitute "a local authority"; and
    (ii) for "council" substitute "authority";
(b) in subsection (2)(b), for "council" substitute "local authority"; and
(c) in subsection (3), for "council"—
    (i) where it first occurs, substitute "local authority"; and
    (ii) where it secondly occurs, substitute "authority".
(8) In section 24(1) (provision of gardening assistance for certain persons), for "An islands or district council" substitute "A local authority".
(9) In section 25 (local authority's functions in relation to cleansing of land)—
(a) in subsection (2), for "An islands or district council" substitute "A local authority"; and
(b) in subsection (3), for "islands or as the case may be district council" substitute "local authority".
(10) In section 26(1) (local authority's functions in relation to the provision of public conveniences), for "An islands or district council" substitute "A local authority".
(11) In section 27 (local authority's functions in relation to provision of a market)—
(a) in subsection (1)—
    (i) for "An islands or district council" substitute "A local authority"; and
    (ii) in paragraph (b)(i), for "council" substitute "authority";
(b) in subsection (3), for "An islands or district council" substitute "A local authority"; and
(c) in subsection (4), the words from "Without" to "Act" shall cease to have effect.
(12) In section 28 (local authority's functions in relation to the provision of clocks)—
(a) for "An islands or district council" substitute "A local authority"; and
(b) in paragraph (b), for "council" substitute "authority".
(13) In section 30(1), for the words from "an islands" to "may", where it first occurs, substitute "a local authority may, with the consent of the roads authority".
(14) In section 67 (interpretation), immediately before the definition of "the 1972 Act" insert—
    ""local authority" means a council constituted under section 2 of the Local Government etc. (Scotland) Act 1994;".
(15) Part I of Schedule 1 (which re-allocates certain functions relating to the countryside) shall cease to have effect.

The Civic Government (Scotland) Act 1982 (c. 45)

129.—(1) The Civic Government (Scotland) Act 1982 shall be amended in accordance with this paragraph.

(2) In section 2 (licensing authorities)—

(a) in subsection (1), for "each district and islands area" substitute "the area of each local authority"; and

(b) in each of subsections (2) and (3), for "district or islands council", wherever it occurs, substitute "local authority".

(3) In section 45 (control of sex shops)—

(a) in subsection (1), for "district or islands council" substitute "local authority"; and

(b) in subsection (2)—

(i) for "district or islands council" substitute "local authority"; and

(ii) for "council's" substitute "authority's".

(4) In section 62 (notification of processions)—

(a) in subsection (1)—

(i) for "regional or islands council" substitute "local authority"; and

(ii) for "council", where it secondly and thirdly occurs, substitute "authority";

(b) in each of subsections (2), (4), (7), (9) and (11), for "regional or islands council", wherever it occurs, substitute "local authority";

(c) in subsection (6)—

(i) for "regional or islands council" substitute "local authority"; and

(ii) for "council", where it secondly occurs, substitute "authority"; and

(d) in subsection (12), in the definition of "chief constable"—

(i) for "regional or islands council" substitute "local authority"; and

(ii) for "council", where it secondly occurs, substitute "authority".

(5) In section 63 (functions of authorities in relation to processions), in each of subsections (1), (1A)(a), (3) and (4), for "regional or islands council", wherever it occurs, substitute "local authority".

(6) In section 64 (appeals against orders under section 63)—

(a) in subsection (4), for "regional or islands council" substitute "local authority";

(b) in subsection (6)—

(i) in paragraph (a)(i), for "regional or islands council" substitute "local authority"; and

(ii) for "council", where it secondly and thirdly occurs, substitute "authority"; and

(c) in subsection (7), for "council" substitute "authority".

(7) In section 87 (local authorities' powers in relation to buildings in need of repair), subsection (6) shall cease to have effect.

(8) In section 89 (safety of platforms etc.), subsection (10) shall cease to have effect.

(9) In section 90 (lighting of common stairs etc.)—

(a) in each of subsections (2), (3), (4), (5), (6), (7), (8) and (9), for "district or islands council", wherever it occurs, substitute "local authority"; and

(b) in each of subsections (8) and (9), for "council", where it secondly occurs, substitute "authority".

(10) In section 91 (installation of lights in private property)—

(a) in subsection (1)—

(i) for "district or islands council" substitute "local authority"; and

(ii) for "council", where it secondly occurs, substitute "authority";

(b) in subsection (2), for "district or islands council" substitute "local authority"; and

(c) in subsection (3)—

(i) for "district or islands council" substitute "local authority"; and

(ii) for "council", where it secondly and thirdly occurs, substitute "authority".

(11) In section 92 (cleaning and painting of common stairs etc.)—

(a) in each of subsections (2), (3), (4), (6), (7) and (8), for "district or islands council", wherever it occurs, substitute "local authority"; and

(b) in subsection (8), for "council", where it secondly and thirdly occurs, substitute "authority".

(12) In section 94 (disused petrol containers)—

(a) in subsection (2), for "regional or islands council" substitute "local authority"; and

(b) in subsection (3)—

(i) for "regional or islands council" substitute "local authority"; and

(ii) for "council", where it secondly occurs, substitute "authority".

(13) In section 95 (private open spaces), in each of subsections (2) and (3)(b), for "district or islands council" substitute "local authority".

(14) In section 96(1) (statues and monuments)—

(a) for "district or island council" substitute "local authority"; and

(b) for "council", where it secondly occurs, substitute "authority".

(15) In section 97 (street names and house numbers), for "district or islands council" substitute "local authority".

(16) In section 119 (regulation of charitable collections)—

(a) in each of subsections (1), (3), (4), (5), (6), (7), (8), (9), (10)(a) and (b) and (12), for "district or islands council", wherever it occurs, substitute "local authority"; and

(b) in subsection (3), for "council", where it secondly occurs, substitute "authority".

(17) In section 120 (savings for Crown and other rights), for "district or islands council" substitute "local authority".

(18) In section 121 (control of the seashore, adjacent waters and inland waters)—

(a) in each of subsections (1), (3), (4), (5)(a) and (c), (6), (7), (8), (9), (10) and (11), for "district or islands council", wherever it occurs, substitute "local authority"; and

(b) in subsection (7), for "council", where it secondly occurs, substitute "authority".

(19) In section 122 (power to execute works on seashore)—

(a) in each of subsections (1), (3), (4) and (5), for "district or islands council", wherever it occurs, substitute "local authority";

(b) in subsection (2)—

    (i) in paragraph (a), for "council" substitute "local authority"; and

    (ii) in paragraph (b)—

        (A) after sub-paragraph (i) insert "and";

        (B) in sub-paragraph (ii), for "the district council" substitute "any local authority other than the authority for Orkney Islands, Shetland Islands or Western Isles"; and

        (C) sub-paragraph (iii) and the word "and" immediately preceding it shall cease to have effect;

(c) in subsection (5), for "council", where it secondly occurs, substitute "local authority".

(20) In section 123 (interpretation of sections 120 to 122)—

(a) in subsection (1), in the definition of "adjacent waters", in paragraph (b), for "district council" substitute "local authority"; and

(b) in subsection (2), after the words "purposes of", where they secondly occur, insert "giving notice or, as the case may be,".

(21) In section 133 (interpretation), in the definition of "local authority", for "regional, islands or district council" substitute "council constituted under section 2 of the Local Government etc. (Scotland) Act 1994".

(22) In Schedule 2 (control of sex shops)—

(a) in each of paragraphs 3, 4, 5(1), (3), (4), (5), (6), (7) and (8), 7(2), (7), (8) and (10) and 8(1), (2), (3), (4), (5), (6), (7) and (8), for "district or islands council", wherever it occurs, substitute "local authority";

(b) in paragraph 6—

    (i) in sub-paragraph (1), for "district or islands council" substitute "local authority"; and

    (ii) in sub-paragraph (6), for "islands or district council" substitute "local authority";

(c) in paragraph 9—

    (i) in sub-paragraphs (1), (2), (4) and (5), for "district or islands council", wherever it occurs, substitute "local authority"; and

    (ii) in sub-paragraphs (3)(g) and (h), for "council", in each place where it occurs, substitute "local authority";

(d) in paragraph 10—

    (i) in sub-paragraphs (1), (2) and (3), for "district or islands council", wherever it occurs, substitute "local authority"; and

    (ii) in sub-paragraph (3), for "council", where it secondly and thirdly occurs, substitute "authority";

(e) in paragraph 12(1), (2)(b), (3), (4) and (6) for "district or islands council", wherever it occurs, substitute "local authority";

(f) in paragraph 13—

    (i) in sub-paragraphs (1), (2), (4), (5), (6), (7), (8), (9) and (10), for "district or islands council", wherever it occurs, substitute "local authority"; and

    (ii) in sub-paragraphs (6) and (9), for "council", where it secondly occurs in each of those paragraphs, substitute "authority";

(g) in paragraph 14—

    (i) in sub-paragraph (1), for "islands or district council" substitute "local authority"; and

(ii) in sub-paragraphs (2), (3), (4), (5), (6) and (7), for "district or islands council", wherever it occurs, substitute "local authority";

(h) in paragraph 15—

(i) in sub-paragraphs (1), (2), (3) and (5), for "district or islands council", wherever it occurs, substitute "local authority";

(ii) in sub-paragraph (2)(b), for "council" substitute "authority"; and

(iii) in sub-paragraph (3), for "council", where it secondly occurs, substitute "local authority";

(i) in paragraph 16(1), (2), (3) and (4), for "district or islands council", wherever it occurs, substitute "local authority";

(j) in paragraph 17—

(i) in sub-paragraphs (1), (2) and (4), for "district or islands council", wherever it occurs, substitute "local authority"; and

(ii) in sub-paragraph (4), for "council", where it secondly occurs, substitute "authority";

(k) in paragraph 18—

(i) in sub-paragraphs (1) and (2), for "district or islands council" substitute "local authority";

(ii) in sub-paragraph (1), for "council", where it secondly occurs, substitute "authority"; and

(iii) in sub-paragraph (2), for "council", where it secondly and thirdly occurs, substitute "authority";

(l) in each of paragraphs 19(8) and 20(1), (3) and (5), for "district or islands council", wherever it occurs, substitute "local authority";

(m) in paragraph 22—

(i) for "district or islands council" substitute "local authority"; and

(ii) for "its" substitute "their";

(n) in paragraph 23—

(i) in sub-paragraphs (1), (2) and (3), for "district or islands council", wherever it occurs, substitute "local authority";

(ii) in sub-paragraph (2), for "council", where it secondly occurs, substitute "authority"; and

(iii) in sub-paragraph (4)(c), for "council" substitute "local authority";

(o) in paragraph 24—

(i) in sub-paragraphs (1), (2)(a), (3), (6), (7) and (9), for "district or islands council", wherever it occurs, substitute "local authority";

(ii) in sub-paragraph (6), for "council", where it secondly, thirdly and fourthly occurs, substitute "authority"; and

(iii) in sub-paragraph (9)(b), for "council" substitute "authority"; and

(p) in paragraph 25(1) and (3), for "district or islands council", wherever it occurs, substitute "local authority".

The Representation of the People Act 1983 (c. 2)

130.—(1) The Representation of the People Act 1983 shall be amended in accordance with this paragraph.

(2) In section 8 (registration officers), for subsection (3) substitute—

"(3) In Scotland, every local authority shall appoint an officer of the authority for their area or for any adjoining area, or an officer appointed by any combination of local authorities, to be registration officer for any constituency or part of a constituency which is situated within their area.".

(3) In section 25 (returning officers: Scotland)—

(a) in subsection (1)—

(i) for "region or islands", in both places where it occurs, substitute "local government"; and

(ii) for "regional or islands council" substitute "local authority for that area";

(b) in subsection (2)—

(i) for the words from "The council" where they first occur, to "area", where it first occurs, substitute "Every local authority";

(ii) for "that region or islands" substitute "their"; and

(iii) for "council", where it secondly occurs, substitute "authority"; and

(c) subsection (3) shall cease to have effect.

(4) In section 31(2) (polling districts in Scotland)—

(a) for "regional or islands", where it first occurs, substitute "local authority";

(b) for "regional or islands council" substitute "local authority";

(c) for "division" substitute "ward"; and
(d) the words from "and for" to "polling district", where it secondly occurs, shall cease to
have effect.

(5) In section 52(4)(b) (provision of officers of local authority to assist registration officer), for
the words from "the" to "area" substitute "every local authority".

(6) In section 82(4)(b) (declaration as to election expenses), for "regional, islands or district
council" substitute "local authority".

(7) In section 96(3)(b) (meeting rooms for local election meetings), for the words from "the
council" to "district" substitute "a local authority".

(8) In section 204 (general application to Scotland)—
(a) in the definition of "electoral area", the words "division or" shall cease to have effect;
(b) for the definition of "local authority" substitute—
     " "local authority" means a council constituted under section 2 of the Local Govern-
         ment etc. (Scotland) Act 1994"; and
(c) for the definition of "local government area" substitute—
     " "local government area" means the area of a local authority;".

(9) In Schedule 5 (use for parliamentary election meetings of rooms in school premises and of
meeting rooms), in paragraph 6(b), for "the council of every islands area and district" substitute
"every local authority".

The Level Crossings Act 1983 (c. 16)

131. In section 1(11) of the Level Crossings Act 1983 (safety arrangements at level crossings:
interpretation), in the definition of "local authority", for "regional, islands or district council"
substitute "council constituted under section 2 of the Local Government etc. (Scotland) Act
1994".

The Litter Act 1983 (c. 35)

132.—(1) The Litter Act 1983 shall be amended in accordance with this paragraph.
(2) In section 4 (consultation and proposals for abatement of litter), for subsection (4)
substitute—
     "(4) In Scotland, it shall be the duty of each local authority to consult from time to time
with such voluntary bodies as the local authority consider appropriate and as agree to participate in the consultations about the steps which the authority and each of the bodies with
which they consulted are to take for the purpose of abating litter in the authority's area; and
it shall be the duty of the local authority—
     (a) to prepare and from time to time revise a statement of the steps which the authority
         and each of the bodies agree to take for the purpose,
     (b) to take such steps as in their opinion will give adequate publicity in their area to the
         statement, and
     (c) to keep a copy of the statement available at their principal office for inspection by the
         public free of charge at all reasonable hours.
     (4A) In subsection (4) above "local authority" means a council constituted under section
2 of the Local Government etc. (Scotland) Act 1994.".

(3) In section 8(7) (interpretation of sections 7 and 8), in the definition of "local authority", for
"regional, islands or district council" substitute "council constituted under section 2 of the Local
Government etc. (Scotland) Act 1994".

The Telecommunications Act 1984 (c. 12)

133.—(1) The Telecommunications Act 1984 shall be amended in accordance with this
paragraph.
(2) In section 97(3)(b) (contributions by local authorities towards provision of facilities:
interpretation), for "regional, islands or district council" substitute "council constituted under
section 2 of the Local Government etc. (Scotland) Act 1994".
(3) In section 98(9) (interpretation of section)—
(a) in the definition of "public sewer", in paragraph (b), for "regional or islands council"
substitute "sewerage authority";
(b) after that definition insert—
     " "sewerage authority" shall be construed in accordance with section 62 of the Local
     Government etc. (Scotland) Act 1994;"; and

(c) in the definition of "water authority", in paragraph (b), for the words from "means" to "1980" substitute "shall be construed in accordance with section 62 of the Local Government etc. (Scotland) Act 1994".

The Road Traffic Regulation Act 1984 (c. 27)

134.—(1) The Road Traffic Regulation Act 1984 shall be amended in accordance with this paragraph.

(2) In section 19(3)(b) (local authority in Scotland empowered to regulate use of roads by public service vehicles), for "regional or islands council" substitute "council constituted under section 2 of the Local Government etc. (Scotland) Act 1994".

(3) In section 26 (arrangements for patrolling school crossings)—

(a) in subsection (2), for "regional or islands council" substitute "council constituted under section 2 of the Local Government etc. (Scotland) Act 1994";

(b) in subsection (4)—

(i) the letter "(a)"; and

(ii) paragraph (b) and the word "and" immediately before it,

shall cease to have effect; and

(c) in subsection (5)—

(i) the letter "(a)";

(ii) paragraph (b) and the word "or" immediately before it; and

(iii) the words "or, in Scotland, the district council",

shall cease to have effect.

(4) In section 32(4)(a) (meaning of certain expressions for purposes of sections 33 to 41), for "regional or islands council" substitute "council constituted under section 2 of the Local Government etc. (Scotland) Act 1994".

(5) In section 37(1)(b) (orders made by local authorities in Scotland for purposes of general scheme of traffic control), for "regional or islands council" substitute "council constituted under section 2 of the Local Government etc. (Scotland) Act 1994".

(6) In section 44(1)(b) (control of off–street parking), for the words from "regions" to "council" substitute "local authority areas, by the council (constituted under section 2 of the Local Government etc. (Scotland) Act 1994) for the area".

(7) In section 45(7)(c) (meaning of "local authority" for purposes of sections 45 to 55), for "the regional or islands council" substitute "a council constituted under section 2 of the Local Government etc. (Scotland) Act 1994".

(8) In section 100(5)(c) (meaning of "local authority" in Scotland for purposes of section), for "regional or islands council" substitute "council constituted under section 2 of the Local Government etc. (Scotland) Act 1994".

(9) In section 121A(4) (traffic authorities), for "regional or islands council" substitute "council constituted under section 2 of the Local Government etc. (Scotland) Act 1994".

The Roads (Scotland) Act 1984 (c. 54)

135.—(1) The Roads (Scotland) Act 1984 shall be amended in accordance with this paragraph.

(2) In section 9(1)(e) (supplementary orders relating to special roads)—

(a) for "regional council", in both places where it occurs, substitute "local authority"; and

(b) after "that", where it secondly occurs, insert "special road".

(3) In section 55(3) (arrangements for provision of meals etc. on picnic sites), for "regional, islands or district council" substitute "local authority".

(4) In section 93(3)(a) (protection of road users from dangers near a road), for the words from "ratepayer" to "islands" substitute "person, being a ratepayer or person liable to pay council tax within their".

(5) In section 95(2) (recovery of expenses by road authority where contravention of section), the words "or by the district council" shall cease to have effect.

(6) In section 97(6) (trading: meanings of certain expressions)—

(a) in the definition of "relevant public market", in paragraph (b), for "regional, islands, or district council" substitute "local authority"; and

(b) in the proviso to that definition, for "council", in both places where it occurs, substitute "local authority".

(7) In section 113(1)(c) (transfer of property and liabilities in connection with special roads etc.), for "regional council" substitute "local authority".

(8) In section 135 (restriction on powers of authority in which sewers and sewage disposal works are vested), in each of subsections (1) and (2), for "local" substitute "sewerage".

(9) In section 143(2)(a)(ii) (procedure for orders), after "section 8" insert "113A".

(10) In section 151 (interpretation)—

(a) in subsection (1)—

(i) in the definition of "local authority", for "regional or islands council" substitute "council constituted under section 2 of the Local Government etc. (Scotland) Act 1994";

(ii) in the definition of "maintenance", in paragraph (b), for "an islands or district council" substitute "a local authority";

(iii) in the definition of "roads authority"—

(A) for "regional or islands council" substitute "council constituted under section 2 of the Local Government etc. (Scotland) Act 1994"; and

(B) for "council", where it secondly occurs, substitute "local authority";

(iv) after the definition of "roads authority" insert—

"sewerage authority" shall be construed in accordance with section 62 of the Local Government etc. (Scotland) Act 1994;"; and

(v) in the definition of "water authority", for "3 of the Water (Scotland) Act 1980" substitute "62 of the Local Government etc. (Scotland) Act 1994"; and

(b) in subsection (3)(c), for "an islands or district council" substitute "a local authority".

(11) In Schedule I (procedures for making or confirming certain orders and schemes)—

(a) in paragraph 3, in the Table—

(i) in entry (i), in column 2, for the words from "The council" to "in which" substitute "Every local authority in whose area";

(ii) in entry (iii), in column 2, for the words from "The council" to "district" substitute "Every local authority";

(iii) in entry (v), in column 2, for the words from "The council" to "which" substitute "Every local authority in whose area"; and

(iv) in entry (vii), in column 2, for the words from "The council" to "which" substitute "Every local authority in whose area"; and

(b) in paragraph 10(a), for the words from "the council" to "district" substitute "every local authority".

The Foster Children (Scotland) Act 1984 (c. 56)

136. In section 21(1) of the Foster Children (Scotland) Act 1984 (interpretation), in the definition of "local authority", for the words from "the" to "area" substitute "a council constituted under section 2 of the Local Government etc. (Scotland) Act 1994".

The Rent (Scotland) Act 1984 (c. 58)

137.—(1) The Rent (Scotland) Act 1984 shall be amended in accordance with this paragraph.

(2) In section 5(2) (no protected or statutory tenancy where landlord's interest belongs to local authority etc.)—

(a) in paragraph (a) for—

(i) "regional, islands or district council", in both places where it occurs; and

(ii) "an islands or district council",

substitute "local authority"; and

(b) after paragraph (a) insert—

"(aa) a water authority or sewerage authority;".

(3) In section 43(1) (registration areas for purposes of Part V), for "districts and islands areas" substitute "areas of local authorities".

(4) In section 62(1) (registration areas for purposes of Part VII), for "districts and islands areas" substitute "areas of local authorities".

(5) In section 63(4) (bodies for purposes of subsection (3)(b)), for paragraph (a) substitute—

"(a) a council constituted under section 2 of the Local Government etc. (Scotland) Act 1994, or a joint board or joint committee of two or more such councils, or the common good of such a council or any trust under the control of such a council;

(aa) a water authority or sewerage authority;".

(6) In section 115(1) (interpretation)—

(a) in the definition of "local authority", for "an islands council or district council" substitute "a council constituted under section 2 of the Local Government etc. (Scotland) Act 1994";

(b) after the definition of "rent assessment committee" insert—
" "sewerage authority" shall be construed in accordance with section 62 of the Local Government etc. (Scotland) Act 1994;"; and
(c) after the definition of "tenant" insert—
" "water authority" shall be construed in accordance with section 62 of the Local Government etc. (Scotland) Act 1994.".

The Cinemas Act 1985 (c. 13)

138. In section 21(1) of the Cinemas Act 1985 (interpretation), in the definition of "local authority", in paragraph (b), for "an islands or district council" substitute "a council constituted under section 2 of the Local Government etc. (Scotland) Act 1994".

The Child Abduction and Custody Act 1985 (c. 60)

139. In section 27(3)(b) of the Child Abduction and Custody Act 1985 (interpretation), for "regional or islands council" substitute "council constituted under section 2 of the Local Government etc. (Scotland) Act 1994".

The Water (Fluoridation) Act 1985 (c. 63)

140.—(1) The Water (Fluoridation) Act 1985 shall be amended in accordance with this paragraph.
(2) In section 1 (fluoridation of water supplies at request of health authority)—
(a) in subsection (6), after "conferred by" insert "subsections (1) to (5) of"; and
(b) in subsection (7), for "water undertaker in exercise of the power conferred by section 87 of the Water Industry Act 1991" substitute "water undertaker (within the meaning of the Water Industry Act 1991) in exercise of the power conferred by section 87 of that Act; and where a water undertaker (within that meaning) is operating a fluoridation scheme by virtue of Schedule 7 to that Act, subsection (6) shall apply in relation to the scheme as that subsection applies, by virtue of the foregoing provisions of this subsection, to fluoridation in exercise of the power so conferred.".
(3) Section 3 (continuity of existing fluoridation schemes) shall cease to have effect.
(4) In section 4 (publicity and consultation)—
(a) in subsection (1), for paragraphs (a) and (b) substitute "to make or withdraw an application";
(b) in subsection (2), for paragraph (b), substitute—
    "(b) give notice of the proposal to—
        (i) the Customers Council; and
        (ii) every local authority whose area falls wholly or partly within the area affected by the proposal.";
(c) in subsection (3), for "local authorities (if any) to whom they are required by subsection (2)(b)" substitute "bodies to whom they are required by subsection (2)(b)(i) and (ii)"; and
(d) in subsection (6), the words "or to terminate a preserved scheme" and in subsection (7) the words "or terminate a preserved scheme" shall cease to have effect.
(5) In section 5 (interpretation)—
(a) for the definition of "appropriate authority" substitute—
" "Customers Council" means the Scottish Water and Sewerage Customers Council;";
(b) for the definition of "local authority" (and the word "and" immediately following that definition) substitute—
" "local authority" means a council constituted under section 2 of the Local Government etc. (Scotland) Act 1994;"; and
(c) for the definition of "statutory water undertaker" substitute—
" "statutory water undertaker" means a water authority; and
"water authority" shall be construed in accordance with section 62 of the Local Government etc. (Scotland) Act 1994;".

The Transport Act 1985 (c. 67)

141. In section 93 of the Transport Act 1985 (travel concession schemes)—
(a) in subsection (8)(b)—
    (i) after "also" insert "—
        (i) "; and
    (ii) after "authority" insert "; and
        (ii) in relation to Scotland, Strathclyde Passenger Transport Authority"; and

(b) in subsection (9)—
    (i) in paragraph (a), after "paragraph (b)" insert "or (c)"; and
    (ii) in paragraph (b), after "jointly" insert "; or
    (c) where the authority or one of the authorities concerned in establishing the scheme are Strathclyde Passenger Transport Authority, to Strathclyde Passenger Transport Executive or (as the case may require) to that Executive and the other authority or authorities so concerned acting jointly.".

The Housing Act 1985 (c. 68)

142.—(1) The Housing Act 1985 shall be amended in accordance with this paragraph.
(2) In section 76(3) (application of Part III of Act to Scotland)—
(a) in paragraph (a), for "district or islands council" substitute "council constituted under section 2 of the Local Government etc. (Scotland) Act 1994"; and
(b) in paragraph (b), for "regional or islands council" substitute "council constituted under section 2 of the Local Government etc. (Scotland) Act 1994".
(3) In Schedule 4 (qualifying period for right to buy and discount)—
(a) in paragraph 7(2), for "regional, islands or district council" substitute "council constituted under section 2 of the Local Government etc. (Scotland) Act 1994"; and
(b) in paragraph 7A(1)(b), for "an islands or district council" substitute "a local housing authority".

The Housing Associations Act 1985 (c. 69)

143.—(1) The Housing Associations Act 1985 shall be amended in accordance with this paragraph.
(2) In section 59(1) and (2) (powers of local authorities to promote and assist housing associations: Scotland), the words "or regional council", wherever they occur, shall cease to have effect.
(3) In section 104 (local housing authorities)—
(a) in subsection (1)(b), for "an islands or district council" substitute "a council constituted under section 2 of the Local Government etc. (Scotland) Act 1994"; and
(b) in subsection (2)(b), for the words from "islands" to "be" substitute "area of a council mentioned in subsection (1)(b) above".
(4) In section 106(2) (minor definitions), in the definition of "local authority", for "an islands council or district council" substitute "a council constituted under section 2 of the Local Government etc. (Scotland) Act 1994".

The Weights and Measures Act 1985 (c. 72)

144. In section 69(3) of the Weights and Measures Act 1985 (local weights and measures authorities: Scotland), for the words from "each" to "council" substitute "the area of each council constituted under section 2 of the Local Government etc. (Scotland) Act 1994 shall be the council for that area".

The Local Government Act 1986 (c. 10)

145. In section 6(2)(b) of the Local Government Act 1986 (interpretation and application of Part II), for "regional, islands or district council" substitute "council constituted under section 2 of the Local Government etc. (Scotland) Act 1994".

The Civil Protection in Peacetime Act 1986 (c. 22)

146. In section 1(1) of the Civil Protection in Peacetime Act 1986 (application of Act)—
(a) after "that Act" insert "including, by virtue of section 4A of that Act, any two or more local authorities jointly and a joint board and joint committee"; and
(b) after "authority", where it thirdly occurs, insert "or, as the case may be, the local authorities, joint board or joint committee".

The Airports Act 1986 (c. 31)

147. In section 12(1) of the Airports Act 1986 (interpretation of Part II), in the definition of—
(a) "local authority", in paragraph (b), for the words from "has" to "1973" substitute "means a council constituted under section 2 of the Local Government etc. (Scotland) Act 1994"; and
(b) "principal council", in paragraph (b), for "regional or islands council" substitute "local authority".

The Disabled Persons (Services, Consultation and Representation) Act 1986 (c. 33)

148.—(1) The Disabled Persons (Services, Consultation and Representation) Act 1986 shall be amended in accordance with this paragraph.

(2) In section 2(9) (rights of authorised representatives of disabled persons: definitions), in the definition of "local authority", in paragraph (b), for "regional, islands or district council" substitute "council constituted under section 2 of the Local Government etc. (Scotland) Act 1994".

(3) In section 16 (interpretation), in the definition of "local authority", in paragraph (b)—

(a) for "regional or islands council" substitute "council constituted under section 2 of the Local Government etc. (Scotland) Act 1994";

(b) the words ", as read with section 2," shall cease to have effect; and

(c) after "Act" insert "or any of the enactments mentioned in section 5(1B) of that Act".

The Gas Act 1986 (c. 44)

149. In Schedule 7 to the Gas Act 1986 (minor and consequential amendments), in paragraph 5(5), in the definition of "local authority", for "an islands or district council" substitute "a council constituted under section 2 of the Local Government etc. (Scotland) Act 1994".

The Parliamentary Constituencies Act 1986 (c. 56)

150. In section 6(4)(b) of the Parliamentary Constituencies Act 1986 (definitions for purposes of section 6(2)), for the words from "the" to "district" substitute "a council constituted under section 2 of the Local Government etc. (Scotland) Act 1994".

The Debtors (Scotland) Act 1987 (c. 18)

151.—(1) The Debtors (Scotland) Act 1987 shall be amended in accordance with this paragraph.

(2) In each of sections 1(5)(e) (competence of time to pay direction) and 5(4)(e) (competence of time to pay order), after sub-paragraph (ii) (and before the word "or" immediately following that sub-paragraph), insert—

"(iia) a collecting authority (within the meaning of section 79 of the Local Government etc. (Scotland) Act 1994) in respect of any charges payable to them by virtue of that section;".

(3) In section 106 (interpretation), for the definition of "summary warrant" substitute—

" "summary warrant" means a summary warrant granted under or, as the case may be, by virtue of—

(a) paragraph 7 of Schedule 2 to the Abolition of Domestic Rates Etc. (Scotland) Act 1987;

(b) paragraph 2 of Schedule 8 to the Local Government Finance Act 1992;

(c) paragraph 2 of Schedule 10 to the Local Government etc. (Scotland) Act 1994; or

(d) any of the enactments mentioned in Schedule 4 to this Act;".

(4) In paragraph 35 of Schedule 5 (interpretation), in the definition of "creditor", after paragraph (e) add—

"; and

(f) for the purposes of paragraph 2 of Schedule 10 to the Local Government etc. (Scotland) Act 1994, the collecting authority (within the meaning of section 79 of that Act).".

The Housing (Scotland) Act 1987 (c. 26)

152.—(1) The Housing (Scotland) Act 1987 shall be amended in accordance with this paragraph.

(2) In section 61 (secure tenant's right to purchase)—

(a) in subsection (2)(a), for sub-paragraphs (i) and (ii) substitute—

"(i) a local authority, or a joint board or joint committee of two or more local authorities, or the common good of a local authority or any trust under the control of a local authority; or

(iia) a water authority or sewerage authority;";

(b) in subsection (11)(a)—

(i) for "a regional, islands or district council" substitute "any local authority";

(ii) the words "council or", where they first occur, shall cease to have effect; and

(iii) for "council", where it thirdly and fourthly occurs, substitute "authority"; and

(c) in subsection (11)(1), after "a water authority" insert "or sewerage authority".

(3) In section 64(6) (conditions of sale: houses in designated rural areas), for "islands or district council", in both places where it occurs, substitute "local authority".

(4) In section 70 (power to refuse to sell certain houses required for educational purposes)—
(a) in subsection (1), for "an islands" substitute "a"; and
(b) after subsection (2) insert—
 "(3) In this section "council" means the local authority for Orkney Islands, Shetland Islands or Western Isles.".
(5) In section 212(4) (authorities empowered to give rent increase notices)—
(a) in paragraph (a), for "regional, islands or district council" substitute "local authority"; and
(b) in paragraph (e), the words "or a water development board" shall cease to have effect.
(6) In section 300(1)(a) (meaning of "public sector authority"), for "regional, islands or district council" substitute "council constituted under section 2 of the Local Government etc. (Scotland) Act 1994".
(7) In section 338(1) (interpretation)—
(a) for the definition of "local authority" substitute—
 " "local authority" means a council constituted under section 2 of the Local Government etc. (Scotland) Act 1994, and the district of a local authority means the area of such a council;";
(b) after the definition of "a service charge" insert—
 " "sewerage authority" shall be construed in accordance with section 62 of the Local Government etc. (Scotland) Act 1994;"; and
(c) for the definitions of "water authority" and "water development board" substitute—
 " "water authority" shall be construed in accordance with section 62 of the Local Government etc. (Scotland) Act 1994;".
(8) In Part I of Schedule 3 (grounds on which court may order recovery of possession), in paragraph 15(a), for "an islands council" substitute "the council (constituted under section 2 of the Local Government etc. (Scotland) Act 1994) for Orkney Islands, Shetland Islands or Western Isles".

The Fire Safety and Safety of Places of Sport Act 1987 (c. 27)

153. In section 41 of the Fire Safety and Safety of Places of Sport Act 1987 (interpretation), in the definition of "local authority", in paragraph (d), for "regional or islands council" substitute "council constituted under section 2 of the Local Government etc. (Scotland) Act 1994".

The Access to Personal Files Act 1987 (c. 37)

154. In Schedule 2 to the Access to Personal Files Act 1987 (accessible personal information: Scotland)—
(a) in paragraph 1, in the table, in the entry relating to "Social work authority", for "section 2(2)" substitute "section 5(1B)"; and
(b) in paragraph 2(2), for "regional, islands or district council" substitute "council constituted under section 2 of the Local Government etc. (Scotland) Act 1994".

The Income and Corporation Taxes Act 1988 (c. 1)

155. In section 842A(3) of the Income and Corporation Taxes Act 1988 (local authorities)—
(a) for paragraphs (a), (b) and (c) substitute—
 "(a) a council constituted under section 2 of the Local Government etc. (Scotland) Act 1994"; and
(b) in paragraph (e), for the words from "falling" to the end substitute "such as is mentioned in paragraph (a) above".

The Local Government Act 1988 (c. 9)

156.—(1) The Local Government Act 1988 shall be amended in accordance with this paragraph.
(2) In section 1 (interpretation)—
(a) in subsection (1)—
 (i) after paragraph (h) insert "and"; and
 (ii) paragraph (k) and the word "and" immediately preceding it shall cease to have effect; and
(b) in subsection (3)(a) for "regional, islands or district council" substitute "council constituted under section 2 of the Local Government etc. (Scotland) Act 1994".
(3) In section 2 (defined activities), after subsection (9) insert—
 "(10) Without prejudice to his powers to make orders or regulations under any other provision of this Part of this Act, the Secretary of State may by order provide that, from 31st

March 1995 or such later date as may be specified in the order until such date as may be so specified, being a date not later than 31st December 2001, the provisions of this Part of this Act shall apply in relation to local authorities subject to such modifications as may be so specified.".

(4) In section 15 (orders, regulations etc.), in each of subsections (2) and (5), after "section 2(9)" insert "or 2(10)".

(5) In section 24(6) (interpretation of Part III of Act), in the definition of—

(a) "local authority", in paragraph (b), for "regional, islands or district council" substitute "council constituted under section 2 of the Local Government etc. (Scotland) Act 1994"; and

(b) "local housing authority", in paragraph (b), for "an islands or district council" substitute "a local authority".

(6) In Schedule 2 (public supply or works contracts: the public authorities)—

(a) after the entry relating to the Peak Park Joint Planning Board insert—

"The Strathclyde Passenger Transport Authority."; and

(b) for "regional, islands or district council" substitute "council constituted under section 2 of the Local Government etc. (Scotland) Act 1994".

The Housing (Scotland) Act 1988 (c. 43)

157.—(1) The Housing (Scotland) Act 1988 shall be amended in accordance with this paragraph.

(2) In section 43(3)(a) (certain tenancies secure where interest of landlord belongs to local authority etc,), for sub-paragraphs (i) and (ii) substitute—

"(i) a council constituted under section 2 of the Local Government etc. (Scotland) Act 1994, or a joint board or joint committee of two or more such councils, or the common good of such a council or any trust under the control of such a council; or

(ia) a water authority or sewerage authority;".

(3) In section 45(4) (transfer of existing tenancies: public bodies), for paragraphs (a) and (b) substitute—

"(a) it belongs to a council constituted under section 2 of the Local Government etc. (Scotland) Act 1994, or a joint board or joint committee of two or more such councils, or the common good of such a council or any trust under the control of such a council; or

(aa) it belongs to a water authority or sewerage authority;".

(4) In section 55(1) (interpretation of Part II of the Act)—

(a) after the definition of "prescribed" insert—

" "sewerage authority" shall be construed in accordance with section 62 of the Local Government etc. (Scotland) Act 1994;";

(b) the word "and", where it occurs immediately after the definition of "tenancy", shall cease to have effect; and

(c) after the definition of "tenant" insert—

"; and

"water authority" shall be construed in accordance with the said section 62.".

(5) In section 56 (right conferred by Part III)—

(a) in subsection (3), for paragraph (a) substitute—

"(a) a council constituted under section 2 of the Local Government etc. (Scotland) Act 1994, or a joint board or joint committee of two or more such councils, or the common good of such a council or any trust under the control of such a council";

(b) in subsection (5)(c), for "islands or district council" substitute "council constituted under section 2 of the Local Government etc. (Scotland) Act 1994";

(c) in subsection (6)(a), for "an islands council" substitute "the council for Orkney Islands, Shetland Islands or Western Isles"; and

(d) in subsection (9)(a), for "islands or district council" substitute "council constituted under section 2 of the Local Government etc. (Scotland) Act 1994".

(6) In section 57(1) (persons by whom right may be exercised)—

(a) the word "neither" shall cease to have effect;

(b) the words from "nor" to "council", where it thirdly occurs, shall cease to have effect; and

(c) after "may" insert "not".

(7) In Schedule 4 (tenancies which cannot be assured tenancies), in paragraph 11—

(a) for sub-paragraph (a) substitute—

"(a) a council constituted under section 2 of the Local Government etc. (Scotland) Act 1994, or a joint board or joint committee of two or more such councils, or the common good of such a council or any trust under the control of such a council;

(aa) a water authority or sewerage authority;"; and

(b) for the word "and", where it occurs immediately after sub-paragraph (e), substitute "or".

The School Boards (Scotland) Act 1988 (c. 47)

158.—(1) The School Boards (Scotland) Act 1988 shall be amended in accordance with this paragraph.

(2) In section 5 (persons entitled to attend Board meetings, etc.)—

(a) in subsection (1), for the words from "The Director" to "purpose" substitute the words "An officer of an education authority"; and

(b) in subsection (2), for the words from "The regional" to "division" substitute the words "The councillor for the electoral ward".

(3) In subsection (2) of section 22 (interpretation)—

(a) after the definition of "co-opted members" insert—

" "councillor" means a councillor elected under section 5 of the Local Government etc. (Scotland) Act 1994";

(b) for the definition of "electoral division" substitute—

" "electoral ward" shall be construed in accordance with section 5 of the Local Government etc. (Scotland) Act 1994"; and

(c) the definitions of "islands councillor" and "regional councillor" shall cease to have effect.

(4) In Schedule 2 (application of 1973 Act to appointment committees)—

(a) in paragraph 5 the words "Schedule 10 to" and "and Schedule 10 to" shall cease to have effect;

(b) in paragraph 14(a) for the words "Director of Education" substitute the words "education authority"; and

(c) in paragraph 15 for the words from "The Director" to "purpose" substitute the words "An officer of the education authority".

The Road Traffic Act 1988 (c. 52)

159.—(1) The Road Traffic Act 1988 shall be amended in accordance with this paragraph.

(2) In section 27(7)(b) (local authorities who may designate roads, etc.), for "regional or islands council" substitute "council constituted under section 2 of the Local Government etc. (Scotland) Act 1994".

(3) In section 33(5)(b) (local authorities who may authorise certain motor vehicle trials), for "regional or islands council" substitute "council constituted under section 2 of the Local Government etc. (Scotland) Act 1994".

(4) In section 39(4)(b) (powers of local authorities as to giving road safety information etc.), for "regional or islands council" substitute "council constituted under section 2 of the Local Government etc. (Scotland) Act 1994".

(5) In section 45(3)(c) (inspectors appointed by designated councils to carry out vehicle tests), for "the council of a region or islands area" substitute "a council constituted under section 2 of the Local Government etc. (Scotland) Act 1994".

(6) In section 67B(2) (tests to check whether defects have been remedied), for "a region or islands area" substitute "the area of a council constituted under section 2 of the Local Government etc. (Scotland) Act 1994".

(7) In section 124(2) (exemption of police instructors from prohibition imposed by section 123), in the definition of "local authority", in paragraph (b), for "regional or islands council" substitute "council constituted under section 2 of the Local Government etc. (Scotland) Act 1994".

(8) In section 144(2)(a)(ii) (local authority exempt from requirement for third-party insurance or security), for "regional, islands or district council" substitute "council constituted under section 2 of the Local Government etc. (Scotland) Act 1994".

(9) In Schedule 2 (deferred tests of condition of vehicles), in paragraph 1(b), for "an islands area or district" substitute "the area of a council constituted under section 2 of the Local Government etc. (Scotland) Act 1994".

The Electricity Act 1989 (c. 29)

160.—(1) Schedule 5 to the Electricity Act 1989 (water rights for hydro-electric generating stations in Scotland) shall be amended in accordance with this paragraph.

(2) In paragraph 8(a)—

(a) after "authority;" insert "and";

(b) for "regional and district councils or the islands council" substitute "council constituted under section 2 of the Local Government etc. (Scotland) Act 1994"; and

(c) the words "; and (iii) the water development board" shall cease to have effect.

(3) In paragraph 9, the words "and the water development board" shall cease to have effect.

(4) In paragraph 14, the words ", or the area of any water development board," shall cease to have effect.

The Local Government and Housing Act 1989 (c. 42)

161.—(1) The Local Government and Housing Act 1989 shall be amended in accordance with this paragraph.

(2) In section 2(6) (politically restricted posts)

(a) in paragraph (a), the words "or director of education" and the words from "or section" to "1980" shall cease to have effect; and

(b) in paragraph (c), for "director of social work" substitute "chief social work officer".

(3) In section 4 (designation and reports of head of paid service)—

(a) in subsection (5), the words ", or Schedule 10 or 20 to," shall cease to have effect; and

(b) in subsection (6)(b), for "regional, islands or district council" substitute "council constituted under section 2 of the Local Government etc. (Scotland) Act 1994".

(4) In section 5(5) (reports of monitoring officer etc.), the words ", or Schedule 10 or 20 to," shall cease to have effect.

(5) In section 8(5)(b) (local authorities to adopt standing orders with respect to staff), for "regional, islands or district council" substitute "council constituted under section 2 of the Local Government etc. (Scotland) Act 1994".

(6) In section 9 (assistants for political groups)—

(a) in subsection (8)(b), the words ", or Schedule 10 or 20 to," shall cease to have effect; and

(b) in subsection (11), in the definition of "relevant authority", in paragraph (b), for "regional, islands or district council" substitute "council constituted under section 2 of the Local Government etc. (Scotland) Act 1994".

(7) In section 14 (voting rights of members of certain committees: Scotland)—

(a) subsections (2) and (3) shall cease to have effect;

(b) in subsection (4), for the words "subsections (1) to (3)" substitute "subsection (1)";

(c) in subsection (5)(d), after "paragraph 3" insert ", or a joint advisory committee formed under paragraph 5B";

(d) for subsection (6) substitute—

"(6) Nothing in this section shall prevent the appointment as a voting member of—

(a) a committee such as is mentioned in subsection (1) of section 124 of the Local Government (Scotland) Act 1973 (committees appointed by education authority); or

(b) a joint committee of two or more authorities whose purposes include either of those mentioned in paragraphs (a) and (b) of that subsection; or

(c) any sub-committee of such a committee or joint committee,

of a person such as is mentioned in subsection (4) of the said section 124.";

(e) in subsection (8), after paragraph (a) insert—

"(aa) section 124(5);"; and

(f) in subsection (9), for "regional, islands or district council" substitute "council constituted under section 2 of the Local Government etc. (Scotland) Act 1994".

(8) In section 21(2) (interpretation of Part I), for "regional, islands or district council" substitute "council constituted under section 2 of the Local Government etc. (Scotland) Act 1994".

(9) In section 31(8) (National Code of Local Government Conduct), in the definition of "local authority", in paragraph (b), for "regional, islands or district council" substitute "council constituted under section 2 of the Local Government etc. (Scotland) Act 1994".

(10) In section 151(4) (power to amend provisions about charges), for paragraphs (b) and (c) substitute—

"or

(b) it is a charge amounting to local taxation.".

(11) In section 152(3) (application of certain provisions as respects Scotland)—

(a) for paragraphs (a), (b) and (c) substitute—

"(a) a council constituted under section 2 of the Local Government etc. (Scotland) Act 1994"; and

(b) for paragraphs (e) and (f) substitute—

"and

(e) a joint board or joint committee within the meaning of section 235(1) of the Local Government (Scotland) Act 1973.".

(12) In section 155(5) (emergency financial assistance to local authorities)—

(a) for paragraphs (a), (b) and (c) substitute "a council constituted under section 2 of the Local Government etc. (Scotland) Act 1994"; and

(b) the letter "(d)" shall cease to have effect.

(13) In section 157(6) (commutation of, and interest on, periodic payments of grants etc. to local authorities), for "regional, islands or district council" substitute "a council constituted under section 2 of the Local Government etc. (Scotland) Act 1994".

(14) In section 170(9) (authorities empowered to provide services etc. for owners or occupiers of houses as respects certain works), for "regional, islands or district council" substitute "council constituted under section 2 of the Local Government etc. (Scotland) Act 1994".

The Prisons (Scotland) Act 1989 (c. 45)

162.—(1) The Prisons (Scotland) Act 1989 shall be amended in accordance with this paragraph.

(2) In section 8(1) (visiting committees), for "regional, island and district councils" substitute "councils constituted under section 2 of the Local Government etc. (Scotland) Act 1994".

(3) In section 14 (legalised police cells)—
(a) in subsection (2)—
    (i) for "any region or islands area" substitute "the area of a council"; and
    (ii) the words "region or islands", where they secondly occur, shall cease to have effect;
(b) in subsection (5), for "any region or islands area" substitute "the area of a council";
(c) in subsection (6), for "islands area of Orkney or of Shetland" substitute "areas of the councils for Orkney Islands and Shetland Islands";
(d) in subsection (7)—
    (i) for "the council of a region or islands area" substitute "a council"; and
    (ii) for "committee" substitute "board"; and
(e) after subsection (8) insert—
    "(9) In this section, 'council' means a council constituted under section 2 of the Local Government etc. (Scotland) Act 1994.".

(4) In section 16 (discharge of prisoners)—
(a) in subsection (2), the words "district or islands", in both places where they occur, shall cease to have effect; and
(b) after subsection (2) insert—
    "(3) In this section, "area" means the area of a council constituted under section 2 of the Local Government etc. (Scotland) Act 1994.".

The Food Safety Act 1990 (c. 16)

163.—(1) The Food Safety Act 1990 shall be amended in accordance with this paragraph.

(2) In section 5(2) (food authorities in Scotland), for "islands or district councils" substitute "councils constituted under section 2 of the Local Government etc. (Scotland) Act 1994".

(3) In section 27(1) (appointment of public analysts), for "regional or islands council" substitute "council constituted under section 2 of the Local Government etc. (Scotland) Act 1994".

(4) In section 28(1) (provision of facilities for examinations), for "regional council" substitute "council constituted under section 2 of the Local Government etc. (Scotland) Act 1994".

The Enterprise and New Towns (Scotland) Act 1990 (c. 35)

164.—(1) The Enterprise and New Towns (Scotland) Act 1990 shall be amended in accordance with this paragraph.

(2) In section 21 (areas of operation of Highlands and Islands Enterprise)—
(a) in subsection (1)—
    (i) for paragraph (a) substitute—
    "(a) the local government areas of Highland, Western Isles, Orkney Islands, Shetland Islands and that part of Argyll and Bute which is the area of the former Argyll and Bute District Council and the islands of Arran, Great Cumbrae and Little Cumbrae;" and
    (ii) in paragraph (b), for "Moray District" substitute "local government area of Moray,"; and
(b) after subsection (4) insert—
    "(5) In this section references to local government areas are references to the new local government areas within the meaning of Part 1 of the Local Government etc. (Scotland) Act 1994.".

(3) In section 36(1) (interpretation), in the definition of "local authority", for "regional, islands or district council" substitute "council constituted under section 2 of the Local Government etc. (Scotland) Act 1994".

The Law Reform (Miscellaneous Provisions) (Scotland) Act 1990 (c. 40)

165.—(1) The Law Reform (Miscellaneous Provisions) (Scotland) Act 1990 shall be amended in accordance with this paragraph.

(2) In section 62(6) (local authorities for purposes of supervised attendance orders), for "regional or islands council" substitute "council constituted under section 2 of the Local Government etc. (Scotland) Act 1994".

(3) In Schedule 6 (supervised attendance orders), in paragraph 2(3)(b), for "director of social work" substitute "chief social work officer".

The Broadcasting Act 1990 (c. 42)

166. In Schedule 2 to the Broadcasting Act 1990 (restrictions on the holding of licences), in paragraph 1(1), in the definition of "local authority", in paragraph (b), for "regional, islands or district council" substitute "council constituted under section 2 of the Local Government etc. (Scotland) Act 1994".

The Environmental Protection Act 1990 (c. 43)

167.—(1) The Environmental Protection Act 1990 shall be amended in accordance with this paragraph.

(2) In section 4(11)(c) (meaning of "local authority" in Scotland for purposes of Part I), for "an islands or district council" substitute "a council constituted under section 2 of the Local Government etc. (Scotland) Act 1994".

(3) In section 30 (authorities for purposes of Part II), in each of subsections (1)(g), (2)(g) and (3)(c), for "an islands or district council" substitute "a council constituted under section 2 of the Local Government etc. (Scotland) Act 1994".

(4) In section 36 (procedures to be carried out where proposal to issue waste management licence)—
   (a) in subsection (6), the words "(other than an islands council)" shall cease to have effect;
   (b) in subsection (6)(a)—
       (i) after "(i)" insert "where the authority is not the council (constituted under section 2 of the Local Government etc. (Scotland) Act 1994) for Orkney Islands, Shetland Islands or Western Isles";
       (ii) after sub-paragraph (ii) insert "and"; and
       (iii) sub-paragraph (iii) shall cease to have effect;
   (c) in subsection (6)(b)—
       (i) after "purification authority" insert "or"; and
       (ii) the words "or the general planning authority" shall cease to have effect;
   (d) in subsection (10)—
       (i) after "conservancy body" insert "or";
       (ii) the words "or general planning authority" shall cease to have effect;
       (iii) after "the body" insert "or"; and
       (iv) the words "or the general planning authority" shall cease to have effect.

(5) In section 39(8) (procedures to be carried out where proposal to accept surrender of licence)—
   (a) the words "(not being an islands council)" shall cease to have effect;
   (b) for paragraph (a) substitute—
       "(a) where the authority is not the council (constituted under section 2 of the Local Government etc. (Scotland) Act 1994) for Orkney Islands, Shetland Islands or Western Isles, refer the proposal to the river purification authority whose area includes any of the relevant land;"; and
   (c) in paragraph (b), the words "or the general planning authority" shall cease to have effect.

(6) In section 45(10) (application to Scotland of certain sections of the 1968 Act for purposes connected with the collection of controlled waste), for paragraphs (a) and (b) substitute—
   "(a) the said section 2 conferred a power on a waste collection authority rather than a duty on a sewerage authority;
   (b) in the said section 3—
       (i) references to a sewerage authority were references to a waste collection authority; and
       (ii) in references to public sewers and public sewage works the word "public" were omitted;

(c) in the said section 4, the reference to a sewerage authority were a reference to a waste collection authority and the words from "by virtue" to the end were omitted; and

(d) in the said section 41, the reference to a sewerage authority were a reference to a waste collection authority,".

(7) In section 50(5)(a) (bodies to be consulted where waste disposal plan being prepared), sub-paragraph (iv) shall cease to have effect.

(8) In section 53 (duties of authorities as respects disposal of waste collected: Scotland)—

(a) in subsection (4)—

(i) the words "(other than an islands council)" shall cease to have effect; and

(ii) in paragraphs (a) and (b), for "regional council", wherever it occurs, substitute "sewerage authority";

(b) in subsection (5)—

(i) for "regional council", in both places where it occurs, substitute "sewerage authority"; and

(ii) for "council", where it thirdly occurs, substitute "sewerage authority"; and

(c) after subsection (5) insert—

"(5A) In this section "sewerage authority" shall be construed in accordance with section 62 of the Local Government etc. (Scotland) Act 1994."

(9) In section 54 (special provisions for land occupied by disposal authorities: Scotland)—

(a) in subsection (4)—

(i) in paragraph (b), for sub-paragraphs (i) to (iv) substitute—

"(i) where the authority is not the council (constituted under section 2 of the Local Government etc. (Scotland) Act 1994) for Orkney Islands, Shetland Islands or Western Isles, to the river purification authority whose area includes any of the land in question;

(ii) to the Health and Safety Executive; and

(iii) where the authority is not the council (constituted under section 2 of the Local Government etc. (Scotland) Act 1994) for Orkney Islands, Shetland Islands or Western Isles, in the case of a proposal to operate mobile plant, to the river purification authority whose area includes the area of the waste disposal authority;"

(ii) in paragraph (c)—

(a) after "purification authority" insert "or"; and

(b) the words "or the general planning authority" shall cease to have effect; and

(b) in subsection (5)—

(i) for the words from "above" to "(d)" substitute "(d)"; and

(ii) for the words "an islands council" substitute "the council (constituted under section 2 of the Local Government etc. (Scotland) Act 1994) for Orkney Islands, Shetland Islands or Western Isles".

(10) In section 86 (preliminary provisions relating to litter)—

(a) in subsection (3), for paragraphs (a) and (b) substitute—

"(a) a council constituted under section 2 of the Local Government etc. (Scotland) Act 1994"; and

(b) in subsection (10)—

(i) for "its" substitute "their"; and

(ii) for the words from "the district" to the end substitute "the council constituted under section 2 of the Local Government etc. (Scotland) Act 1994".

(11) In section 88(9) ("litter authorities" for purposes of section)—

(a) in paragraph (a), the words ", a regional council"; and

(b) in paragraph (b), the words ", regional council",

shall cease to have effect.

(12) In section 90(3) (power to designate litter control areas), the words ", regional council" shall cease to have effect.

(13) In section 92(1) (summary proceedings by litter authorities), the words ", regional council" shall cease to have effect.

(14) In section 93(1) (street litter control notices), the words ", regional council" shall cease to have effect.

(15) In section 95(1) (public registers), the words ", regional council" shall cease to have effect.

(16) In section 99(5)(e) (local authority in Scotland having powers in relation to abandoned trolleys), for "an islands or district council" substitute "a council constituted under section 2 of the Local Government etc. (Scotland) Act 1994".

(17) In section 149(11) (seizure of stray dogs: interpretation), in the definition of "local authority", for "an islands or district council" substitute "a council constituted under section 2 of the Local Government etc. (Scotland) Act 1994".

The New Roads and Street Works Act 1991 (c. 22)

168.—(1) The New Roads and Street Works Act 1991 shall be amended in accordance with this paragraph.

(2) In section 108(6)(a) (relevant authorities in relation to road works including the breaking up or opening in the road of a sewer), for "the local authority, that local" substitute "a sewerage authority, that".

(3) In each of sections 109(6)(a) (notice before granting permission to execute certain road works), 117(3)(a) (notice restricting certain road works) and 149(4)(a) (responsible authority as respects reinstatement of sewers, drains or tunnels) and of paragraphs 7(3)(b) and 9 of Schedule 6 (roads with special engineering difficulties), for "local" substitute "sewerage".

(4) In section 148 (particular and,general provisions as respects sewers)—
(a) in each of subsections (1) and (4), for "local" substitute "sewerage"; and
(b) for subsection (3) substitute—
"(3) References in this Part to an undertaker having apparatus shall, where the apparatus is a sewer, drain or tunnel, be construed—
(a) in the case of apparatus vested in a sewerage authority, as references to that authority; and
(b) in any other case, as references to the authority, body or person having the management or control of the apparatus.".

(5) In section 153 (power of road works authority to undertake road works)—
(a) in subsection (1), the words—
(i) "or district council"; and
(ii) "or council",
shall cease to have effect; and
(b) in subsection (3), the words "or council" shall cease to have effect.

(6) In section 164(1) (interpretation), after the definition of "reinstatement" insert—
" "sewerage authority" shall be construed in accordance with section 62 of the Local Government etc. (Scotland) Act 1994;".

The Children and Young Persons (Protection from Tobacco) Act 1991 (c. 23)

169. In section 6(1) of the Children and Young Persons (Protection from Tobacco) Act 1991 (enforcement action by local authorities in Scotland), for "regional or islands council" substitute "council constituted under section 2 of the Local Government etc. (Scotland) Act 1994".

The Natural Heritage (Scotland) Act 1991 (c. 28)

170.—(1) The Natural Heritage (Scotland) Act 1991 shall be amended in accordance with this paragraph.

(2) In section 20 (making of drought orders), for subsection (3) substitute—
"(3) A drought order may only be made on the application of a water authority.".

(3) In section 22(1) (interpretation), in the definition of "compensation water", the words "or water development board" shall cease to have effect.

(4) In section 24 (rights of entry and inspection)—
(a) in subsection (1)—
(i) for ", a water authority or a water development board" substitute "or a water authority"; and
(ii) in paragraph (a), the words "or board" shall cease to have effect; and
(b) in subsection (9)—
(i) for ", water authority or water development board" substitute "or water authority"; and
(ii) in paragraph (a), the words "or board" shall cease to have effect.

(5) In Schedule 7 (further provisions regarding drought orders)—
(a) in paragraph 5—
(i) in sub-paragraph (1), the words "or a water development board" and (in head (a)) "or board";
(ii) in sub-paragraph (2), the words ", or water development board"; and
(iii) in sub-paragraph (3), the words "or water development board" and "or board",
shall cease to have effect;
(b) in paragraph 6, the words from ", including" to the end shall cease to have effect; and
(c) in paragraph 7, the words "or a water development board" shall cease to have effect.

(6) In Schedule 8 (procedure for making drought orders), in paragraph 1(3), in the second column of the Table—
(a) for "regional, islands or district council", wherever it occurs, substitute "council constituted under section 2 of the Local Government etc. (Scotland) Act 1994"; and

(b) in paragraph (a) of the entry relating to "All Orders", the words "or water development board (not being the applicant)" shall cease to have effect.

The Road Traffic Act 1991 (c. 40)

171. In Schedule 3 to the Road Traffic Act 1991 (permitted and special parking areas outside London), in paragraphs 1(1)(d) and 2(1)(c), for "regional or islands council" substitute "council constituted under section 2 of the Local Government etc. (Scotland) Act 1994".

The Coal Mining Subsidence Act 1991 (c. 45)

172. In section 47(6)(b) of the Coal Mining Subsidence Act 1991 (notices to local authorities), for "district or islands council" substitute "council constituted under section 2 of the Local Government etc. (Scotland) Act 1994".

The Criminal Justice Act 1991 (c. 53)

173. In Schedule 3 to the Criminal Justice Act 1991 (reciprocal enforcement of certain orders), in paragraph 1, in subsection (1A) in sub-paragraph (1), in sub-paragraph (2)(b) and in sub-paragraph (3)(a), and in paragraphs 3(3)(b) and 6(8), for "regional or islands council" substitute "council constituted under section 2 of the Local Government etc. (Scotland) Act 1994".

The Social Security Contributions and Benefits Act 1992 (c. 4)

174.—(1) The Social Security Contributions and Benefits Act 1992 shall be amended in accordance with this paragraph.

(2) In section 28(6)(d) ("local education authority" in Scotland), for "regional or islands council" substitute "council constituted under section 2 of the Local Government etc. (Scotland) Act 1994".

(3) In section 58(4) (incapacity for work: work as councillor to be disregarded), in the definition of "councillor", in paragraph (b), for "regional, islands or district council" substitute "council constituted under section 2 of the Local Government etc. (Scotland) Act 1994".

(4) In sections 123(4) and 130(2) for the words "levying authority" substitute "local authority in Scotland".

(5) In section 137(1) (interpretation), the definition of "levying authority" shall cease to have effect.

The Social Security Administration Act 1992 (c. 5)

175.—(1) The Social Security Administration Act 1992 shall be amended in accordance with this paragraph.

(2) In section 15A(3) ("qualifying lenders" for purposes of section)—

(a) in paragraph (d), the words ", islands council" shall cease to have effect; and

(b) after paragraph (e) insert—

"(ee) any council constituted under section 2 of the Local Government etc. (Scotland) Act 1994".

(3) For the words "levying authority" or "levying authorities" where they appear in sections 76(1), 77(1), 128(1), (2), and (3), 138(1), 139(2), (5) and (6) and 140(1), (2), (4) and (7), substitute "local authority in Scotland" or "local authorities in Scotland" respectively.

(4) In section 138(2) (nature of benefits in Scotland), for "regional, islands or district council' substitute "council constituted under section 2 of the Local Government etc. (Scotland) Act 1994".

(5) In section 191 (interpretation)—

(a) the definition of "levying authority" shall cease to have effect;

(b) in the definition of "local authority", for the words "an islands or district council" substitute "a council constituted under section 2 of the Local Government etc. (Scotland) Act 1994."; and

(c) in the definition of "rating authority", for the words from "the meaning" to "1973" substitute "shall be construed in accordance with section 30 of the Local Government etc. (Scotland) Act 1994".

The Local Government Finance Act 1992 (c. 14)

176.—(1) The Local Government Finance Act 1992 shall be amended in accordance with this paragraph.

(2) In section 70 (council tax in respect of dwellings), for subsection (1)(a) substitute—

"(a) shall be known as the council tax of the council which set it;".

(3) In section 78 (basic amounts payable)—

(a) for "levying" substitute "local"; and

(b) for the definition of "A" substitute—

"A is the amount which, for the financial year in which the day falls and for dwellings in the valuation band listed for the dwelling, has been imposed by the local authority in whose area the dwelling is situated;".

(4) In section 80 (reduced amounts)—

(a) in subsections (1)(a) and (8)(c), for "levying" substitute "local"; and

(b) for subsection (5)(c)(i) substitute—

"(i) relating to the local authority whose council tax constitutes the amount referred to in subsection (1) above;".

(5) In section 81 (appeal to valuation appeal committee), in subsections (1)(a) and (b) and (5), for "levying" substitute "local".

(6) In section 84 (compilation and maintenance of valuation lists), for subsection (10) substitute—

"(10) In this Part "local assessor" means the assessor appointed under section 27 (appointment of assessors) of the Local Government etc. (Scotland) Act 1994 for each valuation area; and any depute assessor appointed under that section shall have all the functions of a local assessor under this Part.".

(7) In section 90 (information about properties), in subsection (8) for "levying" substitute "local".

(8) In section 91 (information about lists), in subsections (2) and (3) for "levying" substitute "local".

(9) In section 94 (substituted and reduced settings) in subsection (8), for "levying" substitute "local".

(10) In section 97 (levying and collection of council tax)—

(a) for subsection (1) substitute—

"(1) A local authority shall levy and collect the council tax set by them in respect of their area."; and

(b) subsection (2) shall cease to have effect.

(11) In subsection (1) of section 98 (information required by Secretary of State), for "levying" substitute "local".

(12) In section 99 (interpretation of Part II)—

(a) the definition of "levying authority" shall cease to have effect;

(b) for the definition of "local authority" substitute—

" "local authority" means a council constituted under section 2 of the Local Government etc. (Scotland) Act 1994; and "council" shall be construed accordingly;";

(c) in the definition of "housing body", paragraph (a) shall cease to have effect; and

(d) for the definition of "valuation appeal committee" substitute—

" "valuation appeal committee" means a valuation appeal committee established under section 29 of the Local Government etc. (Scotland) Act 1994;".

(13) In section 107 (water and sewerage charges)—

(a) subsection (1) shall cease to have effect; and

(b) in subsection (2), for "that Schedule" substitute "Schedule 11 to this Act".

(14) In section 109(1) (council tax grants), for "levying" substitute "local".

(15) In section 111 (references to rateable values), after subsection (10) insert—

"(10A) For the purposes of subsection (10) above, on and after 1st April 1996 the valuation roll which an assessor for a valuation area constituted under section 27 of the Local Government etc. (Scotland) Act 1994 is required to retain shall be the valuation roll for every valuation area existing before that date any part of which lies within his valuation area.".

(16) In Schedule 2 (administration)—

(a) in paragraph 1(2), for "a levying" substitute ", in Scotland, a local";

(b) in paragraph 12(1), for "levying" substitute "local";

(c) in paragraph 13, for "levying", in each place where it occurs, substitute "local"; and

(d) in paragraph 19—

(i) for "levying", in each place where it occurs, substitute "local"; and

(ii) for sub-paragraph (3) substitute—

"(3) Arrangements made under this paragraph for the exercise of functions under Schedule 8 to this Act may not include arrangements for the exercise of functions under paragraph 2(1)(a) of that Schedule.".

(17) In Schedule 3, in paragraph 2, for "levying" in each place where it occurs, substitute "local".

(18) In Schedule 8 (enforcement: Scotland), in paragraphs 1, 2, 3, 4 and 6, for "levying", in each place where it occurs, substitute "local".

(19) In Schedule 12 (payments to local authorities by Secretary of State: Scotland)—

(a) in paragraph 10(1) for "levying" substitute "local";

(b) in paragraph 10(3)(a)—

(i) for sub-head (i) substitute—

"(i) section 24A (lands and heritages partly unoccupied for a short time) of the Local Government (Scotland) Act 1966;" and

(ii) for sub-head (ii) substitute—

"(ii) section 25A (remission of rates on account of hardship) of that Act;";

(c) for paragraph 11(2) substitute—

"(2) Before such date in relation to each financial year as the Secretary of State may direct, each relevant authority shall calculate the amount of their non–domestic rating contribution for that year, and shall inform the Secretary of State of the amount so calculated in respect of them; and, for the purposes of this paragraph, "relevant authority" means, in relation to any financial year prior to and including the financial year 1995–96, a regional or islands council and, in relation to financial years after that year, a local authority."; and

(d) in paragraph 11(3), for "notified to them" substitute "notified by them".

The Local Government Act 1992 (c. 19)

177. In subsection (4)(c) of section 30 of the Local Government Act 1992 (extent), for the words from "Schedule" to "Part II" there shall be substituted the words "Part II of Schedule 4, apart from so much of that Part".

The Tribunals and Inquiries Act 1992 (c. 53)

178. In Part II of Schedule 1 to the Tribunals and Inquiries Act 1992, in paragraph 58 (the entry relating to rates) for the words from "section 4" to the end substitute "section 29 of the Local Government etc. (Scotland) Act 1994.".

The Prisoners and Criminal Proceedings (Scotland) Act 1993 (c. 9)

179.—(1) The Prisoners and Criminal Proceedings (Scotland) Act 1993 shall be amended in accordance with this paragraph.

(2) In section 18(6) (statement on oath by appropriate officer where supervised release order breached etc.)—

(a) in paragraph (b), for "director of social work" substitute "chief social work officer"; and

(b) in paragraph (c), for "director" substitute "chief social work officer".

(3) In section 27(1) (interpretation), in the definition of "local authority", for "regional or islands council" substitute "council constituted under section 2 of the Local Government etc. (Scotland) Act 1994".

The Clean Air Act 1993 (c. 11)

180. In section 64(1) of the Clean Air Act 1993 (interpretation), in the definition of "local authority", in paragraph (b), for "an islands or district council" substitute "a council constituted under section 2 of the Local Government etc. (Scotland) Act 1994".

The Radioactive Substances Act 1993 (c. 12)

181. In section 47(1) of the Radioactive Substances Act 1993 (interpretation)—

(a) in the definition of "local authority", in paragraph (b), for "regional, islands or district council" substitute "council constituted under section 2 of the Local Government etc. (Scotland) Act 1994"; and

(b) in the definition of "relevant water body", in paragraph (b), for "a water authority within the meaning of the Water (Scotland) Act 1980" substitute "a water and sewerage authority established by section 62 of the Local Government etc. (Scotland) Act 1994".

The Local Government (Overseas Assistance) Act 1993 (c. 25)

182. In section l(9)(b) of the Local Government (Overseas Assistance) Act 1993 (local authorities empowered to provide advice and assistance), for "regional, islands or district council" substitute "council constituted under section 2 of the Local Government etc. (Scotland) Act 1994".

The Noise and Statutory Nuisance Act 1993 (c. 40)

183.—(1) The Noise and Statutory Nuisance Act 1993 shall be amended in accordance with this paragraph.

(2) In section 8(5)(b) (local authorities in Scotland who may consent to the operation of loud-speakers in roads), for "district or islands council" substitute "council constituted under section 2 of the Local Government etc. (Scotland) Act 1994".

(3) In section 9(7) (interpretation of certain expressions for purposes of section), in the definition of "local authority", in paragraph (b), for "district or islands council" substitute "council constituted under section 2 of the Local Government etc. (Scotland) Act 1994".

The Railways Act 1993 (c. 43)

184.—(1) The Railways Act 1993 shall be amended in accordance with this paragraph.

(2) In section 136(3) (grants and subsidies), in paragraph (d)(i), for "regional or islands council" substitute "council constituted under section 2 of the Local Government etc. (Scotland) Act 1994".

(3) In section 151(1) (general interpretation), in the definition of "local authority"—

(a) the words "regional council, islands council" shall cease to have effect;

(b) for "London or" substitute "London,"; and

(c) after "Scilly" insert "or any council constituted under section 2 of the Local Government etc. (Scotland) Act 1994".

Section 180(2)   SCHEDULE 14

REPEALS

Chapter	Short title	Extent of repeal
18 and 19 Vict. c. 68.	The Burial Grounds (Scotland) Act 1855.	In section 10, the words "any of the Lords Ordinary of" and the the the words from "And provided" to "such dwelling house". In section 11, the words from "but no ground" to the end.
49 and 50 Vict. c. 15.	The Sporting Lands Rating (Scotland) Act 1886.	The whole Act.
7 and 8 Geo. 6 c. 26.	The Rural Water Supplies and Sewerage Act 1944.	The whole Act.
10 and 11 Geo. 6 c. 41.	The Fire Services Act 1947.	In section 15(2), the proviso. In section 36, in subsection (2), the words "and thirty-six" and "and twenty-three and subsections (3) and (6).
10 and 11 Geo. 6 c. 43.	The Local Government (Scotland) Act 1947.	In section 237(2)(b), the words from "and, if" to "determined". Sections 243, 243A, 243B and 244.
11 and 12 Geo. 6 c. 29.	The National Assistance Act 1948.	In section 33, subsection (2). In the Third Schedule, paragraphs 9 to 13.
12, 13 and 14 Geo. 6 c. 74.	The Coast Protection Act 1949.	In section 20(5), the words "or the council of a district in Scotland".
12, 13 and 14 Geo. 6 c. 97.	The National Parks and Access to the Countryside Act 1949.	In section 21(1), the words "general or district".
3 and 4 Eliz. 2 c. 13.	The Rural Water Supplies and Sewerage Act 1955.	The whole Act.
4 and 5 Eliz. 2 c. 60.	The Valuation and Rating (Scotland) Act 1956.	Section 1. Section 3. Section 22A.

Chapter	Short title	Extent of repeal
		In section 43(1), the definition of "Advisory Council".
6 and 7 Eliz. 2 c. 64.	The Local Government and Miscellaneous Financial Provisions (Scotland) Act 1958.	Section 7.
7 and 8 Eliz. 2 c. 40.	The Deer (Scotland) Act 1959.	In section 25A, in subsection (2), the words "islands and district", and in subsections (4) and (5) the words "islands or district". In section 25D, in subsection (8), the words "islands or district".
1960 c. 62.	The Caravan Sites and Control of Development Act 1960.	Section 24(8A).
1961 c. 41.	The Flood Prevention (Scotland) Act 1961.	In section 42(2) the words "(whether a different authority from the local authority or not)". Section 12(2).
1965 c. 49.	The Registration of Births, Deaths and Marriages (Scotland) Act 1965.	Section 15(4).
1966 c. 51.	The Local Government (Scotland) Act 1966.	Section 17. Section 20. In section 25, in subsection (1), the words "the determination of rateable values," and subsections (3), (4) and (5). In section 46(1), the definition of "rate". In Schedule 3, paragraph 1, in paragraph 3(1), the words from "and that" to "heritages", in paragraph 5, the word "relevant", in both places where it occurs, paragraphs 6 and 7, in paragraph 8, the words from "relevant lands" to "Act" and the words from "included"to "heritages", where it second occurs. In Schedule 5, paragraph 3.
1967 c. 77.	The Police (Scotland) Act 1967.	Section 19(5). Section 21A.
1967 c. 78.	The Water (Scotland) Act 1967.	The whole Act.
1967 c. 86.	The Countryside (Scotland) Act 1967.	In section 49, subsection (5). In section 61, in each of subsections (5), (6) and (8), the word "local". In section 63, in each of subsections (2) and (4) to (9), the word "local" wherever it occurs; and in subsection (11), the word "local" where it first occurs and the words from "and any reference" to the end. In section 65(5), paragraph (c) and in paragraph (f), the words "within the meaning of section 109(1) of the Water (Scotland) Act 1980"; and paragraph (g).
1968 c. 16.	The New Towns (Scotland) Act 1968.	In section 34(1)(a), the words "water, sewerage or other".
1968 c. 46.	The Health Services and Public Health Act 1968.	In section 71, subsection (3).
1968 c. 47.	The Sewerage (Scotland) Act 1968.	Section 18. Section 40. Section 47. Section 52.

Chapter	Short title	Extent of repeal
		In section 59(1), the definitions of "authorised officer", "local authority" and "trunk road".
1968 c. 49.	The Social Work (Scotland) Act 1968.	Section 2.
		In section 5A(3), paragraph (b).
		Section 34(3).
		In section 36, subsections (1), (4) and (6).
		In section 76(2), the words "to which the case stands referred".
		In Schedule 3, in paragraph 3, sub-paragraph (i) and, in sub-paragraph (ii), the words "in any other case".
1968 c. 73.	The Transport Act 1968.	In section 9A(9)(b), the words "regional or islands".
		In section 56(4)(b), the words "regional or islands".
1970 c. 6.	The Rural Water Supplies and Sewerage (Scotland) Act 1970.	The whole Act.
1971 c. 49.	The Rural Water Supplies and Sewerage Act 1971.	The whole Act.
1972 c. 52.	The Town and Country Planning (Scotland) Act 1972.	Section 4(5).
		Section 5(5) and (7).
		In section 8(1) the words from "and may provide for" to the end.
		In section 15(1), the words from "or of the provisions of Part IX" to "to be carried out or", the words ", after holding a local inquiry or other hearing," and the words "carrying out the survey or are not".
		In section 22, the word "(1)" and subsection (2).
		Section 25(4).
		Section 28(3).
		Section 32(7).
		Section 49G.
		Section 50(4).
		In section 52(4), the words "regional, general or district".
		In section 56F(1), the words from "and section 179" to "1973".
		In section 56K(10), the words "and section 179 of the Local Government (Scotland) Act 1973".
		Section 84A.
		In section 87A(1), the words "general and district".
		In section 102, in subsection (1) the words "to whom this subsection applies", and subsection (5).
		Section 169(8).
		Section 229A.
		In paragraphs (a) and (b) of section 231(2), the words "or as applied under section 181 of the Local Government (Scotland) Act 1973.
		Section 254(4).
		Section 265(9).
		In section 275(1), the definition of "district planning functions".

Chapter	Short title	Extent of repeal
		In Part II of Schedule 21, the words from "In section 25(3)(c)" to the end of the paragraph.
1973 c. 65.	The Local Government (Scotland) Act 1973.	Section 1.
		Section 2.
		Section 3.
		Section 3A.
		Section 4.
		Section 5.
		Section 11.
		In section 24(5)(f), the words "regional, islands or district".
		Section 31(4).
		In section 47, in subsection (4), the words ", other than a water development board within the meaning of the Water (Scotland) Act 1980"; and subsection (5).
		In section 51, in subsection (1), the words "within the meaning of this Part of this Act" and subsection (3).
		In section 56(6), paragraphs (a) and (c).
		In section 56(9), paragraph (c).
		In section 63, in subsection (2), the words "or a district council" and, in subsection (5)(a), the words "or district council".
		In section 64(5), paragraphs (c) and (f).
		Section 69(4).
		Section 74(3).
		In section 83, in subsection (2), the words, ", subject to subsection (3A) below,"; subsections (2A), (2B) and (3A); and in subsection (4B)(d), the word "Economic".
		In section 84, subsections (2) and (4).
		In section 87, in subsection (1), the words "any other local authority in the area", in subsection (2), the words from "and where" to the end, and subsection (3).
		Section 90A.
		In section 96(5), the words from, ", so however that" to "31st March 1976".
		In section 100(3), the words from "and to an additional fine" to the end.
		In section 106(1), paragraph (c) and the proviso.
		Section 109.
		In section 111(1)(e), the words "or to a water development board within the meaning of the Water (Scotland) Act 1980,".
		Section 116.
		In section 118, in subsection (1), the words "(a)" and paragraph (b) and, in subsection (5), the words "or any water development board within the meaning of the Water (Scotland) Act 1980".
		Section 127.
		Sections 131 and 132.
		In section 133, subsection (1).
		Section 134(1).

Chapter	Short title	Extent of repeal
		In section 135, in subsection (5), in paragraph (a), the words from "not" to the end, in subsection (6)(d), the word "regional" and subsection (8).
		Sections 137(1) and 138(1).
		Section 140.
		Sections 142 and 143.
		Section 146(7).
		Section 148(1).
		In section 153, in subsection (1), the words "regional or islands", in subsection (2), the words "regional or islands" and, wherever it occurs, "such" and, in subsection (3), the words "regional or islands" and, where it first occurs, "such".
		In section 154, in subsection (1), the words "Subject to subsection (3A) below" and "regional or islands", in subsection (2), the word "regional", in both places where it occurs, in subsection (3), the words "regional or islands" and "such" and subsections (3A) and (3B).
		Sections 154A and 154B.
		Sections 155(1), 156(1) and 157.
		Section 159.
		Section 161.
		In section 163, subsection (1), in subsection (2), the words "as aforesaid" and subsection (3).
		In section 166, subsection (1) and, in subsection (2), paragraphs (a), (e) and (f).
		Section 168.
		Section 170A(5)(a).
		In section 170B(2), the words "or water development boards" where they first occur.
		Section 171(1) and (2).
		Section 173.
		Section 174.
		Section 176.
		Section 177.
		Section 179.
		Section 181.
		Section 182.
		Section 183.
		Section 193(2).
		In section 200, subsections (1) to (6), (8), (9) and (11)(b).
		In section 202, in subsection (1), the words "Subject to subsection (1A) below"; and subsections (1A) and (13).
		In section 215, subsections (3) to (7).
		Sections 222 to 226.
		Section 230.
		In section 235(1), the definition of "area", "college council", "school council", "education committee" and "water authority".
		In section 236(2), the words "Subject to section 74(3) of this Act and to section 20 of the Water (Scotland) Act 1980,"; and paragraph (e).

Chapter	Short title	Extent of repeal
		Schedules 1 and 2.
		In Schedule 6, in paragraph 2, the letter "(a)".
		In Schedule 9, paragraphs 11 and 53.
		Schedule 10.
		Schedules 13 and 14.
		In Schedule 17, in paragraph 1(1)(a), the words "or to a constituent board" and "or to a constituent water authority"; and paragraph 2,
		Schedule 20.
		Schedule 22.
		In Part II of Schedule 27, paragraphs 159, 180 and 182.
1974 c. 40.	The Control of Pollution Act 1974.	Section 32(6).
		Section 106(3).
1975 c. 20.	The District Courts (Scotland) Act 1975.	Section 7(3).
		Section 18(3).
1975 c. 21.	The Criminal Procedure (Scotland) Act 1975.	In Schedule 7D, paragraph 59.
1975 c. 24.	The House of Commons Disqualification Act 1975.	In Schedule 1, in Part IV, the entry relating to Her Majesty's Lord-Lieutenant or Lieutenant for an islands area in Scotland and, in the entry relating to Her Majesty's Lord-Lieutenant or Lieutenant for the district of the city of Aberdeen, Dundee, Edinburgh, or Glasgow, the words "the district of".
1975 c. 30.	The Local Government (Scotland) Act 1975.	In section 1, in subsection (3)(b), the words, ", after consultation with the Advisory Council,", subsection (3)(c), and subsection (7).
		Section 4.
		Section 6(1A).
		In section 7(1A), the words "and, in case of the non-domestic water rate, the net annual value and the apportioned net annual value of part residential subjects".
		Section 7A(3).
		Section 13
		In section 16, the words ", water development boards".
		In section 23, subsections 1(c) and (d) and (2)(c).
		In section 29A, in subsection (3)(a), the words from "or under" to "committees".
		In Schedule 3, paragraphs 1 to 21; in paragraph 22, in sub-paragraph (1), head (c) and, in sub-paragraph (2), the words from "(a)" to "or", where it occurs immediately following sub-paragraph (b); paragraphs 24A and 26; in paragraph 28(1) the words "paragraph 1(4) above and" and ", a water development board"; and paragraphs 29 and 30.
		In Part II of Schedule 6, paragraphs 6, 13, 23, 34 and 53.
1975 c. 72.	The Children Act 1975.	In section 99(1), the word "or" immediately preceding paragraph (e).

Chapter	Short title	Extent of repeal
1976 c. 66.	The Licensing (Scotland) Act 1976.	In section 1, subsection (3), in subsection (4), the words "district or islands" and, in subsection (5), the words "or electoral division". In section 3(2), the words "of the district or islands area". In section 5(8), the words "district or islands". In section 7, in subsection (1), the words "district and islands" and subsection (2).
1976 c. 71.	The Supplementary Benefits Act 1976.	In Schedule 5, in paragraph 2(2), the words "and of", "regions, islands areas", and "and", where it thirdly occurs, and, in paragraph 4(2), the words ", a region, an islands area" and "or", where it secondly occurs.
1978 c. 29.	The National Health Service (Scotland) Act 1978.	In section 16A(1), in paragraph (b), the words "of a regional or islands council's", in paragraph (c), the words "of a district or islands council's" and in paragraph (d), the words "of a regional or islands council's".
1978 c. 50.	The Inner Urban Areas Act 1978.	In section 1(2), the words "or region". In section 2(1), the words "or region", in both places where they occur. In section 7(1)(a), the words "or region".
1980 c. 9.	The Reserve Forces Act 1980.	In section 131, in subsection (2), the words "the district of", subsections (3) and (4) and, in subsection (5), the words "the districts of".
1980 c. 44.	The Education (Scotland) Act 1980.	In section 4, the words "regional or island authority". In section 6, in subsection (2), the letter "(a)" and paragraph (b) and subsection (3). Section 78. In section 86, in paragraph (a), the words from "or" to "authority", where thirdly occurring and in paragraph (e), the words "or by the director of education".
1980 c. 45.	The Water (Scotland) Act 1980.	Sections 3 to 5. In section 10, in subsection (1), the words "or water development board"; in subsection (1A) the words "onto agricultural land or forestry land" and "or as the case may be water development board's"; and subsection (6). In section 11, in subsection (1), in paragraph (a), the words "or a water development board" and in paragraph (b) the words "or board"; in subsection (2), the words "or board"; in subsection (3), the words "or board" wherever they occur; in subsection (4), the words "or board" wherever they occur and "or "the transferee board" "; and in subsections (5) to (7), the words "or board" wherever they occur. In section 13, in subsection (1), the words "or water development board", in both places where they occur, "or board", in both places where they occur and "or ar-

Chapter	Short title	Extent of repeal
		ea"; in subsection (2), the words "or water development board", "or board" wherever they occur, "or area" and "or boards"; in subsection (3), the words "or water development board" and "or area, as the case may be"; and in subsection (6), the words "or water development board". Section 15. In section 16, in subsection (1), the words "or water development board"; and in each of subsections (2), (3) and (8), the words "or board" wherever they occur. In section 17, in subsection (1), the words "or water development board"; in subsection (2), the words "or water development board" and "or board"; in subsection (3), the words "or water development board" and, in both places where they occur, "or board"; and in subsection (4), the words "or water development board". In section 18, the words "or board" in both places where they occur. Section 20. In section 22, the words "or water development board". In section 23, in subsection (1), the words "or water development board"; in subsection (2), the words "or board"; and in subsection (3), the words "or water development board". In section 25(2), the words "or district", where they secondly occur. In section 27(1), the words "or district" where they secondly occur. In section 28, in subsection (1), the words "or a water development board"; and in subsection (2), the words "or water development board". In section 29, in subsection (2), the words "or water development board"; and in subsection (3), the words "or board". Section 30. In section 32, in subsection (1)(b), the words "subject to subsection (2),"; and subsection (2). In section 33, in subsection (1), the words "or water development board", "or their area, as the case may be" and "or board"; in subsection (3), the words "or water development board" in both places where they occur; and in each of subsections (4), (6)(b), (7), (8), (9) and (11), the words "or board" wherever they occur. Section 35(4). In section 38(1), the words "or water development board" and in each of paragraphs (a), (c) and (d), "or board". Sections 40 and 41. Sections 42 to 46. In section 47(3), the word "and" where it first occurs.

Chapter	Short title	Extent of repeal
		Sections 48 and 49.
		In section 54, subsection (2); and in subsection (3)(b), the words from "and in the case" to the end.
		In section 58, in subsection (6), the words "or the district of a district council"and "or by that district council"; and subsection (8).
		Sections 60 and 61.
		Section 63(6).
		Sections 64 to 67.
		In section 68, in subsection (1), the words "or water development board" and "or board"; in the proviso to that subsection the words "or board"; and subsection (3).
		In section 70, in subsection (1), the words "or water development board"; in subsection (2), the words "or board"; in subsection (4), the words "or water development board"; and in the proviso to subsection (4), the words ", or as the case may be the Board,".
		In section 71, in subsection (1), the words "or water development board"; in subsection (5), the words "or board" and, where they secondly occur "or boards"; and in subsection (6) the words "or boards".
		In section 72(2), the words "and water development board".
		In section 73, in subsection (1), the words "or water development board" and "or board"; and in each of subsections (2) and (3), the words "or board" wherever they occur.
		In section 76, in subsection (1), the words "or water development board" and "or board"; in subsection (2), the words "or water development board" and (wherever they occur, both in the subsection and in its proviso) "or board"; in subsection (3), the words "or water development board", "or their area" and "or board"; and in the proviso to subsection (3), the words "or board" and "or the area of that board".
		In section 76H(8), the words from "; and section 65" to the end.
		In section 76L(1), the definitions of "local authority" and "wholesome".
		Sections 80 to 92.
		In section 103, the words "or water development board" in both places where they occur.
		In section 107, in subsection (1)(b), the words "or a water development board" and "or board"; and in subsection (5), the words "or a water development board".
		In section 109, in subsection (1), the definitions of "the 1992 Act", "apportionment scheme", "apportionment note",

Chapter	Short title	Extent of repeal
		"Central Board", "constituent water authority", "contributing authority", "council water charge", "net annual value" and "part residential subjects" and in the definition of "owner", the words ", save in sections 64 to 67,"; and in subsection (3), the words "and water development board".
		In Schedule 1, in paragraph 3, the words "and the area of the water development board"; in paragraph 11, the words "where the river purification authority are not the same authority as the water authority"; in paragraph 12, the words "and the area of the board"; in paragraph 13, the words "not exceeding 10 pence"; in paragraph 14, the words "or board"; in paragraph 17, the words "or board" and "or boards"; in paragraph 19, the words "or water development board" in both places where they occur and "or area"; in paragraph 20, the words "or water development board"; in paragraph 23, the words "or board" and "or boards"; in each of paragraphs 24, 26 and 27, the words "or water development board"; in paragraph 30, the words "or water development board" and "or board"; and in paragraph 31, the words "or board" in both places where they occur.
		In Schedule 2, in each of paragraphs 4 and 6, the words "or water development board" wherever they occur.
		In Schedule 3, in paragraph 1, the words "and water development board", "within their limits of supply of area" and from "and outside" to "removing mains" where they secondly occur; in paragraph 2(2), the words "or board" in both places where they occur; in paragraph 4(1), the words, "within their limits of supply" and "within the said limits"; in paragraph 5, the words "within the limits of supply"; and paragraph 8.
		Schedules 7 and 8.
		In Schedule 10, Part II in so far as relating to the Local Government (Scotland) Act 1973.
1980 c. 65.	The Local Government, Planning and Land Act 1980.	In section 8(1)(b), the words "(ii) a water authority; or".
		In section 20, in subsection (1), in the definition of "development body", sub-paragraph (i) of paragraph (b); and subsection (2A)
		In section 87(2), the word "(a)" and paragraph (b).
		In section 148(2), the words "exercising district planning functions".
		In Schedule 32, in paragraph 33, in sub-paragraph (2), head (a), sub-paragraph (3) and, in sub-paragraph (4), the definitions of "private garage", "private storage premises" and "rates".

Chapter	Short title	Extent of repeal
1981 c. 23.	The Local Government (Miscellaneous Provisions) (Scotland) Act 1981.	Section 6. Section 11. Section 27. In Schedule 2, paragraphs 41 and 42. In Schedule 3, paragraphs 24, 26, 28, 36 and 38.
1982 c. 16.	The Civil Aviation Act 1982.	In section 30, in subsection (1), the words ", other than a district council in Scotland", and the words from "and a" to "above" and, in subsection (2), the words ", other than a district council in Scotland," and, in section 88(10), the words "other than a district council in Scotland,".
1982 c. 41.	The Stock Transfer Act 1982.	Section 5(2).
1982 c. 43.	The Local Government and Planning (Scotland) Act 1982.	Section 4. Sections 6 and 7. In section 14(2), the words "regional or islands councils as". In section 27(4), the words from "Without" to "Act". Sections 33 and 34. In section 50, paragraph (c). Section 56. In Schedule 1, Part I. In Schedule 3, paragraph 16.
1982 c. 45.	The Civic Government (Scotland) Act 1982.	Section 87(6). Section 89(10). In section 121, in subsection (6), the words from "and of" to "that proposal" and, in subsection (7), the words from "but the" to "his consent" and the word "nevertheless". In section 122(2)(b), sub-paragraph (iii) and the word "and" immediately preceding it.
1983 c. 2.	The Representation of the People Act 1983.	In section 18, in subsection (5), the words "any interested authority or", "(or in Scotland, the returning officer)", "or returning officer" in both places where they occur and in the definition of "interested authority", sub-paragraph (iii) and, in subsection (6), the words "or returning officer". Section 25(3). In Section 31(2), the words from "and for" to "polling district", where it secondly occurs. In section 204(1), in the definition of "electoral area", the words "division or".
1984. c. 27.	The Road Traffic Regulation Act 1984.	In section 26(4), paragraph (b) and the word "and" immediately preceding it. In section 26(5), paragraph (b) and the word "or" immediately preceding it and the words "or, in Scotland, the district council".
1984 c. 31.	The Rating and Valuation (Amendment) (Scotland) Act 1984.	Sections 6 and 7. In Schedule 2, paragraph 7.

Chapter	Short title	Extent of repeal
1984 c. 54.	The Roads (Scotland) Act 1984.	In section 4(1), the words "or, in relation to cleansing, with a district council," and the words "or council". In section 95(2), the words "or by the district council". In Schedule 9, paragraphs 27(3)(a) and 64(5)(c).
1985 c. 63.	The Water (Fluoridation) Act 1985.	Section 3. In section 4, in subsection (6), the words "or to terminate a preserved scheme"; and in subsection (7), the words "or terminate a preserved scheme".
1985 c. 69.	The Housing Associations Act 1985.	In section 59, in subsections (1) and (2), the words "or regional council", wherever they appear.
1986 c. 33.	The Disabled Persons (Services, Consultation and Representation) Act 1986.	In section 16, in the definition of "local authority", in paragraph (b), the words ", as read with section 2,".
1987 c. 26.	The Housing (Scotland) Act 1987.	In section 61(11)(a), the words "council or", where first occurring. In section 212(4)(e), the words "or water development board". Section 235. In Schedule 15 in paragraph 2(1), head (f). In Schedule 23, paragraph 23.
1988 c. 9.	The Local Government Act 1988.	In section 1, in subsection (1), the words "and (k) a water development board in Scotland,"; and in subsection (3), the words "and (b) "water development board" has the same meaning as in section 109(1) of the Water (Scotland) Act 1980". In Schedule 2, the words "A water development board in Scotland" and ", and (b) "water development board" has the same meaning as in section 109(1) of the Water (Scotland) Act 1980". In Schedule 6, in paragraph 11, the words from "and", where it first occurs, to the end.
1988 c. 41.	The Local Government Finance Act 1988.	Section 128. In Part II of Schedule 12, paragraph 6.
1988 c. 43.	The Housing (Scotland) Act 1988.	In section 55(1), the word "and" where it occurs immediately after the definition of "tenancy". In section 57(1), the word "neither" and the words from "nor" to "council", where thirdly occurring.
1988 c. 47.	The School Boards (Scotland) Act 1988.	In section 22, in subsection (2), the definitions of "islands councillor" and "regional councillor". In Schedule 2, in paragraph 5, the words "Schedule 10 to" and "and Schedule 10 to".
1989 c. 15.	The Water Act 1989.	In Schedule 25, paragraphs 22 and 60(2).
1989 c. 29.	The Electricity Act 1989.	In Schedule 5, in paragraph 8(a), the words "; and (iii) the water development board"; in paragraph 9, the words "and the water development board"; and in paragraph 14, the words ", or the area of any water development board,".

Chapter	Short title	Extent of repeal
1989 c. 42.	The Local Government and Housing Act 1989.	In section 2(6)(a), the words "or director of education" and the words from "or section" to "1980". In section 4(5), the words ", or Schedule 10 or 20 to,". In section 5(5), the words ", or Schedule 10 or 20 to,". In section 9(8)(b), the words ", or Schedule 10 or 20 to,". In section 14, subsections (2) and (3) and, in subsection (8), paragraphs (b), (c) and (d). In section 155(5), the letter "(d)". In Schedule 1, in paragraph 4, in sub-paragraph (1), in the definition of "ordinary committee", in paragraph (b), the words from "the authority's" to "or" and in sub-paragraph (2), the definition of "social work committee" and the word "and" immediately preceding it. In Schedule 6, paragraphs 7 and 16 to 19. In Schedule 11, paragraph 43.
1989 c. 45.	The Prisons (Scotland) Act 1989.	In section 14(2), the words "region or islands", where secondly occurring and, in section 16(2), the words "district or islands", in both places where they occur.
1990 c. 43.	The Evironmental Protection Act 1990.	In section 36, in subsection (6), the words "(other than an islands council)", paragraph (a)(iii) and in paragraph (b), the words "or the general planning authority" and, in subsection (10), the words "or general planning authority" and "or the general planning authority". In section 39(8), the words "(not being an islands council)" and in paragraph (b) the words "or the general planning authority". In section 50(5)(a), sub-paragraph (iv). In section 53, in subsection (4), the words "(other than an islands council)". In section 54(4)(c), the words "or the general planning authority". In section 88(9), in paragraph (a), the words ", a regional council" and, in paragraph (b), the words ", regional council". In section 90(3), the words ", regional council". In section 92(1), the words ", regional council". In section 93(1), the words ", regional council". In section 95(1), the words ", regional council".
1991 c. 22.	The New Roads and Street Works Act 1991.	In section 153, in subsection (1), the words "of district council" and "or council" and, in subsection (3), the words "or council".
1991 c. 28.	The National Heritage (Scotland) Act 1991.	In section 22(1), in the definition of "compensation water", the words "or water development board". In section 24, in each of subsections (1)(a) and (9)(a), the words "or board".

Chapter	Short title	Extent of repeal
		In Schedule 7, in paragraph 5, in sub-paragraph (1), the words "or a water development board" and (in head (a)) "or board", in sub-paragraph (2), the words "or water development board" and sub-paragraph (3), the words "or water development board" and "or board"; in paragraph 6, the words from ", including" to the end; and in paragraph 7, the words "or a water development board".
		In Schedule 8, in paragraph 1, in sub-paragraph (3), in the second column of the Table in paragraph (a) of the entry relating to "All Orders", the words "or water development board (not being the applicant)".
1991 c. 34.	The Planning and Compensation Act 1991.	In Schedule 13, paragraph 44.
1992 c. 4.	The Social Security Contributions and Benefits Act 1992.	In section 137(1), the definition of "levying authority".
1992 c. 5.	The Social Security Administration Act 1992.	In section 15A(3)(d), the words ", islands council".
		In section 191, the definition of "levying authority".
1992 c. 14.	The Local Government Finance Act 1992.	In section 74(1), the words "regional, islands or district".
		In section 84, in subsection (1), the words "regional and islands" and, in subsection (2)(a), the words "regional or islands".
		In section 85, subsection (2), in subsections (3) and (5) the words "regional or islands" and, in subsection (4), the words "(a)" and "and" and paragraph (b).
		In section 86, in subsection (4) the words "regional or islands" and, in subsections (10) and (1)), the words "regional or islands".
		In section 87(9)(a), the words "regional or islands".
		In section 90(3)(a), the words "regional, islands or district".
		In section 93(1)(a) the words "regional, islands or district" and "as appropriate".
		In section 94(9) the word "regional" and the words from "and may recover" to the end.
		Section 95.
		Section 97(2).
		In section 99, in subsection (1), the definition of "the 1968 Act", council water charge", "levying authority", "public sewage treatment works", "public sewer" and "water authority" and in the definition of "housing body", paragraph (a); and in subsection (2), paragraphs (a)(ii) and (iii), (c) and (d).
		Section 107(1).
		Section 112(2)(d).

Chapter	Short title	Extent of repeal
		In Schedule 2, in paragraph 8(5)(b), the words "or, where the authority is a regional council, each amount set under section 93 of this Act" and, in paragraph 12(2), sub-sub-paragraph (b) and, in sub-sub-paragraph (e) and (f), the word "levying", and paragraph 19(7)(b).
		In Schedule 7, paragraph 1(6).
		In Schedule 8, in paragraph 3(2) the words "or council water charge"; and in paragraph 4(2) the words "or council water charge".
		In Schedule 9, paragraphs 9(c) and 25(d).
		In Schedule 11, Parts I to III; and in Part IV, paragraphs 31 to 34, 36, 37 and 38(a) to (c) and (e).
		In Schedule 13, paragraphs 37, 44(a), (b) and (d), 75 and 93.
1993 c. 43.	The Railways Act 1993.	In section 151(1), in the definition of "local authority", the words "regional council, islands council".

INDEX

References are to sections and schedules

AMENDMENTS, 180(1), Sched. 13

AREA TOURIST BOARDS,
  assistance by old authorities, 176
  schemes establishing,
    amending schemes submitted by local authority, 174
    amendment and revocation by Secretary of State, 173
    purpose of, 172
  tourism-related activities: local authorities' powers, 176

AREAS, 1, Sched. 1; (2000) *see also* COUNCILS; WATER AND SEWERAGE REORGANISATION

ASSETS: RESTRICTION ON DISPOSAL BY EXISTING AUTHORITIES, 55

ASSISTANCE TO NEW AUTHORITIES, 57

BIRTHS, DEATHS AND MARRIAGES: REGISTRATION, 51

BYELAWS, 142

CENTRAL SCOTLAND WATER DEVELOPMENT BOARD, 90

CHILDREN, *see* SCOTTISH CHILDREN'S REPORTER ADMINISTRATION; SOCIAL WORK

COMMENCEMENT, 184(2)–(3)

COMMUNITY COUNCILS, 22

CONSEQUENTIAL AND SUPPLEMENTARY PROVISIONS, 181

CONTRACTS,
  for carrying out functions of local authorities, 58
  restriction on existing authorities entering, 55

COUNCILS,
  constitution, 2
  convenor and deputy convenor, 4
  elections and term of office of councillors, 5–6
  establishment of new local authorities, 7, Sched. 2
  Orkney, Shetland and Western Isles, 3
  see also AREAS; LOCAL AUTHORITIES

COURTS AND ADMINISTRATION OF JUSTICE,
  applications in case of difficulty, 60
  district courts, 47–8
  justices of the peace, 49
  stipendiary magistrates, 50

DECENTRALISATION SCHEMES, 23

DEER FORESTS, 151

DIRECT LABOUR ORGANISATIONS/DIRECT SERVICES ORGANISATION ACCOUNTS, 168

DISTRICT COURTS,
  sittings: expense and inconvenience of, 48
  transitional provisions, 47

EAST OF SCOTLAND WATER AUTHORITY, 62; *see also* WATER AND SEWERAGE REORGANISATION

ECONOMIC DEVELOPMENT, PROMOTION OF, 171

EDUCATION,
  co-operation between education authorities, 32
  committee membership, 31
  denominational schools, 144
  educational endowments, 17
  school transport, 145
  self-governing schools, 143

ENVIRONMENTAL PROTECTION, 73

ETHNIC MINORITIES: GRANTS, 167

EXTENT, 184(4)

FINANCE,
  financial provisions relating to this Act, 178
  local authorities,
    borrowing and lending powers, 165
    Direct Labour Organisations/Direct Services Organisation Accounts, 168
    financing of new authorities prior to 1st April 1996, 25
    grants,
      ethnic minorities, for, 166
      special, 167
    limits on spending, 164
    support services: costs, 169
  transitional provisions, 24
  valuation and rating,
    appeal panels and committees, 29
    areas and authorities, 27
    assessors, appointment of, 27
    enterprise zones, 159
    hybrid orders, 157
    lands and heritages,
      combination and division of, 161
      definition of term, 152
      partly unoccupied for a short time, 155
      unoccupied, 154
    prescribed amount of non-domestic rate, 1543
    rate rebates: grants, 158
    rating authorities, 30
    remission of rates on account of hardship, 156
    rolls, 28
    Scottish Valuation Advisory Council: abolition, 162

FINANCE—*cont.*
  valuation and rating—*cont.*
    shootings, deer forests, fishings and fish counters: exclusion, 151
    valuation by formula, 160
    valuation lists, 26
    Water Authorities, *see* WATER AND SEWERAGE REORGANISATION
FIRE SERVICES, 36
FISHING AND FISH COUNTERS, 151

INFORMATION,
  new authorities, provision to, 56
  see also WATER AND SEWERAGE REORGANISATION
INTERPRETATION, 183

JOINT COMMITTEES AND JOINT BOARDS, 20–21
JUSTICES OF THE PEACE, 49

LANDS AND HERITAGES, *see* FINANCE, valuation and rating,
LICENSING BOARDS, 46
LOCAL ACTS AND INSTRUMENTS, 59
LOCAL AUTHORITIES,
  assets: restriction on disposal by existing authorities, 55
  community councils, 22
  contracts, restriction on entering by existing authorities, 55
  decentralisation schemes, 23
  difficulty in carrying out this Act: applications to Sheriff or court, 60
  Direct Labour Organisations/Direct Services Organisation Accounts, 168
  duties of existing authorities,
    assistance to new authorities, 57
    information for new authorities, 56
  economic development: function to promote, 171
  employees, *see* STAFF OF LOCAL AUTHORITIES
  finance, *see* FINANCE
  functions,
    education, *see* EDUCATION
    fire services, 36
    police, *see* POLICE
    public transport, 40–41
    rivers, 3737
    roads, *see* ROADS
    social work, *see* SOCIAL WORK
    structure plans, 33, Sched. 4
    supplying authority contracted to carry out, 58
    traffic, *see* TRAFFIC
  interpretation, 61
  joint committees and joint boards, 20–21
  licensing boards, 46
  Local Acts and instruments, 59
  new, establishment of, 7, Sched. 2
  property, *see* PROPERTY OF LOCAL AUTHORITIES

LOCAL AUTHORITIES—*cont.*
  records, *see* RECORDS
  resources, effective use of, 170
  support services: costs, 169
  tourism, *see* AREA TOURIST BOARDS
  Water Authorities, supply of goods to, 122
  water charges,
    collection of, 79
    member's arrears, 82
    see also WATER AND SEWERAGE REORGANISATION
  see also AREAS; COUNCILS
LOCAL GOVERNMENT AREAS, 1, Sched. 1, *see also* COUNCILS

MONOPOLIES AND MERGERS COMMISSION, 72

NORTH OF SCOTLAND WATER AUTHORITY, 62; *see also* WATER AND SEWERAGE REORGANISATION

ORDERS UNDER THIS ACT, 181
ORKNEY ISLANDS COUNCIL, 3

PARLIAMENTARY DISQUALIFICATION, 177
PLANNING: STRUCTURE PLANS, 33, Sched. 4
POLICE,
  amalgamation schemes, 35
  reorganisation of police areas, 34
POLLING DISTRICTS, 142
PRINCIPAL REPORTER, *see* SCOTTISH CHILDREN'S REPORTER ADMINISTRATION
PROPERTY COMMISSION, 19
PROPERTY OF LOCAL AUTHORITIES,
  educational endowments, 17
  property commission, 19
  residuary bodies, 18, Sched. 3
  transfer of, 15
  trust property, 16
PUBLIC TRANSPORT,
  Strathclyde Passenger Transport Authority, 40–41, Sched. 5

RATING, *see* FINANCE
RECORDS,
  preservation and management, 53
  use, acquisition and disposal of, 54
  Water Authorities, 119
REGISTRATION OF BIRTHS, DEATHS AND MARRIAGES, 51
REPEALS, 180(2), Sched. 14
RESIDUARY BODIES, 18, Sched. 3
RIVER PURIFICATION BOARDS, 37
ROADS,
  boundary bridges, roads authority for, 39
  definition of "road," 146
  road works register, 149
  special road orders, 147
  toll orders, 148
  traffic signs, 150; *see also* TRAFFIC
  transitory provisions, 38

Savings, 179
Schools, *see* Education
Scottish Children's Reporter
  Administration,
  accounts, 136
  establishment of, 128(1)
  finances: government grants, 135
  functions of,
    ancillary powers, 133
    children's hearings, accommodation for,
      132
    directions by Secretary of State, 134
  officers,
    appointment, 128(5)
    dismissal, appeal against, 129
    management of, 128(7)
  Principal Reporter,
    appointment, 127(2), 128(4)
    dismissal, appeal against, 129
    establishment of office, 127(1)
    functions,
      annual report, 130
      chief officer, 128(2)
      delegation of, 131
      performance of, 128(8)
  property, rights, liabilities and obligations,
    138
  purpose of, 128(3)
  reports, 136
  staff: transfers and continuity of employ-
    ment, 137
  status, constitution and proceedings,
    128(6), Sched. 12
  see also Social Work
Sheriff, Applications to, 60
Shetland Islands Council, 3
Shootings, 151
Short Title, 184(1)
Social Work,
  chief social work officer, 45
  report by local authority preliminary to
    children's hearing, 139
  see also Scottish Children's Reporter
    Administration
Staff of Local Authorities,
  compensation for loss of office or dimin-
    ution of emoluments, 13
  continuity of employment, 10
  new authorities, employment by, 14
  orders and schemes as to, 9
  remuneration, 11
  staff commission, 12
  transfer of employees: orders and schemes
    as to, 8–9
Stipendiary Magistrates, 50
Strathclyde Passenger Transport
  Authority,
  establishment of, 40, Sched. 5
  grants and payments, 41
  guarantees by, 163
Structure plans, 33, Sched. 4

Tourism, *see* Area Tourist Boards

Traffic,
  guidance as to exercise of powers, 43
  order-making powers, restrictions on, 44
  signs, 150
  traffic control schemes, management of, 42
  see also Roads
Transitional Provisions, 182
Transport, *see* Strathclyde Passenger
  Transport Authority
Trust Property, 16
Tweed Fisheries Commission, 52, Sched. 6

Valuation and Rating, *see* Finance
Voluntary Organisations: Assistance, 140

Water and Sewerage Reorganisation,
  Central Scotland Water Development
    Board: dissolution, 90
  charges,
    arrears of member of local authority:
      restriction on voting, 82
    collection by local authority, 79, Sched.
      10
    duty to maintain supply when unpaid, 80
    maximum, 75
    occupiers' liability for, 78
    reduced, 81
    schemes, 76–7
    services provided, for, 74
  Customers Council,
    annual reports, 70
    constitution and proceedings, 67(2),
      Sched. 9
    establishment, 67(1)
    functions, 68
    funding of, 71
    information,
      power to acquire, 69
      provision of, 70
  environmental protection duties, 73
  interpretation, 125
  Monopolies and Mergers Commission, ref-
    erences to, 72
  orders, 126
  sewerage in rural localities: cancellation of
    contribution towards expenses, 124
  Sewerage (Scotland) Act 1968:
    amendments,
      disclosure of information: disapplication
        of restrictions, 104
      private sewers: authorisation, 101
      septic tanks: emptying, 102
      trade effluents register, 103
  Water Authorities,
    advice and assistance, provision of,
      89(2)(b)
    areas,
      alteration, 63
      described by reference to administrat-
        ive areas, 62(3), Sched. 8
      maps of, 64
    codes of practice, 66

WATER AND SEWERAGE REORGANISATION—
cont.
  Water Authorities—cont.
    collaboration: duties of new authorities,
      120
    company formation, 89(2)(a)
    constitution, 62(2), Sched. 7
    establishment, 62
    finances,
      accounts, 87
        audit of, 88
      borrowing powers, 84
      directions as to payment and invest-
        ment, 86
      duties and powers, 83
      grants, 84(1)
      guarantees, 85
    information,
      for new authorities, 123
      for Secretary of State, 118
    land transactions,
      acquisition by agreement, 98
      compulsory acquisition, 99
      disposals, 100
    private legislation, 121
    records held by new authorities, 119
    research by, 89(1)
    Secretary of State,
      directions to new authorities,
        general, 116
        national security interests, 117
      duties as to, 65

WATER AND SEWERAGE REORGANISATION—
cont.
  Water Authorities—cont.
    subsidiary powers, 89
    supply of goods by local authorities, 122
    transfer of property etc: schemes,
      generally, 92
      information as to, 94
      preparations for, 93
      supplementary provisions, 95, Sched.
        11
      vesting, 91
    transfer of staff, 97
  Water (Scotland) Act 1980: further
    amendments,
    mains,
      map to be kept, 111
      objection to proposed laying, 109
    Secretary of State,
      acting in default, 113
      references to, 105
    supply,
      metered, 112
      from premises outwith limits of supply,
        105
      quality: information on, 114
      for use outwith Scotland, 107–8
      vesting of pipes, 110
WEST OF SCOTLAND WATER AUTHORITY, 62; see
  also WATER AND SEWERAGE
  REORGANISATION
WESTERN ISLES COUNCIL, 3

DEREGULATION AND CONTRACTING OUT ACT 1994*

(1994 c. 40)

ARRANGEMENT OF SECTIONS

PART I

DEREGULATION

CHAPTER I

GENERAL

Removal or reduction of burdens

SECT.
1. Power to remove or reduce certain statutory burdens on businesses, individuals etc.
2. Limitations on the power under section 1.
3. Preliminary consultation.
4. Parliamentary consideration of proposals.

Enforcement procedures and appeals

5. Powers to improve enforcement procedures.
6. Model provisions with respect to appeals.

CHAPTER II

MISCELLANEOUS DEREGULATORY PROVISIONS

7. Undertakings as alternative to monopoly reference by Director General of Fair Trading.
8. Newspaper mergers: meaning of "newspaper proprietor" etc.
9. Undertakings as alternative to merger reference: non-divestment matters.
10. Restrictive trade practices: non-notifiable agreements.
11. Restrictive trade practices: registration of commercially sensitive information.
12. Anti-competitive practices: competition references.
13. Striking off of non-trading private companies.
14. Repeal of section 43 of the Weights and Measures Act 1985.
15. Building societies: issue of deferred shares at a premium.
16. Building societies: class 1 and 2 advances—third party mortgages.
17. Building societies: direct participation in syndicated lending.
18. Licensed premises at international ports: permitted hours.
19. Bars in licensed premises in England and Wales: children's certificates.
20. Betting on Sundays.
21. Sporting events and activities on Sundays.
22. Sunday opening of certain licensed premises in Scotland.
23. Repeal of Part I of the Shops Act 1950.
24. Repeal of remainder of the Shops Act 1950.
25. Controls on fund-raising for charitable institutions: exclusion of connected companies.
26. Offences under section 63 of the Charities Act 1992: creation of statutory defence.
27. Applications for permits to conduct public charitable collections: time-limits.
28. Annual audit or examination of charity accounts.
29. Annual reports of charities.
30. Annual returns by charities.
31. Slaughterhouses and knackers' yards: uniting of enforcement functions.
32. Building regulations: power to repeal or modify provisions of local Acts.
33. Amendment of duty of care etc. as respects waste.
34. Controls on London lorries: replacement of discretionary exceptions.
35. Employment agencies etc.: replacement of licensing.
36. Unfair dismissal: selection for redundancy.
37. Power to repeal certain health and safety provisions.
38. Inspection of independent schools.
39. Chapter II: consequential amendments.
40. Extent of Chapter II.

---

* Annotations by Professor Alan Page, Professor of Public Law, University of Dundee.

CHAPTER III

GOODS VEHICLE OPERATOR LICENSING

41. The 1968 Act.
42. Use of vehicles under licences.
43. Objections to grant or variation of licences.
44. Determination of applications for licences.
45. Conditions for securing road safety.
46. Duration of licences and grant of interim licences.
47. Variation of licences.
48. Revocation, suspension and curtailment of licences.
49. Publication of applications.
50. Review and transfer of operating centres.
51. Assessors.
52. Review of decisions.
53. Appeals.
54. Partnerships.
55. Operators' licences not to be transferable etc.
56. Fees.
57. Chapter III: minor and consequential amendments.

CHAPTER IV

PUBLIC SERVICE VEHICLE OPERATOR LICENSING ETC.

58. The 1981 Act.
59. Undertakings given on applications.
60. Objections to applications for licences.
61. Duration of licences.
62. Suspension of licences.
63. Operators' discs.
64. Repeal of section 27 of the 1981 Act.
65. Review of decisions and correction of errors.
66. Fees.
67. Disqualification of PSV operators.
68. Chapter IV: minor and consequential amendments.

PART II

CONTRACTING OUT

Contracting out of functions

69. Functions of Ministers and office-holders.
70. Functions of local authorities.
71. Functions excluded from sections 69 and 70.
72. Effect of contracting out.
73. Termination of contracting out.

Provisions for facilitating contracting out

74. Powers of certain office-holders.
75. Restrictions on disclosure of information.
76. Amendments of enactments etc.

Supplemental

77. Provisions with respect to orders.
78. Extent of Part II.
79. Interpretation of Part II.

PART III

SUPPLEMENTARY

80. Financial provisions.
81. Repeals.
82. Short title, commencement and extent.

SCHEDULES:
    Schedule 1—Powers to improve enforcement procedures.
    Schedule 2—Section 7: sectoral regulators.
    Schedule 3—Non-notifiable agreements: modifications of the Restrictive Trade Practices Act 1976.
    Schedule 4—Section 12: sectoral regulators and transition.
    Schedule 5—Striking off of non-trading private companies: Great Britain.
    Schedule 6—Striking off of non-trading private companies: Northern Ireland.
    Schedule 7—Children's certificates: supplementary provisions.
    Schedule 8—Schedule to be inserted in the Betting, Gaming and Lotteries Act 1963 after Schedule 5.
    Schedule 9—Slaughterhouses and knackers' yards: uniting of enforcement functions.
    Schedule 10—Employment agencies etc.: replacement of licensing.
        Part I—General.
        Part II—Seamen.
    Schedule 11—Miscellaneous deregulatory provisions: consequential amendments.
    Schedule 12—Schedule to be inserted in the Transport Act 1968 after Schedule 8.
    Schedule 13—Goods vehicle operator licensing: minor and consequential amendments.
        Part I—Amendment of the Transport Act 1968.
        Part II—Amendment of other enactments.
    Schedule 14—PSV operator licensing etc.: minor and consequential amendments.
    Schedule 15—Restrictions on disclosure of information.
    Schedule 16—Amendments etc. for facilitating contracting out.
    Schedule 17—Repeals.

An Act to amend, and make provision for the amendment of, statutory provisions and rules of law in order to remove or reduce certain burdens affecting persons in the carrying on of trades, businesses or professions or otherwise, and for other deregulatory purposes; to make further provision in connection with the licensing of operators of goods vehicles; to make provision for and in connection with the contracting out of certain functions vested in Ministers of the Crown, local authorities, certain governmental bodies and the holders of certain offices; and for purposes connected therewith.   [3rd November 1994]

PARLIAMENTARY DEBATES
    Hansard, H.C. Vol. 236, col. 147; Vol. 237, col. 245; Vol. 243, col. 161; Vol. 244, col. 25; Vol. 248, cols. 143, 1496; H.L. Vol. 555, cols. 952, 1440; Vol. 556, cols. 418, 475, 531, 560, 598, 778, 1006, 1072, 1279, 1303, 1352; Vol. 557, cols. 252, 318, 360, 594, 820, 1007; Vol. 558, cols. 126, 540, 842.
    The Bill was discussed in Standing Committee F between February 15 and April 28, 1994.

INTRODUCTION AND GENERAL NOTE
    The Deregulation and Contracting Out Act 1994 arises out of the Government's Deregulation and Competing for Quality initiatives. The aim of the Deregulation initiative is to reduce significantly the level of government regulation of business. The aim of the Competing for Quality Initiative is to "find new ways of mobilising the private sector to meet needs which traditionally have been met only by the public sector". (*The Citizen's Charter First Report* Cm. 2101 (1992), p. 58). Contracting out is one of the principal mechanisms by which the Government has sought to enlist the assistance of the private sector in the provision of public services.

Part I: Deregulation
Chapter I of Pt. I of the Act confers two sets of extra-ordinary powers on Ministers for the purpose of reducing the burdens on business. The first is a power to amend or repeal by ministerial order primary legislation that imposes an unnecessary burden on business, a power which the House of Lords Delegated Powers Scrutiny Committee described as "unprecedented in time of peace" (1993/94; H.L. 60, para. 1). The second is a power to "improve" the fairness, transparency and consistency of enforcement procedures. The Chapter also imposes a duty on the Government to draw up model appeal provisions with a view to their incorporation in legislation imposing burdens on business.

Deregulation orders. The repeal or simplification of regulation which is perceived to be unnecessarily burdensome has been an aim of the Government's Deregulation initiative since its launch in 1985 (*Burdens on Business* (1985), para. 7.2.2; *Lifting the Burden* Cmnd. 9571 (1985), para. 1.2). Under a "concordat" drawn up by the Enterprise and Deregulation Unit (now the Deregulation Unit) on how deregulation should be handled centrally, regulatory departments were asked to review the impact on business of the regulations for which they were responsible (*Building Businesses ... Not Barriers* Cmnd. 9794 (1986), Annex 3, para. 9). A White Paper, *Releasing Enterprise*, Cm. 512 (1988) published three years later, announced that this aspect of the initiative would benefit from "a more systematic approach". Each department would now nominate one or two areas of its responsibilities, of significance for business, to be examined as part of a rolling annual programme of work (para. 1.4). Even so, an efficiency scrutiny reported later, "radical examination of existing legislation was rare, in part because resources had not been allocated for such activity and also because any change would often require primary legislation which was not expected to be available". (*Review of the Implementation and Enforcement of E.C. Law in the U.K.* (July 1993), para. 5.2.)

When the Initiative was relaunched in October 1992, departments were required "to identify and set up programmes to review comprehensively all existing legislation". At the same time, seven business task forces, later increased to eight, were set up to advise Ministers, *inter alia*, "on priorities for the repeal or simplification of existing regulations and enforcement methods so as to minimise the costs on business ... bearing in mind the considerations of public health, safety and security which underlie the regulatory system". (The task forces were on: retail, tourism and other services; food, drink and agriculture; construction; chemicals and pharmaceutical; engineering; financial services; transport and communications; and charities and voluntary organisations. The Health and Safety Commission established its own task forces to review health and safety legislation.) Explaining the decision to set up the task forces, the President of the Board of Trade said:

> "Our deregulation initiative put in place a system to scrutinise the regulations that affect the wealth creating process ... We were not prepared, in the exercise, to rely on the advice of the people who had drafted the regulations in the first place. Therefore, we invited Lord Sainsbury to chair eight task forces, which were drawn largely from the public sector, as they began to work their way through the thousands of regulations that actually exist". (*Hansard*, H.C. Vol. 237, col. 150).

The task forces made more than 600 proposals for reducing the burden of regulation (*Deregulation. Task Forces Proposals for Reform* (January 1994)). The immediate difficulty the Government faced in giving effect to those proposals it accepted was the need in many cases for primary legislation. "If we needed to find time for primary legislation for every ... change [that could usefully reduce burdens and would not remove any necessary protection] change would take years." (*Hansard*, H.C. Vol. 237, col. 151). The solution it has adopted is to create the power under s.1 of the Act to amend or repeal by order primary legislation passed before the end of the 1993–1994 session which imposes a burden on business, *i.e.* a burden affecting any person in the carrying on of any trade, business or profession or otherwise, provided that necessary protection is not removed.

As well as representing an advance for the Government in its efforts to promote deregulation at minimum cost to itself in terms of parliamentary time, the deregulation order-making power also puts the review of existing regulation on a new footing by removing one of the "excuses" for not undertaking a radical examination of existing requirements, namely that there was little point to such an exercise since change would require primary legislation which was not expected to be available (*Review of the Implementation and Enforcement*, paras. 5.2 and 5.5). The Government's assumption of this power was widely opposed. The root of the opposition was the fact that the necessity or otherwise of protection – the test employed by the Act – is a matter that can only be determined by making political and hence conflict-ridden judgments:

> "... [V]irtually all hon. Members recognised that some regulation is necessary for good business standards, good consumer protection, good health and safety at work and good employee relations. Good regulation is an essential part of business. The difference is where we draw the line". (*Hansard*, H.C. Vol. 237, cols. 226–227).

By taking the power to decide where the line should be drawn by ministerial order, the Government, in the eyes of its critics, was thus arrogating to itself the power to decide matters which ought to be subject to the safeguards against the abuse of power inherent in the legislative process rather than to the (by common consent) unsatisfactory procedures for the scrutiny of subordinate legislation:

> "The first four clauses will substitute well-tried safeguards, which only primary legislation can provide with instruments of secondary legislation, with all its limitations and the lack of

debate and deliberation in Committee … Ministers may claim that their intention is to cut through red tape and to speed up the removal of troublesome legislation … but they are removing the constitutional safeguards that act as a check on headstrong Ministers and that should prevent hasty, ill-judged and ill-considered reforms. These safeguards are being replaced with something much less secure and of a weaker constitutional pedigree". (Standing Committee F, col. 36, February 17, 1994).

The Government sought to counter this criticism by agreeing to the provision of an additional opportunity for the parliamentary scrutiny of deregulation proposals. The starting point for this scrutiny will be the laying before each House of a draft of the order and an explanatory document giving details of the proposal and the consultation undertaken (see s.3(3)). The proposal will then be examined by a specially constituted Deregulation Committee in the House of Commons and by the Delegated Powers Scrutiny Committee in the House of Lords. (The Committees will assume the functions of the Joint Committee on Statutory Instruments in relation to draft orders.) It is only through the mechanism of select committee scrutiny, the House of Commons Procedure Committee suggested, that the House and the general public can be certain that primary legislation is not being casually set aside by the Government". (Fourth Report from the select committee on Procedure *Parliamentary Scrutiny of Deregulation Orders*, *Hansard*, H.C. Vol. 238, col. 33).

Special parliamentary scrutiny will be preceded by consultation with affected interests and followed, where the Government decides to proceed, by the laying of a draft of the order before each House for approval together with a statement of any changes made to the proposal as a result of representations made, or resolutions or reports of either House or their Committees during the scrutiny period. The Commons Select Committee on Procedure proposed that the Deregulation Committee should be able to prevent the procedure being used for unsuitable proposals, but the Government resisted this in favour of an alternative proposal whereby a motion to approve a draft order will not be moved unless the House has disagreed with an adverse report in a three hour debate on an amendable motion. A similar procedure will apply in the House of Lords.

Enforcement. The "better" enforcement of regulation in the sense of "ensuring local authorities and national inspectorates apply regulations consistently and provide simple and accessible guidance to make it easier for business to comply" has also been an aim of the Deregulation Initiative from the outset (*Burdens on Business*, paras. 5.1.1–5.2.1, 5.3.1–5.3.2; *Lifting the Burden*, paras. 7.14–7.15). In contrast to the deregulation order-making power, however, the powers to improve the fairness, transparency and consistency of enforcement procedures did not feature in the original version of the Bill but were inserted in response to the criticism that the Bill did not address the over-zealous or unreasonable application of regulatory requirements. (Standing Committee F, cols. 1197–1229; *Hansard*, H.C. Vol. 244, cols. 49–72; *Hansard*, H.L. Vol. 556, cols. 531–545; *Hansard*, H.L. Vol. 557, cols. 832–849, April 28, 1994.)

Five powers are conferred by Sched. 1 to the Act for the purpose of improving the fairness, transparency and consistency of enforcement procedures:

(i) A power to require that when an enforcement officer advises a business to take some remedial action, the business should be entitled on request to a written statement making it clear why that action is required. Unless immediate action is thought necessary, the intention is that the officer will not be able to take enforcement action until the business has had an opportunity to consider the statement. Explaining the assumption of this power, Earl Ferrers said:

"Businesses often value informal advice from enforcement officers, and we very much want to see that continue. But the distinction between advice on best practice and a legal requirement as to what should be done, with which a business has to comply, is an important one. Blurring this distinction can lead to unnecessary costs and indecision for business. An enforcement officer needs to be clear whether a particular requirement is really necessary in order to secure compliance with the legislation and to make clear in advance to the business when he is advising that action is legally required" (*Hansard*, H.L. Vol. 557, col. 833).

(ii) A power to require an enforcement officer, when he takes immediate enforcement action against a business, to provide as soon as practicable a statement explaining why immediate action was necessary. "… [W]e believe that businesses should be entitled to an explanation as to why the enforcement officer considers that immediate action is required in the particular case" (*ibid.*).

(iii) A power to require an enforcement officer minded to take enforcement action against a business so to notify the business, to afford it an opportunity to make representations, and to consider those representations. "It is helpful for business to be able to challenge an enforcement decision which it believes to be unreasonable before any formal action is taken against the business. Defending a prosecution, for example, is risky for the business both in financial terms and in relation to its reputation. The opportunity for an informal review could prevent matters getting to that stage". (*Ibid.*, cols. 833–834).

(iv) A power to require that, when formal action is taken, the business should be told what rights it has to appeal, including the grounds on which an appeal can be made, to whom an appeal should be addressed, the time within which an appeal must be made and whether the enforcement decision can be stayed (in Scotland, suspended) during the appeal. "Most legislation provides for some right of appeal against formal enforcement action – with a stay of execution except in cases of danger. But not all enforcement officers make a point of telling the business clearly what its rights are when the enforcement action is taken". (*Ibid.*, col. 834).

(v) A power to extend the above requirements to third parties who have a direct economic interest in enforcement proceedings. "… [A]n enforcement decision can sometimes have a serious impact on a particular third party who may not even be informed of the decision. For example, action may be taken against a retailer in respect of the products of a particular manufacturer. The retailer will clearly be told, but the manufacturer, who may be significantly affected, may not". (*Ibid.*, col. 834).

These powers fall short of the speedy and effective means of challenging "unreasonable" enforcement action sought by the Bill's critics. Here, all the Government has committed itself to doing is drawing up a model appeals procedure with a view to its incorporation, with or without modifications, in future legislation imposing burdens on business (see s.6).

Chapter II of Pt. I is a package of miscellaneous deregulatory proposals. (Clause 21 of the original Bill which sought to remove the power of local authorities who own market rights to object to a proposal to establish another market within a six and two thirds mile radius of their own was withdrawn on Commons report.) Chapters III and IV amend, and in some cases clarify, the law relating to goods and public service vehicle operator licensing. They principally provide for a system of continuous licensing in place of the present system under which licences must be renewed every five years.

Part II: Contracting Out

Part II of the Act provides for the removal of certain obstacles which prevent the use of private contractors in carrying out certain functions of Ministers, office holders and local authorities. In the Citizen's Charter the Government announced its intention of removing the "remaining obstacles" to the successful contracting out of central government functions (Cm. 1599 (1991), p. 33). In its second report on the Charter it revealed that some activities had had to be withdrawn from the current Competing for Quality programme because of statutory obstacles to contracting them out (Cm. 2540 (1994), p. 95).

The principal obstacle to the contracting out of functions addressed by ss.69 and 70 is the general presumption of law against the delegation of functions conferred by legislation on a minister, office holder or local authority, so that another person may only carry out those functions if specifically authorised to do so. The law already makes exceptions to this presumption for civil servants (the so-called *Carltona* doctrine), local government officers (Local Government Act 1972 (c. 70), s.101; Local Government (Scotland) Act 1973 (c. 65), s.56) and the staff of many office holders. The effect of orders made under these sections will be to extend this principle so that private sector contractors can also carry out functions on behalf of Ministers, office-holders or local authorities.

<small>COMMENCEMENT</small>
See s.82 and S.I. 1994 Nos. 3037 (C. 70) and 3188 (C. 76).

PART I

DEREGULATION

CHAPTER I

GENERAL

Removal or reduction of burdens

Power to remove or reduce certain statutory burdens on businesses, individuals etc.

1.—(1) If, with respect to any provision made by an enactment, a Minister of the Crown is of the opinion—

(a) that the effect of the provision is such as to impose, or authorise or require the imposition of, a burden affecting any person in the carrying on of any trade, business or profession or otherwise, and

(b) that, by amending or repealing the enactment concerned and, where appropriate, by making such other provision as is referred to in subsection (4)(a) below, it would be possible, without removing any necessary protection, to remove or reduce the burden or, as the case may be, the authorisation or requirement by virtue of which the burden may be imposed,

he may, subject to the following provisions of this section and sections 2 to 4 below, by order amend or repeal that enactment.

(2) The reference in subsection (1)(b) above to reducing the authorisation or requirement by virtue of which a burden may be imposed includes a reference to shortening any period of time within which the burden may be so imposed.

(3) In this section and sections 2 to 4 below, in relation to an order under this section,—

(a) "the existing provision" means the provision by which the burden concerned is imposed or, as the case may be, is authorised or required to be imposed; and

(b) "the relevant enactment" means the enactment containing the existing provision.

(4) An order under this section shall be made by statutory instrument and may do all or any of the following—

(a) make provision (whether by amending any enactment or otherwise) creating a burden which relates to the subject matter of, but is less onerous than that imposed by, the existing provision;

(b) make such modifications of enactments as, in the opinion of the Minister concerned, are consequential upon, or incidental to, the amendment or repeal of the relevant enactment;

(c) contain such transitional provisions and savings as appear to the Minister to be appropriate;

(d) make different provision for different cases or different areas;

but no order shall be made under this section unless a draft of the order has been laid before and approved by a resolution of each House of Parliament.

(5) In this section and sections 2 to 4 below—

(a) "Minister of the Crown" has the same meaning as in the Ministers of the Crown Act 1975 and "Minister" shall be construed accordingly;

(b) "burden" includes a restriction, requirement or condition (including one requiring the payment of fees), together with—

(i) any sanction (whether criminal or otherwise) for failure to observe the restriction or to comply with the requirement or condition; and

(ii) any procedural provisions (including provisions for appeal) relevant to that sanction; and

(c) "enactment", subject to subsection (6) below, means an enactment contained in this Act or in any other Act passed before or in the same Session as this Act, or any provision of an order under this section.

(6) In paragraph (c) of subsection (5) above—

(a) "Act" does not include anything contained in Northern Ireland legislation, within the meaning of section 24 of the Interpretation Act 1978; and

(b) the reference to an enactment is a reference to an enactment as for the time being amended, extended or applied by or under any Act mentioned in that paragraph.

(7) Where a restriction, requirement or condition is subject to a criminal sanction (as mentioned in subsection (5)(b)(i) above), nothing in this section

shall authorise the making of an amendment which would have the effect of leaving the restriction, requirement or condition in place but producing a different criminal sanction or altering any procedural provisions relevant to the criminal sanction.

DEFINITIONS
"burden": s.1(5)(b).
"enactment": s.1(5)(c)(6).
"the existing provision": s.1(3)(a).
"Minister of the Crown": Ministers of the Crown Act 1975 (c. 26), s.8(1).
"the relevant enactment": s.1(3)(b).

GENERAL NOTE
This section enables a Minister by order to amend or repeal primary legislation passed before the end of session 1993–1994 which imposes (or authorises or requires the imposition of) a burden on business, *i.e.* a burden affecting any person in the carrying on of any trade, business or profession or otherwise, provided that necessary protection is not removed. If appropriate an existing regulatory regime may be replaced by a less onerous one. On third reading in the House of Lords it was suggested that the power may also be used to write into enactments a power to waive requirements in individual cases (*Hansard*, H.L. Vol. 558, col. 559; for an example of a statutory dispensing power see the Financial Services Act 1986 (c. 60), s.50). An order under this section is made by statutory instrument subject to the affirmative resolution procedure, *i.e.* it must be laid (in draft) and approved by resolution of both Houses before it is made.

The Government has identified over 50 measures which it believes are suitable for implementation by the deregulation order-making power, subject to consultation with the representatives of those likely to be substantially affected. Because of the rolling nature of the Deregulation Initiative more measures are expected to be identified. The booklet *Deregulation: Cutting Red Tape* (Department of Trade and Industry, January 1994) contains an illustrative list of 55 measures which, subject to consultation, the Government intend to bring forward in the form of deregulation proposals. The list contains measures from eight departments covering 29 policy areas.

Subs. (1)
    is of the opinion. The test is a subjective rather than an objective one.
    or otherwise. The power applies to burdens on persons either carrying on businesses, trades or professions or otherwise. It thus covers burdens on charities, voluntary organisations and individuals as well as commercial enterprises (Standing Committee F, col. 62, February 17, 1994). "It covers what people do and it covers what they do other than in the carrying on of a trade, business or profession", *e.g.* as consumers (*Hansard*, H.L. Vol. 556, col. 494).
    necessary protection. In order to make the safeguard "both rigorous and comprehensive" the term "necessary protection" was left deliberately undefined (Standing Committee F, cols. 26 and 91–92, February 15 and 17, 1994; *Hansard*, H.L. Vol. 556, col. 481). "Necessary protection has been left deliberately undefined to ensure that it has the widest possible meaning. It would certainly encompass protection for flora, fauna and the national heritage". (*Hansard*, H.L. Vol. 557, col. 874). It also includes protection for tenants from unlawful eviction and harassment (*ibid.*, col. 878).

Subs. (4)(a)
    This sub-section would allow a regulatory regime to be replaced by a less onerous one.

Subs. (5)
    enactment. The definition of enactment means that the power cannot be exercised in respect of post 1993/94 legislation.

Subs. (7)
    An order cannot be used to change the level of criminal penalties, or the procedural provisions relevant to a criminal sanction, unless the order also changes the nature of the offence concerned.

Limitations on the power under section 1

2.—(1) If an order under section 1 creates a new criminal offence, then, subject to subsections (2) and (3) below, that offence shall not be punishable—
    (a) on indictment with imprisonment for a term of more than two years; or

  (b) on summary conviction with imprisonment for a term exceeding six months or a fine exceeding level 5 on the standard scale or both.

  (2) In the case of an offence which, if committed by an adult, is triable either on indictment or summarily and is not an offence triable on indictment only by virtue of—

    (a) Part V of the Criminal Justice Act 1988, or

    (b) section 457A(4) of the Criminal Procedure (Scotland) Act 1975,

the reference in subsection (1)(b) above to level 5 on the standard scale shall be construed as a reference to the statutory maximum.

  (3) If an order under section 1 above abolishes an offence contained in the relevant enactment and the maximum penalties for that offence are greater than those specified in subsection (1) above, the order may create a new criminal offence having maximum penalties not exceeding those applicable to the offence which is abolished.

  (4) An order under section 1 above shall not contain any provision—

    (a) providing for any forcible entry, search or seizure, or

    (b) compelling the giving of evidence,

unless, and then only to the extent that, a provision to that effect is contained in the relevant enactment and is abolished by the order.

DEFINITIONS
"the relevant enactment": s.1(3)(b).

GENERAL NOTE
  This section places limits on the penalties that may be imposed as part of a replacement regulatory regime unless higher penalties are a feature of the regime being replaced. It also prevents the provision of certain enforcement powers unless such powers are a feature of the regime being replaced.

Subs. (3)
  Where a new offence replaces an existing offence carrying higher penalties than those specified in subs. 1, the limit is the level of the existing penalties.

Preliminary consultation

  3.—(1) Before a Minister makes an order under section 1 above, he shall—

    (a) consult such organisations as appear to him to be representative of interests substantially affected by his proposals; and

    (b) consult such other persons as he considers appropriate.

  (2) If it appears to the Minister, as a result of the consultation required by subsection (1) above, that it is appropriate to vary the whole or any part of his proposals, he shall undertake such further consultation with respect to the variations as appears to him to be appropriate.

  (3) If, after the conclusion of—

    (a) the consultation required by subsection (1) above, and

    (b) any further consultation undertaken as mentioned in subsection (2) above,

the Minister considers it appropriate to proceed with the making of an order under section 1 above, he shall lay before Parliament a document containing his proposals in the form of a draft of the order, together with details of the matters specified in subsection (4) below.

  (4) The matters referred to in subsection (3) above are—

    (a) the burden, authorisation or requirement which it is proposed to remove or reduce;

    (b) whether the existing provision affords any necessary protection and, if so, how that protection is to be continued if the burden, authorisation or requirement is removed or reduced;

    (c) whether any savings in cost are estimated to result from the proposals and, if so, either the estimated amount or the reasons why savings should be expected;

(d) any other benefits which are expected to flow from the removal or reduction of the burden, authorisation or requirement;

(e) any consultation undertaken as required by subsection (1) or subsection (2) above;

(f) any representations received as a result of that consultation; and

(g) the changes (if any) which the Minister has made to his original proposals in the light of those representations.

(5) In giving details of the representations referred to in subsection (4)(f) above, the Minister shall not disclose any information relating to a particular person or business except—

(a) with the consent of that person or of the person carrying on that business; or

(b) in such a manner as not to identify that person or business.

(6) If, before the day on which this section comes into force, any consultation was undertaken which, had it been undertaken after that day, would to any extent have satisfied the requirements of subsection (1) above, those requirements shall to that extent be taken to have been satisfied.

DEFINITIONS
"burden": s.1(5)(b).
"the existing provision": s.1(3)(a).
"Minister": s.1(5)(a).

GENERAL NOTE
This section imposes two obligations on a Minister who proposes to make a deregulation order. The first is an obligation to consult representatives of affected interests and such other persons as he considers appropriate, and to undertake such further consultation as appears appropriate where his proposals are varied as a result of the initial consultation (subss. (1) and (2)). The second is an obligation to lay before Parliament a draft of the order and an explanatory document giving details of the matters specified in subs. (4) (subs. (3)).

Parliamentary consideration of proposals

4.—(1) Where a document has been laid before Parliament under section 3(3) above, no draft of an order under section 1 above to give effect (with or without variations) to proposals in that document shall be laid before Parliament until after the expiry of the period for Parliamentary consideration, as defined in subsection (2) below.

(2) In this section "the period for Parliamentary consideration", in relation to a document, means the period of sixty days beginning on the day on which it was laid before Parliament.

(3) In reckoning the period of sixty days referred to in subsection (2) above, no account shall be taken of any time during which Parliament is dissolved or prorogued or during which either House is adjourned for more than four days.

(4) In preparing a draft of an order under section 1 above to give effect, with or without variations, to proposals in a document laid before Parliament under section 3(3) above, the Minister concerned shall have regard to any representations made during the period for Parliamentary consideration and, in particular, to any resolution or report of, or of any committee of, either House of Parliament with regard to the document.

(5) Together with a draft of an order laid before Parliament under section 1(4) above, the Minister concerned shall lay a statement giving details of—

(a) any representations, resolution or report falling within subsection (4) above; and

(b) the changes (if any) which, in the light of any such representations, resolution or report, the Minister has made to his proposals as contained in the document previously laid before Parliament under section 3(3) above.

(6) Subsection (5) of section 3 above shall apply in relation to the representations referred to in subsection (5)(a) above as it applies in relation to the representations referred to in subsection (4)(f) of that section.

DEFINITIONS
"the period for Parliamentary consideration": s.4(2).

GENERAL NOTE
This section provides a period for the additional parliamentary scrutiny of deregulation proposals before the affirmative resolution debate. By making provision for such scrutiny the Government sought to counter the criticism that the exercise of the deregulation order-making power would be subject to insufficient safeguards. After a deregulation proposal has been laid before Parliament under s.3(3), at least 60 days must elapse before an order to give effect to the proposal may be laid before Parliament. Regard must be had to any representations made during this period and, in particular, to any resolution or report of either House or their Committees with regard to the proposal. A report must also be made to Parliament concerning any changes made to a proposal as a result of representations made, or resolutions or reports of either House or their Committees during the period.

The form that additional scrutiny should take was the subject of extensive consideration: Fourth Report from the Select Committee on Procedure *Parliamentary Scrutiny of Deregulation Orders* 1993/94, H.C. 238; First Special Report from the Select Committee on Procedure *Parliamentary Scrutiny of Deregulation Orders: Government Response to the Fourth Report* 1993/94, H.C. 238; debated H.C. Vol. 243, cols. 380–418; *Second Report from the Select Committee on Procedure of the House* 1993/94, H.L. 58; Select Committee on the Scrutiny of Delegated Powers, *Deregulation and Contracting Out Bill Initial and Further Report* 1993/94, H.L. 60 and 63.

The outcome of that consideration is that deregulation proposals will be examined by a specially constituted Deregulation Committee in the House of Commons and by the Delegated Powers Committee in the House of Lords. (The Committees will assume the functions of the Joint Committee on Statutory Instruments in relation to draft orders.) It is only through the mechanism of select committee scrutiny, the House of Commons Procedure Committee argued, "that the House and the general public can be certain that primary legislation is not being casually set aside by Government" (H.C. 238, para. 33).

The House of Commons Procedure Committee and the Government disagreed over whether the Deregulation Committee should have the power to prevent the order-making power being used to implement specific proposals. The power to veto proposals, the Committee argued, "would be an important check on inappropriate use of delegated legislation to repeal or amend primary legislation, without hindering the House's power to legislate on any matter". (H.C. 238, para. 63). In reply the Government stressed that an adverse report would be treated with the "utmost seriousness", so that in normal circumstances it would expect to submit a revised proposal or to withdraw the proposal altogether. But it reserved the right to lay a draft order in the face of an adverse report. Where it did so, it undertook not to move the motion to approve the draft order unless the House had first rejected the Committee's report (H.C. 404, paras. 16–18, 33–34).

In the House of Lords the Government made a similar undertaking to the effect that if the outcome of a debate on a motion in respect of a report from the Delegated Powers Committee on a draft order were to be a resolution of the House to the effect that the order should not be approved, the motion to approve the order would not be moved. This would leave the Minister with the option of bringing forward his proposals in the form of a Bill, changing his proposals, or not proceeding at all (*Hansard*, H.L. Vol. 555, col. 956; reaffirmed *Hansard*, H.L. Vol. 556, col. 490; *Hansard*, H.L. Vol. 557, cols. 867–868).

Subs. (4)
This subsection requires a Minister, in preparing a draft order to give effect to a deregulation proposal, to have regard to, *inter alia*, any resolution or report of either House or their committees with regard to the proposal, but only during the 60 day period provided for parliamentary consideration. The Minister need not pay heed to reports (and representations) made after the sixtieth day.

Subs. (5)
This subsection gives effect to an undertaking given in committee (Standing Committee E, col. 232, February 24, 1994). It requires a Minister to lay before Parliament, together with the final draft of an order, a statement of any changes made to the proposal as a result of any representations made, or the resolutions or reports of either House or their committees during the scrutiny period.

Enforcement procedures and appeals

Powers to improve enforcement procedures

5.—(1) If, with respect to any provision made by an enactment, a Minister of the Crown is of the opinion—

(a) that the effect of the provision is such as to impose, or authorise or require the imposition of, a restriction, requirement or condition affecting any person in the carrying on of any trade, business or profession or otherwise, and

(b) that, by exercising any one or more of the powers conferred by Schedule 1 to this Act, it would be possible, without jeopardising any necessary protection, to improve (so far as fairness, transparency and consistency are concerned) the procedures for enforcing the restriction, requirement or condition,

he may, subject to the following provisions of this section, by order exercise the power or powers accordingly.

(2) No order shall be made under this section in any case where the sole or main effect which the restriction, requirement or condition may be expected to have on each person on whom it is imposed is an effect on him in his personal capacity, and not as a person carrying on a trade, business or profession.

(3) Where the relevant enactment—

(a) contains a power for the Minister to make regulations or orders; and

(b) provides for that power to be exercisable so as to give effect, with or without modifications, to proposals submitted by some other person,

the Minister shall consult with that person before he makes an order under this section.

(4) An order under this section shall be made by statutory instrument and may do all or any of the following—

(a) make provision as to the consequences of any failure to comply with a provision made by the order;

(b) contain provisions (including provisions modifying enactments relating to the periods within which proceedings must be brought) which are consequential upon, or supplemental or incidental to, the provisions made by the order;

(c) contain such transitional provisions and savings as appear to the Minister to be appropriate;

(d) make different provision for different cases or different areas;

and a statutory instrument containing an order under this section shall be subject to annulment in pursuance of a resolution of either House of Parliament.

(5) Nothing in any order made under this section shall—

(a) preclude an enforcement officer from taking immediate enforcement action against any person, or from requiring any person to take immediate remedial action, in any case where it appears to the officer to be necessary to take such action or impose such a requirement; or

(b) require such an officer to disclose any information the disclosure of which would be contrary to the public interest.

(6) In this section and Schedule 1 to this Act—

"enactment" means an enactment within the meaning of section 1 above, and any subordinate legislation made under such an enactment;

"enforcement action"—

(a) in relation to any restriction, requirement or condition, means any action taken with a view to or in connection with imposing any sanction (whether criminal or otherwise) for failure to observe or comply with it; and

(b) in relation to a restriction, requirement or condition relating to the grant or renewal of licences, includes any refusal to grant, renew or vary a licence, the imposition of any condition on the grant or renewal of a licence and any variation or revocation of a licence;

"enforcement officer" does not include—
    (a) the Director of Public Prosecutions;
    (b) the Lord Advocate or a procurator fiscal; or
    (c) the Director of Public Prosecutions for Northern Ireland,
but, subject to that, means any person who is authorised, whether by or under the relevant enactment or otherwise, to take enforcement action;

"licence" includes any authorisation (by whatever name called) to do anything which would otherwise be unlawful;

"Minister of the Crown" and "Minister" have the same meanings as in section 1 above;

"the relevant enactment" means the enactment containing the provision by which the restriction, requirement or condition is imposed or, as the case may be, is authorised or required to be imposed;

"remedial action" means action taken by any person in order to avoid enforcement action being taken against him;

"subordinate legislation" has the same meaning as in the Interpretation Act 1978.

DEFINITIONS
    "enactment": s.5(6).
    "enforcement action": s.5(6).
    "enforcement officer": s.5(6).
    "licence": s.5(6).
    "Minister of the Crown": s.1(5)(a).
    "the relevant enactment": s.5(6).
    "remedial action": s.5(6).
    "subordinate legislation": Interpretation Act 1978 (c. 30), s.21(1).

GENERAL NOTE
    This section and Sched. 1 were inserted at the report stage in the House of Lords. They address the problem of the allegedly over-zealous or unreasonable application of requirements. A minister may exercise the powers conferred by Sched. 1 if he is of the opinion that by doing so it would be possible, without jeopardising any necessary protection, to improve the fairness, transparency and consistency of enforcement procedures. Introducing the powers, Earl Ferrers said: "... it is important for business to be able to clarify the status of, to understand the reasons for, and to be able to challenge, decisions at as early a stage as possible. The provisions provide an important means of ensuring that they can" (*Hansard*, H.C. Vol. 247, col. 1497).

Subs. (1)
    is of the opinion. The test is a subjective rather than an objective one.
    fairness. Attempts to write proportionality into the legislation were resisted on the ground that, in the sense that the sanction applied should be no greater than is necessary to achieve the objective, it is covered by "fairness" (*Hansard*, H.L. Vol. 557, col. 846; Vol. 558, cols. 559–560).

Subs. (2)
    personal capacity. The effect of this provision is that the power may not be exercised in respect of burdens imposed on individuals which affect them in their capacity as individuals and not in their capacity as persons carrying on a trade, business or profession. The powers do not apply therefore to legislation which solely or mainly affects individuals in a personal capacity.

Subs. (5)
    An order does not preclude an enforcement officer from either taking immediate enforcement action against a person, or requiring a person to take immediate remedial action, where necessary. Nor does it require the disclosure of information contrary to the public interest.

Subs. (6)
enactment. Like the power conferred by s.1, the powers conferred by Sched. 1 cannot be exercised in respect of post-1993–1994 legislation.

Model provisions with respect to appeals

6.—(1) The Secretary of State shall by order prescribe model provisions with respect to appeals against enforcement action with a view to their being incorporated, if thought fit and with or without modifications, in enactments to which subsection (2) below applies.

(2) This subsection applies to enactments which include provision the effect of which is to impose, or authorise or require the imposition of, a restriction, requirement or condition affecting any person in the carrying on of any trade, business or profession or otherwise.

(3) The Secretary of State shall perform his duty under this section in the manner which he considers is best calculated to secure—

  (a) that appeals determined in accordance with the model provisions are determined without unnecessary delay; and

  (b) that the costs or expenses incurred by the parties to appeals so determined are kept to the minimum.

(4) Model provisions prescribed by an order under this section may provide for the appointment of persons to hear and determine appeals and confer powers on persons so appointed, including in particular—

  (a) power to appoint experts and their own counsel or solicitor;

  (b) power to require respondents to disclose documents and other material;

  (c) power to summon or, in Scotland, to cite witnesses;

  (d) power to make interim orders, including orders staying or, in Scotland, suspending enforcement action; and

  (e) power to award costs or expenses to appellants and, in certain cases, against them.

(5) Model provisions so prescribed may also—

  (a) confer a right for interested persons to make representations before enforcement action is taken;

  (b) require the giving of reasons to such persons for any decision to take such action;

  (c) require appellants to state their grounds of appeal and respondents to furnish statements by way of answer;

  (d) enable appellants to amend their grounds of appeal before the hearing;

  (e) require appeals to be determined on the merits rather than by way of review; and

  (f) provide for further appeals to courts on points of law.

(6) An order under this section shall be made by statutory instrument which shall be subject to annulment in pursuance of a resolution of either House of Parliament.

(7) In this section—

  "enactment" does not include anything contained in Northern Ireland legislation but, subject to that, includes an enactment contained in an Act (whenever passed) and an enactment contained in subordinate legislation (whenever made);

  "enforcement action" has the same meaning as in section 5 above;

  "interested person" means—

    (a) the person against whom enforcement action may be or has been taken; and

    (b) any other person in respect of whom either of the conditions mentioned in paragraph 5(1) of Schedule 1 to this Act is fulfilled;

"Northern Ireland legislation" means—
  (a) Northern Ireland legislation within the meaning of section 24 of the Interpretation Act 1978; and
  (b) instruments, within the meaning of the Interpretation Act (Northern Ireland) 1954, made under such legislation;
"subordinate legislation" has the same meaning as in the Interpretation Act 1978.

DEFINITIONS
"enactment": s.6(7).
"enforcement action": s.5(6).
"interested person": s.6(7).
"Northern Ireland legislation": s.6(7).
"subordinate legislation": Interpretation Act 1978 (c. 30), s.21(1).

GENERAL NOTE
This section requires the Secretary of State to draw up model appeal provisions with a view to their incorporation in legislation imposing burdens on business. "The sheer diversity of current appeal mechanisms can, we believe, in itself be a problem for business. Some of the differences in appeal mechanisms arise from the nature of the legislation in question, but in other cases diversity has arisen because of the piecemeal development of the legislation". (*Hansard*, H.L. Vol. 557, col. 834). In truth, however, this commits the Government to very little – only to the prescribing of model provisions, not to their incorporation in legislation imposing burdens on business.

Subs. (2)
The obligation under subs. (1) is an obligation to prescribe model provisions with a view to their being incorporated in enactments to which this subsection applies, *i.e.* enactments which impose burdens on business. Since the incorporation of the model provisions will require separate legislative action ("These provisions could then be used where thought fit when legislation is being drawn up or revised" *Hansard*, H.L. Vol. 557, col. 834; "The model appeal mechanism would be available to be incorporated into future legislation as appropriate ..." *Hansard*, H.C. Vol. 248, cols. 1496–1497) there is no reason why their application should be so confined. The legal as opposed to political significance of this subsection is not therefore immediately apparent.

Subs. (3)
This subsection, which was inserted on third reading in the House of Lords, recognises that the timescales and costs involved in an appeal mechanism are important factors in determining its value to business.

Subs. (7)
Enactment. In contrast to ss.1 and 5 the enactments in which model provisions may be incorporated include post-1993–1994 enactments, but since their incorporation requires separate legislative action, it is not immediately obvious why it should have been thought necessary so to stipulate.

CHAPTER II

MISCELLANEOUS DEREGULATORY PROVISIONS

Undertakings as alternative to monopoly reference by Director General of Fair Trading

7.—(1) In the Fair Trading Act 1973, after section 56 there shall be inserted—

   "*Undertakings as alternative to monopoly reference by Director*

   Proposals by Director
      56A.—(1) The Director may propose that the Secretary of State accept undertakings in lieu of the Director making a monopoly reference if—

(a) he considers that a monopoly situation exists and that there are facts relating to the monopoly situation which may now or in future operate against the public interest,

(b) he intends, apart from the question of undertakings being accepted in lieu, to make a monopoly reference with respect to the existence of the monopoly situation and that the reference should be a monopoly reference not limited to the facts, and

(c) he considers that undertakings offered to be given by particular persons would be sufficient to deal with such of the relevant adverse effects of the monopoly situation as he thinks need to be dealt with.

(2) A proposal under this section shall include—

(a) a statement of the terms of the proposed undertakings and the persons by whom they are proposed to be given,·

(b) a statement of the facts relating to the monopoly situation which the Director considers may now or in future operate against the public interest, and

(c) a statement of the effects identified by the Director as the relevant adverse effects of the monopoly situation.

(3) For the purposes of the law relating to defamation, absolute privilege shall attach to anything included in a proposal under this section pursuant to subsection (2)(b) or (c) of this section.

(4) In this section, references to the relevant adverse effects of a monopoly situation are to the particular effects, adverse to the public interest, which the facts relating to the monopoly situation may now or in future have.

Proposals under section 56A: preparatory steps
56B.—(1) The Director may only make a proposal under section 56A of this Act if—

(a) the first or second condition is met, and

(b) the third condition is met.

(2) The first condition is that the Director has published in an appropriate manner a notice containing—

(a) each of the matters mentioned in subsection (5) of this section, and

(b) the invitation mentioned in subsection (6) of this section.

(3) The second condition is that the Director has published in an appropriate manner—

(a) a notice containing the matters mentioned in paragraphs (a) and (b) of subsection (5) of this section, and

(b) a notice containing—

  (i) the matters mentioned in paragraphs (c), (d), (e) and (f) of that subsection, and

  (ii) the invitation mentioned in subsection (6) of this section.

(4) The third condition is that the Director has considered any representations made to him in accordance with the notice under this section which contains the invitation mentioned in subsection (6) of this section.

(5) The matters referred to above are—

(a) the identity of the person or persons in whose favour the Director considers the monopoly situation exists,

(b) the terms of the proposed monopoly reference,

(c) the facts relating to the monopoly situation which the Director considers may now or in future operate against the public interest,

(d) the effects identified by the Director as the particular effects, adverse to the public interest, which the facts relating to the monopoly situation may now or in future have,

(e) the terms of the undertakings which the Director is, at the time of the notice, considering proposing the Secretary of State accept in lieu of the Director making the proposed monopoly reference ("the potential undertakings"), and

(f) the identity of the persons by whom the potential undertakings would be given.

(6) The invitation referred to above is an invitation to make representations to the Director, within such time as he may specify, about the potential undertakings being the subject of a proposal under section 56A of this Act.

(7) For the purposes of the law relating to defamation, absolute privilege shall attach to anything contained in a notice published under this section.

(8) In this section, references to an appropriate manner, in relation to the publication of a notice by the Director, are to such manner as he considers most suitable for the purpose of bringing the notice to the attention of persons who, in his opinion, are likely to be interested in it.

Proposals under section 56A: exclusion of sensitive information

56C.—(1) The Director shall—

(a) in formulating the statement required by section 56A(2)(b) or (c) of this Act, and

(b) in publishing a notice under section 56B of this Act containing the matters mentioned in subsection (5)(c) and (d) of that section,

have regard to the need for excluding, so far as practicable, any matter to which subsection (2) or (3) of this section applies.

(2) This subsection applies to any matter which relates to the private affairs of an individual, where publication of that matter would or might, in the opinion of the Director, seriously and prejudicially affect the interests of that individual.

(3) This subsection applies to any matter which relates specifically to the affairs of a particular body of persons, whether corporate or unincorporate, where publication of that matter would or might, in the opinion of the Director, seriously and prejudicially affect the interests of that body, unless in his opinion the inclusion of that matter relating specifically to that body is necessary for the purposes of the statement or notice, as the case may be.

Acceptance by Secretary of State of proposals under section 56A

56D.—(1) Where the Secretary of State accepts a proposal under section 56A of this Act, then, within the period of twelve months from the date of acceptance of the undertakings to which the proposal relates, no monopoly reference may be made in the same, or substantially the same, terms as those published by the Director under section 56B of this Act preparatory to making the proposal.

(2) Subsection (I) of this section shall not prevent a reference being made if the Director—

(a) considers that any of the undertakings has been breached, or needs to be varied or superseded, and

(b) has given notice of that fact to the person responsible for giving the undertaking.

(3) The Secretary of State shall send to the Director a copy of every undertaking accepted pursuant to a proposal under section 56A of this Act.

(4) For the purposes of subsection (1) of this section, the Secretary of State shall be treated as accepting a proposal under section 56A of this Act if he accepts the undertakings to which the proposal relates, either in the form in which they were proposed or with such modifications as he

thinks fit; and references in this Act to an undertaking accepted pursuant to a proposal under that section shall be construed accordingly.

Review of undertakings

56E.—(1) The Director shall keep the carrying out of an undertaking to which this section applies under review, and from time to time consider whether, by reason of any change of circumstances, the undertaking is no longer appropriate and either—

(a) one or more of the parties to it can be released from it, or

(b) it needs to be varied or to be superseded by a new undertaking.

(2) If it appears to the Director—

(a) that any one or more of the parties to an undertaking to which this section applies can be released from it,

(b) that such an undertaking needs to be varied or to be superseded by a new undertaking, or

(c) that there has been any failure to carry out such an undertaking, he shall give to the Secretary of State such advice as he may think proper in the circumstances.

(3) Where the Director advises the Secretary of State under subsection (2) of this section that an undertaking needs to be varied or to be superseded by a new undertaking, he shall propose the terms of variation or, as the case may be, the new undertaking.

(4) The Director shall, if the Secretary of State so requests, give him advice with respect to the release, variation or superseding of an undertaking to which this section applies.

(5) In this section, references to an undertaking to which this section applies are to an undertaking accepted—

(a) pursuant to a proposal under section 56A of this Act, or

(b) under section 56F of this Act.

Release, variation and replacement of undertakings

56F.—(1) The Secretary of State may only—

(a) accept a new undertaking in place of an undertaking to which this section applies,

(b) release a person from such an undertaking, or

(c) agree to the variation of such an undertaking,

after considering the advice of the Director on the subject.

(2) The Secretary of State shall send to the Director—

(a) a copy of every undertaking accepted under this section,

(b) particulars of every variation of an undertaking agreed under this section, and

(c) particulars of every release of a person from an undertaking under this section.

(3) In this section, references to an undertaking to which this section applies are to an undertaking accepted—

(a) pursuant to a proposal under section 56A of this Act, or

(b) under this section.

Publication of undertakings etc.

56G.—(1) The Secretary of State shall arrange for the publication in such manner as he considers appropriate of—

(a) every undertaking accepted—

(i) pursuant to a proposal under section 56A of this Act, or

(ii) under section 56F of this Act, and

(b) every variation or release under that section.

(2) Where the Secretary of State accepts undertakings pursuant to a proposal under section 56A of this Act, he shall arrange for the statements included in the proposal under subsection (2)(b) and (c) of that section to be published in such manner as he considers appropriate.

(3) If it appears to the Secretary of State that the publication of any matter contained in a statement which falls to be published under sub-section (2) of this section would be against the public interest, he shall exclude that matter from the statement as published under that subsection.

(4) Without prejudice to subsection (3) of this section, if the Secretary of State considers that it would not be in the public interest to disclose—

(a) any matter contained in a statement which falls to be published under subsection (2) of this section relating to the private affairs of an individual whose interests would, in the opinion of the Secretary of State, be seriously and prejudicially affected by the publication of that matter, or

(b) any matter contained in such a statement relating specifically to the affairs of a particular person whose interests would, in the opinion of the Secretary of State, be seriously and prejudicially affected by the publication of that matter,

the Secretary of State shall exclude that matter from the statement as published under subsection (2) of this section."

(2) Schedule 2 to this Act (sectoral regulators) shall have effect.

GENERAL NOTE

This section and Sched. 2 amend the Fair Trading Act 1973 (c. 41) to permit the Secretary of State to accept undertakings from companies as an alternative to a monopoly reference to the Monopolies and Mergers Commission by the Director General of Fair Trading (DGFT) or by the Directors General of Telecommunications, Electricity Supply and Water Services or the Rail Regulator, *i.e.* those sectoral regulators having concurrent powers with the DGFT.

Newspaper mergers: meaning of "newspaper proprietor" etc.

8.—(1) Section 57 of the Fair Trading Act 1973 shall be amended as follows.

(2) In subsection (1) (which defines "newspaper proprietor" and explains references to the newspapers of a newspaper proprietor) for the words from the beginning of paragraph (b) to the end of the subsection there shall be substituted—

"(b) "newspaper proprietor" includes (in addition to an actual proprietor of a newspaper) any member of a group of persons of which another member is an actual proprietor of a newspaper.

(1A) In this Part of this Act, any reference to the newspapers of a newspaper proprietor ("NP") is to—

(a) all newspapers of which NP is an actual proprietor, and

(b) all newspapers of which a member of a group of persons of which NP is a member is an actual proprietor."

(3) In subsection (2) (definition of "transfer of a newspaper or of newspaper assets") in paragraph (a), for ", a newspaper proprietor in relation to a newspaper;" there shall be substituted "—

(i) an actual proprietor of a newspaper, or

(ii) a person with a primary or secondary controlling interest in an actual proprietor of a newspaper;".

(4) In subsection (4) (definition of "controlling interest") before "controlling" there shall be inserted "primary".

(5) After that subsection there shall be inserted—

"(5) For the purposes of this section a person ("A") has a secondary controlling interest in a body corporate ("B") if, without having a primary controlling interest in B—

(a) A has a primary controlling interest in a body corporate which has a primary controlling interest in B, or

    (b) A is connected to B by a chain of any number of other bodies corporate, in the first of which A has a primary controlling interest, in the second of which the first has a primary controlling interest, and so on, the last such body corporate having a primary controlling interest in B.

    (6) For the purposes of this section a group of persons consists of any number of persons of whom the first is—

    (a) a person other than a body corporate, or

    (b) a body corporate in which no other person has a primary controlling interest,

and the others are the bodies corporate in which the first has a primary or secondary controlling interest.

    (7) In determining for the purposes of subsection (6)(b) of this section whether a body corporate ("X") is one in which another person has a primary controlling interest, there shall be disregarded any body corporate in which X has a primary or secondary controlling interest."

    (6) Subsections (1) to (5) above shall be deemed always to have had effect.

    (7) Section 8 of the Monopolies and Mergers Act 1965 shall be deemed never to have applied to a transaction to which it would not have applied had there been in force at the time of the transaction amendments of that Act corresponding to the amendments of the Fair Trading Act 1973 made by this section.

GENERAL NOTE

    Under the newspaper merger provisions of the Fair Trading Act 1973 (c. 41), the transfer of a newspaper to a "newspaper proprietor" requires the consent of the Secretary of State if the resulting combined circulation of all the relevant newspapers is 500,000 or more copies. As originally enacted these provisions were thought to catch innocent transactions, in particular joint ventures with or between newspaper companies that did not involve the transfer of a newspaper. This section amends the definition of "newspaper proprietor" in s.57 of the Act so as to remove such transactions from the special newspaper regime.

Undertakings as alternative to merger reference: non-divestment matters

    9.—(1) In section 75G of the Fair Trading Act 1973 (acceptance of undertakings) subsections (2) and (3) (under which undertakings are limited to divestment matters) shall cease to have effect.

    (2) In section 75K of that Act (order of Secretary of State where undertaking not fulfilled) in subsection (2) (powers which he may exercise by order) for "powers specified in paragraphs 9A and 12 to 12C and Part II of Schedule 8 to this Act" there shall be substituted "relevant powers".

    (3) In that section, there shall be inserted at the end—

    "(6) In subsection (2) of this section, the relevant powers" means—

    (a) in relation to an undertaking to which subsection (7) of this section applies ("a divestment undertaking"), the powers specified in paragraphs 9A and 12 to 12C and Part II of Schedule 8 to this Act, and

    (b) in relation to an undertaking which is not a divestment undertaking, the powers specified in that Schedule.

    (7) This subsection applies to an undertaking which provides for—

    (a) the division of a business by the sale of any part of the undertaking or assets or otherwise (for which purpose all the activities carried on by way of business by any one person or by any two or more interconnected bodies corporate may be treated as a single business),

    (b) the division of a group of interconnected bodies corporate, or

    (c) the separation, by the sale of any part of the undertaking or assets concerned or other means, of enterprises which are under common control otherwise than by reason of their being enterprises of interconnected bodies corporate.

(8) Schedule 8 to this Act shall, to such extent as is necessary for the purpose of giving effect to subsection (2) of this section, have effect as if, in paragraph 1 of that Schedule, after "section 73" there were inserted "or section 75K"."

GENERAL NOTE
This section empowers the Secretary of State to accept non-divestment undertakings as an alternative to making a merger reference to the Monopolies and Mergers Commission. At present the only undertakings he has power to accept are undertakings to dispose of parts of the business. It also extends his power to make an order under s.75K of the Fair Trading Act 1973 (c. 41) so that if non-divestment undertakings accepted as an alternative to a merger reference are not fulfilled, he will be able to exercise any of the powers in Sched. 8 to the Fair Trading Act to remedy or prevent those adverse effects of the merger on the public interest identified by the DGFT.

Restrictive trade practices: non-notifiable agreements

10.—(1) In the Restrictive Trade Practices Act 1976, after section 27 there shall be inserted—

"Non-notifiable agreements

Non-notifiable agreements
27A.—(1) For the purposes of this Act, a non-notifiable agreement is one which—
(a) is subject to registration under this Act,
(b) is, and has always been, of a description specified for the purposes of this section by order made by the Secretary of State,
(c) is not, and has never been, a price-fixing agreement, and
(d) is not an agreement in respect of which the Director has entered or filed particulars under section 1(2)(b) above.
(2) Without prejudice to the generality of paragraph (b) of subsection (1) above, an order under that paragraph may frame a description by reference—
(a) to the size of the businesses of the parties to an agreement, whether expressed by reference to turnover, as defined in the order, or to market share, as so defined, or in any other manner, or
(b) to exemption under, or any steps taken or decision given under or for the purpose of, any directly applicable Community provision (including any such provision as it has effect from time to time).
(3) In subsection (1)(c) above, the reference to a price-fixing agreement is to an agreement to which this Act applies by virtue of—
(a) a restriction in respect of any of the matters set out in section 6(1)(a) or (b) or 11(2)(a) above, or
(b) an information provision in respect of any of the matters set out in section 7(1)(a) or (b) or 12(2)(a) above.
(4) An order under subsection (1)(b) above shall be made by statutory instrument and may contain such transitional provisions as the Secretary of State considers appropriate."

(2) In section 42(1) of that Act (statutory instruments subject to negative resolution procedure) in paragraph (a) (orders) after "18(5)" there shall be inserted ", 27A(1)(b)".

(3) In section 43(1) of that Act (interpretation) there shall be inserted at the appropriate place—
    " "non-notifiable agreement" has the meaning given by section 27A(1) above;".

(4) Schedule 3 to this Act (which modifies the 1976 Act in relation to non-notifiable agreements) shall have effect.

GENERAL NOTE

This section and Sched. 3 to the Act amend the Restrictive Trade Practices Act 1976 (c. 34) so as to introduce a power to exempt certain categories of restrictive agreement – those that are unlikely to raise competition concerns – from mandatory notification to the DGFT. "Non-notifiable" agreements remain subject to registration under the Act, but are exempt from the requirement to furnish particulars to the DGFT, unless he requests them.

Restrictive trade practices: registration of commercially sensitive information

11. In section 23(3) of the Restrictive Trade Practices Act 1976 (certain categories of information to be entered or filed in a special section of the register of agreements) for paragraph (b) there shall be substituted—

"(b) particulars containing information whose publication would, in the Secretary of State's opinion, substantially damage the legitimate business interests of any person, not being information whose publication is, in the Secretary of State's opinion, in the public interest."

GENERAL NOTE

This section amends the Restrictive Trade Practices Act 1976 (c. 34) in order to widen the range of commercially sensitive information which the Secretary of State may order to be withheld from the public register.

Anti-competitive practices: competition references

12.—(1) In section 5 of the Competition Act 1980 (grounds for competition reference) for subsection (1)(a) there shall be substituted—

"(a) there are reasonable grounds for believing that any person is pursuing, or has pursued, a course of conduct which constitutes an anti-competitive practice,".

(2) In consequence of subsection (1) above, that Act shall be amended as mentioned in subsections (3) to (6) below.

(3) In section 3 of that Act (preliminary investigation by Director General of Fair Trading of possible anti-competitive practice) subsections (2) to (6), (9) and (10) (which provide for the formal constitution, carrying out and discontinuation of an investigation and the publication by the Director of a report following completion of an investigation) shall cease to have effect.

(4) In section 4 of that Act (undertakings) for substances (1) to (3) there shall be substituted—

"(1) Where it appears to the Director—

(a) that there are reasonable grounds for believing that any person is pursuing, or has pursued, a course of conduct which constitutes an anti-competitive practice,

(b) that the practice may operate, now or in future, or have operated, against the public interest, and

(c) that an undertaking offered to be given to the Director by that person, or by a person associated with that person, would remedy or prevent effects adverse to the public interest which the practice may now or in future have,

he may, at any time before making a reference under section 5(1)(a) below in relation to the course of conduct in question, accept the undertaking by giving notice to the person by whom it is offered.

(2) The Director may not accept an undertaking under subsection (1) above unless he has—

(a) arranged for the publication of an appropriate notice, and
(b) considered any representations made to him in accordance with the notice.

(3) Publication under subsection (2)(a) above shall be in such manner as the Director considers most suitable for bringing the notice to the attention of persons who, in his opinion, would, if the course of conduct in question were the subject of a reference under section 5(1)(a) below, be affected by the reference or be likely to have an interest in it.

(3A) In subsection (2)(a) above, the reference to an appropriate notice is to a notice which—

(a) states that the Director is proposing to exercise his power under subsection (1) above,
(b) identifies the course of conduct whose pursuit prompts the exercise of that power,
(c) identifies the person who the Director believes is pursuing, or has pursued, that course of conduct,
(d) identifies the goods or services in relation to which the Director believes that person is pursuing, or has pursued, that course of conduct,
(e) specifies the effects which the Director has identified as effects adverse to the public interest which that course of conduct may now or in future have,
(f) sets out the terms of the undertaking which the Director is proposing to accept,
(g) identifies the person by whom the undertaking is to be given, and
(h) specifies a deadline for the making to the Director of representations about what he proposes to do.

(3B) Once the Director has considered any representations made to him in accordance with a notice under paragraph (a) of subsection (2) above, that subsection shall not apply to the acceptance of a modified version of the undertaking set out in the notice."

(5) In that section, at the end there shall be inserted—

"(10) Subsection (6) of section 2 above shall apply for the purposes of this section as it applies for the purposes of that."

(6) In section 6 of that Act (scope of competition references) for subsections (3) and (4) there shall be substituted—

"(3) Where the Director has accepted an undertaking under section 4 above with respect to the pursuit by any person of a course of conduct in relation to any goods or services, the Director may not, while the undertaking is in force, make a competition reference by virtue of section 5(1) (a) above with respect to the pursuit by that person of that course of conduct in relation to those goods or services."

(7) Schedule 4 to this Act (which makes provision about sectoral regulators and with respect to transition) shall have effect.

GENERAL NOTE

Under the Competition Act 1980 (c. 21) the DGFT must carry out a formal preliminary investigation and publish a report before he can ask the Monopolies and Mergers Commission to investigate an anti-competitive practice or accept undertakings from companies which satisfy his concerns. This section and Sched. 4 to the Act amend the Competition Act 1980 by removing the requirement for a formal investigation and report by the DGFT (or those sectoral regulators having concurrent powers with the DGFT) before undertakings can be accepted or references to the Monopolies and Mergers Commission made.

Striking off of non-trading private companies

13.—(1) Schedule 5 to this Act (which amends the Companies Act 1985 for the purpose of facilitating the striking off of non-trading private companies registered in Great Britain) shall have effect.

(2) Schedule 6 to this Act (which amends the Companies (Northern Ireland) Order 1986 for the purpose of facilitating the striking off of non-trading companies registered in Northern Ireland) shall have effect.

GENERAL NOTE
This section and Sched. 5 insert a new procedure into the Companies Act 1985 (c. 6) which allows private companies that are not trading but still "in operation" to apply to be struck off the register of companies and dissolved, thus relieving their directors of obligations, *e.g.* to file accounts, under the Act. The new procedure provides certain safeguards for those dealing or involved with the company. Schedule 6 makes corresponding provision for Northern Ireland.

Repeal of section 43 of the Weights and Measures Act 1985

14. Section 43 of the Weights and Measures Act 1985 (which provides for the gas comprised in any foam on beer or cider to be disregarded for certain purposes) shall cease to have effect.

GENERAL NOTE
This section repeals s.43 of the Weights and Measures Act 1985 (c. 72). Section 43 provided for the "head" to be disregarded for the purpose of measuring a pint of beer or cider, but was never brought into force. A pint of beer or cider may thus continue to include a reasonable head.

Building societies: issue of deferred shares at a premium

15. In section 7 of the Building Societies Act 1986 (power to raise funds) after subsection (2) there shall be inserted—
"(2A) In the case of deferred shares, the power to raise funds by the issue of shares includes the issue of shares at a premium.
(2B) If a building society issues deferred shares at a premium, whether for cash or otherwise, a sum equal to the aggregate amount or value of the premiums on those shares shall be transferred to the society's reserves."

GENERAL NOTE
This section amends the Building Societies Act 1986 (c. 53) to permit building societies to issue deferred shares at a premium.

Building societies: class 1 and 2 advances—third party mortgages

16.—(1) The Building Societies Act 1986 shall be amended as follows.
(2) In section 10 (advances secured on land), after subsection (4) there shall be inserted—
"(4A) The power to make an advance secured on land incudes power to make an advance which is secured as mentioned in subsection (1) above by virtue of security granted otherwise than by the borrower (in this Act referred to as "an advance secured on third party land")."
(3) In section 11, in subsection (2) (definition of class 1 advances)—
(a) in paragraph (b), at the beginning there shall be inserted "where the advance is not an advance secured on third party land,",
(b) after that paragraph, there shall be inserted—
"(ba) where the advance is an advance secured on third party land—
(i) the borrower intends that the advance will be used for the purpose of acquiring land for the residential use of himself or a dependant of his of a prescribed description; and
(ii) the land on which the advance is secured is for the residential use of the mortgagor or a dependant of his of a prescribed description;", and
(c) in paragraph (c), for the words from "mortgage debt" to "land)" there shall be substituted "outstanding amount secured by a mortgage of the land in favour of the society)".

(4) In subsection (3) of that section (when requirement as to use of land for residential purposes to be treated as satisfied) the words from "the requirement" to the end shall become paragraph (a) and at the end there shall be inserted—

"(b) the requirement in subsection (2)(ba)(i) above shall be treated as satisfied if the borrower intends that no less than 40 per cent. of the area of the land will be for the residential use of himself or a dependant of his of a prescribed description; and

(c) the requirement in subsection (2)(ba)(ii) above shall be treated as satisfied if no less than 40 per cent. of the area of the land is used for residential purposes by the mortgagor or a dependant of his of a prescribed description."

(5) In subsection (4) of that section (definition of class 2 advances) in paragraph (c), for the words from "mortgage debt" to "land)"there shall be substituted "outstanding amount secured by a mortgage of the land)".

(6) In section 12 (class 1 and class 2 advances: supplementary provisions) after subsection (5) there shall be inserted—

"(5A) Subsection (5) above shall also apply as respects advances secured on third party land which is to any extent used for the residential use of mortgagors or persons who are dependants of theirs for the purposes of section 11(2)."

(7) In section 12(10) (reclassification of class 1 and class 2 advances following a material change of circumstances)—

(a) in paragraph (c), there shall be inserted at the beginning "in the case of an advance which is not an advance secured on third party land", and

(b) for "or" at the end of that paragraph there shall be substituted—

"(ca) in the case of an advance which is an advance secured on third party land—

(i) is satisfied on notice given to it by the borrower that there has been a change in the use of the land acquired with the advance, or

(ii) is satisfied on notice given to it by the mortgagor that there has been a change in the use of the land on which the advance is secured, or".

(8) In section 16 (power to lend to individuals otherwise than by class 1 or 2 advances) in subsection (15) (reclassification of loans under section 16 as class 1 or 2 advances)—

(a) in paragraph (b), there shall be inserted at the beginning "where the mortgage is granted by the borrower,", and

(b) for the words from "or" at the end of paragraph (b) to "notice" in paragraph (c) there shall be substituted—

"(c) where the mortgage is granted otherwise than by the borrower and the loan has been used to purchase land—

(i) on notice given to it by the borrower that there has been a change in the use of the land purchased, or

(ii) on notice given to it by the mortgagor that there has been a change in the use of the mortgaged land, or

(d) on notice given to it—

(i) where the mortgage is granted by the borrower, by him, and

(ii) where the mortgage is granted otherwise than by the borrower, by the mortgagor,".

GENERAL NOTE

This section is designed to help ease the problem of negative equity among owner-occupiers and to improve the supply of funding for small businesses. It amends the Building Societies Act 1986 (c. 53) to permit building societies to lend money to borrowers on the security of land owned by third parties. A building society may thus lend to a borrower whose house is worth less than the outstanding mortgage, using a parent's home as additional security, lend to a company on the security of the owner's house, or lend to a company on the security of the property of a sister company in the same group.

Building societies: direct participation in syndicated lending

17.—(1) In the Building Societies Act 1986, after section 14 there shall be inserted—

> **"Power to participate in secured syndicated lending**
> 14A.—(1) Subject to subsection (2) below, a building society may participate in syndicated lending—
>> (a) as a member of the lending syndicate, or
>> (b) as a person whose rights as a participant arise under an arrangement with a member of the lending syndicate ("a sub-participant").
>
> (2) Subsection (1) above only applies if—
>> (a) the syndicated lending is appropriately secured, and
>> (b) where the society's participation is as a sub-participant, the society's rights as such a participant are appropriately secured.
>
> (3) The Commission may, with the consent of the Treasury, by order—
>> (a) make provision with respect to what constitutes appropriate security for the purposes of subsection (2)(a) or (b) above;
>> (b) make provision with respect to the classification, for the purposes of the requirements of this Part for the structure of commercial assets, of a society's participation under this section in syndicated lending; and
>> (c) provide for the application of the provisions of this Part, with such modifications as appear to the Commission to be appropriate, to a society's participation under this section in syndicated lending.
>
> (4) The power conferred by subsection (3) above shall be exercisable by statutory instrument subject to annulment in pursuance of a resolution of either House of Parliament.
>
> (5) A building society may only exercise the power conferred by this section if it has adopted it."

(2) Where, immediately before the day on which this section comes into force, a building society is entitled to exercise powers conferred by section 18 of the Building Societies Act 1986 in relation to—

(a) bodies of the description specified in Part I of the Schedule to the Building Societies (Designation of Qualifying Bodies) Order 1992 (appropriate lending vehicle), or

(b) bodies of the description specified in item 9 of Part I of the Schedule to the Building Societies (Designation of Qualifying Bodies) (No. 3) Order 1993 (lending body),

the society shall be deemed to have adopted the power conferred by section 14A of that Act in accordance with sub-paragraph (1) of paragraph 4 of Schedule 2 to that Act (alteration of powers by the adoption of an adoptable power) and to have determined under sub-paragraph (3) of that paragraph (duty to determine the date on which it intends the alteration to take effect) that it intends the alteration to take effect on the day on which this section comes into force.

(3) In relation to a deemed alteration under subsection (2) above, Schedule 2 to the Building Societies Act 1986 shall have effect with the following modifications—

(a) in paragraph 4(2)(b) (statutory declaration by secretary with respect to alteration) for the words from "a resolution" to the end there shall be substituted "section 17(2) of the Deregulation and Contracting Out Act 1994 and that the record is a true record of the alteration",

(b) in paragraph 4(4) (functions of central office on receipt of record of alteration) the words from "and the central office" to "under it" shall be omitted, and

(c) in paragraph 16(3) (declaration by society of non-anticipation of powers) in paragraphs (a) and (b), the words "and expired with the date of the meeting at which the power was adopted" shall be omitted.

GENERAL NOTE

This section amends the Building Societies Act 1986 (c. 53) to allow building societies to participate directly in syndicated lending, either as an actual member of the lending syndicate or as a "sub-participant".

Licensed premises at international ports: permitted hours

18.—(1) In the Licensing Act 1964, after section 86 there shall be inserted—

"International ports

86A.—(1) At a port where this section is in operation section 59 of this Act shall not apply to licensed premises within an approved wharf.

(2) The Secretary of State may by order bring this section into operation at any port which appears to him to be one at which there is a substantial amount of international passenger traffic.

(3) Before the Secretary of State makes an order bringing this section into operation at a port, he shall satisfy himself that arrangements have been made for affording reasonable facilities on licensed premises within any approved wharf at that port for obtaining hot and cold beverages other than intoxicating liquor at all times when intoxicating liquor is obtainable on those premises.

(4) If it appears to the Secretary of State that at any port where this section is in operation such arrangements as are mentioned in subsection (3) of this section are not being maintained, he shall revoke the order bringing this section into operation at that port, but without prejudice to his power of making a further order with respect to that port.

(5) In this section, "approved wharf" has the same meaning as in the Customs and Excise Management Act 1979."

(2) In the Licensing (Scotland) Act 1976, after section 63 there shall be inserted—

"Exemption of international ports from restrictions on permitted hours

63A.—(1) The Secretary of State may by order made by statutory instrument bring this section into operation at any port which appears to him to be a port at which there is a substantial amount of international passenger traffic.

(2) At a port where this section is in operation, neither section 54 nor section 119 of this Act nor any provision or rule of law prohibiting or restricting the sale or supply of alcoholic liquor on Sunday shall apply to licensed premises which are within an approved wharf.

(3) Before the Secretary of State makes an order bringing this section into operation at a port, he shall satisfy himself that arrangements have been made for affording reasonable facilities in licensed premises within any approved wharf at that port for obtaining hot and cold beverages other than alcoholic liquor at all times when alcoholic liquor is obtainable for consumption in those premises.

(4) If it appears to the Secretary of State that at any port where this section is in operation such arrangements as are mentioned in subsection (3) above are not being maintained, he shall revoke the order bring-

ing this section into operation as respects that port, but without prejudice to his power of making a further order with respect to that port.

(5) In this section, "approved wharf" has the same meaning as in the Customs and Excise Management Act 1979."

GENERAL NOTE

This section empowers the Secretary of State to grant international seaports the same exemption from the licensing laws as airports and hoverports as regards the sale of duty paid and duty free alcohol. The exercise of this power will allow SeaCat terminals to offer comprehensive duty free facilities at the convenience of passengers, regardless of time of sailing, thereby enabling SeaCat operators to compete on an equal footing with the operators of conventional ferries.

Bars in licensed premises in England and Wales: children's certificates

19.—(1) In section 168 of the Licensing Act 1964 (children prohibited from bars) after subsection (3) there shall be inserted—

"(3A) No offence shall be committed under subsection (1) of this section if—

(a) the person under fourteen is in the bar in the company of a person who is eighteen or over,

(b) there is in force a certificate under section 168A(1) of this Act relating to the bar, and

(c) the certificate is operational or subsection (3B) of this section applies.

(3B) This subsection applies where—

(a) the person under fourteen, or a person in whose company he is, is consuming a meal purchased before the certificate ceased to be operational, and

(b) no more than thirty minutes have elapsed since the certificate ceased to be operational.

(3C) No offence shall be committed under subsection (2) of this section if the person causes or procures, or attempts to cause or procure, the person under fourteen to be in the bar in the circumstances mentioned in paragraphs (a) to (c) of subsection (3A) of this section."

(2) After that section there shall be inserted—

"Children's certificates

168A.—(1) The holder of a justices' licence may apply to the licensing justices for the grant of a certificate in relation to any area of the premises for which the licence is in force which consists of or includes a bar.

(2) Licensing justices may grant an application for a certificate under subsection (1) of this section ("a children's certificate") if it appears to them to be appropriate to do so, but shall not do so unless they are satisfied—

(a) that the area to which the application relates constitutes an environment in which it is suitable for persons under fourteen to be present, and

(b) that meals and beverages other than intoxicating liquor will be available for sale for consumption in that area.

(3) Where a children's certificate is in force, the holder of the justices' licence for the licensed premises to which the certificate relates shall keep posted in some conspicuous place in the area to which the certificate relates a notice which—

(a) states that a children's certificate is in force in relation to the area, and

(b) explains the effect of the certificate and of any conditions attached to it.

(4) A person who fails to perform the duty imposed on him by subsection (3) of this section shall be guilty of an offence and liable on summary conviction to a fine of an amount not exceeding level 1 on the standard scale.

(5) In any proceedings for an offence under subsection (4) of this section, it shall be a defence for the accused to prove that he took all reasonable precautions, and exercised all due diligence, to avoid the commission of the offence.

(6) Schedule 12A to this Act (supplementary provisions) shall have effect.

(7) Subsection (1) of this section shall apply to an applicant for a justices' licence as it applies to the holder of a justices' licence, and, in its application by virtue of this subsection, shall have effect as if the reference to the premises for which the licence is in force were to the premises which are the subject of the application for a justices' licence."

(3) After Schedule 12 to that Act there shall be inserted the Schedule set out in Schedule 7 to this Act (supplementary provisions).

GENERAL NOTE

This section and Sched. 7 relax the general prohibition on the admission of children under 14 years of age to the bars of licensed premises in England and Wales by empowering the licensing justices, on application, to grant a children's certificate for bar premises if they are satisfied that the premises constitute an environment in which it is suitable for children to be present and that meals and non-alcoholic beverages will be available.

Betting on Sundays

20.—(1) The Betting, Gaming and Lotteries Act 1963 shall be amended as set out in subsections (2) to (5) below.

(2) In section 5(1), for "Good Friday, Christmas Day or Sunday" there shall be substituted "Good Friday or Christmas Day".

(3) After section 31 there shall be inserted—

"Betting workers: Sunday working

Rights of betting workers as respects Sunday working

31A. Schedule 5A to this Act shall have effect for the purpose of making provision about the rights of betting workers as respects Sunday working."

(4) In Schedule 4, in paragraph 1, for "Good Friday, Christmas Day and every Sunday" there shall be substituted "Good Friday and Christmas Day".

(5) After Schedule 5 there shall be inserted the Schedule set out in Schedule 8 to this Act.

GENERAL NOTE

This section amends the Betting, Gaming and Lotteries Act 1963 (c. 2) so as to remove the prohibition on the opening of betting offices on Sundays and the prohibition on on-course betting on Sundays. Schedule 8 makes provision in relation to the rights of betting office workers as regards Sunday working.

Sporting events and activities on Sundays

21. The entertainments and amusements to which the Sunday Observance Act 1780 applies shall not include any sporting event or activity.

GENERAL NOTE

This section disapplies the Sunday Observance Act 1780 (c. 49) to Sunday sporting events and activities. Charges may thus be made for admission to places used for sporting events and activities on Sundays and such events and activities may be advertised.

Sunday opening of certain licensed premises in Scotland

22. For section 119(3) of the Licensing (Scotland) Act 1976 (trading hours for off-sale premises and off-sale parts of public houses and hotels and prohibition of Sunday opening), there shall be substituted the following subsection—

"(3) Off-sale premises and the off-sale part of premises shall not be opened for the serving of customers with alcoholic liquor—

(a) on a day other than a Sunday, earlier than eight in the morning, and

(b) on a Sunday, earlier than half past twelve in the afternoon,

and shall be closed for the serving of customers with such liquor not later than ten in the evening."

GENERAL NOTE

This section amends s.119(3) of the Licensing (Scotland) Act 1976 (c. 66) to permit off-licences in Scotland to open on Sundays. It was the subject of a free vote on Commons report.

Repeal of Part I of the Shops Act 1950

23. Part I of the Shops Act 1950 (hours of closing) shall cease to have effect.

GENERAL NOTE

This section repeals Pt. I of the Shops Act 1950 (c. 28) which provides for shop closing times and requires shops to close early on one day of the week.

Repeal of remainder of the Shops Act 1950

24. In the Shops Act 1950—
(a) Part II (conditions of employment), and
(b) section 67 (business of hairdresser or barber not to be carried on in Scotland on Sunday),
shall cease to have effect.

GENERAL NOTE

This section repeals the remaining provisions of Pt. II of the Shops Act 1950 (c. 28), most of which was repealed by the Employment Act 1989 (c. 38), and s.67 of the 1950 Act which prohibits hairdressers and barbers in Scotland from carrying on business on Sundays. The Government had already announced their intention to repeal s.67 by way of the deregulation order-making power conferred by s.1 of this Act.

Controls on fund-raising for charitable institutions: exclusion of connected companies

25.—(1) In Part II of the Charities Act 1992 (control of fund-raising for charitable institutions) section 58(1) (definitions) shall be amended as follows.

(2) In the definition of "commercial participator", after "person" there shall be inserted "(apart from a company connected with the institution)".

(3) In paragraph (a) of the definition of "professional fund-raiser", after "institution" there shall be inserted "or a company connected with such an institution".

GENERAL NOTE

This section amends s.58 of the Charities Act 1992 (c. 41) to exclude connected companies, *i.e.* companies that are wholly owned or controlled by charities, from the definition of "professional fund raiser" and "commercial participator" in Part II of that Act. The intention is to make it clear that the controls which Part II introduces on professional and commercial involvement in fund raising for charitable institutions do not apply to such companies (*Hansard*, H.C. Vol. 243, cols. 161–163).

Offences under section 63 of the Charities Act 1992: creation of statutory defence

26.—(1) Section 63 of the Charities Act 1992 (which makes it an offence to solicit property for an institution while falsely representing that it is a registered charity) shall be amended as follows.

(2) After subsection (1) there shall be inserted—

"(1A) In any proceedings for an offence under subsection (1), it shall be a defence for the accused to prove that he believed on reasonable grounds that the institution was a registered charity."

(3) In subsection (2) (meaning of "registered charity") for the words "subsection (1)" there shall be substituted "this section".

GENERAL NOTE

This section creates a defence of reasonable belief to the offence in s.63 of the Charities Act 1992 (c. 41).

Applications for permits to conduct public charitable collections: time-limits

27. In section 67 of the Charities Act 1992 (applications for permits to conduct public charitable collections) paragraph (b) of subsection (3) (which provides that an application shall not be made more than six months before the relevant day) and the word "but" immediately preceding it shall be omitted.

GENERAL NOTE

This section removes the statutory restriction on applications to conduct public charitable collections more than six months in advance. The Government's policy remains that charities should not reserve the most favourable dates for public collections a long time in advance. It intends to issue guidance to that effect to local authorities (*Hansard*, H.L. Vol. 556, col. 820).

Annual audit or examination of charity accounts

28.—(1) Section 43 of the Charities Act 1993 (annual audit or examination of charity accounts) shall be amended as follows.

(2) In subsection (3) (which requires a charity's accounts for a financial year to be audited or independently examined if its gross income and total expenditure in that year, and each of the two previous financial years, is £100,000 or less) after "a charity" there shall be inserted "and its gross income or total expenditure in that year exceeds £10,000".

(3) In subsection (8) (power of Secretary of State to amend sum specified in subsection (1)) after "(1)" there shall be inserted "or (3)".

GENERAL NOTE

This section introduces the first of a "light touch" band of reporting requirements for small charities, *i.e.* charities whose annual income and expenditure do not exceed £10,000. Under this section a charity's accounts for a financial year no longer have to be audited or independently examined if neither its gross income nor total expenditure in that year exceed £10,000.

Annual reports of charities

29.—(1) In section 45 of the Charities Act 1993 (annual reports) in subsection (3) (automatic duty to transmit annual report to the Commissioners) for the words from the beginning to "a charity" there shall be substituted "Where in any financial year of a charity its gross income or total expenditure exceeds £10,000, the annual report required to be prepared under this section in respect of that year".

(2) After that subsection there shall be inserted—

"(3A) Where in any financial year of a charity neither its gross income nor its total expenditure exceeds £10,000, the annual report required to be prepared under this section in respect of that year shall, if the Commissioners so request, be transmitted to them by the charity trustees—

(a) in the case of a request made before the end of seven months from the end of the financial year to which the report relates, within ten months from the end of that year, and

(b) in the case of a request not so made, within three months from the date of the request,

or, in either case, within such longer period as the Commissioners may for any special reason allow in the case of that report."

(3) In subsection (4) of that section, for "any such annual report" there shall be substituted "any annual report transmitted to the Commissioners under this section".

(4) In subsection (5) of that section, for "subsection (3) above" there shall be substituted "this section".

(5) In subsection (6) of that section, for "subsection (3) above" there shall be substituted "this section".

(6) At the end of that section there shall be inserted—

"(7) The charity trustees of a charity shall preserve, for at least six years from the end of the financial year to which it relates, any annual report prepared by them under subsection (1) above which they have not been required to transmit to the Commissioners.

(8) Subsection (4) of section 41 above shall apply in relation to the preservation of any such annual report as it applies in relation to the preservation of any accounting records (the references in subsection (3) of that section being read as references to subsection (7) above).

(9) The Secretary of State may by order amend subsection (3) or (3A) above by substituting a different sum for the sum for the time being specified there."

(7) In section 46(7) of that Act (application of section 45(3) to (6) to annual reports under section 46(5)) after "section 45" there shall be inserted "(as originally enacted)".

(8) In section 49 of that Act (penalty for persistent default in relation to certain requirements) in paragraph (a), after "45(3)" there shall be inserted "or (3A)".

GENERAL NOTE

This section relieves the trustees of a charity whose annual income and expenditure do not exceed £10,000 of the obligation to transmit the annual report to the Commissioners, replacing it with an obligation to transmit the report to the Commissioners if they so request.

Annual returns by charities

30.—(1) Section 48 of the Charities Act 1993 (annual returns by registered charities) shall be amended as follows.

(2) In subsection (1) (duty to prepare annual return) at the beginning there shall be inserted "Subject to subsection (1A) below,".

(3) After subsection (1) there shall be inserted—

"(1A) Subsection (1) above shall not apply in relation to any financial year of a charity in which neither the gross income nor the total expenditure of the charity exceeds £10,000."

(4) At the end there shall be inserted—

"(4) The Secretary of State may by order amend subsection (1A) above by substituting a different sum for the sum for the time being specified there."

GENERAL NOTE

This section relieves the trustees of a charity whose annual income and expenditure do not exceed £10,000 of the obligation to prepare an annual return.

Slaughterhouses and knackers' yards: uniting of enforcement functions

31. Schedule 9 to this Act (which contains provisions designed to facilitate the uniting of enforcement functions relating to slaughterhouses and knackers' yards) shall have effect.

GENERAL NOTE

Meat hygiene duties in slaughterhouses, currently undertaken by local authorities, are to be undertaken by agriculture ministers acting through the Meat Hygiene Service with effect from April 1, 1995. This section and Sched. 9 enable the Meat Hygiene Service also to assume the functions of local authorities in relation to the enforcement of welfare at slaughterhouses and the licensing of slaughtermen, thereby avoiding what would otherwise be a duplication of enforcement authorities in slaughterhouses.

Building regulations: power to repeal or modify provisions of local Acts

32.—(1) In Schedule 1 to the Building Act 1984 (building regulations) in paragraph 11(1), after paragraph (b) there shall be inserted "or
    (c) any provision of a local Act passed before the day on which the Deregulation and Contracting Out Act 1994 is passed,".

(2) In section 14 of that Act (consultation) there shall be inserted at the end—

"(4) Before making any building regulations containing provision of the kind authorised by paragraph 11(1)(c) of Schedule 1 to this Act, the Secretary of State shall consult—
    (a) the Building Regulations Advisory Committee,
    (b) such persons or bodies as appear to him to be representative of local authorities, and
    (c) such other bodies as appear to him to be representative of the interests concerned."

GENERAL NOTE

This section, which extends to England and Wales only, enables provisions of local Acts, passed before the enactment of this Act, to be modified or repealed if they conflict with national building regulations.

Amendment of duty of care etc. as respects waste

33.—(1) In section 34 of the Environmental Protection Act 1990 (duty of care etc. as respects controlled waste), after subsection (4) there shall be inserted—

"(4A) For the purposes of subsection (1)(c)(ii) above—
    (a) a transfer of waste in stages shall be treated as taking place when the first stage of the transfer takes place, and
    (b) a series of transfers between the same parties of waste of the same description shall be treated as a single transfer taking place when the first of the transfers in the series takes place."

(2) Subsection (1) above shall be deemed always to have had effect, except in relation to any proceedings for failure to comply with the duty imposed by section 34(1) of that Act which were commenced before the coming into force of subsection (1) above.

(3) Where any such proceedings have not been disposed of before the coming into force of subsection (1) above, it shall be a defence to show that the conduct in question would not have constituted a breach of the duty concerned had subsection (1) above been in force at the time.

GENERAL NOTE

This section amends s.34 of the Environmental Protection Act 1990 (c. 43). It clarifies the responsibilities of parties to repeated transfers of waste in relation to the provision of descriptions of that waste.

Controls on London lorries: replacement of discretionary exceptions

34.—(1) Subsection (3) below applies to any order having effect under or by virtue of section 6 (orders similar to traffic regulation orders) or 9 (experimental traffic orders) of the Road Traffic Regulation Act 1984 ("the 1984 Act") which provides for a relevant traffic control to be subject to a relevant exception, being an order in relation to which the appropriate authority is a London borough council or the Common Council of the City of London.

(2) For the purposes of this section—

(a) a relevant traffic control is a prohibition or restriction on the use of a road for traffic which does not apply to motor vehicles generally but applies to some or all heavy commercial vehicles, and

(b) a relevant exception is an exception whose application, in the case of any heavy commercial vehicles, depends to any extent on the exercise of a delegated discretion.

(3) The Secretary of State may, for the purpose of replacing a relevant exception to a relevant traffic control with such other exception as he thinks fit, by order make any such variation of an order to which this subsection applies as the appropriate authority may make.

(4) The Secretary of State shall only exercise the power conferred by subsection (3) above if he is satisfied that doing so—

(a) will have the effect that less of a burden is imposed on the carrying on of business, and

(b) will not have the effect of removing any necessary protection.

(5) The Secretary of State may, for the purpose of amending as he thinks fit an exception introduced under subsection (3) above (including such an exception as amended), by order make any such variation of the order varied under that subsection as the appropriate authority may make.

(6) The Secretary of State may, for the purpose of amending as he thinks fit a provision of an order having effect under or by virtue of section 6 or 9 of the 1984 Act which re-enacts (with or without modification) an exception introduced under subsection (3) above (including such an exception as amended) ("a re-enactment order"), by order make any such variation of the order as the appropriate authority may make.

(7) The Secretary of State shall only exercise the power conferred by subsection (5) or (6) above if he is satisfied—

(a) that, if he does so, it will still be the case that less of a burden is imposed on the carrying on of business than was imposed before the replacement under subsection (3) above, and

(b) that doing so will not have the effect of removing any necessary protection.

(8) Paragraphs 35 to 37 of Part VI of Schedule 9 to the 1984 Act (validity of certain orders) shall apply to an order under this section as they apply to an order to which that Part applies; and in those paragraphs, in their application by virtue of this subsection—

(a) "the relevant powers" means the powers conferred by this section with respect to the order in question, and

(b) "the relevant requirements" means the requirements of this section with respect to that order.

(9) Before making any order under this section, the Secretary of State shall consult with such representative organisations as he thinks fit; and any such order shall be made by statutory instrument which shall be subject to annulment in pursuance of a resolution of either House of Parliament.

(10) Where in the case of any order proposed to be made by the council of a London borough or the Common Council of the City of London under or by virtue of section 6 or 9 of the 1984 Act, it is proposed to include in the order any provision—

(a) varying or revoking an order under this section,

(b) varying or revoking an order having effect under or by virtue of section 6 or 9 of that Act which is varied by an order under this section, or

(c) varying or revoking a re-enactment order,

the order shall not be made except with the consent of the Secretary of State.

(11) Where, in the case of any order proposed to be made by the council of a London borough or the Common Council of the City of London under or by virtue of section 9 of the 1984 Act, it is proposed to include in the order provision under section 10(1)(a) of that Act relating to—

(a) an order under this section,

(b) an order having effect under or by virtue of section 6 or 9 of that Act which is varied by an order under this section, or

(c) a re-enactment order,

the order shall not be made except with the consent of the Secretary of State.

(12) In this section—

"appropriate authority", in relation to an order having effect under or by virtue of section 6 or 9 of the 1984 Act, means the authority by which the order is, or is deemed to be, made;

"heavy commercial vehicle" and "road" have the same meanings as in the 1984 Act;

"motor vehicle" means a vehicle treated as a motor vehicle for the purposes of the 1984 Act;

"re-enactment order" has the meaning given by subsection (6) above; and

"the 1984 Act" has the meaning given by subsection (1) above.

DEFINITIONS

"appropriate authority": s.34(12).
"heavy commercial vehicle": s.34(12).
"motor vehicle": s.34(12).
"re-enactment order": s.34(6).
"relevant exception": s.34(2)(b).
"relevant traffic control": s.34(2)(a).
"road": s.34(12).

GENERAL NOTE

This section amends the system for controlling the movement of heavy lorries in London at night and during weekends (the London lorry ban). It gives the Secretary of State the power, exercisable by order, to amend local authority traffic orders in Greater London which impose a prohibition or restriction on the use of a road by heavy lorries unless a permit is granted. It also gives the Secretary of State power to make consequential amendments to such orders and prevents local authorities from making further amendments to those orders without the Secretary of State's consent.

Subss. (4)–(7)

The Secretary of State may only make an order under subs. (3) (and subss. (5) and (6)) if he is satisfied (a) that a lesser burden will be imposed on business as a result and (b) that necessary protection will not be removed. The latter condition, which was inserted on report in the House of Lords, ensures that the Secretary of State cannot make an amending order unless he is satisfied that the London lorry ban will be capable of proper enforcement in its amended form (*Hansard*, H.L. Vol. 558, col. 573).

Employment agencies etc.: replacement of licensing

35. Schedule 10 to this Act (which provides for the replacement of licensing in relation to employment agencies etc.) shall have effect.

GENERAL NOTE

This section and Sched. 10 remove the requirement for employment agencies and employment businesses to be licensed by the Secretary of State (or, in Northern Ireland, the Department of Economic Development). The power to refuse or revoke licences on specified grounds is replaced by a power to prohibit persons from carrying on agencies or businesses on similar grounds. Seamen's agencies (previously the subject of separate provision under the Merchant Shipping Act 1894 (c. 60)) are also brought within the scope of the new regime.

Unfair dismissal: selection for redundancy

36.—(1) In section 59(1) of the Employment Protection (Consolidation) Act 1978 (circumstances in which dismissal for redundancy to be regarded as unfair) paragraph (b) (selection for dismissal in contravention of customary arrangement or agreed procedure) shall be omitted.

(2) Article 22C(1)(e) of the Industrial Relations (Northern Ireland) Order 1976 (corresponding provision for Northern Ireland) shall be omitted.

GENERAL NOTE
   This section repeals s.59(1)(b) of the Employment Protection (Consolidation) Act 1978 (c. 44) (and the corresponding Northern Ireland provision), which provides that a person should be regarded as unfairly dismissed if selected for redundancy in breach of a customary arrangement or agreed procedure.

Power to repeal certain health and safety provisions

37.—(1) The appropriate authority may by regulations repeal or, as the case may be, revoke—

(a) any provision which is an existing statutory provision for the purposes of Part I of the Health and Safety at Work etc. Act 1974 ("the 1974 Act"),

(b) any provision of regulations under section 15 of the 1974 Act (health and safety regulations) which has effect in place of a provision which was an existing statutory provision for the purposes of that Part,

(c) any provision which is an existing statutory provision for the purposes of the Health and Safety at Work (Northern Ireland) Order 1978 ("the 1978 Order"), or

(d) any provision of regulations under Article 17 of the 1978 Order (health and safety regulations) which has effect in place of a provision which was an existing statutory provision for the purposes of that Order.

(2) Before making regulations under subsection (1) above, the appropriate authority shall consult—

(a) in the case of regulations under paragraph (a) or (b) of that subsection, the Health and Safety Commission,

(b) in the case of regulations under paragraph (c) or (d) of that subsection, the Health and Safety Agency for Northern Ireland,

and, in either case, such other persons as the appropriate authority considers appropriate.

(3) Instead of consulting such other persons as the appropriate authority considers it appropriate to consult under subsection (2) above, the authority may require the Health and Safety Commission or, as the case may be, the Health and Safety Agency for Northern Ireland to consult such persons as it considers appropriate for the purpose of deciding how it should respond to consultation under that subsection.

(4) Instead of consulting a person whom the appropriate authority considers it appropriate to consult under subsection (2) above, the authority may require the Health and Safety Commission or, as the case may be, the Health and Safety Agency for Northern Ireland to consult the person for the purpose of deciding how it should respond to consultation under that subsection.

(5) The appropriate authority may require consultation under subsection (3) or (4) above to be carried out in accordance with the authority's directions.

(6) Regulations under subsection (1) above may contain such transitional provisions and savings as the appropriate authority considers appropriate.

(7) Regulations under paragraph (a) or (b) of subsection (1) above shall be made by statutory instrument, and no instrument shall be made under that paragraph unless a draft of it has been laid before, and approved by a resolution of, each House of Parliament.

(8) Regulations under subsection (1)(c) or (d) above—

(a) shall be statutory rules for the purposes of the Statutory Rules (Northern Ireland) Order 1979, and

(b) shall be subject to affirmative resolution, as defined in section 41(4) of the Interpretation Act (Northern Ireland) 1954, as if they were statutory instruments within the meaning of that Act.

(9) In this section, "appropriate authority"—

(a) in relation to regulations under subsection (1)(a) or (b) above, means the Secretary of State, and

(b) in relation to regulations under subsection (1)(c) or (d) above, means the Department concerned (within the meaning of the 1978 Order, but as if any reference to that Order included a reference to this section).

DEFINITIONS
"appropriate authority": s.37(9).

GENERAL NOTE
This section gives the Secretary of State the power, exercisable by order subject to affirmative resolution procedure, to repeal or revoke pre-1974 health and safety standards that no longer serve a useful purpose. Currently, post-1974 health and safety legislation can be repealed without replacement, but it is doubtful whether the Health and Safety at Work etc. Act 1974 (c. 37) allows for the repeal of pre-1974 legislation without replacement. Use of this power is subject to consultation with the Health and Safety Commission (or, in Northern Ireland, the Health and Safety Agency for Northern Ireland) and other appropriate persons.

Subss. (3) and (4)
These subsections empower the Secretary of State to require the Health and Safety Commission to carry out consultation on his behalf.

Inspection of independent schools

38. After section 87 of the Children Act 1989 there shall be inserted—

"Suspension of duty under section 87(3)

87A.—(1) The Secretary of State may appoint a person to be an inspector for the purposes of this section if—

(a) that person already acts as an inspector for other purposes in relation to independent schools to which section 87(1) applies, and

(b) the Secretary of State is satisfied that the person is an appropriate person to determine whether the welfare of children provided with accommodation by such schools is adequately safeguarded and promoted while they are accommodated by them.

(2) Where—

(a) the proprietor of an independent school to which section 87(1) applies enters into an agreement in writing with a person appointed under subsection (1),

(b) the agreement provides for the person so appointed to have in relation to the school the function of determining whether section 87(1) is being complied with, and

(c) the local authority in whose area the school is situated receive from the person with whom the proprietor of the school has entered into the agreement notice in writing that the agreement has come into effect,

the authority's duty under section 87(3) in relation to the school shall be suspended.

(3) Where a local authority's duty under section 87(3) in relation to any school is suspended under this section, it shall cease to be so suspended if the authority receive—

(a) a notice under subsection (4) relating to the person with whom the proprietor of the school entered into the relevant agreement, or

(b) a notice under subsection (5) relating to that agreement.

(4) The Secretary of State shall terminate a person's appointment under subsection (1) if—

(a) that person so requests, or

(b) the Secretary of State ceases, in relation to that person, to be satisfied that he is such a person as is mentioned in paragraph (b) of that subsection,

and shall give notice of the termination of that person's appointment to every local authority.

(5) Where—

(a) a local authority's duty under section 87(3) in relation to any school is suspended under this section, and

(b) the relevant agreement ceases to have effect,

the person with whom the proprietor of the school entered into that agreement shall give to the authority notice in writing of the fact that it has ceased to have effect.

(6) In this section—

(a) "proprietor" has the same meaning as in the Education Act 1944, and

(b) references to the relevant agreement, in relation to the suspension of a local authority's duty under section 87(3) as regards any school, are to the agreement by virtue of which the authority's duty under that provision as regards that school is suspended.

Duties of inspectors under section 87A

87B.—(1) The Secretary of State may impose on a person appointed under section 87A(1) ("an authorised inspector") such requirements relating to, or in connection with, the carrying out under substitution agreements of the function mentioned in section 87A(2)(b) as the Secretary of State thinks fit.

(2) Where, in the course of carrying out under a substitution agreement the function mentioned in section 87A(2)(b), it appears to an authorised inspector that there has been a failure to comply with section 87(1) in the case of a child provided with accommodation by the school to which the agreement relates, the inspector shall give notice of that fact to the Secretary of State.

(3) Where, in the course of carrying out under a substitution agreement the function mentioned in section 87A(2)(b), it appears to an authorised inspector that a child provided with accommodation by the school to which the agreement relates is suffering, or is likely to suffer, significant harm, the inspector shall—

(a) give notice of that fact to the local authority in whose area the school is situated, and

(b) where the inspector is required to make inspection reports to the Secretary of State, supply that local authority with a copy of the latest inspection report to have been made by the inspector to the Secretary of State in relation to the school.

(4) In this section—

(a) "proprietor" has the same meaning as in the Education Act 1944, and

(b) references to substitution agreement are to an agreement between an authorised inspector and the proprietor of an independent school by virtue of which the local authority's duty in relation to the school under section 87(3) is suspended."

GENERAL NOTE
This section empowers the Secretary of State to appoint an organisation that already inspects independent schools for other purposes to undertake the welfare inspection functions in relation to independent schools currently undertaken by local authority social service departments. The effect will be to enable an independent school to opt for inspection for welfare purposes by an organisation other than the local authority in whose area the school is situated.

Chapter II: consequential amendments

39. Schedule 11 to this Act (which contains amendments consequential on certain provisions of this Chapter) shall have effect.

GENERAL NOTE
This section gives effect to Sched. 11 which contains amendments consequential on certain provisions in Chap. II.

Extent of Chapter II

40.—(1) The following provisions of this Chapter extend to England and Wales only—
> sections 18(1), 19, 20(3), 21, 25 to 30, 32, 34 and 38,
> paragraphs 8 to 10 of Schedule 2,
> Schedules 7 and 8, and
> paragraph 2 of Schedule 9.

(2) Sections 18(2), 22 and 24(b) and paragraph 3 of Schedule 9 extend to Scotland only.

(3) The following provisions of this Chapter extend to Northern Ireland only—
> sections 13(2) and 36(2),
> paragraphs 5, 6(2) and 7(2) of Schedule 2,
> Schedule 6, and
> paragraphs 2 and 5 of Schedule 10.

(4) The following provisions of this Chapter also extend to Northern Ireland—
> sections 7 to 12,
> sections 15 to 17,
> sections 35, 37 and 39,
> this section,
> paragraphs 1 to 3 and 15 of Schedule 2,
> Schedule 3,
> paragraphs 1 and 5 to 8 of Schedule 4, and
> paragraph 3 of Schedule 10.

(5) The extent of any amendment of an enactment in paragraph 2 or 3 of Schedule 4 to this Act or Schedule 11 to this Act is the same as that of the enactment amended.

(6) Subject to subsections (3) to (5) above, this Chapter does not extend to Northern Ireland.

GENERAL NOTE
This section defines the territorial extent of Chap. II.

CHAPTER III

GOODS VEHICLE OPERATOR LICENSING

The 1968 Act

41. In this Chapter "the 1968 Act" means the Transport Act 1968.

Use of vehicles under licences

42.—(1) In section 61 of the 1968 Act (authorised vehicles) for subsection (1) there shall be substituted—

"(1) Subject to the following provisions of this section, the vehicles authorised to be used under an operator's licence are—

(a) any motor vehicle in the lawful possession of the licence-holder that is specified in the licence;

(b) any trailer in the lawful possession of the licence-holder; and

(c) any motor vehicle in the lawful possession of the licence-holder that is not specified in the licence.

(1A) An operator's licence may provide that—

(a) no motor vehicle the relevant weight of which exceeds a weight specified in the licence is authorised to be used under it;

(b) no trailer the relevant weight of which exceeds a weight specified in the licence is authorised to be used under it;

(c) no trailers are authorised to be used under it;

(d) no vehicles are authorised to be used under it by virtue of subsection (1)(c) of this section.

(1B) In subsection (1A) of this section "relevant weight", in relation to a motor vehicle or trailer of any prescribed class, means a weight of the description specified in relation to motor vehicles or trailers of that class by regulations."

(2) For subsections (3) and (4) of that section there shall be substituted—

"(3) A vehicle is not authorised to be used under an operator's licence by virtue of subsection (1)(c) of this section after the period of one month beginning with—

(a) the day on which the vehicle was first in the lawful possession of the licence-holder; or

(b) if later, the day on which the licence came into force,

unless during that period the licence-holder has given to the licensing authority by whom the licence was granted a notice, in such form and containing such information about the vehicle as the authority may require, and has paid a prescribed fee to the authority.

(4) Where notice of a vehicle has been duly given and the prescribed fee has been duly paid under subsection (3) of this section, the licensing authority shall vary the licence by directing that the vehicle be specified in it."

(3) After that section there shall be inserted—

"**Maximum numbers of vehicles**

61A.—(1) An operator's licence—

(a) shall specify a maximum number for motor vehicles; and

(b) may specify a maximum number for motor vehicles the relevant weight of which exceeds a weight specified in the licence.

(2) An operator's licence that does not contain a provision such as is mentioned in section 61(1A)(c) of this Act—

(a) shall specify a maximum number for trailers; and

(b) may specify a maximum number for trailers the relevant weight of which exceeds a weight specified in the licence.

(3) The number of vehicles being used under an operator's licence by virtue of section 61(1)(c) of this Act at any one time may not exceed the maximum number specified in the licence under subsection (1)(a) of this section, less however many motor vehicles are specified in the licence.

(4) Where under subsection (1)(b) of this section an operator's licence specifies a maximum number for motor vehicles the relevant weight of which exceeds a specified weight—

  (a) the number of such vehicles being used under the licence by virtue of section 61(1)(c) of this Act at any one time may not exceed
that maximum number, less however many motor vehicles the
relevant weight of which exceeds the specified weight are specified in the licence; and

  (b) the number of such vehicles that are specified in the licence and
being used under it at any one time may not exceed that maximum number.

(5) The number of trailers being used under an operator's licence at
any one time may not exceed the maximum number specified in the
licence under subsection (2)(a) of this section.

(6) Where under subsection (2)(b) of this section an operator's
licence specifies a maximum number for trailers the relevant weight of
which exceeds a specified weight, the number of such trailers being used
under the licence at any one time may not exceed that maximum
number.

(7) The definition of "relevant weight" in section 61(1B) of this Act
applies for the purposes of this section as it applies for the purposes of
section 61(1A).

(8) If subsection (3), (4)(a) or (b), (5) or (6) of this section is contravened, the licence-holder shall be liable on summary conviction to a fine
not exceeding level 4 on the standard scale."

Definitions
  "the 1968 Act": s.41.

General Note
  This section provides an amended description of the categories and numbers of vehicles authorised to be used under a goods vehicle operator's licence. It makes consequential provision for
penalties for contravening restrictions on vehicle numbers.

Objections to grant or variation of licences

43. After section 63(4) of the 1968 Act (which requires objections to the
grant or variation of operators' licences to be made within the prescribed
time and in the prescribed manner) there shall be inserted—

    "(4A) Where the licensing authority considers there to be exceptional
circumstances that justify his doing so, he may direct that an objection be
treated for the purposes of this Part of this Act as duly made under this
section, notwithstanding that it was not made within the prescribed time
or in the prescribed manner."

Definitions
  "the 1968 Act": s.41.

General Note
  This section permits a licensing authority to accept objections, where it considers there are
exceptional circumstances that justify its doing so, notwithstanding that they were not made
within the prescribed time or in the prescribed manner.

Determination of applications for licences

44.—(1) For section 64 of the 1968 Act there shall be substituted—

"Determination of applications for operators' licences

    64.—(1) Subject to sections 69E and 89(2) of this Act, on an appli-
cation for an operator's licence the licensing authority shall consider—

    (a) whether the requirements of subsections (2) and (3) of this section are satisfied; and

    (b) if he thinks fit, whether the requirements of subsection (4) of this section are satisfied.

(2) The applicant must not by reason—

    (a) of any activities or convictions of which particulars may be required to be given under section 62(4)(d) or (e) of this Act; or

    (b) of any conviction required to be notified in accordance with section 62(4A) of this Act,

be unfit to hold an operator's licence.

(3) It must be possible (taking into account the licensing authority's powers under section 64A(3) of this Act) to issue a licence on the application in relation to which paragraphs (a) to (d) of this subsection will apply—

    (a) there are satisfactory arrangements for securing that Part VI of this Act is complied with in the case of the vehicles used under the licence and for securing that those vehicles are not overloaded;

    (b) there are satisfactory facilities and arrangements for maintaining the vehicles used under the licence in a fit and serviceable condition;

    (c) at least one place in the licensing authority's area is specified in the licence as an operating centre of the licence-holder and each place so specified is available and suitable for use as such an operating centre (disregarding any respect in which it may be unsuitable on environmental grounds);

    (d) the capacity of the place so specified (if there is only one) or of both or all the places so specified taken together (if there are more than one) is sufficient to provide an operating centre for all the vehicles used under the licence.

(4) The provision of such facilities and arrangements as are mentioned in subsection (3)(b) of this section must not be prejudiced by reason of the applicant's having insufficient financial resources for that purpose.

(5) In considering whether any of the requirements of subsections (2) to (4) of this section are satisfied, the licensing authority shall have regard to any objection duly made under section 63 of this Act in respect of the application.

(6) In considering whether the requirements of subsection (3) of this section are satisfied, the licensing authority may take into account any undertakings given by the applicant (or procured by him to be given) for the purposes of the application, and may assume that those undertakings will be fulfilled.

(7) In considering whether subsection (3)(c) of this section will apply in relation to a licence, the licensing authority may take into account any conditions that under section 64B of this Act could be attached to the licence, and may assume that any conditions so attached will not be contravened.

(8) In considering whether subsection (3)(c) or (d) of this section will apply in relation to a licence, the licensing authority may take into account (if such be the case) that any proposed operating centre of the applicant would be used—

    (a) as an operating centre of the holders of other operators' licences as well as of the applicant; or

    (b) by the applicant or by other persons for purposes other than keeping vehicles used under the licence.

(9) If the licensing authority determines that any of the requirements that he has taken into consideration in accordance with subsection (1) of

this section are not satisfied, he shall refuse the application, but in any other case he shall, subject to sections 69B and 89(2) of this Act, grant the application.

Issue of operators' licences

64A.—(1) Subject to subsection (2) of this section and to sections 64B, 66, 69B, 69C and 89(2) of this Act, on granting an application for an operator's licence, the licensing authority shall issue that licence in the terms applied for.

(2) If the authority has determined that any of the requirements of section 64(3) or (4) of this Act that he has taken into consideration in accordance with section 64(1) of this Act would not be satisfied unless he exercised any of his powers under subsection (3) of this section, he shall exercise those powers accordingly.

(3) The authority may issue the licence in terms that differ from the terms applied for in any of the following respects—

(a) more or fewer motor vehicles are specified in the licence;

(b) different motor vehicles are specified in it;

(c) it includes a provision such as is mentioned in section 61(1A) of this Act;

(d) it includes a provision such as is mentioned in section 61A(1)(b) or (2)(b) of this Act;

(e) higher or lower maximum numbers are specified in it under section 61A of this Act;

(f) fewer places are specified in it as operating centres of the licence-holder.

(4) Any undertakings taken into account by the authority under section 64(6) of this Act that he considers to be material to the granting of the application shall be recorded in the licence issued."

(2) In section 69B of the 1968 Act (objection to, and refusal or modification of, applications for operators' licences on environmental grounds) for subsection (5) there shall be substituted—

"(5) The licensing authority may not refuse an application for an operator's licence on the ground that any place would be unsuitable as mentioned in subsection (4) of this section if—

(a) on the date the application was made, that place was already specified in an operator's licence granted by the authority as an operating centre of the holder of that licence; or

(b) the applicant has produced to the authority a certificate in force in respect of that place under section 191 or 192 of the Town and Country Planning Act 1990 or section 90 or 90A of the Town and Country Planning (Scotland) Act 1972, stating that its use as an operating centre for vehicles used under any operator's licence is or would be lawful.

(5A) Subsection (5) of this section does not apply in relation to any place that, at the time the application is determined by the licensing authority, is specified in an operator's licence as an operating centre of the holder of that licence.

(5B) In paragraph (a) of subsection (5) of this section "operator's licence" does not include a licence granted under section 67A of this Act, and the reference in that paragraph to a place being specified in an operator's licence does not include a place being so specified—

(a) by virtue of an interim direction such as is mentioned in section 68A of this Act;

(b) if such conditions as may be prescribed in relation to the exercise of the right of any person to appeal against that place being so specified are not satisfied;

   (c) if such conditions as may be prescribed in relation to the review under section 69J of this Act of the decision so to specify that place are not satisfied; or

   (d) by reason of being situated within a place that is so specified."

DEFINITIONS
"the 1968 Act": s.41.

GENERAL NOTE
   This section clarifies the provisions for determining applications for an operator's licence and makes new ones.

Conditions for securing road safety

   45. After section 64A of the 1968 Act (set out in section 44 above) there shall be inserted—

    "Conditions for securing road safety
    64B.—(1) A licensing authority, on granting an operator's licence or on varying such a licence under section 68 of this Act, may attach to it such conditions as he thinks fit for preventing vehicles that are authorised to be used under the licence from causing danger to the public—

     (a) at any point where vehicles first join a public road on their way from an operating centre of the licence-holder (or last leave a public road on their way to such an operating centre); and

     (b) on any road (other than a public road) along which vehicles are driven between such a point and the operating centre.

    (2) On varying an operator's licence under section 68 of this Act, the licensing authority may vary or remove any condition attached to the licence under this section.

    (3) The licensing authority shall not—

     (a) attach to an operator's licence any condition such as is mentioned in this section; or

     (b) vary in such manner as imposes new or further restrictions or requirements any condition attached to an operator's licence under this section,

without first giving the applicant for the licence or (as the case may be) the licence-holder an opportunity of making representations to the authority with respect to the effect on his business of the proposed condition or variation.

    (4) The licensing authority shall give special consideration to any representations made under subsection (3) of this section in determining whether to attach the proposed condition or make the proposed variation.

    (5) In this section as it applies in relation to England and Wales, "public road" means a highway maintainable at the public expense for the purposes of the Highways Act 1980.

    (6) Any person who contravenes any condition attached under this section to a licence of which he is the holder shall be liable on summary conviction to a fine not exceeding level 4 on the standard scale."

DEFINITIONS
"the 1968 Act": s.41.

GENERAL NOTE
   This section empowers a licensing authority to attach conditions to an operator's licence for reasons of road safety. This would enable approval to be given to an otherwise unacceptable operating centre.

Duration of licences and grant of interim licences

46. For section 67 of the 1968 Act there shall be substituted—

"Duration of operators' licences

67.—(1) The date on which an operator's licence is to come into force shall be specified in the licence.

(2) Subject to its revocation or other termination under any provision of this Act or another statutory provision, an operator's licence (other than one granted under section 67A of this Act) shall continue in force indefinitely.

(3) If the holder of an operator's licence requests the licensing authority by whom it was granted to terminate it at any time, the authority shall, subject to subsection (4) of this section, comply with the request.

(4) The licensing authority may refuse to comply with the request if he is considering giving a direction in respect of the licence under section 69(1) of this Act or revoking the licence under Regulation 9(1) of the Goods Vehicles (Operators' Licences, Qualifications and Fees) Regulations 1984.

(5) An operator's licence held by an individual terminates if he dies or becomes a patient within the meaning of Part VII of the Mental Health Act 1983.

Interim licences

67A.—(1) Where on any application for an operator's licence (a "full" licence) the applicant so requests, the licensing authority may grant to him an interim licence.

(2) An interim licence is an operator's licence that (subject to its revocation or other termination under any provision of this Act or another statutory provision) will continue in force until it terminates under subsection (3), (4) or (5) of this section.

(3) If the licensing authority grants the application and issues to the applicant a full licence—

    (a) that is in the terms applied for; or

    (b) that is in those terms, subject only to the attachment under section 64B, 66 or 69C of this Act of any conditions that are also attached to the interim licence,

the interim licence shall terminate on the date on which the full licence comes into force.

(4) If, on an appeal arising out of the application, the Transport Tribunal orders the licensing authority to issue a full licence to the applicant, the interim licence shall terminate—

    (a) on the date on which the full licence issued in pursuance of the order comes into force; or

    (b) at the time at which the application is withdrawn or treated as withdrawn under section 89(3) of this Act.

(5) If neither subsection (3) nor subsection (4) of this section applies, the interim licence shall terminate on the date on which the application is finally disposed of or such earlier date as the applicant may specify in a written request to the licensing authority.

(6) In a case within subsection (5) of this section where the application is granted, the full licence issued to the applicant shall (notwithstanding any statement in it to the contrary) be of no effect before the interim licence terminates.

(7) A request for the grant of an interim licence shall not for the purposes of section 63, 64, 64A, 69B, 69E, 69J or 70 of, or Schedule 8A to, this Act be treated as an application for an operator's licence, but shall

be treated as such an application for any other purposes of this Part of this Act.

(8) The licensing authority may issue an interim licence in the same terms as those applied for in relation to the full licence or in terms that differ from those terms in any of the respects mentioned in section 64A (3) of this Act."

DEFINITIONS
"the 1968 Act": s.41.

GENERAL NOTE
This section provides for licences to continue in force indefinitely unless revoked or otherwise terminated. It also clarifies the position as regards the duration of interim licences.

Variation of licences

47.—(1) For section 68 of the 1968 Act there shall be substituted—

"Variation of operators' licences

68.—(1) Subject to section 69E of this Act, on the application of the holder of an operator's licence, the licensing authority by whom the licence was granted may vary the licence by directing—

(a) that additional motor vehicles be specified in the licence or that any maximum number specified in it under section 61A of this Act be increased;

(b) that any vehicle cease to be specified in the licence or that any maximum number specified in it under section 61A of this Act be reduced;

(c) that any provision in the licence such as is mentioned in section 61(1A) of this Act cease to have effect;

(d) that a provision such as is mentioned in section 61(1A) of this Act be included in the licence;

(e) that any provision in the licence such as is mentioned in section 61A(1)(b) or (2)(b) of this Act cease to have effect;

(f) that a provision such as is mentioned in section 61A(1)(b) or (2) (b) of this Act be included in the licence;

(g) that a new place in the licensing authority's area be specified in the licence as an operating centre of the licence-holder, or that any place cease to be so specified;

(h) that any undertaking recorded in the licence be varied or removed;

(i) that any condition attached to the licence be varied or removed;

(j) in the case of a restricted licence, that it be converted into a standard licence or, in the case of a standard licence, that it be converted into a restricted licence;

(k) in the case of a standard licence, that it cover both international and national transport operations instead of national transport operations only, or vice versa.

(2) In subsection (1) of this section "restricted licence" and "standard licence" mean the same as in the Goods Vehicles (Operators' Licences, Qualifications and Fees) Regulations 1984.

(3) A person applying for the variation of an operator's licence under this section shall give to the licensing authority, in such form as he may require, such information as he may reasonably require for disposing of the application.

(4) Except in the cases mentioned in subsection (5) of this section, the licensing authority shall publish notice of any application for the variation of an operator's licence under this section in the manner prescribed for the publication of notices under section 63(1) of this Act.

(5) The excepted cases are—

 (a) where the application is for a direction under subsection (1)(a) of this section that additional motor vehicles be specified in a licence;

 (b) where the application is for a direction under subsection (1)(b), (d) or (f) of this section;

 (c) where the application is for a direction under subsection (1)(g) of this section that a place cease to be specified in a licence as an operating centre of the licence-holder;

 (d) where the application is for a direction under subsection (1)(j) of this section that a standard licence be converted into a restricted licence;

 (e) where the application is for a direction under subsection (1)(k) of this section that a licence cover national transport operations only instead of both international and national transport operations;

 (f) where the licensing authority is satisfied that the application is of so trivial a nature that it is not necessary that an opportunity should be given for objecting to it or making representations against it.

 (6) Where notice of an application is published under subsection (4) of this section, sections 63, 64 and 64A of this Act shall, with any necessary modifications and subject to section 69D of this Act, apply in relation to that application as they apply in relation to an application for an operator's licence of which notice is published under section 63(1) of this Act.

Interim variations

 68A.—(1) Where an applicant for the variation of an operator's licence under section 68 of this Act so requests, the licensing authority may, before he has determined the application, vary the licence by giving an interim direction in respect of it.

 (2) An interim direction is a direction under section 68(1) of this Act that is expressed to continue in force until it ceases to have effect under subsection (3) or (4) of this section.

 (3) If on determining the application the licensing authority varies the licence by giving a direction in the terms applied for (and does not also under section 64B(1) or (2) or 69C(1) or (3) of this Act attach or vary any conditions), the interim direction shall cease to have effect on the date on which the direction given on the application comes into force.

 (4) If subsection (3) of this section does not apply, the interim direction shall cease to have effect on the date on which the application is finally disposed of or such earlier date as the applicant may specify in a written request to the licensing authority.

 (5) In a case within subsection (4) of this section where on determining the application the licensing authority gives a direction varying the licence, that direction shall be of no effect before the interim direction ceases to have effect.

 (6) A request for an interim direction to be given shall not for the purposes of section 68(4) or 70 of, or Schedule 8A to, this Act be treated as an application for the variation of an operator's licence, but shall be treated as such an application for any other purposes of this Part of this Act."

(2) For section 69D of the 1968 Act there shall be substituted—

"Objection to, and refusal of, applications for variation of operators' licences on environmental grounds

 69D.—(1) This section applies where notice of an application for the variation of an operator's licence has been published under section 68(4) of this Act.

(2) Where the application relates to an existing operating centre of the licence-holder in the licensing authority's area—

(a) any of the persons mentioned in section 63(3) of this Act may object to the grant of the application on the ground that the use of that operating centre in any manner which would be permitted if the application were granted would cause adverse effects on environmental conditions in the vicinity of that centre;

(b) subject to subsection (5) of this section, any person who is the owner or occupier of any land in the vicinity of that operating centre may make representations on that ground against the grant of the application; and

(c) (whether or not anyone objects or makes representations under paragraph (a) or (b) of this subsection) the authority may refuse the application on that ground.

(3) For the purposes of subsection (2) of this section, an application shall be taken to relate to an operating centre if—

(a) granting it would or could result in an increase in the number of vehicles, or the number of vehicles above a certain weight, that have that centre as their operating centre; or

(b) any undertaking recorded in or condition attached to the licence that the application seeks to have varied or removed relates to that centre.

(4) Where the application is for a place in the licensing authority's area to be specified in the licence as an operating centre of the licence-holder—

(a) any of the persons mentioned in section 63(3) of this Act may object to the grant of the application on the ground that that place will be unsuitable on environmental grounds for use as an operating centre of the licence-holder; and

(b) subject to subsection (5) of this section, any person who is the owner or occupier of any land in the vicinity of that place may make representations against the grant of the application on that ground.

(5) A person may not make representations under subsection (2)(b) or (4)(b) of this section unless any adverse effects on environmental conditions arising from the use of the operating centre or place in question would be capable of prejudicially affecting the use or enjoyment of the land there mentioned.

(6) If any person duly objects or makes representations under subsection (4) of this section against an application for a place in the licensing authority's area to be specified in the licence as an operating centre of the licence-holder, the authority may refuse the application—

(a) on the ground that the parking of vehicles used under the licence at or in the vicinity of that place would cause adverse effects on environmental conditions in the vicinity of that place;

(b) subject to subsection (7) of this section, on the ground that that place would be unsuitable on environmental grounds other than the ground mentioned in paragraph (a) of this subsection for use as an operating centre of the licence-holder.

(7) The authority may not refuse the application on the ground mentioned in subsection (6)(b) of this section if—

(a) on the date the application was made, the place in question was already specified in an operator's licence granted by the authority as an operating centre of the holder of that licence; or

(b) the applicant has produced to the authority a certificate in force in respect of that place under section 191 or 192 of the Town and Country Planning Act 1990 or section 90 or 90A of the Town and

Country Planning (Scotland) Act 1972, stating that its use as an operating centre for vehicles used under any operator's licence is or would be lawful.

(8) Subsection (7) of this section does not apply in relation to any place that, at the time the application is determined by the licensing authority, is specified in an operator's licence as an operating centre of the holder of that licence.

(9) In paragraph (a) of subsection (7) of this section "operator's licence" does not include a licence granted under section 67A of this Act, and the reference in that paragraph to a place being specified in an operator's licence does not include a place being so specified—

(a) by virtue of an interim direction such as is mentioned in section 68A of this Act;

(b) if such conditions as may be prescribed in relation to the exercise of the right of any person to appeal against that place being so specified are not satisfied;

(c) if such conditions as may be prescribed in relation to the review under section 69J of this Act of the decision so to specify that place are not satisfied; or

(d) by reason of being situated within a place that is so specified."

<small>DEFINITIONS</small>
"the 1968 Act": s.41.

<small>GENERAL NOTE</small>
This section clarifies and combines the existing provisions for varying licences. It also clarifies the position as regards the duration of interim variations.

Revocation, suspension and curtailment of licences

48.—(1) Section 69 of the 1968 Act (revocation, suspension and curtailment of operators' licences) shall be amended as follows.

(2) For subsections (1) and (2) there shall be substituted—

"(1) Subject to the following provisions of this section, the licensing authority by whom an operator's licence was granted may direct that it be revoked, suspended or curtailed on any of the following grounds—

(a) that a place in the authority's area has, at a time when it was not specified in the licence as an operating centre of the licence-holder, been used as an operating centre for vehicles authorised to be used under the licence;

(b) that the licence-holder has contravened any condition attached to the licence;

(c) that during the five years ending with the date on which the direction is given there has been a conviction such as is mentioned in subsection (4)(a) to (ffff) of this section or a prohibition such as is mentioned in subsection (4)(h) of this section;

(d) that during those five years, on occasions appearing to the authority to be sufficiently numerous to justify the giving of a direction under this subsection, there has been a conviction such as is mentioned in subsection (4)(g) of this section;

(e) that the licence-holder made or procured to be made for the purposes of his application for the licence, an application for the variation of the licence or a request for a direction under paragraph 1 or 3 of Schedule 8A to this Act a statement of fact that (whether to his knowledge or not) was false or a statement of expectation that has not been fulfilled;

(f) that any undertaking recorded in the licence has not been fulfilled;

(g) that the licence-holder, being an individual, has been adjudged bankrupt, or, being a company, has gone into liquidation (other than voluntary liquidation for the purpose of reconstruction);

(h) that since the licence was granted or varied there has been a material change in any of the circumstances of the licence-holder that were relevant to the grant or variation of the licence;

(i) that the licence is liable to revocation, suspension or curtailment by virtue of a direction under subsection (6) of this section.

(2) Where the licensing authority has power to give a direction in respect of a licence under subsection (1) of this section, the authority also has power to direct that a condition, or additional condition, such as is mentioned in section 66 of this Act be attached to the licence.

(2A) In this Part of this Act any reference, in relation to an operator's licence, to a condition attached to the licence under section 66 of this Act includes any condition that was attached to the licence under subsection (2) of this section."

(3) For subsection (5) there shall be substituted—

"(5) Where the licensing authority directs that an operator's licence be revoked, the authority may order the person who was the holder of the licence to be disqualified, indefinitely or for such period as the authority thinks fit, from holding or obtaining an operator's licence, and so long as the disqualification is in force—

(a) any operator's licence held by him at the date of the making of the order (other than the licence revoked) shall be suspended; and

(b) notwithstanding anything in section 64 or 67A of this Act, no operator's licence may be granted to him.

(5A) If a person applies for or obtains an operator's licence while he is disqualified under subsection (5) of this section—

(a) he shall be liable on summary conviction to a fine not exceeding level 4 on the standard scale; and

(b) any operator's licence granted to him on the application or (as the case may be) the operator's licence obtained by him shall be void.

(5B) An order under subsection (5) of this section may be limited so as to apply only to the holding or obtaining of an operator's licence in respect of the area of one or more specified licensing authorities and, if the order is so limited—

(a) paragraphs (a) and (b) of that subsection and subsection (5A) of this section shall apply only to any operator's licence to which the order applies; but

(b) notwithstanding section 61(2)(b) of this Act, no other operator's licence held by the person in question shall authorise the use by him of any vehicle at a time when its operating centre is in an area in respect of which he is disqualified by virtue of the order."

(4) At the end of subsection (7) there shall be added "; and any reference below in this section to subsection (5) or to subsection (6) includes that subsection as it applies by virtue of this subsection."

(5) For subsection (8) there shall be substituted—

"(8) The licensing authority by whom any direction suspending or curtailing a licence under subsection (1) of this section was given may at any time—

(a) cancel the direction together with any order under subsection (7A) of this section that was made when the direction was given;

(b) cancel any such order; or

(c) with the consent of the licence-holder, vary the direction or any such order (or both the direction and any such order).

(8A) The licensing authority by whom any order disqualifying a person was made under subsection (5) of this section may at any time—

(a) cancel that order together with any direction that was given under subsection (6) of this section when the order was made;

(b) cancel any such direction; or

(c) with the consent of the person disqualified, vary the order or any such direction (or both the order and any such direction)."

DEFINITIONS
"the 1968 Act": s.41.

GENERAL NOTE
This section clarifies and combines the existing provisions for the revocation, suspension or curtailment of licences, inserts a new ground consequential on other provisions in this Part of the Act, and enables suspensions, curtailments and other disciplinary decisions to be varied or cancelled by the licensing authority.

Publication of applications

49. For section 69E of the 1968 Act there shall be substituted—

"Publication of notice of application for licences and variations in localities affected

69E.—(1) Subject to subsection (4) of this section, the licensing authority to whom—

(a) any application for an operator's licence; or

(b) any application for a direction such as is mentioned in subsection (2) of this section,

is made shall refuse the application without considering its merits, unless he is satisfied that subsection (3) of this section has been complied with in respect of each locality affected by the application.

(2) The directions referred to in subsection (1)(b) of this section are—

(a) any direction under section 68(1)(a) of this Act that a maximum number specified in a licence under section 61A of this Act be increased;

(b) any direction under section 68(1)(c) or (e) of this Act;

(c) any direction under section 68(1)(g) of this Act that a new place be specified in a licence as an operating centre of the licence-holder; and

(d) any direction under section 68(1)(h) or (i) of this Act which might result in a material change in the use of any operating centre of the licence-holder in the licensing authority's area.

(3) This subsection has been complied with in respect of a locality affected by an application if, within the period beginning twenty-one days before the date on which the application is made and ending twenty-one days after that date, notice of the application in such form and containing such information as may be prescribed has been published in one or more local newspapers circulating in the locality.

(4) The licensing authority is not required by this section to refuse an application if—

(a) he is satisfied as mentioned in subsection (1) of this section, save only that the form or contents of the notice of application as published in any newspaper did not comply with the prescribed requirements; and

(b) he is satisfied that no person's interests are likely to have been prejudiced by the failure to comply with those requirements.

(5) For the purposes of this section a locality is affected by an application for, or for the variation of, an operator's licence if—

(a) it contains any place in the area of the licensing authority that will be an operating centre of the licence-holder if the application is granted; or

   (b) (in the case of an application for variation) it contains an existing operating centre of the licence-holder in the area of the authority and—

      (i) the granting of the application would or could result in an increase in the number of vehicles, or the number of vehicles above a certain weight, that have that centre as their operating centre; or

      (ii) any undertaking recorded in or condition attached to the licence that the application seeks to have varied or removed relates to that centre."

DEFINITIONS
  "the 1968 Act": s.41.

GENERAL NOTE
  This section sets out the circumstances in which an application for an operator's licence or for the variation of an operator's licence must be advertised in a newspaper.

Review and transfer of operating centres

50.—(1) After section 69E of the 1968 Act there shall be inserted—

"Further provisions about operating centres

Periods of review for operating centres

69EA.—(1) Within such time after any period of review as may be prescribed, the licensing authority by whom an operator's licence was granted may serve a notice on the licence-holder stating that the authority is considering whether to exercise any of his powers under sections 69EB and 69EC of this Act in relation to a place specified in the licence as an operating centre of the licence-holder.

(2) The periods of review in relation to an operator's licence are—

  (a) the period of five years beginning with the date specified in the licence as the date on which it came into force; and

  (b) each consecutive period of five years.

(3) Regulations may amend subsection (2) of this section by substituting a higher or lower number (but not a number lower than five) for the number of years currently mentioned in paragraphs (a) and (b).

(4) Regulations may make provision as to the manner in which notices under this section are to be or may be served, including provision as to the circumstances in which and time at which any such notice is to be treated as having been duly served (whether or not it has in fact been served).

Power to remove operating centres on review

69EB.—(1) If, having served notice under section 69EA of this Act in respect of a place specified in an operator's licence, the licensing authority determines that the place is unsuitable—

  (a) on grounds other than environmental grounds; or

  (b) on the ground mentioned in subsection (2) of this section,

for use as an operating centre of the licence-holder, he may (subject to subsection (3) of this section) direct that it cease to be specified in the licence.

(2) The ground referred to in subsection (1)(b) of this section is that the parking of vehicles used under the licence at or in the vicinity of the place causes adverse effects on environmental conditions in that vicinity.

(3) Where the only ground for giving a direction under subsection (1) of this section is the ground mentioned in subsection (2) of this section,

the authority may not give such a direction unless during the period of review in question representations were made to him—

    (a) by a person such as is mentioned in section 63(3) of this Act; or

    (b) by a person who is the owner or occupier of any land in the vicinity of the place in question,

as to the place's unsuitability on environmental grounds for continued use as an operating centre for vehicles used under any operator's licence.

(4) Representations made by a person such as is mentioned in subsection (3)(b) of this section shall be disregarded for the purposes of this section if, when they were made, any adverse effects on environmental conditions arising from the continued use of the place in question would not have been capable of prejudicially affecting the use or enjoyment of the land mentioned in subsection (3)(b).

Powers to attach conditions etc. on review

69EC.—(1) If, having served notice under section 69EA of this Act in respect of a place specified in an operator's licence, the licensing authority does not give a direction in respect of the place under section 69EB of this Act, he may direct—

    (a) that conditions (or additional conditions) such as are mentioned in section 64B, 66(1)(c) or 69C of this Act be attached to the licence;

    (b) that any conditions already attached to the licence under section 64B, 66(1)(c) or 69C be varied.

(2) Any conditions attached to the licence under subsection (1)(a) of this section shall relate (or in the case of conditions such as are mentioned in section 66(1)(c) of this Act, only require the authority to be informed of events that relate) only to the place referred to in subsection (1) of this section (or only to that place and any other places in respect of which the authority has power to attach conditions under that subsection).

(3) Any variation under subsection (1)(b) of this section shall be such as imposes new or further restrictions or requirements in relation to that place, and only that place (or only that place and any other such places).

(4) Where the licensing authority gives a direction in respect of an operator's licence under section 69EB of this Act or subsection (1)(a) of this section, he may also vary the licence by directing—

    (a) that any vehicle cease to be specified in the licence;

    (b) that any maximum number specified in the licence under section 61A of this Act be reduced;

    (c) that a provision such as is mentioned in section 61(1A) of this Act be included in the licence;

    (d) that a provision such as is mentioned in section 61A(1)(b) or (2)(b) of this Act be included in the licence.

(5) In this Part of this Act any reference, in relation to an operator's licence, to a condition attached to the licence under section 64B, 66, or 69C of this Act includes any condition such as is mentioned in section 64B, 66 or (as the case may be) 69C that was attached to the licence under subsection (1)(a) of this section.

Transfer of operating centres

69ED. Schedule 8A to this Act (which makes provision in relation to certain applications for, or for the variation of, operators' licences where the proposed operating centres of the applicant are already specified in an operator's licence) shall have effect."

(2) After Schedule 8 to the 1968 Act there shall be inserted the Schedule set out in Schedule 12 to this Act.

<small>DEFINITIONS</small>
"the 1968 Act": s.41.

<small>GENERAL NOTE</small>
This section and Sched. 12 make provision consequent on the introduction of the continuous licensing system. This section provides for operating centres to be reviewed at five yearly intervals. On a review conditions may be imposed for environmental or road safety reasons, and in certain circumstances an operating centre may be removed from an operator's licence. Sched. 12 introduces a simplified procedure for licence applications where an operating centre to be included in the licence is already specified in another licence.

Assessors

51. After section 69H of the 1968 Act (set out in Schedule 13 to this Act) there shall be inserted—

"Operators' licences: supplementary provisions

Assessors
69I.—(1) In considering any financial question which appears to him to arise in relation to the exercise of his functions under this Part of this Act or the Goods Vehicles (Operators' Licences, Qualifications and Fees) Regulations 1984, the licensing authority may be assisted by an assessor drawn from a panel of persons appointed for that purpose by the Secretary of State.

(2) The Secretary of State shall pay to any such assessor in respect of his services such remuneration as may be determined by the Secretary of State with the consent of the Treasury."

<small>DEFINITIONS</small>
"the 1968 Act": s.41.

<small>GENERAL NOTE</small>
This section empowers a licensing authority to appoint a financial assessor to assist it in considering financial questions.

Review of decisions

52. After section 69I of the 1968 Act (set out in section 51 above) there shall be inserted—

"Review of decisions
69J.—(1) Subject to subsection (2) of this section, the licensing authority may review and, if he thinks fit, vary or revoke any decision of his to grant or refuse—
 (a) an application for an operator's licence; or
 (b) an application for the variation of such a licence in a case where section 68(4) of this Act required notice of the application to be published,
if he is satisfied that a procedural requirement imposed by or under any enactment has not been complied with in relation to the decision.

(2) The licensing authority may only review a decision under subsection (1) of this section—
 (a) if, within such period after taking the decision as may be prescribed, he has given notice to the applicant or (as the case may be) the licence-holder that he intends to review the decision;
 (b) if, within that period, a person who appears to him to have an interest in the decision has requested him to review it; or
 (c) where neither paragraph (a) nor paragraph (b) of this subsection applies, if he considers there to be exceptional circumstances that justify the review.

(3) Regulations may make provision as to the manner in which notices under subsection (2)(a) of this section are to be or may be served, including provision as to the circumstances in which and time at which any such notice is to be treated as having been duly served (whether or not it has in fact been served).

(4) The variation or revocation of a decision under this section shall not make unlawful anything done in reliance on the decision before the variation or revocation takes effect."

DEFINITIONS
"the 1968 Act": s.41.

GENERAL NOTE
This section empowers a licensing authority to review decisions where there has been a procedural irregularity and to correct errors in documents.

Appeals

53. For section 70 of the 1968 Act there shall be substituted—

"Rights of appeal in connection with operators' licences

70.—(1) In the following provisions of this section "appeal" means appeal to the Transport Tribunal.

(2) An applicant for, or for the variation of, an operator's licence may appeal against the refusal of the application or (as the case may be) against the terms of the licence or of the variation.

(3) The holder of an operator's licence may appeal against any direction given under section 61(6), 69(1) or (2), 69EB or 69EC of this Act in respect of the licence.

(4) The holder of an operator's licence may appeal against any order made under section 69(7A) of this Act on the suspension or curtailment of the licence.

(5) A person in respect of whom an order has been made under section 69(5) of this Act (including section 69(5) as it applies by virtue of section 69(7) of this Act) may appeal against that order and against any direction given under section 69(6) of this Act (including section 69(6) as it so applies) when the order was made.

(6) A person who has duly made an objection to an application for, or for the variation of, an operator's licence may appeal against the grant of the application.

(7) A person who—
(a) within the prescribed period has made an application for a review under section 69J of this Act; and
(b) has been certified by the licensing authority as a person such as is mentioned in subsection (2)(b) of that section,
may appeal against the refusal of the application.

(8) In subsections (2) and (3) of this section "operator's licence" does not include a licence granted under section 67A of this Act."

DEFINITIONS
"the 1968 Act": s.41.

GENERAL NOTE
This section restates and extends the rights of appeal in connection with operators' licences.

Partnerships

54. After section 85 of the 1968 Act there shall be inserted—

"Partnerships
85A. Regulations may provide for this Part of this Act to apply in relation to partnerships with such modifications as may be specified in the regulations."

DEFINITIONS
"the 1968 Act": s.41.

GENERAL NOTE
This section makes provision for the operator licensing provisions to be modified in their application to partnerships.

Operators' licences not to be transferable etc.

55. For section 86 of the 1968 Act there shall be substituted—

"Operators' licences not to be transferable etc.
86.—(1) Subject to any regulations under section 85 of this Act, an operator's licence is not transferable or assignable.

(2) Regulations may make provision enabling the licensing authority, where the holder of an operator's licence granted by him has died or become a patient within the meaning of Part VII of the Mental Health Act 1983, to direct that the licence be treated—

(a) as not having terminated at the time the licence-holder died or became such a patient but as having been suspended (that is, as having remained in force subject to the limitation that no vehicles were authorised to be used under it) from that time until the time the direction comes into force; and

(b) as having effect from the time the direction comes into force for a specified period and as being held during that period (for such purposes and to such extent as may be specified) not by the person to whom it was granted but by such other person carrying on that person's business, or part of that person's business, as may be specified.

(3) Regulations may make provision enabling the licensing authority in prescribed circumstances to direct that any operator's licence granted by him be treated (for such purposes, for such period and to such extent as may be specified) as held not by the person to whom it was granted but by such other person carrying on that person's business, or part of that person's business, as may be specified.

(4) Regulations may make provision enabling the licensing authority to direct, for the purpose of giving effect to or supplementing a direction given by him by virtue of subsection (2) or (3) of this section, that this Part of this Act apply with specified modifications in relation to the person who is to be treated under the direction as the holder of an operator's licence.

(5) In this section "specified", in relation to a direction, means specified—

(a) in the regulations under which the direction was given; or

(b) in the direction in accordance with those regulations."

DEFINITIONS
"the 1968 Act": s.41.

GENERAL NOTE
This section makes provision for allowing a person operating goods vehicles to do so under a licence that would otherwise have terminated on the death, incapacity, bankruptcy or liquidation of the licence-holder.

Fees

56. For section 89 of the 1968 Act there shall be substituted—

"Fees

89.—(1) Such fees, payable at such times, and whether in one sum or by instalments, as may be prescribed shall be charged by the licensing authority in respect of—

(a) applications for or for the variation of operators' licences;
(b) the issue or variation of operators' licences;
(c) the continuation in force of operators' licences;
(d) any arrangements made with the holder of an operator's licence to treat the licence for certain administrative purposes as if it were two or more licences.

(2) The licensing authority may decline to proceed with—

(a) any application for or for the variation of an operator's licence; or
(b) the issue or variation of any operator's licence,

until any fee or instalment of a fee in respect of the applications issue or variation (as the case may be) is duly paid.

(3) If, in the case of any application for or for the variation of an operator's licence, any fee or instalment of a fee in respect of the application or the issue or variation of the licence is not duly paid by the prescribed time—

(a) the application shall be treated as withdrawn at that time; and
(b) any decision made or direction given on the application, and any licence issued or variation effected in pursuance of such a decision or direction, ceases to have effect or terminates at that time.

(4) If any fee or instalment of a fee in respect of the continuation in force of an operator's licence is not duly paid by the prescribed time, the licence terminates at that time.

(5) The licensing authority may, if he considers there to be exceptional circumstances that justify his doing so, in any case where subsection (3) or (4) of this section has applied, direct that as from the time mentioned in that subsection its effect in that case be disregarded.

(6) Where, by virtue of such a direction, the effect of subsection (3)(a) of this section is to be disregarded in any case, any termination—

(a) of a licence under section 67A(4)(b) or (5) of this Act; or
(b) of a direction under section 68A(4) of this Act,

by virtue of the operation of subsection (3)(a) in that case before the direction was given shall be cancelled with effect from the same time.

(7) Where such a direction is given in respect of an operator's licence—

(a) any condition attached to the licence under section 66 of this Act shall be treated as having been of no effect during the period beginning with the time the licence terminated by virtue of subsection (3) or (4) of this section and ending with the time the direction comes into force; and
(b) subject to paragraph (a) of this subsection, the licensing authority may vary any such condition as it applies in relation to events occurring before the direction comes into force.

(8) All fees payable under this Part of this Act shall be paid into the Consolidated Fund in such manner as the Treasury may direct."

DEFINITIONS
"the 1968 Act": s.41.

GENERAL NOTE
This section provides for a revised fee system consequent upon the introduction of continuous licences. In particular it introduces a charge for processing an application and a charge for the

continuation in force of a licence. It also permits a licensing authority to decline to proceed with an application and provides for a continuous licence to lapse if fees have not been paid.

Chapter III: minor and consequential amendments

57.—(1) The 1968 Act shall have effect with the further amendments set out in Part I of Schedule 13 to this Act.

(2) The enactments mentioned in Part II of that Schedule shall have effect with the amendments set out in that Part.

DEFINITIONS
   "the 1968 Act": s.41.

GENERAL NOTE
   This section and Sched. 13 make minor and consequential amendments.

CHAPTER IV

PUBLIC SERVICE VEHICLE OPERATOR LICENSING ETC.

The 1981 Act

58. In this Chapter "the 1981 Act" means the Public Passenger Vehicles Act 1981.

Undertakings given on applications

59.—(1) The 1981 Act shall be amended as follows.

(2) After section 14(3) (which provides that an application for a PSV operator's licence shall not be granted unless there will be adequate facilities or arrangements for maintaining the vehicles proposed to be used under the licence etc.) there shall be inserted—

   "(3A) In considering on an application for a PSV operator's licence whether the requirements mentioned in subsection (3) above are satisfied, the traffic commissioner may take into account any undertakings given by the applicant (or procured by him to be given) for the purposes of the application and may assume that those undertakings will be fulfilled."

(3) After section 14(4) there shall be inserted—

   "(5) In any case where the traffic commissioner grants an application for a PSV operator's licence, any undertakings taken into account by him under subsection (3A) above that he considers to be material to the granting of the application shall be recorded in the licence issued to the applicant."

(4) In section 16(6) (which provides that, on the application of the holder of a PSV operator's licence, a traffic commissioner may vary or remove conditions attached to the licence) after paragraph (b) there shall be inserted—

   "or
   (c) vary or remove any undertaking recorded in the licence;".

(5) After section 16(6) there shall be inserted—

   "(6A) In considering whether to grant an application under subsection (6) above, the traffic commissioner may take into account any undertakings given by the applicant (or procured by him to be given) for the purposes of the application, and may assume that those undertakings will be fulfilled.

   (6B) In any case where the traffic commissioner grants an application under subsection (6) above, any undertakings taken into account by him under subsection (6A) above that he considers to be material to the granting of the application shall be recorded in the licence as varied."

(6) In section 17(3) (which sets out the grounds on which a licence may be revoked, suspended or varied under section 17(2)) after paragraph (a) there shall be inserted—
> "(aa) that any undertaking recorded in the licence has not been fulfilled;".

DEFINITIONS
"the 1981 Act": s.58.

GENERAL NOTE
This section provides for the recording in a Public Service Vehicle operator's licence of any material undertakings given by the applicant for the licence.

Objections to applications for licences

60. After section 14A(2) of the 1981 Act (which requires objections to applications for PSV operators' licences to be made within the prescribed time and in the prescribed manner) there shall be inserted—
> "(2A) Where the traffic commissioner considers there to be exceptional circumstances that justify his doing so, he may direct that an objection be treated for the purposes of this Part of this Act as duly made under this section, notwithstanding that it was not made within the prescribed time or in the prescribed manner."

DEFINITIONS
"the 1981 Act": s.58.

GENERAL NOTE
This section provides for objections to applications for licences to be accepted by the traffic commissioner in exceptional circumstances as having been duly made notwithstanding that they were not.

Duration of licences

61. In section 15 of the 1981 Act (duration of licences) for the words from "and the date on which it is to expire" to the end there shall be substituted—
> "(2) Subject to its revocation or other termination under any provision of this Act or another statutory provision, a PSV operator's licence shall continue in force indefinitely.
> (3) If the holder of a PSV operator's licence requests the traffic commissioner by whom it was granted to terminate it at any time, the commissioner shall, subject to subsection (4) below, comply with the request.
> (4) The traffic commissioner may refuse to comply with the request if he is considering taking action in respect of the licence under section 17(1) or (2) of this Act."

DEFINITIONS
"the 1981 Act": s.58.

GENERAL NOTE
This section provides for licences to continue in force indefinitely unless revoked or otherwise terminated.

Suspension of licences

62.—(1) Section 17 of the 1981 Act (revocation, suspension etc. of licences) shall be amended as follows.

(2) In subsection (2)(b) (traffic commissioner's power to suspend a licence for such period as he directs) the words "(during which time it shall be of no effect)" shall be omitted.

(3) After subsection (5) there shall be inserted—

"(5A) Where a licence is suspended under this section, it remains in force during the time of its suspension subject to the limitation that no vehicles are authorised to be used under it.

(5B) A traffic commissioner who has suspended a licence under this section may at any time—

(a) cancel the suspension; or

(b) with the consent of the holder of the licence, vary the period for which it is suspended."

DEFINITIONS
"the 1981 Act": s.58.

GENERAL NOTE

This section enables the traffic commissioner to cancel a suspension or to vary the period of suspension of an operator's licence.

Operators' discs

63.—(1) Section 18 of the 1981 Act (duty to exhibit operator's disc) shall be amended as follows.

(2) For subsection (2) (which requires the holder of a PSV operator's licence to be supplied with a number of operators' discs equal to the maximum number of vehicles that he may use under the licence) there shall be substituted—

"(2) A traffic commissioner on granting a PSV operator's licence shall supply the person to whom the licence is granted—

(a) with a number of operators' discs equal to the maximum number of vehicles that he may use under the licence in accordance with the condition or conditions attached to the licence under section 16(1) of this Act; or

(b) with such lesser number of operators' discs as he may request.

(2A) Where, in the case of any PSV operator's licence, the maximum number referred to in subsection (2)(a) above is increased on the variation of one or more of the conditions there referred to, the traffic commissioner on making the variation shall supply the holder of the licence—

(a) with such number of additional operators' discs as will bring the total number of operators' discs held by him in respect of the licence to that maximum number, or

(b) with such lesser number of additional operators' discs as he may request.

(2B) Where the number of operators' discs currently held in respect of a PSV operator's licence is less than the maximum number referred to in subsection (2)(a) above, the traffic commissioner by whom the licence was granted shall on the application of the holder of the licence supply him with such number of additional operators' discs as is mentioned in subsection (2A)(a) or (b) above.

(2C) Where, in accordance with regulations under subsection (3)(aa) below, all the operators' discs held in respect of a PSV operator's licence expire at the same time, the traffic commissioner by whom the licence was granted shall supply the holder of the licence with a number of new operators' discs equal to the number of discs that have expired."

(3) In subsection (3) (provision that may be made by regulations)—

(a) after paragraph (a) there shall be inserted—

"(aa) as to the expiry of operators' discs;", and

(b) at the end there shall be added—

"(e) for the voluntary return of operators' discs by the holder of a PSV operator's licence."

DEFINITIONS
  "the 1981 Act": s.58.

GENERAL NOTE
  This section allows operators, if they so wish, to be supplied with a lesser number of discs than the maximum number of vehicles they may use under the licence and makes provision for the voluntary return of discs.

Repeal of section 27 of the 1981 Act

64. Section 27 of the 1981 Act (returns to be provided by persons operating public service vehicles) shall cease to have effect.

DEFINITIONS
  "the 1981 Act": s.58.

GENERAL NOTE
  This section repeals s.27 of the Public Passenger Vehicles Act 1981 (c. 14) (returns to be provided by persons operating public service vehicles). Statistical returns are now provided for under the Statistics of Trade Act 1947 (c. 39).

Review of decisions and correction of errors

65.—(1) After section 49 of the 1981 Act there shall be inserted—

"**Review of decisions**
  49A.—(1) Subject to subsection (2) below, a traffic commissioner may review and, if he thinks fit, vary or revoke any decision of his—
  (a) to grant or refuse an application for a PSV operator's licence; or
  (b) to grant or refuse an application for the variation of a PSV operator's licence,
if he is satisfied that a procedural requirement imposed by or under this Act has not been complied with in relation to the decision.
  (2) A traffic commissioner may only review a decision under subsection (1) above—
  (a) if, within such period after taking the decision as may be prescribed, he has given notice to the applicant or (as the case may be) the licence holder that he intends to review the decision;
  (b) if, within that period, a person who appears to him to have an interest in the decision has requested him to review it; or
  (c) where neither paragraph (a) nor paragraph (b) above applies, if he considers there to be exceptional circumstances that justify the review.
  (3) Regulations may make provision as to the manner in which notices under subsection (2)(a) above are to be or may be served, including provision as to the circumstances in which and time at which any such notice is to be treated as having been duly served (whether or not it has in fact been served).
  (4) The variation or revocation of a decision under this section shall not make unlawful anything done in reliance on the decision before the variation or revocation takes effect."
  (2) In section 50 of the 1981 Act (appeals to the Transport Tribunal) after subsection (4) there shall be inserted—
  "(4A) A person who—
  (a) within the prescribed period has made an application for a review under section 49A of this Act; and
  (b) has been certified by the traffic commissioner as a person such as is mentioned in subsection (2)(b) of that section,
  may appeal to the Transport Tribunal against the refusal of the application."
  (3) After section 56 of the 1981 Act there shall be inserted—

"Correction of errors

56A. Where it appears to the traffic commissioner for a traffic area that a document purporting to record, or issued in consequence of, a decision taken in the exercise of his functions contains a clerical error, he may issue a corrected document or a notice in writing that the document is to have effect with such corrections as are stated in the notice."

DEFINITIONS

"the 1981 Act": s.58.

GENERAL NOTE

This section empowers a traffic commissioner to review decisions in respect of the grant or variation of a Public Service Vehicle operator's licence where there has been a procedural error. It also empowers a traffic commissioner to correct clerical errors in documents issued in the exercise of his functions.

Fees

66.—(1) The 1981 Act shall be amended as follows.

(2) In section 52(1)(a) (which sets out matters in respect of which the traffic commissioner for an area is to charge fees) after sub-paragraph (i) there shall be inserted—

> "(ia) applications under section 16(6) of this Act and the grant of such applications;
>
> (ib) the continuation in force of PSV operators' licences;".

(3) For section 52(2)(b) there shall be substituted—

> "(b) the grant of any PSV operator's licence or of any application under section 16(6) of this Act;
>
> (bb) the issue of any certificate, disc or other document referred to in subsection (1) above; or".

(4) After section 52(2) there shall be inserted—

> "(2A) If, in the case of any application for a PSV operator's licence, any fee or instalment of a fee in respect of the application, the grant of the licence or the issue of operators' discs under section 18(2) of this Act is not duly paid by the prescribed time—
>
> (a) the application shall be treated as withdrawn at that time;
>
> (b) any decision made on the application ceases to have effect at that time; and
>
> (c) any licence granted in pursuance of such a decision terminates at that time.
>
> (2B) If, in the case of any application under section 16(6) of this Act, any fee or instalment of a fee in respect of the application, the grant of the application or the issue of operators' discs under section 18(2A) of this Act is not duly paid by the prescribed time—
>
> (a) the application shall be treated as withdrawn at that time;
>
> (b) any decision made on the application, and any variation effected in pursuance of such a decision, ceases to have effect at that time.
>
> (2C) If, in the case of any PSV operator's licence, any fee or instalment of a fee in respect of—
>
> (a) the continuation in force of the licence; or
>
> (b) the issue of operators' discs under section 18(2C) of this Act,
>
> is not duly paid by the prescribed time, the licence terminates at that time.
>
> (2D) If any fee or instalment of a fee in respect of any operators' discs that have been issued under section 18 of this Act is not duly paid by the prescribed time, the discs cease to have effect at that time.
>
> (2E) The traffic commissioner by whom a PSV operator's licence was granted may, if he considers there to be exceptional circumstances that

justify his doing so in any case where subsection (2A), (2B), (2C) or (2D) above has applied, direct that as from the time mentioned in that subsection its effect in that case be disregarded.

(2F) Where the traffic commissioner has given a direction under subsection (2E) above in respect of a PSV operator's licence in a case where subsection (2A) or (2C) above has applied, it shall not for the purposes of section 20(1) or (2) of this Act be regarded as having been practicable for the licence-holder to—

(a) report any matter to the Secretary of State; or

(b) give him notice of any alteration,

during the period beginning with the time mentioned in subsection (2A) or (2C) and ending when the direction came into force."

(5) In section 60 (general power to make regulations for purposes of Act) for subsection (1)(e) there shall be substituted—

"(e) the fees to be payable under this Act, the persons liable to pay them, and the repayment (or partial repayment), in prescribed circumstances, of fees paid under this Act;".

DEFINITIONS
"the 1981 Act": s.58.

GENERAL NOTE
This section introduces a charge for the continuation in force of a continuous licence, and provides for a continuous licence to terminate if fees have not been paid. It also extends the power to make regulations for the repayment of fees.

Disqualification of PSV operators

67.—(1) Section 28 of the Transport Act 1985 (power to disqualify PSV operators) shall be amended as follows.

(2) In subsection (2) (so long as a person is disqualified, no licence shall be granted to him and any obtained by him shall be of no effect) for the words from "no PSV" to the end there shall be substituted—

"(a) any PSV operator's licence held by him at the date of the making of the order under subsection (1) above (other than the licence revoked) shall be suspended (that is, shall remain in force subject to the limitation that no vehicles are authorised to be used under it); and

(b) notwithstanding section 14(4) of the 1981 Act, no PSV operator's licence may be granted to him."

(3) After subsection (2) there shall be inserted—

"(2A) If a person obtains a PSV operator's licence while he is disqualified under subsection (1) above, the licence shall be void."

(4) At the end of subsection (5) (the traffic commissioner may exercise his powers under section 28 in relation to officers of corporate licence-holders and partners of licence-holders) there shall be added—

"and any reference in subsection (6A) below to subsection (1) above or to subsection (4) above includes that subsection as it applies by virtue of this subsection."

(5) After subsection (6) there shall be inserted—

"(6A) The traffic commissioner by whom any order disqualifying a person was made under subsection (1) above may at any time—

(a) cancel that order together with any direction that was given under subsection (4) above when the order was made;

(b) cancel any such direction; or

(c) with the consent of the person disqualified, vary the order or any such direction (or both the order and any such direction)."

DEFINITIONS
"the 1981 Act": s.58.

GENERAL NOTE

This section enables the traffic commissioner to vary or cancel an order disqualifying an operator from holding a licence.

Chapter IV: minor and consequential amendments

68. The 1981 Act and the Transport Act 1985 shall have effect with the further amendments set out in Schedule 14 to this Act.

DEFINITIONS

"the 1981 Act": s.58.

GENERAL NOTE

This section and Sched. 14 make minor and consequential amendments.

PART II

CONTRACTING OUT

Contracting out of functions

Functions of Ministers and office-holders

69.—(1) This section applies to any function of a Minister or office-holder—

(a) which is conferred by or under any enactment; and

(b) which, by virtue of any enactment or rule of law, may be exercised by an officer of his; and

(c) which is not excluded by section 71 below.

(2) If a Minister by order so provides, a function to which this section applies may be exercised by, or by employees of, such person (if any) as may be authorised in that behalf by the office-holder or Minister whose function it is.

(3) A Minister shall not make an order under this section in relation to an office-holder without first consulting him.

(4) An order under this section may provide that a function to which this section applies may be exercised, and an authorisation given by virtue of such an order may (subject to the provisions of the order) authorise the exercise of such a function—

(a) either wholly or to such extent as may be specified in the order or authorisation;

(b) either generally or in such cases or areas as may be so specified; and

(c) either unconditionally or subject to the fulfilment of such conditions as may be so specified.

(5) An authorisation given by virtue of an order under this section—

(a) shall be for such period, not exceeding 10 years, as is specified in the authorisation;

(b) may be revoked at any time by the Minister or office-holder by whom the authorisation is given; and

(c) shall not prevent that Minister or office-holder or any other person from exercising the function to which the authorisation relates.

DEFINITIONS

"employees": s.79(1).

"enactment": s.79(1).

"Minister": s.79(1)(3)(4).

"office-holder": s.79(1).

"officer": s.79(1).

   This section empowers a Minister to make an order specifying which functions of Ministers and office-holders may be contracted out. The functions that may be specified are defined in subs. (1). To mark the constitutional separation of Parliament and the Executive, the functions of office-holders such as the Comptroller and Auditor General are excluded. This was done by an amendment to s.79 which excludes from the definition of "office-holder" the officers of either House of Parliament, the Parliamentary Commissioner for Administration and the Health Service Commissioners. The courts are also excluded, again on grounds of constitutional principle (s.71(1)(a)). The effect of an order is to authorise a Minister or office-holder to contract out a specified function but not to compel him to do so. A function of an office-holder cannot be contracted out, therefore, without an order being made and without the office-holder authorising the contractor to carry out the function. Before making an order specifying the functions of an office-holder, the Minister must first consult him. An order under this section is made by statutory instrument subject to affirmative resolution procedure.

Subs. (1)
   Para. (a): i.e. statutory functions, in contrast to those functions which involve the exercise of prerogative powers.
   Para. (b): in contrast to those functions which must be exercised by the Minister or office-holder personally.

Subs. (2)
   The contracting out of an office-holder's functions is a matter for the discretion of the office-holder: "we shall ensure that office holders … cannot be compelled to contract out by the making of an order as it will be for them and them alone to give authority to any contractor appointed to carry out their functions, and that they could refuse to do" (*Hansard*, H.C. Vol. 237, col. 254).

Functions of local authorities

   70.—(1) This section applies to any function of a local authority—
   (a) which is conferred by or under any enactment; and
   (b) which, by virtue of section 101 of the Local Government Act 1972 or section 56 of the Local Government (Scotland) Act 1973 (arrangements for discharge of functions by local authorities), may be exercised by an officer of the authority; and
   (c) which is not excluded by section 71 below.
   (2) If a Minister by order so provides, a function to which this section applies may be exercised by, or by employees of, such person (if any) as may be authorised in that behalf by the local authority whose function it is.
   (3) A Minister shall not make an order under this section in relation to a local authority without first consulting—
   (a) in the case of an authority in England or Wales, such representatives of local government;
   (b) in the case of an authority in Scotland, such associations of local authorities,
as he considers appropriate.
   (4) Subsections (4) and (5) of section 69 above shall apply for the purposes of this section as they apply for the purposes of that section; and in subsection (5) of that section as so applied any reference to the Minister or office-holder by whom the authorisation is given shall be construed as a reference to the local authority by which the authorisation is given.
   (5) Where at any time—
   (a) an order is in force under this section in relation to any function of a local authority ("authority A"); and
   (b) arrangements are in force under section 101 of the Local Government Act 1972 or section 56 of the Local Government (Scotland) Act 1973 for the exercise of that function by another local authority ("authority B"),
it shall be an implied term of those arrangements that, except with the consent of authority A, authority B shall not give any authorisation by virtue of the order in relation to that function.

DEFINITIONS
"enactment": s.79(1).
"function": s.79(1).
"local authority": s.79(1)(2)(3)(b).
"Minister": s.79(1).
"office-holder": s.79(1).
"officer": s.79(1).

GENERAL NOTE
This section empowers a Minister to make an order specifying those local authority functions which may be contracted out. Again, a local authority will be enabled to contract out but not compelled to do so. The order-making power is subject to the same safeguards as those contained in the equivalent provision in respect of the functions of Ministers and office-holders. An order may be laid only after consultation with representatives of local authorities. An order under this section is made by statutory instrument subject to affirmative resolution procedure.

Planning and licensing functions come within the scope of the order-making power, but there are no plans at present to contract out those functions: "the only functions of which I am aware that have been designated as suitable for the use of the power are local revenue collection and investment management". (Standing Committee F, col. 1017, April 19, 1994).

Subs. (1)
Para. (b): in contrast to those functions that must be exercised by members of the authority itself.

Subs. (2)
It is for the local authority to authorise a contractor to exercise a function which is the subject of a contracting out order.

Functions excluded from sections 69 and 70

71.—(1) Subject to subsections (2) and (3) below, a function is excluded from sections 69 and 70 above if—
   (a) its exercise would constitute the exercise of jurisdiction of any court or of any tribunal which exercises the judicial power of the State; or
   (b) its exercise, or a failure to exercise it, would necessarily interfere with or otherwise affect the liberty of any individual; or
   (c) it is a power or right of entry, search or seizure into or of any property; or
   (d) it is a power or duty to make subordinate legislation.
   (2) Subsection (1)(b) and (c) above shall not exclude any function of the official receiver attached to any court.
   (3) Subsection (1)(c) above shall not exclude any function of a local authority under, or under regulations made under, any of the following enactments, namely—
   (a) section 247 of the Local Government (Scotland) Act 1947 (enforcement of non-domestic rates);
   (b) Part VI of the General Rate Act 1967 (distress for general rates);
   (c) paragraphs 7 and 7A of Schedule 2 and paragraph 11 of Schedule 5 to the Abolition of Domestic Rates Etc. (Scotland) Act 1987 (enforcement of community charges and community water charges);
   (d) paragraphs 5 to 7 of Schedule 4 to the Local Government Finance Act 1988 (enforcement of community charge);
   (e) paragraph 3(2)(b) of Schedule 9 to that Act (enforcement of non-domestic rates);
   (f) paragraphs 5 to 7 of Schedule 4 to the Local Government Finance Act 1992 (enforcement of council tax);
   (g) paragraphs 2 and 6 of Schedule 8 and paragraph 11 of Schedule 11 to that Act (enforcement of council tax and council water charge); and
   (h) paragraph 2 of Schedule 10 to the Local Government etc. (Scotland) Act 1994 (enforcement of water and sewerage charges).

DEFINITIONS
"function": s.79(1).
"local authority": s.79(1)(2)(3)(b).
"subordinate legislation": s.79(1).

GENERAL NOTE
This section limits the scope of the functions that may be specified under ss.69 and 70 as eligible for contracting out.

Subs. (1)
Para. (a): This exception aims to avoid any conflict between the contracting out of functions and the principle of judicial independence. As originally drafted the legislation excluded functions involving the exercise of the jurisdiction of certain courts from the scope of the order-making power. However, the adequacy of the list of courts and the absence of any exclusion for tribunals provoked widespread criticism in response to which the Government introduced this paragraph "to make it clear that any exercise by an office-holder of the jurisdiction of any court or tribunal which exercises the judicial power of the state could not be the subject of an order under [s.69] and could not, by that means, become susceptible to contracting out" (*Hansard*, H.L. Vol. 557, col. 127). The phrase "the judicial power of the State" is taken from s.19 of the Contempt of Court Act 1981 (c. 49).
Para. (b): "liberty" means physical liberty (Standing Committee F, col. 1024); "The reference to an individual makes it clear that only the physical liberty of natural persons, and not a legal body such as a company, is the subject of the paragraph" (*Hansard*, H.L. Vol. 557, col. 376).

Effect of contracting out

72.—(1) This section applies where by virtue of an order made under section 69 or 70 above a person is authorised to exercise any function of a Minister, office-holder or local authority.

(2) Subject to subsection (3) below, anything done or omitted to be done by or in relation to the authorised person (or an employee of his) in, or in connection with, the exercise or purported exercise of the function shall be treated for all purposes as done or omitted to be done—

(a) in the case of a function of a Minister or office-holder, by or in relation to the Minister or office-holder in his capacity as such;

(b) in the case of a function of a local authority, by or in relation to that authority.

(3) Subsection (2) above shall not apply—

(a) for the purposes of so much of any contract made between the authorised person and the Minister, office-holder or local authority as relates to the exercise of the function, or

(b) for the purposes of any criminal proceedings brought in respect of anything done or omitted to be done by the authorised person (or an employee of his).

DEFINITIONS
"employee": s.79(1).
"local authority": s.79(1)(2)(3)(b).
"Minister": s.79(1)(3)(4).
"office-holder": s.79(1).

GENERAL NOTE
This section provides that for all purposes, except those relating to criminal proceedings or contractual relations between the Minister, office-holder, local authority and the contractor, the acts of the contractor are, in effect, the acts of the Minister, office-holder, or local authority. The contracting out of functions therefore does not diminish the accountability or legal liability of a Minister, office-holder or local authority for the exercise or non-exercise of those functions (*Hansard*, H.L. Vol. 557, col. 384).

Termination of contracting out

73.—(1) This section applies where—

(a) by virtue of an order made under section 69 or 70 above a person is

authorised to exercise any function of a Minister, office-holder or local authority; and
(b) the order or authorisation is revoked at a time when a relevant contract is subsisting.

(2) The authorised person shall be entitled to treat the relevant contract as repudiated by the Minister, office-holder or local authority (and not as frustrated by reason of the revocation).

(3) In this section "relevant contract" means so much of any contract made between the authorised person and the Minister, office-holder or local authority as relates to the exercise of the function.

DEFINITIONS
"local authority": s.79(1)(2)(3)(b).
"Minister": s.79(1)(3)(a)(4).
"office-holder": s.79(1).
"relevant contract": s.73(3).

GENERAL NOTE
This section "is designed to ensure that if an order or authorisation is revoked during the life of a contract, through no fault of the contractor, the contractor will not be placed at an undue disadvantage. In other words, it prevents the technical possibility that revoking the order or authorisation could be used to terminate a contract and avoid the agreed arrangements for termination that would normally form part of the contract. ... [it] does not ... prevent the termination of a contract without liability should the contractor be at fault" (Standing Committee F, col. 1087).

Provisions for facilitating contracting out

Powers of certain office-holders

74.—(1) In so far as an office-holder to whom this section applies does not already have power to do so, he may authorise an officer of his to exercise any function of his which is conferred by or under any enactment.

(2) Subject to subsection (3) below, anything done or omitted to be done by an officer so authorised in, or in connection with, the exercise or purported exercise of the function shall be treated for all purposes as done or omitted to be done by the office-holder in his capacity as such.

(3) Subsection (2) above shall not apply for the purposes of any criminal proceedings brought in respect of anything done or omitted to be done as mentioned in that subsection.

(4) The office-holders to whom this section applies are—
(a) the registrar of companies for England and Wales and the registrar of companies for Scotland;
(b) the official receiver attached to any court;
(c) the Comptroller-General of Patents, Designs and Trade Marks;
(d) the Public Trustee;
(e) the traffic commissioner for any traffic area;
(f) the registrar of approved driving instructors;
(g) the Registrar General of Births, Deaths and Marriages for Scotland;
(h) the Keeper of the Registers of Scotland; and
(i) the Keeper of the Records of Scotland.

DEFINITIONS
"enactment": s.79(1).
"officer": s.79(1).
"registrar of approved driving instructors": s.79(1).

GENERAL NOTE
By giving the named office-holders power to authorise their staff to exercise their statutory functions, this section brings those functions within the scope of the contracting out order-making power in s.69.

"The *Carltona* doctrine acknowledges that the volume of work and variety of functions conferred on a Minister means that he cannot always exercise each function personally. ... The clause acknowledges a similar difficulty for the office-holders listed ..." (Standing Committee F, col. 1089).

Restrictions on disclosure of information

75. Schedule 15 to this Act (which contains provisions modifying certain restrictions on the disclosure of information where functions of Ministers, office-holders or local authorities are contracted out) shall have effect.

GENERAL NOTE

   This section gives effect to Sched. 15, which makes provision for the disclosure of information, access to which is restricted by statute or by an obligation of confidentiality, to a contractor if it is necessary to enable him to carry out the work. It also subjects contractors to equivalent restrictions on disclosure of the information and to any sanctions or penalties prescribed for unlawful disclosure.

Amendments of enactments etc.

76. Schedule 16 to this Act (which contains amendments and other provisions for facilitating or otherwise in connection with the contracting out of particular functions, whether in pursuance of an order made under section 69 or 70 above or otherwise) shall have effect.

GENERAL NOTE

   This section gives effect to Sched. 16 to this Act.

Supplemental

Provisions with respect to orders

77.—(1) An order under section 69 or 70 above—
   (a) shall be made by statutory instrument;
   (b) may contain provisions (including provisions modifying enactments) which are consequential upon, or supplemental or incidental to, the provisions made by the order which fall within subsection (2) of that section; and
   (c) may contain such transitional provisions and savings as appear to the Minister by whom the order is made to be appropriate.

   (2) No order shall be made under section 69 or 70 above unless a draft of the order has been laid before, and approved by a resolution of, each House of Parliament.

GENERAL NOTE

   This section provides that an order made under ss.69 or 70 is to be made by statutory instrument, subject to affirmative resolution procedure.

Extent of Part II

78.—(1) The following provisions of this Part extend to Northern Ireland, namely—
   (a) sections 69 and 74 above;
   (b) the other provisions of this Part in so far as they relate to orders under section 69 or to functions of Ministers or office-holders; and
   (c) paragraphs 4, 24 and 25 of Schedule 16.

(2) In so far as they relate to functions under enactments relating to patents, registered designs or trade marks, the provisions of this Part also extend to the Isle of Man, subject to such exceptions and modifications as Her Majesty may specify by Order in Council.

GENERAL NOTE
This section defines the territorial extent of Pt. II of this Act.

Interpretation of Part II

79.—(1) In this Part—
"employee", in relation to a body corporate, includes any director or other officer of that body;
"enactment" does not include an enactment contained in Northern Ireland legislation but, subject to that, includes an enactment contained in an Act (whenever passed) and an enactment contained in subordinate legislation (whenever made);
"function", in relation to a local authority, includes any power to do any thing which is calculated to facilitate, or is conducive or incidental to, the exercise of a function;
"joint board"—
(a) in relation to England and Wales, means a joint or special planning board constituted for a National Park by order under paragraph 1,3 or 3A of Schedule 17 to the Local Government Act 1972, or a joint planning board within the meaning of section 2 of the Town and Country Planning Act 1990;
(b) in relation to Scotland, has the same meaning as in the Local Government (Scotland) Act 1973;
"joint committee"—
(a) in relation to England and Wales, means a joint committee appointed under section 102(1)(b) of the Local Government Act 1972;
(b) in relation to Scotland, has the same meaning as in the Local Government (Scotland) Act 1973;
"local authority"—
(a) in relation to England, means a county council, district council or London borough council, the Common Council of the City of London, the sub-treasurer of the Inner Temple, the under treasurer of the Middle Temple, the Council of the Isles of Scilly or a parish council;
(b) in relation to Wales, means a county council, county borough council or community council;
(c) in relation to Scotland, has the same meaning as in the Local Government (Scotland) Act 1973;
"Minister" has the same meaning as Minister of the Crown has in the Ministers of the Crown Act 1975;
"Northern Ireland legislation" means—
(a) Northern Ireland legislation within the meaning of section 24 of the Interpretation Act 1978; and
(b) instruments, within the meaning of the Interpretation Act (Northern Ireland) 1954, made under such legislation;
"office-holder" does not include a Minister, an officer of either House of Parliament, the Parliamentary Commissioner for Administration or the Health Service Commissioner for England, for Wales or for Scotland but, subject to that, means—
(a) the holder of an office created or continued in existence by a public general Act of Parliament;
(b) the holder of an office the remuneration in respect of which is paid out of money provided by Parliament;

(c) the registrar of companies for England and Wales and the registrar of companies for Scotland; and

(d) the registrar of approved driving instructors;

"officer"—

(a) in relation to a Minister, means any person in the civil service of the Crown who is serving in his department;

(b) in relation to an office-holder, means any member of his staff, or any person in the civil service of the Crown who has been assigned or appointed to assist him in the exercise of his functions;

"the registrar of approved driving instructors" means the officer of the Secretary of State by whom the register of approved driving instructors established in pursuance of section 23 of the Road Traffic Act 1962 is compiled and maintained;

"subordinate legislation" has the same meaning as in the Interpretation Act 1978.

(2) In relation to any time before 1st April 1996, subsection (1) above shall have effect as if, in paragraph (b) of the definition of "local authority", for the words "county borough" there were substituted the word "district".

(3) Subject to subsection (4) below, this Part shall have effect as if—

(a) any reference to a Minister included references to the Forestry Commissioners and the Intervention Board for Agricultural Produce; and

(b) any reference to a local authority included references to a joint board and a joint committee.

(4) Nothing in subsection (3) above shall be construed as enabling those Commissioners or that Board to make an order under section 69 or 70 above; and any order under section 69 above which relates to a function of that Board shall be made by the Ministers (within the meaning of Part I of the Agriculture Act 1957).

(5) Subject to subsection (6) below, any function of an examiner or other officer of the Patent Office which is conferred by or under any enactment shall be treated for all purposes of this Part as if it were a function of the Comptroller-General of Patents, Designs and Trade Marks.

(6) In any case where by virtue of an order made under section 69 above a person is authorised by that Comptroller to exercise any such function as is mentioned in subsection (5) above, section 72(2) above shall have effect as if for paragraphs (a) and (b) there were substituted the words "by or in relation to an examiner or other officer of the Patent Office in his capacity as such".

PART III

SUPPLEMENTARY

Financial provisions

80.—(1) There shall be paid out of money provided by Parliament—

(a) any sums required by a Minister of the Crown, an office-holder, the Forestry Commissioners or the Intervention Board for Agricultural Produce for making payments under contracts entered into under or by virtue of Part II of this Act;

(b) any administrative expenses incurred by a Minister of the Crown or office-holder in consequence of the provisions of this Act; and

(c) any increase attributable to this Act in the sums so payable under any other Act.

(2) In this section—

"Minister of the Crown" has the same meaning as in the Ministers of the Crown Act 1975;

"office-holder" has the same meaning as in Part II of this Act.

DEFINITIONS
"Minister of the Crown": s.80(2) of the Ministers of the Crown Act 1975 (c. 26).
"office-holder": s.79(1).

Repeals

81.—(1) The enactments mentioned in Schedule 17 to this Act (which include enactments which are spent) are hereby repealed to the extent specified in the third column of that Schedule.

(2) The extent of any repeal in that Schedule of an enactment is the same as that of the enactment repealed.

Short title, commencement and extent

82.—(1) This Act may be cited as the Deregulation and Contracting Out Act 1994.

(2) The provisions of this Act set out below shall come into force at the end of the period of two months beginning with the day on which this Act is passed, that is to say—
  (a) sections 7, 9, 10, 12, 15, 16, 17, 20, 21 and 31,
  (b) Schedules 2 to 4,
  (c) Schedule 8,
  (d) Schedule 9,
  (e) section 39 and Schedule 11 so far as relating to sections 93A and 133 of the Fair Trading Act 1973, the Energy Act 1976, the Competition Act 1980, the Building Societies Act 1986, the Financial Services Act 1986, the Companies Act 1989 and the Companies (Northern Ireland) Order 1990,
  (f) Part II, and
  (g) section 81 and Schedule 17 so far as relating to the Fair Trading Act 1973, the Competition Act 1980, the Telecommunications Act 1984, the Gas Act 1986, the Building Societies Act 1986, the Financial Services Act 1986, the Electricity Act 1989, the Companies Act 1989, the Companies (Northern Ireland) Order 1990, the Electricity (Northern Ireland) Order 1992 and the Railways Act 1993.

(3) The provisions of this Act set out below shall come into force on the day on which this Act is passed, that is to say—
  (a) Chapter I of Part I,
  (b) sections 14, 18, 25 to 30, 32 to 34 and 37,
  (c) section 39 and Schedule 11 so far as relating to the Road Traffic Regulation Act 1984 and the Charities Act 1993,
  (d) section 40,
  (e) sections 41, 54 and 55,
  (f) section 57(1) so far as relating to paragraph 14(1)(c) and (d) of Schedule 13, and paragraph 14(1)(c) and (d) of Schedule 13,
  (g) section 81 and Schedule 17 so far as relating to the Road Traffic Regulation Act 1984, the Weights and Measures Act 1985, the Charities Act 1992 and the Charities Act 1993, and
  (h) this section.

(4) The remaining provisions of this Act, other than section 36(2), shall come into force on such day as the Secretary of State may by order made by statutory instrument appoint; and different days may be so appointed for different purposes.

(5) An order under subsection (4) above may include such transitional provisions and savings as appear to the Secretary of State to be necessary or expedient in connection with the coming into force of section 36(1) or Chapters III and IV of Part I of this Act.

(6) Section 36(2) shall come into force on such day as the Department of Economic Development in Northern Ireland may by order appoint.

(7) An order under subsection (6) above—

(a) may contain such transitional provisions as appear to the Department of Economic Development in Northern Ireland to be necessary or expedient in connection with the coming into force of section 36(2), and

(b) shall be a statutory rule for the purposes of the Statutory Rules (Northern Ireland) Order 1979.

(8) Except in so far as any provision of this Act otherwise provides, this Act, other than Chapter I of Part I and this section, does not extend to Northern Ireland.

SCHEDULES

Section 5   SCHEDULE 1

POWERS TO IMPROVE ENFORCEMENT PROCEDURES

Explanation of suggested remedial action

1.—(1) This paragraph confers power to provide that, where an enforcement officer expresses to any person any opinion as to what remedial action should be taken by that person, then, if that person so requests, the officer—

(a) shall as soon as practicable give to him a written notice which satisfies the requirements of sub-paragraph (2) below; and

(b) shall not take any enforcement action against him until after the end of such period beginning with the giving of the notice as may be determined by or under the order.

(2) A notice satisfies the requirements of this sub-paragraph if it—

(a) states the nature of the remedial action which in the officer's opinion should be taken, and explains why and within what period;

(b) explains what constitutes the failure to observe the restriction or to comply with the requirement or condition; and

(c) states the nature of the enforcement action which could be taken and states whether there is a right to make representations before, or a right of appeal against, the taking of such action.

Explanation of immediate enforcement action etc.

2.—(1) This paragraph confers power to provide that, where an enforcement officer—

(a) takes immediate enforcement action against any person; or

(b) requires any person to take immediate remedial action,

the officer shall as soon as practicable give to that person a written notice explaining why it appeared to him to be necessary to take such action or impose such a requirement.

(2) The power conferred by this paragraph shall not be exercisable unless the restriction, requirement or condition is such that observance of or compliance with it would be likely to involve expenditure of a significant amount.

Right to make representations

3. This paragraph confers power to provide that, before an enforcement officer takes any enforcement action against any person, the officer—

(a) shall give to that person a written notice stating—

(i) that he is considering taking the action and the reasons why he is considering it; and

(ii) that the person may, within a period specified in the notice, make written representations to him or, if the person so requests, make oral representations to him in the presence of a person determined by or under the order; and

(b) shall consider any representations which are duly made and not withdrawn.

Explanation of right of appeal

4. This paragraph confers power to provide that, where—

(a) an enforcement officer has taken enforcement action against any person; and

(b) the relevant enactment contains any provision conferring a right of appeal against such action, the officer shall as soon as practicable give to that person a written notice explaining how, where, within what period, and on what grounds, an appeal may be brought, and whether the enforcement action would be stayed or, in Scotland, suspended while an appeal were pending.

Application of provisions to other interested persons

5.—(1) This paragraph confers power to provide that, where—
(a) a third person will or may be required to meet or make a significant contribution towards the cost of observing the restriction or complying with the requirement or condition; or
(b) the enforcement action which may be or has been taken specifically relates to goods or services which are to be or have been supplied by a third person,
any relevant provision shall, with any modifications specified in the order, apply in relation to that person.
(2) In this paragraph—
"relevant provision" means any provision made by virtue of paragraphs 1 to 4 above or any provision of the relevant enactment which is to the like effect;
"third person" means any person other than the one against whom enforcement action may be or has been taken.

DEFINITIONS
"enforcement action": s.5(6).
"enforcement officer": s.5(6).
"remedial action": s.5(6).
"the relevant enactment": s.5(6).

GENERAL NOTE
This Schedule confers five powers on Ministers for the purpose of improving the fairness, transparency and consistency of enforcement procedures. These powers were assumed in response to the criticism that the legislation in its original form did not address the over-zealous or unreasonable enforcement of regulatory requirements.

Para. 1
An enforcement officer who advises a business to take remedial action may be required in the exercise of the power conferred by this paragraph (a) to notify the business in writing of the requirement of which it is in breach, the remedial action advised and the enforcement action that could be taken against it were it not to take the action advised, and (b) to refrain from taking enforcement action against the business until after the end of a specified period. Neither requirement applies where immediate remedial or enforcement action is thought necessary (s.5(5)).

Para. 2
An enforcement officer who takes immediate enforcement action against a business, or requires a business to take immediate remedial action, may be required in the exercise of the power conferred by this paragraph to notify the business in writing why immediate action was thought necessary.

Para. 3
Before taking enforcement action against a business, an enforcement officer may be required in the exercise of the power conferred by this paragraph (a) to notify the business that he is minded to take action against it, (b) to afford the business an opportunity to make representations to him, and (c) to consider any representations made. These requirements do not apply where immediate enforcement action is thought necessary (s.5(5)).

Para. 4
Where enforcement action has been taken against a business, and the legislation under which the action has been taken confers a right of appeal against such action, the enforcement officer may be required in the exercise of the power conferred by this paragraph to give the business details of its right of appeal against the action taken.

Para. 5
In the exercise of the power conferred by this paragraph, the requirements that may be imposed under the preceding four paragraphs to notify *etc.* businesses against which enforcement action may be or has been taken may be extended to third parties who have a direct economic interest in the outcome of that action.

Section 7   SCHEDULE 2

Section 7: Sectoral Regulators

Telecommunications

1.—(1) The Director General of Telecommunications shall be entitled to exercise, concurrently with the Director General of Fair Trading, the functions of that Director under the provisions inserted in the Fair Trading Act 1973 by section 7 above, so far as relating to monopoly situations which exist or may exist in relation to commercial activities connected with telecommunications; and references in those provisions to that Director shall be construed accordingly.

(2) In sub-paragraph (1) above, "commercial activities connected with telecommunications" has the same meaning as in the Telecommunications Act 1984.

2. In section 50(4) of the Telecommunications Act 1984 (which makes provision about the exercise of functions exercised concurrently by the Director General of Fair Trading and the Director General of Telecommunications) after paragraph (c) there shall be inserted "and

(d) paragraph 1 of Schedule 2 to the Deregulation and Contracting Out Act 1994,"

3. In section 50(6) of the Telecommunications Act 1984 (power of Secretary of State to determine any question as to the application of certain provisions) after "above" there shall be inserted "or paragraph 1 of Schedule 2 to the Deregulation and Contracting Out Act 1994".

Electricity

4.—(1) The Director General of Electricity Supply shall be entitled to exercise, concurrently with the Director General of Fair Trading, the functions of that Director under the provisions inserted in the Fair Trading Act 1973 by section 7 above, so far as relating to monopoly situations which exist or may exist in relation to commercial activities connected with the generation, transmission or supply of electricity; and references in those provisions to that Director shall be construed accordingly.

(2) In sub-paragraph (1) above, "commercial activities connected with the generation, transmission or supply of electricity" has the same meaning as in section 43(2) of the Electricity Act 1989.

5.—(1) The Director General of Electricity Supply for Northern Ireland shall be entitled to exercise, concurrently with the Director General of Fair Trading, the functions of that Director under the provisions inserted in the Fair Trading Act 1973 by section 7 above, so far as relating to monopoly situations which exist or may exist in relation to commercial activities connected with the generation, transmission or supply of electricity; and references in those provisions to that Director shall be construed accordingly.

(2) In sub-paragraph (1) above, "commercial activities connected with the generation, transmission or supply of electricity" has the same meaning as in Article 46(2) of the Electricity (Northern Ireland) Order 1992.

6.—(1) In section 43(4) of the Electricity Act 1989 (which makes provision about the exercise of functions exercised concurrently by the Director General of Fair Trading and the Director General of Electricity Supply) after paragraph (c) there shall be inserted "and

(d) paragraph 4 of Schedule 2 to the Deregulation and Contracting Out Act 1994,".

(2) In Article 46(4) of the Electricity (Northern Ireland) Order 1992 (which makes similar provision in relation to the Director General of Fair Trading and the Director General of Electricity Supply for Northern Ireland) after sub-paragraph (c) there shall be inserted "and

(d) paragraph 5 of Schedule 2 to the Deregulation and Contracting Out Act 1994,".

7.—(1) In section 43(6) of the Electricity Act 1989 (power of Secretary of State to determine any question as to the application of certain provisions) after "above" there shall be inserted "or paragraph 4 of Schedule 2 to the Deregulation and Contracting Out Act 1994".

(2) In Article 46(6) of the Electricity (Northern Ireland) Order 1992 (corresponding power of Department of Economic Development) after "(3)" there shall be inserted "or paragraph 5 of Schedule 2 to the Deregulation and Contracting Out Act 1994".

Water

8.—(1) The Director General of Water Services shall be entitled to exercise, concurrently with the Director General of Fair Trading, the functions of that Director under the provisions inserted in the Fair Trading Act 1973 by section 7 above, so far as relating to monopoly situations which exist or may exist in relation to commercial activities connected with the supply of water or the provision of sewerage services.

(2) In sub-paragraph (1) above, "commercial activities connected with the supply of water or the provision of sewerage services" has the same meaning as in section 31(2) of the Water Industry Act 1991.

9. So far as necessary for the purposes of, or in connection with, sub-paragraph (1) of paragraph 8 above, the references to the Director General of Fair Trading in the provisions mentioned in that sub-paragraph shall be construed as if they were or, as the case may require, as if they included references to the Director General of Water Services.

10.—(1) Section 31 of the Water Industry Act 1991 shall be amended as follows.

(2) In subsection (5) (duty to consult other Director in case of functions exercisable concurrently by Director General of Water Services and Director General of Fair Trading) after "subsection (3) above" there shall be inserted "or in paragraph 8 of Schedule 2 to the Deregulation and Contracting Out Act 1994".

(3) In subsection (6) (exercise of function by one Director to exclude exercise in the same matter by the other Director)—

(a) after the words "subsection (3) above", in the first place where they occur, there shall be inserted "or in paragraph 8 of Schedule 2 to the Deregulation and Contracting Out Act 1994", and

(b) for "that paragraph or, as the case may be, in subsection (3) above" there shall be substituted "that provision".

(4) In subsection (8) (power of Secretary of State to determine any question as to the application of certain provisions) after "above" there shall be inserted "or paragraph 8 of Schedule 2 to the Deregulation and Contracting Out Act 1994".

Railways

11.—(1) The Rail Regulator shall be entitled to exercise, concurrently with the Director General of Fair Trading, the functions of that Director under the provisions inserted in the Fair Trading Act 1973 by section 7 above, so far as relating to monopoly situations which exist or may exist in relation to the supply of railway services; and references in those provisions to the Director shall be construed accordingly.

(2) In sub-paragraph (1) above, "the supply of railway services" has the same meaning as in section 67(2) of the Railways Act 1993.

12. In section 67(4) of the Railways Act 1993 (which makes provision about the exercise of functions exercised concurrently by the Director General of Fair Trading and the Rail Regulator) after paragraph (c) there shall be inserted "and

(d) paragraph 11 of Schedule 2 to the Deregulation and Contracting Out Act 1994,".

13. In section 67(8) of the Railways Act 1993 (power of Secretary of State to determine any question as to the application of certain provisions) after "above" there shall be inserted "or paragraph 11 of Schedule 2 to the Deregulation and Contracting Out Act 1994".

14. Section 93B of the Fair Trading Act 1973 (offences of furnishing false or misleading information in connection with functions of the Director General of Fair Trading under Part IV of that Act) shall have effect, so far as relating to functions exercisable by the Rail Regulator by virtue of paragraph 11 above, as if the reference in subsection (1)(a) of that section to the Director included a reference to the Rail Regulator.

Interpretation

15. Expressions used in this Schedule which are also used in the Fair Trading Act 1973 have the same meanings as in that Act.

GENERAL NOTE

This Schedule empowers the utility regulators to propose that the Secretary of State accept undertakings in lieu of the referral to the Monopolies and Mergers Commission of monopoly situations which exist or may exist in relation to commercial activities connected with telecommunications (para. 1), the generation, transmission or supply of electricity (paras. 4 and 5), the supply of water or the provision of sewerage services (para. 8), and the supply of railway services (para. 11).

Section 10   SCHEDULE 3

NON-NOTIFIABLE AGREEMENTS: MODIFICATIONS OF THE RESTRICTIVE TRADE PRACTICES ACT 1976

1. The Restrictive Trade Practices Act 1976 shall be amended as follows.

2. In section 1 (registration of agreements) after subsection (2) there shall be inserted—

"(2A) In the case of a non-notifiable agreement, subsection (2)(a) and (b) above shall only apply where the Director considers that any restrictions or information provisions by virtue of which this Act applies to the agreement are of such significance as to call for investigation by the Court."

3.—(1) Section 24 (particulars and time for registration) shall be amended as follows.

(2) In subsection (1) (duty to furnish particulars of agreements subject to registration under the Act) after "under this Act" there shall be inserted ", other than a non-notifiable agreement,".

(3) In subsection (2) (additional provisions about particulars to be furnished)—

(a) in paragraph (a), after "under this Act" there shall be inserted "and is not a non-notifiable agreement", and

(b) in paragraph (b), for "such an agreement" there shall be substituted "an agreement which, at the time of the variation or determination, falls within paragraph (a) above".

(4) After that subsection there shall be inserted—

"(2A) Subsections (1) and (2)(a) above shall not apply in relation to an agreement which ceases to be a non-notifiable agreement by virtue of the Director entering or filing particulars of it under section 1(2)(b) above."

4. After section 25 there shall be inserted—

"Registration of non-notifiable agreement: duty to inform parties

25A.—(1) Where an agreement ceases to be a non-notifiable agreement by virtue of the Director entering or filing particulars of it under section 1(2)(b) above, he shall give notice of that fact to each of the parties to the agreement.

(2) Regulations under section 27 below may prescribe how notice under subsection (1) above is to be given and who is to be treated as a party to an agreement for the purposes of that subsection."

5.—(1) Section 26 shall be amended as follows.

(2) In subsection (2) (power of the Restrictive Practices Court to make declarations as to certain matters) for the words from "and" to the end there shall be substituted ", declare whether or not it is subject to registration under this Act and declare whether or not it is a non-notifiable agreement."

(3) For subsection (3) there shall be substituted—

"(3) Where a party to an agreement makes an application for a declaration under subsection (2) above, the Director shall not enter or file particulars of the agreement in the register during the time during which the proceedings and any appeal therein are pending.

(3A) Subsection (3) above shall not apply where—

(a) the only question in relation to which the declaration is sought is whether or not the agreement is a non-notifiable agreement, and

(b) the Director considers that any restrictions or information provisions by virtue of which this Act applies to the agreement are of such significance as to call for investigation by the Court.

(3B) Where—

(a) a party to an agreement makes an application for a declaration under subsection (2) above,

(b) the question in relation to which the declaration is sought is relevant to the existence of a duty to furnish particulars of the agreement under section 24 above, and

(c) the application is made before the expiry of the time within which particulars of the agreement are required to be furnished if the duty to furnish particulars under that section applies,

then, if particulars of the agreement have not been furnished under that section before the commencement of the proceedings, that time shall be extended by a time equal to the time during which the proceedings and any appeal therein are pending, and such further time, if any, as the Court may direct."

6. In section 36 (Director's power to obtain information) after subsection (3) there shall be inserted—

"(3A) The Director may give notice to any person being party to an agreement which—

(a) is a non-notifiable agreement, or

(b) has ceased to be a non-notifiable agreement by virtue of the Director entering or filing particulars of it under section 1(2)(b) above,

requiring him to furnish such documents or information in his possession or control as the Director considers expedient for the purposes of, or in connection with, the registration of the agreement."

7.—(1) Schedule 2 (furnishing of particulars of agreements) shall be amended as follows.

(2) In paragraph 1, for sub-paragraph (1) there shall be substituted—

"(1) Subject to paragraph 2 below, no duty to furnish particulars in respect of an agreement which is subject to registration shall be affected by any subsequent variation or determination of the agreement."

(3) In paragraph 2, in sub-paragraph (1), for "an agreement becomes subject to registration after it is made" there shall be substituted ", after an agreement is made, it becomes an agreement in respect of which particulars fall to be furnished under section 24 above".

(4) In that paragraph, in sub-paragraph (2), after "section 24(1) above" there shall be inserted "(so far as applicable)".

(5) In that paragraph, in sub-paragraph (3), for "24" there shall be substituted "24(1)".

(6) In paragraph 5(1) after entry (c) in the Table there shall be inserted—

"(ca) Agreement which ceases to be   Within 1 month from the day on
a non-notifiable agreement.   which the agreement so ceases."

DEFINITIONS

    "non-notifiable agreement": Restrictive Trade Practices Act 1976 (c. 34), s.27A(1).

GENERAL NOTE

    This Schedule modifies the Restrictive Trade Practices Act 1976 (c. 34) in relation to non-notifiable agreements.

Para. 2

    This paragraph amends the 1976 Act to relieve the DGFT of the obligation to register a non-notifiable agreement except where its provisions merit investigation by the Restrictive Practices Court.

Para. 3

    This paragraph amends the 1976 Act to relieve the parties to a non-notifiable agreement of the obligation to furnish particulars of the agreement unless it is registered.

Para. 4

    This paragraph amends the 1976 Act to impose an obligation on the DGFT to inform the parties to a non-notifiable agreement that it has been registered and as a result has ceased to be non-notifiable.

Para. 5

    This paragraph amends the 1976 Act to give the Restrictive Practices Court jurisdiction to determine whether or not an agreement is a non-notifiable agreement.

Para. 6

    This paragraph amends the 1976 Act to give the DGFT power to require information from parties to agreements that are non-notifiable or have ceased to be non-notifiable.

Section 12   SCHEDULE 4

SECTION 12: SECTORAL REGULATORS AND TRANSITION

Sectoral regulators

1. The amendments of the Competition Act 1980 made by section 12(1) to (6) above, together with the consequential amendments of that Act made by paragraph 4(2) to (6) of Schedule 11 to this Act, shall have effect, not only in relation to the jurisdiction of the Director General of Fair Trading under the provisions amended, but also in relation to the jurisdiction under those provisions of each of the following—
    (a) the Director General of Telecommunications,
    (b) the Director General of Electricity Supply,
    (c) the Director General of Electricity Supply for Northern Ireland,
    (d) the Director General of Water Services, and
    (e) the Rail Regulator.

2. In each of the following, namely—
    (a) section 50(4) of the Telecommunications Act 1984,
    (b) section 43(4) of the Electricity Act 1989,
    (c) Article 46(4) of the Electricity (Northern Ireland) Order 1992, and
    (d) section 67(4) of the Railways Act 1993,
(which make provision about the exercise of functions exercised concurrently by the Director General of Fair Trading and the sectoral regulator concerned) for "transferred by", in each place, there shall be substituted "mentioned in".

3. In each of the following, namely—

(a) section 50(6) of the Telecommunications Act 1984,

(b) section 43(6) of the Electricity Act 1989, and

(c) Article 46(6) of the Electricity (Northern Ireland) Order 1992,

(which provide for the Secretary of State or, in Northern Ireland, the Department of Economic Development to determine certain questions in connection with the jurisdictions of the sectoral regulators concerned) for "as to whether" there shall be substituted "in any particular case as to the jurisdiction of the Director under any of the provisions mentioned in" and the words "applies to any particular case" shall be omitted.

4. In section 67(8) of the Railways Act 1993 (corresponding provision in relation to the jurisdiction of the Rail Regulator) for "as to whether" there shall be substituted "in any particular case as to the jurisdiction of the Regulator under any of the provisions mentioned in" and the words "applies to any particular case" shall be omitted.

Transition

5.—(1) Where, immediately before the relevant day, an investigation under section 3 of the Competition Act 1980 has commenced and is being proceeded with, that Act shall, so far as concerns—

(a) further proceeding with the investigation,

(b) publishing, after completion of the investigation, such a report as is mentioned in subsection (10) of that section, and

(c) taking action in consequence of the report,

have effect as if this Act had not been passed.

(2) For the purposes of this paragraph, an investigation under section 3 of the Competition Act 1980 shall be taken to have commenced once the authority by whom it is to be carried out has performed the duties which subsection (2) of that section requires him to perform before carrying out the investigation.

6. Where, immediately before the relevant day, an investigation has been completed, but no such report as is mentioned in section 3(10) of the Competition Act 1980 has yet been published, that Act shall, so far as concerns—

(a) publishing such a report, and

(b) taking action in consequence of it,

have effect as if this Act had not been passed.

7. Where, immediately before the relevant day, the authority by whom an investigation under section 3 of the Competition Act 1980 has been carried out is considering what action to take in consequence of a report published under subsection (10) of that section, that Act shall, so far as concerns taking action in consequence of the report, have effect as if this Act had not been passed.

8. In paragraphs 5 to 7 above, "relevant day" means the day on which section 12 above comes into force.

GENERAL NOTE

This Schedule relieves the utility regulators of the need to undertake a formal investigation and to issue a report before they can ask the Monopolies and Mergers Commission to investigate anti-competitive practices or accept undertakings which address their concerns.

Section 13(1) SCHEDULE 5

STRIKING OFF OF NON-TRADING PRIVATE COMPANIES: GREAT BRITAIN

1. The Companies Act 1985 shall be amended as follows.

2. After section 652 there shall be inserted—

"Registrar may strike private company off register on application

652A.–(1) On application by a private company, the registrar of companies may strike the company's name off the register.

(2) An application by a company under this section shall—

(a) be made on its behalf by its directors or by a majority of them,

(b) be in the prescribed form, and

(c) contain the prescribed information.

(3) The registrar shall not strike a company off under this section until after the expiration of 3 months from the publication by him in the Gazette of a notice—

(a) stating that he may exercise his power under this section in relation to the company, and

(b) inviting any person to show cause why he should not do so.

(4) Where the registrar strikes a company off under this section, he shall publish notice of that fact in the Gazette.

(5) On the publication in the Gazette of a notice under subsection (4), the company to which the notice relates is dissolved.

(6) However, the liability (if any) of every director, managing officer and member of the company continues and may be enforced as if the company had not been dissolved.

(7) Nothing in this section affects the power of the court to wind up a company the name of which has been struck off the register.

Duties in connection with making application under section 652A

652B.—(1) A person shall not make an application under section 652A on behalf of a company if, at any time in the previous 3 months, the company has—

(a) changed its name,

(b) traded or otherwise carried on business,

(c) made a disposal for value of property or rights which, immediately before ceasing to trade or otherwise carry on business, it held for the purpose of disposal for gain in the normal course of trading or otherwise carrying on business, or

(d) engaged in any other activity, except one which is—

(i) necessary or expedient for the purpose of making an application under section 652A, or deciding whether to do so,

(ii) necessary or expedient for the purpose of concluding the affairs of the company,

(iii) necessary or expedient for the purpose of complying with any statutory requirement, or

(iv) specified by the Secretary of State by order for the purposes of this sub-paragraph.

(2) For the purposes of subsection (1), a company shall not be treated as trading or otherwise carrying on business by virtue only of the fact that it makes a payment in respect of a liability incurred in the course of trading or otherwise carrying on business.

(3) A person shall not make an application under section 652A on behalf of a company at a time when any of the following is the case—

(a) an application has been made to the court under section 425 on behalf of the company for the sanctioning of a compromise or arrangement and the matter has not been finally concluded;

(b) a voluntary arrangement in relation to the company has been proposed under Part I of the Insolvency Act 1986 and the matter has not been finally concluded;

(c) an administration order in relation to the company is in force under Part II of that Act or a petition for such an order has been presented and not finally dealt with or withdrawn;

(d) the company is being wound up under Part IV of that Act, whether voluntarily or by the court, or a petition under that Part for the winding up of the company by the court has been presented and not finally dealt with or withdrawn;

(e) there is a receiver or manager of the company's property;

(f) the company's estate is being administered by a judicial factor.

(4) For the purposes of subsection (3)(a), the matter is finally concluded if—

(a) the application has been withdrawn,

(b) the application has been finally dealt with without a compromise or arrangement being sanctioned by the court, or

(c) a compromise or arrangement has been sanctioned by the court and has, together with anything required to be done under any provision made in relation to the matter by order of the court, been fully carried out.

(5) For the purposes of subsection (3)(b), the matter is finally concluded if—

(a) no meetings are to be summoned under section 3 of the Insolvency Act 1986,

(b) meetings summoned under that section fail to approve the arrangement with no, or the same, modifications,

(c) an arrangement approved by meetings summoned under that section, or in consequence of a direction under section 6(4)(b) of that Act, has been fully implemented, or

(d) the court makes an order under subsection (5) of section 6 of that Act revoking approval given at previous meetings and, if the court gives any directions under subsection (6) of that section, the company has done whatever it is required to do under those directions.

(6) A person who makes an application under section 652A on behalf of a company shall secure that a copy of the application is given, within 7 days from the day on which the application is made, to every person who, at any time on that day, is—

(a) a member of the company,

(b) an employee of the company,

(c) a creditor of the company,

(d) a director of the company,

(e) a manager or trustee of any pension fund established for the benefit of employees of the company, or

(f) a person of a description specified for the purposes of this paragraph by regulations made by the Secretary of State.

(7) Subsection (6) shall not require a copy of the application to be given to a director who is a party to the application.

(8) The duty imposed by subsection (6) shall cease to apply if the application is withdrawn before the end of the period for giving the copy application.

(9) The Secretary of State may by order amend subsection (1) for the purpose of altering the period in relation to which the doing of the things mentioned in paragraphs (a) to (d) of that subsection is relevant.

Directors' duties following application under section 652A

652C.—(1) Subsection (2) applies in relation to any time after the day on which a company makes an application under section 652A and before the day on which the application is finally dealt with or withdrawn.

(2) A person who is a director of the company at the end of a day on which a person other than himself becomes—

(a) a member of the company,

(b) an employee of the company,

(c) a creditor of the company,

(d) a director of the company,

(e) a manager or trustee of any pension fund established for the benefit of employees of the company, or

(f) a person of a description specified for the purposes of this paragraph by regulations made by the Secretary of State,

shall secure that a copy of the application is given to that person within 7 days from that day.

(3) The duty imposed by subsection (2) shall cease to apply if the application is finally dealt with or withdrawn before the end of the period for giving the copy application.

(4) Subsection (5) applies where, at any time on or after the day on which a company makes an application under section 652A and before the day on which the application is finally dealt with or withdrawn—

(a) the company—

(i) changes its name,

(ii) trades or otherwise carries on business,

(iii) makes a disposal for value of any property or rights other than those which it was necessary or expedient for it to hold for the purpose of making, or proceeding with, an application under section 652A, or

(iv) engages in any other activity, except one to which subsection (6) applies;

(b) an application is made to the court under section 425 on behalf of the company for the sanctioning of a compromise or arrangement;

(c) a voluntary arrangement in relation to the company is proposed under Part I of the Insolvency Act 1986;

(d) a petition is presented for the making of an administration order under Part II of that Act in relation to the company;

(e) there arise any of the circumstances in which, under section 84(1) of that Act, the company may be voluntarily wound up;

(f) a petition is presented for the winding up of the company by the court under Part IV of that Act;

(g) a receiver or manager of the company's property is appointed; or

(h) a judicial factor is appointed to administer the company's estate.

(5) A person who, at the end of a day on which an event mentioned in any of paragraphs (a) to (h) of subsection (4) occurs, is a director of the company shall secure that the company's application is withdrawn forthwith.

(6) This subsection applies to any activity which is—

(a) necessary or expedient for the purpose of making, or proceeding with, an application under section 652A,

(b) necessary or expedient for the purpose of concluding affairs of the company which are outstanding because of what has been necessary or expedient for the purpose of making, or proceeding with, such an application,

(c) necessary or expedient for the purpose of complying with any statutory requirement, or

(d) specified by the Secretary of State by order for the purposes of this subsection.

(7) For the purposes of subsection (4)(a), a company shall not be treated as trading or otherwise carrying on business by virtue only of the fact that it makes a payment in respect of a liability incurred in the course of trading or otherwise carrying on business.

Sections 652B and 652C: supplementary provisions

652D.—(1) For the purposes of sections 652B(6) and 652C(2), a document shall be treated as given to a person if it is delivered to him or left at his proper address or sent by post to him at that address.

(2) For the purposes of subsection (1) and section 7 of the Interpretation Act 1978 (which relates to the service of documents by post) in its application to that subsection, the proper address of any person shall be his last known address, except that—

(a) in the case of a body corporate, other than one to which subsection (3) applies, it shall be the address of its registered or principal office,

(b) in the case of a partnership, other than one to which subsection (3) applies, it shall be the address of its principal office, and

(c) in the case of a body corporate or partnership to which subsection (3) applies, it shall be the address of its principal office in the United Kingdom.

(3) This subsection applies to a body corporate or partnership which—

(a) is incorporated or formed under the law of a country or territory outside the United Kingdom, and

(b) has a place of business in the United Kingdom.

(4) Where a creditor of the company has more than one place of business, subsection (1) shall have effect, so far as concerns the giving of a document to him, as if for the words from "delivered" to the end there were substituted "left, or sent by post to him, at each place of business of his with which the company has had dealings in relation to a matter by virtue of which he is a creditor of the company."

(5) Any power to make an order or regulations under section 652B or 652C shall—

(a) include power to make different provision for different cases or classes of case,

(b) include power to make such transitional provisions as the Secretary of State considers appropriate, and

(c) be exercisable by statutory instrument subject to annulment in pursuance of a resolution of either House of Parliament.

(6) For the purposes of sections 652B and 652C, an application under section 652A is withdrawn if notice of withdrawal in the prescribed form is given to the registrar of companies.

(7) In sections 652B and 652C, "disposal" includes part disposal.

(8) In sections 652B and 652C and this section, "creditor" includes a contingent or prospective creditor.

Sections 652B and 652C: enforcement

652E.—(1) A person who breaches or fails to perform a duty imposed on him by section 652B or 652C is guilty of an offence and liable to a fine.

(2) A person who fails to perform a duty imposed on him by section 652B(6) or 652C(2) with the intention of concealing the making of the application in question from the person concerned is guilty of an offence and liable to imprisonment or a fine, or both.

(3) In any proceedings for an offence under subsection (1) consisting of breach of a duty imposed by section 652B(1) or (3), it shall be a defence for the accused to prove that he did not know, and could not reasonably have known, of the existence of the facts which led to the breach.

(4) In any proceedings for an offence under subsection (1) consisting of failure to perform the duty imposed by section 652B(6), it shall be a defence for the accused to prove that he took all reasonable steps to perform the duty.

(5) In any proceedings for an offence under subsection (1) consisting of failure to perform a duty imposed by section 652C(2) or (5), it shall be a defence for the accused to prove—

(a) that at the time of the failure he was not aware of the fact that the company had made an application under section 652A, or

(b) that he took all reasonable steps to perform the duty.

Other offences connected with section 652A

652F.—(1) Where a company makes an application under section 652A, any person who, in connection with the application, knowingly or recklessly furnishes any information to the registrar of companies which is false or misleading in a material particular is guilty of an offence and liable to a fine.

(2) Any person who knowingly or recklessly makes an application to the registrar of companies which purports to be an application under section 652A, but which is not, is guilty of an offence and liable to a fine."

3.—(1) Section 653 (objection to striking off by persons aggrieved) shall be amended as follows.

(2) In subsection (1)—

(a) for "The following" there shall be substituted "Subsection (2)", and

(b) at the end there shall be inserted "under section 652."

(3) After subsection (2) there shall be inserted—

"(2A) Subsections (2B) and (2D) apply if a company has been struck off the register under section 652A.

(2B) The court, on an application by a notifiable person made before the expiration of 20 years from publication in the Gazette of notice under section 652A(4), may, if satisfied—

(a) that any duty under section 652B or 652C with respect to the giving to that person of a copy of the company's application under section 652A was not performed,

(b) that the making of the company's application under section 652A involved a breach of duty under section 652B(1) or (3), or

(c) that it is for some other reason just to do so,

order the company's name to be restored to the register.

(2C) In subsection (2B), "notifiable person" means a person to whom a copy of the company's application under section 652A was required to be given under section 652B or 652C.

(2D) The court, on an application by the Secretary of State made before the expiration of 20 years from publication in the Gazette of notice under section 652A(4), may, if satisfied that it is in the public interest to do so, order the company's name to be restored."

(4) In subsection (3)—

(a) for "the order" there shall be substituted "an order under subsection (2), (2B) or (2D)", and

(b) after "company", in the first place where it occurs, there shall be inserted "to which the order relates".

4. In Schedule 24 (punishment of offences), there shall be inserted at the appropriate places—

"652E(1)	Person breaching or failing to perform duty imposed by section 652B or 652C.	1. On indictment. 2. Summary.	A fine. The statutory maximum.
652E(2)	Person failing to perform duty imposed by section 652B(6) or 652C(2) with intent to conceal the making of application under section 652A.	1. On indictment. 2. Summary.	7 years or a fine; or both. 6 months or the statutory maximum; or both.
652F(1)	Person furnishing false or misleading information in connection with application under section 652A.	1. On indictment. 2. Summary.	A fine. The statutory maximum.
652F(2)	Person making false application under section 652A.	1. On indictment. 2. Summary.	A fine. The statutory maximum."

GENERAL NOTE

This Schedule inserts a new procedure in the Companies Act 1985 (c. 6) to allow private companies that are not trading to apply to be struck off the register of companies and dissolved, thus relieving their directors of obligations under the Companies Act 1985. Safeguards are provided for those dealing or involved with the company.

Para. 2

The conditions that must be satisfied before an application can be made are set out in s.652B(1) and (3). Where any of these conditions ceases to be satisfied the application must be withdrawn (s.652C(4)).

A copy of an application must be given to the persons dealing or involved with the company described in s.652B(6) and to any person who deals or becomes involved with the company after the application is made (s.652C(2)).

Before a company can be struck off, notice must be given and objections invited (s.652A(3)).

A company that is struck off is dissolved, but its dissolution does not affect the liability of its directors, management and members which may be enforced as if the company had not been dissolved (s.652A(6)).

Para. 3

Provision is made for the restoration of companies that have been struck off to the register (s.653(2D)).

Section 13(2)   SCHEDULE 6

STRIKING OFF OF NON-TRADING PRIVATE COMPANIES: NORTHERN IRELAND

1. The Companies (Northern Ireland) Order 1986 shall be amended as follows.
2. After Article 603 there shall be inserted—

"*Registrar may strike private company off register on application*

603A.—(1) On application by a private company, the registrar may strike the company's name off the register.

(2) An application by a company under this Article shall—

(a) be made on its behalf by its directors or by a majority of them,

(b) be in the prescribed form, and

(c) contain the prescribed information.

(3) The registrar shall not strike a company off under this Article until after the expiration of 3 months from the publication by him in the Belfast Gazette of a notice—

(a) stating that he may exercise his power under this Article in relation to the company, and

(b) inviting any person to show cause why he should not do so.

(4) Where the registrar strikes a company off under this Article, he shall publish notice of that fact in the Belfast Gazette.

(5) On the publication in the Belfast Gazette of a notice under paragraph (4), the company to which the notice relates is dissolved.

(6) However, the liability (if any) of every director, managing officer and member of the company continues and may be enforced as if the company had not been dissolved.

(7) Nothing in this Article affects the power of the court to wind up a company the name of which has been struck off the register.

Duties in connection with making application under Article 603A

603B.—(1) A person shall not make an application under Article 603A on behalf of a company if, at any time in the previous 3 months, the company has—

(a) changed its name,

(b) traded or otherwise carried on business,

(c) made a disposal for value of property or rights which, immediately before ceasing to trade or otherwise carry on business, it held for the purpose of disposal for gain in the normal course of trading or otherwise carrying on business, or

(d) engaged in any other activity, except one which is—

(i) necessary or expedient for the purpose of making an application under Article 603A, or deciding whether to do so,

(ii) necessary or expedient for the purpose of concluding the affairs of the company,

(iii) necessary or expedient for the purpose of complying with any statutory requirement, or

(iv) specified for the purposes of this head by the Department by order made subject to negative resolution.

(2) For the purposes of paragraph (1), a company shall not be treated as trading or otherwise carrying on business by virtue only of the fact that it makes a payment in respect of a liability incurred in the course of trading or otherwise carrying on business.

(3) A person shall not make an application under Article 603A on behalf of a company at a time when any of the following is the case—

(a) an application has been made to the court under Article 418 on behalf of the company for the sanctioning of a compromise or arrangement and the matter has not been finally concluded;

(b) a voluntary arrangement in relation to the company has been proposed under Part II of the Insolvency (Northern Ireland) Order 1989 and the matter has not been finally concluded;

(c) an administration order in relation to the company is in force under Part III of that Order or a petition for such an order has been presented and not finally dealt with or withdrawn;

(d) the company is being wound up under Part V of that Order, whether voluntarily or by the court, or a petition under that Part for the winding up of the company by the court has been presented and not finally dealt with or withdrawn;

(e) there is a receiver or manager of the company's property.

(4) For the purposes of paragraph (3)(a), the matter is finally concluded if—

(a) the application has been withdrawn,

(b) the application has been finally dealt with without a compromise or arrangement being sanctioned by the court, or

(c) a compromise or arrangement has been sanctioned by the court and has, together with anything required to be done under any provision made in relation to the matter by order of the court, been fully carried out.

(5) For the purposes of paragraph (3)(b), the matter is finally concluded if—

(a) no meetings are to be summoned under Article 16 of the Insolvency (Northern Ireland) Order 1989,

(b) meetings summoned under that Article fail to approve the arrangement with no, or the same, modifications,

(c) an arrangement approved by meetings summoned under that Article, or in consequence of a direction under Article 19(4)(b) of that Order, has been fully implemented, or

(d) the court makes an order under paragraph (5) of Article 19 of that Order revoking approval given at previous meetings and, if the court gives any directions under paragraph (6) of that Article, the company has done whatever it is required to do under those directions.

(6) A person who makes an application under Article 603A on behalf of a company shall secure that a copy of the application is given, within 7 days from the day on which the application is made, to every person who, at any time on that day, is—

(a) a member of the company,

(b) an employee of the company,

(c) a creditor of the company,

(d) a director of the company,

(e) a manager or trustee of any pension fund established for the benefit of employees of the company, or

(f) a person of a description specified for the purposes of this sub-paragraph by regulations made by the Department.

(7) Paragraph (6) shall not require a copy of the application to be given to a director who is a party to the application.

(8) The duty imposed by paragraph (6) shall cease to apply if the application is withdrawn before the end of the period for giving the copy application.

(9) The Department may by order, made subject to negative resolution, amend paragraph (1) for the purpose of altering the period in relation to which the doing of the things mentioned in sub-paragraphs (a) to (d) of that paragraph is relevant.

Directors' duties following application under Article 603A

603C.—(1) Paragraph (2) applies in relation to any time after the day on which a company makes an application under Article 603A and before the day on which the application is finally dealt with or withdrawn.

(2) A person who is a director of the company at the end of a day on which a person other than himself becomes—

(a) a member of the company,

(b) an employee of the company,

(c) a creditor of the company,

(d) a director of the company,

(e) a manager or trustee of any pension fund established for the benefit of employees of the company, or

(f) a person of a description specified for the purposes of this sub-paragraph by regulations made by the Department,

shall secure that a copy of the application is given to that person within 7 days from that day.

(3) The duty imposed by paragraph (2) shall cease to apply if the application is finally dealt with or withdrawn before the end of the period for giving the copy application.

(4) Paragraph (5) applies where, at any time on or after the day on which a company makes an application under Article 603A and before the day on which the application is finally dealt with or withdrawn—

(a) the company—

    (i) changes its name,

    (ii) trades or otherwise carries on business,

    (iii) makes a disposal for value of any property or rights other than those which it was necessary or expedient for it to hold for the purpose of making, or proceeding with, an application under Article 603A, or

    (iv) engages in any other activity, except one to which paragraph (6) applies;

(b) an application is made to the court under Article 418 on behalf of the company for the sanctioning of a compromise or arrangement;

(c) a voluntary arrangement in relation to the company is proposed under Part II of the Insolvency (Northern Ireland) Order 1989;

(d) a petition is presented for the making of an administration order under Part III of that Order in relation to the company;

(e) there arise any of the circumstances in which, under Article 70(1) of that Order, the company may be voluntarily wound up;

(f) a petition is presented for the winding up of the company by the court under Part V of that Order; or

(g) a receiver or manager of the company's property is appointed.

(5) A person who, at the end of a day on which an event mentioned in any of sub-paragraphs (a) to (g) of paragraph (4) occurs, is a director of the company shall secure that the company's application is withdrawn forthwith.

(6) This paragraph applies to any activity which is—

(a) necessary or expedient for the purpose of making, or proceeding with, an application under Article 603A,

(b) necessary or expedient for the purpose of concluding affairs of the company which are outstanding because of what has been necessary or expedient for the purpose of making, or proceeding with, such an application,

(c) necessary or expedient for the purpose of complying with any statutory requirement, or

(d) specified for the purposes of this paragraph by the Department by order made subject to negative resolution.

(7) For the purposes of paragraph (4)(a), a company shall not be treated as trading or otherwise carrying on business by virtue only of the fact that it makes a payment in respect of a liability incurred in the course of trading or otherwise carrying on business.

Articles 603B and 603C: supplementary provisions

603D.—(1) For the purposes of section 24 of the Interpretation Act (Northern Ireland) 1954 (which relates to the service of documents by post) in its application to a document required to be given to any person under Article 603B(6) or 603C(2), the principal office of a body corporate or partnership which—

(a) is incorporated or formed under the law of a country or territory outside the United Kingdom, and

(b) has a place of business in the United Kingdom,

shall be taken to be its principal office in the United Kingdom.

(2) Where a creditor of the company has more than one place of business, section 24(2) of the Act of 1954 shall have effect, so far as concerns the giving of a document to him under Article 603B(6) or 603C(2), as if for paragraphs (b) and (c) there were substituted—

"(b) it is left, or sent by post to him in accordance with subsection (1), at each place of business of his with which the company has had dealings in relation to a matter by virtue of which he is a creditor of the company."

(3) An order or regulations under Article 603B or 603C may make such transitional provisions as the Department considers appropriate.

(4) For the purposes of Articles 603B and 603C, an application under Article 603A is withdrawn if notice of withdrawal in the prescribed form is given to the registrar.

(5) In Articles 603B and 603C, "disposal" includes part disposal.

(6) In Articles 603B and 603C and this Article, "creditor" includes a contingent or prospective creditor.

Articles 603B and 603C: enforcement

603E.—(1) A person who breaches or fails to perform a duty imposed on him by Article 603B or 603C is guilty of an offence and liable to a fine.

(2) A person who fails to perform a duty imposed on him by Article 603B(6) or 603C(2) with the intention of concealing the making of the application in question from the person concerned is guilty of an offence and liable to imprisonment or a fine, or both.

(3) In any proceedings for an offence under paragraph (1) consisting of breach of a duty imposed by Article 603B(1) or (3), it shall be a defence for the accused to prove that he did not know, and could not reasonably have known, of the existence of the facts which led to the breach.

(4) In any proceedings for an offence under paragraph (1) consisting of failure to perform the duty imposed by Article 603B(6), it shall be a defence for the accused to prove that he took all reasonable steps to perform the duty.

(5) In any proceedings for an offence under paragraph (1) consisting of failure to perform a duty imposed by Article 603C(2) or (5) it shall be a defence for the accused to prove—

(a) that at the time of the failure he was not aware of the fact that the company had made an application under Article 603A, or

(b) that he took all reasonable steps to perform the duty.

Other offences connected with Article 603A

603F.—(1) Where a company makes an application under Article 603A, any person who, in connection with the application, knowingly or recklessly furnishes any information to the registrar which is false or misleading in a material particular is guilty of an offence and liable to a fine.

(2) Any person who knowingly or recklessly makes an application to the registrar which purports to be an application under Article 603A, but which is not, is guilty of an offence and liable to a fine."

3.—(1) Article 604 (objection to striking off by persons aggrieved) shall be amended as follows.

(2) In paragraph (1)—

(a) for "The following" there shall be substituted "Paragraph (2)", and

(b) at the end there shall be inserted "under Article 603."

(3) After paragraph (2) there shall be inserted—

"(2A) Paragraphs (2B) and (2D) apply if a company has been struck off the register under Article 603A.

(2B) The court, on an application by a notifiable person made before the expiration of 20 years from publication in the Belfast Gazette of notice under Article 603A(4), may, if satisfied—

(a) that any duty under Article 603B or 603C with respect to the giving to that person of a copy of the company's application under Article 603A was not performed,

(b) that the making of the company's application under Article 603A involved a breach of duty under Article 603B(1) or (3), or

(c) that it is for some other reason just to do so,

order the company's name to be restored to the register.

(2C) In paragraph (2B), "notifiable person" means a person to whom a copy of the company's application under Article 603A was required to be given under Article 603B or 603C.

(2D) The court, on an application by the Department made before the expiration of 20 years from publication in the Belfast Gazette of notice under Article 603A(4), may, if satisfied that it is in the public interest to do so, order the company's name to be restored."

(4) In paragraph (3)—

(a) for "the order" there shall be substituted "an order under paragraph (2), (2B) or (2D)", and

(b) after "company", in the first place where it occurs, there shall be inserted "to which the order relates".

4. In Schedule 23 (punishment of offences), there shall be inserted at the appropriate places—

"603E(1)	Person breaching or failing to perform duty imposed by Article 603B or 603C.	1. On indictment. 2. Summary.	A fine. The statutory maximum.
603E(2)	Person failing to perform duty imposed by Article 603B(6) or 603C(2) with intent to conceal the making of application under Article 603A.	1. On indictment. 2. Summary.	7 years or a fine; or both. 6 months or the statutory maximum; or both.
603F(1)	Person furnishing false or misleading information in connection with application under Article 603A.	1. On indictment. 2. Summary.	A fine. The statutory maximum.
603F(2)	Person making false application under Article 603A.	1. On indictment. 2. Summary.	A fine. The statutory maximum."

GENERAL NOTE

This Schedule makes provision for Northern Ireland corresponding to Sched. 5.

Section 19   SCHEDULE 7

CHILDREN'S CERTIFICATES: SUPPLEMENTARY PROVISIONS

"SCHEDULE 12A

CHILDREN'S CERTIFICATES: SUPPLEMENTARY PROVISIONS

Applications

1.—(1) Licensing justices shall not entertain an application for a children's certificate unless the applicant has, at least 21 days before the commencement of the licensing sessions at which the application is to be made, given to the clerk to the justices and to the chief officer of police notice of his intention to make the application.

(2) Notice under sub-paragraph (1) of this paragraph shall—

(a) be in writing and be signed by the applicant or his authorised agent, and

(b) state the situation of the premises where the area to which the application relates is to be found.

(3) If the premises mentioned in sub-paragraph (2)(b) of this paragraph include a bar which is not included in the area to which the application relates, licensing justices may decline to entertain the application until the applicant has lodged a plan of the premises indicating the area to which the application relates.

2.—(1) Where a chief officer of police wishes to oppose an application for a children's certificate, he must give notice of his intention to do so to the applicant and to the clerk to the licensing justices at least 7 days before the commencement of the licensing sessions at which the application is to be made.

(2) Notice under sub-paragraph (1) of this paragraph shall be in writing and specify in general terms the grounds of the opposition.

Refusal

3. Where licensing justices refuse an application for a children's certificate, they shall specify their reasons in writing to the applicant.

Conditions

4.—(1) It shall be a condition of the grant of a children's certificate that meals and beverages other than intoxicating liquor are available for sale for consumption in the area to which the certificate relates at all times when the certificate is operational.

(2) Licensing justices may impose such other conditions on the grant of a children's certificate as they think fit.

(3) Without prejudice to the generality of sub-paragraph (2) of this paragraph, conditions under that sub-paragraph may restrict the hours during which, or days on which, the certificate is operational.

When operational

5.—(1) Subject to any condition attached by the licensing justices and to sub-paragraph (2) of this paragraph, a children's certificate shall be operational at any time up to nine in the evening.

(2) Licensing justices may, in relation to a children's certificate, approve a later time than nine in the evening as the time when the certificate ceases to be operational, and may do so either generally or for particular days or periods.

(3) Licensing justices may only act under sub-paragraph (2) of this paragraph on the application of the appropriate person, but an approval under that provision need not correspond with the applicant's proposals.

(4) In sub-paragraph (3) of this paragraph, the reference to the appropriate person is—

(a) in the case of an application with respect to an existing children's certificate, to the holder of the justices' licence for the licensed premises to which the certificate relates, and

(b) in the case of an application made in conjunction with an application for a children's certificate, to the applicant for the certificate.

Duration

6. A children's certificate shall remain in force until revoked.

7.—(1) Licensing justices may, on their own motion or on application by the chief officer of police, revoke a children's certificate if they are satisfied—

(a) that the area to which the certificate relates does not constitute an environment in which it is suitable for persons under fourteen to be present, or

(b) that there has been a serious or persistent failure to comply with one or more conditions attached to the certificate.

(2) When acting on their own motion, licensing justices may only revoke a children's certificate if, at least 21 days before the commencement of the licensing sessions at which they propose to revoke the certificate, they have given notice of their intention to do so to the holder of the justices' licence for the licensed premises to which the certificate relates.

(3) When acting on application by the chief officer of police, licensing justices may only revoke a children's certificate if, at least 21 days before the commencement of the licensing sessions at which the application is to be made, the chief officer of police has given—

(a) to the clerk to the licensing justices, and

(b) to the holder of the justices' licence for the licensed premises to which the certificate relates,

notice of his intention to apply for the revocation of the certificate.

(4) Notice under sub-paragraph (2) or (3) of this paragraph shall be in writing and specify in general terms the grounds for the proposed revocation.

8. If the holder of the justices' licence for the licensed premises to which a children's certificate relates gives—

(a) to the clerk to the licensing justices, and

(b) to the chief officer of police,

at least fourteen days notice in writing of a day on which he wishes the certificate to cease to be in force, it shall be treated as revoked on that day.

9. A children's certificate shall be treated as revoked on the day on which the area to which it relates ceases to be comprised in premises for which a justices' licence is in force.

Appeals

10.—(1) Any applicant for a children's certificate who is aggrieved by a decision of licensing justices—

(a) refusing to grant a certificate, or

(b) as to the conditions attached to the grant of a certificate,
may appeal to the Crown Court against the decision.

(2) Any applicant for an extension of the time when a children's certificate is operational who is aggrieved by a decision of licensing justices with respect to his application may appeal to the Crown Court against the decision.

(3) Any holder of a justices' licence who is aggrieved by a decision of licensing justices revoking a children's certificate relating to the licensed premises may appeal to the Crown Court against the decision.

(4) The judgment of the Crown Court on any appeal under this paragraph shall be final.

11. Where the Crown Court—

(a) has awarded costs against an appellant under paragraph 10 of this Schedule, and

(b) is satisfied that the licensing justices cannot recover those costs from him,

it shall order payment out of central funds of such sums as appear to it sufficient to indemnify the licensing justices from all costs and charges whatever to which they have been put in consequence of the appellant's notice of appeal."

General Note

This Schedule makes supplementary provision with regard to children's certificates.

Para. 1

Notice of intention to apply for a children's certificate must be given at least 21 days before the commencement of the licensing sessions at which the application is to be made. If the premises include a bar which is not covered by the application the justices may decline to entertain the application until a plan of the premises has been lodged.

Para. 2

Where an application is opposed, notice must be given in writing, specifying in general terms the grounds of the opposition, at least seven days before the commencement of the licensing sessions at which the application is to be made.

Para. 3

Where an application is refused, reasons must be given in writing.

Para. 4

Licensing justices may impose such conditions on the grant of a certificate "as they think fit".

Para. 7

A certificate may be revoked on the licensing justices' own motion or on application by the chief officer of police. In either case notice must be given in writing specifying in general terms the grounds for the proposed revocation.

Para. 11

This paragraph gives applicants and licence holders a right of appeal against licensing justices' decisions.

Section 20   SCHEDULE 8

SCHEDULE TO BE INSERTED IN THE BETTING, GAMING AND LOTTERIES ACT 1963 AFTER SCHEDULE 5

"SCHEDULE 5A

Rights of Betting Workers as Respects Sunday Working

General interpretation

1.—(1) In this Schedule, except where a contrary intention appears—

"the 1978 Act" means the Employment Protection (Consolidation) Act 1978;

"betting transaction" includes the collection or payment of winnings on a bet and any transaction in which one or more of the parties is acting as a bookmaker;

"betting work" means—

(a) work at a track in England or Wales for a bookmaker on a day on which the bookmaker acts as such at the track, being work which consists of or includes dealing with betting transactions, and

(b) work in a licensed betting office in England or Wales on a day on which the
office is open for use for the effecting of betting transactions;
"betting worker" means an employee who, under his contract of employment, is required to
do betting work or may be required to do such work;
"bookmaker" means any person who—
(a) whether on his own account or as servant or agent to any other person, carries
on, whether occasionally or regularly, the business of receiving or negotiating bets or
conducting pool betting operations; or
(b) by way of business in any manner holds himself out, or permits himself to be
held out, as a person who receives or negotiates bets or conducts such operations;
"the commencement date" means the day on which this Schedule comes into force;
"dismissal" has the same meaning as in Part V of the 1978 Act;
"notice period", in relation to an opting-out notice, has the meaning given by paragraph 6
below;
"opted-out", in relation to a betting worker, shall be construed in accordance with paragraph 5 below;
"opting-in notice" has the meaning given by paragraph 3(2) below;
"opting-out notice" has the meaning given by paragraph 4(3) below;
"protected", in relation to a betting worker, shall be construed in accordance with paragraphs 2 and 3 below.
(2) Subject to sub–paragraph (3) below, the following provisions of the 1978 Act—
section 151(1) and (2) (computation of period of continuous employment), and
section 153 (general interpretation),
shall have effect for the purposes of this Schedule as they have effect for the purposes of that Act.
(3) For the purposes of this Schedule, section 151(2) of the 1978 Act shall have effect with the
omission of the words from "but" onwards and Schedule 13 to that Act shall have effect with the
following modifications—
(a) in paragraph 1 for the words "paragraphs 3 to 12" there shall be substituted "paragraph 4
or paragraphs 9 to 12",
(b) paragraph 3 and paragraphs 5 to 8 shall be omitted, and
(c) in paragraph 4 the words "which normally involves employment for sixteen hours or more
weekly" shall be omitted.
(4) Where section 56 of the 1978 Act (failure to permit women to return to work after child-
birth treated as dismissal) applies to an employee who was employed as a betting worker under
her contract of employment on the last day of her maternity leave period, she shall be treated for
the purposes of this Schedule as if she had been employed as a betting worker on the day with
effect from which she is treated as dismissed under that section.

Meaning of "protected betting worker"

2.—(1) Subject to paragraph 3 below, a betting worker is to be regarded for the purposes of
this Schedule as "protected" if, and only if, sub-paragraph (2) or (3) below applies to him.
(2) This sub-paragraph applies to any betting worker if—
(a) on the day before the commencement date, he was employed as a betting worker,
(b) on that day, he was not employed to work only on Sunday,
(c) he has been continuously employed during the period beginning with that day and ending
with the appropriate date, and
(d) throughout that period, or throughout every part of it during which his relations with his
employer were governed by a contract of employment, he was a betting worker.
(3) This sub-paragraph applies to any betting worker whose contract of employment is such
that under it he—
(a) is not, and may not be, required to work on Sunday, and
(b) could not be so required even if the provisions of this Schedule were disregarded.
(4) In sub-paragraph (2)(c) above "the appropriate date" means—
(a) in relation to paragraphs 7 and 8 below, the effective date of termination,
(b) in relation to paragraph 10 below, the date of the act or failure to act,
(c) in relation to sub-paragraph (2) or (3) of paragraph 12 below, the day on which the agreement is entered into,
(d) in relation to sub-paragraph (4) of that paragraph, the day on which the employee returns
to work,
(e) in relation to paragraph 14 below, any time in relation to which the contract is to be
enforced, and
(f) in relation to paragraph 15 below, the end of the period in respect of which the remuneration is paid or the benefit accrues.

(5) For the purposes of sub-paragraph (4)(a) above, "the effective date of termination", in any case falling within paragraph 1(4) above, means the day with effect from which the employee is treated by section 56 of the 1978 Act as being dismissed.

(6) For the purposes of sub-paragraph (4)(b) above—

(a) where an act extends over a period, the "date of the act" means the first day of the period, and

(b) a deliberate failure to act shall be treated as done when it was decided on,

and in the absence of evidence establishing the contrary, an employer shall be taken to decide on a failure to act when he does an act inconsistent with doing the failed act or, if he has done no such inconsistent act, when the period expires within which he might reasonably have been expected to do the failed act if it was to be done.

(7) Where on the day before the commencement date an employee's relations with his employer have ceased to be governed by a contract of employment, he shall be regarded as satisfying the conditions in sub-paragraph (2)(a) and (b) above if—

(a) that day falls in a week which counts as a period of employment with that employer under paragraph 9 or 10 of Schedule 13 to the 1978 Act (absence from work because of sickness, pregnancy etc.) or under regulations made under paragraph 20 of that Schedule (reinstatement or re-engagement of dismissed employee), and

(b) on the last day before the commencement date on which his relations with his employer were governed by a contract of employment, the employee was a betting worker and was not employed to work only on Sunday.

3.—(1) A betting worker is not a protected betting worker if—

(a) on or after the commencement date, he has given his employer an opting-in notice, and

(b) after giving that notice, he has expressly agreed with his employer to do betting work on Sunday or on a particular Sunday.

(2) In this Schedule "opting-in notice" means a written notice, signed and dated by the betting worker, in which the betting worker expressly states that he wishes to work on Sunday or that he does not object to Sunday working.

Notice of objection to Sunday working

4.—(1) This paragraph applies to any betting worker who, under his contract of employment—

(a) is or may be required to work on Sunday (whether or not as a result of previously giving an opting-in notice), but

(b) is not employed to work only on Sunday.

(2) A betting worker to whom this paragraph applies may at any time give his employer written notice, signed and dated by the betting worker, to the effect that the betting worker objects to Sunday working.

(3) In this Schedule "opting-out notice" means a notice given under sub-paragraph (2) above by a betting worker to whom this paragraph applies.

Meaning of "opted-out betting worker"

5.—(1) Subject to sub-paragraph (5) below, a betting worker is to be regarded for the purposes of this Schedule as "opted-out" if, and only if—

(a) he has given his employer an opting-out notice,

(b) he has been continuously employed during the period beginning with the day on which the notice was given and ending with the appropriate date, and

(c) throughout that period, or throughout every part of it during which his relations with his employer were governed by a contract of employment, he was a betting worker.

(2) In sub-paragraph (1) above "the appropriate date" means—

(a) in relation to paragraphs 7 and 8 below, the effective date of termination,

(b) in relation to paragraph 10 below, the date of the act or failure to act,

(c) in relation to sub-paragraph (2) or (3) of paragraph 13 below, the day on which the agreement is entered into, and

(d) in relation to sub-paragraph (4) of that paragraph, the day on which the employee returns to work.

(3) For the purposes of sub-paragraph (2)(a) above, "the effective date of termination", in any case falling within paragraph 1(4) above, means the day with effect from which the employee is treated by section 56 of the 1978 Act as being dismissed.

(4) For the purposes of sub-paragraph (2)(b) above—

(a) where an act extends over a period, the "date of the act" means the first day of the period, and

(b) a deliberate failure to act shall be treated as done when it was decided on,
and in the absence of evidence establishing the contrary, an employer shall be taken to decide on a failure to act when he does an act inconsistent with doing the failed act or, if hc has done no such inconsistent act, when the period expires within which he might reasonably have been expected to do the failed act if it was to be done.

(5) A betting worker is not an opted-out betting worker if—

(a) after giving the opting-out notice concerned, he has given his employer an opting-in notice, and

(b) after giving that opting-in notice, he has expressly agreed with his employer to do betting work on Sunday or on a particular Sunday.

Meaning of "notice period"

6. In this Schedule "notice period", in relation to an opted-out betting worker, means, subject to paragraph 11(2) below, the period of three months beginning with the day on which the opting-out notice concerned was given.

Right not to be dismissed for refusing Sunday work

7.—(1) Subject to sub-paragraph (2) below, the dismissal of a protected or opted-out betting worker by his employer shall be regarded for the purposes of Part V of the 1978 Act as unfair if the reason for it (or, if more than one, the principal reason) was that the betting worker refused, or proposed to refuse, to do betting work on Sunday or on a particular Sunday.

(2) Sub-paragraph (1) above does not apply in relation to an opted-out betting worker where the reason (or principal reason) for the dismissal was that he refused, or proposed to refuse, to do betting work on any Sunday or Sundays falling before the end of the notice period.

(3) The dismissal of a betting worker by his employer shall be regarded for the purposes of Part V of the 1978 Act as unfair if the reason for it (or, if more than one, the principal reason) was that the betting worker gave, or proposed to give, an opting-out notice to the employer.

(4) Section 142 of the 1978 Act (contracts for a fixed term) shall not exclude the application of section 54 of that Act (right of employee not to be unfairly dismissed) in relation to any dismissal which is unfair by virtue of sub-paragraph (1) or (3) above.

8.—(1) Where the reason or principal reason for the dismissal of a protected or opted-out betting worker was that he was redundant, but it is shown—

(a) that the circumstances constituting the redundancy applied equally to one or more other employees in the same undertaking who held positions similar to that held by him and who have not been dismissed by the employer, and

(b) that the reason (or, if more than one, the principal reason) for which he was selected for dismissal was that specified in paragraph 7(1) above,

then, for the purposes of Part V of the 1978 Act, the dismissal shall be regarded as unfair.

(2) Sub-paragraph (1) above does not apply in relation to an opted-out betting worker where the reason (or principal reason) for which he was selected for dismissal was that specified in paragraph 7(2) above.

(3) Where the reason or principal reason for the dismissal of a betting worker was that he was redundant, but it is shown—

(a) that the circumstances constituting the redundancy applied equally to one or more other employees in the same undertaking who held positions similar to that held by him and who have not been dismissed by the employer, and

(b) that the reason (or, if more than one, the principal reason) for which he was selected for dismissal was that specified in paragraph 7(3) above,

then, for the purposes of Part V of the 1978 Act, the dismissal shall be regarded as unfair.

Exclusion of section 64(1) of Employment Protection (Consolidation) Act 1978

9. Section 54 of the 1978 Act (right of employee not to be unfairly dismissed) shall apply to a dismissal regarded as unfair by virtue of paragraph 7 or 8 above regardless of the period for which the employee has been employed and of his age; and accordingly section 64(1) of that Act (which provides a qualifying period and an upper age limit) shall not apply to such a dismissal.

Right not to suffer detriment for refusing Sunday work

10.—(1) Subject to sub-paragraphs (2) and (4) below, a protected or opted-out betting worker has the right not to be subjected to any detriment by any act, or any deliberate failure to act, by his employer done on the ground that the betting worker refused, or proposed to refuse, to do betting work on Sunday or on a particular Sunday.

(2) Sub-paragraph (1) above does not apply to anything done in relation to an opted-out betting worker on the ground that he refused, or proposed to refuse, to do betting work on any Sunday or Sundays falling before the end of the notice period.

(3) Subject to sub-paragraph (4) below, a betting worker has the right not to be subjected to any detriment by any act, or any deliberate failure to act, by his employer done on the ground that he gave, or proposed to give, an opting-out notice to his employer.

(4) Sub-paragraphs (1) and (3) above do not apply where the detriment in question amounts to dismissal.

(5) For the purposes of this paragraph a betting worker who does not work on Sunday or on a particular Sunday is not to be regarded as having been subjected to any detriment by—

(a) any failure to pay remuneration in respect of betting work on a Sunday which he has not done,

(b) any failure to provide him with any other benefit, where that failure results from the application, in relation to a Sunday on which the employee has not done betting work, of a contractual term under which the extent of that benefit varies according to the number of hours worked by the employee or the remuneration of the employee, or

(c) any failure to provide him with any work, remuneration or other benefit which by virtue of paragraph 14 or 15 below the employer is not obliged to provide.

(6) Where an employer offers to pay a sum specified in the offer to any one or more employees who are protected or opted-out betting workers or who, under their contracts of employment, are not obliged to do betting work on Sunday, if they agree to do betting work on Sunday or on a particular Sunday—

(a) an employee to whom the offer is not made is not to be regarded for the purposes of this paragraph as having been subjected to any detriment by any failure to make the offer to him or to pay him that sum, and

(b) an employee who does not accept the offer is not to be regarded for those purposes as having been subjected to any detriment by any failure to pay him that sum.

Employer's duty to give explanatory statement

11.—(1) Where a person becomes a betting worker to whom paragraph 4 above applies, his employer shall, before the end of the period of two months beginning with the day on which that person becomes such a betting worker, give him a written statement in the prescribed form.

(2) If—

(a) an employer fails to comply with sub-paragraph (1) above in relation to any betting worker, and

(b) the betting worker, on giving the employer an opting-out notice, becomes an opted-out betting worker,

paragraph 6 above shall have effect, in relation to the betting worker, with the substitution for "three months" of "one month".

(3) An employer shall not be regarded as failing to comply with sub-paragraph (1) above in any case where, before the end of the period referred to in that sub-paragraph, the betting worker has given him an opting-out notice.

(4) Subject to sub-paragraph (5) below, the prescribed form is as follows—

"STATUTORY RIGHTS IN RELATION TO SUNDAY BETTING WORK

You have become employed under a contract of employment under which you are or can be required to do Sunday betting work, that is to say, work—

at a track on a Sunday on which your employer is taking bets at the track, or
in a licensed betting office on a Sunday on which it is open for business.

However, if you wish, you can give a notice, as described in the next paragraph, to your employer and you will then have the right not to do Sunday betting work once three months have passed from the date on which you gave the notice.

Your notice must—

be in writing;
be signed and dated by you;
say that you object to doing Sunday betting work.

For three months after you give the notice, your employer can still require you to do all the Sunday betting work your contract provides for. After the three month period has ended, you have the right to complain to an industrial tribunal if, because of your refusal to do Sunday betting work, your employer—

dismisses you, or

does something else detrimental to you, for example, failing to promote you.

Once you have the rights described, you can surrender them only by giving your employer a further notice, signed and dated by you, saying that you wish to do Sunday betting work or that you do not object to doing Sunday betting work and then agreeing with your employer to do such work on Sundays or on a particular Sunday."

(5) The Secretary of State may by order amend the prescribed form set out in sub-paragraph (4) above.

(6) An order under sub-paragraph (5) above shall be made by statutory instrument which shall be subject to annulment in pursuance of a resolution of either House of Parliament.

Effect of rights on contracts of employment

12.—(1) Any contract of employment under which a betting worker who satisfies the conditions in paragraph 2(2)(a) and (b) above was employed on the day before the commencement date is unenforceable to the extent that it—

(a) requires the betting worker to do betting work on Sunday on or after the commencement date, or

(b) requires the employer to provide the betting worker with betting work on Sunday on or after that date.

(2) Except as provided by sub-paragraph (3) below, any agreement entered into after the commencement date between a protected betting worker and his employer is unenforceable to the extent that it—

(a) requires the betting worker to do betting work on Sunday, or

(b) requires the employer to provide the betting worker with betting work on Sunday.

(3) Where, after giving an opting-in notice, a protected betting worker expressly agrees as mentioned in paragraph 3(1)(b) above (and so ceases to be protected), his contract of employment shall be taken to be varied to the extent necessary to give effect to the terms of the agreement.

(4) The reference in sub-paragraph (2) above to a protected betting worker includes a reference to an employee who, although not a protected betting worker for the purposes of that sub-paragraph at the time when the agreement is entered into, is a protected betting worker on the day on which she returns to work as mentioned in paragraph 10 of Schedule 13 to the 1978 Act (maternity).

13.—(1) Where a betting worker gives his employer an opting-out notice, the contract of employment under which he was employed immediately before he gave that notice becomes unenforceable to the extent that it—

(a) requires the betting worker to do betting work on Sunday after the end of the notice period, or

(b) requires the employer to provide the betting worker with betting work on Sunday after the end of that period.

(2) Except as provided by sub-paragraph (3) below, any agreement entered into between an opted-out betting worker and his employer is unenforceable to the extent that it—

(a) requires the betting worker to do betting work on Sunday after the end of the notice period, or

(b) requires the employer to provide the betting worker with betting work on Sunday after the end of that period.

(3) Where, after giving an opting-in notice, an opted-out betting worker expressly agrees as mentioned in paragraph 5(5)(b) above (and so ceases to be opted-out), his contract of employment shall be taken to be varied to the extent necessary to give effect to the terms of the agreement.

(4) The reference in sub-paragraph (2) above to an opted-out betting worker includes a reference to an employee who, although not an opted-out betting worker for the purposes of that sub-paragraph at the time when the agreement is entered into, had given her employer an opting-out notice before that time and is an opted-out betting worker on the day on which she returns to work as mentioned in paragraph 10 of Schedule 13 to the 1978 Act (maternity).

14. If—

(a) under the contract of employment under which a betting worker who satisfies the conditions in paragraph 2(2)(a) and (b) above was employed on the day before the commencement date, the employer is, or may be, required to provide him with betting work for a specified number of hours each week,

(b) under that contract, the betting worker was or might have been required to work on Sunday before the commencement date, and

(c) the betting worker has done betting work on Sunday in that employment (whether or not before the commencement date) but has, on or after the commencement date, ceased to do so, then, so long as the betting worker remains a protected betting worker, that contract shall not be regarded as requiring the employer to provide him with betting work on weekdays in excess of the hours normally worked by the betting worker on weekdays before he ceased to do betting work on Sunday.

15.—(1) If—

(a) under the contract of employment under which a betting worker who satisfies the conditions in paragraph 2(2)(a) and (b) above was employed on the day before the commencement date, the betting worker was or might have been required to work on Sunday before that date,

(b) the betting worker has done betting work on Sunday in that employment (whether or not before the commencement date) but has, on or after the commencement date, ceased to do so, and

(c) it is not apparent from the contract what part of the remuneration payable, or of any other benefit accruing, to the betting worker was intended to be attributable to betting work on Sunday,

then, so long as the betting worker remains a protected betting worker, that contract shall be regarded as enabling the employer to reduce the amount of remuneration paid, or the extent of the other benefit provided, to the betting worker in respect of any period by the proportion which the hours of betting work which (apart from this Schedule) the betting worker could have been required to do on Sunday in the period (in this paragraph referred to as "the contractual Sunday hours") bears to the aggregate of those hours and the hours of work actually done by the betting worker in the period.

(2) Where, under the contract of employment, the hours of work actually done on weekdays in any period would be taken into account in determining the contractual Sunday hours, they shall be taken into account in determining the contractual Sunday hours for the purposes of sub-paragraph (1) above.

Proceedings for contravention of paragraph 10

16. Sections 22B and 22C of the 1978 Act (which relate to proceedings brought by an employee on the ground that he has been subjected to a detriment in contravention of section 22A of that Act) shall have effect as if the reference in section 22B(1) to section 22A included a reference to paragraph 10 above.

Restrictions on contracting out of Schedule

17.—(1) Any provision in an agreement (whether a contract of employment or not) shall be void in so far as it purports—

(a) to exclude or limit the operation of any provision of this Schedule, or

(b) to preclude any person from presenting a complaint to an industrial tribunal by virtue of any provision of this Schedule.

(2) Sub-paragraph (1) above does not apply to an agreement to refrain from presenting or continuing with a complaint where—

(a) a conciliation officer has taken action under section 133(2) or (3) of the 1978 Act (general provisions as to conciliation) or under section 134(1), (2) or (3) (conciliation in case of unfair dismissal) of that Act, or

(b) the conditions regulating compromise agreements under the 1978 Act (as set out in section 140(3) of that Act) are satisfied in relation to the agreement.

Transitional modifications relating to maternity cases

18.—(1) Where—

(a) an employee exercises a right to return to work under Part III of the 1978 Act (maternity), and

(b) because amendments of that Part made by the Trade Union Reform and Employment Rights Act 1993 (in this paragraph referred to as "the 1993 Act") do not have effect in her case, her right is a right to return to work in the job in which she was employed under the original contract of employment,

the preceding provisions of this Schedule shall have effect subject to the modifications in sub-paragraphs (2) and (3) below.

(2) In paragraph 1(4), for "her contract of employment on the last day of her maternity leave period" there shall be substituted "her original contract of employment".

(3) In paragraph 2(7), for paragraph (b) there shall be substituted—

"(b) under her original contract of employment, she was a betting worker and was not employed to work only on Sunday."

(4) In this paragraph and in paragraphs 1 and 2 above as modified by sub-paragraphs (2) and (3) above, "original contract of employment" has the meaning given by section 153(1) of the 1978 Act as originally enacted.

Dismissal on grounds of assertion of statutory right

19. In section 60A of the 1978 Act (dismissal on grounds of assertion of statutory right) in subsection (4)(a), after "or" at the end of paragraph (i) there shall be inserted—
    "(ia) Schedule 5A to the Betting, Gaming and Lotteries Act 1963, or".

Dismissal procedures agreements

20. In section 65 of the 1978 Act (exclusion in respect of dismissal procedures agreement) in subsection (4), after "section 60A(1)" there shall be inserted "or the right conferred by paragraph 7 or 8 of Schedule 5A to the Betting, Gaming and Lotteries Act 1963".

Conciliation

21. In section 133 of the 1978 Act (general provisions as to conciliation officers) after "or" at the end of paragraph (a) there shall be inserted—
    "(aa) arising out of a contravention, or alleged contravention, of paragraph 10 of Schedule 5A to the Betting, Gaming and Lotteries Act 1963; or".

Application of certain other provisions of 1978 Act

22. In the following provisions of the 1978 Act—
    section 129 (remedy for infringement of certain rights),
    section 141(2) (employee ordinarily working outside Great Britain), and
    section 150 and Schedule 12 (death of employee or employer),
any reference to Part II of the 1978 Act includes a reference to paragraph 10 of this Schedule.

GENERAL NOTE
This Schedule makes provision for the protection of betting workers with regard to Sunday working. It is based on Sched. 4 to the Sunday Trading Act 1994 (c. 20).

Para. 1
The first limb of the definition of "betting work" means that only those who work for a bookmaker or tote operator are covered; those employed by others are not covered. The second limb means that ancillary workers in betting shops, such as cleaners, are covered (*Hansard*, H.L. Vol. 556, col. 787).

Para. 2
This paragraph defines "protected betting worker". Sub-paragraph (3) extends the definition to include betting workers whose contracts of employment do not require Sunday working. Such workers therefore enjoy automatically the protections against unfair dismissal and other detrimental action afforded by the Schedule (*Hansard*, H.L. Vol. 556, col. 788).

Para. 3
Under this paragraph a worker may opt-in to Sunday working by giving his employer notice and agreeing to work on Sunday.

Para. 4
Under this paragraph a worker who may or may not be required to work on a Sunday may opt-out of Sunday working.

Para. 5
This paragraph defines an "opted-out betting worker" and gives him the same rights as a protected worker.

Para. 7
This paragraph gives a worker who is dismissed for refusing to work on Sunday or for opting-out of Sunday working a claim for unfair dismissal.

Para. 8

This paragraph gives a worker who has been made redundant for refusing to work on Sunday or for opting-out of Sunday working a claim for unfair dismissal.

Para. 10

This paragraph seeks to ensure that a worker who has refused to work on Sunday or opted-out of Sunday working is not "subjected to any detriment".

Para. 11

This paragraph imposes a duty on employers to notify employees who are or may be required to work on Sundays of their rights.

Paras. 12–15

These paragraphs make consequential variations to existing contracts of employment or those affected by opting-in or opting-out notices.

Para. 17

This paragraph ensures that a provision in an agreement between a betting worker and his employer cannot generally exclude the provisions of this Schedule or prevent a betting worker from pursuing a complaint under it (*Hansard*, H.L. Vol. 556, col. 790).

Para. 18

This paragraph ensures that all betting workers who are subject to the statutory provisions on maternity absence will not fail to have protected status under the Schedule when they return to work, by virtue of being temporarily employed under a different contract to their normal contract (*Hansard*, H.L. Vol. 556, col. 791).

Para. 19

This paragraph provides that the remedy by way of complaint to an industrial tribunal in respect of the right not to be dismissed for refusing Sunday work, set out in paras. 7 and 8 of the Schedule, is not replaced by the provisions of a dismissal procedures agreement designated by the Secretary of State under s.65 of the Employment Protection (Consolidation) Act 1978 (c. 44) (*Hansard*, H.L. Vol. 556, col. 790).

Section 31   SCHEDULE 9

SLAUGHTERHOUSES AND KNACKERS' YARDS: UNITING OF ENFORCEMENT FUNCTIONS

Powers to transfer enforcement functions to agriculture Ministers

1.—(1) This paragraph applies to the following provisions of the Slaughter of Poultry Act 1967—

(a) section 3 (power to make regulations for securing humane conditions of slaughter),
(b) section 4 (power to authorise persons to exercise rights of entry), and
(c) section 6 (duty to execute and enforce the provisions of that Act and of regulations under section 3 of that Act).

(2) The Minister of Agriculture, Fisheries and Food, the Secretary of State for Scotland and the Secretary of State for Wales acting jointly may by regulations provide for any functions under a provision to which this paragraph applies, so far as exercisable by local authorities, to be transferred—

(a) so far as exercisable by local authorities in England, to the Minister of Agriculture, Fisheries and Food, and
(b) so far as exercisable by local authorities in Scotland or Wales, to the Secretary of State.

2.—(1) This paragraph applies to the following provisions of the Slaughterhouses Act 1974—

(a) section 36 (power to make regulations with respect to additional means of rendering animals insensible to pain until death supervenes),
(b) section 38 (power to make regulations for securing humane conditions of slaughter),
(c) section 39 (function of granting licences for slaughtermen),
(d) section 40 (other functions with respect to licences for slaughtermen),
(e) section 41 (duty to execute and enforce the provisions of, and of regulations under, Part II of that Act), and
(f) section 42(1) (power to appoint persons for the purpose of exercising powers of entry).

(2) The Minister of Agriculture, Fisheries and Food and the Secretary of State acting jointly may by regulations provide for any functions under a provision to which this paragraph applies, so far as exercisable by local authorities, to be transferred—

(a) so far as exercisable by local authorities in England, to the Minister of Agriculture, Fisheries and Food, and

(b) so far as exercisable by local authorities in Wales, to the Secretary of State.

3.—(1) This paragraph applies to the following provisions of the Slaughter of Animals (Scotland) Act 1980 (which correspond to the provisions to which paragraph 2 above applies)—

(a) section 9,

(b) section 10,

(c) section 14(3)(c),

(d) section 15,

(e) section 16, and

(f) section 19(1).

(2) The Secretary of State may by regulations provide for any functions under a provision to which this paragraph applies, so far as exercisable by local authorities, to be transferred to the Secretary of State.

4. No functions under the Slaughterhouses Act 1974 or the Slaughter of Animals (Scotland) Act 1980 relating to knackers' yards (within the meaning of the Act concerned) shall be transferred under this Schedule unless the transferee has, in relation to the yards to which the transferred functions relate, functions with respect to the enforcement of law relating to animal health.

5.—(1) Regulations under paragraph 1(2), 2(2) or 3(2) above may contain such supplemental, incidental, consequential and transitional provisions and savings as the authority making the regulations considers appropriate and may, in particular, contain such amendments or repeals of any enactment or subordinate legislation (within the meaning of the Interpretation Act 1978) as that authority considers appropriate in consequence of a transfer of functions under that sub-paragraph.

(2) The power to make regulations under paragraph 1(2), 2(2) or 3(2) above shall be exercisable by statutory instrument which shall be subject to annulment in pursuance of a resolution of either House of Parliament.

Territorial division of enforcement functions under the Food Safety Act 1990

6. In section 6(4)(a) of the Food Safety Act 1990 (which lists authorities from which regulations or orders under the Act must select the authority to enforce and execute them) for "the Minister" there shall be substituted "the Minister of Agriculture, Fisheries and Food, the Secretary of State".

GENERAL NOTE

This Schedule makes provision for the transfer of enforcement functions relating to slaughterhouses and knackers' yards from local authorities to the Minister of Agriculture, Fisheries and Food in England or to the Secretary of State in Scotland and Wales.

Section 35   SCHEDULE 10

EMPLOYMENT AGENCIES ETC.: REPLACEMENT OF LICENSING

PART I

GENERAL

Great Britain

1.—(1) The Employment Agencies Act 1973 shall be amended as follows.

(2) Sections 1 to 3 (licences) shall cease to have effect.

(3) After section 3 there shall be inserted—

"Prohibition orders

Power to make orders

3A.—(1) On application by the Secretary of State, an industrial tribunal may by order prohibit a person from carrying on, or being concerned with the carrying on of—

(a) any employment agency or employment business; or

(b) any specified description of employment agency or employment business.

(2) An order under subsection (1) of this section (in this Act referred to as "a prohibition order") may either prohibit a person from engaging in an activity altogether or prohibit him from doing so otherwise than in accordance with specified conditions.

(3) A prohibition order shall be made for a period beginning with the date of the order and ending—

(a) on a specified date, or

(b) on the happening of a specified event,

in either case, not more than ten years later.

(4) Subject to subsections (5) and (6) of this section, an industrial tribunal shall not make a prohibition order in relation to any person unless it is satisfied that he is, on account of his misconduct or for any other sufficient reason, unsuitable to do what the order prohibits.

(5) An industrial tribunal may make a prohibition order in relation to a body corporate if it is satisfied that—

(a) any director, secretary, manager or similar officer of the body corporate,

(b) any person who performs on behalf of the body corporate the functions of a director, secretary, manager or similar officer, or

(c) any person in accordance with whose directions or instructions the directors of the body corporate are accustomed to act,

is unsuitable, on account of his misconduct or for any other sufficient reason, to do what the order prohibits.

(6) An industrial tribunal may make a prohibition order in relation to a partnership if it is satisfied that any member of the partnership, or any manager employed by the partnership, is unsuitable, on account of his misconduct or for any other sufficient reason, to do what the order prohibits.

(7) For the purposes of subsection (4) of this section, where an employment agency or employment business has been improperly conducted, each person who was carrying on, or concerned with the carrying on of, the agency or business at the time, shall be deemed to have been responsible for what happened unless he can show that it happened without his connivance or consent and was not attributable to any neglect on his part.

(8) A person shall not be deemed to fall within subsection (5)(c) of this section by reason only that the directors act on advice given by him in a professional capacity.

(9) In this section—

"director", in relation to a body corporate whose affairs are controlled by its members, means a member of the body corporate; and

"specified", in relation to a prohibition order, means specified in the order.

Enforcement

3B. Any person who, without reasonable excuse, fails to comply with a prohibition order shall be guilty of an offence and liable on summary conviction to a fine not exceeding level 5 on the standard scale.

Variation and revocation of orders

3C.—(1) On application by the person to whom a prohibition order applies, an industrial tribunal may vary or revoke the order if the tribunal is satisfied that there has been a material change of circumstances since the order was last considered.

(2) An industrial tribunal may not, on an application under this section, so vary a prohibition order as to make it more restrictive.

(3) The Secretary of State shall be a party to any proceedings before an industrial tribunal with respect to an application under this section, and be entitled to appear and be heard accordingly.

(4) When making a prohibition order or disposing of an application under this section, an industrial tribunal may, with a view to preventing the making of vexatious or frivolous applications, by order prohibit the making of an application, or further application, under this section in relation to the prohibition order before such date as the tribunal may specify in the order under this subsection.

Appeals

3D.—(1) An appeal shall lie to the Employment Appeal Tribunal on a question of law arising from any decision of, or arising in proceedings before, an industrial tribunal under section 3A or 3C of this Act.

(2) No other appeal shall lie from a decision of an industrial tribunal under section 3A or 3C of this Act; and section 11 of the Tribunals and Inquiries Act 1992 (appeals from certain tribunals to High Court or Court of Session) shall not apply to proceedings before an industrial tribunal under section 3A or 3C of this Act."

(4) In section 9(4)(a)(iv) (circumstances in which information obtained in exercise of statutory powers may be disclosed) for "hearing under section 3(7) of this Act" there shall be substituted "proceedings under section 3A, 3C or 3D of this Act".

(5) In section 13(1) (interpretation) after the definition of "prescribed" there shall be inserted—

" "prohibition order" has the meaning given by section 3A(2) of this Act;".

Northern Ireland

2.—(1) Articles 3 to 5 of the Employment (Miscellaneous Provisions) (Northern Ireland) Order 1981 shall cease to have effect.

(2) After Article 5 of that Order there shall be inserted—

"Prohibition orders

Power to make orders

5A.—(1) On application by the Department, an industrial tribunal may by order prohibit a person from carrying on, or being concerned with the carrying on of—

(a) any employment agency or employment business; or

(b) any specified description of employment agency or employment business.

(2) An order under paragraph (1) (in this Order referred to as "a prohibition order") may either prohibit a person from engaging in an activity altogether or prohibit him from doing so otherwise than in accordance with specified conditions.

(3) A prohibition order shall be made for a period beginning with the date of the order and ending—

(a) on a specified date, or

(b) on the happening of a specified event,

in either case, not more than ten years later.

(4) Subject to paragraphs (5) and (6), an industrial tribunal shall not make a prohibition order in relation to any person unless it is satisfied that he is, on account of his misconduct or for any other sufficient reason, unsuitable to do what the order prohibits.

(5) An industrial tribunal may make a prohibition order in relation to a body corporate if it is satisfied that—

(a) any director, secretary, manager or similar officer of the body corporate,

(b) any person who performs on behalf of the body corporate the functions of a director, secretary, manager or similar officer, or

(c) any person in accordance with whose directions or instructions the directors of the body corporate are accustomed to act,

is unsuitable, on account of his misconduct or for any other sufficient reason, to do what the order prohibits.

(6) An industrial tribunal may make a prohibition order in relation to a partnership if it is satisfied that any member of the partnership, or any manager employed by the partnership, is unsuitable, on account of his misconduct or for any other sufficient reason, to do what the order prohibits.

(7) For the purposes of paragraph (4), where an employment agency or employment business has been improperly conducted, each person who was carrying on, or concerned with the carrying on of, the agency or business at the time, shall be deemed to have been responsible for what happened unless he can show that it happened without his connivance or consent and was not attributable to any neglect on his part.

(8) A person shall not be deemed to fall within paragraph (5)(c) by reason only that the directors act on advice given by him in a professional capacity.

(9) In this Article—

"director", in relation to a body corporate whose affairs are controlled by its members, means a member of the body corporate; and

"specified", in relation to a prohibition order, means specified in the order.

Enforcement

5B. Any person who, without reasonable excuse, fails to comply with a prohibition order shall be guilty of an offence and liable on summary conviction to a fine not exceeding level 5 on the standard scale.

Variation and revocation of orders

5C.—(1) On application by the person to whom a prohibition order applies, an industrial tribunal may vary or revoke the order if the tribunal is satisfied that there has been a material change of circumstances since the order was last considered.

(2) An industrial tribunal may not, on an application under this Article, so vary a prohibition order as to make it more restrictive.

(3) The Department shall be a party to any proceedings before an industrial tribunal with respect to an application under this Article, and be entitled to appear and be heard accordingly.

(4) When making a prohibition order or disposing of an application under this Article, an industrial tribunal may, with a view to preventing the making of vexatious or frivolous applications, by order prohibit the making of an application, or further application, under this Article in relation to the prohibition order before such date as the tribunal may specify in the order under this paragraph."

(3) In Article 11(1) of that Order (interpretation) after the definition of "prescribed" there shall be inserted—

" "prohibition order" has the meaning given by Article 5A(2);".

PART II

SEAMEN

United Kingdom

3. Sections 110 to 112 of the Merchant Shipping Act 1894 (licences to supply seamen) shall cease to have effect.

Great Britain

4. In the Employment Agencies Act 1973, in section 13(7) (exceptions from the Act) paragraph (e) (exception for the making of arrangements for finding seamen for persons to employ or for finding employment for seamen) shall be omitted.

Northern Ireland

5. In the Employment (Miscellaneous Provisions) (Northern Ireland) Order 1981, in Article 11(5) (exceptions from Part II of the Order), sub-paragraph (d) shall be omitted.

GENERAL NOTE

This Schedule makes provision for the replacement of the licensing requirement for employment agencies under the Employment Agencies Act 1973 (c. 35).

Para. 1

This paragraph replaces the power under the Employment Agencies Act 1973 (c. 35) to refuse or revoke licences on specified grounds with a power to prohibit the carrying on of an employment agency or business on similar grounds. Section 3A(5) of the Employment Agencies Act 1973 is intended to enable an industrial tribunal to make a prohibition order against a body corporate if any of the people in charge are unsuitable to run an employment agency or business (Standing Committee F, col. 670).

Para. 2

This paragraph makes corresponding provision for Northern Ireland.

Paras. 3–5

These paragraphs bring seamen's agencies within the scope of the negative licensing regime.

Section 39   SCHEDULE 11

MISCELLANEOUS DEREGULATORY PROVISIONS: CONSEQUENTIAL AMENDMENTS

Licensing Act 1964 (c. 26)

1.—(1) The Licensing Act 1964 shall be amended as follows.

(2) In section 179(1)(b), after "if" there shall be inserted "subsections (3A) to (3C) of section 168, section 168A,".

(3) In section 196A(1)—

(a) in paragraph (a), after sub-paragraph (iii) there shall be inserted "or

(iv) for the grant or revocation of a children's certificate;", and

(b) in paragraph (b), for "or canteen licence" there shall be substituted ", canteen licence or children's certificate".

(4) In section 201(1), there shall be inserted at the appropriate place in alphabetical order—

" "children's certificate" has the meaning assigned to it by section 168A(2) of this Act;".

(5) In section 202(1)(b), after "Part III of this Act" there shall be inserted ", under section 168A of this Act".

Fair Trading Act 1973 (c. 41)

2.—(1) The Fair Trading Act 1973 shall be amended as follows.

(2) In section 77—

(a) in subsection (1)(a), after "57(1)" there shall be inserted "or (1A)", and

(b) in subsection (5)(a), after "having a" there shall be inserted "primary".

(3) In section 93A(1)(a), for "under section" there shall be substituted "pursuant to a proposal under section 56A of this Act or under section 56F or".

(4) In section 133(4)(a), there shall be inserted at the end "or a notice published by the Director under section 56B of this Act".

Energy Act 1976 (c. 76)

3. In section 5(6) of the Energy Act 1976, for "under", in the third place where it occurs, there shall be substituted "in accordance with section 24 of and Schedule 2 to".

Competition Act 1980 (c. 21)

4.—(1) The Competition Act 1980 shall be amended as follows.

(2) Section 2(5) shall cease to have effect.

(3) In section 5(3)—

(a) after "made" there shall be inserted "by virtue of subsection (1)(b) or (c) above",

(b) after "reference be" there shall be inserted "so", and

(c) the words from the beginning of paragraph (a) to "notice reference" shall be omitted.

(4) In section 15(4) for the words from the beginning to "that investigation" there shall be substituted "On making a competition reference in relation to any course of conduct being pursued by a person falling within section 11(3)(d) above".

(5) In section 16, at the end there shall be inserted—

"(3) For the purposes of this section, the publication by the Director of a notice under section 4(2)(a) above shall be treated as the making by him of a report under this Act."

(6) In section 19(5)(a), after "Act" there shall be inserted "or in anything published under section 4(2)(a) above".

(7) In section 29(1)—

(a) before paragraph (a) there shall be inserted—

"(za) accepted pursuant to a proposal under section 56A of the Fair Trading Act 1973 (within the meaning of that Act) or under section 56F of that Act, or", and

(b) in that paragraph, for "the Fair Trading Act 1973" there shall be substituted "the said Act of 1973".

Road Traffic Regulation Act 1984 (c. 27)

5. In Schedule 9 to the Road Traffic Regulation Act 1984, in paragraph 28, after sub-paragraph (d) there shall be inserted "; or

(e) an order under section 34 of the Deregulation and Contracting Out Act 1994."

Company Directors Disqualification Act 1986 (c. 46)

6. In the Company Directors Disqualification Act 1986, in section 2(1), for "or liquidation" there shall be substituted ", liquidation or striking off".

Building Societies Act 1986 (c. 53)

7.—(1) The Building Societies Act 1986 shall be amended as follows.

(2) In section 10(5) for "borrower" there shall be substituted "mortgagor".

(3) In section 11(7), after "(2)(b)" there shall be inserted "or (2)(ba)(i) or (ii)".

(4) In section 13(2), at the end there shall be inserted—

"(e) where the advance is to be made in connection with a disposition of other land to the borrower, any person having a financial interest in the disposition of the other land and any director, other officer or employee of his or of an associated employer; and

(f) where the advance is to be made in connection with a disposition of other land to the borrower, any person receiving a commission for introducing the parties to the transaction involving the disposition and any director, other officer or employee of his."

(5) In section 13(3)—

(a) after "following a disposition of the land" there shall be inserted "or in connection with a disposition of other land to the borrower", and

(b) in paragraph (a), the words "of the land" shall be omitted.

(6) In section 119(1), there shall be inserted at the appropriate place in alphabetical order—

" "advance secured on third party land" has the meaning given by section 10(4A);".

Financial Services Act 1986 (c. 60)

8. In section 125(7) of the Financial Services Act 1986, the words "section 24 of" shall be omitted.

Companies Act 1989 (c. 40)

9. In Schedule 14 to the Companies Act 1989, in paragraph 9(6), the words "section 24 of" shall be omitted.

Companies (Northern Ireland) Order 1989 (N.I. 18)

10. In the Companies (Northern Ireland) Order 1989, in Article 5(1), for "or liquidation" there shall be substituted ", liquidation or striking off".

Companies (Northern Ireland) Order 1990 (N.I. 5)

11. In Schedule 14 to the Companies (Northern Ireland) Order 1990, in paragraph 9(6), the words "section 24 of" shall be omitted.

Charities Act 1993 (c. 10)

12. In section 47(3) of the Charities Act 1993—
(a) paragraph (a) shall be omitted, and
(b) in paragraph (b), for the words from "such" to "46(3) above" there shall be substituted "a charity other than one falling within paragraph (c) or (d) below".

Section 50   SCHEDULE 12

SCHEDULE TO BE INSERTED IN THE TRANSPORT ACT 1968 AFTER SCHEDULE 8

"SCHEDULE 8A

TRANSFER OF OPERATING CENTRES

Applications for new licences

1.—(1) Where in the case of any application for an operator's licence—
(a) the requirements of sub-paragraphs (2) to (5) of this paragraph are satisfied at the time when the application is made; and
(b) the applicant so requests,
the licensing authority may direct that paragraph 2 of this Schedule is to apply in relation to the application.

(2) Each place referred to in the statement under section 69A(2) of this Act as a proposed operating centre of the applicant must already be specified in an operator's licence as an operating centre of its holder.

(3) That licence must be the same in the case of each such place, and no such place may be specified in more than the one operator's licence.

(4) Where any conditions under section 64B or 69C of this Act relating to any such place are attached to that licence, the applicant must have consented to conditions in the same terms being attached to the licence he is applying for.

(5) Where any undertakings relating to any such place are recorded in that licence, undertakings in the same terms must have been given by the applicant (or have been procured by him to be given) for the purposes of the application.

(6) In determining whether to give a direction under this paragraph, the licensing authority shall take account of whether any new adverse effects on environmental conditions are likely to arise from the use as an operating centre of the applicant of any such place (and may take account of any other matters he considers relevant).

(7) In this paragraph "operator's licence" does not include a licence granted under section 67A of this Act, and the reference in sub-paragraph (2) to a place being specified in an operator's licence does not include a place being so specified—
(a) by virtue of an interim direction such as is mentioned in section 68A of this Act;
(b) if such conditions as may be prescribed in relation to the exercise of the right of any person to appeal against that place being so specified are not satisfied;

   (c) if such conditions as may be prescribed in relation to the review under section 69J of this Act of the decision so to specify that place are not satisfied; or

   (d) by reason of being situated within a place that is so specified.

2.—(1) The following provisions have effect in relation to any application for an operator's licence in respect of which a direction has been given under paragraph 1 of this Schedule.

(2) The notice published under section 63(1) of this Act shall state that the direction has been given.

(3) The following provisions of this Act shall not apply—

      section 64(3)(c) so far as relating to the suitability of any place specified in the licence
         for use as an operating centre of the licence-holder;

      section 64A(3)(f);

      section 69B; and

      section 69E.

(4) Notwithstanding anything in section 64(9) of this Act, the licensing authority may refuse the application if—

   (a) any statement of fact made by the applicant (or procured by him to be made) for the purposes of the request for the direction under paragraph 1 of this Schedule was false (whether to his knowledge or not); or

   (b) any undertaking given or statement of expectation made by the applicant (or procured by him to be given or made) for those purposes has not been fulfilled.

(5) If the application is granted, the licensing authority—

   (a) shall attach to the licence issued to the applicant any conditions in respect of which the applicant has consented under paragraph 1(4) of this Schedule; and

   (b) shall not attach any other conditions to the licence under section 64B or 69C of this Act.

(6) If the application is granted, the licensing authority shall record in the licence—

   (a) any undertakings given or procured to be given under paragraph 1(5) of this Schedule; and

   (b) any other undertakings given by the applicant (or procured by him to be given), whether for the purposes of the application or for the purposes of the request for the direction under paragraph 1 of this Schedule, that the licensing authority considers to be material to his decision to give the direction (and that would not otherwise be required by section 64A(4) of this Act to be recorded in the licence).

Applications for the variation of licences

3.—(1) Where in the case of an application for the variation of an operator's licence under section 68 of this Act—

   (a) the only direction applied for is one under subsection (1)(g) of that section that one or more new places be specified in the licence as an operating centre of the licence-holder;

   (b) the requirements of sub-paragraphs (2) to (5) of this paragraph are satisfied at the time when the application is made; and

   (c) the applicant so requests,

the licensing authority may direct that paragraph 4 of this Schedule is to apply in relation to the application.

(2) Each new place that is proposed to be specified in the licence must already be specified in another operator's licence as an operating centre of its holder.

(3) That other licence must be the same in the case of each such place, and no such place may be specified in more than the one other operator's licence.

(4) Where any conditions under section 64B or 69C of this Act relating to any such place are attached to that other licence, the applicant must have consented to conditions in the same terms being attached to the licence he is applying to have varied.

(5) Where any undertakings relating to any such place are recorded in that other licence, undertakings in the same terms must have been given by the applicant (or have been procured by him to be given) for the purposes of the application.

(6) In determining whether to give a direction under this paragraph, the licensing authority shall take account of whether any new adverse effects on environmental conditions are likely to arise from the use as an operating centre of the applicant of any such place (and may take account of any other matters he considers relevant).

(7) In this paragraph "operator's licence" does not include a licence granted under section 67A of this Act, and the reference in sub-paragraph (2) to a place being specified in an operator's licence does not include a place being so specified—

   (a) by virtue of an interim direction such as is mentioned in section 68A of this Act;

(b) if such conditions as may be prescribed in relation to the exercise of the right of any person to appeal against that place being so specified are not satisfied;

(c) if such conditions as may be prescribed in relation to the review under section 69J of this Act of the decision so to specify that place are not satisfied; or

(d) by reason of being situated within a place that is so specified.

4.—(1) The following provisions have effect in relation to any application for an operator's licence in respect of which a direction has been given under paragraph 3 of this Schedule.

(2) Sections 68(4) and 69E of this Act shall not apply.

(3) If the application is granted, the licensing authority—

(a) shall attach to the licence as varied any conditions in respect of which the applicant has consented under paragraph 3(4) of this Schedule; and

(b) shall not attach any other conditions to the licence under section 64B or 69C of this Act.

(4) If the application is granted, the licensing authority shall record in the licence as varied—

(a) any undertakings given or procured to be given under paragraph 3(5) of this Schedule; and

(b) any other undertakings given by the applicant (or procured by him to be given), whether for the purposes of the application or for the purposes of the request for the direction under paragraph 3 of this Schedule, that the licensing authority considers to be material to his decision to give the direction."

GENERAL NOTE

This Schedule provides a simplified procedure for the transfer of operating centres from one licence to another in circumstances where there is no change other than the identity of the user.

Section 57   SCHEDULE 13

GOODS VEHICLE OPERATOR LICENSING: MINOR AND CONSEQUENTIAL AMENDMENTS

PART I

AMENDMENT OF THE TRANSPORT ACT 1968 (1968 C. 73)

1.—(1) In section 62(2) the words from "which" to the end of paragraph (c) shall be omitted.

(2) In section 62(4)(g) for "authorised vehicles" there shall be substituted "vehicles referred to in the statement under subsection (2) of this section".

2.—(1) In section 63(3) after "64(2)" there shall be inserted "to (4)".

(2) Section 63(5) shall be omitted.

(3) In section 63(6) the definition of "statutory provision" shall be omitted.

3. In section 66(1)(a) for "the authorised vehicles are used" there shall be substituted "vehicles are used under the licence (or, if the licence is at any time suspended under section 69 of this Act, were used under the licence immediately before its suspension)".

4.—(1) In section 69(4) for "(1)(b)" there shall be substituted "(1)(c) and (d)".

(2) In section 69(6) the words "premature termination" shall be omitted.

(3) In section 69(7) for "the authorised vehicles" there shall be substituted "vehicles under the licence".

(4) In section 69(7A) for the words from "if" to the end there shall be substituted "if before that date the licence which is directed to be suspended or curtailed ceases to be in force, on the date on which it ceases to be in force".

(5) In section 69(9) for "(5), (6) or (7)" there shall be substituted "(5) or (6)".

(6) In section 69(10) for "(7) or (7A)" there shall be substituted "or (7A)".

(7) After section 69(10) there shall be inserted—

"(10A) Where an operator's licence is suspended under this section, the licence remains in force during the time of its suspension subject to the limitation that no vehicles are authorised to be used under it."

5.—(1) In section 69A(1)—

(a) for "authorised vehicles" there shall be substituted "vehicles authorised to be used"; and

(b) after "specified" there shall be inserted "as an operating centre of his".

(2) In section 69A(3) for "authorised vehicles" there shall be substituted "vehicles used".

(3) after section 69A(3) there shall be inserted—

"(3A) The statement under subsection (2) of this section and any particulars required under subsection (3) of this section shall be given to the licensing authority in such form as he may require."

6.—(1) In section 69B(1) and (2)—

(a) after "any place" there shall be inserted "in the licensing authority's area", and

(b) for "is unsuitable" there shall be substituted "will be unsuitable".

(2) In section 69B(3)—

(a) for "authorised vehicles" there shall be substituted "vehicles used", and

(b) after "any place" there shall be inserted "in the authority's area".

(3) In section 69B(4)—

(a) after "any place" there shall be inserted "in the authority's area", and

(b) for "is unsuitable" there shall be substituted "would be unsuitable".

(4) For section 69B(6) there shall be substituted—

"(6) Where in the case of any application for an operator's licence—

(a) the licensing authority has power to refuse the application under subsection (3) or (4) of this section; and

(b) any place other than a place that will be unsuitable for use as an operating centre is referred to in the statement under section 69A(2) of this Act as a proposed operating centre of the applicant,

the authority may, instead of refusing the application, issue the licence specifying in it only such place or places referred to in that statement as will not be unsuitable for use as an operating centre.

(6A) For the purposes of subsection (6) of this section, a place will be unsuitable for use as an operating centre if the licensing authority has power to refuse the application under subsection (3) or (4) of this section in consequence of the proposed use of that place as an operating centre."

(5) Section 69B(7) shall be omitted.

7.—(1) For section 69C(1) there shall be substituted—

"(1) A licensing authority, on granting an operator's licence or on varying such a licence on an application of which notice has been published under section 68(4) of this Act, may attach to it such conditions as he thinks fit for preventing or minimising any adverse effects on environmental conditions arising from the use of a place in the area of the authority as an operating centre of the licence-holder."

(2) For section 69C(3) and (4) there shall be substituted—

"(3) On varying an operator's licence on an application of which notice has been published under section 68(4) of this Act, the licensing authority may vary or remove any condition attached to the licence under this section."

(3) For section 69C(5) there shall be substituted—

"(5) The licensing authority shall not—

(a) attach any condition such as is mentioned in this section to an operator's licence; or

(b) vary in such manner as imposes new or further restrictions or requirements any condition attached to an operator's licence under this section,

without first giving the applicant for the licence or (as the case may be) the licence-holder an opportunity of making representations to the authority with respect to the effect on his business of the proposed condition or variation.

(5A) The licensing authority shall give special consideration to any representations made under subsection (5) of this section in determining whether to attach the proposed condition or make the proposed variation."

8. Section 69F shall be omitted.

9. For section 69G there shall be substituted—

"Objections and representations: supplementary provisions

69G.—(1) Any objection or representations under section 69B, 69D or 69EB of this Act shall contain particulars of any matters alleged by the person making the objection or representations to be relevant to the issue to which the objection or representations relate.

(2) Any such objection or representations shall be made in the prescribed manner and, in the case of an objection or representations under section 69B or 69D of this Act, within the prescribed time after the making of the application to which the objection or representations relate.

(3) In the case of an objection or representations under section 69B or 69D of this Act, the prescribed manner and prescribed time shall be stated in the notice of the application published under section 63(1) or (as the case may be) 68(4) of this Act.

(4) Where the licensing authority considers there to be exceptional circumstances that justify his doing so, he may direct that for the purposes of this Part of this Act—

    (a) objections or representations be treated as duly made under section 69B or 69D of this Act, notwithstanding that they were not made in the prescribed manner or within the prescribed time;

    (b) representations be treated as duly made under section 69EB of this Act, notwithstanding that they were not made in the prescribed manner or within the period of review in question.

Determinations as to environmental matters: supplementary provisions

69H.—(1) In making any determination of a description mentioned in subsection (2) of this section, the licensing authority shall have regard to such considerations as may be prescribed as relevant to determinations of that description.

(2) The determinations referred to are—

    (a) any determination with respect to the suitability of any place on environmental grounds for use as an operating centre of the holder of an operator's licence;

    (b) any determination with respect to attaching any condition such as is mentioned in section 69C of this Act to an operator's licence or varying or removing any such condition attached to an operator's licence; and

    (c) any determination with respect to the effect on environmental conditions in any locality of the use in any particular manner of any operating centre of the holder of an operator's licence.

(3) In making any such determination for the purposes of exercising—

    (a) any of his functions in relation to an application for, or for the variation of, an operator's licence; or

    (b) any of his functions under sections 69EA to 69EC of this Act,

the licensing authority may take into account any undertakings given by the applicant or licence-holder (or procured by him to be given) for the purposes of the application or the review under sections 69EA to 69EC, and may assume that those undertakings will be fulfilled.

(4) In making for those purposes a determination of a description mentioned in subsection (2)(a) or (c) of this section, the licensing authority may take into account any conditions such as are mentioned in section 69C of this Act that could be attached to the licence in question, and may assume that any conditions so attached will not be contravened.

(5) Where the licensing authority—

    (a) grants an application for, or for the variation of, an operator's licence; or

    (b) having served notice under section 69EA of this Act in respect of any place specified in such a licence, exercises or determines not to exercise any of his powers under sections 69EB and 69EC of this Act in relation to that place,

any undertakings taken into account by the authority under subsection (4) of this section that the authority considers to be material to the application or (as the case may be) to his decision under sections 69EB and 69EC shall be recorded in the licence in question."

10. In section 82(4) for "authorised vehicles" there shall be substituted "vehicles used under the licence".

11.—(1) After section 84(a) there shall be inserted—

"(aa) that, by virtue of a direction given by the authority under regulations made under section 86(2)(b) or (3) of this Act, a person is to be treated as having been the holder of an operator's licence on any date;".

(2) For section 84(b) there shall be substituted—

"(b) the date of the coming into force of any operator's licence granted by the authority;

(bb) the date on which any operator's licence granted by the authority ceased to be in force;".

(3) For section 84(f) there shall be substituted—

"(f) that an operator's licence was on any date or during any specified period suspended by virtue of a direction given by the authority under section 69(1) of this Act;

(g) that, by virtue of a direction given by the authority under regulations made under section 86(2)(a) of this Act, an operator's licence is to be treated as having been suspended on any date or during any specified period,".

12. In section 85(1) for "authorised vehicles" there shall be substituted "vehicles authorised to be used".

13. In section 87(3) the words "or 69F" shall be omitted.

14.—(1) In section 91(1)—

    (a) in paragraph (a) for "69 and 69F" there shall be substituted "69, 69EA to 69EC and 69J",

(b) in paragraph (c) for "authorised vehicles" there shall be substituted "authorised to be used under any operator's licence or as being used under such a licence",

(c) for paragraph (d) there shall be substituted—

"(d) the custody, production, return and cancellation of operators' licences and of documents, plates and any other means of identification prescribed under paragraph (c) of this subsection;

(dd) the payment of a prescribed fee in respect of any document, plate or such other means of identification that has been lost, defaced or broken;"

(d) in paragraph (f) after "repayment" there shall be inserted "(or partial repayment)", and

(e) the words following paragraph (g) shall be omitted.

(2) In section 91(2) for "authorised vehicles" there shall be substituted "authorised to be used under an operator's licence".

(3) In section 91(4) the words from "and different" to the end shall be omitted.

(4) After section 91(4) there shall be inserted—

"(4A) Any regulations under this Part of this Act may make—

(a) different provision for different cases or classes of case and different circumstances; and

(b) transitional provision;

and regulations made by virtue of subsection (1)(c) of this section may make different provision for the areas of different licensing authorities."

(5) After section 91(6) there shall be inserted—

"(6A) No regulations shall be made under section 69EA(3) of this Act unless a draft of them has been laid before, and approved by a resolution of, each House of Parliament.".

(6) In section 91(7) after "of this Act" there shall be inserted ", other than regulations under section 69EA (3),".

15.—(1) In section 92(1)—

(a) the definition of "authorised vehicle" shall be omitted,

(b) after the definition of "large goods vehicle" there shall be inserted—

" "modification" includes addition, omission and alteration, and related expressions shall be construed accordingly;",

(c) in the definition of "operating centre", for "authorised vehicles" there shall be substituted "vehicles used", and

(d) after the definition of "regulations" there shall be inserted—

" "statutory provision" means a provision contained in an Act or in subordinate legislation within the meaning of the Interpretation Act 1978;".

(2) After section 92(2) there shall be inserted—

"(2A) In this Part of this Act references to vehicles being authorised to be used under an operator's licence are to be read in accordance with section 61 of this Act.

(2B) In this Part of this Act references to the date on which an application is finally disposed of are references—

(a) subject to paragraph (b) of this subsection, to the earliest date by which the application and any appeal to the Transport Tribunal arising out of the application have been determined and any time for bringing such an appeal has expired; or

(b) if the application is withdrawn or any such appeal is abandoned, to the date of the withdrawal or abandonment."

(3) For section 92(3)(b) and (c) there shall be substituted—

"(b) that a provision such as is mentioned in section 61(1A) or 61A(1)(b) or (2)(b) of this Act be included in the licence;

(c) that any maximum number specified in the licence under section 61A of this Act be reduced;".

(4) After section 92(4) there shall be inserted—

"(4A) In this Part of this Act, references to a person becoming a patient within the meaning of Part VII of the Mental Health Act 1983 include references to a curator bonis being appointed in respect of him in Scotland on the ground that he is incapable, by reason of mental disorder, of adequately managing and administering his property and affairs."

(5) In section 92(5) for the words from "operated under" to the end there shall be substituted ", within the meaning of the Road Traffic Act 1988".

PART II

AMENDMENT OF OTHER ENACTMENTS

16. In section 233(1)(c) of the Road Traffic Act 1960—

(a) for "or mark" there shall be substituted ", mark or other thing", and

(b) for "an authorised vehicle" there shall be substituted "authorised to be used, or as being used, under an operator's licence".

17. In section 2(2) of the Road Traffic (Drivers' Ages and Hours of Work) Act 1976 for "64(2)(c)" there shall be substituted "64(3)(a)".

18.—(1) Section 73 of the Road Traffic Act 1988 shall be amended as follows.

(2) In subsection (1)—

(a) for "an authorised vehicle" there shall be substituted "by virtue of section 61 of the Transport Act 1968 authorised to be used under an operator's licence", and

(b) for "the operator's licence was granted for the vehicle" there shall be substituted "the licence was granted".

(3) After subsection (1) there shall be inserted—

"(1ZA) Where in a case within subsection (1) above it appears to the person giving the notice that the vehicle is authorised to be used under two or more operators' licences—

(a) if those licences were granted by different traffic commissioners, his duty under paragraph (a) of that subsection may be discharged by taking steps to bring the contents of the notice to the attention of any one of those commissioners,

(b) if those licences are held by different persons and none of those persons is in charge of the vehicle at the time when the notice is given, his duty under paragraph (b) of that subsection may be discharged by taking steps to bring the contents of the notice to the attention of any one of those persons, and

(c) if those licences are held by different persons and any of those persons is in charge of the vehicle at the time when the notice is given, no steps need be taken under that subsection to bring the contents of the notice to the attention of the others."

(4) In subsection (4) for the words from "and section 72" to "have" there shall be substituted " "operator's licence" has".

Section 68 SCHEDULE 14

PSV Operator Licensing etc: Minor and Consequential Amendments

1. The 1981 Act shall be amended as follows.

2. In section 14(4) for "the provisions of sections 15 and 16" there shall be substituted "section 16".

3. Section 14A(3) shall be omitted.

4. In section 16(6) the word "or" immediately before paragraph (b) shall be omitted.

5.—(1) Section 17(2)(c) shall be omitted.

(2) In section 17(3)—

(a) in paragraph (a) the words "intention or" shall be omitted, and

(b) in paragraph (c) for "section 9 of this Act" there shall be substituted "section 69 of the Road Traffic Act 1988" and for "subsection (9) of that section" there shall be substituted "section 71(1)(a) or (b) of that Act arising out of the contravention of such a prohibition".

6. In section 18(3)(d)—

(a) after "discs" there shall be inserted "on their expiry or otherwise ceasing to have effect,", and

(b) for "expiration" there shall be substituted "termination".

7.—(1) Section 50(2) shall be omitted.

(2) In section 50(4)—

(a) at the end of paragraph (a) there shall be added "or any undertaking recorded in it", and

(b) in paragraph (c) the words "or to curtail its period of validity" shall be omitted.

8. In section 12 of the Transport Act 1985 subsection (3) shall be omitted.

Section 75 SCHEDULE 15

Restrictions on Disclosure of Information

Preliminary

1.—(1) Paragraphs 2 to 5, 7 and 8 below apply where—

(a) a person (contractor A) is authorised, whether by virtue of an order made under section 69 or 70 above or otherwise, to exercise any function (the relevant function) of a Minister, office-holder or local authority (authority A); and

(b) the disclosure of relevant information, that is, information obtained, whether before or after the commencement of this Part of this Act, in or in connection with the exercise of the relevant function or a related function, is restricted by any enactment or by any obligation of confidentiality.

(2) Paragraphs 6 to 8 below apply where—
(a) a person (contractor A) is authorised, whether by virtue of an order made under section 69 or 70 above or otherwise, to exercise any function (the relevant function) of a Minister, office-holder or local authority (authority A); and
(b) the disclosure of relevant information, that is, information obtained, whether before or after the commencement of this Part of this Act, in or in connection with the exercise of any function of another Minister, office-holder or local authority (authority E), is restricted by any enactment or by any obligation of confidentiality.

Disclosures between contracting parties etc.

2. The enactment or obligation shall not prevent or penalise the disclosure of relevant information—
(a) between contractor A or an employee of his and authority A or an authorised officer of that authority;
(b) between contractor A and an employee of his or between one such employee and another; or
(c) where the relevant function has been delegated to authority A by another Minister, office-holder or local authority (authority B), between contractor A or an employee of his and authority B or an authorised officer of that authority,
if the disclosure is necessary or expedient in or in connection with, or for the purpose of facilitating, the exercise of the relevant function or a related function, or the performance of ancillary services.

Disclosures by contracting parties to contractor B

3.—(1) This paragraph applies where another person (contractor B) is authorised, whether by virtue of an order under section 69 or 70 above or otherwise, to exercise the relevant function or a related function.
(2) The enactment or obligation shall not prevent or penalise the disclosure of relevant information by contractor A or an employee of his, or authority A or an authorised officer of that authority, to contractor B or an employee of his if—
(a) the disclosure is necessary or expedient for the purpose of facilitating the exercise of the relevant function or a related function; and
(b) where the disclosure is by contractor A or an employee of his, the disclosure falls within a description of disclosures certified by authority A (whether in the authorisation or otherwise) to be capable of being so necessary or expedient.

Disclosures by contracting parties to contractor C

4.—(1) This paragraph applies where another person (contractor C) is authorised, whether by virtue of an order under section 69 or 70 above or otherwise, to exercise a function of another Minister, office-holder or local authority (authority C).
(2) The enactment or obligation shall not prevent or penalise the disclosure of relevant information by contractor A or an employee of his, or authority A or an authorised officer of that authority, to contractor C or an employee of his if—
(a) the disclosure is necessary or expedient for the purpose of facilitating the exercise of the relevant function, a related function or a function of authority C;
(b) where the disclosure is by contractor A or an employee of his, the disclosure falls within a description of disclosures certified by authority A (whether in the authorisation or otherwise) to be capable of being so necessary or expedient; and
(c) the information could be lawfully disclosed, for that purpose, by authority A to authority C.

Disclosures by contractor A to authority D

5. The enactment or obligation shall not prevent or penalise the disclosure of relevant information by contractor A or an employee of his to another Minister, office-holder or local authority (authority D) or an authorised officer of that authority if—
(a) the disclosure is necessary or expedient for the purpose of facilitating the exercise of the relevant function, a related function or a function of authority D;
(b) the disclosure falls within a description of disclosures certified by authority A (whether in the authorisation or otherwise) to be capable of being so necessary or expedient; and
(c) the information could be lawfully disclosed, for that purpose, by authority A to authority D.

Disclosures to contractor A by authority E

6. The enactment or obligation shall not prevent or penalise the disclosure of relevant information by authority E or an authorised officer of that authority to contractor A or an employee of his if—
(a) the disclosure is necessary or expedient for the purpose of facilitating the exercise of the relevant function, a related function or a function of authority E; and
(b) the information could be lawfully disclosed, for that purpose, by authority E to authority A.

Disclosures for audit purposes

7.—(1) Where authority A is a Minister or office-holder, the enactment or obligation shall not prevent or penalise the disclosure of relevant information by contractor A or an employee of his if—
(a) the disclosure is to the Comptroller, or a person exercising an audit function of his, and the information could lawfully be disclosed to the Comptroller or that person by authority A; or
(b) the disclosure is to an accounting officer, or a person exercising an audit function of his, and the information could lawfully be disclosed to that officer or person by authority A.
(2) Where authority A is a local authority, the enactment or obligation shall not prevent or penalise the disclosure of relevant information by contractor A or an employee of his if—
(a) the disclosure is to the authority's chief finance officer, or a person exercising an audit function of his; and
(b) the information could lawfully be disclosed to that officer or person by the authority.
(3) In this paragraph—
"accounting officer" means an officer appointed by the Treasury under section 22 of the Exchequer and Audit Departments Act 1866 or section 4 of the Government Trading Funds Act 1973;
"audit function", in relation to the Comptroller, includes any function under Part II of the National Audit Act 1983 or Part III of the Audit (Northern Ireland) Order 1987 (examinations into economy, efficiency and effectiveness);
"chief finance officer" has the same meaning as in section 5 of the Local Government and Housing Act 1989;
"Comptroller" means the Comptroller and Auditor General or the Comptroller and Auditor General for Northern Ireland.

Implied term of contractor A's contract

8. It shall be an implied term of any contract made between contractor A and authority A and relating to the exercise of the relevant function that contractor A shall take all reasonable steps to secure that any relevant information—
(a) which is obtained by him or an employee of his; and
(b) the disclosure of which is restricted by any enactment or obligation,
is not disclosed at any time (whether or not during the subsistence of the contract) to any other person in contravention of the enactment or in breach of the obligation.

Unauthorised disclosures

9.—(1) This paragraph applies where—
(a) any information is disclosed to any person in accordance with paragraphs 2 to 7 above (the original disclosure); and
(b) that person, or any other person to whom the information is subsequently so disclosed, discloses the information otherwise than in accordance with paragraphs 2 to 7 above (the unauthorised disclosure).
(2) If the original disclosure was restricted by an enactment, the enactment shall apply in relation to the person making the unauthorised disclosure as if—
(a) he had obtained the information by virtue of the same provision as the person who made the original disclosure; and
(b) where the enactment would not have restricted that disclosure if the person who made it had not fallen within a particular class, he fell within that class.
(3) If the original disclosure was restricted by an obligation, the person making the unauthorised disclosure shall be treated for all purposes as if he were subject to that obligation.

Interpretation: general

10.—(1) In this Schedule—

"ancillary services" means services certified by authority A (whether in the authorisation or otherwise) to be services appearing to it to be calculated to facilitate, or to be conducive or incidental to, the exercise of the relevant function;

"authorised officer", in relation to a Minister, office-holder or local authority, means any officer of the Minister, office-holder or local authority who is authorised by him or it to disclose or (as the case may be) obtain the information in question;

"employee", in relation to contractor A, includes any person who performs ancillary services for that contractor, and any employee of such a person;

"related function" means any function of authority A which is certified by that authority (whether in the authorisation or otherwise) to be a function appearing to it to be a function which is related to the relevant function.

(2) For the purposes of sub-paragraph (1) above a function of authority A is related to another function of that authority if information—

(a) which is obtained in or in connection with the exercise of either function; and

(b) the disclosure of which is restricted by any enactment or by any obligation of confidentiality,

can lawfully be used by that authority for the purpose of facilitating the exercise of the other function.

(3) In this Schedule—

(a) any reference to another person is a reference to a person other than contractor A; and

(b) any reference to another Minister, office-holder or local authority is a reference to a Minister, office-holder or local authority other than authority A.

GENERAL NOTE

This Schedule addresses a major obstacle to the contracting out of functions in the form of statutory and other restrictions on the disclosure of information. Its purpose is to ensure that restricted information can be disclosed to contractors and that contractors are subject to the same restrictions on its disclosure as its original recipients.

Section 76   SCHEDULE 16

AMENDMENTS ETC. FOR FACILITATING CONTRACTING OUT

Newspaper Libel and Registration Act 1881 (c. 60) and Limited Partnerships Act 1907 (c. 24)

1.—(1) This paragraph applies where by virtue of an order made under section 69 of this Act a person is authorised by the registrar of companies to accept delivery of any class of documents which are under any provision of the Newspaper Libel and Registration Act 1881 or the Limited Partnerships Act 1907 to be delivered to the registrar.

(2) If—

(a) the registrar directs that documents of that class shall be delivered to a specified address of the authorised person; and

(b) the direction is printed and made available to the public (with or without payment),

any document of that class which is delivered to an address other than the specified address shall be treated for the purposes of that Act as not having been delivered.

(3) In this paragraph "the registrar of companies" and "the registrar" have the same meanings as in the Companies Act 1985.

Courts Act 1971 (c. 23)

2. For section 27 of the Courts Act 1971 there shall be substituted the following section—

"Administrative and other court staff

27.—(1) The Lord Chancellor may, with the concurrence of the Treasury as to numbers and salaries, appoint such officers and other staff for the Supreme Court and county courts as appear to him appropriate for the following purposes, namely—

(a) maintaining an administrative court service;

(b) discharging any functions in those courts conferred by or under this or any other Act on officers so appointed; and

(c) generally carrying out the administrative work of those courts.

(2) The principal civil service pension scheme within the meaning of section 2 of the Superannuation Act 1972 and for the time being in force shall, with the necessary adaptations, apply to officers and staff appointed under subsection (1) above as it applies to other persons employed in the civil service of the State.

(3) If and to the extent that an order made by the Lord Chancellor so provides, the Lord Chancellor may enter into contracts with other persons for the provision for the purposes mentioned in subsection (1) above, whether by those persons or by sub-contractors of theirs, of officers and staff for the Supreme Court and county courts.

(4) No order under subsection (3) above shall authorise the contracting out of any functions the discharge of which would constitute—

(a) making judicial decisions or advising persons making such decisions;
(b) exercising any judicial discretion or advising persons exercising any such discretion; or
(c) exercising any power of arrest.

(5) An order under subsection (3) above may authorise the contracting out of any functions—

(a) either wholly or to such extent as may be specified in the order;
(b) either generally or in such cases or areas as may be so specified; and
(c) either unconditionally or subject to the fulfilment of such conditions as may be so specified.

(6) Before making an order under subsection (3) above, the Lord Chancellor shall consult with the senior judges as to what effect (if any) the order might have on the proper and efficient administration of justice.

(7) An order under subsection (3) above shall be made by statutory instrument which shall be subject to annulment in pursuance of a resolution of either House of Parliament.

(8) References in this section to the contracting out of any functions are references to the Lord Chancellor entering into contracts for the provision of officers and staff for the purpose of discharging those functions.

(9) In this section—

"the senior judges" means the Lord Chief Justice, the Master of the Rolls, the Vice-Chancellor and the President of the Family Division;

"the Supreme Court" includes the district probate registries."

Local Government Act 1972 (c. 70)

3. If and to the extent that an order under section 70 of this Act so provides, section 223 of the Local Government Act 1972 (appearance of local authorities in legal proceedings) shall have effect as if—

(a) any person authorised by virtue of the order to exercise a function of a local authority, and
(b) any employee of a person so authorised,

were an officer of the authority.

Patents Act 1977 (c. 37)

4. If and to the extent that an order under section 69 of this Act so provides, section 112 of the Patents Act 1977 (misuse of title "Patent Office") shall not apply in relation to anything done by a person who is authorised by virtue of the order to exercise any function of the Comptroller-General of Patents, Designs and Trade Marks.

Rent (Scotland) Act 1984 (c. 58)

5. At the beginning of subsection (3) of section 43 of the Rent (Scotland) Act 1984 (registration of rents under regulated tenancies) there shall be inserted the words "Subject to section 43A below,".

6. After section 43 of that Act there shall be inserted the following section—

"Rent registration service providers

43A.—(1) The Secretary of State may, if he thinks fit, make arrangements ("rent registration arrangements") with another person (a "rent registration service provider") for the performance by that person in accordance with the arrangements of the functions mentioned in subsection (2) below.

(2) Those functions are the functions, under this Part of this Act and section 70 of the Housing (Scotland) Act 1988, of the rent officer for such registration area or areas as are specified in the rent registration arrangements.

(3) While rent registration arrangements are in force in relation to a registration area, section 43(3) above shall not apply in respect of that area.

(4) The appointment of any rent officer appointed for a registration area in relation to which rent registration arrangements have been made shall terminate on the date on which the arrangements come into force.

(5) Rent registration arrangements shall not include any provision calculated to influence the exercise of the rent registration service provider's judgment in the performance of his functions.

(6) A rent registration service provider performing functions in pursuance of rent registration arrangements shall not be regarded as a servant or agent of the Crown and shall not have any status, immunity or privilege of the Crown.

(7) References in this Part of this Act (other than sections 43, 43B, 43C and this section), section 70 of the Housing (Scotland) Act 1988 and any other enactment (including an enactment contained in subordinate legislation) to a rent officer shall, as respects a registration area in relation to which rent registration arrangements are in force, be construed as references to the rent registration service provider responsible for the performance of the functions of the rent officer for that area.

(8) A rent registration service provider may perform his functions through an employee or agent and, if he does so—

(a) any decision of, and anything else done or omitted to be done by or in relation to, the employee or agent shall, for the purposes of any enactment (including an enactment contained in subordinate legislation), be deemed to be a decision of or, as the case may be, done or omitted to be done by or in relation to the rent registration service provider; and

(b) where any enactment refers to the personal knowledge, experience or opinion of a rent officer the knowledge, experience or opinion of the employee or agent shall be deemed to be that of the rent registration service provider.

(9) Subsection (8)(a) above is without prejudice to section 43C below."

7. After section 43A of that Act there shall be inserted the following sections—

"Supplementary provisions regarding rent registration service providers

43B.—(1) Where—

(a) rent registration arrangements are in force in relation to a registration area ("existing arrangements"); and

(b) the Secretary of State decides not to make further such arrangements in relation to that area in respect of the period following the expiry or termination of the existing arrangements,

then, notwithstanding section 43A(3) above, he may under section 43(3) above appoint rent officers for the area, such appointments taking effect on the expiry or, as the case may be, the termination of the existing arrangements.

(2) For the purposes of subsections 5(3) and (4) below, a change of responsibility takes place where—

(a) under rent registration arrangements in relation to a registration area, a rent registration service provider assumes responsibility for the performance of functions which, immediately prior to the coming into force of the arrangements, were performed by a rent officer for the area or by another rent registration service provider; or

(b) a rent officer is appointed for a registration area in relation to which, immediately prior to the coming into force of the appointment, rent registration arrangements were in force.

(3) Where a change of responsibility takes place the Secretary of State shall publish, in such manner as he considers appropriate, a notice specifying—

(a) the registration area concerned;

(b) the date when the change takes effect; and

(c) the name and official address of the person who is rent officer or, as the case may be, rent registration service provider after that date.

(4) Where a change of responsibility takes place—

(a) any decision taken, and anything else done or omitted to be done in the performance of the functions mentioned in section 43A(2) above by or in relation to the person previously responsible for the performance of those functions shall have effect as if taken or, as the case may be, done or omitted to be done by or in relation to the person currently so responsible; and

(b) any court proceedings by or against the person previously so responsible and relating to the performance by him of those functions shall continue by or against the person currently so responsible.

Rent registration service providers: restrictions on disclosure of information

43C.—(1) Schedule 15 to the Deregulation and Contracting Out Act 1994 (restrictions on disclosure of information) shall, where contractor A within the meaning of that Schedule is a rent registration service provider, apply with the following modifications.

(2) Without prejudice to paragraph 10(1), references to an employee of contractor A and, where contractor B within the meaning of that Schedule is also a rent registration service provider, to an employee of contractor B shall be taken to include references to an agent, and the employee of an agent, of contractor A or, as the case may be, of contractor B.

(3) Subject to subsections (4) to (6) below, references to authority A shall be taken to be references to the rent officer for any registration area specified in the rent registration arrangements.

(4) In paragraph 2(a), the reference to authority A shall be taken to be a reference to such a rent officer or the Secretary of State.

(5) In paragraphs 3(2)(b), 4(2)(b), 5(b) and 8 and, in paragraph 10(1), in the definition of "ancillary services", the reference to authority A shall be taken to be a reference to the Secretary of State.

(6) In the definition of "related function" in paragraph 10(1), the reference to a function of authority A which is certified by that authority shall be taken to be a reference to a function of a rent officer which is certified by the Secretary of State."

Companies Act 1985 (c. 6)

8. After subsection (6) of section 704 of the Companies Act 1985 (registration offices) there shall be inserted the following subsections—

"(7) Subsection (8) below applies where by virtue of an order made under section 69 of the Deregulation and Contracting Out Act 1994 a person is authorised by the registrar of companies to accept delivery of any class of documents which are under any provision of the Companies Acts to be delivered to the registrar.

(8) If—

(a) the registrar directs that documents of that class shall be delivered to a specified address of the authorised person; and

(b) the direction is printed and made available to the public (with or without payment),

any document of that class which is delivered to an address other than the specified address shall be treated for the purposes of those Acts as not having been delivered."

9. In section 735A(2) of that Act (relationship of Act to Insolvency Act), for the words "sections 704(5)" there shall be substituted the words "sections 704(5), (7) and (8)".

10. In section 735B of that Act (relationship of Act to Parts IV and V of Financial Services Act 1986), for the words "sections 704(5)" there shall be substituted the words "sections 704(5), (7) and (8)".

Gas Act 1986 (c. 44)

11.—(1) In subsection (5) of section 13 of the Gas Act 1986 (alternative method of charge), for the words "the persons appointed under subsection (3) above" there shall be substituted the words "persons appointed under subsection (3) above who are in the civil service of the Crown".

(2) In subsection (6) of that section, after the words "such proportion" there shall be inserted the words "(if any)".

12.—(1) In subsection (5) of section 16 of that Act (standards of quality), for the words "the persons appointed under subsection (3) above" there shall be substituted the words "persons appointed under subsection (3) above who are in the civil service of the Crown".

(2) In subsection (6) of that section, after the words "such proportion" there shall be inserted the words "(if any)".

13.—(1) In subsection (2) of section 17 of that Act (meter testing and stamping)—

(a) after the words "meter examiner" there shall be inserted the words "who is in the civil service of the Crown"; and

(b) for the words "the prescribed fee" there shall be substituted the words "the requisite fee".

(2) In subsection (6) and (7) of that section, after the words "meter examiners" there shall be inserted the words "who are in the civil service of the Crown".

(3) In subsection (8) of that section, paragraph (d) and the word "and" immediately preceding that paragraph shall cease to have effect.

(4) After that subsection there shall be inserted the following subsection—

"(8A) The fees to be paid to meter examiners who are in the civil service of the Crown for examining, stamping and re-examining meters, and the persons by whom they are to be paid, shall be such as the Secretary of State may, with the approval of the Treasury, from time to time determine; and a determination under this subsection may—

(a) make different provision for different areas or in relation to different cases or different circumstances; and

(b) make such supplementary, incidental or transitional provision as the Secretary of State considers necessary or expedient."

Agriculture Act 1986 (c. 49)

14. For subsection (3) of section 1 of the Agriculture Act 1986 (provision of services and goods connected with agriculture and countryside) there shall be substituted the following subsection—

"(3) The provision which may be made under this section includes provision for any services or goods mentioned in subsection (1) above to be supplied—

(a) through any person with whom the Minister enters into a contract for the making of the supply; or

(b) through any organisation established by him for the purposes of this section."

European Economic Interest Grouping Regulations 1989

15. In paragraph 16 of Schedule 4 to the European Economic Interest Grouping Regulations 1989 (provisions of Companies Act 1985 applying to EEIGs and their establishments), for the words "section 704(5)" there shall be substituted the words "section 704(5), (7) and (8)".

Food Safety Act 1990 (c. 16)

16. After subsection (5) of section 6 of the Food Safety Act 1990 (enforcement of Act) there shall be inserted the following subsection—

"(6) In this Act "authorised officer", in relation to an enforcement authority, means any person (whether or not an officer of the authority) who is authorised by the authority in writing, either generally or specially, to act in matters arising under this Act and regulations and orders made under it; but if regulations made by the Ministers so provide, no person shall be so authorised unless he has such qualifications as may be prescribed by the regulations."

17. In subsection (1) of section 42 of that Act (default powers)—

(a) for the words "one of his officers" there shall be substituted the words "a person (whether or not an officer of his) who is authorised by him in writing to do so"; and

(b) there shall be inserted at the end the words "but if regulations made by the Ministers so provide, no person shall be so authorised unless he has such qualifications as may be prescribed by the regulations."

18. In subsection (1) of section 50 of that Act (service of documents), for the words "any officer" there shall be substituted the words "an authorised officer".

19. In subsection (2) of section 53 of that Act (general interpretation), after the first entry there shall be inserted the following entry—

"Authorised officer of an   section 6(6)".
enforcement authority

Social Security Administration Act 1992 (c. 5)

20.—(1) After subsection (7) of section 54 of the Social Security Administration Act 1992 (claims relating to attendance allowance, disability living allowance and disability working allowance) there shall be inserted the following subsection—

"(7A) Any reference in subsections (3) to (7) above to a medical practitioner who is an officer of the Secretary of State includes a reference to a medical practitioner who is provided by any person in pursuance of a contract entered into with the Secretary of State."

(2) Sub-paragraph (3) below applies where a consent given before the commencement of this Part authorises the disclosure of any information to the Secretary of State, or to a medical practitioner who is an officer of the Secretary of State.

(3) The consent shall have effect as if it also authorised the disclosure of the information—

(a) to a medical practitioner who is provided by any person in pursuance of a contract entered into with the Secretary of State, and

(b) if and to the extent that the Secretary of State so directs, to any employee of such a practitioner.

(4) In this paragraph—

"employee", in relation to a medical practitioner, includes any person who performs ancillary services for the practitioner, and any employee of such a person;

"medical practitioner" has the same meaning as in that Act.

21. After subsection (6) of section 123 of that Act (disclosure of information relating to particular persons) there shall be inserted the following subsection—

"(6A) Subsection (6) above shall have effect as if any medical practitioner who, for the purposes of section 54 above, is provided by any person in pursuance of a contract entered into with the Secretary of State were specified in Part I of Schedule 4 to this Act."

22. After subsection (3) of section 127 of that Act (housing benefit) there shall be inserted the following subsection—

"(4) Where, whether by virtue of an order made under section 70 of the Deregulation and Contracting Out Act 1994 or otherwise, a person is authorised by an authority to exercise any of their functions relating to housing benefit—

(a) subsection (1) above shall have effect in relation to information required in connection with the exercise of those functions, and

(b) subsection (2) above shall have effect in relation to information obtained by reason of their exercise,

as if the authorised person were an authority."

23. After subsection (3) of section 128 of that Act (council tax benefit) there shall be inserted the following subsection—

"(4) Where, whether by virtue of an order made under section 70 of the Deregulation and Contracting Out Act 1994 or otherwise, a person is authorised by a billing or charging authority to exercise any of their functions relating to council tax benefit—

(a) subsection (1) above shall have effect in relation to information required in connection with the exercise of those functions, and

(b) subsection (2) above shall have effect in relation to information obtained by reason of their exercise,

as if the authorised person were such an authority."

Social Security Administration (Northern Ireland) Act 1992 (c. 8)

24.—(1) After subsection (7) of section 52 of the Social Security Administration (Northern Ireland) Act 1992 (claims relating to attendance allowance, disability living allowance and disability working allowance) there shall be inserted the following subsection—

"(7A) Any reference in subsections (3) to (7) above to a medical practitioner who is an officer of the Department includes a reference to a medical practitioner who is provided by any person in pursuance of a contract entered into with the Department."

(2) Sub-paragraph (3) below applies where a consent given before the commencement of this Part authorises the disclosure of any information to the Department, or to a medical practitioner who is an officer of the Department.

(3) The consent shall have effect as if it also authorised the disclosure of the information—

(a) to a medical practitioner who is provided by any person in pursuance of a contract entered into with the Department, and

(b) if and to the extent that the Department so directs, to any employee of such a practitioner.

(4) In this paragraph—

"the Department" means the Department of Health and Social Services for Northern Ireland;

"employee", in relation to a medical practitioner, includes any person who performs ancillary services for the practitioner, and any employee of such a person;

"medical practitioner" has the same meaning as in that Act.

25. After subsection (6) of section 117 of that Act (disclosure of information relating to particular persons) there shall be inserted the following subsection—

"(6A) Subsection (6) above shall have effect as if any medical practitioner who, for the purposes of section 52 above, is provided by any person in pursuance of a contract entered into with the Department were specified in Part I of Schedule 4 to this Act".

GENERAL NOTE

This Schedule makes provisions for facilitating the contracting out of certain functions, whether in pursuance of an order made under s.69 or s.70 or otherwise.

SCHEDULE 17

REPEALS

Chapter or Number	Title	Extent of repeal
57 & 58 Vict. c. 60.	The Merchant Shipping Act 1894.	Sections 110 to 112.
14 Geo. 6. c. 28.	The Shops Act 1950.	The whole Act.
1962 c. 35.	The Shops (Airports) Act 1962.	The whole Act.
1964 c. 26.	The Licensing Act 1964.	In section 196A(1), the word "or" at the end of paragraph (a)(ii).
1965 c. 35.	The Shops (Early Closing Days) Act 1965.	The whole Act.
1968 c. 73.	The Transport Act 1968.	In section 62(2), the words from "which" to the end of paragraph (c). In section 62(4)(b), the words "(or, so long as those sections remain in force, sections 73 and 186 of the Act of 1960)". Section 63(5). In section 63(6), the definition of "statutory provision". In section 69(4), in paragraph (b)(ii) the word "authorisations" and in paragraph (c) the words "or section 73 or 186 of the Act of 1960". In section 69(6), the words "premature termination". Section 69B(7). Section 69F. In section 87(3), the words "or 69F". In section 91(1), the words following paragraph (g). In section 91(4), the words from "and different" to the end. In section 92(1), the definition of "authorised vehicle". Sections 93 and 94(1), (2), (9) and (10).
1969 c. 48.	The Post Office Act 1969.	In Schedule 4, paragraph 51.
1972 c. 70.	The Local Government Act 1972.	In Schedule 29, paragraph 43.
1973 c. 35.	The Employment Agencies Act 1973.	Sections 1 to 3 and 7. In section 9(1)(a), the words from "by" to "Act". Section 10(1). In section 13, in subsection (1), the definitions of "current licence", "holder" and "seaman", and subsection (7)(e).
1973 c. 41.	The Fair Trading Act 1973.	In section 75G, in subsection (1), the words "complying with subsections (2) and (3) of this section", and subsections (2) and (3).
1973 c. 65.	The Local Government (Scotland) Act 1973.	Section 157.
1974 c. 50.	The Road Traffic Act 1974.	In Schedule 4, paragraphs 2, 3, 4(1), (3) and (5), and 5.
1975 c. 24.	The House of Commons Disqualification Act 1975.	In Part III of Schedule 1, the entry relating to persons appointed under section 3(4)(b) of the Employment Agencies Act 1973.
1975 c. 71.	The Employment Protection Act 1975.	In Schedule 13, paragraphs 1 to 4, and, in paragraph 6(3), the words from "and in sub-paragraph (iv)" to the end.

Chapter or Number	Title	Extent of repeal
S.I. 1976/1043 (N.I. 9).	The Industrial Relations (Northern Ireland) Order 1976.	In Article 22C(1), the word "or" immediately preceding sub-paragraph (e) and that sub-paragraph.
1978 c. 44.	The Employment Protection (Consolidation) Act 1978.	In section 59(1), the word "either", the word "or" immediately preceding paragraph (b) and that paragraph.
1979 c. 39.	The Merchant Shipping Act 1979.	In Schedule 6, in Part I, the entries relating to sections 111(4) and 112(2) of the Merchant Shipping Act 1894.
1980 c. 21.	The Competition Act 1980.	Section 2(5). Section 3(2) to (6), (9) and (10). In section 5, subsection (2), in subsection (3), the words from the beginning of paragraph (a) to "notice reference" and subsection (5). Section 6(2). In section 13(1), the words "(subject to subsection (5) of that section)". In section 15(2), paragraph (a) and the word "or" immediately following it.
1980 c. 65.	The Local Government, Planning and Land Act 1980.	In Schedule 4, paragraph 1(4).
1981 c. 14.	The Public Passenger Vehicles Act 1981.	Section 14A(3). In section 16(6), the word "or" immediately before paragraph (b). In section 17(2)(b), the words "(during which time it shall be of no effect)". Section 17(2)(c). In section 17(3)(a), the words "intention or". Section 27. Section 50(2). In section 50(4)(c), the words "or to curtail its period of validity".
S.I. 1981/839 (N.I. 20).	The Employment (Miscellaneous Provisions) (Northern Ireland) Order 1981.	Articles 3 to 5 and 8. Article 9(1). In Article 11, in paragraph (1), the definitions of "current licence", "holder" and "seaman" and paragraph (5)(d).
1982 c. 49.	The Transport Act 1982.	Section 21(5). In Schedule 4, in Part II, paragraphs 2 to 5 and 6(b).
1984 c. 12.	The Telecommunications Act 1984.	In section 50(6), the words "applied to any particular case".
1984 c. 27.	The Road Traffic Regulation Act 1984.	In Schedule 9, in paragraph 28, the word "or" immediately preceding sub-paragraph (d).
1984 c. 32.	The London Regional Transport Act 1984.	In Schedule 6, paragraph 22.
1985 c. 13.	The Cinemas Act 1985.	In Schedule 2, paragraphs 4 and 5.
1985 c. 65.	The Insolvency Act 1985.	In Schedule 8, paragraph 16.
1985 c. 67.	The Transport Act 1985.	Section 12(3). Section 24(2). In Schedule 2, paragraph 4(6) and (9).
1985 c. 72.	The Weights and Measures Act 1985.	Section 43. In section 86, in subsections 2(a) and (5), "43(2),". In section 99(2), the words "Except as provided by section 43(2) above,".

Chapter or Number	Title	Extent of repeal
1986 c. 44.	The Gas Act 1986.	In section 17(8), paragraph (d) and the word "and" immediately preceding that paragraph.
1986 c. 53.	The Building Societies Act 1986.	In section 13, in subsection (2), the word "and" immediately preceding paragraph (d), and in subsection (3)(a), the words "of the land".
1986 c. 60.	The Financial Services Act 1986.	In section 125(7), the words "section 24 of".
1988 c. 1.	The Income and Corporation Taxes Act 1988.	In section 201A, in subsection (2)(c), the words "and holds a current licence for the agency", and, in subsection (3), paragraph (b) and the word "and" immediately preceding it.
1988 c. 54.	The Road Traffic (Consequential Provisions) Act 1988.	In Schedule 3, paragraph 6(4).
1989 c. 29.	The Electricity Act 1989.	In section 43(6), the words "applies to any particular case".
1989 c. 38.	The Employment Act 1989.	In Schedule 6, paragraphs 3 to 5.
1989 c. 40.	The Companies Act 1989.	In Schedule 14, in paragraph 9(6), the words "section 24 of".
1990 c. 43.	The Environmental Protection Act 1990.	In Schedule 15, paragraph 10(2)(a).
S.I. 1990/593 (N.I. 5).	The Companies (Northern Ireland) Order 1990.	In Schedule 14, in paragraph 9(6), the words "section 24 of".
1992 c. 41.	The Charities Act 1992.	Section 67(3)(b) and the word "but" immediately preceding it.
S.I. 1992/231 (N.I. 1).	The Electricity (Northern Ireland) Order 1992.	In Article 46(6), the words "applies to any particular case".
1993 c. 10.	The Charities Act 1993.	Section 47(3)(a).
1993 c. 19.	The Trade Union Reform and Employment Rights Act 1993.	In Schedule 8, paragraph 14(b).
1993 c. 43.	The Railways Act 1993.	In section 67(8), the words "applies to any particular case".
1994 c. 20.	The Sunday Trading Act 1994.	Section 5. In Schedule 4, paragraph 23.

INDEX

References are to sections and schedules

BEER AND CIDER, 14
BETTING ON SUNDAY, 20, Sched. 8
BUILDING REGULATIONS, 32
BUILDING SOCIETIES,
    syndicated lending: participation in, 17
    third party mortgages, 16

CHARITIES,
    annual reports, 29
    annual returns, 30
    audits, 28
    control of fund-raising: connected companies, 25
    public collections: time-limits, 27
    soliciting for non-registered charity: defence, 26
CHILDREN'S CERTIFICATES: LICENSING, 19, Sched. 7
COMMENCEMENT, 82(2)–(7)
CONTRACTING OUT,
    effect of, 72
    extent of provisions, 78
    functions,
        exclusions, 71
        of local authorities, 70
        of Ministers and office-holders, 69
    interpretation, 79
    orders, provisions as to, 77
    provisions for facilitating amendments, 76, Sched. 16
    information: restrictions on disclosure, 75, Sched. 15
    powers of certain office-holders, 74
    termination of, 73

DEREGULATION,
    beer and cider: gas in foam, 14
    betting on Sunday, 20, Sched. 8
    building regulations, 32
    building societies, see BUILDING SOCIETIES
    charities, see CHARITIES
    consequential amendments, 39, Sched. 11
    controlled waste, 33
    employment agencies: replacement of licensing, 35
    enforcement procedure,
        appeals against enforcement action: model provisions, 6
        power to improve, 5, Sched. 1
    extent, 40
    fair trading, see FAIR TRADING
    health and safety provisions, 37
    independent schools: inspection, 38
    licensed premises, see LICENSED PREMISES

DEREGULATION—cont.
    lorries in London, 34
    non-trading companies: striking off, 13, Scheds. 5, 6
    orders for removal or reduction of burdens,
        creating new criminal offence, 2
        limitations on, 2
        parliamentary consideration of proposals, 4
        power as to, 1
        preliminary consultation, 3
    redundancy: unfair dismissal, 36
    restrictive trade practices, see RESTRICTIVE TRADE PRACTICES
    shops, see SHOPS
    slaughterhouses and knackers' yards, 31, Sched. 9
    sporting events on Sunday, 21
    traffic control, 34
    vehicle licensing, see GOODS VEHICLE OPERATOR LICENSING; PUBLIC SERVICE VEHICLE OPERATOR LICENSING

EMPLOYMENT AGENCIES,
    replacement of licensing, 35, Sched. 10
ENVIRONMENTAL PROTECTION: CONTROLLED WASTE, 33
EXTENT, 82(8)

FAIR TRADING,
    newspaper mergers, 8
    undertakings,
        as alternative to merger reference: non-divestment matters, 9
        as alternative to monopoly reference, 7, Sched. 2
FINANCIAL PROVISIONS, 80

GOODS VEHICLE OPERATOR LICENSING,
    appeals, 53
    applications,
        determination of, 44
        publication of, 49
    assessors, 51
    duration of licence, 46
    fees, 56
    interim licences, 46
    issue of licences, 44
    maximum number of vehicles, 42
    minor and consequential amendments, 57, Sched. 13
    not transferable, 55
    objections to grant or variation of licences, 43

GOODS VEHICLE OPERATOR LICENSING—*cont.*
  operating centres,
    review of,
      conditions attached on, 50
      periods of, 50
      power to remove, 50
    transfer of, 50, Sched. 12
  partnerships, 54
  review of decisions, 52
  revocation, suspension and curtailment of
    licences, 48
  road safety, conditions for securing, 45
  use of vehicles under licensing, 42
  variation of licences,
    conditions for, 47
    interim, 47
    objection to and refusal of applications
      for: environmental grounds, 47

HEALTH AND SAFETY, 37

INDEPENDENT SCHOOLS: INSPECTION, 38

LENDING SYNDICATES, 17
LICENSED PREMISES,
  children's certificates, 19, Sched. 7
  international ports: permitted hours, 18
  Sunday opening (Scotland), 22
LONDON LORRIES, 34

MONOPOLIES, *see* FAIR TRADING
MORTGAGES, *see* BUILDING SOCIETIES

NEWSPAPER MERGERS, 8
NON-TRADING COMPANIES: STRIKING OFF, 13,
  Sched. 5, 6
NORTHERN IRELAND,
  non-trading companies: striking off, 13(2),
    Sched. 6
  redundancy: unfair dismissal, 36

PUBLIC SERVICE VEHICLE OPERATOR LICENSING,
  applications,
    objections to, 60

PUBLIC SERVICE VEHICLE OPERATOR
  LICENSING—*cont.*
  applications—*cont.*
    undertakings given on, 59
  disqualification of PSV operators, 67
  duration of licences, 60
  fees, 66
  minor and consequential amendments, 68,
    Sched. 14
  operators' discs, 63
  returns of operators, 64
  review of decisions, 65
  suspension of licences, 62
  undertakings given, 59

REDUNDANCY, 36
REPEALS, 81, Sched. 17
RESTRICTIVE TRADE PRACTICES,
  anti-competitive practices: competition ref-
    erences, 12, Sched. 4
  non-notifiable agreements, 10, Sched. 3
  registration of commercially sensitive infor-
    mation, 11
  sectoral regulators and transition, 7, 12,
    Scheds. 2, 4

SCOTLAND: SUNDAY OPENING, 22, 24(b)
SHOPS,
  barbers in Scotland, 24(b)
  conditions of employment, 24(a)
  hours of closing, 23
SHORT TITLE, 82(1)
SLAUGHTERHOUSES AND KNACKER'S YARDS, 31,
  Sched. 9
SUNDAY,
  betting, 20, Sched. 8
  licensed premises opening (Scotland), 22
  sporting events, 21

TRAFFIC CONTROL, 34; *see also* GOODS VEHICLE
  OPERATOR LICENSING; PUBLIC SERVICE
  VEHICLE OPERATOR LICENSING

UNFAIR DISMISSAL, 36

WASTE; DUTY OF CARE AS TO, 33
WEIGHTS AND MEASURES, 14

CONSOLIDATED FUND (NO. 2) ACT 1994

(1994 c. 41)

An Act to apply certain sums out of the Consolidated Fund to the service of the years ending on 31st March 1995 and 1996.　　[16th December 1994]

PARLIAMENTARY DEBATES
Hansard, H.C. Vol. 251, col. 1165; H.L. Vol. 559, col. 1481.

INTRODUCTION

This Act makes provision for the application of £1,276,707,000 from the Consolidated Fund for the service of the year ending March 31, 1995 and for the application of £95,397,951,000 for the service of the year ending on March 31, 1996.

Issue out of the Consolidated Fund for the year ending 31st March 1995

1. The Treasury may issue out of the Consolidated Fund of the United Kingdom and apply towards making good the supply granted to Her Majesty for the service of the year ending on 31st March 1995 the sum of £1,276,707,000.

Issue out of the Consolidated Fund for the year ending 31st March 1996

2. The Treasury may issue out of the Consolidated Fund of the United Kingdom and apply towards making good the supply granted to Her Majesty for the service of the year ending on 31st March 1996 the sum of £95,397,951,000.

Short title

3. This Act may be cited as the Consolidated Fund (No. 2) Act 1994.

INDEX

References are to section number

CONSOLIDATED FUND, 1
application from, 2, 3

SERVICE OF THE YEAR, 1, 2
SHORT TITLE, 3